A volume of a series in English,
edited by ERNEST BERNBAUM

Victorian Prose

A Companion Volume to
VICTORIAN POETRY
Edited by E. K. Brown

VICTORIAN PROSE

PROSE

Selected and Edited
With Introductions, Bibliographies,
and Notes

By

FREDERICK WILLIAM ROE

EMERITUS PROFESSOR OF ENGLISH
THE UNIVERSITY OF WISCONSIN

THE RONALD PRESS COMPANY • NEW YORK

To

NANCY ROBERTS ROE

"No age hitherto lived out upon the world's surface has been so multiform or so busy; none defies the art of the historian to such a bewildering degree."

SIR EDMOND GOSSE (1918)

"The general mind is seething strangely, and to those who watch the signs of the times, it seems plain that this Nineteenth Century will see revolutions of thought and practice as great as those which the sixteenth witnessed. Through what trials and sore contests the civilized world will have to pass in the course of this new reformation, who can tell?"

T. H. HUXLEY (1860)

"Whatever changes may be before us, the nineteenth century can never cease to be interesting to the future student."

J. A. FROUDE (1874)

PREFACE

It has been the purpose and effort of the editor of this anthology to offer for college courses covering the period such a body of non-fictional prose from major Victorian masters as may fairly represent not only the ideas and style of each writer in turn, but outstanding movements of thought in a great and complex age as well. The writers are grouped in chronological order. Selections and essays of individual authors, in most cases, are likewise arranged in the order of publication, though in a few instances (notably Ruskin and Arnold) it has seemed preferable to present the material in another sequence, so that the student may, if he choose, consider the author's ideas in their logical rather than chronological order. However, the date of publication is printed at the end of every essay or connected series of selections, so that each unit of prose can readily be studied in its time order if that approach be preferred, as may be the case if one should wish, for example, to make a special examination of style. The five autobiographical selections in each instance introduce their respective writers, regardless of dates.

But any scheme of arrangement that an editor adopts may be (and often should be) abandoned by teacher and student in favor of a reading "here and there," according to subject matter, whether it be social philosophy and criticism, education, literary theory, art, religion, speculation, science, history; for all the main streams of Victorian thought are more or less reflected in these pages, and no reasonable editor would, if he could, attempt to fix any reader's approach to such riches.

But whatever wealth of material is accumulated, some readers may fail to find in it all that they look for; an essay, a favorite selection or passage, or even a sequence of pieces, which certain teachers (especially) deem all but indispensable, will be missed. This editor (like most other editors in similar tasks) is well aware that he has had to depend mainly upon his own imperfect judgment and experience. He has perforce been mindful, too, of primary *objectives* in such an anthology, and also unavoidable limitation of space. It would not have been difficult to project a volume of impractical and excessive bulk. The present collection, therefore, cannot be expected to meet all the demands of "outside reading." Should readers have an appetite for more of *Sartor Resartus* or *Marius the Epicurean,* for examples, they may find such material in separate and readily accessible editions.

The editor is bold to say in conclusion that he would be well pleased if his readers, in receptive moods, might take time out from their study of the *text* to read the *gloss,* to wit, the general introduction, the separate critical appreciations, and the annotations! These things are not *meant* to be impedimenta, but, rather, useful guides for younger travelers upon Victorian highways, who, when they in their turn become familiar with their surroundings, will no longer need to be told where they are. And some of them at least may be prompted to explore on their own many a Victorian byway, less familiar to the older scholar, and so, in their time, make better guides for those who come after.

Finally, a personal word of gratitude to the "generations" of students whose interest and cooperation in Victorian studies have been a constant stimulus to me through the years; and to the always helpful library staff who have guided me to sources of information otherwise inaccessible or unknown. I am happy to express special thanks to my friend, Professor E. K. Brown of the University of Chicago, whose *Victorian Poetry*, as companion-piece, has preceded my contribution. To him the plan and production of *Victorian Prose* owe innumerable suggestions. It is a pleasure, also, to express here my sense of obligation to Wisconsin friends and former colleagues,—to Professors George S. Bryan, Lowell E. Noland, William H. Kiekhofer, Friedrich Bruns, Joseph L. Russo, C. D. Zdanowicz, Paul M. Fulcher, Harry Hayden Clark, Ralph A. McCanse, all of whom have given me generous help in particular problems, mainly of annotation, in their fields of specialization.

Acknowledgments are due to Charles Scribner's Sons and to Longmans, Green and Company for their kind permissions to use the essays of Robert Louis Stevenson and of William Morris, respectively.

F. W. R.

Madison, Wisconsin
May 26, 1947

CONTENTS

THE VICTORIAN AGE

THE TWELVE MEN whose work is represented in this volume are masters of non-fictional prose, the most eminent, all in all, in a time of great writers. In thought, style, and influence taken together they reflect the vast range of Victorian thought and movement more effectively than any other group of prose masters could do, even though the members chosen were twice as many. They tell us, in their various ways, something of the main currents of life and thought running through the period, a period so complex and many-sided and so rich in source materials as to baffle even the most expert and comprehensive of students. Lytton Strachey, for example, who has written about the Victorian age with devastating irony and also with subtlety and brilliance, assures us that no writer can hope to see very much of so vast a spectacle. "He will row out over that great ocean of material, and lower down into it, here and there, a little bucket, which will bring up to the light of day some characteristic specimen, from those far depths, to be examined with careful curiosity." Such specimens are the works of these twelve men. They wrote essays, treatises, and sometimes massive studies in the fields of society, politics, economics, education, art, science, history, and religion; and since they were all men of pronounced individuality their compositions possess unique characteristics. There are, of course, broad contrasts between the manners of Macaulay and Carlyle, of Newman and Pater, of Mill and Ruskin, of Arnold and Morris, for examples, but all of them were great personalities living in a great age, who had something to say and knew how to say it; and who therefore commanded in their written speech the kind of expressiveness which the world calls style.

It is impossible fairly to understand these Victorians without some acquaintance with their age, an age that has been severely and often condescendingly handled by many social and literary critics of the twentieth century, who have condemned its religion as narrow and hypocritical, its morals as pharisaic and prudish, its economics as dryly theoretical and inhuman, its politics as muddled and compromising, its art as stuffy and commonplace, its literature as romantic and unrealistic, and its life generally as an incongruous mixture of mammon-worship and sentimental idealism. All this and more, until recently, was repeated *ad nauseam,* until superficial minds whose reading and information were vastly remote from the center came to think of Victorian *literature* as synonymous with *Victorianism,* and of Victorianism as synonymous with "plaster saints and stuffed shirts." But the severest critics of the age were Victorians themselves, who ruthlessly battered the images of false gods long before the twentieth century iconoclasts got out their hammers, as any considerate reader will find for himself in the pages of this book. And today, when mechanized armies and mechanized navies of sea and air have rained death and destruction upon mankind in global war, both critics and general readers alike look back to the accomplishments of the Victorian age with a more just appreciation of their greatness. As an editor of a famous metropolitan newspaper has written (1940): "Nowadays, when people speak of the nineteenth century it is not of a world dominated by Mrs. Grundy and the antimacassar.... What we once upon a time called their stuffiness we now enviously describe as their security. What we once upon a time called their materialism we are now inclined to describe as their civilization."

Although there were deep shadows, as we shall see, the Victorian age, in contrast with our own times, does indeed seem like a long day of continuous sunshine, where prosperity and progress were the high lights. It was an era of peace. There were British wars in China, in India, in the Crimea, in South Africa, and there was vigilant concern over conflicts in continental Europe and in the United States, but none of these disturbances ever seriously interrupted Great Britain's advance at home along the road to industrial and commercial primacy of the world. During the Queen's reign men for the most part "concentrated their efforts upon the improvement of the mechanism of industry and communications," until England became the richest country on earth, sending to the ends of it the products of her factories in the largest mercantile fleet that had ever sailed the seas. To show what British industry and invention had done and to glorify the machine as the instrument of an unparalleled material progress, Prince Albert promoted the Great Exhibition of 1851, only fourteen years after the Queen had taken her throne. A vast structure of glass was erected, the Crystal Palace, and within it were assembled the arts and crafts of the empire and the world. People by the millions (six millions in six months) came to see this symbol of modern civilization, symbol of "a golden age of wealth and concord," symbol of a new epoch in the progress of mankind. Under a "blazing arch of lucid glass," as Thackeray described it, the London *Times* saw a spectacle that foreshadowed universal peace. Lord Macaulay was in raptures over "a most gorgeous sight, vast, graceful, beyond the dreams of the Arabian romances," all of which seemed to him the realization of doctrines he had preached for a lifetime,— liberalism, laissez-faire, free-trade; and he came away thinking, he said, that "there is just as much chance of a revolution in England as of the falling of the moon."

Forty-six years later, in 1897, the British staged in London an even more splendid spectacle. This time it was Queen Victoria's diamond jubilee, the celebration of her sixty years as sovereign and of Britain's continued prosperity and progress since the Great Exhibition of nearly half a century before. Again millions of people gathered to see the show and to pay homage to a great ruler. "A wonderful sight," wrote Paderewski, "of a splendor hardly to be imagined. I saw the pageant, that procession of all the vassals of the Empire, the Maharajahs, the Governors of Dominions, the Prime Ministers, all following the carriage of the Queen." "As the procession passed along," said Lytton Strachey, "escorting Victoria through the thronged re-echoing streets of London on her progress of thanksgiving to St. Paul's Cathedral, the greatness of her realm and the adoration of her subjects blazed out together." To the British everywhere the aged Queen was the still-living emblem of their pride, their wealth, their security, and, above all, their sense of peaceful continuity amidst cycles of momentous change.

The Victorians had abundant reason to believe in progress, if by progress is meant an ever-increasing command and use of the resources of the earth for man's material well-being and enjoyment. And that was exactly its meaning to typical Englishmen, such as John Bright and Lord Macaulay, whose eloquence and literary powers were often displayed in descriptions of Britain's achievements. "Our fields are cultivated," said Macaulay, "with a skill unknown elsewhere, with a skill which has extracted rich harvests from moors and morasses. Our houses are filled with conveniences which the kings of former times might have envied. Our bridges, our canals, our roads, our modes of communication fill every stranger with wonder. Nowhere are manufactures carried to such perfection. Nowhere does man exercise such dominion over matter."

The beginnings of this development, of course, reach back to pre-Victorian days and the later years of the eighteenth century, during which time the application of steam to the uses of industry by means of new machinery made possible the factory system and a new social order. But the greatest expansion and acceleration of these novel forces came after 1837. Before then the railroad was an experimental thing and was received with contemptuous opposition and distrust by many, as when Lord Brougham spoke "of the folly of seven hundred people going fifteen miles an hour in seven carriages." In a very few years, however, railroads became "a fashion and a frenzy" for builders, investors, and travellers. "By December 31, 1848," says Clapham, "there were 5,127 miles of railway open in the United Kingdom, and over 2,000 miles more were under construction by an army of about 175,000 navvies and miscellaneous work-people. Coaches were extinct on all the main routes. . . . By 1865 the great companies had almost reached their final form. . . . This was much more than a financial and engineering feat; it carried with it a social revolution." Like the railroad, steamboats up to 1837 were more of a curiosity than a utility, small wooden paddle-wheelers they were, plying between coast towns or along the Clyde and the Thames. In 1838 the Great Western weighed anchor at Bristol and fourteen days later, in Carlyle's phrase, bounded "through the gullets of the Hudson and threw her cable out on the capstan of New York." Earlier in the same year, the paddle-wheeler Sirius, 700 tons, had made the crossing in eighteen days. "In the fifties and sixties," says Trevelyan, "the great ocean-going ships were increasingly propelled by steam, and built first of iron and then of steel. The change coincided with the enormous development of English iron and steel output, and the increased use of steam and metal in every sort of manufacturing process and product. In 1848 Britain already produced about half the pig iron of the world: in the next thirty years her output was trebled." Along with these mighty changes came the telegraph (1837), the submarine cable (1866), and the telephone (1876); and between 1840 and 1861 the penny post, the use of stamps for letters, letter-boxes in the streets, and Post Office Savings banks, to which may be added as parts of the total picture the lucifer match, free public libraries, photography, cheap daily newspapers, anaesthetics, and antiseptics. To quote Carlyle again: "The huge demon of mechanism smokes and thunders, panting at his great task, in all sections of English land."

The earlier period of this transformation from handicrafts to machine-made goods, from domestic manufacture to mass production, was a time of confusion and social upheaval, when crowds of workers were migrating from the south to the north of England, from Ireland to England, from the highlands of Scotland to the lowlands, and from the country to the city. But after 1850 British industry went forward for many years in almost uninterrupted and altogether unprecedented progress. Population and wealth increased enormously. Towns became cities, and in cities like Manchester, Sheffield, Liverpool, Leeds, Birmingham, and London, with their ugly, sprawling suburbs, the incoming tides of humanity rose to a flood. "The census of 1851," says Trevelyan, "showed that already half the population of the island was urban, 'a situation that had probably not existed before, in a great country, at any time in the world's history.'" Like the legendary King Midas, the British manufacturer seemed to touch nothing that did not turn to gold. For fifty years of Victoria's reign (1837-1887), experts record fabulous increases in export and import trade and in national income, resulting, withal, in increased wages and improved standards of living among the artisan classes, and in decreased pauperism and serious crime among the lowest classes.

The vast material expansion, we may be sure, meant concomitant changes and problems affecting the whole structure of society. No previous social order in all history had seen such rapid and revolutionary mutation as the Victorians saw unfolding before their astonished eyes. A little before this age began, the ways of human life were not radically different from what they had been for centuries, even among ancient peoples; at the end of it our modern world had arrived. A new and gigantic industrialism like this was certain to lead, as Lord Morley said, "to new currents of thought on property, wealth, and the rights of man." In 1837 Great Britain was still an agricultural nation; her land and the surrounding seas produced most of her food. The land, then and for years thereafter, was largely owned by the old aristocracy, a territorial nobility and squirearchy that had ruled England since 1689 and expected to rule until time was no more. "Are you aware," asked John Bright of a Glasgow audience in 1866, "that half the land of England is in the possession of fewer than one hundred and fifty men? Are you aware of the fact that half the land in Scotland is in the possession of not more than ten or twelve men?" A government report in 1874 estimated that all the enclosed land of England and Wales was held by 2,250 persons, thousands of acres of which, much of it waste, were given over to deer parks and hunting preserves. The Reform Bill of 1832 had left the landlords in control of parliament, and for years thereafter cabinets were made up mostly of peers or sons of peers. The reactionary effects of the French Revolution continued for decades beyond Waterloo, and the aristocracy from 1832 to 1867 vigorously resisted all political reform. The stability of the social framework, they held, depended upon its present fixity, wherein property interests, more particularly the landed interests of an hereditary and privileged class, were paramount. So long as this order of things could be maintained its members naturally felt secure and contented; and well they might, for they seemed to have, as Matthew Arnold said, a "monopoly of the world of enjoyment."

But all down the century, emphatically in Victorian times, other classes were emerging into prominence and power. The first of these was the plutocracy or manufacturing class, Carlyle's captains of industry. These were men who, with the advent and aid of the machine, built the factories, the trades, the ships that made Victorian England the commercial and financial center of the world. They were energetic, hardheaded, often ruthless individualists, unashamed Mammon-worshippers, thrusting themselves up from the ranks in a time, probably the fiercest ever known, of the free play of competitive forces. For laissez-faire was their gospel, a gospel laid down by the classical economists and utilitarians, Adam Smith, Malthus, Bentham, James Mill, and Ricardo; eloquently proclaimed by the great leaders of the Manchester School (as Disraeli called it), Richard Cobden and John Bright; and adopted by the manufacturers themselves as something fixed and universal, like the law of gravitation. Morally, this was the doctrine of self-interest as the driving-power of human endeavor; politically, it was, as someone has said, "the creed of the minimized state," the exclusive business of government being the protection of property and the maintenance of order among free competing forces; economically, it meant freedom of trade, unrestricted competition, the liberty of factory-owners to carry on their affairs as they pleased, to buy their labor in the cheapest markets, to determine hours and conditions of work for their workers, and to sell their products wherever prices were highest; for, like the grandees of the land, the captains of industry believed that they should have undisputed right to do as they would with their own, and like them, too, they stubbornly opposed restrictions and interference from the outside.

Up to 1850, or until the final establishment of free trade by the abolition of the Corn Laws (1846) and Navigation Acts (1849) under the leadership of Sir Robert Peel, there was an "epic struggle," as J. L. Hammond says, "between the spirit of feudalism (the landlords) and the spirit of commerce (the manufacturers)." Thereafter contentions subsided. The aristocracy became increasingly plutocratic, and the plutocracy became increasingly aristocratic. Profit was everything. Money was glorified. Between 1850 and 1875 Britain reached newer and higher peaks of prosperity, under an almost totally uncontrolled capitalistic regime. "We feel a-tiptoe with confidence," says one writer; another speaks of "the mighty fabric of English prosperity"; "hearts are uplifted with hope," writes a third. Gladstone described the growth of wealth as "intoxicating," and Disraeli, the country's resources as "inexhaustible." By 1870 the new-rich had many members in Parliament, who were rapidly adopting the political conservatism of the aristocracy; or, as Morley put the matter, by the time the manufacturer "owns a mansion and a piece of land he has a feeling as of blue blood tingling in his veins." Undoubtedly the higher social structure was changing, and not too favorably. The simpler and gentler courtesies of the old aristocracy at its best gave place to the snobbery and smugness of a class unaccustomed to the responsibilities of wealth and position. Senseless luxury and display increased. Class distinctions became sharper. The gulf between the rich and the poor widened. It was the golden age of the philistine, Matthew Arnold's philistine, who had no love of the things of the mind, no love of beautiful things, only "a love of industry, trade and wealth. Can any life be imagined," Arnold asks, "more hideous, more dismal, more unenviable?"

But there were other sides to the life of this vanished Victorian time, well known to readers of Trollope's novels, especially the Barchester series, which move, as Hugh Walpole has said "in a land where it is always afternoon," a land of security, comfort, and peace. All in all, whatever else it was, existence for the prosperous people of those days was a very solid reality; they had no need of a historic sense to interpret the past or to anticipate the future; they neither desired nor dreamed of anything better than the paradisal present. Winston Churchill has brilliantly summarized (1937) their situation: "They never had to face, as we have done, and still do, the possibility of national ruin. Their main foundations were never shaken. They dwelt in an age of British splendor and unchallenged leadership. The art of government was exercised within a limited sphere. World-revolution, mortal defeat, national subjugation, chaotic degeneration, or even national bankruptcy, had not laid steel claws upon their sedate, serene, complacent life."

But while Victorian Britain was a "paradise for the well-to-do," as Morley wrote in 1870, it was a "purgatory for the able, and a hell for the poor." As Carlyle and other "able" men saw it, the wealth of Britain was enchanted: "in the midst of plethoric plenty the people perish; with gold walls, and full barns, no man feels himself safe or satisfied." "The relations of the working-classes of England to its privileged orders," said Disraeli in *Sybil* (1845), "are relations of enmity, and therefore of peril." The prosperity and complacency of the aristocracy and the new-rich blinded them to the frightful abuses and evils among the toilers at the base of the social structure; and if they were not blinded they were generally either indifferent or hostile. The West End of London knew nothing of the horrors of East London. The palaces of the rich and the hovels of the poor multiplied in relative proximity over urban and rural areas, but their occupants were about as far apart as were the gods of Epicurus from the affairs of mortals on earth below. Queen Victoria herself, who meant to overlook nothing within her royal purview, "neither saw nor heard anything to any purpose" (the phrase is E. F. Benson's) concerning the dim millions in factory, field, pottery and mine. Charities there were, of course, for the poor, who would always be poor,—occasional and ineffectual largesses from the private purses of ladies and gentlemen bountiful, who the while remained staunch believers in the permanence of their own social order and its economical system, and who were deaf to the fulminations of that "demagogue," John Bright, as when he said: "it is not benevolence but justice that can deal with giant evils."

And what were those evils? To the special student the Dantesque picture of life and labor in the factories, mines, and homes of the early Victorian workers is only too familiar. Here a brief sketch, more suggestive than detailed and mostly in the words of authorities and contemporaries, must suffice. The Hammonds, in *The Rise of Modern Industry*, say that the industrial system "was exercised at first under conditions that reproduced the degradation of the slave trade." And John Morley, speaking at Newcastle as late as 1883, gave it as his opinion that "the over-crowded debris of our destitute and neglected classes in the great towns was living a life distinctly more degraded than that of the savages in the Pacific Islands." A writer in the *Saturday Review* (an intellectualist and anti-democratic weekly) sounds a warning note about the brutalized workers (1865): "Now and then we get horrid glimpses of a foul current of life running like a pestilential sewer beneath the smooth surface of society, which makes us doubt whether all our boasts about the superior morality of our domestic relations are not just a trifle immature." In the coal and iron mines the working day was eleven to twelve hours, often longer, and the nearly naked women and children who dragged carriages of coal from pit to shaft toiled under conditions of almost total darkness and solitary confinement. "In the Potteries, children were set to work at six years old, and in times of pressure they were employed from half-past six in the morning till eight or nine at night." Child labor was universal in the textile mills, where (after 1833) the hours ranged from six and one-half hours up to eight until the thirteenth year, after which they were twelve up to the eighteenth year, when the working day became for thousands of adults fourteen to sixteen hours, or even more. Wages are described in government reports as starvation wages, the worst probably being in the hosiery mills, where with a working day of sixteen to eighteen hours the pay was from $1.25 to $2.00 per week. Factories were overheated and unventilated, rank with smells and filled with floating dust; machinery was unprotected and accidents were common; there was no compensation for mutilation, no allowance for sickness; work was stupefyingly monotonous from childhood; disease, deformity, immorality were rampant; and most workers were used up at forty. Their homes, if possible, were worse than the factories. Along narrow, dark streets thousands upon thousands of houses were built back to back,—the dark, overcrowded, disgusting, pestilential warrens of the poor. Large populations lived pell-mell in cellars, beyond the pale of elementary decencies, "embedded in material filth." There were no public sanitary services in early Victorian times, no water supply, no sewage disposal, no control of building operations. All things went forward in unregulated, uncontrolled freedom; it was, in Carlyle's phrase, "Laissez-faire and Devil take the hindmost." With inclusive truth and brevity Sir James Graham, in the House of Commons in 1847, described the life of the workers as "eating, drinking, sleeping, working, and dying."

It is to be remembered that as late as 1850 upwards of half the population of Great Britain was illiterate, and that factory, mine, and field workers had no vote. A mass of barbarism (for so it was described) surging chaotically up from below was inevitably an increasing menace not only to industry but to the entire social structure. Signs of revolt were sure to appear as groups of men, here and there, began to sense the desperateness of their situation. Year after year outbreaks of lawlessness occurred in the form of riots, burnings, smashings of machinery, murders, and promiscuous sabotage, mainly the mischief of hot-heads; while workers generally remained law-abiding, and sought to find ways out of their misery by peaceful rather than violent means. Gradually by their own united efforts, by the publicity of government inquiries, by direct government action, and with the help of upper-class leaders whose sympathies were aroused, ways were organized to fight these giant evils of the industrial system.

One was the Chartist Movement. It was launched in 1838-39 and continued through ups and downs for a decade. The famous "Charter" was an instrument of six points (universal manhood suffrage, vote by ballot, equal electoral districts, annual parliaments, payment of members, abolition of property qualifications), by which the workers hoped to right their wrongs according to constitutional procedures. Public meetings were held in every part of the kingdom, addressed by fiery orators, and three times, in 1839, in 1842, and again in 1848, monster petitions were presented to Parliament and rejected by overwhelming and derisive majorities, except the last petition, which died in committee. The upper classes, frightened by uprisings across the Channel, and not forgetful of the French Revolution and the excesses of Jacobinism—"the blind hysterics of the Celt," said Tennyson—raised mountains of opposition and prejudice. But Chartism though ineffectual and premature was not a total failure, for it accelerated collective action among the workers and announced to the public that the laboring millions would not submissively endure a life of inhuman degradation. Responsible leaders now turned their attention to unionism as a way out. Organizations of workers to improve their conditions had been multiplying since the repeal of the Combination Acts in 1824 (which outlawed unions), until tens of thousands of members were enrolled. It was only after Chartism had failed to provide political remedies, however, that operatives, with new vision and purpose, began to extend and consolidate their associations and to look "forward to the establishment of conciliation boards in which their capable officials would be able to deal on equal terms with employers, and, in effect, to share a sort of co-operative control of industrial policy." But public opinion, the Press, members of Parliament, above all the manufacturers fought unionism for decades as a "restriction upon the free circulation of labor" and a violation of the sacred principles of laissez-faire. Such was the position of Bright and Cobden, both leading democrats, and of the Earl of Shaftesbury, who, as Lord Ashley, was England's foremost proponent of factory reform. "All the single despots," he said, "and all the aristocracies that ever were or ever will be are as a puff of wind compared with these tornadoes, the Trade Unions." But at last, in 1875, the government gave way and, in the words of Sidney and Beatrice Webb, "collective bargaining, with all its necessary accompaniments, was, after fifty years of legislative struggle, finally recognized as the law of the land."

Another step forward for the worker in mid-Victorian times was factory reform. There had been various official investigations and reports, followed by certain measures, before 1837, the most important of which was the Factory Act of 1833, with the appointment of four inspectors and some limitations to working hours for children and youths; but every enactment was mostly a dead letter because of persistent and formidable opposition from operators and even from many parents of children whose slender earnings were necessary to prevent starvation. The Mines Bill of 1842, however, effectively prohibited underground employment in mines of girls and women and of boys under ten. The disclosures of the Royal Commission of 1840, say the Hammonds, "took England by storm." Even so, the Bill was hotly opposed in the House of Lords, who in the end were afraid to vote it down. Lord Ashley declared that he had never seen "such a display of selfishness, such frigidity to every human sentiment." Then came the Ten Hours Bill of 1847, the climax of years of struggle by Lord Ashley, an act which fixed to ten hours the daily work of women and youths in textile factories, and, as it was supposed, would automatically fix to the same time the work of adult men; a supposition which was found to be fallacious, because of tricky evasions that made the act ineffective until a supplementary measure was put through twenty-seven years later. In 1878 as a crowning piece of factory legislation the Consolidating Act was passed, bringing all factories and workshops under uniform regulations, providing a single system of government inspection, and creating rules to guarantee safety, protect health and morals, and afford time out for some schooling.

In this same year (1878) John Morley, thinking of Chartism and Trade Unions, but thinking more particularly of the Reform Bill of 1867, expressed his opinion that the real movement of the century was the "rise of the workman to a decisive share in the control of his own destinies." What the worker wanted was justice, not charity; and all through the darkest years of the industrial revolution he had a growing sense of the hopelessness of his situation unless as a citizen he could participate in the affairs of the state by means of the ballot. The basic reform for him was political reform. But opposition was profound and continuous. As the upper classes saw them, we must remember, the workers were a vast, chaotic, almost barbaric mass of creatures, gross, selfish, ignorant, immeasurably corruptible. To give them the ballot was to confer political power upon a mob and so to precipitate anarchy and finally military despotism. So thought Macaulay, Carlyle, Dickens, Ruskin. So thought the Earl of Shaftesbury, who looked upon the Reform Bill of 1867 as "a catastrophe." "Most statesmen," says Christie in his *Transition to Democracy*, "would have agreed with Burke that 'a perfect democracy is the most shameless thing in the world.'" It is to be remembered, too, that the ruling classes, generally, believed that the English political and social system was a system of privilege and that, as a writer in the *Saturday Review* (1864) voiced the belief, "society rests on the existence of a vast population born to do mean things, born to perform the rudest labor, and engaged in nothing else from birth to death. England is a government of a minority, resting on the subjection of a majority forced by circumstances to fulfill all the coarser tasks and most repulsive duties of the common race."

The time-spirit, however, was resistlessly working on the side of the populace, as we have seen. What looked like a very revolutionary form of republicanism, according to the *Pall Mall Gazette,* was steadily flooding in. The poor, said John Stuart Mill in 1852, "have come out of leading strings." In 1858, England's most powerful popular orator, John Bright, began to campaign for political reform. "Wherever you go in Great Britain or Ireland," he said at Birmingham, "five out of every six men you meet have no vote." The millions of unfranchised men, he later insisted, would not be content with a political system in which three per cent of the voters elected more than one-half of the members of Parliament. Gladstone now joined Bright, and in 1864 shocked the public and his Oxford constituents by a declaration in favor of suffrage for the working classes; and two years later he proposed a moderate reform in the electorate. Disraeli attacked the measure, saying that Gladstone had "revived the doctrine of Tom Paine"; but the next year Disraeli himself, always an opportunist and aware that the franchise question, as the historian Trevelyan says, "was now raging like a fever in the nation's blood," put through the Reform Bill of 1867, which gave the franchise to most industrial workers and added approximately a million voters to the electorate. "A leap in the dark," said the Prime Minister, Lord Derby. "Shooting Niagara," wailed Carlyle from the sound-proof study at the top of his house. But democracy was on the march. In 1872, under Gladstone, vote by ballot (i.e., secret voting) became the law of the land; and in 1884, again under Gladstone, the third of England's great Reform Bills was passed, admitting agricultural laborers, many miners, and some other workers to the ballot, and increasing the electorate by about two million voters: an extension of the franchise that meant practical manhood suffrage for Great Britain. Introducing the Bill Gladstone said: "We are firm in the faith that enfranchisement is a good, that the people may be trusted, that the voters under the Constitution are the strength of the Constitution."

Only liberal statesmen and thinkers entertained such confidence—liberals of the future, as Arnold called them. Political power, by these reform measures, was now no longer the exclusive possession of a privileged order; it passed to the people as a whole, the majority of whom could not read a newspaper, tens of thousands of whom could not write their own names. The nobility and gentry had long regarded education as unnecessary for the poor, and many aristocrats, like Lord Melbourne, believed it to be "positively dangerous." Voluntary schools there were, created by the Church, especially in the villages, and, since 1833, aided by the state. Their concern perforce was far more religious than educational, whereby the children were taught to be good and to be content to remain as they were born, a servant class. There were other schools, too,—for examples, the "common day schools" and the so-called Factory Schools set up by employers on government order, but they are described as "altogether inefficient," some of them being, in Lord Shaftesbury's words, "more fitted to be sties or coal holes." Notwithstanding even these various ineffectual efforts to do something, educationally, for the poor, there were (so Morley estimated in 1869) two million children who had no schooling whatsoever. The Hammonds in their *Life* of Lord Shaftesbury go further when they note the prolonged opposition of religious interests to the cause of secular education. "This meant," they say, "that until the Evangelicals and High Churchmen, the Non-Conformists and the Anglicans, could compose their interminable quarrels, twelve out of thirteen of the children of England were to go without education at all." It became sun-clear after the passage of the Reform Bill of 1867 that such conditions could not be continued. As Robert Lowe said in the House of Commons: "Now we must educate our masters." Accordingly in 1870 under Gladstone, the Elementary Education Bill was passed, a measure which for the first time made such education national, and made it compulsory for all children between five and twelve years of age who were unprovided for in the voluntary schools. In 1876 primary education was made compulsory for all schools, and in 1891 it was made free. Experience soon proved to the British that the education of the poor was not a curse but a blessing. On the great issues which have arisen in recent times, says Marvin (in *The Century of Hope*) "the enfranchised millions have given the right answers."

Thoughtful men in the seventies and eighties now realized that a revolution had been going on in their midst for thirty years and more. "We are at the end of a period," said Arnold in 1882; "the traditional, existing social arrangements, which satisfied before, satisfy no longer." Democracy had indeed arrived, though to most landlords and captains of industry it still looked like "a barbarous invasion." The old gospel of rampant individualism, it was now clear, could not solve the problems of the new industrial age. Laissez-faire as a fixed doctrine had to go. Collectivism, in the form of state interference for the common good, had to come and did come. But was collectivism really a right solution of the evils of a new and complex civilization, and, if so, how far should it go? To Herbert Spencer increasing state control, or statism, as he called it, meant increasing bureaucracy, decreasing individual initiative and freedom, and eventual slavery. To liberals, like Gladstone and Morley and Matthew Arnold, intervention of the state in the interests of social justice was the only alternative to anarchy. One thing seemed certain—the upper classes must henceforth maintain their prestige through service and no longer through privilege. So much at least had the Victorians won in the never-ending conflict between the demands of individual freedom and of social control.

But the economic, political and social problems that surged up in the wake of revolutionary industrialism were not the only major concerns of thoughtful Victorians. The most urgent and pervasive they undoubtedly were, for they directly affected the material well-being of all classes of people. But other movements were hardly less revolutionary, since they profoundly agitated the spiritual and intellectual life of educated classes everywhere, changing or obliterating old horizons for some, creating new horizons for others, and sooner or later altering for most minds their conceptions and feelings about the world of which they were a part. These movements of thought and discovery were mainly in the fields of religion and science.

The Victorians, generally speaking, were a religious people. Even the Agnostics, as later they came to be called, were predominantly "puritan in feeling and outlook." And apart from these the great majority of British, in the mid-Victorian period at least, regarded themselves as orthodox Christians, whether they were High Churchmen or Low or Broad, whether they were Non-Conformists of one sect or other; and all alike accepted the Bible as an inspired book, literally true from cover to cover. As an English Dean once put the matter: "The Bible is none other than the voice of Him that sitteth on the throne. Every book of it, every chapter of it, every verse of it, every syllable of it, every letter of it, is the direct utterance of the Most High." This meant that the Scriptures were "infallibly accurate," not only on the side of spiritual truth, but on the sides of scientific and of historical truth as well. Such a religion, like all other forces which find their outlet through human channels, had its strength and its weakness. It produced great characters and great servants of state and society. Its works of charity in the aggregate, all down the period, were undoubtedly far more abundant and helpful than any record will ever reveal. Goodness and kindness must have flowed in a continuous stream from the piety of tens of thousands who, all their lives, regularly worshipped in church or chapel.

But Victorian religion was less a religion of love than of fear. Strict Sabbath observance, while it lasted, was an excessively severe and gloomy thing, joyless for youth and often monotonous and perfunctory for age. There were also, as students of the time have somewhat clamorously proclaimed, not a little complacence, compromise, and hypocrisy—frailties on which the Victorians had no monopoly. Where rank and wealth bestowed their blessings of security and luxury in ever larger measures, it was not difficult for the prosperous to receive them as gifts of a Divine Providence in recognition of the superior worthiness of the British, and thus to create an atmosphere congenial to the spread of smugness and snobbery. It is an ancient human infirmity to wish to make the best of both worlds, only the Victorians wished more zealously, it may be, than their predecessors. Well-to-do laity vigorously opposed any interference on the part of the Church with economic problems and social evils; and when men like Maurice and Kingsley undertook to apply Christian ideals to social problems the Church itself rose in opposition and sometimes to abuse. Religious orthodoxy, on the whole and for the earlier half of the Victorian era, at least, remained fixed within its own narrow bounds, while in the world beyond the Church, under the impact of the new and mighty industrialism, the new science and the higher criticism of the Bible, secularization, spiritual unrest, doubt, agnosticism steadily increased and precipitated momentous issues.

Religion in England and Scotland since the Reformation has of course been predominantly Protestant. Up to the Emancipation Act of 1829 Catholics had no civic equality, and though Irish immigration of workers increased their numbers, they remained a minority group; in matters of Christian orthodoxy they represented the extreme right. A far larger body were the Non-Conformists or Dissenters, that is, all Protestant groups outside of the Established Church. In politics and social reform during the Victorian Period, they were liberal; they consistently and militantly opposed the Tory Anglicans and, broadly speaking, were made up of workers, small tradesmen, and the new-rich in the big towns. In religion they were somberly orthodox in their own various ways, clinging to an infallible Bible, as the Catholics clung to an infallible Church. Oxford-bred Matthew Arnold, who was for many years a government inspector of schools among these people, poured scorn upon their narrow, unlovely religious organizations, with their "jealousy of the Establishment, tea meetings, openings of chapels, sermons."

Between the Dissenters and the Catholics, in a kind of middle way (*via media*), was the Establishment, the Anglican Church, supported by the state, stiffly Tory in politics, representing the upper and middle classes of society and altogether the strongest religious organization in the British Empire. For what it was in early and middle Victorian times historians describe it as cold, conventional, worldly, steeped in self-satisfaction, spiritually deadened. Lytton Strachey in mordant phrases has pictured the Church and its parsons in the days before the Oxford Movement: "For many generations the Church of England had slept the sleep of the — comfortable, the sullen murmurings of dissent, the loud battle-cry of Revolution, had hardly disturbed her slumbers. Portly divines subscribed with a sigh or a smile to the Thirty-Nine Articles, sank quietly into easy livings, rode gaily to hounds of a morning as gentlemen should, and, as gentlemen should, carried their two bottles of an evening." For years the Establishment seemed to regard major social problems as outside its sphere of influence, and, accordingly, restricted its attention to individual charities rather than to the large impersonal sources of trouble. It scarcely touched the masses. The intellectual currents of the age swept past, while the Church remained aloof, "sleekly devout" (as Maurice said), "the child of regal and aristocratical selfishness and unprincipled tyranny" (as Dr. Arnold said, who, like Maurice, was a loyal Churchman). Up to the middle of our period the Anglican clergy, Morley correctly stated, "held education in the hollow of their hands." Oxford and Cambridge were virtually in the exclusive possession of the Church, since no student, up to the Act of 1854, could proceed to the bachelor's degree unless he subscribed to the Thirty-Nine Articles, and he could not even enter Oxford without such subscription; and without a university degree young men found it all but impossible to enter the learned professions. Seventeen years later (1871) another Act of Parliament at last removed all tests from scholarships, fellowships, and higher degrees, "except the theological fellowships and degrees in divinity." The great public schools, Eton, Harrow, and others, in spirit and control were also practically educational corporations of the Establishment. Thinking of these time-hallowed institutions, Matthew Arnold said in 1887: "English secondary education—a chaos when her Majesty's reign began—remains a chaos still, because the upper class amongst us do not want to be disturbed in their preponderance, or the middle class in their vulgarity."

The Anglican Church with all its prestige and power was a loose organization, sheltering under its wide and hospitable roof Christians of various degrees and shades of orthodoxy. There were the Evangelicals, or Low Church people, as they came to be called, who, Trevelyan says, "cared less about the Church as an institution than about the saving of souls." Influenced by the Wesleyan Methodism of an earlier day, they focussed their thought upon individual salvation and blessedness in the world to come, rather than upon social justice here; though Evangelicalism did produce great humanitarians, such as William Wilberforce and the seventh Earl of Shaftesbury. There was the Broad Church, so named because its members understood their theology broadly, not too narrowly and traditionally, and looked forward to the place of the Church in the modern world rather than backward to its place in the fourth and fifth centuries. It was friendly to the new, critical methods of biblical study. It sought to apply the teachings of Jesus and St. Paul to the problems of contemporary life and, in contrast to the Low Church, it stressed the love of God rather than the wickedness of man. Charles Kingsley and Frederick Denison Maurice, the founders of Christian Socialism, were Broad churchmen, as were Dr. Thomas Arnold and Arthur Penrhyn Stanley, Dean of Westminster, all of whom (especially Maurice) and many others acknowledge the influence of Coleridge, who stood for a national Church broad enough to care for the cultural and spiritual interests of all the people, and who believed, as he said, that Christianity was "not a theory, or a speculation; but a life;—not a philosophy of life, but a life and a living process." Another great English churchman, Dean Inge, has said that "the credit of awakening a social conscience in the Church of England belongs chiefly to the mid-Victorian Broad Church group headed by Charles Kingsley and Frederick Denison Maurice."

There was, finally, a third group that traced their ecclesiastical lineage to Archbishop Laud and other theologians of the seventeenth century, divines who "upheld the continuity of the Church of England with the primitive church" and who are known as High Church because they stressed "the ecclesiastical, liturgical, and sacerdotal aspects of Anglicanism." It was this section of the Church, particularly, that provoked the criticisms of Dr. Arnold and Maurice, who were revolted by the condescension and aristocratical aloofness of its clergy and the complacent worldliness of its laity. It was this section, too, that rising young liberals like John Morley, Frederic Harrison, and Leslie Stephen, and scientists like Tyndall and Huxley, had most in mind when they vigorously attacked the English Church as "the champion of intellectual bondage," as the "inveterate foe to new social hope and new scientific truth." Alarmed by the inertia and secularity within the Church and by this aggressive liberalism without, conditions which seemed to threaten universal infidelity, a company of young Oxford men, of whom John Henry Newman was the real leader, organized a counter-attack known as Tractarianism or, more commonly, the Oxford Movement (to which further reference is made in the critical introduction to Newman's prose). They wrote tracts and preached sermons, and thereby sought to arouse the Anglican clergy to a new sense of the Church as a divine institution, "the concrete representation of things invisible" (said Newman); and they succeeded in stirring up storms of controversy that swept the Establishment from end to end. Influenced slightly by the Romantic revival of medievalism of a previous generation, but influenced far more by their own independent theological and historical studies, they upheld, as Newman put the matter, "that primitive Christianity which was delivered for all time by the early teachers of the Church." Many professing

Christians, said Newman, in one of his parochial sermons at St. Mary's Church, Oxford, were so lukewarm that they "have no sense of the authority of religion as external to the mind." To him their Christianity was vague sentiment rather than a fixed belief in dogma, "the backbone of religion." The Tractarians, therefore, endeavored to revive a moribund church by a return to ancient traditional orthodoxy and ritualism. "Black gowns disappeared from the pulpits, choirs began to wear surplices and to turn to the east for the Creed; candles and crucifixes appeared on altars." The rank and file of Anglican laymen, tenaciously Protestant, were unmoved or hostile, and since, like their Queen, they instinctively recoiled "from the intricate ecstasies of High Anglicanism," they probably felt as did the diarist, Crabb Robinson, when in 1842 he wrote to his brother: "The Church as you are aware is now much more than *Religion* the subject of general interest." But when Newman in 1845 went into the Catholic Church he was followed by "an unrivalled band of recruits, principally clerical but not without a lay fraction," said Gladstone, the High Churchman, to whom the secession was "a conspicuous event of the first order in the Anglican religious history of a very remarkable time."

Nevertheless the tides of liberalism rose irresistibly both within and without the churches. From Germany, through Coleridge and his disciples and through others at later periods, there came the higher criticism of the Bible and the use of scientific, comparative, and historical methods in the study of religious documents and phenomena. In Germany the scriptures were being submitted "to the same rules of criticism" as were applied to secular records. Early narratives of the Old Testament were treated as myths and legends, while the human side of the New Testament was stressed and the supernatural side was rejected. Strauss's *Life of Jesus* (1835), translated by George Eliot in 1845, dismissed miracles, critically examined the contemporary backgrounds, and substituted an historical Jesus for the Christ of the theologians. In the sixties, in England, appeared a series of works that reflected in various degrees the spirit and method of this new criticism: *Essays and Reviews* (1860); Bishop Colenso's *Commentary on St. Paul's Epistle to the Romans* (1861) and *Critical Commentary on the Pentateuch* (1862-3); Seeley's *Ecce Homo* (1865), published anonymously; to which may be added Renan's *Vie de Jésus* (1863), translated and widely read in England. There followed scholarly studies in the Greek text of the New Testament, in St. Paul's Epistles, and in the Fathers of the early Church. The winds of controversy rose and orthodoxy seemed threatened with shipwreck. For many, belief in the plenary inspiration of the Bible and in traditional supernaturalism and theology was swept away, and their minds were tossed and troubled as they drifted out into strange seas of thought. Others retreated into a deeper dogmatism and a more inclusive ritualism. Still others, yielding to the "all-dissolving skepticism of the intellect in religious matters" and taking the empirical and social philosophy of John Stuart Mill and the new science as their inspirations, plus some strong tonic from the pages of Carlyle, found an outlet for their idealism in practical efforts to raise the standards of living for all members of society. Meanwhile many churchmen, clergy and laity alike, who remained loyal to the spirit if not to the letter of their faith, gradually enlarged their views, acquired tolerance, accepted the new methods of higher criticism, and gave increasing attention to problems of social welfare.

An even more powerful dissolvent of Victorian religious orthodoxy than the higher biblical criticism was the new science, to which reference has just been made. It is not possible for the student today, without the help of an historical imagination, resting upon a solid foundation of reading, to make real to himself the sweep and bitterness of the conflict between science and religious orthodoxy in Victorian days, especially from 1860 onwards. "There is not a creed which is not shaken," said Matthew Arnold in 1880, "not an accredited dogma which is not shown to be questionable, not a received tradition which does not threaten to dissolve. Our religion has materialized itself in the fact, in the supposed fact; it has attached its emotion to the fact, and now the fact is failing it."

intimations that nature's processes everywhere were fluid and not fixed and that species were not immutable; and Erasmus Darwin (1794) and Lamarck (1809) already had announced their belief in the inheritance of acquired characters. Then came (1844) Chamber's *Vestiges of the Natural History of Creation,* a book that provoked vast discussion and ran through twelve editions in twenty years; in which the anonymous author, beginning with the solar system, presented the view that all natural forms, organic as well as inorganic, were not the products of special creation but of a secular evolutionary process unfolding from lower to higher and culminating at last in man. Herbert Spencer in an article (1852) on the *Development of Hypothesis* and later in his *Principles of Psychology* (1855) expressed "the belief that life under all its forms has arisen by an unbroken evolution, and through the instrumentality of what are called natural forces." Thus the idea of mutability of species, or the development of living forms from other and simpler living forms, steadily gained ground, but no one had yet reached an explanation of the process, though Spencer had come close to one.

When Darwin went out on his famous voyage in the Beagle he too believed in the permanence of species. Happily he took with him a passionate interest in geology, intensified by Lyell's *Principles,* which he read while on his way. Before long the study of geological formations, of fossils, and of living animal forms began to bring up suggestive generalizations. "It was evident," he said, "that such facts as these, as well as many others, could only be explained on the supposition that species gradually became modified; and the subject haunted me." When he returned to England he began to collect facts "on a wholesale scale," particularly facts on domesticated animals and plants, and soon perceived, he said, "that selection was the keystone of man's success in making" useful varieties. "But how selection could be applied to organisms in a state of nature remained for some time a mystery to me." Then quite by chance he read Malthus on *Population* and "it at once struck me that under these circumstance (i.e. of struggle for existence) favorable variations would tend to be preserved, and unfavorable ones destroyed." For the next twenty-one years (1838-1859) Darwin worked on his theory, collecting and marshalling data and examining them from all sides in the light of the principle by which he believed they could be interpreted. In 1859 he published his epochal book, *The Origin of Species,* which Wallace described as "the crowning achievement of the nineteenth century." *

For many years Darwin and darwinism were attacked by clergy and scientists alike. Eminent men from both camps took up arms and fought against the new theory with arrogant dogmatism. Religious leaders found in darwinism "a brutal philosophy," "incompatible with the word of God," and altogether "a huge imposture": while most senior scientists the world over, in the years immediately following publication of *The Origin,* declined to accept Darwin's conclusions, until the perplexed but gentle spirit of the great man wrote to Hooker: "Nearly all men past a moderate age, either in actual years or in mind, are, I am fully convinced, incapable of looking at facts under a new point of view." But time brought its revenges and Darwin lived to see his theory, as Huxley said, "chiefly by his own efforts, irrefragably established in science, inseparably incorporated with the common thoughts of men."

Only expert scientists can properly describe the powerful impulse given to biological research by darwinism. Before the end of the century the flora and fauna of the earth, it would seem, came under the investigation of an army of trained observers, whose researches carried the light of knowledge ever farther into nature's mysteries. The new science, said Huxley, completely changed "the fundamental conceptions and aims of

---

* One of the most interesting circumstances in the history of science is the coincident experience of Alfred Russel Wallace, who, lying sick in a far-off island of the South Pacific (Ternate), read Malthus and then sketched his theory of natural selection, identical with Darwin's. Their two papers, first announcing the theory, were read in London, July 1, 1858.

the students of living nature.... Psychology, ethics, cosmology were stirred to their foundations"; a statement in part suggesting the influence of Victorian science, all of it, upon the conceptions and convictions of intelligent people everywhere. Its most immediate effect was upon religious thought. It undermined "belief in special creation" and in miracles, or the capricious supernatural interference with the laws of nature. For thousands of reflective minds naturalism now dethroned traditional supernaturalism. This meant, as we have seen, a prolonged and bitter conflict between science and religion; but as the period drew to its end it was increasingly recognized that the Bible interpreted life from one point of view, the spiritual and ethical, while science interpreted it from another, the physical, and that warfare was both senseless and futile.

Nevertheless the discoveries and conclusions of the new science brought despair to many and complete skepticism to others. Traditional beliefs upon which men and their fathers had long rested for consolation and hope could not be swept away without leaving wreckage behind. Agnosticism and materialism increased. In the sixteenth and seventeenth centuries the religious conflict was largely a conflict of faiths; in the nineteenth century it was a conflict between faith and no faith. And if the science of the older day took "from man and his world their importance in space," the science of the newer day "took from them their importance in time." Man and nature were now pushed back to beginnings that stretched to distances beyond the reach of the most daring imaginations. It seemed therefore more difficult than ever before for the intelligent individual when contemplating this "dusky spot," the peopled earth around him, ages old, and "the vast sun-clusters" drifting through the illimitable skies above him,—more difficult than ever not to be bowed down with a sense of his nothingness, a sense of the brevity of his puny existence.

But the healthy human mind recovers its lost balance and finds new reasons for believing in its importance when old reasons have failed. With the new science came a new and inspiring awareness of the unity of nature, a realization that no part of the vast panorama of forces, all under the reign of law, was alien from any other part. The atoms and the remotest galaxies were now found to be segments of the same whole, made of the same stuff, and finding their highest manifestations in man. And if that stuff was called matter and if matter, as Tyndall declared in his famous Belfast address (1874), contained "the promise and potency of all terrestrial life," then matter, as Huxley wrote in essays no less famous, was basically as mysterious as spirit. Both, as man experiences them in himself, while inter-dependent, elude final analysis, and if the one, which Huxley preferred to call self-consciousness, is the surest of all facts, the other is not matter as matter "is commonly understood." So far the philosophical scientists. To the religious mind the unity of nature, the omnipresence of its laws, and its mysterious unfathomable potencies broke down the traditional antithesis not only between nature and man but also between the natural and the supernatural, and gave new and deeper meaning to the conception of an imminent deity, whose dwelling is at once in the light of setting suns and in the mind of man,

> A motion and a spirit, that impels
> All thinking things, all objects of all thought,
> And rolls through all things.

The new science, in reality, wrought transformations in the entire mental framework of Victorians and their successors. The effect was revolutionary not in religion alone but in every field of thought unexceptionally. Men of the Romantic period, passionately moved by events in France, had thought of a new society that should come about suddenly, catastrophically, "in England's green and pleasant land." So at first thought Wordsworth and Coleridge; so thought Godwin and Shelley. The Victorians, too, believed in change; the idea of progress was their "secular faith," as Dean Inge has observed. But for them, in consequence of the new geology and the new biology, change was seen as evolutionary, the slow result of mighty onward forces whose origins were hidden in a remote past that had to be explored before directions for the future could confidently be charted. "Every modification of society," said Morley, "is one of the slow growths of time.... Where organic growths are concerned, patience is the sovereign law."

From the new point of view nothing was final, nothing absolute, all was relative; society was infinitely complex and no one formula could explain everything; masses of fact must be weighed and assessed before generalizations and procedures would be warranted. Ineluctably in this aspect of things the spirit of optimism came to be pervasive. The new science gave the Victorians perspective in their outlook; man had come so far through struggle—he would go farther and higher. Herbert Spencer reflected this thought, and Darwin, in his conclusion to *The Origin,* expressed it in words that must appear unusual from a mind so characteristically reserved and cautious: "Hence we may look," he said, weighing the lessons of the past, "with some confidence to a secure future of equally inappreciable length. And as natural selection works solely by and for the good of each being, all corporeal and mental endowments will tend to progress toward perfection." Huxley, on the contrary, could not see in evolution "a constant tendency to increased perfection." The cosmic process is indifferent to progress; its methods are methods of the ape and tiger; for it there must be substituted the ethical process, which "in place of ruthless self-assertion, demands self-restraint." Thus the progress of civilization means continuous interference with the cosmic process, whereby man, if actuated by right ideals, may bring about justice, order, and love in human society and so "modify the conditions of existence for a period longer than now covered by history." And, concludes Huxley, "much may be done to change the nature of man himself." But since (as Huxley recognized) the ethical process is itself a human creation and thus, like all else in man, a product of nature and nature's evolutionary method, one may say that those Victorians were not mistaken who assumed that the survival of the fittest in the struggle for existence at long last must mean the survival of the ethically strongest and best.

———————

Thus the Victorian Era witnessed "revolutions of thought and practice" unparalleled in the previous history of mankind. Professor Gilbert Murray, in the Romanes Lecture for 1935, at Oxford, looking back to the well-remembered time of the 'seventies and 'eighties of the nineteenth century, notes the *order* then as contrasted with the *chaos* now: There was "an approximate unanimity among reasonable educated people about the fundamentals of life. We had an agreed cosmology: we accepted the nebular hypothesis and the doctrine of evolution. We even saw in it a vista of infinite hope for mankind, such as suited our general cheerfulness of outlook. We had a generally agreed system of ethics.... There was another faith—a profound belief in the value and rightness of Western Civilization with its characteristic attributes—its faith in progress, its liberalized Christianity, its humanitarian ethics, its free democratic institutions, its common sense, its obedience to law, its triumphs of applied science, and its vast and ever-increasing wealth. To men of my youth Western, and especially British, civilization was simply the right road of human progress."

This is a candid and true picture of Great Britain as it must have looked in the 'eighties and 'nineties to young men of Professor Murray's class. The England of that day was the conscious center of a vast and expanding Empire, preeminently powerful and prosperous, an England transformed from the England of 1837 and destined to still further changes, some of them ominous. The tempo of life, urban life especially, was greatly accelerated. The ways of making money multiplied, and the new-rich increased in numbers and influence. Old severities and rigidities began to disappear even before the aging Victoria had faded from the scene. Wealth brought more luxury, more leisure, more gaiety, more idleness and parasitism. The portals of London palaces of the older aristocracy opened to members of the opulent middle classes and to artists as well, particularly if their gifts were well supported with wit and sophistication, as was true of Whistler, Oscar Wilde and others of their kind. The world of this later Victorian period comes back to us, says the social historian, quite accurately, from the plays of Pinero, Henry Arthur Jones, and Oscar Wilde; and he finds, too, many suggestions of the time in the famous Gilbert and Sullivan operas which were played before crowded audiences night after night: "It is the music," he says, "the dialogue, of a society that feels itself too secure to be serious or angry or troubled about anything."

But this brilliant urban life of later Victorian England, the flower or the froth of wealth and leisure, was only one part, relatively a small part, of the whole. Commerce and industry, characteristically aggressive, ruthless, and self-centered, had built up a civilization from which beauty seemed to have vanished, alike from cities and countrysides. "The nineteenth century," says Dean Inge, "with its marvels of applied science, has produced the ugliest of all civilizations." "The Age of Victoria," echoes Lytton Strachey, "was, somehow or other, unaesthetic to its marrow-bones." "Neither machine industry nor evangelical religion," says the historian, Trevelyan, "had any use for art and beauty which was despised as effeminate by the makers of the great factory towns of the North." Soames Forsyte, the man of property, in Galsworthy's novel, *The Forsyte Saga*, a typical philistine of the period, enjoyed his pictures not for their aesthetic but for their cash value. Lovers of beauty, minds of refined sensibility were not slow to express their horror of the unsightliness which the new industrialism left in its wake. They were among the first and most violent anti-Victorians. Ruskin had said of the Crystal Palace of 1851 that it "was built in order to exhibit the paltry arts of our fashionable luxury"; and much later he cried out: "Think what it is for men of sensitive faculty to live in such a city as London is now!" His descriptions, in the 'eighties, of the hideousness of contemporary civilization are, as his readers well know, often clothed in the lurid language of the professional pamphleteer, reminding one of the intemperate outbursts of Milton and Burke in their moments of overheated wrath. "The leading passion of my life," William Morris wrote in 1894, "has been and is hatred of modern civilization, ... its eyeless vulgarity, which has destroyed art." "Man's instinct for beauty," said Arnold in 1882, "has been maltreated and starved."

Beyond question ugliness was rampant and unashamed. Houses of prosperous philistines, externally and internally, may have been spacious and comfortable, but they were not lovely. Rooms were crowded with miscellaneous objects which the occupants doubtless called art but which persons of taste, then as now, have called "junk." The massive horsehair sofas and chairs, the ubiquitous antimacassars, the heavy mahogany wardrobes, the corner whatnots loaded with useless absurdities, these and much else probably sustained a sense of solidity and comfort but never of beauty. It was a day of imitations, too, when wallpaper was made to look like marble, wood like bronze, and when furniture legs were carved to resemble flowers and animals and nearly everything was fashioned to appear like something else. For an object to be showy, pretentious, and expensive was enough to suit the unintelligent liking of the new rich.

In such a world art—whose function is to add beauty and significance to man's daily life—had no place. It withdrew to build its own "shadowy isles of bliss" apart. Artists became escapists or rebels, or both. Morris, for example, who could not, as he said, "dissociate art from morality, politics, and religion," and who saw that it was sickening "under selfishness and luxury," was first an escapist and later a revolutionary rebel. For others it was quite enough to retire into their private imaginative towers of ivory above "the roar of machinery and the bustle about wealth," like Morris's friend, the painter, Burne-Jones, to whom a picture meant, he said, "a beautiful romantic dream of something that never was, never will be—in a light better than any light that ever shone—in a land no one can define or remember, only desire—and the forms divinely beautiful."

The story of art's refusal to traffic with Victorian philistinism, particularly in the later decades, is too long and complicated to tell in a general introduction. A few reminders and comments must suffice. The Oxford Movement was itself in part a retreat from the mounting ugliness of the contemporary scene. Undoubtedly in the Gothic churches, old and new, the pageantry of the service, the music, the painted and storied windows, the soaring arches drew many worshippers whose hunger for beauty was satisfied by these things. The revival of medievalism, moreover, which had owed much to the earlier romanticism of Scott, Coleridge, and Keats, and to other influences farther back, was immensely quickened not only by the Oxford Movement, but by Ruskin, Morris, the great architect Augustus Welby Pugin, and by the Pre-Raphaelites; and medievalism, thus broadly considered, gave a powerful momentum to the flight of art and artists from the oppressive materialism of an industrial epoch. Ruskin and Morris, we know, were drawn to Gothic for reasons other than narrowly aesthetic, but its beauty alone evoked from them repeated outbursts of lyrical prose. Pugin, a professional architect and a "consummate Gothicist," who "saw the middle ages as a period of pageantry and color," probably did more by his buildings and his writings to revive the glory of Gothic than any other man in the Victorian period. Under the leadership of Rossetti the Pre-Raphaelites, disgusted with the sentimentalism and sterile conventionalism of much Victorian art, and even more with the increasing vulgarity of the world about them, turned for inspiration mainly to the Middle Ages, and painted poetic pictures and wrote pictorial poetry that pointed the way straight to the ivory tower and the new aestheticism.

"If Rossetti was a subconscious influence, and perhaps the most powerful of all, we looked consciously to Pater for our philosophy," said William Butler Yeats, when speaking of the young poets of the 'nineties, members of the Rhymers Club, who foregathered for a time at the Cheshire Cheese, famous old London inn. Pater, however, was never in the truest sense an "aesthete," since for him as for Plato aesthetics, basically and characteristically, was "ever in close connection with ethics"; but he had, like his Gaston de Latour, "a sober taste for delicate things" and, as he thought scholars and cultivated people should do, he looked upon art as "a refuge, a sort of cloistral refuge, from a certain vulgarity in the actual world." And when he expressed his views in extreme and somewhat ambiguous language, as he sometimes did, particularly in the Conclusion to his *Renaissance,* Pater became the hierophant of the aesthetes, to whom (notably to one of their most brilliant and conspicuous exemplars, Oscar Wilde) art was more real the farther it retreated from a colorless and confused workaday world. (Though it should be said that these young men took their direction far more from French influences than from Pater or the Pre-Raphaelites.) "Art," said Whistler, "is selfishly occupied with her own perfection only." "Art," echoed Wilde, "has no influence upon action.... (It is) simply a method of procuring extraordinary sensations." Upon such principles the descent was easy from art to artifice, to the "purple patch, preciosity, epigram, paradox and conceit," to "elaborate ingenuities" and trivialities, and finally to extreme or unnatural indulgences in sensual excitement,—in short, to decadence, "a spiritual and moral perversity," as Arthur Symons pronounced it. Thus a movement which to many lovers of the beautiful had meant no more than a not unnatural revolt and retreat ended for a brilliant few in absurdity and abnormality. An art completely severed from the everyday concerns of men is in danger of death, for it rarely escapes internal corruption.

But this aestheticism, whether normal or abnormal, natural or artificial, had no effect upon "the solid kind of Briton," to whom, says the sober historian, even the work of the Pre-Raphaelites "was maundering and unhealthy"; and to whom, if he knew anything about them at all, the art and artists of the decadence—*The Yellow Book, The Savoy,* the drawings of Aubrey Beardsley, and the paradoxes and lurid passions of Oscar Wilde—were disgusting and contemptible, only fortifying his faith in his own respectability and way of life. For he was at once the complacent witness and producer of Britain's growing prosperity during these closing decades of the century. Interruptions of material advance in the form of bad harvests or labor troubles were relatively temporary—they did not stay the forward march. New gods of progress were electricity, the motor car, and wireless; communications encircled the earth; British capital investments abroad steadily increased, though competition for world markets as steadily stiffened; the boundaries of empire expanded and its resources multiplied. The solid Briton put his energy and interest into these things, not into anything so trivial and useless to him as art.

The skies above, however, were not always cloudless. Now as before storms came up, often darker and more threatening than ever to those whose eyes could read the signs of the times. William Morris was not alone in thinking, as he said, that "the fabric of society has done its work, and is going to change into something else." Luxury increased, but so did poverty and unemployment, with their inevitable accompaniments of "despair, disease, and filth," as Frederic Harrison saw the social situation in 1882. Masses of people continued to be drawn to the cities from the countrysides, swelling slum districts into plague-spots, where the worst of diseases of modern industrialized society pullulated and festered. Charles Booth, in his monumental study of the London poor (1887-92) "found over thirty per cent of the people of London living in a state of poverty." Conditions were similar in other large industrial centers. "It is simply impossible," wrote Froude (1885), "that the English men and women of the future generations can equal or approach the famous race that has overspread the globe, if they are to be bred in towns such as Birmingham and Glasgow now are, and to rear their families under the conditions which now prevail in these places. Morally and physically they must and will decline." A minority report of the Royal Commission on Labor (1885) stated that "notwithstanding a great increase in national wealth, whole sections of the population ... are unable to obtain a subsistence compatible with health or efficiency. ... Of all who survive to the age of seventy, one out of every three is believed to be in receipt of poor relief."

Agitation against these social diseases (for they were increasingly recognized as such) intensified and spread, and strikes were frequent, the most important being the great London Dock Strike in 1889, involving thousands of casual workers and awakening widespread sympathy and help among civilians generally. Demonstrations were staged recurrently in the form of giant mass meetings in London and smaller meetings elsewhere, and in a steady stream of information and discussion from the daily press, from periodicals, special pamphlets and party magazines. Government, itself, in its handling of domestic problems gave more attention to the "social question" than to all others, excepting only (for part of the period) Gladstone's political activity for Irish Home Rule.

While the majority of church members continued to look "upon the poor as objects for compassion and benevolence," as Cardinal Newman confessed that he had always done, a growing number became actively interested in social welfare. There had been the Christian Socialism of Maurice, Kingsley and Ludlow, which was started in 1848 and ran for some six years, and which owed much to the inspiration of Coleridge and Carlyle. An individualist effort it was, to Christianize society without change in its basic structure and to socialize Christianity,—"brotherhood in heart and fellowship in work," as Maurice had declared. Its influence lived in Friendly Societies, sanitary reforms, better housing, and especially in the Working Men's College, established in London in 1854, where Ruskin taught drawing classes until 1860 and where Ford Madox Brown, Kingsley and others participated.

But religious humanitarianism in the 'eighties and 'nineties was far more extensive and influential than was this earlier pioneering movement, since it was better organized, better informed, better supported. The Salvation Army, created in 1878 by William Booth for conversion of the outcast, soon realized the interdependence of character and environment, and gave its attention to social work, setting up shelters and food depots for the thousands of casuals that now drifted about in the darkest areas of London and other cities, a menace to health and safety. University settlements came into being as concrete expressions of the claim of the poor and underprivileged "upon university men for their

personal attention and help." Arnold Toynbee, an Oxford man, disciple of the eminent philosopher, T. H. Green, and one of Ruskin's Hinksey diggers (a quixotic, undergraduate experiment in roadmaking), led the way for several years and inspired other university men by his zealous activities as lecturer and teacher among the unfortunates of East London. Following his untimely death, Canon Barnett in 1884 founded Toynbee Hall, the first of university settlements. In the same year Canon Scott Holland established Oxford House and initiated the organization of the Christian Social Union, the announced object of which was "without taking up any formal propaganda to urge upon the Church the necessity of careful and painstaking study of social questions." These and other settlements and missions made no attempt to alter the underlying structure of society, but rather sought to ameliorate the conditions of the underprivileged in their places and to bring to them some of the benefits of education and culture.

Unquestionably such multiplying humanitarian activities did much direct good for the poor and probably even more indirect good by way of arousing public concern in the masses of distress and corruption incident to a modern industrialized society. Nevertheless they were peripheral in their effects, not central. What was wanted, as Morris said, were "real social changes." And these to him and to others meant socialism. The first British socialist was Robert Owen who, in pre-Victorian days, had dreamed of universal economic and social equality, but whose intolerant and uncompromising temper unfitted him to be an active agent even in half-way political reforms, to say nothing of becoming a builder of earthly paradises; though his teachings did tell heavily upon many leading Chartists and upon the beginnings of trade unionism.

Socialism as a political movement, with a program and a militant following, first came with the Democratic Federation, founded in 1881 by H. N. Hyndman, a Marxist. "It is not too much to say," wrote Hyndman, "that Marx found Socialism a chaos of unco-ordinated ideas, bootless sentiment and utopian experiment, and placed it finally upon a scientific basis." The Democratic Federation (very soon to be called the Social Democratic Federation) was revolutionary in its ideals, aiming at the overthrow of capitalist society, the substitution of "ordered co-operation" in place of "anarchical competition" (the words are Hyndman's), and "the collective ownership of the means of production." For a time Morris and G. B. Shaw were members. Morris, soon disillusioned and disgusted over factional strife, jealousies and palliative measures, and convinced of the danger of revolt without responsible leadership, withdrew with others to form, in 1884, the Socialist League, in which he advocated "education towards revolution." His vision of a better world, the vision of a man of genius, he accurately described as "socialism seen through the eyes of an artist," a socialism which still quickens the superiority complex in uninformed minds. Shaw left the Social Democratic Federation in 1884 to join the Fabians, a company of recently organized middleclass intellectuals of ultraradical temper, keen to investigate social problems systematically. The Fabians, like the S. D. F.'s, were revolutionary at first: "All Fabians and Social Democrats alike," Shaw tells us, "said freely that as gunpowder had destroyed the feudal system, so the capitalist system could not long survive the invention of dynamite.... We thought that the statement about gunpowder was historically true, and that it would do the capitalists good to remind them of it." Sidney Webb soon joined the new society, and a little later came his wife, the former Beatrice Potter. Under their leadership the Fabians became investigators and analysts of social phenomena, and soon recognized that the new order must be progressively realized through peaceful permeation and political action, step by step; though their ultimate objective, in the words of Webb, was to be "the collective ownership and democratic control of the economic resources of the community."

The great city of London in those early 'eighties was seething with new ideas, stirred up by various middleclass groups, composed mostly of young men. Their gods were Mill and Darwin, Tyndall, Huxley, and Spencer. They had read Carlyle, Ruskin, and Shelley; they knew the socialism of Owen; they listened to the lectures of the fiery

American, Henry George, protagonist of the single tax and social reform; they plunged into courses of economic study and toiled through the pages of Marx's *Capital*, unavailable in English until 1886; they scorned orthodoxy and conservative conventionality; and they poured out a steady stream of leaflets, tracts, articles and essays—all meant to keep the public, especially the public of workers (thousands of whom were now readers), informed on new laws and movements or anything that had to do with the extension of democratic control. Liberal and conservative governments alike reflected the new spirit. Discussion of social issues in Parliament was well-nigh paramount at times and many new laws were passed which steadily broadened the areas of state interference and regulation, areas long regarded as belonging to private interests exclusively. "The path of legislative progress in England has been for years, and must continue to be, distinctly Socialistic," wrote Joseph Chamberlain in 1885; and in 1889 Sir William Harcourt, a leading Liberal, exclaimed: "We are all Socialists now." Such language from these statesmen was general rather than specific, meaning mostly an extension of government control and limited collectivism—i.e., municipal ownership of parks, museums, libraries, hospitals, schools, water, gas, transportation; it did not mean complete economic collectivism and social equality in a classless society, whether socialist or communist.

The workers themselves, spurred on by legislative reforms, by the penetration of middleclass ideas (mostly Fabian), and even more by the self-enlightenment of their own leaders, were becoming convinced that their road to ultimate goals was not by way of isolated experiments in collective control, but by their own direct political action according to constitutional procedures. " 'By us and not for us,' must be their motto," said Morris. After the collapse of Chartism they had turned from political agitation to the building up of their own associations, until at the Trade Union Congress in 1880 the delegates represented some 600,000 members. By 1892 union membership counted more than a million and a half men, composed mostly of skilled workers. Following the London Dock Strike in 1889 casual laborers began to organize in masses. Women, too, were unionized, so that before the end of the Victorian era the workers knew that they were a power in the land. "Our ideal is a co-operative commonwealth," said the leaders, Tom Mann and Ben Tillett. As far back as 1879 there had been thirteen labor candidates for election to the House of Commons, of whom two were returned. In 1880 a third member was chosen; in 1885, eight more; in 1892 five others, including two socialists, Kier Hardie and John Burns. The next year, 1893, the Independent Labor Party was formed "with the object (as it said) of securing collective ownership of all the means of production, distribution, and exchange, by means of direct Labor representation in Parliament and on local authorities." "The spirit of social change and upheaval" was in the air, as a historian of the period soberly affirms. Conceptions of human welfare steadily broadened. Defeats and setbacks were accepted as temporary, while the eyes of leaders remained fixed upon a future day when their ideals of social justice should be realized through the orderly expression of a people's will. British individualism led by British aristocracy was still powerful—it had brought Britain to the summit of world supremacy; but British collectivism led by British democracy had come a long way since 1832 and was destined to go further in the coming century.

Meantime in these last two decades of social turmoil and progress at home the Empire entered upon an era of vast territorial expansion. When Disraeli had become Prime Minister in 1874 he announced a policy of imperial consolidation, and in 1875 sent the Prince of Wales on a trip through India and in the next year made Victoria Empress of that great sub-continent. In succeeding years Britain gained control of the entire valley of the Nile to its sources, of the Malay Peninsula, and of "a large section of New Guinea ...and more than one hundred islands in the Pacific." Canada, Australia, and New Zealand became consolidated, self-governing units of the Empire within the Victorian period, and by the end of it were about to proceed to the next step—membership in the British Commonwealth of Nations. Australia and New Zealand, indeed, were ready, says

the historian (Muir) "for those bold and far-reaching experiments in State Socialism which were to attract the attention of the world in the next period." In South Africa colonies had first been established by the British during the war against Napoleon, when Britain took over the Dutch settlements then under French control. Friction and clashes with the natives and Boers (descendants of Dutch settlers) were recurrent for years. Following the discovery of diamonds (1867-8) and later of gold (1884) in the Transvaal tens of thousands of Britishers (English, Scotch, Australian) crowded in, built cities, and began to clamor for political rights, which were denied them by the independent, stubborn Boers, an agricultural people profoundly alarmed by this sudden invasion of detestable modernism. British aggressiveness, inspired by Chamberlain at home and by Cecil Rhodes in South Africa, finally provoked a conflict of arms as the means of settlement. It was not until after the Boer War (1899-1902) that the colonies were brought together into the unity of South Africa, and, later still, into the British Commonwealth of Nations. But before the Queen passed away she saw herself sovereign of the greatest world state in history: "Its 12,000,000 square miles formed nearly one quarter of the world's area, and its 400,000,000 inhabitants nearly one quarter of the world's population."

With the death of Victoria (January 22, 1901) a great age came to an end. Its "calm, complacent, self-satisfied tranquillities" had not yet "exploded into the world convulsions and wars of the terrible twentieth century," to use the vivid words of Winston Churchill. In contrast with the storms that have swept and wasted the earth in our time, movements and men in the Victorian age are bound to appear tranquil and complacent. As we have seen, it was a period of unbroken internal peace and nearly unbroken material prosperity, when the aristocracy and plutocracy finally came to deserve the rebuke of Kipling in his great *Recessional* ode, following the display of pride and pageantry during the Diamond Jubilee. But the poet's solemn warning was after all but an echo of what most of the greater Victorian prose writers had been saying for sixty years. Always above "the tumult and the shouting," while some spoke out passionately against the evil and the ugliness of the age, others dispassionately explored and interpreted its movements in every important field of thought. More than all else they sought to fix the minds of their readers upon the relatively constant ideals of truth, beauty, justice, and goodwill in the midst of momentous and rapid change. The sum-total of their influence upon their contemporaries no man can measure, but it was indubitably immense. And since as masters of style they dealt with the transformations and issues of a period that laid the foundations of our own, students of the convulsed twentieth century will discover in their writings light and direction along the steep road to a better day.

VICTORIAN PROSE

THOMAS CARLYLE

CHRONOLOGY AND INTRODUCTION

1795 Born December 4, at Ecclefechan, Annandale, Scotland.
1809–14 Student at University of Edinburgh.
1814–18 Teacher at Annan and at Kirkcaldy.
1823–25 *Life of Schiller.*
1824 Translation of Goethe's *Wilhelm Meister's Apprenticeship.*
1827 *German Romance,* 4 vols., including *Wilhelm Meister's Travels.*
1828 Settled at Craigenputtock.
1829 *Signs of the Times.*
1831 *Characteristics.*
1833–38 *Sartor Resartus* (in *Frasers' Magazine*) 1833–34; 1st separate ed., Boston, 1835; 1st British ed., 1838.
1834 Removed to London.

1837 *The French Revolution,* 3 vols.
1839 *Critical and Miscellaneous Essays,* 4 vols.; *Chartism.*
1841 *Heroes and Hero-Worship.*
1843 *Past and Present.*
1845 *Oliver Cromwell's Letters and Speeches,* 2 vols.
1850 *Latter-Day Pamphlets.*
1851 *Life of Sterling.*
1856–58 First collected edition of *Works,* 16 vols.
1858–65 *History of Friedrich II of Prussia,* 6 vols.
1875 *The Early Kings of Norway.*
1881 Died, February 4.

From the field of letters the voice that carried farthest and meant most to reflective British readers of 1845-1865 was the voice of Carlyle. In that time of ferment and change, when old ways and landmarks were being swept away before an advancing tide of new thought in politics, industry, science, and religion, Carlyle delivered a message to troubled minds, which, if not completely convincing, was tremendously inspiring. It fired men, more especially young men, with courage and confidence. They saw in him a prophet who spoke out of the depths of a great experience and a great conviction, and who spoke powerfully. John Stuart Mill, Dickens, Ruskin, Tennyson, Browning, Arnold, William Morris, Leslie Stephen, Froude, Huxley, Tyndall, George Meredith were conspicuous among the many who acknowledged the influence of the sage of Chelsea; some of them as disciples sat at his feet. Emerson, temporarily disillusioned and depressed, came over from Boston as early as 1833 to see Carlyle and went away with impressions that were afterward deepened and fixed through forty years of friendship. When word of his death in 1881 reached America, Walt Whitman heard it and went out under the stars to meditate upon the passing of a great man, and later recorded some of his reflections: "The way to test how much he has left his country," Walt wrote, "were to consider, or try to consider the resultant *ensemble* of the last fifty years, as existing today, *but with Carlyle left out.* It would be like an army with no artillery."

The story of Carlyle's rise to fame has been called "the epic of a soul." It is the record of fairly titanic struggles through many years to succeed as a man of letters in the face of almost overwhelming obstacles, both of inward nature and outward circumstance. More than anything else in the world he wanted to live by writing. "If a man taste the magic cup of literature," he said, "he must drink of it forever, though bitter ingredients enough be mixed with the liquor." He was forty-two before he had confidence that he could live by his pen. Born of humble parentage in a stonemason's cottage, educated only by means of the most rigid economies, intended for the ministry by his pious father and mother, Carlyle at nineteen completed his course at the University of Edinburgh with the conviction that he never could preach the orthodox gospel he had been taught at home. His love for that home was perhaps the deepest passion of his life, but his mind was already voyaging through strange seas of thought in search of new havens. For some fourteen years he tried one experiment in living after another, sometimes in desperate mood prompting suicide. The record of his struggles is dramatically set down in the middle book of *Sartor.* Carlyle's letters and reminiscences vividly authenticate the story, but even these do not so impress us as do the burning pages of *The Everlasting No, The Centre of Indifference,* and *The Everlasting Yea.*

The "conversion" came and light broke through, often a lurid light but infinitely better than

3

darkness. He had begun to learn German, and soon he was reporting of the new heaven and new earth that Goethe and Schiller had revealed to him. Goethe became Carlyle's first hero. "The sight of such a man was to me a Gospel of Gospels, and did, literally, I believe, save me from destruction outward and inward." He had already tried his hand at various kinds of writing, but he now enthusiastically began to interpret German literature to English readers, through the medium of biography, translation, and critical essay. In 1826 he married Jane Welsh, and the next year Jeffrey admitted him to the pages of the *Edinburgh Review* with a short article on Jean Paul Richter.

Immensely heartened and longing for a quiet corner in which he might think and write, Carlyle took his wife to Craigenputtock, a lonely farmstead about sixteen miles from Dumfries: "our Patmos, where Silence reigns supreme." Here he did some of his best work, including *Sartor Resartus* and the great essays on Goethe, Burns, Voltaire, and here he began studies in the period of the French Revolution. But he had not yet succeeded financially. His material livelihood was still in the balance. At last in 1834 Carlyle resolved to make one more attempt with an original book, the history of the French Revolution. If he failed he "resolved to give up the game, abandon literature, buy spade and rifle, and make for the backwoods of America."

He moved to London where materials were accessible, and he grimly settled down to his task. When the first volume was completed he loaned the manuscript to John Stuart Mill, who in turn loaned it to his friend, Mrs. Taylor. After an evening's reading, she left the loose sheets on a table and retired. The next morning a servant, thinking them waste paper, threw them into the grate where all but three or four pages went up in flame and smoke. It was a tragic moment for Carlyle. But his great character rose to the situation: "I will not quit the game while faculty is given me to try playing." Nearly two years later, in January 1837, he finished the work and before closing the door behind him as he was about to go forth on one of his nocturnal walks, he said to Mrs. Carlyle: "I know not whether this book is worth anything, nor what the world will do with it, misdo, or entirely forbear to do, as is likeliest; but this I could tell the world: You have not had for a hundred years any book that comes more direct and flamingly from the heart of a living man. Do what you like with it, You." The *History* established Carlyle's reputation, and for the rest of his long life, he went on writing, until the pen dropped from his fingers on account of the palsy of old age.

A few ideas, a highly individual temperament, and a profound sincerity underlie his voluminous work. From the Germans, mainly Kant, Fichte, and Goethe, he learned to be a transcendentalist and to think of all material things as phenomena, or manifestations of an invisible reality which is spiritual. But temperament played a larger part in this conclusion than speculation, for Carlyle was by nature one to whom this solid-seeming world and all its shows appeared but an insubstantial pageant, "a temporary flame-image of the Eternal." The most Dantesque figure of the modern age, to whom "gloom clung like a shadow," he stood, as it were, on the edge of deep eternities, peering through the mists of the past and the present for authentic intimations of a reality surer than fading matter or vanishing time. This he found, as did Browning, in God and the soul of man. This was what he called the "Dynamics" of life.

Fortified with this essentially simple old gospel, he confronted the world around him and saw it in the grasp of "mechanics," a word that for him summed up all the evils of his day—Materialism, Mammonism, Dilettantism, Utilitarianism, and *Laissez-faire*—or the belief that society could be saved by contrivances, arrangements, comforts, and luxuries alone, if government would only keep its hands off. To Carlyle this was the creed of the devil and threatened the destruction of the social order. In democracy as the panacea of the hour he had no faith, for the masses in the mid-Victorian period were densely ignorant and if given the franchise would, he thought, only be tools of windy parliamentary stump-orators. The poverty and misery of the populace wrung his heart ("I found that personal sympathy with suffering lay at the root of all his thoughts," says Froude); but ignorant toilers who might be trusted to rebel if oppression went too far must not be trusted to rule. Carlyle had no clear vision of the gradual elevation of the workers by education, by increased social responsibility, and by resultant collective effort,—forces which count so much in the democracy of the twentieth century. But he did glimpse these things in clairvoyant moments and made more practical suggestions for reform than many of his readers have been aware of or have been willing to admit.

His sovereign remedies were heroes, hero-worship, and work. The Carlylean hero in a day of dictators has been severely condemned, and it must be admitted that, as Carlyle grew older and his fears for the future multiplied, his hero began to resemble a Hohenzollern drill-sergeant whose duty it was to drive men into battle. It must be admitted, too, that he never clearly told us how to find our heroes, although no one else has succeeded where he failed. But he insisted that governments and industries must be directed by an aristocracy of talent, by leaders whose superior powers of courage, sincerity, vision, management, service, are "Forces of Nature," to be used for the good of the people, not for self-aggrandizement. Carlyle's hero is neither Nietzsche's, with his "will to power," nor Stendhal's, with his "lust for power"; nor is he Shaw's Superman, an incarnation of the "egotistical sublime." Least of all would Carlyle have recognized a Mussolini or a Hitler as hero. The Carlylean hero is the friend and servant of his fellow men. To find him and to place him at the top is the supreme responsibility of every member of society, a responsibility that may not be fulfilled "for centuries," or until men, as true workers at their appointed tasks, have acquired "an eye for talent," and, in the words of William James, have learned "to know a good man when they see him." Prophetically envisaging beyond the stormy present a future society of educated and contented toilers under the guidance of wise leaders, Carlyle for that far day did not fear even democracy and the ballot.

The style in which he clothed this message was a rock of offence to many of his readers, more particularly earlier readers who were accustomed to the regularities and elegancies of Georgian prose (in which Carlyle composed his own first work). To some of them like Jeffrey, it was a "gibberish," mainly of German origin. To others, like Macaulay, it was the language of a mystagogue, the "unknown tongue" of a fanatic. It really was none of these things, but rather the speech of a man tremendously in earnest, writing as he talked, with an extraordinary command of diction, metaphor, allusion, and an intense passion for the palpable and colorful concrete. In power of graphic description and portraiture, whether of battle, human incident, or distinguished personality, Carlyle has no superior in English. Moreover, the energy of his utterance, especially in such a work as *The French Revolution*, is the energy of a Titan. There is also his humor, "his mountain mirth," as Emerson called it; for we are not to forget that the wrath of the sage often ended in explosions of laughter over his own extravagances, proving after all that he had more fellowship with Rabelais than with Swift.

Whether we think of his style or his message, Carlyle is the Norse Thor, wielding his hammer and shaking the earth with his tread. Better still, he is our modern Lear let loose "in the center of the world-whirlwind" and calling on the heavens to bring down vengeance upon evildoers.

SIGNS OF THE TIMES

It is no very good symptom either of nations or individuals, that they deal much in vaticination. Happy men are full of the present, for its bounty suffices them; and wise men also, for its duties engage them. Our grand business undoubtedly is, not to *see* what lies dimly at a distance, but to *do* what lies clearly at hand.

Know'st thou *Yesterday*, its aim and reason;
Work'st thou well *Today*, for worthy things?
Calmly wait the *Morrow's* hidden season,
Need'st not fear what hap soe'er it brings.

But man's "large discourse of reason" *will* look "before and after"; and, impatient of the "ignorant present time," will indulge in anticipation far more than profits him. Seldom can the unhappy be persuaded that the evil of the day is sufficient for it; and the ambitious will not be content with present splendour, but paints yet more glorious triumphs, on the cloud-curtain of the future.

The case, however, is still worse with nations. For here the prophets are not one, but many; and each incites and confirms the other; so that the fatidical fury spreads wider and wider, till at last even Saul must join in it. For there is still a real magic in the action and reaction of minds on one another. The casual deliration of a few becomes, by this mysterious reverberation, 10 the frenzy of many; men lose the use, not only of their understandings, but of their bodily senses; while the most obdurate unbelieving hearts melt, like the rest, in the furnace where all are cast as victims and as fuel. It is grievous to think, that this noble omnipotence of Sympathy has been so rarely the Aaron's-rod of Truth and Virtue, and so often the Enchanter's-rod of Wickedness and Folly! No solitary miscreant, 20 scarcely any solitary maniac, would venture on such actions and imaginations, as large communities of sane men have, in such circumstances, entertained as sound wisdom. Witness long scenes of the French Revolution, in these late times! Levity is no protection against such visitations, nor the utmost earnestness of character. The New-England Puritan burns witches, wrestles for months with the horrors of Satan's invisible world, and all ghastly phantasms, the daily and hourly precursors of the Last Day; then suddenly bethinks him that he is frantic, weeps bitterly, prays contritely, and the history of that gloomy season lies behind him like a frightful dream.

Old England too has had her share of such frenzies and panics; though happily, like other old maladies, they have grown milder of late: and since the days of Titus Oates have mostly passed without loss of men's lives; or indeed without much other loss than that of reason, for the time, in the sufferers. In this mitigated form, however, the distemper is of pretty regular recurrence; and may be reckoned on at intervals, like other natural visitations; so that reasonable men deal with it, as the Londoners do with their fogs,—go cautiously out into the groping crowd, and patiently carry lanterns at noon; knowing, by a well-grounded faith, that the sun is still in existence, and will one day reappear. How often have we heard, for the last fifty years, that the country was wrecked, and fast sinking; whereas, up to this date, the country is entire and afloat! The "State in Danger" is a condition of things, which we have witnessed a hundred times; and as for the Church, it has seldom been out of "danger" since we can remember it.

All men are aware that the present is a crisis of this sort; and why it has become so. The repeal of the Test Acts, and then of the Catholic disabilities, has struck many of their admirers with an indescribable astonishment. Those things seemed fixed and immovable; deep as the foundations of the world; and lo, in a moment they have vanished, and their place knows them no more! Our worthy friends mistook the slumbering Leviathan for an island; often as they had been assured, that Intolerance was, and could be nothing but a Monster; and so, mooring under the lee, they had anchored comfortably in his scaly rind, thinking to take good cheer; as for some space they did. But now their Leviathan has suddenly dived under; and they can no longer be fastened in the stream of time; but must drift forward on it, even like the rest of the world: no very appalling fate, we think, could they but understand it; which, however, they will not yet, for a season. Their little island is gone; sunk deep amid confused eddies; and what is left worth caring for in the universe? What is it to them that the great continents of the earth are still standing; and the polestar and all our loadstars, in the heavens, still shining and eternal? Their cherished little haven is gone, and they will not be comforted! And therefore, day after day, in all manner of periodical or perennial publications, the most lugubrious predictions are sent forth. The King has virtually abdicated; the Church is a widow, without jointure; public principle is gone; private honesty is going; society, in short, is fast falling in pieces; and a time of unmixed evil is come on us.

At such a period, it was to be expected that the rage of prophecy should be more than usually excited. Accordingly, the Millennarians have come forth on the right hand, and the Millites on the left. The Fifth-monarchy men prophesy from the Bible, and the Utilitarians from Bentham. The one announces that the last of the seals is to be opened, positively, in the year 1860; and the other assures us that "the greatest-happiness principle" is to make a heaven of earth, in a still shorter time. We know these symptoms too well, to think it necessary or safe to interfere with them. Time and the hours will bring relief to all parties. The grand encourager of Delphic or other noises is—the Echo. Left to themselves, they will the sooner dissipate, and die away in space.

Meanwhile, we too admit that the present is an important time; as all present time necessarily is. The poorest Day that passes over us is the conflux of two Eternities; it is made up of currents that issue from the remotest Past, and flow onwards into the remotest Future. We were wise indeed, could we discern truly the signs of our own time; and by knowledge of its wants and advantages, wisely adjust our own position in it. Let us, instead of gazing idly into the obscure distance, look calmly around us, for a little, on the perplexed scene where we stand. Perhaps, on a more serious inspection, something of its perplexity will disappear, some of its distinctive characters and deeper tendencies more clearly reveal themselves; whereby our own relations to it, our own true aims and endeavours in it, may also become clearer.

Were we required to characterise this age of ours by any single epithet, we should be tempted to call it, not an Heroical, Devotional, Philosophical, or Moral Age, but, above all others, the Mechanical Age. It is the Age of Machinery, in every outward and inward sense of that word; the age which, with its whole undivided might, forwards, teaches and practises the great art of adapting means to ends. Nothing is now done directly, or by hand; all is by rule and calculated contrivance. For the simplest operation, some helps and accompaniments, some cunning abbreviating process is in readiness. Our old modes of exertion are all discredited, and thrown aside. On every hand, the living artisan is driven from his workshop, to make room for a speedier, inanimate one. The shuttle drops from the fingers of the weaver, and falls into iron fingers that ply it faster. The sailor furls his sail, and lays down his oar; and bids a strong, unwearied servant, on vaporous wings, bear him through the waters. Men have crossed oceans by steam; the Birmingham Fire-king has visited the fabulous East; and the genius of the Cape, were there any Camoens now to sing it, has again been alarmed, and with far stranger thunders than Gamas. There is no end to machinery. Even the horse is stripped of his harness, and finds a fleet fire-horse yoked in his stead. Nay, we have an artist that hatches chickens by steam; the very brood-hen is to be superseded! For all earthly, and for some unearthly purposes, we have machines and mechanic furtherances; for mincing our cabbages; for casting us into magnetic sleep. We remove mountains, and make seas our smooth highways; nothing can resist us. We war with rude Nature; and, by our resistless engines, come off always victorious, and loaded with spoils.

What wonderful accessions have thus been made, and are still making, to the physical power of mankind; how much better fed, clothed, lodged and, in all outward respects, accommodated men now are, or might be, by a given quantity of labour, is a grateful reflection which forces itself on every one. What changes, too, this addition of power is introducing into the Social System; how wealth has more and more increased, and at the same time gathered itself more and more into masses, strangely altering the old relations, and increasing the distance between the rich and the poor, will be a question for Political Economists, and a much more complex and important one than any they have yet engaged with.

But leaving these matters for the present, let us observe how the mechanical genius of our time has diffused itself into quite other provinces. Not the external and physical alone is now managed by machinery, but the internal and spiritual also. Here too nothing follows its spontaneous course, nothing is left to be accomplished by old natural methods. Everything has its cunningly devised implements, its preestablished apparatus; it is not done by hand, but by machinery. Thus we have machines for Education: Lancastrian machines; Hamiltonian machines; monitors, maps and emblems. Instruction, that mysterious communing of Wisdom with Ignorance, is no longer an indefinable tentative process, requiring a study of individual aptitudes, and a perpetual variation of means and methods, to attain the same end; but a secure, universal, straightforward business, to be conducted in the gross, by proper mechanism, with such intellect as comes to hand. Then, we have Religious machines, of all imaginable varieties; the Bible-Society, professing a far higher and heavenly structure, is found, on inquiry, to be altogether an earthly contrivance: supported by collection of moneys, by fomenting of vanities, by puffing, intrigue and chicane; a machine for converting the Heathen. It is the same in all other departments. Has any man, or any society of men, a truth to speak, a piece of spiritual work to do; they can nowise proceed at once and with the mere natural organs, but must first call a public meeting, appoint committees, issue prospectuses, eat a public dinner; in a word, construct or borrow machinery, wherewith to speak it and do it. Without machinery they were hopeless, helpless; a colony of Hindoo weavers squatting in the heart of Lancashire. Mark, too, how every machine must have its moving power, in some of the great currents of society; every little sect among us, Unitarians, Utilitarians, Anabaptists, Phrenologists, must have its Periodical, its monthly or quarterly Magazine;—hanging out, like its windmill, into the *popularis aura*,[1] to grind meal for the society.

With individuals, in like manner, natural strength avails little. No individual now hopes to accomplish the poorest enterprise single-handed and without mechanical aids; he must make interest with some existing corporation, and till his field with their oxen. In these days, more emphatically than ever, "to live, signifies to unite with a party, or to make one." Philosophy, Science, Art, Literature, all depend on machinery. No Newton, by silent meditation, now discovers the system of the world from the falling of an apple; but some quite other than Newton stands in his Museum, his Scientific Institution, and behind whole batteries of retorts, digesters, and galvanic piles imperatively "interrogates Nature,"— who, however, shows no haste to answer. In defect of Raphaels, and Angelos, and Mozarts, we have Royal Academies of Painting, Sculpture, Music; whereby the languishing spirits of Art may be strengthened, as by the more generous diet of a Public Kitchen. Literature, too, has its Paternoster-row mechanism, its Trade-dinners, its Editorial conclaves, and huge subterranean, puffing bellows; so that books are not only printed, but, in a great measure, written and sold, by machinery.

National culture, spiritual benefit of all sorts, is under the same management. No Queen Christina, in these times, needs to send for her Descartes; no King Frederick for his Voltaire, and painfully nourish him with pensions and flattery: any sovereign of taste, who wishes to enlighten his people, has only to impose a new tax, and with the proceeds establish Philosophic Institutes.

Hence the Royal and Imperial Societies, the Bibliothèques,[2] Glyptothèques, Technothèques, which front us in all capital cities; like so many well-finished hives, to which it is expected the stray agencies of Wisdom will swarm of their own accord, and hive and make honey. In like manner, among ourselves, when it is thought that religion is declining, we have only to vote half-a-million's worth of bricks and mortar, and build new churches. In Ireland it seems they have gone still farther, having actually established a "Penny-a-week Purgatory-Society"! Thus does the Genius of Mechanism stand by to help us in all difficulties and emergencies, and with his iron back bears all our burdens.

These things, which we state lightly enough here, are yet of deep import, and indicate a mighty change in our whole manner of existence. For the same habit regulates not our modes of action alone, but our modes of thought and feeling. Men are grown mechanical in head and in heart, as well as in hand. They have lost faith in individual endeavour, and in natural force, of any kind. Not for internal perfection, but for external combinations and arrangements, for institutions, constitutions,—for Mechanism of one sort or other, do they hope and struggle. Their whole efforts, attachments, opinions, turn on mechanism, and are of a mechanical character.

We may trace this tendency in all the great manifestations of our time; in its intellectual aspect, the studies it most favours and its manner of conducting them; in its practical aspects, its politics, arts, religion, morals; in the whole sources, and throughout the whole currents, of its spiritual, no less than its material activity.

Consider, for example, the state of Science generally, in Europe, at this period. It is admitted, on all sides, that the Metaphysical and Moral Sciences are falling into decay, while the Physical are engrossing, every day, more respect and attention. In most of the European nations there is now no such thing as a Science of Mind; only

---

[1] *popularis aura*: popular breeze.

[2] *Bibliothèques*, etc.: French names for libraries, museums of sculpture (carvings of all kinds), museums of the arts and crafts, respectively.

more or less advancement in the general science, or the special sciences, of matter. The French were the first to desert Metaphysics; and though they have lately affected to revive their school, it has yet no signs of vitality. The land of Malebranche, Pascal, Descartes and Fénelon, has now only its Cousins and Villemains; while, in the department of Physics, it reckons far other names. Among ourselves, 10 the Philosophy of Mind, after a rickety infancy, which never reached the vigour of manhood, fell suddenly into decay, languished and finally died out, with its last amiable cultivator, Professor Stewart. In no nation but Germany has any decisive effort been made in psychological science; not to speak of any decisive result. The science of the age, in short, is physical, chemical, physiological; in all shapes me- 20 chanical. Our favourite Mathematics, the highly prized exponent of all these other sciences, has also become more and more mechanical. Excellence in what is called its higher departments depends less on natural genius than on acquired expertness in wielding its machinery. Without undervaluing the wonderful results which a Lagrange or Laplace educes by means of it, we may remark, that their calculus, differ- 30 ential and integral, is little else than a more cunningly-constructed arithmetical mill; where the factors, being put in, are, as it were, ground into the true product, under cover, and without other effort on our part than steady turning of the handle. We have more Mathematics than ever; but less Mathesis.[3] Archimedes and Plato could not have read the *Mécanique Céleste;* but neither would the whole French Institute 40 see aught in that saying, "God geometrises!" but a sentimental rodomontade.

Nay, our whole Metaphysics itself, from Locke's time downward, has been physical; not a spiritual philosophy, but a material one. The singular estimation in which his Essay was so long held as a scientific work (an estimation grounded, indeed, on the estimable character of the man) will one

day be thought a curious indication of the spirit of these times. His whole doctrine is mechanical, in its aim and origin, in its method and its results. It is not a philosophy of the mind: it is a mere discussion concerning the origin of our consciousness, or ideas, or whatever else they are called; a genetic history of what we see *in* the mind. The grand secrets of Necessity and Freewill, of the Mind's vital or non-vital dependence on Matter, of our mysterious relations to Time and Space, to God, to the Universe, are not, in the faintest degree touched on in these inquiries; and seem not to have the smallest connexion with them.

The last class of our Scotch Metaphysicians had a dim notion that much of this was wrong; but they knew not how to right it. The school of Reid had also from the first taken a mechanical course, not seeing any other. The singular conclusions at which Hume, setting out from their admitted premises, was arriving, brought this school into being; they let loose Instinct, as an undiscriminating ban-dog, to guard them against these conclusions;—they tugged lustily at the logical chain by which Hume was so coldly towing them and the world into bottomless abysses of Atheism and Fatalism. But the chain somehow snapped between them; and the issue has been that nobody now cares about either,— any more than about Hartley's, Darwin's, or Priestley's contemporaneous doings in England. Hartley's vibrations and vibratiuncles, one would think, were material and mechanical enough; but our Continental neighbours have gone still farther. One of their philosophers has lately discovered, that "as the liver secretes bile, so does the brain secrete thought"; which astonishing discovery Dr. Cabanis, more lately still, in his *Rapports du Physique et du Morale de l'Homme,* has pushed into its minutest developments.

The metaphysical philosophy of this last inquirer is certainly no shadowy or unsubstantial one. He fairly lays open our moral 50 structure with his dissecting-knives and real metal probes; and exhibits it to the inspection of mankind, by Leuwenhoek microscopes, and inflation with the anatomical blowpipe. Thought, he is inclined to hold,

---

[3] Mathesis: Learning, more especially mathematical learning. Carlyle uses the word to mean the pure science of mathematics (with a suggestion of transcendental implication) as opposed to the applied science of it.

is still secreted by the brain; but then Poetry and Religion (and it is really worth knowing) are "a product of the smaller intestines"! We have the greatest admiration for this learned doctor: with what scientific stoicism he walks through the land of wonders, unwondering; like a wise man through some huge, gaudy, imposing Vauxhall, whose fire-works, cascades and symphonies, the vulgar may enjoy and believe in,—but where he finds nothing real but the saltpetre, pasteboard and catgut. His book may be regarded as the ultimatum of mechanical metaphysics in our time; a remarkable realisation of what in Martinus Scriblerus was still only an idea, that "as the jack had a meat-roasting quality, so had the body a thinking quality,"—upon the strength of which the Nurembergers were to build a wood-and-leather man, "who should reason as well as most country parsons." Vaucanson did indeed make a wooden duck, that seemed to eat and digest; but that bold scheme of the Nurembergers remained for a more modern virtuoso.

This condition of the two great departments of knowledge,—the outward, cultivated exclusively on mechanical principles; the inward, finally abandoned, because, cultivated on such principles, it is found to yield no result,—sufficiently indicates the intellectual bias of our time, its all-pervading disposition towards that line of inquiry. In fact, an inward persuasion has long been diffusing itself, and now and then even comes to utterance, That, except the external, there are no true sciences; that to the inward world (if there be any) our only conceivable road is through the outward; that, in short, what cannot be investigated and understood mechanically, cannot be investigated and understood at all. We advert the more particularly to these intellectual propensities, as to prominent symptoms of our age, because Opinion is at all times doubly related to Action, first as cause, then as effect; and the speculative tendency of any age will therefore give us, on the whole, the best indications of its practical tendency.

Nowhere, for example, is the deep, almost exclusive faith we have in Mechanism more visible than in the Politics of this time. Civil government does by its nature include much that is mechanical, and must be treated accordingly. We term it indeed, in ordinary language, the Machine of Society, and talk of it as the grand working wheel from which all private machines must derive, or to which they must adapt, their movements. Considered merely as a metaphor, all this is well enough; but here, as in so many other cases, the "foam hardens itself into a shell," and the shadow we have wantonly evoked stands terrible before us and will not depart at our bidding. Government includes much also that is not mechanical, and cannot be treated mechanically; of which latter truth, as appears to us, the political speculations and exertions of our time are taking less and less cognisance.

Nay, in the very outset, we might note the mighty interest taken in *mere political arrangements,* as itself the sign of a mechanical age. The whole discontent of Europe takes this direction. The deep, strong cry of all civilised nations,—a cry which, every one now sees, must and will be answered, is: Give us a reform of Government! A good structure of legislation, a proper check upon the executive, a wise arrangement of the judiciary, is *all* that is wanting for human happiness. The Philosopher of this age is not a Socrates, a Plato, a Hooker, or Taylor, who inculcates on men the necessity and infinite worth of moral goodness, the great truth that our happiness depends on the mind which is within us, and not on the circumstances which are without us; but a Smith, a De Lolme, a Bentham, who chiefly inculcates the reverse of this,—that our happiness depends entirely on external circumstances; nay, that the strength and dignity of the mind within us is itself the creature and consequence of these. Were the laws, the government, in good order, all were well with us; the rest would care for itself! Dissentients from this opinion, expressed or implied, are now rarely to be met with; widely and angrily as men differ in its application, the principle is admitted by all.

Equally mechanical, and of equal simplicity, are the methods proposed by both parties for completing or securing this all-sufficient perfection of arrangement. It is no longer the moral, religious, spiritual condition of the people that is our concern, but their physical, practical, economical condition, as regulated by public laws. Thus is the Body-politic more than ever worshipped and tendered; but the Soul-politic less than ever. Love of country, in any high or generous sense, in any other than an almost animal sense, or mere habit, has little importance attached to it in such reforms, or in the opposition shown them. Men are to be guided only by their self-interests. Good government is a good balancing of these; and, except a keen eye and appetite for self-interest, requires no virtue in any quarter. To both parties it is emphatically a machine: to the discontented, a "taxing-machine"; to the contented, a "machine for securing property." Its duties and its faults are not those of a father, but of an active parish-constable.

Thus it is by the mere condition of the machine, by preserving it untouched, or else by reconstructing it, and oiling it anew, that man's salvation as a social being is to be ensured and indefinitely promoted. Contrive the fabric of law aright, and without farther effort on your part, that divine spirit of Freedom, which all hearts venerate and long for, will of herself come to inhabit it; and under her healing wings every noxious influence will wither, every good and salutary one more and more expand. Nay, so devoted are we to this principle, and at the same time so curiously mechanical, that a new trade, specially grounded on it, has arisen among us, under the name of "Codification," or codemaking in the abstract; whereby any people, for a reasonable consideration, may be accommodated with a patent code;— more easily than curious individuals with patent breeches, for the people does not need to be measured first.

To us who live in the midst of all this, and see continually the faith, hope and practice of every one founded on Mechanism of one kind or other, it is apt to seem quite natural, and as if it could never have been otherwise. Nevertheless, if we recollect or reflect a little, we shall find both that it has been, and might again be

otherwise. The domain of Mechanism,— meaning thereby political, ecclesiastical or other outward establishments,—was once considered as embracing, and we are persuaded can at any time embrace, but a limited portion of man's interests, and by no means the highest portion.

To speak a little pedantically, there is a science of *Dynamics* in man's fortunes and nature, as well as of *Mechanics*. There is a science which treats of, and practically addresses, the primary, unmodified forces and energies of man, the mysterious springs of Love, and Fear, and Wonder, of Enthusiasm, Poetry, Religion, all which have a truly vital and *infinite* character; as well as a science which practically addresses the finite, modified developments of these, when they take the shape of immediate "motives," as hope of reward, or as fear of punishment.

Now it is certain, that in former times the wise men, the enlightened lovers of their kind, who appeared generally as Moralists, Poets or Priests, did, without neglecting the Mechanical province, deal chiefly with the Dynamical; applying themselves chiefly to regulate, increase and purify the inward primary powers of man; and fancying that herein lay the main difficulty, and the best service they could undertake. But a wide difference is manifest in our age. For the wise men, who now appear as Political Philosophers, deal exclusively with the Mechanical province; and occupying themselves in counting-up and estimating men's motives, strive by curious checking and balancing, and other adjustments of Profit and Loss, to guide them to their true advantage: while, unfortunately, those same "motives" are so innumerable, and so variable in every individual, that no really useful conclusion can ever be drawn from their enumeration. But though Mechanism, wisely contrived, has done much for man in a social and moral point of view, we cannot be persuaded that it has ever been the chief source of his worth or happiness. Consider the great elements of human enjoyment, the attainments and possessions that exalt man's life to its present height, and see what part of these he owes to institutions, to Mechanism of any kind; and what to the instinctive, unbounded force, which Nature herself lent him, and still continues to him. Shall we say, for example, that Science and Art are indebted principally to the founders of Schools and Universities? Did not Science originate rather, and gain advancement, in the obscure closets of the Roger Bacons, Keplers, Newtons; in the workshops of the Fausts and the Watts; wherever, and in what guise soever Nature, from the first times downwards, had sent a gifted spirit upon the earth? Again, were Homer and Shakspeare members of any beneficed guild, or made Poets by means of it? Were Painting and Sculpture created by forethought, brought into the world by institutions for that end? No; Science and Art have, from first to last, been the free gift of Nature; an unsolicited, unexpected gift; often even a fatal one. These things rose up, as it were, by spontaneous growth, in the free soil and sunshine of Nature. They were not planted or grafted, nor even greatly multiplied or improved by the culture or manuring of institutions. Generally speaking, they have derived only partial help from these; often enough have suffered damage. They made constitutions for themselves. They originated in the Dynamical nature of man, not in his Mechanical nature.

Or, to take an infinitely higher instance, that of the Christian Religion, which, under every theory of it, in the believing or unbelieving mind, must ever be regarded as the crowning glory, or rather the life and soul, of our whole modern culture: How did Christianity arise and spread abroad among men? Was it by institutions, and establishments and well-arranged systems of mechanism? Not so; on the contrary, in all past and existing institutions for those ends, its divine spirit has invariably been found to languish and decay. It arose in the mystic deeps of man's soul; and was spread abroad by the "preaching of the word," by simple, altogether natural and individual efforts; and flew, like hallowed fire, from heart to heart, till all were purified and illuminated by it; and its heavenly light shone, as it still shines, and (as sun or star) will ever shine, through the whole dark destinies of man. Here again was no Mechanism;

man's highest attainment was accomplished Dynamically, not Mechanically.

Nay, we will venture to say, that no high attainment, not even any far-extending movement among men, was ever accomplished otherwise. Strange as it may seem, if we read History with any degree of thoughtfulness, we shall find that the checks and balances of Profit and Loss have never been the grand agents with men; that they have never been roused into deep, thorough, all-pervading efforts by any computable prospect of Profit and Loss, for any visible, finite object; but always for some invisible and infinite one. The Crusades took their rise in Religion; their visible object was, commercially speaking, worth nothing. It was the boundless Invisible world that was laid bare in the imaginations of those men; and in its burning light, the visible shrunk as a scroll. Not mechanical, nor produced by mechanical means, was this vast movement. No dining at Freemasons' Tavern, with the other long train of modern machinery; no cunning reconciliation of "vested interests," was required here: only the passionate voice of one man, the rapt soul looking through the eyes of one man; and rugged, steel-clad Europe trembled beneath his words, and followed him whither he listed. In later ages it was still the same. The Reformation had an invisible, mystic and ideal aim; the result was indeed to be embodied in external things; but its spirit, its worth, was internal, invisible, infinite. Our English Revolution too originated in Religion. Men did battle, in those old days, not for Purse-sake, but for Conscience-sake. Nay, in our own days, it is no way different. The French Revolution itself had something higher in it than cheap bread and a Habeas-corpus act. Here too was an Idea; a Dynamic, not a Mechanic force. It was a struggle, though a blind and at last an insane one, for the infinite, divine nature of Right, of Freedom, of Country.

Thus does man, in every age, vindicate, consciously or unconsciously, his celestial birthright. Thus does Nature hold on her wondrous, unquestionable course; and all our systems and theories are but so many froth-eddies or sandbanks, which from time to time she casts up, and washes away. When we can drain the Ocean into mill-ponds, and bottle-up the Force of Gravity, to be sold by retail, in gas jars; then may we hope to comprehend the infinitudes of man's soul under formulas of Profit and Loss; and rule over this too, as over a patent engine, by checks, and valves, and balances.

Nay, even with regard to Government itself, can it be necessary to remind any one that Freedom, without which indeed all spiritual life is impossible, depends on infinitely more complex influences than either the extension or the curtailment of the "democratic interest"? Who is there that, "taking the high *priori* road," shall point out what these influences are; what deep, subtle, inextricably entangled influences they have been and may be? For man is not the creature and product of Mechanism; but, in a far truer sense, its creator and producer: it is the noble People that makes the noble Government; rather than conversely. On the whole, Institutions are much; but they are not all. The freest and highest spirits of the world have often been found under strange outward circumstances: Saint Paul and his brother Apostles were politically slaves; Epictetus was personally one. Again, forget the influences of Chivalry and Religion, and ask: What countries produced Columbus and Las Casas? Or, descending from virtue and heroism to mere energy and spiritual talent: Cortes, Pizarro, Alba, Ximenes? The Spaniards of the sixteenth century were indisputably the noblest nation of Europe: yet they had the Inquisition and Philip II. They have the same government at this day; and are the lowest nation. The Dutch too have retained their old constitution; but no Siege of Leyden, no William the Silent, not even an Egmont or DeWitt any longer appears among them. With ourselves also, where much has changed, effect has nowise followed cause as it should have done: two centuries ago, the Commons Speaker addressed Queen Elizabeth on bended knees, happy that the virago's foot did not even smite him; yet the people were then governed, not by a Castlereagh, but by a Burghley; they had their Shakspeare and Philip Sidney, where

we have our Sheridan Knowles and Beau Brummel.

These and the like facts are so familiar, the truths which they preach so obvious, and have in all past times been so universally believed and acted on, that we should almost feel ashamed for repeating them; were it not that, on every hand, the memory of them seems to have passed away, or at best died into a faint tradition, of no value as a practical principle. To judge by the loud clamour of our Constitution-builders, Statists, Economists, directors, creators, reformers of Public Societies; in a word, all manner of Mechanists, from the Cartwright up to the Code-maker; and by the nearly total silence of all Preachers and Teachers who should give a voice to Poetry, Religion and Morality, we might fancy either that man's Dynamical nature was, to all spiritual intents, extinct, or else so perfected that nothing more was to be made of it by the old means; and henceforth only in his Mechanical contrivances did any hope exist for him.

To define the limits of these two departments of man's activity, which work into one another, and by means of one another, so intricately and inseparably, were by its nature an impossible attempt. Their relative importance, even to the wisest mind, will vary in different times, according to the special wants and dispositions of those times. Meanwhile, it seems clear enough that only in the right coordination of the two, and the vigorous forwarding of *both*, does our true line of action lie. Undue cultivation of the inward or Dynamical province leads to idle, visionary, impracticable courses, and, especially in rude eras, to Superstition and Fanaticism, with their long train of baleful and well-known evils. Undue cultivation of the outward, again, though less immediately prejudicial, and even for the time productive of many palpable benefits, must, in the long-run, by destroying Moral Force, which is the parent of all other Force, prove not less certainly, and perhaps still more hopelessly, pernicious. This, we take it, is the grand characteristic of our age. By our skill in Mechanism, it has come to pass, that in the management of external things we excel all other ages; while in whatever respects the pure moral nature, in true dignity of soul and character, we are perhaps inferior to most civilised ages.

In fact, if we look deeper, we shall find that this faith in Mechanism has now struck its roots down into man's most intimate, primary sources of conviction; and is thence sending up, over his whole life and activity, innumerable stems,—fruit-bearing and poison-bearing. The truth is, men have lost their belief in the Invisible, and believe, and hope, and work only in the Visible; or, to speak it in other words: This is not a Religious age. Only the material, the immediately practical, not the divine and spiritual, is important to us. The infinite, absolute character of Virtue has passed into a finite, conditional one; it is no longer a worship of the Beautiful and Good; but a calculation of the Profitable. Worship, indeed, in any sense, is not recognised among us, or is mechanically explained into Fear of pain, or Hope of pleasure. Our true Deity is Mechanism. It has subdued external Nature for us, and we think it will do all other things. We are Giants in physical power: in a deeper than metaphorical sense, we are Titans, that strive, by heaping mountain on mountain, to conquer Heaven also.

The strong Mechanical character, so visible in the spiritual pursuits and methods of this age, may be traced much farther into the condition and prevailing disposition of our spiritual nature itself. Consider, for example, the general fashion of Intellect in this era. Intellect, the power man has of knowing and believing, is now nearly synonymous with Logic, or the mere power of arranging and communicating. Its implement is not Meditation, but Argument. "Cause and effect" is almost the only category under which we look at, and work with, all Nature. Our first question with regard to any object is not, What is it? but, How is it? We are no longer instinctively driven to apprehend, and lay to heart, what is Good and Lovely, but rather to inquire, as onlookers, how it is produced, whence it comes, whither it goes. Our favourite Philosophers have no love and no hatred; they stand among us not to do, nor to create anything, but as a sort of Logic-mills, to grind out the true causes and effects of all that is done and created. To the eye of a Smith, a Hume or a Constant, all is well that works quietly. An Order of Ignatius Loyola, a Presbyterianism of John Knox, a Wickliffe or a Henry the Eighth, are simply so many mechanical phenomena, caused or causing.

The *Euphuist* of our day differs much from his pleasant predecessors. An intellectual dapperling of these times boasts chiefly of his irresistible perspicacity, his "dwelling in the daylight of truth," and so forth; which, on examination, turns out to be a dwelling in the *rush*-light of "closet-logic," and a deep unconsciousness that there is any other light to dwell in or any other objects to survey with it. Wonder, indeed, is, on all hands, dying out: it is the sign of uncultivation to wonder. Speak to any small man of a high, majestic Reformation, of a high majestic Luther; and forthwith he sets about "accounting" for it; how the "circumstances of the time" called for such a character, and found him, we suppose, standing girt and road-ready, to do its errand; how the "circumstances of the time" created, fashioned, floated him quietly along into the result; how, in short, this small man, had he been there, could have performed the like himself! For it is the "force of circumstances" that does everything; the force of one man can do nothing. Now all this is grounded on little more than a metaphor. We figure Society as a "Machine," and that mind is opposed to mind, as body is to body; whereby two, or at most ten, little minds must be stronger than one great mind. Notable absurdity! For the plain truth, very plain, we think is, that minds are opposed to minds in quite a different way; and *one* man that has a higher Wisdom, a hitherto unknown spiritual Truth in him, is stronger, not than ten men that have it not, or than ten thousand, but than *all* men that have it not; and stands among them with a quite ethereal, angelic power, as with a sword out of Heaven's own armory, sky-tempered, which no buckler, and no tower of brass, will finally withstand.

But to us, in these times, such considerations rarely occur. We enjoy, we see nothing by direct vision; but only by re-

flection, and in anatomical dismember-
ment. Like Sir Hudibras, for every Why
we must have a Wherefore. We have our
little *theory* on all human and divine
things. Poetry, the workings of genius
itself, which in all times, with one or
another meaning, has been called Inspiration, and held to be mysterious and
inscrutable, is no longer without its scientific exposition. The building of the lofty 10
rhyme is like any other masonry or brick-
laying: we have theories of its rise, height,
decline and fall,—which latter, it would
seem, is now near, among all people. Of
our "Theories of Taste," as they are called,
wherein the deep, infinite, unspeakable
Love of Wisdom and Beauty, which dwells
in all men, is "explained," made mechanically visible, from "Association" and the
like, why should we say anything? Hume 20
has written us a "Natural History of Religion"; in which one Natural History all
the rest are included. Strangely too does
the general feeling coincide with Hume's
in this wonderful problem; for whether his
"Natural History" be the right one or not,
that Religion must have a Natural History,
all of us, cleric and laic, seem to be agreed.
He indeed regards it as a Disease, we again
as Health; so far there is a difference; but 30
in our first principle we are at one.

To what extent theological Unbelief, we
mean intellectual dissent from the Church,
in its view of Holy Writ, prevails at this
day, would be a highly important, were it
not, under any circumstances, an almost
impossible inquiry. But the Unbelief,
which is of a still more fundamental
character, every man may see prevailing,
with scarcely any but the faintest contradic- 40
tion, all around him; even in the Pulpit
itself. Religion in most countries, more
or less in every country, is no longer what
it was, and should be,—a thousand-voiced
psalm from the heart of Man to his invisible Father, the fountain of all Goodness,
Beauty, Truth, and revealed in every revelation of these; but for the most part, a
wise prudential feeling grounded on mere
calculation; a matter, as all others now are, 50
of Expediency and Utility; whereby some
smaller quantum of earthly enjoyment may
be exchanged for a far larger quantum of
celestial enjoyment. Thus Religion too is

Profit, a working for wages; not Reverence,
but vulgar Hope or Fear. Many, we know,
very many we hope, are still religious in a
far different sense; were it not so, our case
were too desperate: but to witness that
such is the temper of the times, we take
any calm observant man, who agrees or
disagrees in our feeling on the matter, and
ask him whether our *view* of it is not in
general well-founded.

Literature, too, if we consider it, gives
similar testimony. At no former era has
Literature, the printed communication of
Thought, been of such importance as it
is now. We often hear that the Church
is in danger; and truly so it is,—in a danger
it seems not to know of: for, with its tithes
in the most perfect safety, its functions are
becoming more and more superseded. The
true Church of England, at this moment,
lies in the Editors of its Newspapers.
These preach to the people daily, weekly;
admonishing kings themselves; advising
peace or war, with an authority which only
the first Reformers, and a long-past class
of Popes, were possessed of; inflicting
moral censure; imparting moral encouragement, consolation, edification; in all ways
diligently "administering the Discipline of
the Church." It may be said too, that in
private disposition the new Preachers
somewhat resemble the Mendicant Friars
of old times: outwardly full of holy zeal;
inwardly not without stratagem, and
hunger for terrestrial things. But omitting
this class, and the boundless host of watery
personages who pipe, as they are able, on
so many scrannel straws, let us look at the
higher regions of Literature, where, if anywhere, the pure melodies of Poesy and
Wisdom should be heard. Of natural
talent there is no deficiency: one or two
richly-endowed individuals even give us a
superiority in this respect. But what is the
song they sing? Is it a tone of the Memnon Statue, breathing music as the *light*
first touches it? A "liquid wisdom," dis-
closing to our sense the deep, infinite harmonies of Nature and man's soul? Alas,
no! It is not a matin or vesper hymn to
the Spirit of Beauty, but a fierce clashing
of cymbals, and shouting of multitudes, as
children pass through the fire to Moloch!
Poetry itself has no eye for the Invisible.

Beauty is no longer the god it worships, but some brute image of Strength; which we may call an idol, for true Strength is one and the same with Beauty, and its worship also is a hymn. The meek, silent Light can mould, create and purify all Nature; but the loud Whirlwind, the sign and product of Disunion, of Weakness, passes on, and is forgotten. How widely this veneration for the physically Strongest has spread itself through Literature, any one may judge who reads either criticism or poem. We praise a work, not as "true," but as "strong"; our highest praise is that it has "affected" us, has "terrified" us. All this, it has been well observed, is the "maximum of the Barbarous," the symptom, not of vigorous refinement, but of luxurious corruption. It speaks much, too, for men's indestructible love of truth, that nothing of this kind will abide with them; that even the talent of a Byron cannot permanently seduce us into idol-worship; that he too, with all his wild siren charming, already begins to be disregarded and forgotten.

Again, with respect to our Moral condition: here also he who runs may read that the same physical, mechanical influences are everywhere busy. For the "superior morality," of which we hear so much, we too would desire to be thankful: at the same time, it were but blindness to deny that this "superior morality" is properly rather an "inferior criminality," produced not by greater love of Virtue, but by greater perfection of Police; and of that far subtler and stronger Police, called Public Opinion. This last watches over us with its Argus eyes more keenly than ever; but the "inward eye" seems heavy with sleep. Of any belief in invisible, divine things, we find as few traces in our Morality as elsewhere. It is by tangible, material considerations that we are guided, not by inward and spiritual. Self-denial, the parent of all virtue, in any true sense of that word, has perhaps seldom been rarer: so rare is it, that the most, even in their abstract speculations, regard its existence as a chimera. Virtue is Pleasure, is Profit; no celestial, but an earthly thing. Virtuous men, Philanthropists, Martyrs are happy accidents; their "taste" lies the right way!

In all senses, we worship and follow after Power; which may be called a physical pursuit. No man now loves Truth, as Truth must be loved, with an infinite love; but only with a finite love, as it were *par amours.*[4] Nay, properly speaking, he does not *believe* and know it, but only "*thinks*" it, and that "there is every probability!" He preaches it aloud, and rushes courageously forth with it,—if there is a multitude huzzaing at his back; yet ever keeps looking over his shoulder, and the instant the huzzaing languishes, he too stops short.

In fact, what morality we have takes the shape of Ambition, or "Honour": beyond money and money's worth, our only rational blessedness is Popularity. It were but a fool's trick to die for conscience. Only for "character," by duel, or in case of extremity, by suicide, is the wise man bound to die. By arguing on the "force of circumstances," we have argued away all force from ourselves; and stand leashed together, uniform in dress and movement, like the rowers of some boundless galley. This and that may be right and true; *but we must not do it.* Wonderful "Force of Public Opinion"! We must act and walk in all points as it prescribes; follow the traffic it bids us, realise the sum of money, the degree of "influence" it expects of us, *or* we shall be lightly esteemed; certain mouthfuls of articulate wind will be blown at us, and this what mortal courage can front? Thus, while civil liberty is more and more secured to us, our moral liberty is all but lost. Practically considered, our creed is Fatalism; and, free in hand and foot, we are shackled in heart and soul with far straiter than feudal chains. Truly may we say, with the Philosopher, "the deep meaning of the Laws of Mechanism lies heavy on us"; and in the closet, in the Marketplace, in the temple, by the social hearth, encumbers the whole movements of our mind, and over our noblest faculties is spreading a nightmare sleep.

These dark features, we are aware, belong more or less to other ages, as well as to ours. This faith in Mechanism, in the all-importance of physical things, is in every age the common refuge of Weakness and blind Discontent; of all who believe,

[4] *par amours:* through love; for love's sake.

as many will ever do, that man's true good lies without him, not within. We are aware also, that, as applied to ourselves in all their aggravation, they form but half a picture; that in the whole picture there are bright lights as well as gloomy shadows. If we here dwell chiefly on the latter, let us not be blamed: it is in general more profitable to reckon up our defects than to boast of our attainments.

Neither, with all these evils more or less clearly before us, have we at any time despaired of the fortunes of society. Despair, or even despondency, in that respect, appears to us, in all cases, a groundless feeling. We have a faith in the imperishable dignity of man; in the high vocation to which, throughout this his earthly history, he has been appointed. However it may be with individual nations, whatever melancholic speculators may assert, it seems a well-ascertained fact, that in all times, reckoning even from those of the Heraclides and Pelasgi, the happiness and greatness of mankind at large have been continually progressive. Doubtless this age also is advancing. Its very unrest, its ceaseless activity, its discontent contains matter of promise. Knowledge, education are opening the eyes of the humblest; are increasing the number of thinking minds without limit. This is as it should be; for not in turning back, not in resisting, but only in resolutely struggling forward, does our life consist.

Nay, after all, our spiritual maladies are but of Opinion; we are but fettered by chains of our own forging, and which ourselves also can rend asunder. This deep, paralysed subjection to physical objects comes not from Nature, but from our own unwise mode of *viewing* Nature. Neither can we understand that man wants, at this hour, any faculty of heart, soul or body, that ever belonged to him. 'He, who has been born, has been a First Man'; has had lying before his young eyes, and as yet unhardened into scientific shapes, a world as plastic, infinite, divine, as lay before the eyes of Adam himself. If Mechanism, like some glass bell, encircles and imprisons us; if the soul looks forth on a fair heavenly country which it cannot reach, and pines, and in its scanty atmosphere is ready to perish,—yet the bell is but of glass; 'one bold stroke to break the bell in pieces, and thou art delivered!' Not the invisible world is wanting, for it dwells in man's soul, and this last is still here. Are the solemn temples, in which the Divinity was once visibly revealed among us, crumbling away? We can repair them, we can rebuild them. The wisdom, the heroic worth of our forefathers, which we have lost, we can recover. That admiration of old nobleness, which now so often shows itself as a faint *dilettantism,* will one day become a generous emulation, and man may again be all that he has been, and more than he has been. Nor are these the mere daydreams of fancy; they are clear possibilities; nay, in this time they are even assuming the character of hopes. Indications we do see in other countries and in our own, signs infinitely cheering to us, that Mechanism is not always to be our hard taskmaster, but one day to be our pliant, all-ministering servant; that a new and brighter spiritual era is slowly evolving itself for all man. But on these things our present course forbids us to enter.

Meanwhile, that great outward changes are in progress can be doubtful to no one. The time is sick and out of joint. Many things have reached their height; and it is a wise adage that tells us, "the darkest hour is nearest the dawn." Wherever we can gather indication of the public thought, whether from printed books, as in France or Germany, or from Carbonari rebellions and other political tumults, as in Spain, Portugal, Italy, and Greece, the voice it utters is the same. The thinking minds of all nations call for change. There is a deep-lying struggle in the whole fabric of society; a boundless grinding collision of the New with the Old. The French Revolution, as is now visible enough, was not the parent of this mighty movement, but its offspring. Those two hostile influences, which always exist in human things, and on the constant intercommunion of which depends their health and safety, had lain in separate masses, accumulating through generations, and France was the scene of their fiercest explosion; but the final issue was not unfolded in that country: nay, it is not yet anywhere unfolded. Political freedom is hitherto the object of these efforts; but they will not and cannot stop there. It is towards a higher freedom than mere freedom from oppression by his fellow-mortal, that man dimly aims. Of this higher, heavenly freedom, which is "man's reasonable service," all his noble institutions, his faithful endeavours and loftiest attainments, are but the body, and more and more approximated emblem.

On the whole, as this wondrous planet, Earth, is journeying with its fellows through infinite Space, so are the wondrous destinies embarked on it journeying through infinite Time, under a higher guidance than ours. For the present, as our astronomy informs us, its path lies towards *Hercules,* the constellation of *Physical Powers*: but that is not our most pressing concern. Go where it will, the deep HEAVEN will be around it. Therein let us have hope and sure faith. To reform a world, to reform a nation, no wise man will undertake; and all but foolish men know, that the only solid, though a far slower reformation, is what each begins and perfects on *himself*.   [1829]

SARTOR RESARTUS

THE EVERLASTING NO

Under the strange nebulous envelopment, wherein our Professor has now shrouded himself, no doubt but his spiritual nature is nevertheless progressive, and growing: for how can the "Son of Time," in any case, stand still? We behold him, through those dim years, in a state of crisis, of transition: his mad Pilgrimings, and general solution into aimless Discontinuity, what is all this but a mad Fermentation; wherefrom, the fiercer it is, the clearer product will one day evolve itself?

Such transitions are ever full of pain: thus the Eagle when he moults is sickly; and, to attain his new beak, must harshly dash-off the old one upon rocks. What Stoicism soever our Wanderer, in his individual acts and motions, may affect, it is clear that there is a hot fever of anarchy and misery raving within; and coruscations of which flash out: as, indeed, how could there be other? Have we not seen him disappointed, bemocked of Destiny, through long years? All that the young heart might desire and pray for has been denied; nay, as in the last worst instance, offered and then snatched away. Ever an "excellent Passivity"; but of useful, reasonable Activity, essential to the former as Food to Hunger, nothing granted: till at length, in this wild Pilgrimage, he must forcibly seize for himself an Activity, though useless, unreasonable. Alas, his cup of bitterness, which had been filling drop by drop, ever since the first "ruddy morning" in the Hinterschlag Gymnasium,[1] was at the very lip; and then with that poison-drop, of the Towgood-and-Blumine business, it runs over, and even hisses over in a deluge of foam.

He himself says once, with more justice than originality: "Man is, properly speaking, based upon Hope, he has no other possession but Hope; this world of his is emphatically the Place of Hope." What then was our Professor's possession? We see him, for the present, quite shut-out from Hope; looking not into the golden orient, but vaguely all around into a dim copper firmament, pregnant with earthquake and tornado.

Alas, shut-out from Hope, in a deeper sense than we yet dream of! For, as he wanders wearisomely through this world, he has now lost all tidings of another and higher. Full of religion, or at least of religiosity, as our Friend has since exhibited himself, he hides not that, in those days, he was wholly irreligious: "Doubt had darkened into Unbelief," says he; "shade after shade goes grimly over your soul, till you have the fixed, starless, Tartarean black." To such readers as have reflected, what can be called reflecting, on man's life, and happily discovered, in con-

[1] *Hinterschlag* Gymnasium: Strike-behind Academy, meant for Annan Academy where Carlyle prepared for the University of Edinburgh.—For 'Towgood-and-Blumine' see chapter on 'Romance' in *Sartor* (II, v).

tradiction to much Profit-and-Loss Philosophy, speculative and practical, that Soul is *not* synonymous with Stomach; who understand, therefore, in our Friend's words, "that, for man's well-being, Faith is properly the one thing needful; how, with it, Martyrs, otherwise weak, can cheerfully endure the shame and the cross; and without it, Worldlings puke-up their sick existence, by suicide, in the midst of luxury": to such, it will be clear that, for a pure moral nature, the loss of his religious Belief was the loss of everything. Unhappy young man! All wounds, the crush of long-continued Destitution, the stab of false Friendship, and of false Love, all wounds in thy so genial heart, would have healed again, had not its life-warmth been withdrawn. Well might he exclaim, in his wild way: "Is there no God, then; but at best an absentee God, sitting idle, ever since the first Sabbath, at the outside of his Universe, and *seeing* it go? Has the word Duty no meaning; is what we call Duty no divine Messenger and Guide, but a false earthly Fantasm, made-up of Desire and Fear, of emanations from the Gallows and from Doctor Graham's Celestial Bed? Happiness of an approving Conscience! Did not Paul of Tarsus, whom admiring men have since named Saint, feel that *he* was 'the chief of sinners,' and Nero of Rome, jocund in spirit (*wohlgemuth*), spend much of his time in fiddling? Foolish Wordmonger, and Motive-grinder, who in thy Logic-mill hast an earthly mechanism for the Godlike itself, and wouldst fain grind me out Virtue from the husks of Pleasure,—I tell thee, Nay! To the unregenerate Prometheus Vinctus of a man, it is ever the bitterest aggravation of his wretchedness that he is conscious of Virtue, that he feels himself the victim not of suffering only, but of injustice. What then? Is the heroic inspiration we name Virtue but some Passion; some bubble of the blood, bubbling in the direction others *profit* by? I know not: only this I know, If what thou namest Happiness be our true aim, then are we all astray. With Stupidity and sound digestion man may front much. But what, in these dull unimaginative days are the terrors of Conscience to the diseases of the Liver! Not

on Morality, but on Cookery, let us build our stronghold: there brandishing our frying-pan, as censer, let us offer sweet incense to the Devil, and live at ease on the fat things *he* has provided for his Elect!"

Thus has the bewildered Wanderer to stand, as so many have done, shouting question after question into the Sibyl-cave of Destiny, and receive no Answer but an Echo. It is all a grim Desert, this once-fair world of his; wherein is heard only the howling of wild-beasts, or the shrieks of despairing, hate-filled men; and no Pillar of Cloud by day, and no Pillar of Fire by night, any longer guides the Pilgrim. To such length has the spirit of Inquiry carried him. "But what boots it (*was thut's*)?" cries he; "it is but the common lot in this era. Not having come to spiritual majority prior to the *Siècle de Louis Quinze,* and not being born purely a Loghead (*Dummkopf*), thou hadst no other outlook. The whole world is, like thee, sold to Unbelief; their old Temples of the Godhead, which for long have not been rainproof, crumble down; and men ask now: Where is the Godhead; our eyes never saw him?"

Pitiful enough were it, for all these wild utterances, to call our Diogenes wicked. Unprofitable servants as we all are, perhaps at no era of his life was he more decisively the Servant of Goodness, the Servant of God, than even now when doubting God's existence. "One circumstance I note," says he: "after all the nameless woe that Inquiry, which for me, what it is not always, was genuine Love of Truth, had wrought me, I nevertheless still loved Truth, and would bate no jot of my allegiance to her. 'Truth!' I cried, 'though the Heavens crush me for following her: no Falsehood! though a whole celestial Lubberland were the price of Apostasy.' In conduct it was the same. Had a divine Messenger from the clouds, or miraculous Handwriting on the wall, convincingly proclaimed to me *This thou shalt do,* with what passionate readiness, as I often thought, would I have done it, had it been leaping into the infernal Fire. Thus, in spite of all Motive-grinders, and Mechanical Profit-and-Loss Philosophies, with the sick ophthalmia and hallucination they had brought on, was the Infinite nature of Duty still dimly present to me: living without God in the world, of God's light I was not utterly bereft; if my as yet sealed eyes, with their unspeakable longing, could nowhere see Him, nevertheless in my heart He was present, and His heaven-written Law still stood legible and sacred there."

Meanwhile, under all these tribulations, and temporal and spiritual destitutions, what must the Wanderer, in his silent soul, have endured! "The painfullest feeling," writes he, "is that of your own Feebleness (*Unkraft*); ever, as the English Milton says, to be weak is the true misery. And yet of your Strength there is and can be no clear feeling, save by what you have prospered in, by what you have done. Between vague wavering Capability and fixed indubitable Performance, what a difference! A certain inarticulate Self-consciousness dwells dimly in us; which only our Works can render articulate and decisively discernible. Our Works are the mirror wherein the spirit first sees its natural lineaments. Hence, too, the folly of that impossible Precept, *Know thyself;* till it be translated into this partially possible one, *Know what thou canst work at.*

"But for me, so strangely unprosperous had I been, the net-result of my Workings amounted as yet simply to—Nothing. How then could I believe in my Strength, when there was as yet no mirror to see it in? Ever did this agitating, yet, as I now perceive, quite frivolous question, remain to me insoluble: Hast thou a certain Faculty, a certain Worth, such even as the most have not; or art thou the completest Dullard of these modern times? Alas! the fearful Unbelief is unbelief in yourself; and how could I believe? Had not my first, last Faith in myself, when even to me the Heavens seemed laid open, and I dared to love, been all-too cruelly belied? The speculative Mystery of Life grew ever more mysterious to me; neither in the practical Mystery had I made the slightest progress, but been everywhere buffeted, foiled, and contemptuously cast out. A feeble unit in the middle of a threatening Infinitude, I seemed to have nothing given me but eyes, whereby to discern my own wretchedness.

Invisible yet impenetrable walls, as of Enchantment, divided me from all living: was there, in the wide world, any true bosom I could press trustfully to mine? O Heaven, No, there was none! I kept a lock upon my lips: why should I speak much with that shifting variety of so-called Friends, in whose withered, vain and too-hungry souls, Friendship was but an incredible tradition? In such cases, your resource is to talk little, and that little mostly from the Newspapers. Now when I look back, it was a strange isolation I then lived in. The men and women around me, even speaking with me, were but Figures: I had, practically, forgotten that they were alive, that they were not merely automatic. In the midst of their crowded streets, and assemblages, I walked solitary; and (except as it was my own heart, not another's, that I kept devouring) savage also, as the tiger in his jungle. Some comfort it would have been, could I, like a Faust, have fancied myself tempted and tormented of the Devil; for a Hell, as I imagine, without Life, though only diabolic Life, were more frightful: but in our age of Down-pulling and Disbelief, the very Devil has been pulled down, you cannot so much as believe in a Devil. To me the Universe was all void of Life, of Purpose, of Volition, even of Hostility: it was one huge, dead, immeasurable Steam-engine, rolling on, in its dead indifference, to grind me limb from limb. O, the vast gloomy, solitary Golgotha, and Mill of Death! Why was the Living banished thither companionless, conscious? Why, if there is no Devil; nay, unless the Devil is your God?"

A prey incessantly to such corrosions, might not, moreover, as the worst aggravation to them, the iron constitution even of a Teufelsdröckh threaten to fail? We conjecture that he has known sickness; and, in spite of his locomotive habits, perhaps sickness of the chronic sort. Hear this, for example: "How beautiful to die of broken-heart, on Paper! Quite another thing in practice; every window of your Feeling, even of your Intellect, as it were, begrimed and mud-bespattered, so that no pure ray can enter; a whole Drugshop in your inwards; the foredone soul drowning slowly in quagmires of Disgust!"

Putting all which external and internal miseries together, may we not find in the following sentences, quite in our Professor's still vein, significance enough? "From Suicide a certain aftershine (*Nachschein*) of Christianity withheld me: perhaps also a certain indolence of character; for, was not that a remedy I had at any time within reach? Often, however, was there a question present to me: Should some one now, at the turning of that corner, blow thee suddenly out of Space, into the other World, or other No-world, by pistol-shot,— how were it? On which ground, too, I have often, in sea-storms and sieged cities and other death-scenes, exhibited an imperturbability, which passed, falsely enough, for courage."

"So had it lasted," concludes the Wanderer, "so had it lasted, as in bitter protracted Death-agony, through long years. The heart within me, unvisited by any heavenly dewdrop, was smouldering in sulphurous, slow-consuming fire. Almost since earliest memory I had shed no tear; or once only when I, murmuring half-audibly, recited Faust's Deathsong, that wild *Selig der den er im Siegesglanze findet* (Happy whom *he* finds in Battle's splendour), and thought that of this last Friend even I was not forsaken, that Destiny itself could not doom me not to die. Having no hope, neither had I any definite fear, were it of Man or of Devil: nay, I often felt as if it might be solacing, could the Arch-Devil himself, though in Tartarean terrors, but rise to me, that I might tell him a little of my mind. And yet, strangely enough, I lived in a continual, indefinite, pining fear; tremulous, pusillanimous, apprehensive of I knew not what: it seemed as if all things in the Heavens above and the Earth beneath would hurt me; as if the Heavens and the Earth were but boundless jaws of a devouring monster, wherein I, palpitating, waited to be devoured.

"Full of such humour, and perhaps the miserablest man in the whole French Capital or Suburbs, was I, one sultry Dog-day, after much perambulation, toiling along the dirty little *Rue Saint-Thomas de l'Enfer,* among civic rubbish enough, in a close atmosphere, and over pavements hot as Nebuchadnezzar's Furnace; whereby doubtless my spirits were little cheered; when, all at once, there rose a Thought in me, and I asked myself: 'What *art* thou afraid of? Wherefore, like a coward, dost thou for ever pip and whimper, and go cowering and trembling? Despicable biped! what is the sum-total of the worst that lies before thee? Death? Well, Death; and say the pangs of Tophet too, and all that the Devil and Man may, will, or can do against thee! Hast thou not a heart; canst thou not suffer whatsoever it be; and, as a Child of Freedom, though outcast, trample Tophet itself under thy feet, while it consumes thee? Let it come, then; I will meet it and defy it!' And as I so thought, there rushed like a stream of fire over my whole soul; and I shook base Fear away from me forever. I was strong, of unknown strength; a spirit, almost a god. Ever from that time, the temper of my misery was changed: not Fear or whining Sorrow was it, but Indignation and grim fire-eyed Defiance.

"Thus had the EVERLASTING No (*das ewige Nein*) pealed authoritatively through all the recesses of my Being, of my ME; and then was it that my whole ME stood up, in native God-created majesty, and with emphasis recorded its Protest. Such a Protest, the most important transaction in Life, may that same Indignation and Defiance, in a psychological point of view, be fitly called. The Everlasting No had said: 'Behold, thou art fatherless, outcast, and the Universe is mine (the Devil's);' to which my whole ME now made answer: '*I* am not thine, but Free, and forever hate thee!'

"It is from this hour that I incline to date my Spiritual New-birth, or Baphometic Fire-baptism; perhaps I directly thereupon began to be a Man."

CENTRE OF INDIFFERENCE

Though, after this "Baphometic Fire-baptism" of his, our Wanderer signifies that his Unrest was but increased; as, indeed, "Indignation and Defiance," especially against things in general, are not the most peaceable inmates; yet can the Psychologist surmise that it was no longer a quite hopeless Unrest; that henceforth it had at least a fixed centre to revolve round.

For the fire-baptised soul, long so scathed and thunder-riven, here feels its own Freedom, which feeling is its Baphometic Baptism: the citadel of its whole kingdom it has thus gained by assault; and will keep inexpugnable; outwards from which the remaining dominions, not indeed without hard battling, will doubtless by degrees be conquered and pacificated. Under another figure, we might say, if in that great moment, in the *Rue Saint-Thomas de l'Enfer,* the old inward Satanic School was not yet thrown out of doors, it received peremptory judicial notice to quit;—whereby, for the rest, its howl-chantings, Ernulphus-cursings, and rebellious gnashing of teeth, might, in the mean while, become only the more tumultuous, and difficult to keep secret.

Accordingly, if we scrutinise these Pilgrimings well, there is perhaps discernible henceforth a certain incipient method in their madness. Not wholly as a Spectre does Teufelsdröckh now storm through the world; at worst as a spectre-fighting Man, nay who will one day be a Spectre-queller. If pilgriming restlessly to so many "Saints' Wells," and ever without quenching of his thirst, he nevertheless finds little secular wells, whereby from time to time some alleviation is ministered. In a word, he is now, if not ceasing, yet intermitting to "eat his own heart"; and clutches round him outwardly on the NOT-ME for wholesomer food. Does not the following glimpse exhibit him in a much more natural state?

"Towns also and Cities, especially the ancient, I failed not to look upon with interest. How beautiful to see thereby, as through a long vista, into the remote Time; to have, as it were, an actual section of almost the earliest Past brought safe into the Present, and set before your eyes! There, in that old City, was a live ember of Culinary Fire put down, say only two-thousand years ago; and there, burning more or less triumphantly, with such fuel as the region yielded, it has burnt, and still burns, and thou thyself seest the very smoke thereof. Ah! and the far more mysterious live ember of Vital Fire was then also put down there; and still miraculously burns and spreads; and the smoke and ashes thereof (in these Judgment-Halls and Churchyards), and its bellows-engines (in these Churches), thou still seest; and its flame, looking out from every kind countenance, and every hateful one, still warms thee or scorches thee.

"Of Man's Activity and Attainment the chief results are aeriform, mystic, and preserved in Tradition only: such are his Forms of Government, with the Authority they rest on; his Customs, or Fashions both of Cloth-habits and of Soul-habits; much more his collective stock of Handicrafts, the whole Faculty he has acquired of manipulating Nature: all these things, as indispensable and priceless as they are, cannot in any way be fixed under lock and key, but must flit, spirit-like, on impalpable vehicles, from Father to Son; if you demand sight of them, they are nowhere to be met with. Visible Ploughmen and Hammermen there have been, ever from Cain and Tubalcain downwards: but where does your accumulated Agricultural, Metallurgic, and other Manufacturing SKILL lie warehoused? It transmits itself on the atmospheric air, on the sun's rays (by Hearing and Vision); it is a thing aeriform, impalpable, of quite spiritual sort. In like manner, ask me not, Where are the LAWS; where is the GOVERNMENT? In vain wilt thou go to Schönbrunn, to Downing Street, to the Palais Bourbon: thou findest nothing there, but brick or stone houses, and some bundles of Papers tied with tape. Where, then, is that same cunningly-devised almighty GOVERNMENT of theirs to be laid hands on? Everywhere, yet nowhere: seen only in its works, this too is a thing aeriform, invisible; or if you will, mystic and miraculous. So spiritual (*geistig*) is our whole daily Life: all that we do springs out of Mystery, Spirit, invisible Force; only like a little Cloud-image, or Armida's Palace, air-built, does the Actual body itself forth from the great mystic Deep.

"Visible and tangible products of the Past, again, I reckon-up to the extent of three: Cities, with their Cabinets and Arsenals; then tilled Fields, to either or to both of which divisions Roads with their Bridges may belong; and thirdly —— Books. In which third truly, the last-invented, lies a worth far surpassing that of the two others. Wondrous indeed is the virtue of a true Book. Not like a dead city of stones, yearly crumbling, yearly needing repair; more like a tilled field, but then a spiritual field: like a spiritual tree, let me rather say, it stands from year to year, and from age to age (we have Books that already number some hundred-and-fifty human ages); and yearly comes its new produce of leaves (Commentaries, Deductions, Philosophical, Political Systems; or were it only Sermons, Pamphlets, Journalistic Essays), every one of which is talismanic and thaumaturgic, for it can persuade men. O thou who art able to write a Book, which once in the two centuries or oftener there is a man gifted to do, envy not him whom they name City-builder, and inexpressibly pity him whom they name Conqueror or City-burner! Thou too art a Conqueror and Victor; but of the true sort, namely over the Devil: thou too hast built what will outlast all marble and metal, and be a wonder-bringing City of the Mind, a Temple and Seminary and Prophetic Mount, whereto all kindreds of the Earth will pilgrim. — Fool! why journeyest thou wearisomely, in thy antiquarian fervour, to gaze on the stone pyramids of Geeza or the clay ones of Sacchara? These stand there, as I can tell thee, idle and inert, looking over the Desert, foolishly enough, for the last three-thousand years: but canst thou not open thy Hebrew BIBLE, then, or even Luther's Version thereof?"

No less satisfactory is his sudden appearance not in Battle, yet on some Battlefield; which, we soon gather, must be that of Wagram: so that here, for once, is a certain approximation to distinctness of date. Omitting much, let us impart what follows:

"Horrible enough! A whole Marchfeld strewed with shell-splinters, cannon-shot, ruined tumbrils, and dead men and horses; stragglers still remaining not so much as buried. And those red mould heaps: ay, there lie the Shells of Men, out of which all the Life and Virtue has been blown; and now they are swept together, and crammed-down out of sight, like blown Egg-shells!— Did Nature, when she bade the Donau bring down his mould-cargoes from the Carinthian and Carpathian Heights, and spread them out here into the softest, richest level,—intend thee, O Marchfeld, for a

corn-bearing Nursery, whereon her children might be nursed; or for a Cockpit, wherein they might more commodiously be throttled and tattered? Were thy three broad highways, meeting here from the ends of Europe, made for Ammunition-wagons, then? Were thy Wagrams and Stillfrieds but so many ready-built Casemates, wherein the house of Hapsburg might batter with artillery, and with artillery be battered? König Ottokar, amid yonder hillocks, dies under Rodolf's truncheon; here Kaiser Franz falls a-swoon under Napoleon's: within which five centuries, to omit the others, how hast thy breast, fair Plain, been defaced and defiled! The greensward is torn-up and trampled-down; man's fond care of it, his fruit-trees, hedge-rows, and pleasant dwellings, blown-away with gunpowder; and the kind seed-field lies a desolate, hideous Place of Sculls. —Nevertheless, Nature is at work; neither shall these Powder-Devilkins with their utmost devilry gainsay her: but all that gore and carnage will be shrouded-in, absorbed into manure; and next year the Marchfeld will be green, nay greener. Thrifty unwearied Nature, ever out of our great waste educing some little profit of thy own,—how dost thou, from the very carcass of the Killer, bring Life for the Living!

"What, speaking in quite unofficial language, is the net-purport and upshot of war? To my own knowledge, for example, there dwell and toil, in the British village of Dumdrudge, usually some five-hundred souls. From these, by certain 'Natural Enemies' of the French, there are successively selected, during the French war, say thirty able-bodied men: Dumdrudge, at her own expense, has suckled and nursed them; she has, not without difficulty and sorrow, fed them up to manhood, and even trained them to crafts, so that one can weave, another build, another hammer, and the weakest can stand under thirty stone avoirdupois. Nevertheless, amid much weeping and swearing, they are selected; all dressed in red; and shipped away, at the public charges, some two-thousand miles, or say only to the south of Spain; and fed there till wanted. And now to that same spot in the south of Spain, are thirty similar French artisans, from a French Dumdrudge, in like manner wending: till at length, after infinite effort, the two parties come into actual juxtaposition; and Thirty stands fronting Thirty, each with a gun in his hand. Straightway the word 'Fire!' is given: and they blow the souls out of one another; and in place of sixty brisk useful craftsmen, the world has sixty dead carcasses, which it must bury, and anew shed tears for. Had these men any quarrel? Busy as the Devil is, not the smallest! They lived far enough apart; were the entirest strangers; nay, in so wide a Universe, there was even unconsciously, by Commerce, some mutual helpfulness between them. How then? Simpleton! their Governors had fallen-out; and, instead of shooting one another, had the cunning to make these poor blockheads shoot.—Alas, so is it in Deutschland, and hitherto in all other lands; still as of old, 'what devilry soever Kings do, the Greeks must pay the piper!'—In that fiction of the English Smollett, it is true, the final Cessation of War is perhaps prophetically shadowed forth; where the two Natural Enemies, in person, take each a Tobacco-pipe, filled with Brimstone; light the same, and smoke in one another's faces till the weaker gives in: but from such predicted Peace-Era, what blood-filled trenches, and contentious centuries, may still divide us!"

Thus can the Professor, at least in lucid intervals, look away from his own sorrows, over the many-coloured world, and pertinently enough note what is passing there. We may remark, indeed, that for the matter of spiritual culture, if for nothing else, perhaps few periods of his life were richer than this. Internally, there is the most momentous instructive Course of Practical Philosophy, with Experiments, going on; towards the right comprehension of which his Peripatetic habits, favourable to Meditation, might help him rather than hinder. Externally, again, as he wanders to and fro, there are, if for the longing heart little substance, yet for the seeing eye sights enough: in these so boundless Travels of his, granting that the Satanic School was even partially kept down, what an incredible knowledge of our Planet, and its Inhabitants and their Works, that is to say, of all knowable things, might not Teufelsdröckh acquire!

"I have read in most Public Libraries," says he, "including those of Constantinople and Samarcand: in most Colleges, except the Chinese Mandarin ones, I have studied, or seen that there was no studying. Unknown languages have I oftenest gathered from their natural repertory, the Air, by my organ of Hearing; Statistics, Geographics, Topographics came, through the Eye, almost of their own accord. The ways of Man, how he seeks food, and warmth, and protection for himself, in most regions, are ocularly known to me. Like the great Hadrian, I meted-out much of the terraqueous Globe with a pair of Compasses that belonged to myself only.

"Of great Scenes, why speak? Three summer days, I lingered reflecting, and composing (dichtete), by the Pine-chasms of Vaucluse; and in that clear lakelet moistened my bread. I have sat under the Palm-trees of Tadmor; smoked a pipe among the ruins of Babylon. The great Wall of China I have seen; and can testify that it is of grey brick, coped and covered with granite, and shews only second-rate masonry.—Great events, also, have not I witnessed? Kings sweated-down (ausgemergelt) into Berlin-and-Milan Customhouse-Officers; the World well won, and the World well lost; oftener than once a hundred-thousand individuals shot (by each other) in one day. All kindreds and peoples and nations dashed together, and shifted and shovelled into heaps, that they might ferment there, and in time unite. The birth-pangs of Democracy, wherewith convulsed Europe was groaning in cries that reached Heaven, could not escape me.

"For great Men I have ever had the warmest predilection; and can perhaps boast that few such in this era have wholly escaped me. Great Men are the inspired (speaking and acting) Texts of that divine BOOK OF REVELATIONS, whereof a Chapter is completed from epoch to epoch, and by some named HISTORY; to which inspired Texts your numerous talented men, and your innumerable untalented men, are the better or worse exegetic Commentaries, and wagonload of too-stupid, heretical or orthodox, weekly Sermons. For my study, the inspired Texts themselves! Thus did not I, in very early days, having disguised me as a tavern-waiter, stand behind the field-chairs, under that shady Tree at Treisnitz by the Jena Highway; waiting upon the great Schiller and greater Goethe; and hearing what I have not forgotten. For ——"

—— But at this point the Editor recalls his principle of caution, some time ago laid down, and must suppress much. Let not the sacredness of Laurelled, still more, of Crowned Heads, be tampered with. Should we, at a future day, find circumstances altered, and the time come for Publication, then may these glimpses into the privacy of the Illustrious be conceded; which for the present were little better than treacherous, perhaps traitorous Evesdroppings. Of Lord Byron, therefore, of Pope Pius, Emperor Tarakwang, and the 'White Waterroses' (Chinese Carbonari) with their mysteries, no notice here! Of Napoleon himself we shall only, glancing from afar, remark that Teufelsdröckh's relation to him seems to have been of very varied character. At first we find our poor Professor on the point of being shot as a spy; then taken into private conversation, even pinched on the ear, yet presented with no money; at last indignantly dismissed, almost thrown out of doors, as an "Ideologist." "He himself," says the Professor, "was among the completest Ideologists, at least Ideopraxists: in the Idea (*in der Idee*) he lived, moved and fought. The man was a Divine Missionary, though unconscious of it; and preached, through the cannon's throat, that great doctrine, *La carrière ouverte aux talens* (The Tools to him that can handle them), which is our ultimate Political Evangel, wherein alone can Liberty lie. Madly enough he preached, it is true, as Enthusiasts and first Missionaries are wont, with imperfect utterance, amid much frothy rant; yet as articulately perhaps as the case admitted. Or call him, if you will, an American Backwoodsman, who had to fell unpenetrated forests, and battle with innumerable wolves, and did not entirely forbear strong liquor, rioting, and even theft; whom, notwithstanding, the peaceful Sower will follow, and, as he cuts the boundless harvest, bless."

More legitimate and decisively authentic is Teufelsdröckh's appearance and emergence (we know not well whence) in the solitude of the North Cape, on that June Midnight. He has a "light-blue Spanish cloak" hanging round him, as his "most commodious, principal, indeed sole uppergarment;" and stands there, on the Worldpromontory, looking over the infinite Brine, like a little blue Belfry (as we figure), now motionless indeed, yet ready, if stirred, to ring quaintest changes.

"Silence as of death," writes he; "for Midnight, even in the Arctic latitudes, has its character: nothing but the granite cliffs ruddy-tinged, the peaceable gurgle of that slow-heaving Polar Ocean, over which in the utmost North the great Sun hangs low and lazy, as if he too were slumbering. Yet is his cloud-couch wrought of crimson and cloth-of-gold; yet does his light stream over the mirror of waters, like a tremulous firepillar, shooting downwards to the abyss, and hide itself under my feet. In such moments, Solitude also is invaluable; for who would speak, or be looked on, when behind him lies all Europe and Africa, fast asleep, except the watchmen; and before him the silent Immensity, and Palace of the Eternal, whereof our Sun is but a porch-lamp?

"Nevertheless, in this solemn moment, comes a man, or monster, scrambling from among the rock-hollows; and, shaggy, huge as the Hyperborean Bear, hails me in Russian speech: most probably, therefore, a Russian Smuggler. With courteous brevity, I signify my indifference to contraband trade, my humane intentions, yet strong wish to be private. In vain: the monster, counting doubtless on his superior stature, and minded to make sport for himself, or perhaps profit, were it with murder, continues to advance; ever assailing me with his importunate train-oil breath; and now has advanced, till we stand both on the verge of the rock, the deep Sea rippling greedily down below. What argument will avail? On the thick Hyperborean, cherubic reasoning, seraphic eloquence were lost. Prepared for such extremity, I, deftly enough, whisk aside one step; draw out, from my interior reservoirs, a sufficient Birmingham Horse-pistol, and say, 'Be so obliging as retire, Friend (*Er ziehe sich zurück, Freund*), and with promptitude!'

This logic even the Hyperborean understands: fast enough, with apologetic, petitionary growl, he sidles off; and, except for suicidal as well as homicidal purposes, need not return.

"Such I hold to be the genuine use of Gunpowder: that it makes all men alike tall. Nay, if thou be cooler, cleverer than I, if thou have more *Mind,* though all but no *Body* whatever, then canst thou kill me first, and art the taller. Hereby, at last, is the Goliath powerless, and the David resistless; savage Animalism is nothing, inventive Spiritualism is all.

"With respect to Duels, indeed, I have my own ideas. Few things, in this so surprising world, strike me with more surprise. Two little visual Spectra of men, hovering with insecure enough cohesion in the midst of the UNFATHOMABLE, and to dissolve therein, at any rate, very soon,—make pause at the distance of twelve paces asunder; whirl round; and, simultaneously by the cunningest mechanism, explode one another into Dissolution; and off-hand become Air, and Non-extant! Deuce on it (*verdammt*), the little spitfires!—Nay, I think with old Hugo von Trimberg: 'God must needs laugh outright, could such a thing be, to see his wondrous Manikins here below.' "

But amid these specialties, let us not forget the great generality, which is our chief quest here: How prospered the inner man of Teufelsdröckh under so much outward shifting? Does Legion still lurk in him, though repressed; or has he exorcised that Devil's Brood? We can answer that the symptoms continue promising. Experience is the grand spiritual Doctor; and with him Teufelsdröckh has now been long a patient, swallowing many a bitter bolus. Unless our poor Friend belong to the numerous class of Incurables, which seems not likely, some cure will doubtless be effected. We should rather say that Legion, or the Satanic School, was now pretty well extirpated and cast out, but next to nothing introduced in its room; whereby the heart remains, for the while, in a quiet but no comfortable state.

"At length, after so much roasting," thus writes our Autobiographer, "I was what

you might name calcined. Pray only that it be not rather, as is the more frequent issue, reduced to a *caput-mortuum!* But in any case, by mere dint of practice, I had grown familiar with many things. Wretchedness was still wretched; but I could now partly see through it, and despise it. Which highest mortal, in this inane Existence, had I not found a Shadow-hunter, or Shadow-hunted; and, when I looked through his brave garnitures, miserable enough? Thy wishes have all been sniffed aside, thought I: but what, had they even been all granted! Did not the Boy Alexander weep because he had not two Planets to conquer; or a whole Solar System; or after that, a whole Universe? *Ach Gott,* when I gazed into these Stars, have they not looked-down on me as if with pity, from their serene spaces; like Eyes glistening with heavenly tears over the little lot of man! Thousands of human generations, all as noisy as our own, have been swallowed-up of Time, and there remains no wreck of them any more; and Arcturus and Orion and Sirius and the Pleiades are still shining in their courses, clear and young, as when the Shepherd first noted them in the plain of Shinar. Pshaw; what is this paltry little Dog-cage of an Earth; what art thou that sittest whining there? Thou art still Nothing, Nobody: true; but who, then, is Something, Somebody? For thee the Family of Man has no use; it rejects thee; thou art wholly as a dissevered limb: so be it; perhaps it is better so!"

Too-heavy-laden Teufelsdröckh? Yet surely his bands are loosening; one day he will hurl the burden far from him, and bound forth free and with a second youth.

"This," says our Professor, "was the CENTRE OF INDIFFERENCE I had now reached; through which whoso travels from the Negative Pole to the Positive must necessarily pass."·

THE EVERLASTING YEA

"Temptations in the Wilderness!" exclaims Teufelsdröckh: "Have we not all to be tried with such? Not so easily can the old Adam, lodged in us by birth, be dispossessed. Our Life is compassed round with Necessity; yet is the meaning of Life itself no other than Freedom, than Voluntary Force; thus have we a warfare; in the beginning, especially, a hard-fought battle. For the God-given mandate, *Work thou in Welldoing,* lies mysteriously written, in Promethean Prophetic Characters, in our hearts; and leaves us no rest, night or day, till it be deciphered and obeyed; till it burn forth, in our conduct, a visible, acted Gospel of Freedom. And as the clay-given mandate, *Eat thou and be filled,* at the same time persuasively proclaims itself through every nerve,—must there not be a confusion, a contest, before the better Influence can become the upper?

"To me nothing seems more natural than that the Son of Man, when such God-given mandate first prophetically stirs within him, and the Clay must now be vanquished or vanquish,—should be carried of the spirit into grim Solitudes, and there fronting the Tempter do grimmest battle with him; defiantly setting him at naught, till he yield and fly. Name it as we choose: with or without visible Devil, whether in the natural Desert of rocks and sands, or in the populous moral Desert of selfishness and baseness,—to such Temptation are we all called. Unhappy if we are not! Unhappy if we are but Half-men, in whom that divine handwriting has never blazed forth, all-subduing, in true sun-splendour; but quivers dubiously amid meaner lights: or smoulders, in dull pain, in darkness, under earthly vapours!—Our Wilderness is the wide World in an Atheistic Century; our Forty Days are long years of suffering and fasting: nevertheless, to these also comes an end. Yes, to me also was given, if not Victory, yet the consciousness of Battle, and the resolve to persevere therein while life or faculty is left. To me also, entangled in the enchanted forests, demon-peopled, doleful of sight and of sound, it was given, after weariest wanderings, to work out my way into the higher sunlit slopes—of that Mountain which has no summit, or whose summit is in Heaven only!"

He says elsewhere, under a less ambitious figure; as figures are, once for all, natural to him: "Has not thy Life been that of most sufficient men (*tüchtigen Männer*) thou hast known in this generation? An outflush of foolish young Enthusiasm, like the first fallow-crop, wherein are as many weeds as valuable herbs: this all parched away, under the Droughts of practical and spiritual Unbelief, as Disappointment, in thought and act, often-repeated gave rise to Doubt, and Doubt gradually settled into Denial! If I have had a second-crop, and now see the perennial greensward, and sit under umbrageous cedars, which defy all Drought (and Doubt); herein too, be the Heavens praised, I am not without examples, and even exemplars."

So that, for Teufelsdröckh also, there has been a "glorious revolution:" these mad shadow-hunting and shadow-hunted Pilgrimings of his were but some purifying "Temptation in the Wilderness," before his apostolic work (such as it was) could begin; which Temptation is now happily over, and the Devil once more worsted! Was "that high moment in the *Rue de l'Enfer,*" then, properly the turning-point of the battle; when the Fiend said, *Worship me, or be torn in shreds;* and was answered valiantly with an *Apage Satana?* [1]—Singular Teufelsdröckh, would thou hadst told thy singular story in plain words! But it is fruitless to look there, in those Paper-bags, for such. Nothing but innuendoes, figurative crotchets: a typical Shadow, fitfully wavering, prophetico-satiric; no clear logical Picture. "How paint to the sensual eye," asks he once, "what passes in the Holy-of-Holies of Man's Soul; in what words, known to these profane times, speak even afar-off of the unspeakable?" We ask in turn: Why perplex these times, profane as they are, with needless obscurity, by omission and by commission? Not mystical only is our Professor, but whimsical; and involves himself, now more than ever, in eye-bewildering *chiaroscuro.* [2] Successive glimpses, here faithfully imparted, our more gifted readers must endeavour to combine for their own behoof.

He says: "The hot Harmattan wind had raged itself out; its howl went silent within me; and the long-deafened soul could now hear. I paused in my wild wander-

[1] *Apage Satana:* "Get thee hence, Satan!"— Matthew, IV, 8–10.

[2] *chiaroscuro:* light and shade, i.e. 'clear-obscure'.

ings; and sat me down to wait, and consider; for it was as if the hour of change drew nigh. I seemed to surrender, to renounce utterly, and say: "Fly, then, false shadows of Hope; I will chase you no more, I will believe you no more. And ye too, haggard spectres of Fear, I care not for you; ye too are all shadows and a lie. Let me rest here: for I am way-weary and life-weary; I will rest here, were it but to die: to die or to live is alike to me; alike insignificant."—And again: "Here, then, as I lay in that CENTRE OF INDIFFERENCE; cast, doubtless by benignant upper Influence, into a healing sleep, the heavy dreams rolled gradually away, and I awoke to a new Heaven and a new Earth. The first preliminary moral Act, Annihilation of Self (*Selbsttödtung*), had been happily accomplished; and my mind's eyes were now unsealed, and its hands ungyved."

Might we not also conjecture that the following passage refers to his Locality, during this same "healing sleep"; that his Pilgrim-staff lies cast aside here, on "the high table-land"; and indeed that the repose is already taking wholesome effect on him? If it were not that the tone, in some parts, has more of riancy, even of levity, than we could have expected! However, in Teufelsdröckh, there is always the strangest Dualism: light dancing, with guitar-music, will be going on in the forecourt, while by fits from within comes the faint whimpering of woe and wail. We transcribe the piece entire:

"Beautiful it was to sit there, as in my skyey Tent, musing and meditating; on the high table-land, in front of the Mountains; over me, as roof, the azure Dome, and around me, for walls, four azure-flowing curtains,—namely, of the Four azure Winds, on whose bottom-fringes also I have seen gilding. And then to fancy the fair Castles, that stood sheltered in these Mountain hollows; with their green flower-lawns, and white dames and damosels, lovely enough: or better still, the straw-roofed Cottages, wherein, stood many a Mother baking bread, with her children round her:—all hidden and protectingly folded-up in the valley-folds; yet there and alive, as sure as if I beheld them. Or to see, as well as fancy, the nine Towns and Villages, that lay round my mountain-seat, which, in still weather, were wont to speak to me (by their steeple-bells) with metal tongue; and, in almost all weather, proclaimed their vitality by repeated Smoke-clouds; whereon, as on a culinary horologue, I might read the hour of the day. For it was the smoke of cookery, as kind housewives at morning, midday, eventide, were boiling their husbands' kettles; and ever a blue pillar rose up into the air, successively or simultaneously, from each of the nine, saying, as plainly as smoke could say: Such and such a meal is getting ready here. Not uninteresting! For you have the whole Borough, with all its love-makings and scandal-mongeries, contentions and contentments, as in miniature, and could cover it all with your hat.—If, in my wide Wayfarings, I had learned to look into the business of the World in its details, here perhaps was the place for combining it into general propositions, and deducing inferences therefrom.

"Often also could I see the black Tempest marching in anger through the distance: round some Schreckhorn, as yet grim-blue, would the eddying vapour gather, and there tumultuously eddy, and flow down like a mad witch's hair; till, after a space, it vanished, and, in the clear sunbeam, your Schreckhorn stood smiling grim-white, for the vapour had held snow. How thou fermentest and elaboratest in thy great fermenting-vat and laboratory of an Atmosphere, of a World, O Nature!—Or what is Nature? Ha! why do I not name thee GOD? Art thou not the 'Living Garment of God'? O Heavens, is it, in very deed, HE, then, that ever speaks through thee; that lives and loves in thee, that lives and loves in me?

"Fore-shadows, call them rather fore-splendours, of that Truth, and Beginning of Truths, fell mysteriously over my soul. Sweeter than Dayspring to the Shipwrecked in Nova Zembla; ah, like the mother's voice to her little child that strays bewildered, weeping, in unknown tumults; like soft streamings of celestial music to my too-exasperated heart, came that Evangel. The Universe is not dead and demoniacal, a charnel-house with spectres; but godlike, and my Father's!

"With other eyes, too, could I now look

upon my fellow man: with an infinite Love, an infinite Pity. Poor, wandering, wayward man! Art thou not tried, and beaten with stripes, even as I am? Ever, whether thou bear the royal mantle or the beggar's gabardine, art thou not so weary, so heavy-laden; and thy Bed of Rest is but a Grave. O my Brother, my Brother, why cannot I shelter thee in my bosom, and wipe away all tears from thy eyes!— Truly, the din of many-voiced Life, which, in this solitude, with the mind's organ, I could hear, was no longer a maddening discord, but a melting one; like inarticulate cries, and sobbings of a dumb creature, which in the ear of Heaven are prayers. The poor Earth, with her poor joys, was now my needy Mother, not my cruel Step-dame; Man, with his so mad Wants and so mean Endeavors, had become the dearer to me; and even for his sufferings and his sins, I now first named him Brother. Thus was I standing in the porch of that 'Sanc-tuary of Sorrow'; by strange, steep ways, had I too been guided thither; and ere long its sacred gates would open, and the 'Divine Depth of Sorrow' lie disclosed to me."

The Professor says, he here first got eye on the Knot that had been strangling him, and straightway could unfasten it, and was free. "A vain interminable contro-versy," writes he, "touching what is at present called Origin of Evil, or some such thing, arises in every soul, since the begin-ning of the world; and in every soul, that would pass from idle Suffering into actual Endeavouring, must first be put an end to. The most, in our time, have to go content with a simple, incomplete enough Suppres-sion of this controversy; to a few, some Solution of it is indispensable. In every new era, too, such Solution comes-out in different terms; and ever the Solution of the last era has become obsolete, and is found unserviceable. For it is man's nature to change his Dialect from century to cen-tury; he cannot help it though he would. The authentic Church-Catechism of our present century has not yet fallen into my hands: meanwhile, for my own private behoof, I attempt to elucidate the matter so. Man's Unhappiness, as I construe, comes of his Greatness; it is because there

is an Infinite in him, which with all his cunning he cannot quite bury under the Finite. Will the whole Finance Ministers and Upholsterers and Confectioners of modern Europe undertake, in joint-stock company, to make one Shoeblack HAPPY? They cannot accomplish it, above an hour or two: for the Shoeblack also has a Soul quite other than his Stomach; and would require, if you consider it, for his perma-nent satisfaction and saturation, simply this allotment, no more, and no less: *God's infinite Universe altogether to himself, therein to enjoy infinitely, and fill every wish as fast as it rose.* Oceans of Hoch-heimer, a Throat like that of Ophiuchus: speak not of them; to the infinite Shoeblack they are as nothing. No sooner is your ocean filled, than he grumbles that it might have been of better vintage. Try him with half of a Universe, of an Omnipo-tence, he sets to quarrelling with the pro-prietor of the other half, and declares himself the most maltreated of men.—Al-ways there is a black spot in our sunshine: it is even, as I said, the *Shadow of Our-selves.*

"But the whim we have of Happiness is somewhat thus. By certain valuations, and averages, of our own striking, we come upon some sort of average terrestrial lot; this we fancy belongs to us by nature, and of indefeasible right. It is simple payment of our wages, of our deserts; requires neither thanks nor complaint; only such *overplus* as there may be do we account Happiness; any *deficit* again is Misery. Now consider that we have the valuation of our own deserts ourselves, and what a fund of Self-conceit there is in each of us,— do you wonder that the balance should so often dip the wrong way, and many a Blockhead cry: See there, what a payment; was ever worthy gentleman so used!—I tell thee, Blockhead, it all comes of thy Vanity; of what thou *fanciest* those same deserts of thine to be. Fancy that thou deservest to be hanged (as is most likely), thou wilt feel it happiness to be only shot: fancy that thou deservest to be hanged in a hair-halter, it will be a luxury to die in hemp.

"So true it is, what I then said, that *the Fraction of Life can be increased in value not so much by increasing your Numerator as by lessening your Denominator*. Nay, unless my Algebra deceive me, *Unity* itself divided by *Zero* will give *Infinity*. Make thy claim of wages a zero, then; thou hast the world under thy feet. Well did the Wisest of our time write: 'It is only with Renunciation (*Entsagen*) that Life, properly speaking, can be said to begin.'

"I asked myself: What is this that, ever since earliest years, thou hast been fretting and fuming, and lamenting and self-tormenting, on account of? Say it in a word: is it not because thou art not HAPPY? Because the THOU (sweet gentleman) is not sufficiently honoured, nourished, soft-bedded, and lovingly cared-for? Foolish soul! What Act of Legislature was there that *thou* shouldst be Happy? A little while ago thou hadst no right to *be* at all. What if thou wert born and predestined not to be Happy, but to be Unhappy! Art thou nothing other than a Vulture, then, that fliest through the Universe seeking after somewhat to *eat;* and shrieking dolefully because carrion enough is not given thee? Close thy *Byron;* open thy *Goethe*."

"*Es leuchtet mir ein,* I see a glimpse of it!" cries he elsewhere: "there is in man a HIGHER than Love of Happiness: he can do without Happiness, and instead thereof find Blessedness! Was it not to preach-forth this same HIGHER that sages and martyrs, the Poet and the Priest, in all times, have spoken and suffered; bearing testimony, through life and through death, of the Godlike that is in Man, and how in the Godlike only has he Strength and Freedom? Which God-inspired Doctrine art thou also honoured to be taught; O Heavens! and broken with manifold merciful Afflictions, even till thou become contrite, and learn it! O, thank thy Destiny for these; thankfully bear what yet remain: thou hadst need of them; the Self in thee needed to be annihilated. By benignant fever-paroxysms is Life rooting out the deep-seated chronic Disease, and triumphs over Death. On the roaring billows of Time, thou art not engulfed, but borne aloft into the azure of Eternity. Love not Pleasure; love God. This is the EVERLASTING YEA, wherein all contradiction is solved: wherein whoso walks and works, it is well with him."

And again: "Small is it that thou canst trample the Earth with its injuries under thy feet, as old Greek Zeno trained thee: thou canst love the Earth while it injures thee, and even because it injures thee; for this a Greater than Zeno was needed, and he too was sent. Knowest thou that '*Worship of Sorrow*'? The Temple thereof, founded some eighteen centuries ago, now lies in ruins, overgrown with jungle, the habitation of doleful creatures: nevertheless, venture forward; in a low crypt, arched out of falling fragments, thou findest the Altar still there, and its sacred Lamp perennially burning."

Without pretending to comment on which strange utterances, the Editor will only remark, that there lies beside them much of a still more questionable character; unsuited to the general apprehension; nay, wherein he himself does not see his way. Nebulous disquisitions on Religion, yet not without bursts of splendour; on the "perennial continuance of Inspiration"; on Prophecy; that there are "true Priests, as well as Baal-Priests, in our own day": with more of the like sort. We select some fractions, by way of finish to this farrago.

"Cease, my much-respected Herr von Voltaire," thus apostrophises the Professor: "shut thy sweet voice; for the task appointed thee seems finished. Sufficiently hast thou demonstrated this proposition, considerable or otherwise: That the Mythus of the Christian Religion looks not in the eighteenth century as it did in the eighth. Alas, were thy six-and-thirty quartos, and the six-and-thirty thousand other quartos and folios, and flying sheets or reams, printed before and since on the same subject, all needed to convince us of so little! But what next? Wilt thou help us to embody the divine Spirit of that Religion in a new Mythus, in a new vehicle and vesture, that our Souls, otherwise too like perishing, may live? What! thou hast no faculty in that kind? Only a torch for burning, no hammer for building? Take our thanks, then, and —— thyself away.

"Meanwhile what are antiquated Mythuses to me? Or is the God present, felt in my own heart, a thing which Herr von Voltaire will dispute out of me; or dispute into me? To the '*Worship of Sorrow*' ascribe what origin and genesis thou pleasest, *has* not that Worship originated, and been generated; is it not *here?* Feel it in thy heart, and then say whether it is of God! This is Belief; all else is Opinion,— for which latter whoso will, let him worry and be worried."

"Neither," observes he elsewhere, "shall ye tear-out one another's eyes, struggling over 'Plenary Inspiration,' and such-like: try rather to get a little even Partial Inspiration, each of you for yourself. One BIBLE I know, of whose Plenary Inspiration doubt is not so much as possible; nay with my own eyes I saw the God's-Hand writing it: thereof all other Bibles are but Leaves, —say, in Picture-Writing to assist the weaker faculty."

Or to give the wearied reader relief, and, bring it to an end, let him take the following perhaps more intelligible passage: "To me, in this our life," says the Professor, "which is an internecine warfare with the Time-spirit, other warfare seems questionable. Hast thou in any way a Contention with thy brother, I advise thee, think well what the meaning thereof is. If thou gauge it to the bottom, it is simply this: 'Fellow, see! thou art taking more than thy share of Happiness in the world, something from *my* share: which, by the Heavens, thou shalt not; nay, I will fight thee rather.'—Alas, and the whole lot to be divided is such a beggarly matter, truly a 'feast of shells,' for the substance has been spilled out: not enough to quench one Appetite; and the collective human species clutching at them!—Can we not, in all such cases, rather say: 'Take it, thou too-ravenous individual; take that pitiful additional fraction of a share, which I reckoned mine, but which thou so wantest; take it with a blessing: would to Heaven I had enough for thee!'—If Fichte's *Wissenschaftslehre* be, 'to a certain extent, Applied Christianity,' surely to a still greater extent, so is this. We have here not a Whole Duty of Man, yet a Half Duty, namely, the Passive half: could we but do it, as we can demonstrate it!

"But indeed Conviction, were it never so excellent, is worthless till it convert itself into Conduct. Nay, properly Conviction is not possible till then; inasmuch as all Speculation is by nature endless, formless,

a vortex amid vortices: only by a felt indubitable certainty of Experience does it find any centre to revolve round, and so fashion itself into a system. Most true is it, as a wise man teaches us, that 'Doubt of any sort cannot be removed except by Action.' On which ground, too, let him who gropes painfully in darkness or uncertain light, and prays vehemently that the dawn may ripen into day, lay this other precept well to heart, which to me was of invaluable service: '*Do the Duty which lies nearest thee,*' which thou knowest to be a Duty! Thy second Duty will already have become clearer.

"May we not say, however, that the hour of Spiritual Enfranchisement is even this: When your Ideal World, wherein the whole man has been dimly struggling and inexpressibly languishing to work, becomes revealed and thrown open; and you discover, with amazement enough, like the Lothario in *Wilhelm Meister,* that your "America is here or nowhere"? The Situation that has not its Duty, its Ideal, was never yet occupied by man. Yes here, in this poor, miserable, hampered, despicable Actual, wherein thou even now standest, here or nowhere is thy Ideal: work it out therefrom; and working, believe, live, be free. Fool! the Ideal is in thyself, the impediment too is in thyself: thy Condition is but the stuff thou art to shape that same Ideal out of: what matters whether such stuff be of this sort or that, so the Form thou give it be heroic, be poetic? O thou that pinest in the imprisonment of the Actual, and criest bitterly to the gods for a kingdom wherein to rule and create, know this of a truth: the thing thou seekest is already with thee, "here or nowhere," couldst thou only see!

"But it is with man's Soul as it was with Nature: the beginning of Creation is— Light. Till the eye have vision, the whole members are in bonds. Divine moment, when over the tempest-tost Soul, as once over the wild-weltering Chaos, it is spoken: Let there be light! Ever to the greatest that has felt such moment, is it not miraculous and God-announcing; even as, under simpler figures, to the simplest and least. The mad primeval Discord is hushed; the rudely-jumbled conflicting elements bind themselves into separate Firmaments: deep silent rock-foundations are built beneath; and the skyey vault with its everlasting Luminaries above: instead of a dark wasteful Chaos, we have a blooming, fertile, Heaven-encompassed World.

"I too could now say to myself: Be no longer a Chaos, but a World, or even Worldkin. Produce! Produce! Were it but the pitifullest infinitesimal fraction of a Product, produce it, in God's name! 'Tis the utmost thou hast in thee: out with it, then. Up, up! Whatsoever thy hand findeth to do, do it with thy whole might. Work while it is called Today; for the Night cometh, wherein no man can work."

NATURAL SUPERNATURALISM

It is in his stupendous Section, headed *Natural Supernaturalism,* that the Professor first becomes a Seer; and, after long effort, such as we have witnessed, finally subdues under his feet this refractory Clothes-Philosophy, and takes victorious possession thereof. Phantasms enough he has had to struggle with; "Cloth-webs and Cob-webs," of Imperial Mantles, Superannuated Symbols, and what not: yet still did he courageously pierce through. Nay, worst of all, two quite mysterious, world-embracing Phantasms, TIME and SPACE, have ever hovered round him, perplexing and bewildering: but with these also he now resolutely grapples, these also he victoriously rends asunder. In a word, he has looked fixedly on Existence, till, one after the other, its earthly hulls and garnitures have all melted away; and now, to his rapt vision, the interior celestial Holy of Holies lies disclosed.

Here, therefore, properly it is that the Philosophy of Clothes attains to Transcendentalism; this last leap, can we but clear it, takes us safe into the promised land, where *Palingenesia,*[1] in all senses, may be considered as beginning. "Courage, then!" may our Diogenes exclaim, with better right than Diogenes the First once did. This stupendous Section we, after long painful meditation, have found not to be unintelligible; but, on the contrary, to be clear, nay radiant, and all-

[1] *Palingenesia:* rebirth.

illuminating. Let the reader, turning on it what utmost force of speculative intellect is in him, do his part; as we, by judicious selection and adjustment, shall study to do ours:

"Deep has been, and is, the significance of Miracles," thus quietly begins the Professor; "far deeper perhaps than we imagine. Meanwhile, the question of questions were: What specially is a Miracle? To that Dutch King of Siam, an icicle had been a miracle; whoso had carried with him an air-pump and vial of vitriolic ether, might have worked a miracle. To my Horse, again, who unhappily is still more unscientific, do not I work a miracle, and magical *'Open sesame!'* every time I please to pay twopence, and open for him an impassable *Schlagbaum,* or shut Turnpike?

" 'But is not a real Miracle simply a violation of the Laws of Nature?' ask several. Whom I answer by this new question: What are the Laws of Nature? To me perhaps the rising of one from the dead were no violation of these Laws, but a confirmation; were some far deeper Law, now first penetrated into, and by Spiritual Force, even as the rest have all been, brought to bear on us with its Material Force.

"Here too may some inquire, not without astonishment: On what ground shall one, that can make Iron swim, come and declare that therefore he can teach Religion? To us, truly, of the Nineteenth Century, such declaration were inept enough; which nevertheless to our fathers, of the First Century, was full of meaning.

" 'But is it not the deepest Law of Nature that she be constant?' cries an illuminated class: 'Is not the Machine of the Universe fixed to move by unalterable rules?' Probable enough, good friends: nay, I too, must believe that the God, whom ancient inspired men assert to be 'without variableness or shadow of turning,' does indeed never change; that Nature, that the Universe, which no one whom it so pleases can be prevented from calling a Machine, does move by the most unalterable rules. And now of you too I make the old inquiry: What those same unalterable rules, forming the complete Statute-Book of Nature, may possibly be?

"They stand written in our Works of Science, say you; in the accumulated records of man's Experience?—Was Man with his Experience present at the Creation, then, to see how it all went on? Have any deepest scientific individuals yet dived down to the foundations of the Universe, and gauged everything there? Did the Maker take them into His counsel; that they read His ground-plan of the incomprehensible All; and can say, This stands marked therein, and no more than this? Alas! not in any wise! These scientific individuals have been nowhere but where we also are; have seen some handbreadths deeper than we see into the Deep that is infinite, without bottom as without shore.

"Laplace's Book on the Stars, wherein he exhibits that certain Planets, with their Satellites, gyrate round our worthy Sun, at a rate and in a course, which, by greatest good fortune, he and the like of him have succeeded in detecting,—is to me as precious as to another. But is this what thou namest "Mechanism of the Heavens," and "System of the World;" this, wherein Sirius and the Pleiades, and all Herschel's Fifteen-thousand Suns per minute, being left out, some paltry handful of Moons, and inert Balls had been—looked at, nicknamed, and marked in the Zodiacal Waybill; so that we can now prate of their Whereabout; their How, their Why, their What, being hid from us, as in the signless Inane?

"System of Nature! To the wisest man, wide as is his vision, Nature remains of quite *infinite* depth, of quite infinite expansion; and all Experience thereof limits itself to some few computed centuries, and measured square-miles. The course of Nature's phases, on this our little fraction of a Planet, is partially known to us: but who knows what deeper courses these depend on; what infinitely larger Cycle (of causes) our little Epicycle revolves on? To the Minnow every cranny and pebble, and quality and accident, of its little native Creek may have become familiar: but does the Minnow understand the Ocean Tides and periodic Currents, the Tradewinds, and Monsoons, and Moon's Eclipses; by all which the condition of its little Creek is regulated, and may, from time to time (*un*miraculously enough), be quite overset and reversed? Such a minnow is Man; his Creek this Planet Earth; his Ocean the immeasurable All; his Monsoons and periodic Currents the mysterious Course of Providence through Æons of Æons.

"We speak of the Volume of Nature: and truly a Volume it is,—whose Author and Writer is God. To read it! Dost thou, does man, so much as well know the Alphabet thereof? With its Words, Sentences, and grand descriptive Pages, poetical and philosophical, spread out through Solar Systems, and Thousands of Years, we shall not try thee. It is a Volume written in celestial hieroglyphs, in the true Sacredwriting; of which even Prophets are happy that they can read here a line and there a line. As for your Institutes, and Academies of Science, they strive bravely; and, from amid the thick-crowded, inextricably intertwisted hieroglyphic writing, pick out, by dextrous combination, some Letters in the vulgar Character, and therefrom put together this and the other economic Recipe, of high avail in Practice. That Nature is more than some boundless Volume of such Recipes, or huge, well-nigh inexhaustible Domestic-Cookery Book, of which the whole secret will in this manner one day evolve itself, the fewest dream.

"Custom," continues the Professor, "doth make dotards of us all. Consider well, thou wilt find that Custom is the greatest of Weavers; and weaves air-raiment for all the Spirits of the Universe: whereby indeed these dwell with us visibly, as ministering servants, in our houses and workshops; but their spiritual nature becomes, to the most, forever hidden. Philosophy complains that Custom has hoodwinked us, from the first; that we do everything by Custom, even Believe by it; that our very Axioms, let us boast of Free-thinking as we may, are oftenest simply such Beliefs as we have never heard questioned. Nay, what is Philosophy throughout but a continual battle against Custom; an ever-renewed effort to *transcend* the sphere of blind Custom, and so become Transcendental?

"Innumerable are the illusions and legerdemain-tricks of Custom: but of all these perhaps the cleverest is her knack of persuading us that the Miraculous, by simple repetition, ceases to be Miraculous. True, it is by this means we live; for man must work as well as wonder: and herein is Custom so far a kind nurse, guiding him to his true benefit. But she is a fond foolish nurse, or rather we are false foolish nurslings, when, in our resting and reflecting hours, we prolong the same deception. Am I to view the Stupendous with stupid indifference, because I have seen it twice, or two-hundred, or two-million times? There is no reason in Nature or in Art why I should: unless, indeed, I am a mere Work-Machine, for whom the divine gift of Thought were no other than the terrestrial gift of Steam is to the Steam-engine; a power whereby cotton might be spun, and money and money's worth realised.

"Notable enough too, here as elsewhere, wilt thou find the potency of Names; which indeed are but one kind of such customwoven, wonder-hiding Garments. Witchcraft, and all manner of Spectre-work, and Demonology, we have now named Madness, and Diseases of the Nerves. Seldom reflecting that still the new question comes upon us: What is Madness, what are Nerves? Ever, as before, does Madness remain a mysterious-terrific, altogether *infernal* boiling-up of the Nether Chaotic Deep, through this fair-painted Vision of Creation, which swims thereon, which we name the Real. Was Luther's Picture of the Devil less a Reality, whether it were formed within the bodily eye, or without it? In every the wisest Soul lies a whole world of internal Madness, an authentic Demon-Empire; out of which, indeed, his world of Wisdom has been creatively built together, and now rests there, as on its dark foundations does a habitable flowery Earth-rind.

"But deepest of all illusory Appearances, for hiding Wonder, as for many other ends, are your two grand fundamental worldenveloping appearances, SPACE and TIME. These, as spun and woven for us from before Birth itself, to clothe our celestial ME for dwelling here, and yet to blind it,— lie all-embracing, as the universal canvas, or warp and woof, whereby all minor Illusions, in this Phantasm Existence, weave and paint themselves. In vain, while here on Earth, shall you endeavour to strip them off; you can, at best, but rend them asunder for moments, and look through.

"Fortunatus had a wishing Hat, which when he put on, and wished himself Anywhere, behold he was There. By this means had Fortunatus triumphed over Space, he had annihilated Space; for him there was no Where, but all was Here. Were a Hatter to establish himself, in the Wahngasse of Weissnichtwo,[2] and make felts of this sort for all mankind, what a world we should have of it! Still stranger, should, on the opposite side of the street, another Hatter establish himself; and, as his fellow-craftsman made Space-annihilating Hats, make Time-annihilating! Of both would I purchase, were it with my last groschen; but chiefly of this latter. To clap-on your felt, and, simply by wishing that you were Any*where,* straightway to be *There!* Next to clap-on your other felt, and simply by wishing that you were Any*when,* and straightway to be *Then!* This were indeed the grander: shooting at will from the Fire-Creation of the World to its Fire-Consummation; here historically present in the First Century, conversing face to face with Paul and Seneca; there prophetically in the Thirty-first, conversing also face to face with other Pauls and Senecas, who as yet stand hidden in the depth of that late Time!

"Or thinkest thou, it were impossible, unimaginable? Is the Past annihilated, then, or only past; is the Future non-extant or only future? Those mystic faculties of thine, Memory and Hope, already answer: already through those mystic avenues, thou the Earth-blinded summonest both Past and Future, and communest with them, though as yet darkly, and with mute beckonings. The curtains of Yesterday drop down, the curtains of Tomorrow roll up; but Yesterday and Tomorrow both *are.* Pierce through the Time-Element, glance into the Eternal. Believe what thou findest written in the sanctuaries of Man's Soul, even as all Thinkers, in all ages, have

2 Wahngasse of Weissnichtwo: 'Dream-alley of I-know-not-where', home of Teufelsdröckh.

devoutly read it there: that Time and Space are not God, but creations of God; that with God as it is a universal HERE, so it is an everlasting Now.

"And seest thou therein any glimpse of IMMORTALITY?—O Heaven! Is the white Tomb of our Loved One, who died from our arms, and had to be left behind us there, which rises in the distance, like a pale, mournfully receding Milestone, to tell how many toilsome uncheered miles we have journeyed on alone,—but a pale spectral Illusion! Is the lost Friend still mysteriously Here, even as we are Here mysteriously, with God!—Know of a truth that only the Time-shadows have perished, or are perishable; that the real Being of whatever was, and whatever is, and whatever will be, *is* even now and forever. This, should it unhappily seem new, thou mayst ponder at thy leisure; for the next twenty years, or the next twenty centuries: believe it thou must; understand it thou canst not.

"That the Thought-forms, Space and Time, wherein, once for all, we are sent into this Earth to live, should condition and determine our whole Practical reasonings, conceptions, and imagings or imaginings,—seems altogether fit, just, and unavoidable. But that they should, furthermore, usurp such sway over pure spiritual Meditation, and blind us to the wonder everywhere lying close on us, seems nowise so. Admit Space and Time to their due rank as Forms of Thought; nay, even, if thou wilt, to their quite undue rank of Realities: and consider, then, with thyself how their thin disguises hide from us the brightest God-effulgences! Thus, were it not miraculous, could I stretch forth my hand, and clutch the Sun? Yet thou seest me daily stretch forth my hand and therewith clutch many a thing, and swing it hither and thither. Art thou a grown baby, then, to fancy that the Miracle lies in miles of distance, or in pounds avoirdupois of weight; and not to see that the true inexplicable God-revealing Miracle lies in this, that I can stretch forth my hand at all; that I have free Force to clutch aught therewith? Innumerable other of this sort are the deceptions, and wonder-hiding stupefactions, which Space practises on us.

"Still worse is it with regard to Time. Your grand anti-magician, and universal wonder-hider, is this same lying Time. Had we but the Time-annihilating Hat, to put on for once only, we should see ourselves in a World of Miracles, wherein all fabled or authentic Thaumaturgy, and feats of Magic, were outdone. But unhappily we have not such a Hat; and man, poor fool that he is, can seldom and scantily help himself without one.

"Were it not wonderful, for instance, had Orpheus, or Amphion, built the walls of Thebes by the mere sound of his Lyre? Yet tell me, Who built these walls of Weissnichtwo; summoning out all the sandstone rocks, to dance along from the *Steinbruch* (now a huge Troglodyte Chasm, with frightful green-mantled pools); and shape themselves into Doric and Ionic pillars, squared ashlar houses, and noble streets? Was it not the still higher Orpheus, or Orpheuses, who, in past centuries, by the divine Music of Wisdom, succeeded in civilising man? Our highest Orpheus walked in Judea, eighteen hundred years ago: his sphere-melody, flowing in wild native tones, took captive the ravished souls of men; and, being of a truth sphere-melody, still flows and sounds, though now with thousandfold accompaniments, and rich symphonies, through all our hearts; and modulates, and divinely leads them. Is that a wonder, which happens in two hours; and does it cease to be wonderful if happening in two million? Not only was Thebes built by the music of an Orpheus; but without the music of some inspired Orpheus was no city ever built, no work that man glories in ever done.

"Sweep away the Illusion of Time; glance, if thou have eyes, from the near moving-cause to its far-distant Mover: The stroke that came transmitted through a whole galaxy of elastic balls, was it less a stroke than if the last ball only had been struck, and sent flying? O, could I (with the Time-annihilating Hat) transport thee direct from the Beginnings to the Endings, how were thy eyesight unsealed, and thy heart set flaming in the Light-sea of celestial wonder! Then sawest thou that this fair Universe, were it in the meanest province thereof, is in very deed the star-domed City of God; that through every star, through every grass-blade, and most through every Living Soul, the glory of a present God still beams. But Nature, which is the Time-vesture of God, and reveals Him to the wise, hides Him from the foolish.

"Again, could anything be more miraculous than an actual authentic Ghost? The English Johnson longed, all his life, to see one; but could not, though he went to Cock Lane, and thence to the church-vaults, and tapped on coffins. Foolish Doctor! Did he never, with the mind's eye as well as with the body's, look round him into that full tide of human Life he so loved; did he never so much as look into Himself? The good Doctor was a Ghost, as actual and authentic as heart could wish; well-nigh a million of Ghosts were travelling the streets by his side. Once more I say, sweep away the illusion of Time; compress the threescore years into three minutes: what else was he, what else are we? Are we not Spirits, that are shaped into a body, into an Appearance; and that fade away again into air and Invisibility? This is no metaphor, it is a simple, scientific *fact:* we start out of Nothingness, take figure, and are Apparitions; round us, as round the veriest spectre, is Eternity; and to Eternity minutes are as years and æons. Come there not tones of Love and Faith, as from celestial harp-strings, like the Song of beatified Souls? And again, do not we squeak and gibber (in our discordant, screech-owlish debatings and recriminatings); and glide bodeful and feeble, and fearful; or uproar (*poltern*), and revel in our mad Dance of the Dead,—till the scent of the morning-air summons us to our still Home; and dreamy Night becomes awake and Day? Where now is Alexander of Macedon: does the steel Host, that yelled in fierce battle-shouts at Issus and Arbela, remain behind him; or have they all vanished utterly, even as perturbed Goblins must? Napoleon too, and his Moscow Retreats and Austerlitz Campaigns! Was it all other than the veriest Spectre-hunt; which has now, with its howling tumult that made night hideous, flitted away?—Ghosts! There are nigh a thousand-million walking the Earth openly at noontide; some half-hundred have vanished from it, some half-hundred have arisen in it, ere thy watch ticks once.

"O Heaven, it is mysterious, it is awful to consider that we not only carry each a future Ghost within him; but are, in very deed, Ghosts! These Limbs, whence had we them; this stormy Force; this life-blood with its burning Passion? They are dust and shadow; a Shadow-system gathered round our ME; wherein through some moments or years, the Divine Essence is to be revealed in the Flesh. That warrior on his strong warhorse, fire flashes through his eyes; force dwells in his arm and heart; but warrior and war-horse are a vision; a revealed Force, nothing more. Stately they tread the Earth, as if it were a firm substance: fool! the Earth is but a film; it cracks in twain, and warrior and war-horse sink beyond plummet's sounding. Plummet's? Fantasy herself will not follow them. A little while ago they were not; a little while, and they are not, their very ashes are not.

"So it has been from the beginning, so will it be to the end. Generation after generation takes to itself the Form of a Body; and forth-issuing from Cimmerian Night, on Heaven's mission APPEARS. What Force and Fire is in each he expends: one grinding in the mill of Industry; one hunter-like climbing the giddy Alpine heights of Science; one madly dashed in pieces on the rocks of Strife, in war with his fellow:—and then the Heaven-sent is recalled; his earthly Vesture falls away, and soon even to Sense becomes a vanished Shadow. Thus, like some wild-flaming, wild-thundering train of Heaven's Artillery, does this mysterious MANKIND thunder and flame, in long-drawn, quick-succeeding grandeur, through the unknown Deep. Thus, like a God-created, fire-breathing Spirit-host, we emerge from the Inane; haste stormfully across the astonished Earth; then plunge again into the Inane. Earth's mountains are levelled, and her seas filled up, in our passage: can the

Earth, which is but dead and a vision, resist Spirits which have reality and are alive? On the hardest adamant some foot-print of us is stamped-in; the last Rear of the host will read traces of the earliest Van. But whence?—O Heaven, whither? Sense knows not; Faith knows not; only that it is through Mystery to Mystery, from God and to God.

> We *are such stuff*
> "As Dreams are made on, and our little Life
> Is rounded with a sleep!"

HEROES, HERO-WORSHIP, AND THE HEROIC IN HISTORY

THE HERO AS POET. DANTE; SHAKSPEARE

The Hero as Divinity, the Hero as Prophet, are productions of old ages; not to be repeated in the new. They pre-suppose a certain rudeness of conception, which the progress of mere scientific knowl-edge puts an end to. There needs to be, as it were, a world vacant, or almost vacant of scientific forms, if men in their loving wonder are to fancy their fellow-man either a god or one speaking with the voice of a god. Divinity and Prophet are past. We are now to see our Hero in the less ambi-tious, but also less questionable, character of Poet; a character which does not pass. The Poet is a heroic figure belonging to all ages; whom all ages possess, when once he is produced, whom the newest age as the oldest may produce;—and will produce, always when Nature pleases. Let Nature send a Hero-soul; in no age is it other than possible that he may be shaped into a Poet.

Hero, Prophet, Poet,—many different names, in different times and places, do we give to Great Men; according to varie-ties we note in them, according to the sphere in which they have displayed them-selves! We might give many more names, on this same principle. I will remark again, however, as a fact not unimportant to be understood, that the different *sphere* constitutes the grand origin of such dis-tinction; that the Hero can be Poet, Prophet, King, Priest or what you will, according to the kind of world he finds himself born into. I confess, I have no notion of a truly great man that could not be *all* sorts of men. The Poet who could merely sit on a chair, and compose stanzas, would never make a stanza worth much. He could not sing the Heroic warrior, unless he himself were at least a Heroic warrior too. I fancy there is in him the Politician, the Thinker, Legislator, Philos-opher;—in one or the other degree, he could have been, he is all these. So too I cannot understand how a Mirabeau, with that great glowing heart, with the fire that was in it, with the bursting tears that were in it, could not have written verses, trage-dies, poems, and touched all hearts in that way, had his course of life and education led him thitherward. The grand funda-mental character is that of Great Man; that the man be great. Napoleon has words in him which are like Austerlitz Battles. Louis Fourteenth's Marshals are a kind of poetical men withal; the things Turenne says are full of sagacity and geniality, like sayings of Samuel Johnson. The great heart, the clear deep-seeing eye: there it lies; no man whatever, in what province soever, can prosper at all without these. Petrarch and Boccaccio did diplomatic messages, it seems, quite well: one can easily believe it: they had done things a little harder than these! Burns, a gifted song-writer, might have made a still better Mirabeau. Shakspeare,—one knows not what *he* could not have made, in the supreme degree.

True, there are aptitudes of Nature too. Nature does not make all great men, more than all other men, in the self-same mould. Varieties of aptitude doubtless; but infi-nitely more of circumstance; and far oftenest it is the *latter* only that are looked to. But it is as with common men in the learning of trades. You take any man, as yet a vague capability of a man, who could be any kind of craftsman; and make him into a smith, a carpenter, a mason: he is then and thenceforth that and nothing else. And if, as Addison complains, you sometimes see a street-porter staggering under his load on spindle-shanks, and near at hand a tailor with the frame of a Samson handling a bit of cloth and small Whitechapel needle,—it cannot be considered that aptitude of Nature alone has been consulted here either!—The Great Man also, to what shall he be bound apprentice? Given your Hero, is he to become Conqueror, King, Philosopher, Poet? It is an inexplicably complex controversial-calculation between the world and him! He will read the world and its laws; the world with its laws will be there to be read. What the world, on *this* matter, shall permit and bid is, as we said, the most important fact about the world.—

Poet and Prophet differ greatly in our loose modern notions of them. In some old languages, again, the titles are synonymous; *Vates* means both Prophet and Poet: and indeed at all times, Prophet and Poet, well understood, have much kindred of meaning. Fundamentally indeed they are still the same; in this most important respect especially, That they have penetrated both of them into the sacred mystery of the Universe; what Goethe calls "the open secret." "Which is the great secret?" asks one.—"The *open* secret,"—open to all, seen by almost none! That divine mystery, which lies everywhere in all Beings, "the Divine Idea of the World, that which lies at the bottom of Appearance," as Fichte styles it; of which all Appearance, from the starry sky to the grass of the field, but especially the Appearance of Man and his work, is but the *vesture*, the embodiment that renders it visible. This divine mystery *is* in all times and in all places; veritably is. In most times and places it is greatly overlooked; and the Universe, definable always in one or the other dialect, as the realised Thought of God, is considered a trivial, inert, commonplace matter,—as if, says the Satirist, it were a dead thing, which some upholsterer had put together! It could do no good, at present, to *speak* much about this; but it is a pity for every one of us if we do not know it, live ever

in the knowledge of it. Really a most mournful pity;—a failure to live at all, if we live otherwise!

But now, I say, whoever may forget this divine mystery, the *Vates*, whether Prophet or Poet, has penetrated into it; is a man sent hither to make it more impressively known to us. That always is his message; he is to reveal that to us,—that sacred mystery which he more than others lives ever present with. While others forget it, he knows it;—I might say, he has been driven to know it; without consent asked of *him*, he finds himself living in it, bound to live in it. Once more, here is no Hearsay, but a direct Insight and Belief; this man too could not help being a sincere man! Whosoever may live in the shows of things, it is for him a necessity of nature to live in the very fact of things. A man once more, in earnest with the Universe, though all others were but toying with it. He is a *Vates*, first of all, in virtue of being sincere. So far Poet and Prophet, participators in the "open secret," are one.

With respect to their distinction again: The *Vates* Prophet, we might say, has seized that sacred mystery rather on the moral side, as Good and Evil, Duty and Prohibition; the *Vates* Poet on what the Germans call the æsthetic side, as Beautiful, and the like. The one we may call a revealer of what we are to do, the other of what we are to love. But indeed these two provinces run into one another, and cannot be disjoined. The Prophet too has his eye on what we are to love: how else shall he know what it is we are to do? The highest Voice ever heard on this earth said withal, "Consider the lilies of the field; they toil not, neither do they spin: yet Solomon in all his glory was not arrayed like one of these." A glance, that, into the deepest deep of Beauty. "The lilies of the field,"—dressed finer than earthly princes, springing-up there in the humble furrow-field; a beautiful *eye* looking-out on you, from the great inner Sea of Beauty! How could the rude Earth make these if her Essence, rugged as she looks and is, were not inwardly Beauty? In this point of view, too, a saying of Goethe's, which has staggered several, may have meaning: "The Beautiful," he intimates, "is higher than the Good; the Beautiful includes in it the Good." The *true* Beautiful; which however, I have said somewhere, "differs from the *false* as Heaven does from Vauxhall!" So much for the distinction and identity of Poet and Prophet.—

In ancient and also in modern periods we find a few Poets who are accounted perfect; whom it were a kind of treason to find fault with. This is noteworthy; this is right: yet in strictness it is only an illusion. At bottom, clearly enough, there is no perfect Poet! A vein of Poetry exists in the hearts of all men; no man is made altogether of Poetry. We are all poets when we *read* a poem well. The "imagination that shudders at the Hell of Dante," is not that the same faculty, weaker in degree, as Dante's own? No one but Shakspeare can embody, out of *Saxo Grammaticus,* the story of *Hamlet* as Shakspeare did: but every one models some kind of story out of it; every one embodies it better or worse. We need not spend time in defining. Where there is no specific difference, as between round and square, all definition must be more or less arbitrary. A man that has *so* much more of the poetic element developed in him as to have become noticeable, will be called Poet by his neighbours. World-Poets too, those whom we are to take for perfect Poets, are settled by critics in the same way. One who rises *so* far above the general level of Poets will, to such and such critics, seem a Universal Poet; as he ought to do. And yet it is, and must be, an arbitrary distinction. All Poets, all men, have some touches of the Universal; no man is wholly made of that. Most Poets are very soon forgotten: but not the noblest Shakspeare or Homer of them can be remembered *forever;*—a day comes when he too is not!

Nevertheless, you will say, there must be a difference between true Poetry and true speech not poetical: what is the difference? On this point many things have been written, especially by late German Critics, some of which are not very intelligible at first. They say, for example, that the Poet has an *infinitude* in him; communicates an *Unendlichkeit,* a certain character of "infinitude," to whatsoever he delineates. This, though not very precise, yet on so vague a matter is worth remembering: if well meditated, some meaning will gradually be found in it. For my own part, I find considerable meaning in the old vulgar distinction of Poetry being *metrical,* having music in it, being a Song. Truly, if pressed to give a definition, one might say this as soon as anything else: If your delineation be authentically *musical,* musical not in word only, but in heart and substance, in all the thoughts and utterances of it, in the whole conception of it, then it will be poetical; if not, not.— Musical: how much lies in that! A *musical* thought is one spoken by a mind that has penetrated into the inmost heart of the thing; detected the inmost mystery of it, namely the *melody* that lies hidden in it; the inward harmony of coherence which is its soul, whereby it exists, and has a right to be, here in this world. All inmost things, we may say, are melodious; naturally utter themselves in Song. The meaning of Song goes deep. Who is there that, in logical words, can express the effect music has on us? A kind of inarticulate unfathomable speech, which leads us to the edge of the Infinite, and lets us for moments gaze into that!

Nay all speech, even the commonest speech, has something of song in it: not a parish in the world but has its parish-accent;—the rhythm or *tune* to which the people there *sing* what they have to say! Accent is a kind of chanting; all men have accent of their own,—though they only *notice* that of others. Observe too how all passionate language does of itself become musical,—with a finer music than the mere accent; the speech of a man even in zealous anger becomes a chant, a song. All deep things are Song. It seems somehow the very central essence of us, Song; as if all the rest were but wrappages and hulls! The primal element of us; of us, and of all things. The Greeks fabled of Sphere-Harmonies: it was the feeling they had of the inner structure of Nature: that the soul of all her voices and utterances was perfect music. Poetry, therefore, we will call *musical Thought.* The Poet is he who *thinks* in that manner. At bottom, it turns still on power of intellect; it is a man's sincerity and depth of vision that makes him a Poet. See deep enough, and you see musically; the heart of Nature *being* everywhere music, if you can only reach it.

The *Vates* Poet, with his melodious Apocalypse of Nature, seems to hold a poor rank among us, in comparison with the *Vates* Prophet; his function, and our esteem of him for his function, alike slight. The Hero taken as Divinity; the Hero taken as Prophet; then next the Hero taken only as Poet: does it not look as if our estimate of the Great Man, epoch after epoch, were continually diminishing? We take him first for a god, then for one god-inspired; and now in the next stage of it, his most miraculous word gains from us only the recognition that he is a Poet, beautiful verse-maker, man of genius, or suchlike!—It looks so; but I persuade myself that intrinsically it is not so. If we consider well, it will perhaps appear that in man still there is the *same* altogether peculiar admiration for the Heroic Gift, by what name soever called, that there at any time was.

I should say, if we do not now reckon a Great Man literally divine, it is that our notions of God, of the supreme unattainable Fountain of Splendour, Wisdom, and Heroism, are ever rising *higher;* not altogether that our reverence for these qualities, as manifested in our like, is getting lower. This is worth taking thought of. Sceptical Dilettantism, the curse of these ages, a curse which will not last forever, does indeed in this the highest province of human things, as in all provinces, make sad work; and our reverence for great men, all crippled, blinded, paralytic as it is, comes-out in poor plight, hardly recognisable. Men worship the shows of great men; the most disbelieve that there is any reality of great men to worship. The dreariest, fatalest faith; believing which, one would literally despair of human things. Nevertheless look, for example, at Napoleon! A Corsican lieutenant of artillery; that is the show of *him:* yet is he not obeyed, *worshipped* after his sort, as all the Tiaraed and Diademed of the world put together could not be? High Duchesses, and ostlers of inns, gather round the Scottish rustic, Burns;—a strange feeling dwelling in each that they never heard a man like this; that, on the whole, this is the man! In the secret heart of these people it still dimly reveals itself, though there is no accredited way of uttering it at present, that this rustic, with his black brows and flashing sun-eyes, and strange words moving laughter and tears, is of a dignity far beyond all others, incommensurable with all others. Do not we feel it so? But now, were Dilettantism, Scepticism, Triviality, and all that sorrowful brood, cast-out of us,—as, by God's blessing, they shall one day be; were faith in the shows of things entirely swept-out, replaced by clear faith in the *things,* so that a man acted on the impulse of that only, and counted the other non-extant; what a new livelier feeling towards this Burns were it!

Nay here in these ages, such as they are, have we not two mere Poets, if not deified, yet we may say beatified? Shakspeare and Dante are Saints of Poetry; really, if we will think of it, *canonised,* so that it is impiety to meddle with them. The unguided instinct of the world, working across all these perverse impediments, has arrived at such result. Dante and Shakspeare are a peculiar Two. They dwell apart, in a kind of royal solitude; none equal, none second to them: in the general feeling of the world, a certain transcendentalism, a glory as of complete perfection, invests these two. They *are* canonised, though no Pope or Cardinals took hand in doing it! Such, in spite of every perverting influence, in the most unheroic times, is still our indestructible reverence for heroism.—We will look a little at these Two, the Poet Dante and the Poet Shakspeare: what little it is permitted us to say here of the Hero as Poet will most fitly arrange itself in that fashion.

Many volumes have been written by way of commentary on Dante and his Book; yet, on the whole, with no great result. His Biography is, as it were, irrecoverably lost for us. An unimportant, wandering, sorrow-stricken man, not much note was taken of him while he lived; and the most of that has vanished, in the long space that now intervenes. It is five centuries since he ceased writing and living here. After all commentaries, the Book itself is mainly what we know of him. The Book;—and one might add that Portrait commonly attributed to Giotto, which, looking on it, you cannot help inclining to think genuine, whoever did it. To me it is a most touching face; perhaps of all faces that I know, the most so. Lonely there, painted as on vacancy, with the simple laurel wound round it; the deathless sorrow and pain, the known victory which is also deathless;—significant of the whole history of Dante! I think it is the mournfulest face that ever was painted from reality; an altogether tragic, heart-affecting face. There is in it, as a foundation of it, the softness, tenderness, gentle affection as of a child; but all this is as if congealed into sharp contradiction, into abnegation, isolation, proud hopeless pain. A soft ethereal soul looking-out so stern, implacable, grim-trenchant, as from imprisonment of thick-ribbed ice! Withal it is a silent pain too, a silent scornful one: the lip is curled in a kind of godlike disdain of the thing that is eating-out his heart,—as if it were withal a mean insignificant thing, as if he whom it had power to torture and strangle were greater than it. The face of one wholly in protest, and life-long unsurrendering battle, against the world. Affection all converted into indignation: an implacable indignation; slow, equable, silent, like that of a god! The eye too, it looks-out as in a kind of *surprise,* a kind of inquiry, Why the world was of such a sort? This is Dante: so he looks, this "voice of ten silent centuries," and sings us "his mystic unfathomable song."

The little that we know of Dante's Life corresponds well enough with this Portrait and this Book. He was born at Florence, in the upper class of society, in the year 1265. His education was the best then going; much school-divinity, Aristotelean logic, some Latin classics,—no inconsiderable insight into certain provinces of things: and Dante, with his earnest intelligent nature, we need not doubt, learned better than most all that was learnable. He has a clear cultivated understanding, and of great subtlety; this best fruit of education he had contrived to realise from these scholastics. He knows accurately and well what lies close to him; but, in such a time, without printed books or free intercourse, he could not know well what was distant: the small clear light, most luminous for what is near, breaks itself into singular *chiaroscuro* striking on what is far off. This was Dante's learning from the schools. In life, he had gone through the usual destinies; been twice out campaigning as a soldier for the Florentine State, been on embassy; had in his thirty-fifth year, by natural gradation of talent and service, become one of the Chief Magistrates of Florence. He had met in boyhood a certain Beatrice Portinari, a beautiful little girl of his own age and rank, and grown-up thenceforth in partial sight of her, in some distant intercourse with her. All readers know his graceful affecting account of this; and then of their being parted; of her being wedded to another, and of her death soon after. She makes a great figure in Dante's Poem; seems to have made a great figure in his life. Of all beings it might seem as if she, held apart from him, far apart at last in the dim Eternity, were the only one he had ever with his whole strength of affection loved. She died: Dante himself was wedded; but it seems not happily, far from happily. I fancy, the rigorous earnest man, with his keen excitabilities, was not altogether easy to make happy.

We will not complain of Dante's miseries: had all gone right with him as he wished it, he might have been Prior, Podestà, or whatsoever they call it, of Florence, well accepted among neighbours,—and the world had wanted one of the most notable words ever spoken or sung. Florence would have had another prosperous Lord Mayor; and the ten dumb centuries continued voiceless, and the ten other listening centuries (for there will be ten of them and more) had no *Divina Commedia* to hear! We will complain of nothing. A nobler destiny was appointed for this Dante; and he, struggling like a man led towards death and crucifixion, could not help fulfilling it. Give *him* the choice of his happiness! He knew not, more than we do, what was really happy, what was really miserable.

In Dante's Priorship, the Guelf-Ghibelline, Bianchi-Neri, or some other confused disturbances rose to such a height, that Dante, whose party had seemed the stronger, was with his friends cast unexpectedly forth into banishment; doomed thenceforth to a life of woe and wandering. His property was all confiscated and more; he had the fiercest feeling that it was entirely unjust, nefarious in the sight of God and man. He tried what was in him to get reinstated; tried even by warlike surprisal, with arms in his hand: but it would not do; bad only had become worse. There is a record, I believe, still extant in the Florence Archives, dooming this Dante, wheresoever caught, to be burnt alive. Burnt alive; so it stands, they say: a very curious civic document. Another curious document, some considerable number of years later, is a Letter of Dante's to the Florentine Magistrates, written in answer to a milder proposal of theirs, that he should return on condition of apologising and paying a fine. He answers, with fixed stern pride: "If I cannot return without calling myself guilty, I will never return, *nunquam revertar*."

For Dante there was now no home in this world. He wandered from patron to patron, from place to place; proving, in his own bitter words, "How hard is the path, *Come è duro calle*." The wretched are not cheerful company. Dante, poor and banished, with his proud earnest nature, with his moody humours, was not a man to conciliate men. Petrarch reports of him that being at Can della Scala's court, and blamed one day for his gloom and taciturnity, he answered in no courtier-like way. Della Scala stood among his courtiers, with mimes and buffoons (*nebulones ac histriones*) making him heartily merry; when turning to Dante, he said: "Is it not strange, now, that this poor fool should make himself so entertaining; while you a wise man sit there day after day, and have nothing to amuse us with at all?" Dante answered bitterly: "No, not strange; your Highness is to recollect the Proverb, *Like to Like;*"—given the amuser, the amusee must also be given! Such a man, with his proud silent ways, with his sarcasms and sorrows, was not made to succeed at court. By degrees, it came to be evident to him that he had no longer any

resting-place, or hope of benefit, in this earth. The earthly world had cast him forth, to wander, wander; no living heart to love him now; for his sore miseries there was no solace here.

The deeper naturally would the Eternal World impress itself on him; that awful reality over which, after all, this Time-world, with its Florences and banishments, only flutters as an unreal shadow. Florence thou shalt never see: but Hell and Purgatory and Heaven thou shalt surely see! What is Florence, Can della Scala, and the World and Life altogether? ETERNITY: thither, of a truth, not elsewhither, art thou and all things bound! The great soul of Dante, homeless on earth, made its home more and more in that awful other world. Naturally his thoughts brooded on that, as on the one fact important for him. Bodied or bodiless, it is the one fact important for all men:—but to Dante, in that age, it was bodied in fixed certainty of scientific shape; he no more doubted of that *Malebolge* [1] Pool, that it all lay there with its gloomy circles, with its *alti guai*,[2] and that he himself should see it, than we doubt that we should see Costantinople if we went thither. Dante's heart, long filled with this, brooding over it in speechless thought and awe, bursts forth at length into "mystic unfathomable song;" and this his *Divine Comedy*, the most remarkable of all modern Books, is the result.

It must have been a great solacement to Dante, and was, as we can see, a proud thought for him at times, that he, here in exile, could do this work; that no Florence, nor no man or men, could hinder him from doing it, or even much help him in doing it. He knew too, partly, that it was great; the greatest a man could do. "If thou follow thy star, *Se tu sequi tua stella*," —so could the Hero, in his forsakenness, in his extreme need, still say to himself: "Follow thou thy star, thou shalt not fail of a glorious haven!" The labour of writing, we find, and indeed could know otherwise, was great and painful for him; he says, This Book, "which has made me

---

[1] *Malebolge:* Evil pits,—name of the eighth circle in Dante's *Inferno*.

[2] *alti guai:* 'loud wails',—heard by Dante as he enters Hell (*Inferno*, III, 22–24).

lean for many years." Ah yes, it was won, all of it, with pain and sore toil,—not in sport, but in grim earnest. His Book, as indeed most good Books are, has been written, in many senses, with his heart's blood. It is his whole history, this Book. He died after finishing it; not yet very old, at the age of fifty-six;—broken-hearted rather, as is said. He lies buried in his death-city Ravenna: *Hic claudor Dantes* 10 *patriis extorris ab oris.* The Florentines begged back his body, in a century after; the Ravenna people would not give it. "Here am I Dante laid, shut-out from my native shores."

I said, Dante's Poem was a Song: it is Tieck who calls it "a mystic unfathomable Song"; and such is literally the character of it. Coleridge remarks very pertinently somewhere, that wherever you find a sen- 20 tence musically worded, of true rhythm and melody in the words, there is something deep and good in the meaning too. For body and soul, word and idea, go strangely together here as everywhere. Song: we said before, it was the Heroic of Speech! All *old* Poems, Homer's and the rest, are authentically Songs. I would say, in strictness, that all right Poems are; that whatsoever is not *sung* is properly no Poem, 30 but a piece of Prose cramped into jingling lines,—to the great injury of the grammar, to the great grief of the reader, for most part! What we want to get at is the *thought* the man had, if he had any: why should he twist it into jingle, if he *could* speak it out plainly? It is only when the heart of him is rapt into true passion of melody, and the very tones of him, according to Coleridge's remark, become musical 40 by the greatness, depth and music of his thoughts, that we can give him right to rhyme and sing; that we call him a Poet, and listen to him as the Heroic of Speakers,—whose speech *is* Song. Pretenders to this are many; and to an earnest reader, I doubt, it is for most part a very melancholy, not to say an insupportable business, that of reading rhyme! Rhyme that had no inward necessity to be rhymed:—it ought 50 to have told us plainly, without any jingle, what it was aiming at. I would advise all men who *can* speak their thought, not to sing it; to understand that, in a serious

time, among serious men, there is no vocation in them for singing it. Precisely as we love the true song, and are charmed by it as by something divine, so shall we hate the false song, and account it a mere wooden noise, a thing hollow, superfluous, altogether an insincere and offensive thing.

I give Dante my highest praise when I say of his *Divine Comedy* that it is, in all senses, genuinely a Song. In the very sound of it there is a *canto fermo;* it proceeds as by a chant. The language, his simple *terza rima,*[3] doubtless helped him in this. One reads along naturally with a sort of *lilt.* But I add, that it could not be otherwise; for the essence and material of the work are themselves rhythmic. Its depth, and rapt passion and sincerity, makes it musical;—go *deep* enough, there is music everywhere. A true inward symmetry, what one calls an architectural harmony, reigns in it, proportionates it all: architectural; which also partakes of the character of music. The three kingdoms, *Inferno, Purgatorio, Paradiso,* look-out on one another like compartments of a great edifice; a great supernatural world-cathedral, piled-up there, stern, solemn, awful; Dante's World of Souls! It is, at bottom, the *sincerest* of all Poems; sincerity, here too, we find to be the measure of worth. It came deep out of the author's heart of hearts; and it goes deep, and through long generations, into ours. The people of Verona, when they saw him on the streets, used to say, *"Eccovi l' uom ch' è stato all' Inferno,* See, there is the man that was in Hell!" Ah yes, he had been in Hell;—in Hell enough, in long severe sorrow and struggle; as the like of him is pretty sure to have been. Commedias that come-out *divine* are not accomplished otherwise. Thought, true labour of any kind, highest virtue itself, is it not the daughter of Pain? Born as out of the black whirlwind;—true *effort,* in fact, as of a captive struggling to free himself: that is Thought. In all ways we are "to become perfect through *suffering."* —But, as I say, no work known to me is so elaborated as this of Dante's. It has

[3] *terza rima:* third (or triple) rime. Dante's verse is in eleven-syllable iambic lines, rhyming in interlocked groups of three,—aba, bcb, cdc, etc.

all been as if molten, in the hottest furnace of his soul. It had made him "lean" for many years. Not the general whole only; every compartment of it is worked-out, with intense earnestness, into truth, into clear visuality. Each answers to the other; each fits in its place, like a marble stone accurately hewn and polished. It is the soul of Dante, and in this the soul of the middle ages, rendered forever rhythmically visible there. No light task; a right intense one: but a task which is *done*.

Perhaps one would say, *intensity*, with the much that depends on it, is the prevailing character of Dante's genius. Dante does not come before us as a large catholic mind, rather a narrow, and even sectarian mind: it is partly the fruit of his age and position, but partly too of his own nature. His greatness has, in all senses, concentered itself into fiery emphasis and depth. He is world-great not because he is worldwide, but because he is world-deep. Through all objects he pierces as it were down into the heart of Being. I know nothing so intense as Dante. Consider, for example, to begin with the outermost development of his intensity, consider how he paints. He has a great power of vision; seizes the very type of a thing; presents that and nothing more. You remember that first view he gets of the Hall of Dite: *red* pinnacle, redhot cone of iron glowing through the dim immensity of gloom;—so vivid, so distinct, visible at once and forever! It is as an emblem of the whole genius of Dante. There is a brevity, an abrupt precision in him: Tacitus is not briefer, more condensed; and then in Dante it seems a natural condensation, spontaneous to the man. One smiting word; and then there is silence, nothing more said. His silence is more eloquent than words. It is strange with what a sharp decisive grace he snatches the true likeness of a matter: cuts into the matter as with a pen of fire. Plutus, the blustering giant, collapses at Virgil's rebuke; it is "as the sails sink, the mast being suddenly broken." Or that poor Brunetto Latini, with the *cotto aspetto*, "face *baked*," parched brown and lean; and the "fiery snow" that falls on them there, a "fiery snow without

wind," "slow, deliberate, never-ending!" Or the lids of those Tombs; square sarcophaguses, in that silent dim-burning Hall, each with its Soul in torment; the lids laid open there; they are to be shut at the Day of Judgment, through Eternity. And how Farinata rises; and how Cavalcante falls—at hearing of his Son, and the past tense *"fue"*! The very movements in Dante have something brief; swift, decisive, almost military. It is of the inmost essence of his genius, this sort of painting. The fiery, swift Italian nature of the man, so silent, passionate, with its quick abrupt movements, its silent "pale rages," speaks itself in these things.

For though this of painting is one of the outermost developments of a man, it comes like all else from the essential faculty of him; it is physiognomical of the whole man. Find a man whose words paint you a likeness, you have found a man worth something; mark his manner of doing it, as very characteristic of him. In the first place, he could not have discerned the object at all, or seen the vital type of it, unless he had, what we may call, *sympathised* with it,—had sympathy in him to bestow on objects. He must have been *sincere* about it too; sincere and sympathetic: a man without worth cannot give you the likeness of any object; he dwells in vague outwardness, fallacy and trivial hearsay, about all objects. And indeed may we not say that intellect altogether expresses itself in this power of discerning what an object is? Whatsoever of faculty a man's mind may have will come out here. Is it even of business, a matter to be done? The gifted man is he who *sees* the essential point, and leaves all the rest aside as surplusage: it is his faculty too, the man of business's faculty, that he discern the true *likeness*, not the false superficial one, of the thing he has got to work in. And how much of *morality* is in the kind of insight we get of anything; "the eye seeing in all things what it brought with it the faculty of seeing"! To the mean eye all things are trivial, as certainly as to the jaundiced they are yellow. Raphael, the Painters tell us, is the best of all Portrait-painters withal. No most gifted eye can exhaust the significance of any object. In the commonest human face there lies more than Raphael will take-away with him.

Dante's painting is not graphic only, brief, true, and of a vividness as of fire in dark night; taken on the wider scale, it is everyway noble, and the outcome of a great soul. Francesca and her Lover, what qualities in that! A thing woven as out of rainbows, on a ground of eternal black. A small flute-voice of infinite wail speaks there, into our very heart of hearts. A touch of womanhood in it too: *della bella persona, che mi fu tolta* [4]; and how, even in the Pit of woe, it is a solace that *he* will never part from her! Saddest tragedy in these *alti guai*. And the racking winds, in that *aer bruno*,[5] whirl them away again, to wail forever!—Strange to think: Dante was the friend of this poor Francesca's father; Francesca herself may have sat upon the Poet's knee, as a bright innocent little child. Infinite pity, yet also infinite rigour of law: it is so Nature is made; it is so Dante discerned that she was made. What a paltry notion is that of his *Divine Comedy's* being a poor splenetic impotent terrestrial libel; putting those into Hell whom he could not be avenged-upon on earth! I suppose if ever pity, tender as a mother's, was in the heart of any man, it was in Dante's. But a man who does not know rigour cannot pity either. His very pity will be cowardly, egoistic,—sentimentality, or little better. I know not in the world an affection equal to that of Dante. It is a tenderness, a trembling, longing, pitying love: like the wail of Æolean harps, soft, soft; like a child's young heart;—and then that stern, sore-saddened heart! These longings of his towards his Beatrice; their meeting together in the *Paradiso;* his gazing in her pure transfigured eyes, her that had been purified by death so long, separated from him so far:—one likens it to the song of angels; it is among the purest utterances of affection, perhaps the very purest, that ever came out of a human soul.

For the *intense* Dante is intense in all things; he has got into the essence of all. His intellectual insight as painter, on occasion too as reasoner, is but the result of all other sorts of intensity. Morally great, above all, we must call him; it is the beginning of all. His scorn, his grief are as transcendent as his love;—as indeed, what are they but the *inverse* or *converse* of his love? *"A Dio spiacenti ed a' nemici sui,* Hateful to God and to the enemies of God": lofty scorn, unappeasable silent reprobation and aversion; *"Non ragionam di lor,* We will not speak of *them,* look only and pass." Or think of this; "They have not the *hope* to die, *Non han speranza di morte."* One day, it had risen sternly benign on the scathed heart of Dante, that he, wretched, never-resting, worn as he was, would full surely *die;* "that Destiny itself could not doom him not to die." Such words are in this man. For rigour, earnestness and depth, he is not to be paralleled in the modern world; to seek his parallel we must go into the Hebrew Bible, and live with the antique Prophets there.

I do not agree with much modern criticism, in greatly preferring the *Inferno* to the two other parts of the Divine Commedia. Such preference belongs, I imagine, to our general Byronism of taste, and is like to be a transient feeling. The *Purgatorio* and *Paradiso,* especially the former, one would almost say, is even more excellent than it. It is a noble thing that *Purgatorio,* "Mountain of Purification"; an emblem of the noblest conception of that age. If Sin is so fatal, and Hell is and must be so rigorous, awful, yet in Repentance too is man purified; Repentance is the grand Christian act. It is beautiful how Dante works it out. The *tremolar dell' onde,* that "trembling" of the ocean-waves, under the first pure gleam of morning, dawning afar on the wandering Two, is as the type of an altered mood. Hope has now dawned; never-dying Hope, if in company still with heavy sorrow. The obscure sojourn of dæmons and reprobate is underfoot; a soft breathing of penitence mounts higher and higher, to the Throne of Mercy itself. "Pray for me," the denizens of that Mount of Pain all say to him.

---

[4] *della bella persona,* etc.:
  "Love. . . .
    Seized this man *for the person beautiful*
    That was ta'en from me"
                    (*Inferno,* V, 100–3).
[5] *aer bruno:* 'brown air', *Inferno,* II, 1.

"Tell my Giovanna to pray for me," my daughter Giovanna: "I think her mother loves me no more!" They toil painfully up by that winding steep, "bent-down like corbels of a building," some of them,—crushed-together so "for the sin of pride": yet nevertheless in years, in ages and æons, they shall have reached the top, which is Heaven's gate, and by Mercy shall have been admitted in. The joy too of all, when one has prevailed; the whole Mountain shakes with joy, and a psalm of praise rises, when one soul has perfected repentance and got its sin and misery left behind! I call all this a noble embodiment of a true noble thought.

But indeed the Three compartments mutually support one another, are indispensable to one another. The *Paradiso,* a kind of inarticulate music to me, is the redeeming side of the *Inferno;* the *Inferno* without it were untrue. All three make-up the true Unseen World, as figured in the Christianity of the Middle Ages; a thing forever memorable, forever true in the essence of it, to all men. It was perhaps delineated in no human soul with such depth of veracity as in this of Dante's; a man *sent* to sing it, to keep it long memorable. Very notable with what brief simplicity he passes out of the every-day reality, into the Invisible one; and in the second or third stanza, we find ourselves in the World of Spirits; and dwell there, as among things palpable, indubitable! To Dante they *were* so; the real world, as it is called, and its facts, was but the threshold to an infinitely higher Fact of a World. At bottom, the one was *preter*natural as the other. Has not each man a soul? He will not only be a spirit, but is one. To the earnest Dante it is all one visible Fact; he believes it, sees it; is the Poet of it in virtue of that. Sincerity, I say again, is the saving merit, now as always.

Dante's Hell, Purgatory, Paradise, are a symbol withal, an emblematic representation of his Belief about this Universe:—some Critic in a future age, like those Scandinavian ones the other day, who has ceased altogether to think as Dante did, may find this too all an "Allegory," perhaps an idle Allegory! It is a sublime embodiment, or sublimest, of the soul of Christianity. It expresses, as in huge world-wide architectural emblems, how the Christian Dante felt Good and Evil to be the two polar elements of this Creation, on which it all turns; that these two differ not by *preferability* of one to the other, but by incompatibility absolute and infinite; that the one is excellent and high as light and Heaven, the other hideous, black as Gehenna and the Pit of Hell! Everlasting Justice, yet with Penitence, with everlasting Pity,—all Christianism, as Dante and the Middle Ages had it, is emblemed here. Emblemed: and yet, as I urged the other day, with what entire truth of purpose; how unconscious of any embleming! Hell, Purgatory, Paradise: these things were not fashioned as emblems; was there, in our Modern European Mind, any thought at all of their being emblems! Were they not indubitable awful facts; the whole heart of man taking them for practically true, all Nature everywhere confirming them? So is it always in these things. Men do not believe an Allegory. The future Critic, whatever his new thought may be, who considers this of Dante to have been all got-up as an Allegory, will commit one sore mistake!—Paganism we recognised as a veracious expression of the earnest awe-struck feeling of man towards the Universe; veracious, true once, and still not without worth for us. But mark here the difference of Paganism and Christianism; one great difference. Paganism emblemed chiefly the Operations of Nature; the destinies, efforts, combinations, vicissitudes of things and men in this world; Christianism emblemed the Law of Human Duty, the Moral Law of Man. One was for the sensuous nature: a rude helpless utterance of the *first* Thought of men,—the chief recognised virtue, Courage, Superiority to Fear. The other was not for the sensuous nature, but for the moral. What a progress is here, if in that one respect only!—

And so in this Dante, as we said, had ten silent centuries, in a very strange way, found a voice. The *Divina Commedia* is of Dante's writing; yet in truth *it* belongs to ten Christian centuries, only the finishing of it is Dante's. So always. The craftsman there, the smith with that metal of his, with these tools, with these cunning methods,—how little of all he does is properly *his* work! All past inventive men work there with him;—as indeed with all of us, in all things. Dante is the spokesman of the Middle Ages; the Thought they lived by stands here, in everlasting music. These sublime ideas of his, terrible and beautiful, are the fruit of the Christian Meditation of all the good men who had gone before him. Precious they; but also is not he precious? Much, had not he spoken, would have been dumb; not dead, yet living voiceless.

On the whole, is it not an utterance, this mystic Song, at once of one of the greatest human souls, and of the highest thing that Europe had hitherto realised for itself? Christianism, as Dante sings it, is another than Paganism in the rude Norse mind; another than "Bastard Christianism" half-articulately spoken in the Arab Desert, seven-hundred years before!— The noble *idea* made *real* hitherto among men, is sung, and emblemed-forth abidingly, by one of the noblest men. In the one sense and in the other, are we not right glad to possess it? As I calculate, it may last yet for long thousands of years. For the thing that is uttered from the inmost parts of a man's soul, differs altogether from what is uttered by the outer part. The outer is of the day, under the empire of mode; the outer passes away, in swift endless changes; the inmost is the same yesterday, today and forever. True souls, in all generations of the world, who look on this Dante, will find a brotherhood in him; the deep sincerity of his thoughts, his woes and hopes, will speak likewise to their sincerity; they will feel that this Dante too was a brother. Napoleon in Saint-Helena is charmed with the genial veracity of old Homer. The oldest Hebrew Prophet, under a vesture the most diverse from ours, does yet, because he speaks from the heart of man, speak to all men's hearts. It is the one sole secret of continuing long memorable. Dante, for depth of sincerity, is like an antique Prophet too; his words, like theirs, come from his very heart. One need not wonder if it were predicted that his Poem might be the most enduring thing our Europe has yet made; for nothing so endures as a truly spoken word. All cathedrals, pontificalities, brass and stone, and outer arrangement never so lasting, are brief in comparison to an unfathomable heart-song like this: one feels as if it might survive, still of importance to men, when these had all sunk into new irrecognisable combinations, and had ceased individually to be. Europe has made much; great cities, great empires, encyclopædias, creeds, bodies of opinion and practice: but it has made little of the class of Dante's Thought. Homer yet *is,* veritably present face to face with every open soul of us; and Greece, where is *it?* Desolate for thousands of years; away, vanished; a bewildered heap of stones and rubbish, the life and existence of it all gone. Like a dream; like the dust of King Agamemnon! Greece was; Greece, except in the *words* it spoke, is not.

The uses of this Dante? We will not say much about his "uses." A human soul who has once got into that primal element of *Song,* and sung-forth fitly somewhat therefrom, has worked in the *depths* of our existence; feeding through long times the life-*roots* of all excellent human things whatsoever,—in a way that "utilities" will not succeed well in calculating! We will not estimate the Sun by the quantity of gas-light it saves us; Dante shall be invaluable, or of no value. One remark I may make: the contrast in this respect between the Hero-Poet and the Hero-Prophet. In a hundred years, Mahomet, as we saw, had his Arabians at Grenada and at Delhi; Dante's Italians seem to be yet very much where they were. Shall we say, then, Dante's effect on the world was small in comparison? Not so; his arena is far more restricted; but also it is far nobler, clearer; —perhaps not less but more important. Mahomet speaks to great masses of men, in the coarse dialect adapted to such; a dialect filled with inconsistencies, crudities, follies: on the great masses alone can he act, and there with good and with evil strangely blended. Dante speaks to the noble, the pure and great, in all times and places. Neither does he grow obsolete, as the other does. Dante burns as a pure star, fixed there in the firmament, at which the great and the high of all ages kindle themselves: he is the possession of all the chosen of the world for uncounted time. Dante, one calculates, may long survive Mahomet. In this way the balance may be made straight again.

But, at any rate, it is not by what is called their effect on the world, by what *we* can judge of their effect there, that a man and his work are measured. Effect? Influence? Utility? Let a man *do* his work; the fruit of it is the care of Another than 10 he. It will grow its own fruit; and whether embodied in Caliph Thrones and Arabian Conquests, so that it "fills all Morning and Evening Newspapers," and all Histories, which are a kind of distilled Newspapers; or not embodied so at all;—what matters that? That is not the real fruit of it! The Arabian Caliph, in so far only as he did something, was something. If the great Cause of Man, and Man's work in God's 20 Earth, got no furtherance from the Arabian Caliph, then no matter how many scimitars he drew, how many gold piasters pocketed, and what uproar and blaring he made in this world,—*he* was but a loud-sounding inanity and futility; at bottom, he *was* not at all. Let us honour the great empire of *Silence,* once more! The boundless treasury which we do *not* jingle in our pockets, or count up and present before 30 men! It is perhaps, of all things, the usefulest for each of us to do, in these loud times.——

As Dante, the Italian man, was sent into our world to embody musically the Religion of the Middle Ages, the Religion of our Modern Europe, its Inner Life; so Shakspeare, we may say, embodies for us the Outer Life of our Europe as developed then, its chivalries, courtesies, humours, ambitions, what practical way of thinking, acting, looking at the world, men then had. As in Homer we may still construe Old Greece; so in Shakspeare and Dante, after thousands of years, what our modern Europe was, in Faith and in Practice, will still be legible. Dante has given us the Faith or Soul; Shakspeare, in a not less noble way, has given us the Practice or 50 body. This latter also we were to have; a man was sent for it, the man Shakspeare. Just when that chivalry way of life had reached its last finish, and was on the point

of breaking down into slow or swift dissolution, as we now see it everywhere, this other sovereign Poet, with his seeing eye, with his perennial singing voice was sent to take note of it, to give long-enduring record of it. Two fit men: Dante, deep, fierce as the central fire of the world; Shakspeare, wide, placid, far-seeing, as the Sun, the upper light of the world. Italy produced the one world-voice; we English had the honour of producing the other.

Curious enough how, as it were by mere accident, this man came to us. I think always, so great, quiet, complete and self-sufficing is this Shakspeare, had the Warwickshire Squire not prosecuted him for deer-stealing, we had perhaps never heard of him as a Poet! The woods and skies, the rustic Life of Man in Stratford there, had been enough for this man! But indeed that strange outbudding of our whole English Existence, which we call the Elizabethan Era, did not it too come as of its own accord? The "Tree Igdrasil" buds and withers by its own laws,—too deep for our scanning. Yet it does bud and wither, and every bough and leaf of it is there, by fixed eternal laws; not a Sir Thomas Lucy but comes at the hour fit for him. Curious, I say, and not sufficiently considered: how everything does coöperate with all; not a leaf rotting on the highway but is indissoluble portion of solar and stellar systems; no thought, word or act of man but has sprung withal out of all men, and works sooner or later, recognisably or irrecognisably, on all men! It is all a Tree: circulation of sap and influences, mutual communication of every minutest leaf with the lowest talon of a root, with every other greatest and minutest portion of the whole. The Tree Igdrasil, that has its roots down in the Kingdoms of Hela and Death, and whose boughs overspread the highest Heaven!—

In some sense it may be said that this glorious Elizabethan Era with its Shakspeare, as the outcome and flowerage of all which had preceded it, is itself attributable to the Catholicism of the Middle Ages. The Christian Faith, which was the theme of Dante's Song, had produced this Practical Life which Shakspeare was to sing. For Religion then, as it now and always is, was the soul of Practice; the primary vital fact in men's life. And remark here, as rather curious, that Middle-Age Catholicism was abolished, so far as Acts of Parliament could abolish it, before Shakspeare, the noblest product of it, made his appearance. He did make his appearance nevertheless. Nature at her own time, with Catholicism or what else might be necessary, sent him forth; taking small thought of Acts of Parliament. King-Henrys, Queen-Elizabeths go their way; and Nature too goes hers. Acts of Parliament, on the whole, are small, notwithstanding the noise they make. What Act of Parliament, debate at St. Stephen's, on the hustings or elsewhere, was it that brought this Shakspeare into being? No dining at Freemasons' Tavern, opening subscription-lists, selling of shares, and infinite other jangling and true or false endeavouring! This Elizabethan Era, and all its nobleness and blessedness, came without proclamation, preparation of ours. Priceless Shakspeare was the free gift of Nature; given altogether silently;—received altogether silently, as if it had been a thing of little account. And yet, very literally, it is a priceless thing. One should look at that side of matters too.

Of this Shakspeare of ours, perhaps the opinion one sometimes hears a little idolatrously expressed is, in fact, the right one; I think the best judgment not of this country only, but of Europe at large, is slowly pointing to the conclusion, That Shakspeare is the chief of all Poets hitherto; the greatest intellect who, in our recorded world, has left record of himself in the way of Literature. On the whole, I know not such a power of vision, such a faculty of thought, if we take all the characters of it, in any other man. Such a calmness of depth; placid joyous strength; all things imaged in that great soul of his so true and clear, as in a tranquil unfathomable sea! It has been said, that in the constructing of Shakspeare's Dramas there is, apart from all other "faculties" as they are called, an understanding manifested, equal to that in Bacon's *Novum Organum*. That is true; and it is not a truth that strikes every one. It would become more apparent if we tried, any of us for himself, how, out of Shak-

speare's dramatic materials, *we* could fashion such a result! The built house seems all so fit,—everyway as it should be, as if it came there by its own law and the nature of things,—we forget the rude disorderly quarry it was shaped from. The very perfection of the house, as if Nature herself had made it, hides the builder's merit. Perfect, more perfect than any other man, we may call Shakspeare in this: he discerns, knows as by instinct, what condition he works under, what his materials are, what his own force and its relation to them is. It is not a transitory glance of insight that will suffice; it is deliberate illumination of the whole matter; it is a calmly *seeing* eye; a great intellect, in short. How a man, of some wide thing that he has witnessed, will construct a narrative, what kind of picture and delineation he will give of it,—is the best measure you could get of what intellect is in the man. Which circumstance is vital and shall stand prominent; which unessential, fit to be suppressed; where is the true *beginning*, the true sequence and ending? To find out this, you task the whole force of insight that is in the man. He must *understand* the thing; according to the depth of his understanding, will the fitness of his answer be. You will try him so. Does like join itself to like; does the spirit of method stir in that confusion, so that its embroilment becomes order? Can the man say, *Fiat lux,* Let there be light; and out of chaos make a world? Precisely as there is *light* in himself, will he accomplish this.

Or indeed we may say again, it is in what I called Portrait-painting, delineating of men and things, especially of men, that Shakspeare is great. All the greatness of the man comes out decisively here. It is unexampled, I think, that calm creative perspicacity of Shakspeare. The thing he looks at reveals not this or that face of it, but its inmost heart, and generic secret: it dissolves itself as in light before him, so that he discerns the perfect structure of it. Creative, we said: poetic creation, what is this too but *seeing* the thing sufficiently? The *word* that will describe the thing, follows of itself from such clear intense sight of the thing. And is not Shakspeare's *morality*, his valour, candour, tolerance, truthfulness; his whole victorious strength and greatness, which can triumph over such obstructions, visible there too? Great as the world! No *twisted,* poor convex-concave mirror, reflecting all objects with its own convexities and concavities; a perfectly *level* mirror;—that is to say withal, if we will understand it, a man justly related to all things and men, a good man. It is truly a lordly spectacle how this great soul takes-in all kinds of men and objects, a Falstaff, an Othello, a Juliet, a Coriolanus; sets them all forth to us in their round completeness; loving, just, the equal brother of all. *Novum Organum,* and all the intellect you will find in Bacon, is of a quite secondary order; earthly, material, poor in comparison with this. Among modern men, one finds, in strictness, almost nothing of the same rank. Goethe alone, since the days of Shakspeare, reminds me of it. Of him too you say that he *saw* the object; you may say what he himself says of Shakspeare: "His characters are like watches with dial-plates of transparent crystal; they show you the hour like others, and the inward mechanism also is all visible."

The seeing eye! It is this that discloses the inner harmony of things; what Nature meant, what musical idea Nature has wrapped-up in these often rough embodiments. Something she did mean. To the seeing eye that something were discernible. Are they base, miserable things? You can laugh over them, you can weep over them; you can in some way or other genially relate yourself to them;—you can, at lowest, hold your peace about them, turn away your own and others' face from them, till the hour come for practically exterminating and extinguishing them! At bottom, it is the Poet's first gift, as it is all men's, that he have intellect enough. He will be a Poet if he have: a Poet in word; or failing that, perhaps still better, a Poet in act. Whether he write at all; and if so, whether in prose or in verse, will depend on accidents; who knows on what extremely trivial accidents,—perhaps on his having had a singing-master, on his being taught to sing in his boyhood! But the faculty which enables him to discern the inner heart of things, and the harmony that dwells there (for whatsoever exists has

a harmony in the heart of it, or it would not hold together and exist), is not the result of habits or accidents, but the gift of Nature herself; the primary outfit for a Heroic Man in what sort soever. To the Poet, as to every other, we say first of all, *See.* If you cannot do that, it is of no use to keep stringing rhymes together, jingling sensibilities against each other, and *name* yourself a Poet; there is no hope for you. If you can, there is, in prose or verse, in action or speculation, all manner of hope. The crabbed old Schoolmaster used to ask, when they brought him a new pupil, "But are ye sure he's *not a dunce?*" Why, really one might ask the same thing, in regard to every man proposed for whatsoever function; and consider it as the one inquiry needful: Are ye sure he's not a dunce? There is, in this world, no other entirely fatal person.

For, in fact, I say the degree of vision that dwells in a man is a correct measure of the man. If called to define Shakspeare's faculty, I should say superiority of Intellect, and think I had included all under that. What indeed are faculties? We talk of faculties as if they were distinct, things separable; as if a man had intellect, imagination, fancy, &c., as he has hands, feet and arms. That is a capital error. Then again, we hear of a man's "intellectual nature," and of his "moral nature," as if these again were divisible, and existed apart. Necessities of language do perhaps prescribe such forms of utterance; we must speak, I am aware, in that way, if we are to speak at all. But words ought not to harden into things for us. It seems to me, our apprehension of this matter is, for most part, radically falsified thereby. We ought to know withal, and to keep forever in mind, that these divisions are at bottom but *names;* that man's spiritual nature, the vital Force which dwells in him, is essentially one and indivisible; that what we call imagination, fancy, understanding, and so forth, are but different figures of the same Power of Insight, all indissolubly connected with each other, physiognomically related; that if we knew one of them, we might know all of them. Morality itself, what we call the moral quality of a man, what is this but another *side* of the one vital Force whereby he is and works? All that a man does is physiognomical of him. You may see how a man would fight, by the way in which he sings; his courage, or want of courage, is visible in the word he utters, in the opinion he has formed, no less than in the stroke he strikes. He is *one;* and preaches the same Self abroad in all these ways.

Without hands a man might have feet, and could still walk: but, consider it,—without morality, intellect were impossible for him; a thoroughly immoral *man* could not know anything at all! To know a thing, what we can call knowing, a man must first *love* the thing, sympathise with it: that is, be *virtuously* related to it. If he have not the justice to put down his own selfishness at every turn, the courage to stand by the dangerous-true at every turn, how shall he know? His virtues, all of them, will lie recorded in his knowledge. Nature, with her truth, remains to the bad, to the selfish and the pusillanimous forever a sealed book: what such can know of Nature is mean, superficial, small; for the uses of the day merely.—But does not the very Fox know something of Nature? Exactly so: it knows where the geese lodge! The human Reynard, very frequent everywhere in the world, what more does he know but this and the like of this? Nay, it should be considered too, that if the Fox had not a certain vulpine *morality,* he could not even know where the geese were, or get at the geese! If he spent his time in splenetic atrabiliar reflections on his own misery, his ill usage by Nature, Fortune and other Foxes, and so forth; and had not courage, promptitude, practicality, and other suitable vulpine gifts and graces, he would catch no geese. We may say of the Fox too, that his morality and insight are of the same dimensions; different faces of the same internal unity of vulpine life!— These things are worth stating; for the contrary of them acts with manifold very baleful perversion, in this time: what limitations, modifications they require, your own candour will supply.

If I say, therefore, that Shakspeare is the greatest of Intellects, I have said all concerning him. But there is more in Shakspeare's intellect than we have yet seen. It is what I call an unconscious intellect; there is more virtue in it than he himself is aware of. Novalis beautifully remarks of him, that those Dramas of his are Products of Nature too, deep as Nature herself. I find a great truth in this saying. Shakspeare's Art is not Artifice; the noblest worth of it is not there by plan or precontrivance. It grows-up from the deeps of Nature, through this noble sincere soul, who is a voice of Nature. The latest generations of men will find new meanings in Shakspeare, new elucidations of their own human being; "new harmonies with the infinite structure of the Universe; concurrences with later ideas, affinities with the higher powers and senses of men." This well deserves meditating. It is Nature's highest reward to a true simple great soul, that he get thus to be *a part of herself.* Such a man's works, whatsoever he with utmost conscious exertion and forethought shall accomplish, grow up withal *unconsciously,* from the unknown deeps in him; —as the oak-tree grows from the Earth's bosom, as the mountains and waters shape themselves; with a symmetry grounded on Nature's own laws, comformable to all Truth whatsoever. How much in Shakspeare lies hid; his sorrows, his silent struggles known to himself; much that was not known at all, not speakable at all: like *roots,* like sap and forces working underground! Speech is great; but Silence is greater.

Withal the joyful tranquillity of this man is notable. I will not blame Dante for his misery: it is as battle without victory; but true battle,—the first, indispensable thing. Yet I call Shakspeare greater than Dante, in that he fought truly, and did conquer. Doubt it not, he had his own sorrows: those *Sonnets* of his will even testify expressly in what deep waters he had waded, and swum struggling for his life;—as what man like him ever failed to have to do? It seems to me a heedless notion, our common one, that he sat like a bird on the bough; and sang forth, free and offhand, never knowing the troubles of other men. Not so; with no man is it so. How could a man travel forward from rustic deer-poaching to such tragedy-writing, and not fall-in with sorrows by the way? Or, still better, how could a man delineate a Hamlet, a Coriolanus, a Macbeth, so many suffering heroic hearts, if his own heroic heart had never suffered?—And now, in contrast with all this, observe his mirthfulness, his genuine overflowing love of laughter! You would say, in no point does he *exaggerate* but only in laughter. Fiery objurgations, words that pierce and burn, are to be found in Shakspeare; yet he is always in measure here; never what Johnson would remark as a specially "good hater." But his laughter seems to pour from him in floods; he heaps all manner of ridiculous nicknames on the butt he is bantering, tumbles and tosses him in all sorts of horseplay; you would say, with his whole heart laughs. And then, if not always the finest, it is always a genial laughter. Not at mere weakness, at misery or poverty; never. No man who *can* laugh, what we call laughing, will laugh at these things. It is some poor character only *desiring* to laugh, and have the credit of wit, that does so. Laughter means sympathy; good laughter is not "the crackling of thorns under the pot." Even at stupidity and pretension this Shakspeare does not laugh otherwise than genially. Dogberry and Verges tickle our very hearts; and we dismiss them covered with explosions of laughter: but we like the poor fellows only the better for our laughing; and hope they will get on well there, and continue Presidents of the City-watch. Such laughter, like sunshine on the deep sea, is very beautiful to me.

We have no room to speak of Shakspeare's individual works; though perhaps there is much still waiting to be said on that head. Had we, for instance, all his plays reviewed as *Hamlet,* in *Wilhelm Meister,* is! A thing which might, one day, be done. August Wilhelm Schlegel has a remark on his Historical Plays, *Henry Fifth* and the others, which is worth remembering. He calls them a kind of National Epic. Marlborough, you recollect, said, he knew no English History but what he had learned from Shakspeare. There are really, if we look to it, few as memorable Histories. The great salient points are admirably seized; all rounds itself off, into a kind of rhythmic coherence; it is, as Schle-gel says, *epic;*—as indeed all delineation by a great thinker will be. There are right beautiful things in those Pieces, which indeed together form one beautiful thing. That battle of Agincourt strikes me as one of the most perfect things, in its sort, we anywhere have of Shakspeare's. The description of the two hosts: the worn-out, jaded English; the dread hour, big with destiny, when the battle shall begin; and then that deathless valour: "Ye good yeomen, whose limbs were made in England!" There is a noble Patriotism in it,—far other than the "indifference" you sometimes hear ascribed to Shakspeare. A true English heart breathes, calm and strong, through the whole business; not boisterous, protrusive; all the better for that. There is a sound in it like the ring of steel. This man too had a right stroke in him, had it come to that!

But I will say, of Shakspeare's works generally, that we have no full impress of him there; even as full as we have of many men. His works are so many windows, through which we see a glimpse of the world that was in him. All his works seem, comparatively speaking, cursory, imperfect, written under cramping circumstances; giving only here and there a note of the full utterance of the man. Passages there are that come upon you like splendour out of Heaven; bursts of radiance, illuminating the very heart of the thing: you say, "That is *true,* spoken once and forever; wheresoever and whensoever there is an open human soul, that will be recognised as true!" Such bursts, however, make us feel that the surrounding matter is not radiant; that it is, in part, temporary, conventional. Alas, Shakspeare had to write for the Globe Playhouse: his great soul had to crush itself, as it could, into that and no other mould. It was with him, then, as it is with us all. No man works save under conditions. The sculptor cannot set his own free Thought before us; but his Thought as he could translate it into the stone that was given, with the tools that were given. *Disjecta membra* are all that we find of any Poet, or of any man.

Whoever looks intelligently at this Shakspeare may recognise that he too was a *Prophet,* in his way; of an insight analogous to the Prophetic, though he took it up in another strain. Nature seemed to this man also divine; *un*speakable, deep as Tophet, high as Heaven: "We are such stuff as Dreams are made of!" That scroll in Westminster Abbey, which few read with understanding, is of the depth of any seer. But the man sang; did not preach, except musically. We called Dante the melodious Priest of Middle-Age Catholicism. May we not call Shakspeare the still more melodious Priest of a *true* Catholicism, the "Universal Church" of the Future and of all times? No narrow superstition, harsh asceticism, intolerance, fanatical fierceness or perversion: a Revelation, so far as it goes, that such a thousandfold hidden beauty and divineness dwells in all Nature; which let all men worship as they can! We may say without offence, that there rises a kind of universal Psalm out of this Shakspeare too; not unfit to make itself heard among the still more sacred Psalms. Not in disharmony with these, if we understood them, but in harmony!—I cannot call this Shakspeare a "Sceptic," as some do; his indifference to the creeds and theological quarrels of his time misleading them. No: neither unpatriotic, though he says little about his Patriotism; nor sceptic, though he says little about his Faith. Such "indifference" was the fruit of his greatness withal: his whole heart was in his own grand sphere of worship (we may call it such); these other controversies, vitally important to other men, were not vital to him.

But call it worship, call it what you will, is it not a right glorious thing, and set of things, this that Shakspeare has brought us? For myself, I feel that there is actually a kind of sacredness in the fact of such a man being sent into this Earth. Is he not an eye to us all; a blessed heaven-sent Bringer of Light?—And, at bottom, was it not perhaps far better that this Shakspeare, everyway an unconscious man, was *conscious* of no Heavenly message? He did not feel, like Mahomet, because he saw into those internal Splendours, that he specially was the "Prophet of God": and was he not greater than Mahomet in that? Greater; and also, if we compute strictly,

as we did in Dante's case, more successful. It was intrinsically an error that notion of Mahomet's, of his supreme Prophethood; and has come down to us inextricably involved in error to this day; dragging along with it such a coil of fables, impurities, intolerances, as makes it a questionable step for me here and now to say, as I have done, that Mahomet was a true Speaker at all, and not rather an ambitious charlatan, perversity and simulacrum; no Speaker, but a Babbler! Even in Arabia, as I compute, Mahomet will have exhausted himself and become obsolete, while this Shakspeare, this Dante may still be young;—while this Shakspeare may still pretend to be a Priest of Mankind, of Arabia as of other places, for unlimited periods to come!

Compared with any speaker or singer one knows, even with Æschylus or Homer, why should he not, for veracity and universality, last like them? He is *sincere* as they; reaches deep down like them, to the universal and perennial. But as for Mahomet, I think it had been better for him *not* to be so conscious! Alas, poor Mahomet; all that he was *conscious* of was a mere error; a futility and triviality,—as indeed such ever is. The truly great in him too was the unconscious: that he was a wild Arab lion of the desert, and did speak-out with that great thunder-voice of his, not by words which he *thought* to be great, but by actions, by feelings, by a history which *were* great! His Koran has become a stupid piece of prolix absurdity; we do not believe, like him, that God wrote that! The Great Man here too, as always, is a Force of Nature: whatsoever is truly great in him springs-up from the *in*articulate deeps.

Well: this is our poor Warwickshire Peasant, who rose to be Manager of a Playhouse, so that he could live without begging; whom the Earl of Southampton cast some kind glances on; whom Sir Thomas Lucy, many thanks to him, was for sending to the Treadmill! We did not account him a god, like Odin, while he dwelt with us;—on which point there were much to be said. But I will say rather, or repeat: In spite of the sad state Hero-worship now lies in, consider what this Shakspeare has actually become among us. Which Englishman we ever made, in this land of ours, which million of Englishmen, would we not give-up rather than the Stratford Peasant? There is no regiment of highest Dignitaries that we would sell him for. He is the grandest thing we have yet done. For our honour among foreign nations, as an ornament to our English Household, what item is there that we would not surrender rather than him? Consider now, if they asked us, Will you give-up your Indian Empire or your Shakspeare, you English; never have had any Indian Empire, or never have had any Shakspeare? Really it were a grave question. Official persons would answer doubtless in official language; but we, for our part too, should not we be forced to answer: Indian Empire, or no Indian Empire; we cannot do without Shakspeare! Indian Empire will go, at any rate, some day; but this Shakspeare does not go, he lasts forever with us; we cannot give-up our Shakspeare!

Nay, apart from spiritualities; and considering him merely as a real, marketable, tangibly-useful possession. England, before long, this Island of ours, will hold but a small fraction of the English: in America, in New Holland, east and west to the very Antipodes, there will be a Saxondom covering great spaces of the Globe. And now, what is it that can keep all these together into virtually one Nation, so that they do not fall-out and fight, but live at peace, in brotherlike intercourse, helping one another? This is justly regarded as the greatest practical problem, the thing all manner of sovereignties and governments are here to accomplish: what is it that will accomplish this? Acts of Parliament, administrative prime-ministers cannot. America is parted from us, so far

as Parliament could part it. Call it not fantastic, for there is much reality in it: Here, I say, is an English King, whom no time or chance, Parliament or combination of Parliaments, can dethrone! This King Shakspeare, does not he shine, in crowned sovereignty, over us all, as the noblest, gentlest, yet strongest of rallying-signs; indestructible; really more valuable in that point of view than any other means or appliance whatsoever? We can fancy him as radiant aloft over all the Nations of Englishmen, a thousand years hence. From Paramatta, from New York, wheresoever, under what sort of Parish-Constable soever, English men and women are, they will say to one another: "Yes, this Shakspeare is ours; we produced him, we speak and think by him; we are of one blood and kind with him." The most common-sense politician, too, if he pleases, may think of that.

Yes, truly, it is a great thing for a Nation that it get an articulate voice; that it produce a man who will speak-forth melodiously what the heart of it means! Italy, for example, poor Italy lies dismembered, scattered asunder, not appearing in any protocol or treaty as a unity at all; yet the noble Italy is actually *one:* Italy produced its Dante; Italy can speak! The Czar of all the Russias, he is strong with so many bayonets, Cossacks and cannons; and does a great feat in keeping such a tract of Earth politically together; but he cannot yet speak. Something great in him, but it is a dumb greatness. He has had no voice of genius, to be heard of all men and times. He must learn to speak. He is a great dumb monster hitherto. His cannons and Cossacks will all have rusted into nonentity, while that Dante's voice is still audible. The Nation that has a Dante is bound together as no dumb Russia can be.—We must here end what we had to say of the *Hero-Poet.*   [1841]

PAST AND PRESENT

GOSPEL OF DILETTANTISM

But after all, the Gospel of Dilettantism, producing a Governing Class who do not govern, nor understand in the least that

they are bound or expected to govern, is still mournfuler than that of Mammonism. Mammonism, as we said, at least works; this goes idle. Mammonism has seized some portion of the message of Nature to man; and seizing that, and following it, will seize and appropriate more and more of Nature's message: but Dilettantism has missed it wholly. "Make money": that will mean withal, "Do work in order to make money." But, "Go gracefully idle in Mayfair," what does or can that mean? An idle, game-preserving and even corn-lawing Aristocracy, in such an England as ours: has it seen the world, if we take thought of it, ever seen such a phenomenon till very lately? Can it long continue to see such?

Accordingly the impotent, insolent Donothingism in Practice and Saynothingism in Speech, which we have to witness on that side of our affairs, is altogether amazing. A Corn-Law demonstrating itself openly, for ten years or more, with "arguments" to make the angels, and some other classes of creatures, weep! For men are not ashamed to rise in Parliament and elsewhere, and speak the things they do *not* think. "Expediency," "Necessities of Party," etc., etc.! It is not known that the Tongue of Man is a sacred organ; that Man himself is definable in Philosophy as an "Incarnate *Word*"; the Word not there, you have no Man there either, but a Phantasm instead! In this way it is that Absurdities may live long enough,—still walking, and talking for themselves, years and decades after the brains are quite out! How are the "knaves and dastards" ever to be got "arrested" at that rate?—

"No man in this fashionable London of yours," friend Sauerteig [1] would say, "speaks a plain word to me. Every man feels bound to be something more than plain; to be pungent withal, witty, ornamental. His poor fraction of sense has to be perked into some epigrammatic shape, that it may prick into me;—perhaps (this is the commonest) to be topsyturvied, left standing on its head, that I may remember it the better! Such grinning inanity is very sad to the soul of man. Human faces should not grin on one like masks; they should look on one like faces! I love honest laughter, as I do sunlight; but not

[1] Sauerteig: Sour dough; a German name which Carlyle sometimes assumed in order to give a dramatic emphasis to what he had to say and also to suggest the foreigner's view of English life.

dishonest: most kinds of dancing too; but the St.-Vitus kind not at all! A fashionable wit, *ach Himmel!* if you ask, Which, he or a Death's-head, will be the cheerier company for me? pray send *not* him!"

Insincere Speech, truly, is the prime material of insincere Action. Action hangs, as it were, *dissolved* in Speech, in Thought whereof Speech is the Shadow; and precipitates itself therefrom. The kind of Speech in a man betokens the kind of Action you will get from him. Our Speech, in these modern days, has become amazing. Johnson complained, "Nobody speaks in earnest, Sir; there is no serious conversation." To us all serious speech of men, as that of Seventeenth-Century Puritans, Twelfth-Century Catholics, German Poets of this Century, has become jargon, more or less insane. Cromwell was mad and a quack; Anselm, Becket, Goethe, *ditto, ditto*.

Perhaps few narratives in History or Mythology are more significant than that Moslem one, of Moses and the Dwellers by the Dead Sea. A tribe of men dwelt on the shores of that same Asphaltic Lake; and having forgotten, as we are all too prone to do, the inner facts of Nature, and taken up with the falsities and outer semblances of it, were fallen into sad conditions,— verging indeed towards a certain far deeper Lake. Whereupon it pleased kind Heaven to send them the Prophet Moses, with an instructive word of warning, out of which might have sprung "remedial measures" not a few. But no: the men of the Dead Sea discovered, as the valet-species always does in heroes or prophets, no comeliness in Moses; listened with real tedium to Moses, with light grinning, or with splenetic sniffs and sneers, affecting even to yawn; and signified, in short, that they found him a humbug, and even a bore. Such was the candid theory these men of the Asphalt Lake formed to themselves of Moses, That probably he was a humbug, that certainly he was a bore.

Moses withdrew; but Nature and her rigorous veracities did not withdraw. The men of the Dead Sea, when we next went to visit them, were all "changed into Apes"; sitting on the trees there, grinning now in the most *un*affected manner; gibbering and chattering very genuine nonsense; finding the whole Universe now a most indisputable Humbug! The Universe has *become* a Humbug to these Apes who thought it one. There they sit and chatter, to this hour: only, I believe, every Sabbath there returns to them a bewildered half-consciousness, half-reminiscence; and they sit, with their wizened smoke-dried visages, and such an air of supreme tragicality as Apes may; looking out through those blink- 10 ing smoke-bleared eyes of theirs, into the wonderfulest universal smoky Twilight and undecipherable disordered Dusk of Things; wholly an Uncertainty, Unintelligibility, they and it; and for commentary thereon, here and there an unmusical chatter or mew:—truest, tragicalest Humbug conceivable by the mind of man or ape! They made no use of their souls; and so have lost them. Their worship on the Sabbath 20 now is to roost there, with unmusical screeches, and half-remember that they had souls.

Didst thou never, O Traveller, fall-in with parties of this tribe? Meseems they are grown somewhat numerous in our day.

HAPPY

All work, even cotton-spinning, is noble; 30 work is alone noble: be that here said and asserted once more. And in like manner too, all dignity is painful; a life of ease is not for any man, nor any god. The life of all gods figures itself to us as a Sublime Sadness,—earnestness of Infinite Battle against Infinite Labor. Our highest religion is named the "Worship of Sorrow." For the son of man there is no noble crown, well worn or even ill worn, but is 40 a crown of thorns!—These things, in spoken words, or still better, in felt instincts alive in every heart, were once well known.

Does not the whole wretchedness, the whole *Atheism* as I call it, of man's ways, in these generations, shadow itself for us in that unspeakable Life-philosophy of his: The pretension to be what he calls "happy"? Every pitifulest whipster that 50 walks within a skin has his head filled with the notion that he is, shall be, or by all human and divine laws ought to be "happy." His wishes, the pitifulest whip-

ster's, are to be fulfilled for him; his days, the pitifulest whipster's, are to flow on in ever-gentle current of enjoyment, impossible even for the gods. The prophets preach to us, Thou shalt be happy; thou shalt love pleasant things, and find them. The people clamor, Why have we not found pleasant things?

We construct our theory of Human Duties, not on any Greatest-Nobleness Principle, never so mistaken; no, but on a Greatest-Happiness Principle. "The word Soul with us, as in some Slavonic dialects, seems to be synonymous with *Stomach*." We plead and speak, in our Parliaments and elsewhere, not as from the Soul, but from the Stomach;—wherefore indeed our pleadings are so slow to profit. We plead not for God's Justice; we are not ashamed to stand clamoring and pleading for our own "interests," our own rents and trade-profits; we say, They are the "interests" of so many; there is such an intense desire in us for them! We demand Free-Trade, with much just vociferation and benevolence, That the poorer classes, who are terribly ill-off at present, may have cheaper New-Orleans bacon. Men ask on Free-trade platforms, How can the indomitable spirit of Englishmen be kept up without plenty of bacon? We shall become a ruined Nation!—Surely, my friends, plenty of bacon is good and indispensable: but, I doubt, you will never get even bacon by aiming only at that. You are men, not animals of prey, well-used or ill-used! Your Greatest-Happiness Principle seems to me fast becoming a rather unhappy one.—What if we should cease babbling about "happiness," and leave *it* resting on its own basis, as it used to do!

A gifted Byron rises in his wrath; and feeling too surely that he for his part is not "happy," declares the same in very violent language, as a piece of news that may be interesting. It evidently has surprised him much. One dislikes to see a man and poet reduced to proclaim on the streets such tidings, but on the whole, as matters go, that is not the most dislikeable. Byron speaks the *truth* in this matter. Byron's large audience indicates how true it is felt to be.

"Happy," my brother? First of all, what

difference is it whether thou art happy or not? Today becomes Yesterday so fast, all Tomorrows become Yesterdays; and then there is no question whatever of the "happiness," but quite another question. Nay, thou hast such a sacred pity left at least for thyself, thy very pains, once gone over into Yesterday, become joys to thee. Besides, thou knowest not what heavenly blessedness and indispensable sanative 10 virtue was in them; thou shalt only know it after many days, when thou art wiser!— A benevolent old Surgeon sat once in our company, with a Patient fallen sick by gourmandizing, whom he had just, too briefly in the Patient's judgment, been examining. The foolish Patient still at intervals continued to break in on our discourse, which rather promised to take a philosophic turn: "But I have lost my 20 appetite," said he, objurgatively, with a tone of irritated pathos; "I have no appetite; I can't eat!"—"My dear fellow," answered the Doctor in mildest tone, "it isn't of the slightest consequence";—and, continued his philosophical discoursings with us!

Or does the reader not know the history of that Scottish iron Misanthrope? The inmates of some town-mansion, in those 30 Northern parts, were thrown into the fearfulest alarm by indubitable symptoms of a ghost inhabiting the next house, or perhaps even the partition-wall! Ever at a certain hour, with preternatural gnarring, growling, and screeching, which attended as running bass, there began, in a horrid, semi-articulate, unearthly voice, this song: 'Once I was hap-hap-happy, but now I am meeserable! Clack-clack-clack, gnarr-r-r, 40 whuz-z: Once I was hap-hap-happy, but now I'm meeserable!'—Rest, rest, perturbed spirit;—or indeed, as the good old Doctor said: My dear fellow, it isn't of the slightest consequence! But no; the perturbed spirit could not rest; and to the neighbors, fretted, affrighted, or at least insufferably bored by him, it was of such consequence that they had to go and examine in his haunted chamber. In his haunted cham- 50 ber, they find that the perturbed spirit is an unfortunate—Imitator of Byron? No, is an unfortunate rusty Meat-jack, gnarring and creaking with rust and work; and this,

in Scottish dialect, is *its* Byronian musical Life-philosophy, sung according to ability!

Truly, I think the man who goes about pothering and uproaring for his "happiness,"—pothering, and were it ballot-boxing, poem-making, or in what way soever fussing and exerting himself,—he is not the man that will help us to "get our knaves and dastards arrested"! No; he rather is on the way to increase the number,—by at least one unit and his tail! Observe, too, that this is all a modern affair; belongs not to the old heroic times, but to these dastard new times. "Happiness our being's end and aim," all that very paltry speculation is at bottom, if we will count well, not yet two centuries old in the world.

The only happiness a brave man ever troubled himself with asking much about was, happiness enough to get his work done. Not "I can't eat!" but "I can't work!" that was the burden of all wise complaining among men. It is, after all, the one unhappiness of a man, That he cannot work; that he cannot get his destiny as a man fulfilled. Behold, the day is passing swiftly over, our life is passing swiftly over; and the night cometh, wherein no man can work. The night once come, our happiness, our unhappiness,—it is all abolished, vanished, clean gone: a thing that has been: "not of the slightest consequence" whether we were happy as eupeptic Curtis, as the fattest pig of Epicurus, or unhappy as Job with potsherds, as musical Byron with Giaours and sensibilities of the heart; as the unmusical Meat-jack with hard labor and rust! But our work,—behold, that is not abolished, that has not vanished: our work, behold, it remains, or the want of it remains;—for endless Times and Eternities, remains; and that is now the sole question with us for evermore! Brief brawling Day, with its noisy phantasms, its poor paper-crowns tinsel-gilt, is gone; and divine everlasting Night, with her star-diadems, with her silences and her veracities, is come! What hast thou done, and how? Happiness, unhappiness: all that was but the *wages* thou hadst; thou hast spent all that, in sustaining thyself hitherward; not a coin of it remains with thee, it is all spent, eaten: and now thy work, where is thy work?

Swift, out with it; let us see thy work!

Of a truth, if man were not a poor hungry dastard, and even much of a blockhead withal, he would cease criticising his victuals to such extent; and criticise himself rather, what he does with his victuals!

LABOR

For there is a perennial nobleness, and even sacredness, in Work. Were he never so benighted, forgetful of his high calling, there is always hope in a man that actually and earnestly works: in Idleness alone is there perpetual despair. Work, never so Mammonish, mean, *is* in communication with Nature; the real desire to get Work done will itself lead one more and more to truth, to Nature's appointments and regulations, which are truth.

The latest Gospel in this world is, Know thy work and do it. "Know thyself": long enough has that poor "self" of thine tormented thee; thou wilt never get to "know" it, I believe! Think it not thy business, this of knowing thyself; thou art an unknowable individual: know what thou canst work at; and work at it, like a Hercules! That will be thy better plan.

It has been written, "an endless significance lies in Work"; a man perfects himself by working. Foul jungles are cleared away, fair seedfields rise instead, and stately cities; and withal the man himself first ceases to be a jungle and foul unwholesome desert thereby. Consider how, even in the meanest sorts of Labor, the whole soul of a man is composed into a kind of real harmony, the instant he sets himself to work! Doubt, Desire, Sorrow, Remorse, Indignation, Despair itself, all these like helldogs lie beleaguering the soul of the poor day-worker, as of every man: but he bends himself with free valor against his task, and all these are stilled, all these shrink murmuring far off into their caves. The man is now a man. The blessed glow of Labor in him, is it not as purifying fire, wherein all poison is burnt up, and of sour smoke itself there is made bright blessed flame!

Destiny, on the whole, has no other way of cultivating us. A formless Chaos, once set it *revolving,* grows round and ever rounder; ranges itself, by mere force of gravity, into strata, spherical courses; is no longer a Chaos, but a round compacted World. What would become of the Earth, did she cease to revolve? In the poor old Earth, so long as she revolves, all inequalities, irregularities disperse themselves; all irregularities are incessantly becoming regular. Hast thou looked on the Potter's wheel,—one of the venerablest objects; old as the Prophet Ezechiel and far older? Rude lumps of clay, how they spin themselves up, by mere quick whirling, into beautiful circular dishes. And fancy the most assiduous Potter, but without his wheel; reduced to make dishes, or rather amorphous botches, by mere kneading and baking! Even such a Potter were Destiny, with a human soul that would rest and lie at ease, that would not work and spin! Of an idle unrevolving man the kindest Destiny, like the most assiduous Potter without wheel, can bake and knead nothing other than a botch; let her spend on him what expensive coloring, what gilding and enamelling she will, he is but a botch. Not a dish; no, a bulging, kneaded, crooked, shambling, squint-cornered, amorphous botch,—a mere enamelled vessel of dishonor! Let the idle think of this.

Blessed is he who has found his work; let him ask no other blessedness. He has a work, a life-purpose; he has found it, and will follow it! How, as a free-flowing channel, dug and torn by noble force through the sour mud-swamp of one's existence, like an ever-deepening river there, it runs and flows;—draining-off the sour festering water, gradually from the root of the remotest grass-blade; making, instead of pestilential swamp, a green fruitful meadow with its clear-flowing stream. How blessed for the meadow itself, let the stream and *its* value be great or small! Labor is Life: from the inmost heart of the Worker rises his god-given Force, the sacred celestial Life-essence breathed into him by Almighty God; from his inmost heart awakens him to all nobleness,—to all knowledge, "self-knowledge," and much else, so soon as Work fitly begins. Knowledge? The knowledge that will hold good in working, cleave thou to that; for

Nature herself accredits that, says Yea to that. Properly thou hast no other knowledge but what thou hast got by working: the rest is yet all a hypothesis of knowledge; a thing to be argued of in schools, a thing floating in the clouds, in endless logic-vortices, till we try it and fix it. "Doubt, of whatever kind, can be ended by Action alone."

And again, hast thou valued Patience, Courage, Perseverance, Openness to light; readiness to own thyself mistaken, to do better next time? All these, all virtues, in wrestling with the dim brute Powers of Fact, in ordering of thy fellows in such wrestle, there and elsewhere not at all, thou wilt continually learn. Set down a brave Sir Christopher in the middle of black ruined Stone-heaps, of foolish unarchitectural Bishops, redtape Officials, idle Nell-Gwyn Defenders of the Faith; and see whether he will ever raise a Paul's Cathedral out of all that, yea or no! Rough, rude, contradictory are all things and persons, from the mutinous masons and Irish hodmen, up to the idle Nell-Gwyn Defenders, to blustering redtape Officials, foolish unarchitectural Bishops. All these things and persons are there not for Christopher's sake and his Cathedral's; they are there for their own sake mainly! Christopher will have to conquer and constrain all these,—if he is able. All these are against him. Equitable Nature herself, who carries her mathematics and architectonics not on the face of her, but deep in the hidden heart of her,—Nature herself is but partially for him; will be wholly against him, if he constrain her not! His very money, where is it to come from? The pious munificence of England lies far-scattered, distant, unable to speak, and say, "I am here";—must be spoken to before it can speak. Pious munificence, and all help, is so silent, invisible like the gods; impediment, contradictions manifold are so loud and near! O brave Sir Christopher, trust thou in those notwithstanding, and front all these; understand all these; by valiant patience, noble effort, insight, by man's-strength, vanquish and compel all these,—and, on the whole, strike down victoriously the last topstone of that Paul's Edifice; thy monument for certain centuries, the stamp "Great Man" impressed very legibly on Portland-stone there!—

Yes, all manner of help, and pious response from Men or Nature, is always what we call silent; cannot speak or come to light, till it be seen, till it be spoken to. Every noble work is at first "impossible." In very truth, for every noble work the possibilities will lie diffused through Immensity; inarticulate, undiscoverable except to faith. Like Gideon thou shalt spread out thy fleece at the door of thy tent; see whether under the wide arch of Heaven there be any bounteous moisture, or none. Thy heart and life-purpose shall be as a miraculous Gideon's fleece, spread out in silent appeal to Heaven: and from the kind Immensities, what from the poor unkind Localities and town and country Parishes there never could, blessed dew-moisture to suffice thee shall have fallen!

Work is of a religious nature:—work is of a *brave* nature; which it is the aim of all religion to be. All work of man is as the swimmer's: a waste ocean threatens to devour him; if he front it not bravely, it will keep its word. By incessant wise defiance of it, lusty rebuke and buffet of it, behold how it loyally supports him, bears him as its conqueror along. "It is so," says Goethe, "with all things that man undertakes in this world."

Brave Sea-captain, Norse Sea-king,—Columbus, my hero, royalest Sea-king of all! it is no friendly environment this of thine, in the waste deep waters; around thee mutinous discouraged souls, behind thee disgrace and ruin, before thee the unpenetrated veil of Night. Brother, these wild water-mountains, bounding from their deep bases (ten miles deep, I am told), are not entirely there on thy behalf! Meseems *they* have other work than floating thee forward:—and the huge Winds, that sweep from Ursa Major to the Tropics and Equators, dancing their giant-waltz through the kingdoms of Chaos and Immensity, they care little about filling rightly or filling wrongly the small shoulder-of-mutton sails in this cockle-skiff of thine! Thou art not among articulate-speaking friends, my brother; thou art among immeasurable dumb monsters, tumbling, howling wide as the world here. Secret, far off, invisible to all hearts but thine, there lies a help in them: see how thou wilt get at that. Patiently thou wilt wait till the mad South-wester spend itself, saving thyself by dextrous science of defence, the while: valiantly, with swift decision, wilt thou strike in, when the favoring East, the Possible, springs up. Mutiny of men thou wilt sternly repress; weakness, despondency, thou wilt cheerily encourage: thou wilt swallow down complaint, unreason, weariness, weakness of others and thyself;—how much wilt thou swallow down! There shall be a depth of Silence in thee, deeper than this Sea, which is but ten miles deep: a Silence unsoundable; known to God only. Thou shalt be a Great man. Yes, my World-Soldier, thou of the World Marine-service,—thou wilt have to be greater than this tumultuous unmeasured World here round thee is: thou, in thy strong soul, as with wrestler's arms, shalt embrace it, harness it down; and make it bear thee on,—to new Americas, or whither God wills!

REWARD

"Religion" I said; for, properly speaking, all true Work is Religion: and whatsoever Religion is not Work may go and dwell among the Brahmins, Antinomians, Spinning Dervishes, or where it will; with me it shall have no harbor. Admirable was that of the old Monks, "Laborare est Orare, Work is Worship."

Older than all preached Gospels was this unpreached, inarticulate, but ineradicable, forever-enduring Gospel: Work, and therein have wellbeing. Man, Son of Earth and of Heaven, lies there not, in the innermost heart of thee, a Spirit of active Method, a Force for Work;—and burns like a painfully-smouldering fire, giving thee no rest till thou unfold it, till thou write it down in beneficent Facts around thee! What is immethodic, waste, thou shalt make methodic, regulated, arable; obedient and productive to thee. Wheresoever thou findest Disorder, there is thy eternal enemy; attack him swiftly, subdue him; make Order of him, the subject not of Chaos, but of Intelligence, Divinity and Thee! The thistle that grows in thy path, dig it

out, that a blade of useful grass, a drop of nourishing milk, may grow there instead. The waste cotton-shrub, gather its waste white down, spin it, weave it; that, in place of idle litter, there may be folded webs, and the naked skin of man be covered.

But above all, where thou findest Ignorance, Stupidity, Brute-mindedness,—yes, there, with or without Church-tithes and Shovel-hat, with or without Talfourd-Mahon Copyrights, or were it with mere dungeons and gibbets and crosses, attack it, I say; smite it wisely, unweariedly, and rest not while thou livest and it lives; but smite, smite, in the name of God! The Highest God, as I understand it, does audibly so command thee; still audibly, if thou have ears to hear. He, even He, with his *unspoken* voice, awfuler than any Sinai thunders or syllabled speech of Whirlwinds; for the SILENCE of deep Eternities, of Worlds from beyond the morning-stars, does it not speak to thee? The unborn Ages; the old Graves, with their long-mouldering dust, the very tears that wetted it now all dry,—do not these speak to thee, what ear hath not heard? The deep Death-kingdoms, the Stars in their never-resting courses, all Space and all Time, proclaim it to thee in continual silent admonition. Thou too, if ever man should, shalt work while it is called To-day. For the Night cometh, wherein no man can work.

All true Work is sacred; in all true Work, were it but true hand-labor, there is something of divineness. Labor, wide as the Earth, has its summit in Heaven. Sweat of the brow; and up from that to sweat of the brain, sweat of the heart; which includes all Kepler calculations, Newton meditations, all Sciences, all spoken Epics, all acted Heroisms, Martyrdoms,—up to that "Agony of bloody sweat," which all men have called divine! O brother, if this is not "worship," then I say, the more pity for worship; for this is the noblest thing yet discovered under God's sky. Who art thou that complainest of thy life of toil? Complain not. Look up, my wearied brother; see thy fellow Workmen there, in God's Eternity; surviving there, they alone surviving: sacred Band of the Immortals, celestial Bodyguard of the

Empire of Mankind. Even in the weak Human Memory they survive so long, as saints, as heroes, as gods; they alone surviving; peopling, they alone, the unmeasured solitudes of Time! To thee Heaven, though severe, is *not* unkind; Heaven is kind,—as a noble Mother; as that Spartan Mother, saying while she gave her son his shield, "With it, my son, or upon it!" Thou too shalt return *home* in honor; to thy far-distant Home, in honor; doubt it not,—if in the battle thou keep thy shield! Thou, in the Eternities and deepest Death-kingdoms, are not an alien; thou everywhere art a denizen! Complain not; the very Spartans did not *complain*.

And who art thou that braggest of thy life of Idleness; complacently showest thy bright gilt equipages; sumptuous cushions; appliances for folding of the hands to mere sleep? Looking up, looking down, around, behind or before, discernest thou, if it be not in Mayfair alone, any *idle* hero, saint, god, or even devil? Not a vestige of one. In the Heavens, in the Earth, in the Waters under the Earth, is none like unto thee. Thou art an original figure in this Creation; a denizen in Mayfair alone, in this extraordinary Century or Half-Century alone! One monster there is in the world: the idle man. What is his "Religion"? That Nature is a Phantasm, where cunning beggary or thievery may sometimes find good victual. That God is a lie; and that Man and his Life are a lie.—Alas, alas, who of us *is* there that can say, I have worked? The faithfulest of us are unprofitable servants; the faithfulest of us know that best. The faithfulest of us may say, with sad and true old Samuel, "Much of my life has been trifled away!" But he that has, and except "on public occasions" professes to have, no function but that of going idle in a graceful or graceless manner; and of begetting sons to go idle; and to address Chief Spinners and Diggers, who at least *are* spinning and digging, "Ye scandalous persons who produce too much"—My Corn-Law friends, on what imaginary still richer Eldorados, and true iron-spikes with law of gravitation, are ye rushing!

As to the Wages of Work there might innumerable things be said; there will and must yet innumerable things be said and spoken, in St. Stephen's and out of St. Stephen's; and gradually not a few things be ascertained and written, on Law-parchment, concerning this very matter:—"Fair day's-wages for a fair day's-work" is the most unrefusable demand! Money-wages "to the extent of keeping your worker alive that he may work more"; these, unless you mean to dismiss him straightway out of this world, are indispensable alike to the noblest Worker and to the least noble!

One thing only I will say here, in special reference to the former class, the noble and noblest; but throwing light on all the other classes and their arrangements of this difficult matter: The "wages" of every noble Work do yet lie in Heaven or else Nowhere. Not in Bank-of-England bills, in Owen's Labor-bank, or any the most improved establishment of banking and money-changing, needest thou, heroic soul, present thy account of earnings. Human banks and labor-banks know thee not; or know thee after generations and centuries have passed away, and thou art clean gone from "rewarding,"—all manner of bank-drafts, shop-tills, and Downing-street Exchequers lying very invisible, so far from thee! Nay, at bottom, dost thou need any reward? Was it thy aim and life-purpose to be filled with good things for thy heroism; to have a life of pomp and ease, and be what men call "happy," in this world, or in any other world? I answer for thee deliberately, No. The whole spiritual secret of the new epoch lies in this, that thou canst answer for thyself, with thy whole clearness of head and heart, deliberately, No!

My brother, the brave man has to give his Life away. Give it, I advise thee;—thou dost not expect to *sell* thy Life in an adequate manner? What price, for example, would content thee? The just price of thy LIFE to thee,—why, God's entire Creation to thyself, the whole Universe of Space, the whole Eternity of Time, and what they hold: that is the price which would content thee; that, and if thou wilt be candid, nothing short of that! It is thy all; and for it thou wouldst have all. Thou art an unreasonable mortal;—or rather thou art a poor *infinite* mortal, who, in thy narrow clay-prison here, *seemest* so unreasonable! Thou wilt never sell thy Life, or any part of thy Life, in a satisfactory manner. Give it, like a royal heart; let the price be Nothing: thou *hast* then, in a certain sense, got All for it! The heroic man,—and is not every man, God be thanked, a potential hero?—has to do so, in all times and circumstances. In the most heroic age, as in the most unheroic, he will have to say, as Burns said proudly and humbly of his little Scottish Songs, little dewdrops of Celestial Melody in an age when so much was unmelodious: "By Heaven, they shall either be invaluable or of no value; I do not need your guineas for them!" It is an element which should, and must, enter deeply into all settlements of wages here below. They never will be "satisfactory" otherwise; they cannot, O Mammon Gospel, they never can! Money for my little piece of work "to the extent that will allow me to keep working"; yes, this,—unless you mean that I shall go my ways *before* the work is all taken out of me: but as to "wages"—!—

On the whole, we do entirely agree with those old Monks, *Laborare est Orare*. In a thousand senses, from one end of it to the other, true Work *is* Worship. He that works, whatsoever be his work, he bodies forth the form of Things Unseen; a small Poet every Worker is. The idea, were it but of his poor Delf Platter, how much more of his Epic Poem, is as yet "seen," half-seen, only by himself; to all others it is a thing unseen, impossible; to Nature herself it is a thing unseen, a thing which never hitherto was;—very "impossible," for it is as yet a No-thing! The Unseen Powers had need to watch over such a man; he works in and for the Unseen. Alas, if he look to the Seen Powers only, he may as well quit the business; his No-thing will never rightly issue as a Thing, but as a Deceptivity, a Sham-thing,—which it had better not do!

Thy No-thing of an Intended Poem, O Poet who hast looked merely to reviewers, copyrights, booksellers, popularities, behold it has not yet become a Thing; for the truth is not in it! Though printed, hot-pressed, reviewed, celebrated, sold to the twentieth edition: what is all that? The

Thing, in philosophical uncommercial language, is still a No-thing, mostly semblance and deception of the sight;—benign Oblivion incessantly gnawing at it, impatient till Chaos, to which it belongs, do reabsorb it!—

He who takes not counsel of the Unseen and Silent, from him will never come real visibility and speech. Thou must descend to the *Mothers,* to the *Manes,* and Hercules-like long suffer and labor there, wouldst thou emerge with victory into the sunlight. As in battle and the shock of war,—for is not this a battle?—thou too shalt fear no pain or death, shalt love no ease or life; the voice of festive Lubberlands, the noise of greedy Acheron shall alike lie silent under thy victorious feet. Thy work, like Dante's, shall "make thee lean for many years." The world and its wages, its criticisms, counsels, helps, impediments, shall be as a waste ocean-flood; the chaos through which thou art to swim and sail. Not the waste waves and their weedy gulf-streams, shalt thou take for guidance: thy star alone,—"*Se tu sequi tua stella!*" [1] Thy star alone, now clear-beaming over Chaos, nay now by fits gone out, disastrously eclipsed: this only shalt thou strive to follow. O, it is a business, as I fancy, that of weltering your way through Chaos and the murk of Hell! Green-eyed dragons watching you, three-headed Cerberuses,—not without sympathy of *their* sort! "*Eccovi l' uom ch' è stato all' Inferno.*" [2] For in fine, as Poet Dryden says, you do walk hand in hand with sheer Madness, all the way,—who is by no means pleasant company! You look fixedly into Madness, and *her* undiscovered, boundless, bottomless Night-empire; that you may extort new Wisdom out of it, as an Eurydice from Tartarus. The higher the Wisdom, the closer was its neighborhood and kindred with mere Insanity; literally so;—and thou wilt, with a speechless feeling, observe how highest Wisdom, struggling up into this world, has oftentimes

[1] *Se tu sequi tua Stella:* "If thou follow thy star" (*Inferno,* XV, 55).

[2] *Eccovi l' uom ch' è stato all' Inferno:* 'Behold the man who has been in Hell'. According to Boccaccio in his *Memoir* of Dante, these words were spoken by citizens of Verona as they saw Dante pass.

carried such tinctures and adhesions of Insanity still cleaving to it hither!

All Works, each in their degree, are a making of Madness sane;—truly enough a religious operation; which cannot be carried on without religion. You have not work otherwise; you have eye-service, greedy grasping of wages, swift and ever swifter manufacture of semblances to get hold of wages. Instead of better felt-hats to cover your head, you have bigger lath-and-plaster hats set travelling the streets on wheels. Instead of heavenly and earthly Guidance for the souls of men, you have "Black or White Surplice" Controversies, stuffed hair-and-leather Popes;—terrestrial *Law-wards,* Lords and Law-bringers, "organizing Labor" in these years, by passing Corn-Laws. With all which, alas, this distracted Earth is now full, nigh to bursting. Semblances most smooth to the touch and eye; most accursed, nevertheless, to body and soul. Semblances, be they of Sham-woven Cloth or of Dilettante Legislation, which are *not* real wool or substance, but Devil's-dust, accursed of God and man! No man has worked, or can work, except religiously; not even the poor day-laborer, the weaver of your coat, the sewer of your shoes. All men, if they work not as in a Great Taskmaster's eye, will work wrong, work unhappily for themselves and you.

Industrial work, still under bondage to Mammon, the rational soul of it not yet awakened, is a tragic spectacle. Men in the rapidest motion and self-motion; restless, with convulsive energy, as if driven by Galvanism, as if possessed by a Devil; tearing asunder mountains,—to no purpose, for Mammonism is always Midas-eared! This is sad, on the face of it. Yet courage: the beneficent Destinies, kind in their sternness, are apprising us that this cannot continue. Labor is not a devil, even while encased in Mammonism; Labor is ever an imprisoned god, writhing unconsciously or consciously to escape out of Mammonism! Plugson of Undershot, like Taillefer of Normandy, wants victory; how much happier will even Plugson be to have a chivalrous victory than a Chactaw one! The unredeemed ugliness is that of a slothful People. Show me a People energetically busy; heaving, struggling, all shoulders at the wheel; their heart pulsing, every muscle swelling, with man's energy and will;—I show you a People of whom great good is already predicable; to whom all manner of good is yet certain, if their energy endure. By very working, they will learn; they have, Antæus-like, their foot on Mother Fact: how can they but learn?

The vulgarest Plugson of a Master-Worker, who can command Workers, and get work out of them, is already a considerable man. Blessed and thrice-blessed symptoms I discern of Master-Workers who are not vulgar men; who are Nobles, and begin to feel that they must act as such: all speed to these, they are England's hope at present! But in this Plugson himself, conscious of almost no nobleness whatever, how much is there! Not without man's faculty, insight, courage, hard energy, is this rugged figure. His words none of the wisest; but his actings cannot be altogether foolish. Think, how were it, stoodst thou suddenly in his shoes! He has to command a thousand men. And not imaginary commanding; no, it is real, incessantly practical. The evil passions of so many men (with the Devil in them, as in all of us) he has to vanquish; by manifold force of speech and of silence, to repress or evade. What a force of silence, to say nothing of the others, is in Plugson! For these his thousand men he has to provide raw-material, machinery, arrangement, houseroom; and ever at the week's end, wages by due sale. No Civil-List, or Goulburn-Baring Budget has he to fall back upon, for paying of his regiment; he has to pick his supplies from the confused face of the whole Earth and Contemporaneous History, by his dexterity alone. There will be dry eyes if he fail to do it!—He exclaims, at present, "black in the face," near strangled with Dilettante Legislation; "Let me have elbow-room, throat-room, and I will not fail! No, I will spin yet, and conquer like a giant: what 'sinews of war' lie in me, untold resources toward the Conquest of this Planet, if instead of hanging me, you husband them, and help me!"—My indomitable friend, it is *true;* and thou shalt and must be helped.

This is not a man I would kill and strangle by Corn-Laws, even if I could!

No, I would fling my Corn-Laws and Shot-belts to the Devil; and try to help this man. I would teach him, by noble precept and law-precept, by noble example most of all, that Mammonism was not the essence of his or of my station in God's Universe; but the adscititious excrescence of it; the gross, terrene, godless embodiment of it; which would have to become, more or less, a godlike one. By noble *real* legislation, by true *noble's*-work, by unwearied, valiant, and were it wageless effort, in my Parliament and in my Parish, I would aid, constrain, encourage him to effect more or less this blessed change. I should know that it would have to be effected; that unless it were in some measure effected, he and I and all of us, I first and soonest of all, were doomed to perdition!—Effected it will be; unless it were a Demon that made this Universe; which I, for my own part, do at no moment, under no form, in the least believe.

May it please your Serene Highnesses, your Majesties, Lordships and Law-wardships, the proper Epic of this world is not now "Arms and the Man"; how much less, "Shirt-frills and the Man": no, it is now "Tools and the Man": that, henceforth to all time, is now our Epic;—and you, first of all others, I think, were wise to take note of that!

DEMOCRACY

If the Serene Highnesses and Majesties do not take note of that, then, as I perceive, *that* will take note of itself! The time for levity, insincerity, and idle babble and play-acting, in all kinds, is gone by; it is a serious, grave time. Old long-vexed questions, not yet solved in logical words or parliamentary laws, are fast solving themselves in facts, somewhat unblessed to behold! This largest of questions, this question of Work and Wages, which ought, had we heeded Heaven's voice, to have begun two generations ago or more, cannot be delayed longer without hearing Earth's voice. "Labor" will verily need to be somewhat "organized," as they say,— God knows with what difficulty. Man will actually need to have his debts and earnings a little better paid by man; which, let

Parliaments speak of them or be silent of them, are eternally his due from man, and cannot, without penalty and at length not without death-penalty, be withheld. How much ought to cease among us straightway; how much ought to begin straightway, while the hours yet are!

Truly they are strange results to which this of leaving all to "Cash"; of quietly shutting-up the God's Temple, and gradually opening wide-open the Mammon's Temple, with "Laissez-faire, and Every man for himself,"—have led us in these days! We have Upper, speaking Classes, who indeed do "speak" as never man spake before; the withered flimsiness, the godless baseness and barrenness of whose Speech might of itself indicate what kind of Doing and practical Governing went on under it! For speech is the gaseous element out of which most kinds of Practice and Performance, especially all kinds of moral Performance, condense themselves, and take shape; as the one is, so will the other be. Descending, accordingly, into the Dumb Class in its Stockport Cellars and Poor-Law Bastilles, have we not to announce that they also are hitherto unexampled in the History of Adam's Posterity?

Life was never a May-game for men: in all times the lot of the dumb millions born to toil was defaced with manifold sufferings, injustices, heavy burdens, avoidable and unavoidable; not play at all, but hard work that made the sinews sore and the heart sore. As bond-slaves, *villani, bordarii, sochemanni,* nay indeed as dukes, earls and kings, men were oftentimes made weary of their life; and had to say, in the sweat of their brow and of their soul, Behold, it is not sport, it is grim earnest, and our back can bear no more! Who knows not what massacrings and harryings there have been; grinding, long-continuing, unbearable injustices,—till the heart had to rise in madness, and some *"Eu Sachsen, nimith euer sachses,* You Saxons, out with your gully-knives, then!" You Saxons, some "arrestment," partial "arrestment of the Knaves and Dastards" has become indispensable!— The page of Dryasdust is heavy with such details.

And yet I will venture to believe that in

no time, since the beginnings of Society, was the lot of those same dumb millions of toilers so entirely unbearable as it is even in the days now passing over us. It is not to die, or even to die of hunger, that makes a man wretched; many men have died; all men must die,—the last exit of us all is in a Fire-Chariot of Pain. But it is to live miserable we know not why; to work sore and yet gain nothing: to be heart-worn, weary, yet isolated, unrelated, girt-in with a cold universal Laissez-faire: it is to die slowly all our life long, imprisoned in a deaf, dead, Infinite Injustice, as in the accursed iron belly of a Phalaris' Bull! This is and remains forever intolerable to all men whom God has made. Do we wonder at French Revolutions, Chartisms, Revolts of Three Days? The times, if we will consider them, are really unexampled.

Never before did I hear of an Irish Widow reduced to "prove her sisterhood by dying of typhus-fever and infecting seventeen persons,"—saying in such undeniable way, "You *see* I was your sister!" Sisterhood, brotherhood, was often forgotten; but not till the rise of these ultimate Mammon and Shotbelt Gospels did I ever see it so expressly denied. If no pious Lord or *Law-ward* would remember it, always some pious Lady (*"Hlaf-dig,"* Benefactress, *"Loaf-giveress,"* they say she is,—blessings on her beautiful heart!) was there, with mild mother-voice and hand, to remember it; some pious thoughtful *Elder,* what we now call "Prester," *Presbyter* or "Priest," was there to put all men in mind of it, in the name of the God who had made all.

Not even in Black Dahomey was it ever, I think, forgotten to the typhus-fever length. Mungo Park, resourceless, had sunk down to die under the Negro Village-Tree, a horrible White object in the eyes of all. But in the poor Black Woman, and her daughter who stood aghast at him, whose earthly wealth and funded capital consisted of one small calabash of rice, there lived a heart richer than *Laissez-faire;* they, with a royal munificence, boiled their rice for him; they sang all night to him, spinning assiduous on their cotton distaffs, as he lay to sleep: "Let us pity the poor white man; no mother has he to fetch him milk, no sister to grind him corn!"

Thou poor black Noble One,—thou *Lady* too: did not a God make thee too; was there not in thee too something of a God!—

Gurth, born thrall of Cedric the Saxon, has been greatly pitied by Dryasdust and others. Gurth, with the brass collar round his neck, tending Cedric's pigs in the glades of the wood, is not what I call an exemplar of human felicity: but Gurth, with the sky above him, with the free air and tinted boscage and umbrage round him, and in him at least the certainty of supper and social lodging when he came home; Gurth to me seems happy, in comparison with many a Lancashire and Buckinghamshire man of these days, not born thrall of anybody! Gurth's brass collar did not gall him: Cedric *deserved* to be his master. The pigs were Cedric's, but Gurth too would get his parings of them. Gurth had the inexpressible satisfaction of feeling himself related indissolubly, though in a rude brass-collar way, to his fellow-mortals in this Earth. He had superiors, inferiors, equals. —Gurth is now "emancipated" long since; has what we call "Liberty." Liberty, I am told, is a divine thing. Liberty when it becomes the "Liberty to die by starvation" is not so divine!

Liberty? The true liberty of a man, you would say, consisted in his finding out, or being forced to find out the right path, and to walk thereon. To learn, or to be taught, what work he actually was able for; and then by permission, persuasion, and even compulsion, to set about doing of the same! That is his true blessedness, honor, "liberty" and maximum of wellbeing: if liberty be not that, I for one have small care about liberty. You do not allow a palpable madman to leap over precipices; you violate his liberty, you that are wise; and keep him, were it in strait-waistcoats, away from the precipices! Every stupid, every cowardly and foolish man is but a less palpable madman: his true liberty were that a wiser man, that any and every wiser man, could, by brass collars, or in whatever milder or sharper way, lay hold of him when he was going wrong, and order and compel him to go a little righter. O, if thou really art my *Senior,* Seigneur, my *Elder,* Presbyter or Priest,—if thou art in very deed my *Wiser,* may a beneficent instinct lead and impel thee to "conquer" me, to command me! If thou do know better than I what is good and right, I conjure thee in the name of God, force me to do it; were it by never such brass collars, whips and handcuffs, leave me not to walk over precipices! That I have been called, by all the Newspapers, a "free man" will avail me little, if my pilgrimage have ended in death and wreck. O that the Newspapers had called me slave, coward, fool, or what it pleased their sweet voices to name me, and I had attained not death, but life!—Liberty requires new definitions.

A conscious abhorrence and intolerance of Folly, of Baseness, Stupidity, Poltroonery and all that brood of things, dwells deep in some men: still deeper in others an *unconscious* abhorrence and intolerance, clothed moreover by the beneficent Supreme Powers in what stout appetites, energies, egoisms so-called, are suitable to it; —these latter are your Conquerers, Romans, Normans, Russians, Indo-English; Founders of what we called Aristocracies. Which indeed have they not the most "divine right" to found;—being themselves very truly Ἄριστοι, BRAVEST, BEST; and conquering generally a confused rabble of WORST, or at lowest, clearly enough, of WORSE? I think their divine right, tried, with affirmatory verdict, in the greatest Law-Court known to me, was good! A class of men who are dreadfully exclaimed against by Dryasdust; of whom nevertheless beneficent Nature has oftentimes had need; and may, alas, again have need.

When, across the hundredfold poor scepticisms, trivialisms and constitutional cobwebberies of Dryasdust, you catch any glimpse of a William the Conqueror, a Tancred of Hauteville or suchlike,—do you not discern veritably some rude outline of a true God-made King; whom not the Champion of England cased in tin, but all Nature and the Universe were calling to the throne? It is absolutely necessary that he get thither. Nature does not mean her poor Saxon children to perish, of obesity, stupor or other malady, as yet: a stern Ruler and Line of Rulers therefore is called in,—a stern but most beneficent *perpetual House-Surgeon* is by Nature herself called

in, and even the appropriate *fees* are provided for him! Dryasdust talks lamentably about Hereward and the Fen Counties; fate of Earl Waltheof; Yorkshire and the North reduced to ashes: all which is undoubtedly lamentable. But even Dryasdust apprises me of one fact: "A child, in this William's reign, might have carried a purse of gold from end to end of England." My erudite friend, it is a fact which outweighs a thousand! Sweep away thy constitutional, sentimental and other cobwebberies; look eye to eye, if thou still have any eye, in the face of this big burly William Bastard: thou wilt see a fellow of most flashing discernment, of most strong lion-heart;—in whom, as it were, within a frame of oak and iron, the gods have planted the soul of "a man of genius"! Dost thou call that nothing? I call it an immense thing!—Rage enough was in this Willelmus Conquæstor, rage enough for his occasions;—and yet the essential element of him, as of all such men, is not scorching *fire,* but shining illuminative *light.* Fire and light are strangely interchangeable; nay, at bottom, I have found them different forms of the same most godlike "elementary substance" in our world: a thing worth stating in these days. The essential element of this Conquæstor is, first of all, the most sun-eyed perception of what *is* really what on this God's-Earth;—which, thou wilt find, does mean at bottom "Justice," and "Virtues" not a few: *Conformity* to what the Maker has seen good to make; that, I suppose, will mean Justice and a Virtue or two?—

Dost thou think Willelmus Conquæstor would have tolerated ten years' jargon, one hour's jargon, on the propriety of killing Cotton-manufacturers by partridge Corn-Laws? I fancy, this was not the man to knock out of his night-rest with nothing but a noisy bedlamism in your mouth! "Assist us still better to bush the partridges; strangle Plugson who spins the shirts?"— *"Par la splendeur de Dieu!"* [1]——Dost thou think Willelmus Conquæstor, in this new time, with Steamengine Captains of Industry on one hand of him, and Joe-Manton Captains of Idleness on the other, would

[1] *Par la splendeur de Dieu:* 'By God's Splendor',—said to have been a favorite oath of William.

have doubted which *was* really the BEST; which did deserve strangling, and which not?

I have a certain indestructible regard for Willelmus Conquæstor. A resident House-Surgeon, provided by Nature for her beloved English People, and even furnished with the requisite fees, as I said; for he by no means felt himself doing Nature's work, this Willelmus, but his own work exclusively! And his own work withal it was; informed *"par la Splendeur de Dieu."*—I say, it is necessary to get the work out of such a man, however harsh that be! When a world, not yet doomed for death, is rushing down to ever-deeper Baseness and Confusion, it is a dire necessity of Nature's to bring in her ARISTOCRACIES, her BEST, even by forcible methods. When their descendants or representatives cease entirely to *be* the Best, Nature's poor world will very soon rush down again to Baseness; and it becomes a dire necessity of Nature's to cast them out. Hence French Revolutions, Five-point Charters, Democracies, and a mournful list of *Etceteras,* in these our afflicted times.

To what extent Democracy has now reached, how it advances irresistible with ominous, ever-increasing speed, he that will open his eyes on any province of human affairs may discern. Democracy is everywhere the inexorable demand of these ages, swiftly fulfilling itself. From the thunder of Napoleon battles, to the jabbering of Open-vestry in St. Mary Axe, all things announce Democracy. A distinguished man, whom some of my readers will hear again with pleasure, thus writes to me what in these days he notes from the Wahngasse of Weissnichtwo, where our London fashions seem to be in full vogue. Let us hear the Herr Teufelsdröckh again, were it but the smallest word!

"Democracy, which means despair of finding any Heroes to govern you, and contented putting-up with the want of them,—alas, thou too, *mein Lieber,* seest well how close it is of kin to *Atheism,* and other sad *Isms:* he who discovers no God whatever, how shall he discover Heroes, the visible Temples of God?—Strange enough meanwhile it is, to observe with what thoughtlessness, here in our rigidly Conservative Country, men rush into Democracy with full cry. Beyond doubt, his Excellenz the Titular-Herr Ritter Kauderwälsch von Pferdefuss-Quacksalber,[2] he our distinguished Conservative Premier himself, and all but the thicker-headed of his Party, discern Democracy to be inevitable as death, and are even desperate of delaying it much!

"You cannot walk the streets without beholding Democracy announce itself: the very Tailor has become, if not properly Sansculottic, which to him would be ruinous, yet a Tailor unconsciously symbolizing, and prophesying with his scissors, the reign of Equality. What now is our fashionable coat? A thing of superfinest texture, of deeply meditated cut; with Malines-lace cuffs; quilted with gold; so that a man can carry, without difficulty, an estate of land on his back? *Keineswegs,* By no manner of means! The Sumptuary Laws have fallen into such a state of desuetude as was never before seen. Our fashionable coat is an amphibium between barnsack and drayman's doublet. The cloth of it is studiously coarse; the color a speckled soot-black or rust-brown gray; the nearest approach to a Peasant's. And for shape,—thou shouldst see it! The last consummation of the year now passing over us is definable as Three Bags; a big bag for the body, two small bags for the arms, and by way of collar a hem! The first Antique Cheruscan who, of felt-cloth or bear's-hide, with bone or metal needle, set about making himself a coat, before Tailors had yet awakened out of Nothing,—did not he make it even so? A loose wide poke for body, with two holes to let out the arms; this was his original coat: to which holes it was soon visible that two small loose pokes, or sleeves, easily appended, would be an improvement.

"Thus has the Tailor-art, so to speak, overset itself, like most other things; changed its centre-of-gravity; whirled suddenly over from zenith to nadir. Your Stulz, with huge somerset, vaults from his high shop-board down to the depths of primal savagery,—carrying much along with

<hr>

[2] *Titular—Herr Ritter,* etc.: His Excellency the Titular–Sir Knight Jargon von Horsefoot—Quack doctor.

him! For I will invite thee to reflect that the Tailor, as topmost ultimate froth of Human Society, is indeed swift-passing, evanescent, slippery to decipher; yet significant of much, nay of all. Topmost evanescent froth, he is churned-up from the very lees, and from all intermediate regions of the liquor. The general outcome he, visible to the eye, of what men aimed to do, and were obliged and enabled to do, in this one public department of symbolizing themselves to each other by covering of their skins. A smack of all Human Life lies in the Tailor: its wild struggles toward beauty, dignity, freedom, victory; and how, hemmed-in by Sedan and Huddersfield, by Nescience, Dulness, Prurience, and other sad necessities and laws of Nature, it has attained just to this: Gray savagery of Three Sacks with a hem!

"When the very Tailor verges toward Sansculottism, is it not ominous? The last Divinity of poor mankind dethroning himself; sinking *his* taper too, flame downmost, like the Genius of Sleep or of Death; admonitory that Tailor time shall be no more!—For, little as one could advise Sumptuary Laws at the present epoch, yet nothing is clearer than that where ranks do actually exist, strict division of costumes will also be enforced; that if we ever have a new Hierarchy and Aristocracy, acknowledged veritably as such, for which I daily pray Heaven, the Tailor will reawaken; and be, by volunteering and appointment, consciously and unconsciously, a safeguard of that same."—Certain farther observations, from the same invaluable pen, on our never-ending changes of mode, our "perpetual nomadic and even ape-like appetite for change and mere change" in all the equipments of our existence, and the "fatal revolutionary character" thereby manifested, we suppress for the present. It may be admitted that Democracy, in all meanings of the word, is in full career; irresistible by any Ritter Kauderwälsch or other Son of Adam, as times go. "Liberty" is a thing men are determined to have.

But truly, as I had to remark in the mean while, "the liberty of not being oppressed by your fellow man" is an indispensable, yet one of the most significant fractional parts of Human Liberty. No man oppresses thee, can bid thee fetch or carry, come or go, without reason shown. True; from all men thou art emancipated: but from Thyself and from the Devil—? No man, wiser, unwiser, can make thee come or go: but thy own futilities, bewilderments, thy false appetites for Money, Windsor Georges and suchlike? No man oppresses thee, O free and independent Franchiser: but does not this stupid Porter-pot oppress thee? No Son of Adam can bid thee come or go; but this absurd Pot of Heavy-wet, this can and does! Thou art the thrall not of Cedric the Saxon, but of thy own brutal appetites and this scoured dish of liquor. And thou pratest of thy "liberty"? Thou entire blockhead!

Heavy-wet and gin: alas, these are not the only kinds of thraldom. Thou who walkest in a vain show, looking out with ornamental dilettante sniff and serene supremacy at all Life and all Death; and amblest jauntily; perking up thy poor talk into crotchets, thy poor conduct into fatuous somnambulisms;—and *art* as an "enchanted Ape" under God's sky, where thou mightest have been a man, had proper Schoolmasters and Conquerors, and Constables with cat-o'-nine tails, been vouchsafed thee; dost thou call that "liberty"? Or your unreposing Mammon-worshipper again, driven, as if by Galvanisms, by Devils and Fixed-Ideas, who rises early and sits late, chasing the impossible; straining every faculty to "fill himself with the east wind,"—how merciful were it, could you, by mild persuasion, or by the severest tyranny so-called, check him in his mad path, and turn him into a wiser one! All painful tyranny, in that case again, were but mild "surgery"; the pain of it cheap, as health and life, instead of galvanism and fixed-idea, are cheap at any price.

Sure enough, of all paths a man could strike into, there *is*, at any given moment, a *best path* for every man; a thing which, here and now, it were of all things *wisest* for him to do;—which could he be but led or driven to do, he were then doing "like a man," as we phrase it; all men and gods agreeing with him, the whole Universe virtually exclaiming Well-done to him! His success, in such case, were complete; his

Mock b

felicity a maximum. This path, to find this path and walk in it, is the one thing needful for him. Whatsoever forwards him in that, let it come to him even in the shape of blows and spurnings, is liberty: whatsoever hinders him, were it ward-motes, open-vestries, pollbooths, tremendous cheers, rivers of heavy-wet, is slavery.

The notion that a man's liberty consists in giving his vote at election-hustings, and saying, "Behold, now I too have my twenty-thousandth part of a Talker in our National Palaver; will not all the gods be good to me?"—is one of the pleasantest! Nature nevertheless is kind at present; and puts it into the heads of many, almost of all. The liberty especially which has to purchase itself by social isolation, and each man standing separate from the other, having "no business with him" but a cash-account: this is such a liberty as the Earth seldom saw;—as the Earth will not long put up with, recommend it how you may. This liberty turns out, before it have long continued in action, with all men flinging up their caps round it, to be, for the Working Millions a liberty to die by want of food; for the Idle Thousands and Units, alas, a still more fatal liberty to live in want of work; to have no earnest duty to do in this God's-World any more. What becomes of a man in such predicament? Earth's Laws are silent; and Heaven's speak in a voice which is not heard. No work, and the ineradicable need of work, give rise to new very wondrous life-philosophies, new very wondrous life-practices! Dilettantism, Pococurantism, Beau-Brummelism, with perhaps an occasional, half-mad, protesting burst of Byronism, establish themselves: at the end of a certain period,—if you go back to "the Dead Sea," there is, say our Moslem friends, a very strange "Sabbath-day" transacting itself there!—Brethren, we know but imperfectly yet, after ages of Constitutional Government, what Liberty and Slavery are.

Democracy, the chase of Liberty in that direction shall go its full course; unrestrainable by him of Pferdefuss-Quacksalber, or any of *his* household. The Toiling Millions of Mankind, in most vital need and passionate instinctive desire of Guidance, shall cast away False-Guidance; and hope, for an hour, that No-Guidance will suffice them: but it can be for an hour only. The smallest item of human Slavery is the oppression of man by his Mock-Superiors; the palpablest, but I say at bottom the smallest. Let him shake-off such oppression, trample it indignantly under his feet; I blame him not, I pity and commend him. But oppression by your Mock-Superiors well shaken off, the grand problem yet remains to solve: That of finding government by your Real-Superiors! Alas, how shall we ever learn the solution of that, benighted, bewildered, sniffing, sneering, godforgetting unfortunates as we are? It is a work for centuries; to be taught us by tribulations, confusions, insurrections, obstructions; who knows if not by conflagration and despair! It is a lesson inclusive of all other lessons; the hardest of all lessons to learn.

One thing I do know: Those Apes, chattering on the branches by the Dead Sea, never got it learned; but chatter there to this day. To them no Moses need come a second time; a thousand Moseses would be but so many painted Phantasms, interesting Fellow-Apes of new strange aspect,—whom they would "invite to dinner," be glad to meet with in lion-soirées. To them the voice of Prophecy, of heavenly monition, is quite ended. They chatter there, all Heaven shut to them, to the end of the world. The unfortunates! Oh, what is dying of hunger, with honest tools in your hand, with a manful purpose in your heart, and much real labor lying round you done, in comparison? You honestly quit your tools; quit a most muddy confused coil of sore work, short rations, of sorrows, dispiriments and contradictions, having now honestly done with it all;—and await, not entirely in a distracted manner, what the Supreme Powers, and the Silences and the Eternities may have to say to you.

A second thing I know: This lesson will have to be learned,—under penalties! England will either learn it, or England also will cease to exist among Nations. England will either learn to reverence its Heroes, and discriminate them from its Sham-Heroes and Valets and gaslighted Histrios; and to prize them as the audible God's-voice, amid all inane jargons and temporary market-cries, and say to them with heart-loyalty, "Be ye King and Priest, and Gospel and Guidance for us": or else England will continue to worship new and ever-new forms of Quackhood,—and so, with what resiliences and reboundings matters little, go down to the Father of Quacks! Can I dread such things of England? Wretched, thick-eyed, gross-hearted mortals, why will ye worship lies, and "Stuffed Clothes-suits created by the ninth-parts of men"! It is not your purses that suffer; your farm-rents, your commerces, your mill-revenues, loud as ye lament over these; no, it is not these alone, but a far deeper than these: it is your souls that lie dead, crushed down under despicable Nightmares, Atheisms, Brain-fumes; and are not souls at all, but mere succedanea for *salt* to keep your bodies and their appetites from putrefying!

Your cotton-spinning and thrice-miraculous mechanism, what is this too, by itself, but a larger kind of Animalism? Spiders can spin, Beavers can build and show contrivance; the Ant lays-up accumulation of capital, and has, for aught I know, a Bank of Antland. If there is no soul in man higher than all that, did it reach to sailing on the cloud-rack, and spinning sea-sand; then I say, man is but an animal, a more cunning kind of brute: he has no soul, but only a succedaneum for salt. Whereupon, seeing himself to be truly of the beasts that perish, he ought to admit it, I think;—and also straightway universally to kill himself; and so, in a manlike manner at least *end,* and wave these brute-worlds *his* dignified farewell!—

[1843]

SHOOTING NIAGARA: AND AFTER?

I

There probably never was so hugely critical an epoch in the history of England as this we have now entered upon, with universal self-congratulation and flinging up of caps; nor one in which—with no Norman Invasion now ahead, to lay hold of it, to bridle and regulate it for us (little thinking it was *for us*), and guide it into higher and wider regions,—the question of utter death or of nobler new life for the poor Country was so uncertain. Three things seem to be agreed upon by gods and men, at least by English men and gods; certain to happen, and are now in visible course of fulfilment.

1. *Democracy* to complete itself; to go the full length of its course, towards the Bottomless or into it, no power now extant to prevent it or even considerably retard it,—till we have seen where it will lead us to, and whether there will *then* be any return possible, or none. Complete "liberty" to all persons; Count of Heads to be the Divine Court of Appeal on every question and interest of mankind; Count of Heads to choose a Parliament according to its own heart at last, and sit with Penny Newspapers zealously watching the same;

said Parliament, so chosen and so watched, to do what trifle of legislating and administering may still be needed in such an England, with its hundred and fifty millions "free" more and more to follow each his own nose, by way of guide-post in this intricate world.

2. That, in a limited time, say fifty years hence, the Church, all Churches and so-called religions, the Christian Religion itself, shall have deliquesced,—into "Liberty of Conscience," Progress of Opinion, Progress of Intellect, Philanthropic Movement, and other aqueous residues, of a vapid, badly-scented character;—and shall, like water spilt upon the ground, trouble nobody considerably thenceforth, but evaporate at its leisure.

3. That, in lieu thereof, there shall be Free Trade, in all senses, and to all lengths: unlimited Free Trade—which some take to mean, "Free racing, ere long with unlimited speed, in the career of *Cheap and Nasty*";—this beautiful career, not in shop-goods only, but in all things temporal, spiritual and eternal, to be flung generously open, wide as the portals of the Universe; so that everybody shall start free, and everywhere, "under enlightened popular suffrage," the race shall be to the

swift, and the high office shall fall to him who is ablest if not to do it, at least to get elected for doing it.

These are three altogether new and very considerable achievements, lying visibly ahead of us, not far off—and so extremely considerable, that every thinking English creature is tempted to go into manifold reflections and inquiries upon them. My own have not been wanting, any time these 10 thirty years past, but they have not been of a joyful or triumphant nature; not prone to utter themselves; indeed expecting, till lately, that they might with propriety lie unuttered altogether. But the series of events comes swifter and swifter, at a strange rate; and hastens unexpectedly so that the wisest Prophecy finds it was quite wrong as to date; and, patiently, or even indolently waiting, is astonished to see it- 20 self fulfilled, not in centuries as antici- pated, but in decades and years. It was a clear prophecy, for instance, that Germany would either become honorably Prussian or go to gradual annihilation: but who of us expected that we ourselves, instead of our children's children, should live to be- hold it; that a magnanimous and fortunate Herr von Bismarck, whose dispraise was in all the Newspapers, would, to his own 30 amazement, find the thing now doable; and would do it, do the essential of it, in a few of the current weeks? That England would have to take the Niagara leap of completed Democracy one day, was also a plain prophecy, though uncertain as to time.

II

The prophecy, truly, was plain enough this long while. It is indeed strange how 40 prepossessions and delusions seize upon whole communities of men; no basis in the notion they have formed, yet everybody adopting it, everybody finding the whole world agreed with him in it, and accepting it as an axiom of Euclid; and, in the uni- versal repetition and reverberation, taking all contradiction of it as an insult, and a sign of malicious insanity, hardly to be borne with patience. "For who can change 50 the opinion of these people?" as our Divus Imperator says. No wisest of mortals. This people cannot be convinced out of its "axiom of Euclid" by any reasoning what-

soever; on the contrary, all the world as- senting, and continually repeating and reverberating, there soon comes that singu- lar phenomenon, which the Germans call Schwärmerey ("enthusiasm" is our poor Greek equivalent), which means simply "Swarmery," or the "Gathering of Men in Swarms," and what prodigies they are in the habit of doing and believing, when thrown into that miraculous condition. Some big Queen Bee is in the centre of the swarm; but any commonplace stupidest bee, Cleon the Tanner, Beales, John of Bromwicham, any bee whatever, if he can happen, by noise or otherwise, to be chosen for the function, will straightway get fatted and inflated into bulk, which of itself means complete capacity; no difficulty about your Queen Bee: and the swarm 20 once formed, finds itself impelled to action, as with one heart and one mind. Singular, in the case of human swarms, with what perfection of unanimity and quasi-religious conviction the stupidest absurdities can be received as axioms of Euclid, nay as articles of faith, which you are not only to be- lieve, unless malignantly insane, but are (if you have any honor or morality) to push into practice, and without delay see 30 done, if your soul would live! Divine com- mandment to vote ("Manhood Suffrage"— Horsehood, Doghood ditto not yet treated of); universal "glorious Liberty" (to Sons of the Devil in overwhelming majority, as would appear); Count of Heads the God- appointed way in this Universe, all other ways Devil-appointed; in one brief word, which includes whatever of palpable in- credibility and delirious absurdity, univer- 40 sally believed, can be uttered or imagined on these points, "the equality of men," any man equal to any other; Quashee Nigger to Socrates or Shakspeare; Judas Iscariot to Jesus Christ—and Bedlam and Gehenna equal to the New Jerusalem, shall we say? If these things are taken up, not only as axioms of Euclid, but as articles of religion burning to be put in practice for the sal- vation of the world,—I think you will ad- 50 mit that Swarmery plays a wonderful part in the heads of poor Mankind; and that very considerable results are likely to fol- low from it in our day!

But you will in vain attempt, by argument of human intellect, to contradict or turn aside any of these divine axioms, indisputable as those of Euclid, and of sacred or quasi-celestial quality to boot: if you have neglected the one method (which was a silent one) of dealing with them at an early stage, they are thenceforth invincible; and will plunge more and more madly forward towards practical fulfilment. Once fulfilled, it will then be seen how credible and wise they are. Not even the Queen Bee but will then know what to think of them. Then, and never till then. . . .

In our own country, *Swarmery* has played a great part for many years past; and especially is now playing, in these very days and months. Our accepted axioms about "Liberty," "Constitutional Government," "Reform," and the like objects, are of truly wonderful texture: venerable by antiquity, many of them, and written in all manner of Canonical Books; or else, the newer part of them, celestially clear as perfect unanimity of all tongues, and *Vox populi vox Dei*,[1] can make them: axioms confessed, or even inspirations and gospel verities, to the general mind of man. To the mind of here and there a man it begins to be suspected that perhaps they are only conditionally true; that taken unconditionally, or under changed conditions, they are not true, but false and even disastrously and fatally so. Ask yourself about "Liberty," for example; what you do really mean by it, what in any just and rational soul is that Divine quality of liberty? That a good man be "free," as we call it, be permitted to unfold himself in works of goodness and nobleness, is surely a blessing to him, immense and indispensable;—to him and to those about him. But that a bad man be "free,"—permitted to unfold himself in *his* particular way, is contrariwise the fatalest curse you could inflict on him; curse and nothing else, to him and all his neighbors. Him the very Heavens call upon you to persuade, to urge, induce, compel, into something of well-doing; if you absolutely cannot, if he will continue in ill-doing,— then for him (I can assure you, though you will be shocked to hear it), the one "blessing" left is the speediest gallows you can

lead him to. Speediest, that at least his ill-doing may cease *quam primum*.[2] Oh, my friends, whither are you buzzing and swarming, in this extremely absurd manner? Expecting a Millennium from "extension of the suffrage," laterally, vertically, or in whatever way?

All the Millenniums I ever heard of heretofore were to be preceded by a "chaining of the Devil for a thousand years,"— laying *him* up, tied neck and heels, and put beyond stirring, as the preliminary. You too have been taking preliminary steps, with more and more ardor, for a thirty years back; but they seem to be all in the opposite direction: a cutting asunder of straps and ties, wherever you might find them; pretty indiscriminate of choice in the matter: a general repeal of old regulations, fetters and restrictions (restrictions on the Devil originally, I believe, for most part, but now fallen slack and ineffectual), which had become unpleasant to many of you,—with loud shouting from the multitude, as strap after strap was cut, "Glory, glory, another strap is gone!"—this, I think, has mainly been the sublime legislative industry of Parliament since it became "Reform Parliament"; victoriously successful, and thought sublime and beneficent by some. So that now hardly any limb of the Devil has a thrum or tatter of rope or leather left upon it:—there needs almost superhuman heroism in you to "whip" a garroter; no Fenian taken with the reddest hand is to be meddled with, under penalties; hardly a murderer, never so detestable and hideous, but you find him "insane," and board him at the public expense,—a very peculiar *British* Prytaneum of these days! And in fact, THE DEVIL (he, verily, if you will consider the sense of words) is likewise become an Emancipated Gentleman; lithe of limb, as in Adam and Eve's time, and scarcely a toe or finger of him *tied* any more. And you, my astonishing friends, *you* are certainly getting into a millennium, such as never was before,— hardly even in the dreams of Bedlam. Better luck to you by the way, my poor friends, —a little less of buzzing, humming, *swarming* (*i.e.*, tumbling in infinite noise and darkness), that you might try to look a lit-

[1] *Vox populi vox Dei*: The voice of the people (is) the voice of God.

[2] *quam primum*: as soon as possible.

tle, each for himself, what kind of "way" it is!

But indeed your "Reform" movement, from of old, has been wonderful to me; everybody meaning by it, not "Reformation," practical amendment of his own foul courses, or even of his neighbor's, which is always much welcomer; no thought of that whatever, though that, you would say, is the one thing to be thought of and aimed at;—but meaning simply "Extension of the Suffrage." Bring in more voting; that will clear away the universal rottenness, and quagmire of mendacities, in which poor England is drowning; let England only vote sufficiently, and all is clean and sweet again. A very singular *swarmery* this of the Reform movement, I must say.

III

Inexpressibly delirious seems to me, at present in my solitude, the puddle of Parliament and Public upon what it calls the "Reform Measure"; that is to say, The calling in of new supplies of blockheadism, gullibility, bribability, amenability to beer and balderdash, by way of amending the woes we have had from our previous supplies of that bad article. The intellect of a man who believes in the possibility of "improvement" by such a method is to me a finished-off and shut-up intellect, with which I would not argue: mere waste of wind between us to exchange words on that class of topics. It is not Thought, this which my reforming brother utters to me with such emphasis and eloquence; it is mere "reflex and reverberation," repetition of what he has always heard others imagining to think, and repeating as orthodox, indispensable, and the gospel of our salvation in this world. Does not all Nature groan everywhere, and lie in bondage, till you give it a Parliament? Is one a man at all unless one have a suffrage to Parliament? These are axioms admitted by all English creatures for the last two hundred years. If you have the misfortune not to believe in them at all, but to believe the contrary for a long time past, the inferences and inspirations drawn from them, and the *"swarmeries"* and enthusiasms of mankind thereon, will seem to you not a little marvelous!—

Meanwhile the *good* that lies in this delirious "new Reform Measure,"—as there lies something of good in almost everything,—is perhaps not inconsiderable. It accelerates notably what I have long looked upon as inevitable;—pushes us at once into the Niagara Rapids: irresistibly propelled, with ever-increasing velocity, we shall now arrive; who knows how *soon!* For a generation past, it has been growing more and more evident that there was only this issue; but now the issue itself has become imminent, the distance of it to be guessed by years. Traitorous Politicians, grasping at votes, even votes from the rabble, have brought it on;—one cannot but consider them traitorous; and for one's own poor share, would rather have been shot than been concerned in it. And yet, after all my silent indignation and disgust. I cannot pretend to be clearly sorry that such a consummation is expedited. I say to myself, "Well, perhaps the sooner such a mass of hypocrisies, universal mismanagements and brutal platitudes and infidelities *ends,*—if not in some improvement, then in death and finis,—may it not be the better? The sum of our sins, increasing steadily day by day, will at least be less, the sooner the settlement is!" ...

Perhaps the consummation may be now nearer than is thought. It seems to me sometimes as if everybody had privately now given up serious notion of resisting it. ... The perceptible, but as yet unacknowledged truth is, people are getting dimly sensible that our Social Affairs and Arrangements, all but the money-safe, are pretty universally a Falsehood, an elaborate old-established Hypocrisy, which is even serving its own poor private purpose ill, and is openly mismanaging every public purpose or interest, to a shameful and indefensible extent. For such a Hypocrisy, in any detail of it (except the money-safe), nobody, official or other, is willing to risk his skin; but cautiously looks round whether there is no postern to retire by, and retires accordingly,—leaving any mob-leader, Beales, John of Leyden, Walter the Penniless, or other impotent enough loud individual, with his tail of loud Roughs, to work their own sweet will. Safer to humor the mob than repress them, with the rope about *your* neck. Everybody sees this official slinking off, has a secret fellow-feeling with it; nobody admires it; but the spoken disapproval is languid, and generally from the teeth outwards. "Has not everybody been very good to you?" say the highest Editors, in these current days, admonishing and soothing down Beales and his Roughs.

So that, if loud mobs, supported by one or two Eloquences in the House, choose to proclaim, some day, with vociferation, as some day they will, "Enough of kingship, and its grimacings and futilities! Is it not a Hypocrisy and Humbug, as you yourselves well know? We demand to become *Commonwealth of England;* that will perhaps be better, worse it cannot be!"—in such case, how much of available resistance does the reader think would ensue? From official persons, with the rope round their neck, should you expect a great amount? I do not; or that resistance to the death would anywhere, "within these walls" or without, be the prevailing phenomenon.

For we are a people drowned in Hypocrisy; saturated with it to the bone:—alas, it is even so, in spite of far other intentions at one time, and of a languid, dumb, but ineradicable inward protest against it still: —and we are beginning to be universally conscious of that horrible condition, and by no means disposed to die in behalf of continuing it! . . . Who could regret the finis of such a thing; finis on any terms whatever! Possibly it will not be death eternal, possibly only death temporal, death temporary.

My neighbors, by the million against one, all expect that it will almost certainly be New-birth, a Saturnian time, with gold nuggets themselves more plentiful than ever. As for us, we will say, Rejoice in the *awakening* of poor England even on these terms. To lie torpid, sluttishly gurgling and mumbling, spiritually in soak "in the Devil's Pickle" for above two hundred years: that was the infinitely dismal condition, all others are but finitely so.

IV

Practically the worthiest inquiry, in regard to all this, would be: "What are probably the steps towards consummation all this will now take; what are, in main fea-

tures, the issues it will arrive at, on unexpectedly (with immense surprise to the most) *shooting* Niagara, to the bottom? And above all, what are the possibilities, resources, impediments, conceivable methods and attemptings of its ever getting out again?" Darker subject of Prophecy can be laid before no man; and to be candid with myself, up to this date I have never seriously meditated it, far less grappled with it as a Problem in any sort practical. Let me avoid branch *first* of this inquiry altogether. If "immortal smash," and shooting of the Falls, be the one issue ahead, our and the reformed Parliament's procedures and adventures in arriving there are not worth conjecturing, in comparison!—And yet the inquiry means withal, both branches of it mean, "What are the duties of good citizens in it, now and onwards?" Meditated it must be, and light sought on it, however hard or impossible to find! It is not always the part of the infinitesimally small minority of wise men and good citizens to sit silent; idle they should never sit.

Supposing the *Commonwealth* established, and Democracy rampant, as in America, or in France by fits for 70 odd years past,—it is a favorable fact that our Aristocracy in their essential height of position, and capability (or possibility) of doing good, are not at once likely to be interfered with; that they will be continued farther on their trial, and only the question somewhat more stringently put to them, "What *are* you good for, then? Show us, show us; or else disappear!" I regard this as potentially a great benefit;— springing from what seems a mad enough phenomenon, the fervid zeal in *behalf* of this "new Reform Bill" and all kindred objects, which is manifested by the better kind of our young Lords and Honorables; a thing very curious to me. Somewhat resembling that bet of the impetuous Irish carpenter, astride of his plank firmly stuck out of window in the sixth story. "Two to one, I *can* saw this plank in so many minutes"; and sawing accordingly, fiercely impetuous,—with success! But from the maddest thing, as we said, there usually may come some particle of good withal (if any poor particle of *good* did lie in it, waiting to be disengaged!)—and this is a signal instance of that kind. Our Aristocracy are not hated or disliked by any Class of the People, but on the contrary are looked up to,—with a certain vulgarly human admiration, and spontaneous recognition of their good qualities and good fortune, which is by no means wholly envious or wholly servile,—by all classes, lower and lowest class included. And indeed, in spite of 10 lamentable exceptions too visible all round, my vote would still be, That from *Plebs* to *Princeps*,[3] there was still no Class among us intrinsically so valuable and recommendable.

What the possibilities of our Aristocracy might still be? this is a question I have often asked myself. Surely their possibilities might still be considerable; though I confess they lie in a most abstruse, and as 20 yet quite uninvestigated condition. But a body of brave men, and of beautiful polite women, furnished *gratis* as they are,—some of them (as my Lord Derby, I am told, in a few years will be) with not far from two-thirds of a million sterling annually,—ought to be good for something, in a society mostly fallen vulgar and chaotic like ours! More than once I have been affected with a deep sorrow and respect for noble 30 souls among them, and their high stoicism, and silent resignation to a kind of life which they individually could not alter, and saw to be so empty and paltry; life of giving and receiving Hospitalities in a gracefully splendid manner. "This, then (such mute soliloquy I have read on some noble brow), this, and something of Village-schools, of Consulting with the Parson, care of Peasant Cottages and Eco- 40 nomies, is to be all our task in the world? Well, well; let us at least *do* this, in our most perfect way!"

In past years, I have sometimes thought what a thing it would be, could the Queen "in Council" (in Parliament or wherever it were) pick out some gallant-minded, stout, well-gifted Cadet,—younger Son of a Duke, of an Earl, of a Queen herself; younger Son doomed now to go mainly to the 50 Devil, for absolute want of a career;—and say to him, "Young fellow, if there do lie

in you potentialities of governing, of gradually guiding, leading and coercing to a noble goal, how sad is it they should be all lost! They are the grandest gifts a mortal can have; and they are, of all, the most necessary to other mortals in this world. See, I have scores on scores of 'Colonies,' all ungoverned, and nine-tenths of them full of jungles, boa-constrictors, rattlesnakes, Parliamentary Eloquences, and Emancipated Niggers ripening towards nothing but destruction: one of these *you* shall have, you as Vice-King; on rational conditions, and *ad vitam aut culpam*[4] it shall be yours (and perhaps your posterity's if worthy): go you and buckle with it, in the name of Heaven; and let us see what you will build it to!" To something how much better than the Parliamentary Eloquences are doing,—thinks the reader? Good Heavens, these West-India Islands, some of them, appear to be the richest and most favored spots on the Planet Earth. Jamaica is an angry subject, and I am shy to speak of it. Poor Dominica itself is described to me in a way to kindle a heroic young heart. . . .

v

I almost think, when once we have made the Niagara leap, the better kind of our Nobility, perhaps after experimenting, will more and more withdraw themselves from the Parliamentary, Oratorical or Political element; leaving that to such Cleon the Tanner and Company as it rightfully belongs to; and be far more chary of their speech than now. Speech issuing in no deed is hateful and contemptible:—how can a man have any nobleness who knows not that? In God's name, let us find out what of noble and profitable we can *do*; if it be nothing, let us at least keep silence, and bear gracefully our strange lot!—

The English Nobleman has still left in him, after such sorrowful erosions, something considerable of chivalry and magnanimity: polite he is, in the finest form; politeness, modest, simple, veritable, ineradicable, dwells in him to the bone; I incline to call him the politest kind of nobleman or man, (especially his wife the

---

[3] *Plebs* to *Princeps:* Common people to prince or leader.

[4] *ad vitam aut culpam:* For life or until misbehaviour.

politest and gracefulest kind of woman) you will find in any country. An immense endowment this, if you consider it well! A very great and indispensable help to whatever other faculties of *kingship* a man may have. Indeed it springs from them all (its sources, every kingly faculty lying in you); and is as the beautiful natural skin, and visible sanction, index and outcome of them all. No king can rule without it; none but potential kings can really have it. In the crude, what we call unbred or *Orson* form, all "men of genius" have it; but see what it avails some of them,—your Samuel Johnson, for instance,—in that crude form, who was so rich in it, too, in the crude way!

Withal it is perhaps a fortunate circumstance that the population has no wild notions, no political enthusiasms of a "new Era" or the like. This, though in itself a dreary and ignoble item, in respect of the revolutionary Many, may nevertheless be for good, if the Few *shall* be really high and brave, as things roll on.

Certain it is, there is nothing but vulgarity in our People's expectations, resolutions or desires, in this Epoch. It is all a peaceable mouldering or tumbling down from mere rottenness and decay; whether slowly mouldering or rapidly tumbling, there will be nothing found of real or true in the rubbish-heap, but a most true desire of making money easily, and of eating it pleasantly. A poor ideal for "reformers," sure enough. But it is the fruit of long antecedents, too; and from of old, our habits in regard to "reformation," or repairing what went wrong (as something is always doing), have been strangely didactic! And to such length have we at last brought it, by our wilful, conscious, and now long-continued method of using *varnish,* instead of actual repair by honest *carpentry,* of what we all knew and saw to have gone undeniably wrong in our procedures and affairs! Method deliberately, steadily, and even solemnly continued, with much admiration of it from ourselves and others, as the best and only good one, for above two hundred years.

Ever since that *annus mirabilis*[5] of 1660, when Oliver Cromwell's dead clay was hung on the gibbet, and a much easier "reign of Christ" under the divine gentleman called Charles II was thought the fit thing, this has been our steady method: varnish, varnish; if a thing have grown so rotten that it yawns palpable, and is so inexpressibly ugly that the eyes of the very populace discern it and detest it,—bring out a new pot of varnish, with the requisite supply of putty; and lay it on handsomely. Don't spare varnish; how well it will all look in a few days, if laid on well! Varnish alone is cheap and is safe; avoid carpentering, chiselling, sawing and hammering on the old quiet House;—dry-rot is in it, who knows how deep; don't disturb the old beams and junctures: varnish, varnish, if you will be blessed by gods and men! This is called the Constitutional System, Conservative System, and other fine names; and this at last has its fruits,—such as we see. Mendacity hanging in the very air we breathe; all men become, unconsciously or half or wholly consciously, *liars* to their own souls and to other men's; grimacing, finessing, periphrasing, in continual hypocrisy of *word,* by way of varnish to continual past, present, future misperformance of *thing:*—clearly sincere about nothing whatever, except in silence, about the appetites of their own huge belly, and the readiest method of assuaging these. From a Population of that sunk kind, ardent only in pursuits that are low and in industries that are sensuous and *beaverish,* there is little peril of *human* enthusiasms, or revolutionary transports, such as occurred in 1789, for instance. A low-minded *pecus*[6] all that; essentially torpid and *ignavum,*[6] on all that is high or nobly human in revolutions.

It is true there is in such a population of itself no *help* at all towards reconstruction of the wreck of your Niagara plunge; of themselves they, with whatever cry of "liberty" in their mouths, are inexorably marked by Destiny as *slaves;* and not even the immortal gods could make them free,—except by making them anew and on a different pattern. No help in them at all, to your model Aristocrat, or to any noble man or thing. But then likewise there is no hindrance, or a minimum of it! Nothing

[5] *annus mirabilis:* wonderful year.

[6] *pecus:* cattle; *ignavum:* slothful.

there in *bar* of the noble Few, who we always trust will be born to us, generation after generation; and on whom and whose living of a noble and valiantly cosmic life amid the worst impediments and hugest anarchies, the whole of our hope depends. Yes, on them only! If amid the thickest welter of surrounding gluttony and baseness, and what must be reckoned bottomless anarchy from shore to shore, there be found no man, no small but invincible minority of men, capable of keeping themselves free from all that, and of living a heroically human life, while the millions round them are noisily living a mere beaverish or doglike one, then truly all hope is gone. But we always struggle to believe Not. Aristocracy by title, by fortune and position, who can doubt but there are still precious possibilities among the chosen of that class? And if that fail us, there is still, we hope, the unclassed Aristocracy by nature, not inconsiderable in numbers, and supreme in faculty, in wisdom, human talent, nobleness and courage, "who derive their patent of nobility direct from Almighty God." If indeed these also fail us, and are trodden out under the unanimous torrent of brutish hoofs and hobnails, and cannot vindicate themselves into clearness here and there, but at length cease even to try it,—then indeed it is all ended: national death, scandalous "Copper-Captaincy" as of France, stern Russian Abolition and Erasure as of Poland: in one form or another, well deserved annihilation, and dismissal from God's universe, that and nothing else lies ahead for our once heroic England too.

How many of our Titular Aristocracy will prove real gold when thrown into the crucible? That is always a highly interesting question to me; and my answer, or guess, has still something considerable of hope lurking in it. But the question as to our Aristocracy by Patent from God the Maker, is infinitely interesting. How many of these, amid the ever-increasing bewilderments and welter of impediments, will be able to develop themselves into something of Heroic Well-doing by act and by word? How many of them will be drawn, pushed and seduced, their very docility and lovingness assisting, into the universal vulgar whirlpool of Parliamenteering, Newspapering, Novel-writing, Comte-Philosophy-ing, immortal Verse-writing, etc., etc., (if of *vocal* turn, as they mostly will be, for some time yet)? How many, by their too desperate resistance to the unanimous vulgar of a Public round them, will become spasmodic instead of strong; and will be overset, and trodden out, under the hoofs and hobnails above said? Will there, in short, prove to be a recognizable small nucleus of Invincible Ἄριστοι [7] fighting for the Good Cause, in their various wisest ways, and never ceasing or slackening till they die? This is the question of questions, on which all turns; in the answer to this, could we give it clearly, as no man can, lies the oracle-response, "Life for you," "Death for you!" Looking into this, there are fearful dubitations many. But considering what of Piety, the devoutest and the bravest yet known, there once was in England, and how extensively, in stupid, maundering and degraded forms, it still lingers, one is inclined timidly to hope the best!

The *best:* for if this small Aristocratic nucleus can hold out and work, it is in the sure case to increase and increase; to become (as Oliver once termed it) "a company of poor men, who will spend all their blood rather." An openly belligerent company, capable at last of taking the biggest slave Nation by the beard, and saying to it, "Enough, ye slaves, and servants of the mud gods; all this must cease! Our heart abhors all this; our soul is sick under it; God's curse is on us while this lasts. Behold, we will all die rather than that this last. Rather all die, we say,— what is your view of the corresponding alternative on your own part?" I see well it must at length come to battle; actual fighting, bloody wrestling, and a great deal of it: but were it unit against thousand, or against thousand-thousand, on the above terms, I know the issue, and have no fear about it. That also is an issue which has been often tried in Human History; and, "while God lives"—(I hope the phrase is not yet obsolete, for the fact is eternal, though so many have forgotten it!)—said issue can or will fall only one way.

[7] Ἄριστοι : plural of Ἄριστος, the best, i.e. aristocrats.

VI

What we can expect this Aristocracy of Nature to do for us? They are of two kinds: the Speculative, speaking or vocal; and the Practical or industrial, whose function is silent. These are of brother quality; but they go very different roads: "men of *genius*" they all emphatically are, the "inspired Gift of God" lodged in each of them. They do infinitely concern the world and us; especially that first or speaking class,—provided God *have* "touched their lips with his hallowed fire"! Supreme is the importance of these. They are our inspired speakers and seers, the light of the world; who are to deliver the world from its swarmeries, its superstitions (*political* or other);—priceless and indispensable to us that first Class!

Nevertheless it is not of these I mean to speak at present; the topic is far too wide, nor is the call to it so immediately pressing. These Sons of Wisdom, gifted to speak as with hallowed lips a real God's-message to us,—I don't much expect they will be numerous, for a long while yet, nor even perhaps appear at all in this time of swarmeries, or be disposed to speak their message to such audience as there is. And if they did, I know well it is not from my advice, or any mortal's, that they could learn their feasible way of doing it. For a great while yet, most of them will fly off into "Literature," into what they call Art, Poetry and the like; and will mainly waste themselves in that inane region,—fallen so inane in our mad era. Alas, though born Sons of Wisdom, they are not exempt from all our "Swarmeries," but only from the grosser kinds of them. This of "Art," "Poetry" and so forth, is a refined Swarmery; the most refined now going; and comes to us, in venerable form, from a distance of above a thousand years. And is still undoubtingly sanctioned, canonized and marked sacred, by the unanimous vote of cultivated persons to this hour. How stir such questions in the present limits? Or in fact, what chance is there that a guess of mine, in regard to what these born Sons of Wisdom in a yet unborn section of Time will say, or to how they will say it, should avail in the least my own contemporaries,

much less them or theirs? Merely on a point or two I will hint what my poor wish is; and know well enough that it is the drawing a bow, not at a venture indeed, but into the almost utterly dark.

First, then, with regard to Art, Poetry and the like, which at present is esteemed the supreme of aims for vocal genius, I hope my literary *Aristos* will pause, and seriously make question before embarking on that; and perhaps will end, in spite of the Swarmeries abroad, by devoting his divine faculty to something far higher, far more vital to us. Poetry? It is not pleasant singing that we want, but wise and earnest speaking:—"Art," "High Art," etc., are very fine and ornamental, but only to persons sitting at their ease: to persons still wrestling with deadly chaos, and still fighting for dubious existence, they are a mockery rather. Our *Aristos,* well meditating, will perhaps discover that the genuine "Art" in all times is a higher synonym for God Almighty's Facts,—which come to us direct from Heaven, but in so abstruse a condition, and cannot be read at all till the better intellect interpret them. That is the real function of our *Aristos* and of his divine gift. Let him think well of this! He will find that all real "Art" is definable as Fact, or say as the disimprisoned "Soul of Fact"; that any other kind of Art, Poetry, or High Art is quite idle in comparison.

The *Bible* itself has, in all changes of theory about it, this as its highest distinction, that it is the *truest* of all Books,—Book springing, every word of it, from the intensest convictions, from the very heart's core, of those who penned it. And has not that been a "successful" Book? Did all the Paternoster-Rows of the world ever hear of one so "successful"? Homer's *Iliad,* too, that great Bundle of old Greek Ballads, is nothing of a *Fiction;* it is the *truest* a Patriotic Ballad-singer, rapt into paroxysm and enthusiasm for the honor of his native Country and native Parish, could manage to sing. To "sing," you will observe; always sings—pipe often rusty, at a loss for metre; but with his heart rightly on fire, when the audience goes with him, and "hangs on him with greed" (as he says they often do). Homer's *Iliad* I almost reckon next to the *Bible;* so stubbornly sincere is it too, though in a far different element, and a far shallower.

"Fiction," my friend, you will be surprised to discover at last what alarming cousinship *it* has to *Lying:* don't go into "Fiction," you *Aristos,* nor concern yourself with "Fine Literature," or Coarse ditto, or the unspeakable glories and rewards of pleasing your generation; which you are 10 not sent hither to *please,* first of all! In general, leave "Literature," the thing called "Literature" at present, to run through its rapid fermentations (how more and more rapid they are in these years!), and to fluff itself off into Nothing, in its own way,—like a poor bottle of soda-water with the cork sprung,—it won't be long. In our time it has become all the rage; highest noblemen and dignitaries courting 20 a new still higher glory there; innumerable men, women and children rushing towards it, yearly ever more. It sat painfully in Grub Street, in hungry garrets, so long; some few heroic martyrs always serving in it, among such a miscellany of semi-fatuous worthless ditto, courting the bubble reputation in *worse* than the cannon's mouth; in general, a very flimsy, foolish set. But that little company of martyrs has at last 30 lifted Literature furiously or foamingly high in the world. Goes like the Iceland geysers in our time,—like uncorked soda-water;—and will, as I said, soon have done. Only wait: in fifty years, I should guess, all really serious souls will have quitted that mad province, left it to the roaring populaces; and for any *Noble*-man or useful person it will be a credit rather to declare, "I never tried Literature; believe 40 me, I have not written anything;"—and we of "Literature" by trade, we shall sink again, I perceive, to the rank of streetfiddling; no higher rank, though with endless increase of sixpences flung into the hat. Of "Literature" keep well to windward, my serious friend!—...

VII

Of the second, or silent Industrial Hero, 50 I may now say something, as more within my limits and the reader's....

The Practical "man of genius" will probably *not* be altogether absent from the Reformed Parliament:—his *Make-believe,* the vulgar millionaire (truly a "bloated" specimen this!) is sure to be frequent there; and along with the multitude of *brass* guineas, it will be very salutary to have a *gold* one or two!—In or out of Parliament, our Practical hero will find no end of work ready for him. It is he that has to re-civilize, out of its now utter savagery, the world of Industry;—think what a set of items: To change *nomadic* contract into *permanent;* to annihilate the soot and dirt and squalid horror now defacing this England, once so clean and comely while it was poor; matters sanitary (and that not to the *body* only) for his people; matters governmental for them; no want of work for this Hero, through a great many generations yet!

And indeed Reformed Parliament itself, with or without his presence, will, you would suppose, have to start at once upon the Industrial question and go quite deep into it. That of Trades Union, with assassin pistol in its hand, will at once urge itself on Reformed Parliament: and Reformed Parliament will give us Blue Books upon it, if nothing farther. Nay, almost still more urgent, and what I could reckon,—as touching on our Ark of the Covenant, on sacred "Free Trade" itself,—to be the preliminary of all, there is the immense and universal question of *Cheap and Nasty.* Let me explain it a little.

"Cheap and nasty"; there is a pregnancy in that poor vulgar proverb, which I wish we better saw and valued! It is the rude indignant protest of human nature against a mischief which, in all times and places, haunts it or lies near it, and which never in any time or place was so like utterly overwhelming it as here and now. Understand, if you will consider it, that no good man did, or ever should, encourage "cheapness" at the ruinous expense of *unfitness,* which is always infidelity, and is dishonorable to a man. If I want an article, let it be genuine, at whatever price; if the price is too high for me, I will go without it, unequipped with it for the present,—I shall not have equipped myself with a hypocrisy, at any rate! This, if you will reflect, is primarily the rule of all purchasing and all producing men. They are not permitted to encourage, patronize, or in any form countenance the working, wearing or acting of Hypocrisies in this world. On the contrary, they are to hate all such with a perfect hatred; to do their best in extinguishing them as the poison of mankind. This is the temper for purchasers of work: how much more for that of doers and producers of it! Work, every one of you, like the Demiurgus or Eternal World-builder; work, none of you, like the Diabolus or Denier and Destroyer,—under penalties!

And now, if this is the fact, that you are not to purchase, to make or to vend any ware or product of the "cheap and nasty" genus, and cannot in any case do it without sin, and even treason against the Maker of you,—consider what a *quantity* of sin, of treason, petty and high, must be accumulating in poor England every day! It is certain as the National debt; and what are all National money Debts, in comparison! Do you know the shop, saleshop, workshop, industrial establishment temporal or spiritual, in broad England, where genuine work is to be had? I confess I hardly do; the more is my sorrow! For a whole Pandora's Box of evils lies in that one fact, my friend; that one is enough for us, and may be taken as the sad summary of all. Universal *shoddy* and Devil's-dust cunningly varnished over; that is what you will find presented you in all places, as ware invitingly cheap, if your experience is like mine. Yes; if Free Trade is the new religion, and if Free Trade do mean Free racing with unlimited velocity in the career of *Cheap and Nasty*,—our Practical hero will be not a little anxious to deal with that question. Infinitely anxious to see how "Free Trade," with such a devil in the belly of it, is to be got *tied* again a little, and forbidden to make a very brute of itself at this rate!

Take one small example only. London bricks are reduced to dry clay again in the course of sixty years, or sooner. *Bricks,* burn them rightly, build them faithfully, with mortar faithfully tempered, they will stand, I believe, barring earthquakes and cannon, for 6,000 years if you like! Etruscan Pottery (*baked clay*, but rightly baked) is some 3,000 years of age, and still fresh as

an infant. Nothing I know of is more lasting than a well-made brick;—we have them here, at the head of this Garden (wall once of a Manor Park), which are in their third or fourth century (Henry Eighth's time, I was told), and still perfect in every particular.

Truly the state of London houses and London house-building, at this time, who shall express how detestable it is, how frightful! "Not a house this of mine," said one indignant gentleman, who had searched the London Environs all around for any bit of Villa: "Not a built house, but a congeries of plastered bandboxes; shambling askew in all joints and corners of it; creaking, quaking under every step;—filling you with disgust and despair!" For there lies in it not the Physical mischief only, but the Moral too, which is far more. I have often sadly thought of this. That a fresh human soul should be born in such a place; born in the midst of a concrete mendacity; taught at every moment not to abhor a lie, but to think a lie all proper, the fixed custom and general law of man, and to twine its young affections round that sort of object! . . .

One hears sometimes of religious controversies running very high; about faith, works, grace, prevenient grace,—into none of which do I enter, or concern myself with your entering. One thing I will remind you of, That the essence and outcome of all religions, creeds and liturgies whatsoever is, To do one's work in a faithful manner. Unhappy caitiff, what to you is the use of orthodoxy, if with every stroke of your hammer you are breaking all the Ten Commandments,—operating upon Devil's-dust, and, with constant invocation of the Devil, endeavoring to reap where you have not sown?—

Truly, I think our Practical *Aristos* will address himself to this sad question, almost as the primary one of all. It is impossible that an Industry, national or personal, carried on under "constant invocation of the Devil," can be a blessed or happy one in any fibre or detail of it! Steadily, in every fibre of it, from heart to skin, that is and remains an Industry accursed; nothing but bewilderment, contention, misery, mutual rage, and continually advancing ruin, *can* dwell there. *Cheap and Nasty* is not found on shop-counters alone; but goes down to the centre,—or indeed springs from it. Overend-Gurney Bankruptcies, Chatham-and-Dover Railway Financierings,—Railway "Promoters" . . . all these are diabolic short-cuts towards wages; clutchings at money without just work done; all these are *Cheap and Nasty* in another form. The glory of a workman, still more of a master-workman, That he does his work well, ought to be his most precious possession; like "the honor of a soldier," dearer to him than life. That is the ideal of the matter:—lying, alas, how far away from us at present! But if you yourself *demoralize* your soldier, and teach him continually to invoke the Evil Genius and to *dis*honor himself,—what do you expect your big Army will grow to? . . .

VIII

Schools, for example, schooling and training of *its* young subjects in the way that they should go, and in the things that they should do: what a boundless outlook that of schools, and of improvement in school methods and school purposes, which in these ages lie hitherto all superannuated and to a frightful degree inapplicable? Our schools go all upon the *vocal* hitherto; no clear aim in them but to teach the young creature how he is to *speak,* to utter himself by tongue and pen;—which, supposing him even to *have something to utter,* as he so very rarely has, is by no means the thing he specially wants in our times. How he is to work, to behave and do; that is the question for him, which he seeks the answer of in schools;—in schools, having now so little chance of it elsewhere. In other times, many or most of his neighbors round him, his superiors over him, if he looked well and could take example, and learn by what he saw, were in use to yield him very much of answer to this vitalest of questions: but now they do not, or do it fatally the reverse way! Talent of speaking grows daily commoner among one's neighbors; amounts already to a weariness and a nuisance, so barren is it of great benefit, and liable to be of great hurt: but the talent of right conduct, of wise and useful behavior seems to grow rarer every day,

and is nowhere taught in the streets and thoroughfares any more. Right schools were never more desirable than now. Nor ever more unattainable, by public clamoring and jargoning, than now. Only the wise Ruler (acknowledged king in his own territories), taking counsel with the wise, and earnestly pushing and endeavoring all his days, might do something in it. It is true, I suppose him to be capable of recognizing and searching out "the *wise,*" who are apt *not* to be found on the high roads at present, or only to be transiently passing there, with closed lips, swift step, and possibly a grimmish aspect of countenance, among the crowd of loquacious *sham*-wise. To be capable of actually recognizing and discerning these; and that is no small postulate (how great a one I know well):—in fact, unless our Noble by rank be a Noble by nature, little or no success is possible to us by him.

But granting this great postulate, what a field in the *Non-vocal* School department, such as was not dreamt of before! *Non-vocal;* presided over by whatever of Pious Wisdom this King could eliminate from all corners of the impious world; and could consecrate with means and appliances for making the new generation, by degrees, less impious. Tragical to think of: Every new generation is born to us direct out of Heaven; white as purest writing-paper, white as snow;—everything we please can be written on it;—and our pleasure and our negligence is, To begin blotching it, scrawling, smutching and smearing it, from the first day it sees the sun; towards such a consummation of ugliness, dirt, and blackness of darkness, as is too often visible. Woe on us; there is no woe like this,—if we were not sunk in stupefaction, and had still eyes to discern or souls to feel it! . . .

IX

It is strange to me, stupid creatures of routine as we mostly are, how in all education of mankind, this of simultaneous Drilling into combined rhythmic action, for almost all good purposes, has been overlooked and left neglected by the elaborate and many-sounding Pedagogues and Professorial Persons we have had, for the long centuries past! It really should be set on foot a little; and developed gradually into the multiform opulent results it holds for us. As might well be done, by an acknowledged king in his own territory, if he were wise. To all children of men it is such an entertainment, when you set them to it. I believe the vulgarest Cockney crowd, flung out million-fold on a Whit-Monday, with nothing but beer and dull folly to depend on for amusement, would at once kindle into something human, if you set them to do almost any regulated act in common. And would dismiss their beer and dull foolery, in the silent charm of rhythmic human companionship, in the practical feeling, probably new, that all of us are made on one pattern, and are, in an unfathomable way, brothers to one another.

Soldier-Drill, for fighting purposes, as I have said, would be the last or finishing touch of all these sorts of Drilling; and certainly the acknowledged king would reckon it not the least important to him, but even perhaps the most so, in these peculiar times. Anarchic Parliaments and Penny Newspapers might perhaps grow jealous of him; in any case, he would have to be cautious, punctilious, severely correct, and obey to the letter whatever laws and regulations they emitted on the subject. But that done, how could the most anarchic Parliament, or Penny Editor, think of forbidding any fellow-citizen such a manifest improvement on all the human creatures round him? Our wise hero Aristocrat, or acknowledged king in his own territory, would by no means think of employing his superlative private Field-regiment in levy of war against the most anarchic Parliament; but, on the contrary, might and would loyally help said Parliament in warring down much anarchy worse than its own, and so gain steadily new favor from it. From it, and from all men and gods! And would have silently the consciousness, too, that with every new Disciplined Man he was widening the arena of *Anti*-Anarchy, of God-appointed *Order* in this world and Nation,—and was looking forward to a day, very distant probably, but certain as Fate.

For I suppose it would in no moment be doubtful to him that, between Anarchy and Anti-ditto, it would have to come to sheer fight at last; and that nothing short of duel to the death could ever void that great quarrel. And he would have his hopes, his assurances, as to how the victory would lie. For everywhere in this Universe, and in every Nation that is not *divorced* from it and in the act of perishing forever, Anti-Anarchy is silently on the increase, at all moments: Anarchy not, but contrariwise; having the whole Universe forever set against it; pushing *it* slowly, at all moments, towards suicide and annihilation. To Anarchy, however million-headed, there is no victory possible. Patience, silence, diligence, ye chosen of the world! Slowly or fast, in the course of time, you will grow to a minority that can actually step forth (sword not yet drawn, but sword ready to be drawn), and say: "Here are we, Sirs; we also are now minded to *vote*,—to all lengths, as you may perceive. A company of poor men (as friend Oliver termed us) who will spend all our blood, if needful!" What are ... 50,000 roughs against such; what are the noisiest anarchic Parliaments, in majority of a million to one, against such? Stubble against fire. Fear not, my friend; the issue is very certain when it comes so far as this!

x

Much the readiest likelihood for our Aristocrat by title would be that of coalescing nobly with his two Brothers, the Aristocrats by nature, spoken of above. Both greatly need him; especially the Vocal or Teaching one, wandering now desolate enough, heard only as a *Vox Clamantis e Deserto* [8];—though I suppose, it will be with the Silent or Industrial one, as with the easier of the two, that our Titular first comes into clear coöperation. This Practical hero, Aristocrat by nature, and standing face to face and hand to hand, all his days, in life-battle with Practical Chaos (with dirt, disorder, nomadism, disobedience, folly and confusion), slowly coercing it into Cosmos, will surely be the natural ally for any titular Aristocrat who is bent on being a real one as the business of his life. No other field of activity is half

---

[8] *Vox Clamantis e Deserto:* "The voice of one crying in the wilderness" (*John,* I, 23).

so promising as the united field which those two might occupy. By nature and position they are visibly a kind of Kings, actual British "Peers" (or Vice-Kings, in absence and abeyance of any visible King); and might take manifold counsel together, hold manifold "Parliament" together—and might mature and adjust innumerable things. Were there but Three Aristocrats of each sort in the whole of Britain, what beneficent unreported *"Parliamenta,"*— actual human consultations and earnest deliberations, responsible to no *"Buncombe,"* disturbed by no Penny Editor . . . ! By degrees, there would some beginnings of success and Cosmos be achieved upon this our unspeakable Chaos; by degrees, something of light, of prophetic twilight, would be shot across its unfathomable dark of horrors,—prophetic of victory, sure, though far away.

[1867]

THOMAS BABINGTON MACAULAY

CHRONOLOGY AND INTRODUCTION

1800 Born, October 25 at Rothley Temple, Leicestershire.
1812–18 Prepared for college in private schools.
1818 Entered Trinity College, Cambridge.
1824 Essays in *Knight's Quarterly Review.*
1825 Essay on *Milton* in *Edinburgh Review.*
1826 Called to the bar.
1830 Entered Parliament.
1831 Made first great speech in favor of Reform Bill.
1834–38 Member of *Supreme Council* in India.
1839 Entered Parliament as member for Edinburgh.

1842 *Lays of Ancient Rome.*
1843 *Collected Essays* in 3 volumes.
1847 Defeated at polls.
1848 *History of England,* Vols. I–II.
1849 Lord Rector of University of Glasgow.
1852 Returned to Parliament for Edinburgh.
1855 *History of England,* Vols. III–IV.
1856 Resigned from Parliament.
1857 Made Baron Macaulay of Rothley.
1859 Died, December 28; buried in Westminster Abbey.
1861 *History of England,* Vol. V, edited by Lady Trevelyan.

Macaulay was the first of the greater Victorians to achieve contemporary fame, which descended upon him suddenly with the essay on *Milton* in 1825, written for the *Edinburgh Review* at the request of its distinguished editor, Francis Jeffrey. He seemed predestined for a phenomenal career, since his mind, which matured precociously, displayed in school and university such extraordinary powers as were sure to win him distinction. As a student he read incessantly in the ancient classics, though he rapidly came to know most of the English and European masterpieces of the sixteenth, seventeenth, and eighteenth centuries. And what he read, he seems never to have forgotten, for his memory was one of the most amazing in the records of mankind. He once remarked, for example, that if all the copies of *Paradise Lost* and *Pilgrim's Progress* were destroyed, he would undertake "to reproduce them both from recollection"; and he thought it probable that he could rewrite Richardson's *Sir Charles Grandison* from memory. He not only read and remembered, he talked, discussed, debated, and wrote, so that when he left Cambridge he was in command of an oral and written style that only needed condensation and ripening to be equal to the utterance of his best days.

Macaulay's temperament was an important part of his intellectual equipment. He was superlatively pugnacious and cocksure. Like Samuel Johnson, he delighted in argument, never doubted his ground, and fought to a finish. Like Johnson also (but without Johnson's humor), he was profoundly serious. He inherited from his father a moral earnestness and a liberal spirit of reform which, coupled with his other gifts, were indispensable assets for the brilliant part he was soon to play. Zachary Macaulay was a prominent member of the "Clapham Sect," mostly a group of evangelical churchmen committed to the correction of social evils, more particularly the slave-trade; and he was for years editor of their paper, the *Christian Observer.* His son, consequently, was bred in an atmosphere of humanitarian thought and discussion, an atmosphere (be it said) which, because of certain pieties and dogmatisms that were a part of it, must be held responsible for some of the inflexibility in that son's mind.

After 1825, Macaulay's reputation soared. As a writer of reviews and as a debater in the House of Commons his voice became one of the most popular and powerful of his day. Thousands of readers devoured his essays, and members of the House crowded the benches when he was on his feet. He was a brilliant spokesman of the rising middle classes, of the men who were rapidly making England the workshop of the world and were demanding political recognition commensurate with their growing importance. A life-long Whig, Macaulay belonged to the school of Adam Smith and preached in season and out of season the gospel of *laissez-faire.* He was an evangelist of the steam engine and of British individualism. He gloried in the splendid material progress of that earlier Victorian period (1837–1860), when England, as he boasted, was "now the richest and most civilized spot in the world!" Militantly and consistently he held that the sole business of government was "to protect our persons and our property"; though he did qualify this position somewhat in his later years, when he expressed the view that government should interfere "where the health of the community is concerned" and favored the Ten Hours Bill for youth and women in factories, and also advocated appropriation of funds for the education of the poor. For the most part, however, Macaulay took no such interest in the condition of the working classes as did Carlyle or (later) Ruskin. These classes, he held, might have their distresses and grievances, but their situation was far better than it had ever been in England before or than it was even now anywhere else in Europe.

He looked at the world practically, not speculatively. "An acre of Middlesex," he wrote in a phrase now famous, "is better than a principality in Utopia." He was Matthew Arnold's arch-Philistine. Bacon, not Plato, was his ideal philosopher; the one ended in mere empty disputation, while the other was the great apostle of "Fruit and Progress." The legitimate end of human thought, Macaulay insisted, was the good of mankind, and by this he meant simply and bluntly an extension "of the Empire of man over matter."

One may admire the power and direct commonsense of such a mind, while at the same time recognizing its limitations. What for Hazlitt was the only thing worth remembering in life, namely, the poetry of it, was for Macaulay almost the only thing that he ever forgot; though it is not quite safe to say that the man who could weep over Homer and Catullus, and who knew his Shakespeare and his Milton as he knew them, had no poetry in his constitution. But the subtleties and intensities, the spiritual richness, sense of beauty and feeling of mystery, in a word, the *inwardness* which we commonly associate with the poetical nature—all this was alien to his make-up; at least we do not find it characteristically in his writings. Dryden was probably his favorite English poet after Shakespeare and Milton. The romanticists and most of his contemporary Victorians, including Carlyle and Ruskin, were not in his ken.

But the British public read Macaulay as it had read Scott and Byron in a former day. His works sold by the many thousands, as can be confirmed statistically in Trevelyan's great *Life*. His matter and his manner alike captured his readers. His knowledge is encyclopedic, his human interest is everywhere paramount, and his attitude of mind is typically British middle class,—practical, assertive, unequivocal, boundlessly confident. His style reflects his mind perfectly. Its major qualities are obviously vigor and clarity, conveying always impressions of sincerity, sureness, and speed. Every reader quickly recognizes, besides, certain individualities of expression that are as much a part of Macaulay as the clothes he wore: adverbs such as "utterly," "wholly," "absolutely," "precisely," "never," "no doubt"; superlatives and parallel constructions; sharp contrasts and comparisons with frequent antithesis and paradox. If there are no subtle shadings, neither are there any ambidextrous qualifications. No reader can lose his way in these pages. The sentences and paragraphs have indeed the hardness and surface-lustre of polished metal, and they have also its reality and strength.

Jeffrey wondered where Macaulay had picked up his style. In essentials it was the gift of nature, but a gift which he cultivated with unwearied and disciplined effort all his life. The *Essays*, which were written for his contemporaries, came from his pen more rapidly than the *History*, which was written for posterity as well; but whatever he composed was done as well as he could do it in the circumstances. Of the essay on *Bacon*, for instance, he said: "There is not a sentence in the latter half of the article which has not been repeatedly recast." Modesty was not Macaulay's forte, yet he was humble enough whenever he contrasted his performance with his aims, as when he observed: "I can truly say that I never read again the most popular passages of my own works without painfully feeling how far my execution has fallen short of the standard which is in my mind." He was not only humble concerning his accomplishment as a writer, he was also remarkably and correctly aware of his limitations, as shown when he wrote to Napier, the successor of Jeffrey, at the time Napier had asked him to review Lockhart's *Life of Scott*, then just published: "I am not successful in analysing the effect of works of genius. I have written several things on historical, political, and moral questions, of which, on the fullest consideration, I am not ashamed, and by which I should be willing to be estimated; but I have never written a page of criticism on poetry or the fine arts, which I would not burn if I had the power. Hazlitt used to say of himself, 'I am nothing if not critical.' The case with me is directly the reverse. I have a strong and acute enjoyment of works of the imagination, but I have never habituated myself to dissect them."

But what Macaulay could do he did brilliantly well, and his fame lives on. The *Essays*, with all their faults, will continue to be read, not only because they are models of effective assertion, but because they are extraordinarily vivid expositions of great characters and great events as well as of a point of view that is representative of an important period in British life. The *History*, unfinished and imperfect, is yet the top of his performance, for here the faults of style are less conspicuous and the virtues are more attractive; here Macaulay is not only a master of exposition, he is also a master of narration and portraiture. Page after page has all the charm of romance. The great third chapter is a classic. Along with other parts of this masterwork it is a perfect realization of Macaulay's literary ideals. "After all," he said, "the first law of writing, that law to which all other laws are subordinate, is this, that the words employed shall be such as convey to the reader the meaning of the writer."

SOUTHEY'S COLLOQUIES

Mr. Southey's political system is just what we might expect from a man who regards politics, not as matter of science, but as matter of taste and feeling. All his schemes of government have been inconsistent with themselves. In his youth he was a republican; yet, as he tells us in his preface to these *Colloquies,* he was even then opposed to the Catholic Claims. He is now a violent Ultra-Tory. Yet, while he maintains, with vehemence approaching to ferocity, all the sterner and harsher parts of the Ultra-Tory theory of government, the baser and dirtier part of that theory disgusts him. Exclusion, persecution, severe punishments for libellers and demagogues, proscriptions, massacres, civil war, if necessary, rather than any concession to a discontented people; these are the measures which he seems inclined to recommend. A severe and gloomy tyranny, crushing opposition, silencing remonstrance, drilling the minds of the people into unreasoning obedience, has in it something of grandeur which delights his imagination. But there is nothing fine in the shabby tricks and jobs of office; and Mr. Southey, accordingly, has no toleration for them. When a Jacobin, he did not perceive that his system led logically, and would have led practically, to the removal of religious distinctions. He now commits a similar error. He renounces the abject and paltry part of the creed of his party, without perceiving that it is also an essential part of that creed. He would have tyranny and purity together; though the most superficial observation might have shown him that there can be no tyranny without corruption.

It is high time, however, that we should proceed to the consideration of the work which is our more immediate subject, and which, indeed, illustrates in almost every page our general remarks on Mr. Southey's writings. In the preface, we are informed that the author, notwithstanding some statements to the contrary, was always opposed to the Catholic Claims. We fully believe this; both because we are sure that Mr. Southey is incapable of publishing a deliberate falsehood, and because his assertion is in itself probable. We should have expected that, even in his wildest paroxysms of democratic enthusiasm, Mr. Southey would have felt no wish to see a simple remedy applied to a great practical evil. We should have expected that the only measure which all the great statesmen of two generations have agreed with each other in supporting would be the only measure which Mr. Southey would have agreed with himself in opposing. He has passed from one extreme of political opinion to another, as Satan in Milton went round the globe, contriving constantly to "ride with darkness." Wherever the thickest shadow of the night may at any moment chance to fall, there is Mr. Southey. It is not everybody who could have so dexterously avoided blundering on the daylight in the course of a journey to the antipodes.

Mr. Southey has not been fortunate in the plan of any of his fictitious narratives. But he has never failed so conspicuously as in the work before us; except, indeed, in the wretched *Vision of Judgement.* In November 1817, it seems the Laureate was sitting over his newspaper, and meditating about the death of the Princess Charlotte. An elderly person of very dignified aspect makes his appearance, announces himself as a stranger from a distant country, and apologises very politely for not having provided himself with letters of introduction. Mr. Southey supposes his visitor to be some American gentleman who has come to see the lakes and the lake-poets, and accordingly proceeds to perform, with that grace, which only long practice can give, all the duties which authors owe to starers. He assures his guest that some of the most agreeable visits which he has received have been from Americans, and that he knows men among them whose talents and virtues would do honour to any country. In passing we may observe, to the honour of Mr. Southey, that, though he evidently has no liking for the American institutions, he never speaks of the people of the United States with that pitiful affectation of contempt by which some members of his party have done more than wars or tariffs can do to excite mutual enmity between two communities formed for mutual fellowship. Great as the faults of his mind are, paltry spite like this has no place in it. Indeed it is scarcely conceivable that a man of his sensibility and his imagination should look without pleasure and national pride on the vigorous and splendid youth of a great people, whose veins are filled with our blood, whose minds are nourished with our literature, and on whom is entailed the rich inheritance of our civilisation, our freedom, and our glory.

But we must return to Mr. Southey's study at Keswick. The visitor informs the hospitable poet that he is not an American but a spirit. Mr. Southey, with more frankness than civility, tells him that he is a very queer one. The stranger holds out his hand. It has neither weight nor substance. Mr. Southey upon this becomes more serious; his hair stands on end; and he adjures the spectre to tell him what he is, and why he comes. The ghost turns out to be Sir Thomas More. The traces of martyrdom, it seems, are worn in the other world, as stars and ribands are worn in this. Sir Thomas shows the poet a red streak round his neck, brighter than a ruby, and informs him that Cranmer wears a suit of flames in Paradise, the right hand glove, we suppose, of peculiar brilliancy.

Sir Thomas pays but a short visit on this occasion, but promises to cultivate the new acquaintance which he has formed, and, after begging that his visit may be kept secret from Mrs. Southey, vanishes into air.

The rest of the book consists of conversations between Mr. Southey and the spirit about trade, currency, Catholic emancipation, periodical literature, female nunneries, butchers, snuff, bookstalls, and a hundred other subjects. Mr. Southey very hospitably takes an opportunity to escort the ghost round the lakes, and directs his attention to the most beautiful points of view. Why a spirit was to be evoked for the purpose of talking over such matters and seeing such sights, why the vicar of the parish, a blue-stocking from London, or an American, such as Mr. Southey at first supposed the aerial visitor to be, might not have done as well, we are unable to conceive. Sir Thomas tells Mr. Southey nothing about future events, and indeed absolutely disclaims the gifts of prescience. He has learned to talk modern English. He has read all the new publications, and loves a jest as well as when he jested with the executioner, though we cannot say that the quality of his wit has materially improved in Paradise. His powers of reasoning, too, are by no means in as great vigour as when he sate on the woolsack; and though he boasts that he is "divested of all those passions which cloud the intellects and warp the understandings of men," we think him, we must confess, far less stoical than formerly. As to revelations, he tells Mr. Southey at the outset to expect none from him. The Laureate expresses some doubts, which assuredly will not raise him in the opinion of our modern millennarians, as to the divine authority of the Apocalypse. But the ghost preserves an impenetrable silence. As far as we remember, only one hint about the employment of disembodied spirits escapes him. He encourages Mr. Southey to hope that there is a Paradise Press, at which all the valuable publications of Mr. Murray and Mr. Colburn are reprinted as regularly as at Philadelphia; and delicately insinuates that *Thalaba* and the *Curse of Kehama* are among the number. What a contrast does this absurd fiction present to those charming narratives which Plato and Cicero prefixed to their dialogues! What cost in machinery, yet what poverty of effect! A ghost brought in to say what any man might have said! The glorified spirit of a great statesman and philosopher dawdling, like a bilious old nabob at a watering-place, over quarterly reviews and novels, dropping in to pay long calls, making excursions in search of the picturesque! The scene of St. George and St. Dennis in the *Pucelle* is hardly more ridiculous. We know what Voltaire meant. Nobody, however, can suppose that Mr. Southey means to make game of the mysteries of a higher state of existence. The fact is that, in the work before us, in the *Vision of Judgement,* and in some of his other pieces, his mode of treating the most solemn subjects differs from that of open scoffers only as the extravagant representations of sacred persons and things in some grotesque Italian paintings differ from the caricatures which Carlile exposes in the front of his shop. We interpret the particular act by the general character. What in the window of a convicted blasphemer we call blasphemous, we call only absurd and ill-judged in an altar-piece.

We now come to the conversations which pass between Mr. Southey and Sir Thomas More, or rather between two Southeys, equally eloquent, equally angry, equally unreasonable, and equally given to talking about what they do not understand. Perhaps we could not select a better instance of the spirit which pervades the whole book than the passages in which Mr. Southey gives his opinion of the manufacturing system. There is nothing which he hates so bitterly. It is, according to him, a system more tyrannical than that of the feudal ages, a system of actual servitude, a system which destroys the bodies and degrades the minds of those who are engaged in it. He expresses a hope that the competition of other nations may drive us out of the field; that our foreign trade may decline; and that we may thus enjoy a restoration of national sanity and strength. But he seems to think that the extermination of the whole manufacturing population would be a blessing, if the evil could be removed in no other way.

Mr. Southey does not bring forward a single fact in support of these views; and, as it seems to us, there are facts which lead to a very different conclusion. In the first place, the poor-rate is very decidedly lower in the manufacturing than in the agricultural districts. If Mr. Southey will look over the Parliamentary returns on this subject, he will find that the amount of parochial relief required by the labourers in the different counties of England is almost exactly in inverse proportion to the degree in which the manufacturing system has been introduced into those counties. The returns for the years ending in March 1825, and in March 1828, are now before us. In the former year we find the poor-rate highest in Sussex, about twenty shillings to every inhabitant. Then come Buckinghamshire, Essex, Suffolk, Bedfordshire, Huntingdonshire, Kent, and Norfolk. In all these the rate is above fifteen shillings a head. We will not go through the whole. Even in Westmoreland and the North Riding of Yorkshire, the rate is at more than eight shillings. In Cumberland and Monmouthshire, the most fortunate of all the agricultural districts, it is at six shillings. But in the West Riding of Yorkshire, it is as low as five shillings: and when we come to Lancashire, we find it at four shillings, one-fifth of what it is in Sussex. The returns of the year ending in March 1828 are a little, and but a little, more unfavourable to the manufacturing districts. Lancashire, even in that season of distress, required a smaller poor-rate than any other district, and little more than one-fourth of the poor-rate raised in Sussex. Cumberland alone, of the agricultural districts, was as well off as the West Riding of Yorkshire. These facts seem to indicate that the manufacturer is both in a more comfortable and in a less dependent situation than the agricultural labourer.

As to the effect of the manufacturing system on the bodily health, we must beg leave to estimate it by a standard far too low and vulgar for a mind so imaginative as that of Mr. Southey, the proportion of births and deaths. We know that, during the growth of this atrocious system, this new misery, to use the phrases of Mr. Southey, this new enormity, this birth of a portentous age, this pest which no man can approve whose heart is not seared or whose understanding has not been darkened, there has been a great diminution of mortality, and that this diminution has been greater in the manufacturing towns than anywhere else. The mortality still is, as it always was, greater in towns than in the country. But the difference has diminished in an extraordinary degree. There is the best reason to believe that the annual mortality of Manchester, about the middle of the last century, was one in twenty-eight. It is now reckoned at one in forty-five. In Glasgow and Leeds a similar improvement has taken place. Nay, the rate of mortality in those three great capitals of the manufacturing districts is now considerably less than it was, fifty years ago, over England and Wales, taken together, open country and all. We might with some plausibility maintain that the people live longer because they are better fed, better lodged, better clothed, and better attended in sickness, and that these improvements are owing to that increase of national wealth which the manufacturing system has produced.

Much more might be said on this subject. But to what end? It is not from bills of mortality and statistical tables that Mr. Southey has learned his political creed. He cannot stoop to study the history of the system which he abuses, to strike the balance between the good and evil which it has produced, to compare district with district, or generation with generation. We will give his own reason for his opinion, the only reason which he gives for it, in his own words:—

We remained a while in silence looking upon the assemblage of dwellings below. Here, and in the adjoining hamlet of Millbeck, the effects of manufactures and of agriculture may be seen and compared. The old cottages are such as the poet and the painter equally delight in beholding. Substantially built of the native stone without mortar, dirtied with no white lime, and their long low roofs covered with slate, if they had been raised by the magic of some indigenous Amphion's music, the materials could not have adjusted themselves more beautifully in accord with the surrounding scene; and time has still further harmonized them with weather stains, lichens, and moss, short grasses, and short fern, and stone-plants of various kinds. The ornamented chimneys, round or square, less adorned than those which, like little turrets, crest the houses of the Portuguese peasantry; and yet not less happily suited to their place, the hedge of clipt box beneath the windows, the rose-bushes beside

the door, the little patch of flower-ground, with its tall hollyhocks in front; the garden beside, the bee-hives, and the orchard with its bank of daffodils and snowdrops, the earliest and the profusest in these parts, indicate in the owners some portion of ease and leisure, some regard to neatness and comfort, some sense of natural, and innocent, and healthful enjoyment. The new cottages of the manufacturers are upon the manufacturing pattern—naked, and in a row.

"How is it," said I, "that everything which is connected with manufactures presents such features of unqualified deformity? From the largest of Mammon's temples down to the poorest hovel in which his helotry are stalled, these edifices have all one character. Time will not mellow them; nature will neither clothe nor conceal them; and they will remain always as offensive to the eye as to the mind."

Here is wisdom. Here are the principles on which nations are to be governed. Rose-bushes and poor-rates, rather than steam-engines and independence. Mortality and cottages with weather-stains, rather than health and long life with edifices which time cannot mellow. We are told, that our age has invented atrocities beyond the imagination of our fathers; that society has been brought into a state compared with which extermination would be a blessing; and all because the dwellings of cotton-spinners are naked and rectangular. Mr. Southey has found out a way, he tells us, in which the effects of manufactures and agriculture may be compared. And what is this way? To stand on a hill, to look at a cottage and a factory, and to see which is the prettier. Does Mr. Southey think that the body of the English peasantry live, or ever lived, in substantial or ornamented cottages, with box-hedges, flower-gardens, bee-hives, and orchards? If not, what is his parallel worth? We despise those mock philosophers, who think that they serve the cause of science by depreciating literature and the fine arts. But if anything could excuse their narrowness of mind, it would be such a book as this. It is not strange that, when one enthusiast makes the picturesque the test of political good, another should feel inclined to proscribe altogether the pleasures of taste and imagination.

Thus it is that Mr. Southey reasons

about matters with which he thinks himself perfectly conversant. We cannot, therefore, be surprised to find that he commits extraordinary blunders when he writes on points of which he acknowledges himself to be ignorant. He confesses that he is not versed in political economy, and that he has neither liking nor aptitude for it; and he then proceeds to read the public a lecture concerning it which fully bears out his confession.

"All wealth," says Sir Thomas More, "in former times was tangible. It consisted in land, money, or chattels, which were either of real or conventional value."

Montesinos, as Mr. Southey somewhat affectedly calls himself, answers thus:—

"Jewels, for example, and pictures, as in Holland, where indeed at one time tulip bulbs answered the same purpose."

"That bubble," says Sir Thomas, "was one of those contagious insanities to which communities are subject. All wealth was real, till the extent of commerce rendered a paper currency necessary; which differed from precious stones and pictures in this important point, that there was no limit to its production."

"We regard it," says Montesinos, "as the representative of real wealth; and, therefore, limited always to the amount of what it represents."

"Pursue that notion," answers the ghost, "and you will be in the dark presently. Your provincial banknotes, which constitute almost wholly the circulating medium of certain districts, pass current to-day. To-morrow tidings may come that the house which issued them has stopt payment, and what do they represent then? You will find them the shadow of a shade."

We scarcely know at which end to begin to disentangle this knot of absurdities. We might ask, why it should be a greater proof of insanity in men to set a high value on rare tulips than on rare stones, which are neither more useful nor more beautiful? We might ask how it can be said that there is no limit to the production of paper money, when a man is hanged if he issues any in the name of another, and is forced to cash what he issues in his own? But Mr. Southey's error lies deeper still. "All wealth," says he,

"was tangible and real till paper currency was introduced." Now, was there ever, since men emerged from a state of utter barbarism, an age in which there were no debts? Is not a debt, while the solvency of the debtor is undoubted, always reckoned as part of the wealth of the creditor? Yet is it tangible and real wealth? Does it cease to be wealth, because there is the security of a written acknowledgment for it? And what else is paper currency? Did Mr. Southey ever read a banknote? If he did, he would see that it is a written acknowledgment of a debt, and a promise to pay that debt. The promise may be violated: the debt may remain unpaid: those to whom it was due may suffer: but this is a risk not confined to cases of paper currency: it is a risk inseparable from the relation of debtor and creditor. Every man who sells goods for anything but ready money runs the risk of finding that what he considered as part of his wealth one day is nothing at all the next day. Mr. Southey refers to the picture-galleries of Holland. The pictures were undoubtedly real and tangible possessions. But surely it might happen that a burgomaster might owe a picture-dealer a thousand guilders for a Teniers. What in this case corresponds to our paper money is not the picture, which is tangible, but the claim of the picture-dealer on his customer for the price of the picture; and this claim is not tangible. Now, would not the picture-dealer consider this claim as part of his wealth? Would not a tradesman who knew of the claim give credit to the picture-dealer the more readily on account of the claim? The burgomaster might be ruined. If so, would not those consequences follow which, as Mr. Southey tells us, were never heard of till paper money came into use? Yesterday this claim was worth a thousand guilders. To-day what is it? The shadow of a shade.

It is true that, the more readily claims of this sort are transferred from hand to hand, the more extensive will be the injury produced by a single failure. The laws of all nations sanction, in certain cases, the transfer of rights not yet reduced into possession. Mr. Southey would scarcely wish, we should think, that all indorsements of bills and notes should be declared invalid. Yet even if this were done, the transfer of claims would imperceptibly take place, to a very great extent. When the baker trusts the butcher, for example, he is in fact, though not in form, trusting the butcher's customers. A man who owes large bills to tradesmen, and fails to pay them, almost always produces distress through a very wide circle of people with whom he never dealt.

In short, what Mr. Southey takes for a difference in kind is only a difference of form and degree. In every society men have claims on the property of others. In every society there is a possibility that some debtors may not be able to fulfil their obligations. In every society, therefore, there is wealth which is not tangible, and which may become the shadow of a shade.

Mr. Southey then proceeds to a dissertation on the national debt, which he considers in a new and most consolatory light, as a clear addition to the income of the country.

"You can understand," says Sir Thomas, "that it constitutes a great part of the national wealth."

"So large a part," answers Montesinos, "that the interest amounted, during the prosperous times of agriculture, to as much as the rental of all the land in Great Britain; and at present to the rental of all lands, all houses, and all other fixed property put together."

The Ghost and Laureate agree that it is very desirable that there should be so secure and advantageous a deposit for wealth as the funds afford. Sir Thomas then proceeds:—

"Another and far more momentous benefit must not be overlooked; the expenditure of an annual interest, equalling, as you have stated, the present rental of all fixed property."

"That expenditure," quoth Montesinos, "gives employment to half the industry in the kingdom, and feeds half the mouths. Take, indeed, the weight of the national debt from this great and complicated social machine, and the wheels must stop."

From this passage we should have been inclined to think that Mr. Southey supposes the dividends to be a free gift periodically sent down from heaven to the fundholders, as quails and manna were sent to the Israelites; were it not that he has vouchsafed, in the following question and answer, to give the public some information which, we believe, was very little needed.

"Whence comes the interest?" says Sir Thomas.

"It is raised," answers Montesinos, "by taxation."

Now, has Mr. Southey ever considered what would be done with this sum if it were not paid as interest to the national creditor? If he would think over this matter for a short time, we suspect that the "momentous benefit" of which he talks would appear to him to shrink strangely in amount. A fundholder, we will suppose, spends dividends amounting to five hundred pounds a year; and his ten nearest neighbours pay fifty pounds each to the tax-gatherer, for the purpose of discharging the interest of the national debt. If the debt were wiped out, a measure, be it understood, which we by no means recommend, the fundholder would cease to spend his five hundred pounds a year. He would no longer give employment to industry, or put food into the mouths of labourers. This Mr. Southey thinks a fearful evil. But is there no mitigating circumstance? Each of the ten neighbours of our fundholder has fifty pounds a year more than formerly. Each of them will, as it seems to our feeble understandings, employ more industry and feed more mouths than formerly. The sum is exactly the same. It is in different hands. But on what grounds does Mr. Southey call upon us to believe that it is in the hands of men who will spend it less liberally or less judiciously? He seems to think that nobody but a fundholder can employ the poor; that, if a tax is remitted, those who formerly used to pay it proceed immediately to dig holes in the earth, and to bury the sum which the Government had been accustomed to take; that no money can set industry in motion till such money has been taken by the tax-gatherer out of one man's pocket and put into another man's pocket. We really wish that Mr. Southey would try to prove this principle, which is indeed the foundation of his whole theory of finance: for we think it right to hint to him that our hard-hearted and unimaginative generation will expect some more satisfactory reason than the only one with which he has yet favoured it, namely, a similitude touching evaporation and dew.

Both the theory and the illustration, indeed, are old friends of ours. In every season of distress which we can remember, Mr. Southey has been proclaiming that it is not from economy, but from increased taxation, that the country must expect relief; and he still, we find, places the undoubting faith of a political Diafoirus, in his

Resaignare, repurgare, et reclysterizare.

"A people," he tells us, "may be too rich, but a government cannot be so."

"A state," says he, "cannot have more wealth at its command than may be employed for the general good, a liberal expenditure in national works being one of the surest means of promoting national prosperity; and the benefit being still more obvious, of an expenditure directed to the purposes of national improvement. But a people may be too rich."

We fully admit that a state cannot have at its command more wealth than may be employed for the general good. But neither can individuals, or bodies of individuals, have at their command more wealth than may be employed for the general good. If there be no limit to the sum which may be usefully laid out in public works and national improvement, then wealth, whether in the hands of private men or of the Government, may always, if the possessors choose to spend it usefully, be usefully spent. The only ground, therefore, on which Mr. Southey can possibly maintain that a government cannot be too rich, but that a people may be too rich, must be this, that governments are more likely to spend their money on good objects than private individuals.

But what is useful expenditure? "A liberal expenditure in national works," says Mr. Southey, "is one of the surest means for promoting national prosperity." What does he mean by national prosperity?

Does he mean the wealth of the State? If so, his reasoning runs thus: The more wealth a state has the better; for the more wealth a state has the more wealth it will have. This is surely something like that fallacy, which is ungallantly termed a lady's reason. If by national prosperity he means the wealth of the people, of how gross a contradiction is Mr. Southey guilty. A people, he tells us, may be too rich: a government cannot: for a government can employ its riches in making the people richer. The wealth of the people is to be taken from them, because they have too much, and laid out in works, which will yield them more.

We are really at a loss to determine whether Mr. Southey's reason for recommending large taxation is that it will make the people rich, or that it will make them poor. But we are sure that, if his object is to make them rich, he takes the wrong course. There are two or three principles respecting public works, which, as an experience of vast extent proves, may be trusted in almost every case.

It scarcely ever happens that any private man or body of men will invest property in a canal, a tunnel, or a bridge, but from an expectation that the outlay will be profitable to them. No work of this sort can be profitable to private speculators, unless the public be willing to pay for the use of it. The public will not pay of their own accord for what yields no profit or convenience to them. There is thus a direct and obvious connection between the motive which induces individuals to undertake such a work, and the utility of the work.

Can we find any such connection in the case of a public work executed by a government? If it is useful, are the individuals who rule the country richer? If it is useless, are they poorer? A public man may be solicitous for his credit. But is not he likely to gain more credit by an useless display of ostentatious architecture in a great town than by the best road or the best canal in some remote province? The fame of public works is a much less certain test of their utility than the amount of toll collected at them. In a corrupt age, there will be direct embezzlement. In the purest age, there will be abundance of jobbing.

Never were the statesmen of any country more sensitive to public opinion, and more spotless in pecuniary transactions, than those who have of late governed England. Yet we have only to look at the buildings recently erected in London for a proof of our rule. In a bad age, the fate of the public is to be robbed outright. In a good age, it is merely to have the dearest and the worst of everything.

Buildings for State purposes the State must erect. And here we think that, in general, the State ought to stop. We firmly believe that five hundred thousand pounds subscribed by individuals for railroads or canals would produce more advantage to the public than five millions voted by Parliament for the same purpose. There are certain old saws about the master's eye and about everybody's business, in which we place very great faith.

There is, we have said, no consistency in Mr. Southey's political system. But if there be in his political system any leading principle, any one error which diverges more widely and variously than any other, it is that of which his theory about national works is a ramification. He conceives that the business of the magistrate is, not merely to see that the persons and property of the people are secure from attack, but that he ought to be a jack-of-all-trades, architect, engineer, schoolmaster, merchant, theologian, a Lady Bountiful in every parish, a Paul Pry in every house, spying, eavesdropping, relieving, admonishing, spending our money for us, and choosing our opinions for us. His principle is, if we understand it rightly, that no man can do anything so well for himself as his rulers, be they who they may, can do it for him, and that a government approaches nearer and nearer to perfection, in proportion as it interferes more and more with the habits and notions of individuals.

He seems to be fully convinced that it is in the power of government to relieve all the distresses under which the lower orders labour. Nay, he considers doubt on this subject as impious. We cannot refrain from quoting his argument on this subject. It is a perfect jewel of logic:—

"Many thousands in your metropolis," says Sir Thomas More, "rise every morning without knowing how they are to subsist during the day; as many of them, where they are to lay their heads at night. All men, even the vicious themselves, know that wickedness leads to misery: but many, even among the good and the wise, have yet to learn that misery is almost as often the cause of wickedness."

"There are many," says Montesinos, "who know this, but believe that it is not in the power of human institutions to prevent this misery. They see the effect, but regard the causes as inseparable from the condition of human nature."

"As surely as God is good," replied Sir Thomas, "so surely there is no such thing as necessary evil. For, by the religious mind, sickness, and pain, and death, are not to be accounted evils."

Now if sickness, pain, and death, are not evils, we cannot understand why it should be an evil that thousands should rise without knowing how they are to subsist. The only evil of hunger is that it produces first pain, then sickness, and finally death. If it did not produce these, it would be no calamity. If these are not evils, it is no calamity. We will propose a very plain dilemma: either physical pain is an evil, or it is not an evil. If it is an evil, then there is necessary evil in the universe: if it is not, why should the poor be delivered from it?

Mr. Southey entertains as exaggerated a notion of the wisdom of governments as of their power. He speaks with the greatest disgust of the respect now paid to public opinion. That opinion is, according to him, to be distrusted and dreaded; its usurpation ought to be vigorously resisted; and the practice of yielding to it is likely to ruin the country. To maintain police is, according to him, only one of the ends of government. The duties of a ruler are patriarchal and paternal. He ought to consider the moral discipline of the people as his first object, to establish a religion, to train the whole community in that religion, and to consider all dissenters as his own enemies.

"Nothing," says Sir Thomas, "is more certain, than that religion is the basis upon which civil government rests; that from religion power derives its authority, laws their efficacy, and both their zeal and sanction; and it is necessary that this religion be established as for the security of the state, and for the welfare of the people, who would otherwise be moved to and fro with every wind of doctrine. A state is secure in proportion as the people are attached to its institutions; it is, therefore, the first and plainest rule of sound policy, that the people be trained up in the way they should go. The state that neglects this prepares its own destruction; and they who train them in any other way are undermining it. Nothing in abstract science can be more certain than these positions are."

"All of which," answers Montesinos, "are nevertheless denied by our professors of the arts Babblative and Scribblative: some in the audacity of evil designs, and others in the glorious assurance of impenetrable ignorance."

The greater part of the two volumes before us is merely an amplification of these paragraphs. What does Mr. Southey mean by saying that religion is demonstrably the basis of civil government? He cannot surely mean that men have no motives except those derived from religion for establishing and supporting civil government, that no temporal advantage is derived from civil government, that men would experience no temporal inconvenience from living in a state of anarchy? If he allows, as we think he must allow, that it is for the good of mankind in this world to have civil government, and that the great majority of mankind have always thought it for their good in this world to have civil government, we then have a basis for government quite distinct from religion. It is true that the Christian religion sanctions government, as it sanctions everything which promotes the happiness and virtue of our species. But we are at a loss to conceive in what sense religion can be said to be the basis of government, in which religion is not also the basis of the practices of eating, drinking, and lighting fires in cold weather. Nothing in history is more certain than that government has existed, has received some obedience, and has given some protection, in times in which it derived no support from religion, in times in which there was no religion that influenced the hearts and lives of men. It was not from dread of Tartarus, or from belief in the Elysian fields, that an Athenian wished to have some institutions which might keep Orestes from filching his

cloak, or Midias from breaking his head. "It is from religion," says Mr. Southey, "that power derives its authority, and laws their efficacy." From what religion does our power over the Hindoos derive its authority, or the law in virtue of which we hang Brahmins its efficacy? For thousands of years civil government has existed in almost every corner of the world, in ages of priestcraft, in ages of fanaticism, in ages of Epicurean indifference, in ages of enlightened piety. However pure or impure the faith of the people might be, whether they adored a beneficent or a malignant power, whether they thought the soul mortal or immortal, they have, as soon as they ceased to be absolute savages, found out their need of civil government, and instituted it accordingly. It is as universal as the practice of cookery. Yet, it is as certain, says Mr. Southey, as anything in abstract science, that government is founded on religion. We should like to know what notion Mr. Southey has of the demonstrations of abstract science. A very vague one, we suspect.

The proof proceeds. As religion is the basis of government, and as the State is secure in proportion as the people are attached to public institutions, it is therefore, says Mr. Southey, the first rule of policy, that the government should train the people in the way in which they should go; and it is plain that those who train them in any other way are undermining the State.

Now it does not appear to us to be the first object that people should always believe in the established religion and be attached to the established government. A religion may be false. A government may be oppressive. And whatever support government gives to false religions, or religion to oppressive governments, we consider as a clear evil.

The maxim, that governments ought to train the people in the way in which they should go, sounds well. But is there any reason for believing that a government is more likely to lead the people in the right way than the people to fall into the right way of themselves? Have there not been governments which were blind leaders of the blind? Are there not still such governments? Can it be laid down as a general rule that the movement of political and religious truth is rather downwards from the government to the people than upwards from the people to the government? These are questions which it is of importance to have clearly resolved. Mr. Southey declaims against public opinion, which is now, he tells us, usurping supreme power. Formerly, according to him, the laws governed; now public opinion governs. What are laws but expression of the opinion of some class which has power over the rest of the community? By what was the world ever governed but by the opinion of some person or persons? By what else can it ever be governed? What are all systems, religious, political, or scientific, but opinions resting on evidence more or less satisfactory? The question is not between human opinion and some higher and more certain mode of arriving at truth, but between opinion and opinion, between the opinions of one man and another, or of one class and another, or of one generation and another. Public opinion is not infallible; but can Mr. Southey construct any institutions which shall secure to us the guidance of an infallible opinion? Can Mr. Southey select any family, any profession, any class, in short, distinguished by any plain badge from the rest of the community, whose opinion is more likely to be just than this much abused public opinion? Would he choose the peers, for example? Or the two hundred tallest men in the country? Or the poor Knights of Windsor? Or children who are born with cauls? Or the seventh sons of seventh sons? We cannot suppose that he would recommend popular election; for that is merely an appeal to public opinion. And to say that society ought to be governed by the opinion of the wisest and best, though true, is useless. Whose opinion is to decide who are the wisest and best?

Mr. Southey and many other respectable people seem to think that, when they have once proved the moral and religious training of the people to be a most important object, it follows, of course, that it is an object which the government ought to pursue. They forget that we have to consider, not merely the goodness of the end,

but also the fitness of the means. Neither in the natural nor in the political body have all members the same office. There is surely no contradiction in saying that a certain section of the community may be quite competent to protect the persons and property of the rest, yet quite unfit to direct our opinions, or to superintend our private habits.

So strong is the interest of a ruler to protect his subjects against all depredations and outrages except his own, so clear and simple are the means by which this end is to be effected, that men are probably better off under the worst governments in the world than they would be in a state of anarchy. Even when the appointment of magistrates has been left to chance, as in the Italian Republics, things have gone on far better than if there had been no magistrates at all, and if every man had done what seemed right in his own eyes. But we see no reason for thinking that the opinions of the magistrate on speculative questions are more likely to be right than those of any other man. None of the modes by which a magistrate is appointed, popular election, the accident of the lot, or the accident of birth, affords, as far as we can perceive, much security for his being wiser than any of his neighbours. The chance of his being wiser than all his neighbours together is still smaller. Now we cannot understand how it can be laid down that it is the duty and the right of one class to direct the opinions of another, unless it can be proved that the former class is more likely to form just opinions than the latter.

The duties of government would be, as Mr. Southey says that they are, paternal, if a government were necessarily as much superior in wisdom to a people as the most foolish father, for a time, is to the most intelligent child, and if a government loved a people as fathers generally love their children. But there is no reason to believe that a government will have either the paternal warmth of affection or the paternal superiority of intellect. Mr. Southey might as well say that the duties of the shoemaker are paternal, and that it is an usurpation in any man not of the craft to say that his shoes are bad and to insist on having better. The division of labour would be no blessing, if those by whom a thing is done were to pay no attention to the opinion of those for whom it is done. The shoemaker, in the *Relapse,* tells Lord Foppington that his Lordship is mistaken in supposing that his shoe pinches. "It does not pinch; it cannot pinch; I know my business; and I never made a better shoe." This is the way in which Mr. Southey would have a government treat a people who usurp the privilege of thinking. Nay, the shoemaker of Vanbrugh has the advantage in the comparison. He contented himself with regulating his customer's shoes, about which he had peculiar means of information, and did not presume to dictate about the coat and hat. But Mr. Southey would have the rulers of a country prescribe opinions to the people, not only about politics, but about matters concerning which a government has no peculiar sources of information, and concerning which any man in the streets may know as much and think as justly as the King, namely religion and morals.

Men are never so likely to settle a question rightly as when they discuss it freely. A government can interfere in discussion only by making it less free than it would otherwise be. Men are most likely to form just opinions when they have no other wish than to know the truth, and are exempt from all influence, either of hope or fear. Government, as government, can bring nothing but the influence of hopes and fears to support its doctrines. It carries on controversy, not with reasons, but with threats and bribes. If it employs reasons, it does so, not in virtue of any powers which belong to it as a government. Thus, instead of a contest between argument and argument, we have a contest between argument and force. Instead of a contest in which truth, from the natural constitution of the human mind, has a decided advantage over falsehood, we have a contest in which truth can be victorious only by accident.

And what, after all, is the security which this training gives to governments? Mr. Southey would scarcely propose that discussion should be more effectually shackled, that public opinion should be more strictly disciplined into conformity with established institutions, than in Spain and Italy. Yet we know that the restraints which exist in Spain and Italy have not prevented atheism from spreading among the educated classes, and especially among those whose office it is to minister at the altars of God. All our readers know how, at the time of the French Revolution, priest after priest came forward to declare that his doctrine, his ministry, his whole life, had been a lie, a mummery during which he could scarcely compose his countenance sufficiently to carry on the imposture. This was the case of a false, or at least of a grossly corrupted religion. Let us take then the case of all others most favourable to Mr. Southey's argument. Let us take that form of religion which he holds to be the purest, the system of the Arminian part of the Church of England. Let us take the form of government which he most admires and regrets, the government of England in the time of Charles the First. Would he wish to see a closer connection between Church and State than then existed? Would he wish for more powerful ecclesiastical tribunals? for a more zealous King? for a more active primate? Would he wish to see a more complete monopoly of public instruction given to the Established Church? Could any government do more to train the people in the way in which he would have them go? And in what did all this training end? The Report of the state of the Province of Canterbury, delivered by Laud to his master at the close of 1639, represents the Church of England as in the highest and most palmy state. So effectually had the Government pursued that policy which Mr. Southey wishes to see revived that there was scarcely the least appearance of dissent. Most of the bishops stated that all was well among their flocks. Seven or eight persons in the diocese of Peterborough had seemed refractory to the Church, but had made ample submission. In Norfolk and Suffolk all whom there had been reason to suspect had made profession of conformity, and appeared to observe it strictly. It is confessed that there was a little difficulty in bringing some of the vulgar in Suffolk to take the sacrament at the rails in the chancel. This was the only open instance of nonconformity which the vigilant eye of Laud could detect in all the dioceses of his twenty-one suffragans, on the very eve of a revolution in which primate, and Church, and monarch, and monarchy were to perish together.

At which time would Mr. Southey pronounce the constitution more secure: in 1639, when Laud presented this Report to Charles; or now, when thousands of meetings openly collect millions of dissenters, when designs against the tithes are openly avowed, when books attacking not only the Establishment, but the first principles of Christianity, are openly sold in the streets? The signs of discontent, he tells us, are stronger in England now than in France when the States-General met: and hence he would have us infer that a revolution like that of France may be at hand. Does he not know that the danger of states is to be estimated, not by what breaks out of the public mind, but by what stays in it? Can he conceive anything more terrible than the situation of a government which rules without apprehension over a people of hypocrites, which is flattered by the press and cursed in the inner chambers, which exults in the attachment and obedience of its subjects, and knows not that those subjects are leagued against it in a free-masonry of hatred, the sign of which is every day conveyed in the glance of ten thousand eyes, the pressure of ten thousand hands, and the tone of ten thousand voices? Profound and ingenious policy! Instead of curing the disease, to remove those symptoms by which alone its nature can be known! To leave the serpent his deadly sting, and deprive him only of his warning rattle!

When the people whom Charles had so assiduously trained in the good way had rewarded his paternal care by cutting off his head, a new kind of training came into fashion. Another government arose which, like the former, considered religion as its surest basis, and the religious discipline of the people as its first duty. Sanguinary laws were enacted against libertinism; profane pictures were burned; drapery was put on indecorous statues; the theatres were shut up; fast-days were numerous; and the Parliament resolved that no person should be admitted into any public employment, unless the House should be first satisfied of his vital godliness. We know what was the end of this training. We know that it ended in impiety, in filthy and heartless sensuality, in the dissolution of all ties of honour and morality. We know that at this very day scriptural phrases, scriptural names, perhaps some scriptural doctrines excite disgust and ridicule, solely because they are associated with the austerity of that period.

Thus has the experiment of training the people in established forms of religion been twice tried in England on a large scale, once by Charles and Laud, and once by the Puritans. The High Tories of our time still entertain many of the feelings and opinions of Charles and Laud, though in a mitigated form; nor is it difficult to see that the heirs of the Puritans are still amongst us. It would be desirable that each of these parties should remember how little advantage or honour it formerly derived from the closest alliance with power, that it fell by the support of rulers and rose by their opposition, that of the two systems that in which the people were at any time drilled was always at that time the unpopular system, that the training of the High Church ended in the reign of the Puritans, and that the training of the Puritans ended in the reign of the harlots.

This was quite natural. Nothing is so galling to a people not broken in from the birth as a paternal, or, in other words, a meddling government, a government which tells them what to read, and say, and eat, and drink, and wear. Our fathers could not bear it two hundred year ago; and we are not more patient than they. Mr. Southey thinks that the yoke of the Church is dropping off because it is loose. We feel convinced that it is borne only because it is easy, and that, in the instant in which an attempt is made to tighten it, it will be flung away. It will be neither the first nor the strongest yoke that has been broken asunder and trampled under foot in the day of the vengeance of England.

. . . . .

The signs of the times, Mr. Southey tells us, are very threatening. His fears for the country would decidedly preponderate over his hopes, but for a firm reliance on the mercy of God. Now, as we know that God has once suffered the civilised world to be overrun by savages, and the Christian religion to be corrupted by doctrines which made it, for some ages, almost as bad as Paganism, we cannot think it inconsistent with his attributes that similar calamities should again befall mankind.

We look, however, on the state of the world, and of this kingdom in particular, with much greater satisfaction and with better hopes. Mr. Southey speaks with contempt of those who think the savage state happier than the social. On this subject, he says, Rousseau never imposed on him even in his youth. But he conceives that a community which has advanced a little way in civilisation is happier than one which has made greater progress. The Britons in the time of Cæsar were happier, he suspects, than the English of the nineteenth century. On the whole, he selects the generation which preceded the Reformation as that in which the people of this country were better off than at any time before or since.

This opinion rests on nothing, as far as we can see, except his own individual associations. He is a man of letters; and a life destitute of literary pleasures seems insipid to him. He abhors the spirit of the present generation, the severity of its studies, the boldness of its inquiries, and the disdain with which it regards some old prejudices by which his own mind is held in bondage. He dislikes an utterly unenlightened age; he dislikes an investigating and reforming age. The first twenty years of the sixteenth century would have exactly suited him. They furnished just the quantity of intellectual excitement which he requires. The learned few read and wrote largely. A scholar was held in high estimation. But the rabble did not presume to think; and even the most inquiring and independent of the educated classes paid more reverence to authority, and less to reason, than is usual in our time. This is a state of things in which Mr. Southey would have found himself quite comfortable; and, accordingly, he pronounces it the happiest state of things ever known in the world.

The savages were wretched, says Mr. Southey; but the people in the time of Sir Thomas More were happier than either they or we. Now we think it quite certain that we have the advantage over the contemporaries of Sir Thomas More, in every point in which they had any advantage over savages.

Mr. Southey does not even pretend to maintain that the people in the sixteenth century were better lodged or clothed than at present. He seems to admit that in these respects there has been some little improvement. It is indeed a matter about which scarcely any doubt can exist in the most perverse mind that the improvements of machinery have lowered the price of manufactured articles, and have brought within the reach of the poorest some conveniences which Sir Thomas More or his master could not have obtained at any price.

The labouring classes, however, were, according to Mr. Southey, better fed three hundred years ago than at present. We believe that he is completely in error on this point. The condition of servants in noble and wealthy families, and of scholars at the Universities, must surely have been better in those times than that of day-labourers; and we are sure that it was not better than that of our workhouse paupers. From the household book of the Northumberland family, we find that in one of the greatest establishments of the kingdom the servants lived very much as common sailors live now. In the reign of Edward the Sixth the state of the students at Cambridge is described to us, on the very best authority, as most wretched. Many of them dined on pottage made of a farthing's worth of beef with a little salt and oatmeal, and literally nothing else. This account we have from a contemporary master of St. John's. Our parish poor now eat wheaten bread. In the sixteenth century the labourer was glad to get barley, and was often forced to content himself with poorer fare. In Harrison's introduction to Holinshed we have an account of the state of our working population in the "golden days," as Mr. Southey calls them, "of good Queen Bess." "The gentilitie," says he, "commonly provide themselves sufficiently of wheat for their own tables, whylest their household and poore neighbours in some shires are inforced to content themselves with rye or barleie; yea, and in time of dearth, many with bread made eyther of beanes, peason, or otes, or of altogether, and some acornes among. I will not say that this extremity is oft so well to be seen in time of plentie as of dearth; but if I should I could easily bring my trial: for albeit there be much more grounde eared nowe almost in everye place than hathe beene of late yeares, yet such a price of corne continueth in eache towne and markete, without any just cause, that the artificer and poore labouring man is not able to reach unto it, but is driven to content himself with horse-corne." We should like to see what the effect would be of putting any parish in England now on allowance of "horse-corne." The helotry of Mammon are not, in our day, so easily enforced to content themselves as the peasantry of that happy period, as Mr. Southey considers it, which elapsed between the fall of the feudal and the rise of the commercial tyranny.

"The people," says Mr. Southey, "are worse fed than when they were fishers." And yet in another place he complains that they will not eat fish. "They have contracted," says he, "I know not how, some obstinate prejudice against a kind of food at once wholesome and delicate, and everywhere to be obtained cheaply and in abundance, were the demand for it as general as it ought to be." It is true that the lower orders have an obstinate prejudice against fish. But hunger has no such obstinate prejudices. If what was formerly a common diet is now eaten only in times of severe pressure, the inference is plain. The people must be fed with what they at least think better food than that of their ancestors.

The advice and medicine which the poorest labourer can now obtain, in disease, or after an accident, is far superior to what Henry the Eighth could have commanded. Scarcely any part of the country is out of the reach of practitioners, who are probably not so far inferior to Sir Henry Halford as they are superior to Dr. Butts. That there has been a great improvement in this respect, Mr. Southey allows. Indeed he could not well have denied it. "But," says he, "the evils for which these sciences are the palliative, have increased since the time of the Druids, in a proportion that heavily overweighs the benefit of improved therapeutics." We know nothing either of the diseases or the remedies of the Druids. But we are quite sure that the improvement of medicine has far more than kept pace with the increase of disease during the last three centuries. This is proved by the best possible evidence. The term of human life is decidedly longer in England than in any former age, respecting which we possess any information on which we can rely. All the rants in the world about picturesque cottages and temples of Mammon will not shake this argument. No test of the physical well-being of society can be named so decisive as that which is furnished by bills of mortality. That the lives of the people of this country have been gradually lengthening during the course of several generations, is as certain as any fact in statistics; and that the lives of men should become longer and longer, while their bodily condition during life is becoming worse and worse, is utterly incredible.

Let our readers think over these circumstances. Let them take into the account the sweating sickness and the plague. Let them take into the account that fearful disease which first made its appearance in the generation to which Mr. Southey assigns the palm of felicity, and raged through Europe with a fury at which the physician stood aghast, and before which the people were swept away by myriads. Let them consider the state of the northern counties, constantly the scene of robberies, rapes, massacres, and conflagrations. Let them add to all this the fact that seventy-two thousand persons suffered death by the hands of the executioner during the reign of Henry the Eighth, and judge between the nineteenth and the sixteenth century.

We do not say that the lower orders in England do not suffer severe hardships. But, in spite of Mr. Southey's assertions, and in spite of the assertions of a class of politicians, who, differing from Mr. Southey in every other point, agree with him in this, we are inclined to doubt whether the labouring classes here really suffer greater physical distress than the labouring classes of the most flourishing countries of the Continent.

It will scarcely be maintained that the lazzaroni who sleep under the porticoes of Naples, or the beggars who besiege the convents of Spain, are in a happier situation than the English commonalty. The distress which has lately been experienced in the northern part of Germany, one of the best governed and most prosperous regions of Europe, surpasses, if we have been correctly informed, anything which has of late years been known among us. In Norway and Sweden the peasantry are constantly compelled to mix bark with their bread; and even this expedient has not always preserved whole families and neighbourhoods from perishing together of famine. An experiment has lately been tried in the kingdom of the Netherlands, which has been cited to prove the possibility of establishing agricultural colonies on the waste lands of England, but which proves to our minds nothing so clearly as this, that the rate of subsistence to which the labouring classes are reduced in the Netherlands is miserably low, and very far inferior to that of the English paupers. No distress which the people here have endured for centuries approaches to that which has been felt by the French in our own time. The beginning of the year 1817 was a time of great distress in this island. But the state of the lowest classes here was luxury compared with that of the people of France. We find in Magendie's *Journal de Physiologie Expérimentale* a paper on a point of physiology connected with the distress of that season. It appears that the inhabitants of six departments, Aix, Jura, Doubs, Haute Saone, Vosges, and Saone-et-Loire, were reduced first to oatmeal and potatoes, and at last to nettles, beanstalks, and other kinds of herbage fit only for cattle; that when the next harvest enabled them to eat barley-bread, many of them died from intemperate indulgence in what they thought an exquisite repast; and that a dropsy of a peculiar description was produced by the hard fare of the year. Dead bodies were found on the roads and in the fields. A single surgeon dissected six of these, and found the stomach shrunk, and filled with the unwholesome aliments which hunger had driven men to share with beasts. Such extremity of distress as this is never heard of in England, or even in Ireland. We are, on the whole, inclined to think, though we would speak with diffidence on a point on which it would be rash to pronounce a positive judgment without a much longer and closer investigation than we have bestowed upon it, that the labouring classes of this island, though they have their grievances and distresses, some produced by their own improvidence, some by the errors of their rulers, are on the whole better off as to physical comforts than the inhabitants of an equally extensive district of the old world. For this very reason, suffering is more acutely felt and more loudly bewailed here than elsewhere. We must take into the account the liberty of discussion, and the strong interest which the opponents of a ministry always have to exaggerate the extent of the public disasters. There are countries in which the people quietly endure distress that here would shake the foundations of the State, countries in which the inhabitants of a whole province turn out to eat grass with less clamour than one Spitalfields weaver would make here, if the overseers were to put him on barley-bread. In those new commonwealths in which a civilised population has at its command a boundless extent of the richest soil, the condition of the labourer is probably happier than in any society which has lasted for many centuries. But in the old world we must confess ourselves unable to find any satisfactory record of any great nation, past or present, in which the working classes have been in a more comfortable situation than in England during the last thirty years. When this island was thinly peopled, it was barbarous: there was little capital; and that little was insecure. It is now the richest and most highly civilised spot in the world; but the population is dense. Thus we have never known that golden age which the lower orders in the United States are now enjoying. We have never known an age of liberty, of order, and of education, an age in which the mechanical sciences were carried to a great height, yet in which the people were **not** sufficiently numerous to cultivate even the most fertile valleys. But, when we compare our own condition with that of our ancestors, we think it clear that the advantages arising from the progress of civilisation have far more than counterbalanced the disadvantages arising from the progress of population. While our numbers have increased tenfold, our wealth has increased a hundredfold. Though there are so many more people to share the wealth now existing in the country than there were in the sixteenth century, it seems certain that a greater share falls to almost every individual than fell to the share of any of the corresponding class in the sixteenth century. The King keeps a more splendid court. The establishments of the nobles are more magnificent. The esquires are richer; the merchants are richer; the shopkeepers are richer. The serving-man, the artisan, and the husbandman, have a more copious and palatable supply of food, better clothing, and better furniture. This is no reason for tolerating abuses, or for neglecting any means of ameliorating the condition of our poorer countrymen. But it is a reason against telling them, as some of our philosophers are constantly telling them, that they are the most wretched people who ever existed on the face of the earth.

We have already adverted to Mr. Southey's amusing doctrine about national wealth. A state, says he, cannot be too rich; but a people may be too rich. His reason for thinking this is extremely curious.

"A people may be too rich, because it is the tendency of the commercial, and more especially of the manufacturing system, to collect wealth rather than to diffuse it. Where wealth is necessarily employed in any of the speculations of trade, its increase is in proportion to its amount. Great capitalists become like pikes in a fish-pond who devour the weaker fish; and it is but too certain, that the poverty of one part of the people seems to increase in the same ratio as the riches of another. There are examples of this in history. In Portugal, when the high tide of wealth flowed in from the conquests in Africa and the East, the effect of that great influx was not more visible in the augmented splendour of the court, and the luxury of the higher ranks, than in the distress of the people."

Mr. Southey's instance is not a very fortunate one. The wealth which did so little for the Portuguese was not the fruit either of manufactures or of commerce carried on by private individuals. It was the wealth, not of the people, but of the Government and its creatures, of those who, as Mr. Southey thinks, can never be too rich. The fact is, that Mr. Southey's proposition is opposed to all history, and to the phenomena which surround us on every side. England is the richest country in Europe, the most commercial country, and the country in which manufactures flourish most. Russia and Poland are the poorest countries in Europe. They have scarcely any trade, and none but the rudest manufactures. Is wealth more diffused in Russia and Poland than in England? There are individuals in Russia and Poland whose incomes are probably equal to those of our richest countrymen. It may be doubted whether there are not, in those countries, as many fortunes of eighty thousand a year as here. But are there as many fortunes of two thousand a year, or of one thousand a year? There are parishes in England which contain more people of between three hundred and three thousand pounds a year than could be found in all the dominions of the Emperor Nicholas. The neat and commodious houses which have been built in London and its vicinity, for people of this class, within the last thirty years, would of themselves form a city larger than the capitals of some European kingdoms. And this is the state of society in which the great proprietors have devoured a smaller!

The cure which Mr. Southey thinks that he has discovered is worthy of the sagacity which he has shown in detecting the evil. The calamities arising from the collection of wealth in the hands of a few capitalists are to be remedied by collecting it in the hands of one great captalist, who has no conceivable motive to use it better than other capitalists, the all-devouring State.

It is not strange that, differing so widely from Mr. Southey as to the past progress of society, we should differ from him also as to its probable destiny. He thinks, that to all outward appearance, the country is hastening to destruction; but he relies firmly on the goodness of God. We do not see either the piety or the rationality of thus confidently expecting that the Supreme Being will interfere to disturb the common succession of causes and effects. We, too, rely on his goodness, on his goodness as manifested, not in extraordinary interpositions, but in those general laws which it has pleased him to establish in the physical and in the moral world. We rely on the natural tendency of the human intellect to truth, and on the natural tendency of society to improvement. We know no well-authenticated instance of a people which has decidedly retrograded in civilisation and prosperity, except from the influence of violent and terrible calamities, such as those which laid the Roman Empire in ruins, or those which, about the beginning of the sixteenth century, desolated Italy. We know of no country which, at the end of fifty years of peace and tolerably good government, has been less prosperous than at the beginning of that period. The political importance of a state may decline, as the balance of power is disturbed by the introduction of new forces. Thus the influence of Holland and of Spain is much diminished. But are Holland and Spain poorer than formerly? We doubt it. Other countries have outrun them. But we suspect that they have been positively, though not relatively, advancing. We suspect that Holland is richer than when she sent her navies up the Thames, that Spain is richer than when a French king was brought captive to the footstool of Charles the Fifth.

History is full of the signs of this natural progress of society. We see in almost every part of the annals of mankind how the industry of individuals, struggling up against wars, taxes, famines, conflagrations, mischievous prohibitions, and more mischievous protections, creates faster than governments can squander, and repairs whatever invaders can destroy. We see the wealth of nations increasing, and all the arts of life approaching nearer and nearer to perfection, in spite of the grossest corruption and the wildest profusion on the part of rulers.

The present moment is one of great distress. But how small will that distress appear when we think over the history of the last forty years; a war, compared with which all other wars sink into insignificance; taxation, such as the most heavily taxed people of former times could not have conceived; a debt larger than all the public debts that ever existed in the world added together; the food of the people studiously rendered dear; the currency imprudently debased, and imprudently restored. Yet is the country poorer than in 1790? We firmly believe that, in spite of all the misgovernment of her rulers, she has been almost constantly becoming richer and richer. Now and then there has been a stoppage, now and then a short retrogression; but as to the general tendency there can be no doubt. A single breaker may recede; but the tide is evidently coming in.

If we were to prophesy that in the year 1930 a population of fifty millions, better fed, clad, and lodged than the English of our time, will cover these islands, that Sussex and Huntingdonshire will be wealthier than the wealthiest parts of the West Riding of Yorkshire now are, that cultivation, rich as that of a flower-garden, will be carried up to the very tops of Ben Nevis and Helvellyn, that machines constructed on principles yet undiscovered will be in every house, that there will be no highways but railroads, no travelling but by steam, that our debt, vast as it seems to us, will appear to our great-grandchildren a trifling encumbrance, which might easily be paid off in a year or two, many people would think us insane. We prophesy nothing; but this we say: If any person had told the Parliament which met in perplexity and terror after the crash in 1720 that in 1830 the wealth of England would surpass all their wildest dreams, that the annual revenue would equal the principal of that debt which they considered as an intolerable burden, that for one man of ten thousand pounds then living there would be five men of fifty thousand pounds, that London would be twice as large and twice as populous, and that nevertheless the rate of mortality would have diminished to one-half of what it then was, that the post-office would bring more into the exchequer than the excise and customs had brought in together under Charles the Second, that stage coaches would run from London to York in twenty-four hours, that men would be in the habit of sailing without wind, and would be beginning to ride without horses, our ancestors would have given as much credit to the prediction as they gave to *Gulliver's Travels.* Yet the prediction would have been true; and they would have perceived that it was not altogether absurd, if they had considered that the country was then raising every year a sum which would have purchased the fee-simple of the revenue of the Plantagenets, ten times what supported the Government of Elizabeth, three times what, in the time of Cromwell, had been thought intolerably oppressive. To almost all men the state of things under which they have been used to live seems to be the necessary state of things. We have heard it said that five per cent. is the natural interest of money, that twelve is the natural number of a jury, that forty shillings is the natural qualification of a county voter. Hence it is that, though in every age everybody knows that up to his own time progressive improvement has been taking place, nobody seems to reckon on any improvement during the next generation. We cannot absolutely prove that those are in error who tell us that society has reached a turning point, that we have seen our best days. But so said all who came before us, and with just as much apparent reason. "A million a year will beggar us," said the patriots of 1640. "Two millions a year will grind the country to powder," was the cry in 1660. "Six millions a year, and a debt of fifty millions!" exclaimed Swift; "the high allies have been the ruin of us." "A hundred and forty millions of debt!"

said Junius; "well may we say that we owe Lord Chatham more than we shall ever pay, if we owe him such a load as this." "Two hundred and forty millions of debt!" cried all the statesmen of 1783 in chorus; "what abilities, or what economy on the part of a minister, can save a country so burdened?" We know that if, since 1783, no fresh debt had been incurred, the increased resources of the country would have enabled us to defray that debt at which Pitt, Fox, and Burke stood aghast, nay, to defray it over and over again, and that with much lighter taxation than what we have actually borne. On what principle is it that, when we see nothing but improvement behind us, we are to expect nothing but deterioration before us?

It is not by the intermeddling of Mr. Southey's idol, the omniscient and omnipotent State, but by the prudence and energy of the people, that England has hitherto been carried forward in civilisation; and it is to the same prudence and the same energy that we now look with comfort and good hope. Our rulers will best promote the improvement of the nation by strictly confining themselves to their own legitimate duties, by leaving capital to find its most lucrative course, commodities their fair price, industry and intelligence their natural reward, idleness and folly their natural punishment, by maintaining peace, by defending property, by diminishing the price of law, and by observing strict economy in every department of the State. Let the Government do this: the People will assuredly do the rest.

[1830]

SAMUEL JOHNSON

The *Life of Johnson* is assuredly a great, a very great work. Homer is not more decidedly the first of heroic poets, Shakspeare is not more decidedly the first of dramatists, Demosthenes is not more decidedly the first of orators, than Boswell is the first of biographers. He has no second. He has distanced all his competitors so decidedly that it is not worth while to place them. Eclipse is first, and the rest nowhere.

We are not sure that there is in the

whole history of the human intellect so strange a phænomenon as this book. Many of the greatest men that ever lived have written biography. Boswell was one of the smallest men that ever lived, and he has beaten them all. He was, if we are to give any credit to his own account or to the united testimony of all who knew him, a man of the meanest and feeblest intellect. Johnson described him as a fellow who had missed his only chance of immortality by not having been alive when the *Dunciad* was written. Beauclerk used his name as a proverbial expression for a bore. He was the laughing-stock of the whole of that brilliant society which has owed to him the greater part of its fame. He was always laying himself at the feet of some eminent man, and begging to be spit upon and trampled upon. He was always earning some ridiculous nickname, and then "binding it as a crown unto him," not merely in metaphor, but literally. He exhibited himself at the Shakspeare Jubilee, to all the crowd which filled Stratford-on-Avon, with a placard round his hat bearing the inscription of Corsica Boswell. In his *Tour,* he proclaimed to all the world that at Edinburgh he was known by the appellation of Paoli Boswell. Servile and impertinent, shallow and pedantic, a bigot and a sot; bloated with family pride, and eternally blustering about the dignity of a born gentleman, yet stooping to be a talebearer, an eavesdropper, a common butt in the taverns of London; so curious to know everybody who was talked about, that, Tory and High Churchman as he was, he manoeuvred, we have been told, for an introduction to Tom Paine, so vain of the most childish distinctions, that when he had been to Court, he drove to the office where his book was printing without changing his clothes, and summoned all the printer's devils to admire his new ruffles and sword; such was this man, and such he was content and proud to be. Everything which another man would have hidden, everything the publication of which would have made another man hang himself, was matter of gay and clamorous exultation to his weak and diseased mind. What silly things he said, what bitter retorts he provoked; how at one place he was troubled with evil presentiments which came to nothing; how at another place, on waking from a drunken doze, he read the prayer-book and took a hair of the dog that had bitten him; how he went to see men hanged and came away maudlin; how he added five hundred pounds to the fortune of one of his babies because she was not scared at Johnson's ugly face; how he was frightened out of his wits at sea, and how the sailors quieted him as they would

have quieted a child; how tipsy he was at Lady Cork's one evening, and how much his merriment annoyed the ladies; how impertinent he was to the Duchess of Argyll, and with what stately contempt she put down his impertinence; how Colonel Macleod sneered to his face at his impudent obtrusiveness; how his father and the very wife of his bosom laughed and fretted at his fooleries; all these things he proclaimed to all the world, as if they had been subjects for pride and ostentatious rejoicing. All the caprices of his temper, all the illusions of his vanity, all his hypochondriac whimsies, all his castles in the air, he displayed with a cool self-complacency, a perfect unconsciousness that he was making a fool of himself, to which it is impossible to find a parallel in the whole history of mankind. He has used many people ill; but assuredly he has used nobody so ill as himself.

That such a man should have written one of the best books in the world is strange enough. But this is not all. Many persons who have conducted themselves foolishly in active life, and whose conversation has indicated no superior powers of mind, have left us valuable works. Goldsmith was very justly described by one of his contemporaries as an inspired idiot, and by another as a being

> Who wrote like an angel, and talked like poor Poll.

La Fontaine was in society a mere simpleton. His blunders would not come in amiss among the stories of Hierocles. But these men attained literary eminence in spite of their weaknesses. Boswell attained it by reason of his weaknesses. If he had not been a great fool, he would never have been a great writer. Without all the qualities which made him the jest and the torment of those among whom he lived, without the officiousness, the inquisitiveness, the effrontery, the toad-eating, the insensibility to all reproof, he never could have produced so excellent a book. He was a slave, proud of his servitude; a Paul Pry, convinced that his own curiosity and garrulity were virtues; an unsafe companion who never scrupled to repay the most liberal hospitality by the basest violation of confidence; a man without delicacy, without shame, without sense enough to know when he was hurting the feelings of others or when he was exposing himself to derision; and because he was all this, he has, in an important department of literature, immeasurably surpassed such writers as Tacitus, Clarendon, Alfieri, and his own idol Johnson.

Of the talents which ordinarily raise men to eminence as writers, Boswell had absolutely none. There is not in all his books a single remark of his own on literature, politics, religion, or society, which is not either commonplace or absurd. His dissertations on hereditary gentility, on the slave-trade, and on the entailing of landed estates, may serve as examples. To say that these passages are sophistical would be to pay them an extravagant compliment. They have no pretence to argument, or even to meaning. He has reported innumerable observations made by himself in the course of conversation. Of those observations we do not remember one which is above the intellectual capacity of a boy of fifteen. He has printed many of his own letters, and in these letters he is always ranting or twaddling. Logic, eloquence, wit, taste, all those things which are generally considered as making a book valuable, were utterly wanting to him. He had, indeed, a quick observation and a retentive memory. These qualities, if he had been a man of sense and virtue, would scarcely of themselves have sufficed to make him conspicuous; but because he was a dunce, a parasite, and a coxcomb, they have made him immortal.

Those parts of his book which, considered abstractedly, are most utterly worthless, are delightful when we read them as illustrations of the character of the writer. Bad in themselves, they are good dramatically, like the nonsense of Justice Shallow, the clipped English of Dr. Caius, or the misplaced consonants of Fluellen. Of all confessors, Boswell is the most candid. Other men who have pretended to lay open their own hearts—Rousseau, for example, and Lord Byron—have evidently written with a constant view to effect, and are to be then most distrusted when they seem to be most sincere. There is scarcely any man who would not rather accuse himself of great crimes and of dark and tempestuous passions than proclaim all his little vanities and wild fancies. It would be easier to find a person who would avow actions like those of Cæsar Borgia or Danton, than one who would publish a daydream like those of Alnaschar and Malvolio. Those weaknesses which most men keep covered up in the most secret places of the mind, not to be disclosed to the eye of friendship or of love, were precisely the weaknesses which Boswell paraded before all the world. He was perfectly frank, because the weakness of his understanding and the tumult of his spirits prevented him from knowing when he made himself ridiculous. His book resembles nothing so much as the conversation of the inmates of the Palace of Truth.

His fame is great, and it will, we have no doubt, be lasting; but it is fame of a peculiar kind, and indeed marvellously resembles infamy. We remember no other case in which the world has made so great a distinction between a book and its author. In general, the book and the author are considered as one. To admire the book is to admire the author. The case of Boswell is an exception, we think the only exception, to this rule. His work is universally allowed to be interesting, instructive, eminently original; yet it has brought him nothing but contempt. All the world reads it; all the world delights in it; yet we do not remember ever to have read or ever to have heard any expression of respect and admiration for the man to whom we owe so much instruction and amusement. While edition after edition of his book was coming forth, his son, as Mr. Croker tells us, was ashamed of it, and hated to hear it mentioned. This feeling was natural and reasonable. Sir Alexander saw that in proportion to the celebrity of the work was the degradation of the author. The very editors of this unfortunate gentleman's books have forgotten their allegiance, and, like those Puritan casuists who took arms by the authority of the king against his person, have attacked the writer while doing homage to the writings. Mr. Croker, for example, has published two thousand five hundred notes on the life of Johnson, and yet scarcely ever mentions the biographer whose performance he has taken such pains to illustrate, without some expression of contempt.

An ill-natured man Boswell certainly was not. Yet the malignity of the most malignant satirist could scarcely cut deeper than his thoughtless loquacity. Having himself no sensibility to derision and contempt, he took it for granted that all others were equally callous. He was not ashamed to exhibit himself to the whole world as a common spy, a common tattler, a humble companion without the excuse of poverty, and to tell a hundred stories of his own pertness and folly, and of the insults which his pertness and folly brought upon him. It was natural that he should show little discretion in cases in which the feelings or the honour of others might be concerned. No man, surely, ever published such stories respecting persons whom he professed to love and revere. He would infallibly have made his hero as contemptible as he has made himself, had not his hero really possessed some moral and intellectual qualities of a very high order. The best proof that Johnson was really an extraordinary man is that his character, instead of being degraded, has, on the whole, been decidedly raised by a work in which all his vices and weaknesses are exposed more unsparingly than they ever were exposed by Churchill or by Kenrick.

Johnson grown old, Johnson in the fulness of his fame and in the enjoyment of a competent fortune, is better known to us than any other man in history. Everything about him—his coat, his wig, his figure, his face, his scrofula, his St. Vitus's dance, his rolling walk, his blinking eye, the outward signs which too clearly marked his approbation of his dinner, his insatiable appetite for fish-sauce and veal-pie with plums, his inextinguishable thirst for tea, his trick of touching the posts as he walked, his mysterious practice of treasuring up scraps of orange-peel, his morning slumbers, his midnight disputations, his contortions, his mutterings, his gruntings, his puffings, his vigorous, acute, and ready eloquence, his sarcastic wit, his vehemence, his insolence, his fits of tempestuous rage, his queer inmates, old Mr. Levett and blind Mrs. Williams, the cat Hodge and the negro Frank—all are as familiar to us as the objects by which we have been surrounded from childhood. But we have no minute information respecting those years of Johnson's life during which his character and his manners became immutably fixed. We know him, not as he was known to the men of his own generation, but as he was known to men whose father he might have been. That celebrated club of which he was the most distinguished member contained few persons who could remember a time when his fame was not fully established and his habits completely formed. He had made himself a name in literature while Reynolds and the Wartons were still boys. He was about twenty years older than Burke, Goldsmith, and Gerard Hamilton; about thirty years older than Gibbon, Beauclerk, and Langton; and about forty years older than Lord Stowell, Sir William Jones, and Windham. Boswell and Mrs. Thrale, the two writers from whom we derive most of our knowledge respecting him, never saw him till long after he was fifty years old, till most of his great works had become classical, and till the pension bestowed on him by the Crown had placed him above poverty. Of those eminent men who were his most intimate associates towards the close of his life, the only one, as far as we remember, who knew him during the first ten or twelve years of his residence in the capital, was David Garrick; and it does not appear that, during those years, David Garrick saw much of his fellow-townsman.

Johnson came up to London precisely at the time when the condition of a man of letters was most miserable and degraded. It was a dark night between two sunny days. The age of patronage had passed away. The age of general curiosity and intelligence had not arrived. The number of readers is at present so great that a popular author may subsist in comfort and opulence on the profits of his works. In the reigns of William the Third, of Anne, and of George the First, even such men as Congreve and Addison would scarcely have been able to live like gentlemen by the mere sale of their writings. But the deficiency of the natural demand for literature was, at the close of the seventeenth and at the beginning of the eighteenth century, more than made up by artificial encouragement, by a vast system of bounties and premiums. There was, perhaps, never a time at which the rewards of literary merit were so splendid, at which men who could write well found such easy admittance into the most distinguished society, and to the highest honours of the State. The chiefs of both the great parties into which the kingdom was divided, patronized literature with emulous munificence. Congreve, when he had scarcely attained his majority, was rewarded for his first comedy with places which made him independent for life. Smith, though his *Hippolytus and Phædra* failed, would have been consoled with three hundred a year but for his own folly. Rowe was not only Poet Laureate, but also land-surveyor of the customs in the port of London, clerk of the council to the Prince of Wales, and secretary of the Presentations to the Lord Chancellor. Hughes was secretary to the Commissions of the Peace. Ambrose Philips was judge of the Prerogative Court in Ireland. Locke was Commissioner of Appeals and of the Board of Trade. Newton was Master of the Mint. Stepney and Prior were employed in embassies of high dignity and importance. Gay, who commenced life as apprentice to a silk mercer, became a secretary of legation at five-and-twenty. It was to a poem on the death of Charles the Second, and to the *City and Country Mouse,* that Montague owed his introduction into public life, his earldom, his garter, and his Auditorship of the Exchequer. Swift, but for the unconquerable prejudice of the queen, would have been a bishop. Oxford, with his white staff in his hand, passed through the crowd of his suitors to welcome Parnell, when that ingenious writer deserted the Whigs. Steele was a commissioner of stamps and a member of Parliament. Arthur Mainwaring was a commissioner of the customs, and auditor of the imprest. Tickell was secretary to the Lords Justices of Ireland. Addison was Secretary of State.

This liberal patronage was brought into fashion, as it seems, by the magnificent Dorset, almost the only noble versifier in the Court of Charles the Second who possessed talents for composition which were independent of the aid of a coronet. Montague owed his elevation to the favour of Dorset, and imitated through the whole course of his life the liberality to which he was himself so greatly indebted. The Tory leaders, Harley and Bolingbroke in particular, vied with the chiefs of the Whig party in zeal for the encouragement of letters. But soon after the accession of the House of Hanover a change took place. The supreme power passed to a man who cared little for poetry or eloquence. The importance of the House of Commons was constantly on the increase. The Government was under the necessity of bartering for Parliamentary support much of that patronage which had been employed in fostering literary merit; and Walpole was by no means inclined to divert any part of the fund of corruption to purposes which he considered as idle. He had eminent talents for government and for debate. But he had paid little attention to books, and felt little respect for authors. One of the coarse jokes of his friend, Sir Charles Hanbury Williams, was far more pleasing to him than Thomson's *Seasons* or Richardson's *Pamela*. He had observed that some of the distinguished writers whom the favour of Halifax had turned into statesmen had been mere incumbrances to their party, dawdlers in office and mutes in Parliament. During the whole course of his administration, therefore, he scarcely befriended a single man of genius. The best writers of the age gave all their support to the Opposition, and contributed to excite that discontent which, after plunging the nation into a foolish and unjust war, overthrew the Minister to make room for men less able and equally immoral. The Opposition could reward its eulogists with little more than promises and caresses. St. James's would give nothing: Leicester House had nothing to give.

Thus, at the time when Johnson commenced his literary career, a writer had little to hope from the patronage of powerful individuals. The patronage of the public did not yet furnish the means of comfortable subsistence. The prices paid by booksellers to authors were so low that a man of considerable talents and unremitting industry could do little more than provide for the day which was passing over him. The lean kine had eaten up the fat kine. The thin and withered ears had devoured the good ears. The season of rich harvest was over, and the period of famine had begun. All that is squalid and miserable might now be summed up in the word Poet. That word denoted a creature dressed like a scarecrow, familiar with compters and spunging-houses, and perfectly qualified to decide on the comparative merits of the Common Side in the King's Bench prison and of Mount Scoundrel in the Fleet. Even the poorest pitied him; and they well might pity him. For if their condition was equally abject, their aspirings were not equally high, nor their sense of insult equally acute. To lodge in a garret up four pair of stairs, to dine in a cellar among footmen out of place, to translate ten hours a day for the wages of a ditcher, to be hunted by bailiffs from one haunt of beggary and pestilence to another, from Grub Street to St. George's Fields, and from St. George's Fields to the alleys behind St. Martin's church, to sleep on a bulk in June and amidst the ashes of a glass-house in December, to die in an hospital, and to be buried in a parish vault, was the fate of more than one writer who, if he had lived thirty years earlier, would have been admitted to the sittings of the Kitcat or the Scriblerus Club, would have sat in Parliament, and would have been intrusted with embassies to the High Allies; who, if he had lived in our time, would have found encouragement scarcely less munificent in Albemarle Street or in Paternoster Row.

As every climate has its peculiar diseases, so every walk of life has its peculiar temptations. The literary character, assuredly, has always had its share of faults, vanity, jealousy, morbid sensibility. To these faults were now superadded the faults which are commonly found in men whose livelihood is precarious, and whose principles are exposed to the trial of severe distress. All the vices of the gambler and of the beggar were blended with those of the author. The prizes in the wretched lottery of book-making were scarcely less ruinous than the blanks. If good fortune came, it came in such a manner that it was almost certain to be abused. After months of starvation and despair, a full third night or a well-received dedication filled the pocket of the lean, ragged, unwashed poet with guineas. He hastened to enjoy those luxuries with the images of which his mind had been haunted while he was sleeping amidst the cinders and eating potatoes at the Irish ordinary in Shoe Lane. A week of taverns soon qualified him for another year of night-cellars. Such was the life of Savage, of Boyse, and of a crowd of others. Sometimes blazing in gold-laced hats and waistcoats; sometimes lying in bed because their coats had gone to pieces, or wearing paper cravats because their linen was in pawn; sometimes drinking champagne and Tokay with Betty Careless; sometimes standing at the window of an eatinghouse in Porridge island, to snuff up the scent of what they could not afford to taste; they knew luxury; they knew beggary; but they never knew comfort. These men were irreclaimable. They looked on a regular and frugal life with the same aversion which an old gipsy or a Mohawk hunter feels for a stationary abode, and for the restraints and securities of civilized communities. They were as untameable, as much wedded to their desolate freedom, as the wild ass. They could no more be broken in to the offices of social man than the unicorn could be trained to serve and abide by the crib. It was well if they did not, like beasts of a still fiercer race, tear the hands which ministered to their necessities. To assist them was impossible; and the most benevolent of mankind at length became weary of giving relief which was dissipated with the wildest profusion as soon as it had been received. If a sum was bestowed on the wretched adventurer, such as, properly husbanded, might have supplied him for six months, it was instantly spent in strange freaks of sensuality, and, before forty-eight hours had elapsed, the poet was again pestering all his acquaintance for twopence to get a plate of shin of beef at a subterraneous cookshop. If his friends gave him an asylum in their houses, those houses were forthwith turned into bagnios and taverns. All order was destroyed; all business was suspended. The most good-natured host began to repent of his eagerness to serve a man of genius in distress when he heard his guest roaring for fresh punch at five o'clock in the morning.

A few eminent writers were more fortunate. Pope had been raised above poverty by the active patronage which, in his youth, both the great political parties had extended to his Homer. Young had received the only pension ever bestowed, to the best of our recollection, by Sir Robert Walpole, as the reward of mere literary merit. One or two of the many poets who attached themselves to the Opposition, Thomson in particular and Mallet, obtained, after much severe suffering, the means of subsistence from their political friends. Richardson, like a man of sense, kept his shop, and his shop kept him, which his novels, admirable as they are, would scarcely have done. But nothing could be more deplorable than the state even of the ablest men, who at that time depended for subsistence on their writings. Johnson, Collins, Fielding, and Thomson were certainly four of the most distinguished persons that England produced during the eighteenth century: it is well known that they were all four arrested for debt.

Into calamities and difficulties such as these Johnson plunged in his twenty-eighth year. From that time till he was three or four and fifty, we have little information respecting him; little, we mean, compared with the full and accurate information which we possess respecting his proceedings and habits towards the close of his life. He emerged at length from cocklofts and sixpenny ordinaries into the society of the polished and the opulent. His fame was established. A pension sufficient for his wants had been conferred on him; and he came forth to astonish a generation with which he had almost as little in common as with Frenchmen or Spaniards.

In his early years he had occasionally seen the great; but he had seen them as a beggar. He now came among them as a companion. The demand for amusement and instruction had, during the course of twenty years, been gradually increasing. The price of literary labour had risen; and those rising men of letters with whom

Johnson was henceforth to associate were for the most part persons widely different from those who had walked about with him all night in the streets for want of a lodging. Burke, Robertson, the Wartons, Gray, Mason, Gibbon, Adam Smith, Beattie, Sir William Jones, Goldsmith, and Churchill were the most distinguished writers of what may be called the second generation of the Johnsonian age. Of these men Churchill was the only one in whom we can trace the stronger lineaments of that character which, when Johnson first came up to London, was common among authors. Of the rest, scarcely any had felt the pressure of severe poverty. Almost all had been early admitted into the most respectable society on an equal footing. They were men of quite a different species from the dependants of Curll and Osborne.

Johnson came among them the solitary specimen of a past age, the last survivor of the genuine race of Grub Street hacks; the last of that generation of authors whose abject misery and whose dissolute manners had furnished inexhaustible matter to the satirical genius of Pope. From nature he had received an uncouth figure, a diseased constitution, and an irritable temper. The manner in which the earlier years of his manhood had been passed had given to his demeanour, and even to his moral character, some peculiarities appalling to the civilized beings who were the companions of his old age. The perverse irregularity of his hours, the slovenliness of his person, his fits of strenuous exertion, interrupted by long intervals of sluggishness, his strange abstinence and his equally strange voracity, his active benevolence, contrasted with the constant rudeness and the occasional ferocity of his manners in society, made him, in the opinion of those with whom he lived during the last twenty years of his life, a complete original. An original he was, undoubtedly, in some respects. But if we possessed full information concerning those who shared his early hardships, we should probably find that what we call his singularities of manner were, for the most part, failings which he had in common with the class to which he belonged. He ate at Streatham Park as he had been used to eat behind the screen at St. John's Gate, when he was ashamed to show his ragged clothes. He ate as it was natural that a man should eat, who, during a great part of his life, had passed the morning in doubt whether he should have food for the afternoon. The habits of his early life had accustomed him to bear privation with fortitude, but not to taste pleasure with moderation. He could fast; but, when he did not fast, he tore his dinner like a famished wolf, with the veins swelling on his forehead, and the perspiration running down his cheeks. He scarcely ever took wine; but when he drank it, he drank it greedily and in large tumblers. These were, in fact, mitigated symptoms of that same moral disease which raged with such deadly malignity in his friends Savage and Boyse. The roughness and violence which he showed in society were to be expected from a man whose temper, not naturally gentle, had been long tried by the bitterest calamities, by the want of meat, of fire, and of clothes, by the importunity of creditors, by the insolence of booksellers, by the derision of fools, by the insincerity of patrons, by that bread which is the bitterest of all food, by those stairs which are the most toilsome of all paths, by that deferred hope which makes the heart sick. Through all these things the ill-dressed, coarse, ungainly pedant had struggled manfully up to eminence and command. It was natural that, in the exercise of his power, he should be *"eo immitior, quia toleraverat,"* [1] that, though his heart was undoubtedly generous and humane, his demeanour in society should be harsh and despotic. For severe distress he had sympathy, and not only sympathy, but munificent relief; but for the suffering which a harsh word inflicts upon a delicate mind he had no pity; for it was a kind of suffering which he could scarcely conceive. He would carry home on his shoulders a sick and starving girl from the streets. He turned his house into a place of refuge for a crowd of wretched old creatures who could find no other asylum; nor could all their peevishness and ingratitude weary out his benevolence.

[1] *eo immitior, quia toleraverat:* "all the more pitiless because he has endured" (Tacitus, *Annals*, I, 20).

But the pangs of wounded vanity seemed to him ridiculous; and he scarcely felt sufficient compassion even for the pangs of wounded affection. He had seen and felt so much of sharp misery, that he was not affected by paltry vexations; and he seemed to think that everybody ought to be as much hardened to those vexations as himself. He was angry with Boswell for complaining of a headache, with Mrs. Thrale for grumbling about the dust on the road, or the smell of the kitchen. These were, in his phrase, "foppish lamentations," which people ought to be ashamed to utter in a world so full of sin and sorrow. Goldsmith crying because *The Good-natured Man* had failed, inspired him with no pity. Though his own health was not good, he detested and despised valetudinarians. Pecuniary losses, unless they reduced the loser absolutely to beggary, moved him very little. People whose hearts had been softened by prosperity might weep, he said, for such events; but all that could be expected of a plain man was not to laugh. He was not much moved even by the spectacle of Lady Tavistock dying of a broken heart for the loss of her lord. Such grief he considered as a luxury reserved for the idle and the wealthy. A washer-woman, left a widow with nine small children, would not have sobbed herself to death.

A person who troubled himself so little about small or sentimental grievances was not likely to be very attentive to the feelings of others in the ordinary intercourse of society. He could not understand how a sarcasm or a reprimand could make any man really unhappy. "My dear doctor," said he to Goldsmith, "what harm does it do to a man to call him Holofernes?" "Pooh, ma'am," he exclaimed to Mrs. Carter, "who is the worse for being talked of uncharitably?" Politeness has been well defined as benevolence in small things. Johnson was impolite, not because he wanted benevolence, but because small things appeared smaller to him than to people who had never known what it was to live for fourpence halfpenny a day.

The characteristic peculiarity of his intellect was the union of great powers with low prejudices. If we judged of him by the best parts of his mind, we should place him almost as high as he was placed by the idolatry of Boswell; if by the worst parts of his mind, we should place him even below Boswell himself. Where he was not under the influence of some strange scruple or some domineering passion, which prevented him from boldly and fairly investigating a subject, he was a wary and acute reasoner, a little too much 10 inclined to scepticism, and a little too fond of paradox. No man was less likely to be imposed upon by fallacies in argument or by exaggerated statements of fact. But if, while he was beating down sophisms and exposing false testimony, some childish prejudices, such as would excite laughter in a well-managed nursery, came across him, he was smitten as if by enchantment. His mind dwindled away under the spell 20 from gigantic elevation to dwarfish littleness. Those who had lately been admiring its amplitude and its force were now as much astonished at its strange narrowness and feebleness as the fisherman in the Arabian tale, when he saw the Genie, whose stature had overshadowed the whole seacoast, and whose might seemed equal to a contest with armies, contract himself to the dimensions of his small prison, and lie 30 there the helpless slave of the charm of Solomon.

Johnson was in the habit of sifting with extreme severity the evidence for all stories which were merely odd. But when they were not only odd but miraculous, his severity relaxed. He began to be credulous precisely at the point where the most credulous people begin to be sceptical. It is curious to observe, both in his writings 40 and in his conversation, the contrast between the disdainful manner in which he rejects unauthenticated anecdotes, even when they are consistent with the general laws of nature, and the respectful manner in which he mentions the wildest stories relating to the invisible world. A man who told him of a water-spout or a meteoric stone generally had the lie direct given him for his pains. A man who told him of 50 a prediction or a dream wonderfully accomplished was sure of a courteous hearing. "Johnson," observed Hogarth, "like King David, says in his haste that all men are

liars." "His incredulity," says Mrs. Thrale, "amounted almost to disease." She tells us how he browbeat a gentleman who gave him an account of a hurricane in the West Indies, and a poor Quaker who related some strange circumstance about the redhot balls fired at the siege of Gibraltar. "It is not so. It cannot be true. Don't tell that story again. You cannot think how poor a figure you make in telling it." He once said, half jestingly, we suppose, that for six months he refused to credit the fact of the earthquake at Lisbon, and that he still believed the extent of the calamity to be greatly exaggerated. Yet he related with a grave face how old Mr. Cave of St. John's Gate saw a ghost, and how this ghost was something of a shadowy being. He went himself on a ghost-hunt to Cock Lane, and was angry with John Wesley for not following up another scent of the same kind with proper spirit and perseverance. He rejects the Celtic genealogies and poems without the least hesitation; yet he declares himself willing to believe the stories of the second-sight. If he had examined the claims of the Highland seers with half the severity with which he sifted the evidence for the genuineness of *Fingal,* he would, we suspect, have come away from Scotland with a mind fully made up. In his *Lives of the Poets,* we find that he is unwilling to give credit to the accounts of Lord Roscommon's early proficiency in his studies; but he tells with great solemnity an absurd romance about some intelligence preternaturally impressed on the mind of that nobleman. He avows himself to be in great doubt about the truth of the story, and ends by warning his readers not wholly to slight such impressions.

Many of his sentiments on religious subjects are worthy of a liberal and enlarged mind. He could discern clearly enough the folly and meanness of all bigotry except his own. When he spoke of the scruples of the Puritans, he spoke like a person who had really obtained an insight into the divine philosophy of the New Testament, and who considered Christianity as a noble scheme of government, tending to promote the happiness and to elevate the moral nature of man. The horror which the sectaries felt for cards, Christmas ale, plum-porridge, mince-pies, and dancing bears, excited his contempt. To the arguments urged by some very worthy people against showy dress he replied with admirable sense and spirit, "Let us not be found, when our Master calls us, stripping the lace off our waist-coats, but the spirit of contention from our souls and tongues. Alas! sir, a man who cannot get to heaven in a green coat will not find his way thither the sooner in a grey one." Yet he was himself under the tyranny of scruples as unreasonable as those of Hudibras or Ralpho, and carried his zeal for ceremonies and for ecclesiastical dignities to lengths altogether inconsistent with reason or with Christian charity. He has gravely noted down in his diary that he once committed the sin of drinking coffee on Good Friday. In Scotland, he thought it his duty to pass several months without joining in public worship, solely because the ministers of the Kirk had not been ordained by bishops. His mode of estimating the piety of his neighbours was somewhat singular. "Campbell," said he, "is a good man, a pious man. I am afraid he has not been in the inside of a church for many years; but he never passes a church without pulling off his hat: this shows he has good principles." Spain and Sicily must surely contain many pious robbers and well-principled assassins. Johnson could easily see that a Roundhead who named all his children after Solomon's singers, and talked in the House of Commons about seeking the Lord, might be an unprincipled villain whose religious mummeries only aggravated his guilt. But a man who took off his hat when he passed a church episcopally consecrated must be a good man, a pious man, a man of good principles. Johnson could easily see that those persons who looked on a dance or a laced waistcoat as sinful, deemed most ignobly of the attributes of God and of the ends of revelation. But with what a storm of invective he would have overwhelmed any man who had blamed him for celebrating the redemption of mankind with sugarless tea and butterless buns!

Nobody spoke more contemptuously of the cant of patriotism. Nobody saw more clearly the error of those who regarded liberty, not as a means, but as an end, and who proposed to themselves, as the object of their pursuit, the prosperity of the State as distinct from the prosperity of the individuals who compose the State. His calm and settled opinion seems to have been that forms of government have little or no influence on the happiness of society. This opinion, erroneous as it is, ought at least to have preserved him from all intemperance on political questions. It did not, however, preserve him from the lowest, fiercest, and most absurd extravagances of party spirit, from rants which, in everything but the diction, resembled those of Squire Western. He was, as a politician, half ice and half fire. On the side of his intellect he was a mere Pococurante,[2] far too apathetic about public affairs, far too sceptical as to the good or evil tendency of any form of polity. His passions, on the contrary, were violent even to slaying against all who leaned to Whiggish principles. The well-known lines which he inserted in Goldsmith's *Traveller* express what seems to have been his deliberate judgment:

How small, of all that human hearts endure,
That part which kings or laws can cause or
cure!

He had previously put expressions very similar into the mouth of Rasselas. It is amusing to contrast these passages with the torrents of raving abuse which he poured forth against the Long Parliament and the American Congress. In one of the conversations reported by Boswell this inconsistency displays itself in the most ludicrous manner.

"Sir Adam Ferguson," says Boswell, "suggested that luxury corrupts a people, and destroys the spirit of liberty. JOHNSON: 'Sir, that is all visionary. I would not give half a guinea to live under one form of government rather than another. It is of no moment to the happiness of an individual. Sir, the danger of the abuse of power is nothing to a private man. What Frenchman is prevented passing his life as he pleases?' SIR ADAM: 'But, sir, in the

---

[2] Pococurante: a nonchalant character in Voltaire's *Candide;* the name is Italian, poco curante, 'caring little.'

British constitution it is surely of importance to keep up a spirit in the people, so as to preserve a balance against the Crown.' JOHNSON: 'Sir, I perceive you are a vile Whig. Why all this childish jealousy of the power of the Crown? The Crown has not power enough.' "

One of the old philosophers, Lord Bacon tells us, used to say that life and death were just the same to him. "Why, then," said an objector, "do you not kill yourself?" The philosopher answered, "Because it is just the same." If the difference between two forms of government be not worth half a guinea, it is not easy to see how Whiggism can be viler than Toryism, or how the Crown can have too little power. If the happiness of individuals is not affected by political abuses, zeal for liberty is doubtless ridiculous. But zeal for monarchy must be equally so. No person could have been more quick-sighted than Johnson to such a contradiction as this in the logic of an antagonist.

The judgments which Johnson passed on books were, in his own time, regarded with superstitious veneration, and, in our time, are generally treated with indiscriminate contempt. They are the judgments of a strong but enslaved understanding. The mind of the critic was hedged round by an uninterrupted fence of prejudices and superstitions. Within his narrow limits, he displayed a vigour and an activity which ought to have enabled him to clear the barrier that confined him.

How it chanced that a man who reasoned on his premises so ably, should assume his premises so foolishly, is one of the great mysteries of human nature. The same inconsistency may be observed in the schoolmen of the Middle Ages. Those writers show so much acuteness and force of mind in arguing on their wretched data, that a modern reader is perpetually at a loss to comprehend how such minds came by such data. Not a flaw in the superstructure of the theory which they are rearing escapes their vigilance. Yet they are blind to the obvious unsoundness of the foundation. It is the same with some eminent lawyers. Their legal arguments are intellectual prodigies, abounding with the happiest analogies and the most refined distinctions. The principles of their arbitrary science being once admitted, the statute-book and the reports being once assumed as the foundations of reasoning, these men must be allowed to be perfect masters of logic. But if a question arises as to the postulates on which their whole system rests, if they are called upon to vindicate the fundamental maxims of that system which they have passed their lives in studying, these very men often talk the language of savages or of children. Those who have listened to a man of this class in his own court, and who have witnessed the skill with which he analyzes and digests a vast mass of evidence, or reconciles a crowd of precedents which at first sight seem contradictory, scarcely know him again when, a few hours later, they hear him speaking on the other side of Westminster Hall in his capacity of legislator. They can scarcely believe that the paltry quirks which are faintly heard through a storm of coughing, and which do not impose on the plainest country gentleman, can proceed from the same sharp and vigorous intellect which had excited their admiration under the same roof, and on the same day.

Johnson decided literary questions like a lawyer, not like a legislator. He never examined foundations where a point was already ruled. His whole code of criticism rested on pure assumption, for which he sometimes quoted a precedent or an authority, but rarely troubled himself to give a reason drawn from the nature of things. He took it for granted that the kind of poetry which flourished in his own time, which he had been accustomed to hear praised from his childhood, and which he had himself written with success, was the best kind of poetry. In his biographical work he has repeatedly laid it down as an undeniable proposition that during the latter part of the seventeenth century, and the earlier part of the eighteenth, English poetry had been in a constant progress of improvement. Waller, Denham, Dryden, and Pope had been, according to him, the great reformers. He judged of all works of the imagination by the standard established among his own contemporaries. Though he allowed Homer to have been a greater man than Virgil, he seems to have thought the *Æneid* a greater poem than the *Iliad*. Indeed, he well might have thought so, for he preferred Pope's *Iliad* to Homer's. He pronounced that, after Hoole's translation of Tasso, Fairfax's would hardly be reprinted. He could see no merit in our fine old English ballads, and always spoke with the most provoking contempt of Percy's fondness for them. Of the great original works of imagination which appeared during his time, Richardson's novels alone excited his admiration. He could see little or no merit in *Tom Jones*, in *Gulliver's Travels*, or in *Tristram Shandy*. To Thomson's *Castle of Indolence* he vouchsafed only a line of cold commendation—of commendation much colder than what he has bestowed on the *Creation* of that portentous bore, Sir Richard Blackmore. Gray was, in his dialect, a barren rascal. Churchill was a blockhead. The contempt which he felt for the trash of Macpherson was indeed just; but it was, we suspect, just by chance. He despised the *Fingal* for the very reason which led many men of genius to admire it. He despised it, not because it was essentially commonplace, but because it had a superficial air of originality.

He was undoubtedly an excellent judge of compositions fashioned on his own principles; but when a deeper philosophy was required, when he undertook to pronounce judgment on the works of those great minds which "yield homage only to eternal laws," his failure was ignominious. He criticized Pope's *Epitaphs* excellently; but his observations on Shakspeare's plays and Milton's poems seem to us for the most part as wretched as if they had been written by Rymer himself, whom we take to have been the worst critic that ever lived.

Some of Johnson's whims on literary subjects can be compared only to that strange nervous feeling which made him uneasy if he had not touched every post between the Mitre tavern and his own lodgings. His preference of Latin epitaphs to English epitaphs, he said, would disgrace Smollett. He declared that he would not pollute the walls of Westminster Abbey with an English epitaph on Goldsmith.

What reason there can be for celebrating a British writer in Latin, which there was not for covering the Roman arches of triumph with Greek inscriptions, or for commemorating the deeds of the heroes of Thermopylæ in Egyptian hieroglyphics, we are utterly unable to imagine.

On men and manners, at least on the men and manners of a particular place and a particular age, Johnson had certainly looked with a most observant and discriminating eye. His remarks on the education of children, on marriage, on the economy of families, on the rules of society, are always striking, and generally sound. In his writings, indeed, the knowledge of life which he possessed in an eminent degree is very imperfectly exhibited. Like those unfortunate chiefs of the Middle Ages who were suffocated by their own chain-mail and cloth of gold, his maxims perish under that load of words which was designed for their defence and their ornament. But it is clear from the remains of his conversation that he had more of that homely wisdom which nothing but experience and observation can give than any writer since the time of Swift. If he had been content to write as he talked, he might have left books on the practical art of living superior to the *Directions to Servants*.

Yet even his remarks on society, like his remarks on literature, indicate a mind at least as remarkable for narrowness as for strength. He was no master of the great science of human nature. He had studied, not the genus man, but the species Londoner. Nobody was ever so thoroughly conversant with all the forms of life and all the shades of moral and intellectual character which were to be seen from Islington to the Thames, and from Hyde Park Corner to Mile-End Green. But his philosophy stopped at the first turnpike-gate. Of the rural life of England he knew nothing; and he took it for granted that everybody who lived in the country was either stupid or miserable. "Country gentlemen," said he, "must be unhappy; for they have not enough to keep their lives in motion"; as if all those peculiar habits and associations which made Fleet Street and Charing Cross the finest views in the world to himself had been essential parts of human nature. Of remote countries and past times he talked with wild and ignorant presumption. "The Athenians of the age of Demosthenes," he said to Mrs. Thrale, "were a people of brutes, a barbarous people." In conversation with Sir Adam Ferguson he used similar language. "The boasted Athenians," he said, "were barbarians. The mass of every people must be barbarous where there is 10 no printing." The fact was this: he saw that a Londoner who could not read was a very stupid and brutal fellow: he saw that great refinement of taste and activity of intellect were rarely found in a Londoner who had not read much; and because it was by means of books that people acquired almost all their knowledge in the society with which he was acquainted, he concluded, in defiance of the strongest and 20 clearest evidence, that the human mind can be cultivated by means of books alone. An Athenian citizen might possess very few volumes; and the largest library to which he had access might be much less valuable than Johnson's bookcase in Bolt Court; but the Athenian might pass every morning in conversation with Socrates, and might hear Pericles speak four or five times every month. He saw the plays of 30 Sophocles and Aristophanes; he walked amidst the friezes of Phidias and the paintings of Zeuxis; he knew by heart the choruses of Æschylus; he heard the rhapsodist at the corner of the streets reciting the *Shield of Achilles* or the *Death of Argus;* he was a legislator, conversant with high questions of alliance, revenue, and war; he was a soldier, trained under a liberal and generous discipline; he was a 40 judge compelled every day to weigh the effect of opposite arguments. These things were in themselves an education—an education eminently fitted, not, indeed, to form exact or profound thinkers, but to give quickness to the perceptions, delicacy to the taste, fluency to the expression, and politeness to the manners. All this was overlooked. An Athenian who did not improve his mind by reading was, in John- 50 son's opinion, much such a person as a Cockney who made his mark, much such a person as black Frank before he went to

school, and far inferior to a parish clerk or a printer's devil.

Johnson's friends have allowed that he carried to a ridiculous extreme his unjust contempt for foreigners. He pronounced the French to be a very silly people, much behind us, stupid, ignorant creatures. And this judgment he formed after having been at Paris about a month, during which he would not talk French, for fear of giving the natives an advantage over him in conversation. He pronounced them, also, to be an indelicate people, because a French footman touched the sugar with his fingers. That ingenious and amusing traveller, M. Simond, has defended his countrymen very successfully against Johnson's accusations, and has pointed out some English practices which, to an impartial spectator, would 20 seem at least as inconsistent with physical cleanliness and social decorum as those which Johnson so bitterly reprehended. To the sage, as Boswell loves to call him, it never occurred to doubt that there must be something eternally and immutably good in the usages to which he had been accustomed. In fact, Johnson's remarks on society beyond the bills of mortality are generally of much the same kind with those 30 of honest Tom Dawson, the English footman in Dr. Moore's *Zeluco*. "Suppose the King of France has no sons, but only a daughter; then, when the king dies, this here daughter, according to that there law, cannot be made queen, but the next near relative, provided he is a man, is made king, and not the last king's daughter, which, to be sure, is very unjust. The French footguards are dressed in blue, and 40 all the marching regiments in white, which has a very foolish appearance for soldiers; and as for blue regimentals, it is only fit for the blue horse or the artillery."

Johnson's visit to the Hebrides introduced him to a state of society completely new to him; and a salutary suspicion of his own deficiencies seems on that occasion to have crossed his mind for the first time. He confessed, in the last paragraph of his 50 *Journey*, that his thoughts on national manners were the thoughts of one who had seen but little, of one who had passed his time almost wholly in cities. This feeling, however, soon passed away. It is remarkable that to the last he entertained a fixed contempt for all those modes of life and those studies which tend to emancipate the mind from the prejudices of a particular age or a particular nation. Of foreign travel and of history he spoke with the fierce and boisterous contempt of ignorance. "What does a man learn by travelling? Is Beauclerk the better for travelling? What did Lord Charlemont learn in his travels, except that there was a snake in one of the pyramids of Egypt?" History was, in his opinion, to use the fine expression of Lord Plunkett, an old almanack: historians could, as he conceived, claim no higher dignity than that of almanack-makers; and his favourite historians were those who, like Lord Hailes, aspired to no higher dignity. He always spoke with contempt of Robertson. Hume he would not even read. He affronted one of his friends for talking to him about Catiline's conspiracy, and declared that he never desired to hear of the Punic war again as long as he lived.

Assuredly one fact which does not directly affect our own interests, considered in itself, is no better worth knowing than another fact. The fact that there is a snake in a pyramid, or the fact that Hannibal crossed the Alps, are in themselves as unprofitable to us as the fact that there is a green blind in a particular house in Threadneedle Street, or the fact that a Mr. Smith comes into the city every morning on the top of one of the Blackwall stages. But it is certain that those who will not crack the shell of history will never get at the kernel. Johnson, with hasty arrogance, pronounced the kernel worthless, because he saw no value in the shell. The real use of travelling to distant countries and of studying the annals of past times is to preserve men from the contraction of mind which those can hardly escape whose whole communion is with one generation and one neighbourhood, who arrive at conclusions by means of an induction not sufficiently copious, and who therefore constantly confound exceptions with rules, and accidents with essential properties. In short, the real use of travelling and of studying history is to keep men from being what Tom Dawson was in fiction, and Samuel Johnson in reality.

Johnson, as Mr. Burke most justly observed, appears far greater in Boswell's books than in his own. His conversation appears to have been quite equal to his writings in matter, and far superior to them in manner. When he talked, he clothed his wit and his sense in forcible and natural expressions. As soon as he took his pen in his hand to write for the public, his style became systematically vicious. All his books are written in a learned language—in a language which nobody hears from his mother or his nurse; in a language in which nobody ever quarrels, or drives bargains, or makes love; in a language in which nobody ever thinks. It is clear that Johnson himself did not think in the dialect in which he wrote. The expressions which came first to his tongue were simple, energetic, and picturesque. When he wrote for publication, he did his sentences out of English into Johnsonese. His letters from the Hebrides to Mrs. Thrale are the original of that work of which the *Journey to the Hebrides* is the translation; and it is amusing to compare the two versions. "When we were taken up-stairs," says he in one of his letters, "a dirty fellow bounced out of the bed on which one of us was to lie." This incident is recorded in the *Journey* as follows: "Out of one of the beds on which we were to repose started up, at our entrance, a man black as a Cyclops from the forge." Sometimes Johnson translated aloud. "*The Rehearsal*," he said, very unjustly, "has not wit enough to keep it sweet"; then, after a pause, "it has not vitality enough to preserve it from putrefaction."

Mannerism is pardonable, and is sometimes even agreeable, when the manner, though vicious, is natural. Few readers, for example, would be willing to part with the mannerism of Milton or of Burke. But a mannerism which does not sit easy on the mannerist, which has been adopted on principle, and which can be sustained only by constant effort, is always offensive. And such is the mannerism of Johnson.

The characteristic faults of his style are

so familiar to all our readers, and have been so often burlesqued, that it is almost superfluous to point them out. It is well known that he made less use than any other eminent writer of those strong plain words, Anglo-Saxon or Norman-French, of which the roots lie in the inmost depths of our language; and that he felt a vicious partiality for terms which, long after our own speech had been fixed, were borrowed from the Greek and Latin, and which, therefore, even when lawfully naturalized, must be considered as born aliens, not entitled to rank with the king's English. His constant practice of padding out a sentence with useless epithets till it became as stiff as the bust of an exquisite; his antithetical forms of expression, constantly employed even where there is no opposition in the ideas expressed; his big words wasted on little things; his harsh inversions, so widely different from those graceful and easy inversions which give variety, spirit, and sweetness to the expression of our great old writers; all these peculiarities have been imitated by his admirers and parodied by his assailants, till the public have become sick of the subject.

Goldsmith said to him, very wittily and very justly, "If you were to write a fable about little fishes, doctor, you would make the little fishes talk like whales." No man surely ever had so little talent for personation as Johnson. Whether he wrote in the character of a disappointed legacy-hunter or an empty town fop, of a crazy virtuoso or a flippant coquette, he wrote in the same pompous and unbending style. His speech, like Sir Piercy Shafton's Euphuistic eloquence, bewrayed him under every disguise. Euphelia and Rhodoclea talk as finely as Imlac the poet, or Seged, Emperor of Ethiopia. The gay Cornelia describes her reception at the country-house of her relations in such terms as these: "I was surprised, after the civilities of my first reception, to find, instead of the leisure and tranquillity which a rural life always promises, and, if well conducted, might always afford, a confused wildness of care, and a tumultuous hurry of diligence, by which every face was clouded and every motion agitated." The gentle Tranquilla informs us that she "had not passed the

earlier part of life without the flattery of courtship and the joys of triumph; but had danced the round of gaiety amidst the murmurs of envy and the gratulations of applause; had been attended from pleasure to pleasure by the great, the sprightly, and the vain; and had seen her regard solicited by the obsequiousness of gallantry, the gaiety of wit, and the timidity of love." Surely Sir John Falstaff himself did not wear his petticoats with a worse grace. The reader may well cry out with honest Sir Hugh Evans, "I like not when a 'oman has a great peard: I spy a great peard under her muffler."

We had something more to say; but our article is already too long, and we must close it. We would fain part in good humour from the hero, from the biographer, and even from the editor, who, ill as he has performed his task, has at least this claim to our gratitude, that he has induced us to read Boswell's book again. As we close it, the club-room is before us, and the table on which stands the omelet for Nugent and the lemons for Johnson. There are assembled those heads which live for ever on the canvas of Reynolds. There are the spectacles of Burke and the tall thin form of Langton, the courtly sneer of Beauclerk and the beaming smile of Garrick, Gibbon tapping his snuffbox and Sir Joshua with his trumpet in his ear. In the foreground is that strange figure which is as familiar to us as the figures of those among whom we have been brought up, the gigantic body, the huge massy face, seamed with the scars of disease, the brown coat, the black worsted stockings, the grey wig with the scorched foretop, the dirty hands, the nails bitten and pared to the quick. We see the eyes and mouth moving with convulsive twitches; we see the heavy form rolling; we hear it puffing; and then comes the "Why, sir!" and the "What then, sir?" and the "No, sir!" and the "You don't see your way through the question, sir!"

What a singular destiny has been that of this remarkable man! To be regarded in his own age as a classic, and in ours as a companion. To receive from his contemporaries that full homage which men of genius have in general received only from posterity! To be more intimately known to posterity than other men are known to their contemporaries! That kind of fame which is commonly the most transient is, in his case, the most durable. The reputation of those writings which he probably expected to be immortal is every day fading; while those peculiarities of manner and that careless table-talk, the memory of which, he probably thought, would die with him, are likely to be remembered as long as the English language is spoken in any quarter of the globe.

[1831]

MOORE'S LIFE OF LORD BYRON

We have read this book with the greatest pleasure. Considered merely as a composition, it deserves to be classed among the best specimens of English prose which our age has produced. It contains, indeed, no single passage equal to two or three which we could select from the *Life of Sheridan*. But, as a whole, it is immeasurably superior to that work. The style is agreeable, clear, and manly, and when it rises into elo- 10 quence, rises without effort or ostentation. Nor is the matter inferior to the manner. It would be difficult to name a book which exhibits more kindness, fairness, and modesty. It has evidently been written, not for the purpose of showing, what, however, it often shows, how well its author can write, but for the purpose of vindicating, as far as truth will permit, the memory of a celebrated man who can no longer vin- 20 dicate himself. Mr. Moore never thrusts himself between Lord Byron and the public. With the strongest temptations to egotism, he has said no more about himself than the subject absolutely required.

A great part, indeed the greater part, of these volumes, consists of extracts from the Letters and Journals of Lord Byron; and it is difficult to speak too highly of the skill which has been shown in the selection 30 and arrangements. We will not say that we have not occasionally remarked in these two large quartos an anecdote which should have been omitted, a letter which should have been suppressed, a name which should have been concealed by asterisks, or asterisks which do not answer the purpose of concealing the name. But it is impossible, on a general survey, to deny that the task has been executed with 40 great judgment and great humanity. When we consider the life which Lord Byron had led, his petulance, his irritability, and his communicativeness, we cannot but admire the dexterity with which Mr. Moore has contrived to exhibit so much of the character and opinions of his friend, with so little pain to the feelings of the living.

The extracts from the journals and correspondence of Lord Byron are in the highest degree valuable, not merely on account of the information which they contain respecting the distinguished man by whom they were written, but on account also of their rare merit as compositions. The letters, at least those which were sent from Italy, are among the best in our language. They are less affected than those of Pope and Walpole; they have more matter in them than those of Cowper. Knowing that many of them were not written merely for the person to whom they were directed, but were general epistles, meant to be read by a large circle, we expected to find them clever and spirited, but deficient in ease. We looked with vigilance for instances of stiffness in the language and awkwardness in the transitions. We have been agreeably disappointed; and we must confess that, if the epistolary style of Lord Byron was artificial, it was a rare and admirable instance of that highest art which cannot be distinguished from nature.

Of the deep and painful interest which this book excites no abstract can give a just notion. So sad and dark a story is scarcely to be found in any work of fiction; and we are little disposed to envy the moralist who can read it without being softened.

The pretty fable by which the Duchess of Orleans illustrated the character of her son the Regent might, with little change, be applied to Byron. All the fairies, save one, had been bidden to his cradle. All the gossips had been profuse of their gifts. One had bestowed nobility, another genius, a third beauty. The malignant elf who had been uninvited came last, and, unable to reverse what her sisters had done for their favourite, had mixed up a curse with every blessing. In the rank of Lord Byron, in his understanding, in his character, in his very person, there was a strange union of opposite extremes. He was born to all that men covet and admire. But in every one of those eminent advantages which he possessed over others was mingled something of misery and debasement. He was sprung from a house, ancient indeed and noble, but degraded and impoverished by a series of crimes and follies which had attained a scandalous publicity. The kinsman whom he succeeded had died poor, and, but for merciful judges, would have died upon the gallows. The young peer had great intellectual powers; yet there was an unsound part in his mind. He had naturally a generous and feeling heart: but his temper was wayward and irritable. He had a head which statuaries loved to copy, and a foot the deformity of which the beggars in the streets mimicked. Distinguished at once by the strength and by the weakness of his intellect, affectionate yet perverse, a poor lord, and a handsome cripple, he required, if ever man required, the firmest and the most judicious training. But, capriciously as nature had dealt with him, the parent to whom the office of forming his character was intrusted was more capricious still. She passed from paroxysms of rage to paroxysms of tenderness. At one time she stifled him with her caresses; at another time she insulted his deformity. He came into the world; and the world treated him as his mother had treated him, sometimes with fondness, sometimes with cruelty, never with justice. It indulged him without discrimination, and punished him without discrimination. He was truly a spoiled child, not merely the spoiled child of his parent, but the spoiled child of nature, the spoiled child of fortune, the spoiled child of fame, the spoiled child of society. His first poems were received with a contempt which, feeble as they were, they did not absolutely deserve. The poem which he published on his return from his travels was, on the other hand, extolled far above

its merit. At twenty-four, he found himself on the highest pinnacle of literary fame, with Scott, Wordsworth, Southey, and a crowd of other distinguished writers beneath his feet. There is scarcely an instance in history of so sudden a rise to so dizzy an eminence.

Everything that could stimulate, and everything that could gratify the strongest propensities of our nature, the gaze of a hundred drawing-rooms, the acclamations of the whole nation, the applause of applauded men, the love of lovely women, all this world and all the glory of it were at once offered to a youth to whom nature had given violent passions, and whom education had never taught to control them. He lived as many men live who have no similar excuse to plead for their faults. But his countrymen and his countrywomen would love him and admire him. They were resolved to see in his excesses only the flash and outbreak of that same fiery mind which glowed in his poetry. He attacked religion; yet in religious circles his name was mentioned with fondness, and in many religious publications his works were censured with singular tenderness. He lampooned the Prince Regent; yet he could not alienate the Tories. Everything, it seemed, was to be forgiven to youth, rank, and genius.

Then came the reaction. Society, capricious in its indignation as it had been capricious in its fondness, flew into a rage with its froward and petted darling. He had been worshipped with an irrational idolatry. He was persecuted with an irrational fury. Much has been written about those unhappy domestic occurrences which decided the fate of his life. Yet nothing is, nothing ever was, positively known to the public, but this, that he quarrelled with his lady, and that she refused to live with him. There have been hints in abundance, and shrugs and shakings of the head, and "Well, well, we know," and "We could an if we would," and "If we list to speak," and "There be that might an they list." But we are not aware that there is before the world substantiated by credible, or even by tangible evidence, a single fact indicating that Lord Byron was more to blame than any other man who is on bad terms with his wife. The professional men whom Lady Byron consulted were undoubtedly of opinion that she ought not to live with her husband. But it is to be remembered that they formed that opinion without hearing both sides. We do not say, we do not mean to insinuate, that Lady Byron was in any respect to blame. We think that those who condemn her on the evidence which is now before the public are as rash as those who condemn her husband. We will not pronounce any judgment, we cannot, even in our own minds, form any judgment, on a transaction which is so imperfectly known to us. It would have been well if, at the time of the separation, all those who knew as little about the matter then as we know about it now, had shown that forbearance which, under such circumstances, is but common justice.

We know no spectacle so ridiculous as the British public in one of its periodical fits of morality. In general, elopements, divorces, and family quarrels, pass with little notice. We read the scandal, talk about it for a day, and forget it. But once in six or seven years our virtue becomes outrageous. We cannot suffer the laws of religion and decency to be violated. We must make a stand against vice. We must teach libertines that the English people appreciate the importance of domestic ties. Accordingly some unfortunate man, in no respect more depraved than hundreds whose offences have been treated with lenity, is singled out as an expiatory sacrifice. If he has children, they are to be taken from him. If he has a profession, he is to be driven from it. He is cut by the higher orders, and hissed by the lower. He is, in truth, a sort of whipping-boy, by whose vicarious agonies all the other transgressors of the same class are, it is supposed, sufficiently chastised. We reflect very complacently on our own severity, and compare with great pride the high standard of morals established in England with the Parisian laxity. At length our anger is satiated. Our victim is ruined and heartbroken. And our virtue goes quietly to sleep for seven years more.

It is clear that those vices which destroy domestic happiness ought to be as much as possible repressed. It is equally clear that they cannot be repressed by penal legislation. It is therefore right and desirable that public opinion should be directed against them. But it should be directed against them uniformly, steadily, and temperately, not by sudden fits and starts. There should be one weight and one measure. Decimation is always an objectionable mode of punishment. It is the resource of judges too indolent and hasty to investigate facts and to discriminate nicely between shades of guilt. It is an irrational practice, even when adopted by military tribunals. When adopted by the tribunal of public opinion, it is infinitely more irrational. It is good that a certain portion of disgrace should constantly attend on certain bad actions. But it is not good that the offenders should merely have to stand the risks of a lottery of infamy, that ninety-nine out of every hundred should escape, and that the hundredth, perhaps the most innocent of the hundred, should pay for all. We remember to have seen a mob assembled in Lincoln's Inn to hoot a gentleman against whom the most oppressive proceeding known to the English law was then in progress. He was hooted because he had been an unfaithful husband, as if some of the most popular men of the age, Lord Nelson for example, had not been unfaithful husbands. We remember a still stronger case. Will posterity believe that, in an age in which men whose gallantries were universally known, and had been legally proved, filled some of the highest offices in the State and in the army, presided at the meetings of religious and benevolent institutions, were the delight of every society, and the favourites of the multitude, a crowd of moralists went to the theatre, in order to pelt a poor actor for disturbing the conjugal felicity of an alderman? What there was in the circumstances either of the offender or of the sufferer to vindicate the zeal of the audience, we could never conceive. It has never been supposed that the situation of an actor is peculiarly favourable to the rigid virtues, or that an alderman enjoys any special immunity from injuries such as that which on this occasion roused the anger of the public. But such is the justice of mankind.

In these cases the punishment was excessive; but the offence was known and proved. The case of Lord Byron was harder. True Jedwood justice was dealt out to him. First came the execution, then the investigation, and last of all, or rather not at all, the accusation. The public, without knowing anything whatever about the transactions in his family, flew into a violent passion with him, and proceeded to invent stories which might justify its anger. Ten or twenty different accounts of the separation, inconsistent with each other, with themselves, and with common sense, circulated at the same time. What evidence there might be for any one of these, the virtuous people who repeated them neither knew nor cared. For in fact these stories were not the causes, but the effects of the public indignation. They resembled those loathsome slanders which Lewis Goldsmith, and other abject libellers of the same class, were in the habit of publishing about Bonaparte; such as that he poisoned a girl with arsenic when he was at the military school, that he hired a grenadier to shoot Dessaix at Marengo, that he filled St. Cloud with all the pollutions of Capreæ. There was a time when anecdotes like these obtained some credence from persons who, hating the French emperor without knowing why, were eager to believe anything which might justify their hatred. Lord Byron fared in the same way. His countrymen were in a bad humour with him. His writings and his character had lost the charm of novelty. He had been guilty of the offence which, of all offences, is punished most severely; he had been over-praised; he had excited too warm an interest; and the public, with its usual justice, chastised him for its own folly. The attachments of the multitude bear no small resemblance to those of the wanton enchantress in the Arabian Tales, who, when the forty days of her fondness were over, was not content with dismissing her lovers, but condemned them to expiate, in loathsome shapes, and under cruel penances, the crime of having once pleased her too well.

The obloquy which Byron had to endure was such as might well have shaken a more constant mind. The newspapers were filled with lampoons. The theatres shook with execrations. He was excluded from circles where he had lately been the observed of all observers. All those creeping things that riot in the decay of nobler natures hastened to their repast; and they were right; they did after their kind. It is not every day that the savage envy of aspiring dunces is gratified by the agonies of such a spirit, and the degradation of such a name.

The unhappy man left his country for ever. The howl of contumely followed him across the sea, up the Rhine, over the Alps; it gradually waxed fainter; it died away; those who had raised it began to ask each other, what, after all, was the matter about which they had been so clamorous, and wished to invite back the criminal whom they had just chased from them. His poetry became more popular than it had ever been; and his complaints were read with tears by thousands and tens of thousands who had never seen his face.

He had fixed his home on the shores of the Adriatic, in the most picturesque and interesting of cities, beneath the brightest of skies, and by the brightest of seas. Censoriousness was not the vice of the neighbours whom he had chosen. They were a race corrupted by bad government and a bad religion, long renowned for skill in the arts of voluptuousness, and tolerant of all the caprices of sensuality. From the public opinion of the country of his adoption, he had nothing to dread. With the public opinion of the country of his birth, he was at open war. He plunged into wild and desperate excesses, ennobled by no generous or tender sentiment. From his Venetian harem he sent forth volume after volume, full of eloquence, of wit, of pathos, of ribaldry, and of bitter disdain. His health sank under the effects of his intemperance. His hair turned gray. His food ceased to nourish him. A hectic fever withered him up. It seemed that his body and mind were about to perish together.

From this wretched degradation he was in some measure rescued by a connection, culpable indeed, yet such as, if it were judged by the standard of morality established in the country where he lived, might be called virtuous. But an imagination polluted by vice, a temper embittered by misfortune, and a frame habituated to the fatal excitement of intoxication, prevented him from fully enjoying the happiness which he might have derived from the purest and most tranquil of his many attachments. Midnight draughts of ardent spirits and Rhenish wines had begun to work the ruin of his fine intellect. His verse lost much of the energy and condensation which had distinguished it. But he would not resign, without a struggle, the empire which he had exercised over the men of his generation. A new dream of ambition arose before him; to be the chief of a literary party; to be the great mover of an intellectual revolution; to guide the public mind of England from his Italian retreat, as Voltaire had guided the public mind of France from the villa of Ferney. With this hope, as it should seem, he established *The Liberal*. But, powerfully as he had affected the imaginations of his contemporaries, he mistook his own powers if he hoped to direct their opinions; and he still more grossly mistook his own disposition, if he thought that he could long act in concert with other men of letters. The plan failed, and failed ignominiously. Angry with himself, angry with his coadjutors, he relinquished it, and turned to another project, the last and noblest of his life.

A nation, once the first among the nations, pre-eminent in knowledge, pre-eminent in military glory, the cradle of philosophy, of eloquence, and of the fine arts, had been for ages bowed down under a cruel yoke. All the vices which oppression generates, the abject vices which it generates in those who submit to it, the ferocious vices which it generates in those who struggle against it, had deformed the character of that miserable race. The valour which had won the great battle of human civilisation, which had saved Europe, which had subjugated Asia, lingered only among pirates and robbers. The ingenuity, once so conspicuously displayed in every department of physical and moral science, had been depraved into a timid and servile cunning. On a sudden this degraded people had risen on their oppressors. Discountenanced or betrayed by the surrounding potentates, they had found in

themselves something of that which might well supply the place of all foreign assistance, something of the energy of their fathers.

As a man of letters, Lord Byron could not but be interested in the event of this contest. His political opinions, though, like all his opinions, unsettled, leaned strongly towards the side of liberty. He had assisted the Italian insurgents with his purse, and, if their struggle against the Austrian Government had been prolonged, would probably have assisted them with his sword. But to Greece he was attached by peculiar ties. He had when young resided in that country. Much of his most splendid and popular poetry had been inspired by its scenery and by its history. Sick of inaction, degraded in his own eyes by his private vices and by his literary failures, pining for untried excitement and honourable distinction, he carried his exhausted body and his wounded spirit to the Grecian camp.

His conduct in his new situation showed so much vigour and good sense as to justify us in believing that, if his life had been prolonged, he might have distinguished himself as a soldier and a politician. But pleasure and sorrow had done the work of seventy years upon his delicate frame. The hand of death was upon him: he knew it; and the only wish which he uttered was that he might die sword in hand.

This was denied to him. Anxiety, exertion, exposure, and those fatal stimulants which had become indispensable to him, soon stretched him on a sick-bed, in a strange land, amidst strange faces, without one human being that he loved near him. There, at thirty-six, the most celebrated Englishman of the nineteenth century closed his brilliant and miserable career.

We cannot even now retrace those events without feeling something of what was felt by the nation, when it was first known that the grave had closed over so much sorrow and so much glory; something of what was felt by those who saw the hearse, with its long train of coaches, turn slowly northward, leaving behind it that cemetery which had been consecrated by the dust of so many great poets, but of which the doors were closed against all that remained of Byron. We well remember that on that day, rigid moralists could not refrain from weeping for one so young, so illustrious, so unhappy, gifted with such rare gifts, and tried by such strong temptations. It is unnecessary to make any reflections. The history carries its moral with it. Our age has indeed been fruitful of warnings to the eminent and of consolations to the obscure. Two men have died within our recollection, who, at the time of life at which many people have hardly completed their education, had raised themselves, each in his own department, to the height of glory. One of them died at Longwood; the other at Missolonghi.

It is always difficult to separate the literary character of a man who lives in our own time from his personal character. It is peculiarly difficult to make this separation in the case of Lord Byron. For it is scarcely too much to say, that Lord Byron never wrote without some reference, direct or indirect, to himself. The interest excited by the events of his life mingles itself in our minds, and probably in the minds of almost all our readers, with the interest which properly belongs to his works. A generation must pass away before it will be possible to form a fair judgment of his books, considered merely as books. At present they are not only books but relics. We will however venture, though with unfeigned diffidence, to offer some desultory remarks on his poetry.

His lot was cast in the time of a great literary revolution. That poetical dynasty which had dethroned the successors of Shakspeare and Spenser was, in its turn, dethroned by a race who represented themselves as heirs of the ancient line, so long dispossessed by usurpers. The real nature of this revolution has not, we think, been comprehended by the great majority of those who concurred in it.

Wherein especially does the poetry of our times differ from that of the last century? Ninety-nine persons out of a hundred would answer that the poetry of the last century was correct, but cold and mechanical, and that the poetry of our time, though wild and irregular, presented far more vivid images, and excited the passions far more strongly than that of Parnell, of Addison, or of Pope. In the same manner we constantly hear it said, that the poets of the age of Elizabeth had far more genius, but far less correctness, than those of the age of Anne. It seems to be taken for granted, that there is some incompatibility, some antithesis between correctness and creative power. We rather suspect that this notion arises merely from an abuse of words, and that it has been the parent of many of the fallacies which perplex the science of criticism.

What is meant by correctness in poetry? If by correctness be meant the conforming to rules which have their foundation in truth and in the principles of human nature, then correctness is only another name for excellence. If by correctness be meant the conforming to rules purely arbitrary, correctness may be another name for dulness and absurdity.

A writer who describes visible objects falsely and violates the propriety of character, a writer who makes the mountains "nod their drowsy heads" at night, or a dying man take leave of the world with a rant like that of Maximin, may be said, in the high and just sense of the phrase, to write incorrectly. He violates the first great law of his art. His imitation is altogether unlike the thing imitated. The four poets who are most eminently free from incorrectness of this description are Homer, Dante, Shakspeare, and Milton. They are, therefore, in one sense, and that the best sense, the most correct of poets.

When it is said that Virgil, though he had less genius than Homer, was a more correct writer, what sense is attached to the word correctness? Is it meant that the story of the Æneid is developed more skilfully than that of the Odyssey? that the Roman describes the face of the external world, or the emotions of the mind, more accurately than the Greek? that the characters of Achates and Mnestheus are more nicely discriminated, and more consistently supported, than those of Achilles, of Nestor, and of Ulysses? The fact incontestably is that, for every violation of the fundamental laws of poetry which can be found in Homer, it would be easy to find twenty in Virgil.

Troilus and Cressida is perhaps of all the plays of Shakspeare that which is commonly considered as the most incorrect. Yet it seems to us infinitely more correct, in the sound sense of the term, than what are called the most correct plays of the most correct dramatists. Compare it, for example, with the *Iphigénie* of Racine. We are sure that the Greeks of Shakspeare bear a far greater resemblance than the Greeks of Racine to the real Greeks who besieged Troy; and for this reason, that the Greeks of Shakspeare are human beings, and the Greeks of Racine mere names, mere words printed in capitals at the head of paragraphs of declamation. Racine, it is true, would have shuddered at the thought of making a warrior at the siege of Troy quote Aristotle. But of what use is it to avoid a single anachronism, when the whole play is one anachronism, the sentiments and phrases of Versailles in the camp of Aulis?

In the sense in which we are now using the word correctness, we think that Sir Walter Scott, Mr. Wordsworth, Mr. Coleridge, are far more correct poets than those who are commonly extolled as the models of correctness, Pope, for example, and Addison. The single description of a moonlight night in Pope's *Iliad* contains more inaccuracies than can be found in all the *Excursion*. There is not a single scene in *Cato*, in which all that conduces to poetical illusion, all the propriety of character, of language, of situation, is not more grossly violated than in any part of the *Lay of the Last Minstrel*. No man can possibly think that the Romans of Addison resemble the real Romans so closely as the moss-troopers of Scott resemble the real moss-troopers. Wat Tinlinn and William of Deloraine are not, it is true, persons of so much dignity as Cato. But the dignity of the persons represented has as little to do with the correctness of poetry as with the correctness of painting. We prefer a gipsy by Reynolds to his Majesty's head on a sign-post, and a Borderer by Scott to a Senator by Addison.

In what sense, then, is the word correctness used by those who say, with the author of the *Pursuits of Literature*, that Pope was the most correct of English Poets, and that next to Pope came the late Mr. Gifford? What is the nature and value of that correctness, the praise of which is denied to *Macbeth*, to *Lear*, and to *Othello*, and given to Hoole's translations and to all the Seatonian prize-poems? We can discover no eternal rule, no rule founded in reason and in the nature of things, which Shakspeare does not observe much more strictly than Pope. But if by correctness be meant the conforming to a narrow legislation which while lenient to the *mala in se*,[1] multiplies, without a shadow of a reason, the *mala prohibita*, if by correctness be meant a strict attention to certain ceremonious observances, which are no more essential to poetry than etiquette to good government, or than the washings of a Pharisee to devotion, then, assuredly, Pope may be a more correct poet than Shakspeare; and, if the code were a little altered, Colley Cibber might be a more correct poet than Pope. But it may well be doubted whether this kind of correctness be a merit, nay, whether it be not an absolute fault.

It would be amusing to make a digest of the irrational laws which bad critics have framed for the government of poets. First in celebrity and in absurdity stand the dramatic unities of place and time. No human being has ever been able to find anything that could, even by courtesy, be called an argument for these unities, except that they have been deduced from the general practice of the Greeks. It requires no very profound examination to discover that the Greek dramas, often admirable as compositions, are, as exhibitions of human character and human life, far inferior to the English plays of the age of Elizabeth. Every scholar knows that the dramatic part of the Athenian tragedies was at first subordinate to the lyrical part. It would, therefore, have been little less than a miracle if the laws of the Athenian stage had been found to suit plays in which there was no chorus. All the greatest masterpieces of the dramatic art have been composed in direct violation of the unities, and could never have been composed if the unities had not been violated. It is clear,

[1] *mala in se:* offenses in themselves, i.e., natural; *mala prohibita*, offenses prohibited by law or rule, i.e., artificial.

for example, that such a character as that of Hamlet could never have been developed within the limits to which Alfieri confined himself. Yet such was the reverence of literary men during the last century for these unities that Johnson who, much to his honour, took the opposite side, was, as he says, "frightened at his own temerity," and "afraid to stand against the authorities which might be produced against him."

There are other rules of the same kind without end. "Shakspeare," says Rymer, "ought not to have made Othello black; for the hero of a tragedy ought always to be white." "Milton," says another critic, "ought not to have taken Adam for his hero; for the hero of an epic poem ought always to be victorious." "Milton," says another, "ought not to have put so many similes into his first book; for the first book of an epic poem ought always to be the most unadorned. There are no similes in the first book of the *Iliad*." "Milton," says another, "ought not to have placed in an epic poem such lines as these:

While thus I called, and strayed I knew not whither.

And why not? The critic is ready with a reason, a lady's reason. "Such lines," says he, "are not, it must be allowed, unpleasing to the ear; but the redundant syllable ought to be confined to the drama, and not admitted into epic poetry." As to the redundant syllable in heroic rhyme on serious subjects, it has been, from the time of Pope downward, proscribed by the general consent of all the correct schools. No magazine would have admitted so incorrect a couplet as that of Drayton:

As when we lived untouch'd with these disgraces,
When as our kingdom was our dear embraces.

Another law of heroic rhyme, which, fifty years ago, was considered as fundamental, was, that there should be a pause, a comma at least, at the end of every couplet. It was also provided that there should never be a full stop except at the end of a line. Well do we remember to have heard a most correct judge of poetry revile Mr. Rogers

for the incorrectness of that most sweet and graceful passage,

Such grief was ours,—it seems but yesterday,—
When in thy prime, wishing so much to stay,
'Twas thine, Maria, thine without a sigh
At midnight in a sister's arms to die.
Oh thou wert lovely; lovely was thy frame,
And pure thy spirit as from heaven it came:
And when recall'd to join the blest above
Thou diedst a victim to exceeding love,
Nursing the young to health. In happier hours,
When idle Fancy wove luxuriant flowers,
Once in thy mirth thou badst me write on thee;
And now I write what thou shalt never see.

Sir Roger Newdigate is fairly entitled, we think, to be ranked among the great critics of this school. He made a law that none of the poems written for the prize which he established at Oxford should exceed fifty lines. This law seems to us to have at least as much foundation in reason as any of those which we have mentioned; nay, much more, for the world, we believe, is pretty well agreed in thinking that the shorter a prize-poem is, the better.

We do not see why we should not make a few more rules of the same kind; why we should not enact that the number of scenes in every act shall be three or some multiple of three, that the number of lines in every scene shall be an exact square, that the *dramatis personæ* shall never be more or fewer than sixteen, and that, in heroic rhymes, every thirty-sixth line shall have twelve syllables. If we were to lay down these canons, and to call Pope, Goldsmith, and Addison incorrect writers for not having complied with our whims, we should act precisely as those critics act who find incorrectness in the magnificent imagery and the varied music of Coleridge and Shelley. The correctness which the last century prized so much resembles the correctness of those pictures of the garden of Eden which we see in old Bibles. We have an exact square enclosed by the rivers Pison, Gihon, Hiddekel, and Euphrates, each with a convenient bridge in the centre, rectangular beds of flowers, a long canal, neatly bricked and railed in, the tree of knowledge clipped like one of the limes behind the Tuilleries, standing in the centre of the grand alley, the snake twined round it, the man on the right hand, the woman on the left, and the beasts drawn up in an exact circle round them. In one sense the picture is correct enough. That is to say, the squares are correct; the circles are correct; the man and the woman are in a most correct line with the tree; and the snake forms a most correct spiral.

But if there were a painter so gifted that he could place on the canvas that glorious paradise, seen by the interior eye of him whose outward sight had failed with long watching and labouring for liberty and truth, if there were a painter who could set before us the mazes of the sapphire brook, the lake with its fringe of myrtles, the flowery meadows, the grottoes overhung by vines, the forests shining with Hesperian fruit and with the plumage of gorgeous birds, the massy shade of that nuptial bower which showered down roses on the sleeping lovers, what should we think of a connoisseur, who should tell us that this painting, though finer than the absurd picture in the old Bible, was not so correct. Surely we should answer, It is both finer and more correct; and it is finer because it is more correct. It is not made up of correctly drawn diagrams; but it is a correct painting, a worthy representation of that which it is intended to represent.

It is not in the fine arts alone that this false correctness is prized by narrow-minded men, by men who cannot distinguish means from ends, or what is accidental from what is essential. M. Jourdain admired correctness in fencing. "You had no business to hit me then. You must never thrust in quart till you have thrust in tierce." M. Tomès liked correctness in medical practice. "I stand up for Artemius. That he killed his patient is plain enough. But still he acted quite according to rule. A man dead is a man dead; and there is an end of the matter. But if rules are to be broken, there is no saying what consequences may follow." We have heard of an old German officer, who was a great admirer of correctness in military operations. He used to revile Bonaparte for spoiling the science of war, which had been carried to such exquisite perfection by Marshall Daun. "In my youth we used to march and countermarch all the summer without gaining or losing a square league,

and then we went into winter quarters. And now comes an ignorant, hot-headed young man, who flies about from Boulogne to Ulm, and from Ulm to the middle of Moravia, and fights battles in December. The whole system of his tactics is monstrously incorrect." The world is of opinion in spite of critics like these, that the end of fencing is to hit, that the end of medicine is to cure, that the end of war is to conquer, and that those means are the most correct which best accomplish the ends.

And has poetry no end, no eternal and immutable principles? Is poetry, like heraldry, mere matter of arbitrary regulation? The heralds tell us that certain scutcheons and bearings denote certain conditions, and that to put colours on colours, or metals on metals, is false blazonry. If all this were reversed, if every coat of arms in Europe were new fashioned, if it were decreed that *or* should never be placed but on *argent*, or *argent* but on *or*, that illegitimacy should be denoted by a *lozenge*, and widowhood by a *bend*, the new science would be just as good as the old science, because both the new and the old would be good for nothing. The mummery of Portcullis and Rouge Dragon, as it has no other value than that which caprice has assigned to it, may well submit to any laws which caprice may impose on it. But it is not so with that great imitative art, to the power of which all ages, the rudest and the most enlightened, bear witness. Since its first great masterpieces were produced, everything that is changeable in this world has been changed. Civilisation has been gained, lost, gained again. Religions, and languages, and forms of government, and usages of private life, and modes of thinking, all have undergone a succession of revolutions. Everything has passed away but the great features of nature, and the heart of man, and the miracles of that art of which it is the office to reflect back the heart of man and the features of nature. Those two strange old poems, the wonder of ninety generations, still retain all their freshness. They still command the veneration of minds enriched by the literature of many nations and ages. They are still, even in wretched translations, the delight of school-boys. Having survived ten thousand capricious fashions, having seen successive codes of criticism become obsolete, they still remain to us, immortal with the immortality of truth, the same when perused in the study of an English scholar, as when they were first chanted at the banquets of the Ionian princes.

Poetry is, as was said more than two thousand years ago, imitation. It is an art analogous in many respects to the art of painting, sculpture, and acting. The imitations of the painter, the sculptor, and the actor, are indeed, within certain limits, more perfect than those of the poet. The machinery which the poet employs consists merely of words; and words cannot, even when employed by such an artist as Homer or Dante, present to the mind images of visible objects quite so lively and exact as those which we carry away from looking on the works of the brush and the chisel. But, on the other hand, the range of poetry is infinitely wider than that of any other imitative art, or than that of all the other imitative arts together. The sculptor can imitate only form; the painter only form and colour; the actor, until the poet supplies him with words, only form, colour, and motion. Poetry holds the outer world in common with the other arts. The heart of man is the province of poetry, and of poetry alone. The painter, the sculptor, and the actor can exhibit no more of human passion and character than that small portion which overflows into the gesture and the face, always an imperfect, often a deceitful, sign of that which is within. The deeper and more complex parts of human nature can be exhibited by means of words alone. Thus the objects of the imitation of poetry are the whole external and the whole internal universe, the face of nature, the vicissitudes of fortune, man as he is in himself, man as he appears in society, all things which really exist, all things of which we can form an image in our minds by combining together parts of things which really exist. The domain of this imperial art is commensurate with the imaginative faculty.

An art essentially imitative ought not surely to be subjected to rules which tend to make its imitations less perfect than they otherwise would be; and those who obey such rules ought to be called, not correct, but incorrect artists. The true way to judge of the rules by which English poetry was governed during the last century is to look at the effects which they produced.

It was in 1780 that Johnson completed his *Lives of the Poets*. He tells us in that work that, since the time of Dryden, English poetry had shown no tendency to relapse into its original savageness, that its language had been refined, its numbers tuned, and its sentiments improved. It may perhaps be doubted whether the nation had any great reason to exult in the refinements and improvements which gave it *Douglas* for *Othello*, and the *Triumphs of Temper* for the *Fairy Queen*.

It was during the thirty years which preceded the appearance of Johnson's *Lives* that the diction and versification of English poetry were, in the sense in which the word is commonly used, most correct. Those thirty years are, as respects poetry, the most deplorable part of our literary history. They have indeed bequeathed to us scarcely any poetry which deserves to be remembered. Two or three hundred lines of Gray, twice as many of Goldsmith, a few stanzas of Beattie and Collins, a few strophes of Mason, and a few clever prologues and satires, were the masterpieces of this age of consummate excellence. They may all be printed in one volume, and that volume would be by no means a volume of extraordinary merit. It would contain no poetry of the very highest class, and little which could be placed very high in the second class. The *Paradise Regained* or *Comus* would outweigh it all.

At last, when poetry had fallen into such utter decay that Mr. Hayley was thought a great poet, it began to appear that the excess of the evil was about to work the cure. Men became tired of an insipid conformity to a standard which derived no authority from nature or reason. A shallow criticism had taught them to ascribe a superstitious value to the spurious correctness of poetasters. A deeper criticism brought them back to the true correctness of the first great masters. The eternal laws of poetry regained their power, and the temporary fashions which had super-seded those laws went after the wig of Lovelace and the hoop of Clarissa.

It was in a cold and barren season that the seeds of that rich harvest which we have reaped were first sown. While poetry was every year becoming more feeble and more mechanical, while the monotonous versification which Pope had introduced, no longer redeemed by his brilliant wit and his compactness of expression, palled on the ear of the public, the great works of the old masters were every day attracting more and more of the admiration which they deserved. The plays of Shakspeare were better acted, better edited, and better known than they had ever been. Our fine ancient ballads were again read with pleas-ure, and it became a fashion to imitate them. Many of the imitations were alto-gether contemptible. But they showed that men had at least begun to admire the ex-cellence which they could not rival. A lit-erary revolution was evidently at hand. There was a ferment in the minds of men, a vague craving for something new, a dis-position to hail with delight anything which might at first sight wear the ap-pearance of originality. A reforming age is always fertile of impostors. The same ex-cited state of public feeling which produced the great separation from the see of Rome produced also the excesses of the Anabap-tists. The same stir in the public mind of Europe which overthrew the abuses of the old French Government, produced the Ja-cobins and Theophilanthropists. Macpher-son and Della Crusca were to the true reformers of English poetry what Knipper-doling was to Luther, or Clootz to Turgot. The success of Chatterton's forgeries and of the far more contemptible forgeries of Ireland showed that people had begun to love the old poetry well, though not wisely. The public was never more disposed to believe stories without evidence, and to admire books without merit. Anything which could break the dull monotony of the correct school was acceptable.

The forerunner of the great restoration of our literature was Cowper. His literary career began and ended at nearly the same time with that of Alfieri. A comparison between Alfieri and Cowper may, at first sight, appear as strange as that which a loyal Presbyterian minister is said to have made in 1745 between George the Second and Enoch. It may seem that the gentle, shy, melancholy Calvinist, whose spirit had been broken by fagging at school, who had not courage to earn a livelihood by reading the titles of bills in the House of Lords, and whose favourite associates were a blind old lady and an evangelical divine, could have nothing in common with the haughty, ardent, and voluptuous nobleman, the horse-jockey, the libertine, who fought Lord Ligonier in Hyde Park, and robbed the Pretender of his queen. But though the private lives of these remarkable men pre-sent scarcely any points of resemblance, their literary lives bear a close analogy to each other. They both found poetry in its lowest state of degradation, feeble, artifi-cial, and altogether nerveless. They both possessed precisely the talents which fitted them for the task of raising it from that deep abasement. They cannot, in strict-ness, be called great poets. They had not in any very high degree the creative power,

The vision and the faculty divine:

but they had great vigour of thought, great warmth of feeling, and what, in their cir-cumstances, was above all things important, a manliness of taste which approached to roughness. They did not deal in mechan-ical versification and conventional phrases. They wrote concerning things the thought of which set their hearts on fire; and thus what they wrote, even when it wanted every other grace, had that inimitable grace which sincerity and strong passion impart to the rudest and most homely composi-tions. Each of them sought for inspiration in a noble and affecting subject, fertile of images which had not yet been hackneyed. Liberty was the muse of Alfieri, Religion was the muse of Cowper. The same truth is found in their lighter pieces. They were not among those who deprecated the se-verity, or deplored the absence, of an un-real mistress in melodious commonplaces. Instead of raving about imaginary Chloes and Sylvias, Cowper wrote of Mrs. Un-win's knitting-needles. The only love-verses of Alfieri were addressed to one whom he truly and passionately loved. "Tutte, le rime amorose che seguono," says he, "tutte sono per essa, e ben sue, e di lei solamente; poichè mai d'altra donna per certo non canterò." [2]

These great men were not free from affectation. But their affectation was directly opposed to the affectation which generally prevailed. Each of them expressed, in strong and bitter language, the contempt which he felt for the effeminate poetasters who were in fashion both in England and in Italy. Cowper complains that

Manner is all in all, whate'er is writ,
The substitute for genius, taste, and wit.

He praised Pope; yet he regretted that Pope had

Made poetry a mere mechanic art,
And every warbler had his tune by heart.

Alfieri speaks with similar scorn of the tragedies of his predecessors. "Mi cadevano dalle mani per la languidezza, trivialità e prolissità dei modi e del verso, senza parlare poi della snervatezza dei pensieri. Or perchè mai questa nostra divina lingua, sì maschia anco, ed energica, e feroce, in bocca di Dante, dovra ella farsi così sbiadata ed eunuca nel dialogo tragico?" [3]

To men thus sick of the languid manner of their contemporaries ruggedness seemed a venial fault, or rather a positive merit. In their hatred of meretricious ornament, and of what Cowper calls "creamy smoothness," they erred on the opposite side. Their style was too austere, their versification too harsh. It is not easy, however, to overrate the service which they rendered to literature. The intrinsic value of their poems is considerable. But the example

[2] Tutte le rime, etc.: "All the love rhymes that follow, all are for her, and well her own, and of her only; for certainly I shall never sing about any other lady."

[3] Mi cadevano, etc.: ("Some other tragedies, either our own Italian, or translated from the French, that I wanted to read hoping to learn from them at least something as to style) fell from my hands because of their dullness, banality and prolixity of technique and verse, let alone the weakness of thought. Now why must this divine language of ours, so masculine, too, and energetic and fierce, in the mouth of Dante, become so colorless and emasculated in the tragic dialogue?" (Vita, IV, i, 139, Opere, vol. I, Torino, 1903).

which they set of mutiny against an absurd system was invaluable. The part which they performed was rather that of Moses than that of Joshua. They opened the house of bondage; but they did not enter the promised land.

During the twenty years which followed the death of Cowper, the revolution in English poetry was fully consummated. None of the writers of this period, not even Sir Walter Scott, contributed so much to the consummation as Lord Byron. Yet Lord Byron contributed to it unwillingly, and with constant self-reproach and shame. All his tastes and inclinations led him to take part with the school of poetry which was going out against the school which was coming in. Of Pope himself he spoke with extravagant admiration. He did not venture directly to say that the little man of Twickenham was a greater poet than Shakspeare or Milton; but he hinted pretty clearly that he thought so. Of his contemporaries, scarcely any had so much of his admiration as Mr. Gifford, who, considered as a poet, was merely Pope, without Pope's wit and fancy, and whose satires are decidedly inferior in vigour and poignancy to the very imperfect juvenile performance of Lord Byron himself. He now and then praised Mr. Wordsworth and Mr. Coleridge, but ungraciously and without cordiality. When he attacked them, he brought his whole soul to the work. Of the most elaborate of Mr. Wordsworth's poems he could find nothing to say, but that it was "clumsy, and frowsy, and his aversion." Peter Bell excited his spleen to such a degree that he evoked the shades of Pope and Dryden, and demanded of them whether it were possible that such trash could evade contempt? In his heart he thought his own Pilgrimage of Harold inferior to his Imitation of Horace's Art of Poetry, a feeble echo of Pope and Johnson. This insipid performance he repeatedly designed to publish, and was withheld only by the solicitations of his friends. He has distinctly declared his approbation of the unities, the most absurd laws by which genius was ever held in servitude. In one of his works, we think in his letter to Mr. Bowles, he compares the poetry of the eighteenth century to the Parthenon, and that of the nineteenth to a Turkish mosque, and boasts that, though he had assisted his contemporaries in building their grotesque and barbarous edifice, he had never joined them in defacing the remains of a chaster and more graceful architecture. In another letter he compares the change which had recently passed on English poetry to the decay of Latin poetry after the Augustan age. In the time of Pope, he tells his friend, it was all Horace with us. It is all Claudian now.

For the great old masters of the art he had no very enthusiastic veneration. In his letter to Mr. Bowles he uses expressions which clearly indicate that he preferred Pope's *Iliad* to the original. Mr. Moore confesses that his friend was no very fervent admirer of Shakspeare. Of all the poets of the first class Lord Byron seems to have admired Dante and Milton most. Yet in the fourth canto of *Childe Harold*, he places Tasso, a writer not merely inferior to them, but of quite a different order of mind, on at least a footing of equality with them. Mr. Hunt is, we suspect, quite correct in saying that Lord Byron could see little or no merit in Spenser.

But Byron the critic and Byron the poet were two very different men. The effects of the noble writer's theory may indeed often be traced in his practice. But his disposition led him to accommodate himself to the literary taste of the age in which he lived; and his talents would have enabled him to accommodate himself to the taste of any age. Though he said much of his contempt for mankind, and though he boasted that amidst the inconstancy of fortune and of fame he was all-sufficient to himself, his literary career indicated nothing of that lonely and unsocial pride which he affected. We cannot conceive him, like Milton or Wordsworth, defying the criticism of his contemporaries, retorting their scorn, and labouring on a poem in the full assurance that it would be unpopular, and in the full assurance that it would be immortal. He has said, by the mouth of one of his heroes, in speaking of political greatness, that "he must serve who fain would sway"; and this he assigns as a reason for not entering into political life. He did not consider that the sway which he had exer-

cised in literature had been purchased by servitude, by the sacrifice of his own taste to the taste of the public.

He was the creature of his age; and whenever he had lived he would have been the creature of his age. Under Charles the First Byron would have been more quaint than Donne. Under Charles the Second the rants of Byron's rhyming plays would have pitted it, boxed it, and galleried it, with those of any Bayes or Bilboa. Under George the First, the monotonous smoothness of Byron's versification and the terseness of his expression would have made Pope himself envious.

As it was, he was the man of the last thirteen years of the eighteenth century, and of the first twenty-three years of the nineteenth century. He belonged half to the old, and half to the new school of poetry. His personal taste led him to the former; his thirst of praise to the latter; his talents were equally suited to both. His fame was a common ground on which the zealots on both sides, Gifford for example, and Shelley, might meet. He was the representative, not of either literary party, but of both at once, and of their conflict, and of the victory by which that conflict was terminated. His poetry fills and measures the whole of the vast interval through which our literature has moved since the time of Johnson. It touches the *Essay on Man* at the one extremity, and the *Excursion* at the other.

There are several parallel instances in literary history. Voltaire, for example, was the connecting link between the France of Lewis the Fourteenth and the France of Lewis the Sixteenth, between Racine and Boileau on the one side, and Condorcet and Beaumarchais on the other. He, like Lord Byron, put himself at the head of an intellectual revolution, dreading it all the time, murmuring at it, sneering at it, yet choosing rather to move before his age in any direction than to be left behind and forgotten. Dryden was the connecting link between the literature of the age of James the First, and the literature of the age of Anne. Oromasdes and Arimanes fought for him. Arimanes carried him off. But his heart was to the last with Oromasdes. Lord Byron was, in the same manner, the mediator between two generations, between two hostile poetical sects. Though always sneering at Mr. Wordsworth, he was yet, though perhaps unconsciously, the interpreter between Mr. Wordsworth and the multitude. In the *Lyrical Ballads* and the *Excursion* Mr. Wordsworth appeared as the high priest of a worship, of which nature was the idol. No poems have ever indicated a more exquisite perception of the beauty of the outer world or a more passionate love and reverence for that beauty. Yet they were not popular; and it is not likely that they ever will be popular as the poetry of Sir Walter Scott is popular. The feeling which pervaded them was too deep for general sympathy. Their style was often too mysterious for general comprehension. They made a few esoteric disciples, and many scoffers. Lord Byron founded what may be called an esoteric Lake school; and all the readers of verse in England, we might say in Europe, hastened to sit at his feet. What Mr. Wordsworth had said like a recluse, Lord Byron said like a man of the world, with less profound feeling, but with more perspicuity, energy, and conciseness. We would refer our readers to the last two cantos of *Childe Harold* and to *Manfred,* in proof of these observations.

Lord Byron, like Mr. Wordsworth, had nothing dramatic in his genius. He was indeed the reverse of a great dramatist, the very antithesis to a great dramatist. All his characters, Harold looking on the sky, from which his country and the sun are disappearing together, the Giaour standing apart in the gloom of the side aisle, and casting a haggard scowl from under his long hood at the crucifix and the censer, Conrad leaning on his sword by the watchtower, Lara smiling on the dancers, Alp gazing steadily on the fatal cloud as it passes before the moon, Manfred wandering among the precipices of Berne, Azzo on the judgment-seat, Ugo at the bar, Lambro frowning on the siesta of his daughter and Juan, Cain presenting his unacceptable offering, are essentially the same. The varieties are varieties merely of age, situation, and outward show. If ever Lord Byron attempted to exhibit men of a different kind, he always made them either insipid or unnatural. Selim is nothing. Bonnivart is nothing. Don Juan, in the first and best cantos, is a feeble copy of the Page in the *Marriage of Figaro.* Johnson, the man whom Juan meets in the slave-market, is a most striking failure. How differently would Sir Walter Scott have drawn a bluff, fearless Englishman, in such a situation! The portrait would have seemed to walk out of the canvas.

Sardanapalus is more closely drawn than any dramatic personage that we can remember. His heroism and his effeminacy, his contempt of death and his dread of a weighty helmet, his kingly resolution to be seen in the foremost ranks, and the anxiety with which he calls for a looking-glass that he may be seen to advantage, are contrasted, it is true, with all the point of Juvenal. Indeed the hint of the character seems to have been taken from what Juvenal says of Otho:

> Speculum civilis sarcina belli.
> Nimirum summi ducis est occidere Galbam,
> Et curare cutem summi constantia civis,
> Bebriaci in campo spolium affectare Palati,
> Et pressum in faciem digitis extendere panem.[4]

These are excellent lines in a satire. But it is not the business of the dramatist to exhibit characters in this sharp antithetical way. It is not thus that Shakspeare makes Prince Hal rise from the rake of Eastcheap into the hero of Shrewsbury, and sink again into the rake of Eastcheap. It is not thus that Shakspeare has exhibited the union of effeminacy and valour in Antony. A dramatist cannot commit a greater error than that of following those pointed descriptions of character in which satirists and historians indulge so much. It is by rejecting what is natural that satirists and historians produce these striking characters. Their great object generally is to ascribe to every man as many contradictory qualities as possible: and this is an object easily attained. By judicious selection and judi-

[4] *Speculum civilis,* etc.: "A mirror among the kit of civil war! It needed, in truth, a mighty general to slay Galba, and keep his own skin sleek; it needed a citizen of highest courage to ape the splendors of the Palace on the field of Bebriacum, and plaster his face with dough!" (Juvenal, *Satire* II, 103-7. *Loeb Classics,* trans.)

cious exaggeration, the intellect and the disposition of any human being might be described as being made up of nothing but startling contrasts. If the dramatist attempts to create a being answering to one of these descriptions, he fails, because he reverses an imperfect analytical process. He produces, not a man, but a personified epigram. Very eminent writers have fallen into this snare. Ben Jonson has given us a Hermogenes, taken from the lively lines of Horace; but the inconsistency which is so amusing in the satire appears unnatural and disgusts us in the play. Sir Walter Scott has committed a far more glaring error of the same kind in the novel of *Peveril*. Admiring, as every judicious reader must admire, the keen and vigorous lines in which Dryden satirised the Duke of Buckingham, Sir Walter attempted to make a Duke of Buckingham to suit them, a real living Zimri; and he made, not a man, but the most grotesque of all monsters. A writer who should attempt to introduce into a play or a novel such a Wharton as the Wharton of Pope, or a Lord Hervey answering to Sporus, would fail in the same manner.

But to return to Lord Byron; his women, like his men, are all of one breed. Haidee is a half-savage and girlish Julia; Julia is a civilised and matronly Haidee. Leila is a wedded Zuleika, Zuleika a virgin Leila. Gulnare and Medora appear to have been intentionally opposed to each other. Yet the difference is a difference of situation only. A slight change of circumstances would, it should seem, have sent Gulnare to the lute of Medora, and armed Medora with the dagger of Gulnare.

It is hardly too much to say, that Lord Byron could exhibit only one man and only one woman, a man, proud, moody, cynical, with defiance on his brow, and misery in his heart, a scorner of his kind, implacable in revenge, yet capable of deep and strong affection: a woman all softness and gentleness, loving to caress and to be caressed, but capable of being transformed by passion into a tigress.

Even these two characters, his only two characters, he could not exhibit dramatically. He exhibited them in the manner, not of Shakspeare, but of Clarendon. He

analysed them; he made them analyse themselves; but he did not make them show themselves. We are told, for example, in many lines of great force and spirit, that the speech of Lara was bitterly sarcastic, that he talked little of his travels, that if he was much questioned about them, his answers became short, and his brow gloomy. But we have none of Lara's sarcastic speeches or short answers. It is not thus that the great masters of human nature have portrayed human beings. Homer never tells us that Nestor loved to relate long stories about his youth. Shakspeare never tells us that in the mind of Iago everything that is beautiful and endearing was associated with some filthy and debasing idea.

It is curious to observe the tendency which the dialogue of Lord Byron always has to lose its character of a dialogue, and to become soliloquy. The scenes between Manfred and the Chamois-hunter, between Manfred and the Witch of the Alps, between Manfred and the Abbot, are instances of this tendency. Manfred, after a few unimportant speeches, has all the talk to himself. The other interlocutors are nothing more than good listeners. They drop an occasional question or ejaculation which sets Manfred off again on the inexhaustible topic of his personal feelings. If we examine the fine passages in Lord Byron's dramas, the description of Rome, for example, in *Manfred*, the description of a Venetian revel in *Marino Faliero*, the concluding invective which the old doge pronounces against Venice, we shall find that there is nothing dramatic in these speeches, that they derive none of their effect from the character or situation of the speaker, and that they would have been as fine, or finer, if they had been published as fragments of blank verse by Lord Byron. There is scarcely a speech in Shakspeare of which the same could be said. No skilful reader of the plays of Shakspeare can endure to see what are called the fine things taken out, under the name of "Beauties," or of "Elegant Extracts," or to hear any single passage, "To be or not to be," for example, quoted as a sample of the great poet. "To be or not to be" has merit undoubtedly as a composition. It would have merit if put into the mouth of a chorus. But its merit as a composition vanishes when compared with its merit as belonging to Hamlet. It is not too much to say that the great plays of Shakspeare would lose less by being deprived of all the passages which are commonly called the fine passages, than those passages lose by being read separately from the play. This is perhaps the highest praise which can be given to a dramatist.

On the other hand, it may be doubted whether there is, in all Lord Byron's plays, a single remarkable passage which owes any portion of its interest or effect to its connection with the characters or the action. He has written only one scene, as far as we can recollect, which is dramatic even in manner—the scene between Lucifer and Cain. The conference is animated, and each of the interlocutors has a fair share of it. But this scene, when examined, will be found to be a confirmation of our remarks. It is a dialogue only in form. It is a soliloquy in essence. It is in reality a debate carried on within one single unquiet and sceptical mind. The questions and the answers, the objections and the solutions, all belong to the same character.

A writer who showed so little dramatic skill in works professedly dramatic, was not likely to write narrative with dramatic effect. Nothing could indeed be more rude and careless than the structure of his narrative poems. He seems to have thought, with the hero of the *Rehearsal,* that the plot was good for nothing but to bring in fine things. His two longest works, *Childe Harold* and *Don Juan,* have no plan whatever. Either of them might have been extended to any length, or cut short at any point. The state in which the *Giaour* appears illustrates the manner in which all Byron's poems were constructed. They are all, like the *Giaour,* collections of fragments; and, though there may be no empty spaces marked by asterisks, it is still easy to perceive, by the clumsiness of the joining, where the parts for the sake of which the whole was composed end and begin.

It was in description and meditation that Byron excelled. "Description," as he said in *Don Juan,* "was his forte." His manner is indeed peculiar, and is almost unequalled; rapid, sketchy, full of vigour; the selection happy, the strokes few and bold. In spite of the reverence which we feel for the genius of Mr. Wordsworth we cannot but think that the minuteness of his descriptions often diminishes their effect. He has accustomed himself to gaze on nature with the eye of a lover, to dwell on every feature, and to mark every change of aspect. Those beauties which strike the most negligent observer, and those which only a close attention discovers, are equally familiar to him and are equally prominent in his poetry. The proverb of old Hesiod, that half is often more than the whole, is eminently applicable to description. The policy of the Dutch, who cut down most of the precious trees in the Spice Islands, in order to raise the value of what remained, was a policy which poets would do well to imitate. It was a policy which no poet understood better than Lord Byron. Whatever his faults might be, he was never, while his mind retained its vigour, accused of prolixity.

His descriptions, great as was their intrinsic merit, derived their principal interest from the feeling which always mingled with them. He was himself the beginning, the middle, and the end, of all his own poetry, the hero of every tale, the chief object in every landscape. Harold, Lara, Manfred, and a crowd of other characters, were universally considered merely as loose incognitos of Byron; and there is every reason to believe that he meant them to be so considered. The wonders of the outer world, the Tagus, with the mighty fleets of England riding on its bosom, the towers of Cintra overhanging the shaggy forest of cork-trees and willows, the glaring marble of Pentelicus, the banks of the Rhine, the glaciers of Clarens, the sweet Lake of Leman, the dell of Egeria with its summer-birds and rustling lizards, the shapeless ruins of Rome overgrown with ivy and wall-flowers, the stars, the sea, the mountains, all were mere accessories, the background to one dark and melancholy figure.

Never had any writer so vast a command of the whole eloquence of scorn, misanthropy, and despair. That Marah was never dry. No art could sweeten, no draughts could exhaust, its perennial waters of bitterness. Never was there such variety in monotony as that of Byron. From maniac laughter to piercing lamentation, there was not a single note of human anguish of which he was not master. Year after year, and month after month, he continued to repeat that to be wretched is the destiny of all; that to be eminently 10 wretched is the destiny of the eminent; that all the desires by which we are cursed lead alike to misery,—if they are not gratified, to the misery of disappointment; if they are gratified, to the misery of satiety. His heroes are men who have arrived by different roads at the same goal of despair, who are sick of life, who are at war with society, who are supported in their anguish only by an unconquerable pride resem- 20 bling that of Prometheus on the rock or of Satan in the burning marl, who can master their agonies by the force of their will, and who to the last defy the whole power of earth and heaven. He always described himself as a man of the same kind with his favourite creations, as a man whose heart had been withered, whose capacity for happiness was gone and could not be restored, but whose invincible spirit 30 dared the worst that could befall him here or hereafter.

How much of this morbid feeling sprang from an original disease of the mind, how much from real misfortune, how much from the nervousness of dissipation, how much was fanciful, how much was merely affected, it is impossible for us, and would probably have been impossible for the most intimate friends of Lord Byron, to decide. 40 Whether there ever existed, or can ever exist, a person answering to the description which he gave of himself may be doubted; but that he was not such a person is beyond all doubt. It is ridiculous to imagine that a man whose mind was really imbued with scorn of his fellow-creatures would have published three or four books every year in order to tell them so; or that a man who could say with truth that he 50 neither sought sympathy nor needed it would have admitted all Europe to hear his farewell to his wife, and his blessings on his child. In the second canto of

Childe Harold, he tells us that he is insensible to fame and obloquy:

Ill may such contest now the spirit move,
Which heeds nor keen reproof nor partial
    praise.

Yet we know on the best evidence that, a day or two before he published these lines, he was greatly, indeed childishly, elated by the compliments paid to his maiden speech in the House of Lords.

We are far, however, from thinking that his sadness was altogether feigned. He was naturally a man of great sensibility; he had been ill-educated; his feelings had been early exposed to sharp trials; he had been crossed in his boyish love; he had been mortified by the failure of his first literary efforts; he was straitened in pecuniary circumstances; he was unfortunate in his domestic relations; the public treated him with cruel injustice; his health and spirits suffered from his dissipated habits of life; he was, on the whole, an unhappy man. He early discovered that, by parading his unhappiness before the multitude, he produced an immense sensation. The world gave him every encouragement to talk about his mental sufferings. The interest which his first confessions excited induced him to affect much that he did not feel; and the affectation probably reacted on his feelings. How far the character in which he exhibited himself was genuine, and how far theatrical, it would probably have puzzled himself to say.

There can be no doubt that this remarkable man owed the vast influence which he exercised over his contemporaries at least as much to his gloomy egotism as to the real power of his poetry. We never could very clearly understand how it is that egotism, so unpopular in conversation, should be so popular in writing; or how it is that men who affect in their compositions qualities and feelings which they have not, impose so much more easily on their contemporaries than on posterity. The interest which the loves of Petrarch excited in his own time, and the pitying fondness with which half Europe looked upon Rousseau, are well known. To readers of our age, the love of Petrarch seems to have been love of that kind which breaks no hearts, and the sufferings of Rousseau to have deserved laughter rather than pity, to have been partly counterfeited, and partly the consequences of his own perverseness and vanity.

What our grandchildren may think of the character of Lord Byron, as exhibited in his poetry, we will not pretend to guess. It is certain, that the interest which he excited during his life is without a parallel in literary history. The feeling with which young readers of poetry regarded him can be conceived only by those who have experienced it. To people who are unacquainted with real calamity, "nothing is so dainty sweet as lovely melancholy." This faint image of sorrow has in all ages been considered by young gentlemen as an agreeable excitement. Old gentlemen and middle-aged gentlemen have so many real causes of sadness that they are rarely inclined "to be as sad as night only for wantonness." Indeed they want the power almost as much as the inclination. We know very few persons engaged in active life, who, even if they were to procure stools to be melancholy upon, and were to sit down with all the premeditation of Master Stephen, would be able to enjoy much of what somebody calls the "ecstasy of woe."

Among that large class of young persons whose reading is almost entirely confined to works of imagination, the popularity of Lord Byron was unbounded. They bought pictures of him; they treasured up the smallest relics of him; they learned his poems by heart, and did their best to write like him, and to look like him. Many of them practised at the glass in the hope of catching the curl of the upper lip, and the scowl of the brow, which appear in some of his portraits. A few discarded their neck-cloths in imitation of their great leader. For some years the Minerva press sent forth no novel without a mysterious, unhappy, Lara-like peer. The number of hopeful undergraduates and medical students who became things of dark imaginings, on whom the freshness of the heart ceased to fall like dew, whose passions had consumed themselves to dust, and to whom the relief of tears was denied, passes all calculation. This was not the worst. There was created in the minds of many of these enthusiasts a pernicious and absurd association between intellectual power and moral depravity. From the poetry of Lord Byron they drew a system of ethics, compounded of misanthropy and voluptuousness, a system in which the two great commandments were, to hate your neighbour, and to love your neighbour's wife.

This affectation has passed away; and a few more years will destroy whatever yet remains of that magical potency which once belonged to the name of Byron. To us he is still a man, young, noble, and unhappy. To our children he will be merely a writer; and their impartial judgment will appoint his place among writers; without regard to his rank or to his private history. That his poetry will undergo a severe sifting, that much of what has been admired by his contemporaries will be rejected as worthless, we have little doubt. But we have as little doubt that, after the closest scrutiny, there will still remain much that can only perish with the English language.

[1831]

HISTORY OF ENGLAND (I)

ENGLAND IN 1685

(a) LONDON

Whoever examines the maps of London which were published towards the close of the reign of Charles the Second will see that only the nucleus of the present capital then existed. The town did not, as now, fade by imperceptible degrees into the country. No long avenues of villas, embowered in lilacs and laburnums, extended from the great centre of wealth and civilization almost to the boundaries of Middlesex and far into the heart of Kent and Surrey. In the east, no part of the immense line of ware-houses and artificial lakes which now spreads from the Tower to Blackwall had even been projected. On the west, scarcely one of those stately piles of building which are inhabited by the noble and wealthy was in existence; and Chelsea, which is now peopled by more than forty thousand human beings, was a quiet country village with scarce a thousand inhabitants. On the north, cattle fed and sportsmen wandered with dogs and guns over the site of the borough of Marylebone, and over far the greater part of 10 the space now covered by the boroughs of Finsbury and of the Tower Hamlets. Islington was almost a solitude; and poets loved to contrast its silence and repose with the din and turmoil of the monster London. On the south, the capital is now connected with its suburb by several bridges, not inferior in magnificence and solidity to the noblest works of the Cæsars. In 1685 a single line of irregular arches, 20 overhung by piles of mean and crazy houses, and garnished after a fashion worthy of the naked barbarians of Dahomy, with scores of mouldering heads, impeded the navigation of the river.

Of the metropolis, the City, properly so called, was the most important division. At the time of the Restoration it had been built, for the most part, of wood and plaster; the few bricks that were used were 30 ill baked; the booths where goods were exposed to sale projected far into the streets, and were overhung by the upper stories. A few specimens of this architecture may still be seen in those districts which were not reached by the great fire. That fire had, in a few days, covered a space of little less than a square mile with the ruins of eighty-nine churches and of thirteen thousand houses. But the city 40 had risen again with a celerity which had excited the admiration of neighboring countries. Unfortunately, the old lines of the streets had been to a great extent preserved; and those lines, originally traced in an age when even princesses performed their journeys on horseback, were often too narrow to allow wheeled carriages to pass each other with ease, and were therefore ill adapted for the residence of wealthy 50 persons in an age when a coach and six was a fashionable luxury. The style of building was, however, far superior to that of the city which had perished. The ordi-

nary material was brick, of much better quality than had formerly been used. On the sites of the ancient parish churches had arisen a multitude of new domes, towers, and spires which bore the mark of the fertile genius of Wren. In every place save one the traces of the great devastation had been completely effaced. But the crowds of workmen, the scaffolds, and the masses of hewn stone were still to be seen where the noblest of Protestant temples was slowly rising on the ruins of the old cathedral of St. Paul.

The whole character of the City has, since that time, undergone a complete change. At present the bankers, the merchants, and the chief shopkeepers repair thither on six mornings of every week for the transaction of business; but they reside in other quarters of the metropolis, or at suburban country-seats surrounded by shrubberies and flower gardens. This revolution in private habits has produced a political revolution of no small importance. The City is no longer regarded by the wealthiest traders with that attachment which every man naturally feels for his home. It is no longer associated in their minds with domestic affections and endearments. The fireside, the nursery, the social table, the quiet bed are not there. Lombard Street and Threadneedle Street are merely places where men toil and accumulate. They go elsewhere to enjoy and to expend. On a Sunday or in an evening after the hours of business, some courts and alleys, which a few hours before had been alive with hurrying feet and anxious faces, are as silent as a country churchyard. The chiefs of the mercantile interest are no longer citizens. They avoid, they almost contemn, municipal honors and duties. Those honors and duties are abandoned to men who, though useful and highly respectable, seldom belong to the princely commercial houses of which the names are held in honor throughout the world.

In the seventeenth century the City was the merchant's residence. Those mansions of the great old burghers which still exist have been turned into counting-houses and ware-houses; but it is evident that they were originally not inferior in magnificence to the dwellings which were then inhabited by the nobility. They sometimes stand in retired and gloomy courts, and are accessible only by inconvenient passages; but their dimensions are ample and their aspect stately. The entrances are decorated with richly carved pillars and canopies. The staircases and landing-places are not wanting in grandeur. The floors are sometimes of wood, tessellated after the fashion of France. The palace of Sir Robert Clayton, in the Old Jewry, contained a superb banqueting room wainscoted with cedar and adorned with battles of gods and giants in fresco. Sir Dudley North expended four thousand pounds, a sum which would then have been important to a duke, on the rich furniture of his reception rooms in Basing-hall Street. In such abodes, under the last Stuarts, the heads of the great firms lived splendidly and hospitably. To their dwelling-place they were bound by the strongest ties of interest and affection. There they had passed their youth, had made their friendships, had courted their wives, had seen their children grow up, had laid the remains of their parents in the earth, and expected that their own remains would be laid. That intense patriotism which is peculiar to the members of societies congregated within a narrow space was, in such circumstances, strongly developed. London was, to the Londoner, what Athens was to the Athenian of the age of Pericles, what Florence was to the Florentine of the fifteenth century. The citizen was proud of the grandeur of his city, punctilious about her claims to respect, ambitious of her offices, and zealous for her franchises.

At the close of the reign of Charles the Second the pride of the Londoners was smarting from a cruel mortification. The old charter had been taken away, and the magistracy had been remodelled. All the civic functionaries were Tories; and the Whigs, though in numbers and in wealth superior to their opponents, found themselves excluded from every local dignity. Nevertheless, the external splendor of the municipal government was not diminished, nay, was rather increased by this change. For, under the administration of some Puritans who had lately borne rule, the ancient fame of the City for good cheer had declined; but under the new magistrates, who belonged to a more festive party, and at whose boards guests of rank and fashion from beyond Temple Bar were often seen, the Guildhall and the halls of the great companies were enlivened by many sumptuous banquets. During these repasts, odes, composed by the poet laureate of the corporation, in praise of the king, the duke, and the mayor, were sung to music. The drinking was deep, the shouting loud. An observant Tory, who had often shared in these revels, has remarked that the practice of huzzaing after drinking healths dates from this joyous period.

The magnificence displayed by the first civic magistrate was almost regal. The gilded coach, indeed, which is now annually admired by the crowd, was not yet a part of his state. On great occasions he appeared on horseback, attended by a long cavalcade inferior in magnificence only to that which, before a coronation, escorted the sovereign from the Tower to Westminster. The Lord Mayor was never seen in public without his rich robe, his hood of black velvet, his gold chain, his jewel, and a great attendance of harbingers and guards. Nor did the world find anything ludicrous in the pomp which constantly surrounded him. For it was not more than proportioned to the place which, as wielding the strength and representing the dignity of the city of London, he was entitled to occupy in the state. That city, being then not only without equal in the country, but without second, had, during five and forty years, exercised almost as great an influence on the politics of England as Paris has, in our own time, exercised on the politics of France. In intelligence London was greatly in advance of every other part of the kingdom. A government, supported and trusted by London, could in a day obtain such pecuniary means as it would have taken months to collect from the rest of the island. Nor were the military resources of the capital to be despised. The power which the lord lieutenants exercised in other parts of the kingdom was in London intrusted to a commission of eminent citizens. Under the orders of this commission were twelve regiments of foot and two regiments of horse. An army of drapers' apprentices and journeymen tailors, with common councilmen for captains and aldermen for colonels, might not indeed have been able to stand its ground against regular troops; but there were then very few regular troops in the kingdom. A town, therefore, which could send forth, at an hour's notice, twenty thousand men, abounding in natural courage, provided with tolerable weapons, and not altogether untinctured with martial discipline, could not but be a valuable ally and a formidable enemy. It was not forgotten that Hampden and Pym had been protected from lawless tyranny by the London trainbands; that, in the great crisis of the Civil War, the London trainbands had marched to raise the siege of Gloucester; or that, in the movement against the military tyrants which followed the downfall of Richard Cromwell, the London trainbands had borne a signal part. In truth, it is no exaggeration to say that, but for the hostility of the City, Charles the First would never have been vanquished, and that, without the help of the City, Charles the Second could scarcely have been restored.

These considerations may serve to explain why, in spite of that attraction which had, during a long course of years, gradually drawn the aristocracy westward, a few men of high rank had continued, till a very recent period, to dwell in the vicinity of the Exchange and of the Guildhall. Shaftesbury and Buckingham, while engaged in bitter and unscrupulous opposition to the government, had thought that they could nowhere carry on their intrigues so conveniently or so securely as under the protection of the city magistrates and the city militia. Shaftesbury had therefore lived in Aldersgate Street, at a house which may still easily be known by pilasters and wreaths, the graceful work of Inigo. Buckingham had ordered his mansion near Charing Cross, once the abode of the archbishops of York, to be pulled down; and, while streets and alleys which are still named after him were rising on that site, chose to reside in Dowgate.

These, however, were rare exceptions. Almost all the noble families of England had long migrated beyond the walls. The district where most of their town houses stood lies between the city and the regions which are now considered as fashionable. A few great men still retain their hereditary hotels between the Strand and the river. The stately dwellings on the south and west of Lincoln's Inn Fields, the Piazza of Covent Garden, Southampton Square, which is now called Bloomsbury Square, and King's Square in Soho Fields, which is now called Soho Square, were among the favorite spots. Foreign princes were carried to see Bloomsbury Square as one of the wonders of England. Soho Square, which had just been built, was to our ancestors a subject of pride with which their posterity will hardly sympathize. Monmouth Square had been the name while the fortunes of the Duke of Monmouth flourished, and on the southern side towered his mansion. The front, though ungraceful, was lofty and richly adorned. The walls of the principal apartments were finely sculptured with fruit, foliage, and armorial bearings, and were hung with embroidered satin. Every trace of this magnificence has long disappeared, and no aristocratical mansion is to be found in that once aristocratical quarter. A little way north from Holborn, and on the verge of the pastures and cornfields, rose two celebrated palaces, each with an ample garden. One of them, then called Southampton House and subsequently Bedford House, was removed about fifty years ago to make room for a new city, which now covers, with its squares, streets, and churches, a vast area, renowned in the seventeenth century for peaches and snipes. The other, Montague House, celebrated for its frescoes and furniture, was, a few months after the death of Charles the Second, burned to the ground, and was speedily succeeded by a more magnificent Montague House, which, having been long the repository of such various and precious treasures of art, science, and learning as were scarce ever before assembled under a single roof, has just given place to an edifice more magnificent still.

Nearer to the court, on a space called Saint James's Fields, had just been built Saint James's Square and Jermyn Street.

Saint James's Church had recently been opened for the accommodation of the inhabitants of this new quarter. Golden Square, which was in the next generation inhabited by lords and ministers of state, had not yet been begun. Indeed the only dwellings to be seen on the north of Piccadilly were three or four isolated and almost rural mansions, of which the most celebrated was the costly pile erected by Clarendon, and nicknamed Dunkirk House. It had been purchased after its founder's downfall by the Duke of Albemarle. The Clarendon Hotel and Albemarle Street still preserve the memory of the site.

He who then rambled to what is now the gayest and most crowded part of Regent Street found himself in a solitude, and was sometimes so fortunate as to have a shot at a woodcock. On the north the Oxford Road ran between hedges. Three or four hundred yards to the south were the garden walls of a few great houses, which were considered as quite out of town. On the west was a meadow renowned for a spring from which, long afterwards, Conduit Street was named. On the east was a field not to be passed without a shudder by any Londoner of that age. There, as in a place far from the haunts of men, had been dug, twenty years before, when the great plague was raging, a pit into which the dead carts had nightly shot corpses by scores. It was popularly believed that the earth was deeply tainted with infection, and could not be disturbed without imminent risk to human life. No foundations were laid there till two generations had passed without any return of the pestilence and till the ghastly spot had long been surrounded by buildings.

We should greatly err if we were to suppose that any of the streets and squares then bore the same aspect as at present. The great majority of the houses, indeed, have, since that time, been wholly or in part rebuilt. If the most fashionable parts of the capital could be placed before us, such as they then were, we should be disgusted by their squalid appearance and poisoned by their noisome atmosphere. In Covent Garden a filthy and noisy market was held close to the dwellings of the great.

Fruit women screamed, carters fought, cabbage stalks and rotten apples accumulated in heaps at the thresholds of the Countess of Berkshire and of the Bishop of Durham.

The center of Lincoln's Inn Fields was an open space where the rabble congregated every evening, within a few yards of Cardigan House and Winchester House, to hear mountebanks harangue, to see bears dance, and to set dogs at oxen. Rubbish was shot in every part of the area. Horses were exercised there. The beggars were as noisy and importunate as in the worst governed cities of the Continent. A Lincoln's Inn mumper was a proverb. The whole fraternity knew the arms and liveries of every charitably disposed grandee in the neighborhood, and, as soon as his lordship's coach and six appeared, came hopping and crawling in crowds to persecute him. These disorders lasted, in spite of many accidents and of some legal proceedings, till, in the reign of George the Second, Sir Joseph Jekyll, Master of the Rolls, was knocked down and nearly killed in the middle of the square. Then at length palisades were set up and a pleasant garden laid out.

Saint James's Square was a receptacle for all the offal and cinders, for all the dead cats and dead dogs of Westminster. At one time a cudgel player kept the ring there. At another time an impudent squatter settled himself there, and built a shed for rubbish under the windows of the gilded saloons in which the first magnates of the realm, Norfolks, Ormonds, Kents, and Pembrokes, gave banquets and balls. It was not till these nuisances had lasted through a whole generation and till much had been written about them that the inhabitants applied to parliament for permission to put up rails and to plant trees.

When such was the state of the quarter inhabited by the most luxurious portion of society, we may easily believe that the great body of the population suffered what would now be considered as insupportable grievances. The pavement was detestable; all foreigners cried shame upon it. The drainage was so bad that in rainy weather the gutters soon became torrents. Several facetious poets have commemorated the fury with which these black rivulets roared down Snow Hill and Ludgate Hill, bearing to Fleet Ditch a vast tribute of animal and vegetable filth from the stalls of butchers and greengrocers. This flood was profusely thrown to right and left by coaches and carts. To keep as far from the carriage road as possible was therefore the wish of every pedestrian. The mild and timid gave the wall. The bold and athletic took it. If two roisters met, they cocked their hats in each other's faces and pushed each other about till the weaker was shoved towards the kennel. If he was a mere bully he sneaked off, muttering that he should find a time. If he was pugnacious, the encounter probably ended in a duel behind Montague House.

The houses were not numbered. There would indeed have been little advantage in numbering them; for of the coachmen, chairmen, porters, and errand boys of London, a very small portion could read. It was necessary to use marks which the most ignorant could understand. The shops were therefore distinguished by painted signs, which gave a gay and grotesque aspect to the streets. The walk from Charing Cross to Whitechapel lay through an endless succession of Saracen's Heads, Royal Oaks, Blue Bears, and Golden Lambs, which disappeared when they were no longer required for the direction of the common people.

When the evening closed in, the difficulty and danger of walking about London became serious indeed. The garret windows were opened, and pails were emptied, with little regard to those who were passing below. Falls, bruises, and broken bones were of constant occurrence. For, till the last year of the reign of Charles the Second, most of the streets were left in profound darkness. Thieves and robbers plied their trade with impunity; yet they were hardly so terrible to peaceable citizens as another class of ruffians. It was a favorite amusement of dissolute young gentlemen to swagger by night about the town, breaking windows, upsetting sedans, beating quiet men, and offering rude caresses to pretty women. Several dynasties of these tyrants had, since the Restoration, domineered over the streets. The Muns

and Tityre Tus had given place to the Hectors, and the Hectors had been recently succeeded by the Scourers. At a later period arose the Nicker, the Hawcubite, and the yet more dreaded name of Mohawk. The machinery for keeping the peace was utterly contemptible. There was an act of Common Council which provided that more than a thousand watchmen should be constantly on the alert in the city, from sunset to sunrise, and that every inhabitant should take his turn of duty. But the act was negligently executed. Few of those who were summoned left their homes; and those few generally found it more agreeable to tipple in ale-houses than to pace the streets.

It ought to be noticed that, in the last year of the reign of Charles the Second, began a great change in the police of London,—a change which has perhaps added as much to the happiness of the great body of the people as revolutions of much greater fame. An ingenious projector, named Edward Heming, obtained letters patent conveying to him, for a term of years, the exclusive right of lighting up London. He undertook, for a moderate consideration, to place a light before every tenth door, on moonless nights, from Michaelmas to Lady Day, and from six to twelve of the clock. Those who now see the capital all the year round, from dusk to dawn blazing with a splendor compared with which the illuminations for La Hogue and Blenheim would have looked pale, may perhaps smile to think of Heming's lanterns, which glimmered feebly before one house in ten during a small part of one night in three. But such was not the feeling of his contemporaries. His scheme was enthusiastically applauded and furiously attacked. The friends of improvement extolled him as the greatest of all the benefactors of his city. What, they asked, were the boasted inventions of Archimedes when compared with the achievement of the man who had turned the nocturnal shades into noonday? In spite of these eloquent eulogies, the cause of darkness was not left undefended. There were fools in that age who opposed the introduction of what was called the new light as strenuously as fools in our age have opposed the introduction of vaccination and railroads, as strenuously as the fools of an age anterior to the dawn of history doubtless opposed the introduction of the plough and of alphabetical writing. Many years after the date of Heming's patent, there were extensive districts in which no lamp was seen.

We may easily imagine what, in such times, must have been the state of the quarters peopled by the outcasts of society. Among those quarters one had attained a scandalous preëminence. On the confines of the city and the Temple had been founded, in the thirteenth century, a House of Carmelite Friars, distinguished by their white hoods. The precinct of this house had, before the Reformation, been a sanctuary for criminals, and still retained the privilege of protecting debtors from arrest. Insolvents consequently were to be found in every dwelling, from cellar to garret. Of these a large proportion were knaves and libertines, and were followed to their asylum by women more abandoned than themselves. The civil power was unable to keep order in a district swarming with such inhabitants; and thus White-friars became the favorite resort of all who wished to be emancipated from the restraints of the law. Though the immunities legally belonging to the place extended only to cases of debt, cheats, false witnesses, forgers, and highwaymen found refuge there. For amidst a rabble so desperate no peace officer's life was in safety. At the cry of "Rescue," bullies with swords and cudgels and termagant hags with spits and broomsticks poured forth by hundreds; and the intruder was fortunate if he escaped back into Fleet Street, hustled, stripped, and pumped upon. Even the warrant of the Chief Justice of England could not be executed without the help of a company of musketeers. Such relics of the barbarism of the darkest ages were to be found within a short walk of the chambers where Somers was studying history and law, of the chapel where Tillotson was preaching, of the coffee-house where Dryden was passing judgment on poems and plays, and of the hall where the Royal Society was examining the astronomical system of Isaac Newton.

Each of the two cities which made up the capital of England had its own center of attraction. In the metropolis of commerce the point of convergence was the Exchange; in the metropolis of fashion the Palace. But the Palace did not retain its influence so long as the Exchange. The revolution completely altered the relations between the court and the higher classes of society. It was by degrees discovered that the king, in his individual capacity, had very little to give; that coronets and garters, bishoprics, and embassies, lordships of the treasury, and tellerships of the Exchequer, nay, even charges in the royal stud and bed-chamber, were really bestowed, not by the king, but by his advisers. Every ambitious and covetous man perceived that he would consult his own interest far better by acquiring the dominion of a Cornish borough, and by rendering good service to the ministry during a critical session, than by becoming the companion or even the minion of his prince. It was therefore in the antechambers, not of George the First and of George the Second, but of Walpole and of Pelham, that the daily crowd of courtiers was to be found. It is also to be remarked that the same revolution which made it impossible that our kings should use the patronage of the state, merely for the purpose of gratifying their personal predilections, gave us several kings unfitted by their education and habits to be gracious and affable hosts. They had been born and bred on the Continent. They never felt themselves at home in our island. If they spoke our language they spoke it inelegantly and with effort. Our national character they never fully understood. Our national manners they hardly attempted to acquire. The most important part of their duty they performed better than any ruler who had preceded them, for they governed strictly according to law; but they could not be the first gentlemen of the realm, the heads of polite society. If ever they unbent it was in a very small circle, where hardly an English face was to be seen; and they were never so happy as when they could escape for a summer to their native land. They had indeed their days of reception for our nobility and gentry; but the reception was mere matter of form, and became at last as solemn a ceremony as a funeral.

Not such was the court of Charles the Second. Whitehall, when he dwelt there, was the focus of political intrigue and of fashionable gayety. Half the jobbing and half the flirting of the metropolis went on under his roof. Whoever could make himself agreeable to the prince or could secure the good offices of the mistress might 10 hope to rise in the world without rendering any service to the government, without being even known by sight to any minister of state. This courtier got a frigate, and that a company; a third, the pardon of a rich offender; a fourth, a lease of crown land on easy terms. If the king notified his pleasure that a briefless lawyer should be made judge or that a libertine baronet should be made a peer, the gravest coun- 20 cillors, after a little murmuring, submitted. Interest, therefore, drew a constant press of suitors to the gates of the palace, and those gates always stood wide. The king kept open house every day, and all day long, for the good society of London, the extreme Whigs only excepted. Hardly any gentleman had any difficulty in making his way to the royal presence. The levee was exactly what the word imports. Some 30 men of quality came every morning to stand round their master, to chat with him while his wig was combed and his cravat tied, and to accompany him in his early walk through the park. All persons who had been properly introduced might, without any special invitation, go to see him dine, sup, dance, and play at hazard, and might have the pleasure of hearing him tell stories, which, indeed, he told remark- 40 ably well, about his flight from Worcester, and about the misery which he had endured when he was a state prisoner in the hands of the canting, meddling preachers of Scotland. Bystanders whom his majesty recognized often came in for a courteous word. This proved a far more successful king-craft than any that his father or grandfather had practised. It was not easy for the most austere republican of the 50 school of Marvell to resist the fascination of so much good humor and affability; and many a veteran Cavalier, in whose heart the remembrance of unrequited sacrifices

and services had been festering during a quarter of a century, was compensated in one moment for wounds and sequestrations by his sovereign's kind nod, and "God bless you, my old friend!"

Whitehall naturally became the chief staple of news. Whenever there was a rumor that anything important had happened or was about to happen, people 10 hastened thither to obtain intelligence from the fountain head. The galleries presented the appearance of a modern clubroom at an anxious time. They were full of people inquiring whether the Dutch mail was in, what tidings the express from France had brought, whether John Sobiesky had beaten the Turks, whether the Doge of Genoa was really at Paris. These were matters about which it was safe to 20 talk aloud. But there were subjects concerning which information was asked and given in whispers. Had Halifax got the better of Rochester? Was there to be a parliament? Was the Duke of York really going to Scotland? Had Monmouth really been sent for to the Hague? Men tried to read the countenance of every minister as he went through the throng to and from the royal closet. All sorts of auguries were 30 drawn from the tone in which his majesty spoke to the Lord President, or from the laugh with which his majesty honoured a jest of the Lord Privy Seal; and, in a few hours, the hopes and fears inspired by such slight indications had spread to all the coffee-houses from St. James's to the Tower.

The coffee-house must not be dismissed with a cursory mention. It might indeed, at that time, have been not improperly 40 called a most important political institution. No parliament had sate for years. The municipal council of the city had ceased to speak the sense of the citizens. Public meetings, harangues, resolutions, and the rest of the modern machinery of agitation had not yet come into fashion. Nothing resembling the modern newspaper existed. In such circumstances, the coffee-houses were the chief organs through which 50 the public opinion of the metropolis vented itself.

The first of these establishments had been set up, in the time of the Commonwealth, by a Turkey merchant, who had acquired among the Mahometans a taste for their favorite beverage. The convenience of being able to make appointments in any part of the town, and of being able to pass evenings socially at a very small charge, was so great that the fashion spread fast. Every man of the upper or middle class went daily to his coffee-house to learn the news and to discuss it. Every coffee-house had one or more orators to whose 10 eloquence the crowd listened with admiration, and who soon became, what the journalists of our own time have been called, a fourth estate of the realm. The court had long seen with uneasiness the growth of this new power in the state. An attempt had been made, during Danby's administration, to close the coffee-houses. But men of all parties missed their usual places of resort so much that there was a uni- 20 versal outcry. The government did not venture, in opposition to a feeling so strong and general, to enforce a regulation of which the legality might well be questioned. Since that time ten years had elapsed, and, during those years, the number and influence of the coffee-houses had been constantly increasing. Foreigners remarked that the coffee-house was that which especially distinguished London 30 from all other cities; that the coffee-house was the Londoner's home, and that those who wished to find a gentleman commonly asked, not whether he lived in Fleet Street or Chancery Lane, but whether he frequented the Grecian or the Rainbow. Nobody was excluded from these places who laid down his penny at the bar. Yet every rank and profession and every shade of religious and political opinion had its 40 own headquarters. There were houses near St. James's Park where fops congregated, their heads and shoulders covered with black or flaxen wigs, not less ample than those which are now worn by the chancellor and by the speaker of the House of Commons. The wig came from Paris, and so did the rest of the fine gentleman's ornaments, his embroidered coat, his fringed gloves, and the tassel which upheld 50 his pantaloons. The conversation was in that dialect which, long after it had ceased to be spoken in fashionable circles, continued, in the mouth of Lord Fopping-

ton, to excite the mirth of theatres. The atmosphere was like that of a perfumer's shop. Tobacco in any other form than that of richly scented snuff was held in abomination. If any clown, ignorant of the usages of the house, called for a pipe, the sneers of the whole assembly and the short answers of the waiters soon convinced him that he had better go somewhere else. Nor, indeed, would he have had far to go. For, in general, the coffee-rooms reeked with tobacco like a guard room; and strangers sometimes expressed their surprise that so many people should leave their own firesides to sit in the midst of eternal fog and stench. Nowhere was the smoking more constant than at Will's. That celebrated house, situated between Covent Garden and Bow Street, was sacred 20 to polite letters. There the talk was about poetical justice and the unities of place and time. There was a faction for Perrault and the moderns, a faction for Boileau and the ancients. One group debated whether *Paradise Lost* ought not to have been in rhyme. To another an envious poetaster demonstrated that *Venice Preserved* ought to have been hooted from the stage. Under no roof was a greater variety of 30 figures to be seen,—earls in stars and garters, clergymen in cassocks and bands, pert templars, sheepish lads from the universities, translators and index-makers in ragged coats of frieze. The great press was to get near the chair where John Dryden sate. In winter, that chair was always in the warmest nook by the fire; in summer, it stood in the balcony. To bow to him, and to hear his opinion of Racine's last tragedy or of 40 Bossu's treatise on epic poetry, was thought a privilege. A pinch from his snuff-box was an honor sufficient to turn the head of a young enthusiast. There were coffee-houses where the first medical men might be consulted. Doctor John Radcliffe, who, in the year 1685, rose to the largest practice in London, came daily, at the hour when the Exchange was full, from his house in Bow Street, then a fashionable 50 part of the capital, to Garraway's, and was to be found surrounded by surgeons and apothecaries at a particular table. There were Puritan coffee-houses where no oath was heard, and where lank-haired men discussed election and reprobation through their noses; Jew coffee-houses where dark-eyed money-changers from Venice and Amsterdam greeted each other; and Popish coffee-houses where, as good Protestants believed, Jesuits planned, over their cups, another great fire, and cast silver bullets to shoot the king.

(b) LITERATURE, SCIENCE, AND ART

Literature which could be carried by the post bag then formed the greater part of the intellectual nutriment ruminated by the country divines and country justices. The difficulty and expense of conveying large packets from place to place were so great that an extensive work was longer in making its way from Paternoster Row to Devonshire or Lancashire than it now is in reaching Kentucky. How scantily a rural parsonage was then furnished, even with books the most necessary to a theologian, has already been remarked. The houses of the gentry were not more plentifully supplied. Few knights of the shire had libraries so good as may now perpetually be found in a servant's hall or in the back parlor of a small shopkeeper. An esquire passed among his neighbors for a great scholar if *Hudibras* and *Baker's Chronicle, Tarlton's Jests,* and the *Seven Champions of Christendom* lay in his hall window among the fishing-rods and fowling-pieces. No circulating library, no book society then existed even in the capital; but in the capital those students who could not afford to purchase largely had a resource. The shops of the great booksellers, near Saint Paul's Churchyard, were crowded every day and all day long with readers, and a known customer was often permitted to carry a volume home. In the country there was no such accommodation, and every man was under the necessity of buying whatever he wished to read.

As to the lady of the manor and her daughters, their literary stores generally consisted of a prayer book and a receipt book. But in truth they lost little by living in rural seclusion. For even in the highest ranks and in those situations which afforded the greatest facilities for mental improvement, the English women of that generation were decidedly worse educated

than they have been at any other time since the Revival of Learning. At an earlier period, they had studied the masterpieces of ancient genius. In the present day, they seldom bestow much attention on the dead languages, but they are familiar with the tongue of Pascal and Molière, with the tongue of Dante and Tasso, with the tongue of Goethe and Schiller; nor is there any purer or more graceful English than that which accomplished women now speak and write. But during the latter part of the seventeenth century, the culture of the female mind seems to have been almost entirely neglected. If a damsel had the least smattering of literature, she was regarded as a prodigy. Ladies highly born, highly bred, and naturally quick-witted were unable to write a line in their mother tongue without solecisms and faults of spelling such as a charity girl would now be ashamed to commit.

The explanation may easily be found. Extravagant licentiousness, the natural effect of extravagant austerity, was now the mode; and licentiousness had produced its ordinary effect, the moral and intellectual degradation of women. To their personal beauty it was the fashion to pay rude and impudent homage. But the admiration and desire which they inspired were seldom mingled with respect, with affection, or with any chivalrous sentiment. The qualities which fit them to be companions, advisers, confidential friends, rather repelled than attracted the libertines of Whitehall. In that court, a maid of honor, who dressed in such a manner as to do full justice to a white bosom, who ogled significantly, who danced voluptuously, who excelled in pert repartee, who was not ashamed to romp with lords of the bedchamber and captains of the guards, to sing sly verses with sly expression, or to put on a page's dress for a frolic, was more likely to be followed and admired, more likely to be honored with royal attentions, more likely to win a rich and noble husband than Jane Grey or Lucy Hutchinson would have been. In such circumstances the standard of female attainments was necessarily low; and it was more dangerous to be above that standard than to be beneath it. Extreme ignorance and frivolity were thought less unbecoming in a lady than the slightest tincture of pedantry. Of the too celebrated women whose faces we still admire on the walls of Hampton Court, few indeed were in the habit of reading anything more valuable than acrostics, lampoons, and translations of the *Clelia* and the *Grand Cyrus*.

The literary acquirements, even of the accomplished gentlemen of that genera- 10 tion, seem to have been somewhat less solid and profound than at an earlier or a later period. Greek learning, at least, did not flourish among us in the days of Charles the Second as it had flourished before the Civil War, or as it again flourished long after the Revolution. There were undoubtedly scholars to whom the whole Greek literature from Homer to Photius was familiar; but such scholars were to be 20 found almost exclusively among the clergy resident at the universities, and even at the universities were few, and were not fully appreciated. At Cambridge it was not thought by any means necessary that a divine should be able to read the Gospels in the original. Nor was the standard at Oxford higher. When, in the reign of William the Third, Christ Church rose up as one man to defend the genuineness of the 30 Epistles of Phalaris, that great college, then considered as the first seat of philology in the kingdom, could not muster such a stock of Attic learning as is now possessed by several youths at every great public school. It may easily be supposed that a dead language, neglected at the universities, was not much studied by men of the world. In a former age, the poetry and eloquence of Greece had been the delight of Raleigh 40 and Falkland. In a later age, the poetry and eloquence of Greece were the delight of Pitt and Fox, of Windham and Grenville. But during the latter part of the seventeenth century there was in England scarcely one eminent statesman who could read with enjoyment a page of Sophocles or Plato.

Good Latin scholars were numerous. The language of Rome, indeed, had not al- 50 together lost its imperial character, and was still, in many parts of Europe, almost indispensable to a traveler or a negotiator. To speak it well was therefore a much more common accomplishment than in our time; and neither Oxford nor Cambridge wanted poets who, on a great occasion, could lay at the foot of the throne happy imitations of the verses in which Virgil and Ovid had celebrated the greatness of Augustus.

Yet even the Latin was giving way to a younger rival. France united at that time almost every species of ascendency. Her military glory was at the height. She had vanquished mighty coalitions. She had dictated treaties. She had subjected great cities and provinces. She had forced the Castilian pride to yield her the precedence. She had summoned Italian princes to prostrate themselves at her footstool. Her authority was supreme in all matters of good breeding, from a duel to a minuet. She determined how a gentleman's coat must be cut, how long his peruke must be, whether his heels must be high or low, and whether the lace on his hat must be broad or narrow. In literature she gave law to the world. The fame of her great writers filled Europe. No other country could produce a tragic poet equal to Racine, a comic poet equal to Molière, a trifler so agreeable as La Fontaine, a rhetorician so skillful as Bossuet. The literary glory of Italy and of Spain had set; that of Germany had not yet dawned. The genius, therefore, of the eminent men who adorned Paris shone forth with a splendor which was set off to full advantage by contrast. France, indeed, had at that time an empire over mankind, such as even the Roman Republic never attained. For when Rome was politically dominant, she was in arts and letters the humble pupil of Greece. France had, over the surrounding countries, at once the ascendency which Rome had over Greece, and the ascendency which Greece had over Rome. French was fast becoming the universal language, the language of fashionable society, the language of diplomacy. At several courts princes and nobles spoke it more accurately and politely than their mother tongue. In our island there was less of this servility than on the Continent. Neither our good nor our bad qualities were those of imitators. Yet even here homage was paid, awkwardly indeed and sullenly, to the literary supremacy of our neighbours. The melodious Tuscan, so familiar to the gallants and ladies of the court of Elizabeth, sank into contempt. A gentleman who quoted Horace or Terence was considered in good company as a pompous pedant. But to garnish his conversation with scraps of French was the best proof which he could give of his parts and attainments. New canons of criticism, new models of style came into fashion. The quaint ingenuity which had deformed the verses of Donne and had been a blemish on those of Cowley disappeared from our poetry. Our prose became less majestic, less artfully involved, less variously musical than that of an earlier age, but more lucid, more easy, and better fitted for controversy and narrative. In these changes it is impossible not to recognize the influence of French precept and of French example. Great masters of our language, in their most dignified compositions, affected to use French words when English words, quite as expressive and melodious, were at hand: and from France was imported the tragedy in rhyme, an exotic which, in our soil, drooped and speedily died.

It would have been well if our writers had also copied the decorum which their great French contemporaries, with few exceptions, preserved; for the profligacy of the English plays, satires, songs, and novels of that age is a deep blot on our national fame. The evil may easily be traced to its source. The wits and the Puritans had never been on friendly terms. There was no sympathy between the two classes. They looked on the whole system of human life from different points and in different lights. The earnest of each was the jest of the other. The pleasures of each were the torments of the other. To the stern precisian even the innocent sport of the fancy seemed a crime. To light and festive natures the solemnity of the zealous brethren furnished copious matter of ridicule. From the Reformation to the Civil War, almost every writer, gifted with a fine sense of the ludicrous, had taken some opportunity of assailing the straight-haired, snuffling, whining saints, who christened their children out of the Book of Nehemiah, who groaned in spirit at the sight of Jack in the Green, and who thought it impious to taste plum porridge on Christmas Day. At length a time came when the laughers began to look grave in their turn. The rigid, ungainly zealots, after having furnished much good sport during two generations, rose up in arms, conquered, ruled, and, grimly smiling, trod down under their feet the whole crowd of mockers. The wounds inflicted by gay and petulant malice were retaliated with the gloomy and implacable malice peculiar to bigots who mistake their own rancour for virtue. The theatres were closed. The players were flogged. The press was put under the guardianship of austere licensers. The Muses were banished from their own favorite haunts. Cowley was ejected from Cambridge and Crashaw from Oxford. The young candidate for academical honors was no longer required to write Ovidian epistles or Virgilian pastorals, but was strictly interrogated by a synod of lowering Supralapsarians as to the day and hour when he experienced the new birth. Such a system was of course fruitful of hypocrites. Under sober clothing and under visages composed to the expression of austerity lay hid during several years the intense desire of license and of revenge. At length that desire was gratified. The Restoration emancipated thousands of minds from a yoke which had become insupportable. The old fight recommenced, but with an animosity altogether new. It was now not a sportive combat, but a war to the death. The Roundhead had no better quarter to expect from those whom he had persecuted than a cruel slave-driver can expect from insurgent slaves still bearing the marks of his collars and his scourges.

The war between wit and Puritanism soon became a war between wit and morality. The hostility excited by a grotesque caricature of virtue did not spare virtue herself. Whatever the canting Roundhead had regarded with reverence was insulted. Whatever he had proscribed was favored. Because he had been scrupulous about trifles, all scruples were treated with derision. Because he had covered his failings with the mask of devotion, men were encouraged to obtrude with cynic impudence all their most scandalous vices on the public eye. Because he had punished illicit love with barbarous severity, virgin purity and conjugal fidelity were to be made a jest. To that sanctimonious jargon, which was his shibboleth, was opposed another jargon not less absurd and much more odious. As he never opened his mouth except in Scriptural phrase, the new breed of wits and fine gentlemen never opened their mouths without uttering ribaldry of which a porter would now be ashamed, and without calling on their Maker to curse them, sink them, confound them, blast them, and damn them.

It is not strange, therefore, that our polite literature, when it revived with the revival of the old civil and ecclesiastical polity, should have been profoundly immoral. A few eminent men, who belonged to an earlier and better age, were exempt from the general contagion. The verse of Waller still breathed the sentiments which had animated a more chivalrous generation. Cowley, distinguished at once as a loyalist and as a man of letters, raised his voice courageously against the immorality which disgraced both letters and loyalty. A mightier spirit, unsubdued by pain, danger, poverty, obloquy, and blindness, meditated, undisturbed by the obscene tumult which raged all around, a song so sublime and so holy that it would not have misbecome the lips of those ethereal Virtues whom he saw, what that inner eye which no calamity could darken, flinging down on the jasper pavement their crowns of amaranth and gold. The vigorous and fertile genius of Butler, if it did not altogether escape the prevailing infection, took the disease in a mild form. But these were men whose minds had been trained in a world which had passed away. They gave place in no long time to a younger generation of poets, and of that generation, from Dryden down to Durfey, the common characteristic was hard-hearted, shameless, swaggering licentiousness, at once inelegant and inhuman. The influence of these writers was doubtless noxious, yet less noxious than it would have been had they been less depraved. The poison which they administered was so strong that it was, in no long time, rejected with nausea. None of them understood the dangerous art of associating images of unlawful pleasure with all that is endearing and ennobling. None of them was aware that a certain decorum is essential even to voluptuousness, that drapery may be more alluring than exposure, and that the imagination may be far more powerfully moved by delicate hints which impel it to exert itself than by gross descriptions which it takes in passively.

The spirit of the Anti-Puritan reaction pervades almost the whole polite literature of the reign of Charles the Second. But the very quintessence of that spirit will be found in the comic drama. The playhouses, shut by the meddling fanatic in the day of his power, were again crowded. To their old attractions new and more powerful attractions had been added. Scenery, dresses, and decorations such as would now be thought mean and absurd, but such as would have been esteemed incredibly magnificent by those who, early in the seventeenth century, sat on the filthy benches of the Hope or under the thatched roof of the Rose, dazzled the eyes of the multitude. The fascination of sex was called in to aid the fascination of art; and the young spectator saw, with emotions unknown to the contemporaries of Shakspeare and Jonson, tender and sprightly heroines personified by lovely women. From the day on which the theatres were reopened they became seminaries of vice, and the evil propagated itself. The profligacy of the representations soon drove away sober people. The frivolous and dissolute who remained required every year stronger and stronger stimulants. Thus the artists corrupted the spectators, and the spectators the artists, till the turpitude of the drama became such as must astonish all who are not aware that extreme relaxation is the natural effect of extreme restraint, and that an age of hypocrisy is, in the regular course of things, followed by an age of impudence.

Nothing is more characteristic of the times than the care with which the poets contrived to put all their loosest verses into the mouths of women. The compositions in which the greatest license was taken were the epilogues. They were almost always recited by favorite actresses, and nothing charmed the depraved audience so much as to hear lines grossly indecent repeated by a beautiful girl, who was supposed to have not yet lost her innocence.

Our theatre was indebted in that age for many plots and characters to Spain, to France, and to the old English masters; but whatever our dramatists touched they tainted. In their imitations the houses of Calderon's stately and high spirited Castilian gentlemen became sties of vice, Shakspeare's Viola a procuress, Molière's misanthrope a ravisher, Molière's Agnes an adulteress. Nothing could be so pure or so heroic but that it became foul and ignoble by transfusion through those foul and ignoble minds.

Such was the state of the drama; and the drama was the department of light literature in which a poet had the best chance of obtaining a subsistence by his pen. The sale of books was so small that a man of the greatest name could expect only a pittance for the copyright of the best performance. There cannot be a stronger instance than the fate of Dryden's last production, the *Fables*. That volume was published when he was universally admitted to be the chief of living English poets. It contains about twelve thousand lines. The versification is admirable, the narratives and descriptions full of life. To this day *Palamon and Arcite, Cymon and Iphigenia, Theodore and Honoria* are the delight both of critics and of schoolboys. The collection includes *Alexander's Feast*, the noblest ode in our language. For the copyright Dryden received two hundred and fifty pounds, less than in our days has sometimes been paid for two articles in a review. Nor does the bargain seem to have been a hard one. For the book went off slowly, and a second edition was not required till the author had been ten years in his grave. By writing for the theatre it was possible to earn a much larger sum with much less trouble. Southern made seven hundred pounds by one play. Otway was raised from beggary to temporary affluence by the success of his *Don Carlos*. Shadwell cleared a hundred and thirty pounds by a single representation of the *Squire of Alsatia*. The consequence was that every man who had to live by his wit wrote plays whether he had any internal vocation to write plays or not. It was thus with Dryden. As a satirist he has rivaled Juvenal. As a didactic poet he perhaps might, with care and meditation, have rivaled Lucretius. Of lyric poets he is, if not the most sublime, the most brilliant and spirit-stirring. But nature, profuse to him of many rare gifts, had denied him the dramatic faculty. Nevertheless all the energies of his best years were wasted on dramatic composition. He had too much judgment not to be aware that in the power of exhibiting character by means of dialogue he was deficient. That deficiency he did his best to conceal, sometimes by surprising and amusing incidents, sometimes by stately declamation, sometimes by harmonious numbers, sometimes by ribaldry but too well suited to the taste of a profane and licentious pit. Yet he never obtained any theatrical success equal to that which rewarded the exertions of some men far inferior to him in general powers. He thought himself fortunate if he cleared a hundred guineas by a play; a scanty remuneration, yet apparently larger than he could have earned in any other way by the same quantity of labor.

The recompense which the wits of that age could obtain from the public was so small that they were under the necessity of eking out their incomes by levying contributions on the great. Every rich and good-natured lord was pestered by authors with a mendicancy so importunate, and a flattery so abject, as may in our time seem incredible. The patron to whom a work was inscribed was expected to reward the writer with a purse of gold. The fee paid for the dedication of a book was often much larger than the sum which any bookseller would give for the copyright. Books were therefore often printed merely that they might be dedicated. This traffic in praise completed the degradation of the literary character. Adulation pushed to the verge, sometimes of nonsense and sometimes of impiety, was not thought to disgrace a poet. Independence, veracity, self-respect, were things not expected by the world from him. In truth, he was in morals something between a pandar and a beggar.

To the other vices which degraded the literary character was added, toward the close of the reign of Charles the Second, the most savage intemperance of party spirit. The wits, as a class, had been impelled by their old hatred of Puritanism to take the side of the court, and had been found useful allies. Dryden, in particular, had done good service to the government. His *Absalom and Achitophel*, the greatest satire of modern times, had amazed the town, had made its way with unprecedented rapidity even into rural districts, and had, wherever it appeared, bitterly annoyed the Exclusionists and raised the courage of the Tories. But we must not, in the admiration which we naturally feel for noble diction and versification, forget the great distinctions of good and evil. The spirit by which Dryden and several of his compeers were at this time animated against the Whigs deserves to be called fiendish. The servile judges and sheriffs of those evil days could not shed blood so fast as the poets cried out for it. Calls for more victims, hideous jests on hanging, bitter taunts on those who, having stood by the king in the hour of danger, now advised him to deal mercifully and generously by his vanquished enemies, were publicly recited on the stage, and, that nothing might be wanting to the guilt and the shame, were recited by women, who, having long been taught to discard all modesty, were now taught to discard all compassion.

It is a remarkable fact that, while the lighter literature of England was thus becoming a nuisance and a national disgrace, the English genius was effecting in science a revolution which will, to the end of time, be reckoned among the highest achievements of the human intellect. Bacon had sown the good seed in a sluggish soil and an ungenial season. He had not expected an early crop, and in his last testament had solemnly bequeathed his fame to the next age. During a whole generation his philosophy had, amidst tumults, wars, and proscriptions, been slowly ripening in a few well-constituted minds. While factions were struggling for dominion over each other, a small body of sages had turned away with benevolent disdain from the conflict, and had devoted themselves to the nobler work of extending the dominion of man over matter. As soon as tranquillity was restored, these teachers easily found attentive audience. For the discipline through which the nation had passed had brought the public

mind to a temper well fitted for the reception of the Verulamian doctrine. The civil troubles had stimulated the faculties of the educated classes and had called forth a restless activity and an insatiable curiosity such as had not before been known among us. Yet the effect of those troubles had been that schemes of political and religious reform were generally regarded with suspicion and contempt. During twenty years the chief employment of busy and ingenious men had been to frame constitutions with first magistrates, without first magistrates, with hereditary senates, with senates appointed by lot, with annual senates, with perpetual senates. In these plans nothing was omitted. All the detail, all the nomenclature, all the ceremonial of the imaginary government was fully set forth—Polemarchs and Phylarchs, Tribes and Galaxies, the Lord Archon and the Lord Strategus. Which ballot boxes were to be green and which red, which balls were to be of gold and which of silver, which magistrates were to wear hats and which black velvet caps with peaks, how the mace was to be carried and when the heralds were to uncover,— these and a hundred more such trifles were gravely considered and arranged by men of no common capacity and learning. But the time for these visions had gone by; and, if any steadfast republican still continued to amuse himself with them, fear of public derision and of a criminal information generally induced him to keep his fancies to himself. It was now unpopular and unsafe to mutter a word against the fundamental laws of the monarchy; but daring and ingenious men might indemnify themselves by treating with disdain what had lately been considered as the fundamental laws of nature. The torrent which had been dammed up in one channel rushed violently into another. The revolutionary spirit, ceasing to operate in politics, began to exert itself with unprecedented vigor and hardihood in every department of physics. The year 1660, the era of the restoration of the old constitution, is also the era from which dates the ascendency of the new philosophy. In that year the Royal Society, destined to be a chief agent in a long series of glorious and salutary reforms, began to exist. In a few months experimental science became all the mode. The transfusion of blood, the ponderation of air, the fixation of mercury, succeeded to that place in the public mind which had been lately occupied by the controversies of the Rota. Dreams of perfect forms of government made way for dreams of wings with which men were to fly from the Tower to the Abbey, and of double-keeled ships which were never to founder in the fiercest storm. All classes were hurried along by the prevailing sentiment. Cavalier and Roundhead, Churchman and Puritan were for once allied. Divines, jurists, statesmen, nobles, princes swelled the triumph of the Baconian philosophy. Poets sang with emulous fervor the approach of the golden age. Cowley, in lines weighty with thought and resplendent with wit, urged the chosen seed to take possession of the promised land flowing with milk and honey, that land which their great deliverer and lawgiver had seen as from the summit of Pisgah, but had not been permitted to enter. Dryden, with more zeal than knowledge, joined his voice to the general acclamation, and foretold things which neither he nor anybody else understood. The Royal Society, he predicted, would soon lead us to the extreme verge of the globe, and there delight us with a better view of the moon. Two able and aspiring prelates, Ward, Bishop of Salisbury, and Wilkins, Bishop of Chester, were conspicuous among the leaders of the movement. Its history was eloquently written by a younger divine who was rising to high distinction in his profession, Thomas Sprat, afterwards Bishop of Rochester. Both Chief Justice Hale and Lord Keeper Guildford stole some hours from the business of their courts to write on hydrostatics. Indeed it was under the immediate directions of Guildford that the first barometers ever exposed to sale in London were constructed. Chemistry divided, for a time, with wine and love, with the stage and the gaming-table, with the intrigues of a courtier and the intrigues of a demagogue, the attention of the fickle Buckingham. Rupert has the credit of having invented mezzotinto, and from him is named that curious bubble of glass which has long amused children and puzzled philosophers. Charles himself had a laboratory at Whitehall, and was far more active and attentive there than at the council board. It was almost necessary to the character of a fine gentleman to have something to say about air-pumps and telescopes; and even fine ladies, now and then, thought it becoming to affect a taste for science, went in coaches and six to visit the Gresham curiosities, and broke forth into cries of delight at finding that a magnet really attracted a needle, and that a microscope really made a fly look as large as a sparrow.

In this, as in every great stir of the human mind, there was doubtless something which might well move a smile. It is the universal law that whatever pursuit, whatever doctrine becomes fashionable shall lose a portion of that dignity which it had possessed while it was confined to a small but earnest minority, and was loved for its own sake alone. It is true that the follies of some persons who, without any real aptitude for science, professed a passion for it, furnished matter of contemptuous mirth to a few malignant satirists who belonged to the preceding generation, and were not disposed to unlearn the lore of their youth. But it is not less true that the great work of interpreting nature was performed by the English of that age as it had never before been performed in any age by any nation. The spirit of Francis Bacon was abroad, a spirit admirably compounded of audacity and sobriety. There was a strong persuasion that the whole world was full of secrets of high moment to the happiness of man, and that man had, by his Maker, been intrusted with the key which, rightly used, would give access to them. There was at the same time a conviction that in physics it was impossible to arrive at the knowledge of general laws except by the careful observation of particular facts. Deeply impressed with these great truths, the professors of the new philosophy applied themselves to their task, and before a quarter of a century had expired, they had given ample earnest of what has since been achieved. Already a reform of agriculture had been commenced. New vegetables were cultivated. New implements of husbandry were employed. New manures were applied to the soil. Evelyn had, under the formal sanction of the Royal Society, given instruction to his countrymen in planting. Temple, in his intervals of leisure, had tried many experiments in horticulture, and had proved that many delicate fruits, the natives of more favored climates, might, with the help of art, be grown on English ground. Medicine, which in France was still in abject bondage and afforded an inexhaustible subject of just ridicule to Molière, had in England become an experimental and progressive science, and every day made some new advance, in defiance of Hippocrates and Galen. The attention of speculative men had been, for the first time, directed to the important subject of sanitary police. The great plague of 1665 induced them to consider with care the defective architecture, draining, and ventilation of the capital. The great fire of 1666 afforded an opportunity for effecting extensive improvements. The whole matter was diligently examined by the Royal Society, and to the suggestions of that body must be partly attributed the changes which, though far short of what the public welfare required, yet made a wide difference between the new and the old London, and probably put a final close to the ravages of pestilence in our country. At the same time one of the founders of the society, Sir William Petty, created the science of political arithmetic, the humble but indispensable handmaid of political philosophy. To that period belonged the chemical discoveries of Boyle and the first botanical researches of Sloane. One after another, phantoms which had haunted the world through ages of darkness fled before the light. Astrology and alchemy became jests. Soon there was scarcely a county in which some of the quorum did not smile contemptuously when an old woman was brought before them for riding on broomsticks or giving cattle the murrain. But it was in those noblest and most arduous departments of knowledge in which induction and mathematical demonstration cooperate for the discovery of truth that the English genius won in that age the most memorable triumphs. John Wallis placed the whole system of statics on a new foundation. Edmund Halley investigated the properties of the atmosphere, the ebb and flow of the sea, the laws of magnetism, and the course of the comets; nor did he shrink from toil, peril, and exile in the cause of science. While he, on the rock of St. Helena, mapped the constellations of the southern hemisphere, our national observatory was rising at Greenwich; and John Flamsteed, the first astronomer royal, was commencing that long series of observations which is never mentioned without respect and gratitude in any part of the globe. But the glory of these men, eminent as they were, is cast into the shade by the transcendent luster of one immortal name. In Isaac Newton two kinds of intellectual power which have little in common and which are not often found together in a very high degree of vigor, but which nevertheless are equally necessary in the most sublime departments of natural philosophy, were united as they have never been united before or since. There may have been minds as happily constituted as his for the cultivation of pure mathematical science; there may have been minds as happily constituted for the cultivation of science purely experimental; but in no other mind have the demonstrative faculty and the inductive faculty coexisted in such supreme excellence and perfect harmony. Perhaps in an age of Scotists and Thomists even his intellect might have run to waste, as many intellects ran to waste which were inferior only to his. Happily the spirit of the age on which his lot was cast gave the right direction to his mind; and his mind reacted with tenfold force on the spirit of the age. In the year 1685 his fame, though splendid, was only dawning; but his genius was in the meridian. His great work, that work which effected a revolution in the most important provinces of natural philosophy, had been completed, but was not yet published, and was just about to be submitted to the consideration of the Royal Society.

It is not very easy to explain why the nation which was so far before its neighbors in science should in art have been far behind them all. Yet such was the fact. It is true that in architecture, an art which is half a science, an art in which none but a geometrician can excel, an art which has no standard of grace but what is directly or indirectly dependent on utility, an art of which the creations derive a part, at least, of their majesty from mere bulk, our country could boast of one truly great man, Christopher Wren; and the fire which laid London in ruins had given him an opportunity, unprecedented in modern history, of displaying his powers. The austere beauty of the Athenian portico, the gloomy sublimity of the Gothic arcade, he was, like almost all his contemporaries, incapable of emulating, and perhaps incapable of appreciating; but no man, born on our side of the Alps, has imitated with so much success the magnificence of the palace-like churches of Italy. Even the superb Louis has left to posterity no work which can bear a comparison with Saint Paul's. But at the close of the reign of Charles the Second there was not a single English painter or statuary whose name is now remembered. This sterility is somewhat mysterious, for painters and statuaries were by no means a despised or an ill-paid class. Their social position was at least as high as at present. Their gains, when compared with the wealth of the nation and with the remuneration of other descriptions of intellectual labor, were even larger than at present. Indeed, the munificent patronage which was extended to artists drew them to our shores in multitudes. Lely, who has preserved to us the rich curls, the full lips, and the languishing eyes of the frail beauties celebrated by Hamilton, was a Westphalian. He had died in 1680, having long lived splendidly, having received the honor of knighthood, and having accumulated a good estate out of the fruits of his skill. His noble collection of drawings and pictures was, after his decease, exhibited by the royal permission in the Banqueting House at Whitehall, and sold by auction for the almost incredible sum of twenty-six thousand pounds, a sum which bore a greater proportion to the fortunes of the rich men of that day than a hundred thousand pounds would bear to the fortunes of the rich men of our time. Lely was succeeded by his countryman Godfrey Kneller, who was made first a knight and then a baronet, and who, after keeping up a sumptuous establishment, and after losing much money by unlucky speculations, was still able to bequeath a large fortune

to his family. The two Vandeveldes, natives of Holland, had been induced by English liberality to settle here, and had produced for the king and his nobles some of the finest sea-pieces in the world. Another Dutchman, Simon Varelst, painted glorious sunflowers and tulips for prices such as had never before been known. Verrio, a Neapolitan, covered ceilings and staircases with Gorgons and Muses, Nymphs and Satyrs, Virtues and Vices, Gods quaffing nectar, and laureled princes riding in triumph. The income which he derived from his performances enabled him to keep one of the most expensive tables in England. For his pieces at Windsor alone he received seven thousand pounds, a sum then sufficient to make a gentleman of moderate wishes perfectly easy for life, a sum greatly exceeding all that Dryden, during a literary life of forty years, obtained from the booksellers. Verrio's chief assistant and successor, Lewis Laguerre, came from France. The two most celebrated sculptors of that day were also foreigners. Cibber, whose pathetic emblems of Fury and Melancholy still adorn Bedlam, was a Dane. Gibbons, to whose graceful fancy and delicate touch many of our palaces, colleges, and churches owe their finest decorations, was a Dutchman. Even the designs for the coin were made by French medalists. Indeed, it was not till the reign of George the Second that our country could glory in a great painter, and George the Third was on the throne before she had reason to be proud of any of her sculptors.

(c) PAST AND PRESENT

It is pleasing to reflect that the public mind of England has softened while it has ripened, and that we have, in the course of ages, become not only a wiser, but also a kinder people. There is scarcely a page of the history or lighter literature of the seventeenth century which does not contain some proof that our ancestors were less humane than their posterity. The discipline of workshops, of schools, of private families, though not more efficient than at present, was infinitely harsher. Masters, well born and bred, were in the habit of beating their servants. Pedagogues knew no way of imparting knowledge but by beating their pupils. Husbands, of decent station, were not ashamed to beat their wives. The implacability of hostile factions was such as we can scarcely conceive. Whigs were disposed to murmur because Stafford was suffered to die without seeing his bowels burned before his face. Tories reviled and insulted Russell as his coach passed from the Tower to the scaffold in Lincoln's Inn Fields. As little mercy was shown by the populace to sufferers of an humbler rank. If an offender was put into the pillory, it was well if he escaped with life from the shower of brickbats and paving stones. If he was tied to the cart's tail, the crowd pressed round him, imploring the hangman to give it to the fellow well, and to make him howl. Gentlemen arranged parties of pleasure to Bridewell on court days, for the purpose of seeing the wretched women who beat hemp there whipped. A man pressed to death for refusing to plead, a woman burned for coining excited less sympathy than is now felt for a galled horse or an over-driven ox. Fights, compared with which a boxing match is a refined and humane spectacle, were among the favorite diversions of a large part of the town. Multitudes assembled to see gladiators hack each other to pieces with deadly weapons, and shouted with delight when one of the combatants lost a finger or an eye. The prisons were hells on earth, seminaries of every crime and of every disease. At the assizes the lean and yellow culprits brought with them from their cells to the dock an atmosphere of stench and pestilence which sometimes avenged them signally on bench, bar, and jury. But on all this misery society looked with profound indifference. Nowhere could be found that sensitive and restless compassion which has, in our time, extended a powerful protection to the factory child, to the Hindoo widow, to the negro slave, which pries into the stores and water-casks of every emigrant ship, which winces at every lash laid on the back of a drunken soldier, which will not suffer the thief in the hulks to be ill fed or overworked, and which has repeatedly endeavored to save the life even of the murderer. It is true that compassion ought, like all other feelings, to be under the government of reason, and has, for want of such gov-

ernment, produced some ridiculous and some deplorable effects. But the more we study the annals of the past, the more shall we rejoice that we live in a merciful age, in an age in which cruelty is abhorred, and in which pain, even when deserved, is inflicted reluctantly and from a sense of duty. Every class doubtless has gained largely by this great moral change; but the class which has gained most is the poorest, the most dependent, and the most defenceless.

The general effect of the evidence which has been submitted to the reader seems hardly to admit of doubt. Yet, in spite of evidence, many will still image to themselves the England of the Stuarts as a more pleasant country than the England in which we live. It may at first sight seem strange that society, while constantly moving forward with eager speed, should be constantly looking backward with tender regret. But these two propensities, inconsistent as they may appear, can easily be resolved into the same principle. Both spring from our impatience of the state in which we actually are. That impatience, while it stimulates us to surpass preceding generations, disposes us to overrate their happiness. It is, in some sense, unreasonable and ungrateful in us to be constantly discontented with a condition which is constantly improving. But, in truth, there is constant improvement precisely because there is constant discontent. If we were perfectly satisfied with the present, we should cease to contrive, to labor, and to save with a view to the future. And it is natural that, being dissatisfied with the present, we should form a too favorable estimate of the past.

In truth we are under a deception similar to that which misleads the traveler in the Arabian desert. Beneath the caravan all is dry and bare; but far in advance and far in the rear is the semblance of refreshing waters. The pilgrims hasten forward and find nothing but sand where, an hour before, they had seen a lake. They turn their eyes and see a lake where, an hour before, they were toiling through sand. A similar illusion seems to haunt nations through every stage of the long progress from poverty and barbarism to the highest degrees of opulence and civilization. But if we resolutely chase the mirage backward, we shall find it recede before us into the regions of fabulous antiquity. It is now the fashion to place the golden age of England in times when noblemen were destitute of comforts the want of which would be intolerable to a modern footman, when farmers and shopkeepers breakfasted on loaves the very sight of which would raise a riot in a modern workhouse, when men died faster in the purest country air than they now die in the most pestilential lanes of our towns, and when men died faster in the lanes of our towns than they now die on the coast of Guiana. We too shall, in our turn, be outstripped, and in our turn be envied. It may well be, in the twentieth century, that the peasant of Dorsetshire may think himself miserably paid with fifteen shillings a week; that the carpenter at Greenwich may receive ten shillings a day; that laboring men may be as little used to dine without meat as they now are to eat ryebread; that sanitary police and medical discoveries may have added several more years to the average length of human life; that numerous comforts and luxuries which are now unknown, or confined to a few, may be within the reach of every diligent and thrifty working man. And yet it may then be the mode to assert that the increase of wealth and the progress of science have benefited the few at the expense of the many, and to talk of the reign of Queen Victoria as the time when England was truly merry England, when all classes were bound together by brotherly sympathy, when the rich did not grind the faces of the poor, and when the poor did not envy the splendor of the rich.

[1848]

JOHN HENRY NEWMAN

CHRONOLOGY AND INTRODUCTION

1801 Born in London, February 21.
1808–17 Private schooling.
1817 Entered Oxford at Trinity College.
1820 Graduated, without high honors, because of illness.
1822 Elected Fellow of Oriel College.
1824 Took Holy Orders and accepted the curacy of St. Clements, Oxford.
1826 Appointed Tutor; resigned curacy.
1828 Vicar of St. Mary's, Oxford.
1832 Completed *The Arians of the Fourth Century;* resigned tutorship, made foreign tour and saw Rome, returning July, next year.
1833 Tractarian Movement started in September.
1838 Influence as Oxford preacher at height.
1841 *Tract 90:* Tracts discontinued.
1842 Retirement to Littlemore.
1843 Resigned living of St. Mary's.
1845 Resigned Fellowship at Oriel and received into Catholic Church, Oct. 8, at Littlemore. *The Development of Christian Doctrine.*
1846 Ordained at Rome.

1848 Founded Oratory of St. Philip Neri at Birmingham.
1851 *The Present Position of Catholics in England.* Asked to be Rector of projected Catholic University, Dublin.
1852 *The Idea of a University.*
1854 Installed as Rector.
1855 *Callista.*
1857 Resigned Rectorship.
1864 Kingsley attacked Newman in *Macmillan's Magazine,* January. Newman replied in seven successive pamphlets, April-June, five of which became the *Apologia pro Vita Sua.*
1865 *The Dream of Gerontius.*
1868 *Verses on Various Occasions.*
1870 *A Grammar of Assent.*
1871 *Essays, Critical and Historical* (1828–1846), 2 vols.
1872 *Discussions and Arguments* (1836–1866). *Historical Sketches* (1824–1860), 3 vols.
1878 Elected Honorary Fellow of Trinity College, Oxford.
1879 Created Cardinal by Pope Leo XIII.
1890 Death, August 11.

Though one of the masters of English prose, Newman never thought of himself as a man of letters. He did not live in the society of literary people, nor was he literary in the sense that writing was his profession. A close associate of his later Catholic years, Father Neville, has left the following memorandum: "He once said that if he had had to choose between social intercourse without literary pursuits and literary pursuits without social intercourse, he would, as a student, without hesitation have chosen the former."

From the time of his conversion at the age of fifteen, Newman was a theologian, and he was an ecclesiastic from the age of twenty-two, when he took Holy Orders. He was deeply religious from boyhood, with an absorbing devotion to the services and sacraments of the Church. His books, of which there are nearly forty, are, with few exceptions, *occasional,* written in exposition or defence of religious doctrine and history, according to the needs of the time. "It has been the fortune of the author through life," Newman says of himself, "that the volumes which he has published have grown for the most part out of duties which lay upon him, or out of the circumstances of the moment. Rarely has he been master of his own studies." After the success of the *Apologia* he remarked: "I can never write well without a definite call. But when the real occasion came, I succeeded." The *Apologia* itself, his masterpiece, and *The Idea of a University,* the two works by which he is best known—at least outside the Catholic Church—are intimately connected with his religious life and interests, apart from which they would not have been written. But such was Newman's genius, such his command of the varied resources of verbal expression and his power of informing his material with a subtle, penetrating, wideranging, most lively intelligence, that his position as a writer is not likely to be challenged so long as great English prose is read and admired.

In his own field of religious thought and controversy, he was, by virtue of his voice and pen, the most commanding figure of his day. He rose to fame at Oxford, where for twenty-five years he lived as student, Fellow, Tutor, and Vicar of St. Mary's, or until he "migrated" in 1842 to Littlemore, a small village some two miles outside the city. Oriel College, in which Newman held his Fellowship, was the intellectual center of the University and had drawn into its fold some of the most brilliant and influential minds of the period,—Dr. Thomas Arnold, Keble, Whately and Hurrell Froude among others, all of whom were Fellows for various terms. Newman, declared Whately (afterwards Archbishop), was "the clearest head he knew." A recent biographer has said: "Already there was gathering about him that mysterious veneration which made it seem as if some Ambrose or Augustine of old time had reappeared to walk the ways of men once more"; an opinion confirmed in the tribute of James Anthony Froude, who was a student at Oriel in Newman's time: "The simplest word which dropped from him was treasured as if it had been an intellectual diamond. For hundreds of young men 'credo in Newmanum' was a genuine symbol of faith." As a preacher in the University Church at St. Mary's no description of him is better known than Matthew Arnold's (1883): "Who could resist the charm of that spiritual apparition, gliding in the dim afternoon light through the aisles of St. Mary's, rising into the pulpit, and then, in the most entrancing of voices, breaking the silence with words and thoughts which were a religious music—subtle, sweet, mournful?"

The English Church in those days, as Newman and his associates (particularly Keble and Hurrell Froude) saw it, was in peril. Modernism, liberalism, secularism were in the air and threatened the very existence of the Establishment, as Anglicans call their religious organization. The repeal of the Test and Corporation Acts in 1828, Catholic Emancipation in 1829, and the Reform Bill of 1832 introduced new and alarming problems concerning orthodox Christianity and the relations between Church and State. Dr. Arnold wrote in 1832: "The Church, as it now stands, no human power can save." Archbishop Whately said of the Establishment: "I fear its days are numbered." Newman, Keble, and Froude, with others (mostly Oriel men) determined to save it, not by making it conform to modernism, but by reaffirming its basis in "that primitive Christianity (to use Newman's words) which was delivered for all time by the early teachers of the church and which was registered and attested in the Anglican formularies and by the Anglican divines." They began to write articles which were called *Tracts for the Times* and were widely distributed, especially among the clergy. Thus was inaugurated what we know as Tractarianism or The Oxford Movement. The last and most famous of the Tracts was *Number 90*, from the pen of Newman, dealing with the Thirty-Nine Articles of the Church and showing that they had "a highly Catholic meaning." Anglicanism was rocked to its foundation. Many went over to Rome, and at last in 1845 Newman himself was received into the Catholic Church.

His conversion cannot be described as sudden or revolutionary. It was a progression rather than an abrupt change. He was by nature idealistic and religious. There was in him from the first a sense of the unreality of physical phenomena. In a letter (1828) he exclaims: "What a veil and curtain this world of sense is! beautiful, but still a veil!"—words that might have come from Carlyle. Very early in life he rests "in the thought of two and two only absolute and luminously self-evident beings, myself and my Creator." The presence of God in the individual self is conscience,—again, a Carlylean note. Recognition of these spiritual realities, of which Newman was intuitively certain and which are independent of revealed religion, is the work of what he called "the illative sense," a kind of higher reason much akin to what Coleridge and Wordsworth thought of as imagination or "the faculty divine," common to all, but most conspicuous in creative minds. "It is not too much to say," Newman declared in a University sermon, "that the stepping by which great geniuses scale the mountain of truth is as unsafe and precarious to men in general as the ascent of a skilful mountaineer up a literal crag. It is a way which they alone can take; and its justification lies alone in their success. And such mainly is the way in which all men, gifted or not gifted, commonly reason—not by rule, but by an inward faculty. Reasoning, then, or the exercise of reason, is a living, spontaneous energy within us, not an art."

To authenticate and support this inner vision there is the revelation of God in Christianity, that is to say, in the Bible, in the Apostolic tradition, "the long history of the Church, the Lives of the Saints, and the reasonings, internal collisions, and decisions of the theological Schools." Crystallized into propositions these make up what the Catholic Church calls dogma or a summary of the human knowledge of divine things. "Religion," says Newman, "cannot maintain its ground at all without theology.... Devotion falls back into dogma.... From the age of fifteen, dogma has been the fundamental principle of my religion: I know no other religion; I cannot enter into the idea of any other sort of religion; religion, as a mere sentiment, is to me a dream and a mockery." By 1828 he plunged into a long and exhaustive study of primitive Christianity and the Church Fathers, the great saints of the third and fourth centuries, until he became, according to the German theologian Döllinger, the "living authority on the history of the first three centuries of the Christian era." His researches convinced him that the Bible alone as Revelation was incomplete without the Apostolic tradition and the accompanying historically progressive ecclesiastical interpretation; and thus he came to believe that the Catholic Church, with its teachings and sacraments, was the infallible, continuous, and living expression of Christianity. On this ground Newman remained to the end, inwardly confident and at peace, so far as his Catholic faith was concerned, but outwardly, often in conflict, to the verge of despair, with personalities and movements in the Church; for he was an almost morbidly sensitive man, shy, reserved, scholarly, unworldly,—vastly different from the executive and administrative type of mind exemplified in the career of Cardinal Manning.

Practically everything that he wrote was inspired with a single purpose, namely, to proclaim and uphold the reality of the unseen, the spiritual world of God of which the Church was the visible representative, against the advancing tides of skepticism and infidelity in the contemporary life of the nineteenth century. Science, the "higher criticism" of the Bible, philosophical speculation, the growth of democracy, the all-engrossing industrialism of the age, like a flood, were, he thought, sweeping away belief in revealed religion, and his mind was filled with dread. In old age (1877) he wrote: "I have all that time (i.e., above fifty years) thought that a time of widespread infidelity was coming, and through all those years the waters have in fact been rising as a deluge." These portentous phenomena Newman summed up as *liberalism,* by which he meant "false liberty of thought, or the exercise of thought upon matters, in which, from the constitution of the human mind, thought cannot be brought to any successful issue." (*Apologia.*) Understood in this sense liberalism could be met, he believed, only by the Catholic Church, the *depositum* of Christian faith and revelation, or, in other words, by "an appeal to the wisdom of the ages against the intellectualism of the hour," as his best biographer, Ward, expressed it. When Newman was asked in 1851 to become Rector of the proposed new Catholic University at Dublin, he welcomed the invitation as an opportunity to declare his views upon the relation of religion to modern thought and to liberal education. The great problem of the hour, says Ward, in interpreting Newman's task, was to show "how Christians were to uphold the traditionary theology and yet be fully alive to the changed outlook wrought by science in a new age; how faith was to be definite, yet compatible with breadth of view." And when in 1864 Charles Kingsley attacked him as a liar ("he called me a liar," are Newman's words), Newman felt that at last, as it were providentially, his chance had come to demonstrate his position, so much misunderstood, before the English public. The history of his mind in the great *Apologia* vindicated for all time the sincerity of his convictions.

As the foregoing analysis should suggest, much of Newman's prose is too specialized in subject matter for most readers, if considered as a basis for general discussion. Books dealing with Church history and dogma—tracts, treatises, polemical pamphlets, occasional papers—had once a contemporary importance but have now only a limited appeal; even the twelve volumes of sermons, powerful as was their effect when spoken from the pulpit and still valuable as they are for the scholarly student of Newman's mind, have lost most of their interest today. Such works are rarely among the permanent things in literature. The *Apologia* and *The Idea of a University* ("the perfect handling of a theory," as Pater described it), together with certain occasional essays, lectures, and historical sketches,—these are the writings that sustain Newman's reputation as a stylist. Here we find the expression of his passionate interest in the primitive and medieval Church and in the Church Fathers, St. Basil, St. Augustine, St. Chrysostom, St. Ambrose, St. Jerome; here for him was the true poetry of life. In this work, too, the reader is impressed with the range, abundance, and vigor of Newman's learning, and is convinced by the subtlety and brilliance of his achievement that, had he chosen, he might have become a great historian, one to challenge comparison with Gibbon, Macaulay, or Carlyle.

The secret of his vitality as a writer is of course in his style, which for him as for all truly literary artists, is thought and speech in one,—"a thinking out into language," as he called it. Of all distinguished prose styles, Newman's is the most difficult to describe, for it is the least mannered. Not that he did not sweat and toil for his effects; not that he did not know that genius must often be at sore pains to fashion the fit medium of the inner vision. In this sense all art is artifice or workmanship: "Why may not language be wrought as well as the clay of the modeller?" he asks. "Why may not words be worked up as well as colors? Why should not skill in diction be simply subservient and instrumental to the great prototypal ideas which are the contemplation of a Plato or a Virgil?" But Newman's stylistic effects, though sought with care and wrought with exquisite finish, are subtly veiled and strictly "subservient" to ideas. Everywhere the reader has a sense that his intelligence is addressed rather than his heart, and that all the resources of language are deployed in order to communicate the writer's thought with clarity, simplicity, and a minimum of ornament. Consequently, Newman's prose has not, for the most part, the concreteness and color which are conspicuous, for examples, in styles like Hazlitt's and Carlyle's. And while it moves with the subtlest cadences, these are never so obviously metrical as are, too often, the rhythms of DeQuincey or of Ruskin. But where in English prose shall the reader go for a more finished deliverance, at once simple, flexible, idiomatic, occasionally colloquial, yet always distinctive, always elevated and never commonplace,—the "classic" style of a richly cultivated intelligence speaking to kindred souls? The aim of a writer, Newman said in words that well describe his own practice, "is to give forth what he has within him; and from his very earnestness it comes to pass that, whatever be the splendor of his diction or the harmony of his periods, he has with him the charm of an incommunicable simplicity. Whatever be his subject, high or low, he treats it suitably and for its own sake.... His page is the lucid mirror of his mind and life."

APOLOGIA PRO VITA SUA

HISTORY OF MY RELIGIOUS OPINIONS
TO THE YEAR 1833

It may easily be conceived how great a trial it is to me to write the following history of myself; but I must not shrink from the task. The words *"Secretum meum mihi,"* [1] keep ringing in my ears; but as men draw towards their end, they care less for disclosures. Nor is it the least part of my trial to anticipate that, upon first reading what I have written, my friends may consider much in it irrelevant to my purpose; yet I cannot help thinking that, viewed as a whole, it will effect what I propose to myself in giving it to the public.

I was brought up from a child to take great delight in reading the Bible; but I had no formed religious convictions till I was fifteen. Of course I had a perfect knowledge of my Catechism.

After I was grown up, I put on paper my recollections of the thoughts and feelings on religious subjects which I had at the time that I was a child and a boy—such as had remained on my mind with sufficient prominence to make me consider them worth recording. Out of these, written in the Long Vacation of 1820, and transcribed with additions in 1823, I select two, which are at once the most definite among them, and also have a bearing on my later convictions.

1. "I used to wish the *Arabian Tales* were true; my imagination ran on unknown influences, on magical powers, and talismans.... I thought life might be a dream, or I an Angel, and all this world a deception, my fellow-angels by a playful device concealing themselves from me, and deceiving me with the semblance of a material world."

Again, "Reading in the Spring of 1816 a sentence from [Dr. Watts's] *Remnants of Time*, entitled 'the Saints unknown to the world,' to the effect, that 'there is nothing in their figure or countenance to distinguish them,' etc., etc., I supposed he spoke of Angels who lived in the world, as it were disguised."

2. The other remark is this: "I was very superstitious, and for some time previous to my conversion [when I was fifteen] used constantly to cross myself on going into the dark."

Of course I must have got this practice from some external source or other; but I can make no sort of conjecture whence; and certainly no one had ever spoken to me on the subject of the Catholic religion, which I only knew by name. The French master was an *émigré* [2] Priest, but he was simply made a butt, as French masters too commonly were in that day, and spoke English very imperfectly. There was a Catholic family in the village, old maiden ladies we used to think; but I knew nothing about them. I have of late years heard that there were one or two Catholic boys in the school; but either we were carefully kept from knowing this, or the knowledge of it made simply no impression on our

1 *Secretum meum mihi:* "my secret to myself."

2 *émigré:* a Royalist fugitive from France at time of Revolution.

minds. My brother will bear witness how free the school was from Catholic ideas.

I had once been into Warwick Street Chapel, with my father, who, I believe, wanted to hear some piece of music; all that I bore away from it was the recollection of a pulpit and a preacher, and a boy swinging a censer.

When I was at Littlemore, I was looking over old copybooks of my school days, and I found among them my first Latin versebook; and in the first page of it there was a device which almost took my breath away with surprise. I have the book before me now, and have just been showing it to others. I have written in the first page, in my schoolboy hand, "John H. Newman, February 11th, 1811, Verse Book"; then follow my first Verses. Between "Verse" and "Book" I have drawn the figure of a solid cross upright, and next to it is, what may indeed be meant for a necklace, but what I cannot make out to be anything else than a set of beads suspended, with a little cross attached. At this time I was not quite ten years old. I suppose I got these ideas from some romance, Mrs. Radcliffe's or Miss Porter's; or from some religious picture; but the strange thing is, how, among the thousand objects which meet a boy's eyes, these in particular should so have fixed themselves in my mind that I made them thus practically my own. I am certain there was nothing in the churches I attended, or the prayer books I read, to suggest them. It must be recollected that Anglican churches and prayer books were not decorated in those days as I believe they are now.

When I was fourteen, I read Paine's Tracts against the Old Testament, and found pleasure in thinking of the objections which were contained in them. Also, I read some of Hume's Essays; and perhaps that on Miracles. So at least I gave my father to understand; but perhaps it was a brag. Also, I recollect copying out some French verses, perhaps Voltaire's, in denial of the immortality of the soul, and saying to myself something like "How dreadful, but how plausible!"

When I was fifteen (in the autumn of 1816) a great change of thought took place in me. I fell under the influences of a defi-nite Creed, and received into my intellect impressions of dogma, which, through God's mercy, have never been effaced or obscured. Above and beyond the conversations and sermons of the excellent man, long dead, the Rev. Walter Mayers, of Pembroke College, Oxford, who was the human means of this beginning of divine faith in me, was the effect of the books which he put into my hands, all of the school of Calvin. One of the first books I read was a work of Romaine's; I neither recollect the title nor the contents, except one doctrine, which of course I do not include among those which I believe to have come from a divine source, viz., the doctrine of final perseverance. I received it at once, and believed that the inward conversion of which I was conscious (and of which I still am more certain than that I have hands and feet) would last into the next life, and that I was elected to eternal glory. I have no consciousness that this belief had any tendency whatever to lead me to be careless about pleasing God. I retained it till the age of twenty-one, when it gradually faded away; but I believe that it had some influence on my opinions, in the direction of those childish imaginations which I have already mentioned, viz., in isolating me from the objects which surrounded me, in confirming me in my mistrust of the reality of material phenomena, and making me rest in the thought of two and two only absolute and luminously self-evident beings, myself and my Creator—for while I considered myself predestined to salvation, my mind did not dwell upon others, as fancying them simply passed over, not predestined to eternal death. I only thought of the mercy to myself.

The detestable doctrine last mentioned is simply denied and abjured, unless my memory strangely deceives me, by the writer who made a deeper impression on my mind than any other, and to whom (humanly speaking) I almost owe my soul—Thomas Scott of Aston Sandford. I so admired and delighted in his writings that, when I was an undergraduate, I thought of making a visit to his Parsonage, in order to see a man whom I so deeply revered. I hardly think I could have given up the idea of this expedition, even after I had taken my degree;

for the news of his death in 1821 came upon me as a disappointment as well as a sorrow. I hung upon the lips of Daniel Wilson, afterwards Bishop of Calcutta, as in two sermons at St. John's Chapel he gave the history of Scott's life and death. I had been possessed of his *Force of Truth* and Essays from a boy; his Commentary I bought when I was an undergraduate.

What, I suppose, will strike any reader of Scott's history and writings is his bold unworldliness and vigorous independence of mind. He followed truth wherever it led him, beginning with Unitarianism, and ending in a zealous faith in the Holy Trinity. It was he who first planted deep in my mind that fundamental truth of religion. With the assistance of Scott's Essays, and the admirable work of Jones of Nayland, I made a collection of Scripture texts in proof of the doctrine, with remarks (I think) of my own upon them, before I was sixteen; and a few months later I drew up a series of texts in support of each verse of the Athanasian Creed. These papers I have still.

Besides his unworldliness, what I also admired in Scott was his resolute opposition to Antinomianism, and the minutely practical character of his writings. They show him to be a true Englishman, and I deeply felt his influence; and for years I used almost as proverbs what I considered to be the scope and issue of his doctrine, "Holiness rather than peace," and "Growth the only evidence of life."

Calvinists make a sharp separation between the elect and the world; there is much in this that is cognate or parallel to the Catholic doctrine; but they go on to say, as I understand them, very differently from Catholicism—that the converted and the unconverted can be discriminated by man, that the justified are conscious of their state of justification, and that the regenerate cannot fall away. Catholics on the other hand shade and soften the awful antagonism between good and evil, which is one of their dogmas, by holding that there are different degrees of justification, that there is a great difference in point of gravity between sin and sin, that there is the possibility and the danger of falling away, and that there is no certain knowl-

edge given to anyone that he is simply in a state of grace, and much less that he is to persevere to the end. Of the Calvinistic tenets the only one which took root in my mind was the fact of heaven and hell, divine favor and divine wrath, of the justified and the unjustified. The notion that the regenerate and the justified were one and the same, and that the regenerate, as such, had the gift of perseverance, remained with me not many years, as I have said already.

This main Catholic doctrine of the warfare between the city of God and the powers of darkness was also deeply impressed upon my mind by a work of a character very opposite to Calvinism, Law's *Serious Call*.

From this time I held with a full inward assent and belief the doctrine of eternal punishment, as delivered by our Lord Himself, in as true a sense as I hold that of eternal happiness; though I have tried in various ways to make that truth less terrible to the intellect.

Now I come to two other works which produced a deep impression on me in the same autumn of 1816, when I was fifteen years old, each contrary to each, and planting in me the seeds of an intellectual inconsistency which disabled me for a long course of years. I read Joseph Milner's *Church History*, and was nothing short of enamored of the long extracts from St. Augustine, St. Ambrose, and the other Fathers which I found there. I read them as being the religion of the primitive Christians; but simultaneously with Milner I read Newton on the Prophecies, and in consequence became most firmly convinced that the Pope was the Antichrist predicted by Daniel, St. Paul, and St. John. My imagination was stained by the effects of this doctrine up to the year 1843; it had been obliterated from my reason and judgment at an earlier date; but the thought remained upon me as a sort of false conscience. Hence came that conflict of mind, which so many have felt besides myself—leading some men to make a compromise between two ideas, so inconsistent with each other—driving others to beat out the one idea or the other from their minds—and ending in my own case, after many years of intellectual unrest, in the gradual decay and extinction of one of them—I do not say in its violent death, for why should I not have murdered it sooner, if I murdered it at all?

I am obliged to mention, though I do it with great reluctance, another deep imagination, which at this time, the autumn of 1816, took possession of me—there can be no mistake about the fact—viz., that it would be the will of God that I should lead a single life. This anticipation, which has held its ground almost continuously ever since—with the break of a month now and a month then, up to 1829, and, after that date, without any break at all—was more or less connected, in my mind, with the notion that my calling in life would require such a sacrifice as celibacy involved; as, for instance, missionary work among the heathen, to which I had a great drawing for some years. It also strengthened my feeling of separation from the visible world, of which I have spoken above.

In 1822 I came under very different influences from those to which I had hitherto been subjected. At that time, Mr. Whately, as he was then, afterwards Archbishop of Dublin, for the few months he remained in Oxford, which he was leaving for good, showed great kindness to me. He renewed it in 1825, when he became Principal of Alban Hall, making me his Vice-Principal and Tutor. Of Dr. Whately I will speak presently, for from 1822 to 1825 I saw most of the present Provost of Oriel, Dr. Hawkins, at that time Vicar of St. Mary's; and, when I took orders in 1824 and had a curacy in Oxford, then, during the Long Vacations, I was especially thrown into his company. I can say with a full heart that I love him, and have never ceased to love him; and I thus preface what otherwise might sound rude, that in the course of the many years in which we were together afterwards, he provoked me very much from time to time, though I am perfectly certain that I have provoked him a great deal more. Moreover, in me such provocation was unbecoming, both because he was the Head of my College, and because, in the first years that I knew him, he had been in many ways of great service to my mind.

He was the first who taught me to weigh my words, and to be cautious in my statements. He led me to that mode of limiting and clearing my sense in discussion and in controversy, and of distinguishing between cognate ideas, and of obviating mistakes by anticipation, which to my surprise has been since considered, even in quarters friendly to me, to savor of the polemics of Rome. He is a man of most exact mind himself, and he used to snub me severely, on reading, as he was kind enough to do, the first sermons that I wrote, and other compositions which I was engaged upon.

Then as to doctrine, he was the means of great additions to my belief. As I have noticed elsewhere, he gave me the *Treatise on Apostolical Preaching,* by Sumner, afterwards Archbishop of Canterbury, from which I was led to give up my remaining Calvinism, and to receive the doctrine of Baptismal Regeneration. In many other ways too he was of use to me, on subjects semireligious and semischolastic.

It was Dr. Hawkins too who taught me to anticipate that, before many years were over, there would be an attack made upon the books and the canon of Scripture. I was brought to the same belief by the conversation of Mr. Blanco White, who also led me to have freer views on the subject of inspiration than were usual in the Church of England at the time.

There is one other principle which I gained from Dr. Hawkins, more directly bearing upon Catholicism than any that I have mentioned; and that is the doctrine of Tradition. When I was an undergraduate, I heard him preach in the University Pulpit his celebrated sermon on the subject, and recollect how long it appeared to me, though he was at that time a very striking preacher; but, when I read it and studied it as his gift, it made a most serious impression upon me. He does not go one step, I think, beyond the high Anglican doctrine, nay he does not reach it; but he does his work thoroughly, and his view was in him original, and his subject was a novel one at the time. He lays down a proposition, self-evident as soon as stated, to those who have at all examined the structure of Scripture, viz., that the sacred text was never intended to teach doctrine, but only to prove it, and that, if we would learn doctrine, we must have recourse to the formularies of the Church; for instance, to the Catechism, and to the Creeds. He considers that, after learning from them the doctrines of Christianity, the inquirer must verify them by Scripture. This view, most true in its outline, most fruitful in its consequences, opened upon me a large field of thought. Dr. Whately held it too. One of its effects was to strike at the root of the principle on which the Bible Society was set up. I belonged to its Oxford Association; it became a matter of time when I should withdraw my name from its subscription-list, though I did not do so at once.

It is with pleasure that I pay here a tribute to the memory of the Rev. William James, then Fellow of Oriel; who, about the year 1823, taught me the doctrine of Apostolical Succession, in the course of a walk, I think, round Christ Church Meadow—I recollect being somewhat impatient of the subject at the time.

It was at about this date, I suppose, that I read Bishop Butler's *Analogy;* the study of which has been to so many, as it was to me, an era in their religious opinions. Its inculcation of a visible Church, the oracle of truth and a pattern of sanctity, of the duties of external religion, and of the historical character of Revelation, are characteristics of this great work which strike the reader at once; for myself, if I may attempt to determine what I most gained from it, it lay in two points, which I shall have an opportunity of dwelling on in the sequel; they are the underlying principles of a great portion of my teaching. First, the very idea of an analogy between the separate works of God leads to the conclusion that the system which is of less importance is economically or sacramentally connected with the more momentous system, and of this conclusion the theory, to which I was inclined as a boy, viz., the unreality of material phenomena, is an ultimate resolution. At this time I did not make the distinction between matter itself and its phenomena, which is so necessary and so obvious in discussing the subject. Secondly, Butler's doctrine that Probability is the guide of life, led me,

at least under the teaching to which a few years later I was introduced, to the question of the logical cogency of Faith, on which I have written so much. Thus to Butler I trace those two principles of my teaching which have led to a charge against me both of fancifulness and of skepticism.

And now as to Dr. Whately. I owe him a great deal. He was a man of generous and warm heart. He was particularly loyal to his friends, and to use the common phrase, "all his geese were swans." While I was still awkward and timid in 1822, he took me by the hand, and acted towards me the part of a gentle and encouraging instructor. He, emphatically, opened my mind, and taught me to think and to use my reason. After being first noticed by him in 1822, I became very intimate with him in 1825, when I was his Vice-Principal at Alban Hall. I gave up that office in 1826, when I became Tutor of my College, and his hold upon me gradually relaxed. He had done his work towards me, or nearly so, when he had taught me to see with my own eyes and to walk with my own feet. Not that I had not a good deal to learn from others still, but I influenced them as well as they me, and co-operated rather than merely concurred with them. As to Dr. Whately, his mind was too different from mine for us to remain long on one line. I recollect how dissatisfied he was with an Article of mine in the *London Review,* which Blanco White, good-humoredly, only called Platonic. When I was diverging from him in opinion (which he did not like), I thought of dedicating my first book to him, in words to the effect that he had not only taught me to think, but to think for myself. He left Oxford in 1831; after that, as far as I can recollect, I never saw him but twice—when he visited the University; once in the street in 1834, once in a room in 1838. From the time that he left, I have always felt a real affection for what I must call his memory; for, at least from the year 1834, he made himself dead to me. He had practically indeed given me up from the time that he became Archbishop in 1831; but in 1834 a correspondence took place between us, which, though conducted in the most friendly language on both sides, was the expression of differences of opinion which acted as a final close to our intercourse. My reason told me that it was impossible we could have got on together longer, had he stayed in Oxford; yet I loved him too much to bid him farewell without pain. After a few years had passed, I began to believe that his influence on me in a higher respect than intellectual advance (I will not say through his fault) had not been satisfactory. I believe that he has inserted sharp things in his later works about me. They have never come in my way, and I have not thought it necessary to seek out what would pain me so much in the reading.

What he did for me in point of religious opinion was first to teach me the existence of the Church as a substantive body or corporation; next to fix in me those anti-Erastian views of Church polity which were one of the most prominent features of the Tractarian Movement. On this point, and, as far as I know, on this point alone, he and Hurrell Froude intimately sympathized, though Froude's development of opinion here was of a later date. In the year 1826, in the course of a walk he said much to me about a work then just published, called *Letters on the Church by an Episcopalian.* He said that it would make my blood boil. It was certainly a most powerful composition. One of our common friends told me that, after reading it, he could not keep still, but went on walking up and down his room. It was ascribed at once to Whately; I gave eager expression to the contrary opinion; but I found the belief of Oxford in the affirmative to be too strong for me; rightly or wrongly I yielded to the general voice; and I have never heard, then or since, of any disclaimer of authorship on the part of Dr. Whately.

The main positions of this able essay are these: first, that Church and State should be independent of each other—he speaks of the duty of protesting "against the profanation of Christ's kingdom, by that *double usurpation,* the interference of the Church in temporals, of the State in spirituals," p. 191; and, secondly, that the Church may justly and by right retain its property, though separated from the State. "The clergy," he says, p. 133, "though they ought not to be the hired servants of the Civil Magistrate, may justly retain their revenues; and the State, though it has no right of interference in spiritual concerns, not only is justly entitled to support from the ministers of religion, and from all other Christians, but would, under the system I am recommending, obtain it much more effectually." The author of this work, whoever he may be, argues out both these points with great force and ingenuity, and with a thoroughgoing vehemence, which perhaps we may refer to the circumstance that he wrote, not *in propria persona,*[3] and as thereby answerable for every sentiment he advanced, but in the professed character of a Scotch Episcopalian. His work had a gradual, but a deep effect on my mind.

I am not aware of any other religious opinion which I owe to Dr. Whately. For his special theological tenets I had no sympathy. In the next year, 1827, he told me he considered that I was Arianizing. The case was this: though at that time I had not read Bishop Bull's *Defensio* nor the Fathers, I was just then very strong for that ante-Nicene view of the Trinitarian doctrine which some writers, both Catholic and non-Catholic, have accused of wearing a sort of Arian exterior. This is the meaning of a passage in Froude's *Remains,* in which he seems to accuse me of speaking against the Athanasian Creed. I had contrasted the two aspects of the Trinitarian doctrine which are respectively presented by the Athanasian Creed and the Nicene. My criticisms were to the effect that some of the verses of the former Creed were unnecessarily scientific. This is a specimen of a certain disdain for Antiquity which had been growing on me now for several years. It showed itself in some flippant language against the Fathers in the *Encyclopaedia Metropolitana,* about whom I knew little at the time, except what I had learned as a boy from Joseph Milner. In writing on the Scripture Miracles in 1825–1826, I had read Middleton on the Miracles of the early Church, and had imbibed a portion of his spirit.

The truth is, I was beginning to prefer

3 *in propria persona:* in his own person.

intellectual excellence to moral; I was drifting in the direction of the liberalism of the day. I was rudely awakened from my dream at the end of 1827 by two great blows—illness and bereavement.

In the beginning of 1829 came the formal break between Dr. Whately and me; the affair of Mr. Peel's re-election was the occasion of it. I think in 1828 or 1827 I had voted in the minority when the Petition to Parliament against the Catholic Claims was brought into Convocation. I did so mainly on the views suggested to me by the theory of the *Letters of an Episcopalian.* Also I disliked the bigoted "two bottle orthodox," as they were invidiously called. Accordingly I took part against Mr. Peel, on a simple academical, not at all an ecclesiastical or a political ground; and this I professed at the time. I considered that Mr. Peel had taken the University by surprise, that his friends had no right to call upon us to turn round on a sudden, and to expose ourselves to the imputation of timeserving, and that a great university ought not to be bullied even by a great Duke of Wellington. Also by this time I was under the influence of Keble and Froude; who, in addition to the reasons I have given, disliked the Duke's change of policy as dictated by liberalism.

Whately was considerably annoyed at me, and he took a humorous revenge, of which he had given me due notice beforehand. As head of a house, he had duties of hospitality to men of all parties; he asked a set of the least intellectual men in Oxford to dinner, and men most fond of port; he made me one of this party; placed me between Provost This, and Principal That, and then asked me if I was proud of my friends. However, he had a serious meaning in his act; he saw, more clearly than I could do, that I was separating from his own friends for good and all.

Dr. Whately attributed my leaving his *clientela* [4] to a wish on my part to be the head of a party myself. I do not think that this charge was deserved. My habitual feeling then and since has been that it was not I who sought friends, but friends who sought me. Never man had kinder or more indulgent friends than I have had, but I expressed my own feeling as to the mode in which I gained them, in this very year 1829, in the course of a copy of verses. Speaking of my blessings, I said, "Blessings of friends, which to my door, *unasked, unhoped,* have come." They have come, they have gone; they came to my great joy, they went to my great grief. He who gave, took away. Dr. Whately's impression about me, however, admits of this explanation:

During the first years of my residence at Oriel, though proud of my College, I was not quite at home there. I was very much alone, and I used often to take my daily walk by myself. I recollect once meeting Dr. Copleston, then Provost, with one of the Fellows. He turned round, and with the kind courteousness which sat so well on him, made me a bow and said, *"Nunquam minus solus, quam cum solus."* [5] At that time indeed (from 1823) I had the intimacy of my dear and true friend Dr. Pusey, and could not fail to admire and revere a soul so devoted to the cause of religion, so full of good works, so faithful in his affections; but he left residence when I was getting to know him well. As to Dr. Whately himself, he was too much my superior to allow of my being at my ease with him; and to no one in Oxford at this time did I open my heart fully and familiarly. But things changed in 1826. At that time I became one of the Tutors of my College, and this gave me position; besides, I had written one or two Essays which had been well received. I began to be known. I preached my first University Sermon. Next year I was one of the Public Examiners for the B. A. degree. In 1828 I became Vicar of St. Mary's. It was to me like the feeling of spring weather after winter; and, if I may so speak, I came out of my shell; I remained out of it till 1841.

The two persons who knew me best at that time are still alive, beneficed clergymen, no longer my friends. They could tell better than anyone else what I was in those years. From this time my tongue was, as it were, loosened, and I spoke

---

[4] *clientela:* Latin for clientage or clientele, a group of persons who attach themselves to one for professional service or advice.

[5] *Nunquam,* etc.: "Never less alone than when alone" (Cicero, *Rep.,* I, 17, 27).

spontaneously and without effort. One of the two, a shrewd man, said of me, I have been told, "Here is a fellow who, when he is silent, will never begin to speak; and when he once begins to speak, will never stop." It was at this time that I began to have influence, which steadily increased for a course of years. I gained upon my pupils, and was in particular intimate and affectionate with two of our probationer Fellows, Robert Isaac Wilberforce (afterwards Archdeacon) and Richard Hurrell Froude. Whately then, an acute man, perhaps saw around me the signs of an incipient party, of which I was not conscious myself. And thus we discern the first elements of that movement afterwards called Tractarian.

The true and primary author of it, however, as is usual with great motive-powers, was out of sight. Having carried off as a mere boy the highest honors of the University, he had turned from the admiration which haunted his steps, and sought for a better and holier satisfaction in pastoral work in the country. Need I say that I am speaking of John Keble? The first time that I was in a room with him was on occasion of my election to a Fellowship at Oriel, when I was sent for into the Tower, to shake hands with the Provost and Fellows. How is that hour fixed in my memory after the changes of forty-two years, forty-two this very day on which I write! I have lately had a letter in my hands, which I sent at the time to my great friend, John William Bowden, with whom I passed almost exclusively my undergraduate years. "I had to hasten to the Tower," I say to him, "to receive the congratulations of all the Fellows. I bore it till Keble took my hand, and then felt so abashed and unworthy of the honor done me that I seemed desirous of quite sinking into the ground." His had been the first name which I had heard spoken of, with reverence rather than admiration, when I came up to Oxford. When one day I was walking in High Street with my dear earliest friend just mentioned, with what eagerness did he cry out, "There's Keble!" and with what awe did I look at him! Then at another time I heard a Master of Arts of my college give an account how he had just then had occasion to introduce himself on some business to Keble, and how gentle, courteous, and unaffected Keble had been, so as almost to put him out of countenance. Then too it was reported, truly or falsely, how a rising man of brilliant reputation, the present Dean of St. Paul's, Dr. Milman, admired and loved him, adding that somehow he was strangely unlike anyone else. However, at the time when I was elected Fellow of Oriel he was not in residence, and he was shy of me for years in consequence of the marks which I bore upon me of the evangelical and liberal schools. At least so I have ever thought. Hurrell Froude brought us together about 1828: it is one of the sayings preserved in his *Remains*— "Do you know the story of the murderer who had done one good thing in his life? Well; if I was ever asked what good deed I had ever done, I should say that I had brought Keble and Newman to understand each other."

The Christian Year made its appearance in 1827. It is not necessary, and scarcely becoming, to praise a book which has already become one of the classics of the language. When the general tone of religious literature was so nerveless and impotent, as it was at that time, Keble struck an original note and woke up in the hearts of thousands a new music, the music of a school long unknown in England. Nor can I pretend to analyze, in my own instance, the effect of religious teaching so deep, so pure, so beautiful. I have never till now tried to do so; yet I think I am not wrong in saying that the two main intellectual truths which it brought home to me were the same two which I had learned from Butler, though recast in the creative mind of my new master. The first of these was what may be called, in a large sense of the word, the Sacramental system; that is, the doctrine that material phenomena are both the types and the instruments of real things unseen—a doctrine which embraces in its fullness, not only what Anglicans, as well as Catholics, believe about Sacraments properly so called; but also the article of "the Communion of Saints"; and likewise the Mysteries of the faith. The connection of this philosophy of religion with what is sometimes called "Berkeleyism" has been mentioned above; I knew little of Berkeley at this time except by name; nor have I ever studied him.

On the second intellectual principle which I gained from Mr. Keble, I could say a great deal, if this were the place for it. It runs through very much that I have written, and has gained for me many hard names. Butler teaches us that probability is the guide of life. The danger of this doctrine, in the case of many minds, is its tendency to destroy in them absolute certainty, leading them to consider every conclusion as doubtful, and resolving truth into an opinion, which it is safe indeed to obey or to profess, but not possible to embrace with full internal assent. If this were to be allowed, then the celebrated saying, "O God, if there be a God, save my soul, if I have a soul!" would be the highest measure of devotion—but who can really pray to a Being about whose existence he is seriously in doubt?

I considered that Mr. Keble met this difficulty by ascribing the firmness of assent which we give to religious doctrine, not to the probabilities which introduced it, but to the living power of faith and love which accepted it. In matters of religion, he seemed to say, it is not merely probability which makes us intellectually certain, but probability as it is put to account by faith and love. It is faith and love which give to probability a force which it has not in itself. Faith and love are directed towards an Object; in the vision of that Object they live; it is that Object, received in faith and love, which renders it reasonable to take probability as sufficient for internal conviction. Thus the argument from Probability, in the matter of religion, became an argument from Personality, which in fact is one form of the argument from Authority.

In illustration, Mr. Keble used to quote the words of the Psalm: "I will guide thee with mine *eye*. Be ye not like to horse and mule, which have no understanding; whose mouths must be held with bit and bridle, lest they fall upon thee." This is the very difference, he used to say, between slaves, and friends or children. Friends do not ask for literal commands; but, from their knowledge of the speaker, they understand his half-words, and from love of him they anticipate his wishes. Hence it is that in his poem for St. Bartholomew's Day, he speaks of the "Eye of God's word"; and in the note quotes Mr. Miller, of Worcester College, who remarks, in his Bampton Lectures, on the special power of Scripture, as having "this Eye, like that of a portrait, uniformly fixed upon us, turn where we will." The view thus suggested by Mr. Keble is brought forward in one of the earliest of the *Tracts for the Times*. In No. 8 I say, "The Gospel is a Law of Liberty. We are treated as sons, not as servants; not subjected to a code of formal commandments, but addressed as those who love God, and wish to please Him."

I did not at all dispute this view of the matter, for I made use of it myself; but I was dissatisfied, because it did not go to the root of the difficulty. It was beautiful and religious, but it did not even profess to be logical; and accordingly I tried to complete it by considerations of my own, which are implied in my *University Sermons, Essay on Ecclesiastical Miracles,* and *Essay on Development of Doctrine.* My argument is in outline as follows: that that absolute certitude which we were able to possess, whether as to the truths of natural theology, or as to the fact of a revelation, was the result of an *assemblage* of concurring and converging probabilities, and that, both according to the constitution of the human mind and the will of its Maker; that certitude was a habit of mind, that certainty was a quality of propositions; that probabilities which did not reach to logical certainty, might suffice for a mental certitude; that the certitude thus brought about might equal in measure and strength the certitude which was created by the strictest scientific demonstration; and that to possess such certitude might in given cases and to given individuals be a plain duty, though not to others in other circumstances:—

Moreover, that, as there were probabilities which sufficed for certitude, so there were other probabilities which were legitimately adapted to create opinion; that it might be quite as much a matter of duty in given cases and to given persons to have about a fact an opinion of a definite strength and consistency, as in the case of greater or of more numerous probabilities it was a duty to have a certitude; that accordingly we were bound to be more or less sure, on a sort of (as it were) graduated scale of assent, viz., according as the probabilities attaching to a professed fact were brought home to us, and, as the case might be, to entertain about it a pious belief, or a pious opinion, or a religious conjecture, or at least, a tolerance of such belief, or 10 opinion, or conjecture in others; that on the other hand, as it was a duty to have a belief, of more or less strong texture, in given cases, so in other cases it was a duty not to believe, not to opine, not to conjecture, not even to tolerate the notion that a professed fact was true, inasmuch as it would be credulity or superstition, or some other moral fault, to do so. This was the region of Private Judgment in religion; 20 that is, of a Private Judgment, not formed arbitrarily and according to one's fancy or liking, but conscientiously, and under a sense of duty.

Considerations such as these throw a new light on the subject of Miracles, and they seem to have led me to reconsider the view which I had taken of them in my Essay in 1825–1826. I do not know what was the date of this change in me, nor of the train 30 of ideas on which it was founded. That there had been already great miracles, as those of Scripture, as the Resurrection, was a fact establishing the principle that the laws of nature had sometimes been suspended by their Divine Author; and since what had happened once might happen again, a certain probability, at least no kind of improbability, was attached to the idea, taken in itself, of miraculous inter- 40 vention in later times, and miraculous accounts were to be regarded in connection with the verisimilitude, scope, instrument, character, testimony, and circumstances with which they presented themselves to us; and, according to the final result of those various considerations, it was our duty to be sure, or to believe, or to opine, or to surmise, or to tolerate, or to reject, or to denounce. The main difference be- 50 tween my Essay on Miracles in 1826 and my Essay in 1842 is this: that in 1826 I considered that miracles were sharply divided into two classes, those which were

to be received, and those which were to be rejected; whereas in 1842 I saw that they were to be regarded according to their greater or less probability, which was in some cases sufficient to create certitude about them, in other cases only belief or opinion.

Moreover, the argument from Analogy, on which this view of the question was founded, suggested to me something besides, in recommendation of the Ecclesiastical Miracles. It fastened itself upon the theory of Church History which I had learned as a boy from Joseph Milner. It is Milner's doctrine that upon the visible Church come down from above, at certain intervals, large and temporary *Effusions* of divine grace. This is the leading idea of his work. He begins by speaking of the Day of Pentecost as marking "the first of those *Effusions* of the Spirit of God, which from age to age have visited the earth since the coming of Christ" (Vol. I, p. 3). In a note he adds that "in the term 'Effusion' there is *not* here included the idea of the miraculous or extraordinary operations of the Spirit of God"; but still it was natural for me, admitting Milner's general theory, and applying to it the principle of analogy, not to stop short at his abrupt *ipse dixit*,[6] but boldly to pass forward to the conclusion, on other grounds plausible, that, as miracles accompanied the first effusion of grace, so they might accompany the later. It is surely a natural and, on the whole, a true anticipation (though of course there are exceptions in particular cases), that gifts and graces go together; now, according to the ancient Catholic doctrine, the gift of miracles was viewed as the attendant and shadow of transcendent sanctity; and, moreover, since such sanctity was not of every day's occurrence, nay further, since one period of Church history differed widely from another, and, as Joseph Milner would say, there have been generations or centuries of degeneracy or disorder, and times of revival, and since one region might be in the midday of religious fervor, and another in twilight or gloom, there was no force in the popular argument that, because we did not see

6 *ipse dixit:* he himself has said (it),—a mere say-so.

miracles with our own eyes, miracles had not happened in former times, or were not now at this very time taking place in distant places—but I must not dwell longer on a subject to which in a few words it is impossible to do justice.

Hurrell Froude was a pupil of Keble's, formed by him, and in turn reacting upon him. I knew him first in 1826, and was in 10 the closest and most affectionate friendship with him from about 1829 till his death in 1836. He was a man of the highest gifts— so truly many-sided that it would be presumptuous in me to attempt to describe him except under those aspects in which he came before me. Nor have I here to speak of the gentleness and tenderness of nature, the playfulness, the free elastic force and graceful versatility of mind, and 20 the patient winning considerateness in discussion, which endeared him to those to whom he opened his heart; for I am all along engaged upon matters of belief and opinion, and am introducing others into my narrative, not for their own sake, or because I love and have loved them, so much as because, and so far as, they have influenced my theological views. In this respect, then, I speak of Hurrell Froude— 30 in his intellectual aspect—as a man of high genius, brimful and overflowing with ideas and views, in him original, which were too many and strong even for his bodily strength, and which crowded and jostled against each other in their effort after distinct shape and expression. And he had an intellect as critical and logical as it was speculative and bold. Dying prematurely, as he did, and in the conflict and transi- 40 tion-state of opinion, his religious views never reached their ultimate conclusion, by the very reason of their multitude and their depth. His opinions arrested and influenced me, even when they did not gain my assent. He professed openly his admiration of the Church of Rome, and his hatred of the Reformers. He delighted in the notion of an hierarchical system, of sacerdotal power, and of full ecclesiastical 50 liberty. He felt scorn of the maxim, "The Bible and the Bible only is the religion of Protestants"; and he gloried in accepting Tradition as a main instrument of religious

teaching. He had a high severe idea of the intrinsic excellence of Virginity; and he considered the Blessed Virgin its great Pattern. He delighted in thinking of the Saints; he had a vivid appreciation of the idea of sanctity, its possibility and its heights; and he was more than inclined to believe a large amount of miraculous interference as occurring in the early and middle ages. He embraced the principle of penance and mortification. He had a deep devotion to the Real Presence, in which he had a firm faith. He was powerfully drawn to the Medieval Church, but not to the Primitive.

He had a keen insight into abstract truth; but he was an Englishman to the backbone in his severe adherence to the real and the concrete. He had a most classical taste, and a genius for philosophy and art; and he was fond of historical inquiry, and the politics of religion. He had no turn for theology as such. He set no sufficient value on the writings of the Fathers, on the detail or development of doctrine, on the definite traditions of the Church viewed in their matter, on the teaching of the Ecumenical Councils, or on the controversies out of which they arose. He took an eager, courageous view of things on the whole. I should say that his power of entering into the minds of others did not equal his other gifts; he could not believe, for instance, that I really held the Roman Church to be Antichristian. On many points he would not believe but that I agreed with him when I did not. He seemed not to understand my difficulties. His were of a different kind, the contrariety between theory and fact. He was a high Tory of the Cavalier stamp, and was disgusted with the Toryism of the opponents of the Reform Bill. He was smitten with the love of the Theocratic Church; he went abroad and was shocked by the degeneracy which he thought he saw in the Catholics of Italy.

It is difficult to enumerate the precise additions to my theological creed which I derived from a friend to whom I owe so much. He taught me to look with admiration towards the Church of Rome, and in the same degree to dislike the Reformation. He fixed deep in me the idea of devotion to the Blessed Virgin, and he led me gradually to believe in the Real Presence.

There is one remaining source of my opinions to be mentioned, and that far from the least important. In proportion as I moved out of the shadow of that liberalism which had hung over my course, my early devotion towards the Fathers returned; and in the Long Vacation of 1828 I set about to read them chronologically, beginning with St. Ignatius and St. Justin. About 1830 a proposal was made to me by Mr. Hugh Rose, who with Mr. Lyall (afterwards Dean of Canterbury) was providing writers for a Theological Library, to furnish them with a History of the Principal Councils. I accepted it, and at once set to work on the Council of Nicaea. It was to launch myself on an ocean with currents innumerable; and I was drifted back first to the ante-Nicene history, and then to the Church of Alexandria. The work at last appeared under the title of *The Arians of the Fourth Century;* and of its 422 pages, the first 117 consisted of introductory matter, and the Council of Nicaea did not appear till the 254th, and then occupied at most twenty pages.

I do not know when I first learned to consider that Antiquity was the true exponent of the doctrines of Christianity and the basis of the Church of England; but I take it for granted that the works of Bishop Bull, which at this time I read, were my chief introduction to this principle. The course of reading which I pursued in the composition of my volume was directly adapted to develop it in my mind. What principally attracted me in the ante-Nicene period was the great Church of Alexandria, the historical center of teaching in those times. Of Rome for some centuries comparatively little is known. The battle of Arianism was first fought in Alexandria; Athanasius, the champion of the truth, was Bishop of Alexandria; and in his writings he refers to the great religious names of an earlier date, to Origen, Dionysius, and others who were the glory of its see, or of its school. The broad philosophy of Clement and Origen carried me away; the philosophy, not the theological doctrine; and I have drawn out some features of it

in my volume, with the zeal and freshness, but with the partiality of a neophyte. Some portions of their teaching, magnificent in themselves, came like music to my inward ear, as if the response to ideas which, with little external to encourage them, I had cherished so long. These were based on the mystical or sacramental principle, and spoke of the various Economies or Dispensations of the Eternal. I understood these passages to mean that the exterior world, physical and historical, was but the manifestation to our senses of realities greater than itself. Nature was a parable; Scripture was an allegory; pagan literature, philosophy, and mythology, properly understood, were but a preparation for the Gospel. The Greek poets and sages were in a certain sense prophets; for "thoughts beyond their thought to those high bards were given." There had been a directly divine dispensation granted to the Jews; but there had been in some sense a dispensation carried on in favor of the Gentiles. He who had taken the seed of Jacob for His elect people had not therefore cast the rest of mankind out of His sight. In the fullness of time both Judaism and Paganism had come to naught; the outward framework, which concealed yet suggested the Living Truth, had never been intended to last, and it was dissolving under the beams of the Sun of Justice which shone behind it and through it. The process of change had been slow; it had been done not rashly, but by rule and measure, "at sundry times and in divers manners," first one disclosure and then another, till the whole evangelical doctrine was brought into full manifestation. And thus room was made for the anticipation of further and deeper disclosures, of truths still under the veil of the letter, and in their season to be revealed. The visible world still remains without its divine interpretation; Holy Church in her sacraments and her hierarchical appointments, will remain, even to the end of the world, after all but a symbol of those heavenly facts which fill eternity. Her mysteries are but the expressions in human language of truths to which the human mind is unequal. It is evident how much there was in all this in correspondence with the thoughts which had attracted me when I was young, and with the doctrine which I have already associated with the *Analogy* and the *Christian Year.*

It was, I suppose, to the Alexandrian school and to the early Church that I owe in particular what I definitely held about the Angels. I viewed them, not only as the ministers employed by the Creator in the Jewish and Christian dispensations, as we find on the face of Scripture, but as carrying on, as Scripture also implies, the Economy of the Visible World. I considered them as the real causes of motion, light, and life, and of those elementary principles of the physical universe which, when offered in their developments to our senses, suggest to us the notion of cause and effect, and of what are called the laws of nature. This doctrine I have drawn out in my Sermon for Michaelmas day, written in 1831. I say of the Angels, "Every breath of air and ray of light and heat, every beautiful prospect, is, as it were, the skirts of their garments, the waving of the robes of those whose faces see God." Again, I ask what would be the thoughts of a man who, "when examining a flower, or a herb, or a pebble, or a ray of light, which he treats as something so beneath him in the scale of existence, suddenly discovered that he was in the presence of some powerful being who was hidden behind the visible things he was inspecting—who, though concealing his wise hand, was giving them their beauty, grace, and perfection, as being God's instrument for the purpose—nay, whose robe and ornaments those objects were which he was so eager to analyze"? and I therefore remark that "we may say with grateful and simple hearts with the Three Holy Children, 'O all ye works of the Lord, etc., etc., bless ye the Lord, praise Him, and magnify Him forever.' "

Also, besides the hosts of evil spirits, I considered there was a middle race δαιμόνια, [7] neither in heaven, nor in hell; partially fallen, capricious, wayward; noble or crafty, benevolent or malicious, as the case might be. These beings gave a sort of inspiration

or intelligence to races, nations, and classes of men. Hence the action of bodies politic and associations, which is often so different from that of the individuals who compose them. Hence the character and the instinct of states and governments, of religious communities and communions. I thought these assemblages had their life in certain unseen Powers. My preference of the Personal to the Abstract would naturally lead me to this view. I thought it countenanced by the mention of "the Prince of Persia" in the Prophet Daniel; and I think I considered that it was of such intermediate beings that the Apocalypse spoke, in its notice of "the Angels of the Seven Churches."

In 1837 I made a further development of this doctrine. I said to an intimate and dear friend, Samuel Francis Wood, in a letter which came into my hands on his death, "I have an idea. The mass of the Fathers (Justin, Athenagoras, Irenaeus, Clement, Tertullian, Origen, Lactantius, Sulpicius, Ambrose, Nazianzen) hold that, though Satan fell from the beginning, the Angels fell before the deluge, falling in love with the daughters of men. This has lately come across me as a remarkable solution of a notion which I cannot help holding. Daniel speaks as if each nation had its guardian Angel. I cannot but think that there are beings with a great deal of good in them, yet with great defects, who are the animating principles of certain institutions, etc., etc.... Take England, with many high virtues, and yet a low Catholicism. It seems to me that John Bull is a spirit neither of heaven nor hell.... Has not the Christian Church, in its parts, surrendered itself to one or other of these simulations of the truth?... How are we to avoid Scylla and Charybdis and go straight on to the very image of Christ?" etc., etc.

I am aware that what I have been saying will, with many men, be doing credit to my imagination at the expense of my judgment—"Hippoclides doesn't care"; I am not setting myself up as a pattern of good sense or of anything else; I am but giving a history of my opinions, and that with the view of showing that I have come by them through intelligible processes of thought and honest external means. The

---

[7] δαιμόνια, Greek word meaning daemons, or supernatural powers, intermediary between God (or gods) and man; in the ancient world belief in them was common.

doctrine indeed of the Economy has in some quarters been itself condemned as intrinsically pernicious—as if leading to lying and equivocation when applied, as I have applied it in my remarks upon it in my *History of the Arians,* to matters of conduct. My answer to this imputation I postpone to the concluding pages of my Volume.

While I was engaged in writing my work upon the Arians, great events were happening at home and abroad, which brought out into form and passionate expression the various beliefs which had so gradually been winning their way into my mind. Shortly before, there had been a Revolution in France; the Bourbons had been dismissed; and I held that it was unchristian for nations to cast off their governors, and, much more, sovereigns who had the divine right of inheritance. Again, the great Reform Agitation was going on around me as I wrote. The Whigs had come into power; Lord Grey had told the Bishops to set their house in order, and some of the Prelates had been insulted and threatened in the streets of London. The vital question was how were we to keep the Church from being liberalized? there was such apathy on the subject in some quarters, such imbecile alarm in others; the true principles of Churchmanship seemed so radically decayed, and there was such distraction in the councils of the Clergy. Blomfield, the Bishop of London of the day, an active and open-hearted man, had been for years engaged in diluting the high orthodoxy of the Church by the introduction of members of the Evangelical body into places of influence and trust. He had deeply offended men who agreed in opinion with myself, by an offhand saying (as it was reported) to the effect that belief in the Apostolical succession had gone out with the Non-jurors. "We can count you," he said to some of the gravest and most venerated persons of the old school. And the Evangelical party itself, with their late successes, seemed to have lost that simplicity and unworldliness which I admired so much in Milner and Scott. It was not that I did not venerate such men as Ryder, the then Bishop of Lichfield, and others of

similar sentiments, who were not yet promoted out of the ranks of the Clergy, but I thought little of them as a class. I thought the Evangelicals played into the hands of the Liberals. With the Establishment thus divided and threatened, thus ignorant of its true strength, I compared that fresh vigorous Power of which I was reading in the first centuries. In her triumphant zeal on behalf of that Primeval Mystery to which I had had so great a devotion from my youth, I recognized the movement of my Spiritual Mother, *"Incessu patuit Dea."* [8] The self-conquest of her Ascetics, the patience of her Martyrs, the irresistible determination of her Bishops, the joyous swing of her advance, both exalted and abashed me. I said to myself, "Look on this picture and on that"; I felt affection for my own Church, but not tenderness; I felt dismay at her prospects, anger and scorn at her do-nothing perplexity. I thought that if Liberalism once got a footing within her, it was sure of the victory in the event. I saw that Reformation principles were powerless to rescue her. As to leaving her, the thought never crossed my imagination; still I ever kept before me that there was something greater than the Established Church, and that that was the Church Catholic and Apostolic, set up from the beginning, of which she was but the local presence and the organ. She was nothing, unless she was this. She must be dealt with strongly, or she would be lost. There was need of a second reformation.

At this time I was disengaged from College duties, and my health had suffered from the labor involved in the composition of my Volume. It was ready for the press in July, 1832, though not published till the end of 1833. I was easily persuaded to join Hurrell Froude and his Father, who were going to the south of Europe for the health of the former.

We set out in December, 1832. It was during this expedition that my verses which are in the *Lyra Apostolica* were written—a few indeed before it, but not more than one or two of them after it. Exchanging, as I was, definite Tutorial

8 *Incessu patuit Dea:* "By her step she appeared a goddess" (*Aeneid,* I, 405).

work, and the literary quiet and pleasant friendships of the last six years, for foreign countries and an unknown future, I naturally was led to think that some inward changes, as well as some larger course of action, were coming upon me. At Whitchurch, while waiting for the down mail to Falmouth, I wrote the verses about my Guardian Angel, which begin with these words: "Are these the tracks of some unearthly Friend?" and which go on to speak of "the vision" which haunted me—that vision is more or less brought out in the whole series of these compositions.

I went to various coasts of the Mediterranean, parted with my friends at Rome; went down for the second time to Sicily without companion, at the end of April, and got back to England by Palermo in the early part of July. The strangeness of foreign life threw me back into myself; I found pleasure in historical sites and beautiful scenes, not in men and manners. We kept clear of Catholics throughout our tour. I had a conversation with the Dean of Malta, a most pleasant man, lately dead; but it was about the Fathers, and the Library of the great church. I knew the Abbate Santini, at Rome, who did no more than copy for me the Gregorian tones. Froude and I made two calls upon Monsignore (now Cardinal) Wiseman at the Collegio Inglese, shortly before we left Rome. Once we heard him preach at a church in the Corso. I do not recollect being in a room with any other ecclesiastics, except a priest at Castro-Giovanni in Sicily, who called on me when I was ill, and with whom I wished to hold a controversy. As to Church Services, we attended the Tenebrae, at the Sistine, for the sake of the Miserere; and that was all. My general feeling was, "All, save the spirit of man, is divine." I saw nothing but what was external; of the hidden life of Catholics I knew nothing. I was still more driven back into myself, and felt my isolation. England was in my thoughts solely, and the news from England came rarely and imperfectly. The Bill for the Suppression of the Irish Sees was in progress, and filled my mind. I had fierce thoughts against the Liberals.

It was the success of the Liberal cause

which fretted me inwardly. I became fierce against its instruments and its manifestations. A French vessel was at Algiers; I would not even look at the tricolor. On my return, though forced to stop twenty-four hours at Paris, I kept indoors the whole time, and all that I saw of that beautiful city was what I saw from the Diligence. The Bishop of London had already sounded me as to my filling one of the Whitehall preacherships, which he had just then put on a new footing; but I was indignant at the line which he was taking, and from my Steamer I had sent home a letter declining the appointment by anticipation, should it be offered to me. At this time I was specially annoyed with Dr. Arnold, though it did not last into later years. Someone, I think, asked in conversation at Rome whether a certain interpretation of Scripture was Christian? it was answered that Dr. Arnold took it; I interposed, "But is *he* a Christian?" The subject went out of my head at once; when afterwards I was taxed with it I could say no more in explanation than (what I believe was the fact) that I must have had in mind some free views of Dr. Arnold about the Old Testament—I thought I must have meant, "Arnold answers for the interpretation, but who is to answer for Arnold?" It was at Rome too that we began the *Lyra Apostolica* which appeared monthly in the *British Magazine*. The motto shows the feeling of both Froude and myself at the time; we borrowed from M. Bunsen a Homer, and Froude chose the words in which Achilles, on returning to the battle, says, "You shall know the difference, now that I am back again."

Especially when I was left by myself, the thought came upon me that deliverance is wrought, not by the many but by the few, not by bodies but by persons. Now it was, I think, that I repeated to myself the words, which had ever been dear to me from my school days, *Exoriare aliquis!* [9]—now too, that Southey's beautiful poem of *Thalaba*, for which I had an immense liking, came forcibly to my mind. I began to think that I had a mission. There are sentences of my letters to my friends to

[9] *Exoriare aliquis* ... (ultor): "May some (avenger) arise!" (*Aeneid*, IV, 625).

this effect, if they are not destroyed. When we took leave of Monsignore Wiseman, he had courteously expressed a wish that we might make a second visit to Rome; I said with great gravity, "We have a work to do in England." I went down at once to Sicily, and the presentiment grew stronger. I struck into the middle of the island, and fell ill of a fever at Leonforte. My servant thought I was dying, and begged for my last directions. I gave them, as he wished; but I said, "I shall not die." I repeated, "I shall not die, for I have not sinned against light, I have not sinned against light." I never have been able to make out at all what I meant.

I got to Castro-Giovanni, and was laid up there for nearly three weeks. Towards the end of May I left for Palermo, taking three days for the journey. Before starting from my inn in the morning of May 26th or 27th, I sat down on my bed, and began to sob bitterly. My servant, who had acted as my nurse, asked what ailed me. I could only answer him, "I have a work to do in England."

I was aching to get home; yet for want of a vessel I was kept at Palermo for three weeks. I began to visit the churches, and they calmed my impatience, though I did not attend any services. I knew nothing of the presence of the Blessed Sacrament there. At last I got off in an orange boat, bound for Marseilles. We were becalmed a whole week in the Straits of Bonifacio. Then it was that I wrote the lines, "Lead, kindly light," which have since become well known. I was writing verses the whole time of my passage. At length I got to Marseilles, and set off for England. The fatigue of traveling was too much for me, and I was laid up for several days at Lyons. At last I got off again, and did not stop night or day (excepting the compulsory delay at Paris) till I reached England, and my mother's house. My brother had arrived from Persia only a few hours before. This was on Tuesday. The following Sunday, July 14th, Mr. Keble preached the Assize Sermon in the University Pulpit. It was published under the title of "National Apostasy." I have ever considered and kept the day as the start of the religious movement of 1833.   [1865]

THE TAMWORTH READING ROOM

SECULAR KNOWLEDGE NOT A PRINCIPLE OF ACTION

People say to me, that it is but a dream to suppose that Christianity should regain the organic power in human society which once it possessed. I cannot help that; I never said it could. I am not a politician; I am proposing no measures, but exposing a fallacy, and resisting a pretence. Let Benthamism reign, if men have no aspirations; but do not tell them to be romantic, and then solace them with glory; do not attempt by philosophy what once was done by religion. The ascendency of Faith may be impracticable, but the reign of Knowledge is incomprehensible. The problem for statesmen of this age is how to educate the masses, and literature and science cannot give the solution.

Not so deems Sir Robert Peel; his firm belief and hope is, "that an increased sagacity will administer to an exalted faith; that it will make men not merely believe in the cold doctrines of Natural Religion, but that it will so prepare and temper the spirit and understanding, that they will be better qualified to comprehend the great scheme of human redemption." He certainly thinks that scientific pursuits have some considerable power of impressing religion upon the mind of the multitude. I think not, and will now say why.

Science gives us the grounds or premises from which religious truths are to be inferred; but it does not set about inferring them, much less does it reach the inference;—that is not its province. It brings before us phenomena, and it leaves us, if we will, to call them works of design, wisdom, or benevolence; and further still, if we will, to proceed to confess an Intelligent Creator. We have to take its facts, and to give them a meaning, and to draw our own conclusions from them. First comes Knowledge, then a view, then reasoning, and then belief. This is why Science has so little of a religious tendency; deductions have no power of persuasion. The heart is commonly reached, not through the reason, but through the imagination, by means of direct impressions, by the testimony of facts and events, by history, by description. Persons influence us, voices melt us, looks subdue us, deeds inflame us. Many a man will live and die upon a dogma: no man will be a martyr for a conclusion. A conclusion is but an opinion; it is not a thing which *is*, but which *we are "certain about"*; and it has often been observed, that we never say we are certain without implying that we doubt. To say that a thing *must* be, is to admit that it *may not* be. No one, I say, will die for his own calculations; he dies for realities. This is why a literary religion is so little to be depended upon; it looks well in fair weather, but its doctrines are opinions, and, when called to suffer for them, it slips them between its folios, or burns them at its hearth. And this again is the secret of the distrust and raillery with which moralists have been so commonly visited. They say and do not. Why? Because they are contemplating the fitness of things, and they live by the square, when they should be realizing their high maxims in the concrete. Now Sir Robert thinks better of natural history, chemistry, and astronomy, than of such ethics; but they too, what are they more than divinity *in posse?* [1] He protests against "controversial divinity": is *inferential* much better?

I have no confidence, then, in philosophers who cannot help being religious, and are Christians by implication. They sit at home, and reach forward to distances which astonish us; but they hit without grasping, and are sometimes as confident about shadows as about realities. They have worked out by a calculation the lie of a country which they never saw, and mapped it by means of a gazetteer; and like blind men, though they can put a stranger on his way, they cannot walk straight themselves, and do not feel it quite their business to walk at all.

Logic makes but a sorry rhetoric with

[1] *in posse:* potentially.

the multitude; first shoot round corners, and you may not despair of converting by a syllogism. Tell men to gain notions of a Creator from His works, and, if they were to set about it (which nobody does), they would be jaded and wearied by the labyrinth they were tracing. Their minds would be gorged and surfeited by the logical operation. Logicians are more set upon concluding rightly, than on right conclusions. They cannot see the end for the process. Few men have that power of mind which may hold fast and firmly a variety of thoughts. We ridicule "men of one idea"; but a great many of us are born to be such, and we should be happier if we knew it. To most men argument makes the point in hand only more doubtful, and considerably less impressive. After all man is *not* a reasoning animal; he is a seeing, feeling, contemplating, acting animal. He is influenced by what is direct and precise. It is very well to freshen our impressions and convictions from physics, but to create them we must go elsewhere. Sir Robert Peel "never can think it possible that a mind can be so constituted, that, after being familiarized with the wonderful discoveries which have been made in every part of experimental science, it can retire from such contemplations without more enlarged conceptions of God's providence, and a higher reverence for His name." If he speaks of religious minds, he perpetrates a truism; if of irreligious, he insinuates a paradox.

Life is not long enough for a religion of inferences; we shall never have done beginning, if we determine to begin with proof. We shall ever be laying out foundations; we shall turn theology into evidences, and divines into textuaries. We shall never get at our first principles. Resolve to believe nothing, and you must prove your proofs and analyse your elements, sinking further and further, and finding "in the lowest depth a lower deep," till you come to the broad bosom of scepticism. I would rather be bound to defend the reasonableness of assuming that Christianity is true, than to demonstrate a moral governance from the physical world. Life is for action. If we insist on proofs for everything, we shall never come to action: to act you must assume, and that assumption is faith.

Let no one suppose that in saying this I am maintaining that all proofs are equally difficult, and all propositions equally debatable. Some assumptions are greater than others, and some doctrines involve postulates larger than others, and more numerous. I only say that impressions lead to action, and that reasonings lead from it. Knowledge of premisses, and inferences upon them,—this is not to *live*. It is very well as a matter of liberal curiosity and of philosophy to analyse our modes of thought; but let this come second, and when there is leisure for it, and then our examinations will in many ways even be subservient to action. But if we commence with scientific knowledge and argumentative proof, or lay any great stress upon it as the basis of personal Christianity, or attempt to make man moral and religious by Libraries and Museums, let us in consistency take chemists for our cooks, and mineralogists for our masons.

Now I wish to state all this as matter of fact, to be judged by the candid testimony of any persons whatever. Why we are so constituted that Faith, not Knowledge or Argument, is our principle of action, is a question with which I have nothing to do; but I think it is a fact, and if it be such, we must resign ourselves to it as best we may, unless we take refuge in the intolerable paradox, that the mass of men are created for nothing, and are meant to leave life as they entered it. So well has this practically been understood in all ages of the world, that no Religion has yet been a Religion of physics or of philosophy. It has ever been synonymous with Revelation. It never has been a deduction from what we know: it has ever been an assertion of what we are to believe. It has never lived in a conclusion; it has never been a message, or a history, or a vision. No legislator or priest ever dreamed of educating our moral nature by science or by argument. There is no difference here between true Religions and pretended. Moses was instructed, not to reason from the creation, but to work miracles. Christianity is a history supernatural, and almost scenic: it tells us what its Author is, by telling us what He has done. I have no wish at all to speak otherwise than respectfully of conscientious Dissenters, but I have heard it said by those who were not their enemies, and who had known much of their preaching, that they had often heard narrow-minded and bigoted clergymen, and often Dissenting ministers of a far more intellectual cast; but that Dissenting teaching came to nothing,—that it was dissipated in thoughts which had no point, and inquiries which converged to no centre, that it ended as it began, and sent away its hearers as it found them;—whereas the instruction in the Church, with all its defects and mistakes, comes to some end, for it started from some beginning. Such is the difference between the dogmatism of faith and the speculations of logic.

Lord Brougham himself, as we have already seen, has recognized the force of this principle. He has not left his philosophical religion to argument; he has committed it to the keeping of the imagination. Why should he depict a great republic of letters, and an intellectual Pantheon, but that he feels that instances and patterns, not logical reasonings, are the living conclusions which alone have a hold over the affections, or can form the character?

SECULAR KNOWLEDGE WITHOUT PERSONAL RELIGION TENDS TO UNBELIEF

When Sir Robert Peel assures us from the Town-hall at Tamworth that physical science must lead to religion, it is no bad compliment to him to say that he is unreal. He speaks of what he knows nothing about. To a religious man like him, Science has ever suggested religious thoughts; he colours the phenomena of physics with the hues of his own mind, and mistakes an interpretation for a deduction. "I am sanguine enough to believe," he says, "that that superior sagacity which is most conversant with the course and constitution of Nature will be first to turn a deaf ear to objections and presumptions against Revealed Religion, and to acknowledge the complete harmony of the Christian Dispensation with all that Reason, assisted by

Revelation, tells us of the course and constitution of Nature." Now, considering that we are all of us educated as Christians from infancy, it is not easy to decide at this day whether Science creates Faith, or only confirms it; but we have this remarkable fact in the history of heathen Greece against the former supposition, that her most eminent empirical philosophers were atheists, and that it was their atheism which was the cause of their eminence. "The natural philosophies of Democritus and others," says Lord Bacon, *"who allow no God or mind* in the frame of things, but attribute the structure of the universe to infinite essays and trials of nature, or what they call fate or fortune, and assigned the causes of particular things to the necessity of matter, *without any intermixture of final causes,* seem, as far as we can judge from the remains of their philosophy, *much more solid,* and to have *gone deeper into nature,* with regard to physical causes, than the philosophies of Aristotle or Plato: and this only because they *never meddled with final causes,* which the others were perpetually inculcating."

Lord Bacon gives us both the fact and the reason for it. Physical philosophers are ever inquiring *whence* things are, not *why;* referring them to nature, not to mind; and thus they tend to make a system a substitute for a God. Each pursuit or calling has its own dangers, and each numbers among its professors men who rise superior to them. As the soldier is tempted to dissipation, and the merchant to acquisitiveness, and the lawyer to the sophistical, and the statesman to the expedient, and the country clergyman to ease and comfort, yet there are good clergymen, statesmen, lawyers, merchants, and soldiers notwithstanding; so there are religious experimentalists, though physics, taken by themselves, tend to infidelity; but to have recourse to physics to *make* men religious is like recommending a canonry as a cure for the gout, or giving a youngster a commission as a penance for irregularities.

The whole framework of Nature is confessedly a tissue of antecedents and consequents; we may refer all things forwards to design, or backwards on a physical cause.

La Place is said to have considered he had a formula which solved all the motions of the solar system; shall we say that those motions came from this formula or from a Divine Fiat? Shall we have recourse for our theory to physics or to theology? Shall we assume Matter and its necessary properties to be eternal, or Mind with its divine attributes? Does the sun shine to warm the earth, or is the earth warmed because the sun shines? The one hypothesis will solve the phenomena as well as the other. Say not it is but a puzzle in argument, and that no one ever felt it in fact. So far from it, I believe that the study of Nature, when religious feeling is away, leads the mind, rightly or wrongly, to acquiesce in the atheistic theory, as the simplest and easiest. It is but parallel to that tendency in anatomical studies, which no one will deny, to solve all the phenomena of the human frame into material elements and powers, and to dispense with the soul. To those who are conscious of matter, but not conscious of mind, it seems more rational to refer all things to one origin, such as they know, than to assume the existence of a second origin such as they know not. It is Religion, then, which suggests to Science its true conclusions; the facts come from Knowledge, but the principles come of Faith.

There are two ways, then, of reading Nature—as a machine and as a work. If we come to it with the assumption that it is a creation, we shall study it with awe; if assuming it to be a system, with mere curiosity. Sir Robert does not make this distinction. He subscribes to the belief that the man "accustomed to such contemplations, *struck with awe* by the manifold proofs of infinite power and infinite wisdom, will yield more ready and hearty assent—yes, the assent of the heart, and not only of the understanding, to the pious exclamation, 'O Lord, how glorious are Thy works!'" He considers that greater insight into Nature will lead a man to say, "How great and wise is the Creator, who has done this!" True: but it is possible that his thoughts may take the form of "How clever is the creature who has discovered it!" and self-conceit may stand proxy for adoration. This is no idle apprehension. Sir Robert himself, religious as he is, gives cause for it; for the first reflection that rises in his mind, as expressed in the above passage, *before* his notice of Divine Power and Wisdom, is, that "the man accustomed to such contemplations will feel the *moral dignity of his nature exalted.*" But Lord Brougham speaks out. "The delight," he says, "is inexpressible of *being able to follow,* as it were, with our eyes, the marvellous works of the Great Architect of Nature." And more clearly still: "One of the most *gratifying treats* which science affords us is *the knowledge of the extraordinary powers* with which the human mind is endowed. No man, until he has studied philosophy, can have a just idea of the great things for which Providence has fitted his understanding, the extraordinary disproportion which there is between his natural strength and the powers of his mind, and the force which he derives from these powers. When we survey the marvellous truths of astronomy, we are first of all lost in the feeling of immense space, and of the comparative insignificance of this globe and its inhabitants. But there soon arises a *sense of gratification and of new wonder* at perceiving how so insignificant a creature has been *able to reach such a knowledge* of the unbounded system of the universe." So, this is the religion we are to gain from the study of Nature; how miserable! The god we attain is our own mind; our veneration is even professedly the worship of self.

The truth is that the system of Nature is just as much connected with Religion, where minds are not religious, as a watch or a steam-carriage. The material world, indeed, is infinitely more wonderful than any human contrivance; but wonder is not religion, or we should be worshipping our railroads. What the physical creation presents to us in itself is a piece of machinery, and when men speak of a Divine Intelligence as its Author, this god of theirs is not the Living and True, unless the spring is the god of a watch, or steam the creator of the engine. Their idol, taken at advantage (though it is *not* an idol, for they do not worship it), is the animating principle of a vast and complicated system; it is subjected to laws, and it is con-natural

and co-extensive with matter. Well does Lord Brougham call it "the great architect of nature"; it is an instinct, or a soul of the world, or a vital power; it is not the Almighty God.

It is observable that Lord Brougham does not allude to any *relation* as existing between his *god* and ourselves. He is filled with awe, it seems, at the powers of the human mind, as displayed in their analysis of the vast creation. Is not this a fitting time to say a word about gratitude towards Him who gave them? Not a syllable. What we gain from his contemplation of Nature is "a gratifying treat," the knowledge of the "great things for which Providence has fitted man's understanding"; our admiration terminates in man; it passes on to no prototype. I am not quarrelling with his result as illogical or unfair; it is but consistent with the principles with which he started. Take the system of Nature by itself, detached from the axioms of Religion, and I am willing to confess—nay, I have been expressly urging—that it does not force us to take it for *more* than a system; but why, then, persist in calling the study of it religious, when it can be treated, and is treated, thus atheistically? Say that Religion hallows the study, not that the study is a true ground of Religion. The essence of Religion is the idea of a Moral Governor, and a particular Providence; now let me ask, is the doctrine of moral governance and a particular providence conveyed to us through the physical sciences at all? Would they be physical sciences if they treated of morals? Can physics teach moral matters without ceasing to be physics? But are not virtue and vice, and responsibility, and reward and punishment, anything else than moral matters, and are *they* not of the essence of Religion? In what department, then, of physics are they to be found? Can the problems and principles they involve be expressed in the differential calculus? Is the galvanic battery a whit more akin to conscience and will, than the mechanical powers? What we seek is what concerns us, the traces of a Moral Governor; even religious minds cannot discern these in the physical sciences; astronomy witnesses divine power, and physics divine skill; and all of them divine beneficence; but which teaches of divine holiness, truth, justice, or mercy? Is that much of a Religion which is silent about duty, sin, and its remedies? Was there ever a Religion which was without the idea of an expiation?

Sir Robert Peel tells us, that physical science imparts "pleasure and *consolation*" on a death-bed. Lord Brougham confines himself to the "gratifying treat"; but Sir Robert ventures to speak of "consolation." Now, if we are on trial in this life, and if death be the time when our account is gathered in, is it at all serious or real to be talking of "consoling" ourselves at such a time with scientific subjects? Are these topics to suggest to us the thought of the Creator or not? If not, are they better than story books, to beguile the mind from what lies before it? But, if they are to speak of Him, can a dying man find rest in the mere notion of his Creator, when he knows Him also so awfully as His Moral Governor and his Judge? Meditate indeed on the wonders of Nature on a death-bed! Rather stay your hunger with corn grown in Jupiter, and warm yourself by the Moon.

But enough on this most painful portion of Sir Robert's Address. As I am coming to an end, I suppose I ought to sum up in a few words what I have been saying. I consider, then, that intrinsically excellent and noble as are scientific pursuits, and worthy of a place in a liberal education, and fruitful in temporal benefits to the community, still they are not, and cannot be, *the instrument* of an ethical training; that physics do not supply a basis, but only materials for religious sentiment; that knowledge does but occupy, does not form the mind;

that apprehension of the unseen is the only known principle capable of subduing moral evil, educating the multitude, and organizing society; and that, whereas man is born for action, action flows not from inferences, but from impressions,—not from reasonings, but from Faith.

That Sir Robert would deny these propositions I am far from contending; I do not even contend that he has asserted the contrary at Tamworth. It matters little to me whether he spoke boldly and intelligibly, as the newspapers represent, or guarded his strong sayings with the contradictory matter with which they are intercalated in his own report. In either case the drift and the effect of his Address are the same. He has given his respected name to a sophistical School, and condescended to mimic the gestures and tones of Lord Brougham. How melancholy is it that a man of such exemplary life, such cultivated tastes, such political distinction, such Parliamentary tact, and such varied experience, should have so little confidence in himself, so little faith in his own principles, so little hope of sympathy in others, so little heart for a great venture, so little of romantic aspiration, and of firm resolve, and stern dutifulness to the Unseen! How sad that he who might have had the affections of many, should have thought, in a day like this, that a Statesman's praise lay in preserving the mean, not in aiming at the high; that to be safe was his first merit, and to kindle enthusiasm his most disgraceful blunder! How pitiable that such a man should not have understood that a body without a soul has no life, and a political party without an idea, no unity!

[1841]

THE RISE AND PROGRESS OF UNIVERSITIES

WHAT IS A UNIVERSITY?

If I were asked to describe as briefly and popularly as I could what a University was, I should draw my answer from its ancient designation of a *Studium Generale,* or "School of Universal Learning." This description implies the assemblage of strangers from all parts in one spot—*from all*

parts; else, how will you find professors and students for every department of knowledge? and *in one spot;* else, how can there be any school at all? Accordingly, in its simple and rudimental form, it is a school of knowledge of every kind, consisting of teachers and learners from every quarter. Many things are requisite to complete and satisfy the idea embodied in this description; but such as this a University seems to be in its essence, a place for the communication and circulation of thought, by means of personal intercourse, through a wide extent of country.

There is nothing far-fetched or unreasonable in the idea thus presented to us; and if this be a University, then a University does but contemplate a necessity of our nature, and is but one specimen in a particular medium, out of many which might be adduced in others, of a provision for that necessity. Mutual education, in a large sense of the word, is one of the great and incessant occupations of human society, carried on partly with set purpose, and partly not. One generation forms another; and the existing generation is ever acting and reacting upon itself in the persons of its individual members. Now, in this process, books, I need scarcely say, that is, the *litera scripta*,[1] are one special instrument. It is true; and emphatically so in this age. Considering the prodigious powers of the press, and how they are developed at this time in the never-intermitting issue of periodicals, tracts, pamphlets, works in series, and light literature, we must allow there never was a time which promised fairer for dispensing with every other means of information and instruction. What can we want more, you will say, for the intellectual education of the whole man, and for every man, than so exuberant and diversified and persistent a promulgation of all kinds of knowledge? Why, you will ask, need we go up to knowledge, when knowledge comes down to us? The Sibyl wrote her prophecies upon the leaves of the forest, and wasted them; but here such careless profusion might be prudently indulged, for it can be afforded without loss, in consequence of the almost fabulous fecundity of the instrument which these latter ages have invented. We have sermons in stones, and books in the running brooks; works larger and more comprehensive than those which have gained for ancients an immortality, issue forth every morning, and are projected onwards to the ends of the earth at the rate of hundreds of miles a day. Our seats are strewed, our pavements are powdered, with swarms

1 *litera scripta:* written word.

of little tracts; and the very bricks of our city walls preach wisdom, by informing us by their placards where we can at once cheaply purchase it.

I allow all this, and much more; such certainly is our popular education, and its effects are remarkable. Nevertheless, after all, even in this age, whenever men are really serious about getting what, in the language of trade, is called "a good article," when they aim at something precise, something refined, something really luminous, something really large, something choice, they go to another market; they avail themselves, in some shape or other, of the rival method, the ancient method, of oral instruction, of present communication between man and man, of teachers instead of learning, of the personal influence of a master, and the humble initiation of a disciple, and, in consequence, of great centers of pilgrimage and throng, which such a method of education necessarily involves. This, I think, will be found to hold good in all those departments or aspects of society which possess an interest sufficient to bind men together, or to constitute what is called "a world." It holds in the political world, and in the high world, and in the religious world; and it holds also in the literary and scientific world.

If the actions of men may be taken as any test of their convictions, then we have reason for saying this, viz.: that the province and the inestimable benefit of the *litera scripta* is that of being a record of truth, and an authority of appeal, and an instrument of teaching in the hands of a teacher; but that, if we wish to become exact and fully furnished in any branch of knowledge which is diversified and complicated, we must consult the living man and listen to his living voice. I am not bound to investigate the cause of this, and anything I may say will, I am conscious, be short of its full analysis; perhaps we may suggest, that no books can get through the number of minute questions which it is possible to ask on any extended subject, or can hit upon the very difficulties which are severally felt by each reader in succession. Or again, that no book can convey the special spirit and delicate peculiarities of its subject with that rapidity and certainty which attend on the sympathy of mind with mind, through the eyes, the look, the accent, and the manner, in casual expressions thrown off at the moment, and the unstudied turns of familiar conversation. But I am already dwelling too long on what is but an incidental portion of my main subject. Whatever be the cause, the fact is undeniable. The general principles of any study you may learn by books at home; but the detail, the color, the tone, the air, the life which makes it live in us, you must catch all these from those in whom it lives already. You must imitate the student in French or German, who is not content with his grammar, but goes to Paris or Dresden; you must take example from the young artist, who aspires to visit the great Masters in Florence and in Rome. Till we have discovered some intellectual daguerreotype which takes off the course of thought, and the form, lineaments, and features of truth, as completely and minutely as the optical instrument reproduces the sensible object, we must come to the teachers of wisdom to learn wisdom, we must repair to the fountain, and drink there. Portions of it may go from thence to the ends of the earth by means of books; but the fullness is in one place alone. It is in such assemblages and congregations of intellect that books themselves, the masterpieces of human genius, are written, or at least originated.

The principle on which I have been insisting is so obvious, and instances in point are so ready, that I should think it tiresome to proceed with the subject, except that one or two illustrations may serve to explain my own language about it, which may not have done justice to the doctrine which it has been intended to enforce.

For instance, the polished manners and highbred bearing which are so difficult of attainment, and so strictly personal when attained—which are so much admired in society, from society are acquired. All that goes to constitute a gentleman—the carriage, gait, address, gestures, voice; the ease, the self-possession, the courtesy, the power of conversing, the talent of not offending; the lofty principle, the delicacy of thought, the happiness of expression, the taste and propriety, the generosity and forbearance, the candor and consideration, the openness of hand—these qualities, some of them come by nature, some of them may be found in any rank, some of them are a direct precept of Christianity; but the full assemblage of them, bound up in the unity of an individual character, do we expect they can be learned from books? are they not necessarily acquired, where they are to be found, in high society? The very nature of the case leads us to say so; you cannot fence without an antagonist, nor challenge all comers in disputation before you have supported a thesis; and in like manner, it stands to reason, you cannot learn to converse till you have the world to converse with; you cannot unlearn your natural bashfulness, or awkwardness, or stiffness, or other besetting deformity, till you serve your time in some school of manners. Well, and is it not so in matter of fact? The metropolis, the court, the great houses of the land, are the centers to which at stated times the country comes up, as to shrines of refinement and good taste; and then in due time the country goes back again home, enriched with a portion of the social accomplishments which those very visits serve to call out and heighten in the gracious dispensers of them. We are unable to conceive how the "gentlemanlike" can otherwise be maintained; and maintained in this way it is.

And now a second instance—and here, too, I am going to speak without personal experience of the subject I am introducing. I admit I have not been in Parliament, any more than I have figured in the beau monde; yet I cannot but think that statesmanship, as well as high breeding, is learned, not by books, but in certain centers of education. If it be not presumption to say so, Parliament puts a clever man *au courant* [2] with politics and affairs of state in a way surprising to himself. A member of the Legislature, if tolerably observant, begins to see things with new eyes, even though his views undergo no change. Words have a meaning now, and ideas a reality, such as they had not before. He hears a vast deal in public speeches and

2 *au courant*: 'with the current', i.e. up to date.

private conservation which is never put into print. The bearings of measures and events, the action of parties, and the persons of friends and enemies, are brought out to the man who is in the midst of them with a distinctness which the most diligent perusal of newspapers will fail to impart to them. It is access to the fountainheads of political wisdom and experience, it is daily intercourse, of one kind or another, with the multitude who go up to them, it is familiarity with business, it is access to the contributions of fact and opinion thrown together by many witnesses from many quarters, which does this for him. However, I need not account for a fact, to which it is sufficient to appeal, that the Houses of Parliament and the atmosphere around them are a sort of University of politics.

As regards the world of science, we find a remarkable instance of the principle which I am illustrating in the periodical meetings for its advance, which have arisen in the course of the last twenty years, such as the British Association. Such gatherings would to many persons appear at first sight simply preposterous. Above all subjects of study, Science is conveyed, is propagated, by books, or by private teaching; experiments and investigations are conducted in silence; discoveries are made in solitude. What have philosophers to do with festive celebrities, and panegyrical solemnities with mathematical and physical truth? Yet on a closer attention to the subject, it is found that not even scientific thought can dispense with the suggestions, the instruction, the stimulus, the sympathy, the intercourse with mankind on a large scale, which such meetings secure. A fine time of year is chosen, when days are long, skies are bright, the earth smiles, and all nature rejoices; a city or town is taken by turns, of ancient name or modern opulence, where buildings are spacious and hospitality hearty. The novelty of place and circumstance, the excitement of strange, or the refreshment of well-known faces, the majesty of rank or of genius, the amiable charities of men pleased both with themselves and with each other; the elevated spirits, the circulation of thought, the curiosity; the morning sections, the outdoor exercise, the well-furnished, well-earned board, the not ungraceful hilarity, the evening circle; the brilliant lecture, the discussions or collisions or guesses of great men one with another, the narratives of scientific processes, of hopes, disappointments, conflicts, and successes, the splendid eulogistic orations; these and the like constituents of the annual celebration are considered to do something real and substantial for the advance of knowledge which can be done in no other way. Of course they can but be occasional; they answer to the annual Act, or Commencement, or Commemoration, of a University, not to its ordinary condition; but they are of a University nature; and I can well believe in their utility. They issue in the promotion of a certain living and, as it were, bodily communication of knowledge from one to another, of a general interchange of ideas, and a comparison and adjustment of science with science, of an enlargement of mind, intellectual and social, of an ardent love of the particular study which may be chosen by each individual, and a noble devotion to its interests.

Such meetings, I repeat, are but periodical, and only partially represent the idea of a University. The bustle and whirl which are their usual concomitants are in ill keeping with the order and gravity of earnest intellectual education. We desiderate means of instruction which involve no interruption of our ordinary habits; nor need we seek it long, for the natural course of things brings it about while we debate over it. In every great country, the metropolis itself becomes a sort of necessary University, whether we will or no. As the chief city is the seat of the court, of high society, of politics, and of law, so as a matter of course is it the seat of letters also; and at this time, for a long term of years, London and Paris are in fact and in operation Universities, though in Paris its famous University is no more, and in London a University scarcely exists except as a board of administration. The newspapers, magazines, reviews, journals, and periodicals of all kinds, the publishing trade, the libraries, museums, and academies there found, the learned and scientific societies, necessarily invest it with the functions of a University;

and that atmosphere of intellect which in a former age hung over Oxford or Bologna or Salamanca has, with the change of times, moved away to the center of civil government. Thither come up youths from all parts of the country, the students of law, medicine, and the fine arts, and the *employés* and *attachés* of literature. There they live, as chance determines; and they are satisfied with their temporary home, for they find in it all that was promised to them there. They have not come in vain, as far as their own object in coming is concerned. They have not learned any particular religion, but they have learned their own particular profession well. They have, moreover, become acquainted with the habits, manners, and opinions of their place of sojourn, and done their part in maintaining the tradition of them. We cannot then be without virtual Universities; a metropolis is such—the simple question is, whether the education sought and given should be based on principle, formed upon rule, directed to the highest ends, or left to the random succession of masters and schools, one after another, with a melancholy waste of thought and an extreme hazard of truth.

Religious teaching itself affords us an illustration of our subject to a certain point. It does not, indeed, seat itself merely in centers of the world; this is impossible from the nature of the case. It is intended for the many, not the few; its subject-matter is truth necessary for us, not truth recondite and rare; but it concurs in the principle of a University so far as this, that its great instrument, or rather organ, has ever been that which nature prescribes in all education, the personal presence of a teacher, or, in theological language, Oral Tradition. It is the living voice, the breathing form, the expressive countenance, which preaches, which catechizes. Truth, a subtle, invisible, manifold spirit, is poured into the mind of the scholar by his eyes and ears, through his affections, imagination, and reason; it is poured into his mind and is sealed up there in perpetuity, by propounding and repeating it, by questioning and requestioning, by correcting and explaining, by progressing and then recurring to first principles, by all those ways which are implied in the word "catechizing." In the first ages, it was a work of long time; months, sometimes years, were devoted to the arduous task of disabusing the mind of the incipient Christian of its pagan errors, and of molding it upon the Christian faith. The Scriptures, indeed, were at hand for the study of those who could avail themselves of them; but St. Irenaeus does not hesitate to speak of whole races who had been converted to Christianity without being able to read them. To be unable to read or write was in those times no evidence of want of learning—the hermits of the deserts were, in this sense of the word, illiterate; yet the great St. Anthony, though he knew not letters, was a match in disputation for the learned philosophers who came to try him. Didymus again, the great Alexandrian theologian, was blind. The ancient discipline, called the *Disciplina Arcani* [3] involved the same principle. The more sacred doctrines of Revelation were not committed to books, but passed on by successive tradition. The teaching on the Blessed Trinity and the Eucharist appears to have been so handed down for some hundred years; and when at length reduced to writing, it has filled many folios, yet has not been exhausted.

But I have said more than enough in illustration; I end as I began—a University is a place of concourse, whither students come from every quarter for every kind of knowledge. You cannot have the best of every kind everywhere; you must go to some great city or emporium for it. There you have all the choicest productions of nature and art all together, which you find each in its own separate place elsewhere. All the riches of the land, and of the earth, are carried up thither; there are the best markets, and there the best workmen. It is the center of trade, the supreme court of fashion, the umpire of rival talents, and the standard of things rare and precious. It is the place for seeing galleries of first-rate pictures, and for hearing wonderful

[3] *Disciplina Arcani*: 'The Discipline of the Secret',—a theological term meaning the practice of reticence regarding their religion observed by the early Christians in order to protect the more intimate mysteries of their faith from possible molestation from the pagans.

voices and performers of transcendent skill. It is the place for great preachers, great orators, great nobles, great statesmen. In the nature of things, greatness and unity go together; excellence implies a center. And such, for the third or fourth time, is a University; I hope I do not weary out the reader by repeating it. It is the place to which a thousand schools make contributions; in which the intellect may safely range and speculate, sure to find its equal in some antagonist activity, and its judge in the tribunal of truth. It is a place where inquiry is pushed forward, and discoveries verified and perfected, and rashness rendered innocuous, and error exposed, by the collision of mind with mind, and knowledge with knowledge. It is the place where the professor becomes eloquent, and is a missionary and a preacher, displaying his science in its most complete and most winning form, pouring it forth with the zeal of enthusiasm, and lighting up his own love of it in the breasts of his hearers. It is the place where the catechist makes good his ground as he goes, treading in the truth day by day into the ready memory, and wedging and tightening it into the expanding reason. It is a place which wins the admiration of the young by its celebrity, kindles the affections of the middle-aged by its beauty, and rivets the fidelity of the old by its associations. It is a seat of wisdom, a light of the world, a minister of the faith, an Alma Mater of the rising generation. It is this and a great deal more, and demands a somewhat better head and hand than mine to describe it well.

Such is a University in its idea and in its purpose; such in good measure has it before now been in fact. Shall it ever be again? We are going forward in the strength of the Cross, under the patronage of the Blessed Virgin, in the name of St. Patrick, to attempt it.

[1854]

THE IDEA OF A UNIVERSITY

KNOWLEDGE ITS OWN END

A University may be considered with reference either to its Students or to its Studies; and the principle that all Knowledge is a whole and the separate Sciences parts of one, which I have hitherto been using in behalf of its studies, is equally important when we direct our attention to its students. Now then I turn to the students, and shall consider the education which, by virtue of this principle, a University will give them; and thus I shall be introduced, Gentlemen, to the second question, which I proposed to discuss, viz., whether and in what sense its teaching, viewed relatively to the taught, carries the attribute of Utility along with it.

I

I have said that all branches of knowledge are connected together, because the subject-matter of knowledge is intimately united in itself, as being the acts and the work of the Creator. Hence it is that the Sciences, into which our knowledge may be said to be cast, have multiplied bearings one on another, and an internal sympathy, and admit, or rather demand, comparison and adjustment. They complete, correct, balance each other. This consideration, if well-founded, must be taken into account, not only as regards the attainment of truth, which is their common end, but as regards the influence which they exercise upon those whose education consists in the study of them. I have said already that to give undue prominence to one is to be unjust to another; to neglect or supersede these is to divert those from their proper object. It is to unsettle the boundary lines between science and science, to disturb their action, to destroy the harmony which binds them together. Such a proceeding will have a corresponding effect when introduced into a place of education. There is no science but tells a different tale, when viewed as a portion of a whole, from what it is likely to suggest when taken by itself, without the safeguard, as I may call it, of others.

Let me make use of an illustration. In the combination of colors, very different effects are produced by a difference in their selection and juxtaposition; red, green, and white change their shades, according to the contrast to which they are submitted. And, in like manner, the drift and meaning of a branch of knowledge varies with the company in which it is introduced to the student. If his reading is confined simply to one subject, however such division of labor may favor the advancement of a particular pursuit, a point into which I do not here enter, certainly it has a tendency to contract his mind. If it is incorporated with others, it depends on those others as to the kind of influence which it exerts upon him. Thus the Classics, which in England are the means of refining the taste, have in France subserved the spread of revolutionary and deistical doctrines. In Metaphysics, again, Butler's *Analogy of Religion,* which has had so much to do with the conversion to the Catholic faith of members of the University of Oxford, appeared to Pitt and others, who had received a different training, to operate only in the direction of infidelity. And so again, Watson, Bishop of Llandaff, as I think he tells us in the narrative of his life, felt the science of Mathematics to indispose the mind to religious belief, while others see in its investigations the best defense of the Christian Mysteries. In like manner, I suppose, Arcesilaus would not have handled logic as Aristotle, nor Aristotle have criticized poets as Plato; yet reasoning and poetry are subject to scientific rules.

It is a great point then to enlarge the range of studies which a University professes, even for the sake of the students; and, though they cannot pursue every subject which is open to them, they will be the gainers by living among those and under those who represent the whole circle. This I conceive to be the advantage of a seat of universal learning, considered as a place of education. An assemblage of learned men, zealous for their own sciences, and rivals of each other, are brought, by familiar intercourse and for the sake of intellectual peace, to adjust together the claims and relations of their respective subjects of investigation. They learn to respect, to consult, to aid each other. Thus is created a pure and clear atmosphere of thought, which the student also breathes,

though in his own case he only pursues a few sciences out of the multitude. He profits by an intellectual tradition, which is independent of particular teachers, which guides him in his choice of subjects, and duly interprets for him those which he chooses. He apprehends the great outlines of knowledge, the principles on which it rests, the scale of its parts, its lights and its shades, its great points and its little, as he otherwise cannot apprehend them. Hence it is that his education is called "Liberal." A habit of mind is formed which lasts through life, of which the attributes are freedom, equitableness, calmness, moderation, and wisdom; or what in a former Discourse I have ventured to call a philosophical habit. This, then, I would assign as the special fruit of the education furnished at a University, as contrasted with other places of teaching or modes of teaching. This is the main purpose of a University in its treatment of its students.

And now the question is asked me, What is the *use* of it? and my answer will constitute the main subject of the Discourses which are to follow.

II

Cautious and practical thinkers, I say, will ask of me, what, after all, is the gain of this Philosophy, of which I make such account, and from which I promise so much. Even supposing it to enable us to give the degree of confidence exactly due to every science respectively, and to estimate precisely the value of every truth which is anywhere to be found, how are we better for this master view of things, which I have been extolling? Does it not reverse the principle of the division of labor? will practical objects be obtained better or worse by its cultivation? to what then does it lead? where does it end? what does it do? how does it profit? what does it promise? Particular sciences are respectively the basis of definite arts, which carry on to results tangible and beneficial the truths which are the subjects of the knowledge attained; what is the Art of this science of sciences; what is the fruit of such a Philosophy? what are we proposing to effect, what inducements do we hold out to the Catholic community, when we set about the enterprise of founding a University?

I am asked what is the end of University Education, and of the Liberal or Philosophical Knowledge which I conceive it to impart; I answer that what I have already said has been sufficient to show that it has a very tangible, real, and sufficient end, though the end cannot be divided from that knowledge itself. Knowledge is capable of being its own end. Such is the constitution of the human mind, that any kind of knowledge, if it be really such, is its own reward. And if this is true of all knowledge, it is true also of that special Philosophy which I have made to consist in a comprehensive view of truth in all its branches, of the relations of science to science, of their mutual bearings, and their respective values. What the worth of such an acquirement is, compared with other objects which we seek—wealth or power or honor or the conveniences and comforts of life—I do not profess here to discuss; but I would maintain, and mean to show, that it is an object, in its own nature so really and undeniably good, as to be the compensation of a great deal of thought in the compassing, and a great deal of trouble in the attaining.

Now, when I say that Knowledge is not merely a means to something beyond it, or the preliminary of certain arts into which it naturally resolves, but an end sufficient to rest in and to pursue for its own sake, surely I am uttering no paradox, for I am stating what is both intelligible in itself, and has ever been the common judgment of philosophers and the ordinary feeling of mankind. I am saying what at least the public opinion of this day ought to be slow to deny, considering how much we have heard of late years, in opposition to Religion, of entertaining, curious, and various knowledge. I am but saying what whole volumes have been written to illustrate, by a "selection from the records of Philosophy, Literature, and Art, in all ages and countries, of a body of examples, to show how the most unpropitious circumstances have been unable to conquer an ardent desire for the acquisition of knowledge." That further advantages accrue to us and redound to others by its possession, over and above what it is in itself, I am

very far indeed from denying; but, independent of these, we are satisfying a direct need of our nature in its very acquisition; and, whereas our nature, unlike that of the inferior creation, does not at once reach its perfection, but depends, in order to it, on a number of external aids and appliances, Knowledge, as one of the principal gifts or accessories by which it is completed, is valuable for what its very presence in us does for us after the manner of a habit, even though it be turned to no further account, nor subserve any direct end.

III

Hence it is that Cicero, in enumerating the various heads of mental excellence, lays down the pursuit of Knowledge for its own sake as the first of them. "This pertains most of all to human nature," he says, "for we are all of us drawn to the pursuit of Knowledge; in which to excel we consider excellent, whereas to mistake, to err, to be ignorant, to be deceived, is both an evil and a disgrace." And he considers Knowledge the very first object to which we are attracted, after the supply of our physical wants. After the calls and duties of our animal existence, as they may be termed, as regards ourselves, our family, and our neighbors, follows, he tells us, "the search after truth. Accordingly, as soon as we escape from the pressure of necessary cares, forthwith we desire to see, to hear, to learn; and consider the knowledge of what is hidden or is wonderful a condition of our happiness."

This passage, though it is but one of many similar passages in a multitude of authors, I take for the very reason that it is so familiarly known to us; and I wish you to observe, Gentlemen, how distinctly it separates the pursuit of Knowledge from those ulterior objects to which certainly it can be made to conduce, and which are, I suppose, solely contemplated by the persons who would ask of me the use of a University or Liberal Education. So far from dreaming of the cultivation of Knowledge directly and mainly in order to our physical comfort and enjoyment, for the sake of life and person, of health, of the conjugal and family union, of the social tie and civil security, the great Orator implies that it is only after our physical and political needs are supplied, and when we are "free from necessary duties and cares," that we are in a condition for "desiring to see, to hear, and to learn." Nor does he contemplate in the least degree the reflex or subsequent action of Knowledge, when acquired, upon those material goods which we set out by securing before we seek it; on the contrary, he expressly denies its bearing upon social life altogether, strange as such a procedure is to those who live after the rise of the Baconian philosophy, and he cautions us against such a cultivation of it as will interfere with our duties to our fellow-creatures. "All these methods," he says, "are engaged in the investigation of truth; by the pursuit of which to be carried off from public occupations is a transgression of duty. For the praise of virtue lies altogether in action; yet intermissions often occur, and then we recur to such pursuits; not to say that the incessant activity of the mind is vigorous enough to carry us on in the pursuit of knowledge, even without any exertion of our own." The idea of benefiting society by means of "the pursuit of science and knowledge," did not enter at all into the motives which he would assign for their cultivation.

This was the ground of the opposition which the elder Cato made to the introduction of Greek Philosophy among his countrymen, when Carneades and his companions, on occasion of their embassy, were charming the Roman youth with their eloquent expositions of it. The fit representative of a practical people, Cato estimated everything by what it produced; whereas the Pursuit of Knowledge promised nothing beyond Knowledge itself. He despised that refinement or enlargement of mind of which he had no experience.

IV

Things which can bear to be cut off from everything else and yet persist in living must have life in themselves; pursuits which issue in nothing, and still maintain their ground for ages, which are regarded as admirable, though they have not as yet proved themselves to be useful, must have their sufficient end in them-

selves, whatever it turn out to be. And we are brought to the same conclusion by considering the force of the epithet by which the knowledge under consideration is popularly designated. It is common to speak of *"liberal* knowledge," of the *"liberal* arts and studies," and of a *"liberal* education," as the especial characteristic or property of a University and of a gentleman; what is really meant by the word? Now, first, in its grammatical sense it is opposed to *servile*; and by "servile work" is understood, as our catechisms inform us, bodily labor, mechanical employment, and the like, in which the mind has little or no part. Parallel to such works are those arts, if they deserve the name, of which the poet speaks, which owe their origin and their method to hazard, not to skill; as, for instance, the practice and operations of an empiric. As far as this contrast may be considered as a guide into the meaning of the word, liberal knowledge and liberal pursuits are exercises of mind, of reason, of reflection.

But we want something more for its explanation, for there are bodily exercises which are liberal, and mental exercises which are not so. For instance, in ancient times the practitioners in medicine were commonly slaves; yet it was an art as intellectual in its nature, in spite of the pretense, fraud, and quackery with which it might then, as now, be debased, as it was heavenly in its aim. And so, in like manner, we contrast a liberal education with a commercial education or a professional; yet no one can deny that commerce and the professions afford scope for the highest and most diversified powers of mind. There is then a great variety of intellectual exercises, which are not technically called "liberal"; on the other hand, I say, there are exercises of the body which do receive that appellation.[1] Such, for instance, was the palaestra,[1] in ancient times; such the Olympic games, in which strength and dexterity of body as well as of mind gained the prize. In Xenophon we read of the young Persian nobility being taught to ride on horseback and to speak the truth—both being among the accomplishments of a gentleman. War, too, however rough a profession, has ever been accounted lib-

---

1 *palaestra:* wrestling-school

eral, unless in cases when it becomes heroic, which would introduce us to another subject.

Now, comparing these instances together, we shall have no difficulty in determining the principle of this apparent variation in the application of the term which I am examining. Manly games, or games of skill, of military prowess, though bodily, are, it seems, accounted liberal; on the other hand, what is merely professional, though highly intellectual, nay, though liberal in comparison of trade and manual labor, is not simply called liberal, and mercantile occupations are not liberal at all. Why this distinction? because that alone is liberal knowledge which stands on its own pretensions, which is independent of sequel, expects no complement, refuses to be *informed* (as it is called) by any end, or absorbed into any art, in order duly to present itself to our contemplation. The most ordinary pursuits have this specific character if they are self-sufficient and complete; the highest lose it when they minister to something beyond them. It is absurd to balance, in point of worth and importance, a treatise on reducing fractures with a game of cricket or a fox-chase; yet of the two the bodily exercise has that quality which we call "liberal," and the intellectual has it not. And so of the learned professions altogether, considered merely as professions; although one of them be the most popularly beneficial, and another the most politically important, and the third the most intimately divine of all human pursuits, yet the very greatness of their end, the health of the body, or of the commonwealth, or of the soul, diminishes, not increases, their claim to the appellation "liberal," and that still more if they are cut down to the strict exigencies of that end. If, for instance, Theology, instead of being cultivated as a contemplation, be limited to the purposes of the pulpit or be represented by the catechism, it loses—not its usefulness, not its divine character, not its meritoriousness (rather it increases these qualities by such charitable condescension) —but it does lose the particular attribute which I am illustrating; just as a face worn by tears and fasting loses its beauty, or a laborer's hand loses its delicateness—for

Theology thus exercised is not simple knowledge, but rather is an art or a business making use of Theology. And thus it appears that even what is supernatural need not be liberal, nor need a hero be a gentleman, for the plain reason that one idea is not another idea. And in like manner the Baconian Philosophy, by using its physical sciences in the service of man, does thereby transfer them from the order of Liberal Pursuits to, I do not say the inferior, but the distinct class of the Useful. And, to take a different instance, hence again, as is evident, whenever personal gain is the motive, still more distinctive an effect has it upon the character of a given pursuit; thus racing, which was a liberal exercise in Greece, forfeits its rank in times like these, so far as it is made the occasion of gambling.

All that I have been now saying is summed up in a few characteristic words of the great Philosopher. "Of possessions," he says, "those rather are useful which bear fruit; those *liberal which tend to enjoyment.* By fruitful, I mean, which yield revenue; by enjoyable, where *nothing accrues of consequence beyond the use.*"

V

Do not suppose, Gentlemen, that in thus appealing to the ancients I am throwing back the world two thousand years, and fettering Philosophy with the reasonings of paganism. While the world lasts, will Aristotle's doctrine on these matters last, for he is the oracle of nature and of truth. While we are men, we cannot help, to a great extent, being Aristotelians, for the great Master does but analyze the thoughts, feelings, views, and opinions of humankind. He has told us the meaning of our own words and ideas, before we were born. In many subject-matters, to think correctly is to think like Aristotle; and we are his disciples whether we will or no, though we may not know it. Now, as to the particular instance before us, the word "liberal," as applied to Knowledge and Education, expresses a specific idea, which ever has been, and ever will be, while the nature of man is the same, just as the idea of the Beautiful is specific, or of the Sublime, or of the Ridiculous, or of the Sordid. It is in the world now, it was in the world then; and, as in the case of the dogmas of faith, it is illustrated by a continous historical tradition, and never was out of the world, from the time it came into it. There have indeed been differences of opinion, from time to time, as to what pursuits and what arts came under that idea, but such differences are but an additonal evidence of its reality. That idea must have a substance in it, which has maintained its ground amid these conflicts and changes, which has ever served as a standard to measure things withal, which has passed from mind to mind unchanged, when there was so much to color, so much to influence any notion or thought whatever, which was not founded in our very nature. Were it a mere generalization, it would have varied with the subjects from which it was generalized; but though its subjects vary with the age, it varies not itself. The palaestra may seem a liberal exercise to Lycurgus, and illiberal to Seneca; coach-driving and prize-fighting may be recognized in Elis, and be condemned in England; music may be despicable in the eyes of certain moderns, and be in the highest place with Aristotle and Plato—and the case is the same in the particular application of the idea of Beauty, or of Goodness, or of Moral Virtue; there is a difference of tastes, a difference of judgments—still these variations imply, instead of discrediting, the archetypal idea, which is but a previous hypothesis or condition by means of which issue is joined between contending opinions and without which there would be nothing to dispute about.

I consider, then, that I am chargeable with no paradox when I speak of a Knowledge which is its own end, when I call it liberal knowledge, or a gentleman's knowledge, when I educate for it, and make it the scope of a University. And still less am I incurring such a charge when I make this acquisition consist, not in Knowledge in a vague and ordinary sense, but in that Knowledge which I have especially called Philosophy, or, in an extended sense of the word, Science; for whatever claims Knowledge has to be considered as a good, these it has in a higher degree when it is viewed not vaguely, not popularly, but precisely and transcendently as Philosophy. Knowledge, I say, is then especially liberal, or sufficient for itself, apart from every external and ulterior object when and so far as it is philosophical, and this I proceed to show.

VI

Now bear with me, Gentlemen, if what I am about to say has at first sight a fanciful appearance. Philosophy, then, or Science, is related to Knowledge in this way: Knowledge is called by the name of Science or Philosophy when it is acted upon, informed, or, if I may use a strong figure, impregnated by Reason. Reason is the principle of that intrinsic fecundity of Knowledge which, to those who possess it, is its especial value, and which dispenses with the necessity of their looking abroad for any end to rest upon external to itself. Knowledge, indeed, when thus exalted into a scientific form, is also power; not only is it excellent in itself, but, whatever such excellence may be, it is something more, it has a result beyond itself. Doubtless; but that is a further consideration, with which I am not concerned. I only say that, prior to its being a power, it is a good; that it is not only an instrument but an end. I know well it may resolve itself into an art, and terminate in a mechanical process, and in tangible fruit; but it also may fall back upon that Reason which informs it, and resolve itself into Philosophy. In one case it is called Useful Knowledge, in the other Liberal. The same person may cultivate it in both ways at once; but this again is a matter foreign to my subject; here I do but say that there are two ways of using Knowledge, and in matter of fact those who use it in one way are not likely to use it in the other, or at least in a very limited measure. You see, then, here are two methods of Education; the end of one is to be philosophical, of the other to be mechanical; the one rises towards general ideas, the other is exhausted upon what is particular and external. Let me not be thought to deny the necessity, or to decry the benefit, of such attention to what is particular and practical as belongs to the useful or mechanical arts; life could not go on without them; we owe our daily welfare to them; their exercise is the duty of the many, and we owe to the many a debt of gratitude for fulfilling that duty. I only say that Knowledge, in proportion as it tends more and more to be particular, ceases to be Knowledge. It is a question whether Knowledge can in any proper sense be predicated of the brute creation; without pretending to metaphysical exactness of phraseology, which would be unsuitable to an occasion like this, I say, it seems to me improper to call that passive 10 sensation, or perception of things, which brutes seem to possess, by the name of Knowledge. When I speak of Knowledge, I mean something intellectual, something which grasps what it perceives through the senses; something which takes a view of things; which sees more than the senses convey; which reasons upon what it sees, and while it sees; which invests it with an idea. It expresses itself, not in a mere 20 enunciation, but by an enthymeme—it is of the nature of science from the first, and in this consists its dignity. The principle of real dignity in Knowledge, its worth, its desirableness, considered irrespectively of its results, is this germ within it of a scientific or a philosophical process. This is how it comes to be an end in itself; this is why it admits of being called Liberal. Not to know the relative disposition of things 30 is the state of slaves or children; to have mapped out the Universe is the boast, or at least the ambition, of Philosophy.

Moreover, such knowledge is not a mere extrinsic or accidental advantage, which is ours today and another's tomorrow, which may be got up from a book, and easily forgotten again, which we can command or communicate at our pleasure, which we can borrow for the occasion, carry about in 40 our hand, and take into the market; it is an acquired illumination, it is a habit, a personal possession, and an inward endowment. And this is the reason why it is more correct, as well as more usual, to speak of a University as a place of education, than of instruction, though, when knowledge is concerned, instruction would at first sight have seemed the more appropriate word. We are instructed, for 50 instance, in manual exercises, in the fine and useful arts, in trades, and in ways of business; for these are methods which have little or no effect upon the mind itself, are

contained in rules committed to memory, to tradition, or to use, and bear upon an end external to themselves. But education is a higher word; it implies an action upon our mental nature, and the formation of a character; it is something individual and permanent, and is commonly spoken of in connection with religion and virtue. When, then, we speak of the communica- 10 tion of Knowledge as being Education, we thereby really imply that that Knowledge is a state or condition of mind; and since cultivation of mind is surely worth seeking for its own sake, we are thus brought once more to the conclusion, which the word "Liberal" and the word "Philosophy" have already suggested, that there is a Knowledge which is desirable, though nothing come of it, as being of itself a treasure, and 20 a sufficient remuneration of years of labor.

VII

This, then, is the answer which I am prepared to give to the question with which I opened this Discourse. Before going on to speak of the object of the Church in taking up Philosophy, and the uses to which she puts it, I am prepared to maintain that Philosophy is its own end, and, as I conceive, I have now begun proving it. 30 I am prepared to maintain that there is a knowledge worth possessing for what it is, and not merely for what it does; and what minutes remain to me today I shall devote to the removal of some portion of the indistinctness and confusion with which the subject may in some minds be surrounded.

It may be objected, then, that, when we profess to seek Knowledge for some end or other beyond itself, whatever it be, we 40 speak intelligibly; but that, whatever men may have said, however obstinately the idea may have kept its ground from age to age, still it is simply unmeaning to say that we seek Knowledge for its own sake, and for nothing else; for that it ever leads to something beyond itself, which therefore is its end, and the cause why it is desirable—moreover, that this end is twofold, either of this world or of the next; that all 50 knowledge is cultivated either for secular objects or for eternal; that if it is directed to secular objects, it is called Useful Knowledge, if to eternal, Religious or Christian

Knowledge—in consequence, that if, as I have allowed, this Liberal Knowledge does not benefit the body or estate, it ought to benefit the soul; but if the fact be really so, that it is neither a physical or a secular good on the one hand, nor a moral good on the other, it cannot be a good at all, and is not worth the trouble which is necessary for its acquisition.

And then I may be reminded that the professors of this Liberal or Philosophical Knowledge have themselves, in every age, recognized this exposition of the matter, and have submitted to the issue in which it terminates; for they have ever been attempting to make men virtuous; or, if not, at least have assumed that refinement of mind was virtue, and that they themselves were the virtuous portion of mankind. This they have professed on the one hand; and, on the other, they have utterly failed in their professions, so as ever to make themselves a proverb among men, and a laughingstock both to the grave and the dissipated portion of mankind, in consequence of them. Thus they have furnished against themselves both the ground and the means of their own exposure, without any trouble at all to anyone else. In a word, from the time that Athens was the University of the world, what has Philosophy taught men, but to promise without practicing, and to aspire without attaining? What has the deep and lofty thought of its disciples ended in but eloquent words? Nay, what has its teaching ever meditated, when it was boldest in its remedies for human ill, beyond charming us to sleep by its lessons, that we might feel nothing at all? like some melodious air, or rather like those strong and transporting perfumes which at first spread their sweetness over everything they touch, but in a little while do but offend in proportion as they once pleased us. Did Philosophy support Cicero under the disfavor of the fickle populace, or nerve Seneca to oppose an imperial tyrant? It abandoned Brutus, as he sorrowfully confessed, in his greatest need, and it forced Cato, as his panegyrist strangely boasts, into the false position of defying heaven. How few can be counted among its professors, who, like Polemo, were thereby converted from a profligate

course, or, like Anaxagoras, thought the world well lost in exchange for its possession? The philosopher in *Rasselas* taught a superhuman doctrine, and then succumbed without an effort to a trial of human affection.

"He discoursed," we are told, "with great energy on the government of the passions. His look was venerable, his action graceful, his pronunciation clear, and his diction elegant. He showed, with great strength of sentiment and variety of illustration, that human nature is degraded and debased when the lower faculties predominate over the higher. He communicated the various precepts given, from time to time, for the conquest of passion, and displayed the happiness of those who had obtained the important victory, after which man is no longer the slave of fear, nor the fool of hope.... He enumerated many examples of heroes immovable by pain or pleasure, who looked with indifference on those modes or accidents to which the vulgar give the names of good and evil."

Rasselas in a few days found the philosopher in a room half darkened, with his eyes misty, and his face pale. "Sir," said he, "you have come at a time when all human friendship is useless; what I suffer cannot be remedied, what I have lost cannot be supplied. My daughter, my only daughter, from whose tenderness I expected all the comforts of my age, died last night of a fever." "Sir," said the prince, "mortality is an event by which a wise man can never be surprised; we know that death is always near, and it should therefore always be expected." "Young man," answered the philosopher, "you speak like one who has never felt the pangs of separation." "Have you, then, forgot the precept," said Rasselas, "which you so powerfully enforced?... consider that external things are naturally variable, but truth and reason are always the same." "What comfort," said the mourner, "can truth and reason afford me? Of what effect are they now, but to tell me that my daughter will not be restored?"

VIII

Better, far better, to make no professions, you will say, than to cheat others with what we are not, and to scandalize them with what we are. The sensualist, or the man of the world, at any rate, is not the victim of fine words, but pursues a reality and gains it. The Philosophy of Utility, you will say, Gentlemen, has at least done its work; and I grant it—it aimed low, but it has fulfilled its aim. If that man of great intellect who has been its Prophet in the conduct of life played false to his own professions, he was not bound by his philosophy to be true to his friend or faithful in his trust. Moral virtue was not the line in which he undertook to instruct men; and though, as the poet calls him, he were the "meanest" of mankind, he was so in what may be called his private capacity, and without any prejudice to the theory of induction. He had a right to be so, if he chose, for anything that the Idols of the den or the theatre had to say to the contrary. His mission was the increase of physical enjoyment and social comfort; and most wonderfully, most awfully has he fulfilled his conception and his design. Almost day by day have we fresh and fresh shoots, and buds, and blossoms, which are to ripen into fruit, on that magical tree of Knowledge which he planted, and to which none of us perhaps, except the very poor, but owes, if not his present life, at least his daily food, his health, and general well-being. He was the divinely provided minister of temporal benefits to all of us so great, that, whatever I am forced to think of him as a man, I have not the heart, from mere gratitude, to speak of him severely. And, in spite of the tendencies of his philosophy, which are, as we see at this day, to depreciate, or to trample on Theology, he has himself, in his writings, gone out of his way, as if with a prophetic misgiving of those tendencies, to insist on it as the instrument of that beneficent Father, who, when He came on earth in visible form, took on Him first and most prominently the office of assuaging the bodily wounds of human nature. And truly, like the old mediciner in the tale, "he sat diligently at his work, and hummed, with cheerful countenance, a pious song"; and then in turn "went out singing into the meadows so gaily that those who had seen him from afar might well have thought it was a youth gathering flowers for his beloved, instead of an old physician gathering healing herbs in the morning dew."

Alas, that men, in the action of life or in their heart of hearts, are not what they seem to be in their moments of excitement, or in their trances or intoxications of genius—so good, so noble, so serene! Alas, that Bacon too in his own way should after all be but the fellow of those heathen philosophers who in their disadvantages had some excuse for their inconsistency, and who surprise us rather in what they did say than in what they did not do! Alas, that he too, like Socrates or Seneca, must be stripped of his holy-day coat, which looks so fair, and should be but a mockery amid his most majestic gravity of phrase; and, for all his vast abilities, should in the littleness of his own moral being but typify the intellectual narrowness of his school! However, granting all this—heroism after all was not his philosophy—I cannot deny he has abundantly achieved what he proposed. His is simply a Method whereby bodily discomforts and temporal wants are to be most effectually removed from the greatest number; and already, before it has shown any signs of exhaustion, the gifts of nature, in their most artificial shapes and luxurious profusion and diversity, from all quarters of the earth, are, it is undeniable, by its means brought even to our doors, and we rejoice in them.

IX

Useful Knowledge then, I grant, has done its work; and Liberal Knowledge as certainly has not done its work—supposing, that is, as the objectors assume, its direct end, like Religious Knowledge, is to make men better; but this I will not for an instant allow, and, unless I allow it, those objectors have said nothing to the purpose. I admit, rather I maintain, what they have been urging, for I consider Knowledge to have its end in itself. For all its friends, or its enemies, may say, I insist upon it, that it is as real a mistake to burden it with virtue or religion as with the mechanical arts. Its direct business is not to steel the soul against temptation or to console it in affliction, any more than to set the loom in motion, or to direct the steam carriage;

be it ever so much the means or the condition of both material and moral advancement, still, taken by and in itself, it as little mends our hearts as it improves our temporal circumstances. And if its eulogists claim for it such a power, they commit the very same kind of encroachment on a province not their own as the political economist who should maintain that his science educated him for casuistry or diplomacy. Knowledge is one thing, virtue is another; good sense is not conscience, refinement is not humility, nor is largeness and justness of view faith. Philosophy, however enlightened, however profound, gives no command over the passions, no influential motives, no vivifying principles. Liberal Education makes not the Christian, not the Catholic, but the gentleman. It is well to be a gentleman, it is well to have a cultivated intellect, a delicate taste, a candid, equitable, dispassionate mind, a noble and courteous bearing in the conduct of life—these are the con-natural qualities of a large knowledge; they are the objects of a University; I am advocating, I shall illustrate and insist upon them; but still, I repeat, they are no guarantee for sanctity or even for conscientiousness; they may attach to the man of the world, to the profligate, to the heartless—pleasant, alas, and attractive as he shows when decked out in them. Taken by themselves, they do but seem to be what they are not; they look like virtue at a distance, but they are detected by close observers, and on the long run; and hence it is that they are popularly accused of pretense and hypocrisy, not, I repeat, from their own fault, but because their professors and their admirers persist in taking them for what they are not, and are officious in arrogating for them a praise to which they have no claim. Quarry the granite rock with razors, or moor the vessel with a thread of silk; then may you hope with such keen and delicate instruments as human knowledge and human reason to contend against those giants, the passion and the pride of man.

Surely we are not driven to theories of this kind in order to vindicate the value and dignity of Liberal Knowledge. Surely the real grounds on which its pretensions rest are not so very subtle or abstruse, so very strange or improbable. Surely it is very intelligible to say, and that is what I say here, that Liberal Education, viewed in itself, is simply the cultivation of the intellect as such, and its object is nothing more or less than intellectual excellence. Everything has its own perfection, be it higher or lower in the scale of things; and the perfection of one is not the perfection of another. Things animate, inanimate, visible, invisible, all are good in their kind, and have a *best* of themselves, which is an object of pursuit. Why do you take such pains with your garden or your park? You see to your walks and turf and shrubberies; to your trees and drives; not as if you meant to make an orchard of the one, or corn or pasture land of the other, but because there is a special beauty in all that is goodly in wood, water, plain, and slope, brought all together by art into one shape, and grouped into one whole. Your cities are beautiful, your palaces, your public buildings, your territorial mansions, your churches; and their beauty leads to nothing beyond itself. There is a physical beauty and a moral—there is a beauty of person, there is a beauty of our moral being, which is natural virtue; and in like manner there is a beauty, there is a perfection, of the intellect. There is an ideal perfection in these various subject-matters, towards which individual instances are seen to rise, and which are the standards for all instances whatever. The Greek divinities and demigods, as the statuary has molded them, with their symmetry of figure and their high forehead and their regular features, are the perfection of physical beauty. The heroes, of whom history tells, Alexander, or Caesar, or Scipio, or Saladin, are the representatives of that magnanimity or self-mastery which is the greatness of human nature. Christianity too has its heroes, and in the supernatural order, and we call them Saints. The artist puts before him beauty of feature and form; the poet, beauty of mind; the preacher, the beauty of grace—then intellect too, I repeat, has its beauty, and it has those who aim at it. To open the mind, to correct it, to refine it, to enable it to know, and to digest, master, rule, and use its knowledge, to give it power over its own faculties, application, flexibility, method, critical exactness, sagacity, resource, address, eloquent expression, is an object as intelligible (for here we are inquiring, not what the object of a Liberal Education is worth, nor what use the Church makes of it, but what it is in itself), I say, an object as intelligible as the cultivation of virtue, while, at the same time, it is absolutely distinct from it.

X

This indeed is but a temporal object, and a transitory possession; but so are other things in themselves which we make much of and pursue. The moralist will tell us that man, in all his functions, is but a flower which blossoms and fades, except so far as a higher principle breathes upon him, and makes him and what he is immortal. Body and mind are carried on into an eternal state of being by the gifts of Divine Munificence; but at first they do but fail in a failing world; and if the powers of intellect decay, the powers of the body have decayed before them, and, as an Hospital or an Almshouse, though its end be ephemeral, may be sanctified to the service of religion, so surely may a University, even were it nothing more than I have as yet described it. We attain to heaven by using this world well, though it is to pass away; we perfect our nature, not by undoing it, but by adding to it what is more than nature, and directing it towards aims higher than its own.   [1852]

KNOWLEDGE VIEWED IN RELATION TO LEARNING

I

It were well if the English, like the Greek language, possessed some definite word to express, simply and generally, intellectual proficiency or perfection, such as "health," as used with reference to the animal frame, and "virtue," with reference to our moral nature. I am not able to find such a term; talent, ability, genius, belong distinctly to the raw material, which is the subject-matter, not to that excellence which is the result of exercise and training. When we turn, indeed, to the particular kinds of intellectual perfection, words are forthcoming for our purpose, as, for instance, judgment, taste, and skill; yet even these belong, for the most part, to powers or habits bearing upon practice or upon art, and not to any perfect condition of the intellect, considered in itself. Wisdom, again, is certainly a more comprehensive word than any other, but it has a direct relation to conduct and to human life. Knowledge, indeed, and Science express purely intellectual ideas, but still not a state or quality of the intellect; for knowledge, in its ordinary sense, is but one of its circumstances, denoting a possession or a habit; and science has been appropriated to the subject-matter of the intellect, instead of belonging in English, as it ought to do, to the intellect itself. The consequence is that, on an occasion like this, many words are necessary, in order, first, to bring out and convey what surely is no difficult idea in itself—that of the cultivation of the intellect as an end; next, in order to recommend what surely is no unreasonable object; and, lastly, to describe and make the mind realize the particular perfection in which that object consists. Everyone knows practically what are the constituents of health or of virtue; and everyone recognizes health and virtue as ends to be pursued; it is otherwise with intellectual excellence, and this must be my excuse, if I seem to anyone to be bestowing a good deal of labor on a preliminary matter.

In default of a recognized term, I have called the perfection or virtue of the intellect by the name of philosophy, philosophical knowledge, enlargement of mind, or illumination; terms which are not uncommonly given to it by writers of this day; but, whatever name we bestow on it, it is, I believe, as a matter of history, the business of a University to make this intellectual culture its direct scope, or to employ itself in the education of the intellect—just as the work of a Hospital lies in healing the sick or wounded, of a Riding or Fencing School, or of a Gymnasium, in exercising the limbs, of an Almshouse, in aiding and solacing the old, of an Orphanage, in protecting innocence, of a Penitentiary, in restoring the guilty. I say a University, taken in its bare idea, and

before we view it as an instrument of the
Church, has this object and this mission;
it contemplates neither moral impression
nor mechanical production; it professes to
exercise the mind neither in art nor in
duty; its function is intellectual culture;
here it may leave its scholars, and it has
done its work when it has done as much
as this. It educates the intellect to reason
well in all matters, to reach out towards 10
truth, and to grasp it.

II

This, I said in my foregoing Discourse,
was the object of a University, viewed in
itself, and apart from the Catholic Church,
or from the State, or from any other power
which may use it; and I illustrated this in
various ways. I said that the intellect must
have an excellence of its own, for there 20
was nothing which had not its specific
good; that the word "educate" would not
be used of intellectual culture, as it is used,
had not the intellect had an end of its
own; that, had it not such an end, there
would be no meaning in calling certain
intellectual exercises "liberal," in contrast
with "useful," as is commonly done; that
the very notion of a philosophical temper
implied it, for it threw us back upon re- 30
search and system as ends in themselves,
distinct from effects and works of any kind;
that a philosophical scheme of knowledge,
or system of sciences, could not, from the
nature of the case, issue in any one definite art or pursuit, as its end; and that,
on the other hand, the discovery and contemplation of truth, to which research and
systematizing led, were surely sufficient
ends, though nothing beyond them were 40
added, and that they had ever been accounted sufficient by mankind.

Here then I take up the subject; and,
having determined that the cultivation of
the intellect is an end distinct and sufficient in itself, and that, so far as words
go, it is an enlargement or illumination, I
proceed to inquire what this mental
breadth, or power, or light, or philosophy
consists in. A Hospital heals a broken 50
limb or cures a fever; what does an Institution effect, which professes the health, not
of the body, not of the soul, but of the
intellect? What is this good, which in

former times, as well as our own, has been
found worth the notice, the appropriation,
of the Catholic Church?

I have then to investigate, in the Discourses which follow, those qualities and
characteristics of the intellect in which its
cultivation issues or rather consists; and,
with a view of assisting myself in this undertaking, I shall recur to certain questions
which have already been touched upon.
These questions are three: viz., the relation
of intellectual culture, first, to *mere* knowledge; secondly, to *professional* knowledge;
and thirdly, to *religious* knowledge. In
other words, are *acquirements* and *attainments* the scope of a University Education?
or *expertness in particular arts and pursuits?* or *moral and religious proficiency?*
or something besides these three? These
questions I shall examine in succession,
with the purpose I have mentioned; and
I hope to be excused, if, in this anxious
undertaking, I am led to repeat what,
either in these Discourses or elsewhere, I
have already put upon paper. And first,
of *Mere Knowledge,* or Learning, and its
connection with intellectual illumination
or Philosophy.

III

I suppose the prima-facie view which the
public at large would take of a University,
considering it as a place of Education, is
nothing more or less than a place for acquiring a great deal of knowledge on a
great many subjects. Memory is one of the
first developed of the mental faculties; a
boy's business when he goes to school is to
learn, that is, to store up things in his
memory. For some years his intellect is
little more than an instrument for taking
in facts, or a receptacle for storing them;
he welcomes them as fast as they come to
him; he lives on what is without; he has
his eyes ever about him; he has a lively
susceptibility of impressions; he imbibes
information of every kind; and little does
he make his own in a true sense of the
word, living rather upon his neighbors all
around him. He has opinions, religious,
political, and literary, and, for a boy, is
very positive in them and sure about them;
but he gets them from his schoolfellows, or
his masters, or his parents, as the case may

be. Such as he is in his other relations, such also is he in his school exercises; his mind is observant, sharp, ready, retentive; he is almost passive in the acquisition of knowledge. I say this in no disparagement of the idea of a clever boy. Geography, chronology, history, language, natural history, he heaps up the matter of these studies as treasures for a future day. It is the seven years of plenty with him; he 10 gathers in by handfuls, like the Egyptians, without counting; and though, as time goes on, there is exercise for his argumentative powers in the Elements of Mathematics, and for his taste in the Poets and Orators, still, while at school, or at least, till quite the last years of his time, he acquires, and little more; and when he is leaving for the University, he is mainly the creature of foreign influences and circum- 20 stances, and made up of accidents, homogeneous or not, as the case may be. Moreover, the moral habits, which are a boy's praise, encourage and assist this result; that is, diligence, assiduity, regularity, dispatch, persevering application; for these are the direct conditions of acquisition, and naturally lead to it. Acquirements, again, are emphatically producible, and at a moment; they are a something to show, both 30 for master and scholar; an audience, even though ignorant themselves of the subjects of an examination, can comprehend when questions are answered and when they are not. Here again is a reason why mental culture is in the minds of men identified with the acquisition of knowledge.

The same notion possesses the public mind, when it passes on from the thought of a school to that of a University; and 40 with the best of reasons so far as this, that there is no true culture without acquirements, and that philosophy presupposes knowledge. It requires a great deal of reading, or a wide range of information, to warrant us in putting forth our opinions on any serious subject; and without such learning the most original mind may be able indeed to dazzle, to amuse, to refute, to perplex, but not to come to any useful 50 result or any trustworthy conclusion. There are indeed persons who profess a different view of the matter, and even act upon it. Every now and then you will find

a person of vigorous or fertile mind, who relies upon his own resources, despises all former authors, and gives the world, with the utmost fearlessness, his views upon religion, or history, or any other popular subject. And his works may sell for a while; he may get a name in his day; but this will be all. His readers are sure to find in the long run that his doctrines are 10 mere theories, and not the expression of facts, that they are chaff instead of bread, and then his popularity drops as suddenly as it rose.

Knowledge, then, is the indispensable condition of expansion of mind, and the instrument of attaining to it; this cannot be denied, it is ever to be insisted on; I begin with it as a first principle; however, the very truth of it carries men too far, and 20 confirms to them the notion that it is the whole of the matter. A narrow mind is thought to be that which contains little knowledge; and an enlarged mind, that which holds a great deal; and what seems to put the matter beyond dispute is the fact of the great number of studies which are pursued in a University, by its very profession. Lectures are given on every kind of subject; examinations are held; 30 prizes awarded. There are moral, metaphysical, physical Professors; Professors of languages, of history, of mathematics, of experimental science. Lists of questions are published, wonderful for their range and depth, variety and difficulty; treatises are written, which carry upon their very face the evidence of extensive reading or multifarious information; what then is wanting for mental culture to a person of 40 large reading and scientific attainments? what is grasp of mind but acquirement? where shall philosophical repose be found, but in the consciousness and enjoyment of large intellectual possessions?

And yet this notion is, I conceive, a mistake, and my present business is to show that it is one, and that the end of a Liberal Education is not mere knowledge, or knowledge considered in its *matter;* and I 50 shall best attain my object, by actually setting down some cases, which will be generally granted to be instances of the process of enlightenment or enlargement of mind, and others which are not, and thus, by the comparison, you will be able to judge for yourselves, Gentlemen, whether Knowledge, that is, acquirement, is after all the real principle of the enlargement, or whether that principle is not rather something beyond it.

IV

For instance, let a person whose experience has hitherto been confined to the more calm and unpretending scenery of these islands, whether here or in England, go for the first time into parts where physical nature puts on her wilder and more awful forms, whether at home or abroad, as into mountainous districts; or let one who has ever lived in a quiet village go for the first time to a great metropolis—then I suppose he will have a sensation which perhaps he never had before. He has a feeling not in addition or increase of former feelings, but of something different in its nature. He will perhaps be borne forward, and find for a time that he has lost his bearings. He has made a certain progress, and he has a consciousness of mental enlargement; he does not stand where he did—he has a new center, and a range of thoughts to which he was before a stranger.

Again, the view of the heavens which the telescope opens upon us, if allowed to fill and possess the mind, may almost whirl it round and make it dizzy. It brings in a flood of ideas, and is rightly called an intellectual enlargement, whatever is meant by the term.

And so again, the sight of beasts of prey and other foreign animals, their strangeness, the originality (if I may use the term) of their forms and gestures and habits and their variety and independence of each other, throw us out of ourselves into another creation, and as if under another Creator, if I may so express the temptation which may come on the mind. We seem to have new faculties, or a new exercise for our faculties, by this addition to our knowledge—like a prisoner, who, having been accustomed to wear manacles or fetters, suddenly finds his arms and legs free.

Hence Physical Science generally, in all its departments, as bringing before us the exuberant riches and resources, yet the orderly course, of the Universe, elevates and excites the student, and at first, I may say, almost takes away his breath, while in time it exercises a tranquilizing influence upon him.

Again, the study of history is said to enlarge and enlighten the mind, and why? because, as I conceive, it gives it a power of judging of passing events, and of all events, and a conscious superiority over them, which before it did not possess.

And, in like manner, what is called seeing the world, entering into active life, going into society, traveling, gaining acquaintance with the various classes of the community, coming into contact with the principles and modes of thought of various parties, interests, and races, their views, aims, habits and manners, their religious creeds and forms of worship—gaining experience how various yet how alike men are, how low-minded, how bad, how opposed, yet how confident in their opinions; all this exerts a perceptible influence upon the mind, which it is impossible to mistake, be it good or be it bad, and is popularly called its enlargement.

And then again, the first time the mind comes across the arguments and speculations of unbelievers, and feels what a novel light they cast upon what he has hitherto accounted sacred; and still more, if it gives in to them and embraces them, and throws off as so much prejudice what it has hitherto held, and, as if waking from a dream, begins to realize to its imagination that there is now no such thing as law and the transgression of law, that sin is a phantom, and punishment a bugbear, that it is free to sin, free to enjoy the world and the flesh; and, still further, when it does enjoy them, and reflects that it may think and hold just what it will, that "the world is all before it where to choose," and what system to build up as its own private persuasion; when this torrent of willful thoughts rushes over and inundates it, who will deny that the fruit of the tree of knowledge, or what the mind takes for knowledge, has made it one of the gods, with a sense of expansion and elevation—an intoxication in reality, still, so far as the subjective state of the mind goes, an illumination? Hence the fanaticism of individuals or nations, who suddenly cast off their Maker. Their eyes are opened; and, like the judgment-stricken king in the Tragedy, they see two suns, and a magic universe, out of which they look back upon their former state of faith and innocence with a sort of contempt and indignation, as if they were then but fools, and the dupes of imposture.

On the other hand, Religion has its own enlargement, and an enlargement, not of tumult, but of peace. It is often remarked of uneducated persons, who have hitherto thought little of the unseen world, that, on their turning to God, looking into themselves, regulating their hearts, reforming their conduct, and meditating on death and judgment, heaven and hell, they seem to become, in point of intellect, different beings from what they were. Before, they took things as they came, and thought no more of one thing than another. But now every event has a meaning; they have their own estimate of whatever happens to them; they are mindful of times and seasons, and compare the present with the past; and the world, no longer dull, monotonous, unprofitable, and hopeless, is a various and complicated drama, with parts and an object, and an awful moral.

v

Now from these instances, to which many more might be added, it is plain, first, that the communication of knowledge certainly is either a condition or the means of that sense of enlargement or enlightenment, of which at this day we hear so much in certain quarters. This cannot be denied; but next, it is equally plain that such communication is not the whole of the process. The enlargement consists, not merely in the passive reception into the mind of a number of ideas hitherto unknown to it, but in the mind's energetic and simultaneous action upon and towards and among those new ideas which are rushing in upon it. It is the action of a formative power, reducing to order and meaning the matter of our acquirements; it is a making the objects of our knowledge subjectively our own, or, to use a familiar word, it is a digestion of what we receive, into the substance of our previous state of thought; and

without this no enlargement is said to follow. There is no enlargement, unless there be a comparison of ideas one with another, as they come before the mind, and a systematizing of them. We feel our minds to be growing and expanding *then,* when we not only learn, but refer what we learn to what we know already. It is not the mere addition to our knowledge that is the illumination; but the locomotion, the movement onwards, of that mental center to which both what we know, and what we are learning, the accumulating mass of our acquirements, gravitates. And therefore a truly great intellect, and recognized to be such by the common opinion of mankind, such as the intellect of Aristotle, or of St. Thomas, or of Newton, or of Goethe (I purposely take instances within and without the Catholic pale, when I would speak of the intellect as such) is one which takes a connected view of old and new, past and present, far and near, and which has an insight into the influence of all these one on another; without which there is no whole, and no center. It possesses the knowledge, not only of things, but also of their mutual and true relations; knowledge, not merely considered as acquirement, but as philosophy.

Accordingly, when this analytical, distributive, harmonizing process is away, the mind experiences no enlargement, and is not reckoned as enlightened or comprehensive, whatever it may add to its knowledge. For instance, a great memory, as I have already said, does not make a philosopher, any more than a dictionary can be called a grammar. There are men who embrace in their minds a vast multitude of ideas, but with little sensibility about their real relations towards each other. These may be antiquarians, annalists, naturalists; they may be learned in the law; they may be versed in statistics; they are most useful in their own place; I should shrink from speaking disrespectfully of them; still, there is nothing in such attainments to guarantee the absence of narrowness of mind. If they are nothing more than well-read men, or men of information, they have not what specially deserves the name of culture of mind, or fulfills the type of Liberal Education.

In like manner, we sometimes fall in with persons who have seen much of the world, and of the men who, in their day, have played a conspicuous part in it, but who generalize nothing, and have no observation, in the true sense of the word. They abound in information in detail, curious and entertaining, about men and things; and, having lived under the influence of no very clear or settled principles, religious or political, they speak of everyone and everything, only as so many phenomena, which are complete in themselves, and lead to nothing, not discussing them, or teaching any truth, or instructing the hearer, but simply talking. No one would say that these persons, well informed as they are, had attained to any great culture of intellect or to philosophy.

The case is the same still more strikingly where the persons in question are beyond dispute men of inferior powers and deficient education. Perhaps they have been much in foreign countries, and they receive, in a passive, otiose, unfruitful way, the various facts which are forced upon them there. Seafaring men, for example, range from one end of the earth to the other; but the multiplicity of external objects which they have encountered forms no symmetrical and consistent picture upon their imagination; they see the tapestry of human life, as it were, on the wrong side, and it tells no story. They sleep, and they rise up, and they find themselves, now in Europe, now in Asia; they see visions of great cities and wild regions; they are in the marts of commerce, or amid the islands of the South; they gaze on Pompey's Pillar, or on the Andes; and nothing which meets them carries them forward or backward, to any idea beyond itself. Nothing has a drift or relation; nothing has a history or a promise. Everything stands by itself, and comes and goes in its turn, like the shifting scenes of a show, which leave the spectator where he was. Perhaps you are near such a man on a particular occasion, and expect him to be shocked or perplexed at something which occurs; but one thing is much the same to him as another, or, if he is perplexed, it is as not knowing what to say, whether it is right to admire, or to ridicule, or to disapprove, while conscious that some

expression of opinion is expected from him; for in fact he has no standard of judgment at all, and no landmarks to guide him to a conclusion. Such is mere acquisition, and, I repeat, no one would dream of calling it philosophy.

VI

Instances such as these confirm, by the contrast, the conclusion I have already drawn from those which preceded them. That only is true enlargement of mind which is the power of viewing many things at once as one whole, of referring them severally to their true place in the universal system, of understanding their respective values, and determining their mutual dependence. Thus is that form of Universal Knowledge, of which I have on a former occasion spoken, set up in the individual intellect, and constitutes its perfection. Possessed of this real illumination, the mind never views any part of the extended subject-matter of Knowledge without recollecting that it is but a part, or without the associations which spring from this recollection. It makes everything in some sort lead to everything else; it would communicate the image of the whole to every separate portion, till that whole becomes in imagination like a spirit, everywhere pervading and penetrating its component parts, and giving them one definite meaning. Just as our bodily organs, when mentioned, recall their function in the body, as the word "creation" suggests the Creator, and "subjects" a sovereign, so, in the mind of the Philosopher, as we are abstractedly conceiving of him, the elements of the physical and moral world, sciences, arts, pursuits, ranks, offices, events, opinions, individualities, are all viewed as one, with correlative functions, and as gradually by successive combinations converging, one and all, to the true center.

To have even a portion of this illuminative reason and true philosophy is the highest state to which nature can aspire, in the way of intellect; it puts the mind above the influences of chance and necessity, above anxiety, suspense, unsettlement, and superstition, which is the lot of the many. Men whose minds are possessed with some one object take exaggerated views of its importance, are feverish in the pursuit of it, make it the measure of things which are utterly foreign to it, and are startled and despond if it happens to fail them. They are ever in alarm or in transport. Those, on the other hand, who have no object or principle whatever to hold by, lose their way, every step they take. They are thrown out, and do not know what to think or say, at every fresh juncture; they have no view of persons, or occurrences, or facts, which come suddenly upon them, and they hang upon the opinion of others, for want of internal resources. But the intellect which has been disciplined to the perfection of its powers, which knows, and thinks while it knows, which has learned to leaven the dense mass of facts and events with the elastic force of reason, such an intellect cannot be partial, cannot be exclusive, cannot be impetuous, cannot be at a loss, cannot but be patient, collected, and majestically calm, because it discerns the end in every beginning, the origin in every end, the law in every interruption, the limit in each delay; because it ever knows where it stands, and how its path lies from one point to another. It is the τετράγωνος[1] of the Peripatetic, and has the *"nil admirari"*[2] of the Stoic—

Felix qui potuit rerum cognoscere causas,
Atque metus omnes, et inexorabile fatum,
Subjecit pedibus, strepitumque Acherontis
    avari.[3]

There are men who, when in difficulties, originate at the moment vast ideas or dazzling projects; who, under the influence of excitement, are able to cast a light, almost as if from inspiration, on a subject or course of action which comes before them; who have a sudden presence of mind equal to any emergency, rising with the occasion, and an undaunted magnanimous bearing,

and an energy and keenness which is but made intense by opposition. This is genius, this is heroism; it is the exhibition of a natural gift, which no culture can teach, at which no Institution can aim; here, on the contrary, we are concerned, not with mere nature, but with training and teaching. That perfection of the Intellect, which is the result of Education, and its beau ideal, to be imparted to individuals in their respective measures, is the clear, calm, accurate vision and comprehension of all things, as far as the finite mind can embrace them, each in its place, and with its own characteristics upon it. It is almost prophetic from its knowledge of history; it is almost heart-searching from its knowledge of human nature; it has almost supernatural charity from its freedom from littleness and prejudice; it has almost the repose of faith, because nothing can startle it; it has almost the beauty and harmony of heavenly contemplation, so intimate is it with the eternal order of things and the music of the spheres.

VII

And now, if I may take it for granted that the true and adequate end of intellectual training and of a University is not Learning or Acquirement, but, rather, is Thought or Reason exercised upon Knowledge, or what may be called Philosophy, I shall be in a position to explain the various mistakes which at the present day beset the subject of University Education.

I say, then, if we would improve the intellect, first of all, we must ascend; we cannot gain real knowledge on a level; we must generalize, we must reduce to method, we must have a grasp of principles, and group and shape our acquisitions by means of them. It matters not whether our field of operation be wide or limited; in every case, to command it, is to mount above it. Who has not felt the irritation of mind and impatience created by a deep, rich country, visited for the first time, with winding lanes, and high hedges, and green steeps, and tangled woods, and everything smiling indeed, but in a maze? The same feeling comes upon us in a strange city, when we have no map of its streets. Hence you hear of practiced travelers, when they first

---

[1] τετράγωνος: 'square', an epithet used by Peripatetics to symbolize the fully balanced mind. The Peripatetics were disciples of Aristotle, "who gave his instruction while walking in the Lyceum at Athens."

[2] *nil admirari*: 'to be astonished at nothing', a Stoic maxim (Horace, *Epis.,* I, vi, 1).

[3] *Felix qui potuit,* etc.: "Happy is he who could know the causes of things and put under his feet all fears and inexorable fate and the roar of greedy Acheron" (Virgil's *Georgics* II, 490-93). Acheron is the river of woe in Hades.

come into a place, mounting some high hill or church tower, by way of reconnoitering its neighborhood. In like manner, you must be above your knowledge, not under it, or it will oppress you; and the more you have of it, the greater will be the load. The learning of a Salmasius or a Burmann, unless you are its master, will be your tyrant. *"Imperat aut servit";* [4] if you can wield it with a strong arm, it is a great weapon; otherwise,

> Vis consili expers
> Mole ruit sua.[5]

You will be overwhelmed, like Tarpeia, by the heavy wealth which you have exacted from tributary generations.

Instances abound; there are authors who are as pointless as they are inexhaustible in their literary resources. They measure knowledge by bulk, as it lies in the rude block, without symmetry, without design. How many commentators are there on the Classics, how many on Holy Scripture, from whom we rise up, wondering at the learning which has passed before us, and wondering why it passed! How many writers are there of Ecclesiastical History, such as Mosheim or Du Pin, who, breaking up their subject into details, destroy its life, and defraud us of the whole by their anxiety about the parts! The Sermons, again, of the English Divines in the seventeenth century, how often are they mere repertories of miscellaneous and officious learning! Of course Catholics also may read without thinking; and, in their case, equally as with Protestants, it holds good, that such knowledge is unworthy of the name, knowledge which they have not thought through, and thought out. Such readers are only possessed by their knowledge, not possessed of it; nay, in matter of fact, they are often even carried away by it, without any volition of their own. Recollect, the Memory can tyrannize, as well as the imagination. Derangement, I believe, has been considered as a loss of control over the sequence of ideas. The mind, once set in motion, is henceforth

---

[4] *Imperat aut servit:* 'It rules or it serves'.
[5] *Vis consili expers,* etc.: "Brute force bereft of wisdom falls to ruin by its own weight" (Horace, *Odes,* III, iv, 65).

deprived of the power of initiation, and becomes the victim of a train of associations, one thought suggesting another, in the way of cause and effect, as if by a mechanical process, or some physical necessity. No one who has had experience of men of studious habits but must recognize the existence of a parallel phenomenon in the case of those who have overstimulated the Memory. In such persons Reason acts almost as feebly and as impotently as in the madman; once fairly started on any subject whatever, they have no power of self-control; they passively endure the succession of impulses which are evolved out of the original exciting cause; they are passed on from one idea to another and go steadily forward, plodding along one line of thought in spite of the amplest concessions of the hearer, or wandering from it in endless digression in spite of his remonstrances. Now, if, as is very certain, no one would envy the madman the glow and originality of his own conceptions, why must we extol the cultivation of that intellect which is the prey, not indeed of barren fancies but of barren facts, of random intrusions from without, though not of morbid imaginations from within? And, in thus speaking, I am not denying that a strong and ready memory is in itself a real treasure; I am not disparaging a well-stored mind, though it be nothing besides, provided it be sober, any more than I would despise a bookseller's shop—it is of great value to others, even when not so to the owner. Nor am I banishing, far from it, the possessors of deep and multifarious learning from my ideal University; they adorn it in the eyes of men; I do but say that they constitute no type of the results at which it aims; that it is no great gain to the intellect to have enlarged the memory at the expense of faculties which are indisputably higher.

VIII

Nor, indeed, am I supposing that there is any great danger, at least in this day, of over-education; the danger is on the other side. I will tell you, Gentlemen, what has been the practical error of the last twenty years—not to load the memory of the student with a mass of undigested knowledge, but to force upon him so much that he has rejected all. It has been the error of distracting and enfeebling the mind by an unmeaning profusion of subjects; of implying that a smattering in a dozen branches of study is not shallowness, which it really is, but enlargement, which it is not; of considering an acquaintance with the learned names of things and persons, and the possession of clever duodecimos, and attendance on eloquent lecturers, and membership with scientific institutions, and the sight of the experiments of a platform and the specimens of a museum—that all this was not dissipation of mind, but progress. All things now are to be learned at once, not first one thing, then another, not one well, but many badly. Learning is to be without exertion, without attention, without toil; without grounding, without advance, without finishing. There is to be nothing individual in it; and this, forsooth, is the wonder of the age. What the steam engine does with matter, the printing press is to do with mind; it is to act mechanically, and the population is to be passively, almost unconsciously enlightened, by the mere multiplication and dissemination of volumes. Whether it be the schoolboy, or the schoolgirl, or the youth at college, or the mechanic in the town, or the politician in the senate, all have been the victims in one way or other of this most preposterous and pernicious of delusions. Wise men have lifted up their voices in vain; and, at length, lest their own institutions should be outshone and should disappear in the folly of the hour, they have been obliged, as far as they could with a good conscience, to humor a spirit which they could not withstand, and make temporizing concessions at which they could not but inwardly smile.

It must not be supposed that, because I so speak, therefore I have some sort of fear of the education of the people; on the contrary, the more education they have, the better, so that it is really education. Nor am I an enemy to the cheap publication of scientific and literary works, which is now in vogue; on the contrary, I consider it a great advantage, convenience, and gain; that is, to those to whom education has given a capacity for using them. Further, I consider such innocent recreations as science and literature are able to furnish will be a very fit occupation of the thoughts and the leisure of young persons, and may be made the means of keeping them from bad employments and bad companions. Moreover, as to that superficial acquaintance with chemistry, and geology, and astronomy, and political economy, and modern history, and biography, and other branches of knowledge, which periodical literature and occasional lectures and scientific institutions diffuse through the community, I think it a graceful accomplishment, and a suitable, nay, in this day a necessary accomplishment, in the case of educated men. Nor, lastly, am I disparaging or discouraging the thorough acquisition of any one of these studies, or denying that, as far as it goes, such thorough acquisition is a real education of the mind. All I say is, call things by their right names, and do not confuse together ideas which are essentially different. A thorough knowledge of one science and a superficial acquaintance with many, are not the same thing; a smattering of a hundred things or a memory for detail, is not a philosophical or comprehensive view. Recreations are not education; accomplishments are not education. Do not say, the people must be educated, when, after all, you only mean amused, refreshed, soothed, put into good spirits and good humor, or kept from vicious excesses. I do not say that such amusements, such occupations of mind, are not a great gain; but they are not education. You may as well call drawing and fencing education, as a general knowledge of botany or conchology. Stuffing birds or playing stringed instruments is an elegant pastime, and a resource to the idle, but it is not education; it does not form or cultivate the intellect. Education is a high word; it is the preparation for knowledge, and it is the imparting of knowledge in proportion to that preparation. We require intellectual eyes to know withal, as bodily eyes for sight. We need both objects and organs intellectual; we cannot gain them without setting about it; we cannot gain them in our sleep, or by haphazard. The best telescope does not dispense with eyes; the printing press or the lecture room will assist us greatly, but we must be true to ourselves, we must be parties in the work. A University is, according to the usual designation, an Alma Mater, knowing her children one by one, not a foundry, or a mint, or a treadmill.

IX

I protest to you, Gentlemen, that if I had to choose between a so-called University which dispensed with residence and tutorial superintendence, and gave its degrees to any person who passed an examination in a wide range of subjects, and a University which had no professors or examinations at all, but merely brought a number of young men together for three or four years, and then sent them away as the University of Oxford is said to have done some sixty years since, if I were asked which of these two methods was the better discipline of the intellect—mind, I do not say which is *morally* the better, for it is plain that compulsory study must be a good and idleness an intolerable mischief—but if I must determine which of the two courses was the more successful in training, molding, enlarging the mind, which sent out men the more fitted for their secular duties, which produced better public men, men of the world, men whose names would descend to posterity, I have no hesitation in giving the preference to that University which did nothing, over that which exacted of its members an acquaintance with every science under the sun. And, paradox as this may seem, still if results be the test of systems, the influence of the public schools and colleges of England, in the course of the last century, at least will bear out one side of the contrast as I have drawn it. What would come, on the other hand, of the ideal systems of education which have fascinated the imagination of this age, could they ever take effect, and whether they would not produce a generation frivolous, narrow-minded, and resourceless, intellectually considered, is a fair subject for debate; but so far is certain, that the Universities and scholastic establishments to which I refer, and which did little more than bring together first boys and then youths in large numbers, these institutions, with miserable deformities on the side of morals, with a hollow profession of Christianity, and a heathen code of ethics—I say, at least they can boast of a succession of heroes and statesmen, of literary men and philosophers, of men conspicuous for great natural virtues, for habits of business, for knowledge of life, for practical judgment, for cultivated tastes, for accomplishments, who have made England what it is—able to subdue the earth, able to domineer over Catholics.

How is this to be explained? I suppose as follows: When a multitude of young men, keen, open-hearted, sympathetic, and observant, as young men are, come together and freely mix with each other, they are sure to learn one from another, even if there be no one to teach them; the conversation of all is a series of lectures to each, and they gain for themselves new ideas and views, fresh matter of thought, and distinct principles for judging and acting, day by day. An infant has to learn the meaning of the information which its senses convey to it, and this seems to be its employment. It fancies all that the eye presents to it to be close to it, till it actually learns the contrary, and thus by practice does it ascertain the relations and uses of those first elements of knowledge which are necessary for its animal existence. A parallel teaching is necessary for our social being, and it is secured by a large school or a college; and this effect may be fairly called in its own department an enlargement of mind. It is seeing the world on a small field with little trouble; for the pupils or students come from very different places, and with widely different notions, and there is much to generalize, much to adjust, much to eliminate, there are interrelations to be defined, and conventional rules to be established, in the process by which the whole assemblage is molded together, and gains one tone and one character.

Let it be clearly understood, I repeat it, that I am not taking into account moral or religious considerations; I am but saying that that youthful community will constitute a whole, it will embody a specific idea, it will represent a doctrine, it will administer a code of conduct, and it will furnish principles of thought and action. It will give birth to a living teaching, which in course of time will take the shape of a self-perpetuating tradition, or a *genius loci*,[6] as it is sometimes called; which haunts the home where it has been born, and which imbues and forms, more or less, and one by one, every individual who is successively brought under its shadow. Thus it is that, independent of direct instruction on the part of Superiors, there is a sort of self-education in the academic institutions of Protestant England; a characteristic tone of thought, a recognized standard of judgment is found in them, which, as developed in the individual who is submitted to it, becomes a twofold source of strength to him, both from the distinct stamp it impresses on his mind, and from the bond of union which it creates between him and others—effects which are shared by the authorities of the place, for they themselves have been educated in it, and at all times are exposed to the influence of its ethical atmosphere. Here then is a real teaching, whatever be its standards and principles, true or false; and it at least tends towards cultivation of the intellect; it at least recognizes that knowledge is something more than a sort of passive reception of scraps and details; it is a something, and it does a something, which never will issue from the most strenuous efforts of a set of teachers, with no mutual sympathies and no intercommunion, of a set of examiners with no opinions which they dare profess, and with no common principles, who are teaching or questioning a set of youths who do not know them, and do not know each other, on a large number of subjects, different in kind, and connected by no wide philosophy, three times a week, or three times a year, or once in three years, in chill lecture rooms or on a pompous anniversary.

X

Nay, self-education in any shape, in the most restricted sense, is preferable to a system of teaching which, professing so much, really does so little for the mind. Shut your College gates against the votary of knowledge, throw him back upon the searchings and the efforts of his own mind; he will gain by being spared an entrance into your Babel. Few, indeed, there are

[6] *genius loci:* spirit of the place.

who can dispense with the stimulus and support of instructors, or will do anything at all if left to themselves. And fewer still (though such great minds are to be found) who will not, from such unassisted attempts, contract a self-reliance and a self-esteem which are not only moral evils, but serious hindrances to the attainment of truth. And next to none, perhaps, or none, who will not be reminded from time to time of the disadvantage under which they lie, by their imperfect grounding, by the breaks, deficiencies, and irregularities of their knowledge, by the eccentricity of opinion and the confusion of principle which they exhibit. They will be too often ignorant of what everyone knows and takes for granted, of that multitude of small truths which fall upon the mind like dust, impalpable and ever accumulating; they may be unable to converse, they may argue perversely, they may pride themselves on their worst paradoxes or their grossest truisms, they may be full of their own mode of viewing things, unwilling to be put out of their way, slow to enter into the minds of others—but, with these and whatever other liabilities upon their heads, they are likely to have more thought, more mind, more philosophy, more true enlargement, than those earnest but ill-used persons who are forced to load their minds with a score of subjects against an examination, who have too much on their hands to indulge themselves in thinking or investigation, who devour premise and conclusion together with indiscriminate greediness, who hold whole sciences on faith, and commit demonstrations to memory, and who too often, as might be expected, when their period of education is passed, throw up all they have learned in disgust, having gained nothing really by their anxious labors, except perhaps the habit of application.

Yet such is the better specimen of the fruit of that ambitious system which has of late years been making way among us; for its result on ordinary minds, and on the common run of students, is less satisfactory still; they leave their place of education simply dissipated and relaxed by the multiplicity of subjects, which they have never really mastered, and so shallow as not even to know their shallowness. How much better, I say, is it for the active and thoughtful intellect, where such is to be found, to eschew the College and the University altogether than to submit to drudgery so ignoble, a mockery so contumelious! How much more profitable for the independent mind, after the mere rudiments of education, to range through a library at random, taking down books as they meet him, and pursuing the trains of thought 10 which his mother wit suggests! How much healthier to wander into the fields, and there with the exiled Prince to find "tongues in the trees, books in the running brooks"! How much more genuine an education is that of the poor boy in the Poem —a Poem, whether in conception or in execution, one of the most touching in our language—who, not in the wide world, but

ranging day by day around his widowed mother's home, "a dexterous gleaner" in a narrow field, and with only such slender outfit

> as the village school and books a few Supplied,

contrived from the beach, and the quay, and the fisher's boat, and the inn's fireside, and the tradesman's shop, and the shepherd's walk, and the smuggler's hut, and the mossy moor, and the screaming gulls, and the restless waves, to fashion for himself a philosophy and a poetry of his own!

But in a large subject, I am exceeding my necessary limits. Gentlemen, I must conclude abruptly; and postpone any summing up of my argument, should that be necessary, to another day.   [1852]

UNIVERSITY SUBJECTS

LITERATURE

Here, then, in the first place, I observe, Gentlemen, that Literature, from the derivation of the word, implies writing, not speaking; this, however, arises from the circumstance of the copiousness, variety, and public circulation of the matters of which it consists. What is spoken cannot outrun the range of the speaker's voice, 10 and perishes in the uttering. When words are in demand to express a long course of thought, when they have to be conveyed to the ends of the earth, or perpetuated for the benefit of posterity, they must be written down, that is, reduced to the shape of literature; still, properly speaking, the terms by which we denote this characteristic gift of man belong to its exhibition by means of the voice, not of handwriting. It ad- 20 dresses itself, in its primary idea, to the ear, not to the eye. We call it the power of speech, we call it language, that is, the use of the tongue; and, even when we write, we still keep in mind what was its original instrument, for we use freely such terms in our books as "saying," "speaking," "telling," "talking," "calling"; we use the terms "phraseology" and "diction"; as if we were still addressing ourselves to the ear.

Now I insist on this, because it shows 30

that speech, and therefore literature, which is its permanent record, is essentially a personal work. It is not some production or result, attained by the partnership of several persons, or by machinery, or by any natural process, but in its very idea it proceeds, and must proceed, from some one given individual. Two persons cannot be the authors of the sounds which strike our ear; and, as they cannot be speaking one and the same speech, neither can they be writing one and the same lecture or discourse,—which must certainly belong to some one person or other, and is the expression of that one person's ideas and feelings,—ideas and feelings personal to himself, though others may have parallel and similar ones,—proper to himself, in the same sense as his voice, his air, his countenance, his carriage, and his action, are personal. In other words, Literature expresses, not objective truth, as it is called, but subjective; not things, but thoughts.

Now this doctrine will become clearer by considering another use of words, which does relate to objective truth, or to things; which relates to matters, not personal, not subjective to the individual, but which, even were there no individual man in the whole world to know them or to talk about them, would exist still. Such objects become the matter of Science, and words indeed are used to express them, but such words are rather symbols than language, and however many we use, and however we may perpetuate them by writing, we never could make any kind of literature out of them, or call them by that name. Such, for instance, would be Euclid's elements; they relate to truths universal and eternal; they are not mere thoughts, but things: 10 they exist in themselves, not by virtue of our understanding them, not in dependence upon our will, but in what is called the *nature* of things, or at least on conditions external to us. The words, then, in which they are set forth are not language, speech, literature, but rather, as I have said, symbols. And, as a proof of it, you will recollect that it is possible, nay usual, to set forth the propositions of Euclid in 20 algebraical notation, which, as all would admit, has nothing to do with literature. What is true of mathematics is true also of every study, so far forth as it is scientific; it makes use of words as the mere vehicle of things, and is thereby withdrawn from the province of literature. Thus metaphysics, ethics, law, political economy, chemistry, theology, cease to be literature in the same degree as they are capable of a severe scien- 30 tific treatment. And hence it is that Aristotle's works on the one hand, though at first sight literature, approach in character, at least a great number of them, to mere science; for even though the things which he treats of and exhibits may not always be real and true, yet he treats them as if they were, not as if they were the thoughts of his own mind; that is, he treats them scientifically. On the other hand, 40 Law or Natural History has before now been treated by an author with so much of colouring derived from his own mind as to become a sort of literature; this is especially seen in the instance of Theology, when it takes the shape of Pulpit Eloquence. It is seen, too, in historical composition, which becomes a mere specimen of chronology, or a chronicle, when divested of the philosophy, the skill, or the party and personal 50 feelings of the particular writer. Science, then, has to do with things, literature with thoughts; science is universal, literature is personal; science uses words merely as sym-

bols, but literature uses language in its full compass, as including phraseology, idiom, style, composition, rhythm, eloquence, and whatever other properties are included in it.

Let us then put aside the scientific use of words, when we are to speak of language and literature. Literature is the personal use or exercise of language That this is so 10 is further proved from the fact that one author uses it so differently from another. Language itself in its very origination would seem to be traceable to individuals. Their peculiarities have given it its character. We are often able in fact to trace particular phrases or idioms to individuals; we know the history of their rise. Slang surely, as it is called, comes of, and breathes of the personal. The connection between 20 the force of words in particular languages and the habits and sentiments of the nations speaking them has often been pointed out. And, while the many use language as they find it, the man of genius uses it indeed, but subjects it withal to his own purposes, and moulds it according to his own peculiarities. The throng and succession of ideas, thoughts, feelings, imaginations, aspirations, which pass within him, 30 the abstractions, the juxtapositions, the comparisons, the discriminations, the conceptions, which are so original in him, his views of external things, his judgments upon life, manners, and history, the exercises of his wit, of his humor, of his depth, of his sagacity, all these innumerable and incessant creations, the very pulsation and throbbing of his intellect, does he image forth, to all does he give utterance, in a 40 corresponding language, which is as multiform as this inward mental action itself and analogous to it, the faithful expression of his intense personality, attending on his own inward world of thought as its very shadow: so that we might as well say that one man's shadow is another's as that the style of a really gifted mind can belong to any but himself. It follows him about as a shadow. His thought and feeling are personal, and so his language is personal. 50

Thought and speech are inseparable from each other. Matter and expression are parts of one: style is a thinking out into language. This is what I have been laying down, and this is literature; not *things,* not the verbal symbols of things; not on the other hand mere *words;* but thoughts expressed in language. Call to mind, Gentlemen, the meaning of the Greek word which expresses this special prerogative of man over the feeble intelligence of the inferior animals. It is called Logos: what does Logos mean? it stands both for *reason* and for *speech,* and it is difficult to say which it means more properly. It means both at once: why? because really they cannot be divided,—because they are in a true sense one. When we can separate light and illumination, life and motion, the convex and the concave of a curve, then will it be possible for thought to tread speech under foot, and to hope to do without it—then will it be conceivable that the vigorous and fertile intellect should renounce its own double, its instrument of expression, and the channel of its speculations and emotions.

Critics should consider this view of the subject before they lay down such canons of taste as the writer whose pages I have quoted. Such men as he is consider fine writing to be an *addition from without* to the matter treated of,—a sort of ornament super-induced, or a luxury indulged in, by those who have time and inclination for such vanities. They speak as if *one* man could do the thought, and *another* the style. We read in Persian travels of the way in which young gentlemen go to work in the East, when they would engage in correspondence with those who inspire them with hope or fear. They cannot write one sentence themselves; so they betake themselves to the professional letter-writer. They confide to him the object they have in view. They have a point to gain from a superior, a favour to ask, an evil to deprecate; they have to approach a man in power, or to make court to some beautiful lady. The professional man manufactures words for them, as they are wanted, as a stationer sells them paper, or a schoolmaster might cut their pens. Thought and word are, in their conception, two things, and thus there is a division of labour. The man of thought comes to the man of words; and the man of words, duly instructed in the thought, dips the pen of desire into the ink of de-

votedness, and proceeds to spread it over the page of desolation. Then the nightingale of affection is heard to warble to the rose of loveliness, while the breeze of anxiety plays around the brow of expectation. This is what the Easterns are said to consider fine writing; and it seems pretty much the idea of the school of critics to whom I have been referring.

We have an instance in literary history of this proceeding nearer home, in a great University, in the latter years of the last century. I have referred to it before now in a public lecture elsewhere; but it is too much in point here to be omitted. A learned Arabic scholar had to deliver a set of lectures before its doctors and professors on an historical subject in which his reading had lain. A linguist is conversant with science rather than with literature; but this gentleman felt that his lectures must not be without a style. Being of the opinion of the Orientals, with whose writings he was familiar, he determined to buy a style. He took the step of engaging a person, at a price, to turn the matter which he had got together into ornamental English. Observe, he did not wish for mere grammatical English, but for an elaborate, pretentious style. An artist was found in the person of a country curate, and the job was carried out. His lectures remain to this day, in their own place in the protracted series of annual Discourses to which they belong, distinguished amid a number of heavyish compositions by the rhetorical and ambitious diction for which he went into the market. This learned divine, indeed, and the author I have quoted, differ from each other in the estimate they respectively form of literary composition; but they agree together in this,—in considering such composition a trick and a trade; they put it on a par with the gold plate and the flowers and the music of a banquet, which do not make the viands better, but the entertainment more pleasurable; as if language were the hired servant, the mere mistress of the reason, and not the lawful wife in her own house.

But can they really think that Homer, or Pindar, or Shakespeare, or Dryden, or Walter Scott, were accustomed to aim at diction for its own sake, instead of being inspired with their subject, and pouring forth beautiful words because they had beautiful thoughts? this is surely too great a paradox to be borne. Rather, it is the fire within the author's breast which overflows in the torrent of his burning, irresistible eloquence; it is the poetry of his inner soul, which relieves itself in the Ode or the Elegy; and his mental attitude and bearing, the beauty of his moral countenance, the force and keenness of his logic, are imaged in the tenderness, or energy, or richness of his language. Nay, according to the well-known line, "facit indignatio versus"; [1] not the words alone, but even the rhythm, the metre, the verse, will be the contemporaneous offspring of the emotion or imagination which possesses him. "Poeta nascitur, non fit," [2] says the proverb; and this is in numerous instances true of his poems, as well as of himself. They are born, not framed; they are a strain rather than a composition; and their perfection is the monument, not so much of his skill as of his power. And this is true of prose as well as of verse in its degree: who will not recognize in the vision of Mirza a delicacy and beauty of style which is very difficult to describe, but which is felt to be in exact correspondence to the ideas of which it is the expression?

And, since the thought and reasonings of an author have, as I have said, a personal character, no wonder that his style is not only the image of his subject, but of his mind. That pomp of language, that full and tuneful diction, that felicitousness in the choice and exquisiteness in the collocation of words, which to prosaic writers seem artificial, is nothing else but the mere habit and way of a lofty intellect. Aristotle, in his sketch of the magnanimous man, tells us that his voice is deep, his motions slow, and his stature commanding. In like manner, the elocution of a great intellect is great. His language expresses, not only his great thoughts, but his great self. Certainly he might use fewer words than he uses; but he fertilizes his simplest ideas,

and germinates into a multitude of details, and prolongs the march of his sentences, and sweeps round to the full diapason of his harmony, as if κύδεϊ γαίων, [3] rejoicing in his own vigour and richness of resource. I say, a narrow critic will call it verbiage, when really it is a sort of fulness of heart, parallel to that which makes the merry boy whistle as he walks, or the strong man, like the smith in the novel, flourish his club when there is no one to fight with.

Shakespeare furnishes us with frequent instances of this peculiarity, and all so beautiful, that it is difficult to select for quotation. For instance, in Macbeth:—

Canst thou not minister to a mind diseased,
Pluck from the memory a rooted sorrow,
Raze out the written troubles of the brain,
And, with some sweet oblivious antidote,
Cleanse the foul bosom of that perilous stuff,
Which weighs upon the heart?

Here a simple idea, by a process which belongs to the orator rather than to the poet, but still comes from the native vigour of genius, is expanded into a many-membered period.

The following from Hamlet is of the same kind:—

'Tis not alone my inky cloak, good mother,
Nor customary suits of solemn black,
Nor windy suspiration of forced breath,
No, nor the fruitful river in the eye,
Nor the dejected haviour of the visage,
Together with all forms, modes, shows of grief,
That can denote me truly.

Now, if such declamation, for declamation it is, however noble, be allowable in a poet, whose genius is so far removed from pompousness or pretence, much more is it allowable in an orator, whose very province it is to put forth words to the best advantage he can. Cicero has nothing more redundant in any part of his writings than these passages from Shakespeare. No lover then at least of Shakespeare may fairly accuse Cicero of gorgeousness of phraseology or diffuseness of style. Nor will any sound critic be tempted to do so. As a certain unaffected neatness and propriety and grace of diction may be required

---

[1] facit indignatio versus: indignation makes verses (Juvenal, Satire, I, 79). The Latin text has versum (verse).

[2] poeta nascitur, non fit: the poet is born, not made (old Roman proverb).

[3] κύδεϊ γαίων: "exulting in his glory (or strength)"—Iliad, I, 405.

of any author who lays claim to be a classic, for the same reason that a certain attention to dress is expected of every gentleman, so to Cicero may be allowed the privilege of the "os magna sonaturum," [4] of which the ancient critic speaks. His copious, majestic, musical flow of language, even if sometimes beyond what the subject-matter demands, is never out of keeping with the occasion or with the speaker. It is the expression of lofty sentiments in lofty sentences, the "mens magna in corpore magno." [5] It is the development of the inner man. Cicero vividly realised the *status* of a Roman senator and statesman, and the "pride of place" of Rome, in all the grace and grandeur which attached to her; and he imbibed, and became, what he admired. As the exploits of Scipio or Pompey are the expression of this greatness in deed, so the language of Cicero is the expression of it in word. And, as the acts of the Roman ruler or soldier represent to us, in a manner special to themselves, the characteristic magnanimity of the lords of the earth, so do the speeches or treatises of her accomplished orator bring it home to our imaginations as no other writing could do. Neither Livy, nor Tacitus, nor Terence, nor Seneca, nor Pliny, nor Quintilian, is an adequate spokesman for the Imperial City. They write Latin; Cicero writes Roman.

You will say that Cicero's language is undeniably studied, but that Shakespeare's is as undeniably natural and spontaneous; and that this is what is meant when the Classics are accused of being mere artists of words. Here we are introduced to a further large question, which gives me the opportunity of anticipating a misapprehension of my meaning. I observe, then, that, not only is that lavish richness of style, which I have noticed in Shakespeare, justifiable on the principles which I have been laying down, but, what is less easy to receive, even elaborateness in composition is no mark of trick or artifice in an author. Undoubtedly the works of the Classics, particularly the Latin, *are* elaborate; they have cost a great deal of time, care, and trouble. They have had many rough copies; I grant it. I grant also that there are writers of name, ancient and modern, who really are guilty of the absurdity of making sentences, as the very end of their literary labour. Such was Isocrates; such were some of the sophists; they were set on words, to the neglect of thoughts or things; I cannot defend them. If I must give an English instance of this fault, much as I love and revere the personal character and intellectual vigour of Dr. Johnson, I cannot deny that his style often outruns the sense and the occasion, and is wanting in that simplicity which is the attribute of genius. Still, granting all this, I cannot grant, notwithstanding, that genius never need take pains,—that genius may not improve by practice,—that it never incurs failures, and succeeds the second time,—that it never finishes off at leisure what it has thrown off in the outline at a stroke.

Take the instance of the painter or the sculptor; he has a conception in his mind which he wishes to represent in the medium of his art;—the Madonna and Child, or Innocence, or Fortitude, or some historical character or event. Do you mean to say he does not study his subject? does he not make sketches? does he not even call them "studies"? does he not call his workroom a *studio*? is he not ever designing, rejecting, adopting, correcting, perfecting? Are not the first attempts of Michael Angelo and Raffaelle extant, in the case of some of their most celebrated compositions? Will any one say that the Apollo Belvidere is not a conception patiently elaborated into its proper perfection? These departments of taste are, according to the received notions of the world, the very province of genius, and yet we call them *arts;* they are the "Fine Arts." Why may not that be true of literary composition which is true of painting, sculpture, architecture, and music? Why may not language be wrought as well as the clay of the modeller? why may not words be worked up as well as colours? why should not skill in diction be simply subservient and instrumental to the great prototypal ideas which are the contemplation of a Plato or a Virgil? Our greatest poet tells us,

[4] *"os magna sonaturum"*: a voice destined to utter great things (Horace, *Satires* I, iv, 43-44).
[5] *"mens magna in corpore magno"*: a great mind in a great body.

The poet's eye, in a fine frenzy rolling,
Doth glance from heaven to earth, from earth
    to heaven,
And, as imagination bodies forth
The forms of things unknown, the poet's pen
Turns them to shapes, and gives to airy nothing
A local habitation and a name.

Now, is it wonderful that that pen of his should sometimes be at fault for a while,—that it should pause, write, erase, rewrite, amend, complete, before he satisfies himself that his language has done justice to the conceptions which his mind's eye contemplated?

In this point of view, doubtless, many or most writers are elaborate; and those certainly not the least whose style is furthest removed from ornament, being simple and natural, or vehement, or severely business-like and practical. Who so energetic and manly as Demosthenes? Yet he is said to have transcribed Thucydides many times over in the formation of his style. Who so gracefully natural as Herodotus? yet his very dialect is not his own, but chosen for the sake of the perfection of his narrative. Who exhibits such happy negligence as our own Addison? yet artistic fastidiousness was so notorious in his instance that the report has got abroad, truly or not, that he was too late in his issue of an important state-paper, from his habit of revision and re-composition. Such great authors were working by a model which was before the eyes of their intellect, and they were labouring to say what they had to say, in such a way as would most exactly and suitably express it. It is not wonderful that other authors, whose style is not simple, should be instances of a similar literary diligence. Virgil wishes his Aeneid to be burned, elaborate as is its composition, because he felt it needed more labour still, in order to make it perfect. The historian Gibbon in the last century is another instance in point. You must not suppose I am going to recommend his style for imitation, any more than his principles; but I refer to him as the example of a writer feeling the task which lay before him, feeling that he had to bring out into words for the comprehension of his readers a great and complicated scene, and wishing that those words should be adequate to his

undertaking. I think he wrote the first chapter of his History three times over; it was not that he corrected or improved the first copy; but he put his first essay, and then his second, aside—he recast his matter, till he had hit the precise exhibition of it which he thought demanded by his subject.

Now in all these instances, I wish you to observe, that what I have admitted about literary workmanship differs from the doctrine which I am opposing in this,—that the mere dealer in words cares little or nothing for the subject which he is embellishing, but can paint and gild anything whatever to order; whereas the artist, whom I am acknowledging, has his great or rich visions before him, and his only aim is to bring out what he thinks or what he feels in a way adequate to the thing spoken of, and appropriate to the speaker.

The illustration which I have been borrowing from the Fine Arts will enable me to go a step further. I have been showing the connection of the thought with the language in literary composition; and in doing so I have exposed the unphilosophical notion that the language was an extra which could be dispensed with and provided to order according to the demand. But I have not yet brought out, what immediately follows from this, and which was the second point which I had to show, viz., that to be capable of easy translation is no test of the excellence of a composition. If I must say what I think, I should lay down, with little hesitation, that the truth was almost the reverse of this doctrine. Nor are many words required to show it. Such a doctrine, as is contained in the passage of the author whom I quoted when I began, goes upon the assumption that one language is just like another language,—that every language has all the ideas, turns of thought, delicacies of expression, figures, associations, abstractions, points of view, which every other language has. Now, as far as regards Science, it is true that all languages are pretty much alike for the purposes of Science; but even in this respect some are more suitable than others, which have to coin words, or to borrow them, in order to express scientific ideas. But if languages are not all equally adapted even to furnish symbols for those universal and eternal truths in which Science consists, how can they reasonably be expected to be all equally rich, equally forcible, equally musical, equally exact, equally happy in expressing the idiosyncratic peculiarities of thought of some original and fertile mind, who has availed himself of one of them? A great author takes his native language, masters it, partly throws himself into it, partly moulds and adapts it, and pours out his multitude of ideas through the variously ramified and delicately minute channels of expression which he has found or framed:—does it follow that this his personal presence (as it may be called) can forthwith be transferred to every other language under the sun? Then may we reasonably maintain that Beethoven's piano music is not really beautiful, because it cannot be played on the hurdy-gurdy. Were not this astonishing doctrine maintained by persons far superior to the writer whom I have selected for animadversion, I should find it difficult to be patient under a gratuitous extravagance. It seems that a really great author must admit of translation, and that we have a test of his excellence when he reads to advantage in a foreign language as well as in his own. Then Shakespeare *is* a genius because he can be translated into German, and *not* a genius because he cannot be translated into French. Then the multiplication-table is the most gifted of all conceivable compositions, because it loses nothing by translation, and can hardly be said to belong to any one language whatever. Whereas I should rather have conceived that, in proportion as ideas are novel and recondite, they would be difficult to put into words, and that the very fact of their having insinuated themselves into one language would diminish the chance of that happy accident being repeated in another. In the language of savages you can hardly express any idea or act of the intellect at all: is the tongue of the Hottentot or Esquimaux to be made the measure of the genius of Plato, Pindar, Tacitus, St. Jerome, Dante, or Cervantes?

Let us recur, I say, to the illustration of the Fine Arts. I suppose you can express ideas in painting which you cannot express in sculpture; and the more an artist is of a painter, the less he is likely to be of a sculptor. The more he commits his genius to the methods and conditions of his own art, the less he will be able to throw himself into the circumstances of another. Is the genius of Fra Angelico, of Francia, or of Raffaelle disparaged by the fact that he was able to do that in colours which no man that ever lived, which no Angel, could achieve in wood? Each of the Fine Arts has its own subject-matter; from the nature of the case you can do in one what you cannot do in another; you can do in painting what you cannot do in carving; you can do in oils what you cannot do in fresco; you can do in marble what you cannot do in ivory; you can do in wax what you cannot do in bronze. Then, I repeat, applying this to the case of languages, why should not genius be able to do in Greek what it cannot do in Latin? and why are its Greek and Latin works defective because they will not turn into English? That genius, of which we are speaking, did not make English; it did not make all languages, present, past, and future; it did not make the laws of *any* language: why is it to be judged of by that in which it had no part, over which it has no control?

And now we are naturally brought on to our third point, which is on the characteristics of Holy Scripture as compared with profane literature. Hitherto we have been concerned with the doctrine of these writers, viz., that style is an *extra,* that it is a mere artifice, and that hence it cannot be translated; now we come to their fact, viz., that Scripture has no such artificial style, and that Scripture can easily be translated. Surely their fact is as untenable as their doctrine.

Scripture easy of translation! then why have there been so few good translators? why is it that there has been such great difficulty in combining the two necessary qualities, fidelity to the original and purity in the adopted vernacular? why is it that the authorized versions of the Church are often so inferior to the original as compositions, except that the Church is bound above all things to see that the version is doctrinally correct, and in a difficult problem is obliged to put up with defects in what is of secondary importance, provided she secure what is of first? If it were so easy to transfer the beauty of the original to the copy, she would not have been content with her received version in various languages which could be named.

And then in the next place, Scripture not elaborate! Scripture not ornamented in diction, and musical in cadence! Why, consider the Epistle to the Hebrews—where is there in the classics any composition more carefully, more artificially written? Consider the book of Job—is it not a sacred drama, as artistic, as perfect, as any Greek tragedy of Sophocles or Euripides? Consider the Psalter—are there no ornaments, no rhythm, no studied cadences, no responsive members, in that divinely beautiful book? And is it not hard to understand? are not the Prophets hard to understand? is not St. Paul hard to understand? Who can say that these are popular compositions? who can say that they are level at first reading with the understandings of the multitude?

That there are portions indeed of the inspired volume more simple both in style and in meaning, and that these are the more sacred and sublime passages, as, for instance, parts of the Gospels, I grant at once; but this does not militate against the doctrine I have been laying down. Recollect, Gentlemen, my distinction when I began. I have said Literature is one thing, and that Science is another; that Literature is of a personal character, that Science treats of what is universal and eternal. In proportion, then, as Scripture excludes the personal colouring of its writers, and rises into the region of pure and mere inspiration, when it ceases in any sense to be the writing of man, of St. Paul or St. John, of Moses or Isaias, then it comes to belong to Science, not Literature. Then it conveys the things of heaven, unseen verities, divine manifestations, and them alone—not the ideas, the feelings, the aspirations, of its human instruments, who, for all that they were inspired and infallible, did not cease to be men. St. Paul's epistles, then, I consider to be literature in a real and true sense, as personal, as rich in reflection and emotion, as Demosthenes or Euripides; and, without ceasing to be revelations of objective truth, they are

expressions of the subjective notwithstanding. On the other hand, portions of the Gospels, of the book of Genesis, and other passages of the Sacred Volume, are of the nature of Science. Such is the beginning of St. John's Gospel, which we read at the end of Mass. Such is the Creed. I mean, passages such as these are the mere enunciation of eternal things, without (so to say) the medium of any human mind transmitting them to us. The words used have the grandeur, the majesty, the calm, unimpassioned beauty of Science; they are in no sense Literature, they are in no sense personal; and therefore they are easy to apprehend, and easy to translate.

Did time admit I could show you parallel instances of what I am speaking of in the Classics, inferior to the inspired word in proportion as the subject-matter of the classical authors is immensely inferior to the subjects treated of in Scripture—but parallel, inasmuch as the classical author or speaker ceases for the moment to have to do with Literature, as speaking of things objectively, and rises to the serene sublimity of Science. But I should be carried too far if I began.

I shall then merely sum up what I have said, and come to a conclusion. Reverting, then, to my original question, what is the meaning of Letters, as contained, Gentlemen, in the designation of your Faculty, I have answered, that by Letters or Literature is meant the expression of thought in language, where by "thought" I mean the ideas, feelings, views, reasonings, and other operations of the human mind. And the Art of Letters is the method by which a speaker or writer brings out in words, worthy of his subject, and sufficient for his audience or readers, the thoughts which impress him. Literature, then, is of a personal character; it consists in the enunciations and teachings of those who have a right to speak as representatives of their kind, and in whose words their brethren find an interpretation of their own sentiments, a record of their own experience, and a suggestion for their own judgments. A great author, Gentlemen, is not one who merely has a *copia verborum*,[6] whether in

6 *copia verborum:* plenty of words, i.e. fluency.

prose or verse, and can, as it were, turn on at his will any number of splendid phrases and swelling sentences; but he is one who has something to say and knows how to say it. I do not claim for him, as such, any great depth of thought, or breadth of view, or philosophy, or sagacity, or knowledge of human nature, or experience of human life, though these additional gifts he may have, and the more he has of them the greater he is; but I ascribe to him, as his characteristic gift, in a large sense the faculty of Expression. He is master of the two-fold Logos, the thought and the word, distinct, but inseparable from each other. He may, if so be, elaborate his compositions, or he may pour out his improvisations, but in either case he has but one aim, which he keeps steadily before him, and is conscientious and single-minded in fulfilling. That aim is to give forth what he has within him; and from his very earnestness it comes to pass that, whatever be the splendour of his diction or the harmony of his periods, he has with him the charm of an incommunicable simplicity. Whatever be his subject, high or low, he treats it suitably and for its own sake. If he is a poet, "nil molitur *ineptè*." [7] If he is an orator, then too he speaks, not only "distinctè" and "splendidè," but also "*aptè*." His page is the lucid mirror of his mind and life —

> Quo fit, ut omnis
> Votivâ pateat veluti descripta tabellâ
> Vita senis. [8]

He writes passionately, because he feels keenly; forcibly, because he conceives vividly; he sees too clearly to be vague; he is too serious to be otiose; he can analyze his subject, and therefore he is rich; he embraces it as a whole and in its parts, and therefore he is consistent; he has a firm hold of it, and therefore he is luminous. When his imagination wells up, it overflows in ornament; when his heart is touched, it thrills along his verse. He always has the right word for the right idea, and never a word too much. If he is brief, it is because few words suffice; when he is lavish of them, still each word has its mark, and aids, not embarrasses, the vigorous march of his elocution. He expresses what all feel, but all cannot say; and his sayings pass into proverbs among his people, and his phrases become household words and idioms of their daily speech, which is tesselated with the rich fragments of his language, as we see in foreign lands the marbles of Roman grandeur worked into the walls and pavements of modern palaces.

Such pre-eminently is Shakespeare among ourselves; such pre-eminently Virgil among the Latins; such in their degree are all those writers who in every nation go by the name of Classics. To particular nations they are necessarily attached from the circumstance of the variety of tongues, and the peculiarities of each; but so far they have a catholic and ecumenical character, that what they express is common to the whole race of man, and they alone are able to express it.

If then the power of speech is a gift as great as any that can be named,—if the origin of language is by many philosophers even considered to be nothing short of divine,—if by means of words the secrets of the heart are brought to light, pain of soul is relieved, hidden grief is carried off, sympathy conveyed, counsel imparted, experience recorded, and wisdom perpetuated,—if by great authors the many are drawn up into unity, national character is fixed, a people speaks, the past and the future, the East and the West are brought into communication with each other,—if such men are, in a word, the spokesmen and prophets of the human family,—it will not answer to make light of Literature or to neglect its study; rather we may be sure that, in proportion as we master it in whatever language, and imbibe its spirit, we shall ourselves become in our own measure the ministers of like benefits to others, be they many or few, be they in the obscurer or the more distinguished walks of life,—who are united to us by social ties, and are within the sphere of our personal influence.   [1858]

---

7 *nil molitur ineptè:* he undertakes no aimless task (Horace, *Ars Poetica,* 140).

8 *Quo fit, ut omnis,* etc.: "Whence it comes that the whole life of the old (poet) is open to view as if graven on a votive tablet" (Horace, *Satires,* II, i, 32).

JOHN STUART MILL

CHRONOLOGY AND INTRODUCTION

1806 Born in London, May 20.
1809–20 Early education under father, James Mill.
1820–21 Lived in southern France, a guest of Sir Samuel Bentham, brother of Jeremy B.
1821–22 Continued education at home. Organized "Utilitarian Society."
1823 Appointed clerk with East India Company.
1824 Writer for *Westminster Review* (founded by J. Bentham).
1826 Crisis in mental life.
1830 Visit to Paris after the Revolution of July. Meets Mrs. Taylor in London.
1830–40 Frequent contributor to periodicals. Editor of *London Review* (1835) and of *London and Westminster Review* (1836–40).
1843 *System of Logic.*
1848 *Principles of Political Economy.* Re-edited in six successive and revised editions up to 1871.

1851 Married Mrs. Taylor.
1857 Retired from East India Company on pension of £1500 a year.
1858 Death of wife in Avignon, France, where Mill now lived in retirement for most of each year.
1859 *On Liberty; Thoughts on Parliamentary Reform.*
1861 *Representative Government.*
1863 *Utilitarianism.*
1865 *An Examination of Sir William Hamilton's Philosophy; Auguste Comte and Positivism.*
1865–68 Member of Parliament for Westminster.
1869 *The Subjection of Women.*
1873 Death in Avignon, May 8. *Autobiography.*
1874 *Three Essays on Religion.*
1879 *Chapters on Socialism,* in *Fortnightly Review.*

Mill is not one of the Victorian masters of imaginative prose, like Carlyle, Ruskin or Newman, whose thought is inseparable from a passionate personality and whose style, consequently, reflects the movement and color of a poetic mind. Mill has passion, at times profound passion, but it is so highly intellectualized that it is felt only by those readers most capable of sustained interest in ideas, which are often abstract and are expressed with scrupulous regard for the laws of logic. His life, however, was the opposite of what Carlyle, in a letter to his brother, called it (he had been reading the *Autobiography*): "the life of a logic-chopping engine, little more of human in it than if it had been done by a thing of mechanized iron." Speculation upon the processes and presuppositions of thought were a necessity for Mill, but there never lived a man with a loftier or more disinterested devotion to the public good. His writings, without exception, are dedicated to the enlightenment and emancipation of his fellow men. "He is the only writer in the world," wrote John Morley in an eloquent tribute (*The Death of Mr. Mill*), "whose treatises on highly abstract subjects have been printed during his life-time in editions for the people, and sold at the price of railway novels. . . . Perhaps the sum of all his distinction lies in the union of stern science with infinite aspiration, of rigorous sense of what is real and practicable with bright and luminous hope." And again, upon the anniversary of Mill's birth, Morley wrote (1906): "Nobody who claims to deal as a matter of history with the intellectual fermentation between 1840 and 1870 or a little longer, whatever value the historian may choose to set upon its products, can fail to assign a leading influence to Mill."

The essentials of his personal history are told in the *Autobiography*, a classic in its field. No other boy of whom the world holds record was ever subjected to so rigorous and so methodical a training or ever came out of it so well. There were no school and college, no amusements or skills, little or no intercourse with other youngsters, hardly anything but steady absorption of Greek, Latin, science, history, literature, political economy, logic; until Mill at fifteen was more or less master of all these disciplines. "In the course of instruction which I have partially retraced," he says, "the point most superficially apparent is the great effort to give, during the years of childhood, an amount of knowledge in what was considered the higher branches of education, which is seldom acquired (if acquired at all) until the age of manhood. . . . I started, I may fairly say, with an advantage of a quarter of a century over my contemporaries.... Mine, however, was not an education of cram. My father never permitted anything which I learnt to degenerate into a mere exercise of memory." Of the thoroughness of this experience Mill's Greek is the capital illustration. He could not remember when he began the language but, he says, "I have been told that it was when I was three years old." At eight he "had read" Herodotus, Diogenes Laertius, Xenophon, Lucian, Isocrates; and, at thirteen, six dialogues of Plato. These foundations stood the test of time. In later years, when preparing to review the first two volumes of Grote's *History of Greece,* he re-read in the original the *Iliad* and *Odyssey;* and later still, when getting up an article on Grote's *Plato,* he went through all the dialogues in Greek.

"From the winter of 1821, when I first read Bentham," he tells us, "I had what might truly be called an object in life; to be a reformer of the world." He organized a utilitarian society of rising young liberals, and he began to write for the reviews, all the while from 1823 onwards occupying a position of growing importance in the service of the East India Company. The paternal system of education appeared to be working miracles in this astonishing young man. Then gradually depression settled upon him. He came to realize that his knowledge was speculative merely, that he was only a "reasoning machine," that associationist psychology was too artificial and incomplete an account of experience, and that continual analysis was "a perpetual worm at the root both of the passions and of the virtues." The crisis broke in 1826. "Suppose," he said to himself, "that all your objects in life were realized; that all the changes in institutions and opinions which you are looking forward to, could be completely effected at this very instant: would this be a great joy and happiness to you? And an irrepressible self-consciousness distinctly answered, 'No!' At this my heart sank within me: the whole foundation on which my life was constructed fell down."

Then a happy chance turned him to imaginative literature, especially to Wordsworth, whose poetry came upon him as summer rain upon parched ground. "What made Wordsworth's poems a medicine for my state of mind was that they expressed, not mere outward beauty, but states of feeling, and of thought colored by feeling, under the excitement of beauty. They seemed to be the very culture of the feelings, which I was in quest of." From this momentous experience Mill emerged a changed individual. Introspection and analysis could never again paralyse normal responses of the heart to the appeals of man and nature. Many years later he recorded in his diary the following reflection: "Essentially solitary occupations, as scientific speculation usually is, do tend in some degree to deaden sympathy. For this, among other reasons, speculation never ought to be the sole and exclusive occupation of anyone." About this time, too, new friendships, different from the old, played their part, friendships with Maurice, Sterling, Carlyle, and, most important of all, with Mrs. Taylor, who became, he says, "the presiding principle of my mental progress," and whom he married in 1851. Though Mill remained a logician and became "the saint of rationalism," as Gladstone called him, he never ceased to emphasize the importance of imaginative literature and art as instruments of culture.

In philosophy he was a consistent empiricist of the English school of Hume (and, in part, of Locke). He held that there is no knowledge independent of experience, that the causes of our sensations, or the nature of things in themselves, are hidden and inaccessible to human faculties, and that moral obligations are not innate but acquired. He was opposed to all forms of trans-cendentalism, or the belief that the mind can reach beyond sense-experience to ultimate truth by intuition or special revelation. Hegelian idealism and Platonic ideas were alike "a jungle of metaphysical abstractions." In later speculations he found in the argument from design some ground for belief in a Creator, but a Creator who, if benevolent, is too limited in power to overcome all the wanton cruelty of nature. He saw a sufficient reason for the highest human aspirations in an ideal of the endless improvability of men forever struggling upwards into a better civilization against hostile forces. This is Mill's religion of humanity, which, according to his posthumous essay on theism, permits man to exalt a historical Christ "as the pattern of perfection."

His work in the fields of political, economic, and social theory is so varied and extensive, and at times so specialized, that only a few leading ideas may be suggested. Utility, he held, is the ultimate test of all ethical values, but Mill's utilitarianism is not the narrow, prudential, legalistic thing it was for Bentham. Anything is of course useful only if it makes for happiness, but happiness is a matter of quality as well as quantity. "The test of quality," argued Mill, "is the preference given by those who are acquainted with both (i.e., the higher and the lower kinds). Socrates would rather choose to be Socrates dissatisfied than a pig satisfied. The pig probably would not, but the pig knows only one side of the question." By the standards of this higher utilitarianism, which takes into account the whole of human nature, and the whole of human society, Mill measured the worth of every political and economic principle with which he was concerned.

In politics he called himself an advanced Liberal. He had a passion for equality, both economic and social; but he knew that the realization of it meant a levelling up as well as a levelling down and that these changes would require long years of education and a gradual amelioration of human character. The rich, leisured classes he looked upon as demoralizing, because for one thing they used government to further private rather than public interests, and for another they made material wealth seem to the groups below the only passport to power and social standing. "At present" (1852), he said of the wage workers, "their idea of social reform appears to be simply higher wages and less work for the sake of more sensual indulgence." The middle, or professional and commercial, classes on the side of their faults really belonged either to the upper or the lower classes; on the side of their virtues they were the hope of the future. Mill believed that the mechanical inventions of the age had so far only increased the physical comforts of the wealthy and the miseries of the poor, while hardly lightening "the day's toil of any human being." To remedy these evils he advocated changes in the laws of inheritance, a more equitable distribution of property, complete political emancipation of women, compulsory elementary education for all classes, and representation of labor in parliament.

In economics Mill was educated in the classical school of Adam Smith, Malthus and Ricardo, the school of *laissez-faire*, of immutable "laws," of the hypothetical "economic man." For Mill these were meaningless abstractions when considered apart from man as an ethical, political, and social being. "The old political economy," he said, "assumes private property and inheritance, as indefeasible facts, and freedom of production and exchange as the *dernier mot* of social improvement." Such generalizations were contrary to all his presuppositions since they were based upon the theory of an unalterable social order. Modes of distributing the resources of the earth and the products of labor—a major economic problem—depend upon the will of man, more particularly upon the will of the working man. Mill was well aware of "the stupidity and habitual indifference of the mass of mankind," and of the countless perils along the roads of progress. But he never took a gloomy view of human prospects because of his confidence in man's power to better himself. Paternal and patriarchal systems of government he dismissed: "the poor have come out of leading strings, and cannot any longer be governed like children." Improve their intelligence and establish just laws of distribution, he argued, and the division of humanity into masters and work people will disappear. He viewed with sympathetic interest the various socialistic theories and experiments of his day, and he favored some form of collective ownership, whenever the workers were fit to assume the rights it would confer and discharge the duties it would impose. But "the natural indolence of mankind, their tendency to be passive, to be the slaves of habit," must not be overlooked. Nor would Mill give up the idea that competition is necessary to progress and that individuals must be guaranteed the fruits of their own labor and abstinence. Most of all he insisted that collectivism in any form must provide for a full development of human nature with its diversity of tastes and talents, and must recognize that progress is largely dependent upon the collision of stimulating minds with freedom to think and act.

Mill learned to write very early. On morning walks, for many years, he would give to his father an oral account of the previous day's reading. He made verses, he wrote out his lessons in political economy, and later he drafted digests of innumerable articles in the *Edinburgh Review*. Thus he early acquired precision and clarity of expression. At seventeen he began to contribute papers to the *Westminster Review*, just established by Bentham, and from then onwards his pen was busy. He overcame what he called "the jejuneness of my early compositions" by a course of reading in "Goldsmith, Fielding, Pascal, Voltaire, and Courier," who helped him, he thought, to gain ease and liveliness. Like most successful writers he spared no pains with everything he produced. He tells us that all his books were twice composed,—a first draft, and "then the whole begun again *de novo*." In his *Inaugural Lecture* (1867) he placed great emphasis upon a study of the Greek and Roman classics, which he regarded as supreme achievements in style, wherein every element and quality of expression are "subordinated to matter." Prose that depended for effect upon artifice and ornament, or that failed in clearness, he condemned. Macaulay he found "affected and antithetical," and he did not hesitate to inform Carlyle that the style of *The French Revolution* "would often *tell* better on the reader if what is said in an abrupt, exclamatory, and interjectional manner were said in the ordinary grammatical mode of nominative and verb."

Mill's own prose would be greater, perhaps, if it had, along with its other virtues, Macaulay's vitality or Carlyle's individuality and color. But though he understood that imagination was as essential for literary greatness as pure intellect, he was himself deficient in imagination, as he was in sheer energy. Being, however, one of the clearest and wisest minds of his time, with something to say—"the grand requisite of good writing"—and possessing an extraordinary command of the ordinary resources of language, Mill holds a place with the Victorian masters of prose. It was his mission in life, he said, to "build the bridges and clear the paths," and for this indispensable work his style is eminently adequate.

AUTOBIOGRAPHY

A CRISIS IN MY MENTAL HISTORY.
ONE STAGE ONWARD

For some years after this time I wrote very little, and nothing regularly, for publication: and great were the advantages which I derived from the intermission. It was of no common importance to me, at this period, to be able to digest and mature my thoughts for my own mind only, without any immediate call for giving them out in print. Had I gone on writing, it would have much disturbed the important transformation in my opinions and character, which took place during those years. The origin of this transformation, or at least the process by which I was prepared for it, can only be explained by turning some distance back.

From the winter of 1821, when I first read Bentham, and especially from the commencement of the Westminster Review, I had what might truly be called an object in life; to be a reformer of the world. My conception of my own happiness was entirely identified with this object. The personal sympathies I wished for were those of fellow labourers in this enterprise. I endeavoured to pick up as many flowers as I could by the way; but as a serious and permanent personal satisfaction to rest upon, my whole reliance was placed on this; and I was accustomed to felicitate myself on the certainty of a happy life which I enjoyed, through placing my happiness in something durable and distant, in which some progress might be always making, while it could never be exhausted by complete attainment. This did very well for several years, during which the general improvement going on in the world and the idea of myself as engaged with others in struggling to promote it, seemed enough to fill up an interesting and animated existence. But the time came when I awakened from this as from a dream. It was in the autumn of 1826. I was in a dull state of nerves, such as everybody is occasionally liable to; unsusceptible to enjoyment or pleasurable excitement; one of those moods when what is pleasure at other times, becomes insipid or indifferent; the state, I should think, in which converts to Methodism usually are, when smitten by their first "conviction of sin." In this frame of mind it occurred to me to put the question directly to myself: "Suppose that all your objects in life were realized; that all the changes in institutions and opinions which you are looking forward to, could be completely effected at this very instant: would this be a great joy and happiness to you?" And an irrepressible self-consciousness distinctly answered, "No!" At this my heart sank within me: the whole foundation on which my life was constructed fell down. All my happiness was to have been found in the continual pursuit of this end. The end had ceased to charm, and how could there ever again be any interest in the means? I seemed to have nothing left to live for.

At first I hoped that the cloud would pass away of itself; but it did not. A night's sleep, the sovereign remedy for the smaller vexations of life, had no effect on it. I awoke to a renewed consciousness of the woful fact. I carried it with me into all companies, into all occupations. Hardly anything had power to cause me even a few minutes' oblivion of it. For some months the cloud seemed to grow thicker and thicker. The lines in Coleridge's "Dejection"—I was not then acquainted with them—exactly describe my case:

A grief without a pang, void, dark and drear,
A drowsy, stifled, unimpassioned grief,
Which finds no natural outlet or relief
In word, or sigh, or tear.

In vain I sought relief from my favourite books; those memorials of past nobleness and greatness from which I had always hitherto drawn strength and animation. I read them now without feeling, or with the accustomed feeling *minus* all its charms; and I became persuaded, that my love of mankind, and of excellence for its own sake, had worn itself out. I sought no comfort by speaking to others of what I felt. If I had loved any one sufficiently to make confiding my griefs a necessity, I should not have been in the condition I was. I felt, too, that mine was not an interesting, or in any way respectable distress. There was nothing in it to attract sympathy. Advice, if I had known where to seek it, would have been most precious. The words of Macbeth to the physician often occurred to my thoughts. But there was no one on whom I could build the faintest hope of such assistance. My father, to whom it would have been natural to me to have recourse in any practical difficulties, was the last person to whom, in such a case as this, I looked for help. Everything convinced me that he had no knowledge of any such mental state as I was suffering from, and that even if he could be made to understand it, he was not the physician who could heal it. My education, which was wholly his work, had been conducted without any regard to the possibility of its ending in this result; and I saw no use in giving him the pain of thinking that his plans had failed, when the failure was probably irremediable, and, at all events, beyond the power of *his* remedies. Of other friends, I had at that time none to whom I had any hope of making my condition intelligible. It was however abundantly intelligible to myself; and the more I dwelt upon it, the more hopeless it appeared.

My course of study had led me to believe, that all mental and moral feelings and qualities, whether of a good or of a bad kind, were the results of association; that we love one thing, and hate another, take pleasure in one sort of action or contemplation, and pain in another sort, through the clinging of pleasurable or painful ideas to those things, from the effect of education or of experience. As a corollary from this, I had always heard it maintained by my father, and was myself convinced, that the object of education should be to form the strongest possible associations of the salutary class; associations of pleasure with all things beneficial to the great whole, and of pain with all things hurtful to it. This doctrine appeared inexpugnable; but it now seemed to me, on retrospect, that my teachers had occupied themselves but superficially with the means of forming and keeping up these salutary associations. They seemed to have trusted altogether to the old familiar instruments, praise and blame, reward and punishment. Now, I did not doubt that by these means, begun early, and applied unremittingly, intense associations of pain and pleasure, especially of pain, might be created, and might produce desires and aversions capable of lasting undiminished to the end of life. But there must always be something artificial and casual in associations thus produced. The pains and pleasures thus forcibly associated with things, are not connected with them by any natural tie; and it is therefore, I thought, essential to the durability of these associations, that they should have become so intense and inveterate as to be practically indissoluble, before the habitual exercise of the power of analysis had commenced. For I now saw, or thought I saw, what I had always before received with incredulity—that the habit of analysis has a tendency to wear away the feelings: as indeed it has, when no other mental habit is cultivated, and the analysing spirit remains without its natural complements and correctives. The very excellence of analysis (I argued) is that it tends to weaken and undermine whatever is the result of prejudice; that it enables us mentally to separate ideas which have only casually clung together:

and no associations whatever could ultimately resist this dissolving force, were it not that we owe to analysis our clearest knowledge of the permanent sequences in nature; the real connexions between Things, not dependent on our will and feelings; natural laws, by virtue of which, in many cases, one thing is inseparable from another in fact; which laws, in proportion as they are clearly perceived and imaginatively realized, cause our ideas of things which are always joined together in Nature, to cohere more and more closely in our thoughts. Analytic habits may thus even strengthen the associations between causes and effects, means and ends, but tend altogether to weaken those which are, to speak familiarly, a *mere* matter of feeling. They are therefore (I thought) favourable to prudence and clear-sightedness, but a perpetual worm at the root both of the passions and of the virtues; and, above all, fearfully undermine all desires, and all pleasures, which are the effects of association, that is, according to the theory I held, all except the purely physical and organic; of the entire insufficiency of which to make life desirable, no one had a stronger conviction than I had. These were the laws of human nature, by which, as it seemed to me, I had been brought to my present state. All those to whom I looked up, were of opinion that the pleasure of sympathy with human beings, and the feelings which made the good of others, and especially of mankind on a large scale, the object of existence, were the greatest and surest sources of happiness. Of the truth of this I was convinced, but to know that a feeling would make me happy if I had it, did not give me the feeling. My education, I thought, had failed to create these feelings in sufficient strength to resist the dissolving influence of analysis, while the whole course of my intellectual cultivation had made precocious and premature analysis the inveterate habit of my mind. I was thus, as I said to myself, left stranded at the commencement of my voyage, with a well-equipped ship and a rudder, but no sail; without any real desire for the ends which I had been so carefully fitted out to work for: no delight in virtue, or the general good, but also just as little in anything else. The fountains of vanity and ambition seemed to have dried up within me, as completely as those of benevolence. I had had (as I reflected) some gratification of vanity at too early an age: I had obtained some distinction, and felt myself of some importance, before the desire of distinction and of importance had grown into a passion: and little as it was which I had attained, yet having been attained too early, like all pleasures enjoyed too soon, it had made me *blasé* [1] and indifferent to the pursuit. Thus neither selfish nor unselfish pleasures were pleasures to me. And there seemed no power in nature sufficient to begin the formation of my character anew, and create in a mind now irretrievably analytic, fresh associations of pleasure with any of the objects of human desire.

These were the thoughts which mingled with the dry heavy dejection of the melancholy winter of 1826–7. During this time I was not incapable of my usual occupations. I went on with them mechanically, by the mere force of habit. I had been so drilled in a certain sort of mental exercise, that I could still carry it on when all the spirit had gone out of it. I even composed and spoke several speeches at the debating society, how, or with what degree of success, I know not. Of four years continual speaking at that society, this is the only year of which I remember next to nothing. Two lines of Coleridge, in whom alone of all writers I have found a true description of what I felt, were often in my thoughts, not at this time (for I had never read them), but in a later period of the same mental malady:

Work without hope draws nectar in a sieve,
And hope without an object cannot live.

In all probability my case was by no means so peculiar as I fancied it, and I doubt not that many others have passed through a similar state; but the idiosyncrasies of my education had given to the general phenomenon a special character, which made it seem the natural effect of causes that it was hardly possible for time to remove.

[1] *blasé:* surfeited, blunted to pleasure from excess.

I frequently asked myself, if I could, or if I was bound to go on living, when life must be passed in this manner. I generally answered to myself, that I did not think I could possibly bear it beyond a year. When, however, not more than half that duration of time had elapsed, a small ray of light broke in upon my gloom. I was reading, accidentally, Marmontel's "Memoires," and came to the passage which relates his father's death, the distressed position of the family, and the sudden inspiration by which he, then a mere boy, felt and made them feel that he would be everything to them—would supply the place of all that they had lost. A vivid conception of the scene and its feelings came over me, and I was moved to tears. From this moment my burden grew lighter. The oppression of the thought that all feeling was dead within me, was gone. I was no longer hopeless: I was not a stock or a stone. I had still, it seemed, some of the material out of which all worth of character, and all capacity for happiness, are made. Relieved from my ever present sense of irremediable wretchedness, I gradually found that the ordinary incidents of life could again give me some pleasure; that I could again find enjoyment, not intense, but sufficient for cheerfulness, in sunshine and sky, in books, in conversation, in public affairs; and that there was, once more, excitement, though of a moderate kind, in exerting myself for my opinions, and for the public good. Thus the cloud gradually drew off, and I again enjoyed life: and though I had several relapses, some of which lasted many months, I never again was as miserable as I had been.

The experiences of this period had two very marked effects on my opinions and character. In the first place, they led me to adopt a theory of life, very unlike that on which I had before acted, and having much in common with what at that time I certainly had never heard of, the anti-self-consciousness theory of Carlyle. I never, indeed, wavered in the conviction that happiness is the test of all rules of conduct, and the end of life. But I now thought that this end was only to be attained by not making it the direct end.

Those only are happy (I thought) who have their minds fixed on some object other than their own happiness; on the happiness of others, on the improvement of mankind, even on some art or pursuit, followed not as a means, but as itself an ideal end. Aiming thus at something else, they find happiness by the way. The enjoyments of life (such was now my theory) are sufficient to make it a pleasant thing, when they are taken *en passant*,[2] without being made a principal object. Once make them so, and they are immediately felt to be insufficient. They will not bear a scrutinizing examination. Ask yourself whether you are happy, and you cease to be so. The only chance is to treat, not happiness, but some end external to it, as the purpose of life. Let your self-consciousness, your scrutiny, your self-interrogation, exhaust themselves on that; and if otherwise fortunately circumstanced you will inhale happiness with the air you breathe, without dwelling on it or thinking about it, without either forestalling it in imagination, or putting it to flight by fatal questioning. This theory now became the basis of my philosophy of life. And I still hold to it as the best theory for all those who have but a moderate degree of sensibility and of capacity for enjoyment, that is, for the great majority of mankind.

The other important change which my opinions at this time underwent, was that I, for the first time, gave its proper place, among the prime necessities of human well-being, to the internal culture of the individual. I ceased to attach almost exclusive importance to the ordering of outward circumstances, and the training of the human being for speculation and for action.

I had now learnt by experience that the passive susceptibilities needed to be cultivated as well as the active capacities, and required to be nourished and enriched as well as guided. I did not, for an instant, lose sight of, or undervalue, that part of the truth which I had seen before; I never turned recreant to intellectual culture, or ceased to consider the power and practice of analysis as an essential condition both

2 *en passant:* incidentally.

of individual and of social improvement. But I thought that it had consequences which required to be corrected, by joining other kinds of cultivation with it. The maintenance of a due balance among the faculties, now seemed to me of primary importance. The cultivation of the feelings became one of the cardinal points in my ethical and philosophical creed. And my thoughts and inclinations turned in an increasing degree towards whatever seemed capable of being instrumental to that object.

I now began to find meaning in the things which I had read or heard about the importance of poetry and art as instruments of human culture. But it was some time longer before I began to know this by personal experience. The only one of the imaginative arts in which I had from childhood taken great pleasure, was music; the best effect of which (and in this it surpasses perhaps every other art) consists in exciting enthusiasm; in winding up to a high pitch those feelings of an elevated kind which are already in the character, but to which this excitement gives a glow and a fervour, which, though transitory at its utmost height, is precious for sustaining them at other times. This effect of music I had often experienced; but like all my pleasurable susceptibilities it was suspended during the gloomy period. I had sought relief again and again from this quarter, but found none. After the tide had turned, and I was in process of recovery, I had been helped forward by music, but in a much less elevated manner. I at this time first became acquainted with Weber's Oberon, and the extreme pleasure which I drew from its delicious melodies did me good, by showing me a source of pleasure to which I was as susceptible as ever. The good, however, was much impaired by the thought, that the pleasure of music (as is quite true of such pleasure as this was, that of mere tune) fades with familiarity, and requires either to be revived by intermittence, or fed by continual novelty. And it is very characteristic both of my then state, and of the general tone of my mind at this period of my life, that I was seriously tormented by the thought of the exhaustibility of musi-

cal combinations. The octave consists only of five tones and two semitones, which can be put together in only a limited number of ways, of which but a small proportion are beautiful: most of these, it seemed to me, must have been already discovered, and there could not be room for a long succession of Mozarts and Webers, to strike out, as these had done, entirely new and surpassingly rich veins of musical beauty. This source of anxiety may, perhaps, be thought to resemble that of the philosophers of Laputa, who feared lest the sun should be burnt out. It was, however, connected with the best feature in my character, and the only good point to be found in my very unromantic and in no way honourable distress. For though my dejection, honestly looked at, could not be called other than egotistical, produced by the ruin, as I thought, of my fabric of happiness, yet the destiny of mankind in general was ever in my thoughts, and could not be separated from my own. I felt that the flaw in my life, must be a flaw in life itself; that the question was, whether, if the reformers of society and government could succeed in their objects, and every person in the community were free and in a state of physical comfort, the pleasures of life, being no longer kept up by struggle and privation, would cease to be pleasures. And I felt that unless I could see my way to some better hope than this for human happiness in general, my dejection must continue; but that if I could see such an outlet, I should then look on the world with pleasure; content as far as I was myself concerned, with any fair share of the general lot.

This state of my thoughts and feelings made the fact of my reading Wordsworth for the first time (in the autumn of 1828), an important event in my life. I took up the collection of his poems from curiosity, with no expectation of mental relief from it, though I had before resorted to poetry with that hope. In the worst period of my depression, I had read through the whole of Byron (then new to me), to try whether a poet, whose peculiar department was supposed to be that of the intenser feelings, could rouse any feeling in me. As might be expected, I got no good from this reading, but the reverse. The poet's state of mind was too like my own. His was the lament of a man who had worn out all pleasures, and who seemed to think that life, to all who possess the good things of it, must necessarily be the vapid, uninteresting thing which I found it. His Harold and Manfred had the same burden on them which I had; and I was not in a frame of mind to desire any comfort from the vehement sensual passion of his Giaours, or the sullenness of his Laras. But while Byron was exactly what did not suit my condition, Wordsworth was exactly what did. I had looked into the Excursion two or three years before, and found little in it; and I should probably have found as little, had I read it at this time. But the miscellaneous poems, in the two-volume edition of 1815 (to which little of value was added in the latter part of the author's life), proved to be the precise thing for my mental wants at that particular juncture.

In the first place, these poems addressed themselves powerfully to one of the strongest of my pleasurable susceptibilities, the love of rural objects and natural scenery; to which I had been indebted not only for much of the pleasure of my life, but quite recently for relief from one of my longest relapses into depression. In this power of rural beauty over me, there was a foundation laid for taking pleasure in Wordsworth's poetry; the more so, as his scenery lies mostly among mountains, which, owing to my early Pyrenean excursion, were my ideal of natural beauty. But Wordsworth would never have had any great effect on me, if he had merely placed before me beautiful pictures of natural scenery. Scott does this still better than Wordsworth, and a very second-rate landscape does it more effectually than any poet. What made Wordsworth's poems a medicine for my state of mind, was that they expressed, not mere outward beauty, but states of feeling, and of thought coloured by feeling, under the excitement of beauty. They seemed to be the very culture of the feelings, which I was in quest of. In them I seemed to draw from a source of inward joy, of sympathetic and imaginative pleasure, which could be shared in by all human beings; which had no connexion with struggle or imperfection, but would be made richer by every improvement in the physical or social condition of mankind. From them I seemed to learn what would be the perennial sources of happiness, when all the greater evils of life shall have been removed. And I felt myself at once better and happier as I came under their influence. There have certainly been, even in our own age, greater poets than Wordsworth; but poetry of deeper and loftier feeling could not have done for me at that time what his did. I needed to be made to feel that there was real, permanent happiness in tranquil contemplation. Wordsworth taught me this, not only without turning away from, but with a greatly increased interest in the common feelings and common destiny of human beings. And the delight which these poems gave me, proved that with culture of this sort, there was nothing to dread from the most confirmed habit of analysis. At the conclusion of the Poems came the famous Ode, falsely called Platonic, "Intimations of Immortality": in which, along with more than his usual sweetness of melody and rhythm, and along with the two passages of grand imagery but bad philosophy so often quoted, I found that he too had had similar experience to mine; that he also had felt that the first freshness of youthful enjoyment of life was not lasting; but that he had sought for compensation, and found it, in the way in which he was now teaching me to find it. The result was that I gradually, but completely, emerged from my habitual depression, and was never again subject to it. I long continued to value Wordsworth less according to his intrinsic merits, than by the measure of what he had done for me. Compared with the greatest poets, he may be said to be the poet of unpoetical natures, possessed of quiet and contemplative tastes. But unpoetical natures are precisely those which require poetic cultivation. This cultivation Wordsworth is much more fitted to give, than poets who are intrinsically far more poets than he.

It so fell out that the merits of Wordsworth were the occasion of my first public declaration of my new way of thinking, and separation from those of my habitual companions who had not undergone a similar change. The person with whom at that time I was most in the habit of comparing notes on such subjects was Roebuck, and I induced him to read Wordsworth, in whom he also at first seemed to find much to admire: but I, like most Wordsworthians, threw myself into strong antagonism to Byron, both as a poet and as to his influence on the character. Roebuck, all whose instincts were those of action and struggle, had, on the contrary, a strong relish and great admiration of Byron, whose writings he regarded as the poetry of human life, while Wordsworth's, according to him, was that of flowers and butterflies. We agreed to have the fight out at our Debating Society, where we accordingly discussed for two evenings the comparative merits of Byron and Wordsworth, propounding and illustrating by long recitations our respective theories of poetry: Sterling also, in a brilliant speech, putting forward his particular theory. This was the first debate on any weighty subject in which Roebuck and I had been on opposite sides. The schism between us widened from this time more and more, though we continued for some years longer to be companions. In the beginning, our chief divergence related to the cultivation of the feelings. Roebuck was in many respects very different from the vulgar notion of a Benthamite or Utilitarian. He was a lover of poetry and of most of the fine arts. He took great pleasure in music, in dramatic performances, especially in painting, and himself drew and designed landscapes with great facility and beauty. But he never could be made to see that these things have any value as aids in the formation of character. Personally, instead of being, as Benthamites are supposed to be, void of feeling, he had very quick and strong sensibilities. But, like most Englishmen who have feelings, he found his feelings stand very much in his way. He was much more susceptible to the painful sympathies than to the pleasurable, and

looking for his happiness elsewhere, he wished that his feelings should be deadened rather than quickened. And, in truth, the English character, and English social circumstances, make it so seldom possible to derive happiness from the exercise of the sympathies, that it is not wonderful if they count for little in an Englishman's scheme of life. In most other countries the paramount importance of the sympathies as a constituent of individual happiness is an axiom, taken for granted rather than needing any formal statement; but most English thinkers almost seem to regard them as necessary evils, required for keeping men's actions benevolent and compassionate. Roebuck was, or appeared to be, this kind of Englishman. He saw little good in any cultivation of the feelings, and none at all in cultivating them through the imagination, which he thought was only cultivating illusions. It was in vain I urged on him that the imaginative emotion which an idea, when vividly conceived, excites in us, is not an illusion but a fact, as real as any of the other qualities of objects; and far from implying anything erroneous and delusive in our mental apprehension of the object, is quite consistent with the most accurate knowledge and most perfect practical recognition of all its physical and intellectual laws and relations. The intensest feeling of the beauty of a cloud lighted by the setting sun, is no hindrance to my knowing that the cloud is vapour of water, subject to all the laws of vapours in a state of suspension; and I am just as likely to allow for, and act on, these physical laws whenever there is occasion to do so, as if I had been incapable of perceiving any distinction between beauty and ugliness.

While my intimacy with Roebuck diminished, I fell more and more into friendly intercourse with our Coleridgian adversaries in the Society, Frederick Maurice and John Sterling, both subsequently so well known, the former by his writings, the latter through the biographies by Hare and Carlyle. Of these two friends, Maurice was the thinker, Sterling the orator, and impassioned expositor of thoughts which, at this period, were almost entirely formed for him by Maurice.

With Maurice I had for some time been acquainted through Eyton Tooke, who had known him at Cambridge, and although my discussions with him were almost always disputes, I had carried away from them much that helped to build up my new fabric of thought, in the same way as I was deriving much from Coleridge, and from the writings of Goethe and other German authors which I read during these years. I have so deep a respect for Maurice's character and purposes, as well as for his great mental gifts, that it is with some unwillingness I say anything which may seem to place him on a less high eminence than I would gladly be able to accord to him. But I have always thought that there was more intellectual power wasted in Maurice than in any other of my contemporaries. Few of them certainly have had so much to waste. Great powers of generalization, rare ingenuity and subtlety, and a wide perception of important and unobvious truths, served him not for putting something better into the place of the worthless heap of received opinions on the great subjects of thought, but for proving to his own mind that the Church of England had known everything from the first, that all the truths on the ground of which the Church and orthodoxy have been attacked (many of which he saw as clearly as any one) are not only consistent with the Thirty-nine Articles, but are better understood and expressed in those Articles than by any one who rejects them. I have never been able to find any other explanation of this, than by attributing it to that timidity of conscience, combined with original sensitiveness of temperament, which has so often driven highly gifted men into Romanism from the need of a firmer support than they can find in the independent conclusions of their own judgment. Any more vulgar kind of timidity no one who knew Maurice would ever think of imputing to him, even if he had not given public proof of his freedom from it, by his ultimate collision with some of the opinions commonly regarded as orthodox, and by his noble origination of the Christian Socialist movement. The nearest parallel to him, in a moral point of view, is Coleridge, to whom, in merely intellectual power, apart from poetical genius, I think him decidedly superior. At this time, however, he might be described as a disciple of Coleridge, and Sterling as a disciple of Coleridge and of him. The modifications which were taking place in my old opinions gave me some points of contact with them; and both Maurice and Sterling were of considerable use to my development. With Sterling I soon became very intimate, and was more attached to him than I have ever been to any other man. He was indeed one of the most lovable of men. His frank, cordial, affectionate, and expansive character; a love of truth alike conspicuous in the highest things and the humblest; a generous and ardent nature which threw itself with impetuosity into the opinions it adopted, but was as eager to do justice to the doctrines and the men it was opposed to, as to make war on what it thought their errors; and an equal devotion to the two cardinal points of Liberty and Duty, formed a combination of qualities as attractive to me, as to all others who knew him as well as I did. With his open mind and heart, he found no difficulty in joining hands with me across the gulf which as yet divided our opinions. He told me how he and others had looked upon me (from hearsay information), as a "made" or manufactured man, having had a certain impress of opinion stamped on me which I could only reproduce; and what a change took place in his feelings when he found, in the discussion on Wordsworth and Byron, that Wordsworth, and all which that name implies, "belonged" to me as much as to him and his friends. The failure of his health soon scattered all his plans of life, and compelled him to live at a distance from London, so that after the first year or two of our acquaintance, we only saw each other at distant intervals. But (as he said himself in one of his letters to Carlyle) when we did meet it was like brothers. Though he was never, in the full sense of the word, a profound thinker, his openness of mind, and the moral courage in which he greatly surpassed Maurice, made him outgrow the dominion which Maurice and Coleridge had once exercised over his intellect; though he retained to the last a great but discriminating admiration of both, and towards Maurice a warm affection. Except in that short and transitory phasis of his life, during which he made the mistake of becoming a clergyman, his mind was ever progressive: and the advance he always seemed to have made when I saw him after an interval, made me apply to him what Goethe said of Schiller, "er hatte eine furchtliche Fortschreitung." [3] He and I started from intellectual points almost as wide apart as the poles, but the distance between us was always diminishing: if I made steps towards some of his opinions, he, during his short life, was constantly approximating more and more to several of mine: and if he had lived, and had health and vigour to prosecute his ever assiduous self-culture, there is no knowing how much further this spontaneous assimilation might have proceeded.

After 1829 I withdrew from attendance on the Debating Society. I had had enough of speech-making, and was glad to carry on my private studies and meditations without any immediate call for outward assertion of their results. I found the fabric of my old and taught opinions giving way in many fresh places, and I never allowed it to fall to pieces, but was incessantly occupied in weaving it anew. I never, in the course of my transition, was content to remain, for ever so short a time, confused and unsettled. When I had taken in any new idea, I could not rest till I had adjusted its relation to my old opinions, and ascertained exactly how far its effect ought to extend in modifying or superseding them.

The conflicts which I had so often had to sustain in defending the theory of government laid down in Bentham's and my father's writings, and the acquaintance I had obtained with other schools of political thinking, made me aware of many things which that doctrine, professing to be a theory of government in general, ought to have made room for and did not. But these things, as yet, remained with me rather as corrections to be made in

applying the theory to practice, than as defects in the theory. I felt that politics could not be a science of specific experience; and that the accusations against the Benthamic theory of *being* a theory, of proceeding *à priori* [4] by way of general reasoning, instead of Baconian experiment, showed complete ignorance of Bacon's principles, and of the necessary conditions of experimental investigation. At this juncture appeared in the Edinburgh Review, Macaulay's famous attack on my father's Essay on Government. This gave me much to think about. I saw that Macaulay's conception of the logic of politics was erroneous; that he stood up for the empirical mode of treating political phenomena, against the philosophical; that even in physical science his notions of philosophizing might have recognized Kepler, but would have excluded Newton and Laplace. But I could not help feeling, that though the tone was unbecoming (an error for which the writer, at a later period, made the most ample and honourable amends), there was truth in several of his strictures on my father's treatment of the subject; that my father's premises were really too narrow, and included but a small number of the general truths, on which, in politics, the important consequences depend. Identity of interest between the governing body and the community at large, is not, in any practical sense which can be attached to it, the only thing on which good government depends; neither can this identity of interest be secured by the mere conditions of election. I was not at all satisfied with the mode in which my father met the criticisms of Macaulay. He did not, as I thought he ought to have done, justify himself by saying, "I was not writing a scientific treatise on politics, I was writing an argument for parliamentary reform." He treated Macaulay's argument as simply irrational; an attack upon the reasoning faculty; an example of the saying of Hobbes, that when reason is against a

---

[3] *er hatte eine,* etc.: "he had a terrible progression" (i.e. development).

[4] *à priori:* reasoning from assumed or self-evident definitions or principles derived from reflection as contrasted with the Baconian method of reasoning to principles derived from observation of facts and generalizations from them, i.e. the *à posteriori* procedure.

man, a man will be against reason. This made me think that there was really something more fundamentally erroneous in my father's conception of philosophical method, as applicable to politics, than I had hitherto supposed there was. But I did not at first see clearly what the error might be. At last it flashed upon me all at once in the course of other studies. In the early part of 1830 I had begun to put on paper the ideas on Logic (chiefly on the distinctions among Terms, and the import of Propositions) which had been suggested and in part worked out in the morning conversations already spoken of. Having secured these thoughts from being lost, I pushed on into the other parts of the subject, to try whether I could do anything further towards clearing up the theory of logic generally. I grappled at once with the problem of Induction, postponing that of Reasoning, on the ground that it is necessary to obtain premises before we can reason from them. Now, Induction is mainly a process for finding the causes of effects: and in attempting to fathom the mode of tracing causes and effects in physical science, I soon saw that in the more perfect of the sciences, we ascend, by generalization from particulars, to the tendencies of causes considered singly, and then reason downward from those separate tendencies, to the effect of the same causes when combined. I then asked myself, what is the ultimate analysis of this deductive process; the common theory of the syllogism evidently throwing no light upon it. My practice (learnt from Hobbes and my father) being to study abstract principles by means of the best concrete instances I could find, the Composition of Forces, in dynamics, occurred to me as the most complete example of the logical process I was investigating. On examining, accordingly, what the mind does when it applies the principle of the Composition of Forces, I found that it performs a simple act of addition. It adds the separate effect of the one force to the separate effect of the other, and puts down the sum of these separate effects as the joint effect. But is this a legitimate process? In dynamics, and in all the mathematical branches of physics, it is; but

in some other cases, as in chemistry, it is not; and I then recollected that something not unlike this was pointed out as one of the distinctions between chemical and mechanical phenomena, in the introduction to that favourite of my boyhood, Thomson's System of Chemistry. This distinction at once made my mind clear as to what was perplexing me in respect to the philosophy of politics. I now saw, that a science is either deductive or experimental, according as, in the province it deals with, the effects of causes when conjoined, are or are not the sums of the effects which the same causes produce when separate. It followed that politics must be a deductive science. It thus appeared, that both Macaulay and my father were wrong; the one in assimilating the method of philosophizing in politics to the purely experimental method of chemistry; while the other, though right in adopting a deductive method, had made a wrong selection of one, having taken as the type of deduction, not the appropriate process, that of the deductive branches of natural philosophy, but the inappropriate one of pure geometry, which, not being a science of causation at all, does not require or admit of any summing-up of effects. A foundation was thus laid in my thoughts for the principal chapters of what I afterwards published on the Logic of the Moral Sciences; and my new position in respect to my old political creed, now became perfectly definite.

If I am asked, what system of political philosophy I substituted for that which, as a philosophy, I had abandoned, I answer, No system: only a conviction that the true system was something much more complex and many-sided than I had previously had any idea of, and that its office was to supply, not a set of model institutions, but principles from which the institutions suitable to any given circumstances might be deduced. The influences of European, that is to say, Continental, thought, and especially those of the reaction of the nineteenth century against the eighteenth, were now streaming in upon me. They came from various quarters: from the writings of Coleridge, which I had begun to read with interest even before the change in my opinions; from the Coleridgians with whom I was in personal intercourse; from what I had read of Goethe; from Carlyle's early articles in the Edinburgh and Foreign Reviews, though for a long time I saw nothing in these (as my father saw nothing in them to the last) but insane rhapsody. From these sources, and from the acquaintance I kept up with the French literature of the time, I derived, among other ideas which the general turning upside down of the opinions of European thinkers had brought uppermost, these in particular: That the human mind has a certain order of possible progress, in which some things must precede others, an order which governments and public instructors can modify to some, but not to an unlimited extent: that all questions of political institutions are relative, not absolute, and that different stages of human progress not only *will* have, but *ought* to have, different institutions: that government is always either in the hands, or passing into the hands, of whatever is the strongest power in society, and that what this power is, does not depend on institutions, but institutions on it: that any general theory or philosophy of politics supposes a previous theory of human progress, and that this is the same thing with a philosophy of history. These opinions, true in the main, were held in an exaggerated and violent manner by the thinkers with whom I was now most accustomed to compare notes, and who, as usual with a reaction, ignored that half of the truth which the thinkers of the eighteenth century saw. But though, at one period of my progress, I for some time undervalued that great century, I never joined in the reaction against it, but kept as firm hold of one side of the truth as I took of the other. The fight between the nineteenth century and the eighteenth always reminded me of the battle about the shield, one side of which was white and the other black. I marvelled at the blind rage with which the combatants rushed against one another. I applied to them, and to Coleridge himself, many of Coleridge's sayings about half truths; and Goethe's device, "many-sidedness," was one which I would most willingly, at this period, have taken for mine.

The writers by whom, more than by any others, a new mode of political thinking was brought home to me, were those of the St. Simonian school in France. In 1829 and 1830 I became acquainted with some of their writings. They were then only in the earlier stages of their speculations. They had not yet dressed out their philosophy as a religion, nor had they organized their scheme of Socialism. They were just beginning to question the principle of hereditary property. I was by no means prepared to go with them even this length; but I was greatly struck with the connected view which they for the first time presented to me, of the natural order of human progress; and especially with their division of all history into organic periods and critical periods. During the organic periods (they said) mankind accept with firm conviction some positive creed, claiming jurisdiction over all their actions, and containing more or less of truth and adaptation to the needs of humanity. Under its influence they make all the progress compatible with the creed, and finally outgrow it; when a period follows of criticism and negation, in which mankind lose their old convictions without acquiring any new ones, of a general or authoritative character, except the conviction that the old are false. The period of Greek and Roman polytheism, so long as really believed in by instructed Greeks and Romans, was an organic period, succeeded by the critical or sceptical period of the Greek philosophers. Another organic period came in with Christianity. The corresponding critical period began with the Reformation, has lasted ever since, still lasts, and cannot altogether cease until a new organic period has been inaugurated by the triumph of a yet more advanced creed. These ideas, I knew, were not peculiar to the St. Simonians; on the contrary, they were the general property of Europe, or at least of Germany and France, but they had never, to my knowledge, been so completely systematized as by these writers, nor the distinguishing characteristics of a critical period so powerfully set forth; for I was not then acquainted with Fichte's Lectures on "The Characteristics of the Present Age." In Carlyle, indeed, I found bitter denunciations of an "age of unbelief," and of the present age as such, which I, like most people at that time, supposed to be passionate protests in favour of the old modes of belief. But all that was true in these denunciations, I thought that I found more calmly and philosophically stated by the St. Simonians. Among their publications, too, there was one which seemed to me far superior to the rest; in which the general idea was matured into something much more definite and instructive. This was an early work of Auguste Comte, who then called himself, and even announced himself in the title-page as, a pupil of Saint Simon. In this tract M. Comte first put forth the doctrine, which he afterwards so copiously illustrated, of the natural succession of three stages in every department of human knowledge: first, the theological, next the metaphysical, and lastly, the positive stage; and contended, that social science must be subject to the same law; that the feudal and Catholic system was the concluding phasis of the theological state of the social science, Protestantism the commencement, and the doctrines of the French Revolution the consummation, of the metaphysical; and that its positive state was yet to come. This doctrine harmonized well with my existing notions, to which it seemed to give a scientific shape. I already regarded the methods of physical science as the proper models for political. But the chief benefit which I derived at this time from the trains of thought suggested by the St. Simonians and by Comte, was, that I obtained a clearer conception than ever before of the peculiarities of an era of transition in opinion, and ceased to mistake the moral and intellectual characteristics of such an era, for the normal attributes of humanity. I looked forward, through the present age of loud disputes but generally weak convictions, to a future which shall unite the best qualities of the critical with the best qualities of the organic periods; unchecked liberty of thought, unbounded freedom of individual action in all modes not hurtful to others; but also, convictions as to what is right and wrong, useful and pernicious, deeply engraven on the feelings by early education and general unanimity of sentiment, and so firmly grounded in reason and in the true exigencies of life, that they shall not, like all former and present creeds, religious, ethical, and political, require to be periodically thrown off and replaced by others.

M. Comte soon left the St. Simonians, and I lost sight of him and his writings for a number of years. But the St. Simonians I continued to cultivate. I was kept *au courant* of their progress by one of their most enthusiastic disciples, M. Gustave d'Eichthal, who about that time passed a considerable interval in England. I was introduced to their chiefs, Bazard and Enfantin, in 1830; and as long as their public teachings and proselytism continued, I read nearly everything they wrote. Their criticisms on the common doctrines of Liberalism seemed to me full of important truth; and it was partly by their writings that my eyes were opened to the very limited and temporary value of the old political economy, which assumes private property and inheritance as indefeasible facts, and freedom of production and exchange as the *dernier mot*[5] of social improvement. The scheme gradually unfolded by the St. Simonians, under which the labour and capital of society would be managed for the general account of the community, every individual being required to take a share of labour, either as thinker, teacher, artist, or producer, all being classed according to their capacity, and remunerated according to their work, appeared to me a far superior description of Socialism to Owen's. Their aim seemed to me desirable and rational, however their means might be inefficacious; and though I neither believed in the practicability, nor in the beneficial operation of their social machinery, I felt that the proclamation of such an ideal of human society could not but tend to give a beneficial direction to the efforts of others to bring

5 *dernier mot:* last word.

society, as at present constituted, nearer to some ideal standard. I honoured them most of all for what they have been most cried down for—the boldness and freedom from prejudice with which they treated the subject of family, the most important of any, and needing more fundamental alterations than remain to be made in any other great social institution, but on which scarcely any reformer has the courage to touch. In proclaiming the perfect equality of men and women, and an entirely new order of things in regard to their relations with one another, the St. Simonians, in common with Owen and Fourier, have entitled themselves to the grateful remembrance of future generations.

In giving an account of this period of my life, I have only specified such of my new impressions as appeared to me, both at the time and since, to be a kind of turning points, marking a definite progress in my mode of thought. But these few selected points give a very insufficient idea of the quantity of thinking which I carried on respecting a host of subjects during these years of transition. Much of this, it is true, consisted in rediscovering things known to all the world, which I had previously disbelieved, or disregarded. But the rediscovery was to me a discovery, giving me plenary possession of the truths, not as traditional platitudes, but fresh from their source: and it seldom failed to place them in some new light, by which they were reconciled with, and seemed to confirm while they modified, the truths less generally known which lay in my early opinions, and in no essential part of which I at any time wavered. All my new thinking only laid the foundation of these more deeply and strongly, while it often removed misapprehension and confusion of ideas which had perverted their effect. For example, during the later returns of my dejection, the doctrine of what is called Philosophical Necessity weighed on my existence like an incubus. I felt as if I was scientifically proved to be the helpless slave of antecedent circumstances; as if my character and that of all others had been formed for us by agencies beyond our control, and was wholly out of our own power. I often said to myself, what a relief it would be if I could disbelieve the doctrine of the formation of character by circumstances; and remembering the wish of Fox respecting the doctrine of resistance to governments, that it might never be forgotten by kings, nor remembered by subjects, I said that it would be a blessing if the doctrine of necessity could be believed by all *quoad* [6] the characters of others, and disbelieved in regard to their own. I pondered painfully on the subject, till gradually I saw light through it. I perceived, that the word Necessity, as a name for the doctrine of Cause and Effect applied to human action, carried with it a misleading association; and that this association was the operative force in the depressing and paralysing influence which I had experienced: I saw that though our character is formed by circumstances, our own desires can do much to shape those circumstances; and that what is really inspiriting and ennobling in the doctrine of freewill, is the conviction that we have real power over the formation of our own character; that our will, by influencing some of our circumstances, can modify our future habits or capabilities of willing. All this was entirely consistent with the doctrine of circumstances, or rather, was that doctrine itself, properly understood. From that time I drew in my own mind, a clear distinction between the doctrine of circumstances, and Fatalism; discarding altogether the misleading word Necessity. The theory, which I now for the first time rightly apprehended, ceased altogether to be discouraging, and besides the relief to my spirits, I no longer suffered under the burden, so heavy to one who aims at being a reformer in opinions, of thinking one doctrine true, and the contrary doctrine morally beneficial. The train of thought which had extricated me from this dilemma, seemed to me, in after years, fitted to render a similar service to others; and it now forms the chapter on Liberty and Necessity in the concluding Book of my system of Logic.

Again, in politics, though I no longer accepted the doctrine of the Essay on Government as a scientific theory; though I ceased to consider representative democ-

6 *quoad:* as to.

racy as an absolute principle, and regarded it as a question of time, place, and circumstance; though I now looked upon the choice of political institutions as a moral and educational question more than one of material interests, thinking that it ought to be decided mainly by the consideration, what great improvement in life and culture stands next in order for the people concerned, as the condition of their further progress, and what institutions are most likely to promote that; nevertheless, this change in the premises of my political philosophy did not alter my practical political creed as to the requirements of my own time and country. I was as much as ever a Radical and Democrat for Europe, and especially for England. I thought the predominance of the aristocratic classes, the noble and the rich, in the English constitution, an evil worth any struggle to get rid of; not on account of taxes, or any such comparatively small inconvenience, but as the great demoralizing agency in the country. Demoralizing, first, because it made the conduct of the Government an example of gross public immorality, through the predominance of private over public interests in the State, and the abuse of the powers of legislation for the advantage of classes. Secondly, and in a still greater degree, because the respect of the multitude always attaching itself principally to that which, in the existing state of society, is the chief passport to power; and under English institutions, riches, hereditary or acquired, being the almost exclusive source of political importance; riches, and the signs of riches, were almost the only things really respected, and the life of the people was mainly devoted to the pursuit of them. I thought, that while the higher and richer classes held the power of government, the instruction and improvement of the mass of the people were contrary to the self-interest of those classes, because tending to render the people more powerful for throwing off the yoke: but if the democracy obtained a large, and perhaps the principal share, in the governing power, it would become the interest of the opulent classes to promote their education, in order to ward off really mischievous errors, and especially those which would lead to unjust violations of property. On these grounds I was not only as ardent as ever for democratic institutions, but earnestly hoped that Owenite, St. Simonian, and all other anti-property doctrines might spread widely among the poorer classes; not that I thought those doctrines true, or desired that they should be acted on, but in order that the higher classes might be made to see that they had more to fear from the poor when uneducated, than when educated.

In this frame of mind the French Revolution of July found me. It roused my utmost enthusiasm, and gave me, as it were, a new existence. I went at once to Paris, was introduced to Lafayette, and laid the groundwork of the intercourse I afterwards kept up with several of the active chiefs of the extreme popular party. After my return I entered warmly, as a writer, into the political discussions of the time; which soon became still more exciting, by the coming in of Lord Grey's Ministry, and the proposing of the Reform Bill. For the next few years I wrote copiously in newspapers. It was about this time that Fonblanque, who had for some time written the political articles in the Examiner, became the proprietor and editor of the paper. It is not forgotten with what verve and talent, as well as fine wit, he carried it on, during the whole period of Lord Grey's Ministry, and what importance it assumed as the principal representative, in the newspaper press, of Radical opinions. The distinguishing character of the paper was given to it entirely by his own articles, which formed at least three-fourths of all the original writing contained in it: but of the remaining fourth I contributed during those years a much larger share than any one else. I wrote nearly all the articles on French subjects, including a weekly summary of French politics, often extending to considerable length; together with many leading articles on general politics, commercial and financial legislation, and any miscellaneous subjects in which I felt interested, and which were suitable to the paper, including occasional reviews of books. Mere newspaper articles on the occurrences or questions of the moment, gave no opportunity for the development of any general mode of thought; but I attempted, in the beginning of 1831, to embody in a series of articles, headed "The Spirit of the Age," some of my new opinions, and especially to point out in the character of the present age, the anomalies and evils characteristic of the transition from a system of opinions which had worn out, to another only in process of being formed. These articles were, I fancy, lumbering in style, and not lively or striking enough to be, at any time, acceptable to newspaper readers; but had they been far more attractive, still, at that particular moment, when great political changes were impending, and engrossing all minds, these discussions were ill-timed, and missed fire altogether. The only effect which I know to have been produced by them, was that Carlyle, then living in a secluded part of Scotland, read them in his solitude, and saying to himself (as he afterwards told me) "Here is a new Mystic," inquired on coming to London that autumn respecting their authorship; an inquiry which was the immediate cause of our becoming personally acquainted.

I have already mentioned Carlyle's earlier writings as one of the channels through which I received the influences which enlarged my early narrow creed; but I do not think that those writings, by themselves, would ever have had any effect on my opinions. What truths they contained, though of the very kind which I was already receiving from other quarters, were presented in a form and vesture less suited than any other to give them access to a mind trained as mine had been. They seemed a haze of poetry and German metaphysics, in which almost the only clear thing was a strong animosity to most of the opinions which were the basis of my mode of thought; religious scepticism, utilitarianism, the doctrine of circumstances, and the attaching any importance to democracy, logic, or political economy. Instead of my having been taught anything, in the first instance, by Carlyle, it was only in proportion as I came to see the same truths through media more suited to my mental constitution, that I recognised them in his writings.

Then, indeed, the wonderful power with which he put them forth made a deep impression upon me, and I was during a long period one of his most fervent admirers; but the good his writings did me, was not as philosophy to instruct, but as poetry to animate. Even at the time when our acquaintance commenced, I was not sufficiently advanced in my new modes of thought, to appreciate him fully; a proof of which is, that on his showing me the manuscript of Sartor Resartus, his best and greatest work, which he had just then finished, I made little of it; though when it came out about two years afterwards in Fraser's Magazine I read it with enthusiastic admiration and the keenest delight. I did not seek and cultivate Carlyle less on account of the fundamental differences in our philosophy. He soon found out that I was not "another mystic," and when for the sake of my own integrity I wrote to him a distinct profession of all those of my opinions which I knew he most disliked, he replied that the chief difference between us was that I "was as yet consciously nothing of a mystic." I do not know at what period he gave up the expectation that I was destined to become one; but though both his and my opinions underwent in subsequent years considerable changes, we never approached much nearer to each other's modes of thought than we were in the first years of our acquaintance. I did not, however, deem myself a competent judge of Carlyle. I felt that he was a poet, and that I was not; that he was a man of intuition, which I was not; and that as such, he not only saw many things long before me, which I could, only when they were pointed out to me, hobble after and prove, but that it was highly probable he could see many things which were not visible to me even after they were pointed out. I knew that I could not see round him, and could never be certain that I saw over him; and I never presumed to judge him with any definiteness, until he was interpreted to me by one greatly the superior of us both—who was more a poet than he, and more a thinker than I—whose own mind and nature included his, and infinitely more.

Among the persons of intellect whom I had known of old, the one with whom I had now most points of agreement was the elder Austin. I have mentioned that he always set himself in opposition to our early sectarianism; and latterly he had, like myself, come under new influences. Having been appointed Professor of Jurisprudence in the London University (now University College), he had lived for some time at Bonn to study for his Lectures; and the influences of German literature and of the German character and state of society had made a very perceptible change in his views of life. His personal disposition was much softened; he was less militant and polemic; his tastes had begun to turn themselves towards the poetic and contemplative. He attached much less importance than formerly to outward changes; unless accompanied by a better cultivation of the inward nature. He had a strong distaste for the general meanness of English life, the absence of enlarged thoughts and unselfish desires, the low objects on which the faculties of all classes of the English are intent. Even the kind of public interests which Englishmen care for, he held in very little esteem. He thought that there was more practical good government, and (which is true enough) infinitely more care for the education and mental improvement of all ranks of the people, under the Prussian monarchy, than under the English representative government: and he held, with the French *Economistes,* that the real security for good government is "un peuple éclairé," [7] which is not always the fruit of popular institutions, and which if it could be had without them, would do their work better than they. Though he approved of the Reform Bill, he predicted, what in fact occurred, that it would not produce the great immediate improvements in government, which many expected from it. The men, he said, who could do these great things, did not exist in the country. There were many points of sympathy between him and me, both in the new opinions he had adopted and in the old ones which he retained. Like me, he never ceased to be an utili-

7 *un peuple éclairé:* an enlightened people.

tarian, and with all his love of the Germans, and enjoyment of their literature, never became in the smallest degree reconciled to the innate-principle metaphysics. He cultivated more and more a kind of German religion, a religion of poetry and feeling with little, if anything, of positive dogma; while, in politics (and here it was that I most differed with him) he acquired an indifference, bordering on contempt, for the progress of popular institutions: though he rejoiced in that of Socialism, as the most effectual means of compelling the powerful classes to educate the people, and to impress on them the only real means of permanently improving their material condition, a limitation of their numbers. Neither was he, at this time, fundamentally opposed to Socialism in itself as an ultimate result of improvement. He professed great disrespect for what he called "the universal principles of human nature of the political economists," and insisted on the evidence which history and daily experience afford of the "extraordinary pliability of human nature" (a phrase which I have somewhere borrowed from him); nor did he think it possible to set any positive bounds to the moral capabilities which might unfold themselves in mankind, under an enlightened direction of social and educational influences. Whether he retained all these opinions to the end of life I know not. Certainly the modes of thinking of his later years, and especially of his last publication, were much more Tory in their general character than those which he held at this time.

My father's tone of thought and feeling, I now felt myself at a great distance from: greater, indeed, than a full and calm explanation and reconsideration on both sides, might have shown to exist in reality. But my father was not one with whom calm and full explanations on fundamental points of doctrine could be expected, at least with one whom he might consider as, in some sort, a deserter from his standard. Fortunately we were almost always in strong agreement on the political questions of the day, which engrossed a large part of his interest and of his conversation. On those matters of opinion on which we differed, we talked little. He knew that the habit of thinking for myself, which his mode of education had fostered, sometimes led me to opinions different from his, and he perceived from time to time that I did not always tell him *how* different. I expected no good, but only pain to both of us, from discussing our differences: and I never expressed them but when he gave utterance to some opinion or feeling repugnant to mine, in a manner which would have made it disingenuousness on my part to remain silent.

It remains to speak of what I wrote during these years, which, independently of my contributions to newspapers, was considerable. In 1830 and 1831 I wrote the five Essays since published under the title of "Essays on some Unsettled Questions of Political Economy," almost as they now stand, except that in 1833 I partially rewrote the fifth Essay. They were written with no immediate purpose of publication; and when, some years later, I offered them to a publisher, he declined them. They were only printed in 1844, after the success of the "System of Logic." I also resumed my speculations on this last subject, and puzzled myself, like others before me, with the great paradox of the discovery of new truths by general reasoning. As to the fact, there could be no doubt. As little could it be doubted, that all reasoning is resolvable into syllogisms, and that in every syllogism the conclusion is actually contained and implied in the premises. How, being so contained and implied, it could be new truth, and how the theorems of geometry, so different in appearance from the definitions and axioms, could be all contained in these, was a difficulty which no one, I thought, had sufficiently felt, and which, at all events, no one had succeeded in clearing up. The explanations offered by Whately and others, though they might give a temporary satisfaction, always, in my mind, left a mist still hanging over the subject. At last, when reading a second or third time the chapters on Reasoning in the second volume of Dugald Stewart, interrogating myself on every point, and following out, as far as I knew how, every topic of thought which the book suggested, I came upon an idea of his respecting the use of axioms in ratiocination, which I did not remember to have before noticed, but which now, in meditating on it, seemed to me not only true of axioms, but of all general propositions whatever, and to be the key of the whole perplexity. From this germ grew the theory of the Syllogism propounded in the Second Book of the Logic; which I immediately fixed by writing it out. And now, with greatly increased hope of being able to produce a work on Logic, of some originality and value, I proceeded to write the First Book, from the rough and imperfect draft I had already made. What I now wrote became the basis of that part of the subsequent Treatise; except that it did not contain the Theory of Kinds, which was a later addition, suggested by otherwise inextricable difficulties which met me in my first attempt to work out the subject of some of the concluding chapters of the Third Book. At the point which I had now reached I made a halt, which lasted five years. I had come to the end of my tether; I could make nothing satisfactory of Induction, at this time. I continued to read any book which seemed to promise light on the subject, and appropriated, as well as I could, the results; but for a long time I found nothing which seemed to open to me any very important vein of meditation.

In 1832 I wrote several papers for the first series of Tait's Magazine, and one for a quarterly periodical called the Jurist, which had been founded, and for a short time carried on, by a set of friends, all lawyers and law reformers, with several of whom I was acquainted. The paper in question is the one on the rights and duties of the State respecting Corporation and Church Property, now standing first among the collected "Dissertations and Discussions"; where one of my articles in "Tait," "The Currency Juggle," also appears. In the whole mass of what I wrote previous to these, there is nothing of sufficient permanent value to justify reprinting. The paper in the Jurist, which I still think a very complete discussion of the rights of the State over Foundations, showed both sides of my opinions, asserting as firmly as I should have done at any time, the doctrine that all endowments are national property, which the government may and ought to control; but not, as I should once have done, condemning endowments in themselves, and proposing that they should be taken to pay off the national debt. On the contrary, I urged strenuously the importance of having a provision for education, not dependent on 10 the mere demand of the market, that is, on the knowledge and discernment of average parents, but calculated to establish and keep up a higher standard of instruction than is likely to be spontaneously demanded by the buyers of the article. All these opinions have been confirmed and strengthened by the whole course of my subsequent reflections.

[1873]

THREE ESSAYS ON RELIGION

NATURE

Nature, natural, and the group of words derived from them, or allied to them in etymology, have at all times filled a great place in the thoughts and taken a strong hold on the feelings of mankind. That they should have done so is not surprising, when we consider what the words, in their primitive and most obvious signification, represent; but it is unfortunate that a set of terms which play so great a part in moral and metaphysical speculation, should have acquired many meanings different from the primary one, yet sufficiently allied to it to admit of confusion. The words have thus become entangled in so many foreign associations, mostly of a very powerful and tenacious character, that they have come to excite, and to be 20 the symbols of, feelings which their original meaning will by no means justify; and which have made them one of the most copious sources of false taste, false philosophy, false morality, and even bad law.

The most important application of the Socratic Elenchus, as exhibited and improved by Plato, consists in dissecting large abstractions of this description; fixing down to a precise definition the mean- 30 ing which as properly used they merely shadow forth, and questioning and testing the common maxims and opinions in which they bear a part. It is to be regretted that among the instructive specimens of this kind of investigation which Plato has left, and to which subsequent times have been so much indebted for whatever intellectual clearness they have attained, he has not enriched posterity with a dialogue 40 περὶ φύσεως.[1] If the idea denoted by the word had been subjected to his searching analysis, and the popular commonplaces in which it figures had been submitted to the ordeal of his powerful dialectics, his successors probably would not have rushed, as they speedily did, into modes of thinking and reasoning of which the fallacious use of that word formed the corner stone; a kind of fallacy from which he was himself singularly free.

According to the Platonic method which is still the best type of such investigations, the first thing to be done with so vague a term is to ascertain precisely what it means. It is also a rule of the same method, that the meaning of an abstraction is best sought for in the concrete— of an universal in the particular. Adopting this course with the word Nature, the first question must be, what is meant by the "nature" of a particular object? as of fire, water, or of some individual plant or animal? Evidently the *ensemble* or aggregate of its powers or properties: the modes in which it acts on other things (counting among those things the senses of the observer) and the modes in which other things act upon it; to which, in the case of a sentient being, must be added, its own capacities of feeling, or being conscious. The Nature of the thing means all this; means its entire capacity of exhibiting phenomena. And since the phenomena which a thing exhibits, however much they vary in different circumstances, are always the same in the same circumstances, they admit of being described in general forms of words, which are called

1 περὶ φύσεως: on Nature.

the *laws* of the thing's nature. Thus it is a law of the nature of water that under the mean pressure of the atmosphere at the level of the sea, it boils at 212° Fahrenheit.

As the nature of any given thing is the aggregate of its powers and properties, so Nature in the abstract is the aggregate of the powers and properties of all things. Nature means the sum of all phenomena together with the causes which produce them; including not only all that happens, but all that is capable of happening; the unused capabilities of causes being as much a part of the idea of Nature, as those which take effect. Since all phenomena which have been sufficiently examined are found to take place with regularity, each having certain fixed conditions, positive and negative, on the occurrence of which it invariably happens; mankind have been able to ascertain, either by direct observation or by reasoning processes grounded on it, the conditions of the occurrence of many phenomena; and the progress of science mainly consists in ascertaining those conditions. When discovered they can be expressed in general propositions, which are called laws of the particular phenomenon, and also, more generally, Laws of Nature. Thus, the truth that all material objects tend towards one another with a force directly as their masses and inversely as the square of their distance, is a law of Nature. The proposition that air and food are necessary to animal life, if it be as we have good reason to believe, true without exception, is also a law of nature, though the phenomenon of which it is the law is special, and not, like gravitation, universal.

Nature, then, in this its simplest acceptation, is a collective name for all facts, actual and possible: or (to speak more accurately) a name for the mode, partly known to us and partly unknown, in which all things take place. For the word suggests, not so much the multitudinous detail of the phenomena, as the conception which might be formed of their manner of existence as a mental whole, by a mind possessing a complete knowledge of them: to which conception it is the aim of science to raise itself, by successive steps of generalization from experience.

Such, then, is a correct definition of the word Nature. But this definition corresponds only to one of the senses of that ambiguous term. It is evidently inapplicable to some of the modes in which the word is familiarly employed. For example, it entirely conflicts with the common form of speech by which Nature is opposed to Art, and natural to artificial. For in the sense of the word Nature which has just been defined, and which is the true scientific sense, Art is as much Nature as anything else; and everything which is artificial is natural—Art has no independent powers of its own: Art is but the employment of the powers of Nature for an end. Phenomena produced by human agency, no less than those which as far as we are concerned are spontaneous, depend on the properties of the elementary forces, or of the elementary substances and their compounds. The united powers of the whole human race could not create a new property of matter in general, or of any one of its species. We can only take advantage for our purposes of the properties which we find. A ship floats by the same laws of specific gravity and equilibrium, as a tree uprooted by the wind and thrown into the water. The corn which men raise for food, grows and produces its grain by the same laws of vegetation by which the wild rose and the mountain strawberry bring forth their flowers and fruit. A house stands and holds together by the natural properties, the weight and cohesion of the materials which compose it: a steam engine works by the natural expansive force of steam, exerting a pressure upon one part of a system of arrangements, which pressure, by the mechanical properties of the lever, is transferred from that to another part where it raises the weight or removes the obstacle brought into connexion with it. In these and all other artificial operations the office of man is, as has often been remarked, a very limited one; it consists in moving things into certain places. We move objects, and by doing this, bring some things into contact which were separate, or separate others which were in contact: and by this simple change of place, natural forces previously dormant are called into action, and produce the desired effect. Even the volition which designs, the intelligence which contrives, and the muscular force which executes these movements, are themselves powers of Nature.

It thus appears that we must recognize at least two principal meanings in the word Nature. In one sense, it means all the powers existing in either the outer or the inner world and everything which takes place by means of those powers. In another sense, it means, not everything which happens, but only what takes place without the agency, or without the voluntary and intentional agency, of man. This distinction is far from exhausting the ambiguities of the word; but it is the key to most of those on which important consequences depend.

Such, then, being the two principal senses of the word Nature; in which of these is it taken, or is it taken in either, when the word and its derivatives are used to convey ideas of commendation, approval, and even moral obligation?

It has conveyed such ideas in all ages. *Naturam sequi* [2] was the fundamental principle of morals in many of the most admired schools of philosophy. Among the ancients, especially in the declining period of ancient intellect and thought, it was the test to which all ethical doctrines were brought. The Stoics and the Epicureans, however irreconcilable in the rest of their systems, agreed in holding themselves bound to prove that their respective maxims of conduct were the dictates of nature. Under their influence the Roman jurists, when attempting to systematize jurisprudence, placed in the front of their exposition a certain *Jus Naturale*,[3] "quod natura," as Justinian declares in the Institutes, "omnia animalia docuit": [4] and as the modern systematic writers not only on law but on moral philosophy, have generally taken the Roman jurists for their models, treatises on the so-called Law of Nature have abounded; and references to this Law as a supreme rule and ulti-

mate standard have pervaded literature. The writers on International Law have done more than any others to give currency to this style of ethical speculation; inasmuch as having no positive law to write about, and yet being anxious to invest the most approved opinions respecting international morality with as much as they could of the authority of law, they endeavoured to find such an authority in Nature's imaginary code. The Christian theology during the period of its greatest ascendency, opposed some, though not a complete, hindrance to the modes of thought which erected Nature into the criterion of morals, inasmuch as, according to the creed of most denominations of Christians (though assuredly not of Christ) man is by nature wicked. But this very doctrine, by the reaction which it provoked, has made the deistical moralists almost unanimous in proclaiming the divinity of Nature, and setting up its fancied dictates as an authoritative rule of action. A reference to that supposed standard is the predominant ingredient in the vein of thought and feeling which was opened by Rousseau, and which has infiltrated itself most widely into the modern mind, not excepting that portion of it which calls itself Christian. The doctrines of Christianity have in every age been largely accommodated to the philosophy which happened to be prevalent, and the Christianity of our day has borrowed a considerable part of its colour and flavour from sentimental deism. At the present time it cannot be said that Nature, or any other standard, is applied as it was wont to be, to deduce rules of action with juridical precision, and with an attempt to make its application coextensive with all human agency. The people of this generation do not commonly apply principles with any such studious exactness, nor own such binding allegiance to any standard, but live in a kind of confusion of many standards; a condition not propitious to the formation of steady moral convictions, but convenient enough to those whose moral opinions sit lightly on them, since it gives them a much wider range of arguments for defending the doctrine of the moment. But though perhaps no

---

2 *Naturam sequi:* 'to follow Nature'.

3 *Jus Naturale:* 'Natural Law'.

4 *"quod natura,"* etc.: 'because nature has taught all living things.'

one could now be found who like the institutional writers of former times, adopts the so-called Law of Nature as the foundation of ethics, and endeavours consistently to reason from it, the word and its cognates must still be counted among those which carry great weight in moral argumentation. That any mode of thinking, feeling, or acting, is "according to nature" is usually accepted as a strong argument for its goodness. If it can be said with any plausibility that "nature enjoins" anything, the propriety of obeying the injunction is by most people considered to be made out: and conversely, the imputation of being contrary to nature, is thought to bar the door against any pretension on the part of the thing so designated, to be tolerated or excused; and the word unnatural has not ceased to be one of the most vituperative epithets in the language. Those who deal in these expressions, may avoid making themselves responsible for any fundamental theorem respecting the standard of moral obligation, but they do not the less imply such a theorem, and one which must be the same in substance with that on which the more logical thinkers of a more laborious age grounded their systematic treatises on Natural Law.

Is it necessary to recognize in these forms of speech, another distinct meaning of the word Nature? Or can they be connected, by any rational bond of union, with either of the two meanings already treated of? At first it may seem that we have no option but to admit another ambiguity in the term. All inquiries are either into what is, or into what ought to be: science and history belonging to the first division, art, morals and politics to the second. But the two senses of the word Nature first pointed out, agree in referring only to what is. In the first meaning, Nature is a collective name for everything which is. In the second, it is a name for everything which is of itself, without voluntary human intervention. But the employment of the word Nature as a term of ethics seems to disclose a third meaning, in which Nature does not stand for what is, but for what ought to be; or for the rule or standard of what ought to be. A little consideration, however, will show that this is not a case of ambiguity; there is not here a third sense of the word. Those who set up Nature as a standard of action do not intend a merely verbal proposition; they do not mean that the standard, whatever it be, should be *called* Nature; they think they are giving some information as to what the standard of action really is. Those who say that we ought to act according to Nature do not mean the mere identical proposition that we ought to do what we ought to do. They think that the word Nature affords some external criterion of what we should do; and if they lay down as a rule for what ought to be, a word which in its proper signification denotes what is, they do so because they have a notion, either clearly or confusedly, that what is, constitutes the rule and standard of what ought to be.

The examination of this notion, is the object of the present Essay. It is proposed to inquire into the truth of the doctrines which make Nature a test of right and wrong, good and evil, or which in any mode or degree attach merit or approval to following, imitating, or obeying Nature. To this inquiry the foregoing discussion respecting the meaning of terms, was an indispensable introduction. Language is as it were the atmosphere of philosophical investigation, which must be made transparent before anything can be seen through it in the true figure and position. In the present case it is necessary to guard against a further ambiguity, which though abundantly obvious, has sometimes misled even sagacious minds, and of which it is well to take distinct note before proceeding further. No word is more commonly associated with the word Nature, than Law; and this last word has distinctly two meanings, in one of which it denotes some definite portion of what is, in the other, of what ought to be. We speak of the law of gravitation, the three laws of motion, the law of definite proportions in chemical combination, the vital laws of organized beings. All these are portions of what is. We also speak of the criminal law, the civil law, the law of honour, the law of veracity, the law of justice; all of which are portions of what ought to be, or of somebody's suppositions, feelings, or commands respecting what ought to be. The first kind of laws, such as the laws of motion, and of gravitation, are neither more nor less than the observed uniformities in the occurrence of phenomena: partly uniformities of antecedence and sequence, partly of concomitance. These are what, in science, and even in ordinary parlance, are meant by laws of Nature. Laws in the other sense are the laws of the land, the law of nations, or moral laws; among which, as already noticed, is dragged in, by jurists and publicists, something which they think proper to call the Law of Nature. Of the liability of these two meanings of the word to be confounded there can be no better example than the first chapter of Montesquieu; where he remarks, that the material world has its laws, the inferior animals have their laws, and man has his laws; and calls attention to the much greater strictness with which the first two sets of laws are observed, than the last; as if it were an inconsistency, and a paradox, that things always are what they are, but men not always what they ought to be. A similar confusion of ideas pervades the writings of Mr. George Combe, from whence it has overflowed into a large region of popular literature, and we are now continually reading injunctions to obey the physical laws of the universe, as being obligatory in the same sense and manner as the moral. The conception which the ethical use of the word Nature implies, of a close relation if not absolute identity between what is and what ought to be, certainly derives part of its hold on the mind from the custom of designating what is, by the expression "laws of nature," while the same word Law is also used, and even more familiarly and emphatically, to express what ought to be.

When it is asserted, or implied, that Nature, or the laws of Nature, should be conformed to, is the Nature which is meant, Nature in the first sense of the term, meaning all which is—the powers and properties of all things? But in this signification, there is no need of a recommendation to act according to nature, since it is what nobody can possibly help doing, and equally whether he acts well or ill.

There is no mode of acting which is not conformable to Nature in this sense of the term, and all modes of acting are so in exactly the same degree. Every action is the exertion of some natural power, and its effects of all sorts are so many phenomena of nature, produced by the powers and properties of some of the objects of nature, in exact obedience to some law or laws of nature. When I voluntarily use my organs to take in food, the act, and its consequences, take place according to laws of nature: if instead of food I swallow poison, the case is exactly the same. To bid people conform to the laws of nature when they have no power but what the laws of nature give them—when it is a physical impossibility for them to do the smallest thing otherwise than through some law of nature, is an absurdity. The thing they need to be told is, what particular law of nature they should make use of in a particular case. When, for example, a person is crossing a river by a narrow bridge to which there is no parapet, he will do well to regulate his proceedings by the laws of equilibrium in moving bodies, instead of conforming only to the law of gravitation, and falling into the river.

Yet, idle as it is to exhort people to do what they cannot avoid doing, and absurd as it is to prescribe as a rule of right conduct what agrees exactly as well with wrong; nevertheless a rational rule of conduct *may* be constructed out of the relation which it ought to bear to the laws of nature in this widest acceptation of the term. Man necessarily obeys the laws of nature, or in other words the properties of things, but he does not necessarily *guide* himself by them. Though all conduct is in conformity to laws of nature, all conduct is not grounded on knowledge of them, and intelligently directed to the attainment of purposes by means of them. Though we cannot emancipate ourselves from the laws of nature as a whole, we can escape from any particular law of nature, if we are able to withdraw ourselves from the circumstances in which it acts. Though we can do nothing except through laws of nature, we can use one law to counteract another. According to Bacon's maxim, we can obey nature in such a manner as to command it. Every alteration of circumstances alters more or less the laws of nature under which we act; and by every choice which we make either of ends or of means, we place ourselves to a greater or less extent under one set of laws of nature instead of another. If, therefore, the useless precept to follow nature were changed into a precept to study nature; to know and take heed of the properties of the things we have to deal with, so far as these properties are capable of forwarding or obstructing any given purpose; we should have arrived at the first principle of all intelligent action, or rather at the definition of intelligent action itself. And a confused notion of this true principle, is, I doubt not, in the minds of many of those who set up the unmeaning doctrine which superficially resembles it. They perceive that the essential difference between wise and foolish conduct consists in attending, or not attending, to the particular laws of nature on which some important result depends. And they think, that a person who attends to a law of nature in order to shape his conduct by it, may be said to obey it, while a person who practically disregards it, and acts as if no such law existed, may be said to disobey it: the circumstance being overlooked, that what is thus called disobedience to a law of nature is obedience to some other or perhaps to the very law itself. For example, a person who goes into a powder magazine either not knowing, or carelessly omitting to think of, the explosive force of gunpowder, is likely to do some act which will cause him to be blown to atoms in obedience to the very law which he has disregarded.

But however much of its authority the "Naturam sequi" doctrine may owe to its being confounded with the rational precept "Naturam observare," its favourers and promoters unquestionably intend much more by it than that precept. To acquire knowledge of the properties of things, and make use of the knowledge for guidance, is a rule of prudence, for the adaptation of means to ends; for giving effect to our wishes and intentions whatever they may be. But the maxim of obedience to Nature, or conformity to Nature, is held up not as a simply prudential but as an ethical maxim; and by those who talk of *jus naturae*, even as a law, fit to be administered by tribunals and enforced by sanctions. Right action, must mean something more and other than merely intelligent action: yet no precept beyond this last, can be connected with the word Nature in the wider and more philosophical of its acceptations. We must try it therefore in the other sense, that in which Nature stands distinguished from Art, and denotes, not the whole course of the phenomena which come under our observation, but only their spontaneous course.

Let us then consider whether we can attach any meaning to the supposed practical maxim of following Nature, in this second sense of the word, in which Nature stands for that which takes place without human intervention. In Nature as thus understood, is the spontaneous course of things when left to themselves, the rule to be followed in endeavouring to adapt things to our use? But it is evident at once that the maxim, taken in this sense, is not merely, as it is in the other sense, superfluous and unmeaning, but palpably absurd and self-contradictory. For while human action cannot help conforming to Nature in the one meaning of the term, the very aim and object of action is to alter and improve Nature in the other meaning. If the natural course of things were perfectly right and satisfactory, to act at all would be a gratuitous meddling, which as it could not make things better, must make them worse. Or if action at all could be justified, it would only be when in direct obedience to instincts, since these might perhaps be accounted part of the spontaneous order of Nature; but to do anything with forethought and purpose, would be a violation of that perfect order. If the artificial is not better than the natural, to what end are all the arts of life? To dig, to plough, to build, to wear clothes, are direct infringements of the injunction to follow nature.

Accordingly it would be said by every one, even of those most under the influence of the feelings which prompt the injunction, that to apply it to such cases as those just spoken of, would be to push it too far. Everybody professes to approve and admire many great triumphs of Art over Nature: the junction by bridges of shores which Nature had made separate, the draining of Nature's marshes, the excavation of her wells, the dragging to light of what she has buried at immense depths in the earth; the turning away of her thunderbolts by lightning rods, of her inundations by embankments, of her ocean by breakwaters. But to commend these and similar feats, is to acknowledge that the ways of Nature are to be conquered, not obeyed: that her powers are often towards man in the position of enemies, from whom he must wrest, by force and ingenuity, what little he can for his own use, and deserves to be applauded when that little is rather more than might be expected from his physical weakness in comparison to those gigantic powers. All praise of Civilization, or Art, or Contrivance, is so much dispraise of Nature; an admission of imperfection, which it is man's business, and merit, to be always endeavouring to correct or mitigate.

The consciousness that whatever man does to improve his condition is in so much a censure and a thwarting of the spontaneous order of Nature, has in all ages caused new and unprecedented attempts at improvement to be generally at first under a shade of religious suspicion; as being in any case uncomplimentary, and very probably offensive to the powerful beings (or, when polytheism gave place to monotheism, to the all-powerful Being) supposed to govern the various phenomena of the universe, and of whose will the course of nature was conceived to be the expression. Any attempt to mould natural phenomena to the convenience of mankind might easily appear an interference with the government of those superior beings: and though life could not have been maintained, much less made pleasant, without perpetual interferences of the kind, each new one was doubtless made with fear and trembling, until experience had shown that it could be ventured on without drawing down the vengeance of the Gods. The sagacity of priests showed them a way to reconcile the impunity of particular infringements with the maintenance of the general dread of encroaching on the divine administration. This was effected by representing each of the principal human inventions as the gift and favour of some God. The old religions also afforded many resources for consulting the Gods, and obtaining their express permission for what would otherwise have appeared a breach of their prerogative. When oracles had ceased, any religion which recognized a revelation afforded expedients for the same purpose. The Catholic religion had the resource of an infallible Church, authorized to declare what exertions of human spontaneity were permitted or forbidden; and in default of this, the case was always open to argument from the Bible whether any particular practice had expressly or by implication been sanctioned. The notion remained that this liberty to control Nature was conceded to man only by special indulgence, and as far as required by his necessities; and there was always a tendency, though a diminishing one, to regard any attempt to exercise power over nature, beyond a certain degree, and a certain admitted range, as an impious effort to usurp divine power, and dare more than was permitted to man. The lines of Horace in which the familiar arts of shipbuilding and navigation are reprobated as *vetitum nefas*,[5] indicate even in that sceptical age a still unexhausted vein of the old sentiment. The intensity of the corresponding feeling in the middle ages is not a precise parallel, on account of the superstition about dealing with evil spirits with which it was complicated: but the imputation of prying into the secrets of the Almighty long remained a powerful weapon of attack against unpopular inquirers into nature: and the charge of presumptuously attempting to defeat the designs of Providence, still retains enough of its original force to be thrown in as a make-weight along with other objections when there is a desire to find fault with any new exertion of human forethought and contrivance. No one, indeed, asserts it to be the intention of the Creator that the spontane-

---

[5] *vetitum nefas*: 'forbidden wrong'; "bold to endure all things, mankind rushes even through forbidden wrong" (Horace, *Odes*, I, iii, 5-6).

ous order of the creation should not be altered, or even that it should not be altered in any new way. But there still exists a vague notion that though it is very proper to control this or the other natural phenomenon, the general scheme of nature is a model for us to imitate: that with more or less liberty in details, we should on the whole be guided by the spirit and general conception of nature's own ways: that they are God's work, and as such perfect; that man cannot rival their unapproachable excellence, and can best show his skill and piety by attempting, in however imperfect a way, to reproduce their likeness; and that if not the whole, yet some particular parts of the spontaneous order of nature, selected according to the speaker's predilections, are in a peculiar sense, manifestations of the Creator's will; a sort of finger posts pointing out the direction which things in general, and therefore our voluntary actions, are intended to take. Feelings of this sort, though repressed on ordinary occasions by the contrary current of life, are ready to break out whenever custom is silent, and the native promptings of the mind have nothing opposed to them but reason: and appeals are continually made to them by rhetoricians, with the effect, if not of convincing opponents, at least of making those who already hold the opinion which the rhetorician desires to recommend, better satisfied with it. For in the present day it probably seldom happens that any one is persuaded to approve any course of action because it appears to him to bear an analogy to the divine government of the world, though the argument tells on him with great force, and is felt by him to be a great support, in behalf of anything which he is already inclined to approve.

If this notion of imitating the ways of Providence as manifested in Nature, is seldom expressed plainly and downrightly as a maxim of general application, it also is seldom directly contradicted. Those who find it on their path, prefer to turn the obstacle rather than to attack it, being often themselves not free from the feeling, and in any case afraid of incurring the charge of impiety by saying anything which might be held to disparage the works of the Creator's power. They therefore, for the most part, rather endeavour to show, that they have as much right to the religious argument as their opponents, and that if the course they recommend seems to conflict with some part of the ways of Providence, there is some other part with which it agrees better than what is contended for on the other side. In this mode of dealing with the great à priori fallacies, the progress of improvement clears away particular errors while the causes of errors are still left standing, and very little weakened by each conflict: yet by a long series of such partial victories precedents are accumulated, to which an appeal may be made against these powerful prepossessions, and which afford a growing hope that the misplaced feeling, after having so often learnt to recede, may some day be compelled to an unconditional surrender. For however offensive the proposition may appear to many religious persons, they should be willing to look in the face the undeniable fact, that the order of nature, in so far as unmodified by man, is such as no being, whose attributes are justice and benevolence, would have made, with the intention that his rational creatures should follow it as an example. If made wholly by such a Being, and not partly by beings of very different qualities, it could only be as a designedly imperfect work, which man, in his limited sphere, is to exercise justice and benevolence in amending. The best persons have always held it to be the essence of religion, that the paramount duty of man upon earth is to amend himself: but all except monkish quietists have annexed to this in their inmost minds (though seldom willing to enunciate the obligation with the same clearness) the additional religious duty of amending the world, and not solely the human part of it but the material; the order of physical nature.

In considering this subject it is necessary to divest ourselves of certain preconceptions which may justly be called natural prejudices, being grounded on feelings which, in themselves natural and inevitable, intrude into matters with which they ought to have no concern. One of these feelings is the astonishment, rising into awe, which is inspired (even independently of all religious sentiment) by any of the greater natural phenomena. A hurricane; a mountain precipice; the desert; the ocean, either agitated or at rest; the solar system, and the great cosmic forces which hold it together; the boundless firmament, and to an educated mind any single star; excite feelings which make all human enterprises and powers appear so insignificant, that to a mind thus occupied it seems insufferable presumption in so puny a creature as man to look critically on things so far above him, or dare to measure himself against the grandeur of the universe. But a little interrogation of our own consciousness will suffice to convince us, that what makes these phenomena so impressive is simply their vastness. The enormous extension in space and time, or the enormous power they exemplify, constitutes their sublimity; a feeling in all cases, more allied to terror than to any moral emotion. And though the vast scale of these phenomena may well excite wonder, and sets at defiance all idea of rivalry, the feeling it inspires is of a totally different character from admiration of excellence. Those in whom awe produces admiration may be aesthetically developed, but they are morally uncultivated. It is one of the endowments of the imaginative part of our mental nature that conceptions of greatness and power, vividly realized, produce a feeling which though in its higher degrees closely bordering on pain, we prefer to most of what are accounted pleasures. But we are quite equally capable of experiencing this feeling towards maleficent power; and we never experience it so strongly towards most of the powers of the universe, as when we have most present to our consciousness a vivid sense of their capacity of inflicting evil. Because these natural powers have what we cannot imitate, enormous might, and overawe us by that one attribute, it would be a great error to infer that their other attributes are such as we ought to emulate, or that we should be justified in using our small powers after the example which Nature sets us with her vast forces.

For, how stands the fact? That next to the greatness of these cosmic forces, the quality which most forcibly strikes every one who does not avert his eyes from it, is their perfect and absolute recklessness. They go straight to their end, without regarding what or whom they crush on the road. Optimists, in their attempts to prove that "whatever is, is right," are obliged to maintain, not that Nature ever turns one step from her path to avoid trampling us into destruction, but that it would be very unreasonable in us to expect that she should. Pope's "Shall gravitation cease when you go by?" may be a just rebuke to any one who should be so silly as to expect common human morality from nature. But if the question were between two men, instead of between a man and a natural phenomenon, that triumphant apostrophe would be thought a rare piece of impudence. A man who should persist in hurling stones or firing cannon when another man "goes by," and having killed him should urge a similar plea in exculpation, would very deservedly be found guilty of murder.

In sober truth, nearly all the things which men are hanged or imprisoned for doing to one another, are nature's every day performances. Killing, the most criminal act recognized by human laws, Nature does once to every being that lives; and in a large proportion of cases, after protracted tortures such as only the greatest monsters whom we read of ever purposely inflicted on their living fellow creatures. If, by an arbitrary reservation, we refuse to account anything murder but what abridges a certain term supposed to be allotted to human life, nature also does this to all but a small percentage of lives, and does it in all the modes, violent or insidious, in which the worst human beings take the lives of one another. Nature impales men, breaks them as if on the wheel, casts them to be devoured by wild beasts, burns them to death, crushes them with stones like the first christian martyr, starves them with hunger, freezes them with cold, poisons them by the quick or slow venom of her exhalations, and has hundreds of other hideous deaths in reserve, such as the ingenious cruelty of a Nabis or a Domitian never surpassed. All this, Nature does with the most supercilious disregard both of mercy and of justice, emptying her shafts upon the best and noblest indifferently with the meanest and worst; upon those who are engaged in the highest and worthiest enterprises, and often as the direct consequence of the noblest acts; and it might almost be imagined as a punishment for them. She mows down those on whose existence hangs the well-being of a whole people, perhaps the prospects of the human race for generations to come, with as little compunction as those whose death is a relief to themselves, or a blessing to those under their noxious influence. Such are Nature's dealings with life. Even when she does not intend to kill, she inflicts the same tortures in apparent wantonness. In the clumsy provision which she has made for that perpetual renewal of animal life, rendered ncessary by the prompt termination she puts to it in every individual instance, no human being ever comes into the world but another human being is literally stretched on the rack for hours or days, not unfrequently issuing in death. Next to taking life (equal to it according to a high authority) is taking the means by which we live; and Nature does this too on the largest scale and with most callous indifference. A single hurricane destroys the hopes of a season; a flight of locusts, or an inundation, desolates a district; a trifling chemical change in an edible root starves a million of people. The waves of the sea like banditti seize and appropriate the wealth of the rich and the little all of the poor with the same accompaniments of stripping, wounding, and killing as their human antitypes. Everything in short which the worst men commit either against life or property is perpetrated on a larger scale by natural agents. Nature has Noyades more fatal than those of Carrier; her explosions of fire damp are as destructive as human artillery; her plague and cholera far surpass the poison cups of Borgias. Even the love of "order" which is thought to be a following of the ways of Nature is in fact a contradiction of them. All, which people are accustomed to deprecate as "disorder" and its consequences, is precisely a counterpart of Nature's ways. Anarchy and the Reign of Terror are overmatched in injustice, ruin, and death, by a hurricane and a pestilence.

But, it is said, all these things are for wise and good ends. On this I must first remark that whether they are so or not, is altogether beside the point. Supposing it true that contrary to appearances these horrors when perpetrated by Nature, promote good ends, still as no one believes that good ends would be promoted by our following the example, the course of Nature cannot be a proper model for us to imitate. Either it is right that we should kill because nature kills; torture because nature tortures; ruin and devastate because nature does the like; or we ought not to consider at all what nature does, but what it is good to do. If there is such a thing as a *reductio ad absurdum*,[6] this surely amounts to one. If it is a sufficient reason for doing one thing, that nature does it, why not another thing? If not all things, why anything? The physical government of the world being full of the things which when done by men are deemed the greatest enormities, it cannot be religious or moral in us to guide our actions by the analogy of the course of nature. This proposition remains true, whatever occult quality of producing good may reside in those facts of nature which to our perceptions are most noxious, and which no one considers it other than a crime to produce artificially.

But, in reality, no one consistently believes in any such occult quality. The phrases which ascribe perfection to the course of nature can only be considered as the exaggerations of poetic or devotional feeling, not intended to stand the test of a sober examination. No one, either religious or irreligious, believes that the hurtful agencies of nature, considered as a whole, promote good purposes, in any other way than by inciting human rational creatures to rise up and struggle against them. If we believed that those agencies were appointed by a benevolent Providence as the means of accomplishing wise purposes which could not be compassed if they did not exist, then everything done by mankind which tends to chain up these

6 *reductio ad absurdam:* "Reduction to absurdity".

natural agencies or to restrict their mischievous operation, from draining a pestilential marsh down to curing the toothache, or putting up an umbrella, ought to be accounted impious; which assuredly nobody does account them, notwithstanding an undercurrent of sentiment setting in that direction which is occasionally perceptible. On the contrary, the improvements on which the civilized part of mankind most pride themselves, consist in more successfully warding off those natural calamities which if we really believed what most people profess to believe, we should cherish as medicines provided for our earthly state by infinite wisdom. Inasmuch too as each generation greatly surpasses its predecessors in the amount of natural evil which it succeeds in averting, our condition, if the theory were true, ought by this time to have become a terrible manifestation of some tremendous calamity, against which the physical evils we have learnt to overmaster, had previously operated as a preservative. Any one, however, who acted as if he supposed this to be the case, would be more likely, I think, to be confined as a lunatic, than reverenced as a saint.

It is undoubtedly a very common fact that good comes out of evil, and when it does occur, it is far too agreeable not to find people eager to dilate on it. But in the first place, it is quite as often true of human crimes, as of natural calamities. The fire of London, which is believed to have had so salutary an effect on the healthiness of the city, would have produced that effect just as much if it had been really the work of the "furor papisticus" [7] so long commemorated on the Monument. The deaths of those whom tyrants or persecutors have made martyrs in any noble cause, have done a service to mankind which would not have been obtained if they had died by accident or disease. Yet whatever incidental and unexpected benefits may result from crimes, they are crimes nevertheless. In the second place, if good frequently comes out of evil, the converse fact, evil coming out of good, is equally common. Every event public or private, which, regretted on its occurrence,

was declared providential at a later period on account of some unforeseen good consequence, might be matched by some other event, deemed fortunate at the time, but which proved calamitous or fatal to those whom it appeared to benefit. Such conflicts between the beginning and the end, or between the event and the expectation, are not only as frequent, but as often held up to notice, in the painful cases as in the agreeable; but there is not the same inclination to generalize on them; or at all events they are not regarded by the moderns (though they were by the ancients) as similarly an indication of the divine purposes: men satisfy themselves with moralizing on the imperfect nature of our foresight, the uncertainty of events, and the vanity of human expectations. The simple fact is, human interests are so complicated, and the effects of any incident whatever so multitudinous, that if it touches mankind at all, its influence on them is, in the great majority of cases, both good and bad. If the greater number of personal misfortunes have their good side, hardly any good fortune ever befell any one which did not give either to the same or to some other person, something to regret: and unhappily there are many misfortunes so overwhelming that their favourable side, if it exists, is entirely overshadowed and made insignificant; while the corresponding statement can seldom be made concerning blessings. The effects too of every cause depend so much on the circumstances which accidentally accompany it, that many cases are sure to occur in which even the total result is markedly opposed to the predominant tendency: and thus not only evil has its good and good its evil side, but good often produces an overbalance of evil and evil an overbalance of good. This, however, is by no means the general tendency of either phenomenon. On the contrary, both good and evil naturally tend to fructify, each in its own kind, good producing good, and evil, evil. It is one of Nature's general rules, and part of her habitual injustice, that "to him that hath shall be given, but from him that hath not, shall be taken even that which he hath." The ordinary and predominant tendency of good is towards more good. Health, strength, wealth,

[7] *furor papisticus:* 'papist rage'.

knowledge, virtue, are not only good in themselves but facilitate and promote the acquisition of good, both of the same and of other kinds. The person who can learn easily, is he who already knows much: it is the strong and not the sickly person who can do everything which most conduces to health; those who find it easy to gain money are not the poor but the rich; while health, strength, knowledge, talents, 10 are all means of acquiring riches, and riches are often an indispensable means of acquiring these. Again, e converso,[8] whatever may be said of evil turning into good, the general tendency of evil is towards further evil. Bodily illness renders the body more susceptible of disease; it produces incapacity of exertion, sometimes debility of mind, and often the loss of means of subsistence. All severe pain, either bodily or 20 mental, tends to increase the susceptibilities of pain forever after. Poverty is the parent of a thousand mental and moral evils. What is still worse, to be injured or oppressed, when habitual, lowers the whole tone of the character. One bad action leads to others, both in the agent himself, in the bystanders, and in the sufferers. All bad qualities are strengthened by habit, and all vices and follies tend to spread. Intel- 30 lectual defects generate moral, and moral, intellectual; and every intellectual or moral defect generates others, and so on without end.

That much applauded class of authors, the writers on natural theology, have, I venture to think, entirely lost their way, and missed the sole line of argument which could have made their speculations acceptable to any one who can perceive when 40 two propositions contradict one another. They have exhausted the resources of sophistry to make it appear that all the suffering in the world exists to prevent greater—that misery exists, for fear lest there should be misery: a thesis which if ever so well maintained, could only avail to explain and justify the works of limited beings, compelled to labour under conditions independent of their own will; but 50 can have no application to a Creator assumed to be omnipotent, who, if he bends to a supposed necessity, himself makes the

[8] e converso: 'conversely'.

necessity which he bends to. If the maker of the world can all that he will, he wills misery, and there is no escape from the conclusion. The more consistent of those who have deemed themselves qualified to "vindicate the ways of God to man" have endeavoured to avoid the alternative by hardening their hearts, and denying that misery is an evil. The goodness of God, they say, does not consist in willing the happiness of his creatures, but their virtue; and the universe, if not a happy, is a just, universe. But waiving the objections to this scheme of ethics, it does not at all get rid of the difficulty. If the Creator of mankind willed that they should all be virtuous, his designs are as completely baffled as if he had willed that they should all be happy: and the order of nature is constructed with even less regard to the requirements of justice than to those of benevolence. If the law of all creation were justice and the Creator omnipotent, then in whatever amount suffering and happiness might be dispensed to the world, each person's share of them would be exactly proportioned to that person's good or evil deeds; no human being would have a worse lot than another, without worse deserts; accident or favouritism would have no part in such a world, but every human life would be the playing out of a drama constructed like a perfect moral tale. No one is able to blind himself to the fact that the world we live in is totally different from this; insomuch that the necessity of redressing the balance has been deemed one of the strongest arguments for another life after death, which amounts to an admission that the order of things in this life is often an example of injustice, not justice. If it be said that God does not take sufficient account of pleasure and pain to make them the reward or punishment of the good or the wicked, but that virtue is itself the greatest good and vice the greatest evil, then these at least ought to be dispensed to all according to what they have done to deserve them; instead of which, every kind of moral depravity is entailed upon multitudes by the fatality of their birth; through the fault of their parents, of society, or of uncontrollable circumstances, certainly through no fault of their own. Not even on the most distorted and contracted theory of good which ever was framed by religious or philosophical fanaticism, can the government of Nature be made to resemble the work of a being at once good and omnipotent.

The only admissible moral theory of Creation is that the Principle of Good *cannot* at once and altogether subdue the powers of evil, either physical or moral; could not place mankind in a world free from the necessity of an incessant struggle with the maleficent powers, or make them always victorious in that struggle, but could and did make them capable of carrying on the fight with vigour and with progressively increasing success. Of all the religious explanations of the order of nature, this alone is neither contradictory to itself, nor to the facts for which it attempts to account. According to it, man's duty would consist, not in simply taking care of his own interests by obeying irresistible power, but in standing forward a not ineffectual auxiliary to a Being of perfect beneficence; a faith which seems much better adapted for nerving him to exertion than a vague and inconsistent reliance on an Author of Good who is supposed to be also the author of evil. And I venture to assert that such has really been, though often unconsciously, the faith of all who have drawn strength and support of any worthy kind from trust in a superintending Providence. There is no subject on which men's practical belief is more incorrectly indicated by the words they use to express it, than religion. Many have derived a base confidence from imagining themselves to be favourites of an omnipotent but capricious and despotic Deity. But those who have been strengthened in goodness by relying on the sympathizing support of a powerful and good Governor of the world, have, I am satisfied, never really believed that Governor to be, in the strict sense of the term, omnipotent. They have always saved his goodness at the expense of his power. They have believed, perhaps, that he could, if he willed, remove all the thorns from their individual path, but not without causing greater harm to some one else, or frustrating some purpose of greater

importance to the general well-being. They have believed that he could do any one thing, but not any combination of things: that his government, like human government, was a system of adjustments and compromises; that the world is inevitably imperfect, contrary to his intention. And since the exertion of all his power to make it as little imperfect as possible, leaves it no better than it is, they cannot but regard that power, though vastly beyond human estimate, yet as in itself not merely finite, but extremely limited. They are bound, for example, to suppose that the best he could do for his human creatures was to make an immense majority of all who have yet existed, be born (without any fault of their own) Patagonians, or Esquimaux, or something nearly as brutal and degraded, but to give them capacities which by being cultivated for very many centuries in toil and suffering, and after many of the best specimens of the race have sacrificed their lives for the purpose, have at last enabled some chosen portions of the species to grow into something better, capable of being improved in centuries more into something really good, of which hitherto there are only to be found individual instances. It may be possible to believe with Plato that perfect goodness, limited and thwarted in every direction by the intractableness of the material, has done this because it could do no better. But that the same perfectly wise and good Being had absolute power over the material, and made it, by voluntary choice, what it is; to admit this might have been supposed impossible to any one who has the simplest notions of moral good and evil. Nor can any such person, whatever kind of religious phrases he may use, fail to believe, that if Nature and Man are both the works of a Being of perfect goodness, that Being intended Nature as a scheme to be amended, not imitated, by Man.

But even though unable to believe that Nature, as a whole, is a realization of the designs of perfect wisdom and benevolence, men do not willingly renounce the idea that some part of Nature, at least, must be intended as an exemplar, or type; that on some portion or other of the Creator's works, the image of the moral qualities which they are accustomed to ascribe to him, must be impressed; that if not all which is, yet something which is, must not only be a faultless model of what ought to be, but must be intended to be our guide and standard in rectifying the rest. It does not suffice them to believe, that what tends to good is to be imitated and perfected, and what tends to evil is to be corrected: they are anxious for some more definite indication of the Creator's designs; and being persuaded that this must somewhere be met with in his works, undertake the dangerous responsibility of picking and choosing among them in quest of it. A choice which except so far as directed by the general maxim that he intends all the good and none of the evil, must of necessity be perfectly arbitrary; and if it leads to any conclusions other than such as can be deduced from that maxim, must be, exactly in that proportion, pernicious.

It has never been settled by any accredited doctrine, what particular departments of the order of nature shall be reputed to be designed for our moral instruction and guidance; and accordingly each person's individual predilections, or momentary convenience, have decided to what parts of the divine government the practical conclusions that he was desirous of establishing, should be recommended to approval as being analogous. One such recommendation must be as fallacious as another, for it is impossible to decide that certain of the Creator's works are more truly expressions of his character than the rest; and the only selection which does not lead to immoral results, is the selection of those which most conduce to the general good, in other words, of those which point to an end which if the entire scheme is the expression of a single omnipotent and consistent will, is evidently not the end intended by it.

There is however one particular element in the construction of the world, which to minds on the look-out for special indication of the Creator's will, has appeared, not without plausibility, peculiarly fitted to afford them; viz., the active impulses of human and other animated beings. One can imagine such persons arguing that when the Author of Nature only made circumstances, he may not have meant to indicate the manner in which his rational creatures were to adjust themselves to those circumstances; but that when he implanted positive stimuli in the creatures themselves, stirring them up to a particular kind of action, it is impossible to doubt that he intended that sort of action to be practised by them. This reasoning, followed out consistently, would lead to the conclusion that the Deity intended, and approves, whatever human beings do; since all that they do being the consequence of some of the impulses with which their Creator must have endowed them, all must equally be considered as done in obedience to his will. As this practical conclusion was shrunk from, it was necessary to draw a distinction, and to pronounce that not the whole, but only parts of the active nature of mankind point to a special intention of the Creator in respect to their conduct. These parts it seemed natural to suppose, must be those in which the Creator's hand is manifested rather than the man's own: and hence the frequent antithesis between man as God made him, and man as he has made himself. Since what is done with deliberation seems more the man's own act. and he is held more completely responsible for it than for what he does from sudden impulse, the considerate part of human conduct is apt to be set down as man's share in the business, and the inconsiderate as God's. The result is the vein of sentiment so common in the modern world (though unknown to the philosophic ancients) which exalts instinct at the expense of reason; an aberration rendered still more mischievous by the opinion commonly held in conjunction with it, that every, or almost every, feeling or impulse which acts promptly without waiting to ask questions, is an instinct. Thus almost every variety of unreflecting and uncalculating impulse receives a kind of consecration, except those which, though unreflecting at the moment, owe their origin to previous habits of reflection: these, being evidently not instinctive, do not meet with the favour accorded to the rest; so that all unreflecting impulses are invested with authority over reason, except the only ones which are most probably right. I do not

mean, of course, that this mode of judgment is even pretended to be consistently
carried out: life could not go on if it were
not admitted that impulses must be controlled, and that reason ought to govern
our actions. The pretension is not to drive
Reason from the helm but rather to bind
her by articles to steer only in a particular
way. Instinct is not to govern, but reason
is to practise some vague and unassign- 10
able amount of deference to Instinct.
Though the impression in favour of instinct as being a peculiar manifestation of
the divine purposes, has not been cast into
the form of a consistent general theory, it
remains a standing prejudice, capable of
being stirred up into hostility to reason in
any case in which the dictate of the rational faculty has not acquired the authority of prescription. 20

I shall not here enter into the difficult
psychological question, what are, or are
not instincts: the subject would require a
volume to itself. Without touching upon
any disputed theoretical points, it is possible to judge how little worthy is the instinctive part of human nature to be held
up as its chief excellence—as the part in
which the hand of infinitive goodness and
wisdom is peculiarly visible. Allowing 30
everything to be an instinct which anybody
has ever asserted to be one, it remains true
that nearly every respectable attribute of
humanity is the result not of instinct, but
of a victory over instinct; and that there is
hardly anything valuable in the natural
man except capacities—a whole world of
possibilities, all of them dependent upon
eminently artificial discipline for being
realized. 40

It is only in a highly artificialized condition of human nature that the notion
grew up, or, I believe, ever could have
grown up, that goodness was natural: because only after a long course of artificial
education did good sentiments become so
habitual, and so predominant over bad, as
to arise unprompted when occasion called
for them. In the times when mankind were
nearer to their natural state, cultivated 50
observers regarded the natural man as a
sort of wild animal, distinguished chiefly
by being craftier than the other beasts of
the field; and all worth of character was

deemed the result of a sort of taming; a
phrase often applied by the ancient philosophers to the appropriate discipline of
human beings. The truth is that there is
hardly a single point of excellence belonging to human character, which is not decidedly repugnant to the untutored feelings
of human nature.

If there be a virtue which more than
any other we expect to find, and really do
find, in an uncivilized state, it is the virtue
of courage. Yet this is from first to last a
victory achieved over one of the most
powerful emotions of human nature. If
there is any one feeling or attribute more
natural than all others to human beings,
it is fear; and no greater proof can be
given of the power of artificial discipline
than the conquest which it has at all times
and places shown itself capable of achieving over so mighty and so universal a sentiment. The widest difference no doubt
exists between one human being and another in the facility or difficulty with which
they acquire this virtue. There is hardly
any department of human excellence in
which difference of original temperament
goes so far. But it may fairly be questioned if any human being is naturally
courageous. Many are naturally pugnacious, or irascible, or enthusiastic, and
these passions when strongly excited may
render them insensible to fear. But take
away the conflicting emotion, and fear re-
asserts its dominion: consistent courage is
always the effect of cultivation. The courage which is occasionally though by no
means generally found among tribes of
savages, is as much the result of education
as that of the Spartans or Romans. In all
such tribes there is a most emphatic direction of the public sentiment into every
channel of expression through which
honour can be paid to courage and cowardice held up to contempt and derision.
It will perhaps be said, that as the expression of a sentiment implies the sentiment
itself, the training of the young to courage
presupposed an originally courageous people. It presupposes only what all good
customs presuppose—that there must have
been individuals better than the rest, who
set the customs going. Some individuals,
who like other people had fears to con-

quer, must have had strength of mind and will to conquer them for themselves. These would obtain the influence belonging to heroes, for that which is at once astonishing and obviously useful never fails to be admired: and partly through this admiration, partly through the fear they themselves excite, they would obtain the power of legislators, and could establish whatever customs they pleased.

Let us next consider a quality which forms the most visible, and one of the most radical of the moral distinctions between human beings and most of the lower animals; that of which the absence, more than of anything else, renders men bestial; the quality of cleanliness. Can anything be more entirely artificial? Children, and the lower classes of most countries, seem to be actually fond of dirt: the vast majority of the human race are indifferent to it: whole nations of otherwise civilized and cultivated human beings tolerate it in some of its worst forms, and only a very small minority are consistently offended by it. Indeed the universal law of the subject appears to be, that uncleanliness offends only those to whom it is unfamiliar, so that those who have lived in so artificial a state as to be unused to it in any form, are the sole persons whom it disgusts in all forms. Of all virtues this is the most evidently not instinctive, but a triumph over instinct. Assuredly neither cleanliness nor the love of cleanliness is natural to man, but only the capacity of acquiring a love of cleanliness.

Our examples have thus far been taken from the personal, or as they are called by Bentham, the self regarding virtues, because these, if any, might be supposed to be congenial even to the uncultivated mind. Of the social virtues it is almost superfluous to speak; so completely is it the verdict of all experience that selfishness is natural. By this I do not in any wise mean to deny that sympathy is natural also; I believe on the contrary that on that important fact rests the possibility of any cultivation of goodness and nobleness, and the hope of their ultimate entire ascendancy. But sympathetic characters, left uncultivated, and given up to their sympathetic instincts, are as selfish as others. The difference is in the *kind* of selfishness: theirs is not solitary but sympathetic selfishness; *l'egoïsme à deux, à trois*, or *à quatre*; [9] and they may be very amiable and delightful to those with whom they sympathize, and grossly unjust and unfeeling to the rest of the world. Indeed the finer nervous organizations which are most capable of and most require sympathy, have, from their fineness, so much stronger impulses of all sorts, that they often furnish the most striking examples of selfishness, though of a less repulsive kind than that of colder natures. Whether there ever was a person in whom, apart from all teaching of instructors, friends or books, and from all intentional self-modelling according to an ideal, natural benevolence was a more powerful attribute than selfishness in any of its forms, may remain undecided. That such cases are extremely rare, every one must admit, and this is enough for the argument.

But (to speak no further of self-control for the benefit of others) the commonest self-control for one's own benefit—that power of sacrificing a present desire to a distant object or a general purpose which is indispensable for making the actions of the individual accord with his own notions of his individual good; even this is most unnatural to the undisciplined human being: as may be seen by the long apprenticeship which children serve to it; the very imperfect manner in which it is acquired by persons born to power, whose will is seldom resisted, and by all who have been early and much indulged; and the marked absence of the quality in savages, in soldiers and sailors, and in a somewhat less degree in nearly the whole of the poorer classes in this and many other countries. The principal difference, on the point under consideration, between this virtue and others, is that although, like them, it requires a course of teaching, it is more susceptible than most of them of being self-taught. The axiom is trite that self-control is only learnt by experience: and this endowment is only thus much nearer to being natural than the others we have spoken of, inasmuch as personal

9 *l'egoïsme à deux*, etc.: 'egoism by twos, by threes, by fours.'

experience, without external inculcation, has a certain tendency to engender it. Nature does not of herself bestow this, any more than other virtues; but nature often administers the rewards and punishments which cultivate it, and which in other cases have to be created artificially for the express purpose.

Veracity might seem, of all virtues, to have the most plausible claim to being natural, since in the absence of motives to the contrary, speech usually conforms to, or at least does not intentionally deviate from, fact. Accordingly this is the virtue with which writers like Rousseau delight in decorating savage life, and setting it in advantageous contrast with the treachery and trickery of civilization. Unfortunately this is a mere fancy picture, contradicted by all the realities of savage life. Savages are always liars. They have not the faintest notion of truth as a virtue. They have a notion of not betraying to their hurt, as of not hurting in any other way, persons to whom they are bound by some special tie of obligation; their chief, their guest, perhaps, or their friend: these feelings of obligation being the taught morality of the savage state, growing out of its characteristic circumstances. But of any point of honour respecting truth for truth's sake, they have not the remotest idea; no more than the whole East, and the greater part of Europe: and in the few countries which are sufficiently improved to have such a point of honour, it is confined to a small minority, who alone, under any circumstances of real temptation practice it.

From the general use of the expression "natural justice," it must be presumed that justice is a virtue generally thought to be directly implanted by nature. I believe, however, that the sentiment of justice is entirely of artificial origin; the idea of natural justice not preceding but following that of conventional justice. The farther we look back into the early modes of thinking of the human race, whether we consider ancient times (including those of the Old Testament) or the portions of mankind who are still in no more advanced a condition than that of ancient times, the more completely do we find men's notions of justice defined and bounded by the express appointment of law. A man's just rights, meant the rights which the law gave him: a just man was he who never infringed, nor sought to infringe, the legal property or other legal rights of others. The notion of a higher justice, to which laws themselves are amenable, and by which the conscience is bound without a positive prescripton of law, is a later extension of the idea, suggested by, and following the analogy of, legal justice, to which it maintains a parallel direction through all the shades and varieties of the sentiment, and from which it borrows nearly the whole of its phraseology. The very words *justus* and *justitia* are derived from *jus,* law. Courts of justice, administration of justice, always mean the tribunals.

If it be said, that there must be the germs of all these virtues in human nature, otherwise mankind would be incapable of acquiring them, I am ready, with a certain amount of explanation, to admit the fact. But the weeds that dispute the ground with these beneficent germs, are themselves not germs but rankly luxuriant growths, and would, in all but some one case in a thousand, entirely stifle and destroy the former, were it not so strongly the interest of mankind to cherish the good germs in one another, that they always do so, in as far as their degree of intelligence (in this as in other respects still very imperfect) allows. It is through such fostering, commenced early, and not counteracted by unfavourable influences, that, in some happily circumstanced specimens of the human race, the most elevated sentiments of which humanity is capable become a second nature, stronger than the first, and not so much subduing the original nature as merging it into itself. Even those gifted organizations which have attained the like excellence by self-culture, owe it essentially to the same cause; for what self-culture would be possible without aid from the general sentiment of mankind delivered through books, and from the contemplation of exalted characters real or ideal? This artificially created or at least artificially perfected nature of the best and noblest human beings, is the only nature which it is ever commendable to follow. It is almost superfluous to say that even this cannot be erected into a standard of conduct, since it is itself the fruit of a training and culture the choice of which, if rational and not accidental, must have been determined by a standard already chosen.

This brief survey is amply sufficient to prove that the duty of man is the same in respect to his own nature as in respect to the nature of all other things, namely not to follow but to amend it. Some people however who do not attempt to deny that instinct ought to be subordinate to reason, pay deference to nature so far as to maintain that every natural inclination must have some sphere of action granted to it, some opening left for its gratification. All natural wishes, they say, must have been implanted for a purpose: and this argument is carried so far, that we often hear it maintained that every wish, which it is supposed to be natural to entertain, must have a corresponding provision in the order of the universe for its gratification: insomuch (for instance) that the desire of an indefinite prolongation of existence, is believed by many to be in itself a sufficient proof of the reality of a future life.

I conceive that there is a radical absurdity in all these attempts to discover, in detail, what are the designs of Providence, in order when they are discovered to help Providence in bringing them about. Those who argue, from particular indications, that Providence intends this or that, either believe that the Creator can do all that he will or that he cannot. If the first supposition is adopted—if Providence is omnipotent, Providence intends whatever happens, and the fact of its happening proves that Providence intended it. If so, everything which a human being can do, is predestined by Providence and is a fulfilment of its designs. But if as is the more religious theory, Providence intends not all which happens, but only what is good, then indeed man has it in his power, by his voluntary actions, to aid the intentions of Providence; but he can only learn those intentions by considering what tends to promote the general good, and not what man has a natural inclination to; for, limited as, on this showing, the divine power must be, by inscrutable but insurmountable obstacles, who knows that man *could* have been created without desires which never are to be, and even which never ought to be, fulfilled? The inclinations with which man has been endowed, as well as any of the other contrivances which we observe in Nature, may be the expression not of the divine will, but of the fetters which impede its free action; and to take hints from these for the guidance of our own conduct may be falling into a trap laid by the enemy. The assumption that everything which infinite goodness can desire, actually comes to pass in this universe, or at least that we must never say or suppose that it does not, is worthy only of those whose slavish fears make them offer the homage of lies to a Being who, they profess to think, is incapable of being deceived and holds all falsehood in abomination.

With regard to this particular hypothesis, that all natural impulses, all propensities sufficiently universal and sufficiently spontaneous to be capable of passing for instincts, must exist for good ends and ought to be only regulated, not repressed; this is of course true of the majority of them, for the species could not have continued to exist unless most of its inclinations had been directed to things needful or useful for its preservation. But unless the instincts can be reduced to a very small number indeed, it must be allowed that we have also bad instincts which it should be the aim of education not simply to regulate but to extirpate, or rather (what can be done even to an instinct) to starve them by disuse. Those who are inclined to multiply the number of instincts, usually include among them one which they call destructiveness: an instinct to destroy for destruction's sake. I can conceive no good reason for preserving this, no more than another propensity which if not an instinct is very like one, what has been called the instinct of domination; a delight in exercising despotism, in holding other beings in subjection to our will. The man who takes pleasure in the mere exertion of authority, apart from the purpose for which it is to be employed, is the last person in whose hands one would willingly entrust it. Again, there are persons who are cruel by character, or, as the phrase is, naturally cruel; who have a real pleasure in inflicting, or seeing the infliction of pain. This kind of cruelty is not mere hardheartedness, absence of pity or remorse; it is a positive thing; a particular kind of voluptuous excitement. The East, and Southern Europe, have afforded, and probably still afford, abundant examples of this hateful propensity. I suppose it will be granted that this is not one of the natural inclinations which it would be wrong to suppress. The only question would be whether it is not a duty to suppress the man himself along with it.

But even if it were true that every one of the elementary impulses of human nature has its good side, and may by a sufficient amount of artificial training be made more useful than hurtful; how little would this amount to, when it must in any case be admitted that without such training all of them, even those which are necessary to our preservation, would fill the world with misery, making human life an exaggerated likeness of the odious scene of violence and tyranny which is exhibited by the rest of the animal kingdom, except in so far as tamed and disciplined by man. There, indeed, those who flatter themselves with the notion of reading the purposes of the Creator in his works, ought in consistency to have seen grounds for inferences from which they have shrunk. If there are any marks at all of special design in creation, one of the things most evidently designed is that a large proportion of all animals should pass their existence in tormenting and devouring other animals. They have been lavishly fitted out with the instruments necessary for that purpose; their strongest instincts impel them to it, and many of them seem to have been constructed incapable of supporting themselves by any other food. If a tenth part of the pains which have been expended in finding benevolent adaptations of all nature, had been employed in collecting evidence to blacken the character of the Creator, what scope for comment would not have been found in the entire existence of the lower animals, divided, with scarcely an exception, into devourers and devoured, and a prey to a thousand ills from which they are denied the faculties necessary for protecting themselves! If we are not obliged to believe the animal creation to be the work of a demon, it is because we need not suppose it to have been made by a Being of infinite power. But if imitation of the Creator's will, as revealed in nature, were applied as a rule of action in this case, the most atrocious enormities of the worst men would be more than justified by the apparent intention of Providence that throughout all animated nature the strong should prey upon the weak.

The preceding observations are far from having exhausted the almost infinite variety of modes and occasions in which the idea of conformity to nature is introduced as an element into the ethical appreciation of actions and dispositions. The same favourable prejudgment follows the word nature through the numerous acceptations, in which it is employed as a distinctive term for certain parts of the constitution of humanity as contrasted with other parts. We have hitherto confined ourselves to one of these acceptations, in which it stands as a general designation for those parts of our mental and moral constitution which are supposed to be innate, in contradistinction to those which are acquired; as when nature is contrasted with education; or when a savage state, without laws, arts, or knowledge, is called a state of nature; or when the question is asked whether benevolence, or the moral sentiment, is natural or acquired; or whether some persons are poets or orators by nature and others not. But in another and a more lax sense, any manifestations by human beings are often termed natural, when it is merely intended to say that they are not studied or designedly assumed in the particular case; as when a person is said to move or speak with natural grace; or when it is said that a person's natural manner or character is so and so; meaning that it is so when he does not attempt to control or disguise it. In a still looser acceptation, a person is said to be naturally, that which he was until some special cause had acted upon him, or which it is supposed he would be if some such cause were withdrawn. Thus a person is said to be naturally dull, but to have made himself intelligent by study and perseverance; to be naturally cheerful, but soured by misfortune; naturally ambitious, but kept down by want of opportunity. Finally, the word natural, applied to feelings or conduct, often seems to mean no more than that they are such as are ordinarily found in human beings; as when it is said that a person acted, on some particular occasion, as it was natural to do; or that to be affected in a particular way by some sight, or sound, or thought, or incident in life, is perfectly natural.

In all these senses of the term, the quality called natural is very often confessedly a worse quality than the one contrasted with it; but whenever its being so is not too obvious to be questioned, the idea seems to be entertained that by describing it as natural, something has been said amounting to a considerable presumption in its favour. For my part I can perceive only one sense in which nature, or naturalness, in a human being, are really terms of praise; and then the praise is only negative: namely when used to denote the absence of affectation. Affectation may be defined, the effort to appear what one is not, when the motive or the occasion is not such as either to excuse the attempt, or to stamp it with the more odious name of hypocrisy. It must be added that the deception is often attempted to be practised on the deceiver himself as well as on others; he imitates the external signs of qualities which he would like to have, in hopes to persuade himself that he has them. Whether in the form of deception or of self-deception, or of something hovering between the two, affectation is very rightly accounted a reproach, and naturalness, understood as the reverse of affectation, a merit. But a more proper term by which to express this estimable quality would be sincerity; a term which has fallen from its original elevated meaning, and popularly denotes only a subordinate branch of the cardinal virtue it once designated as a whole.

Sometimes also, in cases where the term affectation would be inappropriate, since the conduct or demeanour spoken of is really praiseworthy, people say in disparagement of the person concerned, that such conduct or demeanour is not natural to him; and make uncomplimentary comparisons between him and some other person, to whom it is natural: meaning that what in the one seemed excellent was the effect of temporary excitement, or of a great victory over himself, while in the other it is the result to be expected from the habitual character. This mode of speech is not open to censure, since nature is here simply a term for the person's ordinary disposition, and if he is praised it is not for being natural, but for being naturally good.

Conformity to nature, has no connection whatever with right and wrong. The idea can never be fitly introduced into ethical discussions at all, except, occasionally and partially, into the question of degrees of culpability. To illustrate this point, let us consider the phrase by which the greatest intensity of condemnatory feeling is conveyed in connection with the idea of nature—the word unnatural. That a thing is unnatural, in any precise meaning which can be attached to the word, is no argument for its being blamable; since the most criminal actions are to a being like man, not more unnatural than most of the virtues. The acquisition of virtue has in all ages been accounted a work of labour and difficulty, while the *descensus Averni* [10] on the contrary is of proverbial facility: and it assuredly requires in most persons a greater conquest over a greater number of natural inclinations to become eminently virtuous than transcendently vicious. But if an action, or an inclination, has been decided on other grounds to be blamable, it may be a circumstance in aggravation that it is unnatural, that is, repugnant to some strong feeling usually found in human beings; since the bad propensity, whatever it be, has afforded evidence of being both strong and deeply rooted, by having overcome that repugnance. This presumption of course fails if the individual never had the repugnance: and the

[10] *descensus Averni:* literally 'descent of Avernus', or descent into Hades. Lake Avernus, near Cumae (an ancient city in Campania, Italy, and home of the Sibyl), because of sulphurous exhalations from its surface, was fabled to be near the entrance to the infernal region (cf. Virgil, *Aeneid*, VI, 125–155).

argument, therefore, is not fit to be urged unless the feeling which is violated by the act, is not only justifiable and reasonable, but is one which it is blamable to be without.

The corresponding plea in extenuation of a culpable act because it was natural, or because it was prompted by a natural feeling, never, I think, ought to be admitted. There is hardly a bad action ever perpetrated which is not perfectly natural, and the motives to which are not perfectly natural feelings. In the eye of reason, therefore, this is no excuse, but it is quite "natural" that it should be so in the eyes of the multitude; because the meaning of the expression is, that they have a fellow feeling with the offender. When they say that something which they cannot help admitting to be blamable, is nevertheless natural, they mean that they can imagine the possibility of their being themselves tempted to commit it. Most people have a considerable amount of indulgence towards all acts of which they feel a possible source within themselves, reserving their rigour for those which, though perhaps really less bad, they cannot in any way understand how it is possible to commit. If an action convinces them (which it often does on very inadequate grounds) that the person who does it must be a being totally unlike themselves, they are seldom particular in examining the precise degree of blame due to it, or even if blame is properly due to it at all. They measure the degree of guilt by the strength of their antipathy; and hence differences of opinion, and even differences of taste, have been objects of as intense moral abhorrence as the most atrocious crimes.

It will be useful to sum up in a few words the leading conclusions of this Essay.

The word Nature has two principal meanings: it either denotes the entire system of things, with the aggregate of all their properties, or it denotes things as they would be, apart from human intervention.

In the first of these senses, the doctrine that man ought to follow nature is unmeaning; since man has no power to do anything else than follow nature; all his actions are done through, and in obedience to, some one or many of nature's physical or mental laws.

In the other sense of the term, the doctrine that men ought to follow nature, or in other words, ought to make the spontaneous course of things the model of his voluntary actions, is equally irrational and immoral.

Irrational, because all human action whatever, consists in altering, and all useful action in improving, the spontaneous course of nature:

Immoral, because the course of natural phenomena being replete with everything which when committed by human beings is most worthy of abhorrence, any one who endeavoured in his actions to imitate the natural course of things would be universally seen and acknowledged to be the wickedest of men.

The scheme of Nature regarded in its whole extent, cannot have had, for its sole or even principal object, the good of human or other sentient beings. What good it brings to them, is mostly the result of their own exertions. Whatsoever, in nature, gives indication of beneficent design, proves this beneficence to be armed only with limited power; and the duty of man is to co-operate with the beneficent powers, not by imitating but by perpetually striving to amend the course of nature—and bringing that part of it over which we can exercise control, more nearly into conformity with a high standard of justice and goodness.   [1874]

CHARLES DARWIN

CHRONOLOGY AND INTRODUCTION

1809 Born in Shrewsbury, Feb. 12.
1817-25 Early schooling at Shrewsbury.
1825-27 Studied medicine at University of Edinburgh.
1828-31 Student at Christ's College, Cambridge; finished B.A., without honors.
1831-36 Naturalist on the *Beagle*, Dec. 27, 1831 to Oct. 2, 1836.
1837 Took lodgings in London and engaged in scientific research.
1839 Marriage, January 29.
1839 *The Voyage of the Beagle.*
1842 Moved to Down, Kent, his home for the rest of his life.
The Structure and Distribution of Coral Reefs.
1846 *Geological Observations on South America.*

1859 *The Origin of Species.*
1862 *Fertilization of Orchids.*
1868 *The Variation of Animals and Plants under Domestication.*
1871 *The Descent of Man.*
1872 *The Expression of the Emotions in Man and Animals.*
1875 *Insectivorous Plants.*
1876 *The Effects of Cross and Self Fertilization in the Vegetable Kingdom.*
1877 Received LL.D. from Cambridge University.
1880 *The Power of Movement in Plants.*
1881 *The Formation of Vegetable Mould, through the Action of Worms.*
1882 Death, April 19.

Among the great scientists of the Victorian age, Darwin was pre-eminent. His name was linked with Newton's. "He is the Newton of natural history," said Alfred Russel Wallace. T. H. Huxley described the *Origin of Species* as the "most potent instrument for the extension of the realm of natural knowledge which has come into men's hands since the publication of Newton's *Principia.*" The theory of evolution, which Darwin was far from the first to enunciate, became through his researches not only "the central generalization of biology," but one of the most fruitful concepts of all time in practically every field of human thought. We no longer think of things and events, whether in the organic or inorganic world, as immutable, fixed; everything is fluid, changing, evolving. Because of Darwin's immense influence in so many directions upon so many minds, his life and work inevitably find their place in any comprehensive view of the period in which he lived.

His inheritance was most favorable. His paternal grandfather was Erasmus Darwin, physician by vocation, and naturalist, poet, philosopher by avocation; his maternal grandfather was Josiah Wedgwood, the great potter. His father was a successful and locally distinguished doctor of medicine,—"the wisest man I ever knew," said the son. Formal education, both in school and university, Darwin looked back upon—with some injustice to himself—as a waste of time: "No one can more truly despise the old stereotyped stupid classical education than I do," he remarked, years later. Yet he was extremely happy. His health was good, his spirits high, his money allowances liberal, and, consequently, he entered enthusiastically but not extravagantly into the sports and convivialities of the life around him. This was especially true of Cambridge days, of which he wrote when far away on the *Beagle* voyage: "I love and treasure up every recollection of dear old Cambridge."

Darwin was naturalist on that famous little ship because at Cambridge he had developed such an expert interest in observing and collecting various forms of plant and animal life that his teacher and friend, Henslow, professor of Botany, recommended him to Captain Fitzroy as a young scientist qualified to study the fauna and flora of the countries to be visited on a voyage that was sent out by the British government "to survey the southern coast of Tierra del Fuego, and afterwards to visit many of the South Sea Islands, and to return by the Indian Archipelago." "The voyage of the *Beagle,*" he has told us, "has been by far the most important event in my life, and has determined my whole career....I have always felt that I owe to the voyage the first real training or education of my mind; I was led to attend closely to several branches of natural history, and thus my powers of observation were improved, though they were always fairly developed." When Darwin embarked on the expedition in December, 1831, he was twenty-two; when he returned in October, 1836, he was many more than five years older in experience, with a passion for scientific research possibly unrivalled in the history of science. His rapturous absorption in the study of natural phenomena is suggested in a rare outburst, written from the *Beagle*, near Rio de Janeiro (May 1832): "My mind has been, since leaving England, in a perfect hurricane of delight and astonishment, and to this hour scarcely a minute has passed in idleness."

He came back with weakened health, a condition which soon became fixed upon him until, as his son and biographer says, "for nearly forty years he never knew one day of the health of ordinary men, and thus his life was one long struggle against the weariness and strain of sickness." Happily, before long, independent means released him from the necessity of professional employment and enabled him to marry and set up his home in a retired spot just outside Down, in Kent, where he spent long years in studious leisure, only interrupted by recurring periods of ill health. From all accounts Darwin must have been an almost ideal husband and father, as he was companion and friend. When his books appeared and his theories were known, his name was heard everywhere and became, indeed, the storm-center of a conflict that swept England and the whole intellectual world. But his modesty, his simplicity, his complete freedom from arrogance or assumption were unchanged. Very different men found Darwin always the same, a delightful personality. Carlyle said of him to Tyndall, "a more charming man I have never met in my life." "There is something almost pathetic in his simplicity and friendliness," is the recorded impression of Leslie Stephen. James Bryce saw Darwin in 1881, not long before his death, and found him "delightfully unconscious of his greatness, . . . perfectly natural and simple, just like anyone else."

The best analysis of his mind and character is the short autobiography which he wrote, not for publication, but for his wife and children. The passage in which he describes the atrophy of his taste for literature and art is famous and need not be repeated here. Doubtless the case is overstated, but there can be no question that exclusive application of the mind through years to scientific and logical analysis does enfeeble or even sometimes destroy normal emotional responses to the appeals of art and nature. The experience of John Stuart Mill, equally well known, is nearly identical, except that Mill made a recovery, while Darwin, intensely alive to beauty and sublimity in the *Beagle* days, lost most of such feeling after he became immersed in scientific research. Not entirely, however, for he delighted in novels all his life if the endings were happy, and, as his son assures us, "his love of scenery remained fresh and strong."

But when a mind is supremely gifted and fruitful in a single direction, undoubtedly it is best for that mind and for the world that it should develop itself on one side, albeit at the expense of other sides. Even Matthew Arnold recognized that the born naturalist is "extremely rare" and may be allowed to go his own way, regardless of the "harmonious" expansion which culture prescribes for most of us. A born naturalist Darwin was, for even in boyhood he took to observing and collecting all sorts of phenomena, especially beetles. The authentic scientific impulse came to him, however, on the voyage of the *Beagle*: "As far as I can judge," he said, "I worked to the utmost during the voyage from the mere pleasure of investigation, and from my strong desire to add a few facts to the great mass of facts in Natural Science." The awakening of that time carried him through forty and more years of "steady and ardent" pursuit of truth. Some of Darwin's characteristics as a worker are enumerated by his son: "his power of never letting exceptions pass unnoticed; his power of sticking to a subject . . . his doggedness; his love of experiment"; and the habit of making generalizations. "Let theory guide your observations," he said, but he warned the investigator to be slow in publishing them. He knew, too, that truth would not penetrate a mind preoccupied with alien interests, such as fame or wealth or position; and it was because he was able to fix all his great powers for long periods upon single objectives that he explored secrets of nature inaccessible to less fortunate searchers.

Darwin's achievement in science is not for the layman to discuss except in the most general terms. He was not a specialist in the present-day sense. He worked in many fields, in geology, botany, zoology, psychology, bringing together enormous masses of material, "huge classes of phenomena," under large generalizations. His fame rests, for the most part, upon his *Origin of Species*, which for all time established the *fact* of evolution and showed the *mechanism* (natural selection) by which it could be explained. When he sailed away on the *Beagle* Darwin, like almost everybody else, believed in the immutability of species. But his experience brought him face to face with many facts that began to shake his faith: the vast slow changes in earth formations; the great fossil animals of the pampas; the savages of Tierra del Fuego; life on the islands of the Galapagos. He returned from the expedition with more than a hint that species were probably not the fixed result of special creation but were due to natural causes slowly operating through long periods of time. He set to work, and gradually, "after many years of weighing puzzles, to myself *alone*," the conclusion was inevitable that species originated "by means of natural selection, or the survival of the fittest" in the struggle of life. "Why should not Nature take a sudden leap from structure to structure?" he asks. "On the theory of natural selection, we can clearly understand why she should not; for natural selection acts only by taking advantage of slight successive variations; she can never take a great and sudden leap, but must advance by short and sure, though slow steps." Darwin fully understood that his conclusions would open important avenues of research in many directions leading to startling results. "Much light," he said unobtrusively at the end of his book, "will be thrown on the origin of man and his history." Twelve years later, in his *Descent of Man*, he applied his generalization to human beings, and thus demonstrated the unity of all organic life, a theory which he had suggested in a remarkable passage in the *Origin:* "On the principle of natural selection with divergence of character, it does not seem incredible that, from some such low and intermediate form (i.e., one of the lower algae), both animals and plants may have been developed; and, if we admit this, we must likewise admit that all organic beings which have ever lived may be descended from some one primordial form." Modern biology in the field of genetics has gone far beyond Darwin, but the principle "that Natural Selection does exist, and that it plays a dominant role in bringing about evolutionary change" remains unshaken.

In his *Voyage of the Beagle,* Darwin speaks of "the philosophical naturalist," a phrase that accurately describes himself in so far as he habitually and successfully sought to bring masses of fact under large generalizations; and this, no doubt, is all that he meant by the expression. Philosophical in the sense of one who engages in speculation on the meaning of such concepts as mind, matter, and God he never was. More exclusively than most of his intellectual kindred, he was a scientist alone, and seemed content to be nothing more. He expressed little or no interest in the great political and social problems of his day. He clearly realized how far-reaching, indeed how shattering, were the effects of his theories upon the minds of contemporaries all over the world. But he could not be drawn into controversy, and he seems rarely to have unveiled his deepest reflections even to friends. No one could be more conscious than he of the grandeur and mystery of the universe of which earth and man are parts; and none better understood how widespread is suffering in the realm of living things. "What a book," he exclaimed, "a devil's chaplain might write on the clumsy, wasteful, blundering, low, and horribly cruel works of nature!" There is nowhere from his pen a clearer or more characteristically candid expression of his deeper view than the following from a letter to Asa Gray, the American botanist, written in 1860 apropos of the *Origin:* "I had no intention to write atheistically. But I own that I cannot see as plainly as others do, and as I should wish to do, evidence of design and beneficence on all sides of us. There seems to me too much misery in the world. I cannot persuade myself that a beneficent and omnipotent God would have designedly created the Ichneumonidae with the express intention of their feeding within the living bodies of Caterpillars, or that a cat should play with mice. Not believing this, I see no necessity in the belief that the eye was expressly designed. On the other hand, I cannot anyhow be contented to view this wonderful universe, and especially the nature of man, and to conclude that everything is the result of brute force. I am inclined to look at everything as resulting from designed laws, with the details, whether good or bad, left to the working out of what we may call chance. Not that this notion *at all* satisfies me. I feel most deeply that the whole subject is too profound for the human intellect."

An impromptu communication such as this extract from a letter is sufficient evidence that Darwin wrote with directness and clarity. He was content if his readers understood him. "No nigger with a lash over him could have worked harder at clearness than I have done," he said to his friend Hooker, the great botanist. Style in any of its special senses of the word, he seems never to have striven for and certainly never achieved; though he could praise Carlyle's "extraordinary power of drawing pictures of things and men," for example, or could delight in the "flesh and colors" of Huxley's "inimitable manner." Writing for him, if not quite a torture, was far from a pleasure. "A naturalist's life," he once remarked, "would be a happy one if he had only to observe and not to write." In his autobiography he has told his readers how much labor he put into the composition of his books, especially the *Origin,* which he wrote over and over, recasting, compressing, before he gave the manuscript to his publisher. Even then no less a man than Huxley found it one of the hardest of books to understand, partly because of faults of exposition which, he said, "was not Darwin's forte."

All in all, however, Darwin's prose has won praise from specialist and layman alike for its modest plainness and effectiveness, its continuous undercurrent of veracity and vitality, qualities which appear strikingly appropriate to Darwin the man and to his theme. He is, too, a master of economy of phrase; there are few wasted words, there is no surplusage. Now and then moreover his writing surprises by its elevation, as in the concluding paragraphs of the *Origin* and the *Descent*. And in his *Voyage of the Beagle* there are many passages of great vividness and beauty, composed before his mind had "become a kind of machine for grinding general laws out of large collections of facts," as, for example, the following description of a phosphorescent sea off the coast of South America: "While sailing a little south of the Plata on one very dark night, the sea presented a wonderful and most beautiful spectacle. There was a fresh breeze, and every part of the surface, which during the day is seen as foam, now glowed with a pale light. The vessel drove before her bows two billows of liquid phosphorus, and in her wake she was followed by a milky train. As far as the eye reached, the crest of every wave was bright, and the sky above the horizon, from the reflected glare of these livid flames, was not so utterly obscure as over the vault of the heavens." In writing such as this, by no means extremely rare, there is for many readers a quiet fascination not easy to define. What Darwin saw, whether something merely factual or touched with beauty, he could describe with simple clarity and often with unexpected charm.

AUTOBIOGRAPHY

(My father's autobiographical recollections, given in the present chapter, were written for his children,—and written without any thought that they would ever be published. To many this may seem an impossibility; but those who knew my father will understand how it was not only possible, but natural. The autobiography bears the heading, "Recollections of the Development of my Mind and Character," and ends with the following note:—"Aug. 3, 1876. This sketch of my life was begun about May 28th at Hopedene, and since then I have written for nearly an hour on most afternoons."—Note by Darwin's son, Francis Darwin.)

A German Editor having written to me for an account of the development of my mind and character with some sketch of my autobiography, I have thought that the attempt would amuse me, and might possibly interest my children or their children. I know that it would have interested me greatly to have read even so short and dull a sketch of the mind of my grandfather, written by himself, and what he thought and did, and how he worked. I have attempted to write the following account of myself, as if I were a dead man in another world looking back at my own life. Nor have I found this difficult, for life is nearly over with me. I have taken no pains about my style of writing.

I was born at Shrewsbury on February 12th, 1809, and my earliest recollection goes back only to when I was a few months over four years old, when we went to near Abergele for sea-bathing, and I recollect some events and places there with some little distinctness.

My mother died in July 1817, when I was a little over eight years old, and it is odd that I can remember hardly anything about her except her death-bed, her black velvet gown, and her curiously constructed work-table. In the spring of this same year I was sent to a day-school in Shrewsbury, where I stayed a year. I have been told that I was much slower in learning than my younger sister Catherine, and I believe that I was in many ways a naughty boy.

By the time I went to this day-school my taste for natural history, and more especially for collecting, was well developed. I tried to make out the name of plants, and collected all sorts of things, shells, seals, franks, coins, and minerals. The passion for collecting which leads a man to be a systematic naturalist, a virtuoso, or a miser, was very strong in me, and was clearly innate, as none of my sisters or brother ever had this taste.

One little event during this year has fixed itself very firmly in my mind, and I hope that it has done so from my conscience having been afterward sorely troubled by it; it is curious as showing that apparently I was interested at this early age in the variability of plants! I told another little boy (I believe it was Leighton, who afterwards became a well-known lichenologist and botanist), that I could produce variously coloured polyanthuses and primroses by watering them with certain coloured fluids, which was of course a monstrous fable, and had never been tried by me. I may here also confess that as a little boy I was much given to inventing deliberate falsehoods, and this was always done for the sake of causing excitement. For instance, I once gathered much valuable fruit from my father's trees and hid it in the shrubbery, and then ran in breathless haste to spread the news that I had discovered a hoard of stolen fruit.

I must have been a very simple little fellow when I first went to the school. A boy of the name of Garnett took me into a cake shop one day, and bought some cakes for which he did not pay, as the shopman trusted him. When we came out I asked him why he did not pay for them, and he instantly answered, "Why, do you not know that my uncle left a great sum of money to the town on condition that every tradesman should give whatever was wanted without payment to any one who wore his old hat and moved (it) in a particular manner?" and he then showed me how it was moved. He then went into another shop where he was trusted, and asked for some small article, moving his hat in the proper manner, and of course obtained it without payment. When we came out he said, "Now if you like to go by yourself into that cake-shop (how well I remember its exact position) I will lend you my hat, and you can get whatever you like if you move the hat on your head properly." I gladly accepted the generous offer, and went in and asked for some cakes, moved the old hat and was walking out of the shop, when the shopman made a rush at me, so I dropped the cakes and ran for dear life, and was astonished by being greeted with shouts of laughter by my false friend Garnett.

I can say in my own favour that I was as a boy humane, but I owed this entirely to the instruction and example of my sisters. I doubt indeed whether humanity is a natural or innate quality. I was very fond of collecting eggs, but I never took more than a single egg out of a bird's nest, except on one single occasion, when I took all, not for their value, but from a sort of bravado.

I had a strong taste for angling, and would sit for any number of hours on the bank of a river or pond watching the float; when at Maer I was told that I could kill the worms with salt and water, and from that day I never spitted a living worm, though at the expense probably of some loss of success.

Once as a very little boy whilst at the day school, or before that time, I acted cruelly, for I beat a puppy, I believe, simply from enjoying the sense of power; but the beating could not have been severe, for the puppy did not howl, of which I feel sure, as the spot was near the house. This act lay heavily on my conscience, as is shown by my remembering the exact spot where the crime was committed. It probably lay all the heavier from my love of dogs being then, and for a long time afterwards, a passion. Dogs seemed to know this, for I was an adept in robbing their love from their masters.

I remember clearly only one other incident during this year whilst at Mr. Case's daily school,—namely, the burial of a dragoon soldier; and it is surprising how clearly I can still see the horse with the man's empty boots and carbine suspended to the saddle, and the firing over the grave. This scene deeply stirred whatever poetic fancy there was in me.

In the summer of 1818 I went to Dr. Butler's great school in Shrewsbury, and remained there for seven years till Midsummer 1825, when I was sixteen years old. I boarded at this school, so that I had the great advantage of living the life of a true schoolboy; but as the distance was hardly more than a mile to my home, I very often ran there in the longer intervals between the callings over and before locking up at night. This, I think, was in many ways advantageous to me by keeping up home affections and interests. I remember in the early part of my school life that I often had to run very quickly to be in time, and from being a fleet runner was generally successful; but when in doubt I prayed earnestly to God to help me, and I well remember that I attributed my success to the prayers and not to my quick running, and marvelled how generally I was aided.

I have heard my father and elder sister say that I had, as a very young boy, a strong taste for long solitary walks; but what I thought about I know not. I often became quite absorbed, and once, whilst returning to school on the summit of the old fortifications round Shrewsbury, which had been converted into a public foot-path with no parapet on one side, I walked off and fell to the ground, but the height was only seven or eight feet. Nevertheless the number of thoughts which passed through my mind during this very short, but sudden and wholly unexpected fall, was astonishing, and seem hardly compatible with what physiologists have, I believe, proved about each thought requiring quite an appreciable amount of time.

Nothing could have been worse for the development of my mind than Dr. Butler's school, as it was strictly classical, nothing else being taught, except a little ancient geography and history. The school as a means of education to me was simply a blank. During my whole life I have been singularly incapable of mastering any language. Especial attention was paid to verse-making, and this I could never do well. I had many friends, and got together a good collection of old verses, which by patching together, sometimes aided by other boys, I could work into any subject. Much attention was paid to learning by heart the lessons of the previous day; this I could effect with great facility, learning forty or fifty lines of Virgil or Homer, whilst I was in morning chapel; but this exercise was utterly useless, for every verse was forgotten in forty-eight hours. I was not idle, and with the exception of versification, generally worked conscientiously at my classics, not using cribs. The sole pleasure I ever received from such studies, was from some of the odes of Horace, which I admired greatly.

When I left the school I was for my age neither high nor low in it; and I believe that I was considered by all my masters and by my father as a very ordinary boy, rather below the common standard in intellect. To my deep mortification my father once said to me, "You care for nothing but shooting, dogs, and rat-catching, and you will be a disgrace to yourself and all your family." But my father, who was the kindest man I ever knew and whose memory I love with all my heart, must have been angry and somewhat unjust when he used such words.

Looking back as well as I can at my character during my school life, the only qualities which at this period promised well for the future, were, that I had strong and diversified tastes, much zeal for whatever interested me, and a keen pleasure in understanding any complex subject or thing. I was taught Euclid by a private tutor, and I distinctly remember the intense satisfaction which the clear geometrical proofs gave me. I remember, with equal distinctness, the delight which my uncle gave me (the father of Francis Galton) by explaining the principle of the vernier of a barometer. With respect to diversified tastes, independently of science, I was fond of reading various books, and I used to sit for hours reading the historical plays of Shakespeare, generally in an old window in the thick walls of the school. I read also other poetry, such as Thomson's "Seasons," and the recently published poems of Byron and Scott. I mention this because later in life I wholly lost, to my great regret, all pleasure from poetry of any kind, including Shakespeare. In connection with pleasure from poetry, I may add that in 1822 a vivid delight in scenery was first awakened in my mind, during a riding tour on the borders of Wales, and this has lasted longer than any other aesthetic pleasure.

Early in my school days a boy had a copy of the "Wonders of the World," which I often read, and disputed with other boys about the veracity of some of the statements; and I believe that this book first gave me a wish to travel in remote countries, which was ultimately fulfilled by the voyage of the *Beagle*. In the latter part of my school life I became passionately fond of shooting; I do not believe that any one could have shown more zeal for the most holy cause that I did for shooting birds. How well I remember killing my first snipe, and my excitement was so great that I had much difficulty in reloading my gun from the trembling of my hands. This taste long continued, and I became a very good shot. When at Cambridge I used to practise throwing up my gun to my shoulder before a looking-glass to see that I threw it up straight. Another and better plan was to get a friend to wave about a lighted candle, and then to fire at it with a cap on the nipple, and if the aim was accurate the little puff of air would blow out the candle. The explosion of the cap caused a sharp crack, and I was told that the tutor of the college remarked, "What an extraordinary thing it is, Mr. Darwin seems to spend hours in cracking a horse-whip in his room, for I often hear the crack when I pass under his windows."

I had many friends amongst the school boys, whom I loved dearly, and I think that my disposition was then very affectionate.

With respect to science, I continued collecting minerals with much zeal, but quite unscientifically—all that I cared about was a new-*named* mineral, and I hardly attempted to classify them. I must have observed insects with some little care, for when ten years old (1819) I went for three weeks to Plas Edwards on the sea-coast in Wales, I was very much interested and surprised at seeing a large black and scarlet Hemipterous insect, many moths (*Zygaena*), and a Cicindela which was not found in Shropshire. I almost made up my mind to begin collecting all the insects which I could find dead, for on consulting my sister I concluded that it was not right to kill insects for the sake of making a collection. From reading White's "Selborne," I took much pleasure in watching the habits of birds, and even made notes on the subject. In my simplicity I remember wondering why every gentleman did not become an ornithologist.

Towards the close of my school life, my brother worked hard at chemistry, and made a fair laboratory with proper apparatus in the tool-house in the garden, and I was allowed to aid him as a servant in most of his experiments. He made all the gases and many compounds, and I read with great care several books on chemistry, such as Henry and Parkes' "Chemical Catechism." The subject interested me greatly, and we often used to go on working till rather late at night. This was the best part of my education at school, for it showed me practically the meaning of experimental science. The fact that we worked at chemistry somehow got known at school, and as it was an unprecedented fact, I was nick-named "Gas." I was also once publicly rebuked by the head-master, Dr. Butler, for thus wasting my time on such useless subjects; and he called me very unjustly a *"poco curante,"* [1] and as I did not understand what he meant, it seemed to me a fearful reproach.

As I was doing no good at school, my father wisely took me away at a rather earlier age than usual, and sent me (Oct. 1825) to Edinburgh University with my brother, where I stayed for two years or sessions. My brother was completing his medical studies, though I do not believe he ever really intended to practice, and I was sent there to commence them. But soon after this period I became convinced from various small circumstances that my father would leave me property enough to subsist on with some comfort, though I never imagined that I should be so rich a man as I am; but my belief was sufficient to check any strenuous efforts to learn medicine.

The instruction at Edinburgh was altogether by lectures, and these were intolerably dull, with the exception of those on chemistry by Hope; but to my mind there are no advantages and many disadvantages in lectures compared with reading. Dr. Duncan's lectures on Materia Medica at 8 o'clock on a winter's morning are something fearful to remember. Dr. ——— made his lectures on human anatomy as dull as he was himself, and the subject disgusted me. It has proved one of the greatest evils in my life that I was not urged to practise dissection, for I should soon have got over my disgust; and the practise would have been invaluable for all my future work.

1 *poco-curante:* indifferent, nonchalant; an Italian word, literally, 'caring little'.

This has been an irremediable evil, as well as my incapacity to draw. I also attended regularly the clinical wards in the hospital. Some of the cases distressed me a good deal, and I still have vivid pictures before me of some of them; but I was not so foolish as to allow this to lessen my attendance. I cannot understand why this part of my medical course did not interest me in a greater degree; for during the summer before coming to Edinburgh I began attending some of the poor people, chiefly children and women in Shrewsbury: I wrote down as full an account as I could of the case with all the symptoms, and read them aloud to my father, who suggested further inquiries and advised me what medicines to give, which I made up myself. At one time I had at least a dozen patients, and I felt a keen interest in the work. My father, who was by far the best judge of character whom I ever knew, declared that I should make a successful physician,—meaning by this one who would get many patients. He maintained that the chief element of success was exciting confidence; but what he saw in me which convinced him that I should create confidence I know not. I also attended on two occasions the operating theatre in the hospital at Edinburgh, and saw two very bad operations, one on a child, but I rushed away before they were completed. Nor did I ever attend again, for hardly any inducement would have been strong enough to make me do so; this being long before the blessed days of chloroform. The two cases fairly haunted me for many a long year.

My brother stayed only one year at the University, so that during the second year I was left to my own resources; and this was an advantage, for I became well acquainted with several young men fond of natural science. One of these was Ainsworth, who afterwards published his travels in Assyria; he was a Wernerian geologist, and knew a little about many subjects. Dr. Coldstream was a very different young man, prim, formal, highly religious, and most kind-hearted; he afterwards published some good zoological articles. A third young man was Hardie, who would, I think, have made a good botanist, but died early in India. Lastly, Dr. Grant, my senior by several years, but how I became acquainted with him I cannot remember; he published some first-rate zoological papers, but after coming to London as Professor in University College, he did nothing more in science, a fact which has always been inexplicable to me. I knew him well; he was dry and formal in manner, with much enthusiasm beneath this outer crust. He one day, when we were walking together, burst forth in high admiration of Lamarck and his views on evolution. I listened in silent astonishment, and as far as I can judge without any effect on my mind. I had previously read the "Zoonomia" of my grandfather, in which similar views are maintained, but without producing any effect on me. Nevertheless it is probable that the hearing rather early in life such views maintained and praised may have favoured my upholding them under a different form in my "Origin of Species." At this time I admired greatly the "Zoonomia"; but on reading it a second time after an interval of ten or fifteen years, I was much disappointed; the proportion of speculation being so large to the facts given.

Drs. Grant and Coldstream attended much to marine Zoology, and I often accompanied the former to collect animals in the tidal pools, which I dissected as well as I could. I also became friends with some of the Newhaven fishermen, and sometimes accompanied them when they trawled for oysters, and thus got many specimens. But from not having had any regular practice in dissection, and from possessing only a wretched microscope, my attempts were very poor. Nevertheless I made one interesting little discovery, and read, about the beginning of the year 1826, a short paper on the subject before the Plinian Society. This was that the so-called ova of Flustra had the power of independent movement by means of cilia, and were in fact larvae. In another short paper I showed that the little globular bodies which had been supposed to be the young state of *Fucas Loreus* were the egg-cases of the wormlike *Pontobdella muricata*.

The Plinian Society was encouraged and, I believe, founded by Professor Jameson: it consisted of students and met in an underground room in the University for the sake of reading papers on natural science and discussing them. I used regularly to attend, and the meetings had a good effect on me in stimulating my zeal and giving me new congenial acquaintances. One evening a poor young man got up, and after stammering for a prodigious length of time, blushing crimson, he at last slowly got out the words, "Mr. President, I have forgotten what I was going to say." The poor fellow looked quite overwhelmed, and all the members were so surprised that no one could think of a word to say to cover his confusion. The papers which were read to our little society were not printed, so that I had not the satisfaction of seeing my paper in print; but I believe Dr. Grant noticed my small discovery in his excellent memoir on Flustra.

I was also a member of the Royal Medical Society, and attended pretty regularly; but as the subjects were exclusively medical, I did not much care about them. Much rubbish was talked there but there were some good speakers, of whom the best was the present Sir J. Kay-Shuttleworth. Dr. Grant took me occasionally to the meetings of the Wernerian Society, where various papers on natural history were read, discussed, and afterwards published in the "Transactions." I heard Audubon deliver there some interesting discourses on the habits of N. American birds, sneering somewhat unjustly at Waterton. By the way, a negro lived in Edinburgh, who had travelled with Waterton, and gained his livelihood by stuffing birds, which he did excellently: he gave me lessons for payment, and I used often to sit with him, for he was a very pleasant and intelligent man.

Mr. Leonard Horner also took me once to a meeting of the Royal Society of Edinburgh, where I saw Sir Walter Scott in the chair as President, and he apologized to the meeting as not feeling fitted for such a position. I looked at him and at the whole scene with some awe and reverence, and I think it was owing to this visit during my youth, and to my having attended the Royal Medical Society, that I felt the honour of being elected a few years ago an honorary member of both these Societies, more than any other similar honour. If I had been told at that time that I should

one day have been thus honoured, I declare that I should have thought it as ridiculous and improbable, as if I had been told that I should be elected King of England.

During my second year at Edinburgh I attended ——'s lectures on Geology and Zoology, but they were incredibly dull. The sole effect they produced on me was the determination never as long as I lived to read a book on Geology, or in any way to study the science. Yet I feel sure that I was prepared for a philosophical treatment of the subject; for an old Mr. Cotton in Shropshire, who knew a good deal about rocks, had pointed out to me two or three years previously a well-known large erratic boulder in the town of Shrewsbury, called the "bell-stone"; he told me that there was no rock of the same kind nearer than Cumberland or Scotland, and he solemnly assured me that the world would come to an end before any one would be able to explain how this stone came where it now lay. This produced a deep impression on me, and I meditated over this wonderful stone. So that I felt the keenest delight when I first read of the action of icebergs in transporting boulders, and I gloried in the progress of Geology. Equally striking is the fact that I, though now only sixty-seven years old, heard the Professor, in a field lecture at Salisbury Craigs, discoursing on a trapdyke, with amygdaloidal margins and the strata indurated on each side, with volcanic rocks all around us, say that it was a fissure filled with sediment from above, adding with a sneer that there were men who maintained that it had been injected from beneath in a molten condition. When I think of this lecture, I do not wonder that I determined never to attend to Geology.

From attending ——'s lecture, I became acquainted with the curator of the museum, Mr. Macgillivray, who afterwards published a large and excellent book on the birds of Scotland. I had much interesting natural-history talk with him, and he was very kind to me. He gave me some rare shells, for I at that time collected marine mollusca, but with no great zeal.

My summer vacations during these two years were wholly given up to amusements, though I always had some book in hand, which I read with interest. During the summer of 1826 I took a long walking tour with two friends with knapsacks on our backs through North Wales. We walked thirty miles most days, including one day the ascent of Snowdon. I also went with my sister on a riding tour in North Wales, a servant with saddle-bags carrying our clothes. The autumns were devoted to shooting chiefly at Mr. Owen's, at Wood-house, and at my Uncle Jos's, at Maer. My zeal was so great that I used to place my shooting-boots open by my bed-side when I went to bed, so as not to lose half a minute in putting them on in the morning; and on one occasion I reached a distant part of the Maer estate, on the 20th of August for black-game shooting, before I could see: I then toiled on with the game-keeper the whole day through thick heath and young Scotch firs.

I kept an exact record of every bird which I shot throughout the whole season. One day when shooting at Woodhouse with Captain Owen, the eldest son, and Major Hill, his cousin, afterwards Lord Berwick, both of whom I liked very much, I thought myself shamefully used, for every time after I had fired and thought that I had killed a bird, one of the two acted as if loading his gun, and cried out, "You must not count that bird, for I fired at the same time," and the gamekeeper, perceiving the joke, backed them up. After some hours they told me the joke, but it was no joke to me, for I had shot a large number of birds, but did not know how many, and could not add them to my list, which I used to do by making a knot in a piece of string tied to a button-hole. This my wicked friends had perceived.

How I did enjoy shooting! but I think that I must have been half-consciously ashamed of my zeal, for I tried to persuade myself that shooting was almost an intellectual employment; it required so much skill to judge where to find most game and to hunt the dogs well.

One of my autumnal visits to Maer in 1827 was memorable from meeting there Sir J. Mackintosh, who was the best converser I ever listened to. I heard afterwards with a glow of pride that he had said, "There is something in that young man that interests me." This must have been chiefly due to his perceiving that I listened with much interest to everything which he said, for I was as ignorant as a pig about his subjects of history, politics, and moral philosophy. To hear of praise from an eminent person, though no doubt apt or certain to excite vanity, is, I think, good for a young man, as it helps to keep him in the right course.

My visits to Maer during these two or three succeeding years were quite delightful, independently of the autumnal shooting. Life there was perfectly free; the country was very pleasant for walking or riding; and in the evening there was much very agreeable conversation, not so personal as it generally is in large family parties, together with music. In the summer the whole family used often to sit on the steps of the old portico, with the flower-garden in front, and with the steep wooded bank opposite the house reflected in the lake, with here and there a fish rising or a water-bird paddling about. Nothing has left a more vivid picture on my mind than these evenings at Maer. I was also attached to and greatly revered my Uucle Jos; he was silent and reserved, so as to be a rather awful man; but he sometimes talked openly with me. He was the very type of an upright man, with the clearest judgment. I do not believe that any power on earth could have made him swerve an inch from what he considered the right course. I used to apply to him in my mind the well-known ode of Horace, now forgotten by me, in which the words "nec vultus tyrrani, &c.," [2] come in.

CAMBRIDGE 1828-1831

After having spent two sessions in Edinburgh, my father perceived, or he heard from my sisters, that I did not like the thought of being a physician, so he proposed that I should become a clergyman. He was very properly vehement against my turning into an idle sporting man, which then seemed my probable destination. I

[2] *nec vultus tyranni*, etc.: "The man tenacious of his purpose in a righteous cause is not shaken from his firm resolve by the frenzy of his fellow citizens bidding what is wrong, *not by the face of threatening tyrant*," etc. (*Odes*, III, iii, 1-4; Loeb trans.).

asked for some time to consider, as from what little I had heard or thought on the subject I had scruples about declaring my belief in all the dogmas of the Church of England; though otherwise I liked the thought of being a country clergyman. Accordingly I read with care "Pearson on the Creeds," and a few other books on divinity; and as I did not then in the least doubt the strict and literal truth of every word in the Bible, I soon persuaded myself that our Creed must be fully accepted.

Considering how fiercely I have been attacked by the orthodox, it seems ludicrous that I once intended to be a clergyman. Nor was this intention and my father's wish ever formally given up, but died a natural death when, on leaving Cambridge, I joined the *Beagle* as naturalist. If the phrenologists are to be trusted, I was well fitted in one respect to be a clergyman. A few years ago the secretaries of a German psychological society asked me earnestly by letter for a photograph of myself; and some time afterwards I received the proceedings of one of the meetings, in which it seemed that the shape of my head had been the subject of a public discussion, and one of the speakers declared that I had the bump of reverence developed enough for ten priests.

As it was decided that I should be a clergyman, it was necessary that I should go to one of the English universities and take a degree; but as I had never opened a classical book since leaving school, I found to my dismay, that in the two intervening years I had actually forgotten, incredible as it may appear, almost everything which I had learnt, even to some few of the Greek letters. I did not therefore proceed to Cambridge at the usual time in October, but worked with a private tutor in Shrewsbury, and went to Cambridge after the Christmas vacation, early in 1828. I soon recovered my school standard of knowledge, and could translate easy Greek books, such as Homer and the Greek Testament, with moderate facility.

During the three years which I spent at Cambridge my time was wasted, as far as the academical studies were concerned, as completely as at Edinburgh and at school. I attempted mathematics, and even went during the summer of 1828 with a private tutor (a very dull man) to Barmouth, but I got on very slowly. The work was repugnant to me, chiefly from my not being able to see any meaning in the early steps of algebra. This impatience was very foolish, and in after years I have deeply regretted that I did not proceed far enough at least to understand something of the great leading principles of mathematics, for men thus endowed seem to have an extra sense. But I do not believe that I should ever have succeeded beyond a very low grade. With respect to Classics I did nothing except attend a few compulsory college lectures, and the attendance was almost nominal. In my second year I had to work for a month or two to pass the Little-Go, which I did easily. Again, in my last year I worked with some earnestness for my final degree of B. A., and brushed up my Classics, together with a little Algebra and Euclid, which latter gave me much pleasure, as it did at school. In order to pass the B. A. examination, it was also necessary to get up Paley's "Evidences of Christianity," and his "Moral Philosophy." This was done in a thorough manner, and I am convinced that I could have written out the whole of the "Evidences" with perfect correctness, but not of course in the clear language of Paley. The logic of this book and, as I may add, of his "Natural Theology," gave me as much delight as did Euclid. The careful study of these works, without attempting to learn any part by rote, was the only part of the academical course which, as I then felt and as I still believe, was of the least use to me in the education of my mind. I did not at that time trouble myself about Paley's premises; and taking these on trust, I was charmed and convinced by the long line of argumentation. By answering well the examination questions in Paley, by doing Euclid well, and by not failing miserably in Classics, I gained a good place among the οἱ πολλοὶ or crowd of men who do not go in for honours. Oddly enough, I cannot remember how high I stood, and my memory fluctuates between the fifth, tenth, or twelfth, name on the list.

Public lectures on several branches were given in the University, attendance being quite voluntary; but I was so sickened with lectures at Edinburgh that I did not even attend Sedgwick's eloquent and interesting lectures. Had I done so I should probably have become a geologist earlier than I did. I attended, however, Henslow's lectures on Botany, and liked them much for their extreme clearness, and the admirable illustrations; but I did not study botany. Henslow used to take his pupils, including several of the older members of the University, field excursions, on foot or in coaches, to distant places, or in a barge down the river, and lectured on the rarer plants and animals which were observed. These excursions were delightful.

Although, as we shall presently see, there were some redeeming features in my life at Cambridge, my time was sadly wasted there, and worse than wasted. From my passion for shooting and for hunting, and, when this failed, for riding across country, I got into a sporting set, including some dissipated low-minded young men. We used often to dine together in the evening, though these dinners often included men of a higher stamp, and we sometimes drank too much, with jolly singing and playing of cards afterwards. I know that I ought to feel ashamed of days and evenings thus spent, but as some of my friends were very pleasant, and we were all in the highest spirits, I cannot help looking back to these times with much pleasure.

But I am glad to think that I had many other friends of a widely different nature. I was very intimate with Whitley, who was afterwards Senior Wrangler, and we used continually to take long walks together. He inoculated me with a taste for pictures and good engravings, of which I bought some. I frequently went to the Fitzwilliam Gallery, and my taste must have been fairly good, for I certainly admired the best pictures, which I discussed with the old curator. I read also with much interest Sir Joshua Reynolds' book. This taste, though not natural to me, lasted for several years, and many of the pictures in the National Gallery in London gave me much pleasure; that of Sebastian del Piombo exciting in me a sense of sublimity.

I also got into a musical set, I believe by means of my warm-hearted friend, Herbert, who took a high wrangler's degree. From associating with these men, and hearing them play, I acquired a strong taste for music, and used very often to time my walks so as to hear on week days the anthem in King's College Chapel. This gave me intense pleasure, so that my backbone would sometimes shiver. I am sure that there was no affectation or mere imitation in this taste, for I used generally to go by myself to King's College, and I sometimes hired the chorister boys to sing in my rooms. Nevertheless I am so utterly destitute of an ear, that I cannot perceive a discord, or keep time and hum a tune correctly; and it is a mystery how I could possibly have derived pleasure from music.

My musical friends soon perceived my state, and sometimes amused themselves by making me pass an examination, which consisted in ascertaining how many tunes I could recognize when they were played rather more quickly or slowly than usual. "God save the King," when thus played, was a sore puzzle. There was another man with almost as bad an ear as I had, and strange to say he played a little on the flute. Once I had the triumph of beating him in one of our musical examinations.

But no pursuit at Cambridge was followed with nearly so much eagerness or gave me so much pleasure as collecting beetles. It was the mere passion for collecting, for I did not dissect them, and rarely compared their external characters with published descriptions, but got them named anyhow. I will give a proof of my zeal: one day, on tearing off some old bark, I saw two rare beetles, and seized one in each hand; then I saw a third and new kind, which I could not bear to lose, so that I popped the one which I held in my right hand into my mouth. Alas! it ejected some intensely acrid fluid, which burnt my tongue so that I was forced to spit the beetle out, which was lost, as was the third one.

I was very successful in collecting, and invented two new methods; I employed a labourer to scrape, during the winter, moss off old trees and place it in a large bag, and likewise to collect the rubbish at the bottom of the barges in which reeds are brought from the fens, and thus I got some very rare species. No poet ever felt more delighted at seeing his first poem published than I did at seeing, in Stephens' "Illustrations of British Insects," the magic words, "captured by C. Darwin, Esq." I was introduced to entomology by my second cousin, W. Darwin Fox, a clever and most pleasant man, who was then at Christ's College, and with whom I became extremely intimate. Afterwards I became well acquainted, and went out collecting, with Albert Way of Trinity, who in after years became a well-known archaeologist; also with H. Thomson of the same College, afterwards a leading agriculturist, chairman of a great railway, and Member of Parliament. It seems therefore that a taste for collecting beetles is some indication of future success in life!

I am surprised what an indelible impression many of the beetles which I caught at Cambridge have left on my mind. I can remember the exact appearance of certain posts, old trees and banks where I made a good capture. The pretty *Panagaeus crux-major* was a treasure in those days, and here at Down I saw a beetle running across a walk, and on picking it up instantly perceived that it differed slightly from *P. crux-major*, and it turned out to be *P. quadripunctatus*, which is only a variety or closely allied species, differing from it very slightly in outline. I had never seen in those old days Licinus alive, which to an uneducated eye hardly differs from many of the black Carabidous beetles; but my sons found here a specimen, and I instantly recognized that it was new to me; yet I had not looked at a British beetle for the last twenty years.

I have not as yet mentioned a circumstance which influenced my whole career more than any other. This was my friendship with Professor Henslow. Before coming up to Cambridge, I had heard of him from my brother as a man who knew every branch of science, and I was accordingly prepared to reverence him. He kept open house once every week when all undergraduates, and some older members of the University, who were attached to science, used to meet in the evening. I soon got, through Fox, an invitation, and went there regularly. Before long I became well acquainted with Henslow, and during the latter half of my time at Cambridge took long walks with him on most days; so that I was called by some of the dons "the man who walks with Henslow"; and in the evening I was very often asked to join his family dinner. His knowledge was great in botany, entomology, chemistry, mineralogy, and geology. His strongest taste was to draw conclusions from long-continued minute observations. His judgment was excellent, and his whole mind well balanced; but I do not suppose that any one would say that he possessed much original genius. He was deeply religious, and so orthodox that he told me one day he should be grieved if a single word of the Thirty-nine Articles were altered. His moral qualities were in every way admirable. He was free from every tinge of vanity or other petty feeling; and I never saw a man who thought so little about himself or his own concerns. His temper was imperturbably good, with the most winning and courteous manners; yet, as I have seen, he could be roused by any bad action to the warmest indignation and prompt action.

I once saw in his company in the streets of Cambridge almost as horrid a scene as could have been witnessed during the French Revolution. Two body-snatchers had been arrested, and whilst being taken to prison had been torn from the constable by a crowd of the roughest men, who dragged them by their legs along the muddy and stony road. They were covered from head to foot with mud, and their faces were bleeding either from having been kicked or from the stones; they looked like corpses, but the crowd was so dense that I got only a few momentary glimpses of the wretched creatures. Never in my life have I seen such wrath painted on a man's face as was shown by Henslow at this horrid scene. He tried repeatedly to penetrate the mob; but it was simply impossible. He then rushed away to the mayor, telling me not to follow him, but to get more policemen. I forget the issue, except that the two men were got into the prison without being killed.

Henslow's benevolence was unbounded, as he proved by his many excellent schemes for his poor parishioners, when in after years he held the living of Hitcham. My intimacy with such a man ought to have been, and I hope was, an inestimable benefit. I cannot resist mentioning a trifling incident, which showed his kind consideration. Whilst examining some pollen-grains on a damp surface, I saw the tubes exserted, and instantly rushed off to communicate my surprising discovery to him. Now I do not suppose any other professor of botany could have helped laughing at my coming in such a hurry to make such a communication. But he agreed how interesting the phenomenon was, and explained its meaning, but made me clearly understand how well it was known; so I left him not in the least mortified, but well pleased at having discovered for myself so remarkable a fact, but determined not to be in such a hurry again to communicate my discoveries.

Dr. Whewell was one of the older and distinguished men who sometimes visited Henslow, and on several occasions I walked home with him at night. Next to Sir J. Mackintosh he was the best converser on grave subjects to whom I ever listened. Leonard Jenyns, who afterwards published some good essays in Natural History, often stayed with Henslow, who was his brother-in-law. I visited him at his parsonage on the borders of the Fens, and had many a good walk and talk with him about Natural History. I became also acquainted with several other men older than me, who did not care much about science, but were friends of Henslow. One was a Scotchman, brother of Sir Alexander Ramsay, and tutor of Jesus College: he was a delightful man, but did not live for many years. Another was Mr. Dawes, afterwards Dean of Hereford, and famous for his success in the education of the poor. These men and others of the same standing, together with Henslow, used sometimes to take distant excursions into the country, which I was allowed to join, and they were most agreeable.

Looking back, I infer that there must have been something in me a little superior to the common run of youths, otherwise the above-mentioned men, so much older than me and higher in academical position,

would never have allowed me to associate with them. Certainly I was not aware of any such superiority, and I remember one of my sporting friends, Turner, who saw me at work with my beetles, saying that I should some day be a Fellow of the Royal Society, and the notion seemed to me preposterous.

During my last year at Cambridge, I read with care and profound interest Humboldt's "Personal Narrative." This work, and Sir J. Herschel's "Introduction to the Study of Natural Philosophy," stirred up in me a burning zeal to add even the most humble contribution to the noble structure of Natural Science. No one or a dozen other books influenced me nearly so much as these two. I copied out from Humboldt long passages about Teneriffe, and read them aloud on one of the above-mentioned excursions, to (I think) Henslow, Ramsay, and Dawes, for on a previous occasion I had talked about the glories of Teneriffe, and some of the party declared they would endeavour to go there; but I think that they were only half in earnest. I was, however, quite in earnest, and got an introduction to a merchant in London to enquire about ships; but the scheme was, of course, knocked on the head by the voyage of the *Beagle*.

My summer vacations were given up to collecting beetles, to some reading, and short tours. In the autumn my whole time was devoted to shooting, chiefly at Woodhouse and Maer, and sometimes with young Eyton of Eyton. Upon the whole the three years which I spent at Cambridge were the most joyful in my happy life; for I was then in excellent health, and almost always in high spirits.

As I had at first come up to Cambridge at Christmas, I was forced to keep two terms after passing my final examinations, at the commencement of 1831; and Henslow then persuaded me to begin the study of geology. Therefore on my return to Shropshire I examined sections and coloured a map of parts round Shrewsbury. Professor Sedgwick intended to visit North Wales in the beginning of August to pursue his famous geological investigations amongst the older rocks, and Henslow asked him to allow me to accompany him.

Accordingly he came and slept at my father's house.

A short conversation with him during this evening produced a strong impression on my mind. Whilst examining an old gravel-pit near Shrewsbury, a labourer told me that he had found in it a large worn tropical Volute shell, such as may be seen on the chimney-pieces of cottages; and as he would not sell the shell, I was convinced that he had really found it in the pit. I told Sedgwick of the fact, and he at once said (no doubt truly) that it must have been thrown away by some one into the pit; but then added, if really embedded there it would be the greatest misfortune to geology, as it would overthrow all that we know about the superficial deposits of the Midland Counties. These gravel-beds belong in fact to the glacial period, and in after years I found in them broken arctic shells. But I was then utterly astonished at Sedgwick not being delighted at so wonderful a fact as a tropical shell being found near the surface in the middle of England. Nothing before had ever made me thoroughly realize, though I had read various scientific books, that science consists in grouping facts so that general laws or conclusions may be drawn from them.

Next morning we started for Llangollen, Conway, Bangor, and Capel Curig. This tour was of decided use in teaching me a little how to make out the geology of a country. Sedgwick often sent me on a line parallel to his, telling me to bring back specimens of the rock and to mark the stratification on a map. I have little doubt that he did this for my good, as I was too ignorant to have aided him. On this tour I had a striking instance of how easy it is to overlook phenomena, however conspicuous, before they have been observed by any one. We spent many hours in Cwm Idwal, examining all the rocks with extreme care, as Sedgwick was anxious to find fossils in them; but neither of us saw a trace of the wonderful glacial phenomena all around us; we did not notice the plainly scored rocks, the perched boulders, the lateral and terminal moraines. Yet these phenomena are so conspicuous that, as I declared in a paper published many years afterwards in the "Philosophical Magazine," a house burnt down by fire did not tell its story more plainly than did this valley. If it had still been filled by a glacier, the phenomena would have been less distinct than they now are.

At Capel Curig I left Sedgwick and went in a straight line by compass and map across the mountains to Barmouth, never following any track unless it coincided with my course. I thus came on some strange wild places, and enjoyed much this matter of travelling. I visited Barmouth to see some Cambridge friends who were reading there, and thence returned to Shrewsbury and to Maer for shooting; for at that time I should have thought myself mad to give up the first days of partridge-shooting for geology or any other science.

VOYAGE OF THE "BEAGLE" FROM DECEMBER 27, 1831, TO OCTOBER 2, 1836

On returning home from my short geological tour in North Wales, I found a letter from Henslow, informing me that Captain Fitz-Roy was willing to give up part of his own cabin to any young man who would volunteer to go with him without pay as naturalist to the Voyage of the *Beagle*. I have given, as I believe, in my MS. Journal an account of all the circumstances which then occurred; I will here only say that I was instantly eager to accept the offer, but my father strongly objected, adding the words, fortunate for me, "If you can find any man of common sense who advises you to go I will give my consent." So I wrote that evening and refused the offer. On the next morning I went to Maer to be ready for September 1st, and, whilst out shooting, my uncle sent for me, offering to drive me over to Shrewsbury and talk with my father, as my uncle thought it would be wise in me to accept the offer. My father always maintained that he was one of the most sensible men in the world, and he at once consented in the kindest manner. I had been rather extravagant at Cambridge, and to console my father, said, "that I should be deuced clever to spend more than my allowance whilst on board the *Beagle*"; but he answered with a smile, "But they tell me you are very clever."

Next day I started for Cambridge to see Henslow, and thence to London to see Fitz-Roy, and all was soon arranged. Afterwards, on becoming very intimate with Fitz-Roy, I heard that I had run a very narrow risk of being rejected, on account of the shape of my nose! He was an ardent disciple of Lavater, and was convinced that he could judge of a man's character by the outline of his features; and he doubted whether any one with my nose could possess sufficient energy and determination for the voyage. But I think he was afterwards well satisfied that my nose had spoken falsely.

Fitz-Roy's character was a singular one, with very many noble features: he was devoted to his duty, generous to a fault, bold, determined, and indomitably energetic and an ardent friend to all under his sway. He would undertake any sort of trouble to assist those whom he thought deserved assistance. He was a handsome man, strikingly like a gentleman, with highly courteous manners, which resembled those of his maternal uncle, the famous Lord Castlereagh, as I was told by the Minister at Rio. Nevertheless he must have inherited much in his appearance from Charles II, for Dr. Wallich gave me a collection of photographs which he had made, and I was struck with the resemblance of one to Fitz-Roy; and on looking at the name, I found it Ch. E. Sobieski Stuart, Count d'Albanie, a descendant of the same monarch.

Fitz-Roy's temper was a most unfortunate one. It was usually worst in the early morning, and with his eagle eye he could generally detect something amiss about the ship, and was then unsparing in his blame. He was very kind to me, but was a man very difficult to live with on the intimate terms which necessarily followed from our messing by ourselves in the same cabin. We had several quarrels; for instance, early in the voyage at Bahia, in Brazil, he defended and praised slavery, which I abominated, and told me that he had just visited a great slave-owner, who had called up many of his slaves and asked them whether they were happy, and whether they wished

to be free, and all answered "No." I then asked him, perhaps with a sneer, whether he thought that the answer of slaves in the presence of their master was worth anything? This made him excessively angry, and he said that as I doubted his word we could not live any longer together. I thought that I should have been compelled to leave the ship; but as soon as the news spread, which it did quickly, as the captain sent for the first lieutenant to assuage his anger by abusing me, I was deeply gratified by receiving an invitation from all the gun-room officers to mess with them. But after a few hours Fitz-Roy showed his usual magnanimity by sending an officer to me with an apology and a request that I would continue to live with him.

His character was in several respects one of the most noble which I have ever known.

The voyage of the *Beagle* has been by far the most important event in my life, and has determined my whole career; yet it depended on so small a circumstance as my uncle offering to drive me thirty miles to Shrewsbury, which few uncles would have done, and on such a trifle as the shape of my nose. I have always felt that I owe to the voyage the first real training or education of my mind; I was led to attend closely to several branches of natural history, and thus my powers of observation were improved, though they were always fairly developed.

The investigation of the geology of all the places visited was far more important as reasoning here comes into play. On first examining a new district nothing can appear more hopeless than the chaos of rocks; but by recording the stratification and nature of the rocks and fossils at many points, always reasoning and predicting what will be found elsewhere, light soon begins to dawn on the district, and the structure of the whole becomes more or less intelligible. I had brought with me the first volume of Lyell's "Principles of Geology," which I studied attentively; and the book was of the highest service to me in many ways. The very first place which I examined, namely St. Jago in the Cape de Verde islands, showed me clearly the wonderful superiority of Lyell's manner of treating geology, compared with that of any other author, whose works I had with me or ever afterwards read.

Another of my occupations was collecting animals of all classes, briefly describing and roughly dissecting many of the marine ones; but from not being able to draw, and from not having sufficient anatomical knowledge, a great pile of MS. which I made during the voyage has proved almost useless. I thus lost much time, with the exception of that spent in acquiring some knowledge of the Crustaceans, as this was of service when in after years I undertook a monograph of the Cirripedia.

During some part of the day I wrote my Journal, and took much pains in describing carefully and vividly all that I had seen; and this was good practice. My Journal served also, in part, as letters to my home, and portions were sent to England whenever there was an opportunity.

The above various special studies were, however, of no importance compared with the habit of energetic industry and of concentrated attention to whatever I was engaged in, which I then acquired. Everything about which I thought or read was made to bear directly on what I had seen or was likely to see; and this habit of mind was continued during the five years of the voyage. I feel sure that it was this training which has enabled me to do whatever I have done in science.

Looking backwards, I can now perceive how my love for science gradually preponderated over every other taste. During the first two years my old passion for shooting survived in nearly full force, and I shot myself all the birds and animals for my collection; but gradually I gave up my gun more and more, and finally altogether, to my servant, as shooting interfered with my work, more especially with making out the geological structure of a country. I discovered, though unconsciously and insensibly, that the pleasure of observing and reasoning was a much higher one than that of skill and sport. That my mind became developed through my pursuits during the voyage is rendered probable by a remark made by my father, who was the most acute observer whom I ever saw, of a sceptical disposition, and far from being a believer in phrenology; for on first seeing me after the voyage, he turned round to my sisters, and exclaimed, "Why, the shape of his head is quite altered."

To return to the voyage. On September 11th (1831), I paid a flying visit with Fitz-Roy to the *Beagle* at Plymouth. Thence to Shrewsbury to wish my father and sisters a long farewell. On October 24th I took up my residence at Plymouth, and remained there until December 27th, when the *Beagle* finally left the shores of England for her circumnavigation of the world. We made two earlier attempts to sail, but were driven back each time by heavy gales. These two months at Plymouth were the most miserable which I ever spent, though I exerted myself in various ways. I was out of spirits at the thought of leaving all my family and friends for so long a time, and the weather seemed to me inexpressibly gloomy. I was also troubled with palpitation and pain about the heart, and like many a young ignorant man, especially one with a smattering of medical knowledge, was convinced that I had heart disease. I did not consult any doctor, as I fully expected to hear the verdict that I was not fit for the voyage, and I was resolved to go at all hazards.

I need not here refer to the events of the voyage—where we went and what we did—as I have given a sufficiently full account in my published Journal. The glories of the vegetation of the Tropics rise before my mind at the present time more vividly than anything else; though the sense of sublimity, which the great deserts of Patagonia and the forest-clad mountains of Tierra del Fuego excited in me, has left an indelible impression on my mind. The sight of a naked savage in his native land is an event which can never be forgotten. Many of my excursions on horseback through wild countries or in the boats, some of which lasted several weeks, were deeply interesting: their discomfort and some degree of danger were at that time hardly a drawback, and none at all afterwards. I also reflect with high satisfaction on some of my scientific work, such as solving the problem of coral islands, and making out the geological structure of certain islands, for instance, St. Helena. Nor must I pass over the discovery of the singular relations of the animals and plants inhabiting the several islands of the Galapagos archipelago, and of all of them to the inhabitants of South America.

As far as I can judge of myself, I worked to the utmost during the voyage from the mere pleasure of investigation, and from my strong desire to add a few facts to the great mass of facts in Natural Science. But I was also ambitous to take a fair place among scientific men,—whether more ambitious or less so than most of my fellow-workers, I can form no opinion.

The geology of St. Jago is very striking, yet simple: a stream of lava formerly flowed over the bed of the sea, formed of triturated recent shells and corals, which it has baked into a hard white rock. Since then the whole island has been upheaved. But the line of white rock revealed to me a new and important fact, namely, that there had been afterwards subsidence round the craters, which had since been in action, and had poured forth lava. It then first dawned on me that I might perhaps write a book on the geology of the various countries visited, and this made me thrill with delight. That was a memorable hour to me, and how distinctly I can call to mind the low cliff of lava beneath which I rested, with the sun glaring hot, a few strange desert plants growing near, and with living corals in the tidal pools at my feet. Later in the voyage, Fitz-Roy asked me to read some of my Journal, and declared it would be worth publishing; so here was a second book in prospect!

Towards the close of our voyage I received a letter whilst at Ascension, in which my sisters told me that Sedgwick had called on my father, and said that I should take a place among the leading scientific men. I could not at the time understand how he could have learnt anything of my proceedings, but I heard (I believe afterwards) that Henslow had read some of the letters which I wrote to him before the Philosophical Society of Cambridge, and had printed them for private distribution. My collection of fossil bones, which had been sent to Henslow, also excited considerable attention amongst palaeontologists. After reading this letter, I clambered over the mountains of Ascension with a bounding step, and made the volcanic rocks resound under my geological hammer. All this shows how ambitious I was; but I think that I can say with truth that in after years, though I cared in the highest degree for the approbation of such men as Lyell and Hooker, who were my friends, I did not care much about the general public. I do not mean to say that a favourable review or a large sale of my books did not please me greatly, but the pleasure was a fleeting one, and I am sure that I have never turned one inch out of my course to gain fame.

• • • • •

From September 1854 I devoted my whole time to arranging my huge pile of notes, to observing, and to experimenting in relation to the transmutation of species. During the voyage of the *Beagle* I had been deeply impressed by discovering in the Pampean formation great fossil animals covered with armour like that on the existing armadillos; secondly, by the manner in which closely allied animals replace one another in proceeding southwards over the Continent; and thirdly, by the South American character of most of the productions of the Galapagos archipelago, and more especially by the manner in which they differ slightly on each island of the group; none of the islands appearing to be very ancient in a geological sense.

It was evident that such facts as these, as well as many others, could only be explained on the supposition that species gradually become modified; and the subject haunted me. But it was equally evident that neither the action of the surrounding conditions, nor the will of the organism (especially in the case of plants) could account for the innumerable cases in which organisms of every kind are beautifully adapted to their habits of life—for instance, a woodpecker or a tree-frog to climb trees, or a seed for dispersal by hooks or plumes. I had always been much struck by such adaptations, and until these could be explained it seemed to me almost useless to endeavour to prove by indirect evidence that species have been modified.

After my return to England it appeared to me that by following the example of

Lyell in Geology, and by collecting all facts which bore in any way on the variation of animals and plants under domestication and nature, some light might perhaps be thrown on the whole subject, My first note-book was opened in July 1837. I worked on true Baconian principles, and without any theory collected facts on a wholesale scale, more especially with respect to domesticated productions, by printed enquiries, by conversation with skilful breeders and gardeners, and by extensive reading. When I see the list of books of all kinds which I read and abstracted, including whole series of Journals and Transactions, I am surprised at my industry. I soon perceived that selection was the keystone of man's success in making useful races of animals and plants. But how selection could be applied to organisms living in a state of nature remained for some time a mystery to me.

In October 1838, that is, fifteen months after I had begun my systematic enquiry, I happened to read for amusement "Malthus on Population," and being well prepared to appreciate the struggle for existence which everywhere goes on from long-continued observation of the habits of animals and plants, it at once struck me that under these circumstances favourable variations would tend to be preserved, and unfavourable ones to be destroyed. The result of this would be the formation of new species. Here then I had at last got a theory by which to work; but I was so anxious to avoid prejudice, that I determined not for some time to write even the briefest sketch of it. In June 1842 I first allowed myself the satisfaction of writing a very brief abstract of my theory in pencil in 35 pages; and this was enlarged during the summer of 1844 into one of 230 pages, which I had fairly copied out and still possess.

But at that time I overlooked one problem of great importance; and it is astonishing to me, except on the principle of Columbus and his egg, how I could have overlooked it and its solution. This problem is the tendency in organic beings descended from the same stock to diverge in character as they become modified. That they have diverged greatly is obvious from the manner in which species of all kinds can be classed under genera, genera under families, families under sub-orders and so forth; and I can remember the very spot in the road, whilst in my carriage, when to my joy the solution occurred to me; and this was long after I had come to Down. The solution, as I believe, is that the modified offspring of all dominant and increasing forms tend to become adapted to many and highly diversified places in the economy of nature.

Early in 1856 Lyell advised me to write out my views pretty fully, and I began at once to do so on a scale three or four times as extensive as that which was afterwards followed in my "Origin of Species"; yet it was only an abstract of the materials which I had collected, and I got through about half the work on this scale. But my plans were overthrown, for early in the summer of 1858 Mr. Wallace, who was then in the Malay archipelago, sent me an essay "On the Tendency of Varieties to depart indefinitely from the Original Type;" and this essay contained exactly the same theory as mine. Mr. Wallace expressed the wish that if I thought well of his essay, I should send it to Lyell for perusal.

The circumstances under which I consented at the request of Lyell and Hooker to allow of an abstract from my MS., together with a letter to Asa Gray, dated September 5, 1857, to be published at the same time with Wallace's Essay, are given in the "Journal of the Proceedings of the Linnean Society," 1858, p. 45. I was at first very unwilling to consent, as I thought Mr. Wallace might consider my doing so unjustifiable, for I did not then know how generous and noble was his disposition. The extract from my MS. and the letter to Asa Gray had neither been intended for publication, and were badly written. Mr. Wallace's essay, on the other hand, was admirably expressed and quite clear. Nevertheless, our joint productions excited very little attention, and the only published notice of them which I can remember was by Professor Haughton of Dublin, whose verdict was that all that was new in them was false, and what was true was old. This shows how necessary it is that any new view should be explained at considerable length in order to arouse public attention.

In September 1858 I set to work by the strong advice of Lyell and Hooker to prepare a volume on the transmutation of species, but was often interrupted by ill-health, and short visits to Dr. Lane's delightful hydropathic establishment at Moor Park. I abstracted the MS. begun on a much larger scale in 1856, and completed the volume on the same reduced scale. It cost me thirteen months and ten days' hard labour. It was published under the title of the "Origin of Species," in November 1859. Though considerably added to and corrected in the later editions, it has remained substantially the same book.

It is no doubt the chief work of my life. It was from the first highly successful. The first small edition of 1250 copies was sold on the day of publication, and a second edition of 3000 copies soon afterwards. Sixteen thousand copies have now (1876) been sold in England; and considering how stiff a book it is, this is a large sale. It has been translated into almost every European tongue, even into such languages as Spanish, Bohemian, Polish, and Russian. It has also, according to Miss Bird, been translated into Japanese,[3] and is there much studied. Even an essay in Hebrew has appeared on it, showing that the theory is contained in the Old Testament! The reviews were very numerous; for some time I collected all that appeared on the "Origin" and on my related books, and these amount (excluding newspaper reviews) to 265; but after a time I gave up the attempt in despair. Many separate essays and books on the subject have appeared; and in Germany a catalogue or bibliography on "Darwinismus"[4] has appeared every year or two.

The success of the "Origin" may, I think, be attributed in large part to my having long before written two condensed sketches, and to my having finally abstracted a much larger manuscript, which was itself an abstract. By this means I was enabled to select the more striking facts and conclusions. I had, also, during many years

[3] Miss Bird is mistaken, as I learn from Prof. Mitsukuri.—F. D.

[4] Darwinismus: German for Darwinism.

followed a golden rule, namely, that whenever a published fact, a new observation or thought came across me, which was opposed to my general results, to make a memorandum of it without fail and at once; for I had found by experience that such facts and thoughts were far more apt to escape from the memory than favourable ones. Owing to this habit, very few objections were raised against my views which I had not at least noticed and attempted to answer.

It has sometimes been said that the success of the "Origin" proved "that the subject was in the air," or "that men's minds were prepared for it." I do not think that this is strictly true, for I occasionally sounded not a few naturalists, and never happened to come across a single one who seemed to doubt about the permanence of species. Even Lyell and Hooker, though they would listen with interest to me, never seemed to agree. I tried once or twice to explain to able men what I meant by Natural Selection, but signally failed. What I believe was strictly true is that innumerable well-observed facts were stored in the minds of naturalists ready to take their proper places as soon as any theory which would receive them was sufficiently explained. Another element in the success of the book was its moderate size; and this I owe to the appearance of Mr. Wallace's essay; had I published on the scale in which I began to write in 1856, the book would have been four or five times as large as the "Origin," and very few would have had the patience to read it.

. . . . . .

I have now mentioned all the books which I have published, and these have been the milestones in my life, so that little remains to be said. I am not conscious of any change in my mind during the last thirty years, excepting in one point presently to be mentioned; nor, indeed, could any change have been expected unless one of general deterioration. But my father lived to his eighty-third year with his mind as lively as ever it was, and all his faculties undimmed; and I hope that I may die before my mind fails to a sensible extent. I think that I have become a little more skilful in guessing right explanations and in devising experimental tests, but this may probably be the result of mere practice, and of a larger store of knowledge. I have as much difficulty as ever in expressing myself clearly and concisely; and this difficulty has caused me a very great loss of time; but it has had the compensating advantage of forcing me to think long and intently about every sentence, and thus I have been led to see errors in reasoning and in my own observations or those of others.

There seems to be a sort of fatality in my mind leading me to put at first my statement or proposition in a wrong or awkward form. Formerly I used to think about my sentences before writing them down; but for several years I have found that it saves time to scribble in a vile hand whole pages as quickly as I possibly can, contracting half the words; and then correct deliberately. Sentences thus scribbled down are often better ones than I could have written deliberately.

Having said thus much about my manner of writing, I will add that with my large books I spend a good deal of time over the general arrangement of the matter. I first make the rudest outline in two or three pages, and then a larger one in several pages, a few words or one word standing for a whole discussion or series of facts. Each one of these headings is again enlarged and often transferred before I begin to write in extenso.[5] As in several of my books facts observed by others have been very extensively used, and as I have always had several quite distinct subjects in hand at the same time, I may mention that I keep from thirty to forty large portfolios, in cabinets with labelled shelves, into which I can at once put a detached reference or memorandum. I have bought many books, and at their ends I make an index of all the facts that concern my work; or, if the book is not my own, write out a separate abstract, and of such abstracts I have a large drawer full. Before beginning on any subject I look to all the short indexes and make a general and classified index, and by taking the one or more proper portfolios I have all the

5 in extenso: at full length.

information collected during my life ready for use.

I have said that in one respect my mind has changed during the last twenty or thirty years. Up to the age of thirty, or beyond it, poetry of many kinds, such as the works of Milton, Gray, Byron, Wordsworth, Coleridge, and Shelley, gave me great pleasure, and even as a schoolboy I took intense delight in Shakespeare, especially in the historical plays. I have also said that formerly pictures gave me considerable, and music very great delight. But now for many years I cannot endure to read a line of poetry: I have tried lately to read Shakespeare, and found it so intolerably dull that it nauseated me. I have also almost lost my taste for pictures or music. Music generally sets me thinking too energetically on what I have been at work on, instead of giving me pleasure. I retain some taste for fine scenery, but it does not cause me the exquisite delight which it formerly did. On the other hand, novels which are works of the imagination, though not of a very high order, have been for years a wonderful relief and pleasure to me, and I often bless all novelists. A surprising number have been read aloud to me, and I like all if moderately good, and if they do not end unhappily—against which a law ought to be passed. A novel, according to my taste, does not come into the first class unless it contains some person whom one can thoroughly love, and if a pretty woman all the better.

This curious and lamentable loss of the higher aesthetic tastes is all the odder, as books on history, biographies, and travels (independently of any scientific facts which they may contain), and essays on all sorts of subjects interest me as much as ever they did. My mind seems to have become a kind of machine for grinding general laws out of large collections of facts, but why this should have caused the atrophy of that part of the brain alone, on which the higher tastes depend, I cannot conceive. A man with a mind more highly organised or better constituted than mine, would not, I suppose, have thus suffered; and if I had to live my life again, I would have made a rule to read some poetry and listen to some music at least once every week; for perhaps the parts of my brain now atrophied would thus have been kept active through use. The loss of these tastes is a loss of happiness, and may possibly be injurious to the intellect, and more probably to the moral character, by enfeebling the emotional part of our nature.

My books have sold largely in England, have been translated into many languages, and passed through several editions in foreign countries. I have heard it said that the success of a work abroad is the best test of its enduring value. I doubt whether this is at all trustworthy; but judged by this standard my name ought to last for a few years. Therefore it may be worth while to try to analyse the mental qualities and the conditions on which my success has depended; though I am aware that no man can do this correctly.

I have no great quickness of apprehension or wit which is so remarkable in some clever men, for instance, Huxley. I am therefore a poor critic: a paper or book, when first read, generally excites my admiration, and it is only after considerable reflection that I perceive the weak points. My power to follow a long and purely abstract train of thought is very limited; and therefore I could never have succeeded with metaphysics or mathematics. My memory is extensive, yet hazy: it suffices to make me cautious by vaguely telling me that I have observed or read something opposed to the conclusion which I am drawing, or on the other hand in favour of it; and after a time I can generally recollect where to search for my authority. So poor in one sense is my memory, that I have never been able to remember for more than a few days a single date or a line of poetry.

Some of my **critics** have said, "Oh, he is a good observer, but he has no power of reasoning!" I do not think that this can be true, for the "Origin of Species" is one long argument from the beginning to the end, and it has convinced not a few able men. No one could have written it without having some power of reasoning. I have a fair share of invention, and of common sense or judgment, such as every fairly successful lawyer or doctor must have, but not, I believe, in any higher degree.

On the favourable side of the balance, I think that I am superior to the common run of men in noticing things which easily escape attention, and in observing them carefully. My industry has been nearly as great as it could have been in the observation and collection of facts. What is far more important, my love of natural science has been steady and ardent.

This pure love has, however, been much aided by the ambition to be esteemd by my fellow naturalists. From my early youth I have had the strongest desire to understand or explain whatever I observed,—that is, to group all facts under some general laws. These causes combined have given me the patience to reflect or ponder for any number of years over any unexplained problem. As far as I can judge, I am not apt to follow blindly the lead of other men. I have steadily endeavoured to keep my mind free so as to give up any hypothesis, however much beloved (and I cannot resist forming one on every subject), as soon as facts are shown to be opposed to it. Indeed, I have had no choice but to act in this manner, for with the exception of the Coral Reefs, I cannot remember a single first-formed hypothesis which had not after a time to be given up or greatly modified. This has naturally led me to distrust greatly deductive reasoning in the mixed sciences. On the other hand, I am not very sceptical,— a frame of mind which I believe to be injurious to the progress of science. A good deal of scepticism in a scientific man is advisable to avoid much loss of time, for I have met with not a few men, who, I feel sure, have often thus been deterred from experiment or observations, which would have proved directly or indirectly serviceable.

• • • • • •

My habits are methodical, and this has been of not a little use for my particular line of work. Lastly, I have had ample leisure from not having to earn my own bread. Even ill-health, though it has annihilated several years of my life, has saved me from the distractions of society and amusement.

Therefore my success as a man of science, whatever this may have amounted to, has been determined, as far as I can judge, by complex and diversified mental qualities and conditions. Of these, the most important have been—the love of science—unbounded patience in long reflecting over any subject—industry in observing and collecting facts—and a fair share of invention as well as of common sense. With such moderate abilities as I possess, it is truly surprising that I should have influenced to a considerable extent the belief of scientific men on some important points.

[1887]

THE ORIGIN OF SPECIES

BY MEANS OF NATURAL SELECTION; OR, THE PRESERVATION OF FAVORED RACES IN THE STRUGGLE FOR LIFE

STRUGGLE FOR EXISTENCE

Before entering on the subject of this chapter, I must make a few preliminary remarks, to show how the struggle for existence bears on Natural Selection. It has been seen in the last chapter that amongst organic beings in a state of nature there is some individual variability; indeed I am not aware that this has ever been disputed. It is immaterial for us whether a multitude of doubtful forms be called species or subspecies or varieties; what rank, for instance, the two or three hundred doubtful forms of British plants are entitled to hold, if the existence of any well-marked varieties be admitted. But the mere existence of individual variability and of some few well-marked varieties, though necessary as the foundation for the work, helps us but little in understanding how species arise in nature. How have all those exquisite adaptations of one part of the organization to another part, and to the conditions of life, and of one organic being to another being, been perfected? We see these beautiful coadaptations most plainly in the woodpecker and the mistletoe; and only a little less plainly in the humblest parasite which clings to the hairs of a quadruped or feathers of a bird; in the structure of the beetle which dives through the water; in the plumed seed which is wafted by the gentlest breeze; in short, we see beautiful adaptations everywhere and in every part of the organic world.

Again, it may be asked, how is it that varieties, which I have called incipient species, become ultimately converted into good and distinct species which in most cases obviously differ from each other far more than do the varieties of the same species? How do those groups of species, which constitute what are called distinct genera, and which differ from each other more than do the species of the same genus, arise? All these results, as we shall more fully see in the next chapter, follow from the struggle for life. Owing to this struggle, variations, however slight and from whatever cause proceeding, if they be in any degree profitable to the individuals of a species, in their infinitely complex relations to other organic beings and to their physical conditions of life, will tend to the preservation of such individuals, and will generally be inherited by the offspring. The offspring, also, will thus have a better chance of surviving, for, of the many individuals of any species which are periodically born, but a small number can survive. I have called this principle, by which each slight variation, if useful, is preserved, by the term Natural Selection, in order to mark its relation to man's power of selection. But the expression often used by Mr. Herbert Spencer of the Survival of the Fittest is more accurate, and is sometimes equally convenient. We have seen that man by selection can certainly produce great results, and can adapt organic beings to his own uses, through the accumulation of slight but useful variations, given to him by the hand of Nature. But Natural Selection, as we shall hereafter see, is a power incessantly ready for action, and is as immeasurably superior to man's feeble efforts as the works of Nature are to those of Art.

We will now discuss in a little more detail the struggle for existence. In my future work this subject will be treated, as it well deserves, at greater length. The elder De Candolle and Lyell have largely and philosophically shown that all organic beings are exposed to severe competition. In regard to plants, no one has treated this subject with more spirit and ability than W. Herbert, Dean of Manchester, evidently the result of his great horticultural knowledge. Nothing is easier than to admit in words the truth of the universal struggle for life, or more difficult—at least I have found it so—than constantly to bear this conclusion in mind. Yet unless it be thoroughly engrained in the mind, the whole economy of nature, with every fact on distribution, rarity, abundance, extinction, and variation, will be dimly seen or quite misunderstood. We behold the face of nature bright with gladness, we often see superabundance of food; we do not see or we forget that the birds which are idly singing round us mostly live on insects or seeds, and are thus constantly destroying life; or we forget how largely these songsters, or their eggs, or their nestlings, are destroyed by birds and beasts of prey; we do not always bear in mind that, though food may be now superabundant, it is not so at all seasons of each recurring year.

THE TERM, STRUGGLE FOR EXISTENCE, USED IN A LARGE SENSE

I should premise that I use this term in a large and metaphorical sense, including dependence of one being on another, and including (which is more important) not only the life of the individual, but success in leaving progeny. Two canine animals, in a time of dearth, may be truly said to struggle with each other which shall get food and live. But a plant on the edge of a desert is said to struggle for life against the drought, though more properly it should be said to be dependent on the moisture. A plant which annually produces a thousand seeds, of which only one of an average comes to maturity, may be more truly said to struggle with the plants of the same and other kinds which already clothe the ground. The mistletoe is dependent on the apple and a few other trees, but can only in a far-fetched sense be said to struggle with these trees, for, if too many of these parasites grow on the same tree, it languishes and dies. But several seedling mistletoes, growing close together on the same branch, may more truly be said to struggle with each other. As the mistletoe is disseminated by birds, its existence depends on them; and it may metaphorically be said to struggle with other fruit-bearing plants, in tempting the birds to devour and thus disseminate its seeds. In these several senses, which pass into each other, I use for convenience' sake the general term of Struggle for Existence.

GEOMETRICAL RATIO OF INCREASE

A struggle for existence inevitably follows from the high rate at which all organic beings tend to increase. Every being, which during its natural lifetime produces several eggs or seeds, must suffer destruction during some period of its life, and during some season or occasional year; otherwise, on the principle of geometrical increase, its numbers would quickly become so inordinately great that no country could support the product. Hence, as more individuals are produced than can possibly survive, there must in every case be a struggle for existence, either one individual with another of the same species, or with the individuals of distinct species, or with the physical conditions of life. It is the doctrine of Malthus applied with manifold force to the whole animal and vegetable kingdoms; for in this case there can be no artificial increase of food, and no prudential restraint from marriage. Although some species may be now increasing, more or less rapidly, in numbers, all cannot do so, for the world would not hold them.

There is no exception to the rule that every organic being naturally increases at so high a rate that, if not destroyed, the earth would soon be covered by the progeny of a single pair. Even slow-breeding man has doubled in twenty-five years, and at this rate, in less than a thousand years, there would literally not be standing-room for his progeny. Linnaeus has calculated that if an annual plant produced only two seeds—and there is no plant so unproductive as this—and their seedlings next year produced two, and so on, then in twenty years there would be a million plants. The elephant is reckoned the slowest breeder of all known animals, and I have taken some pains to estimate its probable minimum rate of natural increase; it will be safest to assume that it begins breeding when thirty years old, and goes on breeding till ninety years old, bringing forth six young in the interval, and surviving till one hundred years old; if this be so, after a period of from 740 to 750 years there would be nearly nineteen million elephants alive descended from the first pair.

But we have better evidence on this subject than mere theoretical calculations, namely, the numerous recorded cases of the astonishingly rapid increase of various animals in a state of nature when circumstances have been favorable to them during two or three following seasons. Still more striking is the evidence from our domestic animals of many kinds which have run wild in several parts of the world; if the statements of the rate of increase of slow-breeding cattle and horses in South America, and latterly in Australia, had not been well authenticated, they would have been incredible. So it is with plants; cases could be given of introduced plants which have become common throughout whole islands in a period of less than ten years. Several of the plants, such as the cardoon and a tall thistle, which are now the commonest over the wide plains of La Plata, clothing square leagues of surface almost to the exclusion of every other plant, have been introduced from Europe; and there are plants which now range in India, as I hear from Dr. Falconer, from Cape Comorin to the Himalaya, which have been imported from America since its discovery. In such cases, and endless others could be given, no one supposes that the fertility of the animals or plants has been suddenly and temporarily increased in any sensible degree. The obvious explanation is that the conditions of life have been highly favorable, and that there has con-

sequently been less destruction of the old and young, and that nearly all the young have been enabled to breed. Their geometrical ratio of increase, the result of which never fails to be surprising, simply explains their extraordinarily rapid increase and wide diffusion in their new homes.

In a state of nature almost every full-grown plant annually produces seed, and amongst animals there are very few which do not annually pair. Hence we may confidently assert that all plants and animals are tending to increase at a geometrical ratio—that all would rapidly stock every station in which they could anyhow exist—and that this geometrical tendency to increase must be checked by destruction at some period of life. Our familiarity with the larger domestic animals tends, I think, to mislead us; we see no great destruction falling on them, but we do not keep in mind that thousands are annually slaughtered for food, and that in a state of nature an equal number would have somehow to be disposed of.

The only difference between organisms which annually produce eggs or seeds by the thousand, and those which produce extremely few, is, that the slow breeders would require a few more years to people, under favorable conditions, a whole district, let it be ever so large. The condor lays a couple of eggs and the ostrich a score, and yet in the same country the condor may be the more numerous of the two. The Fulmar petrel lays but one egg, yet it is believed to be the most numerous bird in the world. One fly deposits hundreds of eggs, and another, like the hippobosca, a single one; but this difference does not determine how many individuals of the two species can be supported in a district. A large number of eggs is of some importance to those species which depend on a fluctuating amount of food, for it allows them rapidly to increase in number. But the real importance of a large number of eggs or seeds is to make up for much destruction at some period of life; and this period in the great majority of cases is an early one. If an animal can in any way protect its own eggs or young, a small number may be produced, and yet the average stock be fully kept up; but if many eggs or young are destroyed, many must be produced, or the species will become extinct. It would suffice to keep up the full number of a tree, which lived on an average for a thousand years, if a single seed were produced once in a thousand years, supposing that this seed were never destroyed and could be insured to germinate in a fitting place; so that, in all cases, the average number of any animal or plant depends only indirectly on the number of its eggs or seeds.

In looking at Nature, it is most necessary to keep the foregoing considerations always in mind—never to forget that every single organic being may be said to be striving to the utmost to increase in numbers; that each lives by a struggle at some period of its life; that heavy destruction inevitably falls either on the young or old, during each generation or at recurrent intervals. Lighten any check, mitigate the destruction ever so little, and the number of the species will almost instantaneously increase to any amount.

NATURE OF THE CHECKS TO INCREASE

The causes which check the natural tendency of each species to increase are most obscure. Look at the most vigorous species; by as much as it swarms in numbers, by so much will it tend to increase still further. We know not exactly what the checks are even in a single instance. Nor will this surprise anyone who reflects how ignorant we are on this head, even in regard to mankind, although so incomparably better known than any other animal. This subject of the checks to increase has been ably treated by several authors, and I hope in a future work to discuss it at considerable length, more especially in regard to the feral animals of South America. Here I will make only a few remarks, just to recall to the reader's mind some of the chief points. Eggs or very young animals seem generally to suffer most, but this is not invariably the case. With plants there is a vast destruction of seeds, but from some observations which I have made it appears that the seedlings suffer most from germinating in ground already thickly stocked with other plants.

Seedlings, also, are destroyed in vast numbers by various enemies; for instance, on a piece of ground three feet long and two wide, dug and cleared, and where there could be no choking from other plants, I marked all the seedlings of our native weeds as they came up, and out of 357 no less than 295 were destroyed, chiefly by slugs and insects. If turf which has long been mown, and the case would be the same with turf closely browsed by quadrupeds, be let to grow, the more vigorous plants gradually kill the less vigorous, though fully grown plants; thus out of twenty species growing on a little plot of mown turf (three feet by four) nine species perished, from the other species being allowed to grow up freely.

The amount of food for each species, of course, gives the extreme limit to which each can increase; but very frequently it is not the obtaining food, but the serving as prey to other animals, which determines the average number of a species. Thus, there seems to be little doubt that the stock of partridges, grouse, and hares on any large estate depends chiefly on the destruction of vermin. If not one head of game were shot during the next twenty years in England, and, at the same time, no vermin were destroyed, there would, in all probability, be less game than at present, although hundreds of thousands of game animals are now annually shot. On the other hand, in some cases, as with the elephant, none are destroyed by beasts of prey; for even the tiger in India most rarely dares to attack a young elephant protected by its dam.

Climate plays an important part in determining the average number of a species, and periodical seasons of extreme cold or drought seem to be the most effective of all checks. I estimated (chiefly from the greatly reduced numbers of nests in the spring) that the winter of 1854-1855 destroyed four-fifths of the birds in my own grounds; and this is a tremendous destruction, when we remember that ten per cent is an extraordinarily severe mortality from epidemics with men. The action of climate seems at first sight to be quite independent of the struggle for existence; but in so far as climate chiefly acts in reducing food, it brings on the most severe struggle between the individuals, whether of the same or of distinct species, which subsist on the same kind of food. Even when climate, for instance, extreme cold, acts directly, it will be the least vigorous individuals, or those which have got least food through the advancing winter, which will suffer most. When we travel from south to north, or from a damp region to a dry, we invariably see some species gradually getting rarer and rarer, and finally disappearing; and the change of climate being conspicuous, we are tempted to attribute the whole effect to its direct action. But this is a false view; we forget that each species, even where it most abounds, is constantly suffering enormous destruction at some period of its life, from enemies or from competitors for the same place and food; and if these enemies or competitors be in the least degree favored by any slight change of climate, they will increase in numbers; and as each area is already fully stocked with inhabitants, the other species must decrease. When we travel southward and see a species decreasing in numbers, we may feel sure that the cause lies quite as much in other species being favored as in this one being hurt. So it is when we travel northward, but in a somewhat lesser degree, for the number of species of all kinds, and therefore of competitors, decreases northwards; hence in going northwards, or in ascending a mountain, we far oftener meet with stunted forms, due to the *directly* injurious action of climate, than we do in proceeding southwards or in descending a mountain. When we reach the Arctic regions, or snow-capped summits, or absolute deserts, the struggle for life is almost exclusively with the elements.

That climate acts in main part indirectly by favoring other species, we clearly see in the prodigious number of plants which in our gardens can perfectly well endure our climate, but which never become naturalized, for they cannot compete with our native plants nor resist destruction by our native animals.

When a species, owing to highly favorable circumstances, increases inordinately in numbers in a small tract, epidemics—at least, this seems generally to occur with our game animals—often ensue; and here we have a limiting check independent of the struggle for life. But even some of these so-called epidemics appear to be due to parasitic worms, which have, from some cause, possibly in part through facility of diffusion amongst the crowded animals, been disproportionately favored; and here comes in a sort of struggle between the parasite and its prey.

On the other hand, in many cases, a large stock of individuals of the same species, relatively to the numbers of its enemies, is absolutely necessary for its preservation. Thus we can easily raise plenty of corn and rapeseed, etc., in our fields, because the seeds are in great excess compared with the number of birds which feed on them; nor can the birds, though having a superabundance of food at this one season, increase in number proportionately to the supply of seed, as their numbers are checked during the winter; but anyone who has tried knows how troublesome it is to get seed from a few wheat or other such plants in a garden; I have in this case lost every single seed. This view of the necessity of a large stock of the same species for its preservation, explains, I believe, some singular facts in nature such as that of very rare plants being sometimes extremely abundant in the few spots where they do exist; and that of some social plants being social, that is abounding in individuals, even on the extreme verge of their range. For, in such cases, we may believe that a plant could exist only where the conditions of its life were so favorable that many could exist together, and thus save the species from utter destruction. I should add that the good effects of intercrossing, and the ill effects of close interbreeding, no doubt come into play in many of these cases; but I will not here enlarge on this subject.

COMPLEX RELATIONS OF ALL ANIMALS AND PLANTS TO EACH OTHER IN THE STRUGGLE FOR EXISTENCE

Many cases are on record showing how complex and unexpected are the checks and relations between organic beings which have to struggle together in the same country. I will give only a single instance, which, though a simple one, interested me. In Staffordshire, on the estate of a relation, where I had ample means of investigation, there was a large and extremely barren heath, which had never been touched by the hand of man; but several hundred acres of exactly the same nature had been enclosed twenty-five years previously and planted with Scotch fir. The change in the native vegetation of the planted part of the heath was most remarkable, more than is generally seen in passing from one quite different soil to another; not only the proportional numbers of the heath-plants were wholly changed, but twelve species of plants (not counting grasses and carices) flourished in the plantations, which could not be found on the heath. The effect on the insects must have been still greater, for six insectivorous birds were very common in the plantations, which were not to be seen on the heath; and the heath was frequented by two or three distinct insectivorous birds. Here we see how potent has been the effect of the introduction of a single tree, nothing whatever else having been done, with the exception of the land having been enclosed, so that cattle could not enter. But how important an element enclosure is, I plainly saw near Farnham, in Surrey. Here there are extensive heaths, with a few clumps of old Scotch firs on the distant hilltops; within the last ten years large spaces have been enclosed, and self-sown firs are now springing up in multitudes, so close together that all cannot live. When I ascertained that these young trees had not been sown or planted, I was so much surprised at their numbers that I went to several points of view, whence I could examine hundreds of acres of the unenclosed heath, and literally I could not see a single Scotch fir, except the old planted clumps. But on looking closely between the stems of the heath, I found a multitude of seedlings and little trees which had been perpetually browsed down by the cattle. In one square yard, at a point some hundred yards distant from one of the old clumps, I counted thirty-two little trees; and one of them, with twenty-six rings of growth, had, during many years, tried to raise its head above the stems of the heath, and had failed. No wonder that, as soon as the land was enclosed, it became thickly clothed with vigorously growing young firs. Yet the heath was so extremely barren and so extensive that no one would ever have imagined that cattle would have so closely and effectually searched it for food.

Here we see that cattle absolutely determine the existence of the Scotch fir; but in several parts of the world insects determine the existence of cattle. Perhaps Paraguay offers the most curious instance of this; for here neither cattle nor horses nor dogs have ever run wild, though they swarm southward and northward in a feral state; and Azara and Rengger have shown that this is caused by the greater number in Paraguay of a certain fly, which lays its eggs in the navels of these animals when first born. The increase of these flies, numerous as they are, must be habitually checked by some means, probably by other parasitic insects. Hence, if certain insectivorous birds were to decrease in Paraguay, the parasitic insects would probably increase; and this would lessen the number of the navel-frequenting flies—then cattle and horses would become feral, and this would certainly greatly alter (as indeed I have observed in parts of South America) the vegetation; this again would largely affect the insects; and this, as we have just seen in Staffordshire, the insectivorous birds; and so onward in ever-increasing circles of complexity. Not that under nature the relations will ever be as simple as this. Battle within battle must be continually recurring with varying success; and yet in the long run the forces are so nicely balanced that the face of nature remains for long periods of time uniform, though assuredly the merest trifle would give the victory to one organic being over another. Nevertheless, so profound is our ignorance, and so high our presumption, that we marvel when we hear of the extinction of an organic being; and as we do not see the cause, we invoke cataclysms to desolate the world, or invent laws on the duration of the forms of life!

I am tempted to give one more instance showing how plants and animals remote in the scale of nature are bound together by a web of complex relations. I shall hereafter have occasion to show that the exotic *Lobelia fulgens* is never visited in my garden by insects, and consequently, from its peculiar structure, never sets a seed. Nearly all our orchidaceous plants absolutely require the visits of insects to remove their pollen-masses and thus to fertilize them. I find from experiments that humblebees are almost indispensable to the fertilization of the heartsease (*Violo tricolor*), for other bees do not visit this flower. I have also found that the visits of bees are necessary for the fertilization of some kinds of clover; for instance, twenty heads of Dutch clover (*Trifolium repens*) yielded 2,290 seeds, but twenty other heads, protected from bees, produced not one. Again, 100 heads of red clover (*T. pratense*) produced 2,700 seeds, but the same number of protected heads produced not a single seed. Humblebees alone visit red clover, as other bees cannot reach the nectar. It has been suggested that moths may fertilize the clovers; but I doubt whether they could do so in the case of the red clover, from their weight not being sufficient to depress the wing petals. Hence we may infer as highly probable that, if the whole genus of humblebees became extinct or very rare in England, the heartsease and red clover would become very rare, or wholly disappear. The number of humblebees in any district depends in a great measure upon the number of fieldmice, which destroy their combs and nests; and Colonel Newman, who has long attended to the habits of humblebees, believes that "more than two-thirds of them are thus destroyed all over England." Now the number of mice is largely dependent, as everyone knows, on the number of cats; and Colonel Newman says, "Near villages and small towns I have found the nests of humblebees more numerous than elsewhere, which I attribute to the number of cats that destroy the mice." Hence it is quite credible that the presence of a feline animal in large numbers in a district might determine, through the intervention first of mice and then of bees, the frequency of certain flowers in that district!

In the case of every species, many different checks, acting at different periods of life and during different seasons or years, probably come into play; some one check or some few being generally the most potent; but all will concur in determining the average number, or even the existence of the species. In some cases it can be shown that widely different checks act on the same species in different districts. When we look at the plants and bushes clothing an entangled bank, we are tempted to attribute their proportional numbers and kinds to what we call chance. But how false a view is this! Everyone has heard that when an American forest is cut down, a very different vegetation springs up; but it has been observed that ancient Indian ruins in the Southern United States, which must formerly have been cleared of trees, now display the same beautiful diversity and proportion of kinds as in the surrounding virgin forests. What a struggle must have gone on during long centuries between the several kinds of trees, each annually scattering its seeds by the thousand; what war between insect and insect—between insects, snails, and other animals with birds and beasts of prey—all striving to increase, all feeding on each other, or on the trees, their seeds and seedlings, or on the other plants which first clothed the ground and thus checked the growth of the trees! Throw up a handful of feathers, and all fall to the ground according to definite laws; but how simple is the problem where each shall fall compared to that of the action and reaction of the innumerable plants and animals which have determined, in the course of centuries, the proportional numbers and kinds of trees now growing on the old Indian ruins!

The dependency of one organic being on another, as of a parasite on its prey, lies generally between beings remote in the scale of nature. This is likewise sometimes the case with those which may be strictly said to struggle with each other for existence, as in the case of locusts and grassfeeding quadrupeds. But the struggle will almost invariably be most severe between the individuals of the same species, for they frequent the same districts, require the same food, and are exposed to the same dangers. In the case of varieties of the same species, the struggle will generally be almost equally severe, and we sometimes see the contest soon decided; for instance, if several varieties of wheat be sown together, and the mixed seed be resown, some of the varieties which best suit the soil or climate, or are naturally the most fertile, will beat the others and so yield more seed, and will consequently in a few years supplant the other varieties. To keep up a mixed stock of even such extremely close varieties as the variously colored sweet peas, they must be each year harvested separately, and the seed then mixed in due proportion; otherwise the weaker kinds will steadily decrease in number and disappear. So again with the varieties of sheep; it has been asserted that certain mountain varieties will starve out other mountain varieties, so that they cannot be kept together. The same result has followed from keeping together different varieties of the medicinal leech. It may even be doubted whether the varieties of any of our domestic plants or animals have so exactly the same strength, habits, and constitution, that the original proportions of a mixed stock (crossing being prevented) could be kept up for a half-a-dozen generations, if they were allowed to struggle together, in the same manner as beings in a state of nature, and if the seed or young were not annually preserved in due proportion.

STRUGGLE FOR LIFE MOST SEVERE BETWEEN INDIVIDUALS AND VARIETIES OF THE SAME SPECIES

As the species of the same genus usually have, though by no means invariably, much similarity in habits and constitution, and always in structure, the struggle will generally be more severe between them, if they come into competition with each other, than between the species of distinct genera. We see this in the recent extension over parts of the United States of one species of swallow having caused the decrease of another species. The recent increase of the missel thrush in parts of Scotland has caused the decrease of the song thrush. How frequently we hear of one species of rat taking the place of another species under the most different climates! In Russia the small Asiatic cockroach has everywhere driven before it its great congener. In Australia the imported hive-bee is rapidly exterminating the small, stingless native bee. One species of charlock has been known to supplant another species; and so in other cases. We can dimly see why the competition should be most severe between allied forms, which fill nearly the same place in the economy of nature; but probably in no one case could we precisely say why one species has been victorious over another in the great battle of life.

A corollary of the highest importance may be deduced from the foregoing remarks, namely, that the structure of every organic being is related, in the most essential yet often hidden manner, to that of all the other organic beings with which it comes into competition for food or residence, or from which it has to escape, or on which it preys. This is obvious in the structure of the teeth and talons of the tiger; and in that of the legs and claws of the parasite which clings to the hair on the tiger's body. But in the beautifully plumed seed of the dandelion, and in the flattened and fringed legs of the water beetle, the relation seems at first confined to the elements of air and water. Yet the advantage of plumed seeds no doubt stands in the closest relation to the land being already thickly clothed with other plants, so that the seeds may be widely distributed and fall on unoccupied ground. In the water beetle, the structure of its legs, so well adapted for diving, allows it to compete with other aquatic insects, to hunt for its own prey, and to escape serving as prey to other animals.

The store of nutriment laid up within the seeds of many plants seems at first sight to have no sort of relation to other plants. But from the strong growth of young plants produced from such seeds, as peas and beans, when sown in the midst of long grass, it may be suspected that the chief use of the nutriment in the seed is to favor the growth of the seedling whilst struggling with other plants growing vigorously all around.

Look at a plant in the midst of its range! Why does it not double or quadruple its numbers? We know that it can perfectly well withstand a little more heat or cold, dampness or dryness, for elsewhere it ranges into slightly hotter or colder, damper or drier districts. In this case we can clearly see that if we wish in imagination to give the plant the power of increasing in numbers, we should have to give it some advantage over its competitors, or over the animals which prey on it. On the confines of its geographical range, a change of constitution with respect to climate would clearly be an advantage to our plant; but we have reason to believe that only a few plants or animals range so far that they are destroyed exclusively by the rigor of the climate. Not until we reach the extreme confines of life, in the Arctic regions or on the borders of an utter desert, will competition cease. The land may be extremely cold or dry, yet there will be competition between some few species, or between the individuals of the same species, for the warmest or dampest spots.

Hence we can see that when a plant or animal is placed in a new country, amongst new competitors, the conditions of its life will generally be changed in an essential manner, although the climate may be exactly the same as in its former home. If its average numbers are to increase in its new home, we should have to modify it in a different way to what we should have had to do in its native country; for we should have to give it some advantage over a different set of competitors or enemies.

It is good thus to try in imagination to give to any one species an advantage over another. Probably in no single instance should we know what to do. This ought to convince us of our ignorance on the mutual relations of all organic beings—a conviction as necessary as it is difficult to acquire. All that we can do is to keep steadily in mind that each organic being is striving to increase in a geometrical ratio; that each, at some period of its life, during some season of the year, during each generation, or at intervals, has to struggle for life and to suffer great destruction. When we reflect on this struggle we may console ourselves with the full belief that the war of nature is not incessant, that no fear is felt, that death is generally prompt, and that the vigorous, the healthy, and the happy survive and multiply.

NATURAL SELECTION; OR THE SURVIVAL OF THE FITTEST

SUMMARY OF CHAPTER

If under changing conditions of life organic beings present individual differences in almost every part of their structure, and this cannot be disputed; if there be, owing to their geometrical rate of increase, a severe struggle for life at some age, season, or year, and this certainly cannot be disputed—then, considering the infinite complexity of the relations of all organic beings to each other and to their conditions of life, causing an infinite diversity in structure, constitution, and habits, to be advantageous to them, it would be a most extraordinary fact if no variations had ever occurred useful to each being's own welfare, in the same manner as so many variations have occurred useful to man. But if variations useful to any organic being ever do occur, assuredly individuals thus characterized will have the best chance of being preserved in the struggle for life; and from the strong principle of inheritance, these will tend to produce offspring similarly characterized. This principle of preservation, or the Survival of the Fittest, I have called Natural Selection. It leads to the improvement of each creature in relation to its organic and inorganic conditions of life; and consequently, in most cases, to what must be regarded as an advance in organization. Nevertheless, low and simple forms will long endure if well fitted for their simple conditions of life.

Natural Selection, on the principle of qualities being inherited at corresponding ages, can modify the egg, seed, or young as easily as the adult. Among many animals sexual selection will have given its aid to ordinary selection by assuring to the most vigorous and best adapted males the greatest number of offspring. Sexual selection will also give characters useful to the males alone in their struggles or rivalry with other males; and these characters will be transmitted to one sex or to both sexes, according to the form of inheritance which prevails.

Whether Natural Selection has really thus acted in adapting the various forms of life to their several conditions and stations must be judged by the general tenor and balance of evidence given in the following chapters. But we have already seen how it entails extinction; and how largely extinction has acted in the world's history, geology plainly declares. Natural Selection, also, leads to divergence of character; for the more organic beings diverge in structure, habits, and constitution, by so much 10 the more can a large number be supported on the area—of which we see proof by looking to the inhabitants of any small spot, and to the productions naturalized in foreign lands. Therefore, during the modification of the descendants of any one species, and during the incessant struggle of all species to increase in numbers, the more diversified the descendants become, the better will be their chance of success in the 20 battle for life. Thus the small differences distinguishing varieties of the same species steadily tend to increase, till they equal the greater differences between species of the same genus, or even of distinct genera.

We have seen that it is the common, the widely diffused and widely ranging species belonging to the larger genera within each class which vary most; and these tend to transmit to their modified offspring that 30 superiority which now makes them dominant in their own countries. Natural Selection, as has just been remarked, leads to divergence of character and to much extinction of the less improved and intermediate forms of life. On these principles, the nature of the affinities, and the generally well-defined distinctions between the innumerable organic beings in each class throughout the world, may be ex- 40 plained. It is a truly wonderful fact—the wonder of which we are apt to overlook from familiarity—that all animals and all plants throughout all time and space should be related to each other in groups, subordinate to groups, in the manner which we everywhere behold—namely, varieties of the same species most closely related, species of the same genus less closely and unequally related, forming sections 50 and subgenera, species of distinct genera much less closely related, and genera related in different degrees, forming subfamilies, families, orders, subclasses, and

classes. The several subordinate groups in any class cannot be ranked in a single file, but seem clustered round points, and these round other points, and so on in almost endless cycles. If species had been independently created, no explanation would have been possible of this kind of classification; but it is explained through inheritance and the complex action of 10 Natural Selection, entailing extinction and divergence of character, as we have seen illustrated in the diagram.

The affinities of all the beings of the same class have sometimes been represented by a great tree. I believe this simile largely speaks the truth. The green and budding twigs may represent existing species; and those produced during former years may represent the long succession of extinct 20 species. At each period of growth all the growing twigs have tried to branch out on all sides, and to overtop and kill the surrounding twigs and branches, in the same manner as species and groups of species have at all times overmastered other species in the great battle for life. The limbs divided into great branches, and these into lesser and lesser branches, were themselves once, when the tree was young, budding 30 twigs; and this connection of the former and present buds by ramifying branches may well represent the classification of all extinct and living species in groups subordinate to groups. Of the many twigs which flourished when the tree was a mere bush, only two or three, now grown into great branches, yet survive and bear the other branches; so, with the species which lived during long-past geological periods, very 40 few have left living and modified descendants. From the first growth of the tree, many a limb and branch has decayed and dropped off; and these fallen branches of various sizes may represent those whole orders, families, and genera which have now no living representatives, and which are known to us only in a fossil state. As we here and there see a thin, straggling branch springing from a fork low down 50 in a tree, and which by some chance has been favored and is still alive on its summit, so we occasionally see an animal like the Ornithorhynchus or Lepidosiren, which in some small degree connects by its affinities two large branches of life, and which has apparently been saved from fatal competition by having inhabited a protected station. As buds give rise by growth to fresh buds, and these, if vigorous, branch out and overtop on all sides many a feebler branch, so by generation I believe it has been with the great Tree of Life, which fills with its dead and broken branches the crust of the earth, and covers the surface with its ever-branching and beautiful ramifications.

[1859]

JAMES ANTHONY FROUDE

CHRONOLOGY AND INTRODUCTION

1818 Born at Dartington, Devonshire, April 23.
1827 Early schooling at Buckfastleigh, five miles from Dartington.
1830 Sent to Westminster School.
1833 Taken from Westminster; lived at home.
1836 Entered Oxford at Oriel College.
1840 Graduated with a second class in classics.
1840–42 Tutored at Oxford and in Ireland.
1842 Returned to Oxford; won Chancellor's prize for English essay; elected fellow of Exeter College.
1843 Graduated M. A.; took Deacon's orders.
1847 *Shadows of the Clouds.*
1849 *The Nemesis of Faith;* resigned fellowship.
1850 Marriage and residence in North Wales.
1856–70 *History of England,* 12 vols.
1858 Restored to fellowship.
1860 Established home in London.
1861 Editor of *Fraser's Magazine:* went to Spain to study sources for history.
1864–70 Freeman delivered series of attacks upon Froude as historian.
1867–83 *Short Studies,* 4 vols.
1868 Chosen Lord Rector of St. Andrews, Aberdeen.
1872 Lectures in America.

1872–74 *The English in Ireland in the Eighteenth Century,* 3 vols.
1874–75 Resigned editorship of *Fraser's Magazine;* travelled in South Africa.
1878 *Bunyan* (English Men of Letters Series).
1879 *Caesar: a Sketch.*
1881 *Carlyle's Reminiscences.*
1882 *Life of Carlyle* (first forty years), 2 vols.
1883 *Letters and Memorials of Jane Welsh Carlyle; Luther: a Short Biography.*
1884 Made honorary LL.D. at Edinburgh; *Life of Carlyle* (in London), 2 vols.
1884–85 Visited Australia and New Zealand on voyage around the world.
1886 *Oceana.*
1886–87 Wintered in West Indies.
1888 *The English in the West Indies.*
1889 *The Two Chiefs of Dunboy.*
1890 *Lord Beaconsfield.*
1892–94 Regius Professor of Modern History at Oxford.
1894 *Life and Letters of Erasmus;* Died October 20, at Salcombe, Devon.
1895 *English Seamen in the Sixteenth Century.*
1896 *Lectures on the Council of Trent.*
1903 *My Relations with Carlyle.*

Though Froude was not one of the most eminent Victorians, he was a commanding figure, both as a writer and as a personality. "In that society of prepotent personages," said Lytton Strachey, "he more than held his own." He was the author of some forty volumes of prose in the fields of history, biography, essay, and travel, most of which were widely read not only for their dramatic and often highly controversial subject matter but for the effortless ease and vitality of their style. A typical Englishman, living in one of the most important periods of his country's history, widely read, widely travelled, he was as much a man of the world as he was a man of books, and when he chose he could be a welcome member of the best company, talking brilliantly on literature, history, politics, and travel, or on fishing, hunting, and sailing.

Froude's father was a country parson in Devonshire, besides being a landowner, a magistrate, and a Tory. "He upheld the Bishop and all established institutions, believing that the way to heaven was to turn to the right and go straight on." A fox-hunting churchman of the old orthodox school, he found that his oldest and his youngest sons were strangely different from him and from each other: Hurrell became one of the early leaders of the Oxford Movement and a follower and friend of Newman, while Anthony grew up to be a disciple of Carlyle and a foe of Anglo-Catholicism. "God gave the Gospel," he said, "the father of lies invented theology." Anthony's early home life was mostly a torment. He was bullied and flogged by his father, while his brother Hurrell (in the acidly accurate phrase of Strachey) "egged on the parental discipline with pious glee." But in boyhood as in maturity happily he found refuge and relief in the outdoors and in books. He learned to be an expert hunter and sailor, and was equally at home on the moors and on the sea. "To wander round the world in a hundred tons schooner," he wrote in later years, "would be my highest realization of human felicity. . . . I like better than most things," he said again, "a day with my dogs in scattered covers, when I know not what may rise—a woodcock, an odd pheasant, a snipe in the outlying willowbed, and perhaps a mallard or a teal."

An even greater passion than sports was books, whether at home, at school, or at the University. One of Froude's most sustained delights was Greek. He had read, says his biographer, "both the *Iliad* and the *Odyssey* twice before he was eleven." Although his first years at Oxford were mostly idled away, because he believed that he would soon die with the disease that already had carried off mother, brothers, and sisters, he never dropped his Greek, reading (besides Homer) Herodotus, Thucydides, the dramatists, and Pindar, who was a special joy. Late in life when voyaging around the world, he found infinite satisfaction in turning from the ship's library of modern fiction to his favorite classics. "After all," he says in *Oceana*, "I had to fall back on my own supply, Homer and Horace, Pindar and Sophocles. These are the immortal lights in the intellectual sky, and shine on unaffected by the wrecks of empires or the changes of creeds. In them you find human nature, the same yesterday, today, and forever."

Modern literature, too, aroused his enthusiasm, though interest in English history before long surpassed every other interest, including his beloved Greeks. At Oxford, when so many others were plunging into theology and ecclesiastical history, Froude turned to the moderns. He had entered at Oriel where Newman was a fellow and where "the controversial fires were beginning to blaze." He felt the power of Newman's preaching at St. Mary's and never ceased in after life to pay tributes of reverence to that strangely magnetic personality, but he was untouched, unless negatively, by Newman's teaching. He undertook to assist him in a proposal to bring out a series of biographies of English saints. Froude soon had enough, and came to the conclusion that all supernatural stories were legendary. "I was thrown on my own resources," he wrote of himself in retrospect, "and began to read hard in modern history, and literature. Carlyle's books came across me; by Carlyle I was led to Goethe. I discovered Lessing for myself, and then Neander and Schleiermacher. The 'Vestiges of the Natural History of Creation,' which came out about that time introduced modern science to us under an unexpected aspect, and opened new avenues of thought."

Whether as an Oxford student, writer, or man of the world, Froude had no interest in ritualistic religion or in metaphysical speculation; and, as for science, it never upset his fundamental convictions, which were, he believed, beyond its reach: "in matters of religion it can say nothing for it knows nothing." The sacraments and observances of Anglo-Catholics he dismissed as superstition. To the problems of speculative philosophy there were, he held, no practical solutions: "in researches into the absolute we are on the road which ends nowhere." While well aware of the storms that were raging around him, his own foundations of thought, once laid, were unshaken. Amid all the encircling gloom, for Froude as for his master, Carlyle, God and the individual soul stood sure. "What the thing is which we call ourselves we know not," he said in his address on Calvinism. "It may be true—I for one care not if it be—that the descent of our mortal bodies may be traced through an ascending series to some glutinous organism on the rocks of the primeval ocean. It is nothing to me how the Maker of me has been pleased to construct the perishable frame which I call my body. It is *mine*, but it is not *Me*." And in the same essay: "Human life at the best is enveloped in darkness; we know not what we are or whither we are bound. Religion is the light by which we are to see our way along the moral pathways without straying into the brake or the morass. We are not to look at religion itself, but at surrounding things with the help of religion. If we fasten our attention upon the light itself, analysing it into its component rays, speculating on the union and composition of the substance of which it is composed, not only will it no longer serve us for a guide, but our dazzled senses lose their natural powers."

Such was the creed, if belief so undogmatic may be called a creed, to which Froude at last came as he went on his way through a long and distinguished career. After the publication of his *Nemesis of Faith* in 1849, a crude but revealing piece of autobiographical fiction, he lost his fellowship at Exeter, and, now cut off by his disappointed and disgusted father, he was left adrift, without a profession and without means of support. He turned to writing, first to miscellaneous articles and then to history and biography. His reputation rests for the most part upon the *History of England* and the *Life of Carlyle*. He spent twenty years upon the *History*, in twelve volumes, from the fall of Wolsey (1529) to the defeat of the Spanish Armada (1588), a short but momentous stretch of sixty years. "To understand the past," he said, "we must look at it always, when we can, through the eyes of contemporaries." True to this precept Froude searchingly examined large masses of source material belonging to his period. "In London and other places in England, in Paris, in Simancas, and in Vienna, I had read something like a hundred thousand manuscript letters and documents in English, French, Latin, Spanish, and Italian." "Froude had mastered the sixteenth century as Macaulay had mastered the seventeenth, with the same minute, patient industry," says his biographer, Herbert Paul, himself a historian. "When he came to write he wrote with such apparent facility that those who did not know the meaning of historical research thought him shallow and superficial."

History, to Froude, was not a science, dealing with exact calculable factors, but the drama of human life made up of imponderable motives, emotions, ideas,—always in flux, always in conflict on a stage "where good and evil fight out their everlasting battle," and where, "in the long run, it is well with the good and ill with the wicked." Great historians, he thought, wrote from their own vision of truth: "Thucydides wrote to expose the vices of Democracy; Tacitus, the historian of the Caesars, to exhibit the hatefulness of Imperialism." So Froude, choosing for his field the most controversial period of English History, wrote to show that the Reformation saved "England from the tyranny of Rome and the proud foot of a Spanish conqueror." The defeat of the Armada established for all time the supremacy of the Crown as against the supremacy of the Pope. Thus his *History* is deliberately partisan. Worse still, in the eyes of modern scholars, Froude was incredibly careless in transcribing his authorities and he made innumerable mistakes. He was never dishonest, however, and he deposited his transcriptions in the British Museum where they could be consulted and checked at will by all and sundry. When all the corrections are made therefore and all the balances are redressed, his work will remain a brilliant and most readable chapter in England's history, with many pages of exciting narrative and vivid portraiture.

More valuable than his *History*, more valuable than "all my books," in Froude's own opinion, was "beyond doubt" the *Life of Carlyle*, one of the greatest biographies in English. He had read Carlyle's books at Oxford, had seen Carlyle for the first time at Emerson's lecture in London in 1848, and the next year had enjoyed the privilege of an introduction, the beginning of a discipleship extending over a period of thirty and more years. His personal intimacy with Carlyle was indeed closer and of longer duration than Boswell's with Johnson. *Sartor Resartus* and *The French Revolution* had guided him out of the wilderness of uncertainty and doubt into a promised land of confidence and belief; and now in his maturity he was admitted into almost filial relations with the old master whom above all other men he reverenced and loved. There never was, there never will be again, so complete a Carlylean as Froude.

His *Life* and his editorial work on Carlyle's *Reminiscences* and Mrs. Carlyle's *Letters and Journals* awoke a storm of controversy which has not yet entirely subsided. Members of the Carlyle family were outraged because the biographer dared to paint in Rembrandtesque manner the dark shadows as well as the high lights of his great figure: and many others took up the cry. Froude well understood what he was about, he knew that Carlyle was "a prickly reality of flesh and blood," a kind of nineteenth century Samuel Johnson; but he knew, too, that "the only 'Life' of a man which is not worse than useless is a 'Life' which tells the truth so far as the biographer knows it,"—a view that exactly squared with Carlyle's. His biography is a superb piece of writing, in spite of faults and Froudian prepossessions, and it presents in vivid and veracious details the massive portrait of a great Victorian who, as Ruskin said, "was born in the clouds and struck by lightning."

Curiously, the only un-Carlylean thing about Froude as a man of letters is his style. Carlyle's manner of writing is one of the most highly individualized in English prose, while the most peculiar feature of Froude's style is its absence of peculiarity. Many scholars, who have severely censured his carelessness and inaccuracy, without exception have praised his expression for its incomparable ease, lucidity, narrative movement, and sustained vitality. Even his arch-enemy, the historian Freeman, called Froude a "master of narrative." Two or three critics have noted that his style belongs to the school of Newman, to whose prose it is, doubtless, nearest akin, without, of course, possessing Newman's intellectual subtlety and penetration. Whatever we may say of it, the charm is irresistible. There is no violence anywhere, whether in vocabulary, order of sentences, color, figures of speech, or assemblage of dramatic detail. All is transparent and lively. "It is," says Herbert Paul, "as smooth as the motion of a ship on a calm sea, and yet it is never flat nor tame."

SHORT STUDIES ON GREAT SUBJECTS (I)

THE SCIENCE OF HISTORY

Ladies and Gentlemen,—I have undertaken to speak to you this evening on what is called the Science of History. I fear it is a dry subject; and there seems, indeed, something incongruous in the very connection of such words as Science and History. It is as if we were to talk of the colour of sound, or the longitude of the rule-of-three. Where it is so difficult to make out the truth of the commonest disputed fact in matters passing under our very eyes, how can we talk of a science in things long past, which come to us only through books? It often seems to me as if History was like a child's box of letters, with which we can spell any word we please. We have only to pick out such letters as we want, arrange them as we like, and say nothing about those which do not suit our purpose.

I will try to make the thing intelligible, and I will try not to weary you; but I am doubtful of my success either way. First, however, I wish to say a word or two about the eminent person whose name is connected with this way of looking at History, and whose premature death struck us all with such a sudden sorrow. Many of you, perhaps, recollect Mr. Buckle as he stood not so long ago in this place. He spoke more than an hour without a note—never repeating himself, never wasting words; laying out his matter as easily and as pleasantly as if he had been talking to us at his own fireside. We might think what we pleased of Mr. Buckle's views, but it was plain enough that he was a man of uncommon power; and he had qualities also —qualities to which he, perhaps, himself attached little value, as rare as they were admirable.

Most of us, when we have hit on something which we are pleased to think important and original, feel as if we should burst with it. We come out into the book-market with our wares in hand, and ask for thanks and recognition. Mr. Buckle, at an early age, conceived the thought which made him famous, but he took the measure of his abilities. He knew that whenever he pleased he could command personal distinction, but he cared more for his subject than for himself. He was contented to work with patient reticence, unknown and unheard of, for twenty years; and then, at middle life, he produced a work which was translated at once into French and German, and, of all places in the world, fluttered the dovecotes of the Imperial Academy of St. Petersburg.

Goethe says somewhere, that as soon as a man has done anything remarkable, there seems to be a general conspiracy to prevent him from doing it again. He is feasted, fêted, caressed; his time is stolen from him by breakfasts, dinners, societies, idle businesses of a thousand kinds. Mr. Buckle had his share of all this; but there are also more dangerous enemies that wait upon success like this. He had scarcely won for himself the place which he deserved, than his health was found shattered by his labours. He had but time to show us how large a man he was—time just to sketch the outlines of his philosophy, and he passed away as suddenly as he appeared. He went abroad to recover strength for his work, but his work was done with and over. He died of a fever at Damascus, vexed only that he was compelled to leave it uncompleted. Almost his last conscious words were, "My book, my book! I shall never finish my book!" He went away as he had lived, nobly careless of himself, and thinking only of the thing which he had undertaken to do.

But his labour had not been thrown away. Disagree with him as we might, the effect which he had already produced was unmistakable, and it is not likely to pass away. What he said was not essentially new. Some such interpretation of human things is as early as the beginning of thought. But Mr. Buckle, on the one hand, had the art which belongs to men of genius; he could present his opinions with peculiar distinctness; and, on the other hand, there is much in the mode of speculation at present current among us for which those opinions have an unusual fascination. They do not please us, but they excite and irritate us. We are angry with them; and we betray, in being so, an uneasy misgiving that there may be more truth in those opinions than we like to allow.

Mr. Buckle's general theory was something of this kind: When human creatures began first to look about them in the world they lived in, there seemed to be no order in anything. Days and nights were not the same length. The air was sometimes hot and sometimes cold. Some of the stars rose and set like the sun; some were almost motionless in the sky; some described circles round a central star above the north horizon. The planets went on principles of their own; and in the elements there seemed nothing but caprice. Sun and moon would at times go out in eclipse. Sometimes the earth itself would shake under men's feet; and they could only suppose that earth and air and sky and water were inhabited and managed by creatures as wayward as themselves.

Time went on, and the disorder began to arrange itself. Certain influences seemed beneficent to men, others malignant and destructive, and the world was supposed to be animated by good spirits and evil spirits, who were continually fighting against each other, in outward nature and in human creatures themselves. Finally, as men observed more and imagined less, these interpretations gave way also. Phenomena the most opposite in effect were seen to be the result of the same natural law. The fire did not burn the house down if the owners of it were careful, but remained on the hearth and boiled the pot; nor did it seem more inclined to burn a bad man's house down than a good man's provided the badness did not take the form of negligence. The phenomena of nature were found for the most part to proceed in an orderly, regular way, and their variations to be such as could be counted upon. From observing the order of things, the step was easy to cause and effect. An eclipse, instead of being a sign of the anger of Heaven, was found to be the necessary and innocent result of the relative position of sun, moon, and earth. The comets became bodies in space, unrelated to the beings who had imagined that all creation

was watching them and their doings. By degrees, caprice, volition, all symptoms of arbitrary action, disappeared out of the universe; and almost every phenomenon in earth or heaven was found attributable to some law, either understood or perceived to exist. Thus nature was reclaimed from the imagination. The first fantastic conception of things gave way before the moral; the moral in turn gave way before the natural; and at last there was left but one small tract of jungle where the theory of law had failed to penetrate—the doings and characters of human creatures themselves.

There, and only there, amidst the conflicts of reason and emotion, conscience and desire, spiritual forces were still conceived to exist. Cause and effect were not traceable when there was a free volition to disturb the connection. In all other things, from a given set of conditions, the consequences necessarily followed. With man, the word law changed its meaning; and instead of a fixed order, which he could not choose but follow, it became a moral precept, which he might disobey if he dared.

This it was which Mr. Buckle disbelieved. The economy which prevailed throughout nature, he thought it very unlikely should admit of this exception. He considered that human beings acted necessarily from the impulse of outward circumstances upon their mental and bodily condition at any given moment. Every man, he said, acted from a motive; and his conduct was determined by the motive which affected him most powerfully. Every man naturally desires what he supposes to be good for him; but to do well, he must know well. He will eat poison, so long as he does not know that it is poison. Let him see that it will kill him, and he will not touch it. The question was not of moral right and wrong. Once let him be thoroughly made to feel that the thing is destructive, and he will leave it alone by the law of his nature. His virtues are the result of knowledge; his faults, the necessary consequence of the want of it. A boy desires to draw. He knows nothing about it: he draws men like trees or houses, with their centre of gravity anywhere. He makes mistakes, because he knows no better. We do not blame him. Till he is better taught he cannot help it. But his instruction begins. He arrives at straight lines; then at solids; then at curves. He learns perspective, and light and shade. He observes more accurately the forms which he wishes to represent. He perceives effects, and he perceives the means by which they are produced. He has learned what to do; and, in part, he has learned how to do it. His after-progress will depend on the amount of force which his nature possesses; but all this is as natural as the growth of an acorn. You do not preach to the acorn that it is its duty to become a large tree; you do not preach to the art-pupil that it is his duty to become a Holbein. You plant your acorn in favourable soil, where it can have light and air, and be sheltered from the wind; you remove the superfluous branches, you train the strength into the leading shoots. The acorn will then become as fine a tree as it has vital force to become. The difference between men and other things is only in the largeness and variety of man's capacities; and in this special capacity, that he alone has the power of observing the circumstances favourable to his own growth, and can apply them for himself. Yet, again, with this condition,—that he is not, as is commonly supposed, free to choose whether he will make use of these appliances or not. When he knows what is good for him, he will choose it; and he will judge what is good for him by the circumstances which have made him what he is.

And what he would do, Mr. Buckle supposed that he always had done. His history had been a natural growth as much as the growth of the acorn. His improvement had followed the progress of his knowledge; and, by a comparison of his outward circumstances with the condition of his mind, his whole proceedings on this planet, his creeds and constitutions, his good deeds and his bad, his arts and his sciences, his empires and his revolutions, would be found all to arrange themselves into clear relations of cause and effect.

If, when Mr. Buckle pressed his conclusions, we objected the difficulty of finding what the truth about past times really was, he would admit it candidly as far as concerned individuals; but there was not the same difficulty, he said, with masses of men. We might disagree about the characters of Julius or Tiberius Cæsar, but we could know well enough the Romans of the Empire. We had their literature to tell us how they thought; we had their laws to tell us how they governed; we had the broad face of the world, the huge mountainous outline of their general doings upon it, to tell us how they acted. He believed it was all reducible to laws, and could be made as intelligible as the growth of the chalk cliffs or the coal measures.

And thus consistently Mr. Buckle cared little for individuals. He did not believe (as some one has said) that the history of mankind is the history of its great men. Great men with him were but larger atoms, obeying the same impulses with the rest, only perhaps a trifle more erratic. With them or without them, the course of things would have been much the same.

As an illustration of the truth of his view, he would point to the new science of Political Economy. Here already was a large area of human activity in which natural laws were found to act unerringly. Men had gone on for centuries trying to regulate trade on moral principles. They would fix wages according to some imaginary rule of fairness; they would fix prices by what they considered things ought to cost; they encouraged one trade or discouraged another, for moral reasons. They might as well have tried to work a steam-engine on moral reasons. The great statesmen whose names were connected with these enterprises might have as well legislated that water should run up-hill. There were natural laws, fixed in the conditions of things: and to contend against them was the old battle of the Titans against the gods.

As it was with political economy, so it was with all other forms of human activity; and as the true laws of political economy explained the troubles which people fell into in old times, because they were ignorant of them, so the true laws of human nature, as soon as we knew them, would explain their mistakes in more serious matters, and enable us to manage better for the future. Geographical position, climate, air, soil, and the like, had their several influences. The northern nations are hardy and industrious, because they must till the earth if they would eat the fruits of it, and because the temperature is too low to make an idle life enjoyable. In the south, the soil is more productive, while less food is wanted and fewer clothes; and in the exquisite air, exertion is not needed to make the sense of existence delightful. Therefore, in the south we find men lazy and indolent.

True, there are difficulties in these views; the home of the languid Italian was the home also of the sternest race of whom the story of mankind retains a record. And again, when we are told that the Spaniards are superstitious, because Spain is a country of earthquakes, we remember Japan, the spot in all the world where earthquakes are most frequent, and where at the same time there is the most serene disbelief in any supernatural agency whatsoever.

Moreover, if men grow into what they are by natural laws, they cannot help being what they are; and if they cannot help being what they are, a good deal will have to be altered in our general view of human obligations and responsibilities.

That, however, in these theories there is a good deal of truth is quite certain; were there but a hope that those who maintain them would be contented with that admission. A man born in a Mahometan country grows up a Mahometan; in a Catholic country, a Catholic; in a Protestant country, a Protestant. His opinions are like his language; he learns to think as he learns to speak; and it is absurd to suppose him responsible for being what nature makes him. We take pains to educate children. There is a good education and a bad education; there are rules well ascertained by which characters are influenced, and, clearly enough, it is no mere matter for a boy's free will whether he turns out well or ill. We try to train him into good habits; we keep him out of the way of temptations; we see that he is well taught; we mix kindness and strictness; we surround him with every good influence we can command. These are what are termed the advantages of a good education: if we fail to provide those under our care with it,

and if they go wrong, the responsibility we feel is as much ours as theirs. This is at once an admission of the power over us of outward circumstances.

In the same way, we allow for the strength of temptations, and the like.

In general, it is perfectly obvious that men do necessarily absorb, out of the influences in which they grow up, something which gives a complexion to their whole after-character.

When historians have to relate great social or speculative changes, the overthrow of a monarchy or the establishment of a creed, they do but half their duty if they merely relate the events. In an account, for instance, of the rise of Mahometanism, it is not enough to describe the character of the Prophet, the ends which he set before him, the means which he made use of, and the effect which he produced; the historian must show what there was in the condition of the Eastern races which enabled Mahomet to act upon them so powerfully; their existing beliefs, their existing moral and political condition.

In our estimate of the past, and in our calculations of the future—in the judgments which we pass upon one another, we measure responsibility, not by the thing done but by the opportunities which people have had of knowing better or worse. In the efforts which we make to keep our children from bad associations or friends we admit that external circumstances have a powerful effect in making men what they are.

But are circumstances everything? That is the whole question. A science of history, if it is more than a misleading name, implies that the relation between cause and effect holds in human things as completely as in all others, that the origin of human actions is not to be looked for in mysterious properties of the mind, but in influences which are palpable and ponderable.

When natural causes are liable to be set aside and neutralised by what is called volition, the word Science is out of place. If it is free to a man to choose what he will do or not do, there is no adequate science of him. If there is a science of him, there is no free choice, and the praise or blame with which we regard one another are impertinent and out of place.

I am trespassing upon these ethical grounds because, unless I do, the subject cannot be made intelligible. Mankind are but an aggregate of individuals—History is but the record of individual action; and what is true of the part, is true of the whole.

We feel keenly about such things, and when the logic becomes perplexing, we are apt to grow rhetorical about them. But rhetoric is only misleading. Whatever the truth may be, it is best that we should know it; and for truth of any kind we should keep our heads and hearts as cool as we can.

I will say at once, that if we had the whole case before us—if we were taken, like Leibnitz's Tarquin, into the council chamber of nature, and were shown what we really were, where we came from, and where we were going, however unpleasant it might be for some of us to find ourselves, like Tarquin, made into villains, from the subtle necessities of "the best of all possible worlds"; nevertheless, some such theory as Mr. Buckle's might possibly turn out to be true. Likely enough, there is some great "equation of the universe" where the value of the unknown quantities can be determined. But we must treat things in relation to our own powers and position; and the question is, whether the sweep of those vast curves can be measured by the intellect of creatures of a day like ourselves.

The "Faust" of Goethe, tired of the barren round of earthly knowledge, calls magic to his aid. He desires, first, to see the spirit of the Macrocosmos, but his heart fails him before he ventures that tremendous experiment, and he summons before him, instead, the spirit of his own race. There he feels at home. The stream of life and the storm of action, the everlasting ocean of existence, the web and the woof, and the roaring loom of time—he gazes upon them all, and in passionate exultation claims fellowship with the awful thing before him. But the majestic vision fades, and a voice comes to him—"Thou art fellow with the spirits which thy mind can grasp—not with me."

Had Mr. Buckle tried to follow his principles into detail, it might have fared no better with him than with "Faust."

What are the conditions of a science? and when may any subject be said to enter the scientific stage? I suppose when the facts of it begin to resolve themselves into groups; when phenomena are no longer isolated experiences, but appear in connection and order; when, after certain antecedents, certain consequences are uniformly seen to follow; when facts enough have been collected to furnish a basis for conjectural explanation, and when conjectures have so far ceased to be utterly vague, that it is possible in some degree to foresee the future by the help of them.

Till a subject has advanced as far as this, to speak of a science of it is an abuse of language. It is not enough to say that there must be a science of human things, because there is a science of all other things. This is like saying the planets must be inhabited, because the only planet of which we have any experience is inhabited. It may or may not be true, but it is not a practical question; it does not affect the practical treatment of the matter in hand. Let us look at the history of Astronomy.

So long as sun, moon, and planets were supposed to be gods or angels; so long as the sword of Orion was not a metaphor, but a fact, and the groups of stars which inlaid the floor of heaven were the glittering trophies of the loves and wars of the Pantheon, so long there was no science of Astronomy. There was fancy, imagination, poetry, perhaps reverence, but no science. As soon, however, as it was observed that the stars retained their relative places —that the times of their rising and setting varied with the seasons—that sun, moon, and planets moved among them in a plane, and the belt of the Zodiac was marked out and divided, then a new order of things began. Traces of the earlier stage remained in the names of the signs and constellations, just as the Scandinavian mythology survives now in the names of the days of the week: but for all that, the understanding was now at work on the thing; Science had begun, and the first triumph of it was the power of foretelling the future. Eclipses were perceived to recur in cycles of nineteen years, and philosophers were able to say when an eclipse was to be looked for. The periods of the planets were determined. Theories were invented to account for their eccentricities; and, false as those theories might be, the position of the planets could be calculated with moderate certainty by them. The very first result of the science, in its most imperfect stage, was a power of foresight; and this was possible before any one true astronomical law had been discovered.

We should not therefore question the possibility of a science of history, because the explanations of its phenomena were rudimentary or imperfect: that they might be, and might long continue to be, and yet enough might be done to show that there was such a thing, and that it was not entirely without use. But how was it that in those rude days, with small knowledge of mathematics, and with no better instruments than flat walls and dial plates, those first astronomers made progress so considerable? Because, I suppose, the phenomena which they were observing recurred, for the most part, within moderate intervals; so that they could collect large experience within the compass of their natural lives; because days and months and years were measurable periods, and within them the more simple phenomena perpetually repeated themselves.

But how would it have been if, instead of turning on its axis once in twenty-four hours, the earth had taken a year about it; if the year had been nearly four hundred years; if man's life had been no longer than it is, and for the initial steps of astronomy there had been nothing to depend upon except observations recorded in history? How many ages would have passed, had this been our condition, before it would have occurred to any one, that, in what they saw night after night, there was any kind of order at all?

We can see to some extent how it would have been, by the present state of those parts of the science which in fact depend on remote recorded observations. The movements of the comets are still extremely uncertain. The times of their return can be calculated only with the greatest vagueness.

And yet such a hypothesis as I have suggested would but inadequately express the position in which we are in fact placed

towards history. There the phenomena never repeat themselves. There we are dependent wholly on the record of things said to have happened once, but which never happen or can happen a second time. There no experiment is possible; we can watch for no recurring fact to test the worth of our conjectures. It has been suggested, fancifully, that if we consider the universe to be infinite, time is the same as eternity, and the past is perpetually present. Light takes nine years to come to us from Sirius; those rays which we may see to-night when we leave this place, left Sirius nine years ago; and could the inhabitants of Sirius see the earth at this moment, they would see the English army in the trenches before Sebastopol; Florence Nightingale watching at Scutari over the wounded at Inkermann; and the peace of England undisturbed by *Essays and Reviews*.

As the stars recede into distance, so time recedes with them, and there may be, and probably are, stars from which Noah might be seen stepping into the ark, Eve listening to the temptation of the serpent, or that older race, eating the oysters and leaving the shell-heaps behind them, when the Baltic was an open sea.

Could we but compare notes, something might be done; but of this there is no present hope, and without it there will be no science of history. Eclipses, recorded in ancient books, can be verified by calculation, and lost dates can be recovered by them, and we can foresee by the laws which they follow when there will be eclipses again. Will a time ever be when the lost secret of the foundation of Rome can be recovered by historic laws? If not, where is our science? It may be said that this is a particular fact, that we can deal satisfactorily with general phenomena affecting eras and cycles. Well, then, let us take some general phenomena. Mahometanism, for instance, or Buddhism. Those are large enough. Can you imagine a science which would have *foretold* such movements as those? The state of things out of which they rose is obscure; but suppose it not obscure, can you conceive that, with any amount of historical insight into the old Oriental beliefs, you could have seen that they were about to transform themselves into those particular forms and no other?

It is not enough to say, that, after the fact, you can understand partially how Mahometanism came to be. All historians worth the name have told us something about that. But when we talk of science, we mean something with more ambitious pretences, we mean something which can foresee as well as explain; and, thus looked at, to state the problem is to show its absurdity. As little could the wisest man have foreseen this mighty revolution, as thirty years ago such a thing as Mormonism could have been anticipated in America; as little as it could have been foreseen that table-turning and spirit-rapping would have been an outcome of the scientific culture of England in the nineteenth century.

The greatest of Roman thinkers, gazing mournfully at the seething mass of moral putrefaction round him, detected and deigned to notice among its elements a certain detestable superstition, so he called it, rising up amidst the offscouring of the Jews, which was named Christianity. Could Tacitus have looked forward nine centuries to the Rome of Gregory VII., could he have beheld the representative of the majesty of the Cæsars holding the stirrup of the Pontiff of that vile and execrated sect, the spectacle would scarcely have appeared to him the fulfilment of a rational expectation, or an intelligible result of the causes in operation round him. Tacitus, indeed, was born before the science of history; but would M. Comte have seen any more clearly?

Nor is the case much better if we are less hard upon our philosophy; if we content ourselves with the past, and require only a scientific explanation of that.

First, for the facts themselves. They come to us through the minds of those who recorded them, neither machines nor angels, but fallible creatures, with human passions and prejudices. Tacitus and Thucydides were perhaps the ablest men who ever gave themselves to writing history; the ablest, and also the most incapable of conscious falsehood. Yet even now, after all these centuries, the truth of what they relate is called in question. Good reasons can be given to show that neither of them can

be confidently trusted. If we doubt with these, whom are we to believe?

Or again, let the facts be granted. To revert to my simile of the box of letters, you have but to select such facts as suit you, you have but to leave alone those which do not suit you, and let your theory of history be what it will, you can find no difficulty in providing facts to prove it. You may have your Hegel's philosophy of history, or you may have your Schlegel's philosophy of history; you may prove from history that the world is governed in detail by a special Providence; you may prove that there is no sign of any moral agent in the universe, except man; you may believe, if you like it, in the old theory of the wisdom of antiquity; you may speak, as was the fashion in the fifteenth century, of "our fathers, who had more wit and wisdom than we"; or you may talk of "our barbarian ancestors," and describe their wars as the scuffling of kites and crows.

You may maintain that the evolution of humanity has been an unbroken progress towards perfection; you may maintain that there has been no progress at all, and that man remains the same poor creature that he ever was; or, lastly, you may say with the author of the *Contrat Social*, that men were purest and best in primeval simplicity—

When wild in woods the noble savage ran.

In all, or any of these views, history will stand your friend. History, in its passive irony, will make no objection. Like Jarno, in Goethe's novel, it will not condescend to argue with you, and will provide you with abundant illustrations of anything which you may wish to believe.

"What is history," said Napoleon, "but a fiction agreed upon?" "My friend," said Faust to the student, who was growing enthusiastic about the spirit of past ages; "my friend, the times which are gone are a book with seven seals; and what you call the spirit of past ages is but the spirit of this or that worthy gentleman in whose mind those ages are reflected."

One lesson, and only one, history may be said to repeat with distinctness; that the world is built somehow on moral foundations; that, in the long run, it is well with the good; in the long run, it is ill with the wicked. But this is no science; it is no more than the old doctrine taught long ago by the Hebrew prophets. The theories of M. Comte and his disciples advance us, after all, not a step beyond the trodden and familiar ground. If men are not entirely animals, they are at least half animals, and are subject in this aspect of them to the conditions of animals. So far as those parts of man's doings are concerned, which neither have, nor need have, anything moral about them, so far the laws of him are calculable. There are laws for his digestion, and laws of the means by which his digestive organs are supplied with matter. But pass beyond them, and where are we? In a world where it would be as easy to calculate men's actions by laws like those of positive philosophy as to measure the orbit of Neptune with a foot-rule, or weigh Sirius in a grocer's scale.

And it is not difficult to see why this should be. The first principle on which the theory of a science of history can be plausibly argued, is that all actions whatsoever arise from self-interest. It may be enlightened self-interest; it may be unenlightened; but it is assumed as an axiom, that every man, in whatever he does, is aiming at something which he considers will promote his happiness. His conduct is not determined by his will; it is determined by the object of his desire. Adam Smith, in laying the foundation of political economy, expressly eliminates every other motive. He does not say that men never act on other motives; still less, that they never ought to act on other motives. He asserts merely that, as far as the arts of production are concerned, and of buying and selling, the action of self-interest may be counted upon as uniform. What Adam Smith says of political economy, Mr. Buckle would extend over the whole circle of human activity.

Now, that which especially distinguishes a high order of man from a low order of man—that which constitutes human goodness, human greatness, human nobleness—is surely not the degree of enlightenment with which men pursue their own advantage; but it is self-forgetfulness—it is self-sacrifice—it is the disregard of personal pleasure, personal indulgence, personal advantages remote or present, because some other line of conduct is more right.

We are sometimes told that this is but another way of expressing the same thing; that when a man prefers doing what is right, it is only because to do right gives him a higher satisfaction. It appears to me, on the contrary, to be a difference in the very heart and nature of things. The martyr goes to the stake, the patriot to the scaffold, not with a view to any future reward to themselves, but because it is a glory to fling away their lives for truth and freedom. And so through all phases of existence, to the smallest details of common life, the beautiful character is the unselfish character. Those whom we most love and admire are those to whom the thought of self seems never to occur; who do simply and with no ulterior aim—with no thought whether it will be pleasant to themselves or unpleasant—that which is good, and right, and generous.

Is this still selfishness, only more enlightened? I do not think so. The essence of true nobility is neglect of self. Let the thought of self pass in, and the beauty of a great action is gone—like the bloom from a soiled flower. Surely it is a paradox to speak of the self-interest of a martyr who dies for a cause, the triumph of which he will never enjoy; and the greatest of that great company in all ages would have done what they did, had their personal prospects closed with the grave. Nay, there have been those so zealous for some glorious principle, as to wish themselves blotted out of the book of Heaven if the cause of Heaven could succeed.

And out of this mysterious quality, whatever it be, arise the higher relations of human life, the higher modes of human obligation. Kant, the philosopher, used to say that there were two things which overwhelmed him with awe as he thought of them. One was the star-sown deep of space, without limit and without end; the other was, right and wrong. Right, the sacrifice of self to good; wrong, the sacrifice of good to self;—not graduated objects of desire, to which we are determined by the degrees of our knowledge, but wide asunder as pole and pole, as light and darkness —one, the object of infinite love; the other, the object of infinite detestation and scorn. It is in this marvellous power in men to do wrong (it is an old story, but none the less true for that)—it is in this power to do wrong—wrong or right, as it lies somehow with ourselves to' choose—that the impossibility stands of forming scientific calculations of what men will do before the fact, or scientific explanations of what they have done after the fact. If men were consistently selfish, you might analyse their motives; if they were consistently noble, they would express in their conduct the laws of the highest perfection. But so long as two natures are mixed together, and the strange creature which results from the combination is now under one influence and now under another, so long you will make nothing of him except from the old-fashioned moral—or, if you please, imaginative—point of view.

Even the laws of political economy itself cease to guide us when they touch moral government. So long as labour is a chattel to be bought and sold, so long, like other commodities, it follows the condition of supply and demand. But if, for his misfortune, an employer considers that he stands in human relations towards his workmen; if he believes, rightly or wrongly, that he is responsible for them; that in return for their labour he is bound to see that their children are decently taught, and they and their families decently fed and clothed and lodged; that he ought to care for them in sickness and in old age; then political economy will no longer direct him, and the relations between himself and his dependents will have to be arranged on quite other principles.

So long as he considers only his own material profit, so long supply and demand will settle every difficulty; but the introduction of a new factor spoils the equation.

And it is precisely in this debatable ground of low motives and noble emotions —in the struggle, ever failing, yet ever renewed, to carry truth and justice into the administration of human society; in the establishment of states and in the overthrow of tyrannies; in the rise and fall of creeds; in the world of ideas; in the character and deeds of the great actors in the drama of life; where good and evil fight out their everlasting battle, now ranged in opposite camps, now and more often in the heart, both of them, of each living man—that the true human interest of history resides. The progress of industries, the growth of material and mechanical civilisation, are interesting, but they are not the most interesting. They have their reward in the increase of material comforts; but, unless we are mistaken about our nature, they do not highly concern us after all.

Once more; not only is there in men this baffling duality of principle, but there is something else in us which still more defies scientific analysis.

Mr. Buckle would deliver himself from the eccentricities of this and that individual by a doctrine of averages. Though he cannot tell whether A, B, or C will cut his throat, he may assure himself that one man in every fifty thousand, or thereabout (I forget the exact proportion), will cut his throat, and with this he consoles himself. No doubt it is a comforting discovery. Unfortunately, the average of one generation need not be the average of the next. We may be converted by the Japanese, for all that we know, and the Japanese methods of taking leave of life may become fashionable among us. Nay, did not Novalis suggest that the whole race of men would at last become so disgusted with their impotence, that they would extinguish themselves by a simultaneous act of suicide, and make room for a better order of beings? Anyhow, the fountain out of which the race is flowing perpetually changes—no two generations are alike. Whether there is a change in the organisation itself, we cannot tell; but this is certain, that as the planet varies with the atmosphere which surrounds it, so each new generation varies from the last, because it inhales as its atmosphere the accumulated experience and knowledge of the whole past of the world. These things form the spiritual air which we breathe as we grow; and in the infinite multiplicity of elements of which that air is now composed, it is for ever matter of conjecture what the minds will be like which expand under its influence.

From the England of Fielding and Richardson to the England of Miss Austen—

from the England of Miss Austen to the England of Railways and Free-trade, how vast the change; yet perhaps Sir Charles Grandison would not seem so strange to us now, as one of ourselves will seem to our great-grandchildren. The world moves faster and faster; and the difference will probably be considerably greater.

The temper of each new generation is a continual surprise. The fates delight to contradict our most confident expectations. Gibbon believed that the era of conquerors was at an end. Had he lived out the full life of man, he would have seen Europe at the feet of Napoleon. But a few years ago we believed the world had grown too civilised for war, and the Crystal Palace in Hyde Park was to be the inauguration of a new era. Battles, bloody as Napoleon's, are now the familiar tale of every day; and the arts which have made greatest progress are the arts of destruction. What next? We may strain our eyes into the future which lies beyond this waning century; but never was conjecture more at fault. It is blank darkness, which even the imagination fails to people.

What then is the use of History? and what are its lessons? If it can tell us little of the past, and nothing of the future, why waste our time over so barren a study?

First, it is a voice for ever sounding across the centuries the laws of right and wrong. Opinions alter, manners change, creeds rise and fall, but the moral law is written on the tablets of eternity. For every false word or unrighteous deed, for cruelty and oppression, for lust or vanity, the price has to be paid at last: not always by the chief offenders, but paid by some one. Justice and truth alone endure and live. Injustice and falsehood may be long-lived, but doomsday comes at last to them, in French revolutions and other terrible ways.

That is one lesson of History. Another is, that we should draw no horoscopes; that we should expect little, for what we expect will not come to pass. Revolutions, reformations—those vast movements into which heroes and saints have flung themselves, in the belief that they were the dawn of the millennium—have not borne the fruit which they looked for. Millen-

niums are still far away. These great convulsions leave the world changed—perhaps improved—but not improved as the actors in them hoped it would be. Luther would have gone to work with less heart, could he have foreseen the Thirty Years' War, and in the distance the theology of Tübingen. Washington might have hesitated to draw the sword against England, could he have seen the country which he made as we see it now.

The most reasonable anticipations fail us —antecedents the most apposite mislead us; because the conditions of human problems never repeat themselves. Some new feature alters everything—some element which we detect only in its after-operation.

But this, it may be said, is but a meagre outcome. Can the long records of humanity, with all its joys and sorrows, its sufferings and its conquests, teach us no more than this? Let us approach the subject from another side.

If you were asked to point out the special features in which Shakespeare's plays are so transcendently excellent, you would mention, perhaps, among others, this, that his stories are not put together, and his characters are not conceived, to illustrate any particular law or principle. They teach many lessons, but not any one prominent above another; and when we have drawn from them all the direct instruction which they contain, there remains still something unresolved—something which the artist gives, and which the philosopher cannot give.

It is in this characteristic that we are accustomed to say Shakespeare's supreme *truth* lies. He represents real life. His dramas teach as life teaches—neither less nor more. He builds his fabrics as nature does, on right and wrong; but he does not struggle to make nature more systematic than she is. In the subtle interflow of good and evil—in the unmerited sufferings of innocence—in the disproportion of penalties to desert—in the seeming blindness with which justice, in attempting to assert itself, overwhelms innocent and guilty in a common ruin—Shakespeare is true to real experience. The mystery of life he leaves as he finds it; and, in his most tremendous positions, he is addressing rather the intellectual emotions than the understanding, —knowing well that the understanding in such things is at fault, and the sage as ignorant as the child.

Only the highest order of genius can represent nature thus. An inferior artist produces either something entirely immoral, where good and evil are names, and nobility of disposition is supposed to show itself in the absolute disregard of them— or else, if he is a better kind of man, he will force on nature a didactic purpose; he composes what are called moral tales, which may edify the conscience, but will only mislead the intellect.

The finest work of this kind produced in modern times is Lessing's play of *Nathan the Wise*. The object of it is to teach religious toleration. The doctrine is admirable—the mode in which it is enforced is interesting; but it has the fatal fault, that it is not true. Nature does not teach religious toleration by any such direct method; and the result is—no one knew it better than Lessing himself—that the play is not poetry but only splendid manufacture. Shakespeare is eternal; Lessing's *Nathan* will pass away with the mode of thought which gave it birth. One is based on fact; the other, on human theory about fact. The theory seems at first sight to contain the most immediate instruction; but it is not really so.

Cibber and others, as you know, wanted to alter Shakespeare. The French king, in *Lear*, was to be got rid of; Cordelia was to marry Edgar, and Lear himself was to be rewarded for his sufferings by a golden old age. They could not bear that Hamlet should suffer for the sins of Claudius. The wicked king was to die, and the wicked mother; and Hamlet and Ophelia were to make a match of it, and live happily ever after. A common novelist would have arranged it thus; and you would have had your comfortable moral that wickedness was fitly punished, and virtue had its due reward, and all would have been well. But Shakespeare would not have it so. Shakespeare knew that crime was not so simple in its consequences, or Providence so paternal. He was contented to take the truth from life; and the effect upon the mind of the most correct theory of what life ought to be, compared to the effect of the life itself, is infinitesimal in comparison.

Again, let us compare the popular historical treatment of remarkable incidents with Shakespeare's treatment of them. Look at *Macbeth*. You may derive abundant instruction from it—instruction of many kinds. There is a moral lesson of profound interest in the steps by which a noble nature glides to perdition. In more modern fashion you may speculate, if you like, on the political conditions represented there, and the temptation presented in absolute monarchies to unscrupulous ambition; you may say, like Doctor Slop, these things could not have happened under a constitutional government; or, again, you may take up your parable against superstition—you may dilate on the frightful consequences of a belief in witches, and reflect on the superior advantages of an age of schools and newspapers. If the bare facts of the story had come down to us from a chronicler, and an ordinary writer of the nineteenth century had undertaken to relate them, his account, we may depend upon it, would have been put together upon one or other of these principles. Yet, by the side of that unfolding of the secrets of the prison-house of the soul, what lean and shrivelled anatomies the best of such descriptions would seem!

Shakespeare himself, I suppose, could not have given us a theory of what he meant—he gave us the thing itself, on which we might make whatever theories we pleased.

Or again, look at Homer.

The *Iliad* is from two to three thousand years older than *Macbeth*, and yet it is as fresh as if it had been written yesterday. We have there no lessons save in the emotions which rise in us as we read. Homer had no philosophy; he never struggles to impress upon us his views about this or that; you can scarcely tell indeed whether his sympathies are Greek or Trojan; but he represents to us faithfully the men and women among whom he lived. He sang the Tale of Troy, he touched his lyre, he drained the golden beaker in the halls of men like those on whom he was conferring immortality. And thus, although no Agamemnon, king of men, ever led a Grecian fleet to Ilium; though no Priam sought the midnight tent of Achilles; though 'Ulysses and Diomed and Nestor were but names, and Helen but a dream, yet, through Homer's power of representing men and women, those old Greeks will still stand out from amidst the darkness of the ancient world with a sharpness of outline which belongs to no period of history except the most recent. For the mere hard purposes of history, the *Iliad* and *Odyssey* are the most effective books which ever were written. We see the Hall of Menelaus, we see the garden of Alcinous, we see Nausicaa among her maidens on the shore, we see the mellow monarch sitting with ivory sceptre in the Market-place dealing out genial justice. Or again, when the wild mood is on, we can hear the crash of the spears, the rattle of the armour as the heroes fall, and the plunging of the horses among the slain. Could we enter the palace of an old Ionian lord, we know what we should see there; we know the words in which he would address us. We could meet Hector as a friend. If we could choose a companion to spend an evening with over a fireside, it would be the man of many counsels, the husband of Penelope.

I am not going into the vexed question whether History or Poetry is the more true. It has been sometimes said that Poetry is the more true, because it can make things more like what our moral sense would prefer they should be. We hear of poetic justice and the like, as if nature and fact were not just enough.

I entirely dissent from that view. So far as Poetry attempts to improve on truth in that way, so far it abandons truth, and is false to itself. Even literal facts, exactly as they were, a great poet will prefer whenever he can get them. Shakespeare in the historical plays is studious, wherever possible, to give the very words which he finds to have been used; and it shows how wisely he was guided in this, that those magnificent speeches of Wolsey are taken exactly, with no more change than the

metre makes necessary, from Cavendish's Life. Marlborough read Shakespeare for English history, and read nothing else. The poet only is not bound, when it is inconvenient, to what may be called the accidents of facts. It was enough for Shakespeare to know that Prince Hal in his youth had lived among loose companions, and the tavern in Eastcheap came in to fill out his picture; although Mrs. Quickly and Falstaff, and Poins and Bardolph were more likely to have been fallen in with by Shakespeare himself at the Mermaid, than to have been comrades of the true Prince Henry. It was enough for Shakespeare to draw real men, and the situation, whatever it might be would sit easy on them. In this sense only it is that Poetry is truer than History, that it can make a picture more complete. It may take liberties with time and space, and give the action distinctness by throwing it into more manageable compass.

But it may not alter the real conditions of things, or represent life as other than it is. The greatness of the poet depends on his being true to nature, without insisting that nature, shall theorise with him, without making her more just, more philosophical, more moral than reality; and, in difficult matters, leaving much to reflection which cannot be explained.

And if this be true of Poetry—if Homer and Shakespeare are what they are, from the absence of everything didactic about them—may we not thus learn something of what History should be, and in what sense it should aspire to teach?

If Poetry must not theorise, much less should the historian theorise, whose obligations to be true to fact are even greater than the poet's. If the drama is grandest when the action is least explicable by laws, because then it best resembles life, then history will be grandest also under the same conditions. *Macbeth,* were it literally true, would be perfect history; and so far as the historian can approach to that kind of model, so far as he can let his story tell itself in the deeds and words of those who act it out, so far is he most successful. His work is no longer the vapour of his own brain, which a breath will scatter; it is the thing itself, which will have interest for all time. A thousand theories may be formed about it—spiritual theories. Pantheistic theories, cause and effect theories; but each age will have its own philosophy of history, and all these in turn will fail and die, Hegel falls out of date, Schlegel falls out of date, and Comte in good time will fall out of date; the thought about the thing must change as we change; but the thing itself can never change; and a history is durable or perishable as it contains more or least of the writer's own speculations. The splendid intellect of Gibbon for the most part kept him true to the right course in this; yet the philosophical chapters for which he has been most admired or censured may hereafter be thought the least interesting in his work. The time has been when they would not have been comprehended: the time may come when they will seem commonplace.

It may be said, that in requiring history to be written like a drama, we require an impossibility.

For history to be written with the complete form of a drama, doubtless is impossible; but there are periods, and these the periods, for the most part, of greatest interest to mankind, the history of which may be so written that the actors shall reveal their characters in their own words; where mind can be seen matched against mind, and the great passions of the epoch not simply be described as existing, but be exhibited at their white heat in the souls and hearts possessed by them. There are all the elements of drama—drama of the highest order—where the huge forces of the times are as the Grecian destiny and the power of the man is seen either stemming the stream till it overwhelms him, or ruling while he seems to yield to it.

It is Nature's drama—not Shakespeare's—but a drama none the less.

So at least it seems to me. Wherever possible, let us not be told *about* this man or that. Let us hear the man himself speak; let us see him act, and let us be left to form our own opinions about him. The historian, we are told, must not leave his readers to themselves. He must not only lay the facts before them—he must tell them what he himself thinks about those facts. In my opinion, this is precisely what he ought not to do.

Bishop Butler says somewhere, that the best book which could be written would be a book consisting only of premises, from which the readers should draw conclusions for themselves. The highest poetry is the very thing which Butler requires, and the highest history ought to be. We should no more ask for a theory of this or that period of history, than we should ask for a theory of *Macbeth* or *Hamlet*. Philosophies of history, sciences of history—all these, there will continue to be; the fashions of them will change, as our habits of thought will change; each new philosopher will find his chief employment in showing that before him no one understood anything; but the drama of history is imperishable, and the lessons of it will be like what we learn from Homer or Shakespeare—lessons for which we have no words.

The address of history is less to the understanding than to the higher emotions. We learn in it to sympathise with what is great and good; we learn to hate what is base. In the anomalies of fortune we feel the mystery of our mortal existence, and in the companionship of the illustrious natures who have shaped the fortunes of the world, we escape from the littlenesses which cling to the round of common life, and our minds are tuned in a higher and nobler key.

For the rest, and for those large questions which I touched in connection with Mr. Buckle, we live in times of disintegration, and none can tell what will be after us. What opinions—what convictions—the infant of to-day will find prevailing on the earth, if he and it live out together to the middle of another century, only a very bold man would undertake to conjecture! "The time will come," said Lichtenberg, in scorn at the materialising tendencies of modern thought; "the time will come when the belief in God will be as the tales with which old women frighten children; when the world will be a machine, the ether a gas, and God will be a force."

Mankind, if they last long enough on the earth, may develop strange things out of themselves; and the growth of what is called the Positive Philosophy is a curious commentary on Lichtenberg's prophecy. But whether the end be seventy years hence, or seven hundred—be the close of the mortal history of humanity as far distant in the future as its shadowy beginnings seem now to lie behind us—this only we may foretell with confidence—that the riddle of man's nature will remain unsolved. There will be that in him yet 10 which physical laws will fail to explain— that something, whatever it be, in himself and in the world, which science cannot fathom, and which suggests the unknown possibilities of his origin and his destiny. There will remain yet

Those obstinate questionings
Of sense and outward things;
Fallings from us, vanishings—
Blank misgivings of a creature
Moving about in worlds not realised—
High instincts, before which our mortal nature
Did tremble like a guilty thing surprised.

There will remain

Those first affections—
Those shadowy recollections—
Which, be they what they may,
Are yet the fountain-light of all our day—
Are yet the master-light of all our seeing—
Uphold us, cherish, and have power to make
Our noisy years seem moments in the being
 Of the Eternal Silence.

[1864]

HISTORY OF ENGLAND (XII)

THE EXECUTION OF MARY QUEEN OF SCOTS

Briefly, solemnly, and sternly they delivered their awful message. They informed her that they had received a commission under the great seal to see her executed, and she was told that she must prepare to suffer on the following morning. She was dreadfully agitated. For a moment she refused to believe them. Then, as the truth forced itself upon her, tossing her head in disdain and struggling to control herself, she called her physician and began to speak to him of money that was owed to her in France. At last it seems that she broke down altogether, and they left her with a fear either that she would destroy herself in the night, or that she would refuse to come to the scaffold, and 20 that it might be necessary to drag her there by violence.

The end had come. She had long professed to expect it, but the clearest expectation is not certainty. The scene for which she had affected to prepare she was to encounter in its dread reality, and all her busy schemes, her dreams of vengeance, her visions of a revolution, with herself ascending out of the convulsion and seating herself on her rival's throne—all were gone. She had played deep, and the dice had gone against her.

Yet in death, if she encountered it bravely, victory was still possible. Could she but sustain to the last the character of a calumniated suppliant accepting heroically for God's sake and her creed's the concluding stroke of a long series of wrongs, she might stir a tempest of indignation which, if it could not save herself, might at least overwhelm her enemy. Per- 10 sisting, as she persisted to the last, in denying all knowledge of Babington, it would be affectation to credit her with a genuine feeling of religion; but the imperfection of her motive exalts the greatness of her fortitude. To an impassioned believer death is comparatively easy.

Her chaplain was lodged in a separate part of the castle. The commissioners, who were as anxious that her execution should wear its real character as she was herself 20 determined to convert it into a martyrdom, refused, perhaps unwisely, to allow him access to her, and offered her again the assistance of an Anglican dean. They gave her an advantage over them which she did not fail to use. She would not let the dean come near her. She sent a note to the chaplain telling him that she had meant to receive the sacrament, but as it might not be she must content herself with a 30 general confession. She bade him watch through the night and pray for her. In the morning when she was brought out she might perhaps see him, and receive his blessing on her knees. She supped cheerfully, giving her last meal with her attendants a character of sacred parting; afterwards she drew aside her apothecary M. Gorion, and asked him if she might depend upon his fidelity. When he satisfied her that she might trust him, she said she had a letter and two diamonds which she wished to send to Mendoza. He undertook to melt some drug and conceal them in it where they would never be looked for, and promised to deliver them faithfully. One of the jewels was for Mendoza himself; the other and the largest was for Philip. It was to be a sign that she was dying for the truth, and was meant also to bespeak his care for her friends and servants. Every one of them so far as she was able, without forgetting a name, she commended to his liberality. Arundel, Paget, Morgan, the Archbishop of Glasgow, Westmoreland, Throgmorton, the Bishop of Ross, her two secretaries, the ladies who had shared the trials of her imprisonment, she remembered them all, and specified the sums which she desired Philip to bestow on them. And as Mary Stuart then and throughout her life never lacked gratitude to those who had been true to her, so then as always she remembered her enemies. There was no cant about her, no unreal talk of forgiveness of injuries. She bade Gorion tell Philip it was her last prayer that he should persevere, notwithstanding her death, in the invasion of England. It was God's quarrel, she said, and worthy of his greatness; and as soon as he had conquered it, she desired him not to forget how she had been treated by Cecil, and Leicester, and Walsingham; by Lord Huntingdon, who had ill-used her fifteen years before at Tutbury; by Sir Amyas Paulet, and Secretary Wade.

Her last night was a busy one. As she said herself, there was much to be done and the time was short. A few lines to the King of France were dated two hours after midnight. They were to insist for the last time that she was innocent of the conspiracy, that she was dying for religion, and for having asserted her right to the crown; and to beg that out of the sum which he owed her, her servants' wages might be paid and masses provided for her soul. After this she slept for three or four hours, and then rose and with the most elaborate care prepared to encounter the end.

At eight in the morning the provost-marshal knocked at the outer door which communicated with her suite of apartments. It was locked and no one answered, and he went back in some trepidation lest the fears might prove true which had been entertained the preceding evening. On his returning with the sheriff however a few minutes later, the door was open, and they were confronted with the tall majestic figure of Mary Stuart standing before them in splendour. The plain grey dress had been exchanged for a robe of black satin; her jacket was of black satin also, looped and slashed and trimmed with velvet. Her false hair was arranged studiously with a coif, and over her head and falling down over her back was a white veil of delicate lawn. A crucifix of gold hung from her neck. In her hand she held a crucifix of ivory, and a number of jewelled paternosters was attached to her girdle. Led by two of Paulet's gentlemen, the sheriff walking before her, she passed to the chamber of presence in which she had been tried, where Shrewsbury, Kent, Paulet, Drury, and others were waiting to receive her. Andrew Melville, Sir Robert's brother, who had been master of her household, was kneeling in tears. "Melville," she said, "you should rather rejoice than weep that the end of my troubles is come. Tell my friends I die a true Catholic. Commend me to my son. Tell him I have done nothing to prejudice his kingdom of Scotland, and so, good Melville, farewell." She kissed him, and turning asked for her chaplain du Preau. He was not present. There had been a fear of some religious melodrame which it was thought well to avoid. Her ladies, who had attempted to follow her, had been kept back also. She could not afford to leave the account of her death to be reported by enemies and Puritans, and she required assistance for the scene which she meditated. Missing them she asked the reason of their absence, and said she wished them to see her die. Kent said he feared they might scream or faint, or attempt perhaps to dip their handkerchiefs in her blood. She undertook that they should be quiet and obedient. "The queen," she said, "would never deny her so slight a request;" and when Kent still hesitated, she added with tears, "You know I am cousin to your queen, of the blood of Henry VII, a married Queen of France, and anointed Queen of Scotland."

It was impossible to refuse. She was allowed to take six of her own people with her, and select them herself. She chose her physician Burgoyne, Andrew Melville, the apothecary Gorion, and her surgeon, with two ladies, Elizabeth Kennedy and Curle's young wife Barbara Mowbray, whose child she had baptised.

"Allons donc," she then said—"Let us go," and passing out attended by the earls, and leaning on the arm of an officer of the guard, she descended the great staircase to the hall. The news had spread far through the country. Thousands of people were collected outside the walls. About three hundred knights and gentlemen of the county had been admitted to witness the execution. The tables and forms had been removed, and a great wood fire was blazing in the chimney. At the upper end of the hall, above the fire-place, but near it, stood the scaffold, twelve feet square and two feet and a half high. It was covered with black cloth; a low rail ran round it covered with black cloth also, and the sheriff's guard of halberdiers were ranged on the floor below on the four sides to keep off the crowd. On the scaffold was the block, black like the rest; a square black cushion was placed behind it, and behind the cushion a black chair; on the right were two other chairs for the earls. The axe leant against the rail, and two masked figures stood like mutes on either side at the back. The Queen of Scots as she swept in seemed as if coming to take a part in some solemn pageant. Not a muscle of her face could be seen to quiver; she ascended the scaffold with absolute composure, looked round her smiling, and sat down. Shrewsbury and Kent followed and took their places, the sheriff stood at her left hand, and Beale then mounted a platform and read the warrant aloud.

In all the assembly Mary Stuart appeared the person least interested in the words which were consigning her to death.

"Madam," said Lord Shrewsbury to her, when the reading was ended, "you hear what we are commanded to do."

"You will do your duty," she answered, and rose as if to kneel and pray.

The Dean of Peterborough, Dr. Fletcher, approached the rail. "Madam," he began, with a low obeisance, "the queen's most excellent majesty;" "madam, the queen's most excellent majesty"—thrice he commenced his sentence, wanting words to pursue it. When he repeated the words a fourth time, she cut him short.

"Mr. Dean," she said, "I am a Catholic, and must die a Catholic. It is useless to attempt to move me, and your prayers will avail me but little."

"Change your opinion, madam," he cried, his tongue being loosed at last; "repent of your sins, settle your faith in Christ, by him to be saved."

"Trouble not yourself further, Mr. Dean," she answered; "I am settled in my own faith, for which I mean to shed my blood."

"I am sorry, madam," said Shrewsbury, "to see you so addicted to popery."

"That image of Christ you hold there," said Kent, "will not profit you if he be not engraved in your heart."

She did not reply, and turning her back on Fletcher, knelt for her own devotions.

He had been evidently instructed to impair the Catholic complexion of the scene, and the Queen of Scots was determined that he should not succeed. When she knelt he commenced an extempore prayer in which the assembly joined. As his voice sounded out in the hall she raised her own, reciting with powerful deep-chested tones the penitential psalms in Latin, introducing English sentences at intervals that the audience might know what she was saying, and praying with especial distinctness for her holy father the pope.

From time to time, with conspicuous vehemence, she struck the crucifix against her bosom, and then, as the dean gave up the struggle, leaving her Latin, she prayed in English wholly, still clear and loud. She prayed for the Church which she had been ready to betray, for her son whom she had disinherited, for the queen whom she had endeavoured to murder. She prayed God to avert his wrath from England, that England which she had sent a last message to Philip to beseech him to invade. She forgave her enemies, whom she had invited Philip not to forget, and then, praying to the saints to intercede for her with Christ, and kissing the crucifix and crossing her own breast, "Even as thy arms, O Jesus," she cried, "were spread upon the cross, so receive me into thy mercy and forgive my sins."

With these words she rose; the black mutes stepped forward, and in the usual form begged her forgiveness.

"I forgive you," she said, "for now I hope you shall end all my troubles." They offered their help in arranging her dress. "Truly, my lords," she said with a smile to the earls, "I never had such grooms waiting on me before." Her ladies were allowed to come up upon the scaffold to assist her; for the work to be done was considerable, and had been prepared with no common thought.

She laid her crucifix on her chair. The chief executioner took it as a perquisite, but was ordered instantly to lay it down. The lawn veil was lifted carefully off, not to disturb the hair, and was hung upon the rail. The black robe was next removed. Below it was a petticoat of crimson velvet. The black jacket followed, and under the jacket was a body of crimson satin. One of her ladies handed her a pair of crimson sleeves, with which she hastily covered her arms; and thus she stood on the black scaffold with the black figures all around her, blood-red from head to foot.

Her reasons for adopting so extraordinary a costume must be left to conjecture. It is only certain that it must have been carefully studied, and that the pictorial effect must have been appalling.

The women, whose firmness had hitherto borne the trial, began now to give way, spasmodic sobs bursting from them which they could not check. "Ne criez vous," she said, "j'ay promis pour vous." [1] Struggling bravely, they crossed their breasts again and again, she crossing them in turn and bidding them pray for her. Then she knelt on the cushion. Barbara Mowbray bound her eyes with a handkerchief. "Adieu," she said, smiling for the last time and waving her hand to them, "Adieu, au revoir." They stepped back from off the scaffold and left her alone. On her knees she repeated the psalm, In te, Domine, confido, "In Thee, O Lord, have I put my trust." Her shoulders being exposed, two scars became visible, one on either side, and the earls being now a little behind her, Kent pointed to them with his white wand and looked inquiringly at his companion. Shrewsbury whispered that they were the remains of two abscesses from which she had suffered while living with him at Sheffield.

When the psalm was finished she felt for the block, and laying down her head muttered: "In manus, Domine tuas, commendo animam meam." [2] The hard wood seemed to hurt her, for she placed her hands under her neck. The executioners gently removed them, lest they should deaden the blow, and then one of them holding her slightly, the other raised the axe and struck. The scene had been too trying even for the practised headsman of the Tower. His arm wandered. The blow fell on the knot of the handkerchief, and scarcely broke the skin. She neither spoke nor moved. He struck again, this time effectively. The head hung by a shred of skin, which he divided without withdrawing the axe; and at once a metamorphosis was witnessed, strange as was ever wrought by wand of fabled enchanter. The coif fell off and the false plaits. The laboured illusion vanished. The lady who had knelt before the block was in the maturity of grace and loveliness. The executioner, when he raised the head, as usual, to show it to the crowd, exposed the withered features of a grizzled, wrinkled old woman.

"So perish all enemies of the queen," said the Dean of Peterborough. A loud Amen rose over the hall. "Such end," said the Earl of Kent, rising and standing over the body, "to the queen's and the Gospel's enemies."

---

[1] Ne criez vous, etc.: "Do not weep; I have promised for you."

[2] In manus, Domine tuas, etc.: "Into thy hands, O Lord, I commend my spirit" (Luke, XXIII, 46).

Orders had been given that everything which she had worn should be immediately destroyed, that no relics should be carried off to work imaginary miracles. Sentinels stood at the doors who allowed no one to pass out without permission; and after the first pause, the earls still keeping their places, the body was stripped. It then appeared that a favourite lapdog had followed its mistress unperceived, and was 10 concealed under her clothes; when discovered it gave a short cry, and seated itself between the head and the neck, from which the blood was still flowing. It was carried away and carefully washed, and then beads, Paternoster, handkerchief— each particle of dress which the blood had touched, with the cloth on the block and on the scaffold, was burnt in the hall fire in the presence of the crowd. The scaffold itself was next removed: a brief account of the execution was drawn up, with which Henry Talbot, Lord Shrewsbury's son, was sent to London, and then every one was dismissed. Silence settled down on Fotheringay, and the last scene of the life of Mary Stuart, in which tragedy and melodrama were so strangely intermingled, was over.   [1870]

THOMAS CARLYLE: THE HISTORY OF HIS LIFE IN LONDON (II)

CARLYLE IN OLD AGE

So far my account of Carlyle has been taken from written memorials, letters, diaries, and autobiographic fragments. For the future the story will form itself round my own personal intercourse with him. Up to 1860 I had lived in the country. I had paid frequent visits to London, and while there had seen as much of Cheyne 10 Row and its inhabitants as Mrs. Carlyle would encourage. I had exchanged letters occasionally with her and her husband, but purely on external subjects, and close personal intimacy between us there had as yet been none. In the autumn of that year, however, London became my home. Late one afternoon, in the middle of the winter, Carlyle called on me, and said that he wished to see more of me—wished me in 20 fact to be his companion, so far as I could, in his daily rides or walks. Ride with him I could not, having no horse; but the walks were most welcome—and from that date, for twenty years, up to his own death, except when either or both of us were out of town, I never ceased to see him twice or three times a week, and to have two or three hours of conversation with him. The first of these walks I well remember, from 30 an incident which happened in the course of it. It was after nightfall. At Hyde Park Corner, we found a blind beggar anxious to cross over from Knightsbridge to Piccadilly, but afraid to trust his dog to lead him through the carts and carriages. Carlyle took the beggar's arm, led him gently over, and offered to help him further on his way. He declined gratefully; we gave him some trifle, and followed him to see what he would do. His dog led him straight to a public-house in Park Lane. We both laughed, and I suppose I made some ill-natured remark. "Poor fellow," was all that Carlyle said; "he perhaps needs warmth and shelter."

This was the first instance that I observed of what I found to be a universal habit with him. Though still far from rich, he never met any poor creature, whose distress was evident, without speaking kindly to him and helping him more or less in one way or another. Archbishop Whately said that to relieve street beggars was a public crime. Carlyle thought only of their misery. "Modern life," he said, "doing its charity by institutions," is a sad hardener of our hearts. "We should give for our own sakes. It is very low water with the wretched beings, one can easily see that."

Even the imps of the gutters he would not treat as reprobates. He would drop a lesson in their way, sometimes with a sixpence to recommend it.... A small vagabond was at some indecency. Carlyle touched him gently on the back with his stick. "Do you not know that you are a little man," he said, "and not a whelp, that you behave in this way?" There was no sixpence this time. Afterwards a lad of fourteen or so stopped us and begged. Carlyle lectured him for beginning so early at such a trade, told him how, if he worked, he might have a worthy and respectable life before him, and gave him sixpence. The boy shot off down the next alley. "There is a sermon fallen on stony ground," Carlyle said, "but we must do what we can." The crowds of children growing up in London affected him with real pain; these small plants, each with its head just out of the ground, with a whole life ahead, and such a training! I noticed another trait too—Scotch thrift showing itself in hatred of waste. If he saw a crust of bread on the roadway he would stop to pick it up and put it on a step or a railing. Some poor devil might be glad of it, or at worst a dog or a sparrow. To destroy wholesome food was a sin. He was very tender about animals, especially dogs, who, like horses, if well treated, were types of loyalty and fidelity. I horrified him with a story of my Oxford days. The hounds had met at Woodstock. They had drawn the covers without finding a fox, and, not caring to have a blank day, one of the whips had caught a passing sheep dog, rubbed its feet with aniseed, and set it to run. It made for Oxford in its terror, the hounds in full cry behind. They caught the wretched creature in a field outside the town, and tore it to pieces. I never saw Carlyle more affected. He said it was like a human soul flying for salvation before a legion of fiends.

Occupied as he had always seemed to be with high-soaring speculations, scornful as he had appeared, in the "Latter-day Pamphlets," of benevolence, philanthropy, and small palliations of enormous evils, I had not expected so much detailed compassion in little things. I found that personal sympathy with suffering lay at the root of all his thoughts; and that attention to little things was as characteristic of his conduct as it was of his intellect.

His conversation when we were alone together was even more surprising to me. I had been accustomed to hear him impatient of contradiction, extravagantly ex-

aggerative, overbearing opposition with bursts of scornful humour. In private I found him impatient of nothing but of being bored; gentle, quiet, tolerant; *sadly*-humoured, but never *ill*-humoured; ironical, but without the savageness, and when speaking of persons always scrupulously just. He saw through the "clothes" of a man into what he actually was. But the sharpest censure was always qualified. He would say, "If we knew how he came to be what he is, poor fellow, we should not be hard with him."

But he talked more of things than of persons, and on every variety of subject. He had read more miscellaneously than any man I have ever known. His memory was extraordinary, and a universal curiosity had led him to inform himself minutely about matters which I might have supposed that he had never heard of. With English literature he was as familiar as Macaulay was. French and German and Italian he knew infinitely better than Macaulay, and there was this peculiarity about him, that if he read a book which struck him he never rested till he had learnt all that could be ascertained about the writer of it. Thus his knowledge was not in points or lines, but complete and solid.

Even in his laughter he was always serious. I never heard a trivial word from him, nor one which he had better have left unuttered. He cared nothing for money, nothing for promotion in the world. If his friends gained a step anywhere he was pleased with it—but only as worldly advancement might give them a chance of wider usefulness. Men should think of their duty, he said;—let them do that, and the rest, as much as was essential, "would be added to them." I was with him one beautiful spring day under the trees in Hyde Park, the grass recovering its green, the elm buds swelling, the scattered crocuses and snowdrops shining in the sun. The spring, the annual resurrection from death to life, was especially affecting to him. "Behold the lilies of the field!" he said to me; "they toil not, neither do they spin. Yet Solomon, in all his glory, was not arrayed like one of these. What a word was that? and the application was quite true too. Take no thought for the morrow—

care only for what you know to be right. That is the rule."

He had a poor opinion of what is called science; of political economy; of utility as the basis of morals; and such-like, when they dealt with human life. He stood on Kant's Categorical Imperative. Right was right, and wrong was wrong, because God had so ordered; and duty and conduct could be brought under analysis only when men had disowned their nobler nature, and were governed by self-interest. Interested motives might be computed, and a science might grow out of a calculation of their forces. But love of Truth, love of Righteousness—these were not calculable, neither these nor the actions proceeding out of them.

Sciences of natural things he always respected. *Facts* of all kinds were sacred to him. A fact, whatever it might be, was part of the constitution of the universe, and so was related to the Author of it. Of all men that have ever lived he honoured few more than Kepler. Kepler's *"laws"* he looked on as the grandest physical discovery ever made by man; and as long as philosophers were content, like Kepler, to find out facts without building theories on them to dispense with God, he had only good to say of them. Science, however, in these latter days, was stepping beyond its proper province, like the young Titans trying to take heaven by storm. He liked *ill* men like Humboldt, Laplace, or the author of the "Vestiges." He refused Darwin's transmutation of species as unproved; he fought against it, though I could see he dreaded that it might turn out true. If man, as explained by Science, was no more than a developed animal, and conscience and intellect but developments of the functions of animals, then God and religion were no more than inferences, and inferences which might be lawfully disputed. That the grandest achievements of human nature had sprung out of beliefs which might be mere illusions, Carlyle could not admit. That intellect and moral sense should have been put into him by a Being which had none of its own was distinctly not conceivable to him. It might perhaps be that these high gifts lay somewhere in the original germ, out of which

organic life had been developed; that they had been intentionally and consciously placed there by the Author of nature, whom religious instincts had been dimly able to discern. It might so turn out, but for the present the tendency of science was not in any such direction. The tendency of science was to Lucretian Atheism; to a belief that no "intention" or intending mind was discoverable in the universe at all. If the life of man was no more than the life of an animal—if he had no relation, or none which he could discern, with any being higher than himself, God would become an unmeaning word to him. Carlyle often spoke of this, and with evident uneasiness. Earlier in his life, while he was young and confident, and the effects of his religious training were fresh in him, he could fling off the whispers of the scientific spirit with angry disdain; the existence, the omnipresence, the omnipotence of God, were then the strongest of his convictions. The faith remained unshaken in him to the end; he never himself doubted; yet he was perplexed by the indifference with which the Supreme Power was allowing its existence to be obscured. I once said to him, not long before his death, that I could only believe in a God which *did* something. With a cry of pain, which I shall never forget, he said, "He does nothing." For himself, however, his faith stood firm. He did not believe in historical Christianity. He did not believe that the facts alleged in the Apostles' creed had ever really happened. The resurrection of Christ was to him only a symbol of a spiritual truth. As Christ rose from the dead, so were we to rise from the death of sin to the life of righteousness. Not that Christ had actually died and had risen again. He was only *believed* to have died and *believed* to have risen in an age when legend was history, when stories were accepted as true from their beauty or their significance. As long as it was supposed that the earth was the centre of the universe, that the sky moved round it, and that sun and moon and stars had been set there for man's convenience, when it was the creed of all nations that gods came down to the earth, and men were taken into heaven, and that between the two regions there was incessant intercourse, it could be believed easily that the Son of God had lived as a man among men, had descended like Hercules into Hades, and had returned again from it. Such a story then presented no internal difficulty at all. It was not so now. The soul of it was eternally true, but it had been bound up in a mortal body. The body of the belief was now perishing, and the soul of it being discredited by its connection with discovered error, was suspected not to be a soul at all; half mankind, betrayed and deserted, were rushing off into materialism. Nor was materialism the worst. Shivering at so blank a prospect, entangled in the institutions which remained standing when the life had gone out of them, the other half were "reconciling faith with reason," pretending to believe, or believing that they believed, becoming hypocrites, conscious or unconscious, the last the worst of the two, not daring to look the facts in the face, so that the very sense of truth was withered in them. It was to make love to delusion, to take falsehood deliberately into their hearts. For such souls there was no hope at all. Centuries of spiritual anarchy lay before the world before sincere belief could again be generally possible among men of knowledge and insight. With the half-educated and ignorant it was otherwise. To them the existing religion might still represent some real truth. There alone was any open teaching of God's existence, and the divine sanction of morality. Each year, each day, as knowledge spread, the power of the established religion was growing less; but it was not yet entirely gone, and it was the only hold that was left on the most vital of all truths. Thus the rapid growth of materialism had in some degree modified the views which Carlyle had held in early and middle life. Then the "Exodus from Houndsditch" had seemed as if it might lead immediately into a brighter region. He had come to see that it would be but an entry into a wilderness, the promised land lying still far away. His own opinions seemed to be taking no hold. He had cast his bread upon the waters and it was not returning to him, and the exodus appeared less entirely desirable. Sometimes the old fierce note revived. Sometimes,

and more often as he grew older, he wished the old shelter to be left standing as long as a roof remained over it—as long as any of us could profess the old faith with complete sincerity. Sincerity, however, was indispensable. For men who said one thing and meant another, who entered the Church as a profession, and throve in the world by it, while they emasculated the creeds, and watered away the histories— for them Carlyle had no toleration. Religion, if not honest, was a horror to him. Those alone he thought had any right to teach Christianity who had no doubts about its truth. Those who were uncertain ought to choose some other profession, and if compelled to speak should show their colours faithfully.

.   .   .   .   .

Literature was another subject on which Carlyle often talked with me. In his Craigenputtock Essays he had spoken of literature as the highest of human occupations, as the modern priesthood, &c., and so to the last he thought of it when it was the employment of men whom nature had furnished gloriously for that special task, like Goethe and Schiller. But for the writing function in the existing generation of Englishmen he had nothing but contempt. A "man of letters," a man who had taken to literature as a means of living, was generally some one who had gone into it because he was unfit for better work, because he was too vain or too self-willed to travel along the beaten highways, and his writings, unless he was one of a million, began and ended in nothing. Life was action, not talk. The speech, the book, the review or newspaper article was so much force expended—force lost to practical usefulness. When a man had *uttered* his thoughts, still more when he was always uttering them, he no longer even attempted to translate them into act. He said once to me that England had produced her greatest men before she began to have a literature at all. Those Barons who signed their charter by dipping the points of their steel gauntlets in the ink, had more *virtue, manhood,* practical force and wisdom than any of their successors, and when the present disintegration had done its work, and healthy organic tissue began to form again, tongues would not clatter as they did now. Those only would speak who had call to speak. Even the Sunday sermons would cease to be necessary. A man was never made wiser or better by talking or being talked to. He was made better by being trained in habits of industry, by being enabled to *do* good useful work and earn an honest living by it. His excuse for his own life was that there had been no alternative. Sometimes he spoke of his writings as having a certain value; generally, however, as if they had little, and now and then as if they had none. "If there be one thing," he said, "for which I have no special talent, it is literature. If I had been taught to *do* the simplest useful thing, I should have been a better and happier man. All that I can say for myself is, that I have done my best." A strange judgment to come from a man who has exerted so vast an influence by writing alone. Yet in a sense it was true. If literature means the expression by thought or emotion, or the representation of facts in completely beautiful *form,* Carlyle *was* inadequately gifted for it. But his function was not to please, but to instruct. Of all human writings, those which perhaps have produced the deepest effect on the history of the world have been St. Paul's Epistles. What Carlyle had he had in common with St. Paul: extraordinary intellectual insight, extraordinary sincerity, extraordinary resolution to speak out the truth as he perceived it, as if driven on by some impelling internal necessity. He and St. Paul—I know not of whom else the same thing could be said—wrote as if they were pregnant with some world-important idea, of which they were labouring to be delivered, and the effect is the more striking from the abruptness and want of artifice in the utterance. Whether Carlyle would have been happier, more useful, had he been otherwise occupied, I cannot say. He had a fine aptitude for all kinds of business. In any practical prob-lem, whether of politics or private life, he had his finger always, as if by instinct, on the point upon which the issue would turn. Arbitrary as his temperament was, he could, if occasion rose, be prudent, forbearing, dexterous, adroit. He would have risen to greatness in any profession which he had chosen, but in such a world as ours he must have submitted, in rising, to the *"half-sincerities,"* which are the condition of success. We should have lost the Carlyle that we know. It is not certain that we should have gained an equivalent of him.

This is the sort of thing which I used daily to hear from Carlyle. His talk was not always, of course, on such grave matters. He was full of stories, anecdotes of his early life, or of people that he had known.

For more than four years after our walks began, he was still engaged with "Frederick." He spoke freely of what was uppermost in his mind, and many scenes in the history were rehearsed to me before they appeared, Voltaire, Maupertuis, Chatham, Wolfe being brought up as living figures. He never helped himself with gestures, but his voice was as flexible as if he had been trained for the stage. He was never tedious, but dropped out picture after picture in inimitable finished sentences. He was so quiet, so unexaggerative, so well-humoured in these private conversations, that I could scarcely believe he was the same person whom I used to hear declaim in the Pamphlet time. Now and then, if he met an acquaintance who might say a foolish thing, there would come an angry sputter or two; but he was generally so patient, so forbearing, that I thought age had softened him, and I said so one day to Mrs. Carlyle. She laughed and told him of it. "I wish," she said, "Froude had seen you an hour or two after you seemed to him so lamblike." But I was relating what he was as I knew him, and as I always found him from first to last.   [1884]

JOHN RUSKIN

CHRONOLOGY AND INTRODUCTION

1819 Born February 8, in London.

1819–33 Early education at home and under private tutors.

1833 First foreign tour.

1835–45 Miscellaneous poems for Keepsakes of the day.

1836 First defence of Turner (unpublished).

1837 Entered Oxford at Christ Church College: finished, 1842.

1837–38 *The Poetry of Architecture* (papers for *Architectural Magazine*).

1843–60 *Modern Painters* I; II, 1846; III–IV, 1856; V, 1860.

1849 *Seven Lamps of Architecture.*

1851–53 *Stones of Venice,* 3 vols.

1851 *Pre-Raphaelitism.*

1854 *Lectures on Architecture and Painting;* Taught drawing at Working Men's College.

1856 *The Harbours of England.*

1857 *The Elements of Drawing.*

1859 *The Elements of Perspective; The Two Paths; Academy Notes.*

1860–62 *Unto This Last:* "Four Essays on the First Principles of Political Economy," *Cornhill Magazine,* Aug.-Nov., 1860: reprinted, 1862.

1862–72 *Munera Pulveris:* "Essays on Political Economy" in *Frazer's Magazine,* 1862–63: reprinted, 1872.

1865 *Sesame and Lilies.*

1866 *Ethics of the Dust; The Crown of Wild Olive.*

1867 *Time and Tide.*

1869 *Queen of the Air.*

1870–78 Slade Professor of Fine Arts, Oxford; published various volumes of lectures.

1871–84 *Fors Clavigera.*

1872 Lived at Brantwood, Coniston Lake.

1878 Resigned Oxford Professorship on account of ill health.

1880 *Fiction, Fair and Foul.*

1883–85 Re-elected Professor at Oxford.

1885–89 *Praeterita.*

1900 Died, January 21.

Ruskin burst into fame in 1843 at the age of twenty-four with the first volume of *Modern Painters.* During the next seventeen years he wrote eight more volumes on painting and architecture, besides delivering a number of lectures on art, and writing two elementary studies on drawing and perspective. By 1860 he reached the summit of his reputation both as a writer and an interpreter who, more than any other critic before or since, awakened the public to a new sense of beauty in nature and in landscape art; and whose mastery of language was so distinguished as to prompt Tennyson (a severe judge) to remark that he considered Ruskin to be one of the six authors in whom he found the stateliest English prose. "You may say what you please about Ruskin, it doesn't matter in the least," declared William Morris; "the truth is, Ruskin has made art possible in this country.... He has let a flood of daylight into the cloud of sham-technical twaddle which was once the whole substance of art-criticism."

For this work it would be difficult to imagine a more fortunate preparation than Ruskin's. He was the only child of a London merchant who became rich in the sherry trade and who was a man of refined and cultivated tastes, capable of putting his son through the first two books of Livy, delighting in architecture and scenery, acquainted with a number of noted artists, and able himself to paint a little. In vivid autobiographical pages, Ruskin has told us of his introduction to English classics under the guidance of his father, who was "an absolutely beautiful reader of the best poetry and prose"; and to the Bible, under the rigid supervision of his mother, who thus taught him to know that "accuracy of diction means accuracy of sensation." He has told us, also, of his introduction to the beauties of nature and of art by means of coaching tours over England, Wales, and lowland Scotland, when his father periodically went out to receive orders for sherry from aristocratic patrons, and took his family with him. They travelled luxuriously and leisurely, and saw everyhing worth seeing along their way,—private galleries, cathedrals, castles, ruins, scenery. "All these sights were a pleasant amazement to me and panoramic apocalypse of a lovely world," says Ruskin of his thrilling experiences, which he punctually recorded in diaries or worked over into juvenile verses by the thousand. Later, when he had learned to draw (drawing lessons began at eleven), he made innumerable "flying scrawls on the road." Thus while he prepared for Oxford under private tutors he was steadily training himself to *see* with both eyes and heart and to *record* with pen and pencil the beauty that he found everywhere in nature and art.

Then came Turner, the man of "magnificent idiosyncrasy," the first of English landscape painters, whose "golden visions, glorious and beautiful" (as the artist Constable called them) had captivated Ruskin from the time when, at the age of thirteen, his father's business partner had given him a copy of Rogers' *Italy* illustrated with Turner's vignettes. By 1842 the painter had passed into what experts have called his third manner, when his canvases were more conspicuous than ever for their splendid colors, their luminous distances, their indistinctness of outline and their atmosphere of mystery. Hostile critics described his pictures in the kind of brutal language that had been used upon Keats more than twenty years before: "lamplight and rockets," "eggs and spinach," "soapsuds and whitewash." Ruskin was in Switzerland, where he had gone for rest and study after his final examination at Oxford, and where he was absorbed in climbing, sketching, or simply looking, exultantly happy in the solitudes of the higher Alps,—when a Turner review reached him. Raised to the "height of a black anger" by what he read, he instantly resolved to write a paper in defense of his idol and "blow the critics out of the water. ...I put off my pamphlet till I got home.... I meditated all the way down the Rhine, found that *demonstration* in matters of art was no such easy matter, and the pamphlet turned into a volume. Before the volume was half way dealt with it hydraized into three heads, and each head became a volume. Finding that nothing could be done except on such enormous scale, I determined to take the hydra by the horns, and produce a complete treatise on landscape art."

Ruskin's exposition of the principles of art, not only in *Modern Painters,* but in *Seven Lamps* and *The Stones of Venice,* is the work of a man who was, as he said, "not engaged in the selfish cultivation of critical acumen, but in ardent endeavor to spread the love and knowledge of art among all classes." He is the inspired evangelist of truth and beauty, as these are interpreted by the artist rather than by the too conventional critic who cannot rise above the jargon and pedantry of the schools. Ruskin came upon a dull world of conventionalists and connoisseurs to declare that art is infinitely more than a plaything of aristocratic collectors. It is, he insisted, something to quicken and refine the sensibilities of men to a new awareness of immaterial values hidden behind the veil of material beauty. It is more: it is "the expression of one soul talking to another, and is precious according to the greatness of the soul that utters it.... Great art is preeminently and finally the expression of the spirits of great men."

It is evident that art, as Ruskin understood it, is a serious thing. It is the very flower of human life, springing out of the whole of it, whether one thinks of art as the creation of the individual, the nation, or the race. Its health depends upon the health and happiness of its makers and of the social order in which they live. Moreover, art is art, whether it be "greater" or "lesser," for no arbitrary line can be drawn between making statues and making toys, between designing cathedrals and designing plows, between painting in oils or water colors, and coloring Christmas cards or lamp shades, between writing plays and writing limericks. "A blacksmith may put soul into the making of a horseshoe, and an architect may put none into the building of a church. Only exactly in proportion as the soul is thrown into it, the art becomes Fine.... Art is the operation of the hand and the intelligence together."

In other words, all art is work, and all work ought to be art: "Life without industry is guilt, and industry without art is brutality." This was the lesson that Ruskin learned from the art of the middle ages, the "magnificently human" Gothic architecture of the twelfth and thirteenth centuries, and all the minor arts that went with it. Here the master builder joined hands with the humblest craftsman to bring beauty into all the uses of life, and here each worker, according to his capacity, realized the joy of creative effort.

But the realization of art in this wider sense as something made by all for all depends, said Ruskin, alike upon a harmonious environment and a sound cooperative life. "The first schools of beauty must be the streets of your cities, and the chief of our fair designs must be to keep the living creatures round us clean, and in human comfort." Look at the world around you, he exclaimed, and see how ugly it is! The giant, Modern Industry, is striding over the landscape, treading down the older order and leaving in his path confusion, dislocation, noise, and squalor! Mills and tenements are springing up everywhere and are swarming with masses of unhappy toilers, overworked, underpaid, degraded into machines! "It is not that men are ill-fed, but that they have no pleasure in the work by which they make their bread, and therefore look to wealth as the only means of pleasure. It is not that men are pained by the scorn of the upper classes, but they cannot endure their own; for they feel that the kind of labor to which they are condemned is verily a degrading one, and makes them less than men." Thus the modern world as Ruskin saw it was increasingly a negation of the ideals of life that he regarded as most sacred.

And so, in the interests of art as the crowning expression of human activity, he plunged into a study of political economy and the ways by which men live. In language that very often suggests the lurid vehemence of Carlyle, he wrote of the "curses of luxury and waste," of the "deforming mechanism" and the squalid misery in modern cities, of "the want of integrity and simplicity in modern life," wherein people have substituted "mechanism for skill, photograph for picture, cast-iron for sculpture," and wherein cities are no longer built but "clotted and coagulated," like the loathsome slums of London and Manchester. He stormed at the strongholds of the so-called orthodox political economy, which upheld a gospel of enlightened selfishness, with its dogmas of laissez-faire, cash-nexus, competition, and freedom from governmental interference,—the old gospel of the soulless economic man. Ruskin would set up a new political economy founded upon the theory that man, potentially, is a creature with a sense of justice in him and a heart that can love its fellows and be loyal to them. "My political economy," he said, "is based on the axiom 'Man is an animal whose physical power depends on its social faith and affection.' ... The economy I have taught, in opposition to the popular view, is the science which not merely ascertains the relation of existing supply and demand, but determines what *ought* to be demanded and what *can* be supplied.... My Principles of Political Economy were all involved in a single phrase spoken three years ago (1857) at Manchester: 'Soldiers of the Ploughshare as well as Soldiers of the Sword'; and they were all summed up in a single sentence in the last volume of *Modern Painters:* 'Government and co-operation are in all things the Laws of Life, Anarchy and competition the Laws of Death.' "

Ruskin's economic and social teaching, shot through with aesthetic and ethical ideals, rests upon a faith that man's character can be changed, that it can and must be educated in the heart as well as in the head, that a sense of human values must be awakened and maintained in business and in industry, that people must be taught to control their desires for luxuries and to have a proper regard for the rights of their fellows everywhere. Finally, there should be established in society as fast and as far as possible a condition of things wherein each worker might realize, according to his ability and according to the nature of his work, that sense of life which is enjoyed in fullest measure by the great artist, who finds in his art an expression of his creative impulses.

In these fields of art and of social and political economy, Ruskin wrote more or less steadily for over sixty years. Like DeQuincey, he took infinite pains with his prose, and consequently some of it, more especially the earlier, has the taint of artifice, to be seen in ornamental flourish of phrase or purple patch. An epithet is forced for the sake of alliteration or a phrase for balance, and paragraphs sometimes wind up with "grand closings," as Ruskin liked to call them. Even his extraordinary "capacity for rhythmic cadence" is at times carried to the length of making his style more regularly measured than is consonant with the nature of prose. His sentences, too, often run to extreme lengths and become overcrowded with details; and in the larger matters of structure he is, again like DeQuincey, one of the most digressive of writers.

But with all allowance for faults, his style remains, at its best, a great style. It moves, in Ruskin's literary life, through at least three phases, though the reader never can be sure when the earlier Ruskin will anticipate the later or the later remind him of the earlier. The earlier style is the most famous. It is the work of a man with a soul of a poet and the eye of the painter. It is rich in color, in imagery, and in rhythm; and it accomplishes marvellously lovely effects with ordinary words in ordinary collocations. There is nothing freakish about it. It is simply the expression of one who has been caught up into a seventh heaven of beauty. The middle style,—the style of *Unto This Last,* for example—is more difficult to describe because its art is better concealed. It has cast aside the earlier rigidities and formal devices. Its sentences as well as its rhythms are shorter, and its thought is more concentrated. The intensity is not less, but it is better controlled. The typical writing of the third manner of which *Fors Clavigera* and some of the later lectures are examples, is a still different thing. It is often flat and uninspired, weakly garrulous and didactic or merely petulant and sometimes hysterical,—the wearisome grumblings of a tired and disappointed old man. But when the imagination of the embattled veteran is aroused his language reminds the reader of Swift or Carlyle. He has then at his command a fierce and merciless satire, a pungent criticism of the stupidity and pusillanimity of mankind, a sweeping denunciation of the shams and corruptions of modern life, such as sometimes come from a writer who has reached an age and an eminence whence he assumes the privilege freely to indulge in "sputters of sulphur" as he lectures humanity. Whatever his manner, Ruskin could and did manage it, repeatedly, with superb mastery.

PRAETERITA (I)

THE SPRINGS OF WANDEL

I am, and my father was before me, a violent Tory of the old school;—Walter Scott's school, that is to say, and Homer's. I name these two out of the numberless great Tory writers, because they were my own two masters. I had Walter Scott's novels, and the *Iliad* (Pope's translation), for constant reading when I was a child, on weekdays: on Sunday, their effect was tempered by *Robinson Crusoe* and the *Pilgrim's Progress;* my mother having it deeply in her heart to make an evangelical clergyman of me. Fortunately, I had an aunt more evangelical than my mother; and my aunt gave me cold mutton for Sunday's dinner, which—as I much preferred it hot—greatly diminished the influence of the *Pilgrim's Progress;* and the end of the matter was, that I got all the noble imaginative teaching of Defoe and Bunyan, and yet—am not an evangelical clergyman.

I had, however, still better teaching than theirs, and that compulsorily, and every day of the week.

Walter Scott and Pope's Homer were reading of my own election, and my mother forced me, by steady daily toil, to learn long chapters of the Bible by heart; as well as to read it every syllable through, aloud, hard names and all, from Genesis to the Apocalypse, about once a year: and to that discipline—patient, accurate, and resolute—I owe, not only a knowledge of the book, which I find occasionally serviceable, but much of my general power of taking pains, and the best part of my taste in literature. From Walter Scott's novels I might easily, as I grew older, have fallen to other people's novels; and Pope might, perhaps, have led me to take Johnson's English, or Gibbon's, as types of language; but once knowing the 32nd of Deuteronomy, the 119th Psalm, the 15th of 1st Corinthians, the Sermon on the Mount, and most of the Apocalypse, every syllable by heart, and having always a way of thinking with myself what words meant, it was not possible for me, even in the foolishest times of youth, to write entirely superficial or formal English; and the affectation of trying to write like Hooker and George Herbert was the most innocent I could have fallen into.

From my own chosen masters, then, Scott and Homer, I learned the Toryism which my best after-thought has only served to confirm.

That is to say, a most sincere love of kings, and dislike of everybody who attempted to disobey them. Only, both by Homer and Scott, I was taught strange ideas about kings, which I find for the present much obsolete; for, I perceived that both the author of the *Iliad* and the author of *Waverley* made their kings, or king-loving persons, do harder work than anybody else. Tydides or Idomeneus always killed twenty Trojans to other people's one, and Redgauntlet speared more salmon than any of the Solway fishermen; and—which was particularly a subject of admiration to me—I observed that they not only did more, but in proportion to their doings *got* less, than other people—nay, that the best of them were even ready to govern for nothing! and let their followers divide any quantity of spoil or profit. Of late it has seemed to me that the idea of a king has become exactly the contrary of this, and that it has been supposed the duty of superior persons generally to govern less, and get more, than anybody else. So that it was, perhaps, quite as well that in those early days my contemplation of existent kingship was a very distant one.

The aunt who gave me cold mutton on Sundays was my father's sister: she lived at Bridge-end, in the town of Perth, and had a garden full of gooseberry-bushes, sloping down to the Tay, with a door opening to the water, which ran past it, clear-brown over the pebbles three or four feet deep; swift-eddying,—an infinite thing for a child to look down into.

My father began business as a wine-merchant, with no capital, and a considerable amount of debts bequeathed him by my grandfather. He accepted the bequest, and paid them all before he began to lay by anything for himself,—for which his best friends called him a fool, and I, without expressing any opinion as to his wisdom, which I knew in such matters to be at least equal to mine, have written on the granite slab over his grave that he was "an entirely honest merchant." As days went on he was able to take a house in Hunter Street, Brunswick Square, No. 54 (the windows of it, fortunately for me, commanded a view of a marvellous iron post, out of which the water-carts were filled through beautiful little trapdoors, by pipes like boa-constrictors; and I was never weary of contemplating that mystery, and the delicious dripping consequent); and as years went on, and I came to be four or five years old, he could command a postchaise and pair for two months in the summer, by help of which, with my mother and me, he went the round of his country customers (who liked to see the principal of the house his own traveller); so that, at a jog-trot pace, and through the panoramic opening of the four windows of a postchaise, made more panoramic still to me because my seat was a little bracket in front (for we used to hire the chaise regularly for the two months out of Long Acre, and so could have it bracketed and pocketed as we liked), I saw all the high-roads, and most of the cross ones, of England and Wales; and great part of lowland Scotland, as far as Perth, where every other year we spent the whole summer: and I used to read the *Abbot* at Kinross, and the *Monastery* in Glen Farg, which I confused with "Glendearg," and thought that the White Lady had as certainly lived by the streamlet in that glen of the Ochils, as the Queen of Scots in the island of Loch Leven.

To my farther great benefit, as I grew older, I thus saw nearly all the noblemen's houses in England; in reverent and healthy delight of uncovetous admiration,—perceiving, as soon as I could perceive any political truth at all, that it was probably much happier to live in a small house, and have Warwick Castle to be astonished at, than to live in Warwick Castle and have nothing to be astonished at; but that, at all events, it would not make Brunswick Square in the least more pleasantly habitable, to pull Warwick Castle down. And at this day, though I have kind invitations enough to visit America, I could not, even for a couple of months, live in a country so miserable as to possess no castles.

Nevertheless, having formed my notion of kinghood chiefly from the FitzJames of the *Lady of the Lake,* and of noblesse from the Douglas there, and the Douglas in *Marmion,* a painful wonder soon arose in my child-mind, why the castles should now be always empty. Tantallon was there; but no Archibald of Angus:—Stirling, but no Knight of Snowdoun. The galleries and gardens of England were beautiful to see— but his Lordship and her Ladyship were always in town, said the housekeepers and gardeners. Deep yearning took hold of me for a kind of "Restoration," which I began slowly to feel that Charles the Second had not altogether effected, though I always wore a gilded oak-apple very piously in my button-hole on the 29th of May. It seemed to me that Charles the Second's Restoration had been, as compared with the Restoration I wanted, much as that gilded oak-apple to a real apple. And as I grew wiser, the desire for sweet pippins instead of bitter ones, and Living Kings instead of dead ones, appeared to me rational as well as romantic; and gradually it has become the main purpose of my life to grow pippins, and its chief hope, to see Kings.

HERNE-HILL ALMOND BLOSSOMS

When I was about four years old my father found himself able to buy the lease of a house on Herne Hill, a rustic eminence four miles south of the "Standard in Cornhill"; of which the leafy seclusion remains, in all essential points of character, unchanged to this day: certain Gothic splendors, lately indulged in by our wealthier neighbors, being the only serious innovations; and these are so graciously concealed by the fine trees of their grounds, that the passing viator remains unappalled by them; and I can still walk up and down the piece of road between the Fox tavern and the Herne Hill station, imagining myself four years old.

Our house was the northernmost of a group which stand accurately on the top or dome of the hill, where the ground is for a small space level, as the snows are (I understand), on the dome of Mont Blanc; presently falling, however, in what may be, in the London clay formation, considered a precipitous slope, to our valley of Chamouni (or of Dulwich) on the east; and with a softer descent into Cold Harbour-lane on the west: on the south, no less beautifully declining to the dale of the Effra (doubtless shortened from Effrena, signifying the "Unbridled" river; recently, I regret to say, bricked over for the convenience of Mr. Biffin, chemist, and others); while on the north, prolonged indeed with slight depression some half mile or so, and receiving, in the parish of Lambeth, the chivalric title of "Champion Hill," it plunges down at last to efface itself in the plains of Peckham, and the rural barbarism of Goose Green.

The group, of which our house was the quarter, consisted of two precisely similar partner-couples of houses, gardens and all to match; still the two highest blocks of buildings seen from Norwood on the crest of the ridge; so that the house itself, three-storied, with garrets above, commanded, in those comparatively smokeless days, a very notable view from its garret windows, of the Norwood hills on one side, and the winter sunrise over them; and of the valley of the Thames on the other, with Windsor telescopically clear in the distance, and Harrow, conspicuous always in fine weather to open vision against the summer sunset. It had front and back garden in sufficient proportion to its size; the front, richly set with old evergreens, and well-grown lilac and laburnum; the back, seventy yards long by twenty wide, renowned over all the hill for its pears and apples, which had been chosen with extreme care by our predecessor (shame on me to forget the name of a man to whom I owe so much!)—and possessing also a strong old mulberry tree, a tall white-heart cherry tree, a black Kentish one, and an almost unbroken hedge, all round, of alternate gooseberry and currant bush; decked, in due season, (for the ground was wholly beneficent,) with magical splendor of abundant fruit: fresh green, soft amber, and rough-bristled crimson bending the spinous branches; clustered pearl and pendent ruby joyfully discoverable under the large leaves that looked like vine.

The differences of primal importance which I observed between the nature of this garden, and that of Eden, as I had imagined it, were, that, in this one, *all* the fruit was forbidden; and there were no companionable beasts: in other respects the little domain answered every purpose of Paradise to me; and the climate, in that cycle of our years, allowed me to pass most of my life in it. My mother never gave me more to learn than she knew I could easily get learned, if I set myself honestly to work, by twelve o'clock. She never allowed anything to disturb me when my task was set; if it was not said rightly by twelve o'clock, I was kept in till I knew it, and in general, even when Latin Grammar came to supplement the Psalms, I was my own master for at least an hour before half-past one dinner, and for the rest of the afternoon.

My mother, herself finding her chief personal pleasure in her flowers, was often planting or pruning beside me, at least if I chose to stay beside *her.* I never thought of doing anything behind her back which I would not have done before her face; and her presence was therefore no restraint to me; but, also, no particular pleasure, for, from having always been left so much alone, I had generally my own little affairs to see after; and, on the whole, by the time I was seven years old, was already getting too independent, mentally, even of my father and mother; and, having nobody else to be dependent upon, began to lead a very small, perky, contented, conceited, Cock-Robinson-Crusoe sort of life, in the central point which it appeared to me, (as it must naturally appear to geometrical animals,) that I occupied in the universe.

This was partly the fault of my father's modesty; and partly of his pride. He had so much more confidence in my mother's judgment as to such matters than in his own, that he never ventured even to help, much less to cross her, in the conduct of my education; on the other hand, in the fixed purpose of making an ecclesiastical gentleman of me, with the superfinest of manners, and access to the highest circles of fleshly and spiritual society, the visits to Croydon, where I entirely loved my aunt, and young baker-cousins, became rarer and more rare: the society of our neighbors on the hill could not be had without breaking up our regular and sweetly selfish manner of living; and on the whole, I had nothing animate to care for, in a childish way, but myself, some nests of ants, which the gardener would never leave undisturbed for me, and a sociable bird or two; though I never had the sense or perseverance to make one really tame. But that was partly because, if ever I managed to bring one to be the least trustful of me, the cats got it.

Under these circumstances, what powers of imagination I possessed, either fastened themselves on inanimate things,—the sky, the leaves, and pebbles, observable within the walls of Eden,—or caught at any opportunity of flight into regions of romance, compatible with the objective realities of existence in the nineteenth century, within a mile and a quarter of Camberwell Green.

Herein my father, happily, though with no definite intention other than of pleasing me, when he found he could do so without infringing any of my mother's rules, became my guide. I was particularly fond of watching him shave; and was always allowed to come into his room in the morning (under the one in which I am now writing), to be the motionless witness of that operation. Over his dressing-table hung one of his own water-color drawings, made under the teaching of the elder Nasmyth; I believe, at the High School of Edinburgh. It was done in the early manner of tinting, which, just about the time when my father was at the High School, Dr. Munro was teaching Turner; namely, in gray under-tints of Prussian blue and British ink, washed with warm color afterward on the lights. It represented Conway Castle, with its Frith, and, in the foreground, a cottage, a fisherman, and a boat at the water's edge.

When my father had finished shaving, he always told me a story about this picture. The custom began without any initial purpose of his, in consequence of my troublesome curiosity whether the fisherman lived in the cottage, and where he was going to in the boat. It being settled, for peace' sake, that he *did* live in the cottage, and was going in the boat to fish near the castle, the plot of the drama afterward gradu-

ally thickened; and became, I believe, involved with that of the tragedy of *Douglas,* and of the *Castle Spectre,* in both of which pieces my father had performed in private theatricals, before my mother, and a select Edinburgh audience, when he was a boy of sixteen, and she, at grave twenty, a model housekeeper, and very scornful and religiously suspicious of theatricals. But she was never weary of telling me, in later years, how beautiful my father looked in his Highland dress, with the high black feathers.

In the afternoons, when my father returned (always punctually) from his business, he dined, at half-past four, in the front parlor, my mother sitting beside him to hear the events of the day, and give counsel and encouragement with respect to the same;—chiefly the last, for my father was apt to be vexed if orders for sherry fell the least short of their due standard, even for a day or two. I was never present at this time, however, and only avouch what I relate by hearsay and probable conjecture; for between four and six it would have been a grave misdemeanor in me if I so much as approached the parlor door. After that, in summer time, we were all in the garden as long as the day lasted; tea under the white-heart cherry tree; or in winter and rough weather, at six o'clock in the drawing-room,—I having my cup of milk, and slice of bread-and-butter, in a little recess, with a table in front of it, wholly sacred to me; and in which I remained in the evenings as an Idol in a niche, while my mother knitted, and my father read to her,—and to me, so far as I chose to listen.

The series of the Waverley novels, then drawing toward its close, was still the chief source of delight in all households caring for literature; and I can no more recollect the time when I did not know them than when I did not know the Bible; but I have still a vivid remembrance of my father's intense expression of sorrow mixed with scorn, as he threw down *Count Robert of Paris,* after reading three or four pages; and knew that the life of Scott was ended: the scorn being a very complex and bitter feeling in him,—partly, indeed, of the book itself, but chiefly of the wretches who were tormenting and selling the wrecked intellect, and not a little, deep down, of the subtle dishonesty which had essentially caused the ruin. My father never could forgive Scott his concealment of the Ballantyne partnership.

Such being the salutary pleasures of Herne Hill, I have next with deeper gratitude to chronicle what I owe to my mother for the resolutely consistent lessons which so exercised me in the Scriptures as to make every word of them familiar to my ear in habitual music,—yet in that familiarity reverenced, as transcending all thought, and ordaining all conduct.

This she effected, not by her own sayings or personal authority; but simply by compelling me to read the book thoroughly, for myself. As soon as I was able to read with fluency, she began a course of Bible work with me, which never ceased till I went to Oxford. She read alternate verses with me, watching, at first, every intonation of my voice, and correcting the false ones, till she made me understand the verse, if within my reach, rightly, and energetically. It might be beyond me altogether; that she did not care about; but she made sure that as soon as I got hold of it at all, I should get hold of it by the right end.

In this way she began with the first verse of Genesis, and went straight through, to the last verse of the Apocalypse; hard names, numbers, Levitical law, and all; and began again at Genesis the next day. If a name was hard, the better the exercise in pronunciation,—if the chapter was tiresome, the better lesson in patience,—if loathsome, the better lesson in faith that there was some use in its being so outspoken. After our chapters, (from two to three a day, according to their length, the first thing after breakfast, and no interruption from servants allowed,—none from visitors, who either joined in the reading or had to stay upstairs,—and none from any visitings or excursions, except real travelling,) I had to learn a few verses by heart, or repeat, to make sure I had not lost, something of what was already known; and, with the chapters thus gradually possessed from the first word to the last, I had to learn the whole body of the fine old Scottish paraphrases, which are good, melodious, and forceful verse; and to which, together with the Bible itself, I owe the first cultivation of my ear in sound.

It is strange that of all the pieces of the Bible which my mother thus taught me, that which cost me most to learn, and which was, to my child's mind, chiefly repulsive—the 119th Psalm—has now become of all the most precious to me, in its overflowing and glorious passion of love for the Law of God, in opposition to the abuse of it by modern preachers of what they imagine to be His gospel.

But it is only by deliberate effort that I recall the long morning hours of toil, as regular as sunrise,—toil on both sides equal—by which, year after year, my mother forced me to learn these paraphrases, and chapters, (the eighth of 1st Kings being one—try it, good reader, in a leisure hour!) allowing not so much as a syllable to be missed or misplaced; while every sentence was required to be said over and over again till she was satisfied with the accent of it. I recollect a struggle between us of about three weeks, concerning the accent of the "of" in the lines

> "Shall any following spring revive
> The ashes of the urn?"—

I insisting, partly in childish obstinacy, and partly in true instinct for rhythm, (being wholly careless on the subject both of urns and their contents,) on reciting it with an accented *of*. It was not, I say, till after three weeks' labor, that my mother got the accent lightened on the "of" and laid on the ashes, to her mind. But had it taken three years she would have done it, having once undertaken to do it. And, assuredly, had she not done it,—well, there's no knowing what would have happened; but I'm very thankful she *did*.

I have just opened my oldest (in use) Bible,—a small, closely, and very neatly printed volume it is, printed in Edinburgh by Sir D. Hunter Blair and J. Bruce, Printers to the King's Most Excellent Majesty, in 1816. Yellow, now, with age; and flexible, but not unclean, with much use; except that the lower corners of the pages at 8th of 1st Kings, and 32d Deuteronomy, are worn somewhat thin and dark, the learning of these two chapters having cost me much pains. My mother's list of the chapters with which, thus learned, she established my soul in life, has just fallen out of it. I will take what indulgence the incurious reader can give me, for printing the list thus accidentally occurrent:—

Exodus,	chapters	15th and 20th.
2 Samuel,	"	1st, from 17th verse to end.
1 Kings,	"	8th.
Psalms,	"	23d, 32d, 90th, 91st, 103d, 112th, 119th, 139th.
Proverbs,	"	2d, 3d, 8th, 12th.
Isaiah,	"	58th.
Matthew,	"	5th, 6th, 7th.
Acts,	"	26th.
1 Corinthians,	"	13th, 15th.
James,	"	4th.
Revelation,	"	5th, 6th.

And, truly, though I have picked up the elements of a little further knowledge—in mathematics, meteorology, and the like, in after life,—and owe not a little to the teaching of many people, this maternal installation of my mind in that property of chapters I count very confidently the most precious, and, on the whole, the one *essential* part of all my education.

And it is perhaps already time to mark what advantage and mischief, by the chances of life up to seven years old, had been irrevocably determined for me.

I will first count my blessings (as a not unwise friend once recommended me to do, continually; whereas I have a bad trick of always numbering the thorns in my fingers and not the bones in them).

And for best and truest beginning of all blessings, I had been taught the perfect meaning of Peace, in thought, act, and word.

I never had heard my father's or mother's voice once raised in any question with each other; nor seen an angry, or even slightly hurt or offended, glance in the eyes of either. I had never heard a servant scolded; nor even suddenly, passionately, or in any severe manner, blamed. I had never seen a moment's trouble or disorder in any household matter; nor anything whatever either done in a hurry, or undone in due time. I had no conception of such a feeling of anxiety; my father's occasional vexation in the afternoons, when he had only got an order for twelve butts after expecting one for fifteen, as I have just stated, was never manifested to *me;* and itself related only to the question whether his name would be a step higher or lower in the year's list of sherry exporters; for he never spent more than half his income, and therefore found himself little incommoded by occasional variations in the total of it. I had never done any wrong that I knew of—beyond occasionally delaying the commitment to heart of some improving sentence, that I might watch a wasp on the window-pane, or a bird in the cherry tree; and I had never seen any grief.

Next to this quite priceless gift of Peace, I had received the perfect understanding of the natures of Obedience and Faith. I obeyed word, or lifted finger, of father or mother, simply as a ship her helm; not only without idea of resistance, but receiving the direction as a part of my own life and force, and helpful law, as necessary to me in every moral action as the law of gravity in leaping. And my practice in Faith was soon complete; nothing was ever promised me that was not given; nothing ever threatened me that was not inflicted, and nothing ever told me that was not true.

Peace, obedience, faith; these three for chief good; next to these, the habit of fixed attention with both eyes and mind—on which I will not further enlarge at this moment, this being the main practical faculty of my life, causing Mazzini to say of me, in conversation authentically reported, a year or two before his death, that I had "the most analytic mind in Europe." An opinion in which, so far as I am acquainted with Europe, I am myself entirely disposed to concur.

Lastly, an extreme perfection in palate and all other bodily senses, given by the utter prohibition of cake, wine, comfits, or, except in carefullest restriction, fruit; and by fine preparation of what food was given me. Such I esteem the main blessings of my childhood;—next, let me count the equally dominant calamities.

First, that I had nothing to love.

My parents were—in a sort—visible powers of nature to me, no more loved than the sun and the moon: only I should have been annoyed and puzzled if either of them had gone out; (how much, now, when both are darkened!)—still less did I love God; not that I had any quarrel with Him, or fear of Him; but simply found what people told me was His service, disagreeable; and what people told me was His book, not entertaining. I had no companions to quarrel with, neither; nobody to assist, and nobody to thank. Not a servant was ever allowed to do anything for me, but what it was their duty to do; and why should I have been grateful to the cook for cooking, or the gardener for gardening,—when the one dared not give me a baked potato without asking leave, and the other would not let my ants' nests alone, because they made the walks untidy? The evil consequence of all this was not, however, what might perhaps have been expected, that I grew up selfish or unaffectionate; but that, when affection did come, it came with violence utterly rampant and unmanageable, at least by me, who never before had anything to manage.

For (second of chief calamities) I had nothing to endure. Danger or pain of any kind I knew not: my strength was never exercised, my patience never tried, and my courage never fortified. Not that I was ever afraid of anything,—either ghosts, thunder, or beasts; and one of the nearest approaches to insubordination which I was ever tempted into as a child, was in passionate effort to get leave to play with the lion's cubs in Wombwell's menagerie.

Thirdly. I was taught no precision nor etiquette of manners; it was enough if, in the little society we saw, I remained unobtrusive, and replied to a question without shyness: but the shyness came later, and increased as I grew conscious of the rudeness arising from the want of social discipline, and found it impossible to acquire, in advanced life, dexterity in any bodily exercise, skill in any pleasing acomplishment, or ease and tact in ordinary behavior.

Lastly, and chief of evils. My judgment of right and wrong, and powers of independent action, were left entirely undeveloped; because the bridle and blinkers were never taken off me. Children should have their times of being off duty, like soldiers; and when once the obedience, if required, is certain, the little creature should be very early put for periods of practice in complete command of itself; set on the barebacked horse of its own will, and left to break it by its own strength. But the ceaseless authority exercised over my youth left me, when cast out at last into the world, unable for some time to do more than drift with its vortices.

My present verdict, therefore, on the general tenor of my education at that time, must be, that it was at once too formal and too luxurious; leaving my character, at the most important moment for its construction, cramped indeed, but not disciplined; and only by protection innocent, instead of by practice virtuous.

[1885]

MODERN PAINTERS (III)

INFLUENCE OF NATURE

The first thing which I remember, as an event in life, was being taken by my nurse to the brow of Friar's Crag on Derwent Water; the intense joy, mingled with awe, that I had in looking through the hollows in the mossy roots, over the crag, into the dark lake, has associated itself more or less with all twining roots of trees ever since. Two other things I remember as, in a sort, beginnings of life;—crossing Shapfells (being let out of the chaise to run up the hills), and going through Glenfarg, near Kinross, in a winter's morning, when the rocks were hung with icicles; these being culminating points in an early life of more travelling than is usually indulged to a child. In such journeyings, whenever they brought me near hills, and in all mountain ground and scenery, I had a pleasure, as early as I can remember, and continuing till I was eighteen or twenty, infinitely greater than any which has been since possible to me in anything; comparable for intensity only to the joy of a lover in being near a noble and kind mistress, but no more explicable or definable than that feeling of love itself. Only thus much I can remember, respecting it, which is important to our present subject.

First: it was never independent of associated thought. Almost as soon as I could see or hear, I had got reading enough to give me associations with all kinds of scenery; and mountains, in particular, were always partly confused with those of my favorite book, Scott's *Monastery;* so that Glenfarg and all other glens were more or less enchanted to me, filled with forms of hesitating creed about Christie of the Clint Hill, and the monk Eustace; and with a general presence of White Lady everywhere. I also generally knew, or was told by my father and mother, such simple facts of history as were necessary to give more definite and justifiable association to other scenes which chiefly interested me, such as the ruins of Lochleven and Kenilworth; and thus my pleasure in mountains or ruins was never, even in earliest childhood, free from a certain awe and melancholy, and general sense of the meaning of death, though, in its principal influence, entirely exhilarating and gladdening.

Secondly, it was partly dependent on contrast with a very simple and unamused mode of general life; I was born in London, and accustomed, for two or three years, to no other prospect than that of the brick walls over the way; had no brothers nor sisters, nor companions; and though I could always make myself happy in a quiet way, the beauty of the mountains had an additional charm of change and adventure which a country-bred child would not have felt.

Thirdly: there was no definite religious feeling mingled with it. I partly believed in ghosts and fairies; but supposed that angels belonged entirely to the Mosaic dispensation, and cannot remember any single thought or feeling connected with them. I believed that God was in heaven, and could hear me and see me; but this gave me neither pleasure nor pain, and I seldom thought of it at all. I never thought of nature as God's work, but as a separate fact or existence.

Fourthly: it was entirely unaccompanied by powers of reflection or invention. Every fancy that I had about nature was put into my head by some book; and I never reflected about anything till I grew older; and then, the more I reflected, the less nature was precious to me: I could then make myself happy, by thinking, in the dark, or in the dullest scenery; and the beautiful scenery became less essential to my pleasure.

Fifthly: it was, according to its strength, inconsistent with every evil feeling, with spite, anger, covetousness, discontent, and every other hateful passion; but would associate itself deeply with every just and noble sorrow, joy, or affection. It had not, however, always the power to repress what was inconsistent with it; and, though only after stout contention, might at last be crushed by what it had partly repressed. And as it only acted by setting one impulse against another, though it had much power in moulding the character, it had hardly any in strengthening it; it formed temperament but never instilled principle; it kept me generally good-humored and kindly, but could not teach me perseverance of self-denial: what firmness or principle I had was quite independent of it; and it came itself nearly as often in the form of a temptation as of a safeguard, leading me to ramble over hills when I should have been learning lessons, and lose days in reveries which I might have spent in doing kindnesses.

Lastly: although there was no definite religious sentiment mingled with it, there was a continual perception of Sanctity in the whole of nature, from the slightest thing to the vastest;—an instinctive awe, mixed with delight; an indefinable thrill, such as we sometimes imagine to indicate the presence of a disembodied spirit. I could only feel this perfectly when I was alone; and then it would often make me shiver from head to foot with the joy and fear of it, when after being some time away from hills, I first got to the shore of a mountain river, where the brown water circled among the pebbles, or when I first saw the swell of distant land against the sunset, or the first low broken wall, covered with mountain moss. I cannot in the least *describe* the feeling; but I do not

think this is my fault, nor that of the English language, for I am afraid, no feeling *is*
describable. If we had to explain even the
sense of bodily hunger to a person who had
never felt it, we should be hard put to it
for words; and the joy in nature seemed to
me to come of a sort of heart-hunger, satisfied with the presence of a Great and Holy
Spirit. These feelings remained in their
full intensity till I was eighteen or twenty, 10
and then, as the reflective and practical
power increased, and the "cares of this
world" gained upon me, faded gradually
away, in the manner described by Wordsworth in his *Intimations of Immortality.*

I cannot, of course, tell how far I am
justified in supposing that these sensations
may be reasoned upon as common to children in general. In the same degree they
are not of course common, otherwise chil- 20

dren would be, most of them, very different from what they are in their choice of
pleasures. But, as far as such feelings exist, I apprehend they are more or less similar in their nature and influence; only
producing different characters according to
the elements with which they are mingled.
Thus, a very religious child may give up
many pleasures to which its instincts lead
it, for the sake of irksome duties; and an
inventive child would mingle its love of
nature with watchfulness of human sayings
and doings; but I believe the feelings I
have endeavored to describe are the pure
landscape-instinct; and the likelihoods of
good or evil resulting from them may be
reasoned upon as generally indicating the
usefulness or danger of the modern love
and study of landscape.

[1856]

MODERN PAINTERS (I)

THE SKIES OF NATURE, MORNING, NOON, SUNSET, SUNRISE

Stand upon the peak of some isolated
mountain at daybreak, when the night
mists first rise from off the plains, and
watch their white and lake-like fields, as
they float in level bays and winding gulfs
about the islanded summits of the lower
hills, untouched yet by more than dawn, 10
colder and more quiet than a windless sea
under the moon of midnight; watch when
the first sunbeam is sent upon the silver
channels, how the foam of their undulating surface parts and passes away, and
down under their depths the glittering city
and green pasture lie like Atlantis, between the white paths of winding rivers;
the flakes of light falling every moment
faster and broader among the starry spires, 20
as the wreathed surges break and vanish
above them, and the confused crests and
ridges of the dark hills shorten their gray
shadows upon the plain.... Wait a little
longer, and you shall see those scattered
mists rallying in the ravines, and floating
up toward you, along the winding valleys,
till they couch in quiet masses, iridescent
with the morning light, upon the broad
breasts of the higher hills, whose leagues 30

of massy undulation will melt back and
back into that robe of material light, until
they fade away, lost in its lustre, to appear
again above, in the serene heaven, like a
wild, bright, impossible dream, foundation-
less and inaccessible, their very bases
vanishing in the unsubstantial and mocking blue of the deep lake below.... Wait
yet a little longer, and you shall see those
mists gather themselves into white towers,
and stand like fortresses along the promontories, massy and motionless, only piled
with every instant higher and higher into
the sky, and casting longer shadows
athwart the rocks; and out of the pale blue
of the horizon you will see forming and
advancing a troop of narrow, dark, pointed
vapors, which will cover the sky, inch by
inch, with their gray network, and take
the light off the landscape with an eclipse
which will stop the singing of the birds
and the motion of the leaves, together; and
then you will see horizontal bars of black
shadow forming under them, and lurid
wreathes create themselves, you know not
how, along the shoulders of the hills; you
never see them form, but when you look
back to a place which was clear an instant
ago, there is a cloud on it, hanging by the
precipices, as a hawk pauses over his

prey.... And then you will hear the sudden rush of the awakened wind, and you will see those watch-towers of vapor swept away from their foundations, and waving curtains of opaque rain let down to the valleys, swinging from the burdened clouds in black bending fringes, or pacing in pale columns along the lake level, grazing its surface into foam as they go. And then, as the sun sinks, you shall see the storm 10 drift for an instant from off the hills, leaving their broad sides smoking, and loaded yet with snow-white, torn, steam-like rags of capricious vapor, now gone, now gathered again; while the smoldering sun, seeming not far away, but burning like a red-hot ball beside you, and as if you could reach it, plunges through the rushing wind and rolling cloud with headlong fall, as if it meant to rise no more, dyeing all the 20 air about it with blood.... And then you shall hear the fainting tempest die in the hollow of the night, and you shall see a green halo kindling on the summit of the eastern hills, brighter—brighter yet, till the large white circle of the slow moon is lifted up among the barred clouds, step by step, line by line; star after star she quenches with her kindling light, setting in their stead an army of pale, penetrable, fleecy 30 wreaths in the heaven, to give light upon the earth, which move together, hand in hand, company by company, troop by troop, so measured in their unity of motion, that the whole heaven seems to roll with them, and the earth to reel under them.... And then wait yet for one hour until the east again becomes purple, and the heaving mountains, rolling against it in darkness, like waves of a wild sea, are 40 drowned one by one in the glory of its burning: watch the white glaciers blaze in their winding paths about the mountains, like mighty serpents with scales of fire: watch the columnar peaks of solitary snow, kindling downward, chasm by chasm, each in itself a new morning; their long avalanches cast down in keen streams brighter than the lightning, sending each his tribute of driven snow, like altar-smoke, up to 50 the heaven; the rose-light of their silent domes flushing that heaven about them and above them, piercing with purer light through its purple lines of lifted cloud,

casting a new glory on every wreath as it passes by, until the whole heaven, one scarlet canopy, is interwoven with a roof of waving flame, and tossing, vault beyond vault, as with the drifted wings of many companies of angels: and then, when you can look no more for gladness, and when you are bowed down with fear and love of the Maker and Doer of this, tell me who has best delivered this His message unto men!

WATER

(a) Of all inorganic substances, acting in their own proper nature, and without assistance or combination, water is the most wonderful. If we think of it as the source of all the changefulness and beauty which we have seen in clouds; then as the instrument by which the earth we have 20 contemplated was modelled into symmetry, and its crags chiselled into grace; then as, in the form of snow, it robes the mountains it has made with that transcendent light which we could not have conceived if we had not seen; then as it exists in the foam of the torrent, in the iris which spans it, in the morning mist which rises from it, in the deep crystalline pools which mirror 30 its hanging shore, in the broad lake and glancing river; finally, in that which is to all human minds the best emblem of unwearied unconquerable power, the wild, various, fantastic, tameless unity of the sea; what shall we compare to this mighty, this universal element, for glory and for beauty? or how shall we follow its eternal changefulness of feeling? It is like trying to paint a soul.

To suggest the ordinary appearance of calm water, to lay on canvas as much evidence of surface and reflection as may make us understand that water is meant, is, perhaps, the easiest task of art; and even ordinary running or falling water may be sufficiently rendered, by observing careful curves of projection with a dark ground, and breaking a little white over it, as we see done with judgment and truth by 50 Ruysdael. But to paint the actual play of hue on the reflective surface, or to give the forms and fury of water when it begins to show itself; to give the flashing and rocket-like velocity of a noble cataract, or the precision and grace of the sea wave, so exquisitely modelled, though so mockingly transient, so mountainous in its form, yet so cloud-like in its motion, with its variety and delicacy of color, when every ripple and wreath has some peculiar passage of reflection upon itself alone, and the radiating and scintillating sunbeams are mixed with the dim hues of transparent depth and dark rock below; to do this perfectly is 10 beyond the power of man; to do it even partially has been granted to but one or two, even of those few who have dared to attempt it....

Now, the fact is, that there is hardly a road-side pond or pool which has not as much landscape *in* it as above it. It is not the brown, muddy, dull thing we suppose it to be; it has a heart like ourselves, and in the bottom of that there are the boughs 20 of the tall trees, and the blades of the shaking grass, and all manner of hues of variable pleasant light out of the sky. Nay, the ugly gutter, that stagnates over the drain-bars in the heart of the foul city, is not altogether base; down in that, if you will look deep enough, you may see the dark serious blue of far-off sky, and the passing of pure clouds. It is at your own will that you see in that despised stream, 30 either the refuse of the street, or the image of the sky. So it is with almost all other things that we unkindly despise.

. . . . .

(b) Stand for half an hour beside the Fall of Schaffhausen, on the north side where the rapids are long, and watch how the vault of water first bends, unbroken, in pure polished velocity, over the arching 40 rocks at the brow of the cataract, covering them with a dome of crystal twenty feet thick, so swift that its motion is unseen except when a foam-globe from above darts over it like a falling star; and how the trees are lighted above it under all their leaves, at the instant that it breaks into foam; and how all the hollows of that foam burn with green fire like so much shattering chrysoprase; and how, ever and anon, 50 startling you with its white flash, a jet of spray leaps hissing out of the fall, like a rocket, bursting in the wind and driven

away in dust, filling the air with light; and how, through the curdling wreaths of the restless crashing abyss below, the blue of the water, paled by the foam in its body, shows purer than the sky through white rain-cloud; while the shuddering iris stoops in tremulous stillness over all, fading and flushing alternately through the choking spray and shattered sunshine, hiding itself at last among the thick golden leaves which toss to and fro in sympathy with the wild water; their dripping masses lifted at intervals, like sheaves of loaded corn, by some stronger gush from the cataract, and bowed again upon the mossy rocks as its roar dies away; the dew gushing from their thick branches through drooping clusters of emerald herbage, and sparkling in white threads along the dark rocks of the shore, feeding the lichens which chase and checker them with purple and silver.

. . . . . .

(c) As the right rendering of the Alps depends on power of drawing snow, so the right painting of the sea must depend, at least in all coast scenery, in no small measure on the power of drawing foam. Yet there are two conditions of foam of invariable occurrence on breaking waves, of which I have never seen the slightest record attempted; first, the thick, creamy, curdling, overlapping, massy foam, which remains for a moment only after the fall of the wave, and is seen in perfection in its running up the beach; and, secondly, the thin white coating into which this subsides, which opens into oval gaps and clefts, marbling the waves over their whole surface, and connecting the breakers on a flat shore by long dragging streams of white.

It is evident that the difficulty of expressing either of these two conditions must be immense. The lapping and curdling foam is difficult enough to catch, even when the lines of its undulation alone are considered; but the lips, so to speak, which lie along these lines, are full, projecting, and marked by beautiful light and shade; each has its high light, a gradation into shadow of indescribable delicacy, a bright reflected light, and a dark cast shadow: to draw all this requires labor and care, and firmness of work, which, as I imagine, must always, however skilfully bestowed, destroy all impressions of wildness, accidentalism, and evanescence, and so kill the sea. Again, the openings in the thin subsided foam, in their irregular modifications of circular and oval shapes dragged hither and thither, would be hard enough to draw, even if they could be seen on a flat surface; instead of which, every one of the openings is seen 10 in undulation on a tossing surface, broken up over small surges and ripples, and so thrown into perspectives of the most hopeless intricacy. Now it is not easy to express the fall of a pattern with oval openings on the folds of drapery. I do not know that anyone under the mark of Veronese or Titian could even do this as it ought to be done, yet in drapery much stiffness and error may be overlooked: not so in 20 sea; the slightest inaccuracy, the slightest want of flow and freedom in the line, is attached by the eye, in a moment, of high treason, and I believe success to be impossible.

Yet there is not a wave, nor any violently agitated sea, on which both these forms do not appear; the latter especially, after some time of storm, extends over their whole surfaces: the reader sees, therefore, 30 why I said that sea could only be painted by means of more or less dexterous conventionalism, since two of its most enduring phenomena cannot be represented at all.

Again, as respects the form of breakers on an even shore, there is difficulty of no less formidable kind. There is in them an irreconcilable mixture of fury and formalism. Their hollow surface is marked by 40 parallel lines, like those of a smooth millweir, and graduated by reflected and transmitted lights of the most wonderful intricacy, its curve being at the same time necessarily of mathematical purity and precision; yet at the top of this curve, when it nods over, there is a sudden laxity and giving way, the water swings and jumps along the ridge like a shaken chain, and the motion runs from part to part as it 50 does through a serpent's body. Then the wind is at work on the extreme edge, and instead of letting it fling itself off naturally,

it supports it, and drives it back, or scrapes it off and carries it bodily away; so that the spray at the top is in a continual transition between forms projected by their own weight, and forms blown and carried off with their weight overcome. Then at last, when it has come down, who shall say what shape that may be called, which "shape has none," of the great crash where it touches 10 the beach....

Seen from the land, the curl of the breakers, even in nature, is somewhat uniform and monotonous; the size of the waves out at sea is uncomprehended; and those nearer the eye seem to succeed and resemble each other, to move slowly to the beach, and to break in the same lines and forms.

Afloat even twenty yards from the shore, 20 we receive a totally different impression. Every wave around us appears vast, every one different from all the rest; and the breakers present, now that we see them with their backs toward us, the grand, extended, and varied lines of long curvature which are peculiarly expressive both of velocity and power. Recklessness, before unfelt, is manifested in the mad, perpetual, changeful, undirected motion, 30 not of wave after wave, as it appears from the shore, but of the very same water rising and falling. Of waves that successively approach and break, each appears to the mind a separate individual, whose part being performed, it perishes, and is succeeded by another; and there is nothing in this to impress us with the idea of restlessness, any more than in any successive and continuous functions of life and death. 40 But it is when we perceive that it is no succession of wave, but the same water, constantly rising, and crashing, and recoiling, and rolling in again in new forms and with fresh fury, that we perceive the perturbed spirit, and feel the intensity of its unwearied rage. The sensation of power is also trebled; for not only is the vastness of apparent size much increased, but the whole action is different; it is not a passive 50 wave, rolling sleepily forward until it tumbles heavily, prostrated upon the beach; but a sweeping exertion of tremendous and living strength, which does

not now appear to *fall,* but to *burst* upon
the shore; which never perishes but recoils
and recovers.

.   .   .   .   .

(d) The noblest sea that Turner has ever
painted, and, if so, the noblest certainly
ever painted by man, is that of the Slave
Ship, the chief Academy picture of the
Exhibition of 1840. It is a sunset on the
Atlantic, after prolonged storm; but the
storm is partially lulled, and the torn and
streaming rain-clouds are moving in scarlet
lines to lose themselves in the hollow of
the night. The whole surface of sea included in the picture is divided into two
ridges of enormous swell, not high, nor
local, but a low broad heaving of the
whole ocean, like the lifting of its bosom
by deep-drawn breath after the torture of
the storm. Between these two ridges the
fire of the sunset falls along the trough of
the sea, dyeing it with an awful but
glorious light, the intense and lurid splendor which burns like gold, and bathes like
blood. Along this fiery path and valley,
the tossing waves by which the swell of the
sea is restlessly divided, lift themselves in
dark, indefinite, fantastic forms, each casting a faint and ghastly shadow behind it
along the illumined foam. They do not
rise everywhere, but three or four together
in wild groups, fitfully and furiously, as
the under strength of the swell compels or
permits them; leaving between them
treacherous spaces of level and whirling
water, now lighted with green and lamp-
like fire, now flashing back the gold of the
declining sun, now fearfully dyed from
above with the undistinguishable images of
the burning clouds, which fall upon them
in flakes of crimson and scarlet, and give
to the reckless waves the added motion of
their own fiery flying. Purple and blue,
the lurid shadows of the hollow breakers
are cast upon the mist of night, which
gathers cold and low, advancing like the
shadow of death upon the guilty ship as
it labors amidst the lightning of the sea,
its thin masts written upon the sky in lines
of blood, girded with condemnation in
that fearful hue which signs the sky with
horror, and mixes its flaming flood with
the sunlight, and, cast far along the desolate heave of the sepulchral waves, incarnadines the multitudinous sea.   [1843]

GREATNESS IN ART

In the 15th Lecture of Sir Joshua Reynolds, incidental notice is taken of the
distinction between those excellences in
the painter which belong to him *as such,*
and those which belong to him in common
with all men of intellect, the general and
exalted powers of which art is the evidence
and expression, not the subject. But the
distinction is not there dwelt upon as it
should be, for it is owing to the slight
attention ordinarily paid to it, that criticism is open to every form of coxcombry,
and liable to every phase of error. It is a
distinction on which depend all sound
judgment of the rank of the artist, and
all just appreciation of the dignity of art.

Painting, or art generally, as such, with
all its technicalities, difficulties, and particular ends, is nothing but a noble and
expressive language, invaluable as the
vehicle of thought, but by itself nothing.
He who has learned what is commonly
considered the whole art of painting, that
is, the art of representing any natural
object faithfully, has as yet only learned
the language by which his thoughts are
to be expressed. He has done just as much
toward being that which we ought to
respect as a great painter, as a man who
has learned how to express himself gram-
matically and melodiously has toward
being a great poet. The language is,
indeed, more difficult of acquirement in
the one case than in the other, and possesses more power of delighting the sense,
while it speaks to the intellect; but it is,
nevertheless, nothing more than language,
and all those excellences which are peculiar
to the painter as such, are merely what
rhythm, melody, precision, and force are
in the words of the orator and the poet,
necessary to their greatness, but not the
test of their greatness. It is not by the
mode of representing and saying, but by
what is represented and said, that the respective greatness either of the painter or
the writer is to be finally determined.

Speaking with strict propriety, therefore,
we should call a man a great painter only

as he excelled in precision and force in the language of lines, and a great versifier, as he excelled in precision and force in the language of words. A great poet would then be a term strictly, and in precisely the same sense, applicable to both, if warranted by the character of the images or thoughts which each in their respective languages conveyed.

Take, for instance, one of the most perfect poems or pictures (I used the words as synonymous) which modern times have seen:—the "Old Shepherd's Chief-mourner." Here the exquisite execution of the glossy and crisp hair of the dog, the bright sharp touching of the green bough beside it, the clear painting of the wood of the coffin and the folds of the blanket, are language—language clear and expressive in the highest degree. But the close pressure of the dog's breast against the wood, the convulsive clinging of the paws, which has dragged the blanket off the trestle, the total powerlessness of the head laid, close and motionless, upon its folds, the fixed and tearful fall of the eye in its utter hopelessness, the rigidity of repose which marks that there has been no motion nor change in the trance of agony since the last blow was struck on the coffin-lid, the quietness and gloom of the chamber, the spectacles marking the place where the Bible was last closed, indicating how lonely has been the life, how unwatched the departure of him who is now laid solitary in his sleep;— these are all thoughts—thoughts by which the picture is separated at once from hundreds of equal merit, as far as mere painting goes, by which it ranks as a work of high art, and stamps its author, not as the neat imitator of the texture of a skin, or the fold of a drapery, but as the Man of Mind.

It is not, however, always easy, either in painting or literature, to determine where the influence of language stops, and where that of thought begins. Many thoughts are so dependent upon the language in which they are clothed, that they would lose half their beauty if otherwise expressed. But the highest thoughts are those which are least dependent on language, and the dignity of any composition, and praise to which it is entitled, are in exact proportion to its independency of language or expression. A composition is indeed usually most perfect, when to such intrinsic dignity is added all that expression can do to attract and adorn; but in every case of supreme excellence this all becomes as nothing. We are more gratified by the simplest lines or words which can suggest the idea in its own naked beauty, than by the robe and the gem which conceal while they decorate; we are better pleased to feel by their absence how little they could bestow, than by their presence how much they can destroy.

There is therefore, a distinction to be made between what is ornamental in language and what is expressive. That part of it which is necessary to the embodying and conveying of the thought is worthy of respect and attention as necessary to excellence, though not the test of it. But that part of it which is decorative has little more to do with the intrinsic excellence of the picture than the frame or the varnishing of it. And this caution in distinguishing between the ornamental and the expressive is peculiarly necessary in painting; for in the language of words it is nearly impossible for that which is not expressive to be beautiful, except by mere rhythm or melody, any sacrifice to which is immediately stigmatized as error. But the beauty of mere language in painting is not only very attractive and entertaining to the spectator, but requires for its attainment no small exertion of mind and devotion of time by the artist. Hence, in art, men have frequently fancied that they were becoming rhetoricians and poets when they were only learning to speak melodiously, and the judge has over and over again advanced to the honor of authors those who were never more than ornamental writing-masters.

Most pictures of the Dutch school, for instance, excepting always those of Rubens, Vandyke, and Rembrandt, are ostentatious exhibitions of the artist's power of speech, the clear and vigorous elocution of useless and senseless words; while the early efforts of Cimabue and Giotto are the burning messages of prophecy, delivered by the stammering lips of infants. It is not by ranking the former as more than mechanics, or the latter as less than artists that the taste of the multitude, always awake to the lowest pleasures which art can bestow, and blunt to the highest, is to be formed or elevated. It must be the part of the judicious critic carefully to distinguish what is language, and what is thought, and to rank and praise pictures chiefly for the latter, considering the former as a totally inferior excellence, and one which cannot be compared with nor weighed against thought in any way nor in any degree whatsoever. The picture which has the nobler and more numerous ideas, however awkwardly expressed, is a greater and a better picture than that which has the less noble and less numerous ideas, however beautifully expressed. No weight, nor mass, nor beauty of execution, can outweigh one grain or fragment of thought. Three penstrokes of Raffaelle are a greater and a better picture than the most finished work that ever Carlo Dolci polished into inanity. A finished work of a great artist is only better than its sketch, if the sources of pleasure belonging to color and realization—valuable in themselves—are so employed as to increase the impressiveness of the thought. But if one atom of thought has vanished, all color, all finish, all execution, all ornament, are too dearly bought. Nothing but thought can pay for thought, and the instant that the increasing refinement or finish of the picture begins to be paid for by the loss of the faintest shadow of an idea, that instant all refinement or finish is an excrescence and a deformity.

Yet although in all our speculations on art, language is thus to be distinguished from, and held subordinate to, that which it conveys, we must still remember that there are certain ideas inherent in language itself, and that, strictly speaking, every pleasure connected with art has in it some reference to the intellect. The mere sensual pleasure of the eye, received from the most brilliant piece of coloring, is as nothing to that which it receives from a crystal prism, except as it depends on our perception of a certain meaning and intended arrangement of color, which has been the subject of intellect. Nay, the term idea, according to Locke's definition of it, will extend even to the sensual impressions themselves as far as they are "things which the mind occupies itself about in thinking"; that is, not as they are felt by the eye only, but as they are received by the mind through the eye. So that, if I say that the greatest picture is that which conveys to the mind of the spectator the greatest number of the greatest ideas, I have a definition which will include as subjects of comparison every pleasure which art is capable of conveying. If I were to say, on the contrary, that the best picture was that which most closely imitated nature, I should assume that art could only please by imitating nature; and I should cast out of the pale of criticism those parts of works of art which are not imitative, that is to say, intrinsic beauties of color and form, and those works of art wholly, which, like the Arabesques of Raffaelle in the Loggias, are not imitative at all. Now, I want a definition of art wide enough to include all its varieties of aim. I do not say, therefore, that the art is greatest which gives most pleasure, because perhaps there is some art whose end is to teach, and not to please. I do not say that the art is greatest which teaches us most, because perhaps there is some art whose end is to please, and not to teach. I do not say that the art is greatest which imitates best, because perhaps there is some art whose end is to create and not to imitate. But I say that the art is greatest which conveys to the mind of the spectator, by any means whatsoever, the greatest number of the greatest ideas; and I call an idea great in proportion as it is received by a higher faculty of the mind, and as it more fully occupies, and in occupying, exercises and exalts, the faculty by which it is received.

If this, then, be the definition of great art, that of a great artist naturally follows. He is the greatest artist who has embodied, in the sum of his works, the greatest number of the greatest ideas.

IDEAS OF TRUTH, BEAUTY, AND RELATION

(a) *Ideas of Truth:* The word Truth, as applied to art, signifies the faithful statement, either to the mind or senses, of any fact of nature.

We receive an idea of truth, then, when we perceive the faithfulness of such a statement.

The difference between ideas of truth and of imitation lies chiefly in the following points:

First,—Imitation can only be of something material, but truth has reference to statements both of the qualities of material things, and of emotions, impressions, and thoughts. There is a moral as well as material truth,—a truth of impression as well as of form,—of thought as well as of matter; and the truth of impression and thought is a thousand times the more important of the two. Hence, truth is a term of universal application, but imitation is limited to that narrow field of art which takes cognizance only of material things.

Secondly,—Truth may be stated by any signs or symbols which have a definite signification in the minds of those to whom they are addressed, although such signs be themselves no image nor likeness of anything. Whatever can excite in the mind the conception of certain facts, can give ideas of truth, though it be in no degree the imitation or resemblance of those facts. If there be—we do not say there is,—but if there be in painting anything which operates, as words do, not by resembling anything, but by being taken as a symbol and substitute for it, and thus inducing the effect of it, then this channel of communication can convey uncorrupted truth, though it do not in any degree resemble the facts whose conception it induces. But ideas of imitation, of course, require the likeness of the object. They speak to the perceptive faculties only: truth to the conceptive.

Thirdly, and in consequence of what is above stated, an idea of truth exists in the statement of *one* attribute of anything, but an idea of imitation requires the resemblance of as many attributes as we are usually cognizant of in its real presence. A pencil outline of the bough of a tree on white paper is a statement of a certain number of facts of form. It does not yet amount to the imitation of anything. The idea of that form is not given in nature by lines at all, still less by black lines with a white space between them. But those lines convey to the mind a distinct impression of a certain number of facts, which it recognizes as agreeable with its previous impressions of the bough of a tree; and it receives, therefore, an idea of truth. If, instead of two lines, we give a dark form with the brush, we convey information of a certain relation of shade between the bough and sky, recognizable for another idea of truth; but we have still no imitation, for the white paper is not the least like air, nor the black shadow like wood. It is not until after a certain number of ideas of truth have been collected together, that we arrive at an idea of imitation.

Hence it might at first sight appear, that an idea of imitation, inasmuch as several ideas of truth are united in it, is nobler than a simple idea of truth. And if it were necessary that the ideas of truth should be perfect, or should be subjects of contemplation *as such,* it would be so. But, observe, we require to produce the effect of imitation only so many and such ideas of truth as the *senses* are usually cognizant of. Now the senses are not usually, nor unless they be especially devoted to the service, cognizant, with accuracy, of any truths but those of space and projection. It requires long study and attention before they give certain evidence of even the simplest truths of form. For instance, the quay on which the figure is sitting, with his hand at his eyes, in Claude's "Seaport," No. 14 in the National Gallery, is egregiously out of perspective. The eye of this artist, with all his study, had thus not acquired the power of taking cognizance of the apparent form even of a simple parallelopiped: how much less of the complicated forms of boughs, leaves, or limbs? Although, therefore, something resembling the real form is necessary to deception, this something is not to be called a *truth* of form; for, strictly speaking, there are no degrees of truth, there are only degrees of approach to it; and an approach to it, whose feebleness and imperfection would instantly offend and give pain to a mind really capable of distinguishing truth, is yet quite sufficient for all the purposes of deceptive imitation. It is the same with regard to color. If we were to paint a tree sky-blue, or a dog rose-pink, the discernment of the public would be keen enough to discover the falsehood; but, so that there be just so much approach to truth of color as may come up to the common idea of it in men's minds, that is to say, if the trees be all bright green, and flesh unbroken buff, and ground unbroken brown, though all the real and refined truths of color be wholly omitted, or rather defied and contradicted, there is yet quite enough for all purposes of imitation. The only facts, then, which we are usually and certainly cognizant of, are those of distance and projection; and if these be tolerably given, with something like truth of form and color to assist them, the idea of imitation is complete. I would undertake to paint an arm, with every muscle out of its place, and every bone of false form and dislocated articulation, and yet to observe certain coarse and broad resemblances of true outline, which, with careful shading, would induce deception, and draw down the praise and delight of the discerning public. The other day at Bruges, while I was endeavoring to set down in my notebook something of the ineffable expression of the Madonna in the Cathedral, a French amateur came up to me, to inquire if I had seen the modern French pictures in a neighboring church. I had not, but felt little inclined to leave my marble for all the canvas that ever suffered from French brushes. My apathy was attacked with gradually increasing energy of praise. Rubens never executed—Titian never colored anything like them. I thought this highly probable, and still sat quiet. The voice continued at my ear. "Parbleu, Monsieur, Michel Ange n'a rien produit de plus beau!" "De plus *beau?*" repeated I, wishing to know what particular excellences of Michael Angelo were to be intimated by this expression. "Monsieur, on ne peut plus—c'est un tableau admirable—inconceivable; Monsieur," [1] said the Frenchman, lifting up his hands to heaven, as he concentrated in one conclusive and overwhelming proposition the qualities which were to outshine Rubens and overpower Buonaroti, —"Monsieur, IL SORT!"

This gentleman could only perceive two truths—flesh color and projection. These constituted his notion of the perfection of painting; because they unite all that is necessary for deception. He was not therefore cognizant of many ideas of truth, though perfectly cognizant of ideas of imitation.

We shall see, in the course of our investigation of ideas of truth, that ideas of imitation not only do not imply their presence, but even are inconsistent with it; and that pictures which imitate so as to deceive, are never true. But this is not the place for the proof of this; at present we have only to insist on the last and greatest distinction between ideas of truth and of imitation—that the mind, in receiving one of the former, dwells upon its own conception of the fact, or form, or feeling stated, and is occupied only with the qualities and character of that fact or form, considering it as real and existing, being all the while totally regardless of the signs or symbols by which the notion of it has been conveyed. These signs have no pretence, nor hypocrisy, nor legerdemain about them;—there is nothing to be found out, or sifted, or surprised in them;—they bear their message simply and clearly, and it is that message which the mind takes from them and dwells upon, regardless of the language in which it is delivered. But the mind, in receiving an idea of imitation, is wholly occupied in finding out that what has been suggested to it is not what it appears to be: it does not dwell on the suggestion, but on the perception that it is a false suggestion: it derives its pleasure, not from the contemplation of a truth, but from the discovery of a falsehood. So that the moment ideas of truth are grouped together, so as to give rise to an idea of imitation, they change their very nature—lose their essence as ideas of truth—and are corrupted and degraded, so as to share in the treachery of what they have produced. Hence, finally, ideas of truth are the foundation, and ideas of imitation, the destruction, of all art. We shall be better able to appreciate their relative dignity after the investigation which we propose of the func-

---

[1] *"Parbleu, Monsieur"*, etc.:
"Zounds, sir, Michelangelo has produced nothing more beautiful."
"More beautiful?"
"Sir, nothing can be more—it is a picture admirable—inconceivable; sir—*sir, it stands out!"*

tions of the former; but we may as well now express the conclusion to which we shall then be led—that no picture can be good which deceives by its imitation, for the very reason that nothing can be beautiful which is not true.

. . . . . .

(b) *Of Ideas of Beauty:* Any material object which can give us pleasure in the simple contemplation of its outward qualities without any direct and definite exertion of the intellect, I call in some way, or in some degree, beautiful. Why we receive pleasure from some forms and colors, and not from others, is no more to be asked or answered than why we like sugar and dislike wormwood. The utmost subtilty of investigation will only lead us to ultimate instincts and principles of human nature, for which no farther reason can be given than the simple will of the Deity that we should be so created. We may indeed perceive, as far as we are acquainted with His nature, that we have been so constructed as, when in a healthy and cultivated state of mind, to derive pleasure from whatever things are illustrative of that nature; but we do not receive pleasure from them *because* they are illustrative of it, nor from any perception that they are illustrative of it, but instinctively and necessarily, as we derive sensual pleasure from the scent of a rose. On these primary principles of our nature, education and accident operate to an unlimited extent; they may be cultivated or checked, directed or diverted, gifted by right guidance with the most acute and faultless sense, or subjected by neglect to every phase of error and disease. He who has followed up these natural laws of aversion and desire, rendering them more and more authoritative by constant obedience, so as to derive pleasure always from that which God originally intended should give him pleasure, and who derives the greatest possible sum of pleasure from any given object, is a man of taste.

This, then, is the real meaning of this disputed word. Perfect taste is the faculty of receiving the greatest possible pleasure from those material sources which are attractive to our moral nature in its purity and perfection. He who receives little pleasure from these sources wants taste; he who receives pleasure from any other sources, has false or bad taste.

And it is thus that the term "taste" is to be distinguished from that of "judgment," with which it is constantly confounded. Judgment is a general term, expressing definite action of the intellect, and applicable to every kind of subject which can be submitted to it. There may be judgment of congruity, judgment of truth, judgment of justice, and judgment of difficulty and excellence. But all these exertions of the intellect are totally distinct from taste, properly so called, which is the instinctive and instant preferring of one material object to another without any obvious reason, except that it is proper to human nature in its perfection so to do.

Observe, however, I do not mean by excluding direct exertion of the intellect from ideas of beauty, to assert that beauty has no effect upon, nor connection with the intellect. All our moral feelings are so inwoven with our intellectual powers, that we cannot affect the one without in some degree addressing the other; and in all high ideas of beauty, it is more than probable that much of the pleasure depends on delicate and untraceable perceptions of fitness, propriety, and relation, which are purely intellectual, and through which we arrive at our noblest ideas of what is commonly and rightly called "intellectual beauty." But there is yet no immediate *exertion* of the intellect; that is to say, if a person receiving even the noblest ideas of simple beauty be asked *why* he likes the object exciting them, he will not be able to give any distinct reason, nor to trace in his mind any formed thought, to which he can appeal as a source of pleasure. He will say that the thing gratifies, fills, hallows, exalts his mind, but he will not be able to say why, or how. If he can, and if he can show that he perceives in the object any expression of distinct thought, he has received more than an idea of beauty—it is an idea of relation.

Ideas of beauty are among the noblest which can be presented to the human mind, invariably exalting and purifying it according to their degree; and it would appear that we are intended by the Deity to be constantly under their influence, because there is not one single object in nature which is not capable of conveying them, and which, to the rightly perceiving mind, does not present an incalculably greater number of beautiful than of deformed parts; there being in fact scarcely anything, in pure undiseased nature, like positive deformity, but only degrees of beauty, or such slight and rare points of permitted contrast as may render all around them more valuable by their opposition—spots of blackness in creation, to make its colors felt.

But although everything in nature is more or less beautiful, every species of object has its own kind and degree of beauty; some being in their own nature more beautiful than others, and few, if any, individuals possessing the utmost degree of beauty of which the species is capable. This utmost degree of specific beauty, necessarily coexistent with the utmost perfection of the object in other respects, is the ideal of the object.

Ideas of beauty, then, be it remembered, are the subjects of moral, but not of intellectual perception. By the investigation of them we shall be led to the knowledge of the ideal subjects of art.

. . . . .

(c) *Of Ideas of Relation:* I use this term rather as one of convenience than as adequately expressive of the vast class of ideas which I wish to be comprehended under it, namely, all those conveyable by art, which are the subjects of distinct intellectual perception and action, and which are therefore worthy of the name of thoughts. But as every thought, or definite exertion of intellect, implies two subjects, and some connection or relation inferred between them, the term "ideas of relation" is not incorrect, though it is inexpressive.

Under this head must be arranged everything productive of expression, sentiment, and character, whether in figures or landscapes, (for there may be as much definite expression and marked carrying out of particular thoughts in the treatment of inanimate as of animate nature,) everything relating to the conception of the subject and to the congruity and relation of its parts; not as they enhance each other's beauty by known and constant laws of composition, but as they give each other expression and meaning, by particular application, requiring distinct thought to discover or to enjoy; the choice, for instance, of a particular lurid or appalling light to illustrate an incident in itself terrible, or of a particular tone of pure color to prepare the mind for the expression of refined and delicate feeling; and, in a still higher sense, the invention of such incidents and thoughts as can be expressed in words as well as on canvas, and are totally independent of any means of art but such as may serve for the bare suggestion of them. The principal object in the foreground of Turner's "Building of Carthage" is a group of children sailing toy boats. The exquisite choice of this incident, as expressive of the ruling passion which was to be the source of future greatness, in preference to the tumult of busy stonemasons or arming soldiers, is quite as appreciable when it is told as when it is seen,—it has nothing to do with the technicalities of painting; a scratch of the pen would have conveyed the idea and spoken to the intellect as much as the elaborate realizations of color. Such a thought as this is something far above all art; it is epic poetry of the highest order. Claude, in subjects of the same kind, commonly introduces people carrying red trunks with iron locks about, and dwells, with infantine delight, on the lustre of the leather and the ornaments of the iron. The intellect can have no occupation here; we must look to the imitation or to nothing. Consequently, Turner rises above Claude in the very first instant of the conception of his picture, and acquires an intellectual superiority which no powers of the draughtsman or the artist (supposing that such existed in his antagonist) could ever wrest from him.

Such are the function and force of ideas of relation. They are what I have asserted in the second chapter of this section to be the noblest subjects of art. Dependent upon it only for expression, they cause all the rest of its complicated sources of pleasure to take, in comparison with them, the place of mere language or decoration; nay, even the noblest ideas of beauty sink at once beside these into subordination and subjection. It would add little to the influence of Landseer's picture above instanced, Chap. II, § 4, that the form of the dog should be conceived with every perfection of curve and color which its nature was capable of, and that the ideal lines should be carried out with the science of a Praxiteles; nay, the instant that the beauty so obtained interfered with the impression of agony and desolation, and drew the mind 10 away from the feeling of the animal to its outward form, that instant would the picture become monstrous and degraded. The utmost glory of the human body is a mean subject of contemplation, compared to the emotion, exertion, and character of that which animates it; the lustre of the limbs of the Aphrodite is faint beside that of the brow of the Madonna; and the divine form of the Greek god, except as it is the incar- 20 nation and expression of divine mind, is degraded beside the passion and the prophecy of the vaults of the Sistine.

Ideas of relation are, of course, with respect to art generally, the most extensive as the most important source of pleasure; and if we proposed entering upon the criticism of historical works, it would be absurd to attempt to do so without further subdivision and arrangement. But the old landscape painters got over so much canvas without either exercise of, or appeal to, the intellect, that we shall be little troubled with the subjects as far as they are concerned; and whatever subdivision we may adopt, as it will therefore have particular reference to the works of modern artists, will be better understood when we have obtained some knowledge of them in less important points.

By the term "ideas of relation," then, I mean in future to express all those sources of pleasure, which involve and require, at the instant of their perception, active exertion of the intellectual powers.

[1843]

THE STONES OF VENICE (II)

THE NATURE OF GOTHIC

If the reader will look back to the division of our subject which was made in the first chapter of the first volume, he will find that we are now about to enter upon the examination of that school of Venetian architecture which forms an intermediate step between the Byzantine and Gothic forms; but which I find may be conveniently 10 considered in its connection with the latter style. In order that we may discern the tendency of each step of this change, it will be wise in the outset to endeavor to form some general idea of its final result. We know already what the Byzantine architecture is from which the transition was made, but we ought to know something of the Gothic architecture into which it led. I shall endeavor therefore to give the reader 20 in this chapter an idea, at once broad and definite, of the true nature of *Gothic* architecture, properly so called; not of that of Venice only, but of universal Gothic: for it will be one of the most interesting parts of our subsequent inquiry to find out how far Venetian architecture reached the universal or perfect type of Gothic, and how far it either fell short of it, or assumed foreign and independent forms.

The principal difficulty in doing this arises from the fact that every building of the Gothic period differs in some important respect from every other; and many include features which, if they occurred in other buildings, would not be considered Gothic at all; so that all we have to reason 10 upon is merely, if I may be allowed so to express it, a greater or less degree of *Gothicness* in each building we examine. And it is this Gothicness,—the character which, according as it is found more or less in a building, makes it more or less Gothic,—of which I want to define the nature;—and I feel the same kind of difficulty in doing so which would be encountered by any one who undertook to 20 explain, for instance, the nature of Redness, without any actually red thing to point to, but only orange and purple things. Suppose he had only a piece of heather and a dead oak-leaf to do it with. He might say, the color which is mixed with the yellow in this oak-leaf, and with the blue in this heather, would be red, if you had it separate; but it would be difficult, nevertheless, to make the abstraction perfectly intelligible: and it is so in a far greater degree to make the abstraction of the Gothic character intelligible, because that character itself is made up of many mingled ideas, and can consist only in their union. That is to say, pointed arches do not constitute Gothic, nor vaulted roofs, nor flying buttresses, nor grotesque sculptures; but all or some of these things, and many other things with them, when they come together so as to have life.

Observe also, that, in the definition proposed, I shall only endeavor to analyze the idea which I suppose already to exist in the reader's mind. We all have some notion, most of us a very determined one, of the meaning of the term Gothic, but I know that many persons have this idea in their minds without being able to define it: that is to say, understanding generally that Westminster Abbey is Gothic, and St. Paul's is not, that Strasburg Cathedral is Gothic, and St. Peter's is not, they have, nevertheless, no clear notion of what it is that they recognize in the one or miss in the other, such as would enable them to say how far the work at Westminster or Strasburg is good and pure of its kind; still less to say of any nondescript building, like St. James's Palace or Windsor Castle, how much right Gothic element there is in it, and how much wanting. And I believe this inquiry to be a pleasant and profitable one; and that there will be found something more than usually interesting in tracing out this gray, shadowy, many-pinnacled image of the Gothic spirit within us; and discerning what fellowship there is between it and our northern hearts. And if, at any point of the inquiry, I should interfere with any of the reader's previously formed conceptions, and use the term Gothic in any sense which he would not willingly attach to it, I do not ask him to accept, but only to examine and understand, my interpretation, as necessary to the intelligibility of what follows in the rest of the work.

We have, then, the Gothic character submitted to our analysis, just as the rough mineral is submitted to that of the chemist, entangled with many other foreign substances, itself perhaps in no place pure, or ever to be obtained or seen in purity for more than an instant; but nevertheless a thing of definite and separate nature, however inextricable or confused in appearance. Now observe: the chemist defines his mineral by two separate kinds of character; one external, its crystalline form, hardness, lustre, etc.; the other internal, the proportions and nature of its constituent atoms. Exactly in the same manner, we shall find that Gothic architecture has external forms and internal elements. Its elements are certain mental tendencies of the builders, legibly expressed in it; as fancifulness, love of variety, love of richness, and such others. Its external forms are pointed arches, vaulted roofs, etc. And unless both the elements and the forms are there, we have no right to call the style Gothic. It is not enough that it has the Form, if it have not also the power and life. It is not enough that it has the Power, if it have not the form. We must therefore inquire into each of these characters successively; and determine first, what is the Mental Expression, and secondly, what the Material Form of Gothic architecture, properly so called.

Mental Power or Expression. What characters, we have to discover, did the Gothic builders love, or instinctively express in their work, as distinguished from all other builders?

Let us go back for a moment to our chemistry, and note that, in defining a mineral by its constituent parts, it is not one nor another of them, that can make up the mineral, but the union of all: for instance, it is neither in charcoal, nor in oxygen, nor in lime, that there is the making of chalk, but in the combination of all three in certain measures; they are all found in very different things from chalk, and there is nothing like chalk either in charcoal or in oxygen, but they are nevertheless necessary to its existence.

So in the various mental characters which make up the soul of Gothic. It is not one nor another that produces it; but their union in certain measures. Each one of them is found in many other architectures besides Gothic; but Gothic cannot exist where they are not found, or, at least, where their place is not in some way supplied. Only there is this great difference between the composition of the mineral and of the architectural style, that if we withdraw one of its elements from the stone, its form is utterly changed, and its existence as such and such a mineral is destroyed; but if we withdraw one of its mental elements from the Gothic style, it is only a little less Gothic than it was before, and the union of two or three of its elements is enough already to bestow a certain Gothicness of character, which gains in intensity as we add the others, and loses as we again withdraw them.

I believe, then, that the characteristic or *moral* elements of Gothic are the following, placed in the order of their importance:

1. Savageness.
2. Changefulness.
3. Naturalism.
4. Grotesqueness.
5. Rigidity.
6. Redundance.

These characters are here expressed as belonging to the building; as belonging to the builder, they would be expressed thus:—1. Savageness or Rudeness. 2. Love of Change. 3. Love of Nature. 4. Disturbed Imagination. 5. Obstinacy. 6. Generosity. And I repeat, that the withdrawal of any one, or any two, will not at once destroy the Gothic character of a building, but the removal of a majority of them will. I shall proceed to examine them in their order.

1. SAVAGENESS.—I am not sure when the word "Gothic" was first generally applied to the architecture of the North; but I presume that, whatever the date of its original usage, it was intended to imply reproach, and express the barbaric character of the nations among whom that architecture arose. It never implied that they were literally of Gothic lineage, far less that their architecture had been originally invented by the Goths themselves; but it did imply that they and their buildings together exhibited a degree of sternness and rudeness, which, in contradistinction to the character of southern and eastern nations, appeared like a perpetual

reflection of the contrast between the Goth and the Roman in their first encounter. And when that fallen Roman, in the utmost impotence of his luxury, and insolence of his guilt, became the model for the imitation of civilized Europe, at the close of the so-called Dark Ages, the word Gothic became a term of unmitigated contempt, not unmixed with aversion. From that contempt, by the exertion of the antiquaries and architects of this century, Gothic architecture has been sufficiently vindicated; and perhaps some among us, in our admiration of the magnificent science of its structure, and sacredness of its expression, might desire that the term of ancient reproach should be withdrawn, and some other, of more apparent honorableness, adopted in its place. There is no chance, as there is no need, of such a substitution. As far as the epithet was used scornfully, it was used falsely; but there is no reproach in the word, rightly understood; on the contrary, there is a profound truth, which the instinct of mankind almost unconsciously recognizes. It is true, greatly and deeply true, that the architecture of the North is rude and wild; but it is not true, that, for this reason, we are to condemn it, or despise. Far otherwise: I believe it is in this very character that it deserves our profoundest reverence.

The charts of the world which have been drawn up by modern science have thrown into a narrow space the expression of a vast amount of knowledge, but I have never yet seen any one pictorial enough to enable the spectator to imagine the kind of contrast in physical character which exists between Northern and Southern countries. We know the differences in detail, but we have not that broad glance and grasp which would enable us to feel them in their fulness. We know that gentians grow on the Alps, and olives on the Apennines; but we do not enough conceive for ourselves that variegated mosaic of the world's surface which a bird sees in its migration, that difference between the district of the gentian and of the olive which the stork and the swallow see far off, as they lean upon the sirocco wind. Let us, for a moment, try to raise ourselves even above the level of their flight, and imagine the Mediterranean lying beneath us like an irregular lake, and all its ancient promontories sleeping in the sun: here and there an angry spot of thunder, a gray stain of storm, moving upon the burning field; and here and there a fixed wreath of white volcano smoke, surrounded by its circle of ashes; but for the most part a great peacefulness of light, Syria and Greece, Italy and Spain, laid like pieces of 10 a golden pavement into the sea-blue, chased, as we stoop nearer to them, with bossy beaten work of mountain chains, and glowing softly with terraced gardens, and flowers heavy with frankincense, mixed among masses of laurel, and orange, and plumy palm, that abate with their gray-green shadows the burning of the marble rocks, and of the ledges of porphyry sloping under lucent sand. Then let us pass 20 farther toward the north, until we see the orient colors change gradually into a vast belt of rainy green, where the pastures of Switzerland, and poplar valleys of France, and dark forests of the Danube and Carpathians stretch from the mouths of the Loire to those of the Volga, seen through clefts in gray swirls of rain-cloud and flaky veils of the mist of the brooks, spreading low along the pasture lands: and then, 30 farther north still, to see the earth heave into mighty masses of leaden rock and heathy moor, bordering with a broad waste of gloomy purple that belt of field and wood, and splintering into irregular and grisly islands amidst the northern seas, beaten by storm, and chilled by ice-drift, and tormented by furious pulses of contending tide, until the roots of the last forests fail from among the hill ravines, 40 and the hunger of the north wind bites their peaks into barrenness; and, at last, the wall of ice, durable like iron, sets, deathlike, its white teeth against us out of the polar twilight. And, having once traversed in thought this gradation of the zoned iris of the earth in all its material vastness, let us go down nearer to it, and watch the parallel change in the belt of animal life; the multitudes of swift and 50 brilliant creatures that glance in the air and sea, or tread the sands of the southern zone; striped zebras and spotted leopards, glistening serpents, and birds arrayed in purple and scarlet. Let us contrast their delicacy and brilliancy of color, and swiftness of motion, with the frost-cramped strength, and shaggy covering, and dusky plumage of the northern tribes; contrast the Arabian horse with the Shetland, the tiger and leopard with the wolf and bear, the antelope with the elk, the bird of paradise with the osprey; and then, submissively acknowledging the great laws by which the earth and all that it bears are ruled throughout their being, let us not condemn but rejoice in the expression by man of his own rest in the statutes of the lands that gave him birth. Let us watch him with reverence as he sets side by side the burning gems, and smooths with soft sculpture the jasper pillars, that are to reflect a ceaseless sunshine, and rise into a cloudless sky: but not with less reverence let us stand by him, when, with rough strength and hurried stroke, he smites an uncouth animation out of the rocks which he has torn from among the moss of the moorland, and heaves into the darkened air the pile of iron buttress and rugged wall, instinct with work of an imagination as wild and wayward as the northern sea; creatures of ungainly shape and rigid limb, but full of wolfish life; fierce as the winds that beat, and changeful as the clouds that shade them.

There is, I repeat, no degradation, no reproach in this, but all dignity and honorableness: and we should err grievously in refusing either to recognize as an essential character of the existing architecture of the North, or to admit as a desirable character in that which it yet may be, this wildness of thought, and roughness of work; this look of mountain brotherhood between the cathedral and the Alp; this magnificence of sturdy power, put forth only the more energetically because the fine finger-touch was chilled away by the frosty wind, and the eye dimmed by the moor-mist, or blinded by the hail; this outspeaking of the strong spirit of men who may not gather redundant fruitage from the earth, nor bask in dreamy benignity of sunshine, but must break the rock for bread, and cleave the forest for fire, and show, even in what they did for their delight, some of the hard habits of the arm and heart that grew on them as they swung the ax or pressed the plough.

If, however, the savageness of Gothic architecture, merely as an expression of its origin among Northern nations, may be considered, in some sort, a noble character, it possesses a higher nobility still, when considered as an index, not of climate, but of religious principle.

In the 13th and 14th paragraphs of Chapter XXI of the first volume of this work, it was noticed that the systems of architectural ornament, properly so called, might be divided into three:—1. Servile ornament, in which the execution or power of the inferior workman is entirely subjected to the intellect of the higher;—2. Constitutional ornament, in which the executive inferior power is, to a certain point, emancipated and independent, having a will of its own, yet confessing its inferiority and rendering obedience to higher powers;—and 3. Revolutionary ornament, in which no executive inferiority is admitted at all. I must here explain the nature of these divisions at somewhat greater length.

Of Servile ornament, the principal schools are the Greek, Ninevite, and Egyptian; but their servility is of different kinds. The Greek master-workman was far advanced in knowledge and power above the Assyrian or Egyptian. Neither he nor those for whom he worked could endure the appearance of imperfection in anything; and, therefore, what ornament he appointed to be done by those beneath him was composed of mere geometrical forms,—balls, ridges, and perfectly symmetrical foliage,—which could be executed with absolute precision by line and rule, and were as perfect in their way, when completed, as his own figure sculpture. The Assyrian and Egyptian, on the contrary, less cognizant of accurate form in anything, were content to allow their figure sculpture to be executed by inferior workmen, but lowered the method of its treatment to a standard which every workman could reach, and then trained him by discipline so rigid, that there was no chance of his falling beneath the standard appointed. The Greek gave to the lower workman no subject which he could not

perfectly execute. The Assyrian gave him subjects which he could only execute imperfectly, but fixed a legal standard for his imperfection. The workman was, in both systems, a slave.

But in the mediæval, or especially Christian, system of ornament, this slavery is done away with altogether; Christianity having recognized, in small things as well as great, the individual value of every soul. But it not only recognizes its value; it confesses its imperfection, in only bestowing dignity upon the acknowledgment of unworthiness. That admission of lost power and fallen nature, which the Greek or Ninevite felt to be intensely painful, and, as far as might be, altogether refused, the Christian makes daily and hourly, contemplating the fact of it without fear, as tending, in the end, to God's greater glory. Therefore, to every spirit which Christianity summons to her service, her exhortation is: Do what you can, and confess frankly what you are unable to do; neither let your effort be shortened for fear of failure, nor your confession silenced for fear of shame. And it is, perhaps, the principal admirableness of the Gothic schools of architecture, that they thus receive the results of the labor of inferior minds; and out of fragments full of imperfection, and betraying that imperfection in every touch, indulgently raise up a stately and unaccusable whole.

But the modern English mind has this much in common with that of the Greek, that it intensely desires, in all things, the utmost completion or perfection compatible with their nature. This is a noble character in the abstract, but becomes ignoble when it causes us to forget the relative dignities of that nature itself, and to prefer the perfectness of the lower nature to the imperfection of the higher; not considering that as, judged by such a rule, all the brute animals would be preferable to man, because more perfect in their functions and kind, and yet are always held inferior to him, so also in the works of man, those which are more perfect in their kind are always inferior to those which are, in their nature, liable to more faults and shortcomings. For the finer the nature, the more flaws it will show through the clearness of it; and it is a law of this universe, that the best things shall be seldomest seen in their best form. The wild grass grows well and strongly, one year with another; but the wheat is, according to the greater nobleness of its nature, liable to the bitterer blight. And therefore, while in all things that we see or do, we are to desire perfection, and strive for it, we are nevertheless not to set the meaner thing, in its narrow accomplishment, above the nobler thing, in its mighty progress; not to esteem smooth minuteness above shattered majesty; not to prefer mean victory to honorable defeat; not to lower the level of our aim, that we may the more surely enjoy the complacency of success. But, above all, in our dealings with the souls of other men, we are to take care how we check, by severe requirement or narrow caution, efforts which might otherwise lead to a noble issue; and, still more, how we withhold our admiration from great excellencies, because they are mingled with rough faults. Now, in the make and nature of every man, however rude or simple, whom we employ in manual labor, there are some powers for better things; some tardy imagination, torpid capacity of emotion, tottering steps of thought, there are, even at the worst; and in most cases it is all our own fault that they *are* tardy or torpid. But they cannot be strengthened, unless we are content to take them in their feebleness, and unless we prize and honor them in their imperfection above the best and most perfect manual skill. And this is what we have to do with all our laborers; to look for the *thoughtful* part of them, and get that out of them, whatever we lose for it, whatever faults and errors we are obliged to take with it. For the best that is in them cannot manifest itself, but in company with much error. Understand this clearly: You can teach a man to draw a straight line, and to cut one; to strike a curved line, and to carve it; and to copy and carve any number of given lines or forms, with admirable speed and perfect precision; and you find his work perfect of its kind: but if you ask him to think about any of those forms, to consider if he cannot find any better in his own head, he stops;

his execution becomes hesitating; he thinks, and ten to one he thinks wrong; ten to one he makes a mistake in the first touch he gives to his work as a thinking being. But you have made a man of him for all that. He was only a machine before, an animated tool.

And observe, you are put to stern choice in this matter. You must either make a tool of the creature, or a man of him. You cannot make both. Men were not intended to work with the accuracy of tools, to be precise and perfect in all their actions. If you will have that precision out of them, and make their fingers measure degrees like cogwheels, and their arms strike curves like compasses, you must unhumanize them. All the energy of their spirits must be given to make cogs and compasses of themselves. All their attention and strength must go to the accomplishment of the mean act. The eye of the soul must be bent upon the fingerpoint, and the soul's force must fill all the invisible nerves that guide it, ten hours a day, that it may not err from its steely precision, and so soul and sight be worn away, and the whole human being be lost at last—a heap of sawdust, so far as its intellectual work in this world is concerned: saved only by its Heart, which cannot go into the form of cogs and compasses, but expands, after the ten hours are over, into fireside humanity. On the other hand, if you will make a man of the working creature, you cannot make a tool. Let him but begin to imagine, to think, to try to do anything worth doing; and the engine-turned precision is lost at once. Out come all his roughness, all his dulness, all his incapability; shame upon shame, failure upon failure, pause after pause: but out comes the whole majesty of him also; and we know the height of it only when we see the clouds settling upon him. And, whether the clouds be bright or dark, there will be transfiguration behind and within them.

And now, reader, look round this English room of yours, about which you have been proud so often, because the work of it was so good and strong, and the ornaments of it so finished. Examine again all those accurate mouldings, and perfect polishings, and unerring adjustments of the seasoned wood and tempered steel. Many a time you have exulted over them, and thought how great England was, because her slightest work was done so thoroughly. Alas! if read rightly, these perfectnesses are signs of a slavery in our England a thousand times more bitter and more degrading than that of the scourged African, or helot Greek. Men may be beaten, chained, tormented, yoked like cattle, slaughtered like summer flies, and yet remain in one sense, and the best sense, free. But to smother their souls within them, to blight and hew into rotting pollards the suckling branches of their human intelligence, to make the flesh and skin which, after the worm's work on it, is to see God, into leathern thongs to yoke machinery with,—this it is to be slave-masters indeed; and there might be more freedom in England, though her feudal lords' lightest words were worth men's lives, and though the blood of the vexed husbandman dropped in the furrows of her fields, than there is while the animation of her multitudes is sent like fuel to feed the factory smoke, and the strength of them is given daily to be wasted into the fineness of a web, or racked into the exactness of a line.

And, on the other hand, go forth again to gaze upon the old cathedral front, where you have smiled so often at the fantastic ignorance of the old sculptors: examine once more those ugly goblins, and formless monsters, and stern statues, anatomiless and rigid; but do not mock at them, for they are signs of the life and liberty of every workman who struck the stone; a freedom of thought, and rank in scale of being, such as no laws, no charters, no charities can secure; but which it must be the first aim of all Europe at this day to regain for her children.

Let me not be thought to speak wildly or extravagantly. It is verily this degradation of the operative into a machine, which, more than any other evil of the times, is leading the mass of the nations everywhere into vain, incoherent, destructive struggling for a freedom of which they cannot explain the nature to themselves. Their universal outcry against wealth, and against nobility, is not forced from them either by the pressure of famine, or the sting of mortified pride. These do much, and have done much in all ages; but the foundations of society were never yet shaken as they are at this day. It is not that men are ill fed, but that they have no pleasure in the work by which they make their bread, and therefore look to wealth as the only means of pleasure. It is not that men are pained by the scorn of the upper classes, but they cannot endure their own; for they feel that the kind of labor to which they are condemned is verily a degrading one, and makes them less than men. Never had the upper classes so much sympathy with the lower, or charity for them, as they have at this day, and yet never were they so much hated by them: for, of old, the separation between the noble and the poor was merely a wall built by law; now it is a veritable difference in level of standing, a precipice between upper and lower grounds in the field of humanity, and there is pestilential air at the bottom of it. I know not if a day is ever to come when the nature of right freedom will be understood, and when men will see that to obey another man, to labor for him, yield reverence to him or to his place, is not slavery. It is often the best kind of liberty,—liberty from care. The man who says to one, Go, and he goeth, and to another, Come, and he cometh, has, in most cases, more sense of restraint and difficulty than the man who obeys him. The movements of the one are hindered by the burden on his shoulder; of the other, by the bridle on his lips: there is no way by which the burden may be lightened; but we need not suffer from the bridle if we do not champ at it. To yield reverence to another, to hold ourselves and our lives at his disposal, is not slavery; often it is the noblest state in which a man can live in this world. There is, indeed, a reverence which is servile, that is to say, irrational or selfish: but there is also noble reverence, that is to say, reasonable and loving; and a man is never so noble as when he is reverent in this kind; nay, even if the feeling pass the bounds of mere reason, so that it be loving, a man is raised by it. Which had, in reality, most of the serf nature in him,—the Irish peasant who was lying in wait yesterday for his landlord, with his musket muzzle thrust through the ragged hedge; or that old mountain servant, who 200 years ago, at Inverkeithing, gave up his own life and the lives of his seven sons for his chief?— as each fell, calling forth his brother to the death, "Another for Hector!" And therefore, in all ages and all countries, reverence has been paid and sacrifice made by men to each other, not only without complaint, but rejoicingly; and famine, and peril, and sword, and all evil, and all shame, have been borne willingly in the causes of masters and kings; for all these gifts of the heart ennobled the men who gave, not less than the men who received them, and nature prompted, and God rewarded the sacrifice. But to feel their souls withering within them, unthanked, to find their whole being sunk into an unrecognized abyss, to be counted off into a heap of mechanism, numbered with its wheels, and weighed with its hammer strokes,— this, nature bade not,—this, God blesses not,—this, humanity for no long time is able to endure.

We have much studied and much perfected, of late, the great civilized invention of the division of labor; only we give it a false name. It is not, truly speaking, the labor that is divided; but the men:— Divided into mere segments of men— broken into small fragments and crumbs of life; so that all the little piece of intelligence that is left in a man is not enough to make a pin, or a nail, but exhausts itself in making the point of a pin or the head of a nail. Now it is a good and desirable thing, truly, to make many pins in a day; but if we could only see with what crystal sand their points were polished,—sand of human soul, much to be magnified before it can be discerned for what it is,—we should think there might be some loss in it also. And the great cry that rises from all our manufacturing cities, louder than their furnace blast, is all in very deed for this,—that we manufacture everything there except men; we blanch cotton, and strengthen steel, and refine sugar, and shape pottery; but to brighten, to strengthen, to refine, or to form a single living spirit, never enters into our estimate of advantages. And all the evil to which that cry is urging our myriads can be met only in one way: not by teaching nor preaching, for to teach them is but to show them their misery, and to preach to them, if we do nothing more than preach, is to mock at it. It can be met only by a right understanding, on the part of all classes, of what kinds of labor are good for men, raising them, and making them happy; by a determined sacrifice of such convenience, or beauty, or cheapness as is to be got only by the degradation of the workman; and by equally determined demand for the products and results of healthy and ennobling labor.

And how, it will be asked, are these products to be recognized, and this demand to be regulated? Easily: by the observance of three broad and simple rules:

1. Never encourage the manufacture of any article not absolutely necessary, in the production of which *Invention* has no share.

2. Never demand an exact finish for its own sake, but only for some practical or noble end.

3. Never encourage imitation or copying of any kind, except for the sake of preserving record of great works.

The second of these principles is the only one which directly rises out of the consideration of our immediate subject; but I shall briefly explain the meaning and extent of the first also, reserving the enforcement of the third for another place.

1. Never encourage the manufacture of anything not necessary, in the production of which invention has no share.

For instance. Glass beads are utterly unnecessary, and there is no design or thought employed in their manufacture. They are formed by first drawing out the glass into rods; these rods are chopped up into fragments of the size of beads by the human hand, and the fragments are then rounded in the furnace. The men who chop up the rods sit at their work all day, their hands vibrating with a perpetual and exquisitely timed palsy, and the beads dropping beneath their vibration like hail. Neither they, nor the men who draw out the rods or fuse the fragments, have the smallest occasion for the use of any single human faculty; and every young lady, therefore, who buys glass beads is engaged in the slave-trade, and in a much more cruel one than that which we have so long been endeavoring to put down.

But glass cups and vessels may become the subjects of exquisite invention; and if in buying these we pay for the invention, that is to say, for the beautiful form, or color, or engraving, and not for mere finish of execution, we are doing good to humanity.

So, again, the cutting of precious stones, in all ordinary cases, requires little exertion of any mental faculty; some tact and judgment in avoiding flaws, and so on, but nothing to bring out the whole mind. Every person who wears cut jewels merely for the sake of their value is, therefore, a slave-driver.

But the working of the goldsmith, and the various designing of grouped jewellery and enamel-work, may become the subject of the most noble human intelligence. Therefore, money spent in the purchase of well-designed plate, of precious engraved vases, cameos, or enamels, does good to humanity; and, in work of this kind, jewels may be employed to heighten its splendor; and their cutting is then a price paid for the attainment of a noble end, and thus perfectly allowable.

I shall perhaps press this law farther elsewhere, but our immediate concern is chiefly with the second, namely, never to demand an exact finish, when it does not lead to a noble end. For observe, I have only dwelt upon the rudeness of Gothic, or any other kind of imperfectness, as admirable, where it was impossible to get design or thought without it. If you are to have the thought of a rough and untaught man, you must have it in a rough and untaught way; but from an educated man, who can without effort express his thoughts in an educated way, take the graceful expression, and be thankful. Only *get* the thought, and do not silence the peasant because he cannot speak good grammar, or until you have taught him his grammar. Grammar and refinement are good things, both, only be sure of the better thing first. And thus in art, delicate finish is desirable

from the greatest masters, and is always given by them. In some places Michael Angelo, Leonardo, Phidias, Perugino, Turner, all finished with the most exquisite care; and the finish they give always leads to the fuller accomplishment of their noble purposes. But lower men than these cannot finish, for it requires consummate knowledge to finish consummately, and then we must take their thoughts as they are able to give them. So the rule is simple: Always look for invention first, and after that, for such execution as will help the invention, and as the inventor is capable of without painful effort, and *no more*. Above all, demand no refinement of execution where there is no thought, for that is slaves' work, unredeemed. Rather choose rough work than smooth work, so only that the practical purpose be answered, and never imagine there is reason to be proud of anything that may be accomplished by patience and sand-paper.

I shall only give one example, which however will show the reader what I mean, from the manufacture already alluded to, that of glass. Our modern glass is exquisitely clear in its substance, true in its form, accurate in its cutting. We are proud of this. We ought to be ashamed of it. The old Venice glass was muddy, inaccurate in all its forms, and clumsily cut, if at all. And the old Venetian was justly proud of it. For there is this difference between the English and Venetian workman, that the former thinks only of accurately matching his patterns, and getting his curves perfectly true and his edges perfectly sharp, and becomes a mere machine for rounding curves and sharpening edges; while the old Venetian cared not a whit whether his edges were sharp or not, but he invented a new design for every glass that he made, and never moulded a handle or a lip without a new fancy in it. And therefore, though some Venetian glass is ugly and clumsy enough when made by clumsy and uninventive workmen, other Venetian glass is so lovely in its forms that no price is too great for it; and we never see the same form in it twice. Now you cannot have the finish and the varied form too. If the workman is thinking about his edges, he cannot be thinking of his design; if of his design, he cannot think of his edges. Choose whether you will pay for the lovely form or the perfect finish, and choose at the same moment whether you will make the worker a man or a grindstone.

Nay, but the reader interrupts me,—"If the workman can design beautifully, I would not have him kept at the furnace. Let him be taken away and made a gentleman, and have a studio, and design his glass there, and I will have it blown and cut for him by common workmen, and so I will have my design and my finish too."

All ideas of this kind are founded upon two mistaken suppositions: the first, that one man's thoughts can be, or ought to be, executed by another man's hands; the second, that manual labor is a degradation, when it is governed by intellect.

On a large scale, and in work determinable by line and rule, it is indeed both possible and necessary that the thoughts of one man should be carried out by the labor of others; in this sense I have already defined the best architecture to be the expression of the mind of manhood by the hands of childhood. But on a smaller scale, and in a design which cannot be mathematically defined, one man's thoughts can never be expressed by another: and the difference between the spirit of touch of the man who is inventing, and of the man who is obeying directions, is often all the difference between a great and a common work of art. How wide the separation is between original and second-hand execution, I shall endeavor to show elsewhere; it is not so much to our purpose here as to mark the other and more fatal error of despising manual labor when governed by intellect; for it is no less fatal an error to despise it when thus regulated by intellect, than to value it for its own sake. We are always in these days endeavoring to separate the two; we want one man to be always thinking, and another to be always working, and we call one a gentleman, and the other an operative; whereas the workman ought often to be thinking, and the thinker often to be working, and both should be gentlemen, in the best sense. As it is, we make both ungentle, the one envying, the other despising, his brother; and the mass of society is made up of morbid thinkers, and miserable workers. Now it is only by labor that thought can be made healthy, and only by thought that labor can be made happy, and the two cannot be separated with impunity. It would be well if all of us were good handicraftsmen in some kind, and the dishonor of manual labor done away with altogether; so that though there should still be a trenchant distinction of race between nobles and commoners, there should not, among the latter, be a trenchant distinction of employment, as between idle and working men, or between men of liberal and illiberal professions. All professions should be liberal, and there should be less pride felt in peculiarity of employment, and more in excellence of achievement. And yet more, in each several profession, no master should be too proud to do its hardest work. The painter should grind his own colors; the architect work in the mason's yard with his men; the master-manufacturer be himself a more skilful operative than any man in his mills; and the distinction between one man and another be only in experience and skill, and the authority and wealth which these must naturally and justly obtain.

I should be led far from the matter in hand, if I were to pursue this interesting subject. Enough, I trust, has been said to show the reader that the rudeness or imperfection which at first rendered the term "Gothic" one of reproach is indeed, when rightly understood, one of the most noble characters of Christian architecture, and not only a noble but an *essential* one. It seems a fantastic paradox, but it is nevertheless a most important truth, that no architecture can be truly noble which is *not* imperfect. And this is easily demonstrable. For since the architect, whom we will suppose capable of doing all in perfection, cannot execute the whole with his own hands, he must either make slaves of his workmen in the old Greek, and present English fashion, and level his work to a slave's capacities, which is to degrade it; or else he must take his workmen as he finds them, and let them show their weaknesses together with their strength, which will involve the Gothic imperfection, but render the whole work as noble as the intellect of the age can make it.

But the principle may be stated more broadly still. I have confined the illustration of it to architecture, but I must not leave it as if true of architecture only. Hitherto I have used the words imperfect and perfect merely to distinguish between work grossly unskilful, and work executed with average precision and science; and I have been pleading that any degree of unskilfulness should be admitted, so only that the laborer's mind had room for expression. But, accurately speaking, no good work whatever can be perfect, and *the demand for perfection is always a sign of a misunderstanding of the ends of art.*

This for two reasons, both based on everlasting laws. The first, that no great man ever stops working till he has reached his point of failure: that is to say, his mind is always far in advance of his powers of execution, and the latter will now and then give way in trying to follow it; besides that he will always give to the inferior portions of his work only such inferior attention as they require; and according to his greatness he becomes so accustomed to the feeling of dissatisfaction with the best he can do, that in moments of lassitude or anger with himself he will not care though the beholder be dissatisfied also. I believe there has only been one man who would not acknowledge this necessity, and strove always to reach perfection, Leonardo; the end of his vain effort being merely that he would take ten years to a picture and leave it unfinished. And therefore, if we are to have great men working at all, or less men doing their best, the work will be imperfect, however beautiful. Of human work none but what is bad can be perfect, in its own bad way.

The second reason is, that imperfection is in some sort essential to all that we know of life. It is the sign of life in a mortal body, that is to say, of a state of progress and change. Nothing that lives is, or can be, rigidly perfect; part of it is decaying, part nascent. The foxglove blossom,—a third part bud, a third part past, a third part in full bloom,—is a type of the life of this world. And in all things that live there are certain irregularities and deficiencies which are not only signs of life, but sources of beauty. No human face is exactly the same in its lines on each side, no leaf perfect in its lobes, no branch in its symmetry. All admit irregularity as they imply change; and to banish imperfection is to destroy expression, to check exertion, to paralyze vitality. All things are literally better, lovelier, and more beloved for the imperfections which have been divinely appointed, that the law of human life may be Effort, and the law of human judgment, Mercy.

Accept this then for a universal law, that neither architecture nor any other noble work of man can be good unless it be imperfect; and let us be prepared for the otherwise strange fact, which we shall discern clearly as we approach the period of the Renaissance, that the first cause of the fall of the arts of Europe was a relentless requirement of perfection, incapable alike either of being silenced by veneration for greatness, or softened into forgiveness of simplicity.

. Thus far then of the Rudeness or Savageness, which is the first mental element of Gothic architecture. It is an element in many other healthy architectures also, as in Byzantine and Romanesque; but true Gothic cannot exist without it.

The second mental element above named was CHANGEFULNESS or Variety.

I have already enforced the allowing independent operation to the inferior workman, simply as a duty *to him,* and as ennobling the architecture by rendering it more Christian. We have now to consider what reward we obtain for the performance of this duty, namely, the perpetual variety of every feature of the building.

Wherever the workman is utterly enslaved, the parts of the building must of course be absolutely like each other; for the perfection of his execution can only be reached by exercising him in doing one thing, and giving him nothing else to do. The degree in which the workman is degraded may be thus known at a glance, by observing whether the several parts of the building are similar or not; and if, as in Greek work, all the capitals are alike, and all the mouldings unvaried, then the degradation is complete; if, as in Egyptian or Ninevite work, though the manner of executing certain figures is always the same, the order of design is perpetually varied, the degradation is less total; if, as in Gothic work, there is perpetual change both in design and execution, the workman must have been altogether set free.

How much the beholder gains from the liberty of the laborer may perhaps be questioned in England, where one of the strongest instincts in nearly every mind is that Love of Order which makes us desire that our house windows should pair like our carriage horses, and allows us to yield our faith unhesitatingly to architectural theories which fix a form for everything, and forbid variation from it. I would not impeach love of order: it is one of the most useful elements of the English mind; it helps us in our commerce and in all purely practical matters; and it is in many cases one of the foundation-stones of morality. Only do not let us suppose that love of order is love of art. It is true that order, in its highest sense, is one of the necessities of art, just as time is a necessity of music; but love of order has no more to do with our right enjoyment of architecture or painting, than love of punctuality with the appreciation of an opera. Experience, I fear, teaches us that accurate and methodical habits in daily life are seldom characteristic of those who either quickly perceive, or richly possess, the creative powers of art; there is, however, nothing inconsistent between the two instincts, and nothing to hinder us from retaining our business habits, and yet fully allowing and enjoying the noblest gifts of Invention. We already do so, in every other branch of art except architecture, and we only do *not* so there because we have been taught that it would be wrong. Our architects gravely inform us that, as there are four rules of arithmetic, there are five orders of architecture; we, in our simplicity, think that this sounds consistent, and believe them. They inform us also that there is one proper form for Corinthian capitals, another for Doric, and another for Ionic. We, considering that there is also a proper form for the letters A, B, and C, think that this also sounds consistent, and accept the proposition. Understanding, therefore, that one form of the said capitals is proper, and no other, and having a conscientious horror of all impropriety, we allow the architect to provide us with the said capitals, of the proper form, in such and such a quantity, and in all other points to take care that the legal forms are observed; which having done, we rest in forced confidence that we are well housed.

But our higher instincts are not deceived. We take no pleasure in the building provided for us, resembling that which we take in a new book or a new picture. We may be proud of its size, complacent in its correctness, and happy in its convenience. We may take the same pleasure in its symmetry and workmanship as in a well-ordered room, or a skilful piece of manufacture. And this we suppose to be all the pleasure that architecture was ever intended to give us. The idea of reading a building as we would read Milton or Dante, and getting the same kind of delight out of the stones as out of the stanzas, never enters our minds for a moment. And for good reason:—There is indeed rhythm in the verses, quite as strict as the symmetries or rhythm of the architecture, and a thousand times more beautiful, but there is something else than rhythm. The verses were neither made to order, nor to match, as the capitals were; and we have therefore a kind of pleasure in them other than a sense of propriety. But it requires a strong effort of common sense to shake ourselves quit of all that we have been taught for the last two centuries, and wake to the perception of a truth just as simple and certain as it is new: that great art, whether expressing itself in words, colors, or stones, does *not* say the same thing over and over again; that the merit of architecture, as of every other art, consists in its saying new and different things; that to repeat itself is no more a characteristic of genius in marble than it is of genius in print; and that we may, without offending any laws of good taste, require of an architect, as we do of a novelist, that he should be not only correct, but entertaining.

Yet all this is true, and self-evident; only hidden from us, as many other self-evident things are, by false teaching. Nothing is a great work of art, for the production of which either rules or models can be given. Exactly so far as architecture works on known rules, and from given models, it is not an art, but a manufacture; and it is, of the two procedures, rather less rational (because more easy) to copy capitals or mouldings from Phidias, and call ourselves architects, than to copy heads and hands from Titian, and call ourselves painters.

Let us then understand at once that change or variety is as much a necessity to the human heart and brain in buildings as in books; that there is no merit, though there is some occasional use, in monotony; and that we must no more expect to derive either pleasure or profit from an architecture whose ornaments are of one pattern, and whose pillars are of one proportion, than we should out of a universe in which the clouds were all of one shape, and the trees all of one size.

And this we confess in deeds, though not in words. All the pleasure which the people of the nineteenth century take in art, is in pictures, sculpture, minor objects of virtù, or mediæval architecture, which we enjoy under the term picturesque: no pleasure is taken anywhere in modern buildings, and we find all men of true feeling delighting to escape out of modern cities into natural scenery: hence, as I shall hereafter show, that peculiar love of landscape, which is characteristic of the age. It would be well, if, in all other matters, we were as ready to put up with what we dislike, for the sake of compliance with established law, as we are in architecture.

How so debased a law ever came to be established, we shall see when we come to describe the Renaissance schools: here we have only to note, as the second most essential element of the Gothic spirit, that it broke through that law wherever it found it in existence; it not only dared, but delighted in, the infringement of every servile principle; and invented a series of forms of which the merit was, not merely they they were new, but that they were *capable of perpetual novelty*. The pointed arch was not merely a bold variation from the round, but it admitted of millions of variations in itself; for the proportions of a pointed arch are changeable to infinity, while a circular arch is always the same. The grouped shaft was not merely a bold variation from the single one, but it admitted of millions of variations in its grouping, and in the proportions resultant from its grouping. The introduction of tracery was not only a startling change in the treatment of window lights, but admitted endless changes in the interlacement of the tracery bars themselves. So that, while in all living Christian architecture, the love of variety exists, the Gothic schools exhibited that love in culminating energy; and their influence, wherever it extended itself, may be sooner and farther traced by this character than by any other; the tendency to the adoption of Gothic types being always first shown by greater irregularity, and richer variation in the forms of the architecture it is about to supersede, long before the appearance of the pointed arch or of any other recognizable *outward* sign of the Gothic mind.

We must, however, herein note carefully what distinction there is between a healthy and a diseased love of change; for as it was in healthy love of change that the Gothic architecture rose, it was partly in consequence of diseased love of change that it was destroyed. In order to understand this clearly, it will be necessary to consider the different ways in which change and monotony are presented to us in nature; both having their use, like darkness and light, and the one incapable of being enjoyed without the other: change being most delightful after some prolongation of monotony, as light appears most brilliant after the eyes have been for some time closed.

I believe that the true relations of monotony and change may be most simply understood by observing them in music. We may therein notice first, that there is a sublimity and majesty in monotony, which there is not in rapid or frequent variation. This is true throughout all nature. The greater part of the sublimity of the sea depends on its monotony; so also that of desolate moor and mountain scenery; and especially the sublimity of motion, as in the quiet, unchanged fall and rise of an engine beam. So also there is sublimity in darkness which there is not in light.

Again, monotony, after a certain time, or beyond a certain degree, becomes either uninteresting or intolerable, and the musician is obliged to break it in one or two ways: either while the air or passage is perpetually repeated, its notes are variously enriched and harmonized; or else, after a certain number of repeated passages, an entirely new passage is introduced, which is more or less delightful according to the length of the previous monotony. Nature, of course, uses both these kinds of variation perpetually. The sea-waves, resembling each other in general mass, but none like its brother in minor divisions and curves, are a monotony of the first kind; the great plain, broken by an emergent rock or clump of trees, is a monotony of the second.

Farther: in order to the enjoyment of the change in either case, a certain degree of patience is required from the hearer or observer. In the first case, he must be satisfied to endure with patience the recurrence of the great masses of sound or form, and to seek for entertainment in a careful watchfulness of the minor details. In the second case, he must bear patiently the infliction of the monotony for some moments, in order to feel the full refreshment of the change. This is true even of the shortest musical passage in which the element of monotony is employed. In cases of more majestic monotony, the patience required is so considerable that it becomes a kind of pain,—a price paid for the future pleasure.

Again: the talent of the composer is not in the monotony, but in the changes: he may show feeling and taste by his use of monotony in certain places or degrees; that is to say, by his *various* employment of it; but it is always in the new arrangement or invention that his intellect is shown, and not in the monotony which relieves it.

Lastly: if the pleasure of change be too often repeated, it ceases to be delightful, for then change itself becomes monotonous, and we are driven to seek delight in extreme and fantastic degrees of it. This is the diseased love of change of which we have above spoken.

From these facts we may gather generally that monotony is, and ought to be, in itself painful to us, just as darkness is; that an architecture which is altogether monotonous is a dark or dead architecture; and of those who love it, it may be truly said, "they love darkness rather than light." But

monotony in certain measure, used in order to give value to change, and above all, that *transparent* monotony, which, like the shadows of a great painter, suffers all manner of dimly suggested form to be seen through the body of it, is an essential in architectural as in all other composition; and the endurance of monotony has about the same place in a healthy mind that the endurance of darkness has: that is to say, as a strong intellect will have pleasure in the solemnities of storm and twilight, and in the broken and mysterious lights that gleam among them, rather than in mere brilliancy and glare, while a frivolous mind will dread the shadow and the storm; and as a great man will be ready to endure much darkness of fortune in order to reach greater eminence of power or felicity, while an inferior man will not pay the price; exactly in like manner a great mind will accept, or even delight in, monotony which would be wearisome to an inferior intellect, because it has more patience and power of expectation, and is ready to pay the full price for the great future pleasure of change. But in all cases it is not that the noble nature loves monotony, any more than it loves darkness or pain. But it can bear with it, and receive a high pleasure in the endurance or patience, a pleasure necessary to the well-being of this world; while those who will not submit to the temporary sameness, but rush from one change to another, gradually dull the edge of change itself, and bring a shadow and weariness over the whole world from which there is no more escape.

From these general uses of variety in the economy of the world, we may at once understand its use and abuse in architecture. The variety of the Gothic schools is the more healthy and beautiful, because in many cases it is entirely unstudied, and results, not from mere love of change, but from practical necessities. For in one point of view Gothic is not only the best, but the *only rational* architecture, as being that which can fit itself most easily to all services, vulgar or noble. Undefined in its slope of roof, height of shaft, breadth of arch, or disposition of ground plan, it can shrink into a turret, expand into a hall, coil into a staircase, or spring into a spire, with undegraded grace and unexhausted energy; and whenever it finds occasion for change in its form or purpose, it submits to it without the slightest sense of loss either to its unity or majesty,—subtle and flexible like a fiery serpent, but ever attentive to the voice of the charmer. And it is one of the chief virtues of the Gothic builders, that they never suffered ideas of outside symmetries and consistencies to interfere with the real use and value of what they did. If they wanted a window, they opened one; a room, they added one; a buttress, they built one; utterly regardless of any established conventionalities of external appearance, knowing (as indeed it always happened) that such daring interruptions of the formal plan would rather give additional interest to its symmetry than injure it. So that, in the best times of Gothic, a useless window would rather have been opened in an unexpected place for the sake of the surprise, than a useful one forbidden for the sake of symmetry. Every successive architect, employed upon a great work, built the pieces he added in his own way, utterly regardless of the style adopted by his predecessors; and if two towers were raised in nominal correspondence at the sides of a cathedral front, one was nearly sure to be different from the other, and in each the style at the top to be different from the style at the bottom.

These marked variations were, however, only permitted as part of the great system of perpetual change which ran through every member of Gothic design, and rendered it as endless a field for the beholder's inquiry as for the builder's imagination: change, which in the best schools is subtle and delicate, and rendered more delightful by intermingling of a noble monotony; in the more barbaric schools is somewhat fantastic and redundant; but, in all, a necessary and constant condition of the life of the school. Sometimes the variety is in one feature, sometimes in another; it may be in the capitals or crockets, in the niches or the traceries, or in all together, but in some one or other of the features it will be found always. If the mouldings are constant, the surface sculpture will change; if the capitals are of a fixed design, the traceries will change; if the traceries are monotonous, the capitals will change; and if even, as in some fine schools, the early English for example, there is the slightest approximation to an unvarying type of mouldings, capitals, and floral decoration, the variety is found in the disposition of the masses, and in the figure sculpture.

I must now refer for a moment, before we quit the consideration of this, the second mental element of Gothic, to the opening of the third chapter of the *Seven Lamps of Architecture,* in which the distinction was drawn (§ 2) between man gathering and man governing; between his acceptance of the sources of delight from nature, and his development of authoritative or imaginative power in their arrangement: for the two mental elements, not only of Gothic, but of all good architecture, which we have just been examining, belong to it, and are admirable in it, chiefly as it is, more than any other subject of art, the work of man, and the expression of the average power of man. A picture or poem is often little more than a feeble utterance of man's admiration of something out of himself; but architecture approaches more to a creation of his own, born of his necessities, and expressive of his nature. It is also, in some sort, the work of the whole race, while the picture or statue is the work of one only, in most cases more highly gifted than his fellows. And therefore we may expect that the first two elements of good architecture should be expressive of some great truths commonly belonging to the whole race, and necessary to be understood or felt by them in all their work that they do under the sun. And observe what they are: the confession of Imperfection, and the confession of Desire of Change. The building of the bird and the bee needs not express anything like this. It is perfect and unchanging. But just because we are something better than birds or bees, our building must confess that we have not reached the perfection we can imagine, and cannot rest in the condition we have attained. If we pretend to have reached either perfection or satisfaction, we have degraded ourselves and our work. God's work only may express that; but ours may never have that sentence written upon it,—"And behold, it was very good." And, observe again, it is not merely as it renders the edifice a book of various knowledge, or a mine of precious thought, that variety is essential to its nobleness. The vital principle is not the love of *Knowledge,* but the love of *Change.* It is that strange *disquietude* of the Gothic spirit that is its greatness; that restlessness of the dreaming mind, that wanders hither and thither among the niches, and flickers feverishly around the pinnacles, and frets and fades in labyrinthine knots and shadows along wall and roof, and yet is not satisfied, nor shall be satisfied. The Greek could stay in his triglyph furrow, and be at peace; but the work of the Gothic heart is fretwork still, and it can neither rest in, nor from, its labor, but must pass on, sleeplessly, until its love of change shall be pacified for ever in the change that must come alike on them that wake and them that sleep. . . .

Last, because the least essential, of the constituent elements of this noble school, was placed that of REDUNDANCE,—the uncalculating bestowal of the wealth of its labor. There is, indeed, much Gothic, and that of the best period, in which this element is hardly traceable, and which depends for its effect almost exclusively on loveliness of simple design and grace of uninvolved proportion; still, in the most characteristic buildings, a certain portion of their effect depends upon accumulation of ornament; and many of those which have most influence on the minds of men, have attained it by means of this attribute alone. And although, by careful study of the school, it is possible to arrive at a condition of taste which shall be better contented by a few perfect lines than by a whole façade covered with fretwork, the building which only satisfies such a taste is not to be considered the best. For the very first requirement of Gothic architecture being, as we saw above, that it shall both admit the aid, and appeal to the admiration, of the rudest as well as the most refined minds, the richness of the work is, paradoxical as the statement may appear, a part of its humility. No architecture is so haughty as that which is simple; which refuses to address the eye, except in a few clear and forceful lines; which implies, in offering so little to our regards, that all it has offered is perfect; and dis-

dains, either by the complexity or the attractiveness of its features, to embarrass our investigation, or betray us into delight. That humility, which is the very life of the Gothic school, is shown not only in the imperfection, but in the accumulation, of ornament. The inferior rank of the workman is often shown as much in the richness, as the roughness, of his work; and if the cooperation of every hand, and the sympathy of every heart, are to be received, we must be content to allow the redundance which disguises the failure of the feeble, and wins the regard of the inattentive. There are, however, far nobler interests mingling, in the Gothic heart, with the rude love of decorative accumulation: a magnificent enthusiasm, which feels as if it never could do enough to reach the fulness of its ideal; an unselfishness of sacrifice, which would rather cast fruitless labor before the altar than stand idle in the market; and, finally, a profound sympathy with the fulness and wealth of the material universe, rising out of that Naturalism whose operation we have already endeavored to define. The sculptor who sought for his models among the forest leaves, could not but quickly and deeply feel that complexity need not involve the loss of grace, nor richness that of repose; and every hour which he spent in the study of the minute and various work of Nature, made him feel more forcibly the barrenness of what was best in that of man: nor is it to be wondered at, that, seeing her perfect and exquisite creations poured forth in a profusion which conception could not grasp nor calculation sum, he should think that it ill became him to be niggardly of his own rude craftsmanship; and where he saw throughout the universe a faultless beauty lavished on measureless spaces of broidered field and blooming mountain, to grudge his poor and imperfect labor to the few stones that he had raised one upon another, for habitation or memorial. The years of his life passed away before his task was accomplished; but generation succeeded generation with unwearied enthusiasm, and the cathedral front was at last lost in the tapestry of its traceries, like a rock among the thickets and herbage of spring.

[1853]

ARATRA PENTELICI (Lecture I)

THE DIVISION OF ARTS

If, as is commonly believed, the subject of study which it is my special function to bring before you had no relation to the great interests of mankind, I should have less courage in asking for your attention to-day than when I first addressed you; though, even then, I did not do so without painful diffidence. For at this moment, even supposing that in other places it were possible for men to pursue their ordinary avocations undisturbed by indignation or pity,—here, at least, in the midst of the deliberative and religious influences of England, only one subject, I am well assured, can seriously occupy your thoughts—the necessity, namely, of determining how it has come to pass that, in these recent days, iniquity the most reckless and monstrous can be committed unanimously, by men more generous than ever yet in the world's history were deceived into deeds of cruelty; and that prolonged agony of body and spirit, such as we should shrink from inflicting wilfully on a single criminal, has become the appointed and accepted portion of unnumbered multitudes of innocent persons, inhabiting the districts of the world which, of all others, as it seemed, were best instructed in the laws of civilization, and most richly invested with the honor, and indulged in the felicity, of peace.

Believe me, however, the subject of Art —instead of being foreign to these deep questions of social duty and peril—is so vitally connected with them, that it would be impossible for me now to pursue the line of thought in which I began these lectures, because so ghastly an emphasis would be given to every sentence by the force of passing events. It is well, then, that in the plan I have laid down for your study, we shall now be led into the examination of technical details, or abstract conditions of sentiment; so that the hours you spend with me may be times of repose from heavier thoughts. But it chances strangely that, in this course of minutely detailed study, I have first to set before you the most essential piece of human workman-ship, the plough, at the very moment when (you may see the announcement in the journals either of yesterday or the day before) the swords of your soldiers have been sent for *to be sharpened,* and not at all to be beaten into ploughshares. I permit myself, therefore, to remind you of the watchword of all my earnest writings—"Soldiers of the Ploughshare, instead of Soldiers of the Sword,"—and I know it my duty to assert to you that the work we enter upon to-day is no trivial one, but full of solemn hope; the hope, namely, that among you there may be found men wise enough to lead the national passions toward the arts of peace, instead of the arts of war.

I say, the work "we enter upon," because the first four lectures I gave in the spring were wholly prefatory; and the following three only defined for you methods of practice. To-day we begin the systematic analysis and progressive study of our subject.

In general, the three great, or fine, Arts of Painting, Sculpture, and Architecture, are thought of as distinct from the lower and more mechanical formative arts, such as carpentry or pottery. But we cannot, either verbally, or with any practical advantage, admit such classification. How are we to distinguish painting on canvas from painting on china?—or painting on china from painting on glass?—or painting on glass from infusion of color into any vitreous substance, such as enamel?—or the infusion of color into glass and enamel from the infusion of color into wool or silk, and weaving of pictures in tapestry, or patterns in dress? You will find that although, in ultimately accurate use of the word, painting must be held to mean only the laying of a pigment on a surface with a soft instrument; yet, in broad comparison of the functions of Art, we must conceive of one and the same great artistic faculty, as governing *every mode of disposing colors in a permanent relation on, or in, a solid substance;* whether it be tinting canvas, or dyeing stuffs; inlaying metals with fused flint, or coating walls with colored stone.

Similarly, the word "Sculpture,"—though in ultimate accuracy it is to be limited to the development of form in hard substances by cutting away portions of their mass—in broad definition, must be held to signify *the reduction of any shapeless mass of solid matter into an intended shape,* whatever the consistence of the substance, or nature of the instrument employed; whether we carve a granite mountain, or a piece of box-wood, and whether we use, for our forming instrument, axe, or hammer, or chisel, or our own hands, or water to soften, or fire to fuse;—whenever and however we bring a shapeless thing into shape, we do so under the laws of the one great art of Sculpture.

Having thus broadly defined painting and sculpture, we shall see that there is, in the third place, a class of work separated from both, in a specific manner, and including a great group of arts which neither, of necessity, *tint,* nor for the sake of form merely, *shape* the substances they deal with; but construct or arrange them with a view to the resistance of some external force. We construct, for instance, a table with a flat top, and some support of prop, or leg, proportioned in strength to such weights as the table is intended to carry. We construct a ship out of planks, or plates of iron, with reference to certain forces of impact to be sustained, and of inertia to be overcome; or we construct a wall or roof with distinct reference to forces of pressure and oscillation, to be sustained or guarded against; and, therefore, in every case, with especial consideration of the strength of our materials, and the nature of that strength, elastic, tenacious, brittle, and the like.

Now, although this group of arts nearly always involves the putting of two or more separate pieces together, we must not define it by that accident. The blade of an oar is not less formed with reference to external force than if it were made of many pieces; and the frame of a boat, whether hollowed out of a tree-trunk, or constructed of planks nailed together, is essentially the same piece of art, to be judged by its buoyancy and capacity of progression. Still, from the most wonderful piece of all architecture, the human skeleton, to this simple one, the ploughshare, on which it depends for its subsistence, *the putting of two or more pieces together* is curiously necessary to the perfectness of every fine instrument; and the peculiar mechanical work of Dædalus,— inlaying,—becomes all the more delightful to us in external aspect, because, as in the jawbone of a Saurian, or the wood of a bow, it is essential to the finest capacities of tension and resistance.

And observe how unbroken the ascent from this, the simplest architecture, to the loftiest. The placing of the timbers in a ship's stem, and the laying of the stones in a bridge buttress, are similar in art to the construction of the ploughshare, differing in no essential point, either in that they deal with other materials, or because, of the three things produced, one has to divide earth by advancing through it, another to divide water by advancing through it, and the third to divide water which advances against it. And again, the buttress of a bridge differs only from that of a cathedral in having less weight to sustain, and more to resist. We can find no term in the gradation, from the ploughshare to the cathedral buttress, at which we can set a logical distinction.

Thus then we have simply three divisions of Art—one, that of giving colors to substance; another, that of giving form to it without question of resistance to force; and the third, that of giving form or position which will make it capable of such resistance. All the fine arts are embraced under these three divisions. Do not think that it is only a logical or scientific affectation to mass them together in this manner; it is, on the contrary, of the first practical importance to understand that the painter's faculty, or masterhood over color, being as subtle as a musician's over sound, must be looked to for the government of every operation in which color is employed; and that, in the same manner, the appliance of any art whatsoever to minor objects cannot be right, unless under the direction of a true master of that art. Under the present system, you keep your Academician occupied only in producing tinted pieces of canvas to be shown in frames, and smooth pieces of marble to be placed in niches; while you expect your builder or constructor to design colored patterns in stone and brick, and your chinaware merchant to keep a separate body of work-women who can paint china, but nothing else. By this division of labor, you ruin all the arts at once. The work of the Academician becomes mean and effeminate, because he is not used to treat color on a grand scale and in rough materials; and your manufacturers become base, because no well-educated person sets hand to them. And therefore it is necessary to understand, not merely as a logical statement, but as a practical necessity, that wherever beautiful color is to be arranged, you need a Master of Painting; and wherever noble form is to be given, a Master of Sculpture; and wherever complex mechanical force is to be resisted, a Master of Architecture.

But over this triple division there must rule another yet more important. Any of these three arts may be either imitative of natural objects or limited to useful appliance. You may either paint a picture that represents a scene, or your street door, to keep it from rotting; you may mould a statue, or a plate; build the resemblance of a cluster of lotus stalks, or only a square pier. Generally speaking, Painting and Sculpture will be imitative, and Architecture merely useful; but there is a great deal of Sculpture—as this crystal ball, for instance, which is not imitative, and a great deal of architecture which, to some extent, is so, as the so-called foils of Gothic apertures; and for many other reasons you will find it necessary to keep distinction clear in your minds between the arts—of whatever kind—which are imitative, and produce a resemblance or image of something which is not present; and those which are limited to the production of some useful reality, as the blade of a knife, or the wall of a house. You will perceive also, as we advance, that sculpture and painting are indeed in this respect only one art; and that we shall have constantly to speak and think of them as simply *graphic,* whether with chisel or color, their principal function being to make us, in the words of Aristotle, «θεωρητικὸι τοῦ περὶ τὰ σώματα κάλλους» (Polit. 8, 3), "having capacity and habit of contemplation of the beauty that is in material things"; while architecture, and its correlative arts, are to be practised under quite other conditions of sentiment.

Now it is obvious that so far as the fine arts consist either in imitation or mechanical construction, the right judgment of them must depend on our knowledge of the things they imitate, and forces they resist: and my function of teaching here would (for instance) so far resolve itself, either into demonstration that this painting of a peach does resemble a peach, or explanation of the way in which this ploughshare (for instance) is shaped so as to throw the earth aside with least force of thrust. And in both of these methods of study, though of course your own diligence must be your chief master, to a certain extent your Professor of Art can always guide you securely, and can show you, either that the image does truly resemble what it attempts to resemble, or that the structure is rightly prepared for the service it has to perform. But there is yet another virtue of fine art which is, perhaps, exactly that about which you will expect your Professor to teach you most, and which, on the contrary, is exactly that about which you must teach yourselves all that it is essential to learn.

I have here in my hand one of the simplest possible examples of the union of the graphic and constructive powers,—one of my breakfast plates. Since all the finely architectural arts, we said, began in the shaping of the cup and the platter, we will begin, ourselves, with the platter.

Why has it been made round? For two structural reasons: first, that the greatest holding surface may be gathered into the smallest space; and secondly, that in being pushed past other things on the table, it may come into least contact with them.

Next, why has it a rim? For two other structural reasons: first, that it is convenient to put salt or mustard upon; but secondly, and chiefly, that the plate may be easily laid hold of. The rim is the simplest form of continuous handle.

Farther, to keep it from soiling the cloth, it will be wise to put this ridge beneath, round the bottom; for as the rim is the simplest possible form of continuous handle, so this is the simplest form of continuous leg. And we get the section given beneath the figure for the essential one of a rightly made platter.

Thus far our art has been strictly utilitarian, having respect to conditions of collision, of carriage, and of support. But now, on the surface of our piece of pottery, here are various bands and spots of color which are presumably set there to make it pleasanter to the eye. Six of the spots, seen closely, you discover are intended to represent flowers. These then have as distinctly a graphic purpose as the other properties of the plate have an architectural one, and the first critical question we have to ask about them is, whether they are like roses or not. I will anticipate what I have to say in subsequent lectures so far as to assure you that, if they are to be like roses at all, the liker they can be, the better. Do not suppose, as many people will tell you, that because this is a common manufactured article, your roses on it are the better for being ill-painted, or half-painted. If they had been painted by the same hand that did this peach, the plate would have been all the better for it; but, as it chanced, there was no hand such as William Hunt's to paint them, and their graphic power is not distinguished. In any case, however, that graphic power must have been subordinate to their effect as pink spots, while the band of green-blue round the plate's edge, and the spots of gold, pretend to no graphic power at all, but are meaningless spaces of color or metal. Still less have they any mechanical office: they add nowise to the serviceableness of the plate; and their agreeableness, if they possess any, depends, therefore, neither on any imitative, nor any structural, character; but on some inherent pleasantness in themselves, either of mere colors to the eye (as of taste to the tongue), or in the placing of those colors in relations which obey some mental principle of order, or physical principle of harmony.

These abstract relations and inherent pleasantnesses, whether in space, number, or time, and whether of colors or sounds, form what we may properly term the musical or harmonic element in every art; and the study of them is an entirely separate science. It is the branch of art-philosophy to which the word "æsthetics" should be strictly limited, being the inquiry into the nature of things that in themselves are pleasant to the human senses or instincts, though they represent nothing, and serve for nothing, their only service *being* their pleasantness. Thus it is the province of æsthetics to tell you (if you did not know it before), that the taste and color of a peach are pleasant, and to ascertain, if it be ascertainable (and you have any curiosity to know), why they are so.

The information would, I presume, to most of you, be gratuitous. If it were not, and you chanced to be in a sick state of body in which you disliked peaches, it would be, for the time, to you false information, and, so far as it was true of other people, to you useless. Nearly the whole study of æsthetics is in like manner either gratuitous or useless. Either you like the right things without being recommended to do so, or, if you dislike them, your mind cannot be changed by lectures on the laws of taste. You recollect the story of Thackeray, provoked, as he was helping himself to strawberries, by a young coxcomb's telling him that "he never took fruit or sweets." "That," replied, or is said to have replied, Thackeray, "is because you are a sot, and a glutton." And the whole science of æsthetics is, in the depth of it, expressed by one passage of Goethe's in the end of the second part of *Faust;*— the notable one that follows the song of the Lemures, when the angels enter to dispute with the fiends for the soul of Faust. They enter singing—"Pardon to sinners and life to the dust." Mephistoph eles hears them first, and exclaims to his troop, "Discord I hear, and filthy jingling" —"Mis-töne höre ich: garstiges Geklimper." This, you see, is the extreme of bad taste in music. Presently the angelic host begin strewing roses, which discomfits the diabolic crowd altogether. Mephistopheles in vain calls to them—"What do you duck and shrink for—is that proper hellish behavior? Stand fast, and let them strew"—"Was duckt und zuckt ihr; ist das Höllenbrauch? So haltet stand, und lasst sie streuen." There you have, also, the extreme of bad taste in sight and smell. And in the whole passage is a brief embodiment for you of the ultimate fact that all æsthetics depend on the health of soul and body, and the proper exercise of both, not only through years, but generations. Only by harmony of both collateral and successive lives can the great doctrine of the Muses be received which enables men «χαίρειν ὀρθῶς,»—"to have pleasure rightly"; and there is no other definition of the beautiful, nor of any subject of delight, to the æsthetic faculty, than that it is what one noble spirit has created, seen and felt by another of similar or equal nobility. So much as there is in you of ox, or of swine, perceives no beauty, and creates none; what is human in you, in exact proportion to the perfectness of its humanity, can create it, and receive.   [1872]

QUEEN OF THE AIR (Lecture III)

ATHENA ERGANE

In different places of my writings, and through many years of endeavor to define the laws of art, I have insisted on this rightness in work, and on its connection with virtue of character, in so many partial ways, that the impression left on the reader's mind—if, indeed, it was ever impressed at all—has been confused and uncertain. 10 In beginning the series of my corrected works, I wish this principle (in my own mind the foundation of every other) to be made plain, if nothing else is: and will try, therefore, to make it so, as far as, by any effort, I can put it into unmistakable words. And, first, here is a very simple statement of it, given lately in a lecture on the Architecture of the Valley of the Somme, which will be better read in this 20 place than in its incidental connection with my account of the porches of Abbeville.

I had used, in a preceding part of the lecture, the expression, "by what faults" this Gothic architecture fell. We continually speak thus of works of art. We talk of their faults and merits, as of virtues and vices. What do we mean by talking of the faults of a picture, or the merits of 30 a piece of stone?

The faults of a work of art are the faults of its workman, and its virtues his virtues. Great art is the expression of the mind of a great man, and mean art, that of the want of mind of a weak man. A foolish person builds foolishly, and a wise one, sensibly; a virtuous one, beautifully; and a vicious one, basely. If stone work is well put together, it means that a thoughtful 40 man planned it, and a careful man cut it, and an honest man cemented it. If it has too much ornament, it means that its carver was too greedy of pleasure; if too little, that he was rude, or insensitive, or stupid, and the like. So that when once you have learned how to spell these most precious of all legends,—pictures and buildings,—you may read the characters of men, and of nations, in their art, as in a mirror; —nay, as in a microscope, and magnified a hundredfold; for the character becomes passionate in the art, and intensifies itself in all its noblest or meanest delights. Nay, not only as in a microscope, but as under a scalpel, and in dissection; for a man may hide himself from you, or misrepresent himself to you, every other way; but he cannot in his work: there, be sure, you have him to the inmost. All that he likes, all that he sees,—all that he can do,—his imagination, his affections, his perseverance, his impatience, his clumsiness, cleverness, everything is there. If the work is a cobweb, you know it was made by a spider; if a honeycomb, by a bee; a worm-cast is thrown up by a worm, and a nest wreathed by a bird; and a house built by a man, worthily, if he is worthy, and ignobly, if he is ignoble.

And always, from the least to the greatest, as the made thing is good or bad, so is the maker of it.

You all use this faculty of judgment more or less, whether you theoretically admit the principle or not. Take that floral gable; you don't suppose the man who built Stonehenge could have built that, or that the man who built that, would have built Stonehenge? Do you think an old Roman would have liked such a piece of filigree work? or that Michael

Angelo would have spent his time in twisting these stems of roses in and out? Or, of modern handicraftsmen, do you think a burglar, or a brute, or a pickpocket could have carved it? Could Bill Sykes have done it? or the Dodger, dexterous with finger and tool? You will find in the end, that *no man could have done it but exactly the man who did it;* and by looking close at it, you may, if you know your letters, read precisely the manner of man he was.

Now I must insist on this matter, for a grave reason. Of all facts concerning art, this is the one most necessary to be known, that, while manufacture is the work of hands only, art is the work of the whole spirit of man; and as that spirit is, so is the deed of it: and by whatever power of vice or virtue any art is produced, the same vice or virtue it reproduces and teaches. That which is born of evil begets evil; and that which is born of valor and honor, teaches valor and honor. All art is either infection or education. It *must* be one or other of these.

This, I repeat, of all truths respecting art, is the one of which understanding is the most precious, and denial the most deadly. And I assert it the more, because it has of late been repeatedly, expressly, and with contumely denied; and that by high authority: and I hold it one of the most sorrowful facts connected with the decline of the arts among us, that English gentlemen, of high standing as scholars and artists, should have been blinded into the acceptance, and betrayed into the assertion of a fallacy which only authority such as theirs could have rendered for an instant credible. For the contrary of it is written in the history of all great nations; it is the one sentence always inscribed on the steps of their thrones; the one concordant voice in which they speak to us out of their dust.

All such nations first manifest themselves as a pure and beautiful animal race, with intense energy and imagination. They live lives of hardship by choice, and by grand instinct of manly discipline: they become fierce and irresistible soldiers; the nation is always its own army, and their king, or chief head of government, is always their first soldier. Pharaoh, or David, or Leonidas, or Valerius, or Bar-

barossa, or Cœur de Lion, or St. Louis, or Dandolo, or Frederick the Great:—Egyptian, Jew, Greek, Roman, German, English, French, Venetian,—that is inviolable law for them all; their king must be their first soldier, or they cannot be in progressive power. Then, after their great military period, comes the domestic period; in which, without betraying the discipline of war, they add to their great soldiership the delights and possessions of a delicate and tender home-life: and then, for all nations, is the time of their perfect art, which is the fruit, the evidence, the reward of their national ideal of character, developed by the finished care of the occupations of peace. That is the history of all true art that ever was, or can be: palpably the history of it,—unmistakably,—written on the forehead of it in letters of light,—in tongues of fire, by which the seal of virtue is branded as deep as ever iron burned into a convict's flesh the seal of crime. But always, hitherto, after the great period, has followed the day of luxury, and pursuit of the arts for pleasure only. And all has so ended.

Thus far of Abbeville building. Now I have here asserted two things,—first, the foundation of art in moral character; next, the foundation of moral character in war. I must make both these assertions clearer, and prove them.

First, of the foundation of art in moral character. Of course art-gift and amiability of disposition are two different things; a good man is not necessarily a painter, nor does an eye for color necessarily imply an honest mind. But great art implies the union of both powers: it is the expression, by an art-gift, of a pure soul. If the gift is not there, we can have no art at all; and if the soul—and a right soul too—is not there, the art is bad, however dexterous.

But also, remember, that the art-gift itself is only the result of the moral character of generations. A bad woman may have a sweet voice; but that sweetness of voice comes of the past morality of her race. That she can sing with it at all, she owes to the determination of laws of music by the morality of the past. Every act, every impulse, of virtue and vice, affects in any creature, face, voice, nervous power, and vigor and harmony of invention, at once. Perseverance in rightness of human conduct, renders, after a certain number of generations, human art possible; every sin clouds it, be it ever so little a one; and persistent vicious living and following of pleasure render, after a certain number of generations, all art impossible. Men are deceived by the long-suffering of the laws of nature; and mistake, in a nation, the reward of the virtue of its sires for the issue of its own sins. The time of their visitation will come, and that inevitably; for, it is always true, that if the fathers have eaten sour grapes, the children's teeth are set on edge. And for the individual, as soon as you have learned to read, you may, as I have said, know him to the heart's core, through his art. Let his art-gift be never so great, and cultivated to the height by the schools of a great race of men; and it is still but a tapestry thrown over his own being and inner soul; and the bearing of it will show, infallibly, whether it hangs on a man, or on a skeleton. If you are dim-eyed, you may not see the difference in the fall of the folds at first, but learn how to look, and the folds themselves will become transparent, and you shall see through them the death's shape, or the divine one, making the tissue above it as a cloud of light, or as a winding-sheet.

Then farther, observe, I have said (and you will find it true, and that to the uttermost) that, as all lovely art is rooted in virtue, so it bears fruit of virtue, and is didactic in its own nature. It is often didactic also in actually expressed thought, as Giotto's, Michael Angelo's, Dürer's, and hundreds more; but that is not its special function,—it is didactic chiefly by being beautiful; but beautiful with haunting thought, no less than with form, and full of myths that can be read only with the heart.

For instance, at this moment there is open beside me as I write, a page of Persian manuscript, wrought with wreathed azure and gold, and soft green, and violet, and ruby and scarlet, into one field of pure resplendence. It is wrought to delight the eyes only; and does delight them; and the man who did it assuredly had eyes in his head; but not much more. It is not didactic art, but its author was happy: and it will do the good, and the harm, that mere pleasure can do. But, opposite me, is an early Turner drawing of the lake of Geneva, taken about two miles from Geneva, on the Lausanne road, with Mont Blanc in the distance. The old city is seen lying beyond the waveless waters, veiled with a sweet misty veil of Athena's weaving: a faint light of morning, peaceful exceedingly, and almost colorless, shed from behind the Voirons, increases into soft amber along the slope of the Salève, and is just seen, and no more, on the fair warm fields of its summit, between the folds of a white cloud that rests upon the grass, but rises, high and towerlike, into the zenith of dawn above.

There is not as much color in that low amber light upon the hill-side as there is in the palest dead leaf. The lake is not blue, but gray in mist, passing into deep shadows beneath the Voirons' pines; a few dark clusters of leaves, a single white flower—scarcely seen—are all the gladness given to the rocks of the shore. One of the ruby spots of the eastern manuscript would give color enough for all the red that is in Turner's entire drawing. For the mere pleasure of the eye, there is not so much in all those lines of his, throughout the entire landscape, as in half an inch square of the Persian's page. What made him take pleasure in the low color that is only like the brown of a dead leaf? in the cold gray of dawn—in the one white flower among the rocks—in these—and no more than these?

He took pleasure in them because he had been bred among English fields and hills; because the gentleness of a great race was in his heart, and its power of thought in his brain; because he knew the stories of the Alps, and of the cities at their feet; because he had read the Homeric legends of the clouds, and beheld the gods of dawn, and the givers of dew to the fields; because he knew the faces of the crags, and the imagery of the passionate mountains, as a man knows the face of his friend; because he had in him the wonder and sorrow concerning life and death, which are the inheritance of the Gothic soul from the days of its first sea kings; and also the compassion and the joy that are woven into the innermost fabric of every great imaginative spirit, born now in countries that have lived by the Christian faith with any courage or truth. And the picture contains also, for us, just this which its maker had in him to give; and can convey it to us, just so far as we are of the temper in which it must be received. It is didactic, if we are worthy to be taught, no otherwise. The pure heart, it will make more pure; the thoughtful, more thoughtful. It has in it no words for the reckless or the base.

[1869]

LECTURES ON ART (Lecture III)

THE RELATION OF ART TO MORALS

You probably recollect that, in the beginning of my last lecture, it was stated that fine art had, and could have, but three functions: the enforcing of the religious sentiments of men, the perfecting their ethical state, and the doing them material service. We have to-day to examine, the mode of its action in the second power—that of perfecting the morality, or ethical state, of men.

Perfecting, observe—not producing.

You must have the right moral state first, or you cannot have the art. But when the art is once obtained, its reflected action enhances and completes the moral state out of which it arose, and, above all, communicates the exultation to other minds which are already morally capable of the like.

For instance, take the art of singing, and the simplest perfect master of it (up to the limits of his nature) whom you can find;—a skylark. From him you may learn what it is to "sing for joy." You must get the moral state first, the pure gladness, then give it finished expression; and it is perfected in itself, and made communicable to other creatures capable of such joy. But it is incommunicable to those who are not prepared to receive it.

Now, all right human song is, similarly, the finished expression, by art, of the joy or grief of noble persons, for right causes. And accurately in proportion to the rightness of the cause, and purity of the emotion, is the possibility of the fine art. A maiden may sing of her lost love, but a miser cannot sing of his lost money. And with absolute precision, from highest to lowest, *the fineness of the possible art is an index of the moral purity and majesty of the emotion it expresses.* You may test it practically at any instant. Question with yourselves respecting any feeling that has taken strong possession of your mind, "Could this be sung by a master, and sung nobly, with a true melody and art?" Then it is a right feeling. Could it not be sung at all, or only sung ludicrously? It is a base one. And that is so in all the arts; so that with mathematical precision, subject to no error or exception, the art of a nation, so far as it exists, is an exponent of its ethical state.

An exponent, observe, and exalting influence; but not the root or cause. You cannot paint or sing yourselves into being good men; you must be good men before you can either paint or sing, and then the colour and sound will complete in you all that is best.

And this it was that I called upon you to hear, saying, "listen to me at least now," in the first lecture, namely, that no art-teaching could be of use to you, but would rather be harmful, unless it was grafted on something deeper than all art. For indeed not only with this, of which it is my function to show you the laws, but much more with the art of all men, which you came here chiefly to learn, that of language, the chief vices of education have arisen from the one great fallacy of supposing that noble language is a communicable trick of grammar and accent, instead of simply the careful expression of right thought. All the virtues of language are, in their roots, moral; it becomes accurate if the speaker desires to be true; clear, if he speaks with sympathy and a desire to be intelligible; powerful, if he has earnestness; pleasant, if he has sense of rhythm and order. There are no other virtues of language producible by art than these: but let me mark more deeply for an instant the significance of one of them. Language, I said, is only clear when it is sympathetic. You can, in truth, understand a man's word only by understanding his temper. Your own word is also as of an unknown tongue to him unless he understands yours. And it is this which makes the art of language, if any one is to be chosen separately from the rest, that which is fittest for the instrument of a gentleman's education. To teach the meaning of a word thoroughly, is to teach the nature of the spirit that coined it; the secret of language is the secret of sympathy, and its full charm is possible only to the gentle. And thus the principles of beautiful speech have all been fixed by sincere and kindly speech. On the laws which have been determined by sincerity, false speech, apparently beautiful, may afterwards be constructed; but all such utterance, whether in oration or poetry, is not only without permanent power, but it is destructive of the principles it has usurped. So long as no words are uttered but in faithfulness, so long the art of language goes on exalting itself; but the moment it is shaped and chiselled on external principles, it falls into frivolity, and perishes. And this truth would have been long ago manifest, had it not been that in periods of advanced academical science there is always a tendency to deny the sincerity of the first masters of language. Once learn to write gracefully in the manner of an ancient author, and we are apt to think that he also wrote in the manner of some one else. But no noble nor right style was ever yet founded but out of a sincere heart.

No man is worth reading to form your style, who does not mean what he says; nor was any great style ever invented but by some man who meant what he said. Find out the beginner of a great manner of writing, and you have also found the declarer of some true facts or sincere passions: and your whole method of reading will thus be quickened, for, being sure that your author really meant what he said, you will be much more careful to ascertain what it is that he means.

And of yet greater importance is it deeply to know that every beauty possessed by the language of a nation is significant of the innermost laws of its being. Keep the temper of the people stern and manly; make their associations grave, courteous, and for worthy objects; occupy them in just deeds; and their tongue must needs be a grand one. Nor is it possible, therefore—observe the necessary reflected action—that any tongue should be a noble one, of which the words are not so many trumpet-calls to action. All great languages invariably utter great things, and command them; they cannot be mimicked but by obedience; the breadth of them is inspiration because it is not only vocal, but vital; and you can only learn to speak as these men spoke, by becoming what these men were.

Now for direct confirmation of this, I want you to think over the relation of expression to character in two great masters of the absolute art of language, Virgil and Pope. You are perhaps surprised at the last name; and indeed you have in English much higher grasp and melody of language from more passionate minds, but you have nothing else, in its range, so perfect. I name, therefore, these two men, because they are the two most accomplished *Artists*, merely as such, whom I know in literature; and because I think you will be afterwards interested in investigating how the infinite grace in the words of the one, and the severity in those of the other, and the precision in those of both, arise wholly out of the moral elements of their minds:—out of the deep tenderness in Virgil which enabled him to write the stories of Nisus and Lausus; and the serene and just benevolence which placed Pope, in his theology, two centuries in advance of his time, and enabled him to sum the law of noble life in two lines which, so far as I know, are the most complete, the most concise, and the most lofty expression of moral temper existing in English words:—

"*Never elated, while one man's oppress'd;*
Never dejected, while another's bless'd."

I wish you also to remember these lines of Pope, and to make yourselves entirely masters of his system of ethics; because, putting Shakespeare aside as rather the world's than ours, I hold Pope to be the most perfect representative we have, since Chaucer, of the true English mind; and I think the Dunciad is the most absolutely chiselled and monumental work "exacted" in our country. You will find, as you study Pope, that he has expressed for you, in the strictest language and within the briefest limits, every law of art, of criticism, of economy, of policy, and, finally, of a benevolence, humble, rational, and resigned, contented with its allotted share of life, and trusting the problem of its salvation to Him in whose hand lies that of the universe.

And now I pass to the arts with which I have special concern, in which, though the facts are exactly the same, I shall have more difficulty in proving my assertion, because very few of us are as cognizant of the merit of painting as we are of that of language; and I can only show you whence that merit springs, after having thoroughly shown you in what it consists. But, in the meantime, I have simply to tell you, that the manual arts are as accurate exponents of ethical state, as other modes of expression; first, with absolute precision, of that of the workman; and then with precision, disguised by many distorting influences, of that of the nation to which it belongs.

And, first, they are a perfect exponent of the mind of the workman; but, being so, remember, if the mind be great or complex, the art is not an easy book to read; for we must ourselves possess all the mental characters of which we are to read the signs. No man can read the evidence of labour who is not himself laborious, for he does not know what the work cost: nor can he read the evidence of true passion if he is not passionate; nor of gentleness if he is not gentle: and the most subtle signs of fault and weakness of character he can only judge by having had the same faults to fight with. I myself, for instance, know impatient work, and tired work, better than most critics, because I am myself always impatient, and often tired:— so also, the patient and indefatigable touch of a mighty master becomes more wonderful to me than to others. Yet, wonderful in no mean measure it will be to you all, when I make it manifest,—and as soon as we begin our real work, and you have

learned what it is to draw a true line, I shall be able to make manifest to you— and indisputably so,—that the day's work of a man like Mantegna or Paul Veronese consists of an unfaltering, uninterrupted succession of movements of the hand more precise than those of the finest fencer: the pencil leaving one point and arriving at another, not only with unerring precision at the extremity of the line, but with an unerring and yet varied course—sometimes over spaces a foot or more in extent—yet a course so determined everywhere, that either of these men could, and Veronese often does, draw a finished profile, or any other portion of the contour of the face, with one line, not afterwards changed. Try, first, to realise to yourselves the muscular precision of that action, and the intellectual strain of it; for the movement of a fencer is perfect in practised monotony; but the movement of the hand of a great painter is at every instant governed by a direct and new intention. Then imagine that muscular firmness and subtlety, and the instantaneously selective and ordinant energy of the brain, sustained all day long, not only without fatigue, but with a visible joy in the exertion, like that which an eagle seems to take in the wave of his wings; and this all life long, and through long life, not only without failure of power, but with visible increase of it, until the actually organic changes of old age. And then consider, so far as you know anything of physiology, what sort of an ethical state of body and mind that means! ethic through ages past! what fineness of race there must be to get it, what exquisite balance and symmetry of the vital powers! And then, finally, determine for yourselves whether a manhood like that is consistent with any viciousness of soul, with any mean anxiety, any gnawing lust, any wretchedness of spite or remorse, any consciousness of rebellion against law of God or man, or any actual, though unconscious violation of even the least law to which obedience is essential for the glory of life and the pleasing of its Giver.

It is, of course, true that many of the strong masters had deep faults of character, but their faults always show in their work. It is true that some could not govern their passions; if so, they died young, or they painted ill when old. But the greater part of our misapprehension in the whole matter is from our not having well known who the great painters were, and taking delight in the petty skill that was bred in the fumes of the taverns of the North, instead of theirs who breathed empyreal air, sons of the morning, under the woods of Assisi and the crags of Cadore.

It is true however also, as I have pointed out long ago, that the strong masters fall into two great divisions, one leading simple and natural lives, the other restrained in a Puritanism of the worship of beauty; and these two manners of life you may recognize in a moment by their work. Generally the naturalists are the strongest; but there are two of the Puritans, whose work if I can succeed in making clearly understandable to you during my three years here, it is all I need care to do. But of these two Puritans one I cannot name to you, and the other I at present will not. One I cannot, for no one knows his name, except the baptismal one, Bernard, or "dear little Bernard"—Bernardino, called from his birthplace, (Luino, on the Lago Maggiore,) Bernard of Luino. The other is a Venetian, of whom many of you probably have never heard, and of whom, through me, you shall not hear, until I have tried to get some picture by him over to England.

Observe then, this Puritanism in the worship of beauty, though sometimes weak, is always honourable and amiable, and the exact reverse of the false Puritanism, which consists in the dread or disdain of beauty. And in order to treat my subject rightly, I ought to proceed from the skill of art to the choice of its subject, and show you how the moral temper of the workman is shown by his seeking lovely forms and thoughts to express, as well as by the force of his hand in expression. But I need not now urge this part of the proof on you, because you are already, I believe, sufficiently conscious of the truth in this matter, and also I have already said enough of it in my writings; whereas I have not at all said enough of the infallibleness of fine technical work as a proof of every other good power. And indeed it was long before I myself understood the true meaning of the pride of the greatest men in their mere execution, shown for a permanent lesson to us, in the stories which, whether true or not, indicate with absolute accuracy the general conviction of great artists;—the stories of the contest of Apelles and Protogenes in a line only, (of which I can promise you, you shall know the meaning to some purpose in a little while)—the story of the circle of Giotto, and especially, which you may perhaps not have observed, the expression of Dürer in his inscription on the drawings sent him by Raphael. These figures, he says, "Raphael drew and sent to Albert Dürer in Nürnberg, to show him"—What? Not his invention, nor his beauty of expression, but "sein Hand zu weisen," "To show him his *hand*." And you will find, as you examine farther, that all inferior artists are continually trying to escape from the necessity of sound work, and either indulging themselves in their delights in subject, or pluming themselves on their noble motives for attempting what they cannot perform; (and observe, by the way, that a great deal of what is mistaken for conscientious motive is nothing but a very pestilent, because very subtle, condition of vanity); whereas the great men always understand at once that the first morality of a painter, as of everybody else, is to know his business; and so earnest are they in this, that many, whose lives you would think, by the results of their work, had been passed in strong emotion, have in reality subdued themselves, though capable of the very strongest passions, into a calm as absolute as that of a deeply sheltered mountain lake, which reflects every agitation of the clouds in the sky, and every change of the shadows on the hills, but is itself motionless.

Finally, you must remember that great obscurity has been brought upon the truth in this matter by the want of integrity and simplicity in our modern life. I mean integrity in the Latin sense, wholeness. Everything is broken up, and mingled in confusion, both in our habits and thoughts; besides being in great part imitative: so that you not only cannot tell what a man is, but sometimes you cannot tell whether he *is,* at all!—whether you have indeed to do with a spirit, or only with an echo. And thus the same inconsistencies appear now, between the work of artists of merit and their personal characters, as those which you find continually disappointing expectation in the lives of men of modern literary power; the same conditions of society having obscured or misdirected the best qualities of the imagination, both in our literature and art. Thus there is no serious question with any of us as to the personal character of Dante and Giotto, of Shakespeare and Holbein; but we pause timidly in the attempt to analyse the moral laws of the art skill in recent poets, novelists, and painters.

Let me assure you once for all, that as you grow older, if you enable yourselves to distinguish, by the truth of your own lives, what is true in those of other men, you will gradually perceive that all good has its origin in good, never in evil; that the fact of either literature or painting being truly fine of their kind, whatever their mistaken aim, or partial error, is proof of their noble origin: and that, if there is indeed sterling value in the thing done, it has come of a sterling worth in the soul that did it, however alloyed or defiled by conditions of sin which are sometimes more appalling or more strange than those which all may detect in their own hearts, because they are part of a personality altogether larger than ours, and as far beyond our judgment in its darkness as beyond our following in its light. And it is sufficient warning against what some might dread as the probable effect of such a conviction on your own minds, namely, that you might permit yourselves in the weaknesses which you imagined to be allied to genius, when they took the form of personal temptations;—it is surely, I say, sufficient warning against so mean a folly, to discern, as you may with little pains, that, of all human existences, the lives of men of that distorted and tainted nobility of intellect are probably the most miserable.

[1870]

THE CROWN OF WILD OLIVE (Lecture II)

TRAFFIC

My good Yorkshire friends, you asked me down here among your hills that I might talk to you about this Exchange you are going to build; but, earnestly and seriously asking you to pardon me, I am going to do nothing of the kind. I cannot talk, or at least can say very little, about this same Exchange. I must talk of quite other things, though not willingly;—I could not deserve your pardon, if, when you invited me to speak on one subject, I *wilfully* spoke on another. But I cannot speak, to purpose, of anything about which I do not care; and most simply and sorrowfully I have to tell you, in the outset, that I do *not* care about this Exchange of yours.

If, however, when you sent me your invitation, I had answered, "I won't come, I don't care about the Exchange of Bradford," you would have been justly offended with me, not knowing the reasons of so blunt a carelessness. So I have come down, hoping that you will patiently let me tell you why, on this, and many other occasions, I now remain silent, when formerly I should have caught at the opportunity of speaking to a gracious audience.

In a word, then, I do not care about this Exchange—because *you* don't; and because you know perfectly well I cannot make you. Look at the essential conditions of the case, which you, as business men, know perfectly well, though perhaps you think I forget them. You are going to spend £30,000, which to you, collectively, is nothing; the buying a new coat is, as to the cost of it, a much more important matter of consideration to me, than building a new Exchange is to you. But you think you may as well have the right thing for your money. You know there are a great many odd styles of architecture about; you don't want to do anything ridiculous; you hear of me, among others, as a respectable architectural man-milliner; and you send for me, that I may tell you the leading fashion; and what is, in our shops, for the moment, the newest and sweetest thing in pinnacles.

Now, pardon me for telling you frankly,

you cannot have good architecture merely by asking people's advice on occasion. All good architecture is the expression of national life and character, and it is produced by a prevalent and eager national taste, or desire for beauty. And I want you to think a little of the deep significance of this word "taste"; for no statement of mine has been more earnestly or oftener controverted than that good taste is essentially a 10 moral quality. "No," say many of my antagonists, "taste is one thing, morality is another. Tell us what is pretty: we shall be glad to know that; but we need no sermons—even were you able to preach them, which may be doubted."

Permit me, therefore, to fortify this old dogma of mine somewhat. Taste is not only a part and an index of morality;—it is the ONLY morality. The first, and 20 last, and closest trial question to any living creature is, "What do you like?" Tell me what you like, and I'll tell you what you are. Go out into the street, and ask the first man or woman you meet, what their "taste" is; and if they answer candidly, you know them, body and soul. "You, my friend in the rags, with the unsteady gait, what do *you* like?" "A pipe and a quartern of gin." I know you. "You, good 30 woman, with the quick step and tidy bonnet, what do you like?" "A swept hearth, and a clean tea-table; and my husband opposite me, and a baby at my breast." Good, I know you also. "You, little girl with the golden hair and the soft eyes, what do you like?" "My canary, and a run among the wood hyacinths." "You, little boy with the dirty hands, and the low forehead, what do you like?" "A shy at the 40 sparrows, and a game at pitch farthing." Good; we know them all now. What more need we ask?

"Nay," perhaps you answer; "we need rather to ask what these people and children do, than what they like. If they *do* right, it is no matter that they like what is wrong; and if they *do* wrong, it is no matter that they like what is right. Doing is the great thing; and it 50 does not matter that the man likes drinking, so that he does not drink; nor that the little girl likes to be kind to her canary, if she will not learn her lessons; nor that the little boy likes throwing stones at the sparrows, if he goes to the Sunday school." Indeed, for a short time, and in a provisional sense, this is true. For if, resolutely, people do what is right, in time to come they like doing it. But they only are in a right moral state when they *have* come to like doing it; and as long as they don't like it, they are still in a vicious state. The man is not in health of body who is always thinking of the bottle in the cupboard, though he bravely bears his thirst; but the man who heartily enjoys water in the morning, and wine in the evening, each in its proper quantity and time. And the entire object of true education is to make people not merely *do* the right things, but *enjoy* the right things:—not merely industrious, but to love industry—not merely learned, but to love knowledge—not merely pure, but to love purity—not merely just, but to hunger and thirst after justice.

But you may answer or think, "Is the liking for outside ornaments,—for pictures, or statues, or furniture, or architecture, a moral quality?" Yes, most surely, if a rightly set liking. Taste for *any* pictures or statues is not a moral quality, but taste for good ones is. Only here again we have to define the word "good." I don't mean by "good," clever—or learned—or difficult in the doing. Take a picture by Teniers, of sots quarrelling over their dice; it is an entirely clever picture; so clever that nothing in its kind has ever been done equal to it; but it is also an entirely base and evil picture. It is an expression of delight in the prolonged contemplation of a vile thing, and delight in that is an "unmannered," or "immoral" quality. It is "bad taste" in the profoundest sense—it is the taste of the devils. On the other hand, a picture of Titian's, or a Greek statue, or a Greek coin, or a Turner landscape, expresses delight in the perpetual contemplation of a good and perfect thing. That is an entirely moral quality—it is the taste of the angels. And all delight in art, and all love of it, resolve themselves into simple love of that which deserves love. That deserving is the quality which we call "loveliness"—(we ought to have an opposite word, hateliness, to be said of the things which deserve to be hated); and it is not an indifferent nor optional thing whether we love this or that; but it is just the vital function of all our being. What we *like* determines what we *are,* and is the sign of what we are; and to teach taste is inevitably to form character.

As I was thinking over this, in walking up Fleet Street the other day, my eye caught the title of a book standing open in a bookseller's window. It was—"On the necessity of the diffusion of taste among all classes." "Ah," I thought to myself, "my classifying friend, when you have diffused your taste, where will your classes be? The man who likes what you like, belongs to the same class with you, I think. Inevitably so. You may put him to other work if you choose; but, by the condition you have brought him into, he will dislike the work as much as you would yourself. You get hold of a scavenger or a coster-monger, who enjoyed the Newgate Calendar for literature, and 'Pop goes the Weasel' for music. You think you can make him like Dante and Beethoven? I wish you joy of your lessons; but if you do, you have made a gentleman of him:—he won't like to go back to his coster-mongering."

And so completely and unexceptionally is this so, that, if I had time to-night, I could show you that a nation cannot be affected by any vice, or weakness, without expressing it, legibly, and forever, either in bad art, or by want of art; and that there is no national virtue, small or great, which is not manifestly expressed in all the art which circumstances enable the people possessing that virtue to produce. Take, for instance, your great English virtue of enduring and patient courage. You have at present in England only one art of any consequence—that is, iron-working. You know thoroughly well how to cast and hammer iron. Now, do you think, in those masses of lava which you build volcanic cones to melt, and which you forge at the mouths of the Infernos you have created; do you think, on those iron plates, your courage and endurance are not written for-ever,—not merely with an iron pen, but on iron parchment? And take also your great English vice—European vice—vice of all the world—vice of all other worlds that roll or shine in heaven, bearing with them yet the atmosphere of hell—the vice of jealousy, which brings competition into your com-merce, treachery into your councils, and dishonor into your wars—that vice which has rendered for you, and for your next neighboring nation, the daily occupations of existence no longer possible, but with the mail upon your breasts and the sword loose in its sheath; so that at last, you have realized for all the multitudes of the two great peoples who lead the so-called civili-zation of the earth,—you have realized for them all, I say, in person and in policy, what was once true only of the rough Border riders of your Cheviot hills—

"They carved at the meal
    With gloves of steel,
And they drank the red wine through the
        helmet barr'd;"—

do you think that this national shame and dastardliness of heart are not written as legibly on every rivet of your iron armor as the strength of the right hands that forged it?

Friends, I know not whether this thing be the more ludicrous or the more melan-choly. It is quite unspeakably both. Suppose, instead of being now sent for by you, I had been sent for by some private gentleman, living in a suburban house, with his garden separated only by a fruit wall from his next door neighbor's; and he had called me to consult with him on the furnishing of his drawing-room. I begin looking about me, and find the walls rather bare; I think such and such a paper might be desirable—perhaps a little fresco here and there on the ceiling—a damask curtain or so at the windows. "Ah," says my employer, "damask curtains, indeed! That's all very fine, but you know I can't afford that kind of thing just now!" "Yet the world credits you with a splendid in-come!" "Ah, yes," says my friend, "but do you know, at present I am obliged to spend it nearly all in steel-traps?" "Steel-traps! for whom?" "Why, for that fellow on the other side the wall, you know: we're very good friends, capital friends; but we are obliged to keep our traps set on both sides of the wall; we could not possibly keep on friendly terms without them, and our spring guns. The worst of it is, we are both clever fellows enough; and there's never a day passes that we don't find out a new trap, or a new gun-barrel, or something; we spend about fifteen millions a year each in our traps, take it altogether; and I don't see how we're to do with less." A highly comic state of life for two private gentlemen! but for two nations, it seems to me, not wholly comic. Bedlam would be comic, perhaps, if there were only one madman in it; and your Christmas pantomime is comic, when there is only one clown in it; but when the whole world turns clown, and paints itself red with its own heart's blood instead of vermilion, it is something else than comic, I think.

Mind, I know a great deal of this is play, and willingly allow for that. You don't know what to do with yourselves for a sensation; fox-hunting and cricketing will not carry you through the whole of this unendurably long mortal life: you liked pop-guns when you were schoolboys, and rifles and Armstrongs are only the same things better made: but then the worst of it is, that what was play to you when boys, was not play to the sparrows; and what is play to you now, is not play to the small birds of State neither; and for the black eagles, you are somewhat shy of taking shots at them, if I mistake not.

I must get back to the matter in hand, however. Believe me, without further instance, I could show you, in all time, that every nation's vice, or virtue, was written in its art: the soldiership of early Greece; the sensuality of late Italy; the visionary religion of Tuscany; the splendid human energy of Venice. I have no time to do this to-night (I have done it elsewhere before now); but I proceed to apply the principle to ourselves in a more searching manner.

I notice that among all the new buildings which cover your once wild hills, churches and schools are mixed in due, that is to say, in large proportion, with your mills and mansions; and I notice also that the churches and schools are almost always Gothic and, the mansions and mills are never Gothic. May I ask the meaning of this? for, remember, it is peculiarly a modern phenomenon. When Gothic was invented, houses were Gothic as well as churches; and when the Italian style superseded the Gothic, churches were Italian as well as houses. If there is a Gothic spire to the cathedral of Antwerp, there is a Gothic belfry to the Hôtel de Ville at Brussels; if Inigo Jones builds an Italian Whitehall, Sir Christopher Wren builds an Italian St. Paul's. But now you live under one school of architecture, and worship under another. What do you mean by doing this? Am I to understand that you are thinking of changing your architecture back to Gothic; and that you treat your churches experimentally, because it does not matter what mistakes you make in a church? Or am I to understand that you consider Gothic a preeminently sacred and beautiful mode of building, which you think, like the fine frankincense, should be mixed for the tabernacle only, and reserved for your religious services? For if this be the feeling, though it may seem at first as if it were graceful and reverent, at the root of the matter, it signifies neither more nor less than that you have separated your religion from your life.

For consider what a wide significance this fact has: and remember that it is not you only, but all the people of England, who are behaving thus, just now.

You have all got into the habit of calling the church "the house of God." I have seen, over the doors of many churches, the legend actually carved, "*This* is the house of God and this is the gate of heaven." Now, note where that legend comes from, and of what place it was first spoken. A boy leaves his father's house to go on a long journey on foot, to visit his uncle: he has to cross a wild hill-desert; just as if one of your own boys had to cross the wolds to visit an uncle at Carlisle. The second or third day your boy finds himself somewhere between Hawes and Brough, in the midst of the moors, at sunset. It is stony ground, and boggy; he cannot go one foot farther that night. Down he lies, to sleep, on Wharnside, where best he may, gathering a few of the stones together to put under his head;—so wild the place is, he cannot get anything but stones. And there, lying under the broad night, he has a dream; and he sees a ladder set up on the earth, and the top of it reaches to heaven, and the angels of God are seen ascending and descending upon it. And when he wakes out of his sleep, he says, "How dreadful is this place; surely this is none other than the house of God, and this is the gate of heaven." This PLACE, observe; not this church; not this city; not this stone, even, which he puts up for a memorial—the piece of flint on which his head has lain. But this *place;* this windy slope of Wharnside; this moorland hollow, torrent-bitten, snow-blighted; this *any* place where God lets down the ladder. And how are you to know where that will be? or how are you to determine where it may be, but by being ready for it always? Do you know where the lightning is to fall next? You *do* know that, partly; you can guide the lightning; but you cannot guide the going forth of the Spirit, which is as that lightning when it shines from the east to the west.

But the perpetual and insolent warping of that strong verse to serve a merely ecclesiastical purpose, is only one of the thousand instances in which we sink back into gross Judaism. We call our churches "temples." Now, you know perfectly well they are *not* temples. They have never had, never can have, anything whatever to do with temples. They are "synagogues"—"gathering places"—where you gather yourselves together as an assembly; and by not calling them so, you again miss the force of another mighty text—"Thou, when thou prayest, shalt not be as the hypocrites are; for they love to pray standing in the *churches*" [we should translate it], "that they may be seen of men. But thou, when thou prayest, enter into thy closet, and when thou hast shut thy door, pray to thy Father,"—which is, not in chancel nor in aisle, but "in secret."

Now, you feel, as I say this to you—I know you feel—as if I were trying to take away the honor of your churches. Not so; I am trying to prove to you the honor of your houses and your hills; not that the Church is not sacred—but that the whole Earth is. I would have you feel what careless, what constant, what infectious sin there is in all modes of thought, whereby, in calling your churches only "holy," you call your hearths and homes "profane"; and have separated yourselves from the heathen by casting all your household gods to the ground, instead of recognizing, in the places of their many and feeble Lares, the presence of your One and Mighty Lord and Lar.

"But what has all this to do with our Exchange?" you ask me, impatiently. My dear friends, it has just everything to do with it; on these inner and great questions depend all the outer and little ones; and if you have asked me down here to speak to you, because you had before been interested in anything I have written, you must know that all I have yet said about architecture was to show this. The book I called *The Seven Lamps* was to show that certain right states of temper and moral feeling were the magic powers by which all good architecture, without exception, had been produced. *The Stones of Venice* had, from beginning to end, no other aim than to show that the Gothic architecture of Venice had arisen out of, and indicated in all its features, a state of pure national faith, and of domestic virtue; and that its Renaissance architecture had arisen out of, and in all its features indicated, a state of concealed national infidelity, and of domestic corruption. And now, you ask me what style is best to build in, and how can I answer, knowing the meaning of the two styles, but by another question—do you mean to build as Christians or as Infidels? And still more—do you mean to build as honest Christians or as honest Infidels? as thoroughly and confessedly either one or the other? You don't like to be asked such rude questions. I cannot help it; they are of much more importance than this Exchange business; and if they can be at once answered, the Exchange business settles itself in a moment. But before I press them farther, I must ask leave to explain one point clearly.

In all my past work, my endeavor has been to show that good architecture is essentially religious—the production of a faithful and virtuous, not of an infidel and corrupted people. But in the course of doing this, I have had also to show that good architecture is not *ecclesiastical*. People are so apt to look upon religion as the business of the clergy, not their own, that the moment they hear of anything depending on "religion," they think it must also have depended on the priesthood; and I have had to take what place was to be occupied between these two errors, and fight both, often with seeming contradiction. Good architecture is the work of good and believing men; therefore, you say, at least some people say, "Good 10 architecture must essentially have been the work of the clergy, not of the laity." No— a thousand times no; good architecture has always been the work of the commonalty, *not* of the clergy. "What," you say, "those glorious cathedrals—the pride of Europe— did their builders not form Gothic architecture?" No; they corrupted Gothic architecture. Gothic was formed in the baron's castle, and the burgher's street. It was 20 formed by the thoughts, and hands, and powers of laboring citizens and warrior kings. By the monk it was used as an instrument for the aid of his superstition: when that superstition became a beautiful madness, and the best hearts of Europe vainly dreamed and pined in the cloister, and vainly raged and perished in the crusade,—through that fury of perverted faith and wasted war, the Gothic rose also 30 to its loveliest, most fantastic, and, finally, most foolish dreams; and in those dreams was lost.

I hope, now, that there is no risk of your misunderstanding me when I come to the gist of what I want to say to-night;—when I repeat, that every great national architecture has been the result and exponent of a great national religion. You can't have bits of it here, bits there—you must have it 40 everywhere or nowhere. It is not the monopoly of a clerical company—it is not the exponent of a theological dogma—it is not the hieroglyphic writing of an initiated priesthood; it is the manly language of a people inspired by resolute and common purpose, and rendering resolute and common fidelity to the legible laws of an undoubted God.

Now there have as yet been three distinct 50 schools of European architecture. I say, European, because Asiatic and African architectures belong so entirely to other races and climates, that there is no ques-tion of them here; only, in passing, I will simply assure you that whatever is good or great in Egypt, and Syria, and India, is just good or great for the same reasons as the buildings on our side of the Bosphorus. We Europeans, then, have had three great religions: the Greek, which was the worship of the God of Wisdom and Power; the Mediæval, which was the worship of the God of Judgment and Consolation; the Renaissance, which was the worship of the God of Pride and Beauty: these three we have had—they are past,—and now, at last, we English have got a fourth religion, and a God of our own, about which I want to ask you. But I must explain these three old ones first.

I repeat, first, the Greeks essentially worshipped the God of Wisdom; so that whatever contended against their religion,—to the Jews a stumbling-block,—was, to the Greeks—*Foolishness*.

The first Greek idea of deity was that expressed in the word, of which we keep the remnant in our words "*Di*-urnal" and "*Di*-vine"—the god of *Day,* Jupiter the revealer. Athena is his daughter, but especially daughter of the Intellect, springing armed from the head. We are only with the help of recent investigation beginning to penetrate the depth of meaning couched under the Athenaic symbols: but I may note rapidly, that her ægis, the mantle with the serpent fringes, in which she often, in the best statues, is represented as folding up her left hand, for better guard; and the Gorgon, on her shield, are both representative mainly of the chilling horror and sadness (turning men to stone, as it were) of the outmost and superficial spheres of knowledge—that knowledge which separates, in bitterness, hardness, and sorrow, the heart of the full-grown man from the heart of the child. For out of imperfect knowledge spring terror, dissension, danger, and disdain; but from perfect knowledge, given by the full-revealed Athena, strength and peace, in sign of which she is crowned with the olive spray, and bears the resistless spear.

This, then, was the Greek conception of purest Deity; and every habit of life, and every form of his art developed themselves from the seeking this bright, serene, resistless wisdom; and setting himself, as a man, to do things evermore rightly and strongly; not with any ardent affection or ultimate hope; but with a resolute and continent energy of will, as knowing that for failure there was no consolation, and for sin there was no remission. And the Greek architecture rose unerring, bright, clearly defined, and self-contained.

Next followed in Europe the great Christian faith, which was essentially the religion of Comfort. Its great doctrine is the remission of sins; for which cause, it happens, too often, in certain phases of Christianity, that sin and sickness themselves are partly glorified, as if, the more you had to be healed of, the more divine was the healing. The practical result of this doctrine, in art, is a continual contemplation of sin and disease, and of imaginary states of purification from them; thus we have an architecture conceived in a mingled sentiment of melancholy and aspiration, partly severe, partly luxuriant, which will bend itself to every one of our needs, and every one of our fancies, and be strong or weak with us, as we are strong or weak ourselves. It is, of all architecture, the basest, when base people build it—of all, the noblest, when built by the noble.

And now note that both these religions— Greek and Mediæval—perished by falsehood in their own main purpose. The Greek religion of Wisdom perished in a false philosophy—"Oppositions of science, falsely so called." The Mediæval religion of Consolation perished in false comfort; in remission of sins given lyingly. It was the selling of absolution that ended the Mediæval faith; and I can tell you more, it is the selling of absolution which, to the end of time, will mark false Christianity. Pure Christianity gives her remission of sins only by ending them; but false Christianity gets her remission of sins by compounding for them. And there are many ways of compounding for them. We English have beautiful little quiet ways of buying absolution, whether in low Church or high, far more cunning than any of Tetzel's trading.

Then, thirdly, there followed the religion of Pleasure, in which all Europe gave itself to luxury, ending in death. First, bals masqués [1] in every saloon, and then guillotines in every square. And all these three worships issue in vast temple building. Your Greek worshipped Wisdom, and built you the Parthenon—the Virgin's temple. The Mediæval worshipped Consolation, and built you Virgin temples also—but to our Lady of Salvation. Then the Revivalist worshipped beauty, of a sort, and built you Versailles and the Vatican. Now, lastly, will you tell me what we worship, and what we build?

You know we are speaking always of the real, active, continual, national worship; that by which men act, while they live; not that which they talk of, when they die. Now, we have, indeed, a nominal religion, to which we pay tithes of property and sevenths of time; but we have also a practical and earnest religion, to which we devote nine-tenths of our property and sixth-sevenths of our time. And we dispute a great deal about the nominal religion: but we are all unanimous about this practical one; of which I think you will admit that the ruling goddess may be best generally described as the "Goddess of Getting-on," or "Britannia of the Market." The Athenians had an "Athena Agoraia," or Athena of the Market; but she was a subordinate type of their goddess, while our Britannia Agoraia is the principal type of ours. And all your great architectural works are, of course, built to her. It is long since you built a great cathedral; and how you would laugh at me if I proposed building a cathedral on the top of one of these hills of yours, to make it an Acropolis! But your railroad mounds, vaster than the walls of Babylon; your railroad stations, vaster than the temple of Ephesus, and innumerable; your chimneys, how much more mighty and costly than cathedral spires! your harbor-piers; your warehouses; your exchanges!—all these are built to your great Goddess of "Getting-on"; and she has formed, and will continue to form, your architecture, as long as you worship her; and it is quite vain to ask me to tell you how to build to her; you know far better than I.

1 bals masqués: masked balls.

There might, indeed, on some theories, be a conceivably good architecture for Exchanges—that is to say, if there were any heroism in the fact or deed of exchange which might be typically carved on the outside of your building. For, you know, all beautiful architecture must be adorned with sculpture or painting; and for sculpture or painting, you must have a subject. And hitherto it has been a received opinion among the nations of the world that the only right subjects for either, were *heroisms* of some sort. Even on his pots and his flagons, the Greek put a Hercules slaying lions, or an Apollo slaying serpents, or Bacchus slaying melancholy giants, and earthborn despondencies. On his temples, the Greek put contests of great warriors in founding states, or of gods with evil spirits. On his houses and temples alike, the Christian put carvings of angels conquering devils; or of hero-martyrs exchanging this world for another; subject inappropriate, I think, to our direction of exchange here. And the Master of Christians not only left His followers without any orders as to the sculpture of affairs of exchange on the outside of buildings, but gave some strong evidence of His dislike of affairs of exchange within them. And yet there might surely be a heroism in such affairs; and all commerce become a kind of selling of doves, not impious. The wonder has always been great to me, that heroism has never been supposed to be in any wise consistent with the practice of supplying people with food, or clothes; but rather with that of quartering one's self upon them for food, and stripping them of their clothes. Spoiling of armor is a heroic deed in all ages; but the selling of clothes, old or new, has never taken any color of magnanimity. Yet one does not see why feeding the hungry and clothing the naked should ever become base businesses, even when engaged in on a large scale. If one could contrive to attach the notion of conquest to them anyhow! so that, supposing there were anywhere an obstinate race, who refused to be comforted, one might take some pride in giving them compulsory comfort! and, as it were, "*occupying* a country" with one's gifts, instead of one's armies? If one could only consider it as much a victory to get a barren field sown, as to get an eared field stripped; and contend who should build villages, instead of who should "carry" them! Are not all forms of heroism conceivable in doing these serviceable deeds? You doubt who is strongest? It might be ascertained by push of spade, as well as push of sword. Who is wisest? There are witty things to be thought of in planning other business than campaigns. Who is bravest? There are always the elements to fight with, stronger than men; and nearly as merciless.

The only absolutely and unapproachable heroic element in the soldier's work seems to be—that he is paid little for it—and regularly: while you traffickers, and exchangers, and others occupied in presumably benevolent business, like to be paid much for it—and by chance. I never can make out how it is that a *knight*-errant does not expect to be paid for his trouble, but a *pedler*-errant always does;—that people are willing to take hard knocks for nothing, but never to sell ribands cheap; that they are ready to go on fervent crusades, to recover the tomb of a buried God, but never on any travels to fulfil the orders of a living one;—that they will go anywhere barefoot to preach their faith, but must be well bribed to practise it, and are perfectly ready to give the Gospel gratis, but never the loaves and fishes.

If you chose to take the matter up on any such soldierly principle; to do your commerce, and your feeding of nations, for fixed salaries; and to be as particular about giving people the best food, and the best cloth, as soldiers are about giving them the best gunpowder, I could carve something for you on your exchange worth looking at. But I can only at present suggest decorating its frieze with pendant purses; and making its pillars broad at the base, for the sticking of bills. And in the innermost chambers of it there might be a statue of Britannia of the Market, who may have, perhaps advisably, a partridge for her crest, typical at once of her courage in fighting for noble ideas, and of her interest in game; and round its neck, the inscription in golden letters, "Perdix fovit quæ non peperit." [2] Then, for her spear, she might have a weaver's beam; and on her shield, instead of St. George's Cross, the Milanese boar, semi-fleeced, with the town of Gennesaret proper, in the field; and the legend, "In the best market," and her corslet, of leather, folded over her heart in the shape of a purse, with thirty slits in it, for a piece of money to go in at, on each day of the month. And I doubt not but that people would come to see your exchange, and its goddess, with applause.

Nevertheless, I want to point out to you certain strange characters in this goddess of yours. She differs from the great Greek and Mediæval deities essentially in two things—first, as to the continuance of her presumed power; secondly, as to the extent of it.

First, as to the Continuance.

The Greek Goddess of Wisdom gave continual increase of wisdom, as the Christian Spirit of Comfort (or Comforter) continual increase of comfort. There was no question, with these, of any limit or cessation of function. But with your Agora Goddess, that is just the most important question. Getting on—but where to? Gathering together—but how much? Do you mean to gather always—never to spend? If so, I wish you joy of your goddess, for I am just as well off as you, without the trouble of worshipping her at all. But if you do not spend, somebody else will—somebody else must. And it is because of this (among many other such errors) that I have fearlessly declared your so-called science of Political Economy to be no science; because, namely, it has omitted the study of exactly the most important branch of the business—the study of *spending*. For spend you must, and as much as you make, ultimately. You gather corn:—will you bury England under a heap of grain; or will you, when you have gathered, finally eat? You gather gold:—will you make your house-roofs of it, or pave your streets with it? That is still one way of

² *Perdix fovit*, etc.: "*As the partridge, fostering what she brought not forth,* so he that getteth riches, not by right, shall leave them in the midst of his days, and at the end shall be a fool" (Ruskin's note). *Jeremiah* XVII, 11. (best in the Vulgate).

spending it. But if you keep it, that you may get more, I'll give you more; I'll give you all the gold you want—all you can imagine—if you can tell me what you'll do with it. You shall have thousands of gold pieces;—thousands of thousands—millions—mountains, of gold: where will you keep them? Will you put an Olympus of silver upon a golden Pelion—make Ossa like a wart? Do you think the rain and dew would then come down to you, in the streams from such mountains, more blessedly than they will down the mountains which God has made for you, of moss and whinstone? But it is not gold that you want to gather! What is it? greenbacks? No; not those neither. What is it then—is it ciphers after a capital I? Cannot you practise writing ciphers, and write as many as you want! Write ciphers for an hour every morning, in a big book, and say every evening, I am worth all those naughts more than I was yesterday. Won't that do? Well, what in the name of Plutus is it you want? Not gold, not greenbacks, not ciphers after a capital I? You will have to answer, after all, "No; we want, somehow or other, money's *worth*." Well, what is that? Let your Goddess of Getting-on discover it, and let her learn to stay therein.

Second. But there is yet another question to be asked respecting this Goddess of Getting-on. The first was of the continuance of her power; the second is of its extent.

Pallas and the Madonna were supposed to be all the world's Pallas, and all the world's Madonna. They could teach all men, and they could comfort all men. But, look strictly into the nature of the power of your Goddess of Getting-on; and you will find she is the Goddess—not of everybody's getting on—but only of somebody's getting on. This is a vital, or rather deathful, distinction. Examine it in your own ideal of the state of national life which this Goddess is to evoke and maintain. I asked you what it was, when I was last here;—you have never told me. Now, shall I try to tell you?

Your ideal of human life then is, I think, that it should be passed in a pleasant undulating world, with iron and coal everywhere underneath it. On each pleasant bank of this world is to be a beautiful mansion, with two wings; and stables, and coach-houses; a moderately-sized park; a large garden and hot-houses; and pleasant carriage drives through the shrubberies. In this mansion are to live the favored votaries of the Goddess; the English gentleman, with his gracious wife, and his beautiful family; be always able to have the boudoir and the jewels for the wife, and the beautiful ball dresses for the daughters, and hunters for the sons, and a shooting in the Highlands for himself. At the bottom of the bank, is to be the mill; not less than a quarter of a mile long, with one steam engine at each end, and two in the middle, and a chimney three hundred feet high. In this mill are to be in constant employment from eight hundred to a thousand workers, who never drink, never strike, always go to church on Sunday, and always express themselves in respectful language.

Is not that, broadly, and in the main features, the kind of thing you propose to yourselves? It is very pretty indeed, seen from above; not at all so pretty, seen from below. For, observe, while to one family this deity is indeed the Goddess of Getting-on, to a thousand families she is the Goddess of *not* Getting-on. "Nay," you say, "they have all their chance." Yes, so has every one in a lottery, but there must always be the same number of blanks. "Ah! but in a lottery it is not skill and intelligence which take the lead, but blind chance." What then! do you think the old practice, that "they should take who have the power, and they should keep who can," is less iniquitous, when the power has become power of brains instead of fists? and that, though we may not take advantage of a child's or a woman's weakness, we may of a man's foolishness? "Nay, but finally, work must be done, and someone must be at the top, someone at the bottom." Granted, my friends. Work must always be, and captains of work must always be; and if you in the least remember the tone of any of my writings, you must know that they are thought unfit for this age, because they are always insisting on need of government, and speaking with scorn of liberty. But I beg you to observe

that there is a wide difference between being captains or governors of work, and taking the profits of it. It does not follow, because you are general of an army, that you are to take all the treasure, or land, it wins (if it fight for treasure or land); neither, because you are king of a nation, that you are to consume all the profits of the nation's work. Real kings, on the contrary, are known invariably by their doing quite the reverse of this,—by their taking the least possible quantity of the nation's work for themselves. There is no test of real kinghood so infallible as that. Does the crowned creature live simply, bravely, unostentatiously? probably he *is* a King. Does he cover his body with jewels, and his table with delicates? in all probability he is *not* a King. It is possible he may be, as Solomon was; but that is when the nation shares his splendor with him. Solomon made gold, not only to be in his own palace as stones, but to be in Jerusalem as stones. But, even so, for the most part, these splendid kinghoods expire in ruin, and only the true kinghoods live, which are of royal laborers governing loyal laborers; who, both leading rough lives, establish the true dynasties. Conclusively you will find that because you are king of a nation, it does not follow that you are to gather for yourself all the wealth of that nation; neither, because you are king of a small part of the nation, and lord over the means of its maintenance—over field, or mill, or mine,—are you to take all the produce of that piece of the foundation of national existence for yourself.

You will tell me I need not preach against these things, for I cannot mend them. No, good friends, I cannot; but you can, and you will; or something else can and will. Even good things have no abiding power—and shall these evil things persist in victorious evil? All history shows, on the contrary, that to be the exact thing they never can do. Change *must* come; but it is ours to determine whether change of growth, or change of death. Shall the Parthenon be in ruins on its rock, and Bolton priory in its meadow, but these mills of yours be the consummation of the buildings of the earth, and their wheels be as the wheels of eternity? Think you that "men may come, and men may go," but—mills—go on forever? Not so; out of these, better or worse shall come; and it is for you to choose which.

I know that none of this wrong is done with deliberate purpose. I know, on the contrary, that you wish your workmen well; that you do much for them, and that you desire to do more for them, if you saw your way to such benevolence safely. I 10 know that even all this wrong and misery are brought about by a warped sense of duty, each of you striving to do his best; but, unhappily, not knowing for whom this best should be done. And all our hearts have been betrayed by the plausible impiety of the modern economist, telling us that, "To do the best for ourselves, is finally to do the best for others." Friends, our great Master said not so; and most 20 absolutely we shall find this world is not made so. Indeed, to do the best for others, is finally to do the best for ourselves; but it will not do to have our eyes fixed on that issue. The Pagans had got beyond that. Hear what a Pagan says of this matter; hear what were, perhaps, the last written words of Plato,—if not the last actually written (for this we cannot know), yet assuredly in fact and power his parting 30 words—in which, endeavoring to give full crowning and harmonious close to all his thoughts, and to speak the sum of them by the imagined sentence of the Great Spirit, his strength and his heart fail him, and the words cease, broken off forever. They are at the close of the dialogue called *Critias,* in which he describes, partly from real tradition, partly in ideal dream, the early state of Athens; and the genesis, and 40 order, and religion, of the fabled isle of Atlantis; in which genesis he conceives the same first perfection and final degeneracy of man, which in our own Scriptural tradition is expressed by saying that the Sons of God intermarried with the daughters of men, for he supposes the earliest race to have been indeed the children of God; and to have corrupted themselves, until "their spot was not the spot of his children." 50 And this, he says, was the end; that indeed "through many generations, so long as the God's nature in them yet was full, they were submissive to the sacred laws, and

carried themselves lovingly to all that had kindred with them in divineness; for their uttermost spirit was faithful and true, and in every wise great; so that, in *all meekness of wisdom, they dealt with each other,* and took all the chances of life; and despising all things except virtue, they cared little what happened day by day, and *bore lightly the burden* of gold and of possessions; for they saw that, if *only their common love and virtue increased, all these things would be increased together with them;* but to set their esteem and ardent pursuit upon material possession would be to lose that first, and their virtue and affection together with it. And by such reasoning, and what of the divine nature remained in them, they gained all this greatness of which we have already told; but when the God's part of them faded and became extinct, being mixed again and again, and effaced by the prevalent mortality; and the human nature at last exceeded, they then became unable to endure the courses of fortune; and fell into shapelessness of life, and baseness in the sight of him who could see, having lost everything that was fairest of their honor; while to the blind hearts which could not discern the true life, tending to happiness, it seemed that they were then chiefly noble and happy, being filled with all iniquity of inordinate possession and power. Whereupon, the God of Gods, whose Kinghood is in laws, beholding a once just nation thus cast into misery, and desiring to lay such punishment upon them as might make them repent into restraining, gathered together all the gods into his dwelling place, which from heaven's centre overlooks whatever has part in creation; and having assembled them, he said"—

The rest is silence. Last words of the chief wisdom of the heathen, spoken of this idol of riches; this idol of yours; this golden image, high by measureless cubits, set up where your green fields of England are furnace-burned into the likeness of the plain of Dura: this idol, forbidden to us, first of all idols, by our own Master and faith; forbidden to us also by every human lip that has ever, in any age or people, been accounted of as able to speak according to the purposes of God. Continue to make that forbidden deity your principal one, and soon no more art, no more science, no more pleasure will be possible. Catastrophe will come; or, worse than catastrophe, slow mouldering and withering into Hades. But if you can fix some conception of a true human state of life to be striven for—life, good for all men, as for yourselves; if you can determine some honest and simple order of existence; following those trodden ways of wisdom, which are pleasantness, and seeking her quiet and withdrawn paths, which are peace;—then, and so sanctifying wealth into "commonwealth," all your art, your literature, your daily labors, your domestic affection, and citizen's duty, will join and increase into one magnificent harmony. You will know then how to build, well enough; you will build with stone well, but with flesh better; temples not made with hands, but riveted of hearts; and that kind of marble, crimson-veined, is indeed eternal.

[1864]

SESAME AND LILIES (Lecture III)

THE MYSTERY OF LIFE AND ITS ARTS

When I accepted the privilege of addressing you today, I was not aware of a restriction with respect to the topics of discussion which may be brought before this Society— a restriction which, though entirely wise and right under the circumstances contemplated in its introduction, would necessarily have disabled me, thinking as I think, from preparing any lecture for you on the subject of art in a form which might be permanently useful. Pardon me, therefore, in so far as I must transgress such limitation; for indeed my infringement will be of the letter—not of the spirit—of your commands. In whatever I may say touching the religion which has been the foundation of art, or the policy which has contributed to its power, if I offend one, I shall offend all; for I shall take no note of any separations in creeds, or antagonisms in parties: neither do I fear that ultimately I shall offend any, by proving—or at least stating as capable of positive proof—the connection of all that is best in the crafts and arts of man, with the simplicity of his faith, and the sincerity of his patriotism.

But I speak to you under another disadvantage, by which I am checked in frankness of utterance, not here only, but everywhere: namely, that I am never fully aware how far my audiences are disposed to give me credit for real knowledge of my subject, or how far they grant me attention only because I have been sometimes thought an ingenious or pleasant essayist upon it. For I have had what, in many respects, I boldly call the misfortune, to set my words sometimes prettily together; not without a foolish vanity in the poor knack that I had of doing so: until I was heavily punished for this pride, by finding that many people thought of the words only, and cared nothing for their meaning. Happily, therefore, the power of using such pleasant language—if indeed it ever were mine—is passing away from me; and whatever I am now able to say at all, I find myself forced to say with great plainness. For my thoughts have changed also, as my words have; and whereas in earlier life, what little influence I obtained was due perhaps chiefly to the enthusiasm with which I was able to dwell on the beauty of the physical clouds, and of their colors in the sky; so all the influence I now desire to retain must be due to the earnestness with which I am endeavoring to trace the form and beauty of another kind of cloud than those; the bright cloud of which it is written—"What is your life? It is even as a vapor that appeareth for a little time, and then vanisheth away."

I suppose few people reach the middle or latter period of their age, without having, at some moment of change or disappointment, felt the truth of those bitter words; and been startled by the fading of the sunshine from the cloud of their life into the sudden agony of the knowledge that the fabric of it was as fragile as a dream, and the endurance of it as transient as the dew. But it is not always that, even at such times of melancholy surprise, we can enter into any true perception that this human life shares in the nature of it, not only the evanescence, but the mystery of the cloud; that its avenues are wreathed in darkness, and its forms and courses no less fantastic, than spectral and obscure; so that not only in the vanity which we cannot grasp, but in the shadow which we cannot pierce, it is true of this cloudy life of ours, that "man walketh in a vain shadow, and disquieteth himself in vain."

And least of all, whatever may have been the eagerness of our passions, or the height of our pride, are we able to understand in its depth the third and most solemn character in which our life is like those clouds of heaven; that to it belongs not only their transcience, not only their mystery, but also their power; that in the cloud of the human soul there is a fire stronger than the lightning, and a grace more precious 20 than the rain; and that though of the good and evil it shall one day be said alike, that the place that knew them knows them no more, there is an infinite separation between those whose brief presence had there been a blessing, like the mist of Eden that went up from the earth to water the garden, and those whose place knew them only as a drifting and changeful shade, of whom the heavenly sentence is, that they are "wells 30 without water; clouds that are carried with a tempest, to whom the mist of darkness is reserved forever."

To those among us, however, who have lived long enough to form some just estimate of the rate of the changes which are, hour by hour in accelerating catastrophe, manifesting themselves in the laws, the arts, and the creeds of men, it seems to me, that now at least, if never at any former time, 40 the thoughts of the true nature of our life, and of its powers and responsibilities, should present themselves with absolute sadness and sternness. And although I know that this feeling is much deepened in my own mind by disappointment, which, by chance, has attended the greater number of my cherished purposes, I do not for that reason distrust the feeling itself, though I am on my guard against an 50 exaggerated degree of it: nay, I rather believe that in periods of new effort and violent change, disappointment is a wholesome medicine; and that in the secret of it,

as in the twilight so-beloved by Titian, we may see the colors of things with deeper truth than in the most dazzling sunshine. And because these truths about the works of men, which I want to bring to-day before you, are most of them sad ones, though at the same time helpful; and because also I believe that your kind Irish hearts will answer more gladly to the truthful expression of a personal feeling, than to the exposition of an abstract principle, I will permit myself so much unreserved speaking of my own causes of regret, as may enable you to make just allowance for what, according to your sympathies, you will call either the bitterness, or the insight, of a mind which has surrendered its best hopes, and been foiled in its favorite aims.

I spent the ten strongest years of my life (from twenty to thirty), in endeavoring to show the excellence of the work of the man whom I believed, and rightly believed, to be the greatest painter of the schools of England since Reynolds. I had then perfect faith in the power of every great truth of beauty to prevail ultimately, and take its right place in usefulness and honor; and I strove to bring the painter's work into this due place, while the painter was yet alive. But he knew, better than I, the uselessness of talking about what people could not see for themselves. He always discouraged me scornfully, even when he thanked me—and he died before even the superficial effect of my work was visible. I went on, however, thinking I could at least be of use to the public, if not to him, in proving his power. My books got talked about a little. The prices of modern pictures, generally, rose, and I was beginning to take some pleasure in a sense of gradual victory, when, fortunately or unfortunately, an opportunity of perfect trial undeceived me at once, and forever. The Trustees of the National Gallery commissioned me to arrange the Turner drawings there, and permitted me to prepare three hundred examples of his studies from nature, for exhibition at Kensington. At Kensington they were, and are, placed for exhibition; but they are not exhibited, for the room in which they hang is always empty.

Well—this showed me at once, that those

ten years of my life had been, in their chief purpose, lost. For that, I did not so much care; I had, at least, learned my own business thoroughly, and should be able, as I fondly supposed, after such a lesson, now to use my knowledge, with better effect. But what I did care for was the—to me frightful—discovery, that the most splendid genius in the arts might be permitted by Providence to labor and perish uselessly; that in the very fineness of it there might be something rendering it invisible to ordinary eyes; but that, with this strange excellence, faults might be mingled which would be as deadly as its virtues were vain; that the glory of it was perishable, as well as invisible, and the gift and grace of it might be to us as snow in summer and as rain in harvest.

That was the first mystery of life to me. But, while my best energy was given to the study of painting, I had put collateral effort, more prudent if less enthusiastic, into that of architecture; and in this I could not complain of meeting with no sympathy. Among several personal reasons which caused me to desire that I might give this, my closing lecture on the subject of art here, in Ireland, one of the chief was, that in reading it, I should stand near the beautiful building,—the engineer's school of your college,—which was the first realization I had the joy to see, of the principles I had, until then, been endeavoring to teach! but which, alas, is now, to me, no more than the richly canopied monument of one of the most earnest souls that ever gave itself to the arts, and one of my truest and most loving friends, Benjamin Woodward. Nor was it here in Ireland only that I received the help of Irish sympathy and genius. When to another friend, Sir Thomas Deane, with Mr. Woodward, was entrusted the building of the museum at Oxford, the best details of the work were executed by sculptors who had been born and trained here; and the first window of the façade of the building, in which was inaugurated the study of natural science in England, in true fellowship with literature, was carved from my design by an Irish sculptor.

You may perhaps think that no man ought to speak of disappointment, to whom, even in one branch of labor, so much success was granted. Had Mr. Woodward now been beside me, I had not so spoken; but his gentle and passionate spirit was cut off from the fulfilment of its purposes, and the work we did together is now become vain. It may not be so in future; but the architecture we endeavored to introduce is inconsistent alike with the reckless luxury, the deforming mechanism, and the squalid misery of modern cities; among the formative fashions of the day, aided, especially in England, by ecclesiastical sentiment, it indeed obtained notoriety; and sometimes behind an engine furnace, or a railroad bank, you may detect the pathetic discord of its momentary grace, and, with toil, decipher its floral carvings choked with soot. I felt answerable to the schools I loved, only for their injury. I perceived that this new portion of my strength had also been spent in vain; and from amidst streets of iron, and palaces of crystal, shrank back at last to the carving of the mountain and color of the flower.

And still I could tell of failure, and failure repeated, as years went on; but I have trespassed enough on your patience to show you, in part, the causes of my discouragement. Now let me more deliberately tell you its results. You know there is a tendency in the minds of many men, when they are heavily disappointed in the main purposes of their life, to feel, and perhaps in warning, perhaps in mockery, to declare, that life itself is a vanity. Because it has disappointed them, they think its nature is of disappointment always, or at best, of pleasure that can be grasped by imagination only; that the cloud of it has no strength nor fire within; but is a painted cloud only, to be delighted in, yet despised. You know how beautifully Pope has expressed this particular phase of thought:—

"Meanwhile opinion gilds, with varying rays,
These painted clouds that beautify our days;
Each want of happiness by hope supplied,
And each vacuity of sense, by pride.
Hope builds as fast as Knowledge can destroy;
In Folly's cup, still laughs the bubble joy.
One pleasure past, another still we gain,
And not a vanity is given in vain."

But the effect of failure upon my own mind has been just the reverse of this.

The more that my life disappointed me, the more solemn and wonderful it became to me. It seemed, contrarily to Pope's saying, that the vanity of it *was* indeed given in vain; but that there was something behind the veil of it, which was not vanity. It became to me not a painted cloud, but a terrible and impenetrable one: not a mirage, which vanished as I drew near, but a pillar of darkness, to which I was for-10 bidden to draw near. For I saw that both my own failure, and such success in petty things as in its poor triumph seemed to me worse than failure, came from the want of sufficiently earnest effort to understand the whole law and meaning of existence, and to bring it to noble and due end; as, on the other hand, I saw more and more clearly that all enduring success in the arts, or in any other occupation, had come from 20 the ruling of lower purposes, not by a conviction of their nothingness, but by a solemn faith in the advancing power of human nature, or in the promise, however dimly apprehended, that the mortal part of it would one day be swallowed up in immortality; and that, indeed, the arts themselves never had reached any vital strength or honor, but in the effort to proclaim this immortality, and in the serv-30 ice either of great and just religion, or of some unselfish patriotism, and law of such national life as must be the foundation of religion.

Nothing that I have ever said is more true or necessary—nothing has been more misunderstood or misapplied—than my strong assertion that the arts can never be right themselves, unless their motive is right. It is misunderstood this way: weak 40 painters, who have never learned their business, and cannot lay a true line, continually come to me, crying out—"Look at this picture of mine; it *must* be good, I had such a lovely motive. I have put my whole heart into it, and taken years to think over its treatment." Well, the only answer for these people is—if one had the cruelty to make it—"Sir, you cannot think over *any*-thing in any number of years,—you haven't 50 the head to do it; and though you had fine motives, strong enough to make you burn yourself in a slow fire, if only first you could paint a picture, you can't paint one,

nor half an inch of one; you haven't the hand to do it."

But, far more decisively we have to say to the men who *do* know their business, or may know it if they choose—"Sir, you have this gift, and a mighty one; see that you serve your nation faithfully with it. It is a greater trust than ships and armies: you might cast *them* away, if you were their 10 captain, with less treason to your people than in casting your own glorious power away, and serving the devil with it instead of men. Ships and armies you may replace if they are lost, but a great intellect, once abused, is a curse to the earth forever."

This, then, I meant by saying that the arts must have noble motive. This also I said respecting them, that they never had prospered, nor could prosper, but when 20 they had such true purpose, and were devoted to the proclamation of divine truth or law. And yet I saw also that they had always failed in this proclamation—that poetry, and sculpture, and painting, though only great when they strove to teach us something about the gods, never had taught us anything trustworthy about the gods, but had always betrayed their trust in the crisis of it, and, with their 30 powers at the full reach, became ministers to pride and to lust. And I felt also, with increasing amazement, the unconquerable apathy in ourselves and hearers, no less than in these the teachers; and that while the wisdom and rightness of every act and art of life could only be consistent with a right understanding of the ends of life, we were all plunged as in a languid dream—our hearts fat, and our eyes heavy, and 40 our ears closed, lest the inspiration of hand or voice should reach us—lest we should see with our eyes, and understand with our hearts, and be healed.

This intense apathy in all of us is the first great mystery of life; it stands in the way of every perception, every virtue. There is no making ourselves feel enough astonishment at it. That the occupations or pastimes of life should have no motive, 50 is understandable; but—That life itself should have no motive—that we neither care to find out what it may lead to, nor to guard against its being forever taken away from us—here is a mystery indeed.

For just suppose I were able to call at this moment to anyone in this audience by name, and to tell him positively that I knew a large estate had been lately left to him on some curious conditions; but that though I knew it was large, I did not know how large, nor even where it was—whether in the East Indies or the West, or in England, or at the Antipodes. I only knew it was a vast estate, and that there was a chance of his losing it altogether if he did not soon find out on what terms it had been left to him. Suppose I were able to say this positively to any single man in this audience, and he knew that I did not speak without warrant, do you think that he would rest content with that vague knowledge, if it were anywise possible to obtain more? Would he not give every energy to find some trace of the facts, and never rest till he had ascertained where this place was, and what it was like? And suppose he were a young man, and all he could discover by his best endeavor was that the estate was never to be his at all, unless he persevered, during certain years of probation, in an orderly and industrious life; but that, according to the rightness of his conduct, the portion of the estate assigned to him would be greater or less, so that it literally depended on his behavior from day to day whether he got ten thousand a year, or thirty thousand a year, or nothing whatever—would you not think it strange if the youth never troubled himself to satisfy the conditions in any way, nor ever to know what was required of him, but lived exactly as he chose, and never inquired whether his chances of the estate were increasing or passing away? Well, you know that this is actually and literally so with the greater number of the educated persons now living in Christian countries. Nearly every man and woman in any company such as this, outwardly professes to believe—and a large number unquestionably think they believe—much more than this; not only that a quite unlimited estate is in prospect for them if they please the Holder of it, but that the infinite contrary of such a possession—an estate of perpetual misery—is in store for them if they displease this great Land-Holder, this great Heaven-Holder. And

yet there is not one in a thousand of these human souls that cares to think, for ten minutes of the day, where this estate is or how beautiful it is, or what kind of life they are to lead in it, or what kind of life they must lead to obtain it.

You fancy that you care to know this: so little do you care that, probably, at this moment many of you are displeased with me for talking of the matter! You came to hear about the Art of this world, not about the Life of the next, and you are provoked with me for talking of what you can hear any Sunday in church. But do not be afraid. I will tell you something before you go about pictures, and carvings, and pottery, and what else you would like better to hear of than the other world. Nay, perhaps you say, "We want you to talk of pictures and pottery, because we are sure that you know something of them, and you know nothing of the other world." Well—I don't. That is quite true. But the very strangeness and mystery of which I urge you to take notice, is in this—that I do not;—nor you either. Can you answer a single bold question unflinchingly about that other world?—Are you sure there is a heaven? Sure there is a hell? Sure that men are dropping before your faces through the pavements of these streets into eternal life, or sure that they are not? Sure that at your own death you are going to be delivered from all sorrow, to be endowed with all virtue, to be gifted with all felicity, and raised into perpetual companionship with a King, compared to whom the kings of the earth are as grasshoppers, and the nations as the dust of His feet? Are you sure of this? or, if not sure, do any of us so much as care to make it sure? and, if not, how can anything that we do be right—how can anything we think be wise? what honor can there be in the arts that amuse us, or what profit in the possessions that please?

Is not this a mystery of life?

But farther, you may, perhaps, think it a beneficent ordinance for the generality of men that they do not, with earnestness or anxiety, dwell on such questions of the future because the business of the day could not be done if this kind of thought were taken by all of us for the morrow.

Be it so: but at least we might anticipate that the greatest and wisest of us, who were evidently the appointed teachers of the rest, would set themselves apart to seek out whatever could be surely known of the future destinies of their race; and to teach this in no rhetorical or ambiguous manner, but in the plainest and most severely earnest words.

Now, the highest representatives of men who have thus endeavored, during the Christian era, to search out these deep things, and relate them, are Dante and Milton. There are none who for earnestness of thought, for mastery of word, can be classed with these. I am not at present, mind you, speaking of persons set apart in any priestly or pastoral office, to deliver creeds to us, or doctrines; but of men who try to discover and set forth, as far as by human intellect is possible, the facts of the other world. Divines may perhaps teach us how to arrive there, but only these two poets have in any powerful manner striven to discover, or in any definite words professed to tell, what we shall see and become there; or how those upper and nether worlds are, and have been, inhabited.

And what have they told us? Milton's account of the most important event in his whole system of the universe, the fall of the angels, is evidently unbelievable to himself; and the more so, that it is wholly founded on, and in a great part spoiled and degraded from, Hesiod's account of the decisive war of the younger gods with the Titans. The rest of his poem is a picturesque drama, in which every artifice of invention is visibly and consciously employed; not a single fact being, for an instant, conceived as tenable by any living faith. Dante's conception is far more intense, and, by himself, for the time, not to be escaped from; it is indeed a vision, but a vision only, and that one of the wildest that ever entranced a soul—a dream in which every grotesque type or phantasy of heathen tradition is renewed, and adorned; and the destinies of the Christian Church, under their most sacred symbols, become literally subordinate to the praise, and are only to be understood by the aid, of one dear Florentine maiden.

I tell you truly that, as I strive more with this strange lethargy and trance in myself, and awake to the meaning and power of life, it seems daily more amazing to me that men such as these should dare to play with the most precious truths (or the most deadly untruths), by which the whole human race listening to them could be informed, or deceived;—all the world their audiences forever, with pleased ear, and passionate heart;—and yet, to this submissive infinitude of souls, and evermore succeeding and succeeding multitude, hungry for bread of life, they do but play upon sweetly modulated pipes; with pompous nomenclature adorn the councils of hell; touch a troubadour's guitar to the courses of the sun; and fill the openings of eternity, before which prophets have veiled their faces, and which angels desire to look into, with idle puppets of their scholastic imagination, and melancholy lights of frantic faith in their lost mortal love.

Is not this a mystery of life?

But more. We have to remember that these two great teachers were both of them warped in their temper, and thwarted in their search for truth. They were men of intellectual war, unable, through darkness of controversy, or stress of personal grief, to discern where their own ambition modified their utterances of the moral law; or their own agony mingled with their anger at its violation. But greater men than these have been—innocent-hearted—too great for contest. Men, like Homer and Shakespeare, of so unrecognized personality, that it disappears in future ages, and becomes ghostly, like the tradition of a lost heathen god. Men, therefore, to whose unoffended, uncondemning sight, the whole of human nature reveals itself in a pathetic weakness, with which they will not strive; or in mournful and transitory strength, which they dare not praise. And all Pagan and Christian Civilization thus becomes subject to them. It does not matter how little, or how much, any of us have read, either of Homer or Shakespeare; everything round us, in substance, or in thought, has been moulded by them. All Greek gentlemen were educated under Homer. All Roman gentlemen, by Greek literature. All Italian, and French, and

English gentlemen, by Roman literature, and by its principles. Of the scope of Shakespeare, I will say only, that the intellectual measure of every man since born, in the domains of creative thought, may be assigned to him, according to the degree in which he has been taught by Shakespeare. Well, what do these two men, centres of mortal intelligence, deliver to us of conviction respecting what it most behooves that intelligence to grasp? What is their hope—their crown of rejoicing? what manner of exhortation have they for us, or of rebuke? what lies next their own hearts, and dictates their undying words? Have they any peace to promise to our unrest— any redemption to our misery?

Take Homer first, and think if there is any sadder image of human fate than the great Homeric story. The main features in the character of Achilles are its intense desire of justice, and its tenderness of affection. And in that bitter song of the *Iliad,* this man, though aided continually by the wisest of the gods, and burning with the desire of justice in his heart, becomes yet, through ill-governed passion, the most unjust of men: and, full of the deepest tenderness in his heart, becomes yet, through ill-governed passion, the most cruel of men. Intense alike in love and in friendship, he loses, first his mistress, and then his friend; for the sake of the one, he surrenders to death the armies of his own land; for the sake of the other, he surrenders all. Will a man lay down his life for his friend? Yea—even for his *dead* friend, this Achilles, though goddess-born, and goddess-taught, gives up his kingdom, his country, and his life—casts alike the innocent and guilty, with himself, into one gulf of slaughter, and dies at last by the hand of the basest of his adversaries.

Is not this a mystery of life?

But what, then, is the message to us of our own poet, and searcher of hearts, after fifteen hundred years of Christian faith have been numbered over the graves of men? Are his words more cheerful than the Heathen's—is his hope more near—his trust more sure—his reading of fate more happy? Ah, no! He differs from the Heathen poet chiefly in this—that he recognizes, for deliverance, no gods nigh at

hand; and that, by petty chance—by momentary folly—by broken message—by fool's tyranny—or traitor's snare, the strongest and most righteous are brought to their ruin, and perish without word of hope. He indeed, as part of his rendering of character, ascribes the power and modesty of habitual devotion to the gentle and the just. The death-bed of Katharine is bright with visions of angels; and the great soldier-king, standing by his few dead, acknowledges the presence of the Hand that can save alike by many or by few. But observe that from those who with deepest spirit, meditate, and with deepest passion, mourn, there are no such words as these; nor in their hearts are any such consolations. Instead of the perpetual sense of the helpful presence of the Deity, which, through all heathen tradition, is the source of heroic strength, in battle, in exile, and in the valley of the shadow of death, we find only in the great Christian poet, the consciousness of a moral law, through which "the gods are just, and of our pleasant vices make instruments to scourge us"; and of the resolved arbitration of the destinies, that conclude into precision of doom what we feebly and blindly began; and force us, when our indiscretion serves us, and our deepest plots do pall, to the confession, that "there's a divinity that shapes our ends, rough hew them how we will."

Is not this a mystery of life?

Be it so, then. About this human life that is to be, or that is, the wise religious men tell us nothing that we can trust; and the wise contemplative men, nothing that can give us peace. But there is yet a third class, to whom we may turn—the wise practical men. We have sat at the feet of the poets who sang of heaven, and they have told us their dreams. We have listened to the poets who sang of earth, and they have chanted to us dirges and words of despair. But there is one class of men more:—men, not capable of vision, nor sensitive to sorrow, but firm of purpose—practised in business; learned in all that can be (by handling,) known. Men, whose hearts and hopes are wholly in this present world, from whom, therefore, we may surely learn, at least, how, at present, conveniently to live in it. What will *they* say to us, or show us by example? These kings—these councillors—these statesmen and builders of kingdoms—these capitalists and men of business, who weigh the earth, and the dust of it, in a balance. They know the world, surely; and what is the mystery of life to us, is none to them. They can surely show us how to live, while we live, and to gather out of the present world what is best.

I think I can best tell you their answer, by telling you a dream I had once. For though I am no poet, I have dreams sometimes:—I dreamed I was at a child's May-day party, in which every means of entertainment had been provided for them, by a wise and kind host. It was in a stately house, with beautiful gardens attached to it; and the children had been set free in the rooms and gardens, with no care whatever but how to pass their afternoon rejoicingly. They did not, indeed, know much about what was to happen next day; and some of them, I thought, were a little frightened, because there was a chance of their being sent to a new school where there were examinations; but they kept the thoughts of that out of their heads as well as they could, and resolved to enjoy themselves. The house, I said, was in a beautiful garden, and in the garden were all kinds of flowers; sweet, grassy banks for rest; and smooth lawns for play; and pleasant streams and woods; and rocky places for climbing. And the children were happy for a little while, but presently they separated themselves into parties; and then each party declared it would have a piece of the garden for its own, and that none of the others should have anything to do with that piece. Next, they quarrelled violently which pieces they would have; and at last the boys took up the thing, as boys should do, "practically," and fought in the flower-beds till there was hardly a flower left standing; then they trampled down each other's bits of the garden out of spite; and the girls cried till they could cry no more; and so they all lay down at last breathless in the ruin, and waited for the time when they were to be taken home in the evening.

Meanwhile, the children in the house had been making themselves happy also in their manner. For them, there had been provided every kind of indoor pleasure: there was music for them to dance to; and the library was open, with all manner of amusing books; and there was a museum full of the most curious shells, and animals, and birds; and there was a workshop, with lathes and carpenter's tools, for the ingenious boys; and there were pretty fantastic dresses, for the girls to dress in; and there were microscopes, and kaleidoscopes; and whatever toys a child could fancy; and a table, in the dining-room, loaded with everything nice to eat.

But, in the midst of all this, it struck two or three of the more "practical" children, that they would like some of the brass-headed nails that studded the chairs; and so they set to work to pull them out. Presently, the others, who were reading, or looking at shells, took a fancy to do the like; and, in a little while, all the children, nearly, were spraining their fingers, in pulling out brass-headed nails. With all that they could pull out, they were not satisfied; and then, everybody wanted some of somebody else's. And at last, the really practical and sensible ones declared, that nothing was of any real consequence, that afternoon, except to get plenty of brass-headed nails; and that the books, and the cakes, and the microscopes were of no use at all in themselves, but only, if they could be exchanged for nail-heads. And at last they began to fight for nail-heads, as the others fought for the bits of garden. Only here and there, a despised one shrank away into a corner, and tried to get a little quiet with a book, in the midst of the noise; but all the practical ones thought of nothing else but counting nail-heads all the afternoon—even though they knew they would not be allowed to carry so much as one brass knob away with them. But no—it was—"who has most nails? I have a hundred, and you have fifty; or, I have a thousand, and you have two. I must have as many as you before I leave the house, or I cannot possibly go home in peace." At last, they made so much noise that I awoke, and thought to myself, "What a false dream that is, of *children!*" The child is the father of the man; and wiser.

Children never do such foolish things. Only men do.

But there is yet one last class of persons to be interrogated. The wise religious men we have asked in vain; the wise contemplative men, in vain; the wise worldly men, in vain. But there is another group yet. In the midst of this vanity of empty religion—of tragic contemplation—of wrathful and wretched ambition, and dispute for dust, there is yet one great group of persons, by whom all these disputers live—the persons who have determined, or have had it by a beneficent Providence determined for them, that they will do something useful; that whatever may be prepared for them hereafter, or happen to them here, they will, at least, deserve the food that God gives them by winning it honorably: and that, however fallen from the purity, or far from the peace, of Eden, they will carry out the duty of human dominion, though they have lost its felicity; and dress and keep the wilderness, though they no more can dress or keep the garden.

These,—hewers of wood, and drawers of water,—these, bent under burdens, or torn of scourges—these, that dig and weave—that plant and build; workers in wood, and in marble, and in iron—by whom all food, clothing, habitation, furniture, and means of delight are produced, for themselves, and for all men besides; men, whose deeds are good, though their words may be few; men, whose lives are serviceable, be they never so short, and worthy of honor, be they never so humble;—from these, surely, at least, we may receive some clear message of teaching; and pierce, for an instant, into the mystery of life, and of its arts.

Yes; from these, at last, we do receive a lesson. But I grieve to say, or rather—for that is the deeper truth of the matter—I rejoice to say—this message of theirs can only be received by joining them—not by thinking about them.

You sent for me to talk of art; and I have obeyed you in coming. But the main thing I have to tell you is,—that art must not be talked about. The fact that there is talk about it at all, signifies that it is ill done, or cannot be done. No true painter ever speaks, or ever has spoken, much of his art. The greatest speak nothing. Even Reynolds is no exception, for he wrote of all that he could not himself do, and was utterly silent respecting all that he himself did.

The moment a man can really do his work he becomes speechless about it. All words become idle to him—all theories.

Does a bird need to theorize about building its nest, or boast of it when built? All good work is essentially done that way—without hesitation, without difficulty, without boasting; and in the doers of the best, there is an inner and involuntary power which approximates literally to the instinct of an animal—nay, I am certain that in the most perfect human artists, reason does *not* supersede instinct, but is added to an instinct as much more divine than that of the lower animals as the human body is more beautiful than theirs; that a great singer sings not with less instinct than the nightingale, but with more—only more various, applicable, and governable; that a great architect does not build with less instinct than the beaver or the bee, but with more—with an innate cunning of proportion that embraces all beauty, and a divine ingenuity of skill that improvises all construction. But be that as it may—be the instinct less or more than that of inferior animals—like or unlike theirs, still the human art is dependent on that first, and then upon an amount of practice, of science,—and of imagination disciplined by thought, which the true possessor of it knows to be incommunicable, and the true critic of it, inexplicable, except through long process of laborious years. That journey of life's conquest, in which hills over hills, and Alps on Alps arose, and sank,—do you think you can make another trace it painlessly by talking? Why, you cannot even carry us up an Alp, by talking. You can guide us up it, step by step, no otherwise—even so, best silently. You girls, who have been among the hills, know how the bad guide chatters and gesticulates, and it is "Put your foot here"; and "Mind how you balance yourself there"; but the good guide walks on quietly, without a word, only with his eyes on you when need is, and his arm like an iron bar, if need be.

In that slow way, also, art can be taught —if you have faith in your guide, and will let his arm be to you as an iron bar when need is. But in what teacher of art have you such faith? Certainly not in me; for, as I told you at first, I know well enough it is only because you think I can talk, not because you think I know my business, that you let me speak to you at all. If I were to tell you anything that seemed to you strange you would not believe it, and yet it would only be in telling you strange things that I could be of use to you. I could be of great use to you—infinite use—with brief saying, if you would believe it; but you would not, just because the thing that would be of real use would displease you. You are all wild, for instance, with admiration of Gustave Doré. Well, suppose I were to tell you, in the strongest terms I could use, that Gustave Doré's art was bad—bad, not in weakness,—not in failure,—but bad with dreadful power—the power of the Furies and the Harpies mingled, enraging, and polluting; that so long as you looked at it, no perception of pure or beautiful art was possible for you. Suppose I were to tell you that! What would be the use? Would you look at Gustave Doré less? Rather, more, I fancy. On the other hand, I could soon put you into good humor with me, if I chose. I know well enough what you like, and how to praise it to your better liking. I could talk to you about moonlight, and twilight, and spring flowers, and autumn leaves, and the Madonnas of Raphael—how motherly! and the Sibyls of Michael Angelo—how majestic! and the Saints of Angelico—how pious! and the Cherubs of Correggio—how delicious! Old as I am, I could play you a tune on the harp yet, that you would dance to. But neither you nor I should be a bit the better or wiser; or, if we were, our increased wisdom could be of no practical effect. For, indeed, the arts, as regards teachableness, differ from the sciences also in this, that their power is founded not merely on facts which can be communicated, but on dispositions which require to be created. Art is neither to be achieved by effort of thinking, nor explained by accuracy of speaking. It is the instinctive and necessary result of power, which can only be developed through the mind of successive generations, and which finally burst into life under social conditions as slow of growth as the faculties they regulate. Whole æras of mighty history are summed, and the passions of dead myriads are concentrated, in the existence of a noble art; and if that noble art were among us, we should feel it and rejoice; not caring in the least to hear lectures on it; and since it is not among us, be assured we have to go back to the root of it, or, at least, to the place where the stock of it is yet alive, and the branches began to die.

And now, may I have your pardon for pointing out, partly with reference to matters which are at this time of greater moment than the arts—that if we undertook such recession to the vital germ of national arts that have decayed, we should find a more singular arrest of their power in Ireland than in any other European country? For in the eighth century Ireland possessed a school of art in her manuscripts and sculpture, which, in many of its qualities—apparently in all essential qualities of decorative invention—was quite without rival; seeming as if it might have advanced to the highest triumphs in architecture and in painting. But there was one fatal flaw in its nature, by which it was stayed, and stayed with a conspicuousness of pause to which there is no parallel: so that, long ago, in tracing the progress of European schools from infancy to strength, I chose for the students of Kensington, in a lecture since published, two characteristic examples of early art, of equal skill; but in the one case, skill which was progressive—in the other, skill which was at pause. In the one case, it was work receptive of correction—hungry for correction; and in the other, work which inherently rejected correction. I chose for them a corrigible Eve, and an incorrigible Angel, and I grieve to say that the incorrigible Angel was also an Irish Angel!

And the fatal difference lay wholly in this. In both pieces of art there was an equal falling short of the needs of fact; but the Lombardic Eve knew she was in the wrong, and the Irish Angel thought himself all right. The eager Lombardic sculptor, though firmly insisting on his childish idea, yet showed in the irregular broken touches of the features, and the imperfect struggle for softer lines in the form, a perception of beauty and law that he could not render; there was the strain of effort, under conscious imperfection, in every line. But the Irish missal-painter had drawn his angel with no sense of failure, in happy complacency, and put red dots into the palm of each hand, and rounded the eyes into perfect circles, and, I regret to say, left the mouth out altogether, with perfect satisfaction to himself.

May I without offence ask you to consider whether this mode of arrest in ancient Irish art may not be indicative of points of character which even yet, in some measure, arrest your national power? I have seen much of Irish character, and have watched it closely, for I have also much loved it. And I think the form of failure to which it is most liable is this,—that being generous-hearted, and wholly intending always to do right, it does not attend to the external laws of right, but thinks it must necessarily do right because it means to do so, and therefore does wrong without finding it out; and then, when the consequences of its wrong come upon it, or upon others connected with it, it cannot conceive that the wrong is in any wise of its causing or of its doing, but flies into wrath, and a strange agony of desire for justice, as feeling itself wholly innocent, which leads it farther astray, until there is nothing that it is not capable of doing with a good conscience.

But mind, I do not mean to say that, in past or present relations between Ireland and England, you have been wrong, and we right. Far from that, I believe that in all great questions of principle, and in all details of administration of law, you have been usually right, and we wrong; sometimes in misunderstanding you, sometimes in resolute iniquity to you. Nevertheless, in all disputes between states, though the stronger is nearly always mainly in the wrong, the weaker is often so in a minor degree; and I think we sometimes admit the possibility of our being in error, and you never do.

And now, returning to the broader question, what these arts and labors of life have to teach us of its mystery, this is the first of their lessons—that the more beautiful the art, the more it is essentially the work of people who *feel themselves wrong;*—who are striving for the fulfilment of a law, and the grasp of a loveliness, which they have not yet attained, which they feel even farther and farther from attaining the more they strive for it. And yet, in still deeper sense, it is the work of people who know also that they are right. The very sense of inevitable error from their purpose marks the perfectness of that purpose, and the continued sense of failure arises from the continued opening of the eyes more clearly to all the sacredest laws of truth.

This is one lesson. The second is a very plain, and greatly precious one: namely—that whenever the arts and labors of life are fulfilled in this spirit of striving against misrule, and doing whatever we have to do, honorably and perfectly, they invariably bring happiness, as much as seems possible to the nature of man. In all other paths by which that happiness is pursued there is disappointment, or destruction: for ambition and for passion there is no rest—no fruition; the fairest pleasures of youth perish in a darkness greater than their past light: and the loftiest and purest love too often does but inflame the cloud of life with endless fire of pain. But, ascending from lowest to highest, through every scale of human industry, that industry worthily followed, gives peace. Ask the laborer in the field, at the forge, or in the mine; ask the patient, delicate-fingered artisan, or the strong-armed, fiery-hearted worker in bronze, and in marble, and with the colors of light; and none of these, who are true workmen, will ever tell you, that they have found the law of heaven an unkind one—that in the sweat of their face they should eat bread, till they return to the ground; nor that they ever found it an unrewarded obedience, if, indeed, it was rendered faithfully to the command—"Whatsoever thy hand findeth to do—do it with thy might."

These are the two great and constant lessons which our laborers teach us of the mystery of life. But there is another, and a sadder one, which they cannot teach us, which we must read on their tombstones. "Do it with thy might." There have been myriads upon myriads of human creatures who have obeyed this law—who have put every breath and nerve of their being into its toil—who have devoted every hour, and exhausted every faculty—who have bequeathed their unaccomplished thoughts at death—who, being dead, have yet spoken, by majesty of memory, and strength of example. And, at last, what has all this "Might" of humanity accomplished, in six thousand years of labor and sorrow? What has it *done?* Take the three chief occupations and arts of men, one by one, and count their achievements. Begin with the first—the lord of them all—Agriculture. Six thousand years have passed since we were set to till the ground, from which we were taken. How much of it is tilled? How much of that which is, wisely or well? In the very centre and chief garden of Europe—where the two forms of parent Christianity have had their fortresses—where the noble Catholics of the Forest Cantons, and the noble Protestants of the Vaudois valleys, have maintained, for dateless ages, their faiths and liberties—there the unchecked Alpine rivers yet run wild in devastation; and the marshes, which a few hundred men could redeem with a year's labor, still blast their helpless inhabitants into fevered idiotism. That is so, in the centre of Europe! While, on the near coast of Africa, once the Garden of the Hesperides, an Arab woman, but a few sunsets since, ate her child, for famine. And, with all the treasures of the East at our feet, we, in our own dominion, could not find a few grains of rice, for a people that asked of us no more; but stood by, and saw five hundred thousand of them perish of hunger.

Then, after agriculture, the art of kings, take the next head of human arts—Weaving; the art of queens, honored of all noble Heathen women, in the person of their virgin goddess—honored of all Hebrew women, by the word of their wisest king— "She layeth her hands to the spindle, and her hands hold the distaff; she stretcheth out her hand to the poor. She is not afraid of the snow for her household, for all her household are clothed with scarlet. She maketh herself covering of tapestry; her clothing is silk and purple. She maketh fine linen, and selleth it, and delivereth girdles to the merchant." What have we done in all these thousands of years with this bright art of Greek maid and Christian matron? Six thousand years of weaving, and have we learned to weave? Might not every naked wall have been purple with tapestry, and every feeble breast fenced with sweet colors from the cold? What have we done? Our fingers are too few, it seems, to twist together some poor covering for our bodies. We set our streams to work for us, and choke the air with fire, to turn our spinning-wheels—and,—*are we yet clothed?* Are not the streets of the capitals of Europe foul with sale of cast clouts and rotten rags? Is not the beauty of your sweet children left in wretchedness of disgrace, while, with better honor, nature clothes the brood of the bird in its nest, and the suckling of the wolf in her den? And does not every winter's snow robe what you have not robed, and shroud what you have not shrouded; and every winter's wind bear up to heaven its wasted souls, to witness against you hereafter, by the voice of their Christ,—"I was naked, and ye clothed me not"?

Lastly—take the Art of Building—the strongest—proudest—most orderly—most enduring of the arts of man; that of which the produce is in the surest manner accumulative, and need not perish, or be replaced; but if once well done, will stand more strongly than the unbalanced rocks— more prevalently than the crumbling hills. The art which is associated with all civic pride and sacred principle; with which men record their power—satisfy their enthusiasm—make sure their defence—define and make dear their habitation. And in six thousand years of building, what have we done? Of the greater part of all that skill and strength, *no* vestige is left, but fallen stones, that encumber the fields and impede the streams. But, from this waste of disorder, and of time, and of rage, what *is* left to us? Constructive and progressive creatures that we are, with ruling brains, and forming hands, capable of fellowship, and thirsting for fame, can we not contend, in comfort, with the insects of the forest, or, in achievement, with the worm of the sea? The white surf rages in vain against the ramparts built by poor atoms of scarcely nascent life; but only ridges of formless ruin mark the places where once dwelt our noblest multitudes. The ant and the moth have cells for each of their young, but our little ones lie in festering heaps, in homes that consume them like graves; and night by night, from the corners of our streets, rises up the cry of the homeless—"I was a stranger, and ye took me not in."

Must it be always thus? Is our life forever to be without profit—without posses-sion? Shall the strength of its generations be as barren as death; or cast away their labor, as the wild fig-tree casts her untimely figs? Is it all a dream then—the desire of the eyes and the pride of life—or, if it be, might we not live in nobler dream than this? The poets and prophets, the wise men, and the scribes, though they have told us nothing about a life to come, have told us much about the life that is now. They have had—they also,—their dreams, and we have laughed at them. They have dreamed of mercy, and of justice; they have dreamed of peace and good-will; they have dreamed of labor undisappointed, and of rest undisturbed; they have dreamed of fulness in harvest, and overflowing in store; they have dreamed of wisdom in council, and of providence in law; of gladness of parents, and strength of children, and glory of gray hairs. And at these visions of theirs we have mocked, and held them for idle and vain, unreal and unaccomplishable. What have we accomplished with our realities? Is this what has come of our worldly wisdom, tried against their folly? this, our mightiest possible, against their impotent ideal? or, have we only wandered among the spectra of a baser felicity, and chased phantoms of the tombs, instead of visions of the Almighty; and walked after the imaginations of our evil hearts, instead of after the counsels of Eternity, until our lives—not in the likeness of the cloud of heaven, but of the smoke of hell—have become "as a vapor, that appeareth for a little time, and then vanisheth away"?

Does it vanish then? Are you sure of that?—sure, that the nothingness of the grave will be a rest from this troubled nothingness; and that the coiling shadow, which disquiets itself in vain, cannot change into the smoke of the torment that ascends forever? Will any answer that they *are* sure of it, and that there is no fear, nor hope, nor desire, nor labor, whither they go? Be it so: will you not, then, make as sure of the Life that now is, as you are of the Death that is to come? Your hearts are wholly in this world—will you not give them to it wisely, as well as perfectly? And see, first of all, that you *have* hearts, and sound hearts, too, to give. Because you have no heaven to look for, is that any reason that you should remain ignorant of this wonderful and infinite earth, which is firmly and instantly given you in posses-sion? Although your days are numbered, and the following darkness sure, is it nec-essary that you should share the de-gradation of the brute, because you are condemned to its mortality; or live the life of the moth, and of the worm, because you are to companion them in the dust? Not so; we may have but a few thousands of days to spend, perhaps hundreds only—perhaps tens; nay, the longest of our time and best, looked back on, will be but as a moment, as the twinkling of an eye; still we are men, not insects; we are living spirits, not passing clouds. "He maketh the winds His messengers; the momentary fire, His minister;" and shall we do less than *these?* Let us do the work of men while we bear the form of them; and, as we snatch our narrow portion of time out of Eternity, snatch also our narrow inherit-ance of passion out of Immortality—even though our lives *be* as a vapor, that appeareth for a little time, and then vanisheth away.

But there are some of you who believe not this—who think this cloud of life has no such close—that it is to float, revealed and illumined, upon the floor of heaven, in the day when He cometh with clouds, and every eye shall see Him. Some day, you believe, within these five, or ten, or twenty years, for every one of us the judg-ment will be set, and the books opened. If that be true, far more than that must be true. Is there but one day of judgment? Why, for us every day is a day of judgment —every day is a Dies Iræ, and writes its irrevocable verdict in the flame of its West. Think you that judgment waits till the doors of the grave are opened? It waits at the doors of your houses—it waits at the corners of your streets; we are in the midst of judgment—the insects that we crush are our judges—the moments we fret away are our judges—the elements that feed us, judge, as they minister—and the pleasures that deceive us, judge, as they indulge. Let us, for our lives, do the work of Men while we bear the form of them, if indeed those lives are *Not* as a vapor, and do *Not* vanish away.

"The work of men"—and what is that? Well, we may any of us know very quickly, on the condition of being wholly ready to do it. But many of us are for the most part thinking, not of what we are to do, but of what we are to get; and the best of us are sunk into the sin of Ananias, and it is a mortal one—we want to keep back part of the price; and we continually talk of taking up our cross, as if the only harm in a cross was the *weight* of it—as if it was only a thing to be carried, instead of to be—crucified upon. "They that are His have crucified the flesh, with the affections and lusts." Does that mean, think you, that in time of national distress, of religious trial, of crisis for every interest and hope of humanity—none of us will cease jesting, none cease idling, none put themselves to any wholesome work, none take so much as a tag of lace off their footmen's coats, to save the world? Or does it rather mean, that they are ready to leave houses, lands, and kindreds—yes, and life, if need be? Life!—some of us are ready enough to throw that away, joyless as we have made it. But *"station* in Life"—how many of us are ready to quit *that?* Is it not always the great objection, where there is question of finding something useful to do—"We cannot leave our stations in Life"?

Those of us who really cannot—that is to say, who can only maintain themselves by continuing in some business or salaried office, have already something to do; and all that they have to see to is, that they do it honestly and with all their might. But with most people who use that apology, "remaining in the station of life to which Providence has called them" means keeping all the carriages, and all the footmen and large houses they can possibly pay for; and, once for all, I say that if ever Providence *did* put them into stations of that

sort—which is not at all a matter of certainty—Providence is just now very distinctly calling them out again. Levi's station in life was the receipt of custom; and Peter's, the shore of Galilee; and Paul's, the ante-chambers of the High Priest,—which "station in life" each had to leave, with brief notice.

And, whatever our station in life may be, at this crisis, those of us who mean to fulfil our duty ought first to live on as little as we can; and, secondly, to do all the wholesome work for it we can, and to spend all we can spare in doing all the sure good we can.

And sure good is, first in feeding people, then in dressing people, then in lodging people, and lastly in rightly pleasing people, with arts, or sciences, or any other subject of thought.

I say first in feeding; and, once for all, do not let yourselves be deceived by any of the common talk of "indiscriminate charity." The order to us is not to feed the deserving hungry, nor the industrious hungry, nor the amiable and well-intentioned hungry, but simply to feed the hungry. It is quite true, infallibly true, that if any man will not work, neither should he eat—think of that, and every time you sit down to your dinner, ladies and gentlemen, say solemnly, before you ask a blessing, "How much work have I done to-day for my dinner?" But the proper way to enforce that order on those below you, as well as on yourselves, is not to leave vagabonds and honest people to starve together, but very distinctly to discern and seize your vagabond; and shut your vagabond up out of honest people's way, and very sternly then see that, until he has worked, he does *not* eat. But the first thing is to be sure you have the food to give; and, therefore, to enforce the organization of vast activities in agriculture and in commerce, for the production of the wholesomest food, and proper storing and distribution of it, so that no famine shall any more be possible among civilized beings. There is plenty of work in this business alone, and at once, for any number of people who like to engage in it.

Secondly, dressing people—that is to say, urging everyone within reach of your influence to be always neat and clean, and giving them means of being so. In so far as they absolutely refuse, you must give up the effort with respect to them, only taking care that no children within your sphere of influence shall any more be brought up with such habits; and that every person who is willing to dress with propriety shall have encouragement to do so. And the first absolutely necessary step toward this is the gradual adoption of a consistent dress for different ranks of persons, so that their rank shall be known by their dress; and the restriction of the changes of fashion within certain limits. All which appears for the present quite impossible; but it is only so far even difficult as it is difficult to conquer our vanity, frivolity, and desire to appear what we are not. And it is not, nor ever shall be, creed of mine, that these mean and shallow vices are unconquerable by Christian women.

And then, thirdly, lodging people, which you may think should have been put first, but I put it third, because we must feed and clothe people where we find them, and lodge them afterward. And providing lodgment for them means a great deal of vigorous legislation, and cutting down of vested interests that stand in the way, and after that, or before that, so far as we can get it, thorough sanitary and remedial action in the houses that we have; and then the building of more, strongly, beautifully, and in groups of limited extent, kept in proportion to their streams, and walled round, so that there may be no festering and wretched suburb anywhere, but clean and busy street within, and the open country without, with a belt of beautiful garden and orchard round the walls, so that from any part of the city perfectly fresh air and grass, and sight of far horizon, might be reachable in a few minutes' walk. This the final aim; but in immediate action every minor and possible good to be instantly done, when, and as, we can; roofs mended that have holes in them—fences patched that have gaps in them—walls buttressed that totter—and floors propped that shake; cleanliness and order enforced with our own hands and eyes, till we are breathless, every day. And all the fine arts will healthily follow. I myself have washed a

flight of stone stairs all down, with bucket and broom, in a Savoy inn, where they hadn't washed their stairs since they first went up them; and I never made a better sketch than that afternoon.

These, then, are the three first needs of civilized life; and the law for every Christian man and woman is, that they shall be in direct service toward one of these three needs, as far as is consistent with their own special occupation, and if they have no special business, then wholly in one of these services. And out of such exertion in plain duty all other good will come; for in this direct contention with material evil, you will find out the real nature of all evil; you will discern by the various kinds of resistance, what is really the fault and main antagonism to good; also you will find the most unexpected helps and profound lessons given, and truths will come thus down to us which the speculation of all our lives would never have raised us up to. You will find nearly every educational problem solved, as soon as you truly want to do something; everybody will become of use in their own fittest way, and will learn what is best for them to know in that use. Competitive examination will then, and not till then, be wholesome, because it will be daily, and calm, and in practice; and on these familiar arts, and minute, but certain and serviceable knowledges, will be surely edified and sustained the greater arts and splendid theoretical sciences.

But much more than this. On such holy and simple practice will be founded, indeed, at last, an infallible religion. The greatest of all the mysteries of life, and the most terrible, is the corruption of even the sincerest religion, which is not daily founded on rational, effective, humble, and helpful action. Helpful action, observe! for there is just one law, which, obeyed, keeps all religions pure—forgotten, makes them all false. Whenever in any religious faith, dark or bright, we allow our minds to dwell upon the points in which we differ from other people, we are wrong, and in the devil's power. That is the essence of the Pharisee's thanksgiving—"Lord, I thank Thee that I am not as other men are." At every moment of our lives we should be trying to find out, not in what we differ from other people, but in what we agree with them; and the moment we find we can agree as to anything that should be done, kind or good (and who but fools couldn't?) then do it; push at it together: you can't quarrel in a side-by-side push; but the moment that even the best men stop pushing, and begin talking, they mistake their pugnacity for piety, and it's all over. I will not speak of the crimes which in past times have been committed in the name of Christ, nor of the follies which are at this hour held to be consistent with obedience to Him; but I *will* speak of the morbid corruption and waste of vital power in religious sentiment, by which the pure strength of that which should be the guiding soul of every nation, the splendor of its youthful manhood, and spotless light of its maidenhood, is averted or cast away. You may see continually girls who have never been taught to do a single useful thing thoroughly; who cannot sew, who cannot cook, who cannot cast an account, nor prepare a medicine, whose whole life has been passed either in play or in pride; you will find girls like these, when they are earnest-hearted, cast all their innate passion of religious spirit, which was meant by God to support them through the irksomeness of daily toil, into grievous and vain meditation over the meaning of the great Book, of which no syllable was ever yet to be understood but through a deed; all the instinctive wisdom and mercy of their womanhood made vain, and the glory of their pure consciences warped into fruitless agony concerning questions which the laws of common serviceable life would have

either solved for them in an instant, or kept out of their way. Give such a girl any true work that will make her active in the dawn, and weary at night, with the consciousness that her fellow-creatures have indeed been the better for her day, and the powerless sorrow of her enthusiasm will transform itself into a majesty of radiant and beneficent peace.

So with our youths. We once taught them to make Latin verses, and called them educated; now we teach them to leap and to row, to hit a ball with a bat, and call them educated. Can they plough, can they sow, can they plant at the right time, or build with a steady hand? Is it the effort of their lives to be chaste, knightly, faithful, holy in thought, lovely in word and deed? Indeed it is, with some, nay, with many, and the strength of England is in them, and the hope; but we have to turn their courage from the toil of war to the toil of mercy; and their intellect from dispute of words to discernment of things; and their knighthood from the errantry of adventure to the state and fidelity of a kingly power. And then, indeed, shall abide, for them and for us, an incorruptible felicity, and an infallible religion; shall abide for us Faith, no more to be assailed by temptation, no more to be defended by wrath and by fear;—shall abide with us Hope, no more to be quenched by the years that overwhelm, or made ashamed by the shadows that betray: —shall abide for us, and with us, the greatest of these; the abiding will, the abiding name of our Father. For the greatest of these is Charity.

[1869]

MATTHEW ARNOLD

CHRONOLOGY AND INTRODUCTION

1822 Born, December 24, Laleham, Middlesex.
1836–41 School days at Winchester and at Rugby.
1841 Entered Oxford at Balliol College.
1843 Won Newdigate prize for poetry (*Cromwell*).
1844 Degree from Oxford, with second class honors in Litterae Humaniores.
1845 Fellow of Oriel College, Oxford.
1847 Private Secretary to Lord Lansdowne.
1849 *The Strayed Reveller and Other Poems*, by A.
1851 Marriage: appointed to an inspectorship of schools.
1852 *Empedocles on Etna, and Other Poems*, by A.
1853 *Poems*, by Matthew Arnold.
1855 *Poems*, second series.
1857–67 Professor of Poetry at Oxford.
1858 *Merope*.
1861 *On Translating Homer*.
   Popular Education in France.

1864 *A French Eton*.
1865 *Essays in Criticism:* first series.
1867 *On the Study of Celtic Literature*.
   New Poems.
1868 *Schools and Universities on the Continent*.
1869 *Culture and Anarchy*.
1870 *St. Paul and Protestantism*.
   D.C.L. at Oxford.
1871 *Friendship's Garland*.
1873 *Literature and Dogma*.
1875 *God and the Bible*.
1877 *Last Essays on Church and Religion*.
1879 *Mixed Essays*.
1882 *Irish Essays, and Others*.
1883–84 Lecture tour in America.
1885 *Discourses in America*.
1886 Resigned Inspectorship.
1888 Death at Liverpool, April 15.
   Essays in Criticism, second series.
1910 *Essays in Criticism*, third series.

In the early eighteen-fifties Matthew Arnold enjoyed as a poet a limited reputation, which gradually increased until today many admirers place him higher in poetry than in prose. To poetry he would have given his best energies in his best years had circumstances permitted. "If the opinion of the general public about my poems," he wrote to his sister in 1858, "were the same as that of the leading literary men, . . . I should gain the stimulus necessary to enable me to produce my best,—all that I have in me, whatever that may be—to produce which is no light matter with an existence so hampered as mine is. . . . Perfection of a certain kind may there be attained, or at least approached, without knocking yourself to pieces, but to attain or approach perfection in the region of thought and feeling, and to write this with perfection of form, demands not merely an effort and a labor, but an actual tearing of oneself to pieces, which one does not readily consent to unless one can devote one's whole life to poetry." To do this was impossible, for he was now an inspector of schools and continued to be one until 1886, within two years of his death. It was his duty to visit grammar schools of England, mainly among Dissenters in the eastern counties, and to examine and report upon the work done in these schools by pupils and teachers. He performed his routine and often purgatorial tasks with conscientious fidelity and enjoyed a growing recognition as an authority in educational matters. He confessed privately, however, his impatience of getting old amidst a press of occupations for which he was not born. "But we are not here," he said, "to have facilities found us for doing the work we like, but to make them." The wonder is, not that Arnold composed so little poetry in these busy years, but that he was able to produce a body of other writing so distinguished that he now ranks with the masters of Victorian prose.

He had shown his hand in the famous *Preface* of 1853. With his sustained interest in poetry as the most perfect speech of man, and in the problems that go with an intelligent enjoyment of it, he naturally began as an essayist in the field of literary criticism; inevitably, too, since he was for a decade (1857-1867) Professor of Poetry at Oxford. Had Arnold done all his prose work in this field, unquestionably his distinction as a critic would be even greater than it is, for he had the rare gift of making his readers feel the significance as well as the charm of literature. But partly because he was a public official, and partly, no doubt, because he was the son of Thomas Arnold and an Englishman, he could not close his mind to other interests.

Like Sophocles, moreover, he aimed to see life not only steadily but to see it whole; and to do this was to regard literature as part of something vastly larger, namely, civilization. Without a high and fine civilization, there could be no high and fine art; and to art Arnold saw that the world round him was increasingly indifferent and even hostile. It is not to be forgotten, further, that, as he used the word, criticism meant an activity far wider than the appreciation of great works of literary art alone. Criticism he defines as a "disinterested endeavor to learn the best that is known and thought in the world." Its business is, "in all branches of knowledge, to see the object as in itself it really is." It tends to establish a new order of ideas, which, if not absolutely true, are yet true in comparison with those it displaces. Desiring to see the best ideas in all fields of human thought and action prevail, and desiring to see human nature, at least for the majority of mankind, develop on all of its important sides and not on one side alone, Arnold determined to combat certain rising tendencies in the national life, which, if not wisely controlled, might destroy civilization and make art impossible.

He lived in the center of the great movements of the Victorian age. New social forces were surging up on all sides, and old social forces were exhausted or slowing down. For the first time in more than a century and a half the aristocracy—the old landholding class of grandees—was losing its position of leadership, and was standing aloof, "materialized" and "inaccessible to ideas." The great middle classes, the Philistines, were "vulgarized" by their worldly prosperity, their smug satisfaction, their enslavement to "machinery," and their low standards of life; while the lower classes, the populace, uneducated and living in hideous conditions, were "brutalized" by their intemperance, their love of "beer, gin, and fun." It was not only the absorbing and debasing influence of this "passionate material progress" that was threatening the stability of society. It was also the new revolutionary stir in science and religion. As Arnold's critical intelligence viewed the situation an exaggerated individualism was rampant, when people gloried in doing as they liked regardless of their neighbors, and when as a consequence standards of thought, achievement, conduct, and manners were melting away, leaving society to drift into anarchy.

To prescribe culture, or sweetness and light, as a cure for these spreading national ills, was to prescribe what a good many of his contemporaries (like many of his later readers) regarded as something superficial and futile or as hopelessly ideal. It was nothing of the kind. "Culture" sums up the content and method of the social philosophy of Arnold, who was one of the truest democrats of his day, as when he declared that "the capital need is that the whole body of society should come to live with a life worthy to be called human"; but who knew that for him, a literary man, direct political action was impossible. "The hard unintelligence, which is just now our bane," he said, "cannot be conquered by storm; it must be supplied and reduced by culture, by growth in the variety, fulness, and sweetness of our spiritual life; and this end can only be reached by studying things that are outside of ourselves, and by studying them disinterestedly."

The aim of culture is a true and full humanity, or the harmonious development of human nature on all its four sides, the side of conduct, of knowledge, of beauty, of social life and manners. But Arnoldian culture is not only a private affair of the individual; it is an eminently social force also. It combats "machinery" when "machinery" is used as an end and not as a means; it seeks to do away with classes and to show inevitable democracy "how to find and keep high ideals" upon which a fine civilization must at last stand. Obviously to make progress towards such ends society will have to be transformed in its education, its religion, and its conception of the state. Education, in all its preparatory stages at least, should in some form eventually reach everyone, and for the *majority* of mankind its emphasis should be upon the humanities rather than upon the sciences, since facts and abstract principles are unsatisfying unless they fitly engage the emotions and so advance us in our progress towards our "full humanity." Religion, too, which in Arnold's time had long been, as he thought, a matter of sects, dogmas, and observances, and which now under the impact of advancing science and "higher criticism" was losing its hold, especially upon the masses,—religion, Arnold insisted, should be disengaged from externals and unverifiable abstractions about which people mostly differ and restored to its place as the universal expression of man's effort to relate his soul to the "power not ourselves that makes for righteousness," that is, to God. "Religion," he said, "springing out of an experience of the power, the grandeur, the necessity of righteousness, is revealed religion, whether we find it in Sophocles or in Isaiah." The Bible, however, is its supreme record, and the Bible is to be treated as literature, because "its words are used, like the words of common life and of poetry and eloquence, approximately, and not like the terms of science, adequately." The essentials of religion should be embodied in a state church, purged of sacerdotalism and superstition, a church wherein the symbols and offices of worship, consecrated by use, like the great classics of literature, should keep alive in man his noblest aspirations.

For the realization of this far-reaching program in a period of vast material expansion and menacing individualism, Arnold urged upon his readers the idea of an enormous extension of authority in the state, which should implement "the collective best self" of the entire community. Unlike many of his fellow-citizens, he had no fear that such a program would lead to socialism. "Rely upon it," he said, "that we English can use the State without danger.... To use the State is simply to use co-operation of a superior kind."

It becomes clear, as we study Arnold's thought, that he discussed contemporary problems with the critical detachment of a man of letters, who looked upon the humanities, more especially upon great literature, as indispensable agents for the civilization of mankind. While not indifferent to its aesthetic appeal, and forever insisting upon an adequate *form*, he stressed the human interest of literature, its power "to interpret life for us, to console us, to sustain us." In a family letter when commenting on his *Essays in Criticism* (1865), he says: "Going through them I am struck by the admirable riches of human nature that are brought to light in the group of persons of whom they treat, and the sort of unity that as a book to stimulate the better humanity in us the volume has." In the greatest poetry, Arnold believed, there is always to be found "a sense of the inward significance of the outward spectacle of the world"; and therefore, he took poetry to be a "criticism of life," or (if the reader prefers to avoid that much-disputed and much-abused phrase), an interpretation of life by the imaginative reason of the poet.

Arnold's equipment for literary criticism was extraordinarily rich. Brought up on the great classics, ancient and modern, he read them in their own languages through a lifetime. Homer, Sophocles, and Marcus Aurelius in the ancient world; Goethe, Wordsworth, and Sainte-Beuve in the modern, were no doubt the greatest influences upon his mind. His knowledge, while not that of an expert, was nearly always adequate in breadth and soundness for the purposes of criticism. He was even fearful lest a too specialized information might interfere with a balanced judgment. He had profound respect for principles and standards; while in curiosity, detachment, sympathy, and tact his endowment was greater than that of most critics who attempt to estimate the achievements of poets. He was not a critic with a system, though criticism for Arnold was never a mere lawless expression of preferences. In the last analysis it was, of course, the "personal sensation of like or dislike," but only in a mind "qualified in a certain manner,"—a mind, that is, possessing "culture," or the power "through reading to estimate the proportion and relation in what is read." Arnold's own judgments on literature and on men of letters are not the estimates of that impossible creature, the perfect critic. His limitations and prepossessions are real, and none of them has been overlooked by later critics, whose repeated attention to Arnold's opinions is evidence of his importance. But few readers can remain long in the company of his various "Essays in Criticism" without recognizing that here is a critic who, preeminently, treats literature as something both significant and delightful.

Though he had theories about many things, including style, Matthew Arnold had no theory about his own way of writing. In the last year of his life, he remarked to his friend, Russell: "People think I can teach them style. What stuff it all is! Have something to say, and say it as clearly as you can. That is the only secret of style." Any difficulty which readers may find in Arnold comes rather from his ideas than from his expression of them. He delights in simplicity, lucidity, orderliness,—"ordo concatenatioque veri," order and linked succession of truth. He shuns any suggestion of pedantry and for the exposition of his thought he resorts far more to examples than to definitions. Indeed the abundance and felicity of his quotations have been the delight of countless readers who have enjoyed, too, the banter and the irony playing over many a page. Extremes of statement and over-luxuriance of phrase he avoided as "Asiatic" or "Corinthian" in style. There are not more than two or three "purple patches" in all his prose. His own ideal was the "Attic" style, or prose of the center, free from eccentricity in any direction, having the tone of the city and having "shades and distinctions"; a style *"lenis minimeque pertinax*—easy and not too violently insisting." His notion of good writing is perfectly expressed in his tribute to Joubert: "The delight of his life he found in truth, and in the satisfaction which the enjoying of truth gives to the spirit; and he thought the truth was never really and worthily said, so long as the least cloud, clumsiness, and repulsiveness hung about the expression of it."

CULTURE AND ANARCHY

SWEETNESS AND LIGHT

The disparagers of culture make its motive curiosity; sometimes, indeed, they make its motive mere exclusiveness and vanity. The culture which is supposed to plume itself on a smattering of Greek and Latin is a culture which is begotten by nothing so intellectual as curiosity; it is valued either out of sheer vanity and ignorance or else as an engine of social and class distinction, separating its holder, like a badge or title, from other people who have not got it. No serious man would call this *culture*, or attach any value to it, as culture, at all. To find the real ground for the very differing estimate which serious people will set upon culture, we must find some motive for culture in the terms of which may lie a real ambiguity; and such a motive the word *curiosity* gives us.

I have before now pointed out that we English do not, like the foreigners, use this word in a good sense as well as in a bad sense. With us the word is always used in a somewhat disapproving sense. A liberal and intelligent eagerness about the things of the mind may be meant by a foreigner when he speaks of curiosity, but with us the word always conveys a certain notion of frivolous and unedifying activity. In the *Quarterly Review,* some little time ago, was an estimate of the celebrated French critic, M. Sainte-Beuve, and a very inadequate estimate it in my judgment was. And its inadequacy consisted chiefly in this: that in our English way it left out of sight the double sense really involved in the word *curiosity,* thinking enough was said to stamp M. Sainte-Beuve with blame if it was said that he was impelled in his operations as a critic by curiosity, and omitting either to perceive that M. Sainte-Beuve himself, and many other people with him, would consider that this was praiseworthy and not blameworthy, or to point out why it ought really to be accounted worthy of blame and not of praise. For as there is a curiosity about intellectual matters which is futile, and merely a disease, so there is certainly a curiosity—a desire after the things of the mind simply for their own sakes and for the pleasure of seeing them as they are—which is, in an intelligent being, natural and laudable. Nay, and the very desire to see things as they are, implies a balance and regulation of mind which is not often attained without fruitful effort, and which is the very opposite of the blind and diseased impulse of mind which is what we mean to blame when we blame curiosity. Montesquieu says: "The first motive which ought to impel us to study is the desire to augment the excellence of our nature, and to render an intelligent being yet more intelligent." This is the true ground to assign for the genuine scientific passion, however manifested, and for culture, viewed simply as a fruit of this passion; and it is a worthy ground, even though we let the term *curiosity* stand to describe it.

But there is of culture another view, in which not solely the scientific passion, the sheer desire to see things as they are, natural and proper in an intelligent being, appears as the ground of it. There is a view in which all the love of our neighbor, the impulses towards action, help, and beneficence, the desire for removing human error, clearing human confusion, and diminishing human misery, the noble aspiration to leave the world better and happier than we found it—motives eminently such as are called social—come in as part of the grounds of culture, and the main and preeminent part. Culture is then properly described not as having its origin in curiosity, but as having its origin in the love of perfection; it is *a study of perfection.* It moves by the force, not merely or primarily of the scientific passion for pure knowledge, but also of the moral and social passion for doing good. As, in the first view of it, we took for its worthy motto Montesquieu's words: "To render an intelligent being yet more intelligent!" so, in the second view of it, there is no better motto which it can have than these words of Bishop Wilson: "To make reason and the will of God prevail!"

Only, whereas the passion for doing good

is apt to be overhasty in determining what reason and the will of God say, because its turn is for acting rather than thinking and it wants to be beginning to act; and whereas it is apt to take its own conceptions, which proceed from its own state of development and share in all the imperfections and immaturities of this, for a basis of action; what distinguishes culture is, that it is possessed by the scientific passion as well as by the passion of doing good; that it demands worthy notions of reason and the will of God, and does not readily suffer its own crude conceptions to substitute themselves for them. And knowing that no action or institution can be salutary and stable which is not based on reason and the will of God, it is not so bent on acting and instituting, even with the great aim of diminishing human error and misery ever before its thoughts, but that it can remember that acting and instituting are of little use, unless we know how and what we ought to act and to institute.

This culture is more interesting and more far-reaching than that other, which is founded solely on the scientific passion for knowing. But it needs times of faith and ardor, times when the intellectual horizon is opening and widening all around us, to flourish in. And is not the close and bounded intellectual horizon within which we have long lived and moved now lifting up, and are not new lights finding free passage to shine in upon us? For a long time there was no passage for them to make their way in upon us, and then it was of no use to think of adapting the world's action to them. Where was the hope of making reason and the will of God prevail among people who had a routine which they had christened reason and the will of God, in which they were inextricably bound, and beyond which they had no power of looking? But now the iron force of adhesion to the old routine—social, political, religious—has wonderfully yielded; the iron force of exclusion of all which is new has wonderfully yielded. The danger now is, not that people should obstinately refuse to allow anything but their old routine to pass for reason and the will of God, but either that they should allow some novelty or other to pass for these too easily, or else that they should underrate the importance of them altogether, and think it enough to follow action for its own sake, without troubling themselves to make reason and the will of God prevail therein. Now, then, is the moment for culture to be of service, culture which believes in making reason and the will of God prevail, believes in perfection, is the study and pursuit of perfection, and is no longer debarred, by a rigid invincible exclusion of whatever is new, from getting acceptance for its ideas, simply because they are new.

The moment this view of culture is seized, the moment it is regarded not solely as the endeavor to see things as they are, to draw towards a knowledge of the universal order which seems to be intended and aimed at in the world, and which it is a man's happiness to go along with or his misery to go counter to—to learn, in short, the will of God—the moment, I say, culture is considered not merely as the endeavor to *see* and *learn* this, but as the endeavor, also, to make it *prevail,* the moral, social, and beneficent character of culture becomes manifest. The mere endeavor to see and learn the truth for our own personal satisfaction is indeed a commencement for making it prevail, a preparing the way for this, which always serves this, and is wrongly, therefore stamped with blame absolutely in itself and not only in its caricature and degeneration. But perhaps it has got stamped with blame, and disparaged with the dubious title of curiosity, because in comparison with this wider endeavor of such great and plain utility it looks selfish, petty, and unprofitable.

And religion, the greatest and most important of the efforts by which the human race has manifested its impulse to perfect itself—religion, that voice of the deepest human experience—does not only enjoin and sanction the aim which is the great aim of culture, the aim of setting ourselves to ascertain what perfection is and to make it prevail; but also, in determining generally in what human perfection consists, religion comes to a conclusion identical with that which culture—culture seeking the determination of this question through all the voices of human experience which have been heard upon it, of art, science, poetry, philosophy, history, as well as of religion, in order to give a greater fulness and certainty to its solution—likewise reaches. Religion says: *The kingdom of God is within you;* and culture, in like manner, places human perfection in an *internal* condition, in the growth and predominance of our humanity proper, as distinguished from our animality. It places it in the ever-increasing efficacy and in the general harmonious expansion of those gifts of thought and feeling, which make the peculiar dignity, wealth, and happiness of human nature. As I have said on a former occasion: "It is in making endless additions to itself, in the endless expansion of its powers, in endless growth in wisdom and beauty, that the spirit of the human race finds its ideal. To reach this ideal, culture is an indispensable aid, and that is the true value of culture." Not a having and a resting, but a growing and a becoming, is the character of perfection as culture conceives it; and here, too, it coincides with religion.

And because men are all members of one great whole, and the sympathy which is in human nature will not allow one member to be indifferent to the rest or to have a perfect welfare independent of the rest, the expansion of our humanity, to suit the idea of perfection which culture forms, must be a *general* expansion. Perfection, as culture conceives it, is not possible while the individual remains isolated. The individual is required, under pain of being stunted and enfeebled in his own development if he disobeys, to carry others along with him in his march towards perfection, to be continually doing all he can to enlarge and increase the volume of the human stream sweeping thitherward. And, here, once more, culture lays on us the same obligation as religion, which says, as Bishop Wilson has admirably put it, that "to promote the kingdom of God is to increase and hasten one's own happiness."

But, finally, perfection—as culture from a thorough disinterested study of human nature and human experience learns to conceive it—is a harmonious expansion of all the powers which make the beauty and worth of human nature, and is not consistent with the over-development of any one power at the expense of the rest. Here culture goes beyond religion as religion is generally conceived by us.

If culture, then, is a study of perfection, and of harmonious perfection, general perfection, and perfection which consists in becoming something rather than in having something, in an inward condition of the mind and spirit, not in an outward set of circumstances—it is clear that culture, instead of being the frivolous and useless thing which Mr. Bright, and Mr. Frederic Harrison, and many other Liberals are apt to call it, has a very important function to fulfil for mankind. And this function is particularly important in our modern world, of which the whole civilization is, to a much greater degree than the civilization of Greece and Rome, mechanical and external, and tends constantly to become more so. But above all in our own country has culture a weighty part to perform, because here that mechanical character, which civilization tends to take everywhere, is shown in the most eminent degree. Indeed nearly all the characters of perfection, as culture teaches us to fix them, meet in this country with some powerful tendency which thwarts them and sets them at defiance. The idea of perfection as an *inward* condition of the mind and spirit is at variance with the mechanical and material civilization in esteem with us, and nowhere, as I have said, so much in esteem as with us. The idea of perfection as a *general* expansion of the human family is at variance with our strong individualism, our hatred of all limits to the unrestrained swing of the individual's personality, our maxim of "every man for himself." Above all, the idea of perfection as a *harmonious* expansion of human nature is at variance with our want of flexibility, with our inaptitude for seeing more than one side of a thing, with our intense energetic absorption in the particular pursuit we happen to be following. So culture has a rough task to achieve in this country. Its preachers have, and are likely long to have, a hard time of it, and they will much oftener be regarded, for a great while to come, as elegant or spurious Jeremiahs than as friends and benefactors. That, however, will not prevent their doing in the end good service if they persevere. And, meanwhile, the mode of action they have to pursue, and the sort of habits they must fight against, ought to be made quite clear for every one to see, who may be willing to look at the matter attentively and dispassionately.

Faith in machinery is, I said, our besetting danger; often in machinery most absurdly disproportioned to the end which this machinery, if it is to do any good at all, is to serve; but always in machinery, as if it had a value in and for itself. What is freedom but machinery? what is population but machinery? what is coal but machinery? what are railroads but machinery? what is wealth but machinery? what are, even, religious organizations but machinery? Now almost every voice in England is accustomed to speak of these things as if they were precious ends in themselves, and therefore had some of the characters of perfection indisputably joined to them. I have before now noticed Mr. Roebuck's stock argument for proving the greatness and happiness of England as she is, and for quite stopping the mouths of all gainsayers. Mr. Roebuck is never weary of reiterating this argument of his, so I do not know why I should be weary of noticing it. "May not every man in England say what he likes?"—Mr. Roebuck perpetually asks; and that, he thinks, is quite sufficient, and when every man may say what he likes, our aspirations ought to be satisfied. But the aspirations of culture, which is the study of perfection, are not satisfied, unless what men say, when they may say what they like, is worth saying—has good in it, and more good than bad. In the same way the *Times*, replying to some foreign strictures on the dress, looks, and behavior of the English abroad, urges that the English ideal is that every one should be free to do and to look just as he likes. But culture indefatigably tries, not to make what each raw person may like, the rule by which he fashions himself; but to draw ever nearer to a sense of what is indeed beautiful, graceful, and becoming, and to get the raw person to like that.

And in the same way with respect to railroads and coal. Every one must have observed the strange language current during the late discussions as to the possible failure of our supplies of coal. Our coal, thousands of people were saying, is the real basis of our national greatness; if our coal runs short, there is an end of the greatness of England. But what *is* greatness?—culture makes us ask. Greatness is a spiritual condition worthy to excite love, interest, and admiration; and the outward proof of possessing greatness is that we excite love, interest, and admiration. If England were swallowed up by the sea tomorrow, which of the two, a hundred years hence, would most excite the love, interest, and admiration of mankind—would most, therefore, show the evidences of having possessed greatness—the England of the last twenty years, or the England of Elizabeth, of a time of splendid spiritual effort, but when our coal, and our industrial operations depending on coal, were very little developed? Well, then, what an unsound habit of mind it must be which makes us talk of things like coal or iron as constituting the greatness of England, and how salutary a friend is culture, bent on seeing things as they are, and thus dissipating delusions of this kind and fixing standards of perfection that are real!

Wealth, again, that end to which our prodigious works for material advantage are directed—the commonest of commonplaces tells us how men are always apt to regard wealth as a precious end in itself; and certainly they have never been so apt thus to regard it as they are in England at the present time. Never did people believe anything more firmly than nine Englishmen out of ten at the present day believe that our greatness and welfare are proved by our being so very rich. Now, the use of culture is that it helps us, by means of its spiritual standard of perfection, to regard wealth as but machinery, and not only to say as a matter of words that we regard wealth as but machinery, but really to perceive and feel that it is so. If it were not for this purging effect wrought upon our minds by culture, the whole world, the future as well as the present, would inevitably belong to the Philistines. The people who believe most that our greatness and welfare are proved by our being very rich, and who most give their lives and thoughts to becoming rich, are just the very people whom we call Philistines. Culture says: "Consider these people, then, their way of life, their habits, their manners, the very tones of their voice; look at them attentively; observe the literature they read, the things which give them pleasure, the words which come forth out of their mouths, the thoughts which make the furniture of their minds; would any amount of wealth be worth having with the condition that one was to become just like these people by having it?" And thus culture begets a dissatisfaction which is of the highest possible value in stemming the common tide of men's thoughts in a wealthy and industrial community, and which saves the future, as one may hope, from being vulgarized, even if it cannot save the present.

Population, again, and bodily health and vigor, are things which are nowhere treated in such an unintelligent, misleading, exaggerated way as in England. Both are really machinery; yet how many people all around us do we see rest in them and fail to look beyond them! Why, one has heard people, fresh from reading certain articles of the *Times* on the Registrar-General's returns of marriages and births in this country, who would talk of our large English families in quite a solemn strain, as if they had something in itself beautiful, elevating, and meritorious in them; as if the British Philistine would have only to present himself before the Great Judge with his twelve children, in order to be received among the sheep as a matter of right!

But bodily health and vigor, it may be said, are not to be classed with wealth and population as mere machinery; they have a more real and essential value. True; but only as they are more intimately connected with a perfect spiritual condition than wealth or population are. The moment we disjoin them from the idea of a perfect spiritual condition, and pursue them, as we do pursue them, for their own sake and as ends in themselves, our worship of them becomes as mere worship of machinery, as our worship of wealth or population, and as unintelligent and vulgarizing a worship as that is. Every one with anything like an adequate idea of human perfection has distinctly marked this subordination to higher and spiritual ends of the cultivation of bodily vigor and activity. "Bodily exercise profiteth little; but godliness is profitable unto all things," says the author of the Epistle to Timothy. And the utilitarian Franklin says just as explicitly: "Eat and drink such an exact quantity as suits the constitution of thy body, *in reference to the services of the mind.*" But the point of view of culture, keeping the mark of human perfection simply and broadly in view, and not assigning to this perfection, as religion or utilitarianism assigns to it, a special and limited character, this point of view, I say, of culture is best given by these words of Epictetus: "It is a sign of ἀφυΐα," says he— that is, of a nature not finely tempered,— "to give yourselves up to things which relate to the body; to make, for instance, a great fuss about exercise, a great fuss about eating, a great fuss about drinking, a great fuss about walking, a great fuss about riding. All these things ought to be done merely by the way: the formation of the spirit and character must be our real concern." This is admirable; and, indeed, the Greek word εὐφυΐα, a finely tempered nature, gives exactly the notion of perfection as culture brings us to conceive it: a harmonious perfection, a perfection in which the characters of beauty and intelligence are both present, which unites "the two noblest of things"—as Swift, who of one of the two, at any rate, had himself all too little, most happily calls them in his "Battle of the Books"—"the two noblest of things, *sweetness and light.*" The εὐφυὴς is the man who tends towards sweetness and light; the ἀφυής, on the other hand, is our Philistine. The immense spiritual significance of the Greeks is due to their having been inspired with this central and happy idea of the essential character of human perfection; and Mr. Bright's misconception of culture, as a smattering of Greek and Latin, comes itself, after all, from this wonderful significance of the Greeks having affected the very machinery of our education, and is in itself a kind of homage to it.

In thus making sweetness and light to be characters of perfection, culture is of like spirit with poetry, follows one law with poetry. Far more than on our freedom, our population, and our industrialism, many amongst us rely upon our religious organizations to save us. I have called religion a yet more important manifesta- 10 tion of human nature than poetry, because it has worked on a broader scale for perfection, and with greater masses of men. But the idea of beauty and of a human nature perfect on all its sides, which is the dominant idea of poetry, is a true and invaluable idea, though it has not yet had the success that the idea of conquering the obvious faults of our animality, and of a human nature perfect on the moral side— 20 which is the dominant idea of religion—has been enabled to have; and it is destined, adding to itself the religious idea of a devout energy, to transform and govern the other.

The best art and poetry of the Greeks, in which religion and poetry are one, in which the idea of beauty and of a human nature perfect on all sides adds to itself a religious and devout energy, and works in 30 the strength of that, is on this account of such surpassing interest and instructiveness for us, though it was—as, having regard to the human race in general, and, indeed, having regard to the Greeks themselves, we must own—a premature attempt, an attempt which for success needed the moral and religious fibre in humanity to be more braced and developed than it had yet been. But Greece did not err in having the idea 40 of beauty, harmony, and complete human perfection, so present and paramount. It is impossible to have this idea too present and paramount; only, the moral fibre must be braced too. And we, because we have braced the moral fibre, are not on that account in the right way, if at the same time the idea of beauty, harmony, and complete human perfection, is wanting or misapprehended amongst us; and evidently 50 it *is* wanting or misapprehended at present. And when we rely as we do on our religious organizations, which in themselves do not and cannot give us this idea, and think we

have done enough if we make them spread and prevail, then, I say, we fall into our common fault of overvaluing machinery.

Nothing is more common than for people to confound the inward peace and satisfaction which follows the subduing of the obvious faults of our animality with what I may call absolute inward peace and satisfaction—the peace and satisfaction which are reached as we draw near to complete spiritual perfection, and not merely to moral perfection, or rather to relative moral perfection. No people in the world have done more and struggled more to attain this relative moral perfection than our English race has. For no people in the world has the command to *resist the devil,* to *overcome the wicked one,* in the nearest and most obvious sense of those words, had such a pressing force and reality. And we have had our reward, not only in the great worldly prosperity which our obedience to this command has brought us, but also, and far more, in great inward peace and satisfaction. But to me few things are more pathetic than to see people, on the strength of the inward peace and satisfaction which their rudimentary efforts towards perfection have brought them, employ, concerning their incomplete perfection and the religious organizations within which they have found it, language which properly applies only to complete perfection, and is a far-off echo of the human soul's prophecy of it. Religion itself, I need hardly say, supplies them in abundance with this grand language. And very freely do they use it; yet it is really the severest possible criticism of such an incomplete perfection as alone we have yet reached through our religious organizations.

The impulse of the English race towards moral development and self-conquest has nowhere so powerfully manifested itself as in Puritanism. Nowhere has Puritanism found so adequate an expression as in the religious organization of the Independents. The modern Independents have a newspaper, the *Nonconformist,* written with great sincerity and ability. The motto, the standard, the profession of faith which this organ of theirs carries aloft, is: "The Dissidence of Dissent and the Protestantism of the Protestant religion." There is sweetness and light, and an ideal of complete harmonious human perfection! One need not go to culture and poetry to find language to judge it. Religion, with its instinct for perfection, supplies language to judge it, language, too, which is in our mouths every day. "Finally, be of one mind, united in feeling," says St. Peter. There is an ideal which judges the Puritan ideal: "The Dissidence of Dissent and the Protestantism of the Protestant religion!" And religious organizations like this are what people believe in, rest in, would give their lives for! Such, I say, is the wonderful virtue of even the beginnings of perfection, of having conquered even the plain faults of our animality, that the religious organization which has helped us to do it can seem to us something precious, salutary, and to be propagated, even when it wears such a brand of imperfection on its forehead as this. And men have got such a habit of giving to the language of religion a special application, of making it a mere jargon, that for the condemnation which religion itself passes on the shortcomings of their religious organizations they have no ear; they are sure to cheat themselves and to explain this condemnation away. They can only be reached by the criticism which culture, like poetry, speaking a language not to be sophisticated, and resolutely testing these organizations by the ideal of a human perfection complete on all sides, applies to them.

But men of culture and poetry, it will be said, are again and again failing, and failing conspicuously, in the necessary first stage to a harmonious perfection, in the subduing of the great obvious faults of our animality, which it is the glory of these religious organizations to have helped us to subdue. True, they do often so fail. They have often been without the virtues as well as the faults of the Puritan; it has been one of their dangers that they so felt the Puritan's faults that they too much neglected the practice of his virtues. I will not, however, exculpate them at the Puritan's expense. They have often failed in morality, and morality is indispensable. And they have been punished for their failure, as the Puritan has been rewarded

for his performance. They have been punished wherein they erred; but their ideal of beauty, of sweetness and light, and a human nature complete on all its sides, remains the true ideal of perfection still; just as the Puritan's ideal of perfection remains narrow and inadequate, although for what he did well he has been richly rewarded. Notwithstanding the mighty results of the Pilgrim Fathers' voyage, they and their standard of perfection are rightly judged when we figure to ourselves Shakespeare or Virgil—souls in whom sweetness and light, and all that in human nature is most humane, were eminent—accompanying them on their voyage, and think what intolerable company Shakespeare and Virgil would have found them! In the same way let us judge the religious organizations which we see all around us. Do not let us deny the good and the happiness which they have accomplished; but do not let us fail to see clearly that their idea of human perfection is narrow and inadequate, and that the Dissidence of Dissent and the Protestantism of the Protestant religion will never bring humanity to its true goal. As I said with regard to wealth; Let us look at the life of those who live in and for it—so I say with regard to the religious organizations. Look at the life imaged in such a newspaper as the *Nonconformist*—a life of jealousy of the Establishment, disputes, tea-meetings, openings of chapels, sermons; and then think of it as an ideal of a human life completing itself on all sides, and aspiring with all its organs after sweetness, light, and perfection!

Another newspaper, representing, like the *Nonconformist*, one of the religious organizations of this country, was a short time ago giving an account of the crowd at Epsom on the Derby day, and of all the vice and hideousness which was to be seen in that crowd; and then the writer turned suddenly round upon Professor Huxley, and asked him how he proposed to cure all this vice and hideousness without religion. I confess I felt disposed to ask the asker this question: and how do you propose to cure it with such a religion as yours? How is the ideal of a life so unlovely, so unattractive, so incomplete, so narrow, so far removed from a true and satisfying ideal of human perfection, as is the life of your religious organization as you yourself reflect it, to conquer and transform all this vice and hideousness? Indeed, the strongest plea for the study of perfection as pursued by culture, the clearest proof of the actual inadequacy of the idea of perfection held by the religious organizations—expressing, as I have said, the most widespread effort which the human race has yet made after perfection—is to be found in the state of our life and society with these in possession of it, and having been in possession of it I know not how many hundred years. We are all of us included in some religious organization or other; we all call ourselves, in the sublime and aspiring language or religion which I have before noticed, *children of God*. Children of God;—it is an immense pretension!—and how are we to justify it? By the works which we do, and the words which we speak. And the work which we collective children of God do, our grand center of life, our *city* which we have builded for us to dwell in, is London! London, with its unutterable external hideousness, and with its internal canker of *publice egestas, privatim opulentia* [1]—to use the words which Sallust puts into Cato's mouth about Rome —unequalled in the world! The word, again, which we children of God speak, the voice which most hits our collective thought, the newspaper with the largest circulation in England, nay, with the largest circulation in the whole world, is the *Daily Telegraph!* I say that when our religious organizations—which I admit to express the most considerable effort after perfection that our race has yet made—land us in no better result than this, it is high time to examine carefully their idea of perfection, to see whether it does not leave out of account sides and forces of human nature which we might turn to great use; whether it would not be more operative if it were more complete. And I say that the English reliance on our religious organizations and on their ideas of human perfec-

tion just as they stand, is like our reliance on freedom, on muscular Christianity, on population, on coal, on wealth—mere belief in machinery, and unfruitful; and that is wholesomely counteracted by culture, bent on seeing things as they are, and on drawing the human race onwards to a more complete, a harmonious perfection.

Culture, however, shows its single-minded love of perfection, its desire simply to make reason and the will of God prevail, its freedom from fanaticism, by its attitude towards all this machinery, even while it insists that it *is* machinery. Fanatics, seeing the mischief men do themselves by their blind belief in some machinery or other—whether it is wealth and industrialism, or whether it is the cultivation of bodily strength and activity, or whether it is a political organization—or whether it is a religious organization—oppose with might and main the tendency to this or that political and religious organization, or to games and athletic exercises, or to wealth and industrialism, and try violently to stop it. But the flexibility which sweetness and light give, and which is one of the rewards of culture pursued in good faith, enables a man to see that a tendency may be necessary, and even, as a preparation for something in the future, salutary, and yet that the generations or individuals who obey this tendency are sacrificed to it, that they fell short of the hope of perfection by following it; and that its mischiefs are to be criticized, lest it should take too firm a hold and last after it has served its purpose.

Mr. Gladstone well pointed out, in a speech at Paris—and others have pointed out the same thing—how necessary is the present great movement towards wealth and industrialism, in order to lay broad foundations of material well-being for the society of the future. The worst of these justifications is, that they are generally addressed to the very people engaged, body and soul, in the movement in question; at all events, that they are always seized with the greatest avidity by these people, and taken by them as quite justifying their life; and that thus they tend to harden them in their sins. Now, culture admits the necessity of the movement towards fortune-making and exaggerated industrialism,

1 *publice egestas,* etc.: public distress and private superfluity. (Sallust's *Cataline,* LII, 22.). Sallust (86–34 B.C.), Roman historian and politician. Cato, the Younger, (95–46 B.C.), Stoic philosopher and statesman.

readily allows that the future may derive benefit from it; but insists, at the same time, that the passing generations of industrialists—forming, for the most part, the stout main body of Philistinism—are sacrificed to it. In the same way, the result of all the games and sports which occupy the passing generation of boys and young men may be the establishment of a better and sounder physical type for the future to work with. Culture does not set itself against the games and sports; it congratulates the future, and hopes it will make a good use of its improved physical basis; but it points out that our passing generation of boys and young men is, meantime, sacrificed. Puritanism was perhaps necessary to develop the moral fibre of the English race, Nonconformity to break the yoke of ecclesiastical domination over men's minds and to prepare the way for freedom of thought in the distant future; still, culture points out that the harmonious perfection of generations of Puritans and Nonconformists has been, in consequence, sacrificed. Freedom of speech may be necessary for the society of the future, but the young lions of the *Daily Telegraph* in the meanwhile are sacrificed. A voice for every man in his country's government may be necessary for the society of the future, but meanwhile Mr. Beales and Mr. Bradlaugh are sacrificed.

Oxford, the Oxford of the past, has many faults; and she has heavily paid for them in defeat, in isolation, in want of hold upon the modern world. Yet we in Oxford, brought up amidst the beauty and sweetness of that beautiful place, have not failed to seize one truth—the truth that beauty and sweetness are essential characters of a complete human perfection. When I insist on this, I am all in the faith and tradition of Oxford. I say boldly that this our sentiment for beauty and sweetness, our sentiment against hideousness and rawness, has been at the bottom of our attachment to so many beaten causes, of our opposition to so many triumphant movements. And the sentiment is true, and has never been wholly defeated, and has shown its power even in its defeat. We have not won our political battles, we have not carried our main points, we have

not stopped our adversaries' advance, we have not marched victoriously with the modern world; but we have told silently upon the mind of the country, we have prepared currents of feeling which sap our adversaries' position when it seems gained, we have kept up our own communications with the future. Look at the course of the great movement which shook Oxford to its center some thirty years ago! It was directed, as any one who reads Dr. Newman's "Apology" may see, against what in one word may be called "Liberalism." Liberalism prevailed; it was the appointed force to do the work of the hour; it was necessary, it was inevitable that it should prevail. The Oxford movement was broken, it failed; our wrecks are scattered on every shore:

Quae regio in terris nostri non plena laboris? [2]

But what was it, this liberalism, as Dr. Newman saw it, and as it really broke the Oxford movement? It was the great middle-class liberalism, which had for the cardinal points of its belief the Reform Bill of 1832, and local self-government, in politics; in the social sphere, free-trade, unrestricted competition, and the making of large industrial fortunes; in the religious sphere, the Dissidence of Dissent and the Protestantism of the Protestant religion. I do not say that other and more intelligent forces than this were not opposed to the Oxford movement: but this was the force which really beat it; this was the force which Dr. Newman felt himself fighting with; this was the force which till only the other day seemed to be the paramount force in this country, and to be in possession of the future; this was the force whose achievements fill Mr. Lowe with such inexpressible admiration, and whose rule he was so horror-struck to see threatened. And where is this great force of Philistinism now? It is thrust into the second rank, it is become a power of yesterday, it has lost the future. A new power has suddenly appeared, a power which it is im-

[2] *Quae regio:* What region of the earth is not full of our work (woe)? (*Aeneid*, I, 460). Aeneas asks the question of Achates as they observe scenes of the Trojan War carved upon Dido's temple at Carthage.

possible yet to judge fully, but which is certainly a wholly different force from middle-class liberalism; different in its cardinal points of belief, different in its tendencies in every sphere. It loves and admires neither the legislation of middle-class Parliaments, nor the local self-government of middle-class vestries, nor the unrestricted competition of middle-class industrialists, nor the dissidence of middle-class Dissent and the Protestantism of middle-class Protestant religion. I am not now praising this new force, or saying that its own ideals are better; all I say is, that they are wholly different. And who will estimate how much the currents of feeling created by Dr. Newman's movements, the keen desire for beauty and sweetness which it nourished, the deep aversion it manifested to the hardness and vulgarity of middle-class liberalism, the strong light it turned on the hideous and grotesque illusions of middle-class Protestantism—who will estimate how much all these contributed to swell the tide of secret dissatisfaction which has mined the ground under self-confident liberalism of the last thirty years, and has prepared the way for its sudden collapse and supersession? It is in this manner that the sentiment of Oxford for beauty and sweetness conquers, and in this manner long may it continue to conquer!

In this manner it works to the same end as culture, and there is plenty of work for it yet to do. I have said that the new and more democratic force which is now superseding our old middle-class liberalism cannot yet be rightly judged. It has its main tendencies still to form. We hear promises of its giving us administrative reform, law reform, reform of education, and I know not what; but those promises come rather from its advocates, wishing to make a good plea for it and to justify it for superseding middle-class liberalism, than from clear tendencies which it has itself yet developed. But meanwhile it has plenty of well-intentioned friends against whom culture may with advantage continue to uphold steadily its ideal of human perfection; that this is *an inward spiritual activity, having for its characters increased sweetness, increased light, increased life, increased sympathy.*

Mr. Bright, who has a foot in both worlds, the world of middle-class liberalism and the world of democracy, but who brings most of his ideas from the world of middle-class liberalism in which he was bred, always inclines to inculcate that faith in machinery to which, as we have seen, Englishmen are so prone, and which has been the bane of middle-class liberalism. He complains with a sorrowful indignation of people who "appear to have no proper estimate of the value of the franchise"; he leads his disciples to believe—what the Englishman is always too ready to believe—that the having a vote, like the having a large family, or a large business, or large muscles, has in itself some edifying and perfecting effect upon human nature. Or else he cries out to the democracy—"the men," as he calls them, "upon whose shoulders the greatness of England rests"—he cries out to them: "See what you have done! I look over this country and see the cities you have built, the railroads you have made, the manufactures you have produced, the cargoes which freight the ships of the greatest mercantile navy the world has ever seen! I see that you have converted by your labors what was once a wilderness, these islands, into a fruitful garden; I know that you have created this wealth, and are a nation whose name is a word of power throughout all the world." Why, this is just the very style of laudation with which Mr. Roebuck or Mr. Lowe debauches the minds of the middle classes, and makes such Philistines of them. It is the same fashion of teaching a man to value himself not on what he *is,* not on his progress in sweetness and light, but on the number of the railroads he has constructed, or the bigness of the tabernacle he has built. Only the middle classes are told they have done it all with their energy, self-reliance, and capital, and the democracy are told they have done it all with their hands and sinews. But teaching the democracy to put its trust in achievements of this kind is merely training them to be Philistines to take the place of the Philistines whom they are superseding; and they, too, like the middle class, will be encouraged to sit down at the banquet of the future without having on a wedding garment, and nothing excellent can then come from them. Those who know their besetting faults, those who have watched them and listened to them, or those who will read the instructive account recently given of them by one of themselves, the *Journeyman Engineer,* will agree that the idea which culture sets before us of perfection—an increased spiritual activity, having for its characters increased sweetness, increased light, increased sympathy—is an idea which the new democracy needs far more than the idea of the blessedness of the franchise, or the wonderfulness of its own industrial performances.

Other well-meaning friends of this new power are for leading it, not in the old ruts of middle-class Philistinism, but in ways which are naturally alluring to the feet of democracy, though in this country they are novel and untried ways. I may call them the ways of Jacobinism. Violent indignation with the past, abstract systems of renovation applied wholesale, a new doctrine drawn up in black and white for elaborating down to the very smallest details a rational society for the future—these are the ways of Jacobinism. Mr. Frederic Harrison and other disciples of Comte—one of them, Mr. Congreve, is an old friend of mine, and I am glad to have an opportunity of publicly expressing my respect for his talents and character—are among the friends of democracy who are for leading it in paths of this kind. Mr. Frederic Harrison is very hostile to culture, and from a natural enough motive; for culture is the eternal opponent of the two things which are the signal marks of Jacobinism—its fierceness, and its addiction to an abstract system. Culture is always assigning to system-makers and systems a smaller share in the bent of human destiny than their friends like. A current in people's minds sets towards new ideas; people are dissatisfied with their old narrow stock of Philistine ideas, Anglo-Saxon ideas, or any other; and some man, some Bentham or Comte, who has the real merit of having early and strongly felt and helped the new current, but who brings plenty of narrowness and mistakes of his own into his feeling and help of it, is credited with being the author of the whole current, the fit person

to be entrusted with its regulation and to guide the human race.

The excellent German historian of the mythology of Rome, Preller, relating the introduction at Rome under the Tarquins of the worship of Apollo, the god of light, healing, and reconciliation, will have us observe that it was not so much the Tarquins who brought to Rome the new worship of Apollo, as a current in the mind of the Roman people which set powerfully at that time towards a new worship of this kind, and away from the old run of Latin and Sabine religious ideas. In a similar way, culture directs our attention to the natural current there is in human affairs, and to its continual working, and will not let us rivet our faith upon any one man and his doings. It makes us see not only his good side, but also how much in him was of necessity limited and transient; nay, it even feels a pleasure, a sense of an increased freedom and of an ampler future, in so doing.

I remember, when I was under the influence of a mind to which I feel the greatest obligations, the mind of a man who was the very incarnation of sanity and clear sense, a man the most considerable, it seems to me, whom America has yet produced—Benjamin Franklin—I remember the relief with which, after long feeling the sway of Franklin's imperturbable commonsense, I came upon a project of his for a new version of the Book of Job, to replace the old version, the style of which, says Franklin, has become obsolete, and thence less agreeable. "I give," he continues, "a few verses, which may serve as a sample of the kind of version I would recommend." We all recollect the famous verse in our translation: "Then Satan answered the Lord and said: 'Doth Job fear God for nought' " Franklin makes this: "Does your Majesty imagine that Job's good conduct is the effect of mere personal attachment and affection?" I well remember how, when first I read that, I drew a deep breath of relief and said to myself: "After all, there is a stretch of humanity beyond Franklin's victorious good sense!" So, after hearing Bentham cried loudly up as the renovator of modern society, and Bentham's mind and ideas proposed as the rules of our future, I open the "Deontology." There I read: "While Xenophon was writing his history and Euclid teaching geometry, Socrates and Plato were talking nonsense under pretense of talking wisdom and morality. This morality of theirs consisted in words; this wisdom of theirs was the denial of matters known to every man's experience." From the moment of reading that, I am delivered from the bondage of Bentham! the fanaticism of his adherents can touch me no longer. I feel the inadequacy of his mind and ideas for supplying the rule of human society, for perfection.

Culture tends always thus to deal with the men of a system, of disciples, of a school; with men like Comte, or the late Mr. Buckle, or Mr. Mill. However much it may find to admire in these personages, or in some of them, it nevertheless remembers the text: "Be not ye called Rabbi!" and it soon passes on from any Rabbi. But Jacobinism loves a Rabbi; it does not want to pass on from its Rabbi in pursuit of a future and still unreached perfection; it wants its Rabbi and his ideas to stand for perfection, that they may with the more authority recast the world; and for Jacobinism, therefore, culture—eternally passing onwards and seeking—is an impertinence and an offence. But culture, just because it resists this tendency of Jacobinism to impose on us a man with limitations and errors of his own along with the true ideas of which he is the organ, really does the world and Jacobinism itself a service.

So, too, Jacobinism, in its fierce hatred of the past and of those whom it makes liable for the sins of the past, cannot away with the inexhaustible indulgence proper to culture, the consideration of circumstances, the severe judgment of actions joined to the merciful judgment of persons. "The man of culture is in politics," cries Mr. Frederic Harrison, "one of the poorest mortals alive!" Mr. Frederic Harrison wants to be doing business, and he complains that the man of culture stops him with a "turn for small fault-finding, love of selfish ease, and indecision in action." Of what use is culture, he asks, except for "a critic of new books or a professor of belles-lettres?" Why, it is of use because, in presence of the fierce exasperation which breathes, or rather, I may say, hisses through the whole production in which Mr. Frederic Harrison asks that question, it reminds us that the perfection of human nature is sweetness and light. It is of use, because, like religion—that other effort after perfection—it testifies that, where bitter envying and strife are, there is confusion and every evil work.

The pursuit of perfection, then, is the pursuit of sweetness and light. He who works for sweetness and light, works to make reason and the will of God prevail. He who works for machinery, he who works for hatred, works only for confusion. Culture looks beyond machinery, culture hates hatred; culture has one great passion, the passion for sweetness and light. It has one even yet greater!—the passion for making them *prevail*. It is not satisfied till we *all* come to a perfect man; it knows that the sweetness and light of the few must be imperfect until the raw and unkindled masses of humanity are touched with sweetness and light. If I have not shrunk from saying that we must work for sweetness and light, so neither have I shrunk from saying that we must have a broad basis, must have sweetness and light for as many as possible. Again and again I have insisted how those are the happy moments of humanity, how those are the marking epochs of a people's life, how those are the flowering times for literature and art and all the creative power of genius, when there is a *national* glow of life and thought, when the whole of society is in the fullest measure permeated by thought, sensible to beauty, intelligent and alive. Only it must be *real* thought and *real* beauty; *real* sweetness and *real* light. Plenty of people will try to give the masses, as they call them, an intellectual food prepared and adapted in the way they think proper for the actual condition of the masses. The ordinary popular literature is an example of this way of working on the masses. Plenty of people will try to indoctrinate the masses with the set of ideas and judgments constituting the creed of their own profession or party. Our religious and political organizations give an example of this way of working on the masses. I condemn neither way; but **culture works differently**. It does not try to teach down to the level of inferior classes; it does not try to win them for this or that sect of its own, with ready-made judgments and watchwords. It seeks to do away with classes; to make the best that has been thought and known in the world current everywhere; to make all men live in an atmosphere of sweetness and light, where they may use ideas, as it uses them itself, freely—nourished, and not 10 bound by them.

This is the *social idea;* and the men of culture are the true apostles of equality. The great men of culture are those who have had a passion for diffusing, for making prevail, for carrying from one end of society to the other, the best knowledge, the best ideas of their time; who have labored to divest knowledge of all that was harsh, uncouth, difficult, abstract, professional, exclusive; to humanize it, to make it efficient outside the clique of the cultivated and learned, yet still remaining the *best* knowledge and thought of the time, and a true source, therefore, of sweetness and light. Such a man was Abelard in the Middle Ages, in spite of all his imperfections; and thence the boundless emotion and enthusiasm which Abelard excited. Such were Lessing and Herder in Germany, 30 at the end of the last century; and their

services to Germany were in this way inestimably precious. Generations will pass, and literary monuments will accumulate, and works far more perfect than the works of Lessing and Herder will be produced in Germany; and yet the names of these two men will fill a German with a reverence and enthusiasm such as the names of the most gifted masters will hardly awaken. And why? Because they *humanized* knowledge; because they broadened the basis of life and intelligence; because they worked powerfully to diffuse sweetness and light, to make reason and the will of God prevail. With Saint Augustine they said: "Let us not leave thee alone to make in the secret of thy knowledge, as thou didst before the creation of the firmament, the division of light from darkness; let the children of thy spirit, placed in their firmament, make their light shine upon the earth, mark the division of night and day, and announce the revolution of the times; for the old order is passed, and the new arises; the night is spent, the day is come forth; and thou shalt crown the year with thy blessing, when thou shalt send forth laborers into thy harvest sown by other hands than theirs; when thou shalt send forth new laborers to new seed-times, whereof the harvest shall be not yet."

[1867]

DISCOURSES IN AMERICA

LITERATURE AND SCIENCE

Practical people talk with a smile of Plato and of his absolute ideas; and it is impossible to deny that Plato's ideas do often seem unpractical and impracticable, and especially when one views them in connection with the life of a great work-a-day world like the United States. The necessary staple of the life of such a world Plato regards with disdain; handicraft and trade and the working professions he regards with disdain; but what becomes of the life of an industrial modern community if you take handicraft and trade and the working professions out of it? The base mechanic arts and handicrafts, says Plato, bring about a natural weakness in the principle of excellence in a man, so that

he cannot govern the ignoble growths in him, but nurses them, and cannot understand fostering any other. Those who exercise such arts and trades, as they have their bodies, he says, marred by their vulgar businesses, so they have their souls, too, bowed and broken by them. And if one of these uncomely people has a mind to seek self-culture and philosophy, Plato compares him to a bald little tinker, who has scraped together money, and has got his release from service, and has had a bath, and bought a new coat, and is rigged out like a bridegroom about to marry the daughter of his master who has fallen into poor and helpless estate.

Nor do the working professions fare any better than trade at the hands of Plato. He draws for us an inimitable picture of the working lawyer, and of his life of bondage; he shows how this bondage from his youth up has stunted and warped him, and made him small and crooked of soul, encompassing him with difficulties which he is not man enough to rely on justice and truth as means to encounter, but has recourse, for help out of them, to falsehood and wrong. And so, says Plato, this poor creature is bent and broken, and 10 grows up from boy to man without a particle of soundness in him, although exceedingly smart and clever in his own esteem.

One cannot refuse to admire the artist who draws these pictures. But we say to ourselves that his ideas show the influence of a primitive and obsolete order of things, when the warrior caste and the priestly caste were alone in honor, and the humble work of the world was done by slaves. We 20 have now changed all that; the modern majesty consists in work, as Emerson declares; and in work, we may add, principally of such plain and dusty kind as the work of cultivators of the ground, handicraftsmen, men of trade and business, men of the working professions. Above all is this true in a great industrious community such as that of the United States.

Now education, many people go on to 30 say, is still mainly governed by the ideas of men like Plato, who lived when the warrior caste and the priestly or philosophical class were alone in honor, and the really useful part of the community were slaves. It is an education fitted for persons of leisure in such a community. This education passed from Greece and Rome to the feudal communities of Europe, where also the warrior caste and the 40 priestly caste were alone held in honor, and where the really useful and working part of the community, though not nominally slaves as in the pagan world, were practically not much better off than slaves, and not more seriously regarded. And how absurd it is, people end by saying, to inflict this education upon an industrious modern community, where very few indeed are persons of leisure, and the mass to be 50 considered has not leisure, but is bound, for its own great good, and for the great good of the world at large, to plain labor and to industrial pursuits, and the educa-

tion in question tends necessarily to make men dissatisfied with these pursuits and unfitted for them!

That is what is said. So far I must defend Plato, as to plead that his view of education and studies is in the general, as it seems to me, sound enough, and fitted for all sorts and conditions of men, whatever their pursuits may be. "An intelligent man," says Plato, "will prize those studies which result in his soul getting soberness, righteousness, and wisdom, and will less value the others." I cannot consider *that* a bad description of the aim of education, and of the motives which should govern us in the choice of studies, whether we are preparing ourselves for a hereditary seat in the English House of Lords or for the pork trade in Chicago.

Still I admit that Plato's world was not ours, that his scorn of trade and handicraft is fantastic, that he had no conception of a great industrial community such as that of the United States, and that such a community must and will shape its education to suit its own needs. If the usual education handed down to it from the past does not suit it, it will certainly before long drop this and try another. The usual education in the past has been mainly literary. The question is whether the studies which were long supposed to be the best for all of us are practically the best now; whether others are not better. The tyranny of the past, many think, weighs on us injuriously in the predominance given to letters in education. The question is raised whether, to meet the needs of our modern life, the predominance ought not now to pass from letters to science; and naturally the question is nowhere raised with more energy than here in the United States. The design of abasing what is called "mere literary instruction and education," and of exalting what is called "sound, extensive, and practical scientific knowledge," is, in this intensely modern world of the United States, even more perhaps than in Europe, a very popular design, and makes great and rapid progress.

I am going to ask whether the present movement for ousting letters from their old predominance in education, and for transferring the predominance in education to the natural sciences, whether this brisk and flourishing movement ought to prevail, and whether it is likely that in the end it really will prevail. An objection may be raised which I will anticipate. My own studies have been almost wholly in letters, and my visits to the field of the natural sciences have been very slight and inadequate, although those sciences have always strong-10 ly moved my curiosity. A man of letters, it will perhaps be said, is not competent to discuss the comparative merits of letters and natural science as means of education. To this objection I reply, first of all, that his incompetence, if he attempts the discussion but is really incompetent for it, will be abundantly visible; nobody will be taken in; he will have plenty of sharp observers and critics to save mankind from 20 that danger. But the line I am going to follow is, as you will soon discover, so extremely simple, that perhaps it may be followed without failure even by one who for a more ambitious line of discussion would be quite incompetent.

Some of you may possibly remember a phrase of mine which has been the object of a good deal of comment; an observation to the effect that in our culture, the aim 30 being *to know ourselves and the world*, we have, as the means to this end, *to know the best which has been thought and said in the world*. A man of science, who is also an excellent writer and the very prince of debaters, Professor Huxley, in a discourse at the opening of Sir Josiah Mason's college at Birmingham, laying hold of this phrase, expanded it by quoting some more words of mine, which are these: "The civil-40 ized world is to be regarded as now being, for intellectual and spiritual purposes, one great confederation, bound to a joint action and working to a common result; and whose members have for their proper outfit a knowledge of Greek, Roman, and Eastern antiquity, and of one another. Special local and temporary advantages being put out of account, that modern nation will in the intellectual and spiritual sphere make 50 most progress, which most thoroughly carries out this programme."

Now on my phrase, thus enlarged, Professor Huxley remarks that when I speak of the above-mentioned knowledge as enabling us to know ourselves and the world, I assert *literature* to contain the materials which suffice for thus making us know ourselves and the world. But it is not by any means clear, says he, that after having learnt all which ancient and modern literatures have to tell us, we have laid a sufficiently broad and deep foundation for that criticism of life, that knowledge of ourselves and the world, which constitutes culture. On the contrary, Professor Huxley declares that he finds himself "wholly unable to admit that either nations or individuals will really advance, if their outfit draws nothing from the stores of physical science. An army without weapons of precision, and with no particular base of operations, might more hopefully enter upon a campaign on the Rhine, than a man, devoid of a knowledge of what physical science has done in the last century, upon a criticism of life."

This shows how needful it is for those who are to discuss any matter together, to have a common understanding as to the sense of the terms they employ—how needful, and how difficult. What Professor Huxley says, implies just the reproach which is so often brought against the study of *belles lettres,* as they are called: that the study is an elegant one, but slight and ineffectual; a smattering of Greek and Latin and other ornamental things, of little use for any one whose object is to get at truth, and to be a practical man. So, too, M. Renan talks of the "superficial humanism" of a school-course which treats us as if we were all going to be poets, writers, preachers, orators, and he opposes this humanism to positive science, or the critical search after truth. And there is always a tendency in those who are remonstrating against the predominance of letters in education, to understand by letters *belles lettres,* and by *belles lettres* a superficial humanism the opposite of science or true knowledge.

But when we talk of knowing Greek and Roman antiquity, for instance, which is the knowledge people have called the humanities, I for my part mean a knowledge which is something more than a superficial humanism, mainly decorative. "I call

all teaching *scientific*," says Wolf, the critic of Homer, "which is systematically laid out and followed up to its original sources. For example: a knowledge of classical antiquity is scientific when the remains of classical antiquity are correctly studied in the original languages." There can be no doubt that Wolf is perfectly right; that all learning is scientific which is systematically laid out and followed up to its original 10 sources, and that a genuine humanism is scientific.

When I speak of knowing Greek and Roman antiquity, therefore, as a help to knowing ourselves and the world, I mean more than a knowledge of so much vocabulary, so much grammar, so many portions of authors in the Greek and Latin languages, I mean knowing the Greeks and Romans, and their life and genius, and 20 what they were and did in the world; what we get from them, and what is its value. That, at least, is the ideal; and when we talk of endeavoring to know Greek and Roman antiquity, as a help to knowing ourselves and the world, we mean endeavoring so to know them as to satisfy this ideal, however much we may still fall short of it.

The same also as to knowing our own 30 and other modern nations, with the like aim of getting to understand ourselves and the world. To know the best that has been thought and said by the modern nations, is to know, says Professor Huxley, "only what modern *literatures* have to tell us; it is the criticism of life contained in modern literature." And yet "the distinctive character of our times," he urges, "lies in the vast and constantly increasing part which 40 is played by natural knowledge." And how, therefore, can a man, devoid of knowledge of what physical science has done in the last century, enter hopefully upon a criticism of modern life?

Let us, I say, be agreed about the meaning of the terms we are using. I talk of knowing the best which has been thought and uttered in the world; Professor Huxley says this means knowing *literature*. Litera- 50 ture is a large word; it may mean everything written with letters or printed in a book. Euclid's "Elements" and Newton's "Principia" are thus literature. All knowl-

edge that reaches us through books is literature. But by literature Professor Huxley means *belles lettres*. He means to make me say, that knowing the best which has been thought and said by the modern nations is knowing their *belles lettres* and no more. And this is no sufficient equipment, he argues, for a criticism of modern life. But as I do not mean, by knowing ancient Rome, knowing merely more or less of Latin *belles lettres*, and taking no account of Rome's military, and political, and legal, and administrative work in the world; and as, by knowing ancient Greece, I understand knowing her as the giver of Greek art, and the guide to a free and right use of reason and to scientific method, and the founder of our mathematics and physics and astronomy and biology—I understand knowing her as all this, and not merely knowing certain Greek poems, and histories, and treatises, and speeches—so as to the knowledge of modern nations also. By knowing modern nations, I mean not merely knowing their *belles lettres*, but knowing also what has been done by such men as Copernicus, Galileo, Newton, Darwin. "Our ancestors learned," says Professor Huxley, "that the earth is the centre of the visible universe, and that man is the cynosure of things terrestrial; and more especially was it inculcated that the course of nature had no fixed order, but that it could be, and constantly was, altered." But for us now, continues Professor Huxley, "the notions of the beginning and the end of the world entertained by our forefathers are no longer credible. It is very certain that the earth is not the chief body in the material universe, and that the world is not subordinated to man's use. It is even more certain that nature is the expression of a definite order, with which nothing interferes." "And yet," he cries, "the purely classical education advocated by the representatives of the humanists in our day gives no inkling of all this!"

In due place and time I will just touch upon that vexed question of classical education; but at present the question is as to what is meant by knowing the best which modern nations have thought and said. It is not knowing their *belles lettres* merely which is meant. To know Italian *belles lettres* is not to know Italy, and to know English *belles lettres* is not to know England. Into knowing Italy and England there comes a great deal more, Galileo and Newton amongst it. The reproach of being a superficial humanism, a tincture of *belles lettres,* may attach rightly enough to some other disciplines; but to the particular discipline recommended when I proposed knowing the best that has been thought and said in the world, it does not apply. In that best I certainly include what in modern times has been thought and said by the great observers and knowers of nature.

There is, therefore, really no question between Professor Huxley and me as to whether knowing the great results of the modern scientific study of nature is not required as a part of our culture, as well as knowing the products of literature and art. But to follow the processes by which those results are reached, ought, say the friends of physical science, to be made the staple of education for the bulk of mankind. And here there does arise a question between those whom Professor Huxley calls with playful sarcasm "the Levites of culture," and those whom the poor humanist is sometimes apt to regard as its Nebuchadnezzars.

The great results of the scientific investigations of nature we are agreed upon knowing, but how much of our study are we bound to give to the processes by which those results are reached? The results have their visible bearing on human life. But all the processes, too, all the items of fact, by which those results are reached and established, are interesting. All knowledge is interesting to a wise man, and the knowledge of nature is interesting to all men. It is very interesting to know, that, from the albuminous white of the egg, the chick in the egg gets the materials for its flesh, bones, blood, and feathers; while from the fatty yolk of the egg, it gets the heat and energy which enable it at length to break its shell and begin the world. It is less interesting, perhaps, but still it is interesting, to know that when a taper burns, the wax is converted into carbonic acid and water. Moreover, it is quite true that the habit of dealing with facts, which is given by the study of nature, is, as the friends of physical science praise it for being, an excellent discipline. The appeal, in the study of nature, is constantly to observation and experiment; not only is it said that the thing is so, but we can be made to see that it is so. Not only does a man tell us that when a taper burns the wax is converted into carbonic acid and water, as a man may tell us, if he likes, that Charon is punting his ferry-boat on the river Styx, or that Victor Hugo is a sublime poet, or Mr. Gladstone the most admirable of statesmen; but we are made to see that the conversion into carbonic acid and water does actually happen. This reality of natural knowledge it is, which makes the friends of physical science contrast it, as a knowledge of things, with the humanist's knowledge, which is, say they, a knowledge of words. And hence Professor Huxley is moved to lay it down that, "for the purpose of attaining real culture, an exclusively scientific education is at least as effectual as an exclusively literary education." And a certain President of the Section of Mechanical Science in the British Association is, in Scripture phrase, "very bold," and declares that if a man, in his mental training, "has substituted literature and history for natural science, he has chosen the less useful alternative." But whether we go these lengths or not, we must all admit that in natural science the habit gained of dealing with facts is a most valuable discipline, and that every one should have some experience of it.

More than this, however, is demanded by the reformers. It is proposed to make the training in natural science the main part of education, for the great majority of mankind at any rate. And here, I confess, I part company with the friends of physical science, with whom up to this point I have been agreeing. In differing from them, however, I wish to proceed with the utmost caution and diffidence. The smallness of my own acquaintance with the disciplines of natural science is ever before my mind, and I am fearful of doing these disciplines an injustice. The ability and pugnacity of the partisans of natural science make them formidable persons to contradict. The tone of tentative inquiry, which befits a being of dim faculties and bounded knowledge, is the tone I would wish to take and not to depart from. At present it seems to me, that those who are for giving to natural knowledge, as they call it, the chief place in the education of the majority of mankind, leave one important thing out of their account: the constitution of human nature. But I put this forward on the strength of some facts not at all recondite, very far from it; facts capable of being stated in the simplest possible fashion, and to which, if I so state them, the man of science will, I am sure, be willing to allow their due weight.

Deny the facts altogether, I think, he hardly can. He can hardly deny, that when we set ourselves to enumerate the powers which go to the building up of human life, and say that they are the power of conduct, the power of intellect and knowledge, the power of beauty, and the power of social life and manners—he can hardly deny that this scheme, though drawn in rough and plain lines enough, and not pretending to scientific exactness, does yet give a fairly true representation of the matter. Human nature is built up by these powers; we have the need for them all. When we have rightly met and adjusted the claims of them all, we shall then be in a fair way for getting soberness, and righteousness with wisdom. This is evident enough, and the friends of physical science would admit it.

But perhaps they may not have sufficiently observed another thing: namely, that the several powers just mentioned are not isolated, but there is, in the generality of mankind, a perpetual tendency to relate them one to another in divers ways. With one such way of relating them I am particularly concerned now. Following our instinct for intellect and knowledge, we acquire pieces of knowledge; and presently in the generality of men, there arises the desire to relate these pieces of knowledge to our sense for conduct, to our sense for beauty—and there is weariness and dissatisfaction if the desire is balked. Now in this desire lies, I think, the strength of that hold which letters have upon us.

All knowledge is, as I said just now, interesting; and even items of knowledge which from the nature of the case cannot well be related, but must stand isolated in our thoughts, have their interest. Even lists of exceptions have their interest. If we are studying Greek accents it is interesting to know that *pais* and *pas,* and some other monosyllables of the same form of declension, do not take the circumflex upon the last syllable of the genitive plural but vary, in this respect, from the common rule. If we are studying physiology, it is interesting to know that the pulmonary artery carries dark blood and the pulmonary vein carries bright blood, departing in this respect from the common rule for the division of labor between the veins and the arteries. But every one knows how we seek naturally to combine the pieces of our knowledge together, to bring them under general rules, to relate them to principles; and how unsatisfactory and tiresome it would be to go on forever learning lists of exceptions, or accumulating items of fact which must stand isolated.

Well, that same need of relating our knowledge, which operates here within the sphere of our knowledge itself, we shall find operating, also, outside that sphere. We experience, as we go on learning and knowing—the vast majority of us experience—the need of relating what we have learnt and known to the sense which we have in us for conduct, to the sense which we have in us for beauty.

A certain Greek prophetess of Mantineia in Arcadia, Diotima by name, once explained to the philosopher Socrates that love, and impulse, and bent of all kinds, is, in fact, nothing else but the desire in men that good should forever be present to them. This desire for good, Diotima assured Socrates, is our fundamental desire, of which fundamental desire every impulse in us is only some one particular form. And therefore this fundamental desire it is, I suppose—this desire in men that good should be forever present to them—which acts in us when we feel the impulse for relating our knowledge to our sense for conduct and to our sense for beauty. At any rate, with men in general the instinct exists. Such is human nature. And the instinct, it will be admitted, is innocent, and human nature is preserved by our following the lead of its innocent instincts. Therefore, in seeking to gratify this instinct in question, we are following the instinct of self-preservation in humanity.

But, no doubt, some kinds of knowledge cannot be made to directly serve the instinct in question, cannot be directly related to the sense for beauty, to the sense for conduct. These are instrument-knowledges; they lead on to other knowledges, which can. A man who passes his life in instrument-knowledges is a specialist. They may be invaluable as instruments to something beyond, for those who have the gift thus to employ them; and they may be disciplines in themselves wherein it is useful for every one to have some schooling. But it is inconceivable that the generality of men should pass all their mental life with Greek accents or with formal logic. My friend Professor Sylvester, who is one of the first mathematicians in the world, holds transcendental doctrines as to the virtue of mathematics, but those doctrines are not for common men. In the very Senate House and heart of our English Cambridge I once ventured, though not without an apology for my profaneness, to hazard the opinion that for the majority of mankind a little of mathematics, even, goes a long way. Of course this is quite consistent with their being of immense importance as an instrument to something else; but it is the few who have the aptitude for thus using them, not the bulk of mankind.

The natural sciences do not, however, stand on the same footing with these instrument-knowledges. Experience shows us that the generality of men will find more interest in learning that, when a taper burns, the wax is converted into carbonic acid and water, or in learning the explanation of the phenomenon of dew, or in learning how the circulation of the blood is carried on, than they find in learning that the genitive plural of *pais* and *pas* does not take the circumflex on the termination. And one piece of natural knowledge is added to another, and others are added to that, and at last we come to propositions so interesting as Mr. Darwin's famous proposition that "our ancestor was a hairy quadruped furnished with a tail and pointed ears, probably arboreal in his habits." Or we come to propositions of such reach and magnitude as those which Professor Huxley delivers, when he says that the notions of our forefathers about the beginning and the end of the world were all wrong, and that nature is the expression of a definite order with which nothing interferes.

Interesting, indeed, these results of science are, important they are, and we should all of us be acquainted with them. But what I now wish you to mark is, that we are still, when they are propounded to us and we receive them, we are still in the sphere of intellect and knowledge. And for the generality of men there will be found, I say, to arise, when they have duly taken in the proposition that their ancestor was "a hairy quadruped furnished with a tail and pointed ears, probably arboreal in his habits," there will be found to arise an invincible desire to relate this proposition to the sense in us for conduct, and to the sense in us for beauty. But this the men of science will not do for us, and will hardly even profess to do. They will give us other pieces of knowledge, other facts, about other animals and their ancestors, or about plants, or about stones, or about stars; and they may finally bring us to those great "general conceptions of the universe, which are forced upon us all," says Professor Huxley, "by the progress of physical science." But still it will be *knowledge* only which they give us; knowledge not put for us into relation with our sense for conduct, our sense for beauty, and touched with emotion by being so put; not thus put for us, and therefore, to the majority of mankind, after a certain while, unsatisfying, wearying.

Not to the born naturalist, I admit. But what do we mean by a born naturalist? We mean a man in whom the zeal for observing nature is so uncommonly strong and eminent, that it marks him off from the bulk of mankind. Such a man will pass his life happily in collecting natural knowledge and reasoning upon it, and will ask for nothing, or hardly anything, more. I have heard it said that the sagacious and admirable naturalist whom we lost not very long ago, Mr. Darwin, once owned to a friend that for his part he did not experience the necessity for two things which most men find so necessary to them—religion and poetry; science and the domestic affections, he thought, were enough. To a born naturalist, I can well understand that this should seem so. So absorbing is his occupation with nature, so strong his love for his occupation, that he goes on acquiring natural knowledge and reasoning upon it, and has little time or inclination for thinking about getting it related to the desire in man for conduct, the desire in man for beauty. He relates it to them for himself as he goes along, so far as he feels the need; and he draws from the domestic affections all the additional solace necessary. But then Darwins are extremely rare. Another great and admirable master of natural knowledge, Faraday, was a Sandemanian. That is to say, he related his knowledge to his instinct for conduct and to his instinct for beauty, by the aid of that respectable Scottish sectary, Robert Sandeman. And so strong, in general, is the demand of religion and poetry to have their share in a man, to associate themselves with his knowing, and to relieve and rejoice it, that, probably, for one man amongst us with the disposition to do as Darwin did in this respect, there are at last fifty with the disposition to do as Faraday.

Education lays hold upon us, in fact, by satisfying this demand. Professor Huxley holds up to scorn mediæval education, with its neglect of the knowledge of nature, its poverty even of literary studies, its formal logic devoted to "showing how and why that which the Church said was true must be true." But the great mediæval Universities were not brought into being, we may be sure, by the zeal for giving a jejune and contemptible education. Kings have been their nursing fathers, and queens have been their nursing mothers, but not for this. The mediæval Universities came into being, because the supposed knowledge, delivered by Scripture and the Church, so deeply engaged men's hearts, by so simply, easily, and powerfully relating itself to their desire for conduct, their desire for beauty. All other knowledge was dominated by this supposed knowledge and was subordinated to it, because of the surpassing strength of the hold which it gained upon the affections of men, by allying itself profoundly with their sense for conduct, their sense for beauty.

But now, says Professor Huxley, conceptions of the universe fatal to the notions held by our forefathers have been forced upon us by physical science. Grant to him that they are thus fatal, that the new conceptions must and will soon become current everywhere, and that every one will finally perceive them to be fatal to the beliefs of our forefathers. The need of humane letters, as they are truly called, because they serve the paramount desire in men that good should be forever present to them—the need of humane letters, to establish a relation between the new conceptions, and our instinct for beauty, our instinct for conduct, is only the more visible. The Middle Age could do without humane letters, as it could do without the study of nature, because its supposed knowledge was made to engage its emotions so powerfully. Grant that the supposed knowledge disappears, its power of being made to engage the emotions will of course disappear along with it—but the emotions themselves, and their claim to be engaged and satisfied, will remain. Now if we find by experience that humane letters have an undeniable power of engaging the emotions, the importance of humane letters in a man's training becomes not less, but greater, in proportion to the success of modern science in extirpating what it calls "mediæval thinking."

Have humane letters, then, have poetry and eloquence, the power here attributed to them of engaging the emotions, and do they exercise it? And if they have it and exercise it, *how* do they exercise it, so as to exert an influence upon man's sense for conduct, his sense for beauty? Finally, even if they both can and do exert an influence upon the senses in question, how are they to relate to them the results—the modern results—of natural science? All these questions may be asked. First, have poetry and eloquence the power of calling out the emotions? The appeal is to experience. Experience shows that for the vast majority of men, for mankind in general, they have the power. Next, do they exercise it? They do. But then, *how* do they exercise it so as to affect man's sense for conduct, his sense for beauty? And this is perhaps a case for applying the Preacher's words: "Though a man labor to seek it out, yet he shall not find it; yea, farther, though a wise man think to know it, yet shall he not be able to find it." Why should it be one thing, in its effect upon the emotions, to say, "Patience is a virtue," and quite another thing, in its effect upon the emotions, to say with Homer,

τλητὸν γὰρ Μοῖραι θυμὸν θέσαν ἀνθρώποι-
σιν—

"for an enduring heart have the destinies appointed to the children of men"? Why should it be one thing, in its effect upon the emotions, to say with the philosopher Spinoza, *Felicitas in ea consistit quod homo suum esse conservare potest*—"Man's happiness consists in his being able to preserve his own essence," and quite another thing, in its effect upon the emotions, to say with the Gospel, "What is a man advantaged, if he gain the whole world, and lose himself, forfeit himself?" How does this difference of effect arise? I cannot tell, and I am not much concerned to know; the important thing is that it does arise, and that we can profit by it. But how, finally, are poetry and eloquence to exercise the power of relating the modern results of natural science to man's instinct for conduct, his instinct for beauty? And here again I answer that I do not know *how* they will exercise it, but that they can and will exercise it I am sure. I do not mean that modern philosophical poets and modern philosophical moralists are to come and relate for us, in express terms, the results of modern scientific research to our instinct for conduct, our instinct for beauty. But I mean that we shall find, as a matter of experience, if we know the best that has been thought and uttered in the world, we shall find that the art and poetry and eloquence of men who lived, perhaps long ago, who had the most limited natural knowledge, who had the most erroneous conceptions about many important matters, we shall find that this art, and poetry, and

eloquence, have in fact not only the power of refreshing and delighting us, they have also the power—such is the strength and worth, in essentials, of their authors' criticism of life—they have a fortifying, and elevating, and quickening, and suggestive power, capable of wonderfully helping us to relate the results of modern science to our need for conduct, our need for beauty. Homer's conceptions of the physical universe were, I imagine, grotesque; but really, under the shock of hearing from modern science that "the world is not subordinated to man's use, and that man is not the cynosure of things terrestrial," I could, for my own part, desire no better comfort than Homer's line which I quoted just now,

τλητὸν γὰρ Μοῖραι θυμὸν θέσαν ἀνθρώποι-
σιν—

"for an enduring heart have the destinies appointed to the children of men"!

And the more that men's minds are cleared, the more that the results of science are frankly accepted, the more that poetry and eloquence come to be received and studied as what in truth they really are—the criticism of life by gifted men, alive and active with extraordinary power at an unusual number of points;—so much the more will the value of humane letters, and of art also, which is an utterance having a like kind of power with theirs, be felt and acknowledged, and their place in education be secured.

Let us, therefore, all of us, avoid indeed as much as possible any invidious comparison between the merits of humane letters, as means of education, and the merits of natural sciences. But when some President of a Section for Mechanical Science insists on making the comparison, and tells us that "he who in his training has substituted literature and history for natural science has chosen the less useful alternative," let us make answer to him that the student of humane letters only, will, at least, know also the great general conceptions brought in by modern physical science: for science, as Professor Huxley says, forces them upon us all. But the student of the natural sciences only, will, by our very hypothesis, know nothing of humane letters; not to mention that in setting himself to be perpetually accumulating natural knowledge, he sets himself to do what only specialists have in general the gift for doing genially. And so he will probably be unsatisfied, or at any rate incomplete, and even more incomplete than the student of humane letters only.

I once mentioned in a school-report, how a young man in one of our English training colleges having to paraphrase the passage in "Macbeth" beginning,

Can'st thou not minister to a mind diseased?

turned this line into, "Can you not wait upon the lunatic?" And I remarked what a curious state of things it would be, if every pupil of our national schools knew, let us say, that the moon is two thousand one hundred and sixty miles in diameter, and thought at the same time that a good paraphrase for

Can'st thou not minister to a mind diseased?

was, "Can you not wait upon the lunatic?" If one is driven to choose, I think I would rather have a young person ignorant about the moon's diameter, but aware that "Can you not wait upon the lunatic?" is bad, than a young person whose education had been such as to manage things the other way.

Or to go higher than the pupils of our national schools. I have in my mind's eye a member of our British Parliament who comes to travel here in America, who afterwards relates his travels, and who shows a really masterly knowledge of the geology of this great country and of its mining capabilities, but who ends by gravely suggesting that the United States should borrow a prince from our Royal Family, and should make him their king, and should create a House of Lords of great landed proprietors after the pattern of ours; and then America, he thinks, would have her future happily and perfectly secured. Surely, in this case, the President of the Section for Mechanical Science would himself hardly say that our member of Parliament, by concentrating himself upon geology and mineralogy, and so on, and not attending to literature and history, had "chosen the more useful alternative."

If then there is to be separation and option between humane letters on the one hand, and the natural sciences on the other, the great majority of mankind, all who have not exceptional and overpowering aptitudes for the study of nature, would do well, I cannot but think, to choose to be educated in humane letters rather than in the natural sciences. Letters will call out their being at more points, will make them live more.

I said that before I ended I would just touch on the question of classical education, and I will keep my word. Even if literature is to retain a large place in our education, yet Latin and Greek, say the friends of progress, will certainly have to go. Greek is the grand offender in the eyes of these gentlemen. The attackers of the established course of study think that against Greek, at any rate, they have irresistible arguments. Literature may perhaps be needed in education, they say; but why on earth should it be Greek literature? Why not French or German? Nay, "has not an Englishman models in his own literature of every kind of excellence?" As before, it is not on any weak pleadings of my own that I rely for convincing the gainsayers; it is on the constitution of human nature itself, and on the instinct of self-preservation in humanity. The instinct for beauty is set in human nature, as surely as the instinct for knowledge is set there, or the instinct for conduct. If the instinct for beauty is served by Greek literature and art as it is served by no other literature and art, we may trust to the instinct of self-preservation in humanity for keeping Greek as part of our culture. We may trust to it for even making the study of Greek more prevalent than it is now. Greek will come, I hope, some day to be studied more rationally than at present; but it will be increasingly studied as men increasingly feel the need in them for beauty, and how powerfully Greek art and Greek literature can serve this need. Women will again study Greek, as Lady Jane Grey did; I believe that in that chain of forts, with which the fair host of the Amazons are now engirdling our English universities, I find that here in America, in colleges like Smith College in Massachusetts, and Vassar College in the State of New York, and in the happy families of the mixed universities out West, they are studying it already.

Defuit una mihi symmetria prisca—"The antique symmetry was the one thing wanting to me," said Leonardo da Vinci; and he was an Italian. I will not presume to speak for the Americans, but I am sure that, in the Englishman, the want of this admirable symmetry of the Greeks is a thousand times more great and crying than in any Italian. The results of the want show themselves most glaringly, perhaps, in our architecture, but they show themselves, also, in all our art. *Fit details strictly combined, in view of a large general result nobly conceived;* that is just the beautiful *symmetria prisca* of the Greeks, and it is just where we English fail, where all our art fails. Striking ideas we have, and well executed details we have; but that high symmetry which, with satisfying and delightful effect, combines them, we seldom or never have. The glorious beauty of the Acropolis at Athens did not come from single fine things stuck about on that hill, a statue here, a gateway there;—no, it arose from all things being perfectly combined for a supreme total effect. What must not an Englishman feel about our deficiencies in this respect, as the sense for beauty, whereof this symmetry is an essential element, awakens and strengthens within him! what will not one day be his respect and desire for Greece and its *symmetria prisca,* when the scales drop from his eyes as he walks the London streets, and he sees such a lesson in meanness, as the Strand, for instance, in its true deformity! But here we are coming to our friend Mr. Ruskin's province, and I will not intrude upon it, for he is its very sufficient guardian.

And so we at last find, it seems, we find flowing in favor of the humanities the natural and necessary stream of things, which seemed against them when we started.

The "hairy quadruped furnished with a tail and pointed ears, probably arboreal in his habits," this good fellow carried hidden in his nature, apparently, something destined to develop into a necessity for humane letters. Nay, more; we seem finally to be even led to the further conclusion that our hairy ancestor carried in his nature, also, a necessity for Greek.

And, therefore, to say the truth, I cannot really think that humane letters are in much actual danger of being thrust out from their leading place in education, in spite of the array of authorities against them at this moment. So long as human nature is what it is, their attractions will remain irresistible. As with Greek, so with letters generally: they will some day come, we may hope, to be studied more rationally, but they will not lose their place. What will happen will rather be that there will be crowded into education other matters besides, far too many; there will be, perhaps, a period of unsettlement and confusion and false tendency; but letters will not in the end lose their leading place. If they lose it for a time, they will get it back again. We shall be brought back to them by our wants and aspirations. And a poor humanist may possess his soul in patience, neither strive nor cry, admit the energy and brilliancy of the partisans of physical science, and their present favor with the public, to be far greater than his own, and still have a happy faith that the nature of things works silently on behalf of the studies which he loves, and that, while we shall all have to acquaint ourselves with the great results reached by modern science, and to give ourselves as much training in its disciplines as we can conveniently carry, yet the majority of men will always require humane letters; and so much the more, as they have the more and the greater results of science to relate to the need in man for conduct, and to the need in him for beauty.

[1882]

PREFACE TO POEMS, 1853

POETRY AND THE CLASSICS

In two small volumes of Poems, published anonymously, one in 1849, the other in 1852, many of the Poems which compose the present volume have already appeared. The rest are now published for the first time.

I have, in the present collection, omitted the poem from which the volume published in 1852 took its title. I have done so, not because the subject of it was a Sicilian Greek born between two and three thousand years ago, although many persons would think this a sufficient reason. Neither have I done so because I had, in my own opinion, failed in the delineation which I intended to effect. I intended to delineate the feelings of one of the last of the Greek religious philosophers, one of the family of Orpheus and Musaeus, having survived his fellows, living on into a time when the habits of Greek thought and feeling had begun fast to change, character to dwindle, the influence of the Sophists to prevail. Into the feelings of a man so situated there are entered much that we are accustomed to consider as exclusively modern; how much, the fragments of Empedocles himself which remain to us are sufficient at least to indicate. What those who are familiar only with the great monuments of early Greek genius suppose to be its exclusive characteristics, have disappeared; the calm, the cheerfulness, the disinterested objectivity have disappeared; the dialogue of the mind with itself has commenced; modern problems have presented themselves; we hear already the doubts, we witness the discouragement, of Hamlet and of Faust.

The representation of such a man's feelings must be interesting, if consistently drawn. We all naturally take pleasure, says Aristotle, in any imitation or representation whatever: this is the basis of our love of poetry: and we take pleasure in them, he adds, because all knowledge is naturally agreeable to us; not to the philosopher only, but to mankind at large. Every representation therefore which is consistently drawn may be supposed to be interesting, inasmuch as it gratifies this natural interest in knowledge of all kinds. What is *not* interesting, is that which does not add to our knowledge of any kind; that which is vaguely conceived and loosely drawn; a representation which is general, indeterminate, and faint, instead of being particular, precise, and firm.

Any accurate representation may therefore be expected to be interesting; but, if the representation be a poetical one, more than this is demanded. It is demanded, not only that it shall interest, but also that it shall inspirit and rejoice the reader: that it shall convey a charm, and infuse delight. For the Muses, as Hesiod says, were born that they might be "a forgetfulness of evils, and a truce from cares": and it is not enough that the poet should add to the knowledge of men, it is required of him also that he should add to their happiness. "All art," says Schiller, "is dedicated to joy, and there is no higher and no more serious problem, than how to make men happy. The right art is that alone, which creates the highest enjoyment."

A poetical work, therefore, is not yet justified when it has been shown to be an accurate, and therefore interesting representation; it has to be shown also that it is a representation from which men can derive enjoyment. In presence of the most tragic circumstances, represented in a work of art, the feeling of enjoyment, as is well known, may still subsist: the representation of the most utter calamity, of the liveliest anguish, is not sufficient to destroy it: the more tragic the situation, the deeper becomes the enjoyment; and the situation is more tragic in proportion as it becomes more terrible.

What then are the situations, from the representation of which, though accurate, no poetical enjoyment can be derived? They are those in which the suffering finds no vent in action; in which a continuous state of mental distress is prolonged, unrelieved by incident, hope, or resistance; in which there is everything to be endured, nothing to be done. In such situations there is inevitably something morbid, in the description of them something monotonous. When they occur in actual life, they are painful, not tragic; the representation of them in poetry is painful also.

To this class of situations, poetically faulty as it appears to me, that of Empedocles, as I have endeavored to represent him, belongs; and I have therefore excluded the poem from the present collection.

And why, it may be asked, have I entered into this explanation respecting a matter so unimportant as the admission or exclusion of the poem in question? I have done so, because I was anxious to avow that the sole reason for its exclusion was that which has been stated above; and that it has not been excluded in deference to the opinion which many critics of the present day appear to entertain against subjects chosen from distant times and countries: against the choice, in short, of any subjects but modern ones.

"The poet," it is said, and by an intelligent critic, "the poet who would really fix the public attention must leave the exhausted past, and draw his subjects from matters of present import, and *therefore* both of interest and novelty."

Now this view I believe to be completely false. It is worth examining, inasmuch as it is a fair sample of a class of critical dicta everywhere current at the present day, having a philosophical form and air, but no real basis in fact; and which are calculated to vitiate the judgment of readers of poetry, while they exert, so far as they are adopted, a misleading influence on the practice of those who make it.

What are the eternal objects of poetry, among all nations and at all times? They are actions; human actions; possessing an inherent interest in themselves, and which are to be communicated in an interesting manner by the art of the poet. Vainly will the latter imagine that he has everything in his own power; that he can make an intrinsically inferior action equally delightful with a more excellent one by his treatment of it: he may indeed compel us to admire his skill, but his work will possess, within itself, an incurable defect.

The poet, then, has in the first place to select an excellent action; and what actions are the most excellent? Those, certainly, which most powerfully appeal to the great primary human affections: to those elementary feelings which subsist permanently in the race, and which are independent of time. These feelings are permanent and the same; that which interests them is permanent and the same also. The modernness or antiquity of an action, therefore, has nothing to do with its fitness for poetical representation; this depends upon its inherent qualities. To the elementary part of our nature, to our passions, that which is great and passionate is eternally interesting; and interesting solely in proportion to its greatness and to its passion. A great human action of a thousand years ago is more interesting to it than a smaller human action of today, even though upon the representation of this last the most consummate skill may have been expended, and though it has the advantage of appealing by its modern language, familiar manners, and contemporary allusions, to all our transient feelings and interests. These, however, have no right to demand of a poetical work that it shall satisfy them; their claims are to be directed elsewhere. Poetical works belong to the domain of our permanent passions: let them interest these, and the voice of all subordinate claims upon them is at once silenced.

Achilles, Prometheus, Clytemnestra, Dido —what modern poem presents personages as interesting, even to us moderns, as these personages of an "exhausted past"? We have the domestic epic dealing with the details of modern life, which pass daily under our eyes; we have poems representing modern personages in contact with the problems of modern life, moral, intellectual, and social; these works have been produced by poets the most distinguished of their nation and time; yet I fearlessly assert that "Hermann and Dorothea," "Childe Harold," "Jocelyn," the "Excursion," leave the reader cold in comparison with the effect produced upon him by the latter books of the "Iliad," by the "Oresteia," or by the episode of Dido. And why is this? Simply because in the three last-named cases the action is greater, the personages nobler, the situations more intense: and this is the true basis of the interest in a poetical work, and this alone.

It may be urged, however, that past actions may be interesting in themselves, but that they are not to be adopted by the modern poet, because it is impossible for him to have them clearly present to his own mind, and he cannot therefore feel them deeply, nor represent them forcibly. But this is not necessarily the case. The externals of a past action, indeed, he cannot know with the precision of a contemporary; but his business is with its essentials. The outward man of Oedipus or of Macbeth, the houses in which they lived, the ceremonies of their courts, he cannot accurately figure to himself; but neither do they essentially concern him. His business is with their inward man; with their feelings and behavior in certain tragic situations, which engage their passions as men; these have in them nothing local and casual; they are as accessible to the modern poet as to a contemporary.

The date of an action, then, signifies nothing: the action itself, its selection and construction, this is what is all-important. This the Greeks understood far more clearly than we do. The radical difference between their poetical theory and ours consists, as it appears to me, in this: that, with them, the poetical character of the action in itself, and the conduct of it, was the first consideration; with us, attention is fixed mainly on the value of the separate thoughts and images which occur in the treatment of an action. They regarded the whole; we regard the parts. With them, the action predominated over the expression of it; with us, the expression predominates over the action. Not that they failed in expression, or were inattentive to it; on the contrary, they are the highest models of expression, the unapproached masters of the *grand style:* but their expression is so excellent because it is so admirably kept in its right degree of prominence; because it is so simple and so well subordinated; because it draws its force directly from the pregnancy of the matter which it conveys. For what reason was the Greek tragic poet confined to so limited a range of subjects? Because there are so few actions which

unite in themselves, in the highest degree, the conditions of excellence; and it was not thought that on any but an excellent subject could an excellent poem be constructed. A few actions, therefore, eminently adapted for tragedy, maintained almost exclusive possession of the Greek tragic stage. Their significance appeared inexhaustible; they were as permanent problems, perpetually offered to the genius of every fresh poet. This too is the reason of what appears to us moderns a certain baldness of expression in Greek tragedy; of the triviality with which we often reproach the remarks of the chorus, where it takes part in the dialogue: that the action itself, the situation of Orestes, or Merope, or Alcmaeon, was to stand the central point of interest, unforgotten, absorbing, principal; that no accessories were for a moment to distract the spectator's attention from this; that the tone of the parts was to be perpetually kept down, in order not to impair the grandiose effect of the whole. The terrible old mythic story on which the drama was founded stood, before he entered the theater, traced in its bare outlines upon the spectator's mind; it stood in his memory, as a group of statuary, faintly seen, at the end of a long and dark vista: then came the poet, embodying outlines, developing situations, not a word wasted, not a sentiment capriciously thrown in; stroke upon stroke, the drama proceeded; the light deepened upon the group; more and more it revealed itself to the riveted gaze of the spectator; until at last, when the final words were spoken, it stood before him in broad sunlight, a model of immortal beauty.

This was what a Greek critic demanded; this was what a Greek poet endeavored to effect. It signified nothing to what time an action belonged. We do not find that the "Persae" occupied a particularly high rank among the dramas of Aeschylus because it represented a matter of contemporary interest: this was not what a cultivated Athenian required. He required that the permanent elements of his nature should be moved; and dramas of which the action, though taken from a long-distant mythic time, yet was calculated to accomplish this in a higher degree than that of the

"Persae," stood higher in his estimation accordingly. The Greeks felt, no doubt, with their exquisite sagacity of taste, that an action of present times was too near them, too much mixed up with what was accidental and passing, to form a sufficiently grand, detached, and self-subsistent object for a tragic poem. Such objects belonged to the domain of the comic poet, and of the lighter kinds of poetry. For the more serious kinds, for *pragmatic* poetry, to use an excellent expression of Polybius, they were more difficult and severe in the range of subjects which they permitted. Their theory and practice alike, the admirable treatise of Aristotle, and the unrivaled works of their poets, exclaim with a thousand tongues—"All depends upon the subject; choose a fitting action, penetrate yourself with the feeling of its situations; this done, everything else will follow."

But for all kinds of poetry alike there was one point on which they were rigidly exacting: the adaptability of the subject to the kind of poetry selected, and the careful construction of the poem.

How different a way of thinking from this is ours! We can hardly at the present day understand what Menander meant, when he told a man who enquired as to the progress of his comedy that he had finished it, not having yet written a single line, because he had constructed the action of it in his mind. A modern critic would have assured him that the merit of his piece depended on the brilliant things which arose under his pen as he went along. We have poems which seem to exist merely for the sake of single lines and passages; not for the sake of producing any total impression. We have critics who seem to direct their attention merely to detached expressions, to the language about the action, not to the action itself. I verily think that the majority of them do not in their hearts believe that there is such a thing as a total impression to be derived from a poem at all, or to be demanded from a poet; they think the term a commonplace of metaphysical criticism. They will permit the poet to select any action he pleases, and to suffer that action to go as it will, provided he gratifies them with occasional bursts of fine writing, and with a shower of isolated thoughts and images. That is, they permit him to leave their poetical sense ungratified, provided that he gratifies their rhetorical sense and their curiosity. Of his neglecting to gratify these, there is little danger; he needs rather to be warned against the danger of attempting to gratify these alone; he needs rather to be perpetually reminded to prefer his action to everything else; so to treat this, as to permit its inherent excellences to develop themselves, without interruption from the intrusion of his personal peculiarities: most fortunate when he most entirely succeeds in effacing himself, and in enabling a noble action to subsist as it did in nature.

But the modern critic not only permits a false practice: he absolutely prescribes false aims. "A true allegory of the state of one's own mind in a representative history," the poet is told, "is perhaps the highest thing that one can attempt in the way of poetry." And accordingly he attempts it. An allegory of the state of one's own mind, the highest problem of an art which imitates actions! No assuredly, it is not, it never can be so: no great poetical work has ever been produced with such an aim. "Faust" itself, in which something of the kind is attempted, wonderful passages as it contains, and in spite of the unsurpassed beauty of the scenes which relate to Margaret, "Faust" itself, judged as a whole, and judged strictly as a poetical work, is defective: its illustrious author, the greatest poet of modern times, the greatest critic of all times, would have been the first to acknowledge it; he only defended his work, indeed, by asserting it to be "something incommensurable."

The confusion of the present times is great, the multitude of voices counseling different things bewildering, the number of existing works capable of attracting a young writer's attention and of becoming his models, immense: what he wants is a hand to guide him through the confusion, a voice to prescribe to him the aim which he should keep in view, and to explain to him that the value of the literary works which offer themselves to his attention is relative to their power of helping him forward on his road towards this aim. Such a guide the English writer at the present day will nowhere find. Failing this, all that can be looked for, all indeed that can be desired, is, that his attention should be fixed on excellent models; that he may reproduce, at any rate, something of their excellence, by penetrating himself with their works and by catching their spirit, if he cannot be taught to produce what is excellent independently.

Foremost among these models for the English writer stands Shakespeare: a name the greatest perhaps of all poetical names; a name never to be mentioned without reverence. I will venture, however, to express a doubt whether the influence of his works, excellent and fruitful for the readers of poetry, for the great majority, has been an unmixed advantage to the writers of it. Shakespeare indeed chose excellent subjects—the world could afford no better than "Macbeth," or "Romeo and Juliet," or "Othello": he had no theory respecting the necessity of choosing subjects of present import, or the paramount interest attaching to allegories of the state of one's own mind; like all great poets, he knew well what constituted a poetical action; like them, wherever he found such an action, he took it; like them, too, he found his best in past times. But to these general characteristics of all great poets he added a special one of his own; a gift, namely, of happy, abundant, and ingenious expression, eminent and unrivaled: so eminent as irresistibly to strike the attention first in him and even to throw into comparative shade his other excellences as a poet. Here has been the mischief. These other excellences were his fundamental excellences as a poet; what distinguishes the artist from the mere amateur, says Goethe, is *Architectonicè* in the highest sense; that power of execution which creates, forms, and constitutes: not the profoundness of single thoughts, not the richness of imagery, not the abundance of illustration. But these attractive accessories of a poetical work being more easily seized than the spirit of the whole, and these accessories being possessed by Shakespeare in an unequaled degree, a young writer having recourse to Shakespeare as his model runs great risk of being vanquished and absorbed by them,

and, in consequence, of reproducing, according to the measure of his power, these, and these alone. Of this preponderating quality of Shakespeare's genius, accordingly, almost the whole of modern English poetry has, it appears to me, felt the influence. To the exclusive attention on the part of his imitators to this, it is in a great degree owing that of the majority of modern poetical works the details alone are valuable, the composition worthless. In reading them one is perpetually reminded of that terrible sentence on a modern French poet—*il dit tout ce qu'il veut, mais malheureusement il n'a rien à dire.*[1]

Let me give an instance of what I mean. I will take it from the works of the very chief among those who seem to have been formed in the school of Shakespeare; of one whose exquisite genius and pathetic death render him forever interesting. I will take the poem of "Isabella," or the "Pot of Basil," by Keats. I choose this rather than the "Endymion," because the latter work (which a modern critic has classed with the "Faery Queen!") although undoubtedly there blows through it the breath of genius, is yet as a whole so utterly incoherent, as not strictly to merit the name of a poem at all. The poem of "Isabella," then, is a perfect treasure-house of graceful and felicitous words and images: almost in every stanza there occurs one of those vivid and picturesque turns of expression, by which the object is made to flash upon the eye of the mind, and which thrill the reader with a sudden delight. This one short poem contains, perhaps, a greater number of happy single expressions which one could quote than all the extant tragedies of Sophocles. But the action, the story? The action in itself is an excellent one; but so feebly is it conceived by the poet, so loosely constructed, that the effect produced by it, in and for itself, is absolutely null. Let the reader, after he has finished the poem of Keats, turn to the same story in the "Decameron": he will then feel how pregnant and interesting the same action has become in the hands of a

---

[1] *il dit tout ce qu'il veut,* etc.: 'he says all that he wishes to, but unfortunately he has nothing to say.' The French poet is, probably, Théophile Gautier (1811–72).

great artist, who above all things delineates his objects; who subordinates expression to that which it is designed to express.

I have said that the imitators of Shakespeare, fixing their attention on his wonderful gifts of expression, have directed their imitation to this, neglecting his other excellences. These excellences, the fundamental excellences of poetical art, Shakespeare no doubt possessed them—possessed many of them in a splendid degree; but it may perhaps be doubted whether even he himself did not sometimes give scope to his faculty of expression to the prejudice of a higher poetical duty. For we must never forget that Shakespeare is the great poet he is from his skill in discerning and firmly conceiving an excellent action, from his power of intensely feeling a situation, of intimately associating himself with a character; not from his gift of expression, which rather even leads him astray, degenerating sometimes into a fondness for curiosity of expression, into an irritability of fancy, which seems to make it impossible for him to say a thing plainly, even when the press of the action demands the very directest language, or its level character the very simplest. Mr. Hallam, than whom it is impossible to find a saner and more judicious critic, has had the courage (for at the present day it needs courage) to remark, how extremely and faultily difficult Shakespeare's language often is. It is so: you may find main scenes in some of his greatest tragedies, "King Lear," for instance, where the language is so artificial, so curiously tortured, and so difficult, that every speech has to be read two or three times before its meaning can be comprehended. This over-curiousness of expression is indeed but the excessive employment of a wonderful gift—of the power of saying a thing in a happier way than any other man; nevertheless, it is carried so far that one understands what M. Guizot meant when he said that Shakespeare appears in his language to have tried all styles except that of simplicity. He has not the severe and scrupulous self-restraint of the ancients, partly, no doubt, because he had a far less cultivated and exacting audience. He has indeed a far wider range than they had, a far richer fertility of thought; in this

respect he rises above them. In his strong conception of his subject, in the genuine way in which he is penetrated with it, he resembles them, and is unlike the moderns. But in the accurate limitation of it, the conscientious rejection of superfluities, the simple and rigorous development of it from the first line of his work to the last, he falls below them, and comes nearer to the moderns. In his chief works, besides what he has of his own, he has the elementary soundness of the ancients; he has their important action and their large and broad manner; but he has not their purity of method. He is therefore a less safe model; for what he has of his own is personal, and inseparable from his own rich nature; it may be imitated and exaggerated, it cannot be learned or applied as an art. He is above all suggestive; more valuable, therefore, to young writers as men than as artists. But clearness of arrangement, rigor of development, simplicity of style—these may to a certain extent be learned: and these may, I am convinced, be learned best from the ancients, who, although infinitely less suggestive than Shakespeare, are thus, to the artist, more instructive.

What then, it will be asked, are the ancients to be our sole models? the ancients with their comparatively narrow range of experience, and their widely different circumstances? Not, certainly, that which is narrow in the ancients, nor that in which we can no longer sympathize. An action like the action of the "Antigone" of Sophocles, which turns upon the conflict between the heroine's duty to her brother's corpse and that to the laws of her country, is no longer one in which it is possible that we should feel a deep interest. I am speaking too, it will be remembered, not of the best sources of intellectual stimulus for the general reader, but of the best models of instruction for the individual writer. This last may certainly learn of the ancients, better than anywhere else, three things which it is vitally important for him to know: the all-importance of the choice of a subject; the necessity of accurate construction; and the subordinate character of expression. He will learn from them how unspeakably superior is the effect of the one moral impression left by a great action treated as a whole, to the effect produced by the most striking single thought or by the happiest image. As he penetrates into the spirit of the great classical works, as he becomes gradually aware of their intense significance, their noble simplicity, and their calm pathos, he will be convinced that it is this effect, unity and profoundness of moral impression, at which the ancient poets aimed; that it is this which constitutes the grandeur of their works, and which makes them immortal. He will desire to direct his own efforts towards producing the same effect. Above all, he will deliver himself from the jargon of modern criticism, and escape the danger of producing poetical works conceived in the spirit of the passing time, and which partake of its transitoriness.

The present age makes great claims upon us: we owe it service, it will not be satisfied without our admiration. I know not how it is, but their commerce with the ancients appears to me to produce, in those who constantly practise it, a steadying and composing effect upon their judgment, not of literary works only, but of men and events in general. They are like persons who have had a very weighty and impressive experience; they are more truly than others under the empire of facts, and more independent of the language current among those with whom they live. They wish neither to applaud nor to revile their age: they wish to know what it is, what it can give them, and whether this is what they want. What they want, they know very well; they want to educe and cultivate what is best and noblest in themselves: they know, too, that this is no easy task— χαλεπὸν, as Pittacus[2] said, χαλεπὸν ἐσθλὸν ἔμμεναι—and they ask themselves sincerely whether their age and its literature can assist them in the attempt. If they are endeavoring to practise any art, they remember the plain and simple proceedings of the old artists, who attained their grand results by penetrating themselves with

some noble and significant action, not by inflating themselves with a belief in the preëminent importance and greatness of their own times. They do not talk of their mission, nor of interpreting their age, nor of the coming poet; all this, they know, is the mere delirium of vanity; their business is not to praise their age, but to afford to the men who live in it the highest pleasure which they are capable of feeling. If asked to afford this by means of subjects drawn from the age itself, they ask what special fitness the present age has for supplying them. They are told that it is an era of progress, an age commissioned to carry out the great ideas of industrial development and social amelioration. They reply that with all this they can do nothing; that the elements they need for the exercise of their art are great actions, calculated powerfully and delightfully to affect what is permanent in the human soul; that so far as the present age can supply such actions, they will gladly make use of them; but that an age wanting in moral grandeur can with difficulty supply such, and an age of spiritual discomfort with difficulty be powerfully and delightfully affected by them.

A host of voices will indignantly rejoin that the present age is inferior to the past neither in moral grandeur nor in spiritual health. He who possesses the discipline I speak of will content himself with remembering the judgments passed upon the present age, in this respect, by the men of strongest head and widest culture whom it has produced; by Goethe and by Niebuhr. It will be sufficient for him that he knows the opinions held by these two great men respecting the present age and its literature; and that he feels assured in his own mind that their aims and demands upon life were such as he would wish, at any rate, his own to be; and their judgment as to what is impeding and disabling such as he may safely follow. He will not, however, maintain a hostile attitude towards the false pretensions of his age; he will content himself with not being overwhelmed by them. He will esteem himself fortunate if he can succeed in banishing from his mind all feelings of contradiction, and irritation, and impatience; in order to delight himself with the contemplation of

2 Pittacus: one of the Seven Wise Men of Greece (*cir.* 600 B. C.), ruler of Mytilene (589-579). The saying—"it is hard to be good" (or excellent)—comes from Diogenes Laertius' *Lives of Eminent Philosophers*, 'Pittacus' (I, i, 76; Loeb trans. I, 79).

some noble action of a heroic time, and to enable others, through his representation of it, to delight in it also.

I am far indeed from making any claim, for myself, that I possess this discipline; or for the following poems, that they breathe its spirit. But I say, that in the sincere endeavor to learn and practise, amid the bewildering confusion of our times, what is sound and true in poetical art, I seemed to myself to find the only sure guidance, the only solid footing, among the ancients. They, at any rate, knew what they wanted in art, and we do not. It is this uncertainty which is disheartening, and not hostile criticism. How often have I felt this when reading words of disparagement or of cavil: that it is the uncertainty as to what is really to be aimed at which makes our difficulty, not the dissatisfaction of the critic, who himself suffers from the same uncertainty. *Non me tua fervida terrent Dicta; ... Dii me terrent, et Jupiter hostis.*[3]

[3] *Non me tua fervida,* etc.: "Thy fierce words dismay me not; ... the gods dismay me, and Jupiter my foe" (Virgil's *Aeneid,* XII, 894–95).

Two kinds of *dilettanti,* says Goethe, there are in poetry: he who neglects the indispensable mechanical part, and thinks he has done enough if he shows spirituality and feeling; and he who seeks to arrive at poetry merely by mechanism, in which he can acquire an artisan's readiness, and is without soul and matter. And he adds, that the first does most harm to art, and the last to himself. If we must be *dilettanti:* if it is impossible for us, under the circumstances amid which we live, to think clearly, to feel nobly, and to delineate firmly: if we cannot attain to the mastery of the great artists—let us, at least, have so much respect for our art as to prefer it to ourselves. Let us not bewilder our successors: let us transmit to them the practice of poetry, with its boundaries and wholesome regulative laws, under which excellent works may again, perhaps, at some future time, be produced, not yet fallen into oblivion through our neglect, not yet condemned and cancelled by the influence of their eternal enemy, caprice.

[1853]

ESSAYS IN CRITICISM

THE STUDY OF POETRY

"The future of poetry is immense, because in poetry, where it is worthy of its high destinies, our race, as time goes on, will find an ever surer and surer stay. There is not a creed which is not shaken, not an accredited dogma which is not shown to be questionable, not a received tradition which does not threaten to dissolve. Our religion has materialized itself in the fact, in the supposed fact; it has attached its emotion to the fact, and now the fact is failing it. But for poetry the idea is everything; the rest is a world of illusion, of divine illusion. Poetry attaches its emotion to the idea; the idea *is* the fact. The strongest part of our religion today is its unconscious poetry."

Let me be permitted to quote these words of my own, as uttering the thought which should, in my opinion, go with us and govern us in all our study of poetry. In the present work it is the course of one great contributory stream to the world-river of poetry that we are invited to follow. We are here invited to trace the stream of English poetry. But whether we set ourselves, as here, to follow only one of the several streams that make the mighty river of poetry, or whether we seek to know them all, our governing thought should be the same. We should conceive of poetry worthily, and more highly than it has been the custom to conceive of it. We should conceive of it as capable of higher uses, and called to higher destinies, than those which in general men have assigned to it hitherto. More and more mankind will discover that we have to turn to poetry to interpret life for us, to console us, to sustain us. Without poetry, our science will appear incomplete; and most of what now passes with us for religion and philosophy will be replaced by poetry. Science, I say, will appear incomplete without it. For finely and truly does Wordsworth call poetry "the impassioned expression which is in the countenance of all science"; and what is a countenance without its expression? Again, Wordsworth finely and truly calls poetry "the breath and finer spirit of all knowledge": our religion, parading evidences such as those on which the popular mind relies now; our philosophy, pluming itself on its reasonings about causation and finite and infinite being; what are they but the shadows and dreams and false shows of knowledge? The day will come when we shall wonder at ourselves for having trusted to them, for having taken them seriously; and the more we perceive their hollowness, the more we shall prize "the breath and finer spirit of knowledge" offered to us by poetry.

But if we conceive thus highly of the destinies of poetry, we must also set our standard for poetry high, since poetry, to be capable of fulfilling such high destinies, must be poetry of a high order of excellence. We must accustom ourselves to a high standard and to a strict judgment. Sainte-Beuve relates that Napoleon one day said, when somebody was spoken of in his presence as a charlatan: "Charlatan as much as you please; but where is there *not* charlatanism?"—"Yes," answers Sainte-Beuve, "in politics, in the art of governing mankind, that is perhaps true. But in the order of thought, in art, the glory, the eternal honor, is that charlatanism shall find no entrance; herein lies the inviolableness of that noble portion of man's being." It is admirably said, and let us hold fast to it. In poetry, which is thought and art in one, it is the glory, the eternal honor, that charlatanism shall find no entrance; that this noble sphere be kept inviolate and inviolable. Charlatanism is for confusing or obliterating the distinctions between excellent and inferior, sound and unsound or only half-sound, true and untrue or only half-true. It is charlatanism, conscious or unconscious, whenever we confuse or obliterate these. And in poetry, more than anywhere else, it is unpermissible to confuse or obliterate them. For in poetry the distinction between excellent and inferior, sound and unsound or only half-sound, true and untrue or only half-true, is of paramount importance. It is of paramount

importance because of the high destinies of poetry. In poetry, as a criticism of life under the conditions fixed for such a criticism by the laws of poetic truth and poetic beauty, the spirit of our race will find, we have said, as time goes on and as other helps fail, its consolation and stay. But the consolation and stay will be of power in proportion to the power of the criticism of life. And the criticism of life will be of power in proportion as the poetry conveying it is excellent rather than inferior, sound rather than unsound or half-sound, true rather than untrue or half-true.

The best poetry is what we want; the best poetry will be found to have a power of forming, sustaining, and delighting us, as nothing else can. A clearer, deeper sense of the best in poetry, and of the strength and joy to be drawn from it, is the most precious benefit which we can gather from a poetical collection such as the present. And yet in the very nature and conduct of such a collection there is inevitably something which tends to obscure in us the consciousness of what our benefit should be, and to distract us from the pursuit of it. We should therefore steadily set it before our minds at the outset, and should compel ourselves to revert constantly to the thought of it as we proceed.

Yes; constantly in reading poetry, a sense for the best, the really excellent, and of the strength and joy to be drawn from it, should be present in our minds and should govern our estimate of what we read. But this real estimate, the only true one, is liable to be superseded, if we are not watchful, by two other kinds of estimate, the historic estimate and the personal estimate, both of which are fallacious. A poet or a poem may count to us historically, they may count to us on grounds personal to ourselves, and they may count to us really. They may count to us historically. The course of development of a nation's language, thought, and poetry, is profoundly interesting; and by regarding a poet's work as a stage in this course of development we may easily bring ourselves to make it of more importance as poetry than in itself it really is, we may come to use a language of quite exaggerated praise in criticizing it; in short, to over-rate it.

So arises in our poetic judgments the fallacy caused by the estimate which we may call historic. Then, again, a poet or a poem may count to us on grounds personal to ourselves. Our personal affinities, likings, and circumstances, have great power to sway our estimate of this or that poet's work, and to make us attach more importance to it as poetry than in itself it really possesses, because to us it is, or has been, of high importance. Here also we over-rate the object of our interest, and apply to it a language of praise which is quite exaggerated. And thus we get the source of a second fallacy in our poetic judgments—the fallacy caused by an estimate which we may call personal.

Both fallacies are natural. It is evident how naturally the study of the history and development of a poetry may incline a man to pause over reputations and works once conspicuous but now obscure, and to quarrel with a careless public for skipping, in obedience to mere tradition and habit, from one famous name or work in its national poetry to another, ignorant of what it misses, and of the reason for keeping what it keeps, and of the whole process of growth in its poetry. The French have become diligent students of their own early poetry, which they long neglected; the study makes many of them dissatisfied with their so-called classical poetry, the court-tragedy of the seventeenth century, a poetry which Pellisson long ago reproached with its want of the true poetic stamp, with its *politesse stérile et rampante*,[1] but which nevertheless has reigned in France as absolutely as if it had been the perfection of classical poetry indeed. The dissatisfaction is natural; yet a lively and accomplished critic, M. Charles d'Héricault, the editor of Clément Marot, goes too far when he says that "the cloud of glory playing round a classic is a mist as dangerous to the future of a literature as it is intolerable for the purposes of history." "It hinders," he goes on, "it hinders us from seeing more than one single point, the culminating and exceptional point; the summary, fictitious and arbitrary, of a thought and of a work. It substitutes a halo for a physiognomy, it puts a statue where there was once a man, and hiding

[1] *politesse*, etc.: sterile and servile politeness.

from us all trace of the labor, the attempts, the weaknesses, the failures, it claims not study but veneration; it does not show us how the thing is done, it imposes upon us a model. Above all, for the historian this creation of classic personages is inadmissible; for it withdraws the poet from his time, from his proper life, it breaks historical relationships, it blinds criticism by conventional admiration, and renders the investigation of literary origins unacceptable. It gives us a human personage no longer, but a God seated immovable amidst His perfect work, like Jupiter on Olympus: and hardly will it be possible for the young student, to whom such work is exhibited at such a distance from him, to believe that it did not issue ready made from that divine head."

All this is brilliantly and tellingly said, but we must plead for a distinction. Everything depends on the reality of a poet's classic character. If he is a dubious classic, let us sift him; if he is a false classic, let us explode him. But if he is a real classic, if his work belongs to the class of the very best (for this is the true and right meaning of the word *classic, classical*), then the great thing for us is to feel and enjoy his work as deeply as ever we can, and to appreciate the wide difference between it and all work which has not the same high character. This is what is salutary, this is what is formative; this is the great benefit to be got from the study of poetry. Everything which interferes with it, which hinders it, is injurious. True, we must read our classic with open eyes, and not with eyes blinded with superstition; we must perceive when his work comes short, when it drops out of the class of the very best, and we must rate it, in such cases, at its proper value. But the use of this negative criticism is not in itself, it is entirely in its enabling us to have a clearer sense and a deeper enjoyment of what is truly excellent. To trace the labor, the attempts, the weaknesses, the failures of a genuine classic, to acquaint oneself with his time and his life and his historical relationships, is mere literary dilettantism unless it has that clear sense and deeper enjoyment for its end. It may be said that the more we know about a classic the better we shall enjoy him; and, if we lived as long as Methuselah and had all of us heads of perfect clearness and wills of perfect steadfastness, this might be true in fact as it is plausible in theory. But the case here is much the same as the case with the Greek and Latin studies of our schoolboys. The elaborate philological groundwork which we require them to lay is in theory an admirable preparation for appreciating the Greek and Latin authors 10 worthily. The more thoroughly we lay the groundwork, the better we shall be able, it may be said, to enjoy the authors. True, if time were not so short, and schoolboys' wits not so soon tired and their power of attention exhausted; only, as it is, the elaborate philological preparation goes on, but the authors are little known and less enjoyed. So with the investigator of "historic origins" in poetry. He ought to enjoy 20 the true classic all the better for his investigations; he often is distracted from the enjoyment of the best, and with the less good he overbusies himself, and is prone to over-rate it in proportion to the trouble which it has cost him.

The idea of tracing historic origins and historical relationships cannot be absent from a compilation, like the present. And naturally the poets to be exhibited in it 30 will be assigned to those persons for exhibition who are known to prize them highly, rather than to those who have no special inclination towards them. Moreover the very occupation with an author, and the business of exhibiting him, disposes us to affirm and amplify his importance. In the present work, therefore, we are sure of frequent temptation to adopt the historic estimate, or the personal estimate, and to 40 forget the real estimate; which latter, nevertheless, we must employ if we are to make poetry yield us its full benefit. So high is that benefit, the benefit of clearly feeling and of deeply enjoying the really excellent, the truly classic in poetry, that we do well, I say, to set it fixedly before our minds as our object in studying poets and poetry, and to make the desire of attaining it the one principle to which, as 50 the "Imitation" says, whatever we may read or come to know, we always return. *Cum multa legeris et cognoveris, ad unum semper oportet redire principium.*

The historic estimate is likely in especial to affect our judgment and our language when we are dealing with ancient poets; the personal estimate when we are dealing with poets our contemporaries, or at any rate modern. The exaggerations due to the historic estimate are not in themselves, perhaps, of very much gravity. Their report hardly enters the general ear; probably they do not always impose even on the literary men who adopt them. But they lead to a dangerous abuse of language. So we hear Caedmon, among our own poets, compared to Milton. I have already noticed the enthusiasm of one accomplished French critic for "historic origins." Another eminent French critic, M. Vitet, comments upon that famous document of the early poetry of his nation, the "Chanson de Roland." It is indeed a most interesting document. The *joculator* or *jongleur* [2] Taillefer, who was with William the Conqueror's army at Hastings, marched before the Norman troops, so said the tradition, singing "of Charlemagne and of Roland and of Oliver, and of the vassals who died at Roncevaux"; and it is suggested that in the "Chanson de Roland" by one Turoldus or Théroulde, a poem preserved in a manuscript of the twelfth century in the Bodleian Library at Oxford, we have certainly the matter, perhaps even some of the words, of the chant which Taillefer sang. The poem has vigor and freshness; it is not without pathos. But M. Vitet is not satisfied with seeing in it a document of some poetic value, and of very high historic and linguistic value; he sees in it a grand and beautiful work, a monument of epic genius. In its general design he finds the grandiose conception, in its details he finds the constant union of simplicity with greatness, which are the marks, he truly says, of the genuine epic, and distinguish it from the artificial epic of literary ages. One thinks of Homer; this is the sort of praise which is given to Homer, and justly given. Higher praise there cannot well be, and it is the praise

[2] *joculator* or *jongleur*: Latin and French names for jester (or entertainer), who in medieval France was a wandering minstrel, singing in castles or at court. Taillefer was such a bard."

due to epic poetry of the highest order only, and to no other. Let us try, then, the "Chanson de Roland" at its best. Roland, mortally wounded, lays himself down under a pine-tree, with his face turned towards Spain and the enemy—

> De plusurs choses à remembrer li prist
> De tantes teres cume li bers cunquist,
> De dulce France, des humes de sun lign,
> De Carlemagne sun seignor ki l'nurrit.[3]

That is primitive work, I repeat, with an undeniable poetic quality of its own. It deserves such praise, and such praise is sufficient for it. But now turn to Homer—

> "Ὡς φάτο· τοὺς δ' ἤδη κατέχεν φυσίζοος αἶα
> ἐ Λακεδαίμονι αὖθι, φίλη ἐν πατρίδι λαίη.[4]

We are here in another world, another order of poetry altogether; here is rightly due such supreme praise as that which M. Vitet gives to the "Chanson de Roland." If our words are to have any meaning, if our judgments are to have any solidity, we must not heap that supreme praise upon poetry of an order immeasurably inferior.

Indeed there can be no more useful help for discovering what poetry belongs to the class of the truly excellent, and can therefore do us most good, than to have always in one's mind lines and expressions of the great masters, and to apply them as a touchstone to other poetry. Of course we are not to require this other poetry to resemble them; it may be very dissimilar. But if we have any tact we shall find them, when we have lodged them well in our minds, an infallible touchstone for detecting the presence or absence of high poetic quality, and also the degree of this quality, in all other poetry which we may place beside them. Short passages, even single lines, will serve our turn quite sufficiently. Take the two lines which I have just quoted from Homer, the poet's comment on Helen's mention of her brothers;—or take his [9]

> Ἀ δειλώ, τί σφῶϊ δόμεν Πηλῆϊ ἄνακτι
> θνητῷ; ὑμεῖς δ' ἐστὸν ἀγήρω τ' ἀθανάτω τε,
> ἦ ἵνα δυστήνοισι μετ' ἀνδράσιν ἄλγε' ἔχητον;[5]

the address of Zeus to the horses of Peleus; —or take finally his

> Καὶ σέ, γέρον, τὸ πρὶν μὲν ἀκούομεν ὄλβιον
> εἶναι·[6]

the words of Achilles to Priam, a suppliant before him. Take that incomparable line and a half of Dante, Ugolino's tremendous words—

> Io no piangeva; sì dentro impietrai.
> Piangevan elli . . .[7]

take the lovely words of Beatrice to Virgil—

> Io son fatta da Dio, sua mercè, tale,
> Che la vostra miseria non mi tange,
> Nè fiamma d'esto incendio non m'assale . . . [8]

take the simple, but perfect, single line—

> In la sua volontade è nostra pace.[9]

Take of Shakespeare a line or two of Henry the Fourth's expostulation with sleep—

---

[3] "De plusurs choses," etc.: 'Then began he to call many things to remembrance,—all the lands which his valor conquered, and pleasant France, and the men of his lineage, and Charlemagne his liege lord who nourished him.'—*Chanson de Roland*, iii, 939-942 (Arnold's note).

[4] now turn to Homer: 'So said she; they long since in Earth's soft arms were reposing, There, in their own dear land, their fatherland, Lacedaemon.'—*Iliad*, iii, 243-4 (translated by Dr. Hawtrey.—Arnold's note).

[5] —or take his: 'Ah, unhappy pair, why gave we you to King Peleus, to a mortal? but ye are without old age, and immortal. Was it that with men born to misery ye might have sorrow?'—*Iliad*, XVII, 443-445 (Arnold's note).

[6] —or take finally his: 'Nay, and thou too, old man, in former days wast, as we hear, happy.'—*Iliad*, XXIV, 543 (Arnold's note).

[7] —Ugolino's tremendous words: 'I wailed not, so of stone grew I within;—they wailed.'—*Inferno*, XXXIII, 39-40. (Arnold's note). The lines are, rather, 49-50. Ugolino was a Pisan noble and political leader of the 13th century, who was imprisoned with his two sons and two grandsons by his enemy, the archbishop Ruggieri. They all died of starvation. Dante describes Ugolino in the *Inferno*, frozen in ice, gnawing the head of his enemy. The little grandsons "wailed."

[8] the lovely words of Beatrice to Virgil: 'Of such sort hath God, thanked be his mercy, made me, that your misery toucheth me not, neither doth the flame of this fire strike me.'—*Inferno*, II, 91-93. (Arnold's note).

[9] perfect, single line: "In his will is our peace."—*Paradiso*, III, 85 (Arnold's note).

Wilt thou upon the high and giddy mast
Seal up the ship-boy's eyes, and rock his brains
In cradle of the rude imperious surge...

and take, as well, Hamlet's dying request to Horatio—

If thou didst ever hold me in thy heart,
Absent thee from felicity awhile,
And in this harsh world draw thy breath in
    pain
To tell my story...

Take of Milton that Miltonic passage—

Darken'd so, yet shone
Above them all the archangel; but his face
Deep scars of thunder had intrench'd, and care
Sat on his faded cheek...

add two such lines as—

And courage never to submit or yield
And what is else not to be overcome...

and finish with the exquisite close to the loss of Proserpine, the loss

...which cost Ceres all that pain
    To seek her through the world.

These few lines, if we have tact and can use them, are enough even of themselves to keep clear and sound our judgments about poetry, to save us from fallacious estimates of it, to conduct us to a real estimate.

The specimens I have quoted differ widely from one another, but they have in common this: the possession of the very highest poetical quality. If we are thoroughly penetrated by their power, we shall find that we have acquired a sense enabling us, whatever poetry may be laid before us, to feel the degree in which a high poetical quality is present or wanting there. Critics give themselves great labor to draw out what in the abstract constitutes the characters of a high quality of poetry. It is much better simply to have recourse to concrete examples;—to take specimens of poetry of the high, the very highest quality, and to say: The characters of a high quality of poetry are what is expressed *there*. They are far better recognized by being felt in the verse of the master, than by being perused in the prose of the critic. Nevertheless if we are urgently pressed to give some critical account of them, we may safely, perhaps, venture on laying down, not

indeed how and why the characters arise, but where and in what they arise. They are in the matter and substance of the poetry, and they are in its manner and style. Both of these, the substance and matter on the one hand, the style and manner on the other, have a mark, an accent, of high beauty, worth, and power. But if we are asked to define this mark and accent in the abstract, our answer must be: No, for we should thereby be darkening the question, not clearing it. The mark and accent are as given by the substance and matter of that poetry, by the style and manner of that poetry, and of all other poetry which is akin to it in quality.

Only one thing we may add as to the substance and matter of poetry, guiding ourselves by Aristotle's profound observation that the superiority of poetry over history consists in its possessing a higher truth and a higher seriousness (φιλοσοφώτερον καὶ σπουδαιότερον). Let us add, therefore, to what we have said, this: that the substance and matter of the best poetry acquire their special character from possessing, in an eminent degree, truth and seriousness. We may add yet further, what is in itself evident, that to the style and manner of the best poetry their special character, their accent, is given by their diction, and, even yet more, by their movement. And though we distinguish between the two characters, the two accents, of superiority, yet they are nevertheless vitally connected one with the other. The superior character of truth and seriousness, in the matter and substance of the best poetry, is inseparable from the superiority of diction and movement marking its style and manner. The two superiorities are closely related, and are in steadfast proportion one to the other. So far as high poetic truth and seriousness are wanting to a poet's matter and substance, so far also, we may be sure, will a high poetic stamp of diction and movement be wanting to his style and manner. In proportion as this high stamp of diction and movement, again, is absent from a poet's style and manner, we shall find, also, that high poetic truth and seriousness are absent from his substance and matter.

So stated, these are but dry generalities;

their whole force lies in their application. And I could wish every student of poetry to make the application of them for himself. Made by himself, the application would impress itself upon his mind far more deeply than made by me. Neither will my limits allow me to make any full application of the generalities above propounded; but in the hope of bringing out, at any rate, some significance in them, and of establishing an important principle more firmly by their means, I will, in the space which remains to me, follow rapidly from the commencement the course of our English poetry with them in my view.

Once more I return to the early poetry of France, with which our own poetry, in its origins, is indissolubly connected. In the twelfth and thirteenth centuries, that seedtime of all modern language and literature, the poetry of France had a clear predominance in Europe. Of the two divisions of that poetry, its productions in the *langue d'oil* and its productions in the *langue d'oc*, the poetry of the *langue d'oc*, of southern France, of the troubadours, is of importance because of its effect on Italian literature;—the first literature of modern Europe to strike the true and grand note, and to bring forth, as in Dante and Petrarch it brought forth, classics. But the predominance of French poetry in Europe, during the twelfth and thirteenth centuries, is due to its poetry of the *langue d'oil*, the poetry of northern France and of the tongue which is now the French language. In the twelfth century the bloom of this romance-poetry was earlier and stronger in England, at the court of our Anglo-Norman kings, than in France itself. But it was a bloom of French poetry; and as our native poetry formed itself, it formed itself out of this. The romance-poems which took possession of the heart and imagination of Europe in the twelfth and thirteenth centuries are French; "they are," as Southey justly says, "the pride of French literature, nor have we anything which can be placed in competition with them." Themes were supplied from all quarters; but the romance-setting which was common to them all, and which gained the ear of Europe, was French. This constituted for the French poetry, literature, and language, at the height of the Middle Age, an unchallenged predominance. The Italian Brunetto Latini, the master of Dante, wrote his "Treasure" in French because, he says, "la parleure en est plus délitable et plus commune à toutes gens." In the same century, the thirteenth, the French romance-writer, Christian of Troyes, formulates the claims, in chivalry and letters, of France, his native country, as follows—

> Or vous ert par ce livre apris,
> Que Gresse ot de chevalerie
> Le premier los et de clergie;
> Puis vint chevalerie à Rome,
> Et de la clergie la some,
> Qui ore est en France venue.
> Diex doinst qu'ele i soit retenue,
> Et que li lius li abelisse
> 'Tant que de France n'isse
> L'onor qui s'i est arestée!

"Now by this book you will learn that first Greece had the renown for chivalry and letters: then chivalry and the primacy in letters passed to Rome, and now it is come to France. God grant it may be kept there; and that the place may please it so well, that the honor which has come to make stay in France may never depart thence!" Yet it is now all gone, this French romance-poetry, of which the weight of substance and the power of style are not unfairly represented by this extract from Christian of Troyes. Only by means of the historic estimate can we persuade ourselves now to think that any of it is of poetical importance.

But in the fourteenth century there comes an Englishman nourished on this poetry; taught his trade by this poetry, getting words, rhyme, meter from this poetry; for even of that stanza which the Italians used, and which Chaucer derived immediately from the Italians, the basis and suggestion was probably given in France. Chaucer (I have already named him) fascinated his contemporaries, but so too did Christian of Troyes and Wolfram of Eschenbach. Chaucer's power of fascination, however, is enduring; his poetical importance does not need the assistance of the historic estimate; it is real. He is a genuine source of joy and strength, which is flowing still for us and will flow always. He will be read, as time goes on, far more generally than he is read now. His language is a cause of difficulty for us; but so also, and I think in quite as great a degree, is the language of Burns. In Chaucer's case, as in that of Burns, it is a difficulty to be unhesitatingly accepted and overcome.

If we ask ourselves wherein consists the immense superiority of Chaucer's poetry over the romance-poetry—why it is that in passing from this to Chaucer we suddenly feel ourselves to be in another world, we shall find that his superiority is both in the substance of his poetry and in the style of his poetry. His superiority in substance is given by his large, free, simple, clear yet kindly view of human life—so unlike the total want, in the romance-poets, of all intelligent command of it. Chaucer has not their helplessness; he has gained the power to survey the world from a central, a truly human point of view. We have only to call to mind the Prologue to "The Canterbury Tales." The right comment upon it is Dryden's: "It is sufficient to say, according to the proverb, that *here is God's plenty.*" And again: "He is a perpetual fountain of good sense." It is by a large, free, sound representation of things, that poetry, this high criticism of life, has truth of substance; and Chaucer's poetry has truth of substance.

Of his style and manner, if we think first of the romance-poetry and then of Chaucer's divine liquidness of diction, his divine fluidity of movement, it is difficult to speak temperately. They are irresistible, and justify all the rapture with which his successors speak of his "gold dew-drops of speech." Johnson misses the point entirely when he finds fault with Dryden for ascribing to Chaucer the first refinement of our numbers, and says that Gower also can show smooth numbers and easy rhymes. The refinement of our numbers means something far more than this. A nation may have versifiers with smooth numbers and easy rhymes, and yet may have no real poetry at all. Chaucer is the father of our splendid English poetry; he is our "well of English undefiled," because by the lovely charm of his diction, the lovely charm of his movement, he makes an epoch and founds a tradition. In Spenser, Shakespeare, Milton, Keats, we can follow the tradition of the liquid diction, the fluid movement, of Chaucer; at one time it is his liquid diction of which in these poets we feel the virtue, and at another time it is his fluid movement. And the virtue is irresistible.

Bounded as is my space, I must yet find room for an example of Chaucer's virtue, as I have given examples to show the virtue of the great classics. I feel disposed to say that a single line is enough to show the charm of Chaucer's verse; that merely one line like this—

O martyr souded in virginitee! [10]

has a virtue of manner and movement such as we shall not find in all the verse of romance-poetry;—but this is saying nothing. The virtue is such as we shall not find, perhaps, in all English poetry, outside the poets whom I have named as the special inheritors of Chaucer's tradition. A single line, however, is too little if we have not the strain of Chaucer's verse well in our memory; let us take a stanza. It is from "The Prioress's Tale," the story of the Christian child murdered in a Jewry—

My throte is cut unto my nekke-bone
Saidè this child, and as by way of kinde
I should have deyd, yea, longè time agone
But Jesu Christ, as ye in bookès finde,
Will that his glory last and be in minde,
And for the worship of his mother dere
Yet may I sing *O Alma* loud and clere.

Wordsworth has modernized this Tale, and to feel how delicate and evanescent is the charm of verse, we have only to read Wordsworth's first three lines of this stanza after Chaucer's—

My throat is cut unto the bone, I trow,
Said this young child, and by the law of kind
I should have died, yea, many hours ago.

The charm is departed. It is often said that the power of liquidness and fluidity in Chaucer's verse was dependent upon a free, a licentious dealing with language, such as is now impossible; upon a liberty, such as Burns too enjoyed, of making words like

[10] *O martyr souded,* etc.: The French *soudé:* soldered, fixed fast (Arnold's note). The quotation is from the *Prioress's Tale,* 127; Chaucer has 'souded to.'

neck, bird, into a dissyllable by adding to them, and words like *cause, rhyme,* into a dissyllable by sounding the *e* mute. It is true that Chaucer's fluidity is conjoined with this liberty, and is admirably served by it; but we ought not to say that it was dependent upon it. It was dependent upon his talent. Other poets with a like liberty do not attain to the fluidity of Chaucer; Burns himself does not attain to it. Poets, again, who have a talent akin to Chaucer's, such as Shakespeare or Keats, have known how to attain to his fluidity without the like liberty.

And yet Chaucer is not one of the great classics. His poetry transcends and effaces, easily and without effort, all the romance-poetry of Catholic Christendom; it transcends and effaces all the English poetry contemporary with it, it transcends and effaces all the English poetry subsequent to it down to the age of Elizabeth. Of such avail is poetic truth of substance, in its natural and necessary union with poetic truth of style. And yet, I say, Chaucer is not one of the great classics. He has not their accent. What is wanting to him is suggested by the mere mention of the name of the first great classic of Christendom, the immortal poet who died eighty years before Chaucer—Dante. The accent of such verse as

In la sua voluntade è nostra pace ...

is altogether beyond Chaucer's reach; we praise him, but we feel that this accent is out of the question for him. It may be said that it was necessarily out of the reach of any poet in the England of that stage of growth. Possibly; but we are to adopt a real, not a historic, estimate of poetry. However we may account for its absence, something is wanting, then, to the poetry of Chaucer, which poetry must have before it can be placed in the glorious class of the best. And there is no doubt what that something is. It is the σπουδαιότης, the high and excellent seriousness, which Aristotle assigns as one of the grand virtues of poetry. The substance of Chaucer's poetry, his view of things and his criticism of life, has largeness, freedom, shrewdness, benignity; but it has not this high seriousness. Homer's criticism of life has it,

Dante's has it, Shakespeare's has it. It is this chiefly which gives to our spirits what they can rest upon; and with the increasing demands of our modern ages upon poetry, this virtue of giving us what we can rest upon will be more and more highly esteemed. A voice from the slums of Paris, fifty or sixty years after Chaucer, the voice of poor Villon out of his life of riot and crime, has at its happy moments (as, for instance, in the last stanza of "La Belle Heaulmière") more of this important poetic virtue of seriousness than all the productions of Chaucer. But its apparition in Villon, and in men like Villon, is fitful; the greatness of the great poets, the power of their criticism of life, is that their virtue is sustained.

To our praise, therefore, of Chaucer as a poet there must be this limitation; he lacks the high seriousness of the great classics, and therewith an important part of their virtue. Still, the main fact for us to bear in mind about Chaucer is his sterling value according to that real estimate which we firmly adopt for all poets. He has poetic truth of substance, though he has not high poetic seriousness, and corresponding to his truth of substance he has an exquisite value of style and manner. With him is born our real poetry.

For my present purpose I need not dwell on our Elizabethan poetry, or on the continuation and close of this poetry in Milton. We all of us profess to be agreed in the estimate of this poetry; we all of us recognize it as great poetry, our greatest, and Shakespeare and Milton as our poetical classics. The real estimate, here, has universal currency. With the next age of our poetry divergency and difficulty began. An historic estimate of that poetry has established itself; and the question is, whether it will be found to coincide with the real estimate.

The age of Dryden, together with our whole eighteenth century which followed it, sincerely believed itself to have produced poetical classics of its own, and even to have made advance, in poetry, beyond all its predecessors. Dryden regards as not seriously disputable the opinion "that the sweetness of English verse was never understood or practised by our fathers." Cowley could see nothing at all in Chaucer's poetry. Dryden heartily admired it, and, as we have seen, praised its matter admirably; but of its exquisite manner and movement all he can find to say is that "there is the rude sweetness of a Scotch tune in it, which is natural and pleasing, though not perfect." Addison, wishing to praise Chaucer's numbers, compares them with Dryden's own. And all through the eighteenth century, and down even into our own times, the stereotyped phrase of approbation for good verse found in our early poetry has been, that it even approached the verse of Dryden, Addison, Pope, and Johnson.

Are Dryden and Pope poetical classics? Is the historic estimate, which represents them as such, and which has been so long established that it cannot easily give way, the real estimate? Wordsworth and Coleridge, as is well known, denied it; but the authority of Wordsworth and Coleridge does not weigh much with the young generation, and there are many signs to show that the eighteenth century and its judgments are coming into favor again. Are the favorite poets of the eighteenth century classics?

It is impossible within my present limits to discuss the question fully. And what man of letters would not shrink from seeming to dispose dictatorially of the claims of two men who are, at any rate, such masters in letters as Dryden and Pope; two men of such admirable talent, both of them, and one of them, Dryden, a man, on all sides, of such energetic and genial power? And yet, if we are to gain the full benefit from poetry, we must have the real estimate of it. I cast about for some mode of arriving, in the present case, at such an estimate without offence. And perhaps the best way is to begin, as it is easy to begin, with cordial praise.

When we find Chapman, the Elizabethan translator of Homer, expressing himself in his preface thus: "Though truth in her very nakedness sits in so deep a pit, that from Gades to Aurora and Ganges few eyes can sound her, I hope yet those few here will so discover and confirm that, the date being out of her darkness in this morning of our poet, he shall now gird his temples with the sun"—we pronounce that such a prose is intolerable. When we find Milton writing: "And long it was not after, when I was confirmed in this opinion, that he, who would not be frustrate of his hope to write well hereafter in laudable things, ought himself to be a true poem"—we pronounce that such a prose has its own grandeur, but that it is obsolete and inconvenient. But when we find Dryden telling us; "What Virgil wrote in the vigor of his age, in plenty and at ease, I have undertaken to translate in my declining years; struggling with wants, oppressed with sickness, curbed in my genius, liable to be misconstrued in all I write"—then we exclaim that here at last we have the true English prose, a prose such as we would all gladly use if we only knew how. Yet Dryden was Milton's contemporary.

But after the Restoration the time had come when our nation felt the imperious need of a fit prose. So, too, the time had likewise come when our nation felt the imperious need of freeing itself from the absorbing preoccupation which religion in the Puritan age had exercised. It was impossible that this freedom should be brought about without some negative excess, without some neglect and impairment of the religious life of the soul; and the spiritual history of the eighteenth century shows us that the freedom was not achieved without them. Still, the freedom was achieved; the preoccupation, an undoubtedly baneful and retarding one if it had continued, was got rid of. And as with religion among us at that period, so it was also with letters. A fit prose was a necessity; but it was impossible that a fit prose should establish itself among us without some touch of frost to the imaginative life of the soul. The needful qualities for a fit prose are regularity, uniformity, precision, balance. The men of letters, whose destiny it may be to bring their nation to the attainment of a fit prose, must of necessity, whether they work in prose or in verse, give a predominating, an almost exclusive attention to the qualities of regularity, uniformity, precision, balance. But an almost exclusive attention to these qualities involves some repression and silencing of poetry.

We are to regard Dryden as the puissant and glorious founder, Pope as the splendid high priest, of our age of prose and reason, of our excellent and indispensable eighteenth century. For the purposes of their mission and destiny their poetry, like their prose, is admirable. Do you ask me whether Dryden's verse, take it almost where you will, is not good?

A milk-white Hind, immortal and unchanged, Fed on the lawns and in the forest ranged.

I answer: Admirable for the purposes of the inaugurator of an age of prose and reason. Do you ask me whether Pope's verse, take it almost where you will, is not good?

To Hounslow Heath I point, and Banstead Down;
Thence comes your mutton, and these chicks my own.

I answer: Admirable for the purposes of the high priest of an age of prose and reason. But do you ask me whether such verse proceeds from men with an adequate poetic criticism of life, from men whose criticism of life has a high seriousness, or even, without that high seriousness, has poetic largeness, freedom, insight, benignity? Do you ask me whether the application of ideas to life in the verse of these men, often a powerful application, no doubt, is a powerful *poetic* application? Do you ask me whether the poetry of these men has either the matter or the inseparable manner of such an adequate poetic criticism; whether it has the accent of

Absent thee from felicity awhile....

or of

And what is else not to be overcome....

or of

O martyr souded in virginitee!

I answer: It has not and cannot have them; it is the poetry of the builders of an age of prose and reason. Though they may write in verse, though they may in a certain sense be masters of the art of versification, Dryden and Pope are not classics of our poetry, they are classics of our prose.

Gray is our poetical classic of that litera-

ture and age; the position of Gray is singular, and demands a word of notice here. He has not the volume or the power of poets who, coming in times more favorable, have attained to an independent criticism of life. But he lived with the great poets, he lived, above all, with the Greeks, through perpetually studying and enjoying them; and he caught their poetic point of view for regarding life, caught their poetic manner. The point of view and the manner are not self-sprung in him, he caught them of others; and he had not the free and abundant use of them. But whereas Addison and Pope never had the use of them, Gray had the use of them at times. He is the scantiest and frailest of classics in our poetry, but he is a classic.

And now, after Gray, we are met, as we draw towards the end of the eighteenth century, we are met by the great name of Burns. We enter now on times where the personal estimate of poets begins to be rife, and where the real estimate of them is not reached without difficulty. But in spite of the disturbing pressures of personal partiality, of national partiality, let us try to reach a real estimate of the poetry of Burns.

By his English poetry Burns in general belongs to the eighteenth century, and has little importance for us.

Mark ruffian Violence, distain'd with crimes
Rousing elate in these degenerate times;
View unsuspecting Innocence a prey,
As guileful Fraud points out the erring way;
While subtle Litigation's pliant tongue
The life-blood equal sucks of Right and Wrong!

Evidently this is not the real Burns, or his name and fame would have disappeared long ago. Nor is Clarinda's love-poet, Sylvander, the real Burns either. But he tells us himself: "These English songs gravel me to death. I have not the command of the language that I have of my native tongue. In fact, I think that my ideas are more barren in English than in Scotch. I have been at 'Duncan Gray' to dress it in English, but all I can do is desperately stupid." We English turn naturally, in Burns, to the poems in our own language, because we can read them easily; but in those poems we have not the real Burns.

The real Burns is of course in his Scotch poems. Let us boldly say that of much of this poetry, a poetry dealing perpetually with Scotch drink, Scotch religion, and Scotch manners, a Scotchman's estimate is apt to be personal. A Scotchman is used to this world of Scotch drink, Scotch religion, and Scotch manners; he has a tenderness for it; he meets its poet half way. In this tender mood he reads pieces like the "Holy Fair" or "Halloween." But this world of Scotch drink, Scotch religion, and Scotch manners is against a poet, not for him, when it is not a partial countryman who reads him; for in itself it is not a beautiful world, and no one can deny that it is of advantage to a poet to deal with a beautiful world. Burns's world of Scotch drink, Scotch religion, and Scotch manners, is often a harsh, a sordid, a repulsive world; even the world of his "Cotter's Saturday Night" is not a beautiful world. No doubt a poet's criticism of life may have such truth and power that it triumphs over its world and delights us. Burns may triumph over his world, often he does triumph over his world, but let us observe how and where. Burns is the first case we have had where the bias of the personal estimate tends to mislead; let us look at him closely, he can bear it.

Many of his admirers will tell us that we have Burns, convivial, genuine, delightful, here—

Leeze me on drink! it gies us mair
  Than either school or college;
It kindles wit, it waukens lair,
  It pangs us fou o' knowledge.
Be 't whisky gill or penny wheep
  Or ony stronger potion,
It never fails, on drinking deep,
  To kittle up our notion
      By night or day.

There is a great deal of that sort of thing in Burns, and it is unsatisfactory, not because it is bacchanalian poetry, but because it has not that accent of sincerity which bacchanalian poetry, to do it justice, very often has. There is something in it of bravado, something which makes us feel that we have not the man speaking to us with his real voice; something, therefore, poetically unsound.

With still more confidence will his admirers tell us that we have the genuine Burns, the great poet, when his strain asserts the independence, equality, dignity, of men, as in the famous song "For a' that and a' that"—

A prince can mak' a belted knight,
  A marquis, duke, and a' that;
But an honest man's aboon his might,
  Guid faith he mauna fa' that!
    For a' that, and a' that,
      Their dignities, and a' that,
    The pith o' sense, and pride o' worth,
      Are higher rank than a' that.

Here they find his grand, genuine touches; and still more, when this puissant genius, who so often set morality at defiance, falls moralizing—

The sacred lowe o' weel-placed love
  Luxuriantly indulge it;
But never tempt th' illicit rove,
  Tho' naething should divulge it.
I waive the quantum o' the sin,
  The hazard o' concealing,
But och! it hardens a' within,
  And petrifies the feeling.

Or in a higher strain—

Who made the heart, 'tis He alone
  Decidedly can try us.
He knows each chord, its various tone;
  Each spring, its various bias.
Then at the balance let's be mute,
  We never can adjust it;
What's *done* we partly may compute,
  But know not what's resisted.

Or in a better strain yet, a strain, his admirers will say, unsurpassable—

To make a happy fire-side clime
    To weans and wife,
That's the true pathos and sublime
    Of human life.

There is criticism of life for you, the admirers of Burns will say to us; there is the application of ideas to life! There is, undoubtedly. The doctrine of the last-quoted lines coincides almost exactly with what was the aim and end, Xenophon tells us, of all the teaching of Socrates. And the application is a powerful one; made by a man of vigorous understanding, and (need I say?), a master of language.

But for the supreme poetical success more is required than the powerful application of ideas to life; it must be an application under the conditions fixed by the laws of poetic truth and poetic beauty. Those laws fix as an essential condition, in the poet's treatment of such matters as are here in question, high seriousness;—the high seriousness which comes from absolute sincerity. The accent of high seriousness, born of absolute sincerity, is what gives to such verse as

In la sua volontade è nostra pace ...

to such criticism of life as Dante's, its power. Is this accent felt in the passages which I have been quoting from Burns? Surely not; surely, if our sense is quick, we must perceive that we have not in those passages a voice from the very inmost soul of the genuine Burns; he is not speaking to us from these depths, he is more or less preaching. And the compensation for admiring such passages less, from missing the perfect poetic accent in them, will be that we shall admire more the poetry where that accent is found.

No; Burns, like Chaucer, comes short of the high seriousness of the great classics, and the virtue of matter and manner which goes with that high seriousness is wanting to his work. At moments he touched it in a profound and passionate melancholy, as in those four immortal lines taken by Byron as a motto for "The Bride of Abydos," but which have in them a depth of poetic quality such as resides in no verse of Byron's own—

Had we never loved sae kindly,
Had we never loved sae blindly,
Never met, or never parted,
We had ne'er been broken-hearted.

But a whole poem of that quality Burns cannot make; the rest, in the "Farewell to Nancy," is verbiage.

We arrive best at the real estimate of Burns, I think, by conceiving his work as having truth of matter and truth of manner, but not the accent or the poetic virtue of the highest masters. His genuine criticism of life, when the sheer poet in him speaks, is ironic; it is not—

Thou Power Supreme, whose mighty scheme
  These woes of mine fulfil,
Here firm I rest, they must be best
  Because they are Thy will!

It is far rather: Whistle owre the lave o't! Yet we may say of him as of Chaucer, that of life and the world, as they come before him, his view is large, free, shrewd, benignant—truly poetic, therefore; and his manner of rendering what he sees is to match. But we must note, at the same time, his great difference from Chaucer. The freedom of Chaucer is heightened, in Burns, by a fiery, reckless energy; the benignity of Chaucer deepens, in Burns, into an overwhelming sense of the pathos of things;—of the pathos of human nature, the pathos, also, of non-human nature. Instead of the fluidity of Chaucer's manner, the manner of Burns has spring, bounding swiftness. Burns is by far the greater force, though he has perhaps less charm. The world of Chaucer is fairer, richer, more significant than that of Burns; but when the largeness and freedom of Burns get full sweep, as in "Tam o' Shanter," or still more in that puissant and splendid production, "The Jolly Beggars," his world may be what it will, his poetic genius triumphs over it. In the world of "The Jolly Beggars" there is more than hideousness and squalor, there is bestiality; yet the piece is a superb poetic success. It has a breadth, truth, and power which make the famous scene in Auerbach's Cellar, of Goethe's "Faust," seem artificial and tame beside it, and which are only matched by Shakespeare and Aristophanes.

Here, where his largeness and freedom serve him so admirably, and also in those poems and songs where to shrewdness he adds infinite archness and wit, and to benignity infinite pathos, where his manner is flawless, and a perfect poetic whole is the result—in things like the address to the mouse whose home he had ruined, in things like "Duncan Gray," "Tam Glen," "Whistle and I'll come to you my Lad," "Auld Lang Syne" (this list might be made much longer)—here we have the genuine Burns, of whom the real estimate must be high indeed. Not a classic, nor with the excellent σπουδαιότης of the great classics, nor with a verse rising to a criticism of life and a virtue like theirs; but a poet with thorough truth of substance and an answering truth of style, giving us a poetry sound to the core. We all of us have a leaning towards the pathetic, and may be inclined perhaps to prize Burns most for his touches of piercing, sometimes almost intolerable, pathos; for verse like—

> We twa hae paidl't i' the burn
> From mornin' sun till dine;
> But seas between us braid hae roar'd
> Sin auld lang syne...

where he is as lovely as he is sound. But perhaps it is by the perfection of soundness of his lighter and archer masterpieces that he is poetically most wholesome for us. For the votary misled by a personal estimate of Shelley, as so many of us have been, are, and will be—of that beautiful spirit building his many-colored haze of words and images

> Pinnacled dim in the intense inane—

no contact can be wholesomer than the contact with Burns at his archest and soundest. Side by side with the

> On the brink of the night and the morning
> My coursers are wont to respire,
> But the Earth has just whispered a warning
> That their flight must be swifter than fire...

of "Prometheus Unbound," how salutary, how very salutary, to place this from "Tam Glen"—

> My minnie does constantly deave me
> And bids me beware o' young men;
> They flatter, she says, to deceive me;
> But wha can think sae o' Tam Glen?

But we enter on burning ground as we approach the poetry of times so near to us—poetry like that of Byron, Shelley, and Wordsworth—of which the estimates are so often not only personal, but personal with passion. For my purpose, it is enough to have taken the single case of Burns, the first poet we come to of whose work the estimate formed is evidently apt to be personal, and to have suggested how we may proceed, using the poetry of the great classics as a sort of touchstone, to correct this estimate, as we had previously corrected by the same means the historic estimate where we met with it. A collection like the present, with its succession of celebrated names and celebrated poems, offers a good opportunity to us for resolutely endeavoring to make our estimates of poetry real. I have sought to point out a method which will help us in making them so, and to exhibit it in use so far as to put any one who likes in a way of applying it for himself.

At any rate the end to which the method and the estimate are designed to lead, and from leading to which, if they do lead to it, they get their whole value—the benefit of being able clearly to feel and deeply to enjoy the best, the truly classic, in poetry—is an end, let me say it once more at parting, of supreme importance. We are often told that an era is opening in which we are to see multitudes of a common sort of readers, and masses of a common sort of literature; that such readers do not want and could not relish anything better than such literature, and that to provide it is becoming a vast and profitable industry. Even if good literature entirely lost currency with the world, it would still be abundantly worth while to continue to enjoy it by oneself. But it never will lose currency with the world, in spite of momentary appearances; it never will lose supremacy. Currency and supremacy are insured to it, not indeed by the world's deliberate and conscious choice, but by something far deeper—by the instinct of self-preservation in humanity.

[1880]

THE FUNCTION OF CRITICISM
AT THE PRESENT TIME

Many objections have been made to a proposition which, in some remarks of mine on translating Homer, I ventured to put forth; a proposition about criticism, and its importance at the present day. I said: "Of the literature of France and Germany, as of the intellect of Europe in general, the main effort, for now many years, has been a critical effort; the endeavor, in all branches of knowledge, theology, philosophy, history, art, science, to see the object as in itself it really is." I added, that owing to the operation in English literature of certain causes, "almost the last thing for which one would come to English literature is just that very thing which now Europe most desires—criticism":

and that the power and value of English literature was thereby impaired. More than one rejoinder declared that the importance I here assigned to criticism was excessive, and asserted the inherent superiority of the creative effort of the human spirit over its critical effort. And the other day, having been led by a Mr. Sharp's excellent notice of Wordsworth to turn again to his biography, I found, in the words of this great man, whom I, for one, must always listen to with the profoundest respect, a sentence passed on the critic's business, which seems to justify every possible disparagement of it. Wordsworth says in one of his letters:

"The writers in these publications" (the Reviews), "while they prosecute their inglorious employment, cannot be supposed to be in a state of mind very favorable for being affected by the finer influences of a thing so pure as genuine poetry."

And a trustworthy reporter of his conversation quotes a more elaborate judgment to the same effect:

"Wordsworth holds the critical power very low, infinitely lower than the inventive; and he said today that if the quantity of time consumed in writing critiques on the works of others were given to original composition, of whatever kind it might be, it would be much better employed; it would make a man find out sooner his own level, and it would do infinitely less mischief. A false or malicious criticism may do much injury to the minds of others, a stupid invention, either in prose or verse, is quite harmless."

It is almost too much to expect of poor human nature, that a man capable of producing some effect in one line of literature, should, for the greater good of society, voluntarily doom himself to impotence and obscurity in another. Still less is this to be expected from men addicted to the composition of the "false or malicious criticism" of which Wordsworth speaks. However, everybody would admit that a false or malicious criticism had better never have been written. Everybody, too, would be willing to admit, as a general proposition, that the critical faculty is lower than the inventive. But is it true that criticism is really, in itself, a baneful and injurious

employment; is it true that all time given to writing critiques on the works of others would be much better employed if it were given to original composition, of whatever kind this may be? Is it true that Johnson had better have gone on producing more "Irenes" instead of writing his "Lives of the Poets"; nay, is it certain that Wordsworth himself was better employed in making his Ecclesiastical Sonnets than when he made his celebrated Preface so full of criticism, and criticism of the works of others? Wordsworth was himself a great critic, and it is to be sincerely regretted that he has not left us more criticism; Goethe was one of the greatest of critics, and we may sincerely congratulate ourselves that he has left us so much criticism. Without wasting time over the exaggeration which Wordsworth's judgment on criticism clearly contains, or over an attempt to trace the causes—not difficult, I think, to be traced—which may have led Wordsworth to this exaggeration, a critic may with advantage seize an occasion for trying his own conscience, and for asking himself of what real service at any given moment the practice of criticism either is or may be made to his own mind and spirit, and to the minds and spirits of others.

The critical power is of lower rank than the creative. True; but in assenting to this proposition, one or two things are to be kept in mind. It is undeniable that the exercise of a creative power, that a free creative activity, is the highest function of man; it is proved to be so by man's finding in it his true happiness. But it is undeniable, also, that men may have the sense of exercising this free creative activity in other ways than in producing great works of literature or art; if it were not so, all but a very few men would be shut out from the true happiness of all men. They may have it in well-doing, they may have it in learning, they may have it even in criticizing. This is one thing to be kept in mind. Another is, that the exercise of the creative power in the production of great works of literature or art, however high this exercise of it may rank, is not at all epochs and under all conditions possible; and that therefore labor may be vainly spent in attempting it, which might with more fruit be used in preparing for it, in rendering it possible. This creative power works with elements, with materials; what if it has not those materials, those elements, ready for its use? In that case it must surely wait till they are ready. Now, in literature—I will limit myself to literature, for it is about literature that the question arises—the elements with which the creative power works are ideas; the best ideas on every matter which literature touches, current at the time. At any rate we may lay it down as certain that in modern literature no manifestation of the creative power not working with these can be very important or fruitful. And I say *current* at the time, not merely accessible at the time; for creative literary genius does not principally show itself in discovering new ideas: that is rather the business of the philosopher. The grand work of literary genius is a work of synthesis and exposition, not of analysis and discovery; its gift lies in the faculty of being happily inspired by a certain intellectual and spiritual atmosphere, by a certain order of ideas, when it finds itself in them; of dealing divinely with these ideas, presenting them in the most effective and attractive combinations—making beautiful works with them, in short. But it must have the atmosphere, it must find itself amid the order of ideas, in order to work freely; and these it is not so easy to command. This is why great creative epochs in literature are so rare, this is why there is so much that is unsatisfactory in the productions of many men of real genius; because, for the creation of a master-work of literature two powers must concur, the power of the man and the power of the moment, and the man is not enough without the moment; the creative power has, for its happy exercise, appointed elements, and those elements are not in its own control.

Nay, they are more within the control of the critical power. It is the business of the critical power, as I said in the words already quoted, "in all branches of knowledge, theology, philosophy, history, art, science, to see the object as in itself it really is." Thus it tends, at last, to make an intellectual situation of which the creative power can profitably avail itself. It

tends to establish an order of ideas, if not absolutely true, yet true by comparison with that which it displaces; to make the best ideas prevail. Presently these new ideas reach society, the touch of truth is the touch of life, and there is a stir and growth everywhere; out of this stir and growth come the creative epochs of literature.

Or, to narrow our range, and quit these considerations of the general march of genius and of society—considerations which are apt to become too abstract and impalpable—every one can see that a poet, for instance, ought to know life and the world before dealing with them in poetry; and life and the world being in modern times very complex things, the creation of a modern poet, to be worth much, implies a great critical effort behind it; else it must be a comparatively poor, barren, and short-lived affair. This is why Byron's poetry had so little endurance in it, and Goethe's so much; both Byron and Goethe had a great productive power, but Goethe's was nourished by a great critical effort providing the true materials for it, and Byron's was not; Goethe knew life and the world, the poet's necessary subjects, much more comprehensively and thoroughly than Byron. He knew a great deal more of them, and he knew them much more as they really are.

It has long seemed to me that the burst of creative activity in our literature, through the first quarter of this century, had about it in fact something premature; and that from this cause its productions are doomed, most of them, in spite of the sanguine hopes which accompanied and do still accompany them, to prove hardly more lasting than the productions of far less splendid epochs. And this prematureness comes from its having proceeded without having its proper data, without sufficient materials to work with. In other words, the English poetry of the first quarter of this century, with plenty of energy, plenty of creative force, did not know enough. This makes Byron so empty of matter, Shelley so incoherent, Wordsworth even, profound as he is, yet so wanting in completeness and variety. Wordsworth cared little for books, and disparaged Goethe.

I admire Wordsworth, as he is, so much that I cannot wish him different; and it is vain, no doubt, to imagine such a man different from what he is, to suppose that he *could* have been different. But surely the one thing wanting to make Wordsworth an even greater poet than he is—his thought richer, and his influence of wider application—was that he should have read more books, among them, no doubt, 10 those of that Goethe whom he disparaged without reading him.

But to speak of books and reading may easily lead to a misunderstanding here. It was not really books and reading that lacked to our poetry at this epoch: Shelley had plenty of reading, Coleridge had immense reading. Pindar and Sophocles—as we all say so glibly, and often with so little discernment of the real import of what we 20 are saying—had not many books; Shakespeare was no deep reader. True; but in the Greece of Pindar and Sophocles, in the England of Shakespeare, the poet lived in a current of ideas in the highest degree animating and nourishing to the creative power; society was, in the fullest measure, permeated by fresh thought, intelligent and alive. And this state of things is the true basis for the creative power's exercise, 30 in this it finds its data, its materials, truly ready for its hand; all the books and reading in the world are only valuable as they are helps to this. Even when this does not actually exist, books and reading may enable a man to construct a kind of semblance of it in his own mind, a world of knowledge and intelligence in which he may live and work. This is by no means an equivalent to the artist for the nation- 40 ally diffused life and thought of the epochs of Sophocles or Shakespeare; but, besides that it may be a means of preparation for such epochs, it does really constitute, if many share in it, a quickening and sustaining atmosphere of great value. Such an atmosphere the many-sided learning and the long and widely combined critical effort of Germany formed for Goethe, when he lived and worked. There was no na- 50 tional glow of life and thought there as in the Athens of Pericles or the England of Elizabeth. That was the poet's weakness. But there was a sort of equivalent for it in

the complete culture and unfettered thinking of a large body of Germans. That was his strength. In the England of the first quarter of this century there was neither a national glow of life and thought, such as we had in the age of Elizabeth, nor yet a culture and a force of learning and criticism such as were to be found in Germany. Therefore the creative power of poetry wanted, for success in the highest sense, materials and a basis; a thorough interpretation of the world was necessarily denied to it.

At first sight it seems strange that out of the immense stir of the French Revolution and its age should not have come a crop of works of genius equal to that which came out of the stir of the great productive time of Greece, or out of that of the Renascence, with its powerful episode the Reformation. But the truth is that the stir of the French Revolution took a character which essentially distinguished it from such movements as these. These were, in the main, disinterestedly intellectual and spiritual movements; movements in which the human spirit looked for its satisfaction in itself and in the increased play of its own activity. The French Revolution took a political, practical character. The movement, which went on in France under the old régime, from 1700 to 1789, was far more really akin than that of the Revolution itself to the movement of the Renascence; the France of Voltaire and Rousseau told far more powerfully upon the mind of Europe than the France of the Revolution. Goethe reproached this last expressly with having "thrown quiet culture back." Nay, and the true key to how much in our Byron, even in our Wordsworth, is this!—that they had their source in a great movement of feeling, not in a great movement of mind. The French Revolution, however—that object of so much blind love and so much blind hatred—found undoubtedly its motive-power in the intelligence of men, and not in their practical sense; this is what distinguishes it from the English Revolution of Charles the First's time. This is what makes it a more spiritual event than our Revolution, an event of much more powerful and world-wide interest, though practically less successful; it appeals to an order of ideas which are universal, certain, permanent. 1789 asked of a thing, Is it rational? 1642 asked of a thing, Is it legal? or, when it went furthest, Is it according to conscience? This is the English fashion, a fashion to be treated, within its own sphere, with the highest respect; for its success, within its own sphere, has been prodigious. But what is law in one place is not law in another; what is law here today is not law even here tomorrow; and as for conscience, what is binding on one man's conscience is not binding on another's. The old woman who threw her stool at the head of the surpliced minister in St. Giles's Church at Edinburgh obeyed an impulse to which millions of the human race may be permitted to remain strangers. But the prescriptions of reason are absolute, unchanging, of universal validity; *to count by tens is the easiest way of counting*—that is a proposition of which every one, from here to the Antipodes, feels the force; at least I should say so if we did not live in a country where it is not impossible that any morning we may find a letter in the *Times* declaring that a decimal coinage is an absurdity. That a whole nation should have been penetrated with an enthusiasm for pure reason, and with an ardent zeal for making its prescriptions triumph, is a very remarkable thing, when we consider how little of mind, or anything so worthy and quickening as mind, comes into the motives which alone, in general, impel great masses of men. In spite of the extravagant direction given to this enthusiasm, in spite of the crimes and follies in which it lost itself, the French Revolution derives from the force, truth, and universality of the ideas which it took for its law, and from the passion with which it could inspire a multitude for these ideas, a unique and still living power; it is—it will probably long remain—the greatest, the most animating event in history. And as no sincere passion for the things of the mind, even though it turn out in many respects an unfortunate passion, is ever quite thrown away and quite barren of good, France has reaped from hers one fruit—the natural and legitimate fruit though not precisely the grand fruit she

expected: she is the country in Europe where *the people* is most alive.

But the mania for giving an immediate political and practical application to all these fine ideas of the reason was fatal. Here an Englishman is in his element: on this theme we can all go on for hours. And all we are in the habit of saying on it has undoubtedly a great deal of truth. Ideas cannot be too much prized in and for themselves, cannot be too much lived with; but to transport them abruptly into the world of politics and practice, violently to revolutionize this world to their bidding —that is quite another thing. There is the world of ideas and there is the world of practice; the French are often for suppressing the one and the English the other; but neither is to be suppressed. A member of the House of Commons said to me the other day: "That a thing is an anomaly, I consider to be no objection to it whatever." I venture to think he was wrong; that a thing is an anomaly *is* an objection to it, but absolutely and in the sphere of ideas: it is not necessarily, under such and such circumstances, or at such and such a moment, an objection to it in the sphere of politics and practice. Joubert has said beautifully: "C'est la force et le droit qui règlent toutes choses dans le monde; la force en attendant le droit." (Force and right are the governors of this world: force till right is ready.) *Force till right is ready;* and till right is ready, force, the existing order of things, is justified, is the legitimate ruler. But right is something moral, and implies inward recognition, free assent of the will; we are not ready for right—*right, so far as we are concerned, is not ready*— until we have attained this sense of seeing it and willing it. The way in which for us it may change and transform force, the existing order of things, and become, in its turn, the legitimate ruler of the world, should depend on the way in which, when our time comes, we see it and will it. Therefore for other people enamored of their own newly discerned right, to attempt to impose it upon us as ours, and violently to substitute their right for our force, is an act of tyranny, and to be resisted. It sets at naught the second great half of our maxim, *force till right is ready*. This was the grand error of the French Revolution; and its movement of ideas, by quitting the intellectual sphere and rushing furiously into the political sphere, ran, indeed, a prodigious and memorable course, but produced no such intellectual fruit as the movement of ideas of the Renascence, and created, in opposition to itself, what I may call an *epoch of concentration*. The great force of that epoch of concentration was England; and the great voice of that epoch of concentration was Burke. It is the fashion to treat Burke's writings on the French Revolution as superannuated and conquered by the event; as the eloquent but unphilosophical tirades of bigotry and prejudice. I will not deny that they are often disfigured by the violence and passion of the moment, and that in some directions Burke's view was bounded, and his observation therefore at fault. But on the whole, and for those who can make the needful corrections, what distinguishes these writings is their profound, permanent, fruitful, philosophical truth. They contain the true philosophy of an epoch of concentration, dissipate the heavy atmosphere which its own nature is apt to engender round it, and make its resistance rational instead of mechanical.

But Burke is so great because, almost alone in England, he brings thought to bear upon politics, he saturates politics with thought. It is his accident that his ideas were at the service of an epoch of concentration, not of an epoch of expansion; it is his characteristic that he so lived by ideas, and had such a source of them welling up within him, that he could float even an epoch of concentration and English Tory politics with them. It does not hurt him that Dr. Price and the Liberals were enraged with him; it does not even hurt him that George the Third and the Tories were enchanted with him. His greatness is that he lived in a world which neither English Liberalism nor English Toryism is apt to enter—the world of ideas, not the world of catchwords and party habits. So far is it from being really true of him that he "to party gave up what was meant for mankind," that at the very end of his fierce struggle with the French Revolution, after all his invectives against its

false pretensions, hollowness, and madness, with his sincere convictions of its mischievousness, he can close a memorandum on the best means of combating it, some of the last pages he ever wrote—the "Thoughts on French Affairs," in December, 1791—with these striking words:

"The evil is stated, in my opinion, as it exists. The remedy must be where power, wisdom, and information, I hope, are more united with good intentions than they can be with me. I have done with this subject, I believe, forever. It has given me many anxious moments for the last two years. *If a great change is to be made in human affairs, the minds of men will be fitted to it; the general opinions and feelings will draw that way. Every fear, every hope will forward it; and then they who persist in opposing this mighty current in human affairs, will appear rather to resist the decrees of Providence itself, than the mere designs of men. They will not be resolute and firm, but perverse and obstinate.*"

That return of Burke upon himself has always seemed to me one of the finest things in English literature, or indeed in any literature. That is what I call living by ideas: when one side of a question has long had your earnest support, when all your feelings are engaged, when you hear all round you no language but one, when your party talks this language like a steam-engine and can imagine no other—still to be able to think, still to be irresistibly carried, if so it be, by the current of thought to the opposite side of the question, and, like Balaam, to be unable to speak anything *but what the Lord has put in your mouth*. I know nothing more striking, and I must add that I know nothing more un-English.

For the Englishman in general is like my friend the Member of Parliament, and believes, point-blank, that for a thing to be an anomaly is absolutely no objection to it whatever. He is like the Lord Auckland of Burke's day, who, in a memorandum on the French Revolution, talks of "certain miscreants, assuming the name of philosophers, who have presumed themselves capable of establishing a new system of society." The Englishman has been called a political animal, and he values what is political and practical so much that ideas easily become objects of dislike in his eyes, and thinkers "miscreants," because ideas and thinkers have rashly meddled with politics and practice. This would be all very well if the dislike and neglect confined themselves to ideas transported out of their own sphere, and meddling rashly with practice; but they are inevitably extended to ideas as such, and to the whole life of intelligence; practice is everything, a free play of the mind is nothing. The notion of the free play of the mind upon all subjects being a pleasure in itself, being an object of desire, being an essential provider of elements without which a nation's spirit, whatever compensations it may have for them, must, in the long run, die of inanition, hardly enters into an Englishman's thoughts. It is noticeable that the word *curiosity*, which in other languages is used in a good sense, to mean, as a high and fine quality of man's nature, just this disinterested love of a free play of the mind on all subjects, for its own sake—it is noticeable, I say, that this word has in our language no sense of the kind, no sense but a rather bad and disparaging one. But criticism, real criticism, is essentially the exercise of this very quality. It obeys an instinct prompting it to try to know the best that is known and thought in the world, irrespectively of practice, politics, and everything of the kind; and to value knowledge and thought as they approach this best, without the intrusion of any other considerations whatever. This is an instinct for which there is, I think, little original sympathy in the practical English nature, and what there was of it has undergone a long benumbing period of blight and suppression in the epoch of concentration which followed the French Revolution.

But epochs of concentration cannot well endure forever; epochs of expansion, in the due course of things, follow them. Such an epoch of expansion seems to be opening in this country. In the first place all danger of a hostile forcible pressure of foreign ideas upon our practice has long disappeared; like the traveller in the fable, therefore, we begin to wear our cloak a little more loosely. Then, with a long peace, the ideas of Europe steal gradually and amicably in, and mingle, though in infinitesimally small quantities at a time, with our own notions. Then, too, in spite of all that is said about the absorbing and brutalizing influence of our passionate material progress, it seems to me indisputable that this progress is likely, though not certain, to lead in the end to an apparition of intellectual life; and that man, after he has made himself perfectly comfortable and has now to determine what to do with himself next, may begin to remember that he has a mind, and that the mind may be made the source of great pleasure. I grant it is mainly the privilege of faith, at present, to discern this end to our railways, our business, and our fortune-making; but we shall see if, here as elsewhere, faith is not in the end the true prophet. Our ease, our travelling, and our unbounded liberty to hold just as hard and securely as we please to the practice to which our notions have given birth, all tend to beget an inclination to deal a little more freely with these notions themselves, to canvass them a little, to penetrate a little into their real nature. Flutterings of curiosity, in the foreign sense of the word, appear among us, and it is in these that criticism must look to find its account. Criticism first; a time of true creative activity, perhaps—which, as I have said, must inevitably be preceded among us by a time of criticism—hereafter, when criticism has done its work.

It is of the last importance that English criticism should clearly discern what rule for its course, in order to avail itself of the field now opening to it, and to produce fruit for the future, it ought to take. The rule may be summed up in one word—*disinterestedness*. And how is criticism to show disinterestedness? By keeping aloof from what is called "the practical view of things"; by resolutely following the law of its own nature, which is to be a free play of the mind on all subjects which it touches. By steadily refusing to lend itself to any of those ulterior, political, practical considerations about ideas, which plenty of people will be sure to attach to them, which perhaps ought often to be attached to them, which in this country at any rate are certain to be attached to them quite sufficiently, but which criticism has really nothing to do with. Its business is, as I have said, simply to know the best that is known and thought in the world, and by in its turn making this known, to create a current of true and fresh ideas. Its business is to do this with inflexible honesty, with due ability; but its business is to do no more, and to leave alone all questions of practical consequences and applications, questions which will never fail to have due prominence given to them. Else criticism, besides being really false to its own nature, merely continues in the old rut which it has hitherto followed in this country, and will certainly miss the chance now given to it. For what is at present the bane of criticism in this country? It is that practical considerations cling to it and stifle it. It subserves interests not its own. Our organs of criticism are organs of men and parties having practical ends to serve, and with them those practical ends are the first thing and the play of mind the second; so much play of mind as is compatible with the prosecution of those practical ends is all that is wanted. An organ like the *Revue des Deux Mondes,* having for its main function to understand and utter the best that is known and thought in the world, existing, it may be said, as just an organ for a free play of the mind, we have not. But we have the *Edinburgh Review,* existing as an organ of the old Whigs, and for as much play of the mind as may suit its being that; we have the *Quarterly Review,* existing as an organ of the Tories, and for as much play of mind as may suit its being that; we have the *British Quarterly Review,* existing as an organ of the political Dissenters, and for as much play of mind as may suit its being that; we have the *Times,* existing as an organ of the common, satisfied, well-to-do Englishman, and for as much play of mind as may suit its being that. And so on through all the various fractions, political and religious, of our society; every fraction has, as such, its organ of criticism, but the notion of combining all fractions in the common pleasure of a free disinterested play of mind meets with no favor. Directly this play of mind wants to have more scope, and to forget the pressure of practical considerations a little, it is checked, it is made to feel the chain. We saw this the other day in the extinction, so much to be regretted, of the *Home and Foreign Review.* Perhaps in no organ of criticism in this country was there so much knowledge, so much play of mind; but these could not save it. The *Dublin Review* subordinates play of mind to the practical business of English and Irish Catholicism, and lives. It must needs be that men should act in sects and parties, that each of these sects and parties should have its organ, and should make this organ subserve the interests of its action; but it would be well, too, that there should be a criticism, not the minister of these interests, not their enemy, but absolutely and entirely independent of them. No other criticism will ever attain any real authority or make any real way towards its end—the creating a current of true and fresh ideas.

It is because criticism has so little kept in the pure intellectual sphere, has so little detached itself from practice, has been so directly polemical and controversial, that it has so ill accomplished, in this country, its best spiritual work; which is to keep man from a self-satisfaction which is retarding and vulgarizing, to lead him towards perfection, by making his mind dwell upon what is excellent in itself, and the absolute beauty and fitness of things. A polemical practical criticism makes men blind even to the ideal imperfection of their practice, makes them willingly assert its ideal perfection, in order the better to secure it against attack: and clearly this is narrowing and baneful for them. If they were reassured on the practical side, speculative considerations of ideal perfection they might be brought to entertain, and their spiritual horizon would thus gradually widen. Sir Charles Adderley says to the Warwickshire farmers:

"Talk of the improvement of breed! Why, the race we ourselves represent, the men and women, the old Anglo-Saxon race, are the best breed in the whole world.... The absence of a too enervating climate, too unclouded skies, and a too luxurious nature, has produced so vigorous a race of people, and has rendered us so superior to all the world."

Mr. Roebuck says to the Sheffield cutlers:

"I look around me and ask what is the state of England? Is not property safe? Is not every man able to say what he likes? Can you not walk from one end of England to the other in perfect security? I ask you whether, the world over or in past history, there is anything like it? Nothing. I pray that our unrivalled happiness may last."

Now obviously there is a peril for poor human nature in words and thoughts of such exuberant self-satisfaction, until we find ourselves safe in the streets of the Celestial City.

"Das wenige verschwindet leicht dem Blicke
  Der vorwärts sieht, wie viel noch übrig bleibt—"

says Goethe; "the little that is done seems nothing when we look forward and see how much we have yet to do." Clearly this is a better line of reflection for weak humanity, so long as it remains on this earthly field of labor and trial.

But neither Sir Charles Adderley nor Mr. Roebuck is by nature inaccessible to considerations of this sort. They only lose sight of them owing to the controversial life we all lead, and the practical form which all speculation takes with us. They have in view opponents whose aim is not ideal, but practical; and in their zeal to uphold their own practice against these innovators, they go so far as even to attribute to this practice an ideal perfection. Somebody has been wanting to introduce a six pound franchise, or to abolish church-rates, or to collect agricultural statistics by force, or to diminish local self-government. How natural, in reply to such proposals, very likely improper or ill-timed, to go a little beyond the mark and to say stoutly, "Such a race of people as we stand, so superior to all the world! The old Anglo-Saxon race, the best breed in the whole world! I pray that our unrivalled happiness may last! I ask you whether, the world over or in past history, there is anything like it?" And so long as criticism answers this dithyramb by insisting that the old Anglo-Saxon race would be still more superior to all others if it had no church-rates, or that our unrivalled happiness would last yet longer with a six pound franchise, so long will the strain, "The best breed in the whole world!" swell louder and louder, everything ideal and refining will be lost out of sight, and both the assailed and their critics will remain in a sphere, to say the truth, perfectly unvital, a sphere in which spiritual progression is impossible. But let criticism leave church-rates and the franchise alone, and in the most candid spirit, without a single lurking thought of practical innovation, confront with our dithyramb this paragraph on which I stumbled in a newspaper immediately after reading Mr. Roebuck:

"A shocking child murder has just been committed at Nottingham. A girl named Wragg left the workhouse there on Saturday morning with her young illegitimate child. The child was soon afterwards found dead on Mapperly Hills, having been strangled. Wragg is in custody."

Nothing but that; but, in juxtaposition with the absolute eulogies of Sir Charles Adderley and Mr. Roebuck, how eloquent, how suggestive are those few lines! "Our old Anglo-Saxon breed, the best in the whole world!"—how much that is harsh and ill-favored there is in this best! *Wragg!* If we are to talk of ideal perfection, of "the best in the whole world," has any one reflected what a touch of grossness in our race, what an original shortcoming in the more delicate spiritual perceptions, is shown by the natural growth among us of such hideous names—Higginbottom, Stiggins, Bugg! In Ionia and Attica they were luckier in this respect than "the best race in the world"; by the Ilissus there was no Wragg, poor thing! And "our unrivalled happiness"—what an element of grimness, bareness, and hideousness mixes with it and blurs it; the workhouse, the dismal Mapperly Hills—how dismal those who have seen them will remember—the gloom, the smoke, the cold, the strangled illegitimate child! "I ask you whether, the world over or in past history, there is anything like it?" Perhaps not, one is inclined to answer; but at any rate, in that case, the world is very much to be pitied. And the final touch—short, bleak and inhuman: *Wragg is in custody*. The sex lost in the confusion of our unrivalled happiness; or (shall I say?) the superfluous Christian name lopped off by the straightforward vigor of our old Anglo-Saxon breed! There is profit for the spirit in such contrasts as this; criticism serves the cause of perfection by establishing them. By eluding sterile conflict, by refusing to remain in the sphere where alone narrow and relative conceptions have any worth and validity, criticism may diminish its momentary importance, but only in this way has it a chance of gaining admittance for those wider and more perfect conceptions to which all its duty is really owed. Mr. Roebuck will have a poor opinion of an adversary who replies to his defiant songs of triumph only by murmuring under his breath, *Wragg is in custody;* but in no other way will these songs of triumph be induced gradually to moderate themselves, to get rid of what in them is excessive and offensive, and to fall into a softer and truer key.

It will be said that it is a very subtle and indirect action which I am thus prescribing for criticism, and that, by embracing in this manner the Indian virtue of detachment and abandoning the sphere of practical life, it condemns itself to a slow and obscure work. Slow and obscure it may be, but it is the only proper work of criticism. The mass of mankind will never have any ardent zeal for seeing things as they are; very inadequate ideas will always satisfy them. On these inadequate ideas reposes, and must repose, the general practice of the world. That is as much as saying that whoever sets himself to see things as they are will find himself one of a very small circle; but it is only by this small circle resolutely doing its own work that adequate ideas will ever get current at all. The rush and roar of practical life will always have a dizzying and attracting effect upon the most collected spectator, and tend to draw him into its vortex; most of all will this be the case where that life is so powerful as it is in England. But it is only by remaining collected, and refusing to lend himself to the point of view of the practical man, that the critic can do the practical man any service; and it is only by the greatest sincerity in pursuing his own course, and by at last convincing even the practical man of his sincerity, that he can escape misunderstandings which perpetually threaten him.

For the practical man is not apt for fine distinctions, and yet in these distinctions truth and the highest culture greatly find their account. But it is not easy to lead a practical man—unless you reassure him as to your practical intentions, you have no chance of leading him—to see that a thing which he has always been used to look at from one side only, which he greatly values, and which, looked at from that side, quite deserves, perhaps, all the prizing and admiring which he bestows upon it—that this thing, looked at from another side, may appear much less beneficent and beautiful, and yet retain all its claims to our practical allegiance. Where shall we find language innocent enough, how shall we make the spotless purity of our intentions evident enough, to enable us to say to the political Englishman that the British Constitution itself, which, seen from the practical side, looks such a magnificent organ of progress and virtue, seen from the speculative side—with its compromises, its love of facts, its horror of theory, its studied avoidance of clear thoughts—that, seen from this side, our august Constitution sometimes looks—forgive me, shade of Lord Somers!—a colossal machine for the manufacture of Philistines? How is Cobbett to say this and not be misunderstood, blackened as he is with the smoke of a lifelong conflict in the field of political practice? how is Mr. Carlyle to say it and not be misunderstood, after his furious raid into this field with his "Latter-day Pamphlets?" how is Mr. Ruskin, after his pugnacious political economy? I say, the critic must keep out of the region of immediate practice in the political, social, humanitarian sphere, if he wants to make a beginning for that more free speculative treatment of things, which may perhaps one day make its benefits felt even in this sphere, but in a natural and thence irresistible manner.

Do what he will, however, the critic will still remain exposed to frequent misunderstandings, and nowhere so much as in this country. For here people are particularly indisposed even to comprehend that without this free disinterested treatment of things, truth and the highest culture are out of the question. So immersed are they in practical life, so accustomed to take all their notions from this life and its processes, that they are apt to think that truth and culture themselves can be reached by the processes of this life, and that it is an impertinent singularity to think of reaching them in any other. "We are all *terræ filii*," [1] cries their eloquent advocate; "all Philistines together. Away with the notion of proceeding by any other course than the course dear to the Philistines; let us have a social movement, let us organize and combine a party to pursue truth and new thought, let us call it *the liberal party,* and let us all stick to each other, and back each other up. Let us have no nonsense about independent criticism, and intellectual delicacy, and the few and the many. Don't let us trouble ourselves about foreign thought; we shall invent the whole thing for ourselves as we go along. If one of us speaks well, applaud him; if one of us speaks ill, applaud him too; we are all in the same movement, we are all liberals, we are all in pursuit of truth." In this way the pursuit of truth becomes really a social, practical, pleasurable affair, almost requiring a chairman, a secretary, and advertisements; with the excitement of an occasional scandal, with a little resistance to give the happy sense of difficulty overcome; but, in general, plenty of bustle and very little thought. To act is so easy, as Goethe says; to think is so hard! It is true that the critic has many temptations to go with the stream, to make one of the party movement, one of these *terrae filii;* it seems ungracious to refuse to be a *terrae filius,* when so many excellent people are; but the critic's duty is to refuse, or, if resistance is vain, at least to cry with Obermann: *Périssons en résistant.* [2]

How serious a matter it is to try and resist, I had ample opportunity of experiencing when I ventured some time ago to criticize the celebrated first volume of Bishop Colenso. The echoes of the storm which was then raised I still, from time to time, hear grumbling round me. That

storm arose out of a misunderstanding almost inevitable. It is a result of no little culture to attain to a clear perception that science and religion are two wholly different things. The multitude will forever confuse them; but happily that is of no great real importance, for while the multitude imagines itself to live by its false science, it does really live by its true religion. Dr. Colenso, however, in his first volume did all he could to strengthen the confusion, and to make it dangerous. He did this with the best intentions, I freely admit, and with the most candid ignorance that this was the natural effect of what he was doing; but, says Joubert, "Ignorance, which in matters of morals extenuates the crime, is itself, in intellectual matters, a crime of the first order." I criticized Bishop Colenso's speculative confusion. Immediately there was a cry raised: "What is this? here is a liberal attacking a liberal. Do not you belong to the movement? are not you a friend of truth? Is not Bishop Colenso in pursuit of truth? then speak with proper respect of his book. Dr. Stanley is another friend of truth, and you speak with proper respect of his book; why make these invidious differences? both books are excellent, admirable, liberal; Bishop Colenso's perhaps the most so, because it is the boldest, and will have the best practical consequences for the liberal cause. Do you want to encourage to the attack of a brother liberal his, and your, and our implacable enemies, the *Church and State Review* or the *Record*—the High Church rhinoceros and the Evangelical hyena? Be silent, therefore; or rather speak, speak as loud as ever you can! and go into ecstasies over the eighty and odd pigeons."

But criticism cannot follow this coarse and indiscriminate method. It is unfortunately possible for a man in pursuit of truth to write a book which reposes upon a false conception. Even the practical consequences of a book are to genuine criticism no recommendation of it, if the book is, in the highest sense, blundering. I see that a lady who herself, too, is in pursuit of truth, and who writes with great ability, but a little too much, perhaps, under the influence of the practical spirit of the Eng-

[1] *terrae filii:* sons of earth.
[2] *perissons en resistant:* Let us perish, resisting.

lish liberal movement, classes Bishop
Colenso's book and M. Renan's together,
in her survey of the religious state of
Europe, as facts of the same order, works,
both of them, of "great importance";
"great ability, power, and skill"; Bishop
Colenso's, perhaps, the most powerful; at
least, Miss Cobbe gives special expression
to her gratitude that to Bishop Colenso
"has been given the strength to grasp, and
the courage to teach, truths of such deep
import." In the same way, more than one
popular writer has compared him to
Luther. Now it is just this kind of false
estimate which the critical spirit is, it seems
to me, bound to resist. It is really the
strongest possible proof of the low ebb at
which, in England, the critical spirit is,
that while the critical hit in the religious
literature of German is Dr. Strauss's book,
in that of France M. Renan's book, the
book of Bishop Colenso is the critical hit
in the religious literature of England.
Bishop Colenso's book reposes on a total
misconception of the essential elements of
the religious problem, as that problem is
now presented for solution. To criticism,
therefore, which seeks to have the best that
is known and thought on this problem, it
is, however well meant, of no importance
whatever. M. Renan's book attempts a
new synthesis of the elements furnished to
us by the Four Gospels. It attempts, in my
opinion, a synthesis, perhaps premature,
perhaps impossible, certainly not successful.
Up to the present time, at any rate, we
must acquiesce in Fleury's sentence on such
recastings of the Gospel story: *Quiconque
s'imagine la pouvoir mieux écrire, ne l'en-
tend pas.*[3] M. Renan had himself passed
by anticipation a like sentence on his own
work, when he said: "If a new presentation
of the character of Jesus were offered to
me, I would not have it; its very clearness
would be, in my opinion, the best proof
of its insufficiency." His friends may with
perfect justice rejoin that at the sight of
the Holy Land, and of the actual scene of
the Gospel story, all the current of M.
Renan's thoughts may have naturally

changed, and a new casting of that story
irresistibly suggested itself to him; and that
this is just a case for applying Cicero's
maxim: Change of mind is not inconsistency—*nemo doctus unquam mutationem
consilii inconstantiam dixit esse.*[4] Nevertheless, for criticism, M. Renan's first
thought must still be the truer one, as long
as his new casting so fails more fully to
commend itself, more fully (to use Coleridge's happy phrase about the Bible) to
find us. Still M. Renan's attempt is, for
criticism, of the most real interest and importance, since, with all its difficulty, a
fresh synthesis of the New Testament *data*
—not a making war on them, in Voltaire's
fashion, not a leaving them out of mind,
in the world's fashion, but the putting a
new construction upon them, the taking
them from under the old, traditional, conventional point of view and placing them
under a new one—is the very essence of the
religious problem, as now presented; and
only by efforts in this direction can it receive a solution.

Again, in the same spirit in which she
judges Bishop Colenso, Miss Cobbe, like
so many earnest liberals of our practical
race, both here and in America, herself sets
vigorously about a positive reconstruction
of religion, about making a religion of the
future out of hand, or at least setting about
making it. We must not rest, she and they
are always thinking and saying, in negative
criticism, we must be creative and constructive; hence we have such works as her
recent "Religious Duty," and works still
more considerable, perhaps, by others,
which will be in every one's mind. These
works often have much ability; they often
spring out of sincere convictions, and a
sincere wish to do good; and they sometimes, perhaps, do good. Their fault is (if
I may be permitted to say so) one which
they have in common with the British
College of Health, in the New Road.
Every one knows the British College of
Health; it is that building with the lion
and the statue of the Goddess Hygeia before it; at least I am sure about the lion,

---

[3] *"Quiconque,"* etc.: 'Whoever thinks he can
write it better, doesn't understand it.' (Fleury's
'Preface' on the Gospel—Arnold's *Notebooks*,
19).

[4] *Cicero's Maxim:* 'No philosopher ever
called a change of plan inconsistency' (*Letters
to Atticus,* XVI, 7; in Loeb Classics ed., III,
397).

though I am not absolutely certain about the Goddess Hygeia. This building does credit, perhaps, to the resources of Dr. Morrison and his disciples; but it falls a good deal short of one's idea of what a British College of Health ought to be. In England where we hate public interference and love individual enterprise, we have a whole crop of places like the British College of Health; the grand name without the grand thing. Unluckily, creditable to individual enterprise as they are, they tend to impair our taste by making us forget what more grandiose, noble, or beautiful character properly belongs to a public institution. The same may be said of the religions of the future of Miss Cobbe and others. Creditable, like the British College of Health, to the resources of their authors, they yet tend to make us forget what more grandiose, noble, or beautiful character properly belongs to religious constructions. The historic religions, with all their faults, have had this; it certainly belongs to the religious sentiment, when it truly flowers, to have this; and we impoverish our spirit if we allow a religion of the future without it. What then is the duty of criticism here? To take the practical point of view, to applaud the liberal movement and all its works—its New Road religions of the future into the bargain—for their general utility's sake? By no means; but to be perpetually dissatisfied with these works, while they perpetually fall short of a high and perfect ideal.

For criticism, these are elementary laws; but they never can be popular, and in this country they have been very little followed, and one meets with immense obstacles in following them. That is a reason for asserting them again and again. Criticism must maintain its independence of the practical spirit and its aims. Even with well-meant efforts of the practical spirit it must express dissatisfaction, if in the sphere of the ideal they seem impoverishing and limiting. It must not hurry on to the goal because of its practical importance. It must be patient, and know how to wait; and flexible, and know how to attach itself to things and how to withdraw from them. It must be apt to study and praise elements that for the fulness of spiritual perfection are wanted, even though they belong to a power which in the practical sphere may be maleficent. It must be apt to discern the spiritual shortcomings or illusions of powers that in the practical sphere may be beneficent. And this without any notion of favoring or injuring, in the practical sphere, one power or the other; without any notion of playing off, in this sphere, one power against the other. When one looks, for instance, at the English Divorce Court—an institution which perhaps has its practical conveniences, but which in the ideal sphere is so hideous; an institution which neither makes divorce impossible nor makes it decent, which allows a man to get rid of his wife, or a wife of her husband, but makes them drag one another first, for the public edification, through a mire of unutterable infamy—when one looks at this charming institution, I say, with its crowded trials, its newspaper reports, and its money compensations, this institution in which the gross unregenerate British Philistine has indeed stamped an image of himself—one may be permitted to find the marriage theory of Catholicism refreshing and elevating. Or when Protestantism, in virtue of its supposed rational and intellectual origin, gives the law to criticism too magisterially, criticism may and must remind it that its pretensions, in this respect, are illusive and do it harm; that the Reformation was a moral rather than an intellectual event; that Luther's theory of grace no more exactly reflects the mind of the spirit than Bossuet's philosophy of history reflects it; and that there is no more antecedent probability of the Bishop of Durham's stock of ideas being agreeable to perfect reason than of Pope Pius the Ninth's. But criticism will not on that account forget the achievements of Protestantism in the practical and moral sphere; nor that, even in the intellectual sphere, Protestantism, though in a blind and stumbling manner, carried forward the Renascence, while Catholicism threw itself violently across its path.

I lately heard a man of thought and energy contrasting the want of ardor and movement which he now found among young men in this country with what he remembered in his own youth, twenty years ago. "What reformers we were then!" he exclaimed; "What a zeal we had! how we canvassed every institution in Church and State, and were prepared to remodel them all on first principles!" He was inclined to regret, as a spiritual flagging, the lull which he saw. I am disposed rather to regard it as a pause in which the turn to a new mode of spiritual progress is being accomplished. Everything was long seen, by the young and ardent among us, in inseparable connection with politics and practical life. We have pretty well exhausted the benefits of seeing things in this connection, we have got all that can be got by so seeing them. Let us try a more disinterested mode of seeing them; let us betake ourselves more to the serener life of the mind and spirit. This life, too, may have its excesses and dangers; but they are not for us at present. Let us think of quietly enlarging our stock of true and fresh ideas, and not, as soon as we get an idea or half an idea, be running out with it into the street, and trying to make it rule there. Our ideas will, in the end, shape the world all the better for maturing a little. Perhaps in fifty years' time it will in the English House of Commons be an objection to an institution that it is an anomaly, and my friend the Member of Parliament will shudder in his grave. But let us in the meanwhile rather endeavor that in twenty years' time it may, in English literature, be an objection to a proposition that it is absurd. That will be a change so vast, that the imagination almost fails to grasp it. *Ab integro saeclorum nascitur ordo.*[5]

If I have insisted so much on the course which criticism must take where politics and religion are concerned, it is because, where these burning matters are in question, it is most likely to go astray. I have wished, above all, to insist on the attitude which criticism should adopt towards things in general; on its right tone and temper of mind. But then comes another question as to the subject-matter which literary

criticism should most seek. Here, in general, its course is determined for it by the idea which is the law of its being: the idea of a disinterested endeavor to learn and propagate the best that is known and thought in the world, and thus to establish a current of fresh and true ideas. By the very nature of things, as England is not all the world, much of the best that is known and thought in the world cannot be of English growth, must be foreign; by the nature of things, again, it is just this that we are least likely to know, while English thought is streaming in upon us from all sides, and takes excellent care that we shall not be ignorant of its existence. The English critic of literature, therefore, must dwell much on foreign thought, and with particular heed on any part of it, which, while significant and fruitful in itself, is for any reason specially likely to escape him. Again, judging is often spoken of as the critic's one business, and so in some sense it is; but the judgment which almost insensibly forms itself in a fair and clear mind, along with fresh knowledge, is the valuable one; and thus knowledge, and ever fresh knowledge, must be the critic's great concern for himself. And it is by communicating fresh knowledge, and letting his own judgment pass along with it— but insensibly, and in the second place, not the first, as a sort of companion and clue, not as an abstract lawgiver—that the critic will generally do most good to his readers. Sometimes, no doubt, for the sake of establishing an author's place in literature, and his relation to a central standard (and if this is not done, how are we to get at our *best in the world?*) criticism may have to deal with a subject-matter so familiar that fresh knowledge is out of the question, and then it must be all judgment; an enunciation and detailed application of principles. Here the great safeguard is never to let oneself become abstract, always to retain an intimate and lively consciousness of the truth of what one is saying, and, the moment this fails us, to be sure that something is wrong. Still under all circumstances, this mere judgment and application of principles is, in itself, not the most satisfactory work to the critic; like mathematics, it is tautological, and cannot well give us,

5 *Ab integro saeclorum,* etc.: 'from a renewal of the ages order is born (Virgil's *Eclogues,* IV, 5); translated by Shelley in *Hellas:* 'The world's great age begins anew'.

like fresh learning, the sense of creative activity.

But stop, some one will say; all this talk is of no practical use to us whatever; this criticism of yours is not what we have in our minds when we speak of criticism; when we speak of critics and criticism, we mean critics and criticism of the current English literature of the day; when you offer to tell criticism its function, it is to this criticism that we expect you to address yourself. I am sorry for it, for I am afraid I must disappoint these expectations. I am bound by my own definition of criticism; *a disinterested endeavor to learn and propagate the best that is known and thought in the world.* How much of current English literature comes into this "best that is known and thought in the world"? Not very much I fear; certainly less, at this moment, than of the current literature of France or Germany. Well, then, am I to alter my definition of criticism, in order to meet the requirements of a number of practising English critics, who, after all, are free in their choice of a business? That would be making criticism lend itself just to one of those alien practical considerations, which, I have said, are so fatal to it. One may say, indeed, to those who have to deal with the mass—so much better disregarded—of current English literature, that they may at all events endeavor, in dealing with this, to try it, so far as they can, by the standard of the best that is known and thought in the world; one may say, that to get anywhere near this standard, every critic should try and possess one great literature, at least, besides his own; and the more unlike his own, the better. But, after all, the criticism I am really concerned with—the criticism which alone can much help us for the future, the criticism which, throughout Europe, is at the present day meant, when so much stress is laid on the importance of criticism and the critical spirit— is a criticism which regards Europe as being, for intellectual and spiritual purposes, one great confederation, bound to a joint action and working to a common result; and whose members have, for their proper outfit, a knowledge of Greek, Roman and Eastern antiquity, and of one another.

Special, local, and temporary advantages being put out of account, that modern nation will in the intellectual and spiritual sphere make most progress, which most thoroughly carries out this program. And what is that but saying that we too, all of us, as individuals, the more thoroughly we carry it out, shall make the more progress?

There is so much inviting us!—what are we to take? what will nourish us in growth towards perfection? That is the question which, with the immense field of life and of literature lying before him, the critic has to answer; for himself first, and afterwards for others. In this idea of the critic's business the essays brought together in the following pages have had their origin; in this idea, widely different as are their subjects, they have, perhaps, their unity.

I conclude with what I said at the beginning: to have the sense of creative activity is the great happiness and the great proof of being alive, and it is not denied to criticism to have it; but then criticism must be sincere, simple, flexible, ardent, ever widening its knowledge. Then it may have, in no contemptible measure, a joyful sense of creative activity; a sense which a man of insight and conscience will prefer to what he might derive from a poor, starved, fragmentary, inadequate creation. And at some epochs no other creation is possible.

Still, in full measure, the sense of creative activity belongs only to genuine creation; in literature we must never forget that. But what true man of letters ever can forget it? It is no such common matter for a gifted nature to come into possession of a current of true and living ideas, and to produce amid the inspiration of them, that we are likely to underrate it. The epochs of Aeschylus and Shakespeare make us feel their preëminence. In an epoch like those is, no doubt, the true life of literature; there is the promised land, towards which criticism can only beckon. That promised land it will not be ours to enter, and we shall die in the wilderness: but to have desired to enter it, to have saluted it from afar, is already, perhaps, the best distinction among contemporaries; it will certainly be the best title to esteem with posterity.

[1864]

WORDSWORTH

I remember hearing Lord Macaulay say, after Wordsworth's death, when subscriptions were being collected to found a memorial of him, that ten years earlier more money could have been raised in Cambridge alone, to do honor to Wordsworth, than was now raised all through the country. Lord Macaulay had, as we know, his own heightened and telling way of putting things, and we must always make allowance for it. But probably it is true that Wordsworth has never, either before or since, been so accepted and popular, so established in possession of the minds of all who profess to care for poetry, as he was between the years 1830 and 1840, and at Cambridge. From the very first, no doubt, he had his believers and witnesses. But I have myself heard him declare that, for he knew not how many years, his poetry had never brought him in enough to buy his shoe-strings. The poetry-reading public was very slow to recognize him, and was very easily drawn away from him. Scott effaced him with this public. Byron effaced him.

The death of Byron seemed, however, to make an opening for Wordsworth. Scott, who had for some time ceased to produce poetry himself, and stood before the public as a great novelist; Scott, too genuine himself not to feel the profound genuineness of Wordsworth, and with an instinctive recognition of his firm hold on nature and of his local truth, always admired him sincerely, and praised him generously. The influence of Coleridge upon young men of ability was then powerful, and was still gathering strength; this influence told entirely in favor of Wordsworth's poetry. Cambridge was a place where Coleridge's influence had great action, and where Wordsworth's poetry, therefore, flourished especially. But even among the general public its sale grew large, the eminence of its author was widely recognized, and Rydal Mount became an object of pilgrimage. I remember Wordsworth relating how one of the pilgrims, a clergyman, asked him if he had ever written anything besides the "Guide to the Lakes." Yes, he answered modestly, he had written verses. Not every pilgrim was a reader, but the vogue was established, and the stream of pilgrims came.

Mr. Tennyson's decisive appearance dates from 1842. One cannot say that he effaced Wordsworth as Scott and Byron had effaced him. The poetry of Wordsworth had been so long before the public, the suffrage of good judges was so steady and so strong in its favor, that by 1842 the verdict of posterity, one may almost say, had been already pronounced, and Wordsworth's English fame was secure. But the vogue, the ear and applause of the great body of poetry-readers, never quite thoroughly perhaps his, he gradually lost more and more, and Mr. Tennyson gained them. Mr. Tennyson drew to himself, and away from Wordsworth, the poetry-reading public, and the new generations. Even in 1850, when Wordsworth died, this diminution of popularity was visible, and occasioned the remark of Lord Macaulay which I quoted at starting.

The diminution has continued. The influence of Coleridge has waned, and Wordsworth's poetry can no longer draw succor from this ally. The poetry has not, however, wanted eulogists; and it may be said to have brought its eulogists luck, for almost every one who has praised Wordsworth's poetry has praised it well. But the public has remained cold, or, at least, undetermined. Even the abundance of Mr. Palgrave's fine and skilfully chosen specimens of Wordsworth, in the "Golden Treasury," surprised many readers, and gave offense to not a few. To tenth-rate critics and compilers, for whom any violent shock to the public taste would be a temerity not to be risked, it is still quite permissible to speak of Wordsworth's poetry, not only with ignorance, but with impertinence. On the Continent he is almost unknown.

I cannot think, then, that Wordsworth has, up to this time, at all obtained his deserts. "Glory," said M. Renan the other day, "glory after all is the thing which has the best chance of not being altogether vanity." Wordsworth was a homely man, and himself would certainly never have thought of talking of glory as that which, after all, has the best chance of not being altogether vanity. Yet we may well allow that few things are less vain than *real* glory. Let us conceive of the whole group of civilized nations as being, for intellectual and spiritual purposes, one great confederation, bound to a joint action and working towards a common result; a confederation whose members have a due knowledge both of the past, out of which they all proceed, and of one another. This was the ideal of Goethe, and it is an ideal which will impose itself upon the thoughts of our modern societies more and more. Then to be recognized by the verdict of such a confederation as a master, or even as a seriously and eminently worthy workman, in one's own line of intellectual or spiritual activity, is indeed glory; a glory which it would be difficult to rate too highly. For what could be more beneficent, more salutary? The world is forwarded by having its attention fixed on the best things; and here is a tribunal, free from all suspicion of national and provincial partiality, putting a stamp on the best things, and recommending them for general honor and acceptance. A nation, again, is furthered by recognition of its real gifts and successes; it is encouraged to develop them further. And here is an honest verdict, telling us which of our supposed successes are really, in the judgment of the great impartial world, and not in our private judgment only, successes, and which are not.

It is so easy to feel pride and satisfaction in one's own things, so hard to make sure that one is right in feeling it! We have a great empire. But so had Nebuchadnezzar. We extol the "unrivalled happiness" of our national civilization. But then comes a candid friend, and remarks that our upper class is materialized, our middle class vulgarized, and our lower class brutalized. We are proud of our painting, our music. But we find that in the judgment of other people our painting is questionable, and our music non-existent. We are proud of our men of science. And here it turns out that the world is with us; we find that in the judgment of other people, too, Newton among the dead, and Mr. Darwin among the living, hold as high a place as they hold in our national opinion.

Finally, we are proud of our poets and poetry. Now poetry is nothing less than the most perfect speech of man, that in which he comes nearest to being able to utter the truth. It is no small thing, therefore, to succeed eminently in poetry. And so much is required for duly estimating success here, that about poetry it is perhaps hardest to arrive at a sure general verdict, and takes longest. Meanwhile, our own conviction of the superiority of our national poets is not decisive, is almost certain to be mingled, as we see constantly in English eulogy of Shakespeare, with much of provincial infatuation. And we know what was the opinion current among our neighbors the French—people of taste, acuteness, and quick literary tact—not a hundred years ago, about our great poets. The old *"Biographie Universelle"* notices the pretension of the English to a place for their poets among the chief poets of the world, and says that this is a pretension which to no one but an Englishman can ever seem admissible. And the scornful, disparaging things said by foreigners about Shakespeare and Milton, and about our national over-estimate of them, have been often quoted, and will be in every one's remembrance.

A great change has taken place, and Shakespeare is now generally recognized, even in France, as one of the greatest of poets. Yes, some anti-Gallican cynic will say, the French rank him with Corneille and with Victor Hugo! But let me have the pleasure of quoting a sentence about Shakespeare, which I met with by accident not long ago in the *Correspondant*, a French review which not a dozen English people, I suppose, look at. The writer is praising Shakespeare's prose. With Shakespeare, he says, "prose comes in whenever the subject, being more familiar, is unsuited to the majestic English iambic." And he goes on: "Shakespeare is the king of poetic rhythm and style, as well as the king of the realm of thought; along with his dazzling prose, Shakespeare has succeeded in giving us the most varied, the most harmonious verse which has ever sounded upon the human ear since the verse of the Greeks." M. Henry Cochin, the writer of this sentence, deserves our gratitude for it; it would not be easy to praise Shakespeare, in a single sentence, more justly. And when a foreigner and a Frenchman writes thus of Shakespeare, and when Goethe says of Milton, in whom there was so much to repel Goethe rather than to attract him, that "nothing has been ever done so entirely in the sense of the Greeks as *Samson Agonistes*," and that "Milton is in very truth a poet whom we must treat with all reverence," then we understand what constitutes a European recognition of poets and poetry as contradistinguished from a merely national recognition, and that in favor both of Milton and of Shakespeare the judgment of the high court of appeal has finally gone.

I come back to M. Renan's praise of glory, from which I started. Yes, real glory is a most serious thing, glory authenticated by the Amphictyonic Court of final appeal, definite glory. And even for poets and poetry, long and difficult as may be the process of arriving at the right award, the right award comes at last, the definitive glory rests where it is deserved. Every establishment of such a real glory is good and wholesome for mankind at large, good and wholesome for the nation which produced the poet crowned with it. To the poet himself it can seldom do harm; for he, poor man, is in his grave, probably, long before his glory crowns him.

Wordsworth has been in his grave for some thirty years, and certainly his lovers and admirers cannot flatter themselves that this great and steady light of glory as yet shines over him. He is not fully recognized at home; he is not recognized at all abroad. Yet I firmly believe that the poetical performance of Wordsworth is, after that of Shakespeare and Milton, of which all the world now recognizes the worth, undoubtedly the most considerable in our language from the Elizabethan age to the present time. Chaucer is anterior; and on other grounds, too, he cannot well be brought into the comparison. But taking the roll of our chief poetical names, besides Shakespeare and Milton, from the age of Elizabeth downwards, and going through it—Spenser, Dryden, Pope, Gray, Goldsmith, Cowper, Burns, Coleridge, Scott, Campbell, Moore, Byron, Shelley, Keats (I

mention those only who are dead)—I think it certain that Wordsworth's name deserves to stand, and will finally stand, above them all. Several of the poets named have gifts and excellences which Wordsworth has not. But taking the performance of each as a whole, I say that Wordsworth seems to me to have left a body of poetical work superior in power, in interest, in the qualities which give enduring freshness, to that which any one of the others has left.

But this is not enough to say. I think it certain, further, that if we take the chief poetical names of the Continent since the death of Molière, and, omitting Goethe, confront the remaining names with that of Wordsworth, the result is the same. Let us take Klopstock, Lessing, Schiller, Uhland, Rückert, and Heine, for Germany; Filicaja, Alfieri, Manzoni, and Leopardi for Italy; Racine, Boileau, Voltaire, André Chénier, Béranger, Lamartine, Musset, M. Victor Hugo (he has been so long celebrated that although he still lives I may be permitted to name him) for France. Several of these, again, have evidently gifts and excellences to which Wordsworth can make no pretension. But in real poetical achievement it seems to me indubitable that to Wordsworth, here again, belongs the palm. It seems to me that Wordsworth has left behind him a body of poetical work which wears, and will wear, better on the whole than the performance of any one of these personages, so far more brilliant and celebrated, most of them, than the homely poet of Rydal. Wordsworth's performance in poetry is on the whole, in power, in interest, in the qualities which give enduring freshness, superior to theirs.

This is a high claim to make for Wordsworth. But if it is a just claim, if Wordsworth's place among the poets who have appeared in the last two or three centuries is after Shakespeare, Molière, Milton, Goethe, indeed, but before all the rest, then in time Wordsworth will have his due. We shall recognize him in his place, as we recognize Shakespeare and Milton; and not only we ourselves shall recognize him, but he will be recognized by Europe also. Meanwhile, those who recognize him already may do well, perhaps, to ask themselves whether there are not in the case of

Wordsworth certain special obstacles which hinder or delay his due recognition by others, and whether these obstacles are not in some measure removable.

The "Excursion" and the "Prelude," his poems of greatest bulk, are by no means Wordsworth's best work. His best work is in his shorter pieces, and many indeed are there of these which are of first-rate excellence. But in his seven volumes the pieces of high merit are mingled with a mass of pieces very inferior to them; so inferior to them that it seems wonderful how the same poet should have produced both. Shakespeare frequently has lines and passages in a strain quite false, and which are entirely unworthy of him. But one can imagine him smiling if one could meet him in the Elysian Fields and tell him so; smiling and replying that he knew it perfectly well himself, and what did it matter? But with Wordsworth the case is different. Work altogether inferior, work quite uninspired, flat and dull, is produced by him with evident unconsciousness of its defects, and he presents it to us with the same faith and seriousness as his best work. Now a drama or an epic fill the mind, and one does not look beyond them; but in a collection of short pieces the impression made by one piece requires to be continued and sustained by the piece following. In reading Wordsworth the impression made by one of his fine pieces is too often dulled and spoiled by a very inferior piece coming after it.

Wordsworth composed verses during a space of some sixty years; and it is no exaggeration to say that within one single decade of those years, between 1798 and 1808, almost all his really first-rate work was produced. A mass of inferior work remains, work done before and after this golden prime, imbedding the first-rate work and clogging it, obstructing our approach to it, chilling, not unfrequently, the high-wrought mood with which we leave it. To be recognized far and wide as a great poet, to be possible and receivable as a classic, Wordsworth needs to be relieved of a great deal of the poetical baggage which now encumbers him. To administer this relief is indispensable, unless he is to continue to be a poet for the few only—a poet valued far below his real worth by the world.

There is another thing. Wordsworth classified his poems not according to any commonly received plan of arrangement, but according to a scheme of mental physiology. He has poems of the fancy, poems of the imagination, poems of sentiment and reflection, and so on. His categories are ingenious but far-fetched, and the result of his employment of them is unsatisfactory. Poems are separated one from another which possess a kinship of subject or of treatment far more vital and deep than the supposed unity of mental origin, which was Wordsworth's reason for joining them with others.

The tact of the Greeks in matters of this kind was infallible. We may rely upon it that we shall not improve upon the classification adopted by the Greeks for kinds of poetry; that their categories of epic, dramatic, lyric, and so forth, have a natural propriety, and should be adhered to. It may sometimes seem doubtful to which of two categories a poem belongs; whether this or that poem is to be called, for instance, narrative or lyric, lyric or elegiac. But there is to be found in every good poem a strain, a predominant note, which determines the poem as belonging to one of these kinds rather than the other; and here is the best proof of the value of the classification, and of the advantage of adhering to it. Wordsworth's poems will never produce their due effect until they are freed from their present artificial arrangement, and grouped more naturally.

Disengaged from the quantity of inferior work which now obscures them, the best poems of Wordsworth, I hear many people say, would indeed stand out in great beauty, but they would prove to be very few in number, scarcely more than a half a dozen. I maintain, on the other hand, that what strikes me with admiration, what establishes in my opinion Wordsworth's superiority, is the great and ample body of powerful work which remains to him, even after all his inferior work has been cleared away. He gives us so much to rest upon, so much which communicates his spirit and engages ours!

This is of very great importance. If it were a comparison of single pieces, or of three or four pieces, by each poet, I do not say that Wordsworth would stand decisively above Gray, or Burns, or Coleridge, or Keats, or Manzoni, or Heine. It is in his ampler body of powerful work that I find his superiority. His good work itself, his work which counts, is not all of it, of course, of equal value. Some kinds of poetry are in themselves lower kinds than others. The ballad kind is a lower kind; the didactic kind, still more, is a lower kind. Poetry of this latter sort counts, too, sometimes, by its biographical interest partly, not by its poetical interest pure and simple; but then this can only be when the poet producing it has the power and importance of Wordsworth, a power and importance which he assuredly did not establish by such didactic poetry alone. Altogether, it is, I say, by the great body of powerful and significant work which remains to him, after every reduction and deduction has been made, that Wordsworth's superiority is proved.

To exhibit this body of Wordsworth's best work, to clear away obstructions from around it, and to let it speak for itself, is what every lover of Wordsworth should desire. Until this has been done, Wordsworth, whom we, to whom he is dear, all of us know and feel to be so great a poet, has not had a fair chance before the world. When once it has been done, he will make his way best, not by our advocacy of him, but by his own worth and power. We may safely leave him to make his way thus, we who believe that a superior worth and power in poetry finds in mankind a sense responsive to it and disposed at last to recognize it. Yet at the outset, before he has been duly known and recognized, we may do Wordsworth a service, perhaps, by indicating in what his superior power and worth will be found to consist, and in what it will not.

Long ago, in speaking of Homer, I said that the noble and profound application of ideas to life is the most essential part of poetic greatness. I said that a great poet receives his distinctive character of superiority from his application, under the conditions immutably fixed by the laws of poetic beauty and poetic truth, from his application, I say, to his subject, whatever it may be, of the ideas

On man, on nature, and on human life,

which he has acquired for himself. The line quoted is Wordsworth's own; and his superiority arises from his powerful use, in his best pieces, his powerful application to his subject, of ideas "on man, on nature and on human life."

Voltaire, with his signal acuteness, most truly remarked that "no nation has treated in poetry moral ideas with more energy and depth than the English nation." And he adds: "There, it seems to me, is the great merit of the English poets." Voltaire does not mean, by "treating in poetry moral ideas," the composing moral and didactic poems;—that brings us but a very little way in poetry. He means just the same thing as was meant when I spoke above "of the noble and profound application of ideas to life"; and he means the application of these ideas under the conditions fixed for us by the laws of poetic beauty and poetic truth. If it is said that to call these ideas *moral* ideas is to introduce a strong and injurious limitation, I answer that it is to do nothing of the kind, because moral ideas are really so main a part of human life. The question, *how to live,* is itself a moral idea; and it is the question which most interests every man, and with which, in some way or other, he is perpetually occupied. A large sense is of course to be given to the term *moral.* Whatever bears upon the question, "how to live," comes under it.

Nor love thy life, nor hate; but, what thou liv'st,
Live well; how long or short, permit to heaven.

In those fine lines Milton utters, as every one at once perceives, a moral idea. Yes, but so too, when Keats consoles the forward-bending lover on the Grecian Urn, the lover arrested and presented in immortal relief by the sculptor's hand before he can kiss, with the line,

Forever wilt thou love, and she be fair—

he utters a moral idea. When Shakespeare says, that

> We are such stuff
> As dreams are made of, and our little life
> Is rounded with a sleep,

he utters a moral idea.

Voltaire was right in thinking that the energetic and profound treatment of moral ideas, in this large sense, is what distinguishes the English poetry. He sincerely meant praise, not dispraise or hint of limitation; and they err who suppose that poetic limitation is a necessary consequence of the fact, the fact being granted as Voltaire states it. If what distinguishes the greatest poets is their powerful and profound application of ideas to life, which surely no good critic will deny, then to prefix to the term ideas here the term moral makes hardly any difference, because human life itself is in so preponderating a degree moral.

It is important, therefore, to hold fast to this: that poetry is at bottom a criticism of life; that the greatness of a poet lies in his powerful and beautiful application of ideas to life—to the question: How to live. Morals are often treated in a narrow and false fashion; they are bound up with systems of thought and belief which have had their day; they are fallen into the hands of pedants and professional dealers; they grow tiresome to some of us. We find attraction, at times, even in a poetry of revolt against them; in a poetry which might take for its motto Omar Khayyám's words: "Let us make up in the tavern for the time which we have wasted in the mosque." Or we find attractions in a poetry indifferent to them; in a poetry where the contents may be what they will, but where the form is studied and exquisite. We delude ourselves in either case; and the best cure for our delusion is to let our minds rest upon that great and inexhaustible word *life*, until we learn to enter into its meaning. A poetry of revolt against moral ideas is a poetry of revolt against *life;* a poetry of indifference towards moral ideas is a poetry of indifference towards *life*.

Epictetus had a happy figure for things like the play of the senses, or literary form and finish, or argumentative ingenuity, in comparison with "the best and master thing" for us, as he called it, the concern, how to live. Some people were afraid of them, he said, or they disliked and undervalued them. Such people were wrong; they were unthankful or cowardly. But the things might also be over-prized, and treated as final when they are not. They bear to life the relation which inns bear to home. "As if a man, journeying home, and finding a nice inn on the road, and liking it, were to stay forever at the inn! Man, thou hast forgotten thine object; thy journey was not *to* this, but *through* this. 'But this inn is taking.' And how many other inns, too, are taking, and how many fields and meadows! but as places of passage merely. You have an object, which is this: to get home, to do your duty to your family, friends, and fellow-countrymen, to attain inward freedom, serenity, happiness, contentment. Style takes your fancy, arguing takes your fancy, and you forget your home and want to make your abode with them and to stay with them, on the plea that they are taking. Who denies that they are taking? but as places of passage, as inns. And when I say this, you suppose me to be attacking the care for style, the care for argument. I am not; I attack the resting in them, the not looking to the end which is beyond them."

Now, when we come across a poet like Théophile Gautier, we have a poet who has taken up his abode at an inn, and never got farther. There may be inducements to this or that one of us, at this or that moment, to find delight in him, to cleave to him; but after all, we do not change the truth about him—we only stay ourselves in his inn along with him. And when we come across a poet like Wordsworth, who sings

> Of truth, of grandeur, beauty, love and hope,
> And melancholy fear subdued by faith,
> Of blessed consolations in distress,
> Of moral strength and intellectual power,
> Of joy in widest commonalty spread—

then we have a poet intent on "the best and master thing," and who prosecutes his journey home. We say, for brevity's sake, that he deals with *life*, because he deals with that in which life really consists. This is what Voltaire means to praise in the English poets—this dealing with what is really life. But always it is the mark of the greatest poets that they deal with it; and to say that the English poets are remarkable for dealing with it, is only another way of saying, what is true, that in poetry the English genius has especially shown its power.

Wordsworth deals with it, and his greatness lies in his dealing with it so powerfully. I have named a number of celebrated poets above all of whom he, in my opinion, deserves to be placed. He is to be placed above poets like Voltaire, Dryden, Pope, Lessing, Schiller, because these famous personages, with a thousand gifts and merits, never, or scarcely ever, attain the distinctive accent and utterance of the high and genuine poets—

Quique pii vates et Phœbo digna locuti, [1]

at all. Burns, Keats, Heine, not to speak of others in our list, have this accent;—who can doubt it? And at the same time they have treasures of humor, felicity, passion, for which in Wordsworth we shall look in vain. Where, then, is Wordsworth's superiority? It is here; he deals with more of *life* than they do; he deals with *life*, as a whole, more powerfully.

No Wordsworthian will doubt this. Nay, the fervent Wordsworthian will add, as Mr. Leslie Stephen does, that Wordsworth's poetry is precious because his philosophy is sound; that his "ethical system is as distinctive and capable of exposition as Bishop Butler's"; that his poetry is informed by ideas which "fall spontaneously into a scientific system of thought." But we must be on our guard against the Wordsworthians, if we want to secure for Wordsworth his due rank as a poet. The Wordsworthians are apt to praise him for the wrong things, and to lay far too much stress upon what they call his philosophy. His poetry is the reality, his philosophy—so far, at least, as it may put on the form and habit of "a scientific system of thought," and the more that it puts them on—is the illusion. Perhaps we shall one day learn to make this proposition general, and to say: Poetry is the reality, philosophy

[1] *Quique pii vates,* etc.: 'And the loyal bards whose speech was meet for Apollo' (Virgil, *Aeneid,* VI, 662).

the illusion. But in Wordsworth's case, at any rate, we cannot do him justice until we dismiss his formal philosophy.

The "Excursion" abounds with philosophy and therefore the "Excursion" is to the Wordsworthian what it never can be to the disinterested lover of poetry—a satisfactory work. "Duty exists," says Wordsworth, in the "Excursion"; and then he proceeds thus—

... Immutably survive,
For our support, the measures and the forms,
Which an abstract Intelligence supplies
Whose kingdom is, where time and space are not.

And the Wordsworthian is delighted, and thinks that here is a sweet union of philosophy and poetry. But the disinterested lover of poetry will feel that the lines carry us really not a step farther than the proposition which they would interpret; that they are a tissue of elevated but abstract verbiage, alien to the very nature of poetry.

Or let us come direct to the center of Wordsworth's philosophy, as "an ethical system, as distinctive and capable of systematical exposition as Bishop Butler's"—

... One adequate support
For the calamities of mortal life
Exists, one only;—an assured belief
That the procession of our fate, howe'er
Sad or disturbed, is ordered by a Being
Of infinite benevolence and power;
Whose everlasting purposes embrace
All accidents, converting them to good.

That is doctrine such as we hear in church too, religious and philosophic doctrine; and the attached Wordsworthian loves passages of such doctrine, and brings them forward in proof of his poet's excellence. But however true the doctrine may be, it has, as here presented, none of the characters of *poetic* truth, the kind of truth which we require from a poet. and in which Wordsworth is really strong.

Even the "intimations" of the famous Ode, those corner-stones of the supposed philosophic system of Wordsworth—the idea of the high instincts and affections coming out in childhood, testifying of a divine home recently left, and fading away as our life proceeds—this idea, of undeniable beauty as a play of fancy, has itself not the character of poetic truth of the best kind; it has no real solidity. The instinct of delight in Nature and her beauty had no doubt extraordinary strength in Wordsworth himself as a child. But to say that universally this instinct is mighty in childhood, and tends to die away afterwards, is to say what is extremely doubtful. In many people, perhaps with the majority of educated persons, the love of nature is 10 nearly imperceptible at ten years old, but strong and operative at thirty. In general we may say of these high instincts of early childhood, the base of the alleged systematic philosophy of Wordsworth, what Thucydides says of the early achievements of the Greek race: "It is impossible to speak with certainty of what is so remote; but from all that we can really investigate, I should say that they were no very great things."   20

Finally, the "scientific system of thought" in Wordsworth gives us at least such poetry as this, which the devout Wordsworthian accepts—

O for the coming of that glorious time
When, prizing knowledge as her noblest wealth
And best protection, this Imperial Realm,
While she exacts allegiance, shall admit
An obligation, on her part, to *teach*
Them who are born to serve her and obey;
Binding herself by statute to secure,
For all the children whom her soil maintains,
The rudiments of letters, and inform
The mind with moral and religious truth.

Wordsworth calls Voltaire dull, and surely the production of these un-Voltairian lines must have been imposed on him as a judgment! One can hear them being quoted at a Social Science Congress; one can call up the whole scene. A great room in one of 40 our dismal provincial towns; dusty air and jaded afternoon daylight; benches full of men with bald heads and women in spectacles; an orator lifting up his face from a manuscript written within and without to declaim these lines of Wordsworth; and in the soul of any poor child of nature who may have wandered in thither, an unutterable sense of lamentation, and mourning, and woe!

"But turn we," as Wordsworth says, "from these bold, bad men," the haunters of Social Science Congresses. And let us be on our guard, too, against the exhibitors and extollers of a "scientific system of thought" in Wordsworth's poetry. The poetry will never be seen aright while they thus exhibit it. The cause of its greatness is simple, and may be told quite simply. Wordsworth's poetry is great because of the extraordinary power with which Wordsworth feels the joy offered to us in nature, the joy offered to us in the simple primary 10 affections and duties; and because of the extraordinary power with which, in case after case, he shows us this joy, and renders it so as to make us share it.

The source of joy from which he thus draws is the truest and most unfailing source of joy accessible to man. It is also accessible universally. Wordsworth brings us word, therefore, according to his own strong and characteristic line, he brings us 20 word

Of joy in widest commonalty spread,

Here is an immense advantage for a poet. Wordsworth tells of what all seek, and tells of it at its truest and best source, and yet a source where all may go and draw for it.

Nevertheless, we are not to suppose that everything is precious which Wordsworth, standing even at this perennial and beautiful source, may give us. Wordsworthians 30 are apt to talk as if it must be. They will speak with the same reverence of "The Sailor's Mother," for example, as of "Lucy Gray." They do their master harm by such lack of discrimination. "Lucy Gray" is a beautiful success; "The Sailor's Mother" is a failure. To give aright what he wishes to give, to interpret and render successfully, is not always within Wordsworth's own command. It is within no poet's command; here is the part of the Muse, the inspiration, the God, the "not ourselves." In Wordsworth's case, the accident, for so it may almost be called, of inspiration, is of peculiar importance. No poet, perhaps, is so evidently filled with a new and sacred energy when the inspiration is upon him; no poet, when it fails him, is so left "weak as is a breaking wave." I remember hear- 50 ing him say that "Goethe's poetry was not inevitable enough." The remark is striking and true; no line in Goethe, as Goethe said himself, but its maker knew well how it came there. Wordsworth is right,

Goethe's poetry is not inevitable; not inevitable enough. But Wordsworth's poetry, when he is at his best, is inevitable, as inevitable as Nature herself. It might seem that Nature not only gave him the matter for his poem, but wrote his poem for him. He has no style. He was too conversant with Milton not to catch at times his master's manner, and he has fine Miltonic lines; but he has no assured poetic style of his own, like Milton. When he seeks to have a style he falls into ponderosity and pomposity. In the "Excursion" we have his style, as an artistic product of his own creation; and although Jeffrey completely failed to recognize Wordsworth's real greatness, he was yet not wrong in saying of the "Excursion," as a work of poetic style: "This will never do." And yet magical as is that power, which Wordsworth has not, of assured and possessed poetic style, he has something which is an equivalent for it.

Every one who has any sense for these things feels the subtle turn, the heightening, which is given to a poet's verse by his genius for style. We can feel it in the

> After life's fitful fever, he sleeps well—

of Shakespeare; in the

> ...though fall'n on evil days,
> On evil days though fall'n, and evil tongues—

of Milton. It is the incomparable charm of Milton's power of poetic style which gives such worth to "Paradise Regained," and makes a great poem of a work in which Milton's imagination does not soar high. Wordsworth has in constant possession, and at command, no style of this kind; but he had too poetic a nature, and had read the great poets too well, not to catch, as I have already remarked, something of it occasionally. We find it not only in his Miltonic lines; we find it in such a phrase as this, where the manner is his own, not Milton's—

> the fierce confederate storm
> Of sorrow barricadoed evermore
> Within the walls of cities;

although even here, perhaps, the power of style which is undeniable, is more properly that of eloquent prose than the subtle heightening and change wrought by gen-uine poetic style. It is style, again, and the elevation given by style, which chiefly makes the effectiveness of "Laodameia." Still the right sort of verse to choose from Wordsworth, if we are to seize his true and most characteristic form of expression, is a line like this from "Michael"—

> And never lifted up a single stone.

There is nothing subtle in it, no heightening, no study of poetic style, strictly so called, at all; yet it is expression of the highest and most truly expressive kind.

Wordsworth owed much to Burns, and a style of perfect plainness, relying for effect solely on the weight and force of that which with entire fidelity it utters, Burns could show him.

> The poor inhabitant below
> Was quick to learn and wise to know,
> And keenly felt the friendly glow
>   And softer flame;
> But thoughtless follies laid him low
> And stain'd his name.

Every one will be conscious of a likeness here to Wordsworth; and if Wordsworth did great things with this nobly plain manner, we must remember, what indeed he himself would always have been forward to acknowledge, that Burns used it before him.

Still Wordsworth's use of it has something unique and unmatchable. Nature herself seems, I say, to take the pen out of his hand, and to write for him with her own bare, sheer, penetrating power. This arises from two causes; from the profound sincereness with which Wordsworth feels his subject, and also from the profoundly sincere and natural character of his subject itself. He can and will treat such a subject with nothing but the most plain, first-hand, almost austere naturalness. His expression may often be called bald, as, for instance, in the poem of "Resolution and Independence"; but it is bald as the bare mountain tops are bald, with a baldness which is full of grandeur.

Wherever we meet with the successful balance, in Wordsworth, of profound truth of subject with profound truth of execution, he is unique. His best poems are those which most perfectly exhibit this balance. I have a warm admiration for "Laodameia" and for the great "Ode"; but if I am to tell the very truth, I find "Laodameia" not wholly free from something artificial, and the great "Ode" not wholly free from something declamatory. If I had to pick out poems of a kind most perfectly to show Wordsworth's unique power, I should rather choose poems such as "Michael," "The Fountain," "The Highland Reaper." And poems with the peculiar and unique beauty which distinguishes these, Wordsworth produced in considerable number; besides very many other poems of which the worth, although not so rare as the worth of these, is still exceedingly high.

On the whole, then, as I said at the beginning, not only is Wordsworth eminent by reason of the goodness of his best work, but he is eminent also by reason of the great body of good work which he has left to us. With the ancients I will not compare him. In many respects the ancients are far above us, and yet there is something that we demand which they can never give. Leaving the ancients, let us come to the poets and poetry of Christendom. Dante, Shakespeare, Molière, Milton, Goethe, are altogether larger and more splendid luminaries in the poetical heaven than Wordsworth. But I know not where else, among the moderns, we are to find his superiors.

To disengage the poems which show his power, and to present them to the English-speaking public and to the world, is the object of this volume. I by no means say that it contains all which in Wordsworth's poems is interesting. Except in the case of "Margaret," a story composed separately from the rest of the "Excursion," and which belongs to a different part of England, I have not ventured on detaching portions of poems, or on giving any piece otherwise than as Wordsworth himself gave it. But under the conditions imposed by this reserve, the volume contains, I think, everything, or nearly everything, which may best serve him with the majority of lovers of poetry, nothing which may disserve him.

I have spoken lightly of Wordsworthians; and if we are to get Wordsworth recognized by the public and by the world, we must recommend him not in the spirit of a clique, but in the spirit of disinterested lovers of poetry. But I am a Wordsworthian myself. I can read with pleasure and edification "Peter Bell," and the whole series of "Ecclesiastical Sonnets," and the address to Mr. Wilkinson's spade, and even the "Thanksgiving Ode"—everything of Wordsworth, I think, except "Vaudracour and Julia." It is not for nothing that one has been brought up in the veneration of a man so truly worthy of homage; that one has seen him and heard him, lived in his neighborhood, and been familiar with his country. No Wordsworthian has a tenderer affection for this pure and sage master than I, or is less really offended by his defects. But Wordsworth is something more than the pure and sage master of a small band of devoted followers, and we ought not to rest satisfied until he is seen to be what he is. He is one of the very chief glories of English Poetry; and by nothing is England so glorious as by her poetry. Let us lay aside every weight which hinders our getting him recognized as this, and let our one study be to bring to pass, as widely as possible and as truly as possible, his own word concerning his poems: "They will coöperate with the benign tendencies in human nature and society, and will, in their degree, be efficacious in making men wiser, better, and happier."

[1879]

THOMAS HENRY HUXLEY

CHRONOLOGY AND INTRODUCTION

1825 Born at Ealing, near London, May 4.

1830–35 Early education at Ealing.

1835–41 Irregular education at Coventry, whither his father moved in 1835.

1841 Went to London to study medicine.

1842 Matriculation at London University.

1845 Graduated M. B.

1846 Qualified for practice of medicine; appointed assistant surgeon to H.M.S. *Rattlesnake*.

1846–50 Voyage on *Rattlesnake*, Dec. 4, 1846 to Nov. 9, 1850.

1851 Elected Fellow of Royal Society.

1854 Left service in Navy; accepted lectureship in natural history at Royal School of Mines, London.

1855 Marriage; Naturalist to the Government Geological Survey.

1860–70 Growing reputation and influence through lectures, technical papers, and books, mainly on scientific subjects.

1860 Famous reply to Bishop of Oxford, at meeting of British Association, in Oxford.

1866 Received LL.D. from Edinburgh University, with Carlyle and Tyndall.

1870–95 Reputation as public official, administrator, and speaker at its height; served on several Royal Commissions and made member of many learned societies, at home and abroad.

1872 Travelled to Italy and Egypt for health.

1872–4 Lord Rector of Aberdeen University.

1876 Visited America on lecture tour.

1878 Received LL.D. from Dublin University.

1879 LL.D. from Cambridge University.

1883 President of the Royal Society.

1885 D.C.L. from Oxford University.

1893 Delivered Romanes Lecture at Oxford on "Evolution and Ethics."

1894 Received the Darwin Medal.

1895 Death, June 29.

One of the greatest achievements of the Victorian age was the advancement of science. There were many distinguished workers, among whom Darwin was first. But in the company of his contemporaries or immediate successors none was more brilliant and famous than Thomas Henry Huxley, who called himself Darwin's bulldog and who became the century's most redoubtable champion of scientific truth and freedom of thought, when both were challenged as they had not been since the time of Galileo. Huxley was not only a first-rate scientist, he was a great humanitarian, whose voice and pen powerfully served the cause of education and social welfare for more than a generation. His mind, indeed, seems to the lay reader of his collected essays as scarcely less philosophical and literary than it was scientific. "Science and literature," he said, "are not two things, but two sides of one thing."

Huxley's early training was irregular. Although in childhood he was not precocious, he soon developed a strong appetite for books, reading by himself in various directions, notably in philosophy, logic, and science. In 1841 he went to London to study medicine and by hard work he rapidly won distinction not only in botany and chemistry, but especially in anatomy and physiology; and he was qualified for medical practice in 1846. Near the end of this year he received an appointment as assistant surgeon on the *Rattlesnake*, a government ship fitted out to make a surveying cruise in the waters between Australia and the Great Barrier Reef. Huxley was twenty-one, eager for adventure, insatiably curious, ready to put up with the rough realities of life on shipboard during a voyage of four years, with much time on his hands to study certain forms of sea life and to read. Among the books that he took with him were Carlyle's *Sartor Resartus* and the *Miscellanies*, both of which, besides other writings of Carlyle at a later date, made an "ineffaceable impression" upon his mind "as a source of intellectual invigoration and moral stimulus." His scientific studies went on continuously, and upon his return to England he published papers which brought him the acquaintance of a number of men in the front rank of contemporary science, and, shortly, membership in the Royal Society. But no opening came whereby he could make his living as a scientist, and the "bread and cheese" problem had to be solved. For a few years the path ahead seemed impenetrable. He was almost in despair. "The spectre of a wasted life has passed before me," he wrote to the Australian girl whom he was to marry in better days, which came at last in 1854 when he was made a lecturer in natural history at the Royal School of Mines, in London.

Huxley rose rapidly to eminence. He was a tireless worker. He developed methods of direct observation and analysis of representative animals, such as made him, in the words of one of his pupils (himself a distinguished scientist) "the father of modern laboratory instruction." As a lecturer, whether before professional or non-professional audiences, he was unrivalled for the accuracy and lucidity of his exposition and for the intellectual stimulation which he gave to his listeners.

He gloried in his profession. "Science seems to me," he said, "to teach in the highest and strongest manner the great truth which is embodied in the Christian conception of entire surrender to the will of God. Sit down before fact as a little child, be prepared to give up every preconceived notion, follow humbly wherever and to whatever abysses nature leads, or you shall learn nothing. I have only begun to learn content and peace of mind since I have resolved at all risks to do this." Huxley was one of the first scientists to consult all available authorities in French and German; and, says his son and biographer, he aspired to know the entire field of biological science "before he would claim to be a master in one department." In the days before modern highly intensified specialization had begun, he ranged over the fields of paleontology, physiology, anatomy, comparative anatomy, and zoology, and obtained, says a later student, "a grasp of nature as a whole second only to that of Darwin."

It was the publication of *The Origin of Species* that brought a kind of philosophic unity to his scattered researches in natural history and "inspired his thought with tenfold vigor." He had known the author before 1859, but from then onwards a friendship grew up which Huxley counted as one of the happiest experiences of his life, for in Darwin he "found something bigger than ordinary humanity—an unequalled simplicity and directness of purpose—a sublime unself-ishness." He rapidly mastered the Darwinian hypothesis, and "with one or two reservations as to the logical completeness of the theory," particularly concerning the causes of variation, he accepted it "as a powerful instrument of research" and wrote to Darwin that he was sharpening his claws and beak in readiness to defend it.

For twenty years and more Huxley was the protagonist in one of the greatest battles ever waged for freedom of thought and for empirical truth against the forces of reactionary orthodoxy, both scientific and ecclesiastical. The burning question concerned the origin of man. "Among my senior contemporaries," he wrote, "men like Lyell, regarded as revolutionaries of the deepest dye, were strongly opposed to anything which tended to break down the barrier between man and the rest of the animal world." The accumulation of evidence from 1859 to 1880, however, finally over-came most of the hesitation or opposition from scientists. It was otherwise with the orthodox clergy and with thousands of educated laymen, who saw in Darwinism a theory of the origin of man that was materialistic, degrading, and contrary to Biblical revelation. They fought long and bitterly against it, and heaped upon Huxley their ridicule, scorn, and wrath. "His name," says his son, "was anathema; he was a terrible example of intellectual pravity beyond redemption, a man with opinions such as cannot be held 'without grave personal sin on his part,' the representative in his single person of rationalism, materialism, atheism." But his courage, his mastery of facts, his lucidity in exposition, his readiness and skill in debate gave him the victory even against such antagonists as the Bishop of Oxford and Gladstone. His opponents, he declared, were attempting to harmonize impossibilities by trying to put the new wine of science into the old bottles of Judaism and to make the first chapter of Genesis the beginning and end of scientific truth. On such terms reconcilement between free thought and traditional authority was un-attainable. Huxley's last appearance on the platform as the champion of evolution was in the summer of 1894, when, before a distinguished audience of scientists of the Royal Society, he rose to second a vote of thanks for the presidential address of Lord Salisbury, in which he heard the doctrine, that he had been "damned for advocating thirty-four years" earlier, now "enun-ciated as a matter of course—disputed by no reasonable man."

His battle was against obscurantist orthodoxy and superstition, never against sincere piety and religion, for he was as passionately devoted to the total welfare of the people as he was to the advance of science. When a member of the newly formed (1870) school board of London he argued for the retention of Bible-reading in the elementary schools, because he believed that the masses should not be deprived of the one great literature open to them as a source of moral training, which he placed even above intellectual. He vigorously opposed the exclusively classical education which dominated the curricula of the public schools and universities in his time, and fought for the admission of scientific studies as equally important with literary in the pursuit of culture by the modern man and woman. And for those young people who were proposing to prepare themselves for medicine, engineering, and experimental and technical fields of work in connection with rapidly expanding commerce and industry, Huxley regarded a thorough scientific training as indispensable. "The modern university," he said, "looks forward, and is a factory of new knowledge: its professors have to be at the top of the wave of progress. Research and criticism must be the breath of their nostrils; laboratory work the main business of the scientific student; books his main helpers." But he never advocated an exclusively scientific education, which, he thought, would "bring about a mental twist as surely as an exclusively literary training." He wanted to see breadth of culture without superficiality and without narrowness. "In the mass of mankind, the aesthetic faculty," he said, "like the reasoning power and the moral sense, needs to be roused, directed, and cultivated; and I know not why the development of that side of his nature, through which man has access to a perennial spring of ennobling pleasure, should be omitted from any comprehensive scheme of university educa- tion. . . . I should like to see Professors of the Fine Arts in every university."

In his middle and later years when his acquaintance with the contemporary world became intimate and extensive, Huxley's interest not only in educational, but in social and political problems deepened. He saw the need of increased governmental action and control as against unrestricted *laissez-faire*. "What gives force to the socialistic movement which is now stirring European society to its depths (1871) but a determination on the part of the naturally able men among the proletariat, to put an end, somehow or other, to the misery and degradation in which a large proportion of their fellows is steeped?" How far state interference should go must never be determined abstractly, but always experimentally. "If individuality has no play, society does not advance," he insisted; "if individuality breaks out of all bounds, society perishes. . . . I take it that the good of mankind means the attainment, by every man, of all the happiness which he can enjoy without diminishing the happiness of his fellow men."

Huxley's humanitarianism was not only practical but speculative. From boyhood to his last days he read extensively in philosophy and probed into the deepest problems which confront the inquiring mind. He came to regard himself as an agnostic, since he could find no basis for knowledge of realities supposed to lie beyond the reach of sense-perception. In earlier days he was a materialist, but it was not long before he thought of matter as no less mysterious than spirit; both concepts were empty as regards empirical results and both involved the thinker in "mere verbal subtleties." Final answers as to the nature of ultimate reality could not, he believed, be reached by the human intellect. Huxley was never dogmatic in his agnosticism and never closed the door to demonstrable evidence from whatever source. But he had a passionate dislike of apriorism or absolutism, and to the end he distrusted the power of man ever to solve the immemorial riddles of existence. Yet he was no pessimist, even though he understood better than most men what he took to be "the passionless impersonality" of the cosmic process. If man the animal has at last, by "ape and tiger methods . . . worked his way to the headship of the sentient world," to this struggle for bare existence there has succeeded the struggle to make existence intelligible and to bring the order of "things" into harmony with the moral sense of man. "Social progress," said Huxley, "means a checking of the cosmic process at every step and the substitution for it of another, which may be called the ethical process. . . . I see no limit to the extent to which intelligence and will, guided by sound prin- ciples of investigation, and organized in common effort, may modify conditions of existence, for a period longer than now covered in history. And much may be done to change the nature of man himself."

If along with this profound insight into many of the major human problems of Huxley's day, we think of his lifelong pleasure in pure literature and his command of language, whether for the platform or for the printed page, we may well consider him to be as much a man of letters as a scientist. It is even possible that he will live longer as a force in letters than as a force in science. He delighted in novels, essays, and poetry. Literary allusions in his collected works are frequent and apposite. Shakespeare and Milton among the older English classics, and Tennyson and Browning among the moderns, were great favorites; and undoubtedly his sensi- tiveness to both matter and form in poetry quickened his feeling for style in his own writing. Certainly his mastery of expression, seemingly so easy, was the fruit of both taste and toil. "Sometimes I write essays half a dozen times before I can get them into proper shape," he said; "and I believe I become more fastidious as I grow older." His experience as a lecturer, inter- preting Darwinism and other scientific subjects to popular audiences, undoubtedly helped him to acquire an unsurpassed lucidity and liveliness. Clearness, indeed, together with simplicity and sincerity, was his highest aim always. He had a constitutional dislike of "copious and per-fervid eloquence" in any form, and he abhorred a "cumbrous and uncouth scholasticism" such as he found in Kant's German style. "Love the truth, think clearly and honestly," Huxley seems to say to the would-be writer, "and the personality will come through if you have one." His own essays, with hardly an exception, are models of what George Bernard Shaw calls style, namely, effectiveness of assertion. Their forward movement is a sure sign of the author's mastery of subject matter and form; they are invariably direct, unambiguous, satisfyingly complete. And, besides, there are, as Darwin exclaimed, "scores of splendid passages, and vivid flashes of wit."

AUTOBIOGRAPHY

And when I consider, in one view, the many things ... which I have upon my hands, I feel the burlesque of being employed in this man-ner at my time of life. But, in another view, and taking in all circumstances, these things, as trifling as they may appear, no less than things of greater importance, seem to be put upon me to do... —*Bishop Butler to the Duchess of Somerset.*

The "many things" to which the Duch-ess's correspondent here refers are the repairs and improvements of the episcopal seat at Auckland. I doubt if the great apologist, greater in nothing than in the simple dignity of his character, would have considered the writing an account of him-self as a thing which could be put upon him to do, whatever circumstances might be taken in. But the good bishop lived in an age when a man might write books and yet be permitted to keep his private exist-ence to himself; in the pre-Boswellian epoch, when the germ of the photographer lay in the womb of the distant future, and the interviewer who pervades our age was an unforeseen, indeed unimaginable, birth of time.

At present, the most convinced believer in the aphorism *"Bene qui latuit, bene vixit,"* [1] is not always able to act up to it. An importunate person informs him that his portrait is about to be published and will be accompanied by a biography which the importunate person proposes to write. The sufferer knows what that means; either he undertakes to revise the "biography" or he does not. In the former case, he makes himself responsible; in the latter, he allows the publication of a mass of more or less

fulsome inaccuracies for which he will be held responsible by those who are familiar with the prevalent art of self-advertisement. On the whole, it may be better to get over the "burlesque of being employed in this manner" and do the thing himself.

It was by reflections of this kind that, some years ago, I was led to write and permit the publication of the subjoined sketch.

I was born about eight o'clock in the morning on the 4th of May, 1825, at Eal-ing, which was, at that time, as quiet a little country village as could be found within half-a-dozen miles of Hyde Park Corner. Now it is a suburb of London with, I believe, 30,000 inhabitants. My father was one of the masters in a large semipublic school which at one time had a high reputation. I am not aware that any portents preceded my arrival in this world, but, in my childhood, I remember hearing a traditional account of the man-ner in which I lost the chance of an endowment of great practical value. The windows of my mother's room were open, in consequence of the unusual warmth of the weather. For the same reason, prob-ably, a neighboring beehive had swarmed, and the new colony, pitching on the win-dow-sill, was making its way into the room when the horrified nurse shut down the sash. If that well-meaning woman had only abstained from her ill-timed interfer-ence, the swarm might have settled on my lips, and I should have been endowed with that mellifluous eloquence which, in this country, leads far more surely than worth, capacity, or honest work, to the highest places in Church and State. But the op-portunity was lost, and I have been obliged to content myself through life with saying what I mean in the plainest of plain lan-

[1] *Bene qui latuit,* etc.: 'He who has well hidden himself has lived well' (Ovid, *Tristia,* III, iv, 25).

guage, than which, I suppose, there is no habit more ruinous to a man's prospects of advancement.

Why I was christened Thomas Henry I do not know; but it is a curious chance that my parents should have fixed for my usual denomination upon the name of that particular Apostle with whom I have always felt most sympathy. Physically and mentally I am the son of my mother so completely—even down to peculiar movements of the hands, which made their appearance in me as I reached the age she had when I noticed them—that I can hardly find any trace of my father in myself, except an inborn faculty for drawing, which unfortunately, in my case, has never been cultivated, a hot temper, and that amount of tenacity of purpose which unfriendly observers sometimes call obstinacy.

My mother was a slender brunette, of an emotional and energetic temperament, and possessed of the most piercing black eyes I ever saw in a woman's head. With no more education than other women of the middle classes in her day, she had an excellent mental capacity. Her most distinguishing characteristic, however, was rapidity of thought. If one ventured to suggest she had not taken much time to arrive at any conclusion, she would say, "I cannot help it, things flash across me." That peculiarity has been passed on to me in full strength; it has often stood me in good stead; it has sometimes played me sad tricks, and it has always been a danger. But, after all, if my time were to come over again, there is nothing I would less willingly part with than my inheritance of mother wit.

I have next to nothing to say about my childhood. In later years my mother, looking at me almost reproachfully, would sometimes say, "Ah! you were such a pretty boy!" whence I had no difficulty in concluding that I had not fulfilled my early promise in the matter of looks. In fact, I have a distinct recollection of certain curls of which I was vain, and of a conviction that I closely resembled that handsome, courtly gentleman, Sir Herbert Oakley, who was vicar of our parish, and who was as a god to us country folk, because he was occasionally visited by the then Prince George of Cambridge. I remember turning my pinafore wrong side forwards in order to represent a surplice, and preaching to my mother's maids in the kitchen as nearly as possible in Sir Herbert's manner one Sunday morning when the rest of the family were at church. That is the earliest indication I can call to mind of the strong clerical affinities which my friend Mr. Herbert Spencer has always ascribed to me, though I fancy they have for the most part remained in a latent state.

My regular school training was of the briefest, perhaps fortunately, for though my way of life has made me acquainted with all sorts and conditions of men, from the highest to the lowest, I deliberately affirm that the society I fell into at school was the worst I have ever known. We boys were average lads, with much the same inherent capacity for good and evil as any others; but the people who were set over us cared about as much for our intellectual and moral welfare as if they were baby-farmers. We were left to the operation of the struggle for existence among ourselves, and bullying was the least of the ill practices current among us. Almost the only cheerful reminiscence in connection with the place which arises in my mind is that of a battle I had with one of my classmates, who had bullied me until I could stand it no longer. I was a very slight lad, but there was a wildcat element in me which, when roused, made up for lack of weight, and I licked my adversary effectually. However, one of my first experiences of the extremely rough-and-ready nature of justice, as exhibited by the course of things in general, arose out of the fact that I—the victor—had a black eye, while he—the vanquished—had none, so that I got into disgrace and he did not. We made it up, and thereafter I was unmolested. One of the greatest shocks I ever received in my life was to be told a dozen years afterwards by the groom who brought me my horse in a stable-yard in Sydney that he was my quondam antagonist. He had a long story of family misfortune to account for his position, but at that time it was necessary to deal very cautiously with mysterious strangers in New South Wales, and on inquiry I found that the unfortunate young man had not only been "sent out," but had undergone more than one colonial conviction.

As I grew older, my great desire was to be a mechanical engineer, but the fates were against this and, while very young, I commenced the study of medicine under a medical brother-in-law. But, though the Institute of Mechanical Engineers would certainly not own me, I am not sure that I have not all along been a sort of mechanical engineer *in partibus infidelium*.[2] I am now occasionally horrified to think how very little I ever knew or cared about medicine as the art of healing. The only part of my professional course which really and deeply interested me was physiology, which is the mechanical engineering of living machines; and, notwithstanding that natural science has been my proper business, I am afraid there is very little of the genuine naturalist in me. I never collected anything, and species work was always a burden to me; what I cared for was the architectural and engineering part of the business, the working out the wonderful unity of plan in the thousands and thousands of diverse living constructions, and the modifications of similar apparatuses to serve diverse ends. The extraordinary attraction I felt towards the study of the intricacies of living structure nearly proved fatal to me at the outset. I was a mere boy—I think between thirteen and fourteen years of age—when I was taken by some older student friends of mine to the first post-mortem examination I ever attended. All my life I have been most unfortunately sensitive to the disagreeables which attend anatomical pursuits, but on this occasion my curiosity overpowered all other feelings, and I spent two or three hours in gratifying it. I did not cut myself, and none of the ordinary symptoms of dissection-poison supervened, but poisoned I was somehow, and I remember sinking into a strange state of apathy. By way of a last chance, I was sent to the care of

some good, kind people, friends of my father's, who lived in a farmhouse in the heart of Warwickshire. I remember staggering from my bed to the window on the bright spring morning after my arrival, and throwing open the casement. Life seemed to come back on the wings of the breeze, and to this day the faint odor of wood-smoke, like that which floated across the farmyard in the early morning, is as good to me as the "sweet south upon a bed of violets." I soon recovered, but for years I suffered from occasional paroxysms of internal pain, and from that time my constant friend, hypochondriacal dyspepsia, commenced his half century of co-tenancy of my fleshly tabernacle.

Looking back on my *Lehrjahre,*[3] I am sorry to say that I do not think that any account of my doings as a student would tend to edification. In fact, I should distinctly warn ingenuous youth to avoid imitating my example. I worked extremely hard when it pleased me, and when it did not—which was a very frequent case—I was extremely idle (unless making caricatures of one's pastors and masters is to be called a branch of industry), or else wasted my energies in wrong directions. I read everything I could lay hands upon, including novels, and took up all sorts of pursuits to drop them again quite as speedily. No doubt it was very largely my own fault, but the only instruction from which I ever obtained the proper effect of education was that which I received from Mr. Wharton Jones, who was the lecturer on physiology at the Charing Cross School of Medicine. The extent and precision of his knowledge impressed me greatly, and the severe exactness of his method of lecturing was quite to my taste. I do not know that I have ever felt so much respect for anybody as a teacher before or since. I worked hard to obtain his approbation, and he was extremely kind and helpful to the youngster who, I am afraid, took up more of his time than he had any right to do. It was he who suggested the publication of my first scientific paper—a very little one—in the *Medical Gazette* of 1845, and most kindly corrected the literary faults which

---

[2] *in partibus infidelium:* 'in the domain of infidels';—a title given to Catholic bishops of defunct sees, "usually in countries under Moslem control." Though Huxley professes no real authority in mechanical engineering, he assumes a kind of titular authority in 'the engineering part' of biological science.

[3] *Lehrjahre:* years of learning, i.e. apprenticeship.

abounded in it, short as it was; for at that time, and for many years afterwards, I detested the trouble of writing, and would take no pains over it.

It was in the early spring of 1846, that, having finished my obligatory medical studies and passed the first M.B. examination at the London University—though I was still too young to qualify at the College of Surgeons—I was talking to a fellow student (the present eminent physician, Sir Joseph Fayrer), and wondering what I should do to meet the imperative necessity for earning my own bread, when my friend suggested that I should write to Sir William Burnett, at that time Director-General for the Medical Service of the Navy, for an appointment. I thought this rather a strong thing to do, as Sir William was personally unknown to me, but my cheery friend would not listen to my scruples, so I went to my lodgings and wrote the best letter I could devise. A few days afterwards I received the usual official circular of acknowledgment, but at the bottom there was written an instruction to call at Somerset House on such a day. I thought that looked like business, so at the appointed time I called and sent in my card, while I waited in Sir William's anteroom. He was a tall, shrewd-looking old gentleman, with a broad Scotch accent—and I think I see him now as he entered with my card in his hand. The first thing he did was to return it, with the frugal reminder that I should probably find it useful on some other occasion. The second was to ask whether I was an Irishman. I suppose the air of modesty about my appeal must have struck him. I satisfied the Director-General that I was English to the backbone, and he made some inquiries as to my student career, finally desiring me to hold myself ready for examination. Having passed this, I was in Her Majesty's Service, and entered on the books of Nelson's old ship, the *Victory*, for duty at Haslar Hospital, about a couple of months after I made my application.

My official chief at Haslar was a very remarkable person, the late Sir John Richardson, an excellent naturalist, and far-famed as an indomitable Arctic traveler. He was a silent, reserved man, outside the circle of his family and intimates; and, having a full share of youthful vanity, I was extremely disgusted to find that "Old John," as we irreverent youngsters called him, took not the slightest notice of my worshipful self either the first time I attended him, as it was my duty to do, or for some weeks afterwards. I am afraid to think of the lengths to which my tongue may have run on the subject of the churlishness of the chief, who was, in truth, one of the kindest-hearted and most considerate of men. But one day, as I was crossing the hospital square, Sir John stopped me, and heaped coals of fire on my head by telling me that he had tried to get me one of the resident appointments, much coveted by the assistant surgeons, but that the Admiralty had put in another man. "However," said he, "I mean to keep you here till I can get you something you will like," and turned upon his heel without waiting for the thanks I stammered out. That explained how it was I had not been packed off to the West Coast of Africa like some of my juniors, and why, eventually, I remained altogether seven months at Haslar.

After a long interval, during which "Old John" ignored my existence almost as completely as before, he stopped me again as we met in a casual way, and describing the service on which the *Rattlesnake* was likely to be employed, said that Captain Owen Stanley, who was to command the ship, had asked him to recommend an assistant surgeon who knew something of science; would I like that? Of course I jumped at the offer. "Very well, I give you leave; go to London at once and see Captain Stanley." I went, saw my future commander, who was very civil to me, and promised to ask that I should be appointed to his ship, as in due time I was. It is a singular thing that, during the few months of my stay at Haslar, I had among my messmates two future Directors-General of the Medical Service of the Navy (Sir Alexander Armstrong and Sir John Watt-Reid), with the present President of the College of Physicians and my kindest of doctors, Sir Andrew Clark.

Life on board Her Majesty's ships in those days was a very different affair from what it is now, and ours was exceptionally rough, as we were often many months without receiving letters or seeing any civilized people but ourselves. In exchange, we had the interest of being about the last voyagers, I suppose, to whom it could be possible to meet with people who knew nothing of firearms—as we did on the south coast of New Guinea—and of making acquaintance with a variety of interesting savage and semicivilized people. But, apart from experience of this kind and the opportunities offered for scientific work, to me, personally, the cruise was extremely valuable. It was good for me to live under sharp discipline; to be down on the realities of existence by living on bare necessaries; to find out how extremely well worth living life seemed to be when one woke up from a night's rest on a soft plank, with the sky for canopy and cocoa and weevily biscuit the sole prospect for breakfast; and, more especially, to learn to work for the sake of what I got for myself out of it, even if it all went to the bottom and I along with it. My brother officers were as good fellows as sailors ought to be and generally are, but, naturally, they neither knew nor cared anything about my pursuits, nor understood why I should be so zealous in pursuit of the objects which my friends, the middies, christened "Buffons," after the title conspicuous on a volume of the *Suites à Buffon*,[4] which stood on my shelf in the chart room.

During the four years of our absence, I sent home communication after communication to the "Linnean Society," with the same result as that obtained by Noah when he sent the raven out of his ark. Tired at last of hearing nothing about them, I determined to do or die, and in 1849 I drew up a more elaborate paper and forwarded it to the Royal Society. This was my dove, if I had only known it. But owing to the movements of the ship, I heard nothing of that either until my return to England in the latter end of the year 1850, when I found that it was printed and published, and that a huge packet of separate copies awaited me. When I hear some of my young friends complain of want of sympathy and encouragement, I am inclined to think that my naval life was not the least valuable part of my education.

Three years after my return were occupied by a battle between my scientific friends on the one hand and the Admiralty on the other, as to whether the latter ought, or ought not, to act up to the spirit of a pledge they had given to encourage officers who had done scientific work by contributing to the expense of publishing mine. At last the Admiralty, getting tired, I suppose, cut short the discussion by ordering me to join a ship, which thing I declined to do, and as Rastignac, in the *Père Goriot*, says to Paris, I said to London, "*à nous deux*."[5] I desired to obtain a Professorship of either Physiology or Comparative Anatomy, and as vacancies occurred I applied, but in vain. My friend, Professor Tyndall, and I were candidates at the same time, he for the Chair of Physics and I for that of Natural History in the University of Toronto, which, fortunately, as it turned out, would not look at either of us. I say fortunately, not from any lack of respect for Toronto, but because I soon made up my mind that London was the place for me, and hence I have steadily declined the inducements to leave it, which have at various times been offered. At last, in 1854, on the translation of my warm friend Edward Forbes, to Edinburgh, Sir Henry De la Beche, the Director-General of the Geological Survey, offered me the post Forbes vacated of Paleontologist and Lecturer on Natural History. I refused the former point-blank, and accepted the latter only provisionally, telling Sir Henry that I did not care for fossils, and that I should give up Natural History as soon as I could get a physiological post. But I held the office for thirty-one years, and a large part of my work has been paleontological.

At that time I disliked public speaking, and had a firm conviction that I should break down every time I opened my mouth. I believe I had every fault a speaker could have (except talking at random or indulging in rhetoric), when I spoke to the first important audience I ever addressed, on a Friday evening at the Royal Institu-

---

[4] *Suites à Buffon*: 'sequels to Buffon', eminent French naturalist (1707–88). The phrase refers to subsequent and related scientific papers in the field of natural history.

[5] *À nous deux*: "(It's) between us two."

tion, in 1852. Yet, I must confess to having been guilty, *malgré moi*,[6] of as much public speaking as most of my contemporaries, and for the last ten years it ceased to be so much of a bugbear to me. I used to pity myself for having to go through this training, but I am now more disposed to compassionate the unfortunate audiences, especially my ever-friendly hearers at the Royal Institution, who were the subjects of my oratorical experiments.

The last thing that it would be proper for me to do would be to speak of the work of my life, or to say at the end of the day whether I think I have earned my wages or not. Men are said to be partial judges of themselves. Young men may be— I doubt if old men are. Life seems terribly foreshortened as they look back, and the mountain they set themselves to climb in youth turns out to be a mere spur of immeasurably higher ranges when, with failing breath, they reached the top. But if I may speak of the objects I have had more or less definitely in view since I began the ascent of my hillock, they are briefly these: To promote the increase of natural knowledge and to forward the application of scientific methods of investigation to all the problems of life to the best of my ability, in the conviction, which has grown with my growth and strengthened with my strength, that there is no alleviation for the sufferings of mankind except veracity of thought and of action, and the resolute facing of the world as it is when the garment of make-believe by which pious hands have hidden its uglier features is stripped off.

It is with this intent that I have subordinated any reasonable, or unreasonable, ambition for scientific fame which I may have permitted myself to entertain to other ends: to the popularization of science; to the development and organization of scientific education; to the endless series of battles and skirmishes over evolution; and to untiring opposition to that ecclesiastical spirit, that clericalism, which in England, as everywhere else, and to whatever denomination it may belong, is the deadly enemy of science.

In striving for the attainment of these

[6] *malgré moi:* in spite of myself.

objects, I have been but one among many, and I shall be well content to be remembered, or even not remembered, as such. Circumstances, among which I am proud to reckon the devoted kindness of many friends, have led to my occupation of various prominent positions, among which the Presidency of the Royal Society is the highest. It would be mock modesty on my part, with these and other scientific honors which have been bestowed upon me, to pretend that I have not succeeded in the career which I have followed, rather because I was driven into it than of my own free will; but I am afraid I should not count even these things as marks of success if I could not hope that I had somewhat helped that movement of opinion which has been called the New Reformation.   [1890]

THE METHOD BY WHICH THE CAUSES OF THE PRESENT AND PAST CONDITIONS OF ORGANIC NATURE ARE TO BE DISCOVERED

In the two preceding lectures I have endeavored to indicate to you the extent of the subject-matter of the inquiry upon which we are engaged; and having thus acquired some conception of the past and present phenomena of organic nature, I must now turn to that which constitutes the great problem which we have set before ourselves—I mean, the question of what knowledge we have of the causes of these phenomena of organic nature, and how such knowledge is obtainable.

Here, on the threshold of the inquiry, an objection meets us. There are in the world a number of extremely worthy, well-meaning persons, whose judgments and opinions are entitled to the utmost respect on account of their sincerity, who are of opinion that vital phenomena, and especially all questions relating to the origin of vital phenomena, are questions quite apart from the ordinary run of inquiry, and are, by their very nature, placed out of our reach. They say that all these phenomena originated miraculously, or in some way totally different from the ordinary course of nature, and that therefore they conceive it to be futile, not to say presumptuous, to attempt to inquire into them.

To such sincere and earnest persons, I would only say that a question of this kind is not to be shelved upon theoretical or speculative grounds. You may remember the story of the Sophist who demonstrated to Diogenes in the most complete and satisfactory manner that he could not walk; that, in fact, all motion was an impossibility; and that Diogenes refuted him by simply getting up and walking round his tub. So, in the same way, the man of science replies to objections of this kind, by simply getting up and walking onward, and showing what science has done and is doing—by pointing to that immense mass of facts which have been ascertained and systematized under the forms of the great doctrines of morphology, of development, of distribution, and the like. He sees an enormous mass of facts and laws relating to organic beings, which stand on the same sound foundation as every other natural law. With this mass of facts and laws before us, therefore, seeing that, as far as organic matters have hitherto been accessible and studied, they have shown themselves capable of yielding to scientific investigation, we may accept this as proof that order and law reign there as well as in the rest of nature. The man of science says nothing to objectors of this sort, but supposes that we can and shall walk to a knowledge of the origin of organic nature, in the same way that we have walked to a knowledge of the laws and principles of the inorganic world.

But there are objectors who say the same from ignorance and ill-will. To such I would reply that the objection comes ill from them, and that the real presumption, I may almost say the real blasphemy, in this matter, is in the attempt to limit that inquiry into the causes of phenomena, which is the source of all human blessings, and from which has sprung all human prosperity and progress; for, after all, we can accomplish comparatively little; the limited range of our own faculties bounds us on every side—the field of our powers of observation is small enough, and he who endeavors to narrow the sphere of our inquiries is only pursuing a course that is likely to produce the greatest harm to his fellow men.

But now, assuming, as we all do, I hope, that these phenomena are properly accessible to inquiry, and setting out upon our search into the causes of the phenomena of organic nature, or, at any rate, setting out to discover how much we at present know upon these abstruse matters, the question arises as to what is to be our course of proceeding, and what method we must lay down for our guidance. I reply to that question that our method must be exactly the same as that which is pursued in any other scientific inquiry, the method of scientific investigation being the same for all orders of facts and phenomena whatsoever.

I must dwell a little on this point, for I wish you to leave this room with a very clear conviction that scientific investigation is not, as many people seem to suppose, some kind of modern black art. I say that you might easily gather this impression from the manner in which many persons speak of scientific inquiry, or talk about inductive and deductive philosophy, or the principles of the "Baconian philosophy." I do protest that, of the vast number of cants in this world, there are none, to my mind, so contemptible as the pseudoscientific cant which is talked about the "Baconian philosophy."

To hear people talk about the great Chancellor—and a very great man he certainly was—you would think that it was he who had invented science, and that there was no such thing as sound reasoning before the time of Queen Elizabeth! Of course, you say, that cannot possibly be true; you perceive, on a moment's reflection, that such an idea is absurdly wrong, and yet, so firmly rooted is this sort of impression—I cannot call it an idea, or conception—the thing is too absurd to be entertained—but so completely does it exist at the bottom of most men's minds, that this has been a matter of observation with me for many years past. There are many men who, though knowing absolutely nothing of the subject with which they may be dealing, wish, nevertheless, to damage the author of some view with which they think fit to disagree. What they do, then, is not to go and learn something about the subject, which one would naturally think the best way of fairly dealing with it; but they abuse the originator of the view they question, in a general manner, and wind up by saying that, "After all, you know, the principles and method of this author are totally opposed to the canons of the Baconian philosophy." Then everybody applauds, as a matter of course, and agrees that it must be so. But if you were to stop them all in the middle of their applause, you would probably find that neither the speaker nor his applauders could tell you how or in what way it was so; neither the one nor the other having the slightest idea of what they mean when they speak of the "Baconian philosophy."

You will understand, I hope, that I have not the slightest desire to join in the outcry against either the morals, the intellect, or the great genius of Lord Chancellor Bacon. He was undoubtedly a very great man, let people say what they will of him; but notwithstanding all that he did for philosophy, it would be entirely wrong to suppose that the methods of modern scientific inquiry originated with him, or with his age; they originated with the first man, whoever he was; and indeed existed long before him, for many of the essential processes of reasoning are exerted by the higher order of brutes as completely and effectively as by ourselves. We see in many of the brute creation the exercise of one, at least, of the same powers of reasoning as that which we ourselves employ.

The method of scientific investigation is nothing but the expression of the necessary mode of working of the human mind. It is simply the mode at which all phenomena are reasoned about, rendered precise and exact. There is no more difference, but there is just the same kind of difference, between the mental operations of a man of science and those of an ordinary person, as there is between the operations and methods of a baker or of a butcher weighing out his goods in common scales, and the operations of a chemist in performing a difficult and complex analysis by means of his balance and finely graduated weights. It is not that the action of the scales in the one case, and the balance in the other, differ in the principles of their construction or manner of working; but the beam of one is set on an infinitely finer axis than the other, and of course turns by the addition of a much smaller weight.

You will understand this better, perhaps, if I give you some familiar example. You have all heard it repeated, I dare say, that men of science work by means of induction and deduction, and that, by the help of these operations, they, in a sort of sense, wring from Nature certain other things, which are called natural laws, and causes, and that out of these, by some cunning skill of their own, they build up hypotheses and theories. And it is imagined by many that the operations of the common mind can be by no means compared with these processes, and that they have to be acquired by a sort of special apprenticeship to the craft. To hear all these large words, you would think that the mind of a man of science must be constituted differently from that of his fellow men; but if you will not be frightened by terms, you will discover that you are quite wrong, and that all these terrible apparatus are being used by yourselves every day and every hour of your lives.

There is a well-known incident in one of Molière's plays, where the author makes the hero express unbounded delight on being told that he had been talking prose during the whole of his life. In the same way, I trust that you will take comfort, and be delighted with yourselves, on the discovery that you have been acting on the principles of inductive and deductive philosophy during the same period. Probably there is not one here who has not in the course of the day had occasion to set in motion a complex train of reasoning, of the very same kind, though differing of course in degree, as that which a scientific man goes through in tracing the causes of natural phenomena.

A very trivial circumstance will serve to exemplify this. Suppose you go into a fruiterer's shop, wanting an apple—you take up one, and, on biting it, you find it is sour; you look at it, and see that it is hard and green. You take up another one, and that too is hard, green, and sour. The shopman offers you a third; but, before biting it, you examine it, and find that it is hard and green, and you immediately say that you will not have it, as it must be sour, like those that you have already tried.

Nothing can be more simple than that, you think; but if you will take the trouble to analyze and trace out into its logical elements what has been done by the mind, you will be greatly surprised. In the first place, you have performed the operation of induction. You found that, in two experiences, hardness and greenness in apples went together with sourness. It was so in the first case, and it was confirmed by the second. True, it is a very small basis, but still it is enough to make an induction from; you generalize the facts, and you expect to find sourness in apples where you get hardness and greenness. You found upon that a general law that all hard and green apples are sour; and that, so far as it goes, is a perfect induction. Well, having got your natural law in this way, when you are offered another apple which you find is hard and green, you say, "All hard and green apples are sour; this apple is hard and green; therefore, this apple is sour." That train of reasoning is what logicians call a syllogism, and has all its various parts and terms—its major premise, its minor premise, and its conclusion. And, by the help of further reasoning, which, if drawn out, would have to be exhibited in two or three other syllogisms, you arrive at your final determination, "I will not have that apple." So that, you see, you have, in the first place, established a law by induction, and upon that you have founded a deduction, and reasoned out the special conclusion of the particular case. Well now, suppose, having got your law, that, at some time afterwards, you are discussing the qualities of apples with a friend: you will say to him, "It is a very curious thing—but I find that all hard and green apples are sour!" Your friend says to you, "But how do you know that?" You at once reply, "Oh, because I have tried them over and over again, and have always found them to be so." Well, if we were talking science instead of common sense, we should call that an experimental verification. And, if still opposed, you go

further, and say, "I have heard from the people in Somersetshire and Devonshire, where a large number of apples are grown, that they have observed the same thing. It is also found to be the case in Normandy, and in North America. In short, I find it to be the universal experience of mankind wherever attention has been directed to the subject." Whereupon, your friend, unless he is a very unreasonable man, agrees with you, and is convinced that you are quite right in the conclusion you have drawn. He believes, although perhaps he does not know he believes it, that the more extensive verifications are—that the more frequently experiments have been made and results of the same kind arrived at—that the more varied the conditions under which the same results are attained, the more certain is the ultimate conclusion, and he disputes the question no further. He sees that the experiment has been tried under all sorts of conditions, as to time, place, and people, with the same result; and he says with you, therefore, that the law you have laid down must be a good one, and he must believe it.

In science we do the same thing—the philosopher exercises precisely the same faculties, though in a much more delicate manner. In scientific inquiry it becomes a matter of duty to expose a supposed law to every possible kind of verification, and to take care, moreover, that this is done intentionally, and not left to a mere accident, as in the case of the apples. And in science, as in common life, our confidence in a law is in exact proportion to the absence of variation in the result of our experimental verifications. For instance, if you let go your grasp of an article you may have in your hand, it will immediately fall to the ground. That is a very common verification of one of the best established laws of nature—that of gravitation. The method by which men of science establish the existence of that law is exactly the same as that by which we have established the trivial proposition about the sourness of hard and green apples. But we believe it in such an extensive, thorough, and unhesitating manner because the universal experience of mankind verifies it, and we can verify it ourselves at any time; and that is the strongest possible foundation on which any natural law can rest.

So much, then, by way of proof that the method of establishing laws in science is exactly the same as that pursued in common life. Let us now turn to another matter (though really it is but another phase of the same question), and that is, the method by which, from the relations of certain phenomena, we prove that some stand in the position of causes towards the others.

I want to put the case clearly before you, and I will therefore show you what I mean by another familiar example. I will suppose that one of you, on coming down in the morning to the parlor of your house, finds that a teapot and some spoons which had been left in the room on the previous evening are gone—the window is open, and you observe the mark of a dirty hand on the window frame, and perhaps, in addition to that, you notice the impress of a hobnailed shoe on the gravel outside. All these phenomena have struck your attention instantly, and before two seconds have passed you say, "Oh, somebody has broken open the window, entered the room, and run off with the spoons and the teapot!" That speech is out of your mouth in a moment. And you will probably add, "I know there has; I am quite sure of it!" You mean to say exactly what you know; but in reality you are giving expression to what is, in all essential particulars, an hypothesis. You do not *know* it at all; it is nothing but an hypothesis rapidly framed in your own mind. And it is an hypothesis founded on a long train of inductions and deductions.

What are those inductions and deductions, and how have you got at this hypothesis? You have observed, in the first place, that the window is open; but by a train of reasoning involving many inductions and deductions, you have probably arrived long before at the general law—and a very good one it is—that windows do not open of themselves; and you therefore conclude that something has opened the window. A second general law that you have arrived at in the same way is, that teapots and spoons do not go out of a window spontaneously, and you are satisfied that,

as they are not now where you left them, they have been removed. In the third place, you look at the marks on the window sill, and the shoe marks outside, and you say that in all previous experience the former kind of mark has never been produced by anything else but the hand of a human being; and the same experience shows that no other animal but man at present wears shoes with hobnails in them such as would produce the marks in the gravel. I do not know, even if we could discover any of those "missing links" that are talked about, that they would help us to any other conclusion! At any rate the law which states our present experience is strong enough for my present purpose. You next reach the conclusion that, as these kinds of marks have not been left by any other animals than men, or are liable to be formed in any other way than by a man's hand and shoe, the marks in question have been formed by a man in that way. You have, further, a general law, founded on observation and experience, and that, too, is, I am sorry to say, a very universal and unimpeachable one—that some men are thieves; and you assume at once from all these premises—and that is what constitutes your hypothesis—that the man who made the marks outside and on the window sill, opened the window, got into the room, and stole your teapot and spoons. You have now arrived at a *vera causa*—you have assumed a cause which, it is plain, is competent to produce all the phenomena you have observed. You can explain all these phenomena only by the hypothesis of a thief. But that is a hypothetical conclusion, of the justice of which you have no absolute proof at all; it is only rendered highly probable by a series of inductive and deductive reasonings.

I suppose your first action, assuming that you are a man of ordinary common sense, and that you have established this hypothesis to your own satisfaction, will very likely be to go off for the police, and set them on the track of the burglar, with the view to the recovery of your property. But just as you are starting with this object, some person comes in, and on learning what you are about, says, "My good friend, you are going on a great deal too fast.

How do you know that the man who really made the marks took the spoons? It might have been a monkey that took them, and the man may have merely looked in afterwards." You would probably reply, "Well, that is all very well, but you see it is contrary to all experience of the way teapots and spoons are abstracted; so that, at any rate, your hypothesis is less probable than mine." While you are talking the thing over in this way, another friend arrives, one of that good kind of people that I was talking of a little while ago. And he might say, "Oh, my dear sir, you are certainly going on a great deal too fast. You are most presumptuous. You admit that all these occurrences took place when you were fast asleep, at a time when you could not possibly have known anything about what was taking place. How do you know that the laws of Nature are not suspended during the night? It may be that there has been some kind of supernatural interference in this case." In point of fact, he declares that your hypothesis is one of which you cannot at all demonstrate the truth, and that you are by no means sure that the laws of Nature are the same when you are asleep as when you are awake.

Well, now, you cannot at the moment answer that kind of reasoning. You feel that your worthy friend has you somewhat at a disadvantage. You will feel perfectly convinced in your own mind, however, that you are quite right, and you say to him, "My good friend, I can only be guided by the natural probabilities of the case, and if you will be kind enough to stand aside and permit me to pass, I will go and fetch the police." Well, we will suppose that your journey is successful, and that by good luck you meet with a policeman; that eventually the burglar is found with your property on his person, and the marks correspond to his hand and to his boots. Probably any jury would consider those facts a very good experimental verification of your hypothesis touching the cause of the abnormal phenomena observed in your parlor, and would act accordingly.

Now, in this supposititious case, I have taken phenomena of a very common kind, in order that you might see what are the different steps in an ordinary process of reasoning, if you will only take the trouble to analyze it carefully. All the operations I have described, you will see, are involved in the mind of any man of sense in leading him to a conclusion as to the course he should take in order to make good a robbery and punish the offender. I say that you are led, in that case, to your conclusion by exactly the same train of reasoning as that which a man of science pursues when he is endeavoring to discover the origin and laws of the most occult phenomena. The process is, and always must be, the same; and precisely the same mode of reasoning was employed by Newton and Laplace in their endeavors to discover and define the causes of the movements of the heavenly bodies, as you, with your own common sense, would employ to detect a burglar. The only difference is that, the nature of the inquiry being more abstruse, every step has to be most carefully watched, so that there may not be a single crack or flaw in your hypothesis. A flaw or crack in many of the hypotheses of daily life may be of little or no moment as affecting the general correctness of the conclusions at which we may arive; but, in a scientific inquiry, a fallacy, great or small, is always of importance, and is sure to be in the long run constantly productive of mischievous, if not fatal, results.

Do not allow yourselves to be misled by the common notion that an hypothesis is untrustworthy simply because it is an hypothesis. It is often urged, in respect to some scientific conclusion, that, after all, it is only an hypothesis. But what more have we to guide us in nine-tenths of the most important affairs of daily life than hypotheses, and often very ill-based ones? So that in science, where the evidence of an hypothesis is subjected to the most rigid examination, we may rightly pursue the same course. You may have hypotheses, and hypotheses. A man may say, if he likes, that the moon is made of green cheese—that is an hypothesis. But another man, who has devoted a great deal of time and attention to the subject, and availed himself of the most powerful telescope and the results of the observations of others, declares that in his opinion it is probably composed of materials very similar to those of which our own earth is made up—and that is also only an hypothesis. But I need not tell you that there is an enormous difference in the value of the two hypotheses. That one which is based on sound scientific knowledge is sure to have a corresponding value; and that which is a mere hasty random guess is likely to have but 10 little value. Every great step in our progress in discovering causes has been made in exactly the same way as that which I have detailed to you. A person observing the occurrence of certain facts and phenomena asks, naturally enough, what process, what kind of operation known to occur in Nature applied to the particular case, will unravel and explain the mystery? Hence you have the scientific hypothesis; and its 20 value will be proportionate to the care and completeness with which its basis has been tested and verified. It is in these matters as in the commonest affairs of practical life: the guess of the fool will be folly, while the guess of the wise man will contain wisdom. In all cases, you see that the value of the result depends on the patience and faithfulness with which the investigator applies to his hypothesis every possible kind of 30 verification.

[1863]

ON THE ADVISABLENESS OF IMPROVING NATURAL KNOWLEDGE

This time two hundred years ago—in the beginning of January, 1666—those of our 40 forefathers who inhabited this great and ancient city, took breath between the shocks of two fearful calamities: one not quite past, although its fury had abated; the other to come.

Within a few yards of the very spot on which we are assembled, so the tradition runs, that painful and deadly malady, the plague, appeared in the latter months of 1664; and, though no new visitor, smote 50 the people of England, and especially of her capital, with a violence unknown before, in the course of the following year.

The hand of a master has pictured what happened in those dismal months; and in that truest of fictions, *The History of the Plague Year,* Defoe shows death, with every accompaniment of pain and terror, stalking through the narrow streets of old London, and changing their busy hum into a silence broken only by the wailing of the mourners of fifty thousand dead; by the woeful denunciations and mad prayers of fanatics; and by the madder yells of despairing profligates.

But, about this time in 1666, the death-rate had sunk to nearly its ordinary amount; a case of plague occurred only here and there, and the richer citizens who had flown from the pest had returned to their dwellings. The remnant of the people began to toil at the accustomed round of duty, or of pleasure; and the stream of city life bid fair to flow back along its old bed, with renewed and uninterrupted vigor.

The newly-kindled hope was deceitful. The great plague, indeed, returned no more; but what it had done for the Londoners, the great fire, which broke out in the autumn of 1666, did for London; and, in September of that year, a heap of ashes and the indestructible energy of the people were all that remained of the glory of five-sixths of the city within the walls.

Our forefathers had their own ways of accounting for each of these calamities. They submitted to the plague in humility and in penitence, for they believed it to be the judgment of God. But, towards the fire they were furiously indignant, interpreting it as the effect of the malice of man,—as the work of the Republicans, or of the Papists, according as their prepossessions ran in favor of loyalty or of Puritanism.

It would, I fancy, have fared but ill with one who, standing where I now stand, in what was then a thickly-peopled and fashionable part of London, should have broached to our ancestors the doctrine which I now propound to you—that all their hypotheses were alike wrong; that the plague was no more, in their sense, Divine judgment, than the fire was the work of any political, or of any religious, sect; but that they were themselves the authors of both plague and fire, and that they must look to themselves to prevent the recurrence of calamities, to all appearance so peculiarly beyond the reach of human control—so evidently the result of the wrath of God, or of the craft and subtlety of an enemy.

And one may picture to one's self how harmoniously the holy cursing of the Puritan of that day would have chimed in with the unholy cursing and the crackling wit of the Rochesters and Sedleys, and with the reviling of the political fanatics, if my imaginary plain dealer had gone on to say that, if the return of such misfortunes were ever rendered impossible, it would not be in virtue of the victory of the faith of Laud, or of that of Milton; and, as little, by the triumph of republicanism, as by that of monarchy. But that the one thing needful for compassing this end was, that the people of England should second the efforts of an insignificant corporation, the establishment of which, a few years before the epoch of the great plague and the great fire, had been as little noticed, as they were conspicuous.

Some twenty years before the outbreak of the plague a few calm and thoughtful students banded themselves together for the purpose, as they phrased it, of "improving natural knowledge." The ends they proposed to attain cannot be stated more clearly than in the words of one of the founders of the organization:—

"Our business was (precluding matters of theology and state affairs) to discourse and consider of philosophical enquiries, and such as related thereunto:—as Physick, Anatomy, Geometry, Astronomy, Navigation, Staticks, Magneticks, Chymicks, Mechanicks, and Natural Experiments; with the state of these studies and their cultivation at home and abroad. We then discoursed of the circulation of the blood, the valves in the veins, the venæ lacteæ,[1] the lymphatic vessels, the Copernican hypothesis, the nature of comets and new stars, the satellites of Jupiter, the oval shape (as it then appeared) of Saturn, the spots on the sun and its turning on its own axis, the inequalities and selenography of the moon, the several phases of Venus and Mercury, the improvement of telescopes and grinding of glasses for that purpose, the weight of air, the possibility or impossibility of vacuities and nature's abhorrence thereof, the Torricellian experiment in quicksilver, the descent of heavy bodies and the degree of acceleration therein, with divers other things of like nature, some of which were then but new discoveries, and others not so generally known and embraced as now they are; with other things appertaining to what hath been called the New Philosophy, which from the times of Galileo at Florence, and Sir Francis Bacon (Lord Verulam) in England, hath been much cultivated in Italy, France, Germany, and other parts abroad, as well as with us in England."

The learned Dr. Wallis, writing in 1696, narrates in these words what happened half a century before, or about 1645. The associates met at Oxford, in the rooms of Dr. Wilkins, who was destined to become a bishop; and subsequently coming together in London, they attracted the notice of the king. And it is a strange evidence of the taste for knowledge which the most obviously worthless of the Stuarts shared with his father and grandfather, that Charles the Second was not content with saying witty things about his philosophers, but did wise things with regard to them. For he not only bestowed upon them such attention as he could spare from his poodles and his mistresses, but, being in his usual state of impecuniosity, begged for them of the Duke of Ormond; and, that step being without effect, gave them Chelsea College, a charter, and a mace: crowning his favors in the best way they could be crowned, by burdening them no further with royal patronage or state interference.

Thus it was that the half-dozen young men, studious of the "New Philosophy," who met in one another's lodgings in Oxford or in London, in the middle of the seventeenth century, grew in numerical and in real strength, until, in its latter part, the "Royal Society for the Improvement of Natural Knowledge" had already become famous, and had acquired a claim

---

[1] *venae lacteae:* lacteal veins.

upon the veneration of Englishmen, which it has ever since retained, as the principal focus of scientific activity in our islands, and the chief champion of the cause it was formed to support.

It was by the aid of the Royal Society that Newton published his *Principia*. If all the books in the world, except the *Philosophical Transactions*, were destroyed, it is safe to say that the foundations of physical science would remain unshaken, and that the vast intellectual progress of the last two centuries would be largely, though incompletely, recorded. Nor have any signs of halting or of decrepitude manifested themselves in our own times. As in Dr. Wallis's days, so in these, "our business is, precluding theology and state affairs, to discourse and consider of philosophical inquiries." But our "Mathematick" is one which Newton would have to go to school to learn; our "Staticks, Mechanicks, Magneticks, Chymicks, and Natural Experiments" constitute a mass of physical and chemical knowledge, a glimpse at which would compensate Galileo for the doings of a score of inquisitorial cardinals; our "Physick" and "Anatomy" have embraced such infinite varieties of beings, have laid open such new worlds in time and space, have grappled, not unsuccessfully, with such complex problems, that the eyes of Vesalius and of Harvey might be dazzled by the sight of the tree that has grown out of their grain of mustard seed.

The fact is perhaps rather too much, than too little, forced upon one's notice, nowadays, that all this marvelous intellectual growth has a no less wonderful expression in practical life; and that, in this respect, if in no other, the movement symbolized by the progress of the Royal Society stands without a parallel in the history of mankind.

A series of volumes as bulky as the *Transactions of the Royal Society* might possibly be filled with the subtle speculations of the Schoolmen; not improbably, the obtaining a mastery over the products of mediæval thought might necessitate an even greater expenditure of time and of energy than the acquirement of the "New Philosophy"; but though such work engrossed the best intellects of Europe for a longer time than has elapsed since the great fire, its effects were "writ in water," so far as our social state is concerned.

On the other hand, if the noble first President of the Royal Society could revisit the upper air and once more gladden his eyes with a sight of the familiar mace, he would find himself in the midst of a material civilization more different from that of his day, than that of the seventeenth was from that of the first century. And if Lord Brouncker's native sagacity had not deserted his ghost, he would need no long reflection to discover that all these great ships, these railways, these telegraphs, these factories, these printing-presses, without which the whole fabric of modern English society would collapse into a mass of stagnant and starving pauperism,—that all these pillars of our State are but the ripples and the bubbles upon the surface of that great spiritual stream, the springs of which only, he and his fellows were privileged to see; and seeing, to recognize as that which it behooved them above all things to keep pure and undefiled.

It may not be too great a flight of imagination to conceive our noble *revenant* not forgetful of the great troubles of his own day, and anxious to know how often London had been burned down since his time, and how often the plague had carried off its thousands. He would have to learn that, although London contains tenfold the inflammable matter that it did in 1666; though, not content with filling our rooms with woodwork and light draperies, we must needs lead inflammable and explosive gases into every corner of our streets and houses, we never allow even a street to burn down. And if he asked how this had come about, we should have to explain that the improvement of natural knowledge has furnished us with dozens of machines for throwing water upon fires, any one of which would have furnished the ingenious Mr. Hooke, the first "curator and experimenter" of the Royal Society, with ample materials for discourse before half a dozen meetings of that body; and that, to say truth, except for the progress of natural knowledge, we should not have been able to make even the tools by which these machines are constructed. And, further, it would be necessary to add, that although severe fires sometimes occur and inflict great damage, the loss is very generally compensated by societies, the operations of which have been rendered possible only by the progress of natural knowledge in the direction of mathematics, and the accumulation of wealth in virtue of other natural knowledge.

But the plague? My Lord Brouncker's observation would not, I fear, lead him to think that Englishmen of the nineteenth century are purer in life, or more fervent in religious faith, than the generation which could produce a Boyle, an Evelyn, and a Milton. He might find the mud of society at the bottom, instead of at the top, but fear that the sum total would be as deserving of swift judgment as at the time of the Restoration. And it would be our duty to explain once more, and this time not without shame, that we have no reason to believe that it is the improvement of our faith, nor that of our morals, which keeps the plague from our city; but, again that it is the improvement of our natural knowledge.

We have learned that pestilences will only take up their abode among those who have prepared unswept and ungarnished residences for them. Their cities must have narrow, unwatered streets, foul with accumulated garbage. Their houses must be ill-drained, ill-lighted, ill-ventilated. Their subjects must be ill-washed, ill-fed, ill-clothed. The London of 1665 was such a city. The cities of the East, where plague has an enduring dwelling, are such cities. We, in later times, have learned somewhat of Nature, and partly obey her. Because of this partial improvement of our natural knowledge and of that fractional obedience, we have no plague; because that knowledge is still very imperfect and that obedience yet incomplete, typhoid is our companion and cholera our visitor. But it is not presumptuous to express the belief that, when our knowledge is more complete and our obedience the expression of our knowledge, London will count her centuries of freedom from typhoid and cholera, as she now gratefully reckons her two hundred years of ignorance of that plague which swooped upon her thrice in the first half of the seventeenth century.

Surely, there is nothing in these explanations which is not fully borne out by the facts? Surely, the principles involved in them are now admitted among the fixed beliefs of all thinking men? Surely, it is true that our countrymen are less subject to fire, famine, pestilence, and all the evils which result from a want of command over and due anticipation of the course of Nature, than were the countrymen of Milton; and health, wealth, and well-being are more abundant with us than with them? But no less certainly is the difference due to the improvement of our knowledge of Nature, and the extent to which that improved knowledge has been incorporated with the household words of men, and has supplied the springs of their daily actions.

Granting for a moment, then, the truth of that which the depreciators of natural knowledge are so fond of urging, that its improvement can only add to the resources of our material civilization; admitting it to be possible that the founders of the Royal Society themselves looked for no other reward than this, I cannot confess that I was guilty of exaggeration when I hinted, that to him who had the gift of distinguishing between prominent events and important events, the origin of a combined effort on the part of mankind to improve natural knowledge might have loomed larger than the Plague and have outshone the glare of the Fire; as a something fraught with a wealth of beneficence to mankind, in comparison with which the damage done by those ghastly evils would shrink into insignificance.

It is very certain that for every victim slain by the plague, hundreds of mankind exist and find a fair share of happiness in the world by the aid of the spinning jenny. And the great fire, at its worst, could not have burned the supply of coal, the daily working of which, in the bowels of the earth, made possible by the steam pump, gives rise to an amount of wealth to which the millions lost in old London are but as an old song.

But spinning jenny and steam pump are, after all, but toys, possessing an accidental value; and natural knowledge creates multitudes of more subtle contrivances, the praises of which do not happen to be sung because they are not directly convertible into instruments for creating wealth. When I contemplate natural knowledge squandering such gifts among men, the only appropriate comparison I can find for her is, to liken her to such a peasant woman as one sees in the Alps, striding ever upward, heavily burdened, and with mind bent only on her home; but yet without effort and without thought, knitting for her children. Now stockings are good and comfortable things, and the children will undoubtedly be much the better for them; but surely it would be short-sighted, to say the least of it, to depreciate this toiling mother as a mere stocking-machine— a mere provider of physical comforts?

However, there are blind leaders of the blind, and not a few of them, who take this view of natural knowledge, and can see nothing in the bountiful mother of humanity but a sort of comfort-grinding machine. According to them, the improvement of natural knowledge always has been, and always must be, synonymous with no more than the improvement of the material resources and the increase of the gratifications of men.

Natural knowledge is, in their eyes, no real mother of mankind, bringing them up with kindness, and, if need be, with sternness, in the way they should go, and instructing them in all things needful for their welfare; but a sort of fairy godmother, ready to furnish her pets with shoes of swiftness, swords of sharpness, and omnipotent Aladdin's lamps, so that they may have telegraphs to Saturn, and see the other side of the moon, and thank God they are better than their benighted ancestors.

If this talk were true, I, for one, should not greatly care to toil in the service of natural knowledge. I think I would just as soon be quietly chipping my own flint axe, after the manner of my forefathers a few thousand years back, as be troubled with the endless malady of thought which now infests us all, for such reward. But I venture to say that such views are contrary alike to reason and to fact. Those who

discourse in such fashion seem to me to be so intent upon trying to see what is above Nature, or what is behind her, that they are blind to what stares them in the face in her.

I should not venture to speak thus strongly if my justification were not to be found in the simplest and most obvious facts,—if it needed more than an appeal to the most notorious truths to justify my assertion, that the improvement of natural knowledge, whatever direction it has taken, and however low the aims of those who may have commenced it—has not only conferred practical benefits on men, but, in so doing, has effected a revolution in their conceptions of the universe and of themselves, and has profoundly altered their modes of thinking and their views of right and wrong. I say that natural knowledge, seeking to satisfy natural wants, has found the ideas which can alone still spiritual cravings. I say that natural knowledge, in desiring to ascertain the laws of comfort, has been driven to discover those of conduct, and to lay the foundations of a new morality.

Let us take these points separately; and first, what great ideas has natural knowledge introduced into men's minds?

I cannot but think that the foundations of all natural knowledge were laid when the reason of man first came face to face with the facts of Nature; when the savage first learned that the fingers of one hand are fewer than those of both; that it is shorter to cross a stream than to head it; that a stone stops where it is unless it be moved, and that it drops from the hand which lets it go; that light and heat come and go with the sun; that sticks burn away in a fire; that plants and animals grow and die; that if he struck his fellow savage a blow he would make him angry, and perhaps get a blow in return, while if he offered him a fruit he would please him, and perhaps receive a fish in exchange. When men had acquired this much knowledge, the outlines, rude though they were, of mathematics, of physics, of chemistry, of biology, of moral, economical, and political science, were sketched. Nor did the germ of religion fail when science began to bud.

Listen to words which, though new, are yet three thousand years old:—

"...When in heaven the stars about the moon
Look beautiful, when all the winds are laid,
And every height comes out, and jutting peak
And valley, and the immeasurable heavens
Break open to their highest, and all the stars
Shine, and the shepherd gladdens in his
    heart."

If the half savage Greek could share our feelings thus far, it is irrational to doubt that he went further, to find as we do, that upon that brief gladness there follows a certain sorrow,—the little light of awakened human intelligence shines so mere a spark amidst the abyss of the unknown and unknowable; seems so insufficient to do more than illuminate the imperfections that cannot be remedied, the aspirations that cannot be realized, of man's own nature. But in this sadness, this consciousness of the limitation of man, this sense of an open secret which he cannot penetrate, lies the essence of all religion; and the attempt to embody it in the forms furnished by the intellect is the origin of the higher theologies.

Thus it seems impossible to imagine but that the foundations of all knowledge— secular or sacred—were laid when intelligence dawned, though the superstructure remained for long ages so slight and feeble as to be compatible with the existence of almost any general view respecting the mode of governance of the universe. No doubt, from the first, there were certain phenomena which, to the rudest mind, presented a constancy of occurrence, and suggested that a fixed order ruled, at any rate, among them. I doubt if the grossest of Fetish worshippers ever imagined that a stone must have a god within it to make it fall, or that a fruit had a god within it to make it taste sweet. With regard to such matters as these, it is hardly questionable that mankind from the first took strictly positive and scientific views.

But, with respect to all the less familiar occurrences which present themselves, uncultured man, no doubt, has always taken himself as the standard of comparison, as the centre and measure of the world; nor

could he well avoid doing so. And finding that his apparently uncaused will has a powerful effect in giving rise to many occurrences, he naturally enough ascribed other and greater events to other and greater volitions, and came to look upon the world and all that therein is, as the product of the volitions of persons like himself, but stronger, and capable of being appeased or angered, as he himself might be soothed or irritated. Through such conceptions of the plan and working of the universe all mankind have passed, or are passing. And we may now consider what has been the effect of the improvement of natural knowledge on the views of men who have reached this stage, and who have begun to cultivate natural knowledge with no desire but that of "increasing God's honor and bettering man's estate."

For example, what could seem wiser, from a mere material point of view, more innocent, from a theological one, to an ancient people, than that they should learn the exact succession of the seasons, as warnings for their husbandmen; or the position of the stars, as guides to their rude navigators? But what has grown out of this search for natural knowledge of so merely useful a character? You all know the reply. Astronomy,—which of all sciences has filled men's minds with general ideas of a character most foreign to their daily experience, and has, more than any other, rendered it impossible for them to accept the beliefs of their fathers. Astronomy,—which tells them that this so vast and seemingly solid earth is but an atom among atoms, whirling, no man knows whither, through illimitable space; which demonstrates that what we call the peaceful heaven above us, is but that space, filled by an infinitely subtle manner whose particles are seething and surging, like the waves of an angry sea; which opens up to us infinite regions where nothing is known, or ever seems to have been known, but matter and force, operating according to rigid rules; which leads us to contemplate phenomena the very nature of which demonstrates that they must have had a beginning, and that they must have an end, but the very nature of which also proves that the beginning was, to our conceptions of time, infinitely remote, and that the end is as immeasurably distant.

But it is not alone those who pursue astronomy who ask for bread and receive ideas. What more harmless than the attempt to lift and distribute water by pumping it; what more absolutely and grossly utilitarian? Yet out of pumps grew the discussions about Nature's abhorrence of a vacuum; and then it was discovered that Nature does not abhor a vacuum, but that air has weight; and that notion paved the way for the doctrine that all matter has weight, and that the force which produces weight is coextensive with the universe,— in short, to the theory of universal gravitation and endless force. While learning how to handle gases led to the discovery of oxygen, and to modern chemistry, and to the notion of the indestructibility of matter.

Again, what simpler, or more absolutely practical, than the attempt to keep the axle of a wheel from heating when the wheel turns around very fast? How useful for carters and gig drivers to know something about this; and how good were it, if any ingenious person would find out the cause of such phenomena, and thence educe a general remedy for them. Such an ingenious person was Count Rumford; and he and his successors have landed us in the theory of the persistence, or indestructibility, of force. And in the infinitely minute, as in the infinitely great, the seekers after natural knowledge of the kinds called physical and chemical, have everywhere found a definite order and succession of events which seem never to be infringed.

And how has it fared with "Physick" and Anatomy? Have the anatomist, the physiologist, or the physician, whose business it has been to devote themselves assiduously to that eminently practical and direct end, the alleviation of the sufferings of mankind,—have they been able to confine their vision more absolutely to the strictly useful? I fear they are the worst offenders of all. For if the astronomer has set before us the infinite magnitude of space, and the practical eternity of the duration of the universe; if the physical and chemical philosophers have demonstrated the infinite minuteness of its constituent parts, and the practical eternity of matter and of force; and if both have alike proclaimed the universality of a definite and predictable order and succession of events, the workers in biology have not only accepted all these, but have added more startling theses of their own. For, as the astronomers discover in the earth no centre of the universe, but an eccentric speck, so the naturalists find man to be no centre of the living world, but one amidst endless modifications of life; and as the astronomer observes the mark of practically endless time set upon the arrangements of the solar system, so the student of life finds the records of ancient forms of existence peopling the world for ages, which, in relation to human experience, are infinite.

Furthermore, the physiologist finds life to be as dependent for its manifestation on particular molecular arrangements as any physical or chemical phenomenon; and wherever he extends his researches, fixed order and unchanging causation reveal themselves, as plainly as in the rest of Nature.

Nor can I find that any other fate has awaited the germ of Religion. Arising, like all other kinds of knowledge, out of the action and interaction of man's mind, with that which is not man's mind, it has taken the intellectual coverings of Fetishism or Polytheism; of Theism or Atheism; of Superstition or Rationalism. With these, and their relative merits and demerits, I have nothing to do; but this it is needful for my purpose to say, that if the religion of the present differs from that of the past, it is because the theology of the present has become more scientific than that of the past; because it has not only renounced idols of wood and idols of stone, but begins to see the necessity of breaking in pieces the idols built up of books and traditions and fine-spun ecclesiastical cobwebs: and of cherishing the noblest and most human of man's emotions, by worship "for the most part of the silent sort" at the Altar of the Unknown.

Such are a few of the new conceptions implanted in our minds by the improvement of natural knowledge. Men have acquired the ideas of the practically infinite extent of the universe and of its practical eternity; they are familiar with the conception that our earth is but an infinitesimal fragment of that part of the universe which can be seen; and that, nevertheless, its duration is, as compared with our standards of time, infinite. They have further acquired the idea that man is but one of innumerable forms of life now existing on the globe, and that the present existences are but the last of an immeasurable series of predecessors. Moreover, every step they have made in natural knowledge has tended to extend and rivet in their minds the conception of a definite order of the universe—which is embodied in what are called, by an unhappy metaphor, the laws of Nature—and to narrow the range and loosen the force of men's belief in spontaneity, or in changes other than such as arise out of that definite order itself.

Whether these ideas are well or ill founded is not the question. No one can deny that they exist, and have been the inevitable outgrowth of the improvement of natural knowledge. And if so, it cannot be doubted that they are changing the form of men's most cherished and most important convictions.

And as regards the second point—the extent to which the improvement of natural knowledge has remodeled and altered what may be termed the intellectual ethics of men,—what are among the moral convictions most fondly held by barbarous and semi-barbarous people?

They are the convictions that authority is the soundest basis of belief; that merit attaches to a readiness to believe; that the doubting disposition is a bad one, and scepticism a sin; that when good authority has pronounced what is to be believed, and faith has accepted it, reason has no further duty. There are many excellent persons who yet hold by these principles, and it is not my present business, or intention, to discuss their views. All I wish to bring clearly before your minds is the unquestionable fact, that the improvement of natural knowledge is effected by methods which directly give the lie to all these convictions, and assume the exact reverse of each to be true.

The improver of natural knowledge absolutely refuses to acknowledge authority, as such. For him, scepticism is the highest of duties; blind faith the one unpardonable sin. And it cannot be otherwise, for every great advance in natural knowledge has involved the absolute rejection of authority, the cherishing of the keenest scepticism, the annihilation of the spirit of blind faith; and the most ardent votary of science holds his firmest convictions, not because the men he most venerates hold them; not because their verity is testified by portents and wonders; but because his experience teaches him that whenever he chooses to bring these convictions into contact with their primary source, Nature—whenever he thinks fit to test them by appealing to experiment and to observation—Nature will confirm them. The man of science has learned to believe in justification, not by faith but by verification.

Thus, without for a moment pretending to despise the practical results of improvement of natural knowledge, and its beneficial influence on material civilization, it must, I think, be admitted that the great ideas, some of which I have indicated, and the ethical spirit which I have endeavored to sketch, in the few moments which remained at my disposal, constitute the real and permanent significance of natural knowledge.

If these ideas be destined, as I believe they are, to be more and more firmly established as the world grows older; if that spirit be fated, as I believe it is, to extend itself into all departments of human thought, and to become co-extensive with the range of knowledge; if, as our race approaches its maturity, it discovers, as I believe it will, that there is but one kind of knowledge and but one method of acquiring it; then we, who are still children, may justly feel it our highest duty to recognize the advisableness of improving natural knowledge, and so to aid ourselves and our successors in our course towards the noble goal which lies before mankind.

[1866]

A LIBERAL EDUCATION, AND WHERE TO FIND IT

The business which the South London Workingmen's College has undertaken is a great work; indeed, I might say, that Education, with which that College proposes to grapple, is the greatest work of all those which lie ready to a man's hand just at present.

And, at length, this fact is becoming generally recognized. You cannot go anywhere without hearing a buzz of more or less confused and contradictory talk on this subject—nor can you fail to notice that, in one point at any rate, there is a very decided advance upon like discussions in former days. Nobody outside the agricultural interest now dares to say that education is a bad thing. If any representative of the once large and powerful party, which, in former days, proclaimed this opinion, still exists in a semifossil state, he keeps his thoughts to himself. In fact, there is a chorus of voices, almost distressing in their harmony, raised in favor of the doctrine that education is the great panacea for human troubles, and that, if the country is not shortly to go to the dogs, everybody must be educated.

The politicians tells us, "You must educate the masses because they are going to be masters." The clergy join in the cry for education, for they affirm that the people are drifting away from church and chapel into the broadest infidelity. The manufacturers and the capitalists swell the chorus lustily. They declare that ignorance makes bad workmen; that England will soon be unable to turn out cotton goods, or steam engines, cheaper than other people; and then, Ichabod! Ichabod! the glory will be departed from us. And a few voices are lifted up in favor of the doctrine that the masses should be educated because they are men and women with unlimited capacities of being, doing, and suffering, and that it is as true now, as ever it was, that the people perish for lack of knowledge.

These members of the minority, with whom I confess I have a good deal of sympathy, are doubtful whether any of the other reasons urged in favor of the education of the people are of much value—whether, indeed, some of them are based upon either wise or noble grounds of action. They question if it be wise to tell people that you will do for them, out of fear of their power, what you have left undone, so long as your only motive was compassion for their weakness and their sorrows. And if ignorance of everything which it is needful a ruler should know is likely to do so much harm in the governing classes of the future, why is it, they ask reasonably enough, that such ignorance in the governing classes of the past has not been viewed with equal horror?

Compare the average artisan and the average country squire, and it may be doubted if you will find a pin to choose between the two in point of ignorance, class feeling, or prejudice. It is true that the ignorance is of a different sort—that the class feeling is in favor of a different class—and that the prejudice has a distinct savor of wrong-headedness in each case—but it is questionable if the one is either a bit better, or a bit worse, than the other. The old protectionist theory is the doctrine of trades unions as applied by the squires, and the modern trades unionism is the doctrine of the squires applied by the artisans. Why should we be worse off under one regime than under the other?

Again, this skeptical minority asks the clergy to think whether it is really want of education which keeps the masses away from their ministrations—whether the most completely educated men are not as open to reproach on this score as the workmen; and whether, perchance, this may not indicate that it is not education which lies at the bottom of the matter?

Once more, these people, whom there is no pleasing, venture to doubt whether the glory, which rests upon being able to undersell all the rest of the world, is a very safe kind of glory—whether we may not purchase it too dear; especially if we allow education, which ought to be directed to the making of men, to be diverted into a process of manufacturing human tools, wonderfully adroit in the exercise of some technical industry, but good for nothing else.

And, finally, these people inquire

whether it is the masses alone who need a reformed and improved education. They ask whether the richest of our public schools might not well be made to supply knowledge, as well as gentlemanly habits, a strong class feeling, and eminent proficiency in cricket. They seem to think that the noble foundations of our old universities are hardly fulfilling their functions in their present posture of half- clerical seminaries, half-racecourses, where men are trained to win a senior wrangler-ship, or a double first, as horses are trained to win a cup, with as little reference to the needs of after-life in the case of the man as in that of the racer. And while as zealous for education as the rest, they affirm that if the education of the richer classes were such as to fit them to be the leaders and the governors of the poorer, and if the education of the poorer classes were such as to enable them to appreciate really wise guidance and good governance, the politicians need not fear mob-law, nor the clergy lament their want of flocks, nor the capitalists prognosticate the annihilation of the prosperity of the country.

Such is the diversity of opinion upon the why and the wherefore of education. And my hearers will be prepared to expect that the practical recommendations which are put forward are not less discordant. There is a loud cry for compulsory education. We English, in spite of constant experience to the contrary, preserve a touching faith in the efficacy of acts of Parliament; and I believe we should have compulsory education in the course of next session if there were the least probability that half a dozen leading statesmen of different parties would agree what that education should be.

Some hold that education without theology is worse than none. Others maintain, quite as strongly, that education with theology is in the same predicament. But this is certain, that those who hold the first opinion can by no means agree what theology should be taught; and that those who maintain the second are in a small minority.

At any rate "make people learn to read, write, and cipher," say a great many; and the advice is undoubtedly sensible as far as it goes. But, as has happened to me in former days, those who, in despair of getting anything better, advocate this measure, are met with the objection that it is very like making a child practice the use of a knife, fork, and spoon, without giving it a particle of meat. I really don't know what reply is to be made to such an objection.

But it would be unprofitable to spend more time in disentangling, or rather in showing up the knots in, the raveled skeins of our neighbors. Much more to the purpose is it to ask if we possess any clue of our own which may guide us among these entanglements. And by way of a beginning, let us ask ourselves— What is education? Above all things, what is our ideal of a thoroughly liberal education?—of that education which, if we could begin life again, we would give ourselves—of that education which, if we could mold the fates to our own will, we would give our children? Well, I know not what may be your conceptions upon this matter, but I will tell you mine, and I hope I shall find that our views are not very discrepant.

Suppose it were perfectly certain that the life and fortune of every one of us would, one day or other, depend upon his winning or losing a game of chess. Don't you think that we should all consider it to be a primary duty to learn at least the names and the moves of the pieces; to have a notion of a gambit, and a keen eye for all the means of giving and getting out of check? Do you not think that we should look with a disapprobation amounting to scorn, upon the father who allowed his son, or the state which allowed its members, to grow up without knowing a pawn from a knight?

Yet, it is a very plain and elementary truth that the life, the fortune, and the happiness of every one of us, and, more or less, of those who are connected with us, do depend upon our knowing something of the rules of a game infinitely more difficult and complicated than chess. It is a game which has been played for untold ages, every man and woman of us being one of the two players in a game of his or her own. The chessboard is the world, the pieces are the phenomena of the universe, the rules of the game are what we call the laws of Nature. The player on the other side is hidden from us. We know that his play is always fair, just, and patient. But also we know, to our cost, that he never overlooks a mistake, or makes the smallest allowance for ignorance. To the man who plays well, the highest stakes are paid, with that sort of overflowing generosity with which the strong shows delight in strength. And one who plays ill is checkmated— without haste, but without remorse.

My metaphor will remind some of you of the famous picture in which Retzsch has depicted Satan playing at chess with man for his soul. Substitute for the mocking fiend in that picture a calm, strong angel who is playing for love, as we say, and would rather lose than win—and I should accept it as an image of human life.

Well, what I mean by Education is learning the rules of this mighty game. In other words, education is the instruction of the intellect in the laws of Nature, under which name I include not merely things and their forces, but men and their ways; and the fashioning of the affections and of the will into an earnest and loving desire to move in harmony with those laws. For me, education means neither more nor less than this. Anything which professes to call itself education must be tried by this standard, and if it fails to stand the test, I will not call it education, whatever may be the force of authority or of numbers upon the other side.

It is important to remember that, in strictness, there is no such thing as an uneducated man. Take an extreme case. Suppose that an adult man, in the full vigor of his faculties, could be suddenly placed in the world, as Adam is said to have been, and then left to do as he best might. How long would he be left uneducated? Not five minutes. Nature would begin to teach him, through the eye, the ear, the touch, the properties of objects. Pain and pleasure would be at his elbow telling him to do this and avoid that; and by slow degrees the man would receive an education which, if narrow, would be thorough, real, and adequate to his circumstances, though there would be no extras and very few accomplishments.

And if to this solitary man entered a second Adam, or, better still, an Eve, a new and greater world, that of social and moral phenomena, would be revealed. Joys and woes, compared with which all others might seem but faint shadows, would spring from the new relations. Happiness and sorrow would take the place of the coarser monitors, pleasure and pain; but conduct would still be shaped by the observation of the natural consequences of actions; or, in other words, by the laws of the nature of man.

To every one of us the world was once as fresh and new as to Adam. And then, long before we were susceptible of any other mode of instruction, Nature took us in hand, and every minute of waking life brought its educational influence, shaping our actions into rough accordance with Nature's laws, so that we might not be ended untimely by too gross disobedience. Nor should I speak of this process of education as past, for anyone, be he as old as he may. For every man the world is as fresh as it was at the first day, and as full of untold novelties for him who has the eyes to see them. And Nature is still continuing her patient education of us in that great university, the universe, of which we are all members—Nature having no Test Acts.

Those who take honors in Nature's university, who learn the laws which govern men and things and obey them, are the really great and successful men in this world. The great mass of mankind are the "Poll," who pick up just enough to get through without much discredit. Those who won't learn at all are plucked; and then you can't come up again. Nature's pluck means extermination.

Thus the question of compulsory education is settled so far as Nature is concerned. Her bill on that question was framed and passed long ago. But, like all compulsory legislation, that of Nature is harsh and wasteful in its operation. Ignorance is visited as sharply as willful disobedience— incapacity meets with the same punishment as crime. Nature's discipline is not even a word and a blow, and the blow first; but the blow without the word. It is left to you to find out why your ears are boxed.

The object of what we commonly call education—that education in which man intervenes and which I shall distinguish as artificial education—is to make good these defects in Nature's methods; to prepare the child to receive Nature's education, neither incapably nor ignorantly, nor with willful disobedience; and to understand the preliminary symptoms of her pleasure, without waiting for the box on the ear. In short, all artificial education ought to be an anticipation of natural education. And a liberal education is an artificial education— which has not only prepared a man to escape the great evils of disobedience to natural laws, but has trained him to appreciate and to seize upon the rewards which Nature scatters with as free a hand as her penalties.

That man, I think, has had a liberal education who has been so trained in youth that his body is the ready servant of his will, and does with ease and pleasure all the work that, as a mechanism, it is capable of; whose intellect is a clear, cold, logic engine, with all its parts of equal strength, and in smooth working order; ready, like a steam engine, to be turned to any kind of work, and spin the gossamers as well as forge the anchors of the mind; whose mind is stored with a knowledge of the great and fundamental truths of Nature and of the laws of her operations; one who, no stunted ascetic, is full of life and fire, but whose passions are trained to come to heel by a vigorous will, the servant of a tender conscience; who has learned to love all beauty, whether of Nature or of art, to hate all vileness, and to respect others as himself.

Such an one and no other, I conceive, has had a liberal education; for he is, as completely as a man can be, in harmony with Nature. He will make the best of her, and she of him. They will get on together rarely; she as his ever-beneficent mother; he as her mouthpiece, her conscious self, her minister and interpreter.

Where is such an education as this to be had? Where is there any approximation to it? Has anyone tried to found such an education? Looking over the length and breadth of these islands, I am afraid that all these questions must receive a negative answer. Consider our primary schools and what is taught in them. A child learns:

1. To read, write, and cipher, more or less well; but in a very large proportion of cases not so well as to take pleasure in reading, or to be able to write the commonest letter properly.

2. A quantity of dogmatic theology, of which the child, nine times out of ten, understands next to nothing.

3. Mixed up with this, so as to seem to stand or fall with it, a few of the broadest and simplest principles of morality. This, to my mind, is much as if a man of science should make the story of the fall of the apple in Newton's garden an integral part of the doctrine of gravitation, and teach it as of equal authority with the law of the inverse squares.

4. A good deal of Jewish history and Syrian geography, and perhaps a little something about English history and the geography of the child's own country. But I doubt if there is a primary school in England in which hangs a map of the hundred in which the village lies, so that the children may be practically taught by it what a map means.

5. A certain amount of regularity, attentive obedience, respect for others—obtained by fear, if the master be incompetent or foolish; by love and reverence, if he be wise.

So far as this school course embraces a training in the theory and practice of obedience to the moral laws of Nature, I gladly admit, not only that it contains a valuable educational element, but that, so far, it deals with the most valuable and important part of all education. Yet, contrast what is done in this direction with what might be done; with the time given to matters of comparatively no importance; with the absence of any attention to things of the highest moment; and one is tempted to think of Falstaff's bill and "the halfpenny worth of bread to all that quantity of sack."

Let us consider what a child thus "educated" knows, and what it does not know. Begin with the most important topic of all—morality, as the guide of conduct. The child knows well enough that some acts meet with approbation and some with disapprobation. But it has never heard that there lies in the nature of things a reason for every moral law, as cogent and as well defined as that which underlies every physical law; that stealing and lying are just as certain to be followed by evil consequences as putting your hand in the fire, or jumping out of a garret window. Again, though the scholar may have been 10 made acquainted, in dogmatic fashion, with the broad laws of morality, he has had no training in the application of those laws to the difficult problems which result from the complex conditions of modern civilization. Would it not be very hard to expect anyone to solve a problem in conic sections who had merely been taught the axioms and definitions of mathematical science?

A workman has to bear hard labor, and 20 perhaps privation, while he sees others rolling in wealth, and feeding their dogs with what would keep his children from starvation. Would it not be well to have helped that man to calm the natural promptings of discontent by showing him, in his youth, the necessary connection of the moral law which prohibits stealing with the stability of society—by proving to him, once for all, that it is better for his own 30 people, better for himself, better for future generations, that he should starve than steal? If you have no foundation of knowledge or habit of thought to work upon, what chance have you of persuading a hungry man that a capitalist is not a thief "with a circumbendibus"? And if he honestly believes that, of what avail is it to quote the commandment against stealing when he proposes to make the capital- 40 ist disgorge?

Again, the child learns absolutely nothing of the history or the political organization of his own country. His general impression is that everything of much importance happened a very long while ago; and that the Queen and the gentlefolks govern the country much after the fashion of King David and the elders and nobles of Israel—his sole models. Will you 50 give a man with this much information a vote? In easy times he sells it for a pot of beer. Why should he not? It is of about as much use to him as a chignon, and he

knows as much what to do with it, for any other purpose. In bad times, on the contrary, he applies his simple theory of government, and believes that his rulers are the cause of his sufferings—a belief which sometimes bears remarkable practical fruits.

Least of all does the child gather from this primary "education" of ours a conception of the laws of the physical world, or of the relations of cause and effect therein. And this is the more to be lamented, as the poor are especially exposed to physical evils, and are more interested in removing them than any other class of the community. If anyone is concerned in knowing the ordinary laws of mechanics one would think it is the hand-laborer, whose daily toil lies among levers and pulleys; or among the other implements of artisan work. And if anyone is interested in the laws of health, it is the poor workman, whose strength is wasted by ill-prepared food, whose health is sapped by bad ventilation and bad drainage, and half whose children are massacred by disorders which might be prevented. Not only does our present primary education carefully abstain from hinting to the poor man that some of his greatest evils are traceable to mere physical agencies, which could be removed by energy, patience, and frugality; but it does worse—it renders him, so far as it can, deaf to those who could help him, and tries to substitute an Oriental submission to what is falsely declared to be the will of God, for his natural tendency to strive after a better condition.

What wonder, then, if very recently an appeal has been made to statistics for the profoundly foolish purpose of showing that education is of no good—that it diminishes neither misery nor crime among the masses of mankind? I reply, why should the thing which has been called education do either the one or the other? If I am a knave or a fool, teaching me to read and write won't make me less of either one or the other—unless somebody shows me how to put my reading and writing to wise and good purposes.

Suppose anyone were to argue that medicine is of no use, because it could be proved statistically that the percentage of death was just the same among people who had been taught how to open a medicine chest and among those who did not so much as know the key by sight. The argument is absurd; but it is not more preposterous than that against which I am contending. The only medicine for suffering, crime, and all the other woes of mankind, is wisdom. Teach a man to read and write, and you have put into his hands the great keys of the wisdom box. But it is quite another matter whether he ever opens the box or not. And he is as likely to poison as to cure himself, if, without guidance, he swallows the first drug that comes to hand. In these times a man may as well be purblind, as unable to read—lame, as unable to write. But I protest that, if I thought the alternative were a necessary one, I would rather that the children of the poor should grow up ignorant of both these mighty arts, than that they should remain ignorant of that knowledge to which these arts are means.

It may be said that all these animadversions may apply to primary schools, but that the higher schools, at any rate, must be allowed to give a liberal education. In fact they professedly sacrifice everything else to this object.

Let us inquire into this matter. What do the higher schools, those to which the great middle class of the country sends its children, teach, over and above the instruction given is the primary schools? There is a little more reading and writing of English. But, for all that, everyone knows that it is a rare thing to find a boy of the middle or upper classes who can read aloud decently, or who can put his thoughts on paper in clear and grammatical (to say nothing of good or elegant) language. The "ciphering" of the lower schools expands into elementary mathematics in the higher; into arithmetic, with a little algebra, a little Euclid. But I doubt if one boy in five hundred has ever heard the explanation of a rule of arithmetic, or knows his Euclid otherwise than by rote.

Of theology, the middle-class schoolboy gets rather less than poorer children, less absolutely and less relatively, because there are so many other claims upon his attention. I venture to say that, in the great majority of cases, his ideas on this subject when he leaves school are of the most shadowy and vague description, and associated with painful impressions of the weary hours spent in learning collects and catechism by heart.

Modern geography, modern history, modern literature; the English language as a language; the whole circle of the sciences, physical, moral, and social, are even more completely ignored in the higher than in the lower schools. Up till within a few years back, a boy might have passed through any one of the great public schools with the greatest distinction and credit, and might never so much as have heard of one of the subjects I have just mentioned. He might never have heard that the earth goes round the sun; that England underwent a great revolution in 1688, and France another in 1789; that there once lived certain notable men called Chaucer, Shakespeare, Milton, Voltaire, Goethe, Schiller. The first might be a German and the last an Englishman for anything he could tell you to the contrary. And as for Science, the only idea the word would suggest to his mind would be dexterity in boxing.

I have said that this was the state of things a few years back, for the sake of the few righteous who are to be found among the educational cities of the plain. But I would not have you too sanguine about the result, if you sound the minds of the existing generation of public-school boys on such topics as those I have mentioned.

Now let us pause to consider this wonderful state of affairs; for the time will come when Englishmen will quote it as the stock example of the stolid stupidity of their ancestors in the nineteenth century. The most thoroughly commercial people, the greatest voluntary wanderers and colonists the world has ever seen, are precisely the middle classes of this country. If there be a people which has been busy making history on a great scale for the last three hundred years—and the most profoundly interesting history—history which, if it happened to be that of Greece or Rome, we should study with avidity—it is the English. If there be a people which, during the same period, has developed a remarkable literature, it is our own. If there be a nation whose prosperity depends absolutely and wholly upon their mastery over the forces of Nature, upon their intelligent apprehension of and obedience to the laws of the creation and distribution of wealth, and of the stable equilibrium of the forces of society, it is precisely this nation. And yet this is what these wonderful people tell their sons: "At the cost of from one to two thousand pounds of our hard-earned money we devote twelve of the most precious years of your lives to school. There you shall toil, or be supposed to toil; but there you shall not learn one single thing of all those you will most want to know directly you leave school and enter upon the practical business of life. You will in all probability go into business, but you shall not know where or how any article of commerce is produced, or the difference between an export or an import, or the meaning of the word *capital*. You will very likely settle in a colony, but you shall not know whether Tasmania is part of New South Wales, or vice versa.

"Very probably you may become a manufacturer, but you shall not be provided with the means of understanding the working of one of your own steam engines, or the nature of the raw products you employ; and, when you are asked to buy a patent, you shall not have the slightest means of judging whether the inventor is an impostor who is contravening the elementary principles of science, or a man who will make you as rich as Croesus.

"You will very likely get into the House of Commons. You will have to take your share in making laws which may prove a blessing or a curse to millions of men. But you shall not hear one word respecting the political organization of your country; the meaning of the controversy between free traders and protectionists shall never have been mentioned to you; you shall not so much as know that there are such things as economical laws.

"The mental power which will be of most importance in your daily life will be the power of seeing things as they are without regard to authority; and of drawing accurate general conclusions from particular facts. But at school and at college you shall know of no source of truth but authority; nor exercise your reasoning faculty upon anything but deductions from that which is laid down by authority.

"You will have to weary your soul with work, and many a time eat your bread in sorrow and in bitterness, and you shall not have learned to take refuge in the great source of pleasure without alloy, the serene resting-place for worn human nature—the world of art."

Said I not rightly that we are a wonderful people? I am quite prepared to allow that education entirely devoted to these omitted subjects might not be a completely liberal education. But is an education which ignores them all a liberal education? Nay, is it too much to say that the education which should embrace these subjects and no others would be a real education, though an incomplete one; while an education which omits them is really not an education at all, but a more or less useful course of intellectual gymnastics?

For what does the middle-class school put in the place of all these things which are left out? It substitutes what is usually comprised under the compendious title of the "classics"—that is to say, the languages, the literature, and the history of the ancient Greeks and Romans, and the geography of so much of the world as was known to these two great nations of antiquity. Now, do not expect me to depreciate the earnest and enlightened pursuit of classical learning. I have not the least desire to speak ill of such occupations, nor any sympathy with those who run them down. On the contrary, if my opportunities had lain in that direction, there is no investigation into which I could have thrown myself with greater delight than that of antiquity.

What science can present greater attractions than philology? How can a lover of literary excellence fail to rejoice in the ancient masterpieces? And with what consistency could I, whose business lies so much in the attempt to decipher the past, and to build up intelligible forms out of the scattered fragments of long-extinct beings, fail to take a sympathetic, though an unlearned, interest in the labors of a

Niebuhr, a Gibbon, or a Grote? Classical history is a great section of the paleontology of man; and I have the same double respect for it as for other kinds of paleontology—that is to say, a respect for the facts which it establishes as for all facts, and a still greater respect for it as a preparation for the discovery of a law of progress.

But if the classics were taught as they might be taught—if boys and girls were instructed in Greek and Latin, not merely as languages, but as illustrations of philological science; if a vivid picture of life on the shores of the Mediterranean two thousand years ago were imprinted on the minds of scholars; if ancient history were taught, not as a weary series of feuds and fights, but traced to its causes in such men placed under such conditions; if, lastly, the study of the classical books were followed in such a manner as to impress boys with their beauties, and with the grand simplicity of their statement of the everlasting problems of human life, instead of with their verbal and grammatical peculiarities—I still think it as little proper that they should form the basis of a liberal education for our contemporaries, as I should think it fitting to make that sort of paleontology with which I am familiar the backbone of modern education.

It is wonderful how close a parallel to classical training could be made out of that paleontology to which I refer. In the first place I could get up an osteological primer so arid, so pedantic in its terminology, so altogether distasteful to the youthful mind, as to beat the recent famous production of the headmasters out of the field in all these excellences. Next, I could exercise my boys upon easy fossils, and bring out all their powers of memory and all their ingenuity in the application of my osteogrammatical rules to the interpretation, or construing, of those fragments. To those who had reached the higher classes, I might supply odd bones to be built up into animals, giving great honor and reward to him who succeeded in fabricating monsters most entirely in accordance with the rules. That would answer to verse-making and essay-writing in the dead languages.

To be sure, if a great comparative anatomist were to look at these fabrications he might shake his head, or laugh. But what then? Would such a catastrophe destroy the parallel? What, think you, would Cicero, or Horace, say to the production of the best sixth form going? And would not Terence stop his ears and run out if he could be present at an English performance of his own plays? Would *Hamlet,* in the mouths of a set of French actors, who should insist on pronouncing English after the fashion of their own tongue, be more hideously ridiculous?

But it will be said that I am forgetting the beauty, and the human interest, which appertain to classical studies. To this I reply that it is only a very strong man who can appreciate the charms of a landscape as he is toiling up a steep hill, along a bad road. What with short-windedness, stones, ruts, and a pervading sense of the wisdom of rest-and-be-thankful, most of us have little enough sense of the beautiful under these circumstances. The ordinary schoolboy is precisely in this case. He finds Parnassus uncommonly steep, and there is no chance of his having much time or inclination to look about him till he gets to the top. And nine times out of ten he does not get to the top.

But if this be a fair picture of the results of classical teaching at its best—and I gather from those who have authority to speak on such matters that it is so—what is to be said of classical teaching at its worst, or, in other words, of the classics of our ordinary middle-class schools? I will tell you. It means getting up endless forms and rules by heart. It means turning Latin and Greek into English, for the mere sake of being able to do it, and without the smallest regard to the worth, or worthlessness, of the author read. It means the learning of innumerable, not always decent, fables in such a shape that the meaning they once had is dried up into utter trash; and the only impression left upon a boy's mind is that the people who believed such things must have been the greatest idiots the world ever saw. And it means, finally, that after a dozen years spent at this kind of work, the sufferer shall be incompetent to interpret a passage in an author he has not already got up; that he shall loathe the sight of a Greek or Latin book; and that he shall never open, or think of, a classical writer again, until, wonderful to relate, he insists upon submitting his sons to the same process.

These be your gods, O Israel! For the sake of this net result (and respectability) the British father denies his children all the knowledge they might turn to account in life, not merely for the achievement of vulgar success, but for guidance in the great crises of human existence. This is the stone he offers to those whom he is bound by the strongest and tenderest ties to feed with bread.

If primary and secondary education are in this unsatisfactory state, what is to be said to the universities? This is an awful subject, and one I almost fear to touch with my unhallowed hands; but I can tell you what those say who have authority to speak.

The Rector of Lincoln College, in his lately published valuable *Suggestions for Academical Organization with Especial Reference to Oxford,* tells us (p. 127):

"The colleges were, in their origin, endowments, not for the elements of a general liberal education, but for the prolonged study of special and professional faculties by men of riper age. The universities embraced both these objects. The colleges, while they incidentally aided in elementary education, were specially devoted to the highest learning. . . .

"This was the theory of the Middle-Age university and the design of collegiate foundations in their origin. Time and circumstances have brought about a total change. The colleges no longer promote the researches of science, or direct professional study. Here and there college walls may shelter an occasional student, but not in larger proportions than may be found in private life. Elementary teaching of youths under twenty is now the only function performed by the university, and almost the only object of college endowments. Colleges were homes for the life-study of the highest and most abstruse parts of knowledge. They have become boarding schools in which the elements of the learned languages are taught to youths."

If Mr. Pattison's high position, and his obvious love and respect for his university, be insufficient to convince the outside world that language so severe is yet no more than just, the authority of the Commissioners who reported on the University of Oxford in 1850 is open to no challenge. Yet they write:

"It is generally acknowledged that both Oxford and the country at large suffer greatly from the absence of a body of learned men devoting their lives to the cultivation of science, and to the direction of academical education.

"The fact that so few books of profound research emanate from the University of Oxford materially impairs its character as a seat of learning, and consequently its hold on the respect of the nation."

Cambridge can claim no exemption from the reproaches addressed to Oxford. And thus there seems no escape from the admission that what we fondly call our great seats of learning are simply "boarding schools" for bigger boys; that learned men are not more numerous in them than out of them; that the advancement of knowledge is not the object of fellows of colleges; that, in the philosophic calm and meditative stillness of their greenswarded courts, philosophy does not thrive, and meditation bears few fruits.

It is my good fortune to reckon amongst my friends resident members of both universities, who are men of learning and research, zealous cultivators of science, keeping before their minds a noble ideal of a university, and doing their best to make that ideal a reality; and, to me, they would necessarily typify the universities, did not the authoritative statements I have quoted compel me to believe that they are exceptional, and not representative men. Indeed, upon calm consideration, several circumstances lead me to think that the Rector of Lincoln College and the Commissioners cannot be far wrong.

I believe there can be no doubt that the foreigner who should wish to become acquainted with the scientific, or the literary, activity of modern England, would simply lose his time and his pains if he visited our universities with that object.

And, as for works of profound research

on any subject, and, above all, in that classical lore for which the universities profess to sacrifice almost everything else, why, a third-rate, poverty-stricken German university turns out more produce of that kind in one year than our vast and wealthy foundations elaborate in ten.

Ask any man who is investigating any question, profoundly and thoroughly—be it historical, philosophical, philological, physical, literary, or theological; who is trying to make himself master of any abstract subject (except, perhaps, political economy and geology, both of which are intensely Anglican sciences)—whether he is not compelled to read half a dozen times as many German as English books? And whether, of these English books, more than one in ten is the work of a fellow of a college, or a professor of an English university?

Is this from any lack of power in the English as compared with the German mind? The countrymen of Grote and of Mill, of Faraday, of Robert Brown, of Lyell, and of Darwin, to go no further back than the contemporaries of men of middle age, can afford to smile at such a suggestion. England can show now, as she has been able to show in every generation since civilization spread over the West, individual men who hold their own against the world, and keep alive the old tradition of her intellectual eminence.

But, in the majority of cases, these men are what they are in virtue of their native intellectual force, and of a strength of character which will not recognize impediments. They are not trained in the courts of the Temple of Science, but storm the walls of that edifice in all sorts of irregular ways, and with much loss of time and power, in order to obtain their legitimate positions.

Our universities not only do not encourage such men; do not offer them positions in which it should be their highest duty to do thoroughly that which they are most capable of doing; but, as far as possible, university training shuts out of the minds of those among them who are subjected to it the prospect that there is anything in the world for which they are specially fitted. Imagine the success of the attempt to still the intellectual hunger of any of the men I have mentioned by putting before him, as the object of existence, the successful mimicry of the measure of a Greek song, or the roll of Ciceronian prose! Imagine how much success would be likely to attend the attempt to persuade such men that the education which leads to perfection in such elegances is alone to be called culture, while the facts of history, the process of thought, the conditions of moral and social existence, and the laws of physical nature are left to be dealt with as they may by outside barbarians!

It is not thus that the German universities, from being beneath notice a century ago, have become what they are now—the the most intensely cultivated and the most productive intellectual corporations the world has ever seen.

The student who repairs to them sees in the list of classes and of professors a fair picture of the world of knowledge. Whatever he needs to know there is someone ready to teach him, someone competent to discipline him in the way of learning; whatever his special bent, let him but be able and diligent, and in due time he shall find distinction and a career. Among his professors he sees men whose names are known and revered throughout the civilized world; and their living example infects him with a noble ambition, and a love for the spirit of work.

The Germans dominate the intellectual world by virtue of the same simple secret as that which made Napoleon the master of old Europe. They have declared *la carrière ouverte aux talents*,[1] and every Bursch marches with a professor's gown in his knapsack. Let him become a great scholar, or man of science, and ministers will compete for his services. In Germany they do not leave the chance of his holding the office he would render illustrious to the tender mercies of a hot canvass, and the final wisdom of a mob of country parsons.

In short, in Germany, the universities are exactly what the Rector of Lincoln and

[1] *la carrière ouverte aux talents:* a favorite saying of Napoleon (as to the meaning of the French Revolution): 'the career (is) open to the talents,' or, as Carlyle translates, 'the tools to him that can use them.'

the Commissioners tell us the English universities are not; that is to say, corporations "of learned men devoting their lives to the cultivation of science, and the direction of academical education." They are not "boarding schools for youths," nor clerical seminaries; but institutions for the higher culture of men, in which the theological faculty is of no more importance or prominence than the rest; and which are 10 truly "universities," since they strive to represent and embody the totality of human knowledge, and to find room for all forms of intellectual activity.

May zealous and clear-headed reformers like Mr. Pattison succeed in their noble endeavors to shape our universites towards some such ideal as this, without losing what is valuable and distinctive in their social tone! But until they have succeeded, a 20 liberal education will be no more obtainable in our Oxford and Cambridge Universities than in our public schools.

If I am justified in my conception of the ideal of a liberal education, and if what I have said about the existing educational institutions of the country is also true, it is clear that the two have no sort of relation to one another; that the best of our schools and the most complete of our university 30 trainings give but a narrow, one-sided, and essentially illiberal education—while the worst give what is really next to no education at all. The South London Workingmen's College could not copy any of these institutions if it would; I am bold enough to express the conviction that it ought not if it could.

For what is wanted is the reality and not the mere name of a liberal education; and 40 this College must steadily set before itself the ambition to be able to give that education sooner or later. At present we are but beginning, sharpening our educational tools, as it were, and, except a modicum of physical science, we are not able to offer much more than is to be found in an ordinary school.

Moral and social science—one of the greatest and most fruitful of our future 50 classes, I hope—at present lacks only one thing in our program, and that is a teacher. A considerable want, no doubt; but it must be recollected that it is much better to want a teacher than to want the desire to learn.

Further, we need what, for want of a better name, I must call Physical Geography. What I mean is that which the Germans call *Erdkunde*. It is a description of the earth, of its place and relation to other bodies; of its general structure, and of its great features—winds, tides, mountains, plains; of the chief forms of the vegetable and animal worlds, of the varieties of man. It is the peg upon which the greatest quantity of useful and entertaining scientific information can be suspended.

Literature is not upon the College program; but I hope some day to see it there. For literature is the greatest of all sources of refined pleasure, and one of the great uses of a liberal education is to enable us to enjoy that pleasure. There is scope enough for the purposes of liberal education in the study of the rich treasures of our own language alone. All that is needed is direction, and the cultivation of a refined taste by attention to sound criticism. But there is no reason why French and German should not be mastered sufficiently to read what is worth reading in those languages with pleasure and with profit.

And finally, by and by, we must have history; treated not as a succession of battles and dynasties; not as a series of biographies; not as evidence that Providence has always been on the side of either Whigs or Tories; but as the development of man in times past, and in other conditions than our own.

But, as it is one of the principles of our College to be self-supporting, the public must lead, and we must follow, in these matters. If my hearers take to heart what I have said about liberal education, they will desire these things, and I doubt not we shall be able to supply them. But we must wait till the demand is made.

[1868]

SCIENCE AND CULTURE

From the time that the first suggestion to introduce physical science into ordinary education was timidly whispered, until now, the advocates of scientific education have met with opposition of two kinds.

On the one hand, they have been pooh-poohed by the men of business who pride themselves on being the representatives of practicality; while, on the other hand, they have been excommunicated by the classical scholars, in their capacity of Levites in charge of the ark of culture and monopolists of liberal education.

The practical men believed that the idol whom they worship—rule of thumb—has been the source of the past prosperity, and will suffice for the future welfare of the arts and manufactures. They are of opinion that science is speculative rubbish; that theory and practice have nothing to do with one another; and that the scientific habit of mind is an impediment, rather than an aid, in the conduct of ordinary affairs.

I have used the past tense in speaking of the practical men—for although they were very formidable thirty years ago, I am not sure that the pure species has not been extirpated. In fact, so far as mere argument goes, they have been subjected to such a *feu d'enfer* [1] that it is a miracle if any have escaped. But I have remarked that your typical practical man has an unexpected resemblance to one of Milton's angels. His spiritual wounds, such as are inflicted by logical weapons, may be as deep as a well and as wide as a church door, but beyond shedding a few drops of ichor, celestial or otherwise, he is no whit the worse. So, if any of these opponents be left, I will not waste time in vain repetition of the demonstrative evidence of the practical value of science; but knowing that a parable will sometimes penetrate where syllogisms fail to effect an entrance, I will offer a story for their consideration.

Once upon a time, a boy, with nothing to depend upon but his own vigorous nature, was thrown into the thick of the struggle for existence in the midst of a great manufacturing population. He seems to have had a hard fight, inasmuch as, by the time he was thirty years of age, his total disposable funds amounted to twenty pounds. Nevertheless, middle life found him giving proof of his comprehension of the practical problems he had been roughly

[1] *feu d'enfer:* fire of hell.

called upon to solve, by a career of remarkable prosperity.

Finally, having reached old age with its well-earned surroundings of "honour, troops of friends," the hero of my story bethought himself of those who were making a like start in life, and how he could stretch out a helping hand to them.

After long and anxious reflection this successful practical man of business could devise nothing better than to provide them with the means of obtaining "sound, extensive, and practical scientific knowledge." And he devoted a large part of his wealth and five years of incessant work to this end.

I need not point the moral of a tale which, as the solid and spacious fabric of the Scientific College assures us, is no fable, nor can anything which I could say intensify the force of this practical answer to practical objections.

We may take it for granted then, that, in the opinion of those best qualified to judge, the diffusion of thorough scientific education is an absolutely essential condition of industrial progress; and that the College which has been opened today will confer an inestimable boon upon those whose livelihood is to be gained by the practise of the arts and manufactures of the district.

The only question worth discussion is, whether the conditions, under which the work of the College is to be carried out, are such as to give it the best possible chance of achieving permanent success.

Sir Josiah Mason, without doubt most wisely, has left very large freedom of action to the trustees, to whom he proposes ultimately to commit the administration of the College, so that they may be able to adjust its arrangements in accordance with the changing conditions of the future. But, with respect to three points, he has laid most explicit injunctions upon both administrators and teachers.

Party politics are forbidden to enter into the minds of either, so far as the work of the College is concerned; theology is as sternly banished from its precincts; and finally, it is especially declared that the College shall make no provision for "mere literary instruction and education."

It does not concern me at present to dwell upon the first two injunctions any longer than may be needful to express my full conviction of their wisdom. But the third prohibition brings us face to face with those other opponents of scientific education, who are by no means in the moribund condition of the practical man, but alive, alert, and formidable.

It is not impossible that we shall hear this express exclusion of "literary instruction and education" from a College which, nevertheless, professes to give a high and efficient education, sharply criticised. Certainly the time was that the Levites of culture would have sounded their trumpets against its walls as against an educational Jericho.

How often have we not been told that the study of physical science is incompetent to confer culture; that it touches none of the higher problems of life; and, what is worse, that the continual devotion to scientific studies tends to generate a narrow and bigoted belief in the applicability of scientific methods to the search after truth of all kinds? How frequently one has reason to observe that no reply to a troublesome argument tells so well as calling its author a "mere scientific specialist." And, as I am afraid it is not permissible to speak of this form of opposition to scientific education in the past tense; may we not expect to be told that this, not only omission, but prohibition, of "mere literary instruction and education" is a patent example of scientific narrow-mindedness?

I am not acquainted with Sir Josiah Mason's reasons for the action which he has taken; but if, as I apprehend is the case, he refers to the ordinary classical course of our schools and universities by the name of "mere literary instruction and education," I venture to offer sundry reasons of my own in support of that action.

For I hold very strongly by two convictions: The first is, that neither the discipline nor the subject-matter of classical education is of such direct value to the student of physical science as to justify the expenditure of valuable time upon either; and the second is, that for the purpose of attaining real culture, an exclusively scientific education is at least as effectual as an exclusively literary education.

I need hardly point out to you that these opinions, especially the latter, are diametrically opposed to those of the great majority of educated Englishmen, influenced as they are by school and university traditions. In their belief, culture is obtainable only by a liberal education; and a liberal education is synonymous, not merely with education and instruction in literature, but in one particular form of literature, namely, that of Greek and Roman antiquity. They hold that the man who has learned Latin and Greek, however little, is educated; while he who is versed in other branches of knowledge, however deeply, is a more or less respectable specialist, not admissible into the cultured caste. The stamp of the educated man, the University degree, is not for him.

I am too well acquainted with the generous catholicity of spirit, the true sympathy with scientific thought, which pervades the writings of our chief apostle of culture to identify him with these opinions; and yet one may cull from one and another of those epistles to the Philistines, which so much delight all who do not answer to that name, sentences which lend them some support.

Mr. Arnold tells us that the meaning of culture is "to know the best that has been thought and said in the world." It is the criticism of life contained in literature. That criticism regards "Europe as being, for intellectual and spiritual purposes, one great confederation, bound to a joint action and working to a common result; and whose members have, for their common outfit, a knowledge of Greek, Roman, and Eastern antiquity, and of one another. Special, local, and temporary advantages being put out of account, that modern nation will in the intellectual and spiritual sphere make most progress, which most thoroughly carries out this programme. And what is that but saying that we too, all of us, as individuals, the more thoroughly we carry it out, shall make the more progress?"

We have here to deal with two distinct propositions. The first, that a criticism of life is the essence of culture; the second, that literature contains the materials which suffice for the construction of such criticism.

I think that we must all assent to the first proposition. For culture certainly means something quite different from learning or technical skill. It implies the possession of an ideal, and the habit of critically estimating the value of things by comparison with a theoretic standard. Perfect culture should supply a complete theory of life, based upon a clear knowledge alike of its possibilities and of its limitations.

But we may agree to all this, and yet strongly dissent from the assumption that literature alone is competent to supply this knowledge. After having learnt all that Greek, Roman, and Eastern antiquity have thought and said, and all that modern literature have to tell us, it is not self-evident that we have laid a sufficiently broad and deep foundation for that criticism of life, which constitutes culture.

Indeed, to any one acquainted with the scope of physical science, it is not at all evident. Considering progress only in the "intellectual and spiritual sphere," I find myself wholly unable to admit that either nations or individuals will really advance, if their common outfit draws nothing from the stores of physical science. I should say that an army, without weapons of precision and with no particular base of operations, might more hopefully enter upon a campaign on the Rhine, than a man, devoid of a knowledge of what physical science has done in the last century, upon a criticism of life.

When a biologist meets with an anomaly, he instinctively turns to the study of development to clear it up. The rationale of contradictory opinions may with equal confidence be sought in history.

It is, happily, no new thing that Englishmen should employ their wealth in building and endowing institutions for educational purposes. But, five or six hundred years ago, deeds of foundation expressed or implied conditions as nearly as possible contrary to those which have been thought expedient by Sir Josiah Mason. That is to say, physical science was practically ignored, while a certain literary training was enjoined as a means to the acquirement of knowledge which was essentially theological.

The reason of this singular contradiction between the actions of men alike animated by a strong and disinterested desire to promote the welfare of their fellows, is easily discovered.

At that time, in fact, if any one desired knowledge beyond such as could be obtained by his own observation, or by common conversation, his first necessity was to learn the Latin language, inasmuch as all the higher knowledge of the western world was contained in works written in that language. Hence, Latin grammar, with logic and rhetoric, studied through Latin, were the fundamentals of education. With respect to the substance of the knowledge imparted through this channel, the Jewish and Christian Scriptures, as interpreted and supplemented by the Romish Church, were held to contain a complete and infallibly true body of information.

Theological dicta were, to the thinkers of those days, that which the axioms and definitions of Euclid are to the geometers of these. The business of the philosophers of the middle ages was to deduce from the data furnished by the theologians, conclusions in accordance with ecclesiastical decrees. They were allowed the high privilege of showing, by logical process, how and why that which the Church said was true, must be true. And if their demonstrations fell short of or exceeded this limit, the Church was materially ready to check their aberrations; if need were, by the help of the secular arm.

Between the two, our ancestors were furnished with a compact and complete criticism of life. They were told how the world began and how it would end; they learned that all material existence was but a base and insignificant blot upon the fair face of the spiritual world, and that nature was, to all intents and purposes, the playground of the devil; they learned that the earth is the centre of the visible universe, and that man is the cynosure of things terrestrial, and more especially was it inculcated that the course of nature had no fixed order, but that it could be, and constantly was, altered by the agency of innumerable spiritual beings, good and bad, according as they were moved by the deeds and prayers of men. The sum and substance of the whole doctrine was to produce the conviction that the only thing really worth knowing in this world was how to secure that place in a better which, under certain conditions, the Church promised.

Our ancestors had a living belief in this theory of life, and acted upon it in their dealings with education, as in all other matters. Culture meant saintliness—after the fashion of the saints of those days; the education that led to it was, of necessity, theological; and the way to theology lay through Latin.

That the study of nature—further than was requisite for the satisfaction of everyday wants—should have any bearing on human life was far from the thoughts of men thus trained. Indeed, as nature had been cursed for man's sake, it was an obvious conclusion that those who meddled with nature were likely to come into pretty close contact with Satan. And, if any born scientific investigator followed his instincts, he might safely reckon upon earning the reputation, and probably upon suffering the fate, of a sorcerer.

Had the western world been left to itself in Chinese isolation, there is no saying how long this state of things might have endured. But, happily, it was not left to itself. Even earlier than the thirteenth century, the development of Moorish civilisation in Spain and the great movement of the Crusades had introduced the leaven which, from that day to this, has never ceased to work. At first, through the intermediation of Arabic translations, afterwards by the study of the originals, the western nations of Europe became acquainted with the writings of the ancient philosophers and poets, and, in time, with the whole of the vast literature of antiquity.

Whatever there was of high intellectual aspiration or dominant capacity in Italy, France, Germany, and England, spent itself for centuries in taking possession of the rich inheritance left by the dead civilisations of Greece and Rome. Marvellously aided by the invention of printing, classical learning spread and flourished. Those who possessed it prided themselves on having attained the highest culture then within the reach of mankind.

And justly. For, saving Dante on his solitary pinnacle, there was no figure in modern literature at the time of the Renascence to compare with the men of antiquity; there was no art to compete with their sculpture; there was no physical science but that which Greece had created. Above all, there was no other example of perfect intellectual freedom—of the unhesitating acceptance of reason as the sole guide to truth and the supreme arbiter of conduct.

The new learning necessarily soon exerted a profound influence upon education. The language of the monks and schoolmen seemed little better than gibberish to scholars fresh from Virgil and Cicero, and the study of Latin was placed upon a new foundation. Moreover, Latin itself ceased to afford the sole key to knowledge. The student who sought the highest thought of antiquity, found only a second-hand reflection of it in Roman literature, and turned his face to the full light of the Greeks. And after a battle, not altogether dissimilar to that which is at present being fought over the teaching of physical science, the study of Greek was recognised as an essential element of all higher education.

Thus the Humanists, as they were called, won the day; and the great reform which they effected was of incalculable service to mankind. But the Nemesis of all reformers is finality; and the reformers of education, like those of religion, fell into the profound, however common, error of mistaking the beginning for the end of the work of reformation.

The representatives of the Humanists, in the nineteenth century, take their stand upon classical education as the sole avenue to culture, as firmly as if we were still in the age of Renaissance. Yet, surely, the present intellectual relations of the modern and the ancient worlds are profoundly different from those which obtained three centuries ago. Leaving aside the existence of a great and characteristically modern literature, of modern painting, and, especially, of modern music, there is one feature of the present state of the civilised world which separates it more widely from the Renascence, than the Renascence was separated from the middle ages.

This distinctive character of our own times lies in the vast and constantly increasing part which is played by natural knowledge. Not only is our daily life shaped by it; not only does the prosperity of millions of men depend upon it, but our whole theory of life has long been influenced, consciously or unconsciously, by the general conceptions of the universe, which have been forced upon us by physical science.

In fact, the most elementary acquaintance with the results of scientific investigation shows us that they offer a broad and striking contradiction to the opinion so implicitly credited and taught in the middle ages.

The notions of the beginning and the end of the world entertained by our forefathers are no longer credible. It is very certain that the earth is not the chief body in the material universe, and that the world is not subordinated to man's use. It is even more certain that nature is the expression of a definite order with which nothing interferes, and that the chief business of mankind is to learn that order and govern themselves accordingly. Moreover this scientific "criticism of life" presents itself to us with different credentials from any other. It appeals not to authority, nor to what anybody may have thought or said, but to nature. It admits that all our interpretations of natural fact are more or less imperfect and symbolic, and bids the learner seek for truth not among words but among things. It warns us that the assertion which outstrips evidence is not only a blunder but a crime.

The purely classical education advocated by the representatives of the Humanists in our day, gives no inkling of all this. A man may be a better scholar than Erasmus, and know no more of the chief causes of the present intellectual fermentation than Erasmus did. Scholarly and pious persons, worthy of all respect, favour us with allocutions upon the sadness of the antagonism of science to their mediæval way of thinking, which betray an ignorance of the first principles of scientific investigation, an incapacity for understanding what a man of science means by veracity, and an unconsciousness of the weight of established scientific truths, which is almost comical.

There is no great force in the *tu quoque* [2] argument, or else the advocates of scientific education might fairly enough retort upon the modern Humanists that they may be learned specialists, but that they possess no such sound foundation for a criticism of life as deserves the name of culture. And, indeed, if we were disposed to be cruel, we might urge that the Humanists have brought this reproach upon themselves, not because they are too full of the spirit of the ancient Greek, but because they lack it.

The period of the Renascence is commonly called that of the "Revival of Letters," as if the influences then brought to bear upon the mind of Western Europe had been wholly exhausted in the field of literature. I think it is very commonly forgotten that the revival of science, effected by the same agency, although less conspicuous, was not less momentous.

In fact, the few and scattered students of nature of that day picked up the clue to her secrets exactly as it fell from the hands of the Greeks a thousand years before. The foundations of mathematics were so well laid by them, that our children learn their geometry from a book written for the schools of Alexandria two thousand years ago. Modern astronomy is the natural continuation and development of the work of Hipparchus and of Ptolemy; modern physics of that of Democritus and of Archimedes; it was long before modern biological science outgrew the knowledge bequeathed to us by Aristotle, by Theophrastus, and by Galen.

We cannot know all the best thoughts and saying of the Greeks unless we know what they thought about natural phenomena. We cannot fully apprehend their criticism of life unless we understand the extent to which that criticism was affected by scientific conceptions. We falsely pre-

2 *tu quoque:* you also.

tend to be the inheritors of their culture, unless we are penetrated, as the best minds among them were, with an unhesitating faith that the free employment of reason, in accordance with scientific method, is the sole method of reaching truth.

Thus I venture to think that the pretensions of our modern Humanists to the possession of the monopoly of culture and to the exclusive inheritance of the spirit 10 of antiquity must be abated, if not abandoned. But I should be very sorry that anything I have said should be taken to imply a desire on my part to depreciate the value of classical education, as it might be and as it sometimes is. The native capacities of mankind vary no less than their opportunities; and while culture is one, the road by which one man may best reach it is widely different from that which 20 is most advantageous to another. Again, while scientific education is yet inchoate and tentative, classical education is thoroughly well organised upon the practical experience of generations of teachers. So that, given ample time for learning and estimation for ordinary life, or for a literary career, I do not think that a young Englishman in search of culture can do better than follow the course usually 30 marked out for him, supplementing its deficiencies by his own efforts.

But for those who mean to make science their serious occupation; or who intend to follow the profession of medicine; or who have to enter early upon the business of life; for all these, in my opinion, classical education is a mistake; and it is for this reason that I am glad to see "mere literary education and instruction" shut 40 out from the curriculum of Sir Josiah Mason's College, seeing that its inclusion would probably lead to the introduction of the ordinary smattering of Latin and Greek.

Nevertheless, I am the last person to question the importance of genuine literary education, or to suppose that intellectual culture can be complete without it. An exclusively scientific training will bring 50 about a mental twist as surely as an exclusively literary training. The value of the cargo does not compensate for a ship's being out of trim; and I should be very

sorry to think that the Scientific College would turn out none but lopsided men.

There is no need, however, that such a catastrophe should happen. Instruction in English, French, and German is provided, and thus the three greatest literatures of the modern world are made accessible to the student.

French and German, and especially the latter language, are absolutely indispensable to those who desire full knowledge in any department of science. But even supposing that the knowledge of these languages acquired is not more than sufficient for purely scientific purposes, every Englishman has, in his native tongue, an almost perfect instrument of literary expression; and, in his own literature, models of every kind of literary excellence. If an Englishman cannot get literary culture out of his Bible, his Shakespeare, his Milton, neither, in my belief, will the profoundest study of Homer and Sophocles, Virgil and Horace, give it to him.

Thus, since the constitution of the College makes sufficient provision for literary as well as for scientific education, and since artistic instruction is also contemplated, it seems to me that a fairly complete culture is offered to all who are willing to take advantage of it.

But I am not sure that at this point the "practical" man, scotched but not slain, may ask what all this talk about culture has to do with an Institution, the object of which is defined to be "to promote the prosperity of the manufactures and the industry of the country." He may suggest that what is wanted for this end is not culture, nor even a purely scientific discipline, but simply a knowledge of applied science.

I often wish that this phrase, "applied science," had never been invented. For it suggests that there is a sort of scientific knowledge of direct practical use, which can be studied apart from another sort of scientific knowledge, which is of no practical utility, and which is termed "pure science." But there is no more complete fallacy than this. What people call applied science is nothing but the application of pure science to particular classes of problems. It consists of deductions from those general principles, established by reasoning and observation, which constitute pure science. No one can safely make these deductions until he has a firm grasp of the principles; and he can obtain that grasp only by personal experience of the operations of observation and of reasoning on which they are founded.

Almost all the processes employed in the arts and manufactures fall within the range either of physics or of chemistry. In order to improve them, one must thoroughly understand them; and no one has a chance of really understanding them, unless he has obtained that mastery of principles and that habit of dealing with facts, which is given by long-continued and well-directed purely scientific training in the physical and the chemical laboratory. So that there really is no question as to the necessity of purely scientific discipline, even if the work of the College were limited by the narrowest interpretation of its stated aims.

And, as to the desirableness of a wider culture than that yielded by science alone, it is to be recollected that the improvement of manufacturing processes is only one of the conditions which contribute to the prosperity of industry. Industry is a means and not an end; and mankind work only to get something which they want. What that something is depends partly on their innate, and partly on their acquired, desires.

If the wealth resulting from prosperous industry is to be spent upon the gratification of unworthy desires, if the increasing perfection of manufacturing processes is to be accompanied by an increasing debasement of those who carry them on, I do not see the good of industry and prosperity.

Now it is perfectly true that men's views of what is desirable depend upon their characters; and that the innate proclivities to which we give that name are not touched by any amount of instruction. But it does not follow that even mere intellectual education may not, to an indefinite extent, modify the practical manifestation of the characters of men in their actions, by supplying them with motives unknown to the ignorant. A pleasure-loving character will have pleasure of some sort; but, if you give him the choice, he may prefer pleasures which do not degrade him to those which do. And this choice is offered to every man, who possesses in literary or artistic culture a never-failing source of pleasures, which are neither withered by age, nor staled by custom, nor embittered in the recollection by the pangs of self-reproach.

If the Institution opened today fulfils the intention of its founder, the picked intelligences among all classes of the population of this district will pass through it. No child born in Birmingham, henceforward, if he have the capacity to profit by the opportunities offered to him, first in the primary and other schools, and afterwards in the Scientific College, need fail to obtain, not merely the instruction, but the culture most appropriate to the conditions of his life.

Within these walls, the future employer and the future artisan may sojourn together for a while, and carry, through all their lives, the stamp of the influences then brought to bear upon them. Hence, it is not beside the mark to remind you, that the prosperity of industry depends not merely upon the improvement of manufacturing processes, not merely upon the ennobling of the individual character, but upon a third condition, namely, a clear understanding of the conditions of social life, on the part of both the capitalist and the operative, and their agreement upon common principles of social action. They must learn that social phenomena are as much the expression of natural laws as any others; that no social arrangements can be permanent unless they harmonise with the requirements of social statics and dynamics; and that, in the nature of things, there is an arbiter whose decisions execute themselves.

But this knowledge is only to be obtained by the application of the methods of investigation adopted in physical researches to the investigation of the phenomena of society. Hence, I confess, I should like to see one addition made to the excellent scheme of education propounded for the College, in the shape of provision for the teaching of Sociology. For though we are all agreed that party politics are to have no place in the instruction of the College; yet in this country, practically governed as it is now by universal suffrage, every man who does his duty must exercise political functions. And, if the evils which are inseparable from the good of political liberty are to be checked, if the perpetual oscillation of nations between anarchy and despotism is to be re- 10 placed by the steady march of self-restraining freedom; it will be because men will gradually bring themselves to deal with political, as they now deal with scientific questions; to be as ashamed of undue haste and partisan prejudice in the one case as in the other; and to believe that the machinery of society is at least as delicate as that of a spinning-jenny, and as little likely to be improved by the med- 20 dling of those who have not taken the trouble to master the principles of its action.

In conclusion, I am sure that I make myself the mouthpiece of all present in offering to the venerable founder of the Institution, which now commences its beneficent career, our congratulations on the completion of his work; and in express- 30 ing the conviction, that the remotest posterity will point to it as a crucial instance of the wisdom which natural piety leads all men to ascribe to their ancestors.

[1880]

THE STRUGGLE FOR EXISTENCE IN HUMAN SOCIETY

The vast and varied procession of events, 40 which we call Nature, affords a sublime spectacle and an inexhaustible wealth of attractive problems to the speculative observer. If we confine our attention to that aspect which engages the attention of the intellect, nature appears a beautiful and harmonious whole, the incarnation of a faultless logical process, from certain premises in the past to an inevitable conclusion in the future. But if it be regarded from 50 a less elevated, though more human, point of view; if our moral sympathies are allowed to influence our judgment, and we permit ourselves to criticize our great

mother as we criticize one another; then our verdict, at least so far as sentient nature is concerned, can hardly be so favorable.

In sober truth, to those who have made a study of the phenomena of life as they are exhibited by the higher forms of the animal world, the optimistic dogma that this is the best of all possible worlds will seem little better than a libel upon possibility. It is really only another instance to be added to the many extant, of the audacity of à priori speculators who, having created God in their own image, find no difficulty in assuming that the Almighty must have been actuated by the same motives as themselves. They are quite sure that, had any other course been practicable, He would no more have made infinite suffering a necessary ingredient of His handiwork than a respectable philosopher would have done the like.

But even the modified optimism of the time-honored thesis of physico-theology, that the sentient world is, on the whole, regulated by principles of benevolence, does but ill stand the test of impartial confrontation with the facts of the case. No doubt it is quite true that sentient nature affords hosts of examples of subtle contrivances directed towards the production of pleasure or the avoidance of pain; and it may be proper to say that these are evidences of benevolence. But if so, why is it not equally proper to say of the equally numerous arrangements, the no less necessary result of which is the production of pain, that they are evidences of malevolence?

If a vast amount of that which, in a piece of human workmanship, we should call skill, is visible in those parts of the organization of a deer to which it owes its ability to escape from beasts of prey, there is at least equal skill displayed in that bodily mechanism of the wolf which enables him to track, and sooner or later to bring down, the deer. Viewed under the dry light of science, deer and wolf are alike admirable; and, if both were nonsentient automata, there would be nothing to qualify our admiration of the action of the one on the other. But the fact that the deer suffers, while the wolf inflicts suffering, engages our moral sympathies. We should call men like the deer innocent and good, men such as the wolf malignant and bad; we should call those who defended the deer and aided him to escape brave and compassionate, and those who helped the wolf in his bloody work base and cruel. Surely, if we transfer these judgments to nature outside the world of man at all, we must do so impartially. In that case, the goodness of the right hand which helps the deer, and the wickedness of the left hand which eggs on the wolf, will neutralize one another—and the course of nature will appear to be neither moral nor immoral, but nonmoral.

This conclusion is thrust upon us by analogous facts in every part of the sentient world; yet, inasmuch as it not only jars upon prevalent prejudices, but arouses the natural dislike to that which is painful, much ingenuity has been exercised in devising an escape from it.

From the theological side, we are told that this is a state of probation, and that the seeming injustices and immoralities of nature will be compensated by and by. But how this compensation is to be effected, in the case of the great majority of sentient things, is not clear. I apprehend that no one is seriously prepared to maintain that the ghosts of all the myriads of generations of herbivorous animals which lived during the millions of years of the earth's duration, before the appearance of man, and which have all that time been tormented and devoured by carnivores, are to be compensated by a perennial existence in clover; while the ghosts of carnivores are to go to some kennel where there is neither a pan of water nor a bone with any meat on it. Besides, from the point of view of morality, the last stage of things would be worse than the first. For the carnivores, however brutal and sanguinary, have only done that which, if there is any evidence of contrivance in the world, they were expressly constructed to do. Moreover, carnivores and herbivores alike have been subject to all the miseries incidental to old age, disease, and overmultiplication, and both might well put in a claim for "compensation" on this score.

On the evolutionist side, on the other hand, we are told to take comfort from the reflection that the terrible struggle for existence tends to final good, and that the suffering of the ancestor is paid for by the increased perfection of the progeny. There would be something in this argument if, in Chinese fashion, the present generation could pay its debts to its ancestors; otherwise it is not clear what compensation the Eohippus gets for his sorrows in the fact that, some millions of years afterwards, one of his descendants wins the Derby. And, again, it is an error to imagine that evolution signifies a constant tendency to increased perfection. That process undoubtedly involves a constant remodeling of the organism in adaptation to new conditions; but it depends on the nature of those conditions whether the direction of the modifications effected shall be upward or downward. Retrogressive is as practical as progressive metamorphosis. If what the physical philosophers tell us, that our globe has been in a state of fusion, and, like the sun, is gradually cooling down, is true, then the time must come when evolution will mean adaptation to an universal winter, and all forms of life will die out, except such low and simple organisms as the Diatom of the arctic and antarctic ice and the Protococcus of the red snow. If our globe is proceeding from a condition in which it was too hot to support any but the lowest living thing to a condition in which it will be too cold to permit of the existence of any others, the course of life upon its surface must describe a trajectory like that of a ball fired from a mortar; and the sinking half of that course is as much a part of the general process of evolution as the rising.

From the point of view of the moralist the animal world is on about the same level as a gladiator's show. The creatures are fairly well treated, and set to fight—whereby the strongest, the swiftest, and the cunningest live to fight another day. The spectator has no need to turn his thumbs down, as no quarter is given. He must admit that the skill and training displayed are wonderful. But he must shut his eyes if he would not see that more or less enduring suffering is the meed of both vanquished and victor. And since the great game is going on in every corner of the world, thousands of times a minute; since, were our ears sharp enough, we need not descend to the gates of hell to hear—

sospiri, pianti, ed alti guai.

. . . . .

Voci alte e fioche, e suon di man con elle [1]

—it seems to follow that, if the world is governed by benevolence, it must be a different sort of benevolence from that of John Howard.

But the old Babylonians wisely symbolized Nature by their great goddess Istar, who combined the attributes of Aphrodite with those of Ares. Her terrible aspect is not to be ignored or covered up with shams; but it is not the only one. If the optimism of Leibnitz is a foolish though pleasant dream, the pessimism of Schopenhauer is a nightmare, the more foolish because of its hideousness. Error which is not pleasant is surely the worst form of wrong.

This may not be the best of all possible worlds, but to say that it is the worst is mere petulant nonsense. A worn-out voluptuary may find nothing good under the sun, or a vain and inexperienced youth, who cannot get the moon he cries for, may vent his irritation in pessimistic moanings; but there can be no doubt in the mind of any reasonable person that mankind could, would, and in fact do, get on fairly well with vastly less happiness and far more misery than find their way into the lives of nine people out of ten. If each and all of us had been visited by an attack of neuralgia, or of extreme mental depression, for one hour in every twenty-four—a supposition which many tolerably vigorous people know, to their cost, is not extravagant—the burden of life would have been immensely increased without much practical hindrance to its general course. Men with any manhood in them find life quite worth living under worse conditions than these.

There is another sufficiently obvious fact, which renders the hypothesis that the course of sentient nature is dictated by malevolence quite untenable. A vast multitude of pleasures, and these among the purest and the best, are superfluities, bits of good which are to all appearances unnecessary as inducements to live, and are, so to speak, thrown into the bargain of life. To those who experience them, few delights can be more entrancing than such as are afforded by natural beauty, or by the arts, and especially by music; but they are products of, rather than factors in, evolution, and it is probable that they are known, in any considerable degree, to but a very small proportion of mankind.

The conclusion of the whole matter seems to be that, if Ormuzd has not had his way in this world, neither has Ahriman. Pessimism is as little consonant with the facts of sentient existence as optimism. If we desire to represent the course of nature in terms of human thought, and assume that it was intended to be that which it is, we must say that its governing principle is intellectual and not moral; that it is a materialized logical process, accompanied by pleasures and pains, the incidence of which, in the majority of cases, has not the slightest reference to moral desert. That the rain falls alike upon the just and the unjust, and that those upon whom the Tower of Siloam fell were no worse than their neighbors, seem to be Oriental modes of expressing the same conclusion.

In the strict sense of the word *nature,* it denotes the sum of the phenomenal world, of that which has been, and is, and will be; and society, like art, is therefore a part of nature. But it is convenient to distinguish those parts of nature in which man plays the part of immediate cause, as something apart; and, therefore, society, like art, is usefully to be considered as distinct from nature. It is the more desirable, and even necessary, to make this distinction, since society differs from nature in having a definite moral object; whence it comes about that the course shaped by the ethical man—the member of society or citizen—necessarily runs counter to that which the non-ethical man—the primitive savage, or

---

[1] *sospiri. . . . con elle:* Dante's *Inferno,* Canto III, 22, 27:
". . . sighs and clamors and shrill wailings.

. . . . .

High voices and hoarse, and sound of hands as well" (Fletcher's trans.).

man as a mere member of the animal kingdom—tends to adopt. The latter fights out the struggle for existence to the bitter end, like any other animal; the former devotes his best energies to the object of setting limits to the struggle.

In the cycle of phenomena presented by the life of man the animal, no more moral end is discernible than in that presented by the lives of the wolf and of the deer. However imperfect the relics of prehistoric men may be, the evidence which they afford clearly tends to the conclusion that, for thousands and thousands of years, before the origin of the oldest known civilizations, men were savages of a very low type. They strove with their enemies and their competitors; they preyed upon things weaker or less cunning than themselves; they were born, multiplied without stint, and died, for thousands of generations alongside the mammoth, the urus, the lion, and the hyena, whose lives were spent in the same way; and they were no more to be praised or blamed, on moral grounds, than their less erect and more hairy compatriots.

As among these, so among primitive men, the weakest and stupidest went to the wall, while the toughest and shrewdest, those who were best fitted to cope with their circumstances, but not the best in any other sense, survived. Life was a continual free fight, and beyond the limited and temporary relations of the family, the Hobbesian war of each against all was the normal state of existence. The human species, like others, plashed and floundered amid the general stream of evolution, keeping its head above water as it best might, and thinking neither of whence nor whither.

The history of civilization—that is, of society—on the other hand, is the record of the attempts which the human race has made to escape from this position. The first men who substituted the state of mutual peace for that of mutual war, whatever the motive which impelled them to take that step, created society. But, in establishing peace, they obviously put a limit upon the struggle for existence. Between the members of that society, at any rate, it was not to be pursued à outrance.[2] And of all the successive shapes which society has taken, that most nearly approaches perfection in which the war of individual against individual is most strictly limited. The primitive savage, tutored by Istar, appropriated whatever took his fancy, and killed whosoever opposed him, if he could. On the contrary, the ideal of the ethical man is to limit his freedom of action to a sphere in which he does not interfere with the freedom of others; he seeks the commonweal as much as his own; and, indeed, as an essential part of his own welfare. Peace is both end and means with him; and he founds his life on a more or less complete self-restraint, which is the negation of the unlimited struggle for existence. He tries to escape from his place in the animal kingdom, founded on the free development of the principle of nonmoral evolution, and to establish a kingdom of Man, governed upon the principle of moral evolution. For society not only has a moral end, but in its perfection, social life, is embodied morality.

But the effort of ethical man to work towards a moral end by no means abolished, perhaps has hardly modified, the deep-seated organic impulses which impel the natural man to follow his nonmoral course. One of the most essential conditions, if not the chief cause, of the struggle for existence, is the tendency to multiply without limit, which man shares with all living things. It is notable that "increase and multiply" is a commandment traditionally much older than the ten; and that it is, perhaps, the only one which has been spontaneously and ex animo[3] obeyed by the great majority of the human race. But, in civilized society, the inevitable result of such obedience is the re-establishment, in all its intensity, of that struggle for existence—the war of each against all—the mitigation or abolition of which was the chief end of social organization.

It is conceivable that, at some period in the history of the fabled Atlantis, the production of food should have been exactly sufficient to meet the wants of the population, that the makers of the commodities

2 *à outrance:* to the utmost (i.e. death).

3 *ex animo:* from the heart (i.e. sincerely).

of the artificer should have amounted to just the number supportable by the surplus food of the agriculturists. And, as there is no harm in adding another monstrous supposition to the 'foregoing, let it be imagined that every man, woman, and child was perfectly virtuous, and aimed at the good of all as the highest personal good. In that happy land, the natural man would have been finally put down by the ethical man. There would have been no competition, but the industry of each would have been serviceable to all; nobody being vain and nobody avaricious, there would have been no rivalries; the struggle for existence would have been abolished, and the millennium would have finally set in. But it is obvious that this state of things could have been permanent only with a stationary population. Add ten fresh mouths; and as, by the supposition, there was only exactly enough before, somebody must go on short rations. The Atlantis society might have been a heaven upon earth, the whole nation might have consisted of just men, needing no repentance, and yet somebody must starve. Reckless Istar, nonmoral Nature, would have riven the ethical fabric. I was once talking with a very eminent physician about the *vis medicatrix naturae*.[4] "Stuff!" said he; "nine times out of ten nature does not want to cure the man; she wants to put him in his coffin." And Istar-Nature appears to have equally little sympathy with the ends of society. "Stuff! she wants nothing but a fair field and free play for her darling the strongest."

Our Atlantis may be an impossible figment, but the antagonistic tendencies which the fable adumbrates have existed in every society which was ever established, and, to all appearance, must strive for the victory in all that will be. Historians point to the greed and ambition of rulers, to the reckless turbulence of the ruled, to the debasing effects of wealth and luxury, and to the devastating wars which have formed a great part of the occupation of mankind, as the causes of the decay of states and the foundering of old civilizations, and thereby point their story with a moral. No doubt

immoral motives of all sorts have figured largely among the minor causes of these events. But beneath all this superficial turmoil lay the deep-seated impulse given by unlimited multiplication. In the swarms of colonies thrown out by Phoenicia and by old Greece; in the *ver sacrum* [5] of the Latin races; in the floods of Gauls and of Teutons which burst over the frontiers of the old civilization of Europe; in the swaying to and fro of the vast Mongolian hordes in late times, the population problem comes to the front in a very visible shape. Nor is it less plainly manifest in the everlasting agrarian questions of ancient Rome than in the Arreoi societies of the Polynesian Islands.

In the ancient world, and in a large part of that in which we live, the practice of infanticide was, or is, a regular and legal custom; famine, pestilence, and war were and are normal factors in the struggle for existence, and they have served, in a gross and brutal fashion, to mitigate the intensity of the effects of its chief cause.

But, in the more advanced civilizations, the progress of private and public morality has steadily tended to remove all these checks. We declare infanticide murder, and punish it as such; we decree, not quite so successfully, that no one shall die of hunger; we regard death from preventable causes of other kinds as a sort of constructive murder, and eliminate pestilence to the best of our ability; we declaim against the curse of war, and the wickedness of the military spirit, and we are never weary of dilating on the blessedness of peace and the innocent beneficence of Industry. In their moments of expansion, even statesmen and men of business go thus far. The finer spirits look to an ideal *civitas Dei* [6]— a state when, every man having reached the point of absolute self-negation, and having nothing but moral perfection to strive after, peace will truly reign, not merely among nations, but among men, and the struggle for existence will be at an end.

4 *vis medicatrix naturæ:* the healing power of nature.

5 *ver sacrum:* 'sacred spring'—an offering of the first fruits of spring: "it sometimes involved the going forth as colonists (when they were grown) of all children born in the sacred season" (Webster's *International*).

6 *civitas Dei:* city of God.

Whether human nature is competent under any circumstances, to reach, or even seriously advance towards, this ideal condition, is a question which need not be discussed. It will be admitted that mankind has not yet reached this stage by a very long way, and my business is with the present. And that which I wish to point out is that, so long as the natural man increases and multiplies without restraint, so long will peace and industry not only permit, but they will necessitate, a struggle for existence as sharp as any that ever went on under the regime of war. If Istar is to reign on the one hand, she will demand her human sacrifices on the other.

Let us look at home. For seventy years peace and industry have had their way among us with less interruption and under more favorable conditions than in any other country on the face of the earth. The wealth of Croesus was nothing to that which we have accumulated, and our prosperity has filled the world with envy. But Nemesis did not forget Croesus—has she forgotten us?

I think not. There are now 36,000,000 of people in our islands, and every year considerably more than 300,000 are added to our numbers. That is to say, about every hundred seconds, or so, a new claimant to a share in the common stock or maintenance presents him or herself among us. At the present time, the produce of the soil does not suffice to feed half its population. The other moiety has to be supplied with food which must be bought from the people of food-producing countries. That is to say, we have to offer them the things which they want in exchange for the things we want. And the things they want and which we can produce better than they can are mainly manufactures—industrial products.

The insolent reproach of the first Napoleon had a very solid foundation. We not only are, but, under penalty of starvation, we are bound to be, a nation of shopkeepers. But other nations also lie under the same necessity of keeping shop, and some of them deal in the same goods as ourselves. Our customers naturally seek to get the most and the best in exchange for their produce. If our goods are inferior to those of our competitors, there is no ground, compatible with the sanity of the buyers, which can be alleged, why they should not prefer the latter. And, if that result should ever take place on a large and general scale, five or six millions of us would soon have nothing to eat. We know what the cotton famine was; and we can therefore form some notion of what a dearth of customers would be.

Judged by an ethical standard, nothing can be less satisfactory than the position in which we find ourselves. In a real, though incomplete, degree we have attained the condition of peace which is the main object of social organization; and, for argument's sake, it may be assumed that we desire nothing but that which is in itself innocent and praiseworthy—namely, the enjoyment of the fruits of honest industry. And lo! in spite of ourselves, we are in reality engaged in an internecine struggle for existence with our presumably no less peaceful and well-meaning neighbors. We seek peace and we do not ensue it. The moral nature in us asks for no more than is compatible with the general good; the nonmoral nature proclaims and acts upon that fine old Scottish family motto, "Thou shalt starve ere I want." Let us be under no illusions, then. So long as unlimited multiplication goes on, no social organization which has ever been devised, or is likely to be devised, no fiddle-faddling with the distribution of wealth, will deliver society from the tendency to be destroyed by the reproduction within itself, in its intensest form, of that struggle for existence the limitation of which is the object of society. And however shocking to the moral sense this eternal competition of man against man and of nation against nation may be; however revolting may be the accumulation of misery at the negative pole of society, in contrast with that of monstrous wealth at the positive pole—this state of things must abide, and grow continually worse, so long as Istar holds her way unchecked. It is the true riddle of the Sphinx; and every nation which does not solve it will sooner or later be devoured by the monster itself has generated.

The practical and pressing question for us, just now, seems to me to be how to gain time. "Time brings counsel," as the Teutonic proverb has it; and wiser folk among our posterity may see their way out of that which at present looks like an impasse.

It would be folly to entertain any ill-feeling towards those neighbors and rivals who, like ourselves, are slaves of Istar; but, if somebody is to be starved, the modern world has no Oracle of Delphi to which the nations can appeal for an indication of the victim. It is open to us to try our fortune; and, if we avoid impending fate, there will be a certain ground for believing that we are the right people to escape. *Securus judicat orbis.*[7]

To this end, it is well to look into the necessary conditions of our salvation by works. They are two, one plain to all the world and hardly needing insistence; the other seemingly not so plain, since too often it has been theoretically and practically left out of sight. The obvious condition is that our produce shall be better than that of others. There is only one reason why our goods should be preferred to those of our rivals—our customers must find them better at the price. That means that we must use more knowledge, skill, and industry in producing them, without a proportionate increase in the cost of production; and, as the price of labor constitutes a large element in that cost, the rate of wages must be restricted within certain limits. It is perfectly true that cheap production and cheap labor are by no means synonymous; but it is also true that wages cannot increase beyond a certain proportion without destroying cheapness. Cheapness, then, with, as part and parcel of cheapness, a moderate price of labor, is essential to our success as competitors in the markets of the world.

The second condition is really quite as plainly indispensable as the first, if one thinks seriously about the matter. It is social stability. Society is stable when the wants of its members obtain as much satisfaction as, life being what it is, common sense and experience show may be reasonably expected. Mankind, in general, care very little for forms of government or ideal considerations of any sort; and nothing really stirs the great multitude to break with custom and incur the manifest perils of revolt except the belief that misery in this world, or damnation in the next, or both, are threatened by the continuance of the state of things in which they have been brought up. But when they do attain that conviction, society becomes as unstable as a package of dynamite, and a very small matter will produce the explosion which sends it back to the chaos of savagery.

It needs no argument to prove that when the price of labor sinks below a certain point, the worker infallibly falls into that condition which the French emphatically call *la misère*—a word for which I do not think there is any exact English equivalent. It is a condition in which the food, warmth, and clothing which are necessary for the mere maintenance of the functions of the body in their normal state cannot be obtained; in which men, women, and children are forced to crowd into dens wherein decency is abolished and the most ordinary conditions of healthful existence are impossible of attainment; in which the pleasures within reach are reduced to bestiality and drunkenness; in which the pains accumulate at compound interest, in the shape of starvation, disease, stunted development, and moral degradation; in which the prospect of even steady and honest industry is a life of unsuccessful battling with hunger, rounded by a pauper's grave.

That a certain proportion of the members of every great aggregation of mankind should constantly tend to establish and populate such a Slough of Despond as this is inevitable, so long as some people are by nature idle and vicious, while others are disabled by sickness or accident, or thrown upon the world by the death of their breadwinners. So long as that proportion is restricted within tolerable limits, it can be dealt with; and, so far as it arises only from such causes, its existence may and must be patiently borne. But, when the organization of society, instead of mitigating this tendency, tends to continue and intensify it; when a given social order plainly makes for evil and not for good, men naturally enough begin to think it high time to try a fresh experiment. The animal man, finding that the ethical man has landed him in such a slough, resumes his ancient sovereignty, and preaches anarchy; which is, substantially, a proposal to reduce the social cosmos to chaos, and begin the brute struggle for existence once again.

Anyone who is acquainted with the state of the population of all great industrial centers, whether in this or other countries, is aware that, amidst a large and increasing body of that population, la misère reigns supreme. I have no pretensions to the character of a philanthropist, and I have a special horror of all sorts of sentimental rhetoric; I am merely trying to deal with facts, to some extent within my own knowl- 20 edge, and further evidenced by abundant testimony, as a naturalist; and I take it to be a mere plain truth that, throughout industrial Europe, there is not a single large manufacturing city which is free from a vast mass of people whose condition is exactly that described; and from a still greater mass who, living just on the edge of the social swamp, are liable to be pre- cipitated into it by any lack of demand 30 for their produce. And, with every addi- tion to the population, the multitude already sunk in the pit and the number of the host sliding towards it continually increase.

Argumentation can hardly be needful to make it clear that no society in which the elements of decomposition are thus swiftly and surely accumulating can hope to win in the race of industries.

Intelligence, knowledge, and skill are un- doubtedly conditions of success; but of what avail are they likely to be unless they are backed up by honesty, energy, good will, and all the physical and moral facul- ties that go to the making of manhood, and unless they are stimulated by hope of such reward as men may fairly look to? And what dweller in the slough of want, dwarfed in body and soul, demoralized, 50 hopeless, can reasonably be expected to possess these qualities?

Any full and permanent development of the productive powers of an industrial pop- ulation, then, must be compatible with and, indeed, based upon a social organiza- tion which will secure a fair amount of physical and moral welfare to that popula- tion; which will make for good and not for evil. Natural science and religious enthusiasm rarely go hand in hand, but on this matter their concord is complete; and the least sympathetic of naturalists can but 10 admire the insight and the devotion of such social reformers as the late Lord Shaftesbury, whose recently published Life and Letters gives a vivid picture of the condition of the working classes fifty years ago, and of the pit which our industry, ignoring these plain truths, was then dig- ing under its own feet.

There is, perhaps, no more hopeful sign of progress among us, in the last half-cen- 20 tury, than the steadily increasing devotion which has been and is directed to measures for promoting physical and moral welfare among the poorer classes. Sanitary re- formers, like most other reformers whom I have had the advantage of knowing, seem to need a good dose of fanaticism, as a sort of moral coca, to keep them up to the mark, and, doubtless, they have made many mistakes; but that the endeavor to improve 30 the condition under which our industrial population live, to amend the drainage of densely peopled streets, to provide baths, washhouses, and gymnasia, to facilitate habits of thrift, to furnish some provision for instruction and amusement in public libraries and the like, is not only desirable from a philanthropic point of view, but an essential condition of safe industrial devel- opment, appears to me to be indisputable. 40 It is by such means alone, so far as I can see, that we can hope to check the constant gravitation of industrial society towards la misère, until the general progress of intelli- gence and morality leads men to grapple with the sources of that tendency. If it is said that the carrying out of such arrange- ments as those indicated must enhance the cost of production, and thus handicap the producer in the race of competition, I ven- 50 ture, in the first place, to doubt the fact; but if it be so, it results that industrial society has to face a dilemma, either alter- native of which threatens destruction.

On the one hand, a population the labor

of which is sufficiently remunerated may be physically and morally healthy and socially stable, but may fail in industrial competition by reason of the dearness of its produce. On the other hand, a population the labor of which is insufficiently remunerated must become physically and morally unhealthy, and socially unstable; and though it may succeed for a while in industrial competition, by reason of the cheapness of its produce, it must in the end fall, through hideous misery and degradation, to utter ruin.

Well, if these are the only possible alternatives, let us for ourselves and our children choose the former, and, if need be, starve like men. But I do not believe that the stable society made up of healthy, vigorous, instructed, and self-ruling people would ever incur serious risk of that fate. They are not likely to be troubled with many competitors of the same character, just yet; and they may be safely trusted to find ways of holding their own.

[1888]

WILLIAM MORRIS

CHRONOLOGY AND INTRODUCTION

1834 Born March 24, at Walthamstow, Essex.
1848 School at Marlborough.
1853–6 At Oxford: *Oxford and Cambridge Magazine:* takes B.A., 1856.
1857 London, with Burne-Jones and Rossetti.
1858 *The Defence of Guinevere and Other Poems.*
1859 Marriage.
1860 Moves into Red House, Upton, Kent.
1861 Establishment of Morris, Marshall, Faulkner and Company, a firm of decorators.
1865 Moves to 26 Queen Square, London, as residence and place of business.
1867 *The Life and Death of Jason.*
1868–70 *The Earthly Paradise.*
1869–70 Translations of Icelandic Sagas.
1871 Kelmscott Manor is summer home: first journey to Iceland.
1872 *Love is Enough.*
1873 Second journey to Iceland.
1875 *The Aeneids of Virgil*—a translation.
1876 *Sigurd the Volsung.*
1878 Removal to Kelmscott House, Hammersmith.

1881 Merton Abbey Works started.
1882 *Hopes and Fears for Art.*
1883 Joins Democratic Federation.
1885 Helps to establish (and joins) Socialist League.
1887 *The Odyssey*—a translation.
1888 *A Dream of John Ball.*
Signs of Change.
The House of the Wolfings.
1889 *The Roots of the Mountains.*
1890 Forms Hammersmith Socialist Society.
1891 *News from Nowhere.*
Poems by the Way.
The Story of the Glittering Plain.
Kelmscott Press started.
1894 *The Wood Beyond the World.*
1895 *Beowulf,*—a translation.
1896 *The Well at the World's End:* The Kelmscott Chaucer.
Death of Morris, Oct. 3.
1897 *The Water of the Wondrous Isles.*
The Sundering Flood.
1914 *Lectures on Art and Industry.*
1915 *Lectures on Socialism.*

William Morris is increasingly accepted as a major Victorian, because of his distinction as a writer, a craftsman, a reformer, and a personality. The range and quality of his total accomplishment are amazing even in an age of eminent artists. His reputation as a poet was first, but he wrote nearly as good prose in his undergraduate days as any that came from his pen in the last years, when he returned to imaginative writing and produced a succession of stories of strange adventures told in language almost as strange. Between this earlier and later writing, during the years when he had become the foremost craftsman of his age and an active agitator for a new social order, Morris turned out many essays and lectures on the arts and crafts and on socialism, always in simple, informal prose, expressed in "homely, every-day words." But these words carried his vision to his hearers and, as Bernard Shaw says, "survive as the best books in the Bible of Socialism." "I have only one subject to lecture on," Morris said,—"the relation of Art to Labor."

Nothing in the records of artists seems more strange than that the author of *The Earthly Paradise, Jason,* and *Sigurd,* and the maker of lovely stained glass and tapestries should at forty-nine become a propagandist of revolutionary radicalism, preaching socialism on street corners, distributing manifestoes from the tail of a cart in Hyde Park, London, and struggling desperately to find a clue to the labyrinth of Marxian economics. Morris was known to his friends and contemporaries as a poet who had written verses of exquisite and exotic beauty, more like dream-pictures than anything else, fashioned out of fragments of scenes and circumstances that lay floating in his brain after reading Malory and Froissart and other medieval and classical narratives. He called himself a dreamer of dreams, born out of his due time. Why should *he* strive to set the crooked straight? His theory of art, so far as the reading public could infer it from his performances, seemed to be that art had nothing to do with contemporary life, but was rather the embodiment of "dreams in a series of pictures" (as he phrased it), such as might have the effect upon older readers that fairy stories have upon children, transporting them for the while away from the monotony, ugliness, and stale familiarity of everyday life into a region of strangeness and beauty. Burne-Jones, his life-long friend, would never admit that Morris's connection with socialism was anything but a "parenthesis" of his life. "Morris was before all things a poet and an artist," he insisted; and the only place for such a man, he thought, was in his studio away from the noisy distractions of the crowd.

But there are currents in the lives of men often invisible even to their closest friends. It was so with Morris. His entrance into socialism was not a break with the past, but a fulfillment. From his Oxford days onward he had a deepening interest in the welfare of humanity. In a letter to his mother in which he first reveals his resolution to forsake Holy Orders for architecture, he seeks to reassure his disappointed family: "I will by no means give up things I have thought of for the bettering of the world in so far as lies in me." The talk at Oxford was not always on Malory and Keats and Tennyson; it was sometimes on Carlyle and Ruskin, on the organization of labor and the re-making of society; and Morris was always in the thick of it, knocking his head with his fists in irrepressible excitement. Throughout his life there are glimpses of this passion of humanity. "Do you know," he said many years later, "when I see a poor devil drunk and brutal I always feel, quite apart from my aesthetical perceptions, a sort of shame, as if I myself had some hand in it. . . . I claim not to be separated from those that are heavy-hearted only because I am well in health and full of pleasant work and eager about it, and not oppressed by desires so as not to be able to take interest in it all."

When he wrote these words Morris was the successful head of a firm of decorators. "The industries immediately taken in hand," says his daughter, "were stained glass, wall-painting, painted tiles, furniture, embroidery, table-glass, metal-work; very soon came chinzes, paperhangings, and woven-hangings; tapestry and carpets were later." Although he called himself "a decorator by profession," he meant by the phrase infinitely more than a description of his business; for he now conceived of art as the very flowering of life, or rather as the distilled essence of beauty made available for the delight of man in his home, in the streets of his cities, and in his places of work and worship. "Beauty," he said, "which is what is meant by art, is, I contend, no mere accident to human life, which people can take or leave, as they choose, but a positive necessity of life, if we are to live as nature meant us to." Art, thus understood, gives pleasure not only to the user but to the maker, for delight in skill is at the root of it, and "the pleasurable exercise of our energies is the only true source of happiness. . . . Art is the expression of joy in labor."

Morris, moreover, like Ruskin, drew no dividing line between an artist and a workman; all art is work and all work is art in so far as it expresses the happiness of the worker. "I must ask you," he said, "to extend the word art beyond those matters which are consciously works of art, to take in not only painting and sculpture, and architecture, but the shapes and colors of all household goods, nay, even the arrangement of the fields for tillage and pasture, the management of towns and of our highways of all kinds; in a word, to extend it to the aspect of all the externals of life." And for illustration of what he wished to see realized in so far as *method* and *spirit of work* were concerned, he turned to the medieval art of the twelfth and thirteenth centuries, to the golden age of handicrafts and co-operative tradition, when "the best artist was a workman still, the humblest workman an artist." (Morris never meant a revival of this art in the nineteenth century; every period, he insisted, must create its own art.)

It becomes evident that, along with Morris's underlying passion of humanity, there was his developing conception of art as a profoundly social matter, involving the happiness or misery of all classes of people. Instead of a civilization that could realize his ideals he now saw in the 'seventies and 'eighties a social order that was "trampling out all the beauty of life and making us less than men." Luxury and idleness were increasing for the rich, want and misery for the poor. Workers were enslaved to machines and were "rubbing through life towards the workhouse and the grave on ten shillings a week." Their homes were dens of filth, and half England was "a foul and greasy cinder-heap." Morris's indignation rose to fever-heat and he deliberately declared: "If our civilization is to carry us no further, to nothing better, I for one wish we had never gone so far." It is to be remembered that he was in the truest sense not only an artist but a democrat: "Over and over again have I asked myself why should not my lot be the common lot. My work is simple enough; much of it, nor that the least pleasant, any man of decent intelligence could do, if he could but get to care about the work and its results. Indeed I have been ashamed when I have thought of the contrast between my happy working hours and the unpraised, unrewarded, monotonous drudgery which most men are condemned to. Nothing shall convince me that such labor as this is good or necessary to civilization." Morris now saw clearly that "the first step towards a new birth of art must be a definite rise in the condition of the workers."

It was a time of stir when he went into socialism. Class consciousness among the wage earners had been gathering power. Society at large had been a good deal shaken out of its complacency by the writings of Carlyle and Ruskin. The young intellectuals, brought up on Spencer and J. S. Mill, were turning to Karl Marx and Henry George and were for the first time setting up organizations with socialism as their working creed, notably the Democratic Federation in 1881 and the Fabians in 1884. Morris could not labor for a better civilization from the outside, as did many of his contemporaries; he must join the rank and file. When, therefore, he united with the Democratic Federation—"as far as I know the only active Socialist Organization in England"—he was ready to sacrifice his time, his money, his reputation, and his superb energies. He sold the greater part of his library in order to devote the proceeds to the "cause," and he freely contributed cash and essays to support *Justice*, the organ of the Federation, and, later, *The Commonweal*, the organ of the Socialist League.

Morris's social ideals cannot adequately be summarized in a paragraph. He faced the whole problem of modern life, and the writings of this period are crowded with criticism, comments, hints, and suggestions which, in the aggregate, however vague and impractical they may be in some directions, must convince his readers of his penetrating insight and profound sincerity, as well as of his amazing range of interest. Although to the last he dreamed of an ideal civilization, he never seriously permitted himself to forecast the society of tomorrow. He was content to attack conditions around him, first. He wanted capitalism, organized for profit, with its competition, mastership, monopoly, exploitation of labor to give place to a communal, co-operative society, made up of associations of workers, each according to his creative capacity producing to satisfy his own needs and the needs of his fellows. It would be a society of equals, economically speaking; private property would be abolished in the sense that no one should have what was not directly the result of his own labor. The resources of the earth and the agencies for their development and use—machinery, capital, means of transit—should belong to the community. No one would be allowed to inherit or store up a surplus sufficient to enable him to exploit the labor of his fellow men, and no one, if restricted to the fruits of his own work, could become rich. Every one in the new order would live in obedience to the law of nature, which commands men to work if they would survive. Machines, in so far as they enslave men, should be given up; to the extent that they are a saving of labor and a means of simplification of life they should be kept. The hours for really repulsive but necessary jobs could be shortened; the jobs themselves could be varied and even made honorable, to be taken up by volunteers under the call for patriotic service.

But when all is said Morris did not look to see the sun rise on a Monday morning over an Earthly Paradise that had been miraculously created out of the corruptly capitalistic society of a Saturday night before. His earlier intransigence changed with time into something more accommodating to circumstances, when he was ready to accept ameliorative measures as stepping stones to a far-distant goal. He came to realize that the most difficult and fundamental change must be a change in human nature; and so in the later years of his socialism he placed the emphasis upon education. But he never lost sight of the distant objective, which was the emancipation of labor and the organization of society into a fellowship of workers, from which would come a rebirth of art: "an art made intelligently by the whole body of those who live by their labor: instinct with their thoughts and aspirations, moving whither they are moving, changing as they change, the genuine expression of their sense of the beauty and mystery of life: an art born with their joy and outliving their sorrow, though tinged by it: an art leaving to future ages living witness of the existence of deft hands and eager minds not too proud to tell us of their imperfect thoughts, and their glimpses of insight into wonders and terrors, as they passed amid the hurry of their daily work through the sunshine and the shadow of their lives."

HOPES AND FEARS FOR ART

THE LESSER ARTS

Hereafter I hope in another lecture to have the pleasure of laying before you an historical survey of the lesser, or, as they are called, the Decorative Arts, and I must con-fess it would have been pleasanter to me to have begun my talk with you by entering at once upon the subject of the history of this great industry; but, as I have something to say in a third lecture about various matters connected with the practice of

Decoration among ourselves in these days, I feel that I should be in a false position before you, and one that might lead to confusion, or overmuch explanation, if I did not let you know what I think on the nature and scope of these arts, on their condition at the present time, and their outlook in times to come. In doing this it is like enough that I shall say things with which you will very much disagree; I must ask you therefore from the outset to believe that whatever I may blame or whatever I may praise, I neither, when I think of what history has been, am inclined to lament the past, to despise the present, or despair of the future; that I believe all the change and stir about us is a sign of the world's life, and that it will lead—by ways, indeed, of which we have no guess—to the bettering of all mankind.

Now as to the scope and nature of these arts I have to say, that though when I come more into the details of my subject I shall not meddle much with the great art of Architecture, and less still with the great arts commonly called Sculpture and Painting, yet I cannot in my own mind quite sever them from those lesser so-called Decorative Arts, which I have to speak about: it is only in latter times, and under the most intricate conditions of life, that they have fallen apart from one another; and I hold that, when they are so parted, it is ill for the Arts altogether: the lesser ones become trivial, mechanical, unintelligent, incapable of resisting the changes pressed upon them by fashion or dishonesty; while the greater, however they may be practised for a while by men of great minds and wonder-working hands, unhelped by the lesser, unhelped by each other, are sure to lose their dignity of popular arts, and become nothing but dull adjuncts to unmeaning pomp, or ingenious toys for a few rich and idle men.

However, I have not undertaken to talk to you of Architecture, Sculpture, and Painting, in the narrower sense of those words, since, most unhappily as I think, these master-arts, these arts more specially of the intellect, are at the present day divorced from decoration in its narrower sense. Our subject is that great body of art, by means of which men have at all times more or less striven to beautify the familiar matters of everyday life: a wide subject, a great industry; both a great part of the history of the world, and a most helpful instrument to the study of that history.

A very great industry indeed, comprising the crafts of house-building, painting, joinery and carpentry, smiths' work, pottery and glass-making, weaving, and many others: a body of art most important to the public in general, but still more so to us handicraftsmen; since there is scarce anything that they use, and that we fashion, but it has always been thought to be unfinished till it has had some touch or other of decoration about it. True it is that in many or most cases we have got so used to this ornament, that we look upon it as if it had grown of itself, and note it no more than the mosses on the dry sticks with which we light our fires. So much the worse! for there *is* the decoration, or some pretence of it, and it has, or ought to have, a use and a meaning. For, and this is at the root of the whole matter, everything made by man's hands has a form, which must be either beautiful or ugly; beautiful if it is in accord with Nature, and helps her; ugly if it is discordant with Nature, and thwarts her; it cannot be indifferent: we, for our parts, are busy or sluggish, eager or unhappy, and our eyes are apt to get dulled to this eventfulness of form in those things which we are always looking at. Now it is one of the chief uses of decoration, the chief part of its alliance with nature, that it has to sharpen our dulled senses in this matter: for this end are those wonders of intricate patterns interwoven, those strange forms invented, which men have so long delighted in: forms and intricacies that do not necessarily imitate nature, but in which the hand of the craftsman is guided to work in the way that she does, till the web, the cup, or the knife, look as natural, nay as lovely, as the green field, the river bank, or the mountain flint.

To give people pleasure in the things they must perforce *use,* that is one great office of decoration; to give people pleasure in the things they must perforce *make,* that is the other use of it.

Does not our subject look important enough now? I say that without these arts, our rest would be vacant and uninteresting, our labour mere endurance, mere wearing away of body and mind.

As for that last use of these arts, the giving us pleasure in our work, I scarcely know how to speak strongly enough of it; and yet if I did not know the value of repeating a truth again and again, I should have to excuse myself to you for saying any more about this, when I remember how a great man now living has spoken of it: I mean my friend Professor John Ruskin: if you read the chapter in the 2nd vol. of his *Stones of Venice* entitled, "On the Nature of Gothic, and the Office of the Workman therein," you will read at once the truest and the most eloquent words that can possibly be said on the subject. What I have to say upon it can scarcely be more than an echo of his words, yet I repeat there is some use in reiterating a truth, lest it be forgotten; so I will say this much further: we all know what people have said about the curse of labour, and what heavy and grievous nonsense are the more part of their words thereupon; whereas indeed the real curses of craftsmen have been the curse of stupidity, and the curse of injustice from within and from without: no, I cannot suppose there is anybody here who would think it either a good life, or an amusing one, to sit with one's hands before one doing nothing—to live like a gentleman, as fools call it.

Nevertheless there *is* dull work to be done, and a weary business it is setting men about such work, and seeing them through it, and I would rather do the work twice over with my own hands than have such a job: but now only let the arts which we are talking of beautify our labour, and be widely spread, intelligent, well understood both by the maker and the user, let them grow in one word *popular,* and there will be pretty much an end of dull work and its wearing slavery; and no man will any longer have an excuse for talking about the curse of labour, no man will any longer have an excuse for evading the blessing of labour. I believe there is nothing that will aid the world's progress so much as the attainment of this; I protest there is nothing in the world that I desire so much as this, wrapped up, as I am sure

it is, with changes political and social, that in one way or another we all desire.

Now if the objection be made, that these arts have been the handmaids of luxury, of tyranny and of superstition, I must needs say that it is true in a sense; they have been so used, as many other excellent things have been. But it is also true that, among some nations, their most vigorous and freest times have been the very blossoming times of art: while at the same time, I must allow that these decorative arts have flourished among oppressed peoples, who have seemed to have no hope of freedom: yet I do not think that we shall be wrong in thinking that at such times, among such peoples, art, at least, was free; when it has not been, when it has really been gripped by superstition, or by luxury, it has straightway begun to sicken under that grip. Nor must you forget that when men say popes, kings, and emperors built such and such buildings, it is a mere way of speaking. You look in your history-books to see who built Westminster Abbey, who built St. Sophia at Constantinople, and they tell you Henry III., Justinian the Emperor. Did they? or, rather, men like you and me, handicraftsmen, who have left no names behind them, nothing but their work?

Now as these arts call people's attention and interest to the matters of every-day life in the present, so also, and that I think is no little matter, they call our attention at every step to that history, of which, I said before, they are so great a part; for no nation, no state of society, however rude, has been wholly without them: nay, there are peoples not a few, of whom we know scarce anything, save that they thought such and such forms beautiful. So strong is the bond between history and decoration, that in the practice of the latter we cannot, if we would, wholly shake off the influence of past times over what we do at present. I do not think it is too much to say that no man, however original he may be, can sit down to-day and draw the ornament of a cloth, or the form of an ordinary vessel or piece of furniture, that will be other than a development or a degradation of forms used hundreds of years ago; and these, too, very often, forms that once had a serious meaning, though they are now become little more than a habit of the hand; forms that were once perhaps the mysterious symbols of worships and beliefs now little remembered or wholly forgotten. Those who have diligently followed the delightful study of these arts are able as if through windows to look upon the life of the past:—the very first beginnings of thought among nations whom we cannot even name; the terrible empires of the ancient East; the free vigour and glory of Greece; the heavy weight, the firm grasp of Rome; the fall of her temporal Empire which spread so wide about the world all that good and evil which men can never forget, and never cease to feel; the clashing of East and West, South and North, about her rich and fruitful daughter Byzantium; the rise, the dissensions, and the waning of Islam; the wanderings of Scandinavia; the Crusades; the foundation of the States of modern Europe; the struggles of free thought with ancient dying system—with all these events and their meaning is the history of popular art interwoven; with all this, I say, the careful student of decoration as an historical industry must be familiar. When I think of this, and the usefulness of all this knowledge, at a time when history has become so earnest a study amongst us as to have given us, as it were, a new sense: at a time when we so long to know the reality of all that has happened, and are to be put off no longer with the dull records of the battles and intrigues of kings and scoundrels,—I say when I think of all this, I hardly know how to say that this interweaving of the Decorative Arts with the history of the past is of less importance than their dealings with the life of the present: for should not these memories also be a part of our daily life?

And now let me recapitulate a little before I go further, before we begin to look into the condition of the arts at the present day. These arts, I have said, are part of a great system invented for the expression of a man's delight in beauty: all peoples and times have used them; they have been the joy of free nations, and the solace of oppressed nations; religion has used and elevated them, has abused and degraded them; they are connected with all history, and are clear teachers of it; and, best of all, they are the sweeteners of human labour, both to the handicraftsman, whose life is spent in working in them, and to people in general who are influenced by the sight of them at every turn of the day's work: they make our toil happy, our rest fruitful.

And now if all I have said seems to you but mere open-mouthed praise of these arts, I must say that it is not for nothing that what I have hitherto put before you has taken that form.

It is because I must now ask you this question: All these good things—will you have them? will you cast them from you?

Are you surprised at my question—you, most of whom, like myself, are engaged in the actual practice of the arts that are, or ought to be, popular?

In explanation, I must somewhat repeat what I have already said. Time was when the mystery and wonder of handicrafts were well acknowledged by the world, when imagination and fancy mingled with all things made by man; and in those days all handicraftsmen were *artists*, as we should now call them. But the thought of man became more intricate, more difficult to express; art grew a heavier thing to deal with, and its labour was more divided among great men, lesser men, and little men; till that art, which was once scarce more than a rest of body and soul, as the hand cast the shuttle or swung the hammer, became to some men so serious a labour, that their working lives have been one long tragedy of hope and fear, joy and trouble. This was the growth of art: like all growth, it was good and fruitful for awhile; like all fruitful growth, it grew into decay; like all decay of what was once fruitful, it will grow into something new.

Into decay; for as the arts sundered into the greater and the lesser, contempt on one side, carelessness on the other arose, both begotten of ignorance of that *philosophy* of the Decorative Arts, a hint of which I have tried just now to put before you. The artist came out from the handicraftsmen, and left them without hope of elevation, while he himself was left without the help of intelligent, industrious sympathy. Both have suffered; the artist no less than the workman. It is with art as it fares with a company of soldiers before a redoubt, when the captain runs forward full of hope and energy, but looks not behind him to see if his men are following, and they hang back, not knowing why they are brought there to die. The captain's life is spent for nothing, and his men are sullen prisoners in the redoubt of Unhappiness and Brutality.

I must in plain words say of the Decorative Arts, of all the arts, that it is not so much that we are inferior in them to all who have gone before us, but rather that they are in a state of anarchy and disorganisation, which makes a sweeping change necessary and certain.

So that again I ask my question, All that good fruit which the arts should bear, will you have it? will you cast it from you? Shall that sweeping change that must come, be the change of loss or of gain?

We who believe in the continuous life of the world, surely we are bound to hope that the change will bring us gain and not loss, and to strive to bring that gain about.

Yet how the world may answer my question, who can say? A man in his short life can see but a little way ahead, and even in mine, wonderful and unexpected things have come to pass. I must needs say that therein lies my hope rather than in all I see going on round about us. Without disputing that if the imaginative arts perish, some new thing, at present unguessed of, *may* be put forward to supply their loss in men's lives, I cannot feel happy in that prospect, nor can I believe that mankind will endure such a loss for ever: but in the meantime the present state of the arts and their dealings with modern life and progress seem to me to point, in appearance at least, to this immediate future; that the world, which has for a long time busied itself about other matters than the arts, and has carelessly let them sink lower and lower, till many not uncultivated men, ignorant of what they once were, and hopeless of what they might yet be, look upon them with mere contempt; that the world, I say, thus busied and hurried, will one day wipe the slate, and be clean rid in her impatience of the whole matter with all this tangle and trouble.

And then—what then?

Even now amid the squalor of London it is hard to imagine what it will be. Architecture, Sculpture, Painting, with the crowd of lesser arts that belong to them, these, together with Music and Poetry, will be dead and forgotten, will no longer excite or amuse people in the least: for, once more, we must not deceive ourselves; the death of one art means the death of all; the only difference in their fate will be that the luckiest will be eaten the last— the luckiest, or the unluckiest: in all that has to do with beauty the invention and ingenuity of man will have come to a dead stop; and all the while Nature will go on with her eternal recurrence of lovely changes—spring, summer, autumn, and winter; sunshine, rain, and snow; storm and fair weather; dawn, noon, and sunset; day and night—ever bearing witness against man that he has deliberately chosen ugliness instead of beauty, and to live where he is strongest amidst squalor or blank emptiness.

You see, sirs, we cannot quite imagine it; any more, perhaps, than our forefathers of ancient London, living in the pretty, carefully whitened houses, with the famous church and its huge spire rising above them,—than they, passing about the fair gardens running down to the broad river, could have imagined a whole county or more covered over with hideous hovels, big, middle-sized, and little, which should one day be called London.

Sirs, I say that this dead blank of the arts that I more than dread is difficult even now to imagine; yet I fear that I must say that if it does not come about, it will be owing to some turn of events which we cannot at present foresee: but I hold that if it does happen, it will only last for a time, that it will be but a burning up of the gathered weeds, so that the field may bear more abundantly. I hold that men would wake up after a while, and look round and find the dullness unbearable, and begin once more inventing, imitating, and imagining, as in earlier days.

That faith comforts me, and I can say calmly, if the blank space must happen, it must, and amidst its darkness the new seed must sprout. So it has been before: first comes birth, and hope scarcely conscious of itself; then the flower and fruit of mastery, with hope more than conscious enough, passing into insolence, as decay follows ripeness; and then—the new birth again.

Meantime it is the plain duty of all who look seriously on the arts to do their best to save the world from what at the best will be a loss, the result of ignorance and unwisdom; to prevent, in fact, that most discouraging of all changes, the supplying the place of an extinct brutality by a new one; nay, even if those who really care for the arts are so weak and few that they can do nothing else, it may be their business to keep alive some tradition, some memory of the past, so that the new life when it comes may not waste itself more than enough in fashioning wholly new forms for its new spirit.

To what side then shall those turn for help, who really understand the gain of a great art in the world, and the loss of peace and good life that must follow from the lack of it? I think that they must begin by acknowledging that the ancient art, the art of unconscious intelligence, as one should call it, which began without a date, at least so long ago as those strange and masterly scratchings on mammoth-bones and the like found but the other day in the drift—that this art of unconscious intelligence is all but dead; that what little of it is left lingers among half-civilised nations, and is growing coarser, feebler, less intelligent year by year; nay, it is mostly at the mercy of some commercial accident, such as the arrival of a few shiploads of European dye-stuffs or a few dozen orders from European merchants: this they must recognise, and must hope to see in time its place filled by a new art of conscious intelligence, the birth of wiser, simpler, freer ways of life than the world leads now, than the world has ever led.

I said, *to see* this in time; I do not mean to say that our own eyes will look upon it: it may be so far off, as indeed it seems to some, that many would scarcely think it worth while thinking of: but there are some of us who cannot turn our faces to the wall, or sit deedless because our hope seems somewhat dim; and, indeed, I think that while the signs of the last decay of the old art with all the evils that must follow in its train are only too obvious about us, so on the other hand there are not wanting signs of the new dawn beyond that possible night of the arts, of which I have before spoken; this sign chiefly, that there are some few at least, who are heartily discontented with things as they are, and crave for something better, or at least some promise of it—this best of signs: for I suppose that if some half-dozen men at any time earnestly set their hearts on something coming about which is not discordant with nature, it will come to pass one day or other; because it is not by accident that an idea comes into the heads of a few; rather they are pushed on, and forced to speak or act by something stirring in the heart of the world which would otherwise be left without expression.

By what means then shall those work who long for reform in the arts, and who shall they seek to kindle into eager desire for possession of beauty, and better still, for the development of the faculty that creates beauty?

People say to me often enough: If you want to make your art succeed and flourish, you must make it the fashion: a phrase which I confess annoys me; for they mean by it that I should spend one day over my work to two days in trying to convince rich, and supposed influential people, that they care very much for what they really do not care in the least, so that it may happen according to the proverb: *Bell-wether took the leap, and we all went over.* Well, such advisers are right if they are content with the thing lasting but a little while; say till you can make a little money—if you don't get pinched by the door shutting too quickly: otherwise they are wrong: the people they are thinking of have too many strings to their bow, and can turn their backs too easily on a thing that fails, for it to be safe work trusting to their whims: it is not their fault, they cannot help it, but they have no chance of spending time enough over the arts to know anything practical of them, and they must of necessity be in the hands of those who spend their time in pushing fashion this way and that for their own advantage.

Sirs, there is no help to be got out of

these latter, or those who let themselves be led by them: the only real help for the decorative arts must come from those who work in them; nor must they be led, they must lead.

You whose hands make those things that should be works of art, you must be all artists, and good artists too, before the public at large can take real interest in such things; and when you have become so, I promise you that you shall lead the fashion; fashion shall follow your hands obediently enough.

That is the only way in which we can get a supply of intelligent popular art: a few artists of the kind so-called now, what can they do working in the teeth of difficulties thrown in their way by what is called Commerce, but which should be called greed of money? working helplessly among the crowd of those who are ridiculously called manufacturers, i.e. handicraftsmen, though the more part of them never did a stroke of hand-work in their lives, and are nothing better than capitalists and salesmen. What can these grains of sand do, I say, amidst the enormous mass of work turned out every year which professes in some way to be decorative art, but the decoration of which no one heeds except the salesmen who have to do with it, and are hard put to it to supply the cravings of the public for something new, not for something pretty?

The remedy, I repeat, is plain if it can be applied; the handicraftsman, left behind by the artist when the arts sundered, must come up with him, must work side by side with him: apart from the difference between a great master and a scholar, apart from the differences of the natural bent of men's minds, which would make one man an imitative, and another an architectural or decorative artist, there should be no difference between those employed on strictly ornamental work; and the body of artists dealing with this should quicken with their art all makers of things into artists also, in proportion to the necessities and uses of the things they would make.

I know what stupendous difficulties, social and economical, there are in the way of this; yet I think that they seem to be greater than they are: and of one thing I am sure, that no real living decorative art is possible if this is impossible.

It is not impossible, on the contrary it is certain to come about, if you are at heart desirous to quicken the arts; if the world will, for the sake of beauty and decency, sacrifice some of the things it is so busy over (many of which I think are not very worthy of its trouble), art will begin to grow again; as for those difficulties above mentioned, some of them I know will in any case melt away before the steady change of the relative conditions of men; the rest, reason and resolute attention to the laws of nature, which are also the laws of art, will dispose of little by little: once more, the way will not be far to seek, if the will be with us.

Yet, granted the will, and though the way lies ready to us, we must not be discouraged if the journey seem barren enough at first, nay, not even if things seem to grow worse for a while: for it is natural enough that the very evil which has forced on the beginning of reform should look uglier, while on the one hand life and wisdom are building up the new, and on the other folly and deadness are hugging the old to them.

In this, as in all other matters, lapse of time will be needed before things seem to straighten, and the courage and patience that does not despise small things lying ready to be done; and care and watchfulness, lest we begin to build the wall ere the footings are well in; and always through all things much humility that is not easily cast down by failure, that seeks to be taught, and is ready to learn.

For your teachers, they must be Nature and History: as for the first, that you must learn of it is so obvious that I need not dwell upon that now: hereafter, when I have to speak more of matters of detail, I may have to speak of the manner in which you must learn of Nature. As to the second I do not think that any man but one of the highest genius could do anything in these days without much study of ancient art, and even he would be much hindered if he lacked it. If you think that this contradicts what I said about the death of that ancient art, and the necessity I implied for an art that should be characteristic of the present day, I can only say that, in these times of plenteous knowledge and meagre performance, if we do not study the ancient work directly and learn to understand it, we shall find ourselves influenced by the feeble work all round us, and shall be copying the better work through the copyists and *without* understanding it, which will by no means bring about intelligent art. Let us therefore study it wisely, be taught by it, kindled by it; all the while determining not to imitate or repeat it; to have either no art at all, or an art which we have made our own.

Yet I am almost brought to a stand-still when bidding you to study nature and the history of art, by remembering that this is London, and what it is like: how can I ask workingmen passing up and down these hideous streets day by day to care about beauty? If it were politics, we must care about that; or science, you could · wrap yourselves up in the study of facts, no doubt, without much caring what goes on about you—but beauty! do you not see what terrible difficulties beset art, owing to a long neglect of art—and neglect of reason, too, in this matter? It is such a heavy question by what effort, by what dead-lift, you can thrust this difficulty from you, that I must perforce set it aside for the present, and must at least hope that the study of history and its monuments will help you somewhat herein. If you can really fill your minds with memories of great works of art, and great times of art, you will, I think, be able to a certain extent to look through the aforesaid ugly surroundings, and will be moved to discontent of what is careless and brutal now, and will, I hope, at last be so much discontented with what is bad, that you will determine to bear no longer that shortsighted, reckless brutality of squalor that so disgraces our intricate civilisation.

Well, at any rate, London is good for this, that it is well off for museums,—which I heartily wish were to be got at seven days in the week instead of six, or at least on the only day on which an ordinarily busy man, one of the taxpayers who support them, can as a rule see them quietly,—and certainly any of us who may have any natural turn for art must get more help from frequenting them than one can well say. It is true, however, that people need some preliminary instruction before they can get all the good possible to be got from the prodigious treasures of art possessed by the country in that form: there also one sees things in a piecemeal way: nor can I deny that there is something melancholy about a museum, such a tale of violence, destruction, and carelessness, as its treasured scraps tell us.

But moreover you may sometimes have an opportunity of studying ancient art in a narrower but a more intimate, a more kindly form, the monuments of our own land. Sometimes only, since we live in the middle of this world of brick and mortar, and there is little else left us amidst it, except the ghost of the great church at Westminster, ruined as its exterior is by the stupidity of the restoring architect, and insulted as its glorious interior is by the pompous undertakers' lies, by the vainglory and ignorance of the last two centuries and a half—little besides that and the matchless Hall near it: but when we can get beyond that smoky world, there, out in the country we may still see the works of our fathers yet alive amidst the very nature they were wrought into, and of which they are so completely a part: for there indeed if anywhere, in the English country, in the days when people cared about such things, was there a full sympathy between the works of man and the land they were made for:—the land is a little land; too much shut up within the narrow seas, as it seems, to have much space for swelling into hugeness: there are no great wastes overwhelming in their dreariness, no great solitudes of forests, no terrible untrodden mountain-walls: all is measured, mingled, varied, gliding easily one thing into another: little rivers, little plains, swelling, speedily-changing up-lands, all beset with handsome orderly trees; little hills, little mountains, netted over with the walls of sheep-walks: all is little; yet not foolish and blank, but serious rather, and abundant of meaning for such as choose to seek it: it is neither prison nor palace, but a decent home.

All which I neither praise nor blame, but say that so it is: some people praise this homeliness overmuch, as if the land were the very axle-tree of the world; so do not I, nor any unblinded by pride in themselves and all that belongs to them: others there are who scorn it and the tameness of it: not I any the more: though it would indeed be hard if there were nothing else in the world, no wonders, no terrors, no unspeakable beauties: yet when we think what a small part of the world's history, past, present, and to come, is this land we live in, and how much smaller still in the history of the arts, and yet how our forefathers clung to it, and with what care and pains they adorned it, this unromantic, uneventful-looking land of England, surely by this too our hearts may be touched, and our hope quickened.

For as was the land, such was the art of it while folk yet troubled themselves about such things; it strove little to impress people either by pomp or ingenuity: not unseldom it fell into commonplace, rarely it rose into majesty; yet was it never oppressive, never a slave's nightmare nor an insolent boast: and at its best it had an inventiveness, an individuality that grander styles have never overpassed: its best too, and that was in its very heart, was given as freely to the yeoman's house, and the humble village church, as to the lord's palace or the mighty cathedral: never coarse, though often rude enough, sweet, natural and unaffected, an art of peasants rather than of merchant-princes or courtiers, it must be a hard heart, I think, that does not love it: whether a man has been born among it like ourselves, or has come wonderingly on its simplicity from all the grandeur overseas. A peasant art, I say, and it clung fast to the life of the people, and still lived among the cottagers and yeomen in many parts of the country while the big houses were being built "French and fine": still lived also in many a quaint pattern of loom and printing-block, and embroiderer's needle, while over-seas stupid pomp had extinguished all nature and freedom, and art was become, in France especially, the mere expression of that successful and exultant rascality, which in the flesh no long time afterwards went down into the pit for ever.

Such was the English art, whose history is in a sense at your doors, grown scarce indeed, and growing scarcer year by year, not only through greedy destruction, of which there is certainly less than there used to be, but also through the attacks of another foe, called nowadays "restoration."

I must not make a long story about this, but also I cannot quite pass it over, since I have pressed on you the study of these ancient monuments. Thus the matter stands: these old buildings have been altered and added to century after century, often beautifully, always historically; their very value, a great part of it, lay in that: they have suffered almost always from neglect also, often from violence (that latter a piece of history often far from uninteresting), but ordinary obvious mending would almost always have kept them standing, pieces of nature and of history.

But of late years a great uprising of ecclesiastical zeal, coinciding with a great increase of study, and consequently of knowledge of mediæval architecture, has driven people into spending their money on these buildings, not merely with the purpose of repairing them, of keeping them safe, clean, and wind- and water-tight, but also of "restoring" them to some ideal state of perfection; sweeping away if possible all signs of what has befallen them at least since the Reformation, and often since dates much earlier: this has sometimes been done with much disregard of art and entirely from ecclesiastical zeal, but oftener it has been well meant enough as regards art: yet you will not have listened to what I have said to-night if you do not see that from my point of view this restoration must be as impossible to bring about, as the attempt at it is destructive to the buildings so dealt with: I scarcely like to think what a great part of them have been made nearly useless to students of art and history: unless you knew a great deal about architecture you perhaps would scarce understand what terrible damage has been done by that dangerous "little knowledge" in this matter: but at least it is easy to be understood, that to deal recklessly with valuable (and national) monuments which, when once gone, can never be replaced by any splendour of modern art, is doing a very sorry service to the State.

You will see by all that I have said on this study of ancient art that I mean by education herein something much wider than the teaching of a definite art in schools of design, and that it must be something that we must do more or less for ourselves: I mean by it a systematic concentration of our thoughts on the matter, a studying of it in all ways, careful and laborious practice of it, and a determination to do nothing but what is known to be good in workmanship and design.

Of course, however, both as an instrument of that study we have been speaking of, as well as of the practice of the arts, all handicraftsmen should be taught to draw very carefully; as indeed all people should be taught drawing who are not physically incapable of learning it: but the art of drawing so taught would not be the art of designing, but only a means towards *this* end, *general capability in dealing with the arts.*

For I wish specially to impress this upon you, that *designing* cannot be taught at all in a school: continued practice will help a man who is naturally a designer, continual notice of nature and of art: no doubt those who have some faculty for designing are still numerous, and they want from a school certain technical teaching, just as they want tools: in these days also, when the best school, the school of successful practice going on around you, is at such a low ebb, they do undoubtedly want instruction in the history of the arts: these two things schools of design can give: but the royal road of a set of rules deduced from a sham science of design, that is itself not a science but another set of rules, will lead nowhere;—or, let us rather say, to beginning again.

As to the kind of drawing that should be taught to men engaged in ornamental work, there is only *one best* way of teaching drawing, and that is teaching the scholar to draw the human figure: both because the lines of a man's body are much more subtle than anything else, and because you can more surely be found out and set right if you go wrong. I do think that such teaching as this, given to all people who care for it, would help the revival of the arts very much: the habit of discriminating between right and wrong, the sense of pleasure in drawing a good line, would really, I think, be education in the due sense of the word for all such people as had the germs of invention in them; yet as aforesaid, in this age of the world it would be mere affectation to pretend to shut one's eyes to the art of past ages: that also we must study. If other circumstances, social and economical, do not stand in our way, that is to say, if the world is not too busy to allow us to have Decorative Arts at all, these two are the *direct* means by which we shall get them; that is, general cultivation of the powers of the mind, general cultivation of the powers of the eye and hand.

Perhaps that seems to you very commonplace advice and a very roundabout road; nevertheless 'tis a certain one, if by any road you desire to come to the new art, which is my subject to-night: if you do not, and if those germs of invention, which, as I said just now, are no doubt still common enough among men, are left neglected and undeveloped, the laws of Nature will assert themselves in this as in other matters, and the faculty of design itself will gradually fade from the race of man. Sirs, shall we approach nearer to perfection by casting away so large a part of that intelligence which makes us *men?*

And now before I make an end, I want to call your attention to certain things, that, owing to our neglect of the arts for other business, bar that good road to us and are such an hindrance, that, till they are dealt with, it is hard even to make a beginning of our endeavour. And if my talk should seem to grow too serious for our subject, as indeed I think it cannot do, I beg you to remember what I said earlier, of how the arts all hang together. Now there is one art of which the old architect of Edward the Third's time was thinking—he who founded New College at Oxford, I mean—when he took this for his motto: "Manners maketh man": he meant by manners the art of morals, the art of living worthily, and like a man. I must needs claim this art also as dealing with my subject.

There is a great deal of sham work in the world, hurtful to the buyer, more hurtful to the seller, if he only knew it, most hurtful to the maker: how good a foundation it would be towards getting good Decorative Art, that is ornamental workmanship, if we craftsmen were to resolve to turn out nothing but excellent workmanship in all things, instead of having, as we too often have now, a very low average standard of work, which we often fall below.

I do not blame either one class or another in this matter, I blame all: to set aside our own class of handicraftsmen, of whose shortcomings you and I know so much that we need talk no more about it, I know that the public in general are set on having things cheap, being so ignorant that they do not know when they get them nasty also; so ignorant that they neither know nor care whether they give a man his due: I know that the manufacturers (so called) are so set on carrying out competition to its utmost, competition of cheapness, not of excellence, that they meet the bargain-hunters half way, and cheerfully furnish them with nasty wares at the cheap rate they are asked for, by means of what can be called by no prettier name than fraud. England has of late been too much busied with the counting-house and not enough with the workshop: with the result that the counting-house at the present moment is rather barren of orders.

I say all classes are to blame in this matter, but also I say that the remedy lies with the handicraftsmen, who are not ignorant of these things like the public, and who have no call to be greedy and isolated like the manufacturers or middlemen; the duty and honour of educating the public lies with them, and they have in them the seeds of order and organisation which make that duty the easier.

When will they see to this and help to make men of us all by insisting on this most weighty piece of manners; so that we may adorn life with the pleasure of cheerfully *buying* goods at their due price; with the pleasure of *selling* goods that we could be proud of both for fair price and fair workmanship: with the pleasure of working soundly and without haste at *making* goods that we could be proud of?—much the greatest pleasure of the three is that last, such a pleasure as, I think, the world has none like it.

You must not say that this piece of manners lies out of my subject: it is essentially a part of it and most important: for I am bidding you learn to be artists, if art is not to come to an end amongst us: and what is an artist but a workman who is determined that, whatever else happens, his work shall be excellent? or, to put it in another way: the decoration of workmanship, what is it but the expression of man's pleasure in successful labour? But what pleasure can there be in *bad* work, in *un*successful labour; why should we decorate *that?* and how can we bear to be always unsuccessful in our labour?

As greed of unfair gain, wanting to be paid for what we have not earned, cumbers our path with this tangle of bad work, of sham work, so that heaped-up money which this greed has brought us (for greed will have its way, like all other strong passions), this money, I say, gathered into heaps little and big, with all the false distinction which so unhappily it yet commands amongst us, has raised up against the arts a barrier of the love of luxury and show, which is of all obvious hindrances the worst to overpass: the highest and most cultivated classes are not free from the vulgarity of it, the lower are not free from its pretence. I beg you to remember both as a remedy against this, and as explaining exactly what I mean, that nothing can be a work of art which is not useful; that is to say, which does not minister to the body when well under command of the mind, or which does not amuse, soothe, or elevate the mind in a healthy state. What tons upon tons of unutterable rubbish pretending to be works of art in some degree would this maxim clear out of our London houses, if it were understood and acted upon! To my mind it is only here and there (out of the kitchen) that you can find in a well-to-do house things that are of any use at all: as a rule all the decoration (so called) that has got there is there for the sake of show, not because anybody likes it. I repeat, this stupidity goes through all classes of society: the silk curtains in my Lord's drawing-room are no more a matter of art to him than the powder in his footman's hair; the kitchen in a country farmhouse is most commonly a pleasant and homelike place, the parlour dreary and useless.

Simplicity of life, begetting simplicity of taste, that is, a love for sweet and lofty things, is of all matters most necessary for the birth of the new and better art we crave for; simplicity everywhere, in the palace as well as in the cottage.

Still more is this necessary, cleanliness and decency everywhere, in the cottage as well as in the palace: the lack of that is a serious piece of *manners* for us to correct: that lack and all the inequalities of life, and the heaped-up thoughtlessness and disorder of so many centuries that cause it: and as yet it is only a very few men who have begun to think about a remedy for it in its widest range: even in its narrower aspect, in the defacements of our big towns by all that commerce brings with it, who heeds it? who tries to control their squalor and hideousness? there is nothing but thoughtlessness and recklessness in the matter: the helplessness of people who don't live long enough to do a thing themselves, and have not manliness and foresight enough to begin the work, and pass it on to those that shall come after them.

Is money to be gathered? cut down the pleasant trees among the houses, pull down ancient and venerable buildings for the money that a few square yards of London dirt will fetch; blacken rivers, hide the sun and poison the air with smoke and worse, and it's nobody's business to see to it or mend it: that is all that modern commerce, the counting-house forgetful of the workshop, will do for us herein.

And Science—we have loved her well, and followed her diligently, what will she do? I fear she is so much in the pay of the counting-house, the counting-house and the drill-sergeant, that she is too busy, and will for the present do nothing. Yet there are matters which I should have thought easy for her; say for example teaching Manchester how to consume its own smoke, or Leeds how to get rid of its superfluous black dye without turning it into the river, which would be as much worth her attention as the production of the heaviest of heavy black silks, or the biggest of useless guns. Anyhow, however it be done, unless people care about carrying on their business without making the world hideous, how can they care about Art? I know it will cost much both of time and money to better these things even a little; but I do not see how these can be better spent than in making life cheerful and honourable for others and for ourselves; and the gain of good life to the country at large that would result from men seriously setting about the bettering of the decency of our big towns would be priceless, even if nothing specially good befell the arts in consequence: I do not know that it would; but I should begin to think matters hopeful if men turned their attention to such things, and I repeat that, unless they do so, we can scarcely even begin with any hope our endeavours for the bettering of the arts.

Unless something or other is done to give all men some pleasure for the eyes and rest for the mind in the aspect of their own and their neighbours' houses, until the contrast is less disgraceful between the fields where beasts live and the streets where men live, I suppose that the practice of the arts must be mainly kept in the hands of a few highly cultivated men, who can go often to beautiful places, whose education enables them, in the contemplation of the past glories of the world, to shut out from their view the everyday squalors that the most of men move in. Sirs, I believe that art has such sympathy with cheerful freedom, openheartedness and reality, so much she sickens under selfishness and luxury, that she will not live thus isolated and exclusive. I will go further than this and say that on such terms I do not wish her to live. I protest that it would be a shame to an honest artist to enjoy what he had huddled up to himself of such art, as it would be for a rich man to sit and eat dainty food amongst starving soldiers in a beleaguered fort.

I do not want art for a few, any more than education for a few, or freedom for a few.

No, rather than art should live this poor thin life among a few exceptional men, despising those beneath them for an ignorance for which they themselves are responsible, for a brutality that they will not struggle with,—rather than this, I would that the world should indeed sweep away all art for awhile, as I said before I thought it possible she might do; rather than the wheat should rot in the miser's granary, I would that the earth had it, that it might yet have a chance to quicken in the dark.

I have a sort of faith, though, that this clearing away of all art will not happen, that men will get wiser, as well as more learned; that many of the intricacies of life, on which we now pride ourselves more than enough, partly because they are new, partly because they have come with the gain of better things, will be cast aside as having played their part, and being useful no longer. I hope that we shall have leisure from war,—war commercial, as well as war of the bullet and the bayonet; leisure from the knowledge that darkens counsel; leisure above all from the greed of money, and the craving for that overwhelming distinction that money now brings: I believe that as we have even now partly achieved LIBERTY, so we shall one day achieve EQUALITY, which, and which only, means FRATERNITY, and so have leisure from poverty and all its griping, sordid cares.

Then having leisure from all these things, amidst renewed simplicity of life we shall have leisure to think about our work, that faithful daily companion, which no man any longer will venture to call the Curse of labour: for surely then we shall be happy in it, each in his place, no man grudging at another; no one bidden to be any man's *servant*, every one scorning to be any man's *master:* men will then assuredly be happy in their work, and that happiness will assuredly bring forth decorative, noble, *popular* art.

That art will make our streets as beautiful as the woods, as elevating as the mountain-sides: it will be a pleasure and a rest, and not a weight upon the spirits to come from the open country into a town; every man's house will be fair and decent, soothing to his mind and helpful to his work: all the works of man that we live amongst and handle will be in harmony with nature, will be reasonable and beautiful: yet all will be simple and inspiriting, not childish nor enervating; for as nothing of beauty and splendour that man's mind and hand may compass shall be wanting from our public buildings, so in no private dwelling will there be any signs of waste, pomp, or insolence, and every man will have his share of the *best*.

It is a dream, you may say, of what has never been and never will be; true, it has never been, and therefore, since the world is alive and moving yet, my hope is the greater that it one day will be: true, it is a dream; but dreams have before now come about of things so good and necessary to us, that we scarcely think of them more than of the daylight, though once people had to live without them, without even the hope of them.

Anyhow, dream as it is, I pray you to pardon my setting it before you, for it lies at the bottom of all my work in the Decorative Arts, nor will it ever be out of my thoughts: and I am here with you to-night to ask you to help me in realising this dream, this *hope*.

[1878]

THE ART OF THE PEOPLE

"And the men of labour spent their strength in daily struggling for bread to maintain the vital strength they labour with: so living in a daily circulation of sorrow, living but to work, and working but to live, as if daily bread were the only end of a wearisome life, and a wearisome life the only occasion of daily bread."— DANIEL DEFOE.

I know that a large proportion of those here present are either already practising the Fine Arts, or are being specially educated to that end, and I feel that I may be expected to address myself specially to these. But since it is not to be doubted that we are *all* met together because of the interest we take in what concerns these arts, I would rather address myself to you *all* as representing the public in general. Indeed, those of you who are specially studying Art could learn little of me that would be useful to yourselves only. You are already learning under competent masters—most competent, I am glad to know—by means of a system which should teach you all you need, if you have been right in making the first step of devoting yourselves to Art; I mean if you are aiming at the right thing, and in some way or another understand what Art means, which you may well do without being able to express it, and if you are resolute to follow on the path which that inborn knowledge has shown to you; if it is otherwise with you than this, no system and no teachers will help you to produce real art of any kind, be it never so humble. Those of you who are real artists know well enough all the special advice I can give you, and in how few words it may be said—follow nature, study antiquity, make your own art, and do not steal it, grudge no expense of trouble, patience, or courage, in the striving to accomplish the hard thing you have set yourselves to do. You have had all that said to you twenty times, I doubt not; and twenty times twenty have said it to yourselves, and now I have said it again to you, and done neither you nor me good nor harm thereby. So true it all is, so well known, and so hard to follow.

But to me, and I hope to you, Art is a very serious thing, and cannot by any means be dissociated from the weighty matters that occupy the thoughts of men; and there are principles underlying the practice of it, on which all serious-minded men, may—nay, must—have their own thoughts. It is on some of these that I ask your leave to speak, and to address myself, not only to those who are consciously interested in the arts, but to all those also who have considered what the progress of civilisation promises and threatens to those who shall come after us: what there is to hope and fear for the future of the arts, which were born with the birth of civilisation and will only die with its death—what on this side of things, the present time of strife and doubt and change is preparing for the better time, when the change shall have come, the strife be lulled, and the doubt cleared: this is a question, I say, which is indeed weighty, and may well interest all thinking men.

Nay, so universally important is it, that I fear lest you should think I am taking too much upon myself to speak to you on so weighty a matter, nor should I have dared to do so, if I did not feel that I am to-night only the mouthpiece of better men than myself, whose hopes and fears I share;

and that being so, I am the more emboldened to speak out, if I can, my full mind on the subject, because I am in a city where, if anywhere, men are not contented to live wholly for themselves and the present, but have fully accepted the duty of keeping their eyes open to whatever new is stirring, so that they may help and be helped by any truth that there may be in it. Nor can I forget, that, since you have done me the great honour of choosing me for the President of your Society of Arts for the past year, and of asking me to speak to you to-night, I should be doing less than my duty if I did not, according to my lights, speak out straightforwardly whatever seemed to me might be in a small degree useful to you. Indeed, I think I am among friends, who may forgive me if I speak rashly, but scarcely if I speak falsely.

The aim of your Society and School of Arts is, as I understand it, to further those arts by education widely spread. A very great object is that, and well worthy of the reputation of this great city; but since Birmingham has also, I rejoice to know, a great reputation for not allowing things to go about shamming life when the brains are knocked out of them, I think you should know and see clearly what it is you have undertaken to further by these institutions, and whether you really care about it, or only languidly acquiesce in it—whether, in short, you know it to the heart, and are indeed part and parcel of it, with your own will, or against it; or else have heard say that it is a good thing if any one care to meddle with it.

If you are surprised at my putting that question for your consideration, I will tell you why I do so. There are some of us who love Art most, and I may say most faithfully, who see for certain that such love is rare nowadays. We cannot help seeing, that besides a vast number of people, who (poor souls!) are sordid and brutal of mind and habits, and have had no chance or choice in the matter, there are many high-minded, thoughtful, and cultivated men who inwardly think the arts to be a foolish accident of civilisation—nay, worse perhaps, a nuisance, a disease, a hindrance to human progress. Some of these, doubtless, are very busy about other sides of thought. They are, as I should put it, so *artistically* engrossed by the study of science, politics, or what not, that they have necessarily narrowed their minds by their hard and praiseworthy labours. But since such men are few, this does not account for a prevalent habit of thought that looks upon Art as at best trifling.

What is wrong, then, with us or the arts, since what was once accounted so glorious, is now deemed paltry?

The question is no light one; for, to put the matter in its clearest light, I will say that the leaders of modern thought do for the most part sincerely and single-mindedly hate and despise the arts; and you know well that as the leaders are, so must the people be; and that means that we who are met together here for the furthering of Art by wide-spread education are either deceiving ourselves and wasting our time, since we shall one day be of the same opinion as the best men among us, or else we represent a small minority that is right, as minorities sometimes are, while those upright men aforesaid, and the great mass of civilised men, have been blinded by untoward circumstances.

That we are of this mind—the minority that is right—is, I hope, the case. I hope we know assuredly that the arts we have met together to further are necessary to the life of man, if the progress of civilisation is not to be as causeless as the turning of a wheel that makes nothing.

How, then, shall we, the minority, carry out the duty which our position thrusts upon us, of striving to grow into a majority?

If we could only explain to those thoughtful men, and the millions of whom they are the flower, what the thing is that we love, which is to us as the bread we eat, and the air we breathe, but about which they know nothing and feel nothing, save a vague instinct of repulsion, then the seed of victory might be sown. This is hard indeed to do; yet if we ponder upon a chapter of ancient or mediæval history, it seems to me some glimmer of a chance of doing so breaks in upon us. Take for example a century of the Byzantine Empire, weary yourselves with reading the names of the pedants, tyrants, and tax-gatherers to whom the terrible chain which long-dead Rome once forged, still gave the power of cheating people into thinking that they were necessary lords of the world. Turn then to the lands they governed, and read and forget a long string of the causeless murders of Northern and Saracen pirates and robbers. That is pretty much the sum of what so-called history has left us of the tale of those days—the stupid languor and the evil deeds of kings and scoundrels. Must we turn away then, and say that all was evil? How then did men live from day to day? How then did Europe grow into intelligence and freedom? It seems there were others than those of whom history (so called) has left us the names and the deeds. These, the raw material for the treasury and the slave-market, we now call "the people," and we know that they were working all that while. Yes, and that their work was not merely slaves' work, the meal-trough before them and the whip behind them; for though history (so called) has forgotten them, yet their work has not been forgotten, but has made another history—the history of Art. There is not an ancient city in the East or the West that does not bear some token of their grief, and joy, and hope. From Ispahan to Northumberland, there is no building built between the seventh and seventeenth centuries that does not show the influence of the labour of that oppressed and neglected herd of men. No one of them, indeed, rose high above his fellows. There was no Plato, or Shakespeare, or Michael Angelo amongst them. Yet scattered as it was among many men, how strong their thought was, how long it abided, how far it travelled!

And so it was ever through all those days when Art was so vigorous and progressive. Who can say how little we should know of many periods, but for their art? History (so called) has remembered the kings and warriors, because they destroyed; Art has remembered the people, because they created.

I think, then, that this knowledge we have of the life of past times gives us some token of the way we should take in meeting those honest and single-hearted men who above all things desire the world's progress, but whose minds are, as it were, sick on this point of the arts. Surely you may say to them: When all is gained that you (and we) so long for, what shall we do then? That great change which we are working for, each in his own way, will come like other changes, as a thief in the night, and will be with us before we know it; but let us imagine that its consummation has come suddenly and dramatically, acknowledged and hailed by all right-minded people; and what shall we do then, lest we begin once more to heap up fresh corruption for the woeful labour of ages once again? I say, as we turn away from the flagstaff where the new banner has been just run up; as we depart, our ears yet ringing with the blare of the heralds' trumpets that have proclaimed the new order of things, what shall we turn to then, what *must* we turn to then?

To what else, save to our work, our daily labour?

With what, then, shall we adorn it when we have become wholly free and reasonable? It is necessary toil, but shall it be toil only? Shall all we can do with it be to shorten the hours of that toil to the utmost, that the hours of leisure may be long beyond what men used to hope for? and what then shall we do with the leisure, if we say that all toil is irksome? Shall we sleep it all away?—Yes, and never wake up again, I should hope, in that case.

What shall we do then? what shall our necessary hours of labour bring forth?

That will be a question for all men in that day when many wrongs are righted, and when there will be no classes of degradation on whom the dirty work of the world can be shovelled; and if men's minds are still sick and loathe the arts, they will not be able to answer that question.

Once men sat under grinding tyrannies, amidst violence and fear so great, that nowadays we wonder how they lived through twenty-four hours of it, till we remember that then, as now, their daily labour was the main part of their lives, and that daily labour was sweetened by the daily creation of Art; and shall we who are delivered from the evils they bore, live drearier days than they did? Shall men, who have come forth from so many tyrannies, bind them-

selves to yet another one, and become the slaves of nature, piling day upon day of hopeless, useless toil? Must this go on worsening till it comes to this at last—that the world shall have come into its inheritance, and with all foes conquered and nought to bind it, shall choose to sit down and labour for ever amidst grim ugliness? How, then, were all our hopes cheated, what a gulf of despair should we tumble into then?

In truth, it cannot be; yet if that sickness of repulsion to the arts were to go on hopelessly, nought else would be, and the extinction of the love of beauty and imagination would prove to be the extinction of civilisation. But that sickness the world will one day throw off, yet will, I believe, pass through many pains in so doing, some of which will look very like the death-throes of Art, and some, perhaps, will be grievous enough to the poor people of the world; since hard necessity, I doubt, works many of the world's changes, rather than the purblind striving to see, which we call the foresight of man.

Meanwhile, remember that I asked just now, what was amiss in Art or in ourselves that this sickness was upon us. Nothing is wrong or can be with Art in the abstract—that must always be good for mankind, or we are all wrong together: but with Art, as we of these latter days have known it, there is much wrong; nay, what are we here for to-night if that is not so? were not the schools of art founded all over the country some thirty years ago because we had found out that popular art was fading—or perhaps had faded out from amongst us?

As to the progress made since then in this country—and in this country only, if at all—it is hard for me to speak without being either ungracious or insincere, and yet speak I must. I say, then, that an apparent external progress in some ways is obvious, but I do not know how far that is hopeful, for time must try it, and prove whether it be a passing fashion or the first token of a real stir among the great mass of civilised men. To speak quite frankly, and as one friend to another, I must needs say that even as I say those words they seem too good to be true. And yet—who knows?—so wont are we to frame history for the future as well as for the past, so often are our eyes blind both when we look backward and when we look forward, because we have been gazing so intently at our own days, our own lines. May all be better than I think it!

At any rate let us count our gains, and set them against less hopeful signs of the times. In England, then—and as far as I know, in England only—painters of pictures have grown, I believe, more numerous, and certainly more conscientious in their work, and in some cases—and this more especially in England—have developed and expressed a sense of beauty which the world has not seen for the last three hundred years. This is certainly a very great gain, which is not easy to overestimate, both for those who make the pictures and those who use them.

Furthermore, in England, and in England only, there has been a great improvement in architecture and the arts that attend it—arts which it was the special province of the afore-mentioned schools to revive and foster. This, also, is a considerable gain to the users of the works so made, but I fear a gain less important to most of those concerned in making them.

Against these gains we must, I am very sorry to say, set the fact not easy to be accounted for, that the rest of the civilised world (so called) seems to have done little more than stand still in these matters; and that among ourselves these improvements have concerned comparatively few people, the mass of our population not being in the least touched by them; so that the great bulk of our architecture—the art which most depends on the taste of the people at large—grows worse and worse every day.

I must speak also of another piece of discouragement before I go further. I daresay many of you will remember how emphatically those who first had to do with the movement of which the foundation of our art-schools was a part, called the attention of our pattern-designers to the beautiful works of the East. This was surely most well judged of them, for they bade us look at an art at once beautiful, orderly, living in our own day, and above all, popular. Now, it is a grievous result of the sickness of civilisation that this art is fast disappearing before the advance of western conquest and commerce—fast, and every day faster. While we are met here in Birmingham to further the spread of education in art, Englishmen in India are, in their short-sightedness, actively destroying the very sources of that education—jewellery, metal-work, pottery, calico-printing, brocade-weaving, carpet-making—all the famous and historical arts of the great peninsula have been for long treated as matters of no importance, to be thrust aside for the advantage of any paltry scrap of so-called commerce; and matters are now speedily coming to an end there. I daresay some of you saw the presents which the native Princes gave to the Prince of Wales on the occasion of his progress through India. I did myself, I will not say with great disappointment, for I guessed what they would be like, but with great grief, since there was scarce here and there a piece of goods among these costly gifts, things given as great treasures, which faintly upheld the ancient fame of the cradle of the industrial arts. Nay, in some cases, it would have been laughable, if it had not been so sad, to see the piteous simplicity with which the conquered race had copied the blank vulgarity of their lords. And this deterioration we are now, as I have said, actively engaged in forwarding. I have read a little book, a handbook to the Indian Court of last year's Paris Exhibition, which takes the occasion of noting the state of manufactures in India one by one. "Art manufactures," you would call them; but, indeed, all manufactures are, or were, "art manufactures" in India. Dr. Birdwood, the author of this book, is of great experience in Indian life, a man of science, and a lover of the arts. His story, by no means a new one to me, or others interested in the East and its labour, is a sad one indeed. The conquered races in their hopelessness are everywhere giving up the genuine practice of their own arts, which we know ourselves, as we have indeed loudly proclaimed, are founded on the truest and most natural principles. The often-praised perfection of these arts is the blossom of many ages of labour and change, but the conquered races are casting it aside as a thing of no value, so that they may conform themselves to the inferior art, or rather the lack of art, of their conquerors. In some parts of the country the genuine arts are quite destroyed; in many others nearly so; in all they have more or less begun to sicken. So much so is this the case, that now for some time the Government has been furthering this deterioration. As for example, no doubt with the best intentions, and certainly in full sympathy with the general English public, both at home and in India, that Government is now manufacturing cheap Indian carpets in the Indian gaols. I do not say that it is a bad thing to turn out real work, or works of art, in gaols; on the contrary, I think it good if it be properly managed. But in this case, the Government, being, as I said, in full sympathy with the English public, has determined that it will make its wares cheap, whether it make them nasty or not. Cheap and nasty they are, I assure you; but, though they are the worst of their kind, they would not be made thus, if everything did not tend the same way. And it is the same everywhere and with all Indian manufactures, till it has come to this—that these poor people have all but lost the one distinction, the one glory that conquest had left them. Their famous wares, so praised by those who thirty year ago began to attempt the restoration of popular art amongst ourselves, are no longer to be bought at reasonable prices in the common market, but must be sought for and treasured as precious relics for the museums we have founded for our art education. In short, their art is dead, and the commerce of modern civilisation has slain it.

What is going on in India is also going on, more or less, all over the East; but I have spoken of India chiefly because I cannot help thinking that we ourselves are responsible for what is happening there. Chance-hap has made us the lords of many millions out there; surely, it behooves us to look to it, lest we give to the people whom we have made helpless scorpions for fish and stones for bread.

But since neither on this side, nor on any other, can art be amended, until the countries that lead civilisation are themselves in a healthy state about it, let us return to the consideration of its condition among ourselves. And again I say, that obvious as is that surface improvement of the arts within the past few years, I fear too much that there is something wrong about the root of the plant to exult over the bursting of its February buds.

I have just shown you for one thing that lovers of Indian and Eastern Art, including as they do the heads of our institutions for art education, and I am sure many among what are called the governing classes, are utterly powerless to stay its downward course. The general tendency of civilisation is against them, and is too strong for them.

Again, though many of us love architecture dearly, and believe that it helps the healthiness both of body and soul to live among beautiful things, we of the big towns are mostly compelled to live in houses which have become a by-word of contempt for their ugliness and inconvenience. The stream of civilisation is against us, and we cannot battle against it.

Once more those devoted men who have upheld the standard of truth and beauty amongst us, and whose pictures, painted amidst difficulties that none but a painter can know, show qualities of mind unsurpassed in any age—these great men have but a narrow circle that can understand their works, and are utterly unknown to the great mass of the people: civilisation is so much against them, that they cannot move the people.

Therefore, looking at all this, I cannot think that all is well with the root of the tree we are cultivating. Indeed, I believe that if other things were but to stand still in the world, this improvement before mentioned would lead to a kind of art which, in that impossible case, would be in a way stable, would perhaps stand still also. This would be an art cultivated professedly by a few, and for a few, who would consider it necessary—a duty, if they could admit duties—to despise the common herd, to hold themselves aloof from all that the world has been struggling for from the first, to guard carefully every approach to their palace of art. It would be a pity to waste many words on the prospect of such a school

of art as this, which does in a way, theoretically at least, exist at present, and has
for its watchword a piece of slang that does
not mean the harmless thing it seems to
mean—art for art's sake. Its fore-doomed
end must be, that art at last will seem too
delicate a thing for even the hands of the
initiated to touch; and the initiated must
at last sit still and do nothing—to the grief
of no one.

Well, certainly, if I thought you were
come here to further such an art as this I
could not have stood up and called you
friends; though such a feeble folk as I have
told you of one could scarce care to call
foes.

Yet, as I say, such men exist, and I have
troubled you with speaking of them, because I know that those honest and intelligent people, who are eager for human
progress, and yet lack part of the human
senses, and are anti-artistic, suppose that
such men are artists, and that this is what
art means, and what it does for people, and
that such a narrow, cowardly life is what
we, fellow-handicraftsmen, aim at. I see this
taken for granted continually, even by
many who, to say truth, ought to know
better, and I long to put the slur from off
us; to make people understand that we,
least of all men, wish to widen the gulf
between the classes, nay, worse still, to
make new classes of elevation, and new
classes of degradation—new lords and new
slaves; that we, least of all men, want to
cultivate the "plant called man" in different ways—here stingily, there wastefully: I
wish people to understand that the art we
are striving for is a good thing which all
can share, which will elevate all; in good
sooth, if all people do not soon share it
there will soon be none to share; if all are
not elevated by it, mankind will lose the
elevation it has gained. Nor is such an art
as we long for a vain dream; such an art
once was in times that were worse than
these, when there was less courage, kindness,
and truth in the world than there is now;
such an art there will be hereafter, when
there will be more courage, kindness, and
truth than there is now in the world.

Let us look backward in history once
more for a short while, and then steadily
forward till my words are done: I began by
saying that part of the common and necessary advice given to Art students was to
study antiquity; and no doubt many of you,
like me, have done so; have wandered, for
instance, through the galleries of the admirable museum of South Kensington, and,
like me, have been filled with wonder and
gratitude at the beauty which has been
born from the brain of man. Now, consider, I pray you, what these wonderful
works are, and how they were made; and
indeed, it is neither in extravagance nor
without due meaning that I use the word
"wonderful" in speaking of them. Well,
these things are just the common household goods of those past days, and that is
one reason why they are so few and so
carefully treasured. They were common
things in their own day, used without fear
of breaking or spoiling—no rarities then—
and yet we have called them "wonderful."

And how were they made? Did a great
artist draw the designs for them—a man of
cultivation, highly paid, daintily fed, carefully housed, wrapped up in cotton wool,
in short, when he was not at work? By
no means. Wonderful as these works are,
they were made by "common fellows," as
the phrase goes, in the common course of
their daily labour. Such were the men we
honour in honouring those works. And
their labour—do you think it was irksome
to them? Those of you who are artists
know very well that it was not; that it
could not be. Many a grin of pleasure, I'll
be bound—and you will not contradict me
—went to the carrying through of those
mazes of mysterious beauty, to the invention of those strange beasts and birds and
flowers that we ourselves have chuckled over
at South Kensington. While they were at
work, at least, these men were not unhappy, and I suppose they worked most
days, and the most part of the day, as we
do.

Or those treasures of architecture that we
study so carefully nowadays—what are they?
how were they made? There are great
minsters among them, indeed, and palaces
of kings and lords, but not many; and, noble and awe-inspiring as these may be, they
differ only in size from the little grey
church that still so often makes the commonplace English landscape beautiful, and

the little grey house that still, in some parts of the country at least, makes an English village a thing apart, to be seen and pondered on by all who love romance and beauty. These form the mass of our architectural treasures, the houses that everyday people lived in, the unregarded churches in which they worshipped.

And, once more, who was it that designed and ornamented them? The great architect, carefully kept for the purpose, and guarded from the common troubles of common men? By no means. Sometimes, perhaps, it was the monk, the ploughman's brother; oftenest his other brother, the village carpenter, smith, mason, what not—"a common fellow," whose common everyday labour fashioned works that are to-day the wonder and despair of many a hard-working "cultivated" architect. And did he loathe his work? No, it is impossible. I have seen, as we most of us have, work done by such men in some out-of-the-way hamlet —where to-day even few strangers ever come, and whose people seldom go five miles from their own doors; in such places, I say, I have seen work so delicate, so careful, and so inventive, that nothing in its way could go further. And I will assert, without fear of contradiction, that no human ingenuity can produce work such as this without pleasure being a third party to the brain that conceived and the hand that fashioned it. Nor are such works rare. The throne of the great Plantagenet, or the great Valois, was no more daintily carved than the seat of the village mass-john, or the chest of the yeoman's good-wife.

So, you see, there was much going on to make life endurable in those times. Not every day, you may be sure, was a day of slaughter and tumult, though the histories read almost as if it were so; but every day the hammer chinked on the anvil, and the chisel played about the oak beam, and never without some beauty and invention being born of it, and consequently some human happiness.

That last word brings me to the very kernel and heart of what I have come here to say to you, and I pray you to think of it most seriously—not as to my words, but as to a thought which is stirring in the world, and will one day grow into something.

That thing which I understand by real art is the expression by man of his pleasure in labour. I do not believe he can be happy in his labour without expressing that happiness; and especially is this so when he is at work at anything in which he specially excels. A most kind gift is this of nature, since all men, nay, it seems all things too, must labour; so that not only does the dog take pleasure in hunting, and the horse in running, and the bird in flying, but so natural does the idea seem to us, that we imagine to ourselves that the earth and the very elements rejoice in doing their appointed work; and the poets have told us of the spring meadows smiling, of the exultation of the fire, of the countless laughter of the sea.

Nor until these latter days has man ever rejected this universal gift, but always, when he has not been too much perplexed, too much bound by disease or beaten down by trouble, has striven to make his work at least happy. Pain he has too often found in his pleasure, and weariness in his rest, to trust to these. What matter if his happiness lie with what must be always with him—his work?

And, once more, shall we, who have gained so much, forego this gain, the earliest, most natural gain of mankind? If we have to a great extent done so, as I verily fear we have, what strange foglights must have misled us; or rather let me say, how hard pressed we must have been in the battle with the evils we have overcome, to have forgotten the greatest of all evils. I cannot call it less than that. If a man has work to do which he despises, which does not satisfy his natural and rightful desire for pleasure, the greater part of his life must pass unhappily and without self-respect. Consider, I beg of you, what that means, and what ruin must come of it in the end.

If I could only persuade you of this, that the chief duty of the civilised world to-day is to set about making labour happy for all, to do its utmost to minimise the amount of unhappy labour—nay, if I could only persuade some two or three of you here present—I should have made a good night's work of it.

Do not, at any rate, shelter yourselves

from any misgiving you may have behind the fallacy that the art-lacking labour of to-day is happy work: for the most of men it is not so. It would take long, perhaps, to show you, and make you fully understand that the would-be art which it produces is joyless. But there is another token of its being most unhappy work, which you cannot fail to understand at once—a grievous thing that token is—and I beg of you to believe that I feel the full shame of it, as I stand here speaking of it; but if we do not admit that we are sick, how can we be healed? This hapless token is, that the work done by the civilised world is mostly dishonest work. Look now: I admit that civilisation does make certain things well, things which it knows, consciously or unconsciously, are necessary to its present unhealthy condition. These things, to speak shortly, are chiefly machines for carrying on the competition in buying and selling, called falsely commerce; and machines for the violent destruction of life—that is to say, materials for two kinds of war; of which kinds the last is no doubt the worst, not so much in itself perhaps, but because on this point the conscience of the world is beginning to be somewhat pricked. But, on the other hand, matters for the carrying on of a dignified daily life, that life of mutual trust, forbearance, and help, which is the only real life of thinking men—these things the civilised world makes ill, and even increasingly worse and worse.

If I am wrong in saying this, you know well I am only saying what is widely thought, nay widely said too, for that matter. Let me give an instance, familiar enough, of that wide-spread opinion. There is a very clever book of pictures now being sold at the railway bookstalls, called "The British Working Man, by one who does not believe in him,"—a title and a book which make me both angry and ashamed, because the two express much injustice, and not a little truth in their quaint, and necessarily exaggerated way. It is quite true, and very sad to say, that if any one nowadays wants a piece of ordinary work done by gardener, carpenter, mason, dyer, weaver, smith, what you will, he will be a lucky rarity if he get it well done. He will, on the contrary, meet on every side with evasion of plain

duties, and disregard of other men's rights; yet I cannot see how the "British Working Man" is to be made to bear the whole burden of this blame, or indeed the chief part of it. I doubt if it be possible for a whole mass of men to do work to which they are driven, and in which there is no hope and no pleasure, without trying to shirk it—at any rate, shirked it has always been under such circumstances. On the other hand, I know that there are some men so rightminded, that they will, in despite of irksomeness and hopelessness, drive right through their work. Such men are the salt of the earth. But must there not be something wrong with a state of society which drives these into that bitter heroism, and the most part into shirking, into the depths often of half-conscious self-contempt and degradation? Be sure that there is, that the blindness and hurry of civilisation, as it now is, have to answer a heavy charge as to that enormous amount of pleasureless work —work that tries every muscle of the body and every atom of the brain, and which is done without pleasure and without aim— work which everybody who has to do with tries to shuffle off in the speediest way that dread of starvation or ruin will allow him.

I am as sure of one thing as that I am living and breathing, and it is this: that the dishonesty in the daily arts of life, complaints of which are in all men's mouths, and which I can answer for it does exist, is the natural and inevitable result of the world in the hurry of the war of the counting-house, and the war of the battlefield, having forgotten—of all men, I say, each for the other, having forgotten, that pleasure in our daily labour, which nature cries out for as its due.

Therefore, I say again, it is necessary to the further progress of civilisation that men should turn their thoughts to some means of limiting, and in the end of doing away with, degrading labour.

I do not think my words hitherto spoken have given you any occasion to think that I mean by this either hard or rough labour; I do not pity men much for their hardships, especially if they be accidental; not necessarily attached to one class or one condition, I mean. Nor do I think (I were crazy or dreaming else) that the work of the world can be carried on without rough labour; but I have seen enough of that to know that it need not be by any means degrading. To plough the earth, to cast the net, to fold the flock—these, and such as these, which are rough occupations enough, and which carry with them many hardships, are good enough for the best of us, certain conditions of leisure, freedom, and due wages being granted. As to the bricklayer, the mason, and the like—these would be artists, and doing not only necessary, but beautiful, and therefore happy work, if art were anything like what it should be. No, it is not such labour as this which we need to do away with, but the toil which makes the thousand and one things which nobody wants, which are used merely as the counters for the competitive buying and selling, falsely called commerce, which I have spoken of before—I know in my heart, and not merely by my reason, that this toil cries out to be done away with. But, besides that, the labour which now makes things good and necessary in themselves, merely as counters for the commercial war aforesaid, needs regulating and reforming. Nor can this reform be brought about save by art; and if we were only come to our right minds, and could see the necessity for making labour sweet to all men, as it is now to very few—the necessity, I repeat; lest discontent, unrest, and despair should at last swallow up all society. If we, then, with our eyes cleared, could but make some sacrifice of things which do us no good, since we unjustly and uneasily possess them, then indeed I believe we should sow the seeds of a happiness which the world has not yet known, of a rest and content which would make it what I cannot help thinking it was meant to be: and with that seed would be sown also the seed of real art, the expression of man's happiness in his labour,—and art made by the people, and for the people, as a happiness to the maker and the user.

That is the only real art there is, the only art which will be an instrument to the progress of the world, and not a hindrance. Nor can I seriously doubt that in your hearts you know that it is so, all of you, at any rate, who have in you an instinct for art. I believe that you agree with me in this, though you may differ from much else that I have said. I think assuredly that this is the art whose welfare we have met together to further, and the necessary instruction in which we have undertaken to spread as widely as may be.

Thus I have told you something of what I think is to be hoped and feared for the future of art; and if you ask me what I expect as a practical outcome of the admission of these opinions, I must say at once that I know, even if we were all of one mind, and that what I think the right mind on this subject, we should still have much work and many hindrances before us; we should still have need of all the prudence, foresight, and industry of the best among us; and, even so, our path would sometimes seem blind enough. And, to-day, when the opinions which we think right, and which one day will be generally thought so, have to struggle sorely to make themselves noticed at all, it is early days for us to try to see our exact and clearly mapped road. I suppose you will think it too commonplace of me to say that the general education that makes men think, will one day make them think rightly upon art. Commonplace as it is, I really believe it, and am indeed encouraged by it, when I remember how obviously this age is one of transition from the old to the new, and what a strange confusion, from out of which we shall one day come, our ignorance and half-ignorance is like to make of the exhausted rubbish of the old and the crude rubbish of the new, both of which lie so ready to our hands.

But, if I must say, furthermore, any words that seem like words of practical advice, I think my task is hard, and I fear I shall offend some of you whatever I say; for this is indeed an affair of morality, rather than of what people call art.

However, I cannot forget that, in my mind, it is not possible to dissociate art from morality, politics, and religion. Truth in these great matters of principle is of one, and it is only in formal treatises that it can be split up diversely. I must also ask you to remember how I have already said, that though my mouth alone speaks, it speaks, however feebly and disjointedly, the thoughts of many men better than myself.

And further, though when things are tending to the best, we shall still, as aforesaid, need our best men to lead us quite right; yet even now surely, when it is far from that, the least of us can do some yeoman's service to the cause, and live and die not without honour.

So I will say that I believe there are two virtues much needed in modern life, if it is ever to become sweet; and I am quite sure 10 that they are absolutely necessary in the sowing the seed of an *art which is to be made by the people and for the people, as a happiness to the maker and the user.* These virtues are honesty, and simplicity of life. To make my meaning clearer I will name the opposing vice of the second of these—luxury to wit. Also I mean by honesty, the careful and eager giving his due to every man, the determination not to gain 20 by any man's loss, which in my experience is not a common virtue.

But note how the practice of either of these virtues will make the other easier to us. For if our wants are few, we shall have but little chance of being driven by our wants into injustice; and if we are fixed in the principle of giving every man his due, how can our self-respect bear that we should give too much to ourselves? 30

And in art, and in that preparation for it without which no art that is stable or worthy can be, the raising, namely, of those classes which have heretofore been degraded, the practice of these virtues would make a new world of it. For if you are rich, your simplicity of life will both go towards smoothing over the dreadful contrast between waste and want, which is the great horror of civilised countries, and will also 40 give an example and standard of dignified life to those classes which you desire to raise, who, as it is indeed, being like enough to rich people, are given both to envy and to imitate the idleness and waste that the possession of much money produces.

Nay, and apart from the morality of the matter, which I am forced to speak to you of, let me tell you that though simplicity in art may be costly as well as uncostly, at 50 least it is not wasteful, and nothing is more destructive to art than the want of it. I have never been in any rich man's house which would not have looked the better for having a bonfire made outside of it of nine-tenths of all that it held. Indeed, our sacrifice on the side of luxury will, it seems to me, be little or nothing: for, as far as I can make out, what people usually mean by it, is either a gathering of possessions which are sheer vexations to the owner, or a chain of pompous circumstance, which checks and annoys the rich man at every step. Yes, luxury cannot exist without slavery of some kind or other, and its abolition will be blessed, like the abolition of other slaveries, by the freeing both of the slaves and of their masters.

Lastly, if, besides attaining to simplicity of life, we attain also to the love of justice, then will all things be ready for the new springtime of the arts. For those of us that are employers of labour, how can we bear to give any man less money than he can decently live on, less leisure than his education and self-respect demand? or those of us who are workmen, how can we bear to fail in the contract we have undertaken, or to make it necessary for a foreman to go up and down spying out our mean tricks and evasions? or we the shopkeepers—can we endure to lie about our wares, that we may shuffle off our losses on to some one else's shoulders? or we the public—how can we bear to pay a price for a piece of goods which will help to trouble one man, to ruin another, and to starve a third? Or, still more, I think, how can we bear to use, how can we enjoy something which has been a pain and a grief for the maker to make?

And now, I think, I have said what I came to say. I confess that there is nothing new in it, but you know the experience of the world is that a thing must be said over and over again before any great number of men can be got to listen to it. Let my words tonight, therefore, pass for one of the necessary times that the thought in them must be spoken out.

For the rest I believe that, however seriously these words may be gainsayed, I have been speaking to an audience in whom any words spoken from a sense of duty and in hearty good-will, as mine have been, will quicken thought and sow some good seed. At any rate, it is good for a man who thinks seriously to face his fellows, and speak out whatever really burns in him, so that men may seem less strange to one another, and misunderstanding, the fruitful cause of aimless strife, may be avoided.

But if to any of you I have seemed to speak hopelessly, my words have been lacking in art; and you must remember that hopelessness would have locked my mouth, not opened it. I am, indeed, hopeful, but can I give a date to the accomplishment of my hope, and say that it will happen in my life or yours?

But I will say at least, Courage! for things wonderful, unhoped-for, glorious, have happened even in this short while I have been alive.

Yes, surely these times are wonderful and fruitful of change, which, as it wears and gathers new life even in its wearing, will one day bring better things for the toiling days of men, who, with freer hearts and clearer eyes, will once more gain the sense of outward beauty, and rejoice in it.

Meanwhile, if these hours be dark, as, indeed, in many ways they are, at least do not let us sit deedless, like fools and fine gentlemen, thinking the common toil not good enough for us, and beaten by the muddle; but rather let us work like good fellows trying by some dim candle-light to set our workshop ready against to-morrow's daylight—that to-morrow, when the civilised world, no longer greedy, strifeful, and destructive, shall have a new art, a glorious art, made by the people and for the people, as a happiness to the maker and the user.

[1879]

THE BEAUTY OF LIFE

"——propter vitam vivendi perdere causas." [1]
—*Juvenal*

I stand before you this evening weighted with a disadvantage that I did not feel last year;—I have little fresh to tell you; I can somewhat enlarge on what I said then; here and there I may make bold to give you a practical suggestion, or I may put what I have to say in a way which will be clearer to some of you perhaps; but my message is really the same as it was when I first had the pleasure of meeting you.

It is true that if all were going smoothly with art, or at all events so smoothly that there were but a few malcontents in the world, you might listen with some pleasure, and perhaps advantage, to the talk of an old hand in the craft concerning ways of work, the snares that beset success, and the shortest road to it, to a tale of workshop receipts and the like: that would be a pleasant talk surely between friends and fellow-workmen; but it seems to me as if it were not for us as yet; nay, maybe we may live long and find no time fit for such restful talk as the cheerful histories of the hopes and fears of our workshops: anyhow to-night I cannot do it, but must once again call the faithful of art to a battle wider and more distracting than that kindly struggle with nature, to which all true craftsmen are born; which is both the building-up and the wearing-away of their lives.

As I look round on this assemblage, and think of all that it represents, I cannot choose but be moved to the soul by the troubles of the life of civilised man, and the hope that thrusts itself through them; I cannot refrain from giving you once again the message with which, as it seems, some chance-hap has charged me: that message is, in short, to call on you to face the latest danger which civilisation is threatened with, a danger of her own breeding: that men in struggling towards the complete attainment of all the luxuries of life for the strongest portion of their race should deprive their whole race of all the beauty of life: a danger that the strongest and wisest of mankind, in striving to attain to a complete mastery over nature, should destroy her simplest and widest-spread gifts, and thereby enslave simple people to them, and themselves to themselves, and so at last drag the world into a second barbarism more ignoble, and a thousand-fold more hopeless, than the first.

Now of you who are listening to me, there are some, I feel sure, who have received this message, and taken it to heart, and are day by day fighting the battle that it calls on you to fight: to you I can say nothing but that if any word I speak dis-

[1] *propter vitam vivendi*, etc.: In *Art and Socialism*, Morris translates: "for the sake of life to destroy the reasons for living." The quotation is from Juvenal's *Satires*, VIII, 84.

courage you, I shall heartily wish I had never spoken at all: but to be shown the enemy, and the castle we have got to storm, is not to be bidden to run from him; nor am I telling you to sit down deedless in the desert because between you and the promised land lies many a trouble, and death itself maybe: the hope before you you know, and nothing that I can say can take it away from you; but friend may with advantage cry out to friend in the battle that a stroke is coming from this side or that: take my hasty words in that sense, I beg of you.

But I think there will be others of you in whom vague discontent is stirring: who are oppressed by the life that surrounds you; confused and troubled by that oppression, and not knowing on which side to seek a remedy, though you are fain to do so: well, we, who have gone further into those troubles, believe that we can help you: true we cannot at once take your trouble from you; nay, we may at first rather add to it; but we can tell you what we think of the way out of it; and then amidst the many things you will have to do to set yourselves and others fairly on that way, you will many days, nay most days, forget your trouble in thinking of the good that lies beyond it, for which you are working.

But, again, there are others amongst you (and to speak plainly, I daresay they are the majority), who are not by any means troubled by doubt of the road the world is going, nor excited by any hope of its bettering that road: to them the cause of civilisation is simple and even commonplace: wonder, hope, and fear no longer hang about it; it has become to us like the rising and setting of the sun; it cannot err, and we have no call to meddle with it, either to complain of its course, or to try to direct it.

There is a ground of reason and wisdom in that way of looking at the matter: surely the world will go on its ways, thrust forward by impulses which we cannot understand or sway: but as it grows in strength for the journey, its necessary food is the life and aspirations of *all* of us: and we discontented strugglers with what at times seems the hurrying blindness of civilisation, no less than those who see nothing but

smooth, unvarying progress in it, are bred of civilisation also, and shall be used up to further it in some way or other, I doubt not: and it may be of some service to those who think themselves the only loyal subjects of progress to hear of our existence, since their not hearing of it would not make an end of it: it may set them a-thinking not unprofitably to hear of burdens that they do not help to bear, but which are nevertheless real and weighty enough to some of their fellow-men, who are helping, even as they are, to form the civilisation that is to be.

The danger that the present course of civilisation will destroy the beauty of life—these are hard words, and I wish I could mend them, but I cannot, while I speak what I believe to be the truth.

That the beauty of life is a thing of no moment, I suppose few people would venture to assert, and yet most civilised people act as if it were of none, and in so doing are wronging both themselves and those that are to come after them; for that beauty, which is what is meant by *art*, using the word in its widest sense, is, I contend, no mere accident to human life, which people can take or leave as they choose, but a positive necessity of life, if we are to live as nature meant us to; that is, unless we are content to be less than men.

Now I ask you, as I have been asking myself this long while, what proportion of the population in civilised countries has any share at all in that necessity of life?

I say that the answer which must be made to that question justifies my fear that modern civilisation is on the road to trample out all the beauty of life, and to make us less than men.

Now if there should be any here who will say: It was always so; there always was a mass of rough ignorance that knew and cared nothing about art; I answer first, that if that be the case, then it was always wrong, and we, as soon as we have become conscious of that wrong, are bound to set it right if we can.

But moreover, strange to say, and in spite of all the suffering that the world has wantonly made for itself, and has in all ages so persistently clung to, as if it were a good and holy thing, this wrong of the mass of men being regardless of art was *not* always so.

So much is now known of the periods of art that have left abundant examples of their work behind them, that we can judge of the art of all periods by comparing these with the remains of times of which less has been left us; and we cannot fail to come to the conclusion that down to very recent days everything that the hand of man touched was more or less beautiful: so that in those days all people who made anything shared in art, as well as all people who used the things so made: that is, *all* people shared in art.

But some people may say: And was that to be wished for? would not this universal spreading of art stop progress in other matters, hinder the work of the world? Would it not make us unmanly? or if not that, would it not be intrusive, and push out other things necessary also for men to study?

Well, I have claimed a necessary place for art, a natural place, and it would be in the very essence of it, that it would apply its own rules of order and fitness to the general ways of life: it seems to me, therefore, that people who are over-anxious of the outward expression of beauty becoming too great a force among the other forces of life, would, if they had had the making of the external world, have been afraid of making an ear of wheat beautiful, lest it should not have been good to eat.

But indeed there seems no chance of art becoming universal, unless on the terms that it shall have little self-consciousness, and for the most part be done with little effort; so that the rough work of the world would be as little hindered by it, as the work of external nature is by the beauty of all her forms and moods: this was the case in the times that I have been speaking of: of art which was made by conscious effort, the result of the individual striving towards perfect expression of their thoughts by men very specially gifted, there was perhaps no more than there is now, except in very wonderful and short periods; though I believe that even for such men the struggle to produce beauty was not so bitter as it now is. But if there were not more great

thinkers than there are now, there was a countless multitude of happy workers whose work did express, and could not choose but express, some original thought, and was consequently both interesting and beautiful: now there is certainly no chance of the more individual art becoming common, and either wearying us by its over-abundance, or by noisy self-assertion preventing highly cultivated men taking their due part in the other work of the world; it is too difficult to do: it will be always but the blossom of all the half-conscious work below it, the fulfilment of the shortcomings of less complete minds: but it will waste much of its power, and have much less influence on men's minds, unless it be surrounded by abundance of that commoner work, in which all men once shared, and which, I say, will, when art has really awakened, be done so easily and constantly, that it will stand in no man's way to hinder him from doing what he will, good or evil. And as, on the one hand, I believe that art made by the people and for the people as a joy both to the maker and the user would further progress in other matters rather than hinder it, so also I firmly believe that that higher art produced only by great brains and miraculously gifted hands cannot exist without it: I believe that the present state of things in which it does exist, while popular art is, let us say, asleep or sick, is a transitional state, which must end at last either in utter defeat or utter victory for the arts.

For whereas all works of craftsmanship were once beautiful, unwittingly or not, they are now divided into two kinds, works of art and non-works of art: now nothing made by man's hand can be indifferent: it must be either beautiful and elevating, or ugly and degrading; and those things that are without art are so aggressively; they wound it by their existence, and they are now so much in the majority that the works of art we are obliged to set ourselves to seek for, whereas the other things are the ordinary companions of our everyday life; so that if those who cultivate art intellectually were inclined never so much to wrap themselves in their special gifts and their high cultivation, and so live happily, apart from other men, and despising them, they could not do so: they are as it were living in an enemy's country; at every turn there is something lying in wait to offend and vex their nicer sense and educated eyes: they must share in the general discomfort—and I am glad of it.

So the matter stands: from the first dawn of history till quite modern times, art, which nature meant to solace all, fulfilled its purpose; all men shared in it; that was what made life romantic, as people call it, in those days; that and not robber-barons and inaccessible kings with their hierarchy of serving-nobles and other such rubbish: but art grew and grew, saw empires sicken and sickened with them; grew hale again, and haler, and grew so great at last, that she seemed in good truth to have conquered everything, and laid the material world under foot. Then came a change at a period of the greatest life and hope in many ways that Europe had known till then: a time of so much and such varied hope that people call it the time of the New Birth: as far as the arts are concerned I deny it that title; rather it seems to me that the great men who lived and glorified the practice of art in those days, were the fruit of the old, not the seed of the new order of things: but a stirring and hopeful time it was, and many things were newborn then which have since brought forth fruit enough: and it is strange and perplexing that from those days forward the lapse of time, which, through plenteous confusion and failure, has on the whole been steadily destroying privilege and exclusiveness in other matters, has delivered up art to be the exclusive privilege of a few, and has taken from the people their birthright; while both wronged and wrongers have been wholly unconscious of what they were doing.

Wholly unconscious—yes, but we are no longer so: there lies the sting of it, and there also the hope.

When the brightness of the so-called Renaissance faded, and it faded very suddenly, a deadly chill fell upon the arts: that New-birth mostly meant looking back to past times, wherein the men of those days thought they saw a perfection of art, which to their minds was different in kind, and not in degree only, from the ruder suggestive art of their own fathers: this perfection they were ambitious to imitate, this alone seemed to be art to them, the rest was childishness: so wonderful was their energy, their success so great, that no doubt to commonplace minds among them, though surely not to the great masters, that perfection seemed to be gained: and, perfection being gained, what are you to do?—you can go no further, you must aim at standing still—which you cannot do.

Art by no means stood still in those latter days of the Renaissance, but took the downward road with terrible swiftness, and tumbled down at the bottom of the hill, where as if bewitched it lay long in great content, believing itself to be the art of Michael Angelo, while it was the art of men whom nobody remembers but those who want to sell their pictures.

Thus it fared with the more individual forms of art. As to the art of the people; in countries and places where the greater art had flourished most, it went step by step on the downward path with that: in more out-of-the-way places, England for instance, it still felt the influence of the life of its earlier and happy days, and in a way lived on a while; but its life was so feeble, and, so to say, illogical, that it could not resist any change in external circumstances, still less could it give birth to anything new; and before this century began, its last flicker had died out. Still, while it was living, in whatever dotage, it did imply something going on in those matters of daily use that we have been thinking of, and doubtless satisfied some cravings for beauty: and when it was dead, for a long time people did not know it, or what had taken its place, crept so to say into its dead body—that pretence of art, to wit, which is done with machines, though sometimes the machines are called men, and doubtless are so out of working hours: nevertheless long before it was quite dead it had fallen so low that the whole subject was usually treated with the utmost contempt by every one who had any pretence of being a sensible man, and in short the whole civilised world had forgotten that there had ever been an art *made by the people for the people as a joy for the maker and the user.*

But now it seems to me that the very

suddenness of the change ought to comfort us, to make us look upon this break in the continuity of the golden chain as an accident only, that itself cannot last: for think how many thousand years it may be since that primæval man graved with a flint splinter on a bone the story of the mammoth he had seen, or told us of the slow uplifting of the heavily-horned heads of the reindeer that he stalked: think I say of the space of time from then till the dimming of the brightness of the Italian Renaissance! whereas from that time till popular art died unnoticed and despised among ourselves is just but two hundred years.

Strange too, that very death is contemporaneous with new-birth of something at all events; for out of all despair sprang a new time of hope lighted by the torch of the French Revolution: and things that have languished with the languishing of art, rose afresh and surely heralded its new birth: in good earnest poetry was born again, and the English Language, which under the hands of sycophantic verse-makers had been reduced to a miserable jargon, whose meaning, if it have a meaning, cannot be made out without translation, flowed clear, pure, and simple, along with the music of Blake and Coleridge: take those names, the earliest in date among ourselves, as a type of the change that has happened in literature since the time of George II.

With that literature in which romance, that is to say humanity, was re-born, there sprang up also a feeling for the romance of external nature, which is surely strong in us now, joined with a longing to know something real of the lives of those who have gone before us; of these feelings united you will find the broadest expression in the pages of Walter Scott: it is curious as showing how sometimes one art will lag behind another in a revival, that the man who wrote the exquisite and wholly unfettered naturalism of the Heart of Midlothian, for instance, thought himself continually bound to seem to feel ashamed of, and to excuse himself for, his love of Gothic Architecture: he felt that it was romantic, and he knew that it gave him pleasure, but somehow he had not found out that it was art, having been taught in many ways that nothing could be art that was not done by a named man under academical rules.

I need not perhaps dwell much on what of change has been since: you know well that one of the master-arts, the art of painting, has been revolutionised. I have a genuine difficulty in speaking to you of men who are my own personal friends, nay my masters: still, since I cannot quite say nothing of them I must say the plain truth, which is this: never in the whole history of art did any set of men come nearer to the feat of making something out of nothing than that little knot of painters who have raised English art from what it was, when as a boy I used to go to the Royal Academy Exhibition, to what it is now.

It would be ungracious indeed for me who have been so much taught by him, that I cannot help feeling continually as I speak that I am echoing his words, to leave out the name of John Ruskin from an account of what has happened since the tide, as we hope, began to turn in the direction of art. True it is, that his unequalled style of English and his wonderful eloquence would, whatever its subject-matter, have gained him some sort of a hearing in a time that has not lost its relish for literature; but surely the influence that he has exercised over cultivated people must be the result of that style and that eloquence expressing what was already stirring in men's minds; he could not have written what he has done unless people were in some sort ready for it: any more than those painters could have begun their crusade against the dullness and incompetency that was the rule in their art thirty years ago unless they had some hope that they would one day move people to understand them.

Well, we find that the gains since the turning-point of the tide are these: that there are some few artists who have, as it were, caught up the golden chain dropped two hundred years ago, and that there are a few highly cultivated people who can understand them; and that beyond these there is a vague feeling abroad among people of the same degree, of discontent at the ignoble ugliness that surrounds them.

That seems to me to mark the advance that we have made since the last of popular art came to an end amongst us, and I do not say, considering where we then were, that it is not a great advance, for it comes to this, that though the battle is still to win, there are those who are ready for the battle.

Indeed it would be a strange shame for this age if it were not so: for as every age of the world has its own troubles to confuse it, and its own follies to cumber it, so has each its own work to do, pointed out to it by unfailing signs of the times; and it is unmanly and stupid for the children of any age to say: We will not set our hands to the work; we did not make the troubles, we will not weary ourselves seeking a remedy for them: so heaping up for their sons a heavier load than they can lift without such struggles as will wound and cripple them sorely. Not thus our fathers served us, who, working late and early, left us at last that seething mass of people so terribly alive and energetic, that we call modern Europe; not thus those served us, who have made for us these present days, so fruitful of change and wondering expectation.

The century that is now beginning to draw to an end, if people were to take to nicknaming centuries, would be called the Century of Commerce; and I do not think I undervalue the work that it has done: it has broken down many a prejudice and taught many a lesson that the world has been hitherto slow to learn: it has made it possible for many a man to live free, who would in other times have been a slave, body or soul, or both: if it has not quite spread peace and justice through the world, as at the end of its first half we fondly hoped it would, it has at least stirred up in many fresh cravings for peace and justice: its work has been good and plenteous, but much of it was roughly done, as needs was; recklessness has commonly gone with its energy, blindness too often with its haste: so that perhaps it may be work enough for the next century to repair the blunders of that recklessness, to clear away the rubbish which that hurried work has piled up; nay even we in the second half of its last quarter may do something towards setting its house in order.

You, of this great and famous town, for instance, which has had so much to do with the Century of Commerce, your gains are obvious to all men, but the price you have paid for them is obvious to many— surely to yourselves most of all: I do not say that they are not worth the price; I know that England and the world could very ill afford to exchange the Birmingham of to-day for the Birmingham of the year 1700: but surely if what you have gained be more than a mockery, you cannot stop at those gains, or even go on always piling up similar ones. Nothing can make me believe that the present condition of your Black Country yonder is an unchangeable necessity of your life and position: such miseries as this were begun and carried on in pure thoughtlessness, and a hundredth part of the energy that was spent in creating them would get rid of them: I do think if we were not all of us too prone to acquiesce in the base byword "after me the deluge," it would soon be something more than an idle dream to hope that your pleasant midland hills and fields might begin to become pleasant again in some way or other, even without depopulating them; or that those once lovely valleys of Yorkshire in the "heavy woollen district," with their sweeping hill-sides and noble rivers, should not need the stroke of ruin to make them once more delightful abodes of men, instead of the dog-holes that the Century of Commerce has made them.

Well, people will not take the trouble or spend the money necessary to beginning this sort of reforms, because they do not feel the evils they live amongst, because they have degraded themselves into something less than men; they are unmanly because they have ceased to have their due share of art.

For again I say that therein rich people have defrauded themselves as well as the poor: you will see a refined and highly educated man nowadays, who has been to Italy and Egypt, and where not, who can talk learnedly enough (and fantastically enough sometimes) about art, and who has at his fingers' ends abundant lore concerning the art and literature of past days, sitting down without signs of discomfort in a house, that with all its surroundings is just brutally vulgar and hideous: all his education has not done more for him than that.

The truth is, that in art, and in other things besides, the laboured education of a few will not raise even those few above the reach of the evils that beset the ignorance of the great mass of the population: the brutality of which such a huge stock has been accumulated lower down, will often show without much peeling through the selfish refinement of those who have let it accumulate. The lack of art, or rather the murder of art, that curses our streets from the sordidness of the surroundings of the lower classes, has its exact counterpart in the dullness and vulgarity of those of the middle classes, and the double-distilled dullness, and scarcely less vulgarity of those of the upper classes.

I say this is as it should be; it is just and fair as far as it goes; and moreover the rich with their leisure are the more like to move if they feel the pinch themselves.

But how shall they and we, and all of us, move? What is the remedy?

What remedy can there be for the blunders of civilisation but further civilisation? You do not by any accident think that we have gone as far in that direction as it is possible to go, do you?—even in England, I mean?

When some changes have come to pass, that perhaps will be speedier than most people think, doubtless education will both grow in quality and in quantity; so that it may be, that as the nineteenth century is to be called the Century of Commerce, the twentieth may be called the Century of Education. But that education does not end when people leave school is now a mere commonplace; and how then can you really educate men who lead the life of machines, who only think for the few hours during which they are not at work, who in short spend almost their whole lives in doing work which is not proper for developing them body and mind in some worthy way? You cannot educate, you cannot civilise men, unless you can give them a share in art.

Yes, and it is hard indeed as things go to give most men that share; for they do not miss it, or ask for it, and it is impossible as things are that they should either miss or ask for it. Nevertheless everything has a beginning, and many great things have had very small ones; and since, as I have said, these ideas are already abroad in more than one form, we must not be too much discouraged at the seemingly boundless weight we have to lift.

After all, we are only bound to play our own parts, and do our own share of the lifting; and as in no case that share can be great, so also in all cases it is called for, it is necessary. Therefore let us work and faint not; remembering that though it be natural, and therefore excusable, amidst doubtful times to feel doubts of success oppress us at whiles, yet not to crush those doubts, and work as if we had them not, is simple cowardice, which is unforgivable. No man has any right to say that all has been done for nothing, that all the faithful unwearying strife of those that have gone before us shall lead us nowhither; that mankind will but go round and round in a circle for ever: no man has a right to say that, and then get up morning after morning to eat his victuals and sleep a-nights, all the while making other people toil to keep his worthless life a-going.

Be sure that some way or other will be found out of the tangle, even when things seem most tangled, and be no less sure that some use will then have come of our work, if it has been faithful, and therefore unsparingly careful and thoughtful.

So once more I say, if in any matters civilisation has gone astray, the remedy lies not in standing still, but in more complete civilisation.

Now whatever discussion there may be about that often used and often misused word, I believe all who hear me will agree with me in believing from their hearts, and not merely in saying in conventional phrase, that the civilisation which does not carry the whole people with it, is doomed to fall, and give place to one which at least aims at doing so.

We talk of the civilisation of the ancient peoples, of the classical times: well, civilised they were no doubt, some of their folk at least: an Athenian citizen for instance led a simple, dignified, almost perfect life; but there were drawbacks to happiness perhaps in the lives of his slaves:

and the civilisation of the ancients was founded on slavery.

Indeed that ancient society did give a model to the world, and showed us for ever what blessings are freedom of life and thought, self-restraint and a generous education: all those blessings the ancient free peoples set forth to the world—and kept them to themselves.

Therefore no tyrant was too base, no pretext too hollow, for enslaving the grandsons of the men of Salamis and Thermopylæ: therefore did the descendants of those stern and self-restrained Romans, who were ready to give up everything, and life as the least of things, to the glory of their commonweal, produce monsters of license and reckless folly. Therefore did a little knot of Galilean peasants overthrow the Roman Empire.

Ancient civilisation was chained to slavery and exclusiveness, and it fell; the barbarism that took its place has delivered us from slavery and grown into modern civilisation; and that in its turn has before it the choice of never-ceasing growth, or destruction by that which has in it the seeds of higher growth.

There is an ugly word for a dreadful fact, which I must make bold to use—the residuum: that word since the time I first saw it used, has had a terrible significance to me, and I have felt from my heart that if this residuum were a necessary part of modern civilisation, as some people openly, and many more tacitly, assume that it is, then this civilisation carries with it the poison that shall one day destroy it, even as its elder sister did: if civilisation is to go no further than this, it had better not have gone so far: if it does not aim at getting rid of this misery and giving some share in the happiness and dignity of life to *all* the people that it has created, and which it spends such unwearying energy in creating, it is simply an organised injustice, a mere instrument for oppression, so much the worse than that which has gone before it, as its pretensions are higher, its slavery subtler, its mastery harder to overthrow, because supported by such a dense mass of commonplace well-being and comfort.

Surely this cannot be: surely there is a distinct feeling abroad of this injustice: so that if the residuum still clogs all the efforts of modern civilisation to rise above mere population-breeding and money-making, the difficulty of dealing with it is the legacy, first of the ages of violence and almost conscious brutal injustice, and next of the ages of thoughtlessness, of hurry and blindness; surely all those who think at all of the future of the world are at work in one way or other in striving to rid it of this shame.

That to my mind is the meaning of what we call National Education, which we have begun, and which is doubtless already bearing its fruits, and will bear greater, when all people are educated, not according to the money which they or their parents possess, but according to the capacity of their minds.

What effect that will have upon the future of the arts, I cannot say, but one would surely think a very great effect; for it will enable people to see clearly many things which are now as completely hidden from them as if they were blind in body and idiotic in mind: and this, I say, will act not only upon those who most directly feel the evils of ignorance, but also upon those who feel them indirectly,— upon us, the educated: the great wave of rising intelligence, rife with so many natural desires and aspirations, will carry all classes along with it, and force us all to see that many things which we have been used to look upon as necessary and eternal evils are merely the accidental and temporary growths of past stupidity, and can be escaped from by due effort, and the exercise of courage, goodwill, and forethought.

And among those evils, I do, and must always, believe will fall that one which last year I told you that I accounted the greatest of all evils, the heaviest of all slaveries; that evil of the greater part of the population being engaged in by far the most part of their lives in work, which at the best cannot interest them, or develop their best faculties, and at the worst (and that is the commonest, too) is mere unmitigated slavish toil, only to be wrung out of them by the sternest compulsion, a toil which they shirk all they can—small blame to them. And this toil degrades them into less than men: and they will some day come to know it, and cry out to be made men again, and art only can do it, and redeem them from this slavery; and I say once more that this is her highest and most glorious end and aim; and it is in her struggle to attain to it that she will most surely purify herself, and quicken her own aspirations towards perfection.

But we—in the meantime we must not sit waiting for obvious signs of these later and glorious days to show themselves on earth, and in the heavens, but rather turn to the commonplace, and maybe often dull work of fitting ourselves in detail to take part in them if we should live to see one of them; or in doing our best to make the path smooth for their coming, if we are to die before they are here.

What, therefore, can we do, to guard traditions of time past that we may not one day have to begin anew from the beginning with none to teach us? What are we to do, that we may take heed to, and spread the decencies of life, so that at the least we may have a field where it will be possible for art to grow when men begin to long for it: what finally can we do, each of us, to cherish some germ of art, so that it may meet with others, and spread and grow little by little into the thing that we need?

Now I cannot pretend to think that the first of these duties is a matter of indifference to you, after my experience of the enthusiastic meeting that I had the honour of addressing here last autumn on the subject of the (so called) restoration of St. Mark's at Venice; you thought, and most justly thought, it seems to me, that the subject was of such moment to art in general, that it was a simple and obvious thing for men who were anxious on the matter to address themselves to those who had the decision of it in their hands; even though the former were called Englishmen, and the latter Italians; for you felt that the name of lovers of art would cover those differences: if you had any misgivings, you remembered that there was but one such building in the world, and that it was worth while risking a breach of etiquette, if any words of ours could do anything towards saving it; well, the Italians were, some of them, very naturally, though surely unreasonably, irritated, for a time, and in some of their prints they bade us look at home; that was no argument in favour of the wisdom of wantonly rebuilding St. Mark's façade: but certainly those of us who have not yet looked at home in this matter had better do so speedily, late and over late though it be: for though we have no golden-pictured interiors like St. Mark's Church at home, we still have many buildings which are both works of ancient art and monuments of history: and just think what is happening to them, and note, since we profess to recognise their value, how helpless art is in the Century of Commerce!

In the first place, many and many a beautiful and ancient building is being destroyed all over civilised Europe as well as in England, because it is supposed to interfere with the convenience of the citizens, while a little forethought might save it without trenching on that convenience; but even apart from that, I say that if we are not prepared to put up with a little inconvenience in our lifetimes for the sake of preserving a monument of art which will elevate and educate, not only ourselves, but our sons, and our sons' sons, it is vain and idle of us to talk about art—or education either. Brutality must be bred of such brutality.

The same thing may be said about enlarging, or otherwise altering for convenience' sake, old buildings still in use for something like their original purposes: in almost all such cases it is really nothing more than a question of a little money for a new site: and then a new building can be built exactly fitted for the uses it is needed for, with such art about it as our own days can furnish; while the old monument is left to tell its tale of change and progress, to hold out example and warning to us in the practice of the arts: and thus the convenience of the public, the progress of modern art, and the cause of education, are all furthered at once at the cost of a little money.

Surely if it be worth while troubling ourselves about the works of art of to-day, of which any amount almost can be done, since we are yet alive, it is worth while spending a little care, forethought, and money in preserving the art of bygone ages, of which (woe worth the while!) so little is left, and of which we can never have any more, whatever good-hap the world may attain to.

No man who consents to the destruction or the mutilation of an ancient building has any right to pretend that he cares about art; or has any excuse to plead in defence of his crime against civilisation and progress, save sheer brutal ignorance.

But before I leave this subject I must say a word or two about the curious invention of our own days called Restoration, a method of dealing with works of bygone days which, though not so degrading in its spirit as downright destruction, is nevertheless little better in its results on the condition of those works of art; it is obvious that I have no time to argue the question out tonight, so I will only make these assertions:

That ancient buildings, being both works of art and monuments of history, must obviously be treated with great care and delicacy: that the imitative art of to-day is not, and cannot be the same thing as ancient art, and cannot replace it; and that therefore if we superimpose this work on the old, we destroy it both as art and as a record of history: lastly, that the natural weathering of the surface of a building is beautiful, and its loss disastrous.

Now the restorers hold the exact contrary of all this: they think that any clever architect to-day can deal off-hand successfully with the ancient work; that while all things else have changed about us since (say) the thirteenth century, art has not changed, and that our workmen can turn out work identical with that of the thirteenth century; and, lastly, that the weather-beaten surface of an ancient building is worthless, and to be got rid of wherever possible.

You see the question is difficult to argue, because there seem to be no common grounds between the restorers and the anti-restorers: I appeal therefore to the public, and bid them note, that though our opinions may be wrong, the action we advise is not rash: let the question be shelved awhile: if, as we are always pressing on people, due care be taken of these monuments, so that they shall not fall into disrepair, they will be always there to "restore" whenever people think proper and when we are proved wrong; but if it should turn out that we are right, how can the "restored" buildings be restored? I beg of you therefore to let the question be shelved, till art has so advanced among us, that we can deal authoritatively with it, till there is no longer any doubt about the matter.

Surely these monuments of our art and history, which, whatever the lawyers may say, belong not to a coterie, or to a rich man here and there, but to the nation at large, are worth this delay: surely the last relics of the life of the "famous men and our fathers that begat us" may justly claim of us the exercise of a little patience.

It will give us trouble no doubt, all this care of our possessions: but there is more trouble to come; for I must now speak of something else, of possessions which should be common to all of us, of the green grass, and the leaves, and the waters, of the very light and air of heaven, which the Century of Commerce has been too busy to pay any heed to. And first let me remind you that I am supposing every one here present professes to care about art.

Well, there are some rich men among us whom we oddly enough call manufacturers, by which we mean capitalists who pay other men to organise manufacturers; these gentlemen, many of whom buy pictures and profess to care about art, burn a deal of coal: there is an Act in existence which was passed to prevent them sometimes and in some places from pouring a dense cloud of smoke over the world, and, to my thinking, a very lame and partial Act it is: but nothing hinders these lovers of art from being a law to themselves, and making it a point of honour with them to minimize the smoke nuisance as far as their own works are concerned; and if they don't do so, when mere money, and even a very little of that, is what it will cost them, I say that their love of art is a mere pretence: how can you care about the image of a landscape when you show by your deeds that you don't care for the landscape itself? or what right have you to shut yourself up with beautiful form and colour when you make it impossible for other people to have any share in these things?

Well, and as to the smoke Act itself: I

don't know what heed you pay to it in Birmingham, but I have seen myself what heed is paid to it in other places; Bradford for instance; though close by them at Saltaire they have an example which I should have thought might have shamed them; for the huge chimney there which serves the acres of weaving and spinning sheds of Sir Titus Salt and his brothers is as guiltless of smoke as an ordinary kitchen chimney. Or Manchester: a gentleman of that city told me that the smoke Act was a mere dead letter there: well, they buy pictures in Manchester and profess to wish to further the arts: but you see it must be idle pretence as far as their rich people are concerned: they only want to talk about it, and have themselves talked of.

I don't know what you are doing about this matter here; but you must forgive my saying, that unless you are beginning to think of some way of dealing with it, you are not beginning yet to pave your way to success in the arts.

Well, I have spoken of a huge nuisance, which is a type of the worst nuisances of what an ill-tempered man might be excused for calling the Century of Nuisances, rather than the Century of Commerce. I will now leave it to the consciences of the rich and influential among us, and speak of a minor nuisance which it is in the power of every one of us to abate, and which, small as it is, is so vexatious, that if I can prevail on a score of you to take heed to it by what I am saying, I shall think my evening's work a good one. Sandwich-papers I mean—of course you laugh: but come now, don't you, civilised as you are in Birmingham, leave them all about the Lickey hills and your public gardens and the like? If you don't I really scarcely know with what words to praise you. When we Londoners go to enjoy ourselves at Hampton Court, for instance, we take special good care to let everybody know that we have had something to eat: so that the park just outside the gates (and a beautiful place it is) looks as if it had been snowing dirty paper. I really think you might promise me one and all who are here present to have done with this sluttish habit, which is the type of many another in its way, just as the smoke nuisance is. I mean such things as scrawling one's name on monuments, tearing down tree boughs, and the like.

I suppose 'tis early days in the revival of the arts to express one's disgust at the daily increasing hideousness of the posters with which all our towns are daubed. Still we ought to be disgusted at such horrors, and I think make up our minds never to buy any of the articles so advertised. I can't believe they can be worth much if they need all that shouting to sell them.

Again, I must ask what do you do with the trees on a site that is going to be built over? do you try to save them, to adapt your houses at all to them? do you understand what treasures they are in a town or a suburb? or what a relief they will be to the hideous dog-holes which (forgive me!) you are probably going to build in their places? I ask this anxiously, and with grief in my soul, for in London and its suburbs we always begin by clearing a site till it is as bare as the pavement: I really think that almost anybody would have been shocked, if I could have shown him some of the trees that have been wantonly murdered in the suburb in which I live (Hammersmith to wit), amongst them some of those magnificent cedars, for which we along the river used to be famous once.

But here again see how helpless those are who care about art or nature amidst the hurry of the Century of Commerce.

Pray do not forget, that any one who cuts down a tree wantonly or carelessly, especially in a great town or its suburbs, need make no pretence of caring about art.

What else can we do to help to educate ourselves and others in the path of art, to be on the road to attaining an *Art made by the people and for the people as a joy to the maker and the user?*

Why, having got to understand something of what art was, having got to look upon its ancient monuments as friends that can tell us something of times bygone, and whose faces we do not wish to alter, even though they be worn by time and grief: having got to spend money and trouble upon matters of decency, great and little; having made it clear that we really do care about nature even in the suburbs of a big town—having got so far, we shall begin to think of the houses in which we live.

For I must tell you that unless you are resolved to have good and rational architecture, it is, once again, useless your thinking about art at all.

I have spoken of the popular arts, but they might all be summed up in that one word Architecture; they are all parts of that great whole, and the art of house-building begins it all: if we did not know how to dye or to weave; if we had neither gold, nor silver, nor silk; and no pigments to paint with but half-a-dozen ochres and umbers, we might yet frame a worthy art that would lead to everything, if we had but timber, stone, and lime, and a few cutting tools to make these common things not only shelter us from wind and weather, but also express the thoughts and aspirations that stir in us.

Architecture would lead us to all the arts, as it did with earlier men: but if we despise it and take no note of how we are housed, the other arts will have a hard time of it indeed.

Now I do not think the greatest of optimists would deny that, taking us one and all, we are at present housed in a perfectly shameful way, and since the greatest part of us have to live in houses already built for us, it must be admitted that it is rather hard to know what to do, beyond waiting till they tumble about our ears.

Only we must not lay the fault upon the builders, as some people seem inclined to do: they are our very humble servants, and will build what we ask for; remember, that rich men are not obliged to live in ugly houses, and yet you see they do; which the builders may be well excused for taking as a sign of what is wanted.

Well, the point is, we must do what we can, and make people understand what we want them to do for us, by letting them see what we do for ourselves.

Hitherto, judging us by that standard, the builders may well say that we want the pretence of a thing rather than the thing itself; that we want a show of petty luxury if we are unrich, a show of insulting stupidity if we are rich: and they are quite clear that as a rule we want to get something that shall look as if it cost twice as much as it really did.

You cannot have Architecture on those terms: simplicity and solidity are the very first requisites of it: just think if it is not so. How we please ourselves with an old building by thinking of all the generations of men that have passed through it! do we not remember how it has received their joy, and borne their sorrow, and not even their folly has left sourness upon it? it still looks as kind to us as it did to them. And the converse of this we ought to feel when we look at a newly-built house if it were as it should be: we should feel a pleasure in thinking how he who had built it had left a piece of his soul behind him to greet the newcomers one after another long and long after he was gone:—but what sentiment can an ordinary modern house move in us, or what thought—save a hope that we may speedily forget its base ugliness?

But if you ask me how we are to pay for this solidity and extra expense, that seems to me a reasonable question; for you must dismiss at once as a delusion the hope that has been sometimes cherished, that you can have a building which is a work of art, and is therefore above all things properly built, at the same price as a building which only pretends to be this: never forget when people talk about cheap art in general, by the way, that all art costs time, trouble, and thought, and that money is only a counter to represent these things.

However, I must try to answer the question I have supposed put, how are we to pay for decent houses?

It seems to me that, by a great piece of good luck, the way to pay for them is by doing that which alone can produce popular art among us: living a simple life, I mean. Once more I say that the greatest foe to art is luxury, art cannot live in its atmosphere.

When you hear of the luxuries of the ancients, you must remember that they were not like our luxuries, they were rather indulgences in pieces of extravagant folly than what we to-day call luxury; which perhaps you would rather call comfort: well I accept the word, and say that a Greek or Roman of the luxurious time would stare astonished could he be brought back again, and shown the comforts of a well-to-do middle-class house.

But some, I know, think that the attainment of these very comforts is what makes the difference between civilisation and un-civilisation, that they are the essence of civilisation. Is it so indeed? Farewell my hope then!—I had thought that civilisation meant the attainment of peace and order and freedom, of goodwill between man and man, of the love of truth and the hatred of injustice, and by consequence the attainment of the good life which these things breed, a life free from craven fear, but full of incident: that was what I thought it meant, not more stuffed chairs and more cushions, and more carpets and gas, and more dainty meat and drink—and therewithal more and sharper differences between class and class.

If that be what it is, I for my part wish I were well out of it, and living in a tent in the Persian desert, or a turf hut on the Iceland hill-side. But however it be, and I think my view is the true view, I tell you that art abhors that side of civilisation, she cannot breathe in the houses that lie under its stuffy slavery.

Believe me, if we want art to begin at home, as it must, we must clear our houses of troublesome superfluities that are for ever in our way: conventional comforts that are no real comforts, and do but make work for servants and doctors: if you want a golden rule that will fit everybody, this is it:

"Have nothing in your houses that you do not know to be useful, or believe to be beautiful."

And if we apply that rule strictly, we shall in the first place show the builders and such-like servants of the public what we really want, we shall create a demand for real art, as the phrase goes; and in the second place, we shall surely have more money to pay for decent houses.

Perhaps it will not try your patience too much if I lay before you my idea of the fittings necessary to the sitting-room of a healthy person: a room, I mean, which he would not have to cook in much, or sleep in generally, or in which he would not have to do any very litter-making manual work. First a book-case with a great many books in it: next a table that will keep steady when you write or work at it: then several chairs that you can move, and a bench that you can sit or lie upon: next a cupboard with drawers: next, unless either the book-case or the cupboard be very beautiful with painting or carving, you will want pictures or engravings, such as you can afford, only not stopgaps, but real works of art on the wall; or else the wall itself must be ornamented with some beautiful and restful pattern: we shall also want a vase or two to put flowers in, which latter you must have sometimes, especially if you live in a town. Then there will be the fireplace of course, which in our climate is bound to be the chief object in the room.

That is all we shall want, especially if the floor be good; if it be not, as, by the way, in a modern house it is pretty certain not to be, I admit that a small carpet which can be bundled out of the room in two minutes will be useful, and we must also take care that it is beautiful, or it will annoy us terribly.

Now unless we are musical, and need a piano (in which case, as far as beauty is concerned, we are in a bad way), that is quite all we want: and we can add very little to these necessaries without troubling ourselves, and hindering our work, our thought, and our rest.

If these things were done at the least cost for which they could be done well and solidly, they ought not to cost much; and they are so few, that those that could afford to have them at all, could afford to spend some trouble to get them fitting and beautiful: and all those who care about art ought to take great trouble to do so, and to take care that there be no sham art amongst them, nothing that it has degraded a man to make or sell. And I feel sure, that if all who care about art were to take this pains, it would make a great impression upon the public.

This simplicity you may make as costly as you please or can, on the other hand: you may hang your walls with tapestry instead of whitewash or paper; or you may cover them with mosaic, or have them frescoed by a great painter: all this is not luxury, if it be done for beauty's sake, and not for show: it does not break our golden rule: *Have nothing in your houses which you do not know to be useful or believe to be beautiful.*

All art starts from this simplicity; and the higher the art rises, the greater the simplicity. I have been speaking of the fittings of a dwelling-house—a place in which we eat and drink, and pass familiar hours; but when you come to places which people want to make more specially beautiful because of the solemnity or dignity of their uses, they will be simpler still, and have little in them save the bare walls made as beautiful as may be. St. Mark's at Venice has very little furniture in it, much less than most Roman Catholic churches: its lovely and stately mother St. Sophia of Constantinople had less still, even when it was a Christian church: but we need not go either to Venice or Stamboul to take note of that: go into one of our own mighty Gothic naves (do any of you remember the first time you did so?) and note how the huge free space satisfies and elevates you, even now when window and wall are stripped of ornament: then think of the meaning of simplicity, and absence of encumbering gew-gaws.

Now after all, for us who are learning art, it is not far to seek what is the surest way to further it; that which most breeds art is art; every piece of work that we do which is well done, is so much help to the cause; every piece of pretence and half-heartedness is so much hurt to it. Most of you who take to the practice of art can find out in no very long time whether you have any gifts for it or not: if you have not, throw the thing up, or you will have a wretched time of it yourselves, and will be damaging the cause by laborious pretence: but if you have gifts of any kind, you are happy indeed beyond most men; for your pleasure is always with you, nor can you be intemperate in the enjoyment of it, and as you use it, it does not lessen, but grows: if you are by chance weary of it at night, you get up in the morning eager for it: or if perhaps in the morning it seems folly to you for a while, yet presently, when your hand has been moving a little in its wonted way, fresh hope has sprung up beneath it and you are happy again. While others are getting through the day like plants thrust into the earth, which cannot turn this way or that but as the wind blows them, you know what you want, and your will is on the alert to find it, and you, whatever happens, whether it be joy or grief, are at least alive.

Now when I spoke to you last year, after I had sat down I was half afraid that I had on some points said too much, that I had spoken too bitterly in my eagerness; that a rash word might have discouraged some of you; I was very far from meaning that: what I wanted to do, what I want to do to-night, is to put definitely before you a cause for which to strive.

That cause is the Democracy of Art, the ennobling of daily and common work, which will one day put hope and pleasure in the place of fear and pain, as the forces which move men to labour and keep the world a-going.

If I have enlisted any one in that cause, rash as my words may have been, or feeble as they may have been, they have done more good than harm; nor do I believe that any words of mine can discourage any who have joined that cause or are ready to do so: their way is too clear before them for that, and every one of us can help the cause whether he be great or little.

I know indeed that men, wearied by the pettiness of the details of the strife, their patience tried by hope deferred, will at whiles, excusably enough, turn back in their hearts to other days, when if the issues were not clearer, the means of trying them were simpler; when, so stirring were the times, one might even have atoned for many a blunder and backsliding by visibly dying for the cause. To have breasted the Spanish pikes at Leyden, to have drawn sword with Oliver: that may well seem to us at times amidst the tangles of to-day a happy fate: for a man to be able to say, I have lived like a fool, but now I will cast away fooling for an hour, and die like a man—there is something in that certainly: and yet 'tis clear that few men can be so lucky as to die for a cause, without having first of all lived for it. And as this is the most that can be asked from the greatest man that follows a cause, so it is the least that can be taken from the smallest.

So to us who have a Cause at heart, our highest ambition and our simplest duty are one and the same thing: for the most part we shall be too busy doing the work that lies ready to our hands, to let impatience for visibly great progress vex us much; but surely since we are servants of a Cause, hope must be ever with us, and sometimes perhaps it will so quicken our vision that it will outrun the slow lapse of time, and show us the victorious days when millions of those who now sit in darkness will be enlightened by an *Art made by the people and for the people, a joy to the maker and the user.*   [1880]

SIGNS OF CHANGE

USEFUL WORK VERSUS USELESS TOIL

The above title may strike some of my readers as strange. It is assumed by most people nowadays that all work is useful, and by most *well-to-do* people that all work is desirable Most people, well-to-do or not, believe that, even when a man is doing work which appears to be useless, he is earning his livelihood by it—he is "em- 10 ployed," as the phrase goes; and most of those who are well-to-do cheer on the happy worker with congratulations and praises, if he is only "industrious" enough and deprives himself of all pleasure and holidays in the sacred cause of labour. In short, it has become an article of the creed of modern morality that all labour is good in itself —a convenient belief to those who live on the labour of others. But as to those on 20 whom they live, I recommend them not to take it on trust, but to look into the matter a little deeper.

Let us grant, first, that the race of man must either labour or perish. Nature does not give us our livelihood gratis; we must win it by toil of some sort or degree. Let us see, then, if she does not give us some compensation for this compulsion to labour, since certainly in other matters she takes 30 care to make the acts necessary to the continuance of life in the individual and the race not only endurable, but even pleasurable.

You may be sure that she does so, that it is of the nature of man, when he is not diseased, to take pleasure in his work under certain conditions. And, yet, we must say in the teeth of the hypocritical praise of all labour, whatsoever it may be, of which I 40 have made mention, that there is some labour which is so far from being a blessing that it is a curse; that it would be better for the community and for the worker if the latter were to fold his hands and refuse to work, and either die or let us pack him off to the workhouse or prison—which you will.

Here, you see, are two kinds of work— one good, the other bad; one not far removed from a blessing, a lightening of life; the other a mere curse, a burden to life.

What is the difference between them, then? This: one has hope in it, the other has not. It is manly to do the one kind of work, and manly also to refuse to do the other.

What is the nature of the hope which, when it is present in work, makes it worth doing?

It is threefold, I think—hope of rest, hope of product, hope of pleasure in the work itself; and hope of these also in some abundance and of good quality; rest enough and good enough to be worth having; product worth having by one who is neither a fool nor an ascetic; pleasure enough for all for us to be conscious of it while we are at work; not a mere habit, the loss of which we shall feel as a fidgety man feels the loss of the bit of string he fidgets with.

I have put the hope of rest first because it is the simplest and most natural part of our hope. Whatever pleasure there is in some work, there is certainly some pain in all work, the beast-like pain of stirring up our slumbering energies to action, the beast-like dread of change when things are pretty well with us; and the compensation for this animal pain is animal rest. We must feel while we are working that the time will come when we shall not have to work. Also the rest, when it comes, must be long enough to allow us to enjoy it; it must be longer than is merely necessary for us to recover the strength we have expended in working, and it must be animal rest also in this, that it must not be disturbed by anxiety, else we shall not be able to enjoy it. If we have this amount and kind of rest we shall, so far, be no worse off than the beasts.

As to the hope of product, I have said that Nature compels us to work for that. It remains for *us* to look to it that we *do* really produce something, and not nothing, or at least nothing that we want or are allowed to use. If we look to this and use our wills we shall, so far, be better than machines.

The hope of pleasure in the work itself: how strange that hope must seem to some of my readers—to most of them! Yet I think that to all living things there is a pleasure in the exercise of their energies, and that even beasts rejoice in being lithe and swift and strong. But a man at work, making something which he feels will exist because he is working at it and wills it, is exercising the energies of his mind and soul as well as of his body. Memory and imagination help him as he works. Not only his own thoughts, but the thoughts of the men of past ages guide his hands; and, as a part of the human race, he creates. If we work thus we shall be men, and our days will be happy and eventful.

Thus worthy work carries with it the hope of pleasure in rest, the hope of the pleasure in our using what it makes, and the hope of pleasure in our daily creative skill.

All other work but this is worthless; it is slaves' work—mere toiling to live, that we may live to toil.

Therefore, since we have, as it were, a pair of scales in which to weigh the work now done in the world, let us use them. Let us estimate the worthiness of the work we do, after so many thousand years of toil, so many promises of hope deferred, such boundless exultation over the progress of civilization and the gain of liberty.

Now, the first thing as to the work done in civilization and the easiest to notice is that it is portioned out very unequally amongst the different classes of society. First, there are people—not a few—who do no work, and make no pretence of doing any. Next, there are people, and very many of them, who work fairly hard, though with abundant easements and holidays, claimed and allowed; and lastly, there are people who work so hard that they may be said to do nothing else than work, and are accordingly called "the working classes," as distinguished from the middle classes and the rich, or aristocracy, whom I have mentioned above.

It is clear that this inequality presses heavily upon the "working class," and must visibly tend to destroy their hope of rest at least, and so, in that particular, make them worse off than mere beasts of the field; but that is not the sum and end of our folly of turning useful work into useless toil, but only the beginning of it.

For first, as to the class of rich people doing no work, we all know that they consume a great deal while they produce nothing. Therefore, clearly, they have to be kept at the expense of those who do work, just as paupers have, and are a mere burden on the community. In these days there are many who have learned to see this, though they can see no further into the evils of our present system, and have formed no idea of any scheme for getting rid of this burden; though perhaps they have a vague hope that changes in the system of voting for members of the House of Commons, may, as if by magic, tend in that direction. With such hopes or superstitions we need not trouble ourselves. Moreover, this class, the aristocracy, once thought most necessary to the State, is scant of numbers, and has now no power of its own, but depends on the support of the class next below it—the middle class. In fact, it is really composed either of the most successful men of that class, or of their immediate descendants.

As to the middle class, including the trading, manufacturing, and professional people of our society, they do, as a rule, seem to work quite hard enough, and so at first sight might be thought to help the community, and not burden it. But by far the greater part of them, though they work, do not produce, and even when they do produce, as in the case of those engaged (wastefully indeed) in the distribution of goods, or doctors, or (genuine) artists and literary men, they consume out of all proportion to their due share. The commercial and manufacturing part of them, the most powerful part, spend their lives and energies in fighting amongst themselves for their respective shares of the wealth which they *force* the genuine workers to provide for them; the others are almost wholly the hangers-on of these; they do not work for the public, but a privileged class: they are the parasites of property, sometimes, as in the case of lawyers, undisguisedly so; sometimes, as the doctors and others above mentioned, professing to be useful, but too often of no use save as supporters of the system of folly, fraud, and tyranny of which they form a part. And all these we must remember have, as a rule, one aim in view; not the production of utilities, but the gaining of a position either for themselves or their children in which they will not have to work at all. It is their ambition and the end of their whole lives to gain, if not for themselves yet at least for their children, the proud position of being obvious burdens on the community. For their work itself, in spite of the sham dignity with which they surround it, they care nothing: save a few enthusiasts, men of science, art or letters, who, if they are not the salt of the earth, are at least (and oh, the pity of it!) the salt of the miserable system of which they are the slaves, which hinders and thwarts them at every turn, and even sometimes corrupts them.

Here then is another class, this time very numerous and all-powerful, which produces very little and consumes enormously, and is therefore in the main supported, as paupers are, by the real producers. The class that remains to be considered produces all that is produced, and supports both itself and the other classes, though it is placed in a position of inferiority to them; real inferiority, mind you, involving a degradation both of mind and body. But it is a necessary consequence of this tyranny and folly that again many of these workers are not producers. A vast number of them once more are merely parasites of property, some of them openly so, as the soldiers by land and sea who are kept on foot for the perpetuating of national rivalries and enmities, and for the purposes of the national struggle for the share of the product of unpaid labour. But besides this obvious burden on the producers and the scarcely less obvious one of domestic servants, there is first the army of clerks, shop-assistants, and so forth, who are engaged in the service of the private war for wealth, which, as above said, is the real occupation of the well-to-do middle class. This is a larger body of workers than might be supposed, for it includes amongst others all those engaged in what I should call competitive salesmanship, or, to use a less dignified word, the puffery of wares, which has now got to such a pitch that there are many things which cost far more to sell than they do to make.

Next there is the mass of people employed in making all those articles of folly and luxury, the demand for which is the outcome of the existence of the rich nonproducing classes; things which people leading a manly and uncorrupted life would not ask for or dream of. These things, whoever may gainsay me, I will for ever refuse to call wealth: they are not wealth, but waste. Wealth is what Nature gives us and what a reasonable man can make out of the gifts of Nature for his reasonable use. The sunlight, the fresh air, the unspoiled face of the earth, food, raiment and housing necessary and decent; the storing up of knowledge of all kinds, and the power of disseminating it; means of free communication between man and man; works of art, the beauty which man creates when he is most a man, most aspiring and thoughtful—all things which serve the pleasure of people, free, manly and uncorrupted. This is wealth. Nor can I think of anything worth having which does not come under one or other of these heads. But think, I beseech you, of the product of England, the workshop of the world, and will you not be bewildered, as I am, at the thought of the mass of things which no sane man could desire, but which our useless toil makes—and sells?

Now, further, there is even a sadder industry yet, which is forced on many, very many, of our workers—the making of wares which are necessary to them and their brethren, *because they are an inferior class.* For if many men live without producing, nay, must live lives so empty and foolish that they *force* a great part of the workers to produce wares which no one needs, not even the rich, it follows that most men must be poor; and, living as they do on wages from those whom they support, cannot get for their use the *goods* which men naturally desire, but must put up with miserable makeshifts for them, with coarse food that does not nourish, with rotten raiment which does not shelter, with wretched houses which may well make a town-dweller in civilization look back with regret to the tent of the nomad tribe, or the cave of the pre-historic savage. Nay, the workers must even lend a hand to the great industrial invention of the age—adulteration, and by its help produce for their own use shams and mockeries of the luxury of the rich; for the wage-earners must always live as the wage-payers bid them, and their very habits of life are *forced* on them by their masters.

But it is waste of time to try to express in words due contempt of the productions of the much-praised cheapness of our epoch. It must be enough to say that this cheapness is necessary to the system of exploiting on which modern manufacture rests. In other words, our society includes a great mass of slaves, who must be fed, clothed, housed and amused as slaves, and that their daily necessity compels them to make the slave-wares whose use is the perpetuation of their slavery.

To sum up, then, concerning the manner of work in civilized States, these States are composed of three classes—a class which does not even pretend to work, a class which pretends to work but which produces nothing, and a class which works, but is compelled by the other two classes to do work which is often unproductive.

Civilization therefore wastes its own resources, and will do so as long as the present system lasts. These are cold words with which to describe the tyranny under which we suffer; try then to consider what they mean.

There is a certain amount of natural material and of natural forces in the world, and a certain amount of labour-power inherent in the persons of the men that inhabit it. Men urged by their necessities and desires have laboured for many thousands of years at the task of subjugating the forces of Nature and of making the natural material useful to them. To our eyes, since we cannot see into the future, that struggle with Nature seems nearly over, and the victory of the human race over her nearly complete. And, looking backwards to the time when history first began, we note that the progress of that victory has been far swifter and more startling within the last two hundred years than ever before. Surely, therefore, we moderns ought to be in all ways vastly better off than any who have gone before us. Surely we ought, one and all of us, to be wealthy, to be well furnished with the good things which our victory over Nature has won for us.

But what is the real fact? Who will dare to deny that the great mass of civilized men are poor? So poor are they that it is mere childishness troubling ourselves to discuss whether perhaps they are in some ways a little better off than their forefathers. They are poor; nor can their poverty be measured by the poverty of a resourceless savage, for he knows of nothing else than his poverty; that he should be cold, hungry, houseless, dirty, ignorant, all that is to him as natural as that he should have a skin. But for us, for the most of us, civilization has bred desires which she forbids us to satisfy, and so is not merely a niggard but a torturer also.

Thus then have the fruits of our victory over Nature been stolen from us, thus has compulsion by Nature to labour in hope of rest, gain, and pleasure been turned into compulsion by man to labour in hope—of living to labour!

What shall we do then, can we mend it?

Well, remember once more that it is not our remote ancestors who achieved the victory over Nature, but our fathers, nay, our very selves. For us to sit hopeless and helpless then would be a strange folly indeed: be sure that we can amend it. What, then, is the first thing to be done?

We have seen that modern society is divided into two classes, one of which is *privileged* to be kept by the labour of the other—that is, it forces the other to work for it and takes from this inferior class everything that it *can* take from it, and uses the wealth so taken to keep its own members in a superior position, to make them beings of a higher order than the others: longer lived, more beautiful, more honoured, more refined than those of the other class. I do not say that it troubles itself about its members being *positively* long lived, beautiful or refined, but merely insists that they shall be so *relatively* to the inferior class. As also it cannot use the labour-power of the inferior class fairly in producing real wealth, it wastes it wholesale in the production of rubbish.

It is this robbery and waste on the part

of the minority which keeps the majority poor; if it could be shown that it is necessary for the preservation of society that this should be submitted to, little more could be said on the matter, save that the despair of the oppressed majority would probably at some time or other destroy Society. But it has been shown, on the contrary, even by such incomplete experiments, for instance, as Co-operation (so called), that the existence of a privileged class is by no means necessary for the production of wealth, but rather for the "government" of the producers of wealth, or, in other words, for the upholding of privilege.

The first step to be taken then is to abolish a class of men privileged to shirk their duties as men, thus forcing others to do the work which they refuse to do. All must work according to their ability, and so produce what they consume—that is, each man should work as well as he can for his own livelihood, and his livelihood should be assured to him; that is to say, all the advantages which society would provide for each and all of its members.

Thus, at last, would true Society be founded. It would rest on equality of condition. No man would be tormented for the benefit of another—nay, no one man would be tormented for the benefit of Society. Nor, indeed, can that order be called Society which is not upheld for the benefit of every one of its members.

But since men live now, badly as they live, when so many people do not produce at all, and when so much work is wasted, it is clear that, under conditions where all produced and no work was wasted, not only would every one work with the certain hope of gaining a due share of wealth by his work, but also he could not miss his due share of rest. Here, then, are two out of the three kinds of hope mentioned above as an essential part of worthy work assured to the worker. When class robbery is abolished, every man will reap the fruits of his labour, every man will have due rest—leisure, that is. Some Socialists might say we need not go any further than this; it is enough that the worker should get the full produce of his work, and that his rest should be abundant. But though the compulsion of man's tyranny is thus abolished, I yet demand compensation for the compulsion of Nature's necessity. As long as the work is repulsive it will still be a burden which must be taken up daily, and even so would mar our life, even though the hours of labour were short. What we want to do is to add to our wealth without diminishing our pleasure. Nature will not be finally conquered till our work becomes a part of the pleasure of our lives.

That first step of freeing people from the compulsion to labour needlessly will at least put us on the way towards this happy end; for we shall then have time and opportunities for bringing it about. As things are now, between the waste of labour-power in mere idleness and its waste in unproductive work, it is clear that the world of civilization is supported by a small part of its people; when all were working usefully for its support, the share of work which each would have to do would be but small, if our standard of life were about on the footing of what well-to-do and refined people now think desirable. We shall have labour-power to spare, and shall in short, be as wealthy as we please. It will be easy to live. If we were to wake up some morning now, under our present system, and find it "easy to live," that system would force us to set to work at once and make it hard to live; we should call that "developing our resources," or some such fine name. The multiplication of labour has become a necessity for us, and as long as that goes on no ingenuity in the invention of machines will be of any real use to us. Each new machine will cause a certain amount of misery among the workers whose special industry it may disturb; so many of them will be reduced from skilled to unskilled workmen, and then gradually matters will slip into their due grooves, and all will work apparently smoothly again; and if it were not that all this is preparing revolution, things would be, for the greater part of men, just as they were before the new wonderful invention.

But when revolution has made it "easy to live," when all are working harmoniously together and there is no one to rob the worker of his time, that is to say, his life; in those coming days there will be no compulsion on us to go on producing things we do not want, no compulsion on us to labour for nothing; we shall be able calmly and thoughtfully to consider what we shall do with our wealth of labour-power. Now, for my part, I think the first use we ought to make of that wealth, of that freedom, should be to make all our labour, even the commonest and most necessary, pleasant to everybody; for thinking over the matter carefully I can see that the one course which will certainly make life happy in the face of all accidents and troubles is to take a pleasurable interest in all the details of life. And lest perchance you think that an assertion too universally accepted to be worth making, let me remind you how entirely modern civilization forbids it; with what sordid, and even terrible, details it surrounds the life of the poor, what a mechanical and empty life she forces on the rich; and how rare a holiday it is for any of us to feel ourselves a part of Nature, and unhurriedly, thoughtfully, and happily to note the course of our lives amidst all the little links of events which connect them with the lives of others, and build up the great whole of humanity.

But such a holiday our whole lives might be, if we were resolute to make all our labour reasonable and pleasant. But we must be resolute indeed; for no half measures will help us here. It has been said already that our present joyless labour, and our lives scared and anxious as the life of a hunted beast, are forced upon us by the present system of producing for the profit of the privileged classes. It is necessary to state what this means. Under the present system of wages and capital the "manufacturer" (most absurdly so called, since a manufacturer means a person who makes with his hands) having a monopoly of the means whereby the power to labour inherent in every man's body can be used for production, is the master of those who are not so privileged; he, and he alone, is able to make use of this labour-power, which, on the other hand, is the only commodity by means of which his "capital," that is to say, the accumulated product of past labour, can be made productive to him. He therefore buys the labour-power of those who are bare of capital and can only live by selling it to him; his purpose in this trans-action is to increase his capital, to make it breed. It is clear that if he paid those with whom he makes his bargain the full value of their labour, that is to say, all that they produced, he would fail in his purpose. But since he is the monopolist of the means of productive labour, he can *compel* them to make a bargain better for him and worse for them than that; which bargain is that after they have earned their livelihood, estimated according to a standard high enough to ensure their peaceable submission to his mastership, the rest (and by far the larger part as a matter of fact) of what they produce shall belong to him, shall be his *property* to do as he likes with, to use or abuse at his pleasure; which property is, as we all know, jealously guarded by army and navy, police and prison; in short, by that huge mass of physical force which superstition, habit, fear of death by starvation—IGNORANCE, in one word, among the propertyless masses enables the propertied classes to use for the subjection of—their slaves.

Now, at other times, other evils resulting from this system may be put forward. What I want to point out now is the impossibility of our attaining to attractive labour under this system, and to repeat that it is this robbery (there is no other word for it) which wastes the available labour-power of the civilized world, forcing many men to do nothing, and many, very many more to do nothing useful; and forcing those who carry on really useful labour to most burdensome over-work. For understand once for all that the "manufacturer" aims primarily at producing, by means of the labour he has stolen from others, not goods but profits, that is, the "wealth" that is produced over and above the livelihood of his workmen, and the wear and tear of his machinery. Whether that "wealth" is real or sham matters nothing to him. If it sells and yields him a "profit" it is all right. I have said that, owing to there being rich people who have more money than they can spend reasonably, and who therefore buy sham wealth, there is waste on that side; and also that, owing to there being poor people who cannot afford to buy things which are worth making, there is waste on that side. So that the "demand" which the capitalist "supplies" is a false demand. The market in which he sells is "rigged" by the miserable inequalities produced by the robbery of the system of Capital and Wages.

It is this system, therefore, which we must be resolute in getting rid of, if we are to attain to happy and useful work for all. The first step towards making labour attractive is to get the means of making labour fruitful, the Capital, including the land, machinery, factories, etc., into the hands of the community, to be used for the good of all alike, so that we might all work at "supplying" the real "demands" of each and all—that is to say, work for livelihood, instead of working to supply the demand of the profit market—instead of working for profit—*i.e.*, the power of compelling other men to work against their will.

When this first step has been taken and men begin to understand that Nature wills all men either to work or starve, and when they are no longer such fools as to allow some the alternative of stealing, when this happy day is come, we shall then be relieved from the tax of waste, and consequently shall find that we have, as aforesaid, a mass of labour-power available, which will enable us to live as we please within reasonable limits. We shall no longer be hurried and driven by the fear of starvation, which at present presses no less on the greater part of men in civilized communities than it does on mere savages. The first and most obvious necessities will be so easily provided for in a community in which there is no waste of labour, that we shall have time to look round and consider what we really do want, that can be obtained without overtaxing our energies; for the often-expressed fear of mere idleness falling upon us when the force supplied by the present hierarchy of compulsion is withdrawn, is a fear which is but generated by the burden of excessive and repulsive labour, which we most of us have to bear at present.

I say once more that, in my belief, the first thing which we shall think so necessary as to be worth sacrificing some idle time for, will be the attractiveness of labour. No very heavy sacrifice will be required for attaining this object, but some *will* be required. For we may hope that men who have just waded through a period of strife and revolution will be the last to put up long with a life of mere utilitarianism, though Socialists are sometimes accused by ignorant persons of aiming at such a life. On the other hand, the ornamental part of modern life is already rotten to the core, and must be utterly swept away before the new order of things is realized. There is nothing of it—there is nothing which could come of it that could satisfy the aspirations of men set free from the tyranny of commercialism.

We must begin to build up the ornamental part of life—its pleasures, bodily and mental, scientific and artistic, social and individual—on the basis of work undertaken willingly and cheerfully, with the consciousness of benefiting ourselves and our neighbours by it. Such absolutely necessary work as we should have to do would in the first place take up but a small part of each day, and so far would not be burdensome; but it would be a task of daily recurrence, and therefore would spoil our day's pleasure unless it were made at least endurable while it lasted. In other words, all labour, even the commonest, must be made attractive.

How can this be done?—is the question the answer to which will take up the rest of this paper. In giving some hints on this question, I know that, while all Socialists will agree with many of the suggestions made, some of them may seem to some strange and venturesome. These must be considered as being given without any intention of dogmatizing, and as merely expressing my own personal opinion.

From all that has been said already it follows that labour, to be attractive, must be directed towards some obviously useful end, unless in cases where it is undertaken voluntarily by each individual as a pastime. This element of obvious usefulness is all the more to be counted on in sweetening tasks otherwise irksome, since social morality, the responsibility of man towards the life of man, will, in the new order of things, take the place of theological morality, or the responsibility of man to some abstract idea. Next, the day's work will be short. This need not be insisted on. It is clear that with work unwasted it *can* be short. It is clear also that much work which is now a torment, would be easily endurable if it were much shortened.

Variety of work is the next point, and a most important one. To compel a man to do day after day the same task, without any hope of escape or change, means nothing short of turning his life into a prison-torment. Nothing but the tyranny of profit-grinding makes this necessary. A man might easily learn and practise at least three crafts, varying sedentary occupation with outdoor—occupation calling for the exercise of strong bodily energy for work in which the mind had more to do. There are few men, for instance, who would not wish to spend part of their lives in the most necessary and pleasantest of all work—cultivating the earth. One thing which will make this variety of employment possible will be the form that education will take in a socially ordered community. At present all education is directed towards the end of fitting people to take their places in the hierarchy of commerce—these as masters, those as workmen. The education of the masters is more ornamental than that of the workmen, but it is commercial still; and even at the ancient universities learning is but little regarded, unless it can in the long run be made *to pay*. Due education is a totally different thing from this, and concerns itself in finding out what different people are fit for, and helping them along the road which they are inclined to take. In a duly ordered society, therefore, young people would be taught such handicrafts as they had a turn for as a part of their education, the discipline of their minds and bodies; and adults would also have opportunities of learning in the same schools, for the development of individual capacities would be of all things chiefly aimed at by education, instead, as now, the subordination of all capacities to the great end of "money-making" for oneself—or one's master. The amount of talent, and even genius, which the present system crushes, and which would be drawn out by such a system, would make our daily work easy and interesting.

Under this head of variety I will note one product of industry which has suffered so much from commercialism that it can scarcely be said to exist, and is, indeed, so foreign from our epoch that I fear there are some who will find it difficult to understand what I have to say on the subject, which I nevertheless must say, since it is really a most important one. I mean that side of art which is, or ought to be, done by the ordinary workman while he is about his ordinary work, and which has got to be called, very properly, Popular Art. This art, I repeat, no longer exists now, having been killed by commercialism. But from the beginning of man's contest with Nature till the rise of the present capitalistic system, it was alive, and generally flourished. While it lasted, everything that was made by man was adorned by man, just as everything made by Nature is adorned by her. The craftsman, as he fashioned the thing he had under his hand, ornamented it so naturally and so entirely without conscious effort, that it is often difficult to distinguish where the mere utilitarian part of his work ended and the ornamental began. Now the origin of this art was the necessity that the workman felt for variety in his work, and though the beauty produced by this desire was a great gift to the world, yet the obtaining variety and pleasure in the work by the workman was a matter of more importance still, for it stamped all labour with the impress of pleasure. All this has now quite disappeared from the work of civilization. If you wish to have ornament, you must pay specially for it, and the workman is compelled to produce ornament, as he is to produce other wares. He is compelled to pretend happiness in his work, so that the beauty produced by man's hand, which was once a solace to his labour, has now become an extra burden to him, and ornament is now but one of the follies of useless toil, and perhaps not the least irksome of its fetters.

Besides the short duration of labour, its conscious usefulness, and the variety which should go with it, there is another thing needed to make it attractive, and that is pleasant surroundings. The misery and squalor which we people of civilization bear with so much complacency as a necessary part of the manufacturing system, is just as necessary to the community at large as a proportionate amount of filth would be in the house of a private rich man. If such a man were to allow the cinders to be raked all over his drawing-room, and a privy to be established in each corner of his dining-room, if he habitually made a dust and refuse heap of his once beautiful garden, never washed his sheets or changed his tablecloth, and made his family sleep five in a bed, he would surely find himself in the claws of a commission *de lunatico*.[1] But such acts of miserly folly are just what our present society is doing daily under the compulsion of a supposed necessity, which is nothing short of madness. I beg you to bring your commission of lunacy against civilization without more delay.

For all our crowded towns and bewildering factories are simply the outcome of the profit system. Capitalistic manufacture, capitalistic land-owning, and capitalistic exchange force men into big cities in order to manipulate them in the interests of capital; the same tyranny contracts the due space of the factory so much that (for instance) the interior of a great weaving-shed is almost as ridiculous a spectacle as it is a horrible one. There is no other necessity for all this, save the necessity for grinding profits out of men's lives, and of producing cheap goods for the use (and subjection) of the slaves who grind. All labour is not yet driven into factories; often where it is there is no necessity for it, save again the profit tyranny. People engaged in all such labour need by no means be compelled to pig together in close city quarters. There is no reason why they should not follow their occupations in quiet country homes, in industrial colleges, in small towns, or, in short, where they find it happiest for them to live.

As to that part of labour which must be associated on a large scale, this very factory system, under a reasonable order of things (though to my mind there might still be drawbacks to it), would at least offer opportunities for a full and eager social life surrounded by many pleasures. The factories might be centres of intellectual activity also, and work in them might well

be varied very much: the tending of the necessary machinery might to each individual be but a short part of the day's work. The other work might vary from raising food from the surrounding country to the study and practice of art and science. It is a matter of course that people engaged in such work, and being the masters of their own lives, would not allow any hurry or want of foresight to force them into enduring dirt, disorder, or want of room. Science duly applied would enable them to get rid of refuse, to minimize, if not wholly to destroy, all the inconveniences which at present attend the use of elaborate machinery, such as smoke, stench and noise; nor would they endure that the buildings in which they worked or lived should be ugly blots on the fair face of the earth. Beginning by making their factories, buildings, and sheds decent and convenient like their homes, they would infallibly go on to make them not merely negatively good, inoffensive merely, but even beautiful, so that the glorious art of architecture, now for some time slain by commercial greed, would be born again and flourish.

So, you see, I claim that work in a duly ordered community should be made attractive by the consciousness of usefulness, by its being carried on with intelligent interest, by variety, and by its being exercised amidst pleasurable surroundings. But I have also claimed, as we all do, that the day's work should not be wearisomely long. It may be said, "How can you make this last claim square with the others? If the work is to be so refined, will not the goods made be very expensive?"

I do admit, as I have said before, that some sacrifice will be necessary in order to make labour attractive. I mean that, if we *could* be contented in a free community to work in the same hurried, dirty, disorderly, heartless way as we do now, we might shorten our day's labour very much more than I suppose we shall do, taking all kinds of labour into account. But if we did, it would mean that our new-won freedom of condition would leave us listless and wretched, if not anxious, as we are now, which I hold is simply impossible. We should be contented to make the sacrifices necessary for raising our condition to the

[1] *de lunatico: de lunatico inquirendo,* a legal phrase meaning (literally) 'for inquiring concerning the lunatic', and used of a writ directing an inquiry as to whether a person named in the writ is insane.

standard called out for as desirable by the whole community. Nor only so. We should, individually, be emulous to sacrifice quite freely still more of our time and our ease towards the raising of the standard of life. Persons, either by themselves or associated for such purposes, would freely, and for the love of the work and for its results— stimulated by the hope of the pleasure of creation—produce those ornaments of life for the service of all, which they are now bribed to produce (or pretend to produce) for the service of a few rich men. The experiment of a civilized community living wholly without art or literature has not yet been tried. The past degradation and corruption of civilization may force this denial of pleasure upon the society which will arise from its ashes. If that must be, we will accept the passing phase of utilitarianism as a foundation for the art which is to be. If the cripple and the starveling disappear from our streets, if the earth nourish us all alike, if the sun shine for all of us alike, if to one and all of us the glorious drama of the earth—day and night, summer and winter—can be presented as a thing to understand and love, we can afford to wait awhile till we are purified from the shame of the past corruption, and till art arises again amongst people freed from the terror of the slave and the shame of the robber.

Meantime, in any case, the refinement, thoughtfulness, and deliberation of labour must indeed be paid for, but not by compulsion to labour long hours. Our epoch has invented machines which would have appeared wild dreams to the men of past ages, and of those machines we have as yet *made no use*.

They are called "labour-saving" machines—a commonly used phrase which implies what we expect of them; but we do not get what we expect. What they really do is to reduce the skilled labourer to the ranks of the unskilled, to increase the number of the "reserve army of labour" —that is, to increase the precariousness of life among the workers and to intensify the labour of those who serve the machines (as slaves their masters). All this they do by the way, while they pile up the profits of the employers of labour, or force them to expend those profits in bitter commercial war with each other. In a true society these miracles of ingenuity would be for the first time used for minimizing the amount of time spent in unattractive labour, which by their means might be so reduced as to be but a very light burden on each individual. All the more as these machines would most certainly be very much improved when it was no longer a question as to whether their improvement would "pay" the individual, but rather whether it would benefit the community.

So much for the ordinary use of machinery, which would probably, after a time, be somewhat restricted when men found out that there was no need for anxiety as to mere subsistence, and learned to take an interest and pleasure in handiwork which, done deliberately and thoughtfully, could be made more attractive than machine work.

Again, as people freed from the daily terror of starvation find out what they really wanted, being no longer compelled by anything but their own needs, they would refuse to produce the mere inanities which are now called luxuries, or the poison and trash now called cheap wares. No one would make plush breeches when there were no flunkies to wear them, nor would anybody waste his time over making oleomargarine when no one was *compelled* to abstain from real butter. Adulteration laws are only needed in a society of thieves—and in such a society they are a dead letter.

Socialists are often asked how work of the rougher and more repulsive kind could be carried out in the new condition of things. To attempt to answer such questions fully or authoritatively would be attempting the impossibility of constructing a scheme of a new society out of the materials of the old, before we knew which of those materials would disappear and which endure through the evolution which is leading us to the great change. Yet it is not difficult to conceive of some arrangement whereby those who did the roughest work should work for the shortest spells. And again, what is said above of the variety of work applies specially here. Once more I say, that for a man to be the whole of his life hopelessly engaged in performing one repulsive and never-ending task, is an arrangement fit enough for the hell imagined by theologians, but scarcely fit for any other form of society. Lastly, if this rougher work were of any special kind, we may suppose that special volunteers would be called on to perform it, who would surely be forthcoming, unless men in a state of freedom should lose the sparks of manliness which they possessed as slaves.

And yet if there be any work which cannot be made other than repulsive, either by the shortness of its duration or the intermittency of its recurrence, or by the sense of special and peculiar usefulness (and therefore honour) in the mind of the man who performs it freely,—if there be any work which cannot be but a torment to the worker, what then? Well, then, let us see if the heavens will fall on us if we leave it undone, for it were better that they should. The produce of such work cannot be worth the price of it.

Now we have seen that the semi-theological dogma that all labour, under any circumstances, is a blessing to the labourer, is hypocritical and false; that, on the other hand, labour is good when due hope of rest and pleasure accompanies it. We have weighed the work of civilization in the balance and found it wanting, since hope is mostly lacking to it, and therefore we see that civilization has bred a dire curse for men. But we have seen also that the work of the world might be carried on in hope and with pleasure if it were not wasted by folly and tyranny, by the perpetual strife of opposing classes.

It is Peace, therefore, which we need in order that we may live and work in hope and with pleasure. Peace so much desired, if we may trust men's words, but which has been so continually and steadily rejected by them in deeds. But for us, let us set our hearts on it and win it at whatever cost.

What the cost may be, who can tell? Will it be possible to win peace peaceably? Alas, how can it be? We are so hemmed in by wrong and folly, that in one way or other we must always be fighting against them: our own lives may see no end to the struggle, perhaps no obvious hope of the end. It may be that the best we can hope to see is that struggle getting sharper and bitterer day by day, until it breaks out openly at last into the slaughter of men by actual warfare instead of by the slower and crueller methods of "peaceful" commerce. If we live to see that, we shall live to see much; for it will mean the rich classes grown conscious of their own wrong and robbery, and consciously defending them by open violence; and then the end will be drawing near.

But in any case, and whatever the nature of our strife for peace may be, if we only aim at it steadily and with singleness of heart, and ever keep it in view, a reflection from that peace of the future will illumine the turmoil and trouble of our lives, whether the trouble be seemingly petty, or obviously tragic; and we shall, in our hopes at least, live the lives of men: nor can the present times give us any reward greater than that.

[1885]

HOW I BECAME A SOCIALIST

I am asked by the Editor to give some sort of a history of the above conversion, and I feel that it may be of some use to do so, if my readers will look upon me as a type of a certain group of people, but not so easy to do clearly, briefly and truly. Let me, however, try. But first, I will say what I mean by being a Socialist, since I am told that the word no longer expresses definitely and with certainty what it did ten years ago. Well, what I mean by Socialism is a condition of society in which there should

be neither rich nor poor, neither master nor master's man, neither idle nor overworked, neither brain-sick brain workers, nor heart-sick hand workers, in a word, in which all men would be living in equality of condition, and would manage their affairs unwastefully, and with the full consciousness that harm to one would mean harm to all—the realisation at last of the meaning of the word COMMONWEALTH.

Now this view of Socialism which I hold to-day, and hope to die holding, is what I began with; I had no transitional period, unless you may call such a brief period of political radicalism during which I saw my ideal clear enough, but had no hope of any realisation of it. That came to an end some months before I joined the (then) Democratic Federation, and the meaning of my joining that body was that I had conceived a hope of the realisation of my ideal. If you ask me how much of a hope, or what I thought we Socialists then living and working would accomplish towards it, or when there would be effected any change in the face of society, I must say, I do not know. I can only say that I did not measure my hope, nor the joy that it brought me at the time. For the rest, when I took that step I was blankly ignorant of economics; I had never so much as opened Adam Smith, or heard of Ricardo, or of Karl Marx. Oddly enough, I had read some of Mill, to wit, those posthumous papers of his (published, was it in the *Westminster Review* or the *Fortnightly*?) in which he attacks Socialism in its Fourierist guise. In those papers he put the arguments, as far as they go, clearly and honestly, and the result, so far as I was concerned, was to convince me that Socialism was a necessary change, and that it was possible to bring it about in our own days. Those papers put the finishing touch to my conversion to Socialism. Well, having joined a Socialist body (for the Federation soon became definitely Socialist), I put some conscience into trying to learn the economical side of Socialism, and even tackled Marx, though I must confess that, whereas I thoroughly enjoyed the historical part of *Capital,* I suffered agonies of confusion of the brain over reading the pure economics of that great work. Anyhow, I read what I could, and will hope that some information stuck to me from my reading; but more, I must think, from continuous conversation with such friends as Bax and Hyndman and Scheu, and the brisk course of propaganda meetings which were going on at the time, and in which I took my share. Such finish to what of education in practical Socialism as I am capable of I received afterwards from some of my Anarchist friends, from whom I learned, quite against their intention, that Anarchism was impossible, much

as I learned from Mill against *his* intention that Socialism was necessary.

But in this telling how I fell into *practical* Socialism I have begun, as I perceive, in the middle, for in my position of a well-to-do man, not suffering from the disabilities which oppress a working man at every step, I feel that I might never have been drawn into the practical side of the question if an ideal had not forced me to seek towards it. For politics as politics, *i.e.,* not regarded as a necessary if cumbersome and disgustful means to an end, would never have attracted me, nor when I had become conscious of the wrongs of society as it now is, and the oppression of poor people, could I have ever believed in the possibility of a *partial* setting right of those wrongs. In other words, I could never have been such a fool as to believe in the happy and "respectable" poor.

If, therefore, my ideal forced me to look for practical Socialism, what was it that forced me to conceive of an ideal? Now, here comes in what I said of my being (in this paper) a type of a certain group of mind.

Before the uprising of *modern* Socialism almost all intelligent people either were, or professed themselves to be, quite contented with the civilisation of this century. Again, almost all of these really were thus contented, and saw nothing to do but to perfect the said civilisation by getting rid of a few ridiculous survivals of the barbarous ages. To be short, this was the *Whig* frame of mind, natural to the modern prosperous middle-class men, who, in fact, as far as mechanical progress is concerned, have nothing to ask for, if only Socialism would leave them alone to enjoy their plentiful style.

But besides these contented ones there were others who were not really contented, but had a vague sentiment of repulsion to the triumph of civilisation, but were coerced into silence by the measureless power of Whiggery. Lastly, there were a few who were in open rebellion against the said Whiggery—a few, say two, Carlyle and Ruskin. The latter, before my days of practical Socialism, was my master towards the ideal aforesaid, and, looking backward, I cannot help saying, by the way, how deadly dull the world would have been twenty years ago but for Ruskin! It was through him that I learned to give form to my discontent, which I must say was not by any means vague. Apart from the desire to produce beautiful things, the leading passion of my life has been and is hatred of modern civilisation. What shall I say of it now, when the words are put into my mouth, my hope of its destruction—what shall I say of its supplanting by Socialism?

What shall I say concerning its mastery of and its waste of mechanical power, its commonwealth so poor, its enemies of the commonwealth so rich, its stupendous organisation—for the misery of life! Its contempt of simple pleasures which everyone could enjoy but for its folly? Its eyeless vulgarity which has destroyed art, the one certain solace of labour? All this I felt then as now, but I did not know why it was so. The hope of the past times was gone, the struggles of mankind for many ages had produced nothing but this sordid, aimless, ugly confusion; the immediate future seemed to me likely to intensify all the present evils by sweeping away the last survivals of the days before the dull squalor of civilisation had settled down on the world. This was a bad look-out indeed, and, if I may mention myself as a personality and not as a mere type, especially so to a man of my disposition, careless of metaphysics and religion, as well as of scientific analysis, but with a deep love of the earth and the life on it, and a passion for the history of the past of mankind. Think of it! Was it all to end in a counting-house on the top of a cinder-heap, with Podsnap's drawing-room in the offing, and a Whig committee dealing out champagne to the rich and margarine to the poor in such convenient proportions as would make all men contented together, though the pleasure of the eyes was gone from the world, and the place of Homer was to be taken by Huxley? Yet, believe me, in my heart, when I really forced myself to look towards the future, that is what I saw in it, and, as far as I could tell, scarce anyone seemed to think it worth while to struggle against such a consummation of civilisation. So there I was in for a fine pessimistic end of life, if it had not somehow dawned on me that amidst all this filth of civilisation

the seeds of a great change, what we others call Social-Revolution, were beginning to germinate. The whole face of things was changed to me by that discovery, and all I had to do then in order to become a Socialist was to hook myself on to the practical movement, which, as before said, I have tried to do as well as I could.

To sum up, then the study of history and the love and practice of art forced me into a hatred of the civilisation which, if things were to stop as they are, would turn history into inconsequent nonsense, and make art a collection of the curiosities of the past, which would have no serious relation to the life of the present.

But the consciousness of revolution stirring amidst our hateful modern society prevented me, luckier than many others of artistic perceptions, from crystallising into a mere railer against "progress" on the one hand, and on the other from wasting time and energy in any of the numerous schemes by which the quasi-artistic of the middle classes hope to make art grow when it has no longer any root, and thus I became a practical Socialist.

A last word or two. Perhaps some of our friends will say, what have we to do with these matters of history and art? We want by means of Social-Democracy to win a decent livelihood, we want in some sort to live, and that at once. Surely any one who professes to think that the question of art and cultivation must go before that of the knife and fork (and there are some who do propose that) does not understand what art means, or how that its roots must have a soil of a thriving and unanxious life. Yet it must be remembered that civilisation has reduced the workman to such a skinny and pitiful existence, that he scarcely knows how to frame a desire for any life much better than that which he now endures perforce. It is the province of art to set the true ideal of a full and reasonable life before him, a life to which the perception and creation of beauty, the enjoyment of real pleasure that is, shall be felt to be as necessary to man as his daily bread, and that no man, and no set of men, can be deprived of this except by mere opposition, which should be resisted to the utmost.

[1894]

WALTER PATER

CHRONOLOGY AND INTRODUCTION

1839 Born, August 4, Shadwell, East London.
1853 Entered King's School, Canterbury.
1858 Entered Queen's College, Oxford.
1862 Took his degree, a second class in *Literae Humaniores.*
1864 Elected Classical Fellow at Brasenose; Wrote *Diaphanèite,* his first work in prose.
1865 Toured Italy.
1866 "Coleridge," in *Westminster Review* for January.
1873 *Studies in the History of the Renaissance.* Five of these essays had previously appeared in periodicals.
1878 "The Child in The House," in *Macmillan's Magazine* for August.
1882 In Rome, to get background for *Marius.*
1885 *Marius the Epicurean.*
1886–93 Lived in London, when not on duty at Oxford.

1887 *Imaginary Portraits,* previously published in separate articles in *Macmillan's Magazine.*
1889 *Appreciations, With An Essay on Style:* all material, except *Shakespeare's English Kings,* previously published.
1893 *Plato and Platonism:* Chapters I, VI, VIII previously published.
1894 Received LL.D. from University of Glasgow.
Death, July 30, at Oxford.
1895 *Greek Studies;*
Miscellaneous Studies.
1896 *Gaston de Latour.*
1897 *Essays from "The Guardian":* privately printed. Published 1901.
1903 *Uncollected Essays.*
1919 *Sketches and Reviews.*

When his *Studies in the History of the Renaissance* appeared in 1873, Pater suddenly became an Oxford celebrity. He had entered the University in 1858 with a scholarship won by ability and hard work. Swinburne, John Addington Symonds, John Richard Green were undergraduates there. In the year before, Matthew Arnold had commenced his professorship in poetry, and Rossetti, Morris, and Burne-Jones were decorating the walls of the Oxford Union Library with scenes from Malory's *Morte d'Arthur.* The enchantments of age-old Oxford (for modernism, though on the way, had not yet arrived) were even more thrilling to Pater than they had been to Arnold, since Pater had already lived for some years as a schoolboy at Canterbury, like his Emerald Uthwart, "under the shadow of medieval church-towers, amid the haunts, the traditions, and with something of the discipline of monasticism." As a student and later as Fellow and Tutor, he was the withdrawn, cloistered scholar, burying himself in philosophy and the classics, though not failing to read the moderns like Goethe and Browning or to hear Arnold's lectures, and to be fired with a love of Plato under the stimulus of Jowett, who once said to him: "You have a mind that will attain eminence."

Though there was no "aestheticism" at Oxford when Pater went up, by the time he published the *Renaissance* a considerable stir had developed and the cry "Art for art's sake" began to be heard. The Pre-Raphaelites in painting, and Rossetti, Morris, and Swinburne in poetry were lifting their banners in a warfare for beauty against lifeless conventions and an all-too-aggressive ugliness. Gautier and the French neo-romantics were being read and translated. In 1870 Ruskin took his Oxford chair as Slade Professor of Fine Arts; and in 1874 Oscar Wilde, to whom Pater's volume was already "the golden book of spirit and sense, the holy writ of beauty," matriculated at Magdalen College, and quickly became a notoriety, talking endlessly to admiring groups on the new aestheticism, and proclaiming Walter Pater as the high priest of the cult of those who wished to "burn with a hard gem-like flame" in their pursuit of exquisite passions in a fleeting world.

Outwardly Pater was unmoved. Inwardly he was embarrassed and troubled. He seems never to have suspected that his *Conclusion* might be misunderstood as the manifesto of a new-paganism such as would lead ardent disciples to think of art as a means of shocking the proprieties and securing for themselves extraordinary sensations, dangerous delights. "I wish they wouldn't call me a 'hedonist'," he said to Edmund Gosse; "it produces such a bad effect on the minds of people who don't know Greek." He suppressed the offending *Conclusion* in a second edition of the *Renaissance* and reprinted it (with some changes) only in 1888, or not until his *Marius the Epicurean* (1885) had clarified his views and corrected the misconceptions of his readers. Since then his reputation has had its ebbs and flows, but nothing in the field of letters seems more certain than that his place is now secure among the prose masters of his time. In an editorial on the centenary of his birth the *London Times Literary Supplement* for August 5, 1939 summed up the matter in these words: "Pater the aesthete and Pater the sentimental dabbler in religious sensations will soon have disappeared, chiefly through natural decay of all that was false in them, partly by absorption of the little core of truth into the just conception of the man as a whole."

Doubtless his work will always have a limited appeal. Though he was well aware of "our wild nineteenth century," as he called it, "the defect of which lies in the direction of intellectual anarchy and confusion," he seems as much aloof from his time as Sir Thomas Browne and Charles Lamb were from theirs. His almost exclusive interest in the arts of painting, architecture, and imaginative literature is probably too special to attract a wide audience. But Pater well understood where his genius lay and was content to use it within its own bounds. It would be difficult to imagine a more retired life than he lived at Oxford, mostly in his carefully ordered rooms at Brasenose College, where he led as scholarly an existence as did Gray at Cambridge a century earlier, devoted to the search and the expression of truth, as he discovered it in his favorite fields.

And this, for him, was imaginative truth,—truth, that is to say, expressed in sensuous forms, made beautiful by the artist, who "steeps his thought again and again into the fire of color." Nothing could be farther from a superficial or frivolous aestheticism. Like his Marius, Pater believed "in a severe intellectual meditation, that salt of poetry, without which all the more serious charm is lacking to the imaginative world." On the other hand he had little concern with colorless abstractions or metaphysical theories about being and non-being, though he knew the value of general ideas and had, like Florian Deleal, "a kind of mystical appetite for sacred things." Rather he looked to the transforming power of art to make the world at once "more deeply sensuous and more deeply ideal," by giving form to the formless and to every obstinate question "of sense and outward things." Plato, a life-long study, was precious to Pater (as were Dante and Rossetti) because, for the most part, he clothed his ideas in the garments of poetry and thus expressed "a sensuous love of the unseen." Wordsworth, in appreciation of whom he wrote one of his most distinguished studies, is recognized as a poet who could convey in splendid verse "the sense of a life in natural objects." Truth thus embodied in sensuous forms becomes beauty, or, more exactly, it is *order*, imposed upon things otherwise shapeless, chaotic. Form and content are inseparably united into an organic whole, like mind and body; and, from this union art, or what Pater chooses to call *form* in the strictest sense, is realized: for in art "in its consummate moments, the end is not distinct from the means, the form from the matter, the subject from the expression."

Such is the essence of Pater's aestheticism. While there are traces of over-sensuousness in its earlier expression, and while mere form and color seem at times to be more important than ideas (we are not to forget his great attention to the visual arts), this aestheticism is for the most part a severely intellectual matter, chiefly the concern of what Pater, along with Coleridge and Arnold, regarded as the highest faculty in man—imaginative reason: "art," he rightly insisted, "addresses not pure sense, still less the pure intellect, but the imaginative reason through the senses." Certainly a writer who is mainly occupied with great names and great themes can never fairly be accused of regarding art as the plaything of "aesthetes," something trivial, exotic, or decadent. Pater's aesthetics, moreover, is "ever in close connection with ethics," even though the immediate purpose of art is never moral. For the beauty, the order, the repose of art, especially great art, passes insensibly into the mind of him who enjoys it; as do the spirit of control and the "boundless sympathy," which it always embodies. The incompleteness of his aesthetics is to be found elsewhere,—in his view that the end of life is contemplation rather than action; since—at least in an imperfect world—vision alone, spectacle alone, can never satisfy the soul, which must somehow live creatively most of the time if it is to experience in rare seasons of detachment the raptures of contemplation.

Pater's theory of art is the basis of his criticism. The poem, the picture, or other beautiful object, possesses a certain "virtue" or "active principle," which is capable of producing "pleasurable impressions" upon the mind of the critic who is qualified by temperament, catholicity of taste, and scholarship to note and to disengage this unique "virtue" and so to tell his readers precisely what the work of art means to him. Since the "essential truth" is no other than essential form (order) or beauty, Pater calls the critic who achieves this result an aesthetic critic; and since it is inseparable from a personality which has diffused through the work of art "a unity of atmosphere," he frequently speaks of the total effect, or central impression, as the *vraie vérité*. To bring this to light, to mark its distinguishing features, Pater will describe and analyze his material with a deliberateness and subtlety unrivalled among critics. While he does not forget that the "artist is a child of his time," nor that one period is different from another period, neither does he forget that "besides these conditions of time and place, and independent of them, there is also an element of permanence, a standard of taste, which genius confesses." This is "the intellectual tradition," by which the scholarly critic's power will be disciplined and guided,—his "power of being deeply moved in the presence of beautiful objects."

To describe such criticism as irresponsible impressionism is to misunderstand it totally. All criticism is impressionist in the sense that it is the critic's answer to the self-imposed question: What, precisely what, is this work of art to me? Everything depends upon the *mind* of the critic,—whether it is enslaved to dead rules or is free, whether it is blown about by caprice and prejudice or is controlled by long familiarity "with the great masters in art or literature." A critical intelligence habitually concerned, as was Pater's, with such matters as Platonism, Stoicism, Epicureanism, Spinozism, Christianity, and with such figures as Plato, Marcus Aurelius, Dante, Montaigne, Leonardo, Michelangelo, Bruno, Pascal, Shakespeare, Coleridge, Wordsworth cannot be described as impressionist in the loose, popular sense of the term. Pater's impressions, generally speaking, have a high quality and authority because they reflect such an intelligence. And if his criticism does not seem to depend upon external standards as criteria of taste, such as philosophical criticism presupposes, or does not directly tell us why the *Odyssey*, for example, is greater than *The Life and Death of Jason*, or *Hamlet* than *Candida*, it is because he employs his standards implicitly, rather than explicitly by the more obvious methods of comparison and contrast. Intent upon the *vraie vérité* of the work of art in question (always a significant work of art), Pater is satisfied if he can in turn fix the mind of his reader upon *that*.

His manner of securing this result, his style, has been a rock of offence for many readers, whose views may be summarized in Prosser Hall Frye's description of his prose as "wholly factitious and opaque." It is an easy matter to point out the limitations, or, if the reader chooses, the faults in Pater's ways of expressing himself. His style is far from simple, nor is it even lucid in the usual sense of lucidity, that is, communicating its meaning easily and quickly. It lacks vigor and movement; rather, it is sometimes languorous and, to some readers, heavy and "dreamy." Though not without color and imagery, it would suffer if compared with the vividness of a style like Carlyle's or Conrad's. Its sentences are not infrequently involved and cumbersome, with qualification upon qualification, until the reader's progress is inevitably retarded. Altogether it is without the gusto and ease of such a style as Hazlitt's.

Nevertheless, Pater wrote distinguished prose, "faithful to the coloring of his own spirit, and in the strictest sense original." He fashioned it with the fastidious care that a Chinese seamstress of the older time must have exercised upon a heavy Mandarin coat. Though a self-conscious artist, he is never insincere, and never permits his manner to get the better of his theme, realizing all the time that the "chief stimulus of a good style is to possess a full, rich, complex matter to grapple with." Pater's material—namely, art, artists, and the influences that played upon them—is one of the most difficult of all subjects to handle, precisely because the shade, the distinction, the nuance are everything. Consequently he was unsatisfied until he had exhausted every resource of word and sentence to bring out, for example, the enigmatical mind of Leonardo, the "egotism" of Montaigne, or the pictorial quality in a painting of Giorgione's. As a result the reader, at least the scholarly reader, receives from Pater the satisfaction that comes from contact with an extraordinarily informed and refined intelligence, an intelligence that knew the significance of beauty and delighted in it; whose style is best described in his own words: "the happy phrase or sentence was really modelled upon a cleanly finished structure of scrupulous thought."

THE RENAISSANCE

PREFACE

Many attempts have been made by writers on art and poetry to define beauty in the abstract, to express it in the most general terms, to find a universal formula for it. The value of these attempts has most often been in the suggestive and penetrating things said by the way. Such discussions help us very little to enjoy what has been 10 well done in art or poetry, to discriminate between what is more and what is less excellent in them, or to use words like beauty, excellence, art, poetry, with a more precise meaning than they would otherwise have. Beauty, like all other qualities presented to human experience, is relative; and the definition of it becomes unmeaning and useless in proportion to its abstractness. To define beauty, not in the most ab- 20 stract, but in the most concrete terms possible, to find, not a universal formula for it, but the formula which expresses most adequately this or that special manifestation of it, is the aim of the true student of æsthetics.

"To see the object as in itself it really is," has been justly said to be the aim of all true criticism whatever; and in æsthetic criticism the first step towards seeing one's 30 object as it really is, is to know one's own impression as it really is, to discriminate it, to realise it distinctly. The objects with which æsthetic criticism deals—music, poetry, artistic and accomplished forms of human life—are indeed receptacles of so many powers or forces: they possess, like the products of nature, so many virtues or qualities. What is this song or picture, this engaging personality presented in life 40 or in a book, to me? What effect does it really produce on me? Does it give me pleasure? and if so, what sort or degree of pleasure? How is my nature modified by its presence, and under its influence? The answers to these questions are the original facts with which the æsthetic critic has to do; and, as in the study of light, of morals, of number, one must realise such primary data for oneself, or not at all. And he who 50 experiences these impressions strongly, and drives directly at the analysis and discrimination of them, has no need to trouble himself with the abstract question what beauty is in itself, or what its exact relation to truth or experience—metaphysical questions, as unprofitable as metaphysical questions elsewhere. He may pass them all by as being, answerable or not, of no interest to him.

The æsthetic critic, then, regards all the objects with which he has to do, all works of art, and the fairer forms of nature and human life, as powers or forces producing pleasurable sensations, each of a more or less peculiar or unique kind. This influence he feels, and wishes to explain, analysing it, and reducing it to its elements. To him, the picture, the landscape, the engaging personality in life or in a book, *La Gioconda,* the hills of Carrara, Pico of Mirandola, are valuable for their virtues, as we say, in speaking of a herb, a wine, a gem; for the property each has of affecting one with a special, a unique, impression of pleasure. Our education becomes complete in proportion as our susceptibility to these impressions increases in depth and variety. And the function of the æsthetic critic is to distinguish, analyse, and separate from its adjuncts, the virtue by which a picture, a landscape, a fair personality in life or in a book, produces this special impression of beauty or pleasure, to indicate what the source of that impression is, and under what conditions it is experienced. His end is reached when he has disengaged that virtue, and noted it, as a chemist notes some natural element, for himself and others; and the rule for those who would reach this end is stated with great exactness in the words of a recent critic of Sainte-Beuve: *De se borner à connaître de près les belles choses, et à s'en nourrir en exquis amateurs, en humanistes accomplis.*[1]

What is important, then, is not that the critic should possess a correct abstract definition of beauty for the intellect, but a

[1] *De se borner,* etc.: 'To limit themselves to know lovely things near at hand, and to nourish themselves upon them, like refined amateurs, like accomplished humanists.'

certain kind of temperament, the power of being deeply moved by the presence of beautiful objects. He will remember always that beauty exists in many forms. To him all periods, types, schools of taste, are in themselves equal. In all ages there have been some excellent workmen, and some excellent work done. The question he asks is always:—In whom did the stir, the genius, the sentiment of the period find itself? where was the receptacle of its refinement, its elevation, its taste? "The ages are all equal," says William Blake, "but genius is always above its age."

Often it will require great nicety to disengage this virtue from the commoner elements with which it may be found in combination. Few artists, not Goethe or Byron even, work quite cleanly, casting off all *débris,* and leaving us only what the heat of their imagination has wholly fused and transformed. Take, for instance, the writings of Wordsworth. The heat of his genius, entering into the substance of his work, has crystallised a part, but only a part, of it; and in that great mass of verse there is much which might well be forgotten. But scattered up and down it, sometimes fusing and transforming entire compositions, like the stanzas on *Resolution and Independence,* and the Ode on the *Recollections of Childhood,* sometimes, as if at random, depositing a fine crystal here or there, in a matter it does not wholly search through and transform, we trace the action of his unique, incommunicable faculty, that strange, mystical sense of a life in natural things, and of man's life as a part of nature, drawing strength and colour and character from local influences, from the hills and streams, and from natural sights and sounds. Well! that is the *virtue,* the active principle in Wordsworth's poetry; and then the function of the critic of Wordsworth is to follow up that active principle, to disengage it, to mark the degree in which it penetrates his verse.

The subjects of the following studies are taken from the history of the Renaissance, and touch what I think the chief points in that complex, many-sided movement. I have explained in the first of them what I understand by the word, giving it a much wider scope than was intended by those who originally used it to denote only that revival of classical antiquity in the fifteenth century which was but one of many results of a general excitement and enlightening of the human mind, of which the great aim and achievements of what, as Christian art, is often falsely opposed to the Renaissance, were another result. This outbreak of the human spirit may be traced far into the Middle Age itself, with its qualities already clearly pronounced, the care for physical beauty, the worship of the body, the breaking down of those limits which the religious system of the Middle Age imposed on the heart and the imagination. I have taken as an example of this movement, this earlier Renaissance within the Middle Age itself, and as an expression of its qualities, two little compositions in early French; not because they constitute the best possible expression of them, but because they help the unity of my series, inasmuch as the Renaissance ends also in France, in French poetry, in a phase of which the writings of Joachim du Bellay are in many ways the most perfect illustration; the Renaissance thus putting forth in France an aftermath, a wonderful later growth, the products of which have to the full that subtle and delicate sweetness which belongs to a refined and comely decadence; just as its earliest phases have the freshness which belongs to all periods of growth in art, the charm of *ascêsis,*[2] of the austere and serious girding of the loins in youth.

But it is in Italy, in the fifteenth century, that the interest of the Renaissance mainly lies,—in that solemn fifteenth century which can hardly be studied too much, not merely for its positive results in the things of the intellect and the imagination, its concrete works of art, its special and prominent personalities, with their profound æsthetic charm, but for its general spirit and character, for the ethical qualities of which it is a consummate type.

The various forms of intellectual activity which together make up the culture of an age, move for the most part from different

---

[2] *ascêsis:* 'severe training'; not exactly synonymous with asceticism as usually understood. In his essay *Style* Pater defines the word as "self-restraint, a skilful economy of means."

starting-points, and by unconnected roads. As products of the same generation they partake, indeed, of a common character, and unconsciously illustrate each other; but of the producers themselves, each group is solitary, gaining what advantage or disadvantage there may be in intellectual isolation. Art and poetry, philosophy and the religious life, and that other life of refined pleasure and action in the open places of the world, are each of them confined to its own circle of ideas, and those who prosecute either of them are generally little curious of the thoughts of others. There come, however, from time to time, eras of more favourable conditions, in which the thoughts of men draw nearer together than is their wont, and the many interests of the intellectual world combine in one complete type of general culture. The fifteenth century in Italy is one of these happier eras; and what is sometimes said of the age of Pericles is true of that of Lorenzo:—it is an age productive in personalities, many-sided, centralised, complete. Here, artists and philosophers and those whom the action of the world has elevated and made keen, do not live in isolation, but breathe a common air, and catch light and heat from each other's thoughts. There is a spirit of general elevation and enlightenment in which all alike communicate. It is the unity of this spirit which gives unity to all the various products of the Renaissance; and it is to this intimate alliance with mind, this participation in the best thoughts which that age produced, that the art of Italy in the fifteenth century owes much of its grave dignity and influence.

I have added an essay on Winckelmann, as not incongruous with the studies which precede it, because Winckelmann, coming in the eighteenth century, really belongs in spirit to an earlier age. By his enthusiasm for the things of the intellect and the imagination for their own sake, by his Hellenism, his life-long struggle to attain to the Greek spirit, he is in sympathy with the humanists of an earlier century. He is the last fruit of the Renaissance, and explains in a striking way its motive and tendencies.

[1873]

LA GIOCONDA

La Gioconda is, in the truest sense, Leonardo's masterpiece, the revealing instance of his mode of thought and work. In suggestiveness, only the Melancholia of Dürer is comparable to it; and no crude symbolism disturbs the effect of its subdued and graceful mystery. We all know the face and hands of the figure, set in its marble chair, in that cirque of fantastic rocks, as in some faint light under the sea. Perhaps of all ancient pictures time has chilled it least. As often happens with works in which invention seems to reach its limit, there is an element in it given to, not invented by, the master. In that inestimable folio of drawings, once in the possession of Vasari, were certain designs by Verrocchio, faces of such impressive beauty that Leonardo in his boyhood copied them many times. It is hard not to connect them with these designs of the elder, by-past master, as with its germinal principle, the unfathomable smile, always with a touch of something sinister in it, which plays over all Leonardo's work. Besides, the picture is a portrait. From childhood we see this image defining itself on the fabric of his dreams; and but for express historical testimony, we might fancy that this was but his ideal lady, embodied and beheld at last. What was the relationship of a living Florentine to this creature of his thought? By means of what strange affinities had the person and the dream grown up thus apart, and yet so closely together? Present from the first incorporeally in Leonardo's thought, dimly traced in the designs of Verrocchio, she is found present at last in Il Giocondo's house. That there is much of mere portraiture in the picture is attested by the legend that by artificial means, the presence of mimes and flute-players, that subtle expression was protracted on the face. Again, was it in four years and by renewed labor never really completed, or in four months and as by stroke of magic, that the image was projected?

The presence that thus rose so strangely beside the waters, is expressive of what in the ways of a thousand years men had come to desire. Hers is the head upon which all "the ends of the world are come," and the eyelids are a little weary. It is a beauty wrought out from within upon the flesh, the deposit, little cell by cell, of strange thoughts and fantastic reveries and exquisite passions. Set it for a moment beside one of those white Greek goddesses or beautiful women of antiquity, and how would they be troubled by this beauty, into which the soul with all its maladies has passed! All the thoughts and experience of the world 10 have etched and moulded there, in that which they have of power to refine and make expressive the outward form, the animalism of Greece, the lust of Rome, the reverie of the middle age with its spiritual ambition and imaginative loves, the return of the Pagan world, the sins of the Borgias. She is older than the rocks among which she sits; like the vampire, she has been dead many times, and learned the secrets of the 20 grave; and has been a diver in deep seas, and keeps their fallen day about her; and trafficked for strange webs with Eastern merchants: and, as Leda, was the mother of Helen of Troy, and, as Saint Anne, the mother of Mary; and all this has been to her but as the sound of lyres and flutes, and lives only in the delicacy with which it has moulded the changing lineaments, and tinged the eyelids and the hands. The 30 fancy of a perpetual life, sweeping together ten thousand experiences, is an old one; and modern thought has conceived the idea of humanity as wrought upon by, and summing up in itself, all modes of thought and life. Certainly Lady Lisa might stand as the embodiment of the old fancy, the symbol of the modern idea.

[1869]

CONCLUSION

Λέγει που Ἡράκλειτος ὅτι πάντα χωρεῖ καὶ οὐδὲν μένει [1]

To regard all things and principles of things as inconstant modes or fashions has more and more become the tendency of modern thought. Let us begin with that which is without—our physical life. Fix

upon it in one of its more exquisite intervals, the moment, for instance, of delicious recoil from the flood of water in summer heat. What is the whole physical life in that moment but a combination of natural elements to which science gives their names? But these elements, phosphorus and lime and delicate fibres, are present not in the human body alone: we detect them in places most remote from it. Our physical life is a perpetual motion of them—the passage of the blood, the wasting and repairing of the lenses of the eye, the modification of the tissues of the brain by every ray of light and sound—processes which science reduces to simpler and more elementary forces. Like the elements of which we are composed, the action of these forces extends beyond us; it rusts iron and ripens corn. Far out on every side of us those elements are broadcast, driven by many forces; and birth and gesture and death and the springing of violets from the grave are but a few out of ten thousand resultant combinations. That clear, perpetual outline of face and limb is but an image of ours, under which we group them—a design in a web, the actual threads of which pass out beyond it. This at least of flame-like our life has, that it is but the concurrence, renewed from moment to moment, of forces parting sooner or later on their ways.

Or if we begin with the inward world of thought and feeling, the whirlpool is still more rapid, the flame more eager and devouring. There it is no longer the gradual darkening of the eye and fading of colour from the wall,—the movement of the shore-side, where the water flows down indeed, though in apparent rest,—but the race of the mid-stream, a drift of momentary acts of sight and passion and thought. At first sight experience seems to bury us under a flood of external objects, pressing upon us with a sharp and importunate reality, calling us out of ourselves in a thousand forms of action. But when reflexion begins to act upon those objects they are dissipated under its influence; the cohesive force seems suspended like a trick of magic; each object is loosed into a group of impressions—colour, odour, texture—in the mind of the observer. And if we continue to dwell in thought on this world, not of objects in the

---

[1] Λέγει που Ἡράκλειτος, etc., from the *Cratylus* of Plato (402 A). In his *Plato and Platonism*, ch. I, Pater translates: "Heraclitus cries out, All things give way: nothing remaineth" (*Library Ed.*, 14).

solidity with which language invests them, but of impressions unstable, flickering, inconsistent, which burn and are extinguished with our consciousness of them, it contracts still further; the whole scope of observation is dwarfed to the narrow chamber of the individual mind. Experience, already reduced to a swarm of impressions, is ringed round for each one of us by that thick wall of personality through which no real voice has ever pierced on its way to us, or from us to that which we can only conjecture to be without. Every one of those impressions is the impression of the individual in his isolation, each mind keeping as a solitary prisoner its own dream of a world.

Analysis goes a step farther still, and assures us that those impressions of the individual mind to which, for each one of us, experience dwindles down, are in perpetual flight; that each of them is limited by time, and that as time is infinitely divisible, each of them is infinitely divisible also; all that is actual in it being a single moment, gone while we try to apprehend it, of which it may ever be more truly said that it has ceased to be than that it is. To such a tremulous wisp constantly reforming itself on the stream, to a single sharp impression, with a sense in it, a relic more or less fleeting, of such moments gone by, what is real in our life fines itself down. It is with this movement, with the passage and dissolution of impressions, images, sensations, that analysis leaves off—that continual vanishing away, that strange, perpetual weaving and unweaving of ourselves.

Philosophiren, says Novalis, *ist dephlegmatisiren, vivificiren.*[2] The service of philosophy, of speculative culture, towards the human spirit is to rouse, to startle it into sharp and eager observation. Every moment some form grows perfect in hand or face; some tone on the hills or the sea is choicer than the rest; some mood of passion or insight or intellectual excitement is irresistibly real and attractive for us,—for that moment only. Not the fruit of experience, but experience itself, is the end.

A counted number of pulses only is given to us of a variegated, dramatic, life. How may we see in them all that is to be seen in them by the finest senses? How shall we pass most swiftly from point to point, and be present always at the focus where the greatest number of vital forces unite in their purest energy?

To burn always with this hard, gemlike flame, to maintain this ecstasy, is success in life. In a sense it might even be said that our failure is to form habits: for, after all, habit is relative to a stereotyped world, and meantime it is only the roughness of the eye that makes any two persons, things, situations, seem alike. While all melts under our feet, we may well catch at any exquisite passion, or any contribution to knowledge that seems by a lifted horizon to set the spirit free for a moment, or any stirring of the senses, strange dyes, strange colours, and curious odours, or work of the artist's hands, or the face of one's friend. Not to discriminate every moment some passionate attitude in those about us, and in the brilliancy of their gifts some tragic dividing of forces on their ways, is, on this short day of frost and sun, to sleep before evening. With this sense of the splendour of our experience and of its awful brevity, gathering all we are into one desperate effort to see and touch, we shall hardly have time to make theories about the things we see and touch. What we have to do is to be for ever curiously testing new opinions and courting new impressions, never acquiescing in a facile orthodoxy of Comte, or of Hegel, or of our own. Philosophical theories or ideas, as points of view, instruments of criticism, may help us to gather up what might otherwise pass unregarded by us. "Philosophy is the microscope of thought." The theory or idea or system which requires of us the sacrifice of any part of this experience, in consideration of some interest into which we cannot enter, or some abstract theory we have not identified with ourselves, or what is only conventional, has no real claim upon us.

One of the most beautiful passages in the writings of Rousseau is that in the sixth book of the *Confessions,* where he describes the awakening in him of the literary sense. An undefinable taint of death had always

---

[2] *Philosophiren,* etc.: "To philosophize is to throw off inertia, to come to life." Novalis is the pseudonym of Friedrich von Hardenberg (1772–1801), German poet and romanticist.

clung about him, and now in early manhood he believed himself smitten by mortal disease. He asked himself how he might make as much as possible of the interval that remained; and he was not biassed by anything in his previous life when he decided that it must be by intellectual excitement, which he found just then in the clear, fresh writings of Voltaire. Well! we are all *condamnés,* as Victor Hugo says: we are all under sentence of death but with a sort of indefinite reprieve—*les hommes sont tous condamnés à mort avec des sursis indéfinis:* we have an interval, and then our place knows us no more. Some spend this interval in listlessness, some in high passions, the wisest, at least among "the children of this world," in art and song. For our one chance lies in expanding that interval, in getting as many pulsations as possible into the given time. Great passions may give us this quickened sense of life, ecstasy and sorrow of love, the various forms of enthusiastic activity, disinterested or otherwise, which come naturally to many of us. Only be sure it is passion—that it does yield you this fruit of a quickened, multiplied consciousness. Of this wisdom, the poetic passion, the desire of beauty, the love of art for art's sake, has most; for art comes to you professing frankly to give nothing but the highest quality to your moments as they pass, and simply for those moments' sake.

[1868]

APPRECIATIONS

WORDSWORTH

Some English critics at the beginning of the present century had a great deal to say concerning a distinction, of much importance, as they thought, in the true estimate of poetry, between the *Fancy,* and another more powerful faculty—the *Imagination.* This metaphysical distinction, borrowed originally from the writings of German philosophers, and perhaps not always clearly apprehended by those who talked of it, involved a far deeper and more vital distinction, with which indeed all true criticism more or less directly has to do, the distinction, namely, between higher and lower degrees of intensity in the poet's perception of his subject, and in his concentration of himself upon his work. Of those who dwelt upon the metaphysical distinction between the Fancy and the Imagination, it was Wordsworth who made the most of it, assuming it as the basis for the final classification of his poetical writings; and it is in these writings that the deeper and more vital distinction, which, as I have said, underlies the metaphysical distinction, is most needed, and may best be illustrated.

For nowhere is there so perplexed a mixture as in Wordsworth's own poetry, of work touched with intense and individual power, with work of almost no character at all. He has much conventional sentiment, and some of that insincere poetic diction, against which his most serious critical efforts were directed: the reaction in his political ideas, consequent on the excesses of 1795, makes him, at times, a mere declaimer on moral and social topics; and he seems, sometimes, to force an unwilling pen, and write by rule. By making the most of these blemishes it is possible to obscure the true æsthetic value of his work, just as his life also, a life of much quiet delicacy and independence, might easily be placed in a false focus, and made to appear a somewhat tame theme in illustration of the more obvious parochial virtues. And those who wish to understand his influence, and experience his peculiar savour, must bear with patience the presence of an alien element in Wordsworth's work, which never coalesced with what is really delightful in it, nor underwent his special power. Who that values his writings most has not felt the intrusion there, from time to time, of something tedious and prosaic? Of all poets equally great, he would gain most by a skilfully made anthology. Such a selection would show, in truth, not so much what he was, or to himself or others seemed to be, as what, by the more energetic and fertile quality in his writings, he was ever tending to become. And the mixture in his work, as it actually stands, is so perplexed, that one fears to miss the least promising composition even, lest some precious morsel should be lying hidden within—the few perfect lines, the phrase, the single word perhaps, to which he often works up mechanically through a poem, almost the whole of which may be tame enough. He who thought that in all creative work the larger part was *given* passively, to the recipient mind, who waited so dutifully upon the gift, to whom so large a measure was sometimes given, had his times also of desertion and relapse; and he has permitted the impress of these too to remain in his work. And this duality there—the fitfulness with which the higher qualities manifest themselves in it, gives the effect in his poetry of a power not altogether his own, or under his control, which comes and goes when it will, lifting or lowering a matter, poor in itself; so that that old fancy which made the poet's art an enthusiasm, a form of divine possession, seems almost literally true of him.

This constant suggestion of an absolute duality between higher and lower moods, and the work done in them, stimulating one always to look below the surface, makes the reading of Wordsworth an excellent sort of training towards the things of art and poetry. It begets in those, who, coming across him in youth, can bear him at all, a habit of reading between the lines, a faith in the effect of concentration and collectedness of mind in the right appreciation of poetry, an expectation of things, in this order, coming to one by means of a right discipline of the temper as well as of the intellect. He meets us with the promise that he has much, and something very peculiar, to give us, if we will follow a certain difficult way, and seems to have the secret of a special and privileged state of mind. And those who have undergone his influence, and followed this difficult way, are like people who have passed through some initiation, a *disciplina arcani*,[1] by submitting to which they become able constantly to distinguish in art, speech, feeling,

[1] *disciplina arcani*: 'discipline of the secret,' a phrase used to describe the practice of reticence by the early Christians regarding their religion, "probably to avoid molestation from the pagans."

manners, that which is organic, animated, expressive, from that which is only conventional, derivative, inexpressive.

But although the necessity of selecting these precious morsels for oneself is an opportunity for the exercise of Wordsworth's peculiar influence, and induces a kind of just criticism and true estimate of it, yet the purely literary product would have been more excellent, had the writer himself purged away that alien element. How perfect would have been the little treasury, shut between the covers of how thin a book! Let us suppose the desired separation made, the electric thread untwined, the golden pieces, great and small, lying apart together. What are the peculiarities of this residue? What special sense does Wordsworth exercise, and what instincts does he satisfy? What are the subjects and the motives which in him excite the imaginative faculty? What are the qualities in things and persons which he values, the impression and sense of which he can convey to others, in an extraordinary way?

An intimate consciousness of the expression of natural things, which weighs, listens, penetrates, where the earlier mind passed roughly by, is a large element in the complexion of modern poetry. It has been remarked as a fact in mental history again and again. It reveals itself in many forms, but is strongest and most attractive in what is strongest and most attractive in modern literature. It is exemplified, almost equally, by writers as unlike each other as Senancour and Théophile Gautier: as a singular chapter in the history of the human mind, its growth might be traced from Rousseau to Chateaubriand, from Chateaubriand to Victor Hugo: it has doubtless some latent connexion with those pantheistic theories which locate an intelligent soul in material things, and have largely exercised men's minds in some modern systems of philosophy: it is traceable even in the graver writings of historians: it makes as much difference between ancient and modern landscape art, as there is between the rough masks of an early mosaic and a portrait by Reynolds or Gainsborough. Of this new sense, the writings of Wordsworth are the central and elementary expression: he is more simply and entirely occupied with it than any other poet, though there are fine expressions of precisely the same thing in so different a poet as Shelley. There was in his own character a certain contentment, a sort of inborn religious placidity, seldom found united with a sensibility so mobile as his, which was favourable to the quiet, habitual observation of inanimate, or imperfectly animate, existence. His life of eighty years is divided by no very profoundly felt incidents: its changes are almost wholly inward, and it falls into broad, untroubled, perhaps somewhat monotonous spaces. What it most resembles is the life of one of those early Italian or Flemish painters, who, just because their minds were full of heavenly visions, passed, some of them, the better part of sixty years in quiet, systematic industry. This placid life matured a quite unusual sensibility, really innate in him, to the sights and sounds of the natural world—the flower and its shadow on the stone, the cuckoo and its echo. The poem of *Resolution and Independence* is a storehouse of such records: for its fulness of imagery it may be compared to Keat's *Saint Agnes' Eve*. To read one of his longer pastoral poems for the first time, is like a day spent in a new country: the memory is crowded for a while with its precise and vivid incidents—

"The pliant harebell swinging in the breeze
On some grey rock";—

"The single sheep and the one blasted tree
And the bleak music from that old stone
   wall";—

"And in the meadows and the lower grounds
Was all the sweetness of a common dawn";—

"And that green corn all day is rustling in
   thine ears."

Clear and delicate at once, as he is in the outlining of visible imagery, he is more clear and delicate still, and finely scrupulous, in the noting of sounds; so that he conceives of noble sound as even moulding the human countenance to nobler types, and as something actually "profaned" by colour, by visible form, or image. He has a power likewise of realising, and conveying to the consciousness of the reader, abstract and elementary impressions—silence, darkness, absolute motionlessness: or, again, the whole complex sentiment of a particular place, the abstract expression of desolation in the long white road, of peacefulness in a particular folding of the hills. In the airy building of the brain, a special day or hour even, comes to have for him a sort of personal identity, a spirit or angel given to it, by which, for its exceptional insight, or the happy light upon it, it has a presence in one's history, and acts there, as a separate power or accomplishment; and he has celebrated in many of his poems the "efficacious spirit," which, as he says, resides in these "particular spots" of time.

It is to such a world, and to a world of congruous meditation thereon, that we see him retiring in his but lately published poem of *The Recluse*—taking leave, without much count of costs, of the world of business, of action and ambition, as also of all that for the majority of mankind counts as sensuous enjoyment.

And so it came about that this sense of a life in natural objects, which in most poetry is but a rhetorical artifice, is with Wordsworth the assertion of what for him is almost literal fact. To him every natural object seemed to possess more or less of a moral or spiritual life, to be capable of a companionship with man, full of expression, of inexplicable affinities and delicacies of intercourse. An emanation, a particular spirit, belonged, not to the moving leaves or water only, but to the distant peak of the hills arising suddenly, by some change of perspective, above the nearer horizon, to the passing space of light across the plain, to the lichened Druidic stone even, for a certain weird fellowship in it with the moods of men. It was like a "survival," in the peculiar intellectual temperament of a man of letters at the end of the eighteenth century, of that primitive condition, which some philosophers have traced in the general history of human culture, wherein all outward objects alike, including even the works of men's hands, were believed to be endowed with animation, and the world was "full of souls"—that mood in which the old Greek gods were first begotten, and which had many strange aftergrowths.

In the early ages, this belief, delightful as its effects on poetry often are, was but the result of a crude intelligence. But, in Wordsworth, such power of seeing life, such perception of a soul, in inanimate things, came of an exceptional suscepti- bility to the impressions of eye and ear, and was, in its essence, a kind of sensuous- ness. At least, it is only in a temperament exceptionally susceptible on the sensuous side, that this sense of the expressiveness of outward things comes to be so large a 10 part of life. That he awakened "a sort of thought in sense," is Shelley's just estimate of this element in Wordsworth's poetry.

And it was through nature, thus enno- bled by a semblance of passion and thought, that he approached the spectacle of human life. Human life, indeed, is for him, at first, only an additional, accidental grace on an expressive landscape. When he thought of man, it was of man as in the 20 presence and under the influence of these effective natural objects, and linked to them by many associations. The close connexion of man with natural objects, the habitual association of his thoughts and feelings with a particular spot of earth, has some- times seemed to degrade those who are subject to its influence, as if it did but reinforce that physical connexion of our nature with the actual lime and clay of the 30 soil, which is always drawing us nearer to our end. But for Wordsworth, these influ- ences tended to the dignity of human na- ture, because they tended to tranquillise it. By raising nature to the level of human thought he gives it power and expression: he subdues man to the level of nature, and gives him thereby a certain breadth and coolness and solemnity. The leech-gatherer on the moor, the woman "stepping west- 40 ward," are for him natural objects, almost in the same sense as the aged thorn, or the lichened rock on the heath. In this sense the leader of the "Lake School," in spite of an earnest preoccupation with man, his thoughts, his destiny, is the poet of nature. And of nature, after all, in its modesty. The English lake country has, of course, its grandeurs. But the peculiar function of Wordsworth's genius, as carrying in it a 50 power to open out the soul of apparently little or familiar things, would have found its true test had he become the poet of Surrey, say! and the prophet of its life.

The glories of Italy and Switzerland, though he did write a little about them, had too potent a material life of their own to serve greatly his poetic purpose.

Religious sentiment, consecrating the af- fections and natural regrets of the human heart, above all, that pitiful awe and care for the perishing human clay, of which relic-worship is but the corruption, has al- ways had much to do with localities, with the thoughts which attach themselves to actual scenes and places. Now what is true of it everywhere, is truest of it in those secluded valleys where one generation after another maintains the same abiding-place; and it was on this side, that Wordsworth apprehended religion most strongly. Con- sisting, as it did so much, in the recognition of local sanctities, in the habit of connect- ing the stones and trees of a particular spot of earth with the great events of life, till the low walls, the green mounds, the half- obliterated epitaphs seemed full of voices, and a sort of natural oracles, the very re- ligion of these people of the dales appeared but as another link between them and the earth, and was literally a religion of nature. It tranquillised them by bringing them under the placid rule of traditional and narrowly localised observances. "Grave livers," they seemed to him, under this as- pect, with stately speech, and something of that natural dignity of manners, which un- derlies the highest courtesy.

And, seeing man thus as a part of nature, elevated and solemnised in proportion as his daily life and occupations brought him into companionship with permanent nat- ural objects, his very religion forming new links for him with the narrow limits of the valley, the low vaults of his church, the rough stones of his home, made intense for him now with profound sentiment, Words- worth was able to appreciate passion in the lowly. He chooses to depict people from humble life, because, being nearer to na- ture than others, they are on the whole more impassioned, certainly more direct in their expression of passion, than other men: it is for this direct expression of passion, that he values their humble words. In much that he said in exaltation of rural life, he was but pleading indirectly for that sincerity, that perfect fidelity to one's own inward presentations, to the precise features of the picture within, without which any profound poetry is impossible. It was not for their tameness, but for this passionate sincerity, that he chose incidents and situations from common life, "related in a selection of language really used by men." He constantly endeavours to bring his language near to the real language of men: to the real language of men, however, not on the dead level of their ordinary intercourse, but in select moments of vivid sensation, when this language is winnowed and ennobled by excitement. There are poets who have chosen rural life as their subject, for the sake of its passionless repose, and times when Wordsworth himself extols the mere calm and dispassionate survey of things as the highest aim of poetical culture. But it was not for such passionless calm that he preferred the scenes of pastoral life; and the meditative poet, sheltering himself, as it might seem, from the agitations of the outward world, is in reality only clearing the scene for the great exhibitions of emotion, and what he values most is the almost elementary expression of elementary feelings.

And so he has much for those who value highly the concentrated presentment of passion, who appraise men and women by their susceptibility to it, and art and poetry as they afford the spectacle of it. Breaking from time to time into the pensive spectacle of their daily toil, their occupations near to nature, come those great elementary feelings, lifting and solemnising their language and giving it a natural music. The great, distinguishing passion came to Michael by the sheepfold, to Ruth by the wayside, adding these humble children of the furrow to the true aristocracy of passionate souls. In this respect, Wordsworth's work resembles most that of George Sand, in those of her novels which depict country life. With a penetrative pathos, which puts him in the same rank with the masters of the sentiment of pity in literature, with Meinhold and Victor Hugo, he collects all the traces of vivid excitement which were to be found in that pastoral world—the girl who rung her father's knell; the unborn infant feeling about its mother's heart; the instinctive touches of children; the sorrows of the wild creatures, even—their homesickness, their strange yearnings; the tales of passionate regret that hang by a ruined farm-building, a heap of stones, a deserted sheepfold; that gay, false, adventurous, outer world, which breaks in from time to time to bewilder and deflower these quiet homes; not "passionate sorrow" only, for the overthrow of the soul's beauty, but the loss of, or carelessness for personal beauty even, in those whom men have wronged—their pathetic wanness; the sailor "who, in his heart, was half a shepherd on the stormy seas"; the wild woman teaching her child to pray for her betrayer; incidents like the making of the shepherd's staff, or that of the young boy laying the first stone of the sheepfold;—all the pathetic episodes of their humble existence, their longing, their wonder at fortune, their poor pathetic pleasures, like the pleasures of children, won so hardly in the struggle for bare existence; their yearning towards each other, in their darkened houses, or at their early toil. A sort of biblical depth and solemnity hangs over this strange, new, passionate, pastoral world, of which he first raised the image, and the reflection of which some of our best modern fiction has caught from him.

He pondered much over the philosophy of his poetry, and reading deeply in the history of his own mind, seems at times to have passed the borders of a world of strange speculations, inconsistent enough, had he cared to note such inconsistencies, with those traditional beliefs, which were otherwise the object of his devout acceptance. Thinking of the high value he set upon customariness, upon all that is habitual, local, rooted in the ground, in matters of religious sentiment, you might sometimes regard him as one tethered down to a world, refined and peaceful indeed, but with no broad outlook, a world protected, but somewhat narrowed, by the influence of received ideas. But he is at times also something very different from this, and something much bolder. A chance expression is overheard and placed in a new connexion, the sudden memory of a thing long past occurs to him, a distant object is relieved for a while by a random gleam of light—accidents turning up for a moment what lies below the surface of our immediate experience—and he passes from the humble graves and lowly arches of "the little rock-like pile" of a Westmoreland church, on bold trains of speculative thought, and comes, from point to point, into strange contact with thoughts which have visited, from time to time, far more venturesome, perhaps errant, spirits.

He had pondered deeply, for instance, on those strange reminiscences and forebodings, which seem to make our lives stretch before and behind us, beyond where we can see or touch anything, or trace the lines of connexion. Following the soul, backwards and forwards, on these endless ways, his sense of man's dim, potential powers became a pledge to him, indeed, of a future life, but carried him back also to that mysterious notion of an earlier state of existence—the fancy of the Platonists—the old heresy of Origen. It was in this mood that he conceived those oft-reiterated regrets for a half-ideal childhood, when the relics of Paradise still clung about the soul —a childhood, as it seemed, full of the fruits of old age, lost for all, in a degree, in the passing away of the youth of the world, lost for each one, over again, in the passing away of actual youth. It is this ideal childhood which he celebrates in his famous *Ode on the Recollections of Childhood,* and some other poems which may be grouped around it, such as the lines on *Tintern Abbey,* and something like what he describes was actually truer of himself than he seems to have understood; for his own most delightful poems were really the instinctive production of earlier life, and most surely for him, "the first diviner influence of this world" passed away, more and more completely, in his contact with experience.

Sometimes as he dwelt upon those moments of profound, imaginative power, in which the outward object appears to take colour and expression, a new nature almost, from the prompting of the observant mind, the actual world would, as it were, dissolve and detach itself, flake by flake, and he himself seemed to be the creator, and when he would the destroyer, of the world in which he lived—that old isolating

thought of many a brain-sick mystic of ancient and modern times.

At other times, again, in those periods of intense susceptibility, in which he appeared to himself as but the passive recipient of external influences, he was attracted by the thought of a spirit of life in outward things, a single, all-pervading mind in them, of which man, and even the poet's imaginative energy, are but moments—that old dream of the *anima mundi* [2], the mother of all things and their grave, in which some had desired to lose themselves, and others had become indifferent to the distinctions of good and evil. It would come, sometimes, like the sign of the *macrocosm* to Faust in his cell: the network of man and nature was seen to be pervaded by a common, universal life: a new, bold thought lifted him above the furrow, above the green turf of the Westmoreland churchyard, to a world altogether different in its vagueness and vastness, and the narrow glen was full of the brooding power of one universal spirit.

And so he has something, also, for those who feel the fascination of bold speculative ideas, who are really capable of rising upon them to conditions of poetical thought. He uses them, indeed, always with a very fine apprehension of the limits within which alone philosophical imaginings have any place in true poetry; and using them only for poetical purposes, is not too careful even to make them consistent with each other. To him, theories which for other men bring a world of technical diction, brought perfect form and expression, as in those two lofty books of *The Prelude,* which describe the decay and the restoration of Imagination and Taste. Skirting the borders of this world of bewildering heights and depths, he got but the first exciting influence of it, that joyful enthusiasm which great imaginative theories prompt, when the mind first comes to have an understanding of them; and it is not under the influence of these thoughts that his poetry becomes tedious or loses its blitheness. He keeps them, too, always within certain ethical bounds,

[2] *anima mundi:* spirit, or vital essence, of the (physical) world.

so that no word of his could offend the simplest of those simple souls which are always the largest portion of mankind. But it is, nevertheless, the contact of these thoughts, the speculative boldness in them, which constitutes, at least for some minds, the secret attraction of much of his best poetry—the sudden passage from lowly thoughts and places to the majestic forms of philosophical imagination, the play of these forms over a world so different, enlarging so strangely the bounds of its humble churchyards, and breaking such a wild light on the graves of christened children.

And these moods always brought with them faultless expression. In regard to expression, as with feeling and thought, the duality of the higher and lower moods was absolute. It belonged to the higher, the imaginative mood, and was the pledge of its reality, to bring the appropriate language with it. In him, when the really poetical motive worked at all, it united, with absolute justice, the word and the idea; each, in the imaginative flame, becoming inseparably one with the other, by that fusion of matter and form, which is the characteristic of the highest poetical expression. His words are themselves thought and feeling; not eloquent, or musical words merely, but that sort of creative language which carries the reality of what it depicts, directly, to the consciousness.

The music of mere metre performs but a limited, yet a very peculiar and subtly ascertained function, in Wordsworth's poetry. With him, metre is but an additional grace, accessory to that deeper music of words and sounds, that moving power, which they exercise in the nobler prose no less than in formal poetry. It is a sedative to that excitement, an excitement sometimes almost painful, under which the language, alike of poetry and prose, attains a rhythmical power, independent of metrical combination, and dependent rather on some subtle adjustment of the elementary sounds of words themselves to the image or feeling they convey. Yet some of his pieces, pieces prompted by a sort of half-playful mysticism, like the *Daffodils* and *The Two April Mornings*, are distinguished by a certain quaint gaiety of metre, and rival by

their perfect execution, in this respect, similar pieces among our own Elizabethan, or contemporary French poetry. And those who take up these poems after an interval of months, or years perhaps, may be surprised at finding how well old favourites wear, how their strange, inventive turns of diction or thought still send through them the old feeling of surprise. Those who lived about Wordsworth were all great lovers of the older English literature, and oftentimes there came out in him a noticeable likeness to our earlier poets. He quotes unconsciously, but with new power of meaning, a clause from one of Shakespeare's sonnets; and, as with some other men's most famous work, the *Ode on the Recollections of Childhood* had its anticipator. He drew something too from the unconscious mysticism of the old English language itself, drawing out the inward significance of its racy idiom, and the not wholly unconscious poetry of the language used by the simplest people under strong excitement—language, therefore, at its origin.

The office of the poet is not that of the moralist, and the first aim of Wordsworth's poetry is to give the reader a peculiar kind of pleasure. But through his poetry, and through this pleasure in it, he does actually convey to the reader an extraordinary wisdom in the things of practice. One lesson, if men must have lessons, he conveys more clearly than all, the supreme importance of contemplation in the conduct of life.

Contemplation—impassioned contemplation—that, is with Wordsworth the end-in-itself, the perfect end. We see the majority of mankind going most often to definite ends, lower or higher ends, as their own instincts may determine; but the end may never be attained, and the means not be quite the right means, great ends and little ones alike being, for the most part, distant, and the ways to them, in this dim world, somewhat vague. Meantime, to higher or lower ends, they move too often with something of a sad countenance, with hurried and ignoble gait, becoming, unconsciously, something like thorns, in their anxiety to bear grapes; it being possible for people, in the pursuit of even great ends, to become themselves thin and impoverished in spirit and temper, thus diminishing the sum of perfection in the world, at its very sources. We understand this when it is a question of mean, or of intensely selfish ends—of Grandet, or Javert. We think it bad morality to say that the end justifies the means, and we know how false to all higher conceptions of the religious life is the type of one who is ready to do evil that good may come. We contrast with such dark, mistaken eagerness, a type like that of Saint Catherine of Siena, who made the means to her ends so attractive, that she has won for herself an undying place in the *House Beautiful,* not by her rectitude of soul only, but by its "fairness"—by those quite different qualities which commend themselves to the poet and the artist.

Yet, for most of us, the conception of means and ends covers the whole of life, and is the exclusive type or figure under which we represent our lives to ourselves. Such a figure, reducing all things to machinery, though it has on its side the authority of that old Greek moralist who has fixed for succeeding generations the outline of the theory of right living, is too like a mere picture or description of men's lives as we actually find them, to be the basis of the higher ethics. It covers the meanness of men's daily lives, and much of the dexterity and the vigour with which they pursue what may seem to them the good of themselves or of others; but not the intangible perfection of those whose ideal is rather in *being* than in *doing*—not those *manners* which are, in the deepest as in the simplest sense, *morals,* and without which one cannot so much as offer a cup of water to a poor man without offence— not the part of "antique Rachel," sitting in the company of Beatrice; and even the moralist might well endeavour rather to withdraw men from the too exclusive consideration of means and ends, in life.

Against this predominance of machinery in our existence, Wordsworth's poetry, like all great art and poetry, is a continual protest. Justify rather the end by the means, it seems to say: whatever may become of the fruit, make sure of the flowers and the leaves. It was justly said, therefore, by one who had meditated very profoundly on the true relation of means to ends in life, and on the distinction between what is desirable in itself and what is desirable only as machinery, that when the battle which he and his friends were waging had been won, the world would need more than ever those qualities which Wordsworth was keeping alive and nourishing.

That the end of life is not action but contemplation—*being* as distinct from *doing* —a certain disposition of the mind: is, in some shape or other, the principle of all the higher morality. In poetry, in art, if you enter into their true spirit at all, you touch this principle, in a measure: these, by their very sterility, are a type of beholding for the mere joy of beholding. To treat life in the spirit of art, is to make life a thing in which means and ends are identified: to encourage such treatment, the true moral significance of art and poetry. Wordsworth, and other poets who have been like him in ancient or more recent times, are the masters, the experts, in this art of impassioned contemplation. Their work is, not to teach lessons, or enforce rules, or even to stimulate us to noble ends: but to withdraw the thoughts for a little while from the mere machinery of life, to fix them, with appropriate emotions, on the spectacle of those great facts in man's existence which no machinery affects, "on the great and universal passions of men, the most general and interesting of their occupations, and the entire world of nature,"—on "the operations of the elements and the appearances of the visible universe, on storm and sunshine, on the revolutions of the seasons, on cold and heat, on loss of friends and kindred, on injuries and resentments, on gratitude and hope, on fear and sorrow." To witness this spectacle with appropriate emotions is the aim of all culture; and of these emotions poetry like Wordsworth's is a great nourisher and stimulant. He sees nature full of sentiment and excitement; he sees men and women as parts of nature, passionate, excited, in strange grouping and connexion with the grandeur and beauty of the natural world:—images, in his own words, "of man suffering, amid awful forms and powers."

Such is the figure of the more powerful and original poet, hidden away, in part, under those weaker elements in Wordsworth's poetry, which for some minds determine their entire character; a poet somewhat bolder and more passionate than might at first sight be supposed, but not too bold for true poetical taste; an unimpassioned writer, you might sometimes fancy, yet thinking the chief aim, in life and art alike, to be a certain deep emotion; seeking most often the great elementary passions in lowly places; having at least this condition of all impassioned work, that he aims always at an absolute sincerity of feeling and diction, so that he is the true forerunner of the deepest and most passionate poetry of our own day; yet going back also, with something of a protest against the conventional fervour of much of the poetry popular in his own time, to those older English poets, whose unconscious likeness often comes out in him.

[1874]

ROMANTICISM

αἰνεῖ δὲ παλαιὸν μὲν οἶνον, ἄνθεα δ' ὕμνων νεωτέρων [1]

The words classical and romantic, although, like many other critical expressions, sometimes abused by those who have understood them too vaguely or too absolutely, yet define two real tendencies in the history of art and literature. Used in an exaggerated sense, to express a greater opposition between those tendencies than really exists, they have at times tended to divide people of taste into opposite camps. But in that House Beautiful which the creative minds of all generations—the artists and those who have treated life in the spirit of art—are always building together, for the refreshment of the human spirit, these oppositions cease; and the Interpreter of the House Beautiful, the true aesthetic critic, uses these divisions only so far as they enable him to enter into the peculiarities of the objects with which he has to do. The term

classical, fixed, as it is, to a well-defined literature and a well-defined group in art, is clear indeed; but then it has often been used in a hard, and merely scholastic sense, by the praisers of what is old and accustomed, at the expense of what is new, by critics who would never have discovered for themselves the charm of any work, whether new or old, who value what is old, in art or literature, for its accessories, and chiefly for the conventional authority that has gathered about it—people who would never really have been made glad by any Venus fresh-risen from the sea, and who praise the Venus of old Greece and Rome only because they fancy her grown now into something staid and tame.

And as the term classical has been used in a too absolute, and therefore in a misleading sense, so the term romantic has been used much too vaguely, in various accidental senses. The sense in which Scott is called a romantic writer is chiefly this: that, in opposition to the literary tradition of the last century, he loved strange adventure, and sought it in the Middle Age. Much later, in a Yorkshire village, the spirit of romanticism bore a more really characteristic fruit in the work of a young girl, Emily Brontë, the romance of Wuthering Heights; the figures of Hareton Earnshaw, of Catherine Linton, and of Heathcliffe—tearing open Catherine's grave, removing one side of her coffin, that he may really lie beside her in death—figures so passionate, yet woven on a background of delicately beautiful moorland scenery, being typical examples of that spirit. In Germany, again, that spirit is shown less in Tieck, its professional representative, than in Meinhold, the author of Sidonia the Sorceress and the Amber-Witch. In Germany and France, within the last hundred years, the term has been used to describe a particular school of writers; and, consequently, when Heine criticizes the Romantic School in Germany—that movement which culminated in Goethe's Goetz von Berlichingen; or when Théophile Gautier criticizes the romantic movement in France, where, indeed, it bore its most characteristic fruits, and its play is hardly yet over—where, by a certain audacity, or bizarrerie of motive, united with faultless

---

[1] "While thou praiseth the wine that is old, thou shalt also praise the flowers of songs that are new." From Pindar, Olympian Odes, IX, 48-9 (trans. Sandys, Loeb Classics, 101).

literary execution, it still shows itself in imaginative literature—they use the word, with an exact sense of special artistic qualities, indeed; but use it, nevertheless, with a limited application to the manifestation of those qualities at a particular period. But the romantic spirit is, in reality, an ever-present, an enduring principle, in the artistic temperament; and the qualities of thought and style which that, and other similar uses of the word *romantic* really indicate, are indeed but symptoms of a very continuous and widely working influence.

Though the words *classical* and *romantic,* then, have acquired an almost technical meaning, in application to certain developments of German and French taste, yet this is but one variation of an old opposition, which may be traced from the very beginning of the formation of European art and literature. From the first formation of anything like a standard of taste in these things, the restless curiosity of their more eager lovers necessarily made itself felt, in the craving for new motives, new subjects of interest, new modifications of style. Hence, the opposition between the classicists and the romanticists—between the adherents, in the culture of beauty, of the principles of liberty, and authority, respectively—of strength, and order or what the Greeks called κοσμιότης.[2]

Sainte-Beuve, in the third volume of the *Causeries du Lundi,* has discussed the question, *What is meant by a classic?* It was a question he was well fitted to answer, having himself lived through many phases of taste, and having been in earlier life an enthusiastic member of the romantic school; he was also a great master of that sort of "philosophy of literature" which delights in tracing traditions in it, and the way in which various phases of thought and sentiment maintain themselves, through successive modifications, from epoch to epoch. His aim, then, is to give the word *classic* a wider and, as he says, a more generous sense than it commonly bears, to make it expressly *grandiose et flottant;*[3] and, in doing this, he develops, in a masterly manner, those qualities of measure, purity

temperance, of which it is the especial function of classical art and literature, whatever meaning, narrower or wider, we attach to the term, to take care.

The charm, therefore, of what is classical, in art or literature, is that of the well-known tale, to which we can, nevertheless, listen over and over again, because it is told so well. To the absolute beauty of its artistic form is added the accidental, tranquil charm of familiarity. There are times, indeed, at which these charms fail to work on our spirits at all, because they fail to excite us. *"Romanticism,"* says Stendhal, "is the art of presenting to people the literary works which, in the actual state of their habits and beliefs, are capable of giving them the greatest possible pleasure; *classicism,* on the contrary, of presenting them with that which gave the greatest possible pleasure to their grandfathers." But then, beneath all changes of habits and beliefs, our love of that mere abstract proportion—of music—which what is classical in literature possesses, still maintains itself in the best of us, and what pleased our grandparents may at least tranquilize us. The "classic" comes to us out of the cool and quiet of other times, as the measure of what a long experience has shown will at least never displease us. And in the classical literature of Greece and Rome, as in the classics of the last century, the essentially classical element is that quality of order in beauty, which they possess, indeed, in a pre-eminent degree, and which impresses some minds to the exclusion of everything else in them.

It is the addition of strangeness to beauty, that constitutes the romantic character in art; and the desire of beauty being a fixed element in every artistic organization, it is the addition of curiosity to this desire of beauty, that constitutes the romantic temper. Curiosity and the desire of beauty have each their place in art, as in all true criticism. When one's curiosity is deficient, when one is not eager enough for new impressions, and new pleasures, one is liable to value mere academical proprieties too highly, to be satisfied with worn-out or conventional types, with the insipid ornament of Racine, or the prettiness of that later Greek sculpture which passed so long for

---

[2] κοσμιότης: decorum propriety.
[3] *grandiose et flottant:* imposing and current.

true Hellenic work; to miss those places where the handiwork of nature, or of the artist, has been most cunning; to find the most stimulating products of art a mere irritation. And when one's curiosity is in excess, when it overbalances the desire of beauty, then one is liable to value in works of art what is inartistic in them; to be satisfied with what is exaggerated in art, with productions like some of those of the romantic school in Germany; not to distinguish, zealously enough, between what is admirably done, and what is done not quite so well, in the writings, for instance, of Jean Paul. And if I had to give instances of these defects, then I should say that Pope, in common with the age of literature to which he belonged, had too little curiosity, so that there is always a certain insipidity in the effect of his work, exquisite as it is; and, coming down to our own time, that Balzac had an excess of curiosity—curiosity not duly tempered with the desire of beauty.

But, however falsely those two tendencies may be opposed by critics, or exaggerated by artists themselves, they are tendencies really at work at all times in art, molding it, with the balance sometimes a little on one side, sometimes a little on the other, generating, respectively, as the balance inclines on this side or that, two principles, two traditions, in art, and in literature so far as it partakes of the spirit of art. If there is a great overbalance of curiosity, then, we have the grotesque in art; if the union of strangeness and beauty, under very difficult and complex conditions, be a successful one, if the union be entire, then the resultant beauty is very exquisite, very attractive. With a passionate care for beauty, the romantic spirit refuses to have it, unless the condition of strangeness be first fulfilled. Its desire is for a beauty born of unlikely elements, by a profound alchemy, by a difficult initiation, by the charm which wrings it even out of terrible things; and a trace of distortion, of the grotesque, may perhaps linger, as an additional element of expression, about its ultimate grace. Its eager, excited spirit will have strength, the grotesque, first of all—the trees shrieking as you tear off the leaves; for Jean Valjean, the long years of

convict life; for Redgauntlet, the quicksands of Solway Moss; then, incorporate with this strangeness, and intensified by restraint, as much sweetness, as much beauty, as is compatible with that. *Énergique, frais, et dispos*—these, according to Sainte-Beuve, are the characteristics of a genuine classic—*les ouvrages anciens ne sont pas classiques parce qu'ils sont vieux, mais parce qu'ils sont énergiques, frais, et dispos.*[4] Energy, freshness, intelligent and masterly disposition—these are characteristics of Victor Hugo when his alchemy is complete, in certain figures, like Marius and Cosette; in certain scenes, like that in the opening of *Les Travailleurs de la Mer*, where Déruchette writes the name of *Gilliatt* in the snow, on Christmas morning; but always there is a certain note of strangeness discernible there, as well.

The essential elements, then, of the romantic spirit are curiosity and the love of beauty; and it is only as an illustration of these qualities that it seeks the Middle Age, because, in the overcharged atmosphere of the Middle Age, there are unworked sources of romantic effect, of a strange beauty, to be won, by strong imagination, out of things unlikely or remote.

Few, probably, now read Madame de Staël's *De l'Allemagne*, though it has its interest, the interest which never quite fades out of work really touched with the enthusiasm of the spiritual adventurer, the pioneer in culture. It was published in 1810, to introduce to French readers a new school of writers—the romantic school, from beyond the Rhine; and it was followed, twenty-three years later, by Heine's *Romantische Schule*, as at once a supplement and a correction. Both these books, then, connect romanticism with Germany, with the names especially of Goethe and Tieck; and, to many English readers, the idea of romanticism is still inseparably connected with Germany—that Germany which, in its quaint old towns, under the spire of Strasbourg or the towers of Heidelberg, was

4 *les ouvrages,* etc.: 'Ancient works are not classics because they are old, but because they are vigorous, fresh, and well ordered.' Sainte-Beuve really quotes Goethe in a conversation with Eckermann, April 2, 1829 (*Everyman's* trans., 305).

always listening in rapt inaction to the melodious, fascinating voices of the Middle Age, and which, now that it has got Strasbourg back again, has, I suppose, almost ceased to exist. But neither Germany, with its Goethe and Tieck, nor England, with its Byron and Scott, is nearly so representative of the romantic temper as France, with Murger, and Gautier, and Victor Hugo. It is in French literature that its most characteristic expression is to be found; and that, as most closely derivative, historically, from such peculiar conditions, as ever reinforce it to the utmost.

For, although temperament has much to do with the generation of the romantic spirit, and although this spirit, with its curiosity, its thirst for a curious beauty, may be always traceable in excellent art (traceable even in Sophocles) yet still, in a limited sense, it may be said to be a product of special epochs. Outbreaks of this spirit, that is, come naturally with particular periods—times, when, in men's approaches towards art and poetry, curiosity may be noticed to take the lead, when men come to art and poetry, with a deep thirst for intellectual excitement, after a long *ennui,* or in reaction against the strain of outward, practical things—in the later Middle Age, for instance; so that medieval poetry, centering in Dante, is often opposed to Greek and Roman poetry, as romantic poetry to the classical. What the romanticism of Dante is may be estimated if we compare the lines in which Virgil describes the hazelwood, from whose broken twigs flows the blood of Polydorus, not without the expression of a real shudder at the ghastly incident, with the whole canto of the *Inferno* into which Dante has expanded them, beautifying and softening it, meanwhile, by a sentiment of profound pity. And it is especially in that period of intellectual disturbance immediately preceding Dante, amid which the romance languages define themselves at last, that this temper is manifested. Here, in the literature of Provence, the very name of *romanticism* is stamped with its true signification; here we have indeed a romantic world, grotesque even, in the strength of its passions, almost insane in its curious expression of them, drawing all things into its sphere, making the birds, nay! lifeless things, its voices and messengers, yet so penetrated with the desire for beauty and sweetness that it begets a wholly new species of poetry, in which the *Renaissance* may be said to begin. The last century was pre-eminently a classical age, an age in which, for art and literature, the element of a comely order was in the ascendant; which, passing away, left a hard battle to be fought between the classical and the romantic schools. Yet, it is in the heart of this century, of Goldsmith and Stothard, of Watteau and the *Siècle de Louis XIV*—in one of its central, if not most characteristic figures, in Rousseau—that the modern or French romanticism really originates. But what in the eighteenth century is but an exceptional phenomenon, breaking through its fair reserve and discretion only at rare intervals, is the habitual guise of the nineteenth, breaking through it perpetually, with a feverishness, an incomprehensible straining and excitement, which all experience to some degree, but yearning also, in the genuine children of the romantic school, to be *énergique, frais, et dispos*—for those qualities of energy, freshness, comely order; and often, as in Murger, in Gautier, in Victor Hugo, for instance, with singular felicity attaining them.

It is in the terrible tragedy of Rousseau, in fact, that French romanticism, with much else, begins; reading his *Confessions* we seem actually to assist at the birth of this new, strong spirit in the French mind. The wildness which has shocked so many and the fascination which has influenced almost everyone in the squalid yet eloquent figure we see and hear so clearly in that book, wandering among the apple-blossoms and under the vines of Neuchâtel or Vevey, actually give it the quality of a very successful romantic invention. His strangeness or distortion, his profound subjectivity, his passionateness—the *cor laceratum* [5]—Rousseau makes all men in love with these. *Je ne suis fait comme aucun de ceux que j'ai sus. Mais si je ne vaux pas mieux, au moins je suis autre*—"I am not made like anyone else I have ever known; yet, if I am not better, at least I am different." These words, from the first page of the

[5] *cor laceratum:* torn heart.

Confessions, anticipate all the Werthers, Renés, Obermanns, of the last hundred years. For Rousseau did but anticipate a trouble in the spirit of the whole world; and thirty years afterwards, what in him was a peculiarity became part of the general consciousness. A storm was coming; Rousseau, with others, felt it in the air, and they helped to bring it down; they introduced a disturbing element into French literature, then so trim and formal, like our own literature of the age of Queen Anne.

In 1815 the storm had come and gone, but had left, in the spirit of "young France," the ennui of an immense disillusion. In the last chapter of Edgar Quinet's *Révolution Française,* a work itself full of irony, of disillusion, he distinguishes two books, Sénancour's *Obermann* and Chateaubriand's *Génie du Christianisme,* as characteristic of the first decade of the present century. In those two books we detect already the disease and the cure—in *Obermann* the irony, refined into° a plaintive philosophy of "indifference"—in Chateaubriand's *Génie du Christianisme,* the refuge from a tarnished actual present, a present of disillusion, into a world of strength and beauty in the Middle Age, as at an earlier period—in *René* and *Atala*—into the free play of them in savage life. It is to minds in this spiritual situation, weary of the present, but yearning for the spectacle of beauty and strength, that the works of French romanticism appeal. They set a positive value on the intense, the exceptional; and a certain distortion is sometimes noticeable in them, as in conceptions like Victor Hugo's *Quasimodo,* or *Gwynplaine,* something of a terrible grotesque, of the *macabre,* as the French themselves call it; though always combined with perfect literary execution, as in Gautier's *La Morte Amoureuse,* or the scene of the "maimed" burial-rites of the player, dead of the frost, in his *Capitaine Fracasse*—true "flowers of the yew." It becomes grim humor in Victor Hugo's combat of Gilliatt with the devilfish, or the incident, with all its ghastly comedy drawn out at length, of the great gun detached from its fastenings on shipboard in *Quatre-Vingt-Treize* (perhaps the most terrible of all accidents that can happen by sea) and in the entire episode, in that book,

of the *Convention.* Not less surely does it reach a genuine pathos; for the habit of noting and distinguishing one's own most intimate passages of sentiment makes one sympathetic, begetting, as it must, the power of entering, by all sorts of finer ways, into the intimate recesses of other minds; so that pity is another quality of romanticism, both Victor Hugo and Gautier being great lovers of animals, and charming writers about them, and Murger being unrivaled in the pathos of his *Scènes de la Vie de Jeunesse.* Penetrating so finely into all situations which appeal to pity, above all, into the special or exceptional phases of such feeling, the romantic humor is not afraid of the quaintness or singularity of its circumstances or expression, pity, indeed, being of the essence of humor; so that Victor Hugo does but turn his romanticism into practice, in his hunger and thirst after practical *Justice!*—a justice which shall no longer wrong children, or animals, for instance, by ignoring in a stupid, mere breadth of view, minute facts about them. Yet the romanticists are antinomian, too, sometimes, because the love of energy and beauty, of distinction in passion, tended naturally to become a little *bizarre,* plunging into the Middle Age, into the secrets of old Italian story. *Are we in the Inferno?* —we are tempted to ask, wondering at something malign in so much beauty. For over all a care for the refreshment of the human spirit by fine art manifests itself, a predominant sense of literary charm, so that, in their search for the secret of exquisite expression, the romantic school went back to the forgotten world of early French poetry, and literature itself became the most delicate of the arts—like "goldsmith's work," says Sainte-Beuve, of Bertrand's *Gaspard de la Nuit*—and that peculiarly French gift, the gift of exquisite speech, *argute loqui,*[6] attained in them a perfection which it had never seen before.

Stendhal, a writer whom I have already quoted, and of whom English readers might well know much more than they do, stands between the earlier and later growths of the romantic spirit. His novels are rich in romantic quality; and his other writings— partly criticism, partly personal reminis-

[6] *argute loqui:* to speak subtly.

cences—are a very curious and interesting illustration of the needs out of which romanticism arose. In his book on *Racine and Shakespeare,* Stendhal argues that all good art was romantic in its day; and this is perhaps true in Stendhal's sense. That little treatise, full of "dry light" and fertile ideas, was published in the year 1823, and its object is to defend an entire independence and liberty in the choice and treatment of subject, both in art and literature, against those who upheld the exclusive authority of precedent. In pleading the cause of romanticism, therefore, it is the novelty, both of form and of motive, in writings like the *Hernani* of Victor Hugo (which soon followed it, raising a storm of criticism) that he is chiefly concerned to justify. To be interesting and really stimulating, to keep us from yawning even, art and literature must follow the subtle movements of that nimbly-shifting *Time-Spirit,* or *Zeit-Geist,* understood by French not less than by German criticism, which is always modifying men's taste, as it modifies their manners and their pleasures. This, he contends, is what all great workmen had always understood. Dante, Shakespeare, Molière, had exercised an absolute independence in their choice of subject and treatment. To turn always with that ever-changing spirit, yet to retain the flavor of what was admirably done in past generations, in the classics, as we say—is the problem of true romanticism. "Dante," he observes, "was pre-eminently the romantic poet. He adored Virgil, yet he wrote the *Divine Comedy,* with the episode of Ugolino, which is as unlike the *Aeneid* as can possibly be. And those who thus obey the fundamental principle of romanticism, one by one become classical, and are joined to that ever-increasing common league, formed by men of all countries, to approach nearer and nearer to perfection."

Romanticism, then, although it has its epochs, is in its essential characteristics rather a spirit which shows itself at all times, in various degrees, in individual workmen and their work, and the amount of which criticism has to estimate in them taken one by one, than the peculiarity of a time or a school. Depending on the varying proportion of curiosity and the desire of beauty, natural tendencies of the artistic spirit at all times, it must always be partly a matter of individual temperament. The eighteenth century in England has been regarded as almost exclusively a classical period; yet William Blake, a type of so much which breaks through what are conventionally thought the influences of that century, is still a noticeable phenomenon in it, and the reaction in favor of naturalism in poetry begins in that century, early. There are, thus, the born romanticists and the born classicists. There are the born classicists who start with *form,* to whose minds the comeliness of the old, immemorial, well-recognized types in art and literature have revealed themselves impressively; who will entertain no matter which will not go easily and flexibly into them; whose work aspires only to be a variation upon, or study from, the older masters. "'Tis art's decline, my son!" they are always saying, to the progressive element in their own generation—to those who care for that which in fifty years' time everyone will be caring for. On the other hand, there are the born romanticists, who start with an original, untried *matter,* still in fusion; who conceive this vividly, and hold by it as the essence of their work; who, by the very vividness and heat of their conception, purge away, sooner or later, all that is not organically appropriate to it, till the whole effect adjusts itself in clear, orderly, proportionate form; which form, after a very little time, becomes classical in its turn.

The romantic or classical character of a picture, a poem, a literary work, depends, then, on the balance of certain qualities in it; and in this sense a very real distinction may be drawn between good classical and good romantic work. But all critical terms are relative; and there is at least a valuable suggestion in that theory of Stendhal's that all good art was romantic in its day. In the beauties of Homer and Phidias, quiet as they now seem, there must have been, for those who confronted them for the first time, excitement and surprise, the sudden, unforeseen satisfaction of the desire of beauty. Yet the *Odyssey,* with its marvelous adventure, is more romantic than the *Iliad,* which nevertheless contains, among many other romantic episodes, that of the immortal horses of Achilles, who weep at the death of Patroclus. Aeschylus is more romantic than Sophocles, whose *Philoctetes,* were it written now, might figure, for the strangeness of its motive and the perfectness of its execution, as typically romantic; while, of Euripides, it may be said that his method in writing his plays is to sacrifice readily almost everything else, so that he may attain the fullness of a single romantic effect. These two tendencies, indeed, might be applied as a measure or standard, all through Greek and Roman art and poetry, with very illuminating results; and for an analyst of the romantic principle in art, no exercise would be more profitable than to walk through the collection of classical antiquities at the Louvre, or the British Museum, or to examine some representative collection of Greek coins, and note how the element of curiosity, of the love of strangeness, insinuates itself into the classical design, and record the effects of the romantic spirit there, the traces of struggle, of the grotesque even, though overbalanced here by sweetness— as in the sculpture of Chartres and Rheims, the real sweetness of mind in the sculptor is often overbalanced by the grotesque, by the rudeness of his strength.

Classicism, then, means for Stendhal, for that younger enthusiastic band of French writers whose unconscious method he formulated into principles, the reign of what is pedantic, conventional, and narrowly academical in art; for him, all good art is romantic. To Sainte-Beuve, who understands the term in a more liberal sense, it is the characteristic of certain epochs, of certain spirits in every epoch, not given to the exercise of original imagination, but rather to the working out of refinements of manner on some authorized matter; and who bring to their perfection, in this way, the elements of sanity, of order and beauty in manner. In general criticism, again, it means the spirit of Greece and Rome, of some phases in literature and art that may seem of equal authority with Greece and Rome, the age of Louis the Fourteenth, the age of Johnson—though this is at best

an uncritical use of the term, because in Greek and Roman work there are typical examples of the romantic spirit. But explain the terms as we may, in application to particular epochs, there are these two elements always recognizable; united in perfect art—in Sophocles, in Dante, in the highest work of Goethe, though not always absolutely balanced there; and these two elements may be not inappropriately termed the classical and romantic tendencies.

Material for the artist, motives of inspiration, are not yet exhausted; our curious, complex, aspiring age still abounds in subjects for aesthetic manipulation by the literary as well as by other forms of art. For the literary art, at all events, the problem just now is, to induce order upon the contorted, proportionless accumulation of our knowledge and experience, our science and history, our hopes and disillusion, and, in effecting this, to do consciously what has been done hitherto for the most part too unconsciously, to write our English language as the Latins wrote theirs, as the French write, as scholars should write. Appealing, as he may, to precedent in this matter, the scholar will still remember that if "the style is the man" it is also the age; that the nineteenth century too will be found to have had its style, justified by necessity—a style very different, alike from the baldness of an impossible "Queen Anne" revival, and an incorrect, incondite exuberance, after the mode of Elizabeth; that we can only return to either at the price of an impoverishment of form or matter, or both, although, an intellectually rich age such as ours being necessarily an eclectic one, we may well cultivate some of the excellences of literary type so different as those; that in literature as in other matters it is well to unite as many diverse elements as may be; that the individual writer or artist, certainly, is to be estimated by the number of graces he combines, and his power of interpenetrating them in a given work. To discriminate schools, of art, of literature, is, of course, part of the obvious business of literary criticism; but, in the work of literary production, it is easy to be overmuch occupied concerning them. For, in truth, the legitimate contention is, not of one age or school of literary art against another, but of all successive schools alike, against the stupidity which is dead to the substance, and the vulgarity which is dead to form.

[1876]

MISCELLANEOUS STUDIES

THE CHILD IN THE HOUSE

As Florian Deleal walked, one hot afternoon, he overtook by the wayside a poor aged man, and, as he seemed weary with the road, helped him on with the burden which he carried, a certain distance. And as the man told his story, it chanced that he named the place, a little place in the neighborhood of a great city, where Florian had passed his earliest years, but which he had never since seen, and, the story told, went forward on his journey comforted. And that night, like a regard for his pity, a dream of that place came to Florian, a dream which did for him the office of the finer sort of memory, bringing its object to mind with a great clearness, yet, as sometimes happens in dreams, raised a little above itself, and above ordinary retrospect. The true aspect of the place, especially of the house there in which he had lived as a child, the fashion of its doors, its hearths, its windows, the very scent upon the air of it, was with him in sleep for a season; only, with tints more musically blent on wall and floor, and some finer light and shadow running in and out along its curves and angles, and with all its little carvings daintier. He awoke with a sigh at the thought of almost thirty years which lay between him and that place, yet with a flutter of pleasure still within him at the fair light, as if it were a smile, upon it. And it happened that this accident of his dream was just the thing needed for the beginning of a certain design he then had in view, the noting, namely, of some things in the story of his spirit—in that process of brain-building by which we are, each one of us, what we are. With the image of the place so clear and favourable upon him, he fell to thinking of himself therein, and how his thoughts had grown up to him. In that half-spiritualised house he could watch the better, over again, the gradual expansion of the soul which had come to be there—of which indeed, through the law which makes the material objects about them so large an element in children's lives, it had actually become a part; inward and outward being woven through and through each other into one inextricable texture—half, tint and trace and accident of homely colour and form, from the wood and the bricks; half, mere soul-stuff, floated thither from who knows how far. In the house and garden of his dream he saw a child moving, and could divide the main streams at least of the winds that had played on him, and study so the first stage in that mental journey.

The *old house,* as when Florian talked of it afterwards he always called it (as all children do, who can recollect a change of home, soon enough but not too soon to mark a period in their lives), really was an old house; and an element of French descent in its inmates—descent from Watteau, the old court-painter, one of whose gallant pieces still hung in one of the rooms —might explain, together with some other things, a noticeable trimness and comely whiteness about everything there—the curtains, the couches, the paint on the walls with which the light and shadow played so delicately; might explain also the tolerance of the great poplar in the garden, a tree most often despised by English people, but which French people love, having observed a certain fresh way its leaves have of dealing with the wind, making it sound, in never so slight a stirring of the air, like running water.

The old-fashioned, low wainscoting went round the rooms, and up the staircase with carved balusters and shadowy angles, landing half-way up at a broad window, with a swallow's nest below the sill, and the blossom of an old pear-tree showing across it in late April, against the blue, below which the perfumed juice of the find of fallen fruit in autumn was so fresh. At the next turning came the closet which held on its deep shelves the best china. Little angel faces and reedy flutings stood out round the fireplace of the children's room. And on the top of the house, above the large attic, where the white mice ran in the twilight—an infinite, unexplored wonderland of childish treasures, glass beads, empty scent-bottles still sweet, thrum of coloured silks, among its lumber—a flat space of roof, railed round, gave a view of the neighbouring steeples; for the house, as I said, stood near a great city, which sent up heavenwards, over the twisting weathervanes, not seldom, its beds of rolling cloud and smoke, touched with storm or sunshine. But the child of whom I am writing did not hate the fog because of the crimson lights which fell from it sometimes upon the chimneys, and the whites which gleamed through its openings, on summer mornings, on turret or pavement. For it is false to suppose that a child's sense of beauty is dependent on any choiceness or special fineness, in the objects which present themselves to it, though this indeed comes to be the rule with most of us in later life; earlier, in some degree, we see inwardly; and the child finds for itself, and with unstinted delight, a difference for the sense, in those whites and reds through the smoke on very homely buildings, and in the gold of the dandelions at the road-side, just beyond the houses, where not a handful of earth is virgin and untouched, in the lack of better ministries to its desire of beauty.

This house then stood not far beyond the gloom and rumours of the town, among high garden-walls, bright all summer-time with Golden-rod, and brown-and-golden Wallflower—*Flos Parietis*,[1] as the children's Latin-reading father taught them to call it, while he was with them. Tracing back the threads of his complex spiritual habit, as he was used in after years to do, Florian found that he owed to the place many tones of sentiment afterwards customary with him, certain inward lights under which things most naturally presented themselves to him. The coming and going of travellers to the town along the way, the shadow of the streets, the sudden breath of the neighbouring gardens, the singular brightness of bright weather there, its singular darknesses

1 *Flos Parietis:* 'flower of the wall.'

which linked themselves in his mind to certain engraved illustrations in the old big Bible at home, the coolness of the dark, cavernous shops round the great church, with its giddy winding stair up to the pigeons and the bells—a citadel of peace in the heart of the trouble—all this acted on his childish fancy, so that ever afterwards the like aspects and incidents never failed to throw him into a well-recognised imaginative mood, seeming actually to have become a part of the texture of his mind. Also, Florian could trace home to this point a pervading preference in himself for a kind of comeliness and dignity, an *urbanity* literally, in modes of life, which he connected with the pale people of towns, and which made him susceptible to a kind of exquisite satisfaction in the trimness and well-considered grace of certain things and persons he afterwards met with, here and there, in his way through the world.

So the child of whom I am writing lived on there quietly; things without thus ministering to him, as he sat daily at the window with the birdcage hanging below it, and his mother taught him to read, wondering at the ease with which he learned, and at the quickness of his memory. The perfume of the little flowers of the lime-tree fell through the air upon them like rain; while time seemed to move ever more slowly to the murmur of the bees in it, till it almost stood still on June afternoons. How insignificant, at the moment, seem the influences of the sensible things which are tossed and fall and lie about us, so, or so, in the environment of early childhood. How indelibly, as we afterwards discover, they affect us; with what capricious attractions and associations they figure themselves on the white paper, the smooth wax, of our ingenuous souls, as "with lead in the rock for ever," giving form and feature, and as it were assigned house-room in our memory, to early experiences of feeling and thought, which abide with us ever afterwards, thus, and not otherwise. The realities and passions, the rumours of the greater world without, steal in upon us, each by its own special little passageway, through the wall of custom about us; and never afterwards quite detach themselves from this or that accident, or trick, in the mode of their first entrance to us. Our susceptibilities, the discovery of our powers, manifold experiences—our various experiences of the coming and going of bodily pain, for instance—belong to this or the other well-remembered place in the material habitation—that little white room with the window across which the heavy blossoms could beat so peevishly in the wind, with just that particular catch or throb, such a sense of teasing in it, on gusty mornings; and the early habitation thus gradually becomes a sort of material shrine or sanctuary of sentiment; a system of visible symbolism interweaves itself through all our thoughts and passions; and irresistibly, little shapes, voices, accidents—the angle at which the sun in the morning fell on the pillow—become parts of the great chain wherewith we are bound.

Thus far, for Florian, what all this had determined was a peculiarly strong sense of home—so forcible a motive with all of us—prompting to us our customary love of the earth, and the larger part of our fear of death, that revulsion we have from it, as from something strange, untried, unfriendly; though lifelong imprisonment, they tell you, and final banishment from home is a thing bitterer still; the looking forward to but a short space, a mere childish *goûter* [2] and dessert of it, before the end, being so great a resource of effort to pilgrims and wayfarers, and the soldier in distant quarters, and lending, in lack of that, some power of solace to the thought of sleep in the home churchyard, at least—dead cheek by dead cheek, and with the rain soaking in upon one from above. So powerful is this instinct, and yet accidents like those I have been speaking of so mechanically determine it; its essence being indeed the early familiar, as constituting our ideal, or typical conception, of rest and security. Out of so many possible conditions, just this for you and that for me, brings ever the unmistakable realisation of the delightful *chez soi;* [3] this for the Englishman, for me and you, with the closely-drawn white curtain and the shaded

lamp; that, quite other, for the wandering Arab, who folds his tent every morning, and makes his sleeping-place among haunted ruins, or in old tombs.

With Florian then the sense of home became singularly intense, his good fortune being that the special character of his home was in itself so essentially home-like. As after many wanderings I have come to fancy that some parts of Surrey and Kent are, for Englishmen, the true landscape, true home-counties, by right, partly, of a certain earthy warmth in the yellow of the sand below their gorse-bushes, and of a certain gray-blue mist after rain, in the hollows of the hills there, welcome to fatigued eyes, and never seen farther south; so I think that the sort of house I have described, with precisely those proportions of red-brick and green, and with a just perceptible monotony in the subdued order of it, for its distinguishing note, is for Englishmen at least typically home-like. And so for Florian that general human instinct was reinforced by this special home-likeness in the place his wandering soul had happened to light on, as, in the second degree, its body and earthly tabernacle; the sense of harmony between his soul and its physical environment became, for a time at least, like perfectly played music, and the life led there singularly tranquil and filled with a curious sense of self-possession. The love of security, of an habitually undisputed standing-ground or sleeping-place, came to count for much in the generation and correcting of his thoughts, and afterwards as a salutary principle of restraint in all his wanderings of spirit. The wistful yearning towards home, in absence from it, as the shadows of evening deepened, and he followed in thought what was doing there from hour to hour, interpreted to him much of a yearning and regret he experienced afterwards, towards he knew not what, out of strange ways of feeling and thought in which, from time to time his spirit found itself alone; and in the tears shed in such absences there seemed always to be some soul-subduing foretaste of what his last tears might be.

And the sense of security could hardly have been deeper, the quiet of the child's soul being one with the quiet of its home,

---

[2] *goûter:* afternoon lunch, especially for children.
[3] *chez soi:* at home.

a place "inclosed" and "sealed." But upon this assured place, upon the child's assured soul which resembled it, there came floating in from the larger world without, as at windows left ajar unknowingly, or over the high garden walls, two streams of impressions, the sentiments of beauty and pain—recognitions of the visible, tangible, audible loveliness of things, as a very real and somewhat tyrannous element in them—and of the sorrow of the world, of grown people and children and animals, as a thing not to be put by in them. From this point he could trace two predominant processes of mental change in him—the growth of an almost diseased sensibility to the spectacle of suffering, and, parallel with this, the rapid growth of a certain capacity of fascination by bright colour and choice form —the sweet curvings, for instance, of the lips of those who seemed to him comely persons, modulated in such delicate unison to the things they said or sang,—marking early the activity in him of a more than customary sensuousness, "the lust of the eye," as the Preacher says, which might lead him, one day, how far! Could he have foreseen the weariness of the way! In music sometimes the two sorts of impressions came together, and he would weep, to the surprise of older people. Tears of joy too the child knew, also to older people's surprise; real tears, once, or relief from long-strung, childish expectation, when he found returned at evening, with new roses in her cheeks, the little sister who had been to a place where there was a wood, and brought back for him a treasure of fallen acorns, and black crow's feathers, and his peace at finding her again near him mingled all night with some intimate sense of the distant forest, the rumour of its breezes, with the glossy blackbirds aslant and the branches lifted in them, and of the perfect nicety of the little cups that fell. So those two elementary apprehensions of the tenderness and of the colour in things grew apace in him, and were seen by him afterwards to send their roots back into the beginnings of life.

Let me note first some of the occasions of his recognition of the element of pain in things—incidents, now and again, which seemed suddenly to awake in him the whole force of the sentiment which Goethe has called the *Weltschmerz*, and in which the concentrated sorrow of the world seemed suddenly to lie heavy upon him. A book lay in an old bookcase, of which he cared to remember one picture—a woman sitting, with hands bound behind her, the dress, the cap, the hair, folded with a simplicity which touched him strangely, as if not by her own hands, but with some ambiguous care at the hands of others— Queen Marie Antoinette, on her way to execution—we all remember David's drawing, meant merely to make her ridiculous. The face that had been so high had learned to be mute and resistless; but out of its very resistlessness, seemed now to call on men to have pity, and forbear; and he took note of that, as he closed the book, as a thing to look at again, if he should at any time find himself tempted to be cruel. Again he would never quite forget the appeal in the small sister's face, in the garden under the lilacs, terrified at a spider lighted on her sleeve. He could trace back to the look then noted a certain mercy he conceived always for people in fear, even of little things, which seemed to make him, though but for a moment, capable of almost any sacrifice of himself. Impressible, susceptible persons, indeed, who had had their sorrows, lived about him; and this sensibility was due in part to the tacit influence of their presence, enforcing upon him habitually the fact that there are those who pass their days, as a matter of course, in a sort of "going quietly." Most poignantly of all he could recall, in unfading minutest circumstance, the cry on the stair, sounding bitterly through the house, and struck into his soul for ever, of an aged woman, his father's sister, come now to announce his death in distant India; how it seemed to make the aged woman like a child again; and, he knew not why, but this fancy was full of pity to him. There were the little sorrows of the dumb animals too—of the white angora, with a dark tail like an ermine's, and a face like a flower, who fell into a lingering sickness, and became quite delicately human in its valetudinarianism, and came to have a hundred different expressions of voice—how it grew worse and worse, till it began to feel the light too much

for it, and at last, after one wild morning of
pain, the little soul flickered away from the
body, quite worn to death already, and
now but feebly retaining it.

So he wanted another pet; and as there
were starlings about the place, which could
be taught to speak, one of them was caught,
and he meant to treat it kindly; but in the
night its young ones could be heard crying
after it, and the responsive cry of the 10
mother-bird towards them; and at last, with
the first light, though not till after some
debate with himself, he went down and
opened the cage, and saw a sharp bound of
the prisoner up to her nestlings; and therewith came the sense of remorse,—that he
too was become an accomplice in moving,
to the limit of his small power, the springs
and handles of that great machine in things,
constructed so ingeniously to play pain- 20
fugues on the delicate nerve-work of living
creatures.

I have remarked how, in the process of
our brain-building, as the house of thought
in which we live gets itself together, like
some airy bird's-nest of floating thistle-down
and chance straws, compact at last, little
accidents have their consequence; and thus
it happened that, as he walked one evening,
a garden gate, usually closed, stood open; 30
and lo! within, a great red hawthorn in full
flower, embossing heavily the bleached and
twisted trunk and branches, so aged that
there were but few green leaves thereon—
a plumage of tender, crimson fire out of
the heart of the dry wood. The perfume
of the tree had now and again reached
him, in the currents of the wind, over the
wall, and he had wondered what might be
behind it, and was now allowed to fill his 40
arms with the flowers—flowers enough for
all the old blue-china pots along the chim-
ney-piece, making *fête*,[4] in the children's
room. Was it some periodic moment in
the expansion of soul within him, or mere
trick of heat in the heavily-laden summer
air? But the beauty of the thing struck home
to him feverishly; and in dreams all night
he loitered along a magic roadway of crimson flowers, which seemed to open ruddily 50
in thick, fresh masses about his feet, and
fill softly all the little hollows in the banks
on either side. Always afterwards, summer

by summer, as the flowers came on, the
blossom of the red hawthorn still seemed
to him absolutely the reddest of all things;
and the goodly crimson, still alive in the
works of old Venetian masters or old
Flemish tapestries, called out always from
afar the recollection of the flame in those
perishing little petals, as it pulsed gradually out of them, kept long in the drawers
of an old cabinet. Also then, for the first
time, he seemed to experience a passionateness in his relation to fair outward objects,
an inexplicable excitement in their presence, which disturbed him, and from which
he half longed to be free. A touch of regret or desire mingled all night with the
remembered presence of the red flowers,
and their perfume in the darkness about
him; and the longing for some undivined,
entire possession of them was the beginning
of a revelation to him, growing ever clearer,
with the coming of the gracious summer
guise of fields and trees and persons in each
succeeding year, of a certain, at times seemingly exclusive, predominance in his interests, of beautiful physical things, a kind of
tyranny of the senses over him.

In later years he came upon philosophies
which occupied him much in the estimate
of the proportion of the sensuous and the
ideal elements in human knowledge, the
relative parts they bear in it; and, in his
intellectual scheme, was led to assign very
little to the abstract thought, and much to
its sensible vehicle or occasion. Such metaphysical speculation did but reinforce what
was instinctive in his way of receiving the
world, and for him, everywhere, that sensible vehicle or occasion became, perhaps
only too surely, the necessary concomitant
of any perception of things, real enough
to be of any weight or reckoning, in his
house of thought. There were times when
he could think of the necessity he was
under of associating all thoughts to touch
and sight, as a sympathetic link between
himself and actual, feeling, living objects;
a protest in favour of real men and women
against mere gray, unreal abstractions; and
he remembered gratefully how the Christian religion, hardly less than the religion
of the ancient Greeks, translating so much
of its spiritual verity into things that may
be seen, condescends in part to sanction

this infirmity, if so it be, of our human existence, wherein the world of sense is so much with us, and welcomed this thought as a kind of keeper and sentinel over his soul therein. But certainly, he came more and more to be unable to care for, or think of soul but as in an actual body, or of any world but that wherein are water and trees, and where men and women look, so or so, and press actual hands. It was the trick even his pity learned, fastening those who suffered in anywise to his affections by a kind of sensible attachments. He would think of Julian, fallen into incurable sickness, as spoiled in the sweet blossom of his skin like pale amber, and his honey-like hair; of Cecil, early dead, as cut off from the lilies, from golden summer days, from women's voices; and then what comforted him a little was the thought of the turning of the child's flesh to violets in the turf above him. And thinking of the very poor, it was not the things which most men care most for that he yearned to give them; but fairer roses, perhaps, and power to taste quite as they will, at their ease and not task-burdened, a certain desirable, clear light in the new morning, through which sometimes he had noticed them, quite unconscious of it, on their way to their early toil.

So he yielded himself to these things, to be played upon by them like a musical instrument, and began to note with deepening watchfulness, but always with some puzzled, unutterable longing in his enjoyment, the phases of the seasons and of the growing or waning day, down even to the shadowy changes wrought on bare wall or ceiling—the light cast up from the snow, bringing out their darkest angles; the brown light in the cloud, which meant rain; that almost too austere clearness, in the protracted light of the lengthening day, before warm weather began, as if it lingered but to make a severer workday, with the school-books opened earlier and later; that beam of June sunshine, at last, as he lay awake before the time, a way of gold-dust across the darkness; all the humming, the freshness, the perfume of the garden seemed to lie upon it—and coming in one afternoon in September, along the red gravel walk, to look for a basket of yellow crabapples left in the cool, old parlour, he remembered it the more, and how the colours struck upon him, because a wasp on one bitten apple stung him, and he felt the passion of sudden, severe pain. For this too brought its curious reflexions; and, in relief from it, he would wonder over it—how it had then been with him—puzzled at the depth of the charm or spell over him, which lay, for a little while at least, in the mere absence of pain; once, especially, when an older boy taught him to make flowers of sealing-wax, and he had burnt his hand badly at the lighted taper, and been unable to sleep. He remembered that also afterwards, as a sort of typical thing—a white vision of heat about him, clinging closely, through the languid scent of the ointments put upon the place to make it well.

Also, as he felt this pressure upon him of the sensible world, then, as often afterwards, there would come another sort of curious questioning how the last impressions of eye and ear might happen to him, how they would find him—the scent of the last flower, the soft yellowness of the last morning, the last recognition of some object of affection, hand or voice; it could not be but that the latest look of the eyes, before their final closing, would be strangely vivid; one would go with the hot tears, the cry, the touch of the wistful bystander, impressed how deeply on one! or would it be, perhaps, a mere frail retiring of all things, great or little, away from one, into a level distance?

For with this desire of physical beauty mingled itself early the fear of death—the fear of death intensified by the desire of beauty. Hitherto he had never gazed upon dead faces, as sometimes, afterwards, at the *Morgue* in Paris, or in that fair cemetery at Munich, where all the dead must go and lie in state before burial, behind glass windows, among the flowers and incense and holy candles—the aged clergy with their sacred ornaments, the young men in their dancing shoes and spotless white linen—after which visits, those waxen, resistless faces would always live with him for many days, making the broadest sunshine sickly. The child had heard indeed of the death of his father, and how, in the Indian station, a fever had taken him, so that though not in action he had yet died as a soldier; and hearing of the "resurrection of the just," he could think of him as still abroad in the world, somehow, for his protection—a grand, though perhaps rather terrible figure, in beautiful soldier's things, like the figure in the picture of Joshua's Vision in the Bible—and of that, round which the mourners moved so softly, and afterwards with such solemn singing, as but a worn-out garment left at a deserted lodging. So it was, until on a summer day he walked with his mother through a fair churchyard. In a bright dress he rambled among the graves, in the gay weather, and so came, in one corner, upon an open grave for a child —a dark space on the brilliant grass—the black mould lying heaped up round it, weighing down the little jewelled branches of the dwarf rose-bushes in flower. And therewith came, full-grown, never wholly to leave him, with the certainty that even children do sometimes die, the physical horror of death, with its wholly selfish recoil from the association of lower forms of life, and the suffocating weight above. No benign, grave figure in beautiful soldier's things any longer abroad in the world for his protection! only a few poor, piteous bones; and above them, possibly, a certain sort of figure he hoped not to see. For sitting one day in the garden below an open window, he heard people talking, and could not but listen, how, in a sleepless hour, a sick woman had seen one of the dead sitting beside her, come to call her hence; and from the broken talk evolved with much clearness the notion that not all those dead people had really departed to the churchyard, nor were quite so motionless as they looked, but led a secret, half-fugitive life in their old homes, quite free by night, though sometimes visible in the day, dodging from room to room, with no great goodwill towards those who shared the place with them. All night the figure sat beside him in the reveries of his broken sleep, and was not quite gone in the morning—an odd, irreconcileable new member of the household, making the sweet familiar chambers unfriendly and suspect by its uncertain presence. He could have hated the

dead he had pitied so, for being thus. Afterwards he came to think of those poor, home-returning ghosts, which all men have fancied to themselves—the *revenants*—pathetically, as crying, or beating with vain hands at the doors, as the wind came, their cries distinguishable in it as a wilder inner note. But, always making death more unfamiliar still, that old experience would ever, from time to time, return to him; even in the living he sometimes caught its likeness; at any time or place, in a moment, the faint atmosphere of the chamber of death would be breathed around him, and the image with the bound chin, the quaint smile, the straight, stiff feet, shed itself across the air upon the bright carpet, amid the gayest company, or happiest communing with himself.

To most children the sombre questioning to which impressions like these attach themselves, if they come at all, are actually suggested by religious books, which therefore they often regard with much secret distaste, and dismiss, as far as possible, from their habitual thoughts as a too depressing element in life. To Florian such impressions, these misgivings as to the ultimate tendency of the years, of the relationship between life and death, had been suggested spontaneously in the natural course of his mental growth by a strong innate sense for the soberer tones in things, further strengthened by actual circumstances; and religious sentiment, that system of biblical ideas in which he had been brought up, presented itself to him as a thing that might soften and dignify, and light up as with a "lively hope," a melancholy already deeply settled in him. So he yielded himself easily to religious impressions, and with a kind of mystical appetite for sacred things; the more as they came to him through a saintly person who loved him tenderly, and believed that this early preoccupation with them already marked the child out for a saint. He began to love, for their own sakes, church lights, holy days, all that belonged to the comely order of the sanctuary, the secrets of its white linen, and holy vessels, and fonts of pure water; and its hieratic purity and simplicity became the type of something he desired always to have about him in actual life. He pored over the pictures in religious books, and knew by heart the exact mode in which the wrestling angel grasped Jacob, how Jacob looked in his mysterious sleep, how the bells and pomegranates were attached to the hem of Aaron's vestment, sounding sweetly as he glided over the turf of the holy place. His way of conceiving religion came then to be in effect what it ever afterwards remained—a sacred history indeed, but still more a sacred ideal, a transcendent version or representation, under intenser and more expressive light and shade, of human life and its familiar or exceptional incidents, birth, death, marriage, youth, age, tears, joy, rest, sleep, waking—a mirror, towards which men might turn away their eyes from vanity and dullness, and see themselves therein as angels, with their daily meat and drink, even, become a kind of sacred transaction—a complementary strain or burden, applied to our every-day existence, whereby the stray snatches of music in it re-set themselves, and fall into the scheme of some higher and more consistent harmony. A place adumbrated itself in his thoughts, wherein those sacred personalities, which are at once the reflex and the pattern of our nobler phases of life, housed themselves; and this region in his intellectual scheme all subsequent experience did but tend still further to realise and define. Some ideal, hieratic persons he would always need to occupy it and keep a warmth there. And he could hardly understand those who felt no such need at all, finding themselves quite happy without such heavenly companionship, and sacred double of their life, beside them.

Thus a constant substitution of the typical for the actual took place in his thoughts. Angels might be met by the way, under English elm or beach-tree; mere messengers seemed like angels, bound on celestial errands; a deep mysticity brooded over real meetings and partings; marriages were made in heaven; and deaths also, with hands of angels thereupon, to bear soul and body quietly asunder, each to its appointed rest. All the acts and accidents of daily life borrowed a sacred colour and significance; the very colours of things became themselves weighty with meanings like the sacred stuffs of Moses' tabernacle, full of penitence or peace. Sentiment, congruous in the first instance only with those divine transactions, the deep, effusive unction of the House of Bethany, was assumed as the due attitude for the reception of our every-day existence; and for a time he walked through the world in a sustained, not unpleasurable awe, generated by the habitual recognition, beside every circumstance and event of life, of its celestial correspondent.

Sensibility—the desire of physical beauty—a strange biblical awe, which made any reference to the unseen act on him like solemn music—these qualities the child took away with him, when, at about the age of twelve years, he left the old house, and was taken to live in another place. He had never left home before, and, anticipating much from this change, had long dreamed over it, jealously counting the days till the time fixed for departure should come; had been a little careless about others even, in his strong desire for it—when Lewis fell sick, for instance, and they must wait still two days longer. At last the morning came, very fine; and all things—the very pavement with its dust, at the roadside—seemed to have a white, pearl-like lustre in them. They were to travel by a favourite road on which he had often walked a certain distance, and on one of those two prisoner days, when Lewis was sick, had walked farther than ever before, in his great desire to reach the new place. They had started and gone a little way when a pet bird was found to have been left behind, and must even now—so it presented itself to him—have already all the appealing fierceness and wild self-pity at heart of one left by others to perish of hunger in a closed house; and he returned to fetch it, himself in hardly less stormy distress. But as he passed in search of it from room to room, lying so pale, with a look of meekness in their denudation, and at last through that little, stripped white room, the aspect of the place touched him like the face of one dead; and a clinging back towards it came over him, so intense that he knew it would last long, and spoiling all his pleasure in the realisation of a thing so eagerly anticipated. And so, with the bird found, but himself in an agony of home-sickness, thus capriciously sprung up within him, he was driven quickly away, far into the rural distance, so fondly speculated on, of that favourite country-road.

[1878]

MARIUS THE EPICUREAN

DIVINE SERVICE

"Wisdom hath builded herself a house; she hath mingled her wine; she hath also prepared for herself a table."

The more highly favored ages of imaginative art present instances of the summing up of an entire world of complex associations under some single form, like the *Zeus* of Olympia, or the series of frescoes which commemorate *The Acts of Saint Francis,* at Assisi, or like the play of *Hamlet* or *Faust.* It was not in an image, or series of images, yet still in a sort of dramatic action, and with the unity of a single appeal to eye and ear, that Marius about this time found all his new impressions set forth, regarding what he had already recognized, intellectually, as for him at least the most beautiful thing in the world.

To understand the influence upon him of what follows the reader must remember that it was an experience which came amid a deep sense of vacuity in life. The fairest products of the earth seemed to be dropping to pieces, as if in men's very hands, around him. How real was their sorrow, and his! "His observation of life" had come to be like the constant telling of a sorrowful rosary, day after day; till, as if taking infection from the cloudy sorrow of the mind, the eye also, the very senses, were grown faint and sick. And now it happened as with the actual morning on which he found himself a spectator of this new thing. The long winter had been a season of unvarying sullenness. At last, on this day he awoke with a sharp flash of lightning in the earliest twilight; in a little while the heavy rain had filtered the air; the clear light was abroad; and, as though the spring had set in with a sudden leap in the heart of things, the whole scene around him lay like some untarnished picture beneath a sky of delicate blue. Under the spell of his late depression, Marius had suddenly determined to leave Rome for a while. But desiring first to advertise Cornelius of his movements, and failing to find him in his lodgings, he had ventured, still early in the day, to seek him in the Cecilian villa. Passing through its silent and empty courtyard he loitered for a moment, to admire. Under the clear but immature light of winter morning after a storm, all the details of form and color in the old marbles were distinctly visible, and with a kind of severity or sadness (so it struck him) amid their beauty—in them, and in all other details of the scene—the cypresses, the bunches of pale daffodils in the grass, the curves of the purple hills of Tusculum, with the drifts of virgin snow still lying in their hollows.

The little open door, through which he passed from the courtyard, admitted him into what was plainly the vast *Lararium,*[1] or domestic sanctuary, of the Cecilian family, transformed in many particulars, but still richly decorated, and retaining much of its ancient furniture in metalwork and costly stone. The peculiar half-light of dawn seemed to be lingering beyond its hour upon the solemn marble walls; and here, though at that moment in absolute silence, a great company of people was assembled. In that brief period of peace, during which the church emerged for a while from her jealously-guarded subterranean life, the rigor of an earlier rule of exclusion had been relaxed. And so it came to pass that on this morning Marius saw for the first time the wonderful spectacle—wonderful, especially, in its evidential power over himself, over his own thoughts—of those who believe.

There were noticeable, among those present, great varieties of rank, of age, of

---

[1] *Lararium:* part of the old Roman home devoted to the worship of the household gods (Lares), whose images were assembled there.

personal type. The Roman *ingenuus*,[2] with the white toga and gold ring, stood side by side with his slave; and the air of the whole company was, above all, a grave one, an air of recollection. Coming thus unexpectedly upon this large assembly, so entirely united, in a silence so profound, for purposes unknown to him, Marius felt for a moment as if he had stumbled by chance upon some great conspiracy. Yet that could scarcely be, for the people here collected might have figured as the earliest handsel, or pattern, of a new world, from the very face of which discontent had passed away. Corresponding to the variety of human type there present was the various expression of every form of human sorrow assuaged. What desire, what fulfillment of desire, had wrought so pathetically on the features of these ranks of aged men and women of humble condition? Those young men, bent down so discreetly on the details of their sacred service, had faced life and were glad, by some science, or light of knowledge they had, to which there had certainly been no parallel in the older world. Was some credible message from beyond "the flaming rampart of the world"—a message of hope, regarding the place of men's souls and their interest in the sum of things—already molding anew their very bodies, and looks, and voices, now and here? At least, there was a cleansing and kindling flame at work in them, which seemed to make everything else Marius had ever known look comparatively vulgar and mean. There were the children, above all—troops of children—reminding him of those pathetic children's graves, like cradles or garden-beds, he had noticed in his first visit to these places; and they more than satisfied the odd curiosity he had then conceived about them, wondering in what quaintly expressive forms they might come forth into the daylight, if awakened from sleep. Children of the Catacombs, some but "a span long," with features not so much beautiful as heroic (that world of new, refining sentiment having set its seal even on childhood); they retained certainly no stain or trace of anything subterranean this morning, in the alacrity of their worship—as ready as if they had been at play—stretching forth their hands, crying, chanting in a resonant voice, and with boldly upturned faces, *Christe Eleison!* [3]

For the silence—silence, amid those lights of early morning to which Marius had always been constitutionally impressible, as having in them a certain reproachful austerity—was broken suddenly by resounding cries of *Kyrie Eleison!* [4] *Christe Eleison!* repeated alternately, again and again, until the bishop, rising from his chair, made sign that this prayer should cease. But the voices burst out once more presently, in richer and more varied melody, though still of an antiphonal character; the men, the women and children, the deacons, the people, answering one another, somewhat after the manner of a Greek chorus. But again with what a novelty of poetic accent; what a genuine expansion of heart; what profound intimations for the intellect, as the meaning of the words grew upon him! *Cum grandi affectu et compunctione dicatur* [5]—says an ancient eucharistic order; and certainly, the mystic tone of this praying and singing was one with the expression of deliverance, of grateful assurance and sincerity, upon the faces of those assembled. As if some searching correction, a regeneration of the body by the spirit, had begun, and was already gone a great way, the countenances of men, women, and children alike had a brightness on them which he could fancy reflected upon himself—an amenity, a mystic amiability and unction, which found its way most readily of all to the hearts of children themselves. The religious poetry of those Hebrew psalms—*Benedixisti Domine terram tuam. Dixit Dominus Domino meo, sede a dextris meis* [6]—was certainly in marvelous accord with the lyrical instinct of his own character. Those august hymns, he thought, must thereafter ever remain by him as among the well-tested powers in

<hr/>

[2] *ingenuus:* Roman noble, freeborn.

[3] *Christe Eleison:* "Christ, have mercy on us!" This and some succeeding quotations are part of the Mass in the Roman Catholic service.

[4] *Kyrie Eleison:* "Lord, have mercy upon us!"

[5] *Cum grandi affectu,* etc.: "Let it be uttered with deep feeling and compassion."

[6] *Benedixisti Domine,* etc.: "Lord, thou hast been well pleased unto thy land" (*Psalms,* LXXXV, 1).—"The Lord said unto my Lord, Sit thou at my right hand" (*Psalms,* CX, 1).

things to soothe and fortify the soul. One could never grow tired of them!

In the old pagan worship there had been little to call the understanding into play. Here, on the other hand, the utterance, the eloquence, the music of worship conveyed, as Marius readily understood, a fact or series of facts, for intellectual reception. That became evident, more especially, in those lessons, or sacred readings, which, like the singing, in broken vernacular Latin, occurred at certain intervals, amid the silence of the assembly. There were readings, again with bursts of chanted invocation between for fuller light on a difficult path, in which many a vagrant voice of human philosophy, haunting men's minds from of old, recurred with clearer accent than had ever belonged to it before, as if lifted, above its first intention, into the harmonies of some supreme system of knowledge or doctrine, at length complete. And last of all came a narrative which, with a thousand tender memories, everyone appeared to know by heart, displaying, in all the vividness of a picture for the eye, the mournful figure of him towards whom this whole act of worship still consistently turned—a figure which seemed to have absorbed, like some rich tincture in his garment, all that was deepfelt and impassioned in the experiences of the past.

It was the anniversary of his birth as a little child they celebrated today. *Astiterunt reges terrae;* so the Gradual, the "Song of Degrees," proceeded, the young men on the steps of the altar responding in deep, clear, antiphon or chorus—

Astiterunt reges terrae—
Adversus sanctum puerum tuum, Jesum;
Nunc, Domine, da servis tuis loqui verbum
    tuum—
Et signa fieri, per nomen sancti pueri Jesu. [7]

And the proper action of the rite itself, like a half-opened book to be read by the duly initiated mind, took up those suggestions, and carried them forward into the present, as having reference to a power still efficacious, still after some mystic sense even now in action among the people there assembled. The entire office, indeed, with its interchange of lessons, hymns, prayer, silence, was itself like a single piece of highly composite, dramatic music; a "song of degrees," rising steadily to a climax. Notwithstanding the absence of any central image visible to the eye, the entire ceremonial process, like the place in which it was enacted, was weighty with symbolic significance, seemed to express a single leading motive. The mystery, if such in fact it was, centered indeed in the actions of one visible person, distinguished among the assistants, who stood ranged in semicircle around him, by the extreme fineness of his white vestments, and the pointed cap with the golden ornaments upon his head.

Nor had Marius ever seen the pontifical character, as he conceived it—*sicut unguentum in capite, descendens in oram vestimenti* [8]—so fully realized, as in the expression, the manner and voice, of this novel pontiff, as he took his seat on the white chair placed for him by the young men, and received his long staff into his hand, or moved his hands—hands which seemed endowed in very deed with some mysterious power—at the *Lavabo*,[9] or at the various benedictions, or to bless certain objects on the table before him, chanting in cadence of a grave sweetness the leading parts of the rite. What profound unction and mysticity! The solemn character of the singing was at its height when he opened his lips. Like some new sort of *rhapsôdos*,[10] it was for the moment as if he alone possessed the words of the office, and they flowed anew from some permanent source of inspiration within him. The table or altar at which he presided, below a canopy on delicate spiral columns, was in fact the tomb of a youthful

---

[7] *Astiterunt reges terrae,* etc.:
"The kings of the earth stood (in his presence),
Before Thy Holy Child, Jesus;
Now, O Lord, pemit Thy servants to speak
    Thy word—
And signs be given in the name of the Holy
    Child Jesus."

[8] *sicut unguentum,* etc.: "like precious ointment upon the head, . . . that went down to the skirts of the garment" (*Psalms,* CXXXIII, 2).

[9] *Lavabo:* "I will wash": the verses 6-12 of *Psalm* XXVI, beginning 'Lavabo' (in the *Vulgate*), recited by the priest in the Mass, following the Offertory, while washing his hands.

[10] *rhapsôdos:* professional reciter of epic poems or songs.

"witness," of the family of the Cecilii, who had shed his blood not many years before, and whose relics were still in this place. It was for his sake the bishop put his lips so often to the surface before him —the regretful memory of that death entwining itself, though not without certain notes of triumph, as a matter of special inward significance, throughout a service, which was, before all else, from first to last, a commemoration of the dead.

A sacrifice also—a sacrifice, it might seem, like the most primitive, the most natural and enduringly significant of old pagan sacrifices, of the simplest fruits of the earth. And in connection with this circumstance again, as in the actual stones of the building so in the rite itself, what Marius observed was not so much new matter as a new spirit, molding, informing, with a new intention, many observances not witnessed for the first time today. Men and women came to the altar successively, in perfect order, and deposited below the latticework of pierced white marble, their baskets of wheat and grapes, incense, oil for the sanctuary lamps; bread and wine especially— pure wheaten bread, the pure white wine of the Tusculan vineyards. There was here a veritable consecration, hopeful and animating, of the earth's gifts, of old dead and dark matter itself, now in some way redeemed at last, of all that we can touch or see, in the midst of a jaded world that had lost the true sense of such things, and in strong contrast to the wise emperor's renunciant and impassive attitude towards them. Certain portions of that bread and wine were taken into the bishop's hands; and thereafter, with an increasing mysticity and effusion, the rite proceeded. Still in a strain of inspired supplication, the antiphonal singing developed, from this point, into a kind of dialogue between the chief minister and the whole assisting company—

SURSUM CORDA!
HABEMUS AD DOMINUM.
GRATIAS AGAMUS DOMINO DEO NOSTRO! [11]—

It might have been thought the business, the duty or service of young men more particularly, as they stood there in long ranks, and in severe and simple vesture of the purest white—a service in which they would seem to be flying for refuge, as with their precious, their treacherous and critical youth in their hands, to one—Yes! one like themselves, who yet claimed their worship, a worship, above all, in the way of Aurelius, in the way of imitation. *Adoramus te Christe, quia per crucem tuam redemisti mundum!* [12]—they cry together. So deep is the emotion that at moments it seems to Marius as if some there present apprehend that prayer prevails, that the very object of this pathetic crying himself draws near. From the first there had been the sense, an increasing assurance, of one coming—actually with them now, according to the oft-repeated affirmation or petition, *Dominus vobiscum!* [13] Some at least were quite sure of it; and the confidence of this remnant fired the hearts, and gave meaning to the bold, ecstatic worship, of all the rest about them.

Prompted especially by the suggestions of that mysterious old Jewish psalmody, so new to him—lesson and hymn—and catching therewith a portion of the enthusiasm of those beside him, Marius could discern dimly, behind the solemn recitation which now followed, at once a narrative and a prayer, the most touching image truly that had ever come within the scope of his mental or physical gaze. It was the image of a young man giving up voluntarily, one by one, for the greatest of ends, the greatest gifts; actually parting with himself, above all, with the serenity, the divine serenity, of his own soul; yet from the midst of his desolation crying out upon the greatness of his success, as if foreseeing this very worship. As center of the supposed facts which for these people were become so constraining a motive of hopefulness, of activity, that image seemed to display itself with an overwhelming claim on human gratitude. What Saint Lewis of France

[11] *Sursum corda!* etc.:
"Lift up your hearts!
We have lifted them unto the Lord!
Let us give thanks to the Lord our God!"

[12] *Adoramus te Christe,* etc.: "We adore thee, O Christ, because by Thy cross Thou hast redeemed the world."
[13] *Dominus vobiscum:* "The Lord be with you!"

discerned, and found so irresistibly touching, across the dimness of many centuries, as a painful thing done for love of him by one he had never seen, was to them almost as a thing of yesterday; and their hearts were whole with it. It had the force, among their interests, of an almost recent event in the career of one whom their fathers' fathers might have known. From memories so sublime, yet so close at 10 hand, had the narrative descended in which these acts of worship centered; though again the names of some more recently dead were mingled in it. And it seemed as if the very dead were aware; to be stirring beneath the slabs of the sepulchers which lay so near, that they might associate themselves to this enthusiasm—to this exalted worship of Jesus.

One by one, at last, the faithful approach 20 to receive from the chief minister morsels of the great, white, wheaten cake he had taken into his hands—*Perducat vos ad vitam aeternam!* [14] he prays, half-silently, as they depart again, after discreet embraces. The Eucharist of those early days was, even more

entirely than at any later or happier time, an act of thanksgiving; and while the remnants of the feast are borne away for the reception of the sick, the sustained gladness of the rite reaches its highest point in the singing of a hymn—a hymn like the spontaneous product of two opposed militant companies, contending accordingly together, heightening, accumulating, their witness, provoking one another's worship, in a kind of sacred rivalry.

Ite! Missa est! [15]—cried the young deacons; and Marius departed from that strange scene along with the rest. What was it?—Was it this made the way of Cornelius so pleasant through the world? As for Marius himself—the natural soul of worship in him had at last been satisfied as never before. He felt, as he left that place, that he must hereafter experience often a longing memory, a kind of thirst, for all this, over again. And it seemed moreover to define what he must require of the powers, whatsoever they might be, that had brought him into the world at all, to make him not unhappy in it.

[1885]

[14] *Perducat vos,* etc.: "May he bring you to life everlasting!"

[15] *Ite! Missa est!:* "Go! It (i.e. the service) is finished!"

ROBERT LOUIS STEVENSON

CHRONOLOGY AND INTRODUCTION

1850 Born, November 13, Edinburgh.

1857–66 Early and irregular schooling in Edinburgh and near London. First book published privately, *The Pentland Rising, A Page of History* (1866).

1867–75 Entered the University of Edinburgh; studied engineering and, later, law; trips to continent for health; called to bar (1875), but never practiced.

1875–79 Contributed essays and stories to various magazines; *An Inland Voyage* (1878); *Travels with a Donkey* (1879).

1879 Sailed for America, August 7.

1880 Married, May 19; returned to Scotland; spent several months in Switzerland for health (1880-1882).

1881 *Virginibus Puerisque; Treasure Island* (serially, in *Young Folks,* October, 1881— January, 1882).

1882 In England, Scotland, and Southern France; *Familiar Studies of Men and Books* (collected essays); *New Arabian Nights.*

1883 *Across the Plains; Black Arrow; The Silverado Squatters.*

1884 Settled in Bournemouth, England.

1885 *Prince Otto; A Child's Garden of Verses; More New Arabian Nights.*

1886 *Strange Case of Dr. Jekyll and Mr. Hyde; Kidnapped.*

1887 Sailed for America; took cottage at Saranac Lake, N. Y. for winter; *Memories and Portraits* (collected essays); *The Merry Men, and Other Tales.*

1888 Twelve essays in *Scribner's Magazine;* sailed, June 7, to South Seas.

1889 *The Master of Ballantrae;* returned to Honolulu and again (June) sailed to South Seas; *The Wrong Box.*

1890 *The South Seas: A Record of Three Cruises;* settled in Samoa.

1891–92 *The Wrecker; Across the Plains* (republished in book form), with *Other Memories and Essays; A Footnote to History: Eight Years of Trouble in Samoa.*

1893 *Catriona* (in America, *David Balfour*).

1894 *The Ebb Tide;* worked on St. Ives, A *Family of Engineers, Weir of Hermiston* (all left unfinished). Died at Vailima, December 3.

Stevenson cannot rank with the greatest masters of Victorian prose, but he holds a distinguished place not very far below them, a place which he seems certain to keep for years to come. His distinction, if not so high as theirs in any one field of writing, is more varied. Some critics think that he is best as an essayist, one of Briton's most delightful; a few give first place to certain short stories; while others are convinced that his reputation rests upon two or three novels. Galsworthy, for example, says that Stevenson is, "next to Dumas, the best of all romantic novelists, certainly the best British romanticist." And as a personality, whether revealed in his letters, in his verse, in his travel notes, or in the records of biographers and intimate friends, he is one of the most appealing figures of his time.

Stevenson was himself the personification of romance at every moment of his life. Though he liked to think that there was Highland blood in his veins, he was a Lowland Scot of Scandinavian descent. Much of his genius came from his father, a man of Calvinistic temper, sombrely, even morbidly, pious,—a passionate, tragic figure who rose to distinction as a builder of lighthouses. From his mother, the daughter of a clergyman, Stevenson inherited his Gallic gayety and laughter. The old family servant, known as Cummie, was a powerful influence upon him in childhood. She taught him the Bible and the shorter catechism, and told him endless stories of warlocks, witches, goblins, fairies, kelpies,—all made vivid in the telling with plenty of "curdling realism," such as put terror into the heart of the susceptible lad; an experience partly offset by happy hours spent at the manse of his maternal grandfather. "Out of my reminiscences of life in that dear place," he wrote in after years, "all the morbid and painful elements have disappeared. That was my golden age." He read independently and passionately from boyhood, one of the most potent charms being Scott, who remained a life-long enthusiasm.

Stevenson's regular education was, as he thought of it, "the merest shadow." He was a congenital truant, "sedulously idle," taking his studies unsystematically, even rebelliously. At Edinburgh University, where he was professedly preparing to be an engineer (later a lawyer), he loafed his way along, made light of the professors, became wilfully eccentric and bohemian in his habits, read Tyndall and Huxley and affected, ostentatiously, agnosticism and atheism in his thinking and talking;—emphatically a problem-youth to his professionally gifted and conventionally orthodox father. But he saw a great deal of "life" and, like Scott in the famous "Liddesdale raids," he was "making" himself all the time. Two friends, moreover, did much for him in these vagabond Edinburgh days. One was Professor Fleeming Jenkin, on the engineering faculty at the University, who shook some of the conceit and posturing out of him; and the other was W. E. Henley, then an invalid in an Edinburgh hospital, whose courage and vivid intelligence were, as Stevenson said, "wine to me." And by now he was determined to live a literary life. Sir Sidney Colvin, who came to know him intimately, says: "He read precociously and omnivorously in the *belles-lettres,* including a very wide range of English poetry, fiction, and essays, and a fairly wide range of French; and was a genuine student of Scottish history.... The art of literature was already his private passion." While a student at the University he became a member of the Speculative Society ("Spec"), a literary club of long and famous memory for which he wrote essays and debated, and of which he was president for two terms. With three other students he founded the *Edinburgh University Magazine,* hardly more than an ephemeral venture but one that gave an outlet to youthful literary ambitions. Outwardly flippant, the Stevenson of this period in his unremitting efforts to learn the art of writing was, as a friend described him, inwardly flint.

By the time he was twenty-three he showed signs of tubercular trouble, an affliction which made of him for the rest of his life a semi-invalid with intervals of joyous vitality. For several years following student days he was a kind of wandering bohemian, now in London, now in Scotland, but mostly in France, canoeing along rivers, travelling alone with a donkey, enjoying a seemingly carefree existence among artists at Barbizon, Grez, Fontainebleau, Paris, doing exactly what he wished to do, the evident embodiment of gayety and insouciance, yet always underneath the dour and determined Scot.

While at Grez, he met Mrs. Osborne, an American woman with whom he fell in love and later married. In 1879 he followed her to California, crossing the continent in an emigrant train, thus breaking with his family for the time and living near to starvation. He settled at last in San Francisco where, says his biographer, he became "a pitiable wreck, ready for the hospital, ready almost for the undertaker." In this lowest ebb of his fortunes, his father came to his rescue with a regular allowance sufficient to enable Stevenson to marry and carry on.

From now to the end he waged battle against the disease that had already laid its fatal hand upon him. Once in Hyères, on the French Riviera, he suffered a terrible illness that nearly swept him away and left "the tabernacle in rags," as he said. In this desperate condition he wrote the famous *Requiem,* now inscribed over his grave on the mountain-top in Samoa:

> Under the wide and starry sky,
> Dig the grave and let me lie,
> Glad did I live and gladly die,
>   And I laid me down with a will.
> This be the verse you grave for me:
> *Here he lies where he longed to be;*
> *Home is the sailor, home from the sea,*
>   *And the hunter home from the hill.*

Stevenson lived dangerously, but he lived courageously and creatively too. In this period much of his best work was done; fame and fortune came to him and passionate happiness. After several years in Europe, following his marriage, he returned to America, a celebrity, received in triumph.

But his inborn dislike of towns and settled society, even more his insatiable thirst for adventurous wandering, shortly found expression in a series of cruises through the South Seas, which had laid their spell upon him from boyhood. Health and energies revived; the romance of living possessed him with intensified freshness. "The sea, islands, the islanders, the island life and climate, make and keep me truly happier," he wrote to Henry James. "These last two years I have been much at sea, and I have *never wearied.*" The first voyage on the yacht *Casco,* out of the Golden Gate, was probably the most thrilling of all. "Day after day," he wrote, "the sun flamed; night after night the moon beaconed, or the stars paraded their lustrous regiment. I was aware of a spiritual change, or perhaps, rather a molecular re-constitution. My bones were sweeter to me. I had come to my own climate, and looked back with pity on those damp and wintry zones miscalled the temperate."

In September 1890, Stevenson settled on one of the islands of the Samoa group, Upolu, and bought a tract of four hundred acres on which he built a spacious house, and became a kind of South Sea laird, "living patriarchally," as he said, lavish in hospitality, interested in all affairs of the island and beloved by the Samoans, to whom he was Tusitala, teller of tales. His home, Vailima, stood on the mountain side, six hundred feet above the sea, where it commanded a prospect of unsurpassed beauty. "Heaven upon earth for sweetness, freshness, depth upon depth of unimaginable color, and a huge silence broken at this moment (he is writing on a morning) only by the far-away murmur of the Pacific and the rich piping of a single bird....I shall never set my foot again upon the heather. Here I am until I die, and here will I be buried." One day after a spell of intense work upon *Weir of Hermiston* his long-beleaguered body suddenly collapsed, and by faithful Samoans it was laid to rest upon the mountain-top, far above his home.

It is unnecessary to dwell at any length upon the romantic personality of Stevenson, for the story of his life, told even in outline, reveals to us the kind of man he was. He made a spectacular figure wherever he went or whatever he did, "this slender, slovenly, nondescript apparition," as Colvin described him. Undoubtedly he had often heard the chimes at midnight in old Edinburgh, and, in Colvin's guarded phrase, would seek "solace among the crude allurements of the city streets." But the zest of life possessed him, if not the deep Hazlittian gusto, and he got out of his experiences as he went along a fund of knowledge and sympathy that made him one of the most tolerant of men, one of the most human of writers. And though he came to understand, as his wife said, "the pitiless cruelty of modern civilization," regardless of what he saw and suffered at any period of his life, he could say when very close to the end of it: "I believe in an ultimate decency of things; ay, and if I woke in hell, should still believe it!"

Had Stevenson known full health he might have been a man of action, very likely a soldier or sailor, for he hungered and thirsted after adventure, and there were many times when deeds meant more to him than words, even beautifully written words. Although fate would not make him (as he once remarked, more than half jestingly, no doubt) "a leader of a great horde of irregular cavalry, devastating whole valleys," he yet refused to allow medicine bottles to color his view of life, or disease to quench his high romantic courage and creativity. The underlying quality of the man is nowhere more truly revealed than in two accounts of himself, one made in a letter to George Meredith in 1893, and one in a late conversation with his stepson, Lloyd Osborne. To Meredith he wrote: "For fourteen years I have not had a day's real health; I have wakened sick and gone to bed weary; and I have done my work unflinchingly. I have written in bed, and written out of it, written in hemorrhages, written in sickness, written torn by coughing, written when my head swam for sickness; and for so long, it seems to me I have won my wager and recovered my glove." And to Osborne he said: "I am not a man of any unusual talent, Lloyd; I started out with very moderate abilities; my success has been due to my really remarkable industry—to developing what I had in me to the extreme limit. When a man begins to sharpen one faculty, and keeps on sharpening it with tireless perseverance, he can achieve wonders. Everybody knows it; it's a commonplace; and yet how rare it is to find anybody doing it—I mean to the uttermost as I did. What genius I had was for *work*."

Probably no writer ever toiled harder to learn his craft than Stevenson. In his youth he composed, as his biographer notes, "essays, tales, sketches, and poems all blindly imitative"; he played the "sedulous ape" to many models, to Montaigne, Bacon, Hazlitt, Lamb, Sir Thomas Browne, Defoe, Hawthorne, Flaubert. He wrote and rewrote, tireless in his determination to master the use of words and the management of sentences, or "the web" of written discourse. "I lived with words," he confessed; "habit and practice sharpen gifts." But passionate zest in the artistry of his art never made him forget its end for him,—communication of "the uncommunicable thrill of things"; an end not to be reached, moreover, without adequate knowledge. *Art* is finally born in a writer, he insisted, only when the "ardor of the blood...is swayed by knowledge and seconded by craft." It was this way to the last with Stevenson. "I sit here and smoke and write and re-write, and destroy, and rage at my own impotence, from six in the morning till eight at night," he told a correspondent only a few months before his death. His deepest concern was to better past efforts: "life is a series of farewells, even in art," whose proper business, he protested, is "to give life to abstractions and significance and charm to facts."

Consequently his style progressively improved until traces of deliberate artifice, to be found sometimes in his earlier prose, are absent from his last work, the splendid unfinished *Weir of Hermiston*. Every reader who knows and enjoys good writing must find delight in one and another of his best things, delight in the precision and felicity of words, in picturesque and cadenced sentences, in sustained animation through paragraph and page, all communicating a healthy and heroic outlook on life.

Stevenson believed that the best a writer has to impart, in the long last, is himself. That is why his essays continue to be read. Like other good essayists he liked to talk about himself; he liked to give expression to his reflections on that highest of all arts, the art of living, more especially since he was, withal, much of a moralist and "something of the Shorter Catechist." Besides, he was vital to his fingertips. No doubt he has been more a favorite with younger readers than with older, who do not see in him what they see in the greater masters of the essay, Montaigne, Bacon, Hazlitt, and Lamb, for examples. But young and old alike will always find in his essays what they find, also, in his novels, stories, sketches, and letters, the revelation of a valiant spirit and a luminous and lovable intelligence, who experienced life as a romantically thrilling adventure and who makes them experience it that way, too.

VIRGINIBUS PUERISQUE

PAN'S PIPES

The world in which we live has been variously said and sung by the most ingenious poets and philosophers—these reducing it to formulae and chemical ingredients, those striking the lyre in high-sounding measures for the handiwork of God. What experience supplies is of a mingled tissue, and the choosing mind has much to reject before it can get together the materials of a theory. Dew and thunder, destroying Attila and the Spring lampkins, belong to an order of contrasts which no repetition can assimilate. There is an uncouth, outlandish strain throughout the web of the world, as from a vexatious planet in the house of life. Things are not congruous and wear strange disguises: the consummate flower is fostered out of dung, and after nourishing itself awhile with heaven's delicate distillations, decays again into indistinguishable soil; and with Caesar's ashes, Hamlet tells us, the urchins make dirt pies and filthily besmear their countenance. Nay, the kindly shine of summer, when tracked home with the scientific spyglass, is found to issue from the most portentous nightmare of the universe—the great, conflagrant sun: a world of hell's squibs, tumultuary, roaring aloud, inimical to life. The sun itself is enough to disgust a human being of the scene which he inhabits; and you would not fancy there was a green or habitable spot in a universe thus awfully lighted up. And yet it is by the blaze of such a conflagration, to which the fire of Rome was but a spark, that we do all our fiddling, and hold domestic tea-parties at the arbor door.

The Greeks figured Pan, the god of Nature, now terribly stamping his foot, so that armies were dispersed; now by the woodside on a summer noon trolling on his pipe till he charmed the hearts of upland plowmen. And the Greeks, in so figuring, uttered the last word in human experience. To certain smoke-dried spirits matter and motion and elastic ethers, and the hypothesis of this or that other spectacled professor, tell a speaking story; but for youth and all ductile and congenial minds, Pan is not dead, but of all the classic hierarchy alone survives in triumph —goat-footed, with a gleeful and an angry look, the type of the shaggy world; and in every wood, if you go with a spirit properly prepared, you shall hear the note of his pipe.

For it is a shaggy world, and yet studded with gardens; where the salt and tumbling sea receives clear rivers running from among reeds and lilies; fruitful and austere; a rustic world; sunshiny, lewd, and cruel. What is it the birds sing among the trees in pairing-time? What means the sound of the rain falling far and wide upon the leafy forest? To what tune does the fisherman whistle, as he hauls in his net at morning, and the bright fish are heaped inside the boat? These are all airs upon Pan's pipe; he it was who gave them breath in the exultation of his heart, and gleefully modulated their outflow with his lips and fingers. The coarse mirth of herdsmen, shaking the dells with laughter and striking out high echoes from the rock; the tune

of moving feet in the lamp-lit city, or on
the smooth ballroom floor; the hoofs of
many horses, beating the wide pastures in
alarm; the song of hurrying rivers; the
color of clear skies; and smiles and the live
touch of hands; and the voice of things,
and their significant look, and the renovat-
ing influence they breathe forth—these are
his joyful measures, to which the whole
earth treads in choral harmony. To this
music the young lambs bound as to a tabor,
and the London shopgirl skips rudely in
the dance. For it puts a spirit of goodness
in all hearts; and to look on the happy
side of nature is common, in their hours,
to all created things. Some are vocal under
a good influence, are pleasing whenever
they are pleased, and hand on their happiness to others, as a child, who, looking
upon lovely things, looks lovely. Some leap
to the strains with unapt foot, and make
a halting figure in the universal dance.
And some, like sour spectators at the play,
receive the music into their hearts with an
unmoved countenance, and walk like
strangers through the general rejoicing.
But let him feign never so carefully, there
is not a man but has his pulses shaken
when Pan trolls out a stave of ecstasy
and sets the world a-singing.

Alas if that were all! But oftentimes the
air is changed; and in the screech of the
night wind, chasing navies, subverting
the tall ships and the rooted cedar of the
hills; in the random deadly levin or
the fury of headlong floods, we recognize
the "dread foundation" of life and the
anger in Pan's heart. Earth wages open
war against her children, and under her
softest touch hides treacherous claws. The
cool waters invite us in to drown; the
domestic hearth burns up in the hour of
sleep, and makes an end of all. Everything is good or bad, helpful or deadly,
not in itself, but by its circumstances.
For a few bright days in England the
hurricane must break forth and the North
Sea pay a toll of populous ships. And
when the universal music has led lovers
into the path of dalliance, confident of
Nature's sympathy, suddenly the air shifts
into a minor, and death makes a clutch
from his ambuscade below the bed of
marriage. For death is given in a kiss;

the dearest kindnesses are fatal; and into
this life, where one thing preys upon
another, the child too often makes its entrance from the mother's corpse. It is no
wonder, with so traitorous a scheme of
things, if the wise people who created
for us the idea of Pan thought that of
all fears the fear of him was the most
terrible, since it embraces all. And still we
preserve the phrase—a panic terror. To
reckon dangers too curiously, to hearken
too intently for the threat that runs through
all the winning music of the world, to
hold back the hand from the rose because
of the thorn, and from life because of
death—this is to be afraid of Pan. Highly
respectable citizens who flee life's pleasures and responsibilities and keep, with
upright hat, upon the midway of custom,
avoiding the right hand and the left, the
ecstasies and the agonies, how surprised
they would be if they could hear their
attitude mythologically expressed, and
knew themselves as tooth-chattering ones,
who flee from Nature because they fear
the hand of Nature's God! Shrilly sound
Pan's pipes; and behold the banker instantly concealed in the bank parlor! For
to distrust one's impulses is to be recreant
to Pan.

There are moments when the mind refuses to be satisfied with evolution, and
demands a ruddier presentation of the
sum of man's experience. Sometimes the
mood is brought about by laughter at
the humorous side of life, as when, ab-
stracting ourselves from earth, we imagine
people plodding on foot, or seated in
ships and speedy trains, with the planet
all the while whirling in the opposite
direction, so that, for all their hurry,
they travel back-foremost through the universe of space. Sometimes it comes by
the spirit of delight, and sometimes by the
spirit of terror. At least, there will always
be hours when we refuse to be put off by
the feint of explanation, nicknamed science; and demand instead some palpitating
image of our estate, that shall represent
the troubled and uncertain element in
which we dwell, and satisfy reason by the
means of art. Science writes of the world
as if with the cold finger of a starfish; it
is all true; but what is it when compared

to the reality of which it discourses? where hearts beat high in April, and death strikes, and hills totter in the earthquake, and there is a glamour over all the objects of sight, and a thrill in all noises for the ear, and Romance herself has made her dwelling among men? So we come back to the old myth, and hear the goat-footed piper making the music which is itself the charm and terror of things; and when a glen invites our visiting footsteps, fancy that Pan leads us thither with a gracious tremolo; or when our hearts quail at the thunder or the cataract, tell ourselves that he has stamped his foot in the nigh thicket.

[1878]

ÆS TRIPLEX

The changes wrought by death are in themselves so sharp and final, and so terrible and melancholy in their consequences, that the thing stands alone in man's experience, and has no parallel upon earth. It outdoes all other accidents because it is the last of them. Sometimes it leaps suddenly upon its victims like a Thug; sometimes it lays a regular siege and creeps upon their citadel during a score of years. And when the business is done, there is sore havoc made in other people's lives, and a pin knocked out by which many subsidiary friendships hung together. There are empty chairs, solitary walks, and single beds at night. Again, in taking away our friends, death does not take them away utterly, but leaves behind a mocking, tragical, and soon intolerable residue, which must be hurriedly concealed. Hence a whole chapter of sights and customs striking to the mind, from the pyramids of Egypt to the gibbets and dule trees of mediæval Europe. The poorest persons have a bit of pageant going toward the tomb; memorial stones are set up over the least memorable; and, in order to preserve some show of respect for what remains of our old loves and friendships, we must accompany it with much grimly ludicrous ceremonial, and the hired undertaker parades before the door. All this, and much more of the same sort, accompanied by the eloquence of poets, has gone a great way to put humanity in error; nay, in many philosophies the error has been embodied and laid down with every circumstance of logic; although in real life the bustle and swiftness, in leaving people little time to think, have not let them time enough to go dangerously wrong in practice.

As a matter of fact, although few things are spoken of with more fearful whisperings than this prospect of death, few have less influence on conduct under healthy circumstances. We have all heard of cities in South America built upon the side of fiery mountains, and how, even in this tremendous neighborhood, the inhabitants are not a jot more impressed by the solemnity of mortal conditions than if they were delving gardens in the greenest corner of England. There are serenades and suppers and much gallantry among the myrtles overhead; and meanwhile the foundation shudders underfoot, the bowels of the mountain growl, and at any moment living ruin may leap sky-high into the moonlight, and tumble man and his merry-making in the dust. In the eyes of very young people, and very dull old ones, there is something indescribably reckless and desperate in such a picture. It seems not credible that respectable married people, with umbrellas, should find appetite for a bit of supper within quite a long distance of a fiery mountain; ordinary life begins to smell of high-handed debauch when it is carried on so close to a catastrophe; and even cheese and salad, it seems, could hardly be relished in such circumstances without something like a defiance of the Creator. It should be a place for nobody but hermits dwelling in prayer and maceration, or mere born-devils drowning care in a perpetual carouse.

And yet, when one comes to think upon it calmly, the situation of these South American citizens forms only a very pale figure for the state of ordinary mankind. This world itself, travelling blindly and swiftly in overcrowded space, among a million other worlds travelling blindly and swiftly in contrary directions, may very well come by a knock that would set it into explosion like a penny squib. And what, pathologically looked at, is the human body with all its organs, but a mere bagful of petards? The least of these is as dangerous to the whole economy as the ship's powder-magazine to the ship; and with every breath we breathe, and every meal we eat, we are putting one or more of them in peril. If we clung as devotedly as some philosophers pretend we do to the abstract idea of life, or were half as frightened as they make out we are, for the subversive accident that ends it all, the trumpets might sound by the hour and no one would follow them into battle—the bluepeter might fly at the truck, but who would climb into a sea-going ship? Think (if these philosophers were right) with what a preparation of spirit we should affront the daily peril of the dinner-table: a deadlier spot than any battle-field in history, where the far greater proportion of our ancestors have miserably left their bones! What woman would ever be lured into marriage, so much more dangerous than the wildest sea? And what would it be to grow old? For, after a certain distance, every step we take in life we find the ice growing thinner below our feet, and all around us and behind us we see our contemporaries going through. By the time a man gets well into the seventies, his continued existence is a mere miracle; and when he lays his old bones in bed for the night, there is an overwhelming probability that he will never see the day. Do the old men mind it, as a matter of fact? Why, no. They were never merrier; they have their grog at night, and tell the raciest stories; they hear of the death of people about their own age, or even younger, not as if it was a grisly warning, but with a simple childlike pleasure at having outlived some one else; and when a draught might puff them out like a guttering candle, or a bit of a stumble shatter them like so much glass, their old hearts keep sound and unaffrighted, and they go on, bubbling with laughter, through years of man's age compared to which the valley at Balaclava was as safe and peaceful as a village cricket-green on Sunday. It may fairly be questioned (if we look to the peril only) whether it was a much more daring feat for Curtius to plunge into the gulf, than for any old gentleman of ninety to doff his clothes and clamber into bed.

Indeed, it is a memorable subject for consideration, with what unconcern and gaiety mankind pricks on along the Valley of the Shadow of Death. The whole way is one wilderness of snares, and the end of it, for those who fear the last pinch, is irrevocable ruin. And yet we go spinning through it all, like a party for the Derby. Perhaps the reader remembers one of the humorous devices of the deified Caligula: how he encouraged a vast concourse of holiday-makers on to his bridge over Baiæ bay; and when they were in the height of their enjoyment, turned loose the Prætorian guards among the company, and had them tossed into the sea. This is no bad miniature of the dealings of nature with the transitory race of man. Only, what a checkered picnic we have of it, even while it lasts! and into what great waters, not to be crossed by any swimmer, God's pale Prætorian throws us over in the end!

We live the time that a match flickers; we pop the cork of a ginger-beer bottle, and the earthquake swallows us on the instant. Is it not odd, is it not incongruous, is it not, in the highest sense of human speech, incredible, that we should think so highly of the ginger-beer, and regard so little the devouring earthquake? The love of Life and the fear of Death are two famous phrases that grow harder to understand the more we think about them. It is a well-known fact that an immense proportion of boat accidents would never happen if people held the sheet in their hands instead of making it fast; and yet, unless it be some martinet of a professional mariner or some landsman with shattered nerves, every one of God's creatures makes it fast. A strange instance of man's unconcern and brazen boldness in the face of death!

We confound ourselves with metaphysical phrases, which we import into daily talk with noble inappropriateness. We have no idea of what death is, apart from its circumstances and some of its consequences to others; and although we have some experience of living, there is not a man on earth who has flown so high into abstraction as to have any practical guess at the meaning of the word *life*. All literature, from Job and Omar Khayyam to Thomas Carlyle or Walt Whitman, is but an attempt to look upon the human state with such largeness of view as shall enable us to rise from the consideration of living to the Definition of Life. And our sages give us about the best satisfaction in their power when they say that it is a vapor, or a show, or made of the same stuff with dreams. Philosophy, in its more rigid 10 sense, has been at the same work for ages; and after a myriad bald heads have wagged over the problem, and piles of words have been heaped one upon another into dry and cloudy volumes without end, philosophy has the honor of laying before us, with modest pride, her contribution toward the subject: that life is a Permanent Possibility of Sensation. Truly a fine result! A man may very well love beef, 20 or hunting, or a woman; but surely, surely, not a Permanent Possibility of Sensation! He may be afraid of a precipice, or a dentist, or a large enemy with a club, or even an undertaker's man; but not certainly of abstract death. We may trick with the word life in its dozen senses until we are weary of tricking; we may argue in terms of all the philosophies on earth, but one fact remains true throughout— 30 that we do not love life, in the sense that we are greatly preoccupied about its conservation—that we do not, properly speaking, love life at all, but living. Into the views of the least careful there will enter some degree of providence; no man's eyes are fixed entirely on the passing hour; but although we have some anticipation of good health, good weather, wine, active employment, love, and self-approval, the 40 sum of these anticipations does not amount to anything like a general view of life's possibilities and issues; nor are those who cherish them most vividly, at all the most scrupulous of their personal safety. To be deeply interested in the accidents of our existence, to enjoy keenly the mixed texture of human experience, rather leads a man to disregard precautions, and risk his neck against a straw. For surely the 50 love of living is stronger in an Alpine climber roping over a peril, or a hunter riding merrily at a stiff fence, than in a creature who lives upon a diet and walks a measured distance in the interest of his constitution.

There is a great deal of very vile nonsense talked upon both sides of the matter: tearing divines reducing life to the dimensions of a mere funeral procession, so short as to be hardly decent; and melancholy unbelievers yearning for the tomb as if it were a world too far away. Both sides must feel a little ashamed of their performances now and again when they draw in their chairs to dinner. Indeed, a good meal and a bottle of wine is an answer to most standard works upon the question. When a man's heart warms to his viands, he forgets a great deal of sophistry, and soars into a rosy zone of contemplation. Death may be knocking at the door, like the Commander's statue; 20 we have something else in hand, thank God, and let him knock. Passing bells are ringing all the world over. All the world over, and every hour, some one is parting company with all his aches and ecstasies. For us also the trap is laid. But we are so fond of life that we have no leisure to entertain the terror of death. It is a honeymoon with us all through, and none of the longest. Small blame to us if we give 30 our whole hearts to this glowing bride of ours, to the appetites, to honor, to the hungry curiosity of the mind, to the pleasure of the eyes in nature, and the pride of our own nimble bodies.

We all of us appreciate the sensations; but as for caring about the Permanence of the Possibility, a man's head is generally very bald, and his senses very dull, before he comes to that. Whether we regard 40 life as a lane leading to a dead wall—a mere bag's end, as the French say—or whether we think of it as a vestibule or gymnasium, where we wait our turn and prepare our faculties for some more noble destiny; whether we thunder in a pulpit, or pule in little atheistic poetry-books, about its vanity and brevity; whether we look justly for years of health and vigor, or are about to mount into a Bath chair, 50 as a step toward the hearse; in each and all of these views and situations there is but one conclusion possible: that a man should stop his ears against paralyzing terror, and run the race that is set before him with a single mind. No one surely could have recoiled with more heartache and terror from the thought of death than our respected lexicographer; and yet we know how little it affected his conduct, how wisely and boldly he walked, and in what a fresh and lively vein he spoke of life. Already an old man, he ventured on his Highland tour; and his heart, bound with triple brass, did not recoil before 10 twenty-seven individual cups of tea. As courage and intelligence are the two qualities best worth a good man's cultivation, so it is the first part of intelligence to recognize our precarious estate in life, and the first part of courage to be not at all abashed before the fact. A frank and somewhat headlong carriage, not looking too anxiously before, not dallying in maudlin regret over the past, stamps the man who 20 is well armored for this world.

And not only well armored for himself, but a good friend and a good citizen to boot. We do not go to cowards for tender dealings; there is nothing so cruel as panic; the man who has least fear for his own carcass, has most time to consider others. That eminent chemist who took his walks abroad in tin shoes, and subsisted wholly upon tepid milk, had all his work cut out 30 for him in considerate dealings with his own digestion. So soon as prudence has begun to grow up in the brain, like a dismal fungus, it finds its first expression in a paralysis of generous acts. The victim begins to shrink spiritually; he develops a fancy for parlors with a regulated temperature, and takes his morality on the principle of tin shoes and tepid milk. The care of one important body or soul becomes 40 so engrossing, that all the noises of the outer world begin to come thin and faint into the parlor with the regulated temperature; and the tin shoes go equably forward over blood and rain. To be otherwise is to ossify; and the scruple-monger ends by standing stock-still. Now the man who has his heart on his sleeve, and a good whirling weathercock of a brain, who reckons his life as a thing to be dashingly used and cheer- 50 fully hazarded, makes a very different acquaintance of the world, keeps all his pulses going true and fast, and gathers impetus as he runs, until, if he be running toward

anything better than wildfire, he may shoot up and become a constellation in the end. Lord, look after his health; Lord, have a care of his soul, says he; and he has at the key of the position, and swashes through incongruity and peril toward his aim. Death is on all sides of him with pointed batteries, as he is on all sides of all of us; unfortunate surprises gird him round; mimmouthed friends and relations hold up their hands in quite a little elegiacal synod about his path: and what cares he for all this? Being a true lover of living, a fellow with something pushing and spontaneous in his inside, he must, like any other soldier, in any other stirring, deadly warfare, push on at his best pace until he touch the goal. "A peerage or Westminster Abbey!" cried Nelson in his bright, boyish, heroic manner. These are great incentives; not for any of these, but for the plain satisfaction of living, of being about their business in some sort or other, do the brave, serviceable men of every nation tread down the nettle danger, and pass flyingly over all the stumbling-blocks of prudence. Think of the heroism of Johnson, think of that superb indifference to mortal limitation that set him upon his dictionary, and carried him through triumphantly until the end! Who, if he were wisely considerate of things at large, would ever embark upon any work much more considerable than a halfpenny post card? Who would project a serial novel, after Thackeray and Dickens had each fallen in mid-course? Who would find heart enough to begin to live, if he dallied with the consideration of death?

And, after all, what sorry and pitiful quibbling all this is! To forego all the issues of living in a parlor with the regulated temperature—as if that were not to die a hundred times over, and for ten years at a stretch! As if it were not to die in one's own lifetime, and without even the sad immunities of death! As if it were not to die, and yet be the patient spectators of our own pitiable change! The Permanent Possibility is preserved, but the sensations carefully held at arm's length, as if one kept a photographic plate in a dark chamber. It is better to lose health like a spendthrift than to waste it like a miser.

It is better to live and be done with it, than to die daily in the sickroom. By all means begin your folio; even if the doctor does not give you a year, even if he hesitates about a month, make one brave push and see what can be accomplished in a week. It is not only in finished undertakings that we ought to honor useful labor. A spirit goes out of the man who means execution, which outlives the most untimely ending. All who have meant good work with their whole hearts, have done good work, although they may die before they have the time to sign it. Every heart that has beat strong and cheerfully has left a hopeful impulse behind it in the world, and bettered the tradition of mankind. And even if death catch people, like an open pitfall, and in mid-career, laying out vast projects, and planning monstrous foundations, flushed with hope, and their mouths full of boastful language, they should be at once tripped up and silenced: is there not something brave and spirited in such a termination? and does not life go down with a better grace, foaming in full body over a precipice, than miserably straggling to an end in sandy deltas? When the Greeks made their fine saying that those whom the gods love die young, I cannot help believing they had this sort of death also in their eye. For surely, at whatever age it overtake the man, this is to die young. Death has not been suffered to take so much as an illusion from his heart. In the hot-fit of life, a-tiptoe on the highest point of being, he passes at a bound on to the other side. The noise of the mallet and chisel is scarcely quenched, the trumpets are hardly done blowing, when, trailing with him clouds of glory, this happy-starred, full-blooded spirit shoots into the spiritual land.

[1878]

MEMORIES AND PORTRAITS

A GOSSIP ON ROMANCE

In anything fit to be called by the name of reading, the process itself should be absorbing and voluptuous; we should gloat over a book, be rapt clean out of ourselves, and rise from the perusal, our mind filled with the busiest, kaleidoscopic dance of images, incapable of sleep or of continuous thought. The words, if the book be eloquent, should run thenceforward in our ears like the noise of breakers, and the story, if it be a story, repeat itself in a thousand colored pictures to the eye. It was for this last pleasure that we read so closely, and loved our books so dearly, in the bright, troubled period of boyhood. Eloquence and thought, character and conversation, were but obstacles to brush aside as we dug blithely after a certain sort of incident, like a pig for truffles. For my part, I liked a story to begin with an old wayside inn where, "toward the close of the year 17–," several gentlemen in three-cocked hats were playing bowls. A friend of mine preferred the Malabar coast in a storm, with a ship beating to windward, and a scowling fellow of herculean proportions striding along the beach; he, to be sure, was a pirate. This was further afield than my home-keeping fancy loved to travel, and designed altogether for a larger canvas than the tales that I affected. Give me a highwayman and I was full to the brim; a Jacobite would do, but the highwayman was my favorite dish. I can still hear that merry clatter of the hoofs along the moonlit lane; night and the coming of the day are still related in my mind with the doings of John Rann or Jerry Abershaw; and the words "post-chaise," the "great North road," "ostler," and "nag" still sound in my ears like poetry. One and all, at least, and each with his particular fancy, we read story-books in childhood, not for eloquence or character or thought, but for some quality of the brute incident. That quality was not mere bloodshed or wonder. Although each of these was welcome in its place, the charm for the sake of which we read depended on something different from either. My elders used to read novels aloud; and I can still remember four different passages which I heard, before I was ten, with the same keen and lasting pleasure. One I discovered long afterward to be the admirable opening of *What Will He Do with It:* it was no wonder I was pleased with that. The other three still remain unidentified. One is a little vague; it was about a dark, tall house at night, and people groping on the stairs by the light that escaped from the open door of a sick-room. In another, a lover left a ball, and went walking in a cool, dewy park, whence he could watch the lighted windows and the figures of the dancers as they moved. This was the most sentimental impression I think I had yet received, for a child is somewhat deaf to the sentimental. In the last, a poet, who had been tragically wrangling with his wife, walked forth on the sea-beach on a tempestuous night and witnessed the horrors of a wreck. Different as they are, all these early favorites have a common note—they have all a touch of the romantic.

Drama is the poetry of conduct, romance the poetry of circumstance. The pleasure that we take in life is of two sorts—the active and the passive. Now we are conscious of a great command over our destiny; anon we are lifted up by circumstance, as by a breaking wave, and dashed we know not how into the future. Now we are pleased by our conduct, anon merely pleased by our surroundings. It would be hard to say which of these modes of satisfaction is the more effective, but the latter is surely the more constant. Conduct is three parts of life, they say; but I think they put it high. There is a vast deal in life and letters both which is not immoral, but simply a-moral; which either does not regard the human will at all, or deals with it in obvious and healthy relations; where the interest turns, not upon what a man shall choose to do, but on how he manages to do it; not on the passionate slips and hesitations of the conscience, but on the problems of the body and of the practical intelligence, in clean, open-air adventure, the shock of arms or the diplomacy of life. With such material as this it is impossible to build a play, for the serious theatre exists solely on moral grounds, and is a standing proof of the dissemination of the human conscience. But it is possible to build, upon this ground, the most joyous of verses, and the most lively, beautiful, and buoyant tales.

One thing in life calls for another; there is a fitness in events and places. The sight of a pleasant arbor puts it in our mind to sit there. One place suggests work, another idleness, a third early rising and long rambles in the dew. The effect of night, of any flowing water, of lighted cities, of the peep of day, of ships, of the open ocean, calls up in the mind an army of anonymous desires and pleasures. Something, we feel, should happen; we know not what, yet we proceed in quest of it. And many of the happiest hours of life fleet by us in this vain attendance on the genius of the place and moment. It is thus that tracts of young fir, and low rocks that reach into deep soundings, particularly torture and delight me. Something must have happened in such places, and perhaps ages back, to members of my race; and when I was a child I tried in vain to invent appropriate games for them, as I still try, just as vainly, to fit them with the proper story. Some places speak distinctly. Certain dank gardens cry aloud for a murder; certain old houses demand to be haunted; certain coasts are set apart for shipwreck. Other spots again seem to abide their destiny, suggestive and impenetrable, "miching mallecho." The inn at Burford Bridge, with its arbors and green gardens and silent, eddying river—though it is known already as the place where Keats wrote some of his *Endymion* and Nelson parted from his Emma—still seems to wait the coming of the appropriate legend. Within these ivied walls, behind these old green shutters, some further business smoulders, waiting for its hour. The old Hawes Inn at the Queen's Ferry makes a similar call upon my fancy. There it stands, apart from the town, beside the pier, in a climate of its own, half inland, half marine—in front, the ferry bubbling with the tide and the guardship swinging to her anchor; behind, the old garden with the trees. Americans seek it already for the sake of Lovel and Oldbuck, who dined there at the beginning of the *Antiquary.* But you need not tell me—that is not all; there is some story, unrecorded or not yet complete, which must express the meaning of that inn more fully. So it is with names and faces; so it is with incidents that are idle and inconclusive in themselves, and yet seem like the beginning of some quaint romance, which the all-careless author leaves untold. How many of these romances have we not seen determined at their birth; how many people have met us with a look of meaning in their eye, and sunk at once into trivial acquaintances; to how many places have we not drawn near, with express intimations—"here my destiny awaits me" —and we have but dined there and passed on! I have lived both at the Hawes and Burford in a perpetual flutter, on the heels, as it seemed, of some adventure that should justify the place; but though the feeling had me to bed at night and called me again at morning in one unbroken round of pleasure and suspense, nothing befell me in either worth remark. The man of the hour had not yet come; but some day, I think, a boat shall put off from the Queen's Ferry, fraught with a dear cargo, and some frosty night a horseman, on a tragic errand, rattle with his whip upon the green shutters of the inn at Burford.

Now, this is one of the natural appetites with which any lively literature has to count. The desire for knowledge, I had almost added the desire for meat, is not more deeply seated than this demand for fit and striking incident. The dullest of clowns tells, or tries to tell, himself a story, as the feeblest of children uses invention in his play; and even as the imaginative grown person, joining in the game, at once enriches it with many delightful circumstances, the great creative writer shows us the realization and the apotheosis of the day-dreams of common men. His stories may be nourished with the realities of life, but their true mark is to satisfy the nameless longings of the reader, and to obey the ideal laws of the day-dream. The right kind of thing should fall out in the right kind of place; the right kind of thing should follow; and not only the characters talk aptly and think naturally, but all the circumstances in a tale answer one to another like notes in music. The threads of a story come from time to time together and make a picture in the web; the characters fall from time to time into some attitude to each other or to nature, which stamps the story home like an illustration. Crusoe recoiling from the footprint, Achilles shouting over against the Trojans, Ulysses bending the great bow, Christian running with his fingers in his ears, these are each culminating moments in the legend, and each has been printed on the mind's eye forever. Other things we may forget; we may forget the words, although they are beautiful; we may forget the author's comment, although perhaps it was ingenious and true; but these epoch-making scenes, which put the last mark of truth upon a story and fill up, at one blow, our capacity for sympathetic pleasure, we so adopt into the very bosom of our mind that neither time nor tide can efface or weaken the impression. This, then, is the plastic part of literature: to embody character, thought, or emotion in some act or attitude that shall be remarkably striking to the mind's eye. This is the highest and hardest thing to do in words; the thing which, once accomplished, equally delights the schoolboy and the sage, and makes, in its own right, the quality of epics. Compared with this, all other purposes in literature, except the purely lyrical or the purely philosophic, are bastard in nature, facile of execution, and feeble in result. It is one thing to write about the inn at Burford, or to describe scenery with the word-painters; it is quite another to seize on the heart of the suggestion and make a country famous with a legend. It is one thing to remark and to dissect, with the most cutting logic, the complications of life, and of the human spirit; it is quite another to give them body and blood in the story of Ajax or of Hamlet. The first is literature, but the second is something besides, for it is likewise art.

English people of the present day are apt, I know not why, to look somewhat down on incident, and reserve their admiration for the clink of teaspoons and the accents of the curate. It is thought clever to write a novel with no story at all, or at least with a very dull one. Reduced even to the lowest terms, a certain interest can be communicated by the art of narrative; a sense of human kinship stirred; and a kind of monotonous fitness, comparable to the words and air of *Sandy's Mull*, preserved among the infinitesimal occurrences recorded. Some people work, in this manner, with even a strong touch. Mr. Trollope's inimitable clergymen naturally arise to the mind in this connection. But even Mr. Trollope does not confine himself to chronicling small beer. Mr. Crawley's collision with the Bishop's wife, Mr. Melnette dallying in the deserted banquet-room, are typical incidents, especially conceived, fitly embodying a crisis. Or again look at Thackeray. If Rawdon Crawley's blow were not delivered, *Vanity Fair* would cease to be a work of art. That scene is the chief ganglion of the tale; and the discharge of energy from Rawdon's fist is the reward and consolation of the reader. The end of *Esmond* is a yet wider excursion from the author's customary fields; the scene at Castlewood is pure Dumas; the great and wily English borrower has here borrowed from the great, unblushing French thief; as usual, he has borrowed admirably well, and the breaking of the sword rounds off the best of all his books with a manly, martial note. But perhaps nothing can more strongly illustrate the necessity for marking incident than to compare the living fame of *Robinson Crusoe* with the discredit of *Clarissa Harlowe*. *Clarissa* is a book of a far more startling import, worked out, on a great canvas, with inimitable courage and unflagging art. It contains wit, character, passion, plot, conversations full of spirit and insight, letters sparkling with unstrained humanity; and if the death of the heroine be somewhat frigid and artificial, the last days of the hero strike the only note of what we now call Byronism, between the Elizabethans and Byron himself. And yet a little story of a shipwrecked sailor, with not a tenth part of the style nor a thousandth part of the wisdom, exploring none of the arcana of humanity and deprived of the perennial interest of love, goes on from edition to edition, ever young, while *Clarissa* lies upon the shelves unread. A friend of mine, a Welsh blacksmith, was twenty-five years old and could neither read nor write, when he heard a chapter of *Robinson* read aloud in a farm kitchen. Up to that moment he had sat content, huddled in his ignorance, but he left that farm another man. There were day-dreams, it appeared, divine day-dreams, written and printed and bound, and to be bought for money and enjoyed at pleasure. Down he sat that day, painfully learned to read Welsh, and returned to borrow the book. It had been lost, nor could he find another copy but one that was in English. Down he sat once more, learned English, and at length, and with entire delight, read *Robinson*. It was like the story of a love-chase. If he had heard a letter from *Clarissa*, would he have been fired with the same chivalrous ardor? I wonder. Yet *Clarissa* has every quality that can be shown in prose, one alone excepted—pictorial or picture-making romance. While *Robinson* depends, for the most part and with the overwhelming majority of its readers, on the charm of circumstance.

In the highest achievements of the art of words, the dramatic and the pictorial, the moral and romantic interest, rise and fall together by a common and organic law. Situation is animated with passion, passion clothed upon with situation. Neither exists for itself, but each inheres indissolubly with the other. This is high art; and not only the highest art possible in words, but the highest art of all, since it combines the greatest mass and diversity of the elements of truth and pleasure. Such are epics, and the few prose tales that have the epic weight. But as from a school of works, aping the creative, incident and romance are ruthlessly discarded, so may character and drama be omitted or subordinated to romance. There is one book, for example, more generally loved than Shakespeare, that captivates in childhood, and still delights in age—I mean the *Arabian Nights*—where you shall look in vain for moral or for intellectual interest. No human face or voice greets us among that wooden crowd of kings and genies, sorcerers and beggarmen. Adventure, on the most naked terms, furnishes forth the entertainment and is found enough. Dumas approaches perhaps nearest of any modern to these Arabian authors in the purely material charm of some of his romances. The early part of *Monte Cristo,* down to the finding of the treasure, is a piece of perfect story-telling; the man never breathed who shared these moving incidents without a tremor; and yet Faria is a thing of packthread and Dantès little more than a name. The sequel is one long-drawn error, gloomy, bloody, unnatural, and dull; but as for these early chapters, I do not believe there is another volume extant where you can breathe the same unmingled atmosphere of romance. It is very thin and light, to be sure, as on a high mountain; but it is brisk and clear and sunny in proportion. I saw the other day, with envy, an old and a very clever lady setting forth on a second or third voyage into *Monte Cristo.* Here are stories which powerfully affect the reader, which can be reperused at any age, and where the characters are no more than puppets. The bony fist of the showman visibly propels them; their springs are an open secret; their faces are of wood, their bellies filled with bran; and yet we thrillingly partake of their adventures. And the point may be illustrated still further. The last interview between Lucy and Richard Feverel is pure drama; more than that, it is the strongest scene, since Shakespeare, in the English tongue. Their first meeting by the river, on the other hand, is pure romance; it has nothing to do with character; it might happen to any other boy and maiden, and be none the less delightful for the change. And yet I think he would be a bold man who should choose between these passages. Thus, in the same book, we may have two scenes, each capital in its order: in the one, human passion, deep calling unto deep, shall utter its genuine voice; in the second, according circumstances, like instruments in tune, shall build up a trivial but desirable incident, such as we love to prefigure for ourselves; and in the end, in spite of the critics, we may hesitate to give the preference to either. The one may ask more genius—I do not say it does; but at least the other dwells as clearly in the memory.

True romantic art, again, makes a romance of all things. It reaches into the highest abstraction of the ideal; it does not refuse the most pedestrian realism. *Robinson Crusoe* is as realistic as it is romantic: both qualities are pushed to an extreme, and neither suffers. Nor does romance depend upon the material importance of the incidents. To deal with strong and deadly elements, banditti, pirates, war and murder, is to conjure with great names, and, in the event of failure, to double the disgrace. The arrival of Haydn and Consuelo at the Canon's villa is a very trifling incident; yet we may read a dozen boisterous stories from beginning to end, and not receive so fresh and stirring an impression of adventure. It was the scene of Crusoe at the wreck, if I remember rightly, that so bewitched my blacksmith. Nor is the fact surprising. Every single article the castaway recovers from the hulk is "a joy forever" to the man who reads of them. They are the things that should be found, and the bare enumeration stirs the blood. I found a glimmer of the same interest the other day in a new book, *The Sailor's Sweetheart,* by Mr. Clark Russell. The whole business of the brig *Morning Star* is very rightly felt and spiritedly written; but the clothes, the books and the money satisfy the reader's mind like things to eat. We are dealing here with the old cut-and-dry, legitimate interest of treasure trove. But even treasure trove can be made dull. There are few people who have not groaned under the plethora of goods that fell to the lot of the *Swiss Family Robinson,* that dreary family. They found article after article, creature after creature, from milk kine to pieces of ordnance, a whole consignment; but no informing taste had presided over the selection, there was no smack or relish in the invoice; and these riches left the fancy cold. The box of goods in Verne's *Mysterious Island* is another case in point; there was no gusto and no glamor about that; it might have come from a shop. But the two hundred and seventy-eight Australian sovereigns on board the *Morning Star* fell upon me like a surprise that I had expected; whole vistas of secondary stories, besides the one in hand, radiated forth from that discovery, as they radiate from a striking particular in life; and I was made for the moment as happy as a reader has the right to be.

To come at all at the nature of this quality of romance, we must bear in mind the peculiarity of our attitude to any art. No art produces illusion; in the theatre we never forget that we are in the theatre; and while we read a story, we sit wavering between two minds, now merely clapping our hands at the merit of the performance, now condescending to take an active part in fancy with the characters. This last is the triumph of romantic story-telling: when the reader consciously plays at being the hero, the scene is a good scene. Now, in character-studies the pleasure that we take is critical; we watch, we approve, we smile at incongruities, we are moved to sudden heats of sympathy with courage, suffering, or virtue. But the characters are still themselves, they are not us; the more clearly they are depicted, the more widely do they stand away from us, the more imperiously do they thrust us back into our place as a spectator. I cannot identify myself with Rawdon Crawley or with Eugène de Rastignac, for I have scarce a hope or fear in common with them. It is not character but incident that woos us out of our reserve. Something happens as we desire to have it happen to ourselves; some situation, that we have long dallied with in fancy, is realized in the story with enticing and appropriate details. Then we forget the characters; then we push the hero aside; then we plunge into the tale in our own person and bathe in fresh experience; and then, and then only, do we say we have been reading a romance. It is not only pleasurable things that we imagine in our day-dreams; there are lights in which we are willing to contemplate even the idea of our own death; ways in which it seems as if it would amuse us to be cheated, wounded, or calumniated. It is thus possible to construct a story, even of tragic import, in which every incident, detail, and trick of circumstance shall be welcome to the reader's thoughts. Fiction is to the grown man what play is to the child; it is there that he changes the atmosphere and tenor of his life; and when the game so chimes with his fancy that he can join in it

with all his heart, when it pleases him with every turn, when he loves to recall it and dwells upon its recollection with entire delight, fiction is called romance.

Walter Scott is out and away the king of the romantics. *The Lady of the Lake* has no indisputable claim to be a poem beyond the inherent fitness and desirability of the tale. It is just such a story as a man would make up for himself, walking, in the best health and temper, through just such scenes as it is laid in. Hence it is that a charm dwells undefinable among these slovenly verses, as the unseen cuckoo fills the mountains with his note; hence, even after we have flung the book aside, the scenery and adventures remain present to the mind, a new and green possession, not unworthy of that beautiful name, *The Lady of the Lake,* or that direct, romantic opening,—one of the most spirited and poetical in literature,— "The stag at eve had drunk his fill." The same strength and the same weaknesses adorn and disfigure the novels. In that ill-written, ragged book, *The Pirate,* the figure of Cleveland—cast up by the sea on the resounding foreland of Dunrossness —moving, with the blood on his hands and the Spanish words on his tongue, among the simple islanders—singing a serenade under the window of his Shetland mistress—is conceived in the very highest manner of romantic invention. The words of his song, "Through groves of palm," sung in such a scene and by such a lover, clench, as in a nutshell, the emphatic contrast upon which the tale is built. In *Guy Mannering,* again, every incident is delightful to the imagination; and the scene when Harry Bertram lands at Ellangowan is a model instance of romantic method.

"'I remember the tune well,' he says, 'though I cannot guess what should at present so strongly recall it to my memory.' He took his flageolet from his pocket and played a simple melody. Apparently the tune awoke the corresponding associations of a damsel.... She immediately took up the song—

"'Are these the links of Forth, she said;
   Or are they the crooks of Dee,
   Or the bonny woods of Warroch Head
   That I so fain would see?'

" 'By heaven!' said Bertram, 'it is the very ballad.' "

On this quotation two remarks fall to be made. First, as an instance of modern feeling for romance, this famous touch of the flageolet and the old song is selected by Miss Braddon for omission. Miss Braddon's idea of a story, like Mrs. Todgers's idea of a wooden leg, were something strange to have expounded. As a matter of personal experience, Meg's appearance to old Mr. Bertram on the road, the ruins of Derncleugh, the scene of the flageolet, and the Dominie's recognition of Harry, are the four strong notes that continue to ring in the mind after the book is laid aside. The second point is still more curious. The reader will observe a mark of excision in the passage as quoted by me. Well, here is how it runs in the original: "A damsel who, close behind a fine spring about half-way down the descent, and which had once supplied the castle with water, was engaged in bleaching linen." A man who gave in such copy would be discharged from the staff of a daily paper. Scott has forgotten to prepare the reader for the presence of the "damsel"; he has forgotten to mention the spring and its relation to the ruin; and now, face to face with his omission, in-stead of trying back and starting fair, crams all this matter, tail foremost, into a single shambling sentence. It is not merely bad English, or bad style; it is abominably bad narrative besides.

Certainly the contrast is remarkable; and it is one that throws a strong light upon the subject of this paper. For here we have a man of the finest creative instinct touching with perfect certainty and charm the romantic junctures of his story; and we find him utterly careless, almost, it would seem, incapable, in the technical matter of style, and not only frequently weak, but frequently wrong in points of drama. In character parts, indeed, and particularly in the Scotch, he was delicate, strong, and truthful; but the trite, obliterated features of too many of his heroes have already wearied two generations of readers. At times his characters will speak with something far beyond propriety with a true heroic note; but on the next page they will be wading wearily forward with an un-grammatical and undramatic rigmarole of words. The man who could conceive and write the character of Elspeth of the Craig-burnfoot, as Scott has conceived and writ-ten it, had not only splendid romantic, but splendid tragic gifts. How comes it, then, that he could so often fob us off with languid, inarticulate twaddle?

It seems to me that the explanation is to be found in the very quality of his sur-prising merits. As his books are play to the reader, so were they play to him. He conjured up the romantic with delight, but he had hardly patience to describe it. He was a great day-dreamer, a seer of fit and beautiful and humorous visions, but hardly a great artist; hardly, in the manful sense, an artist at all. He pleased himself, and so he pleases us. Of the pleasures of his art he tasted fully; but of its toils and vigils and distresses never man knew less. A great romantic—an idle child.

[1882]

ESSAYS ON LITERATURE

BOOKS WHICH HAVE INFLUENCED ME

The Editor has somewhat insidiously laid a trap for his correspondents, the ques-tion put appearing at first so innocent, truly cutting so deep. It is not, indeed, until after some reconnaissance and review that the writer awakes to find himself engaged upon something in the nature of autobiography, or, perhaps worse, upon a chapter in the life of that little, beautiful brother whom we once all had, and whom we have all lost and mourned, the man we ought to have been, the man we hoped to be. But when word has been passed (even to an editor), it should, if possible, be kept; and if sometimes I am wise and say too little, and sometimes weak and say too much, the blame must lie at the door of the person who entrapped me.

The most influential books, and the tru-est in their influence, are works of fiction. They do not pin the reader to a dogma which he must afterward discover to be inexact; they do not teach him a lesson which he must afterward unlearn. They repeat, they rearrange, they clarify the lessons of life; they disengage us from ourselves, they constrain us to the acquaintance of others; and they show us the web of experience, not as we can see it for ourselves, but with a singular change—that monstrous, consuming *ego* of ours being, for the nonce, struck out. To be so, they must be reasonably true to the human comedy; and any work that is so serves the turn of instruction. But the course of our education is answered best by those poems and romances where we breathe a magnanimous atmosphere of thought and meet generous and pious characters. Shakespeare has served me best. Few living friends have had upon me an influence so strong for good as Hamlet or Rosalind. The last character, already well beloved in the reading, I had the good fortune to see, I must think, in an impressionable hour, played by Mrs. Scott Siddons. Nothing has ever more moved, more delighted, more refreshed me; nor has the influence quite passed away. Kent's brief speech over the dying Lear had a great effect upon my mind, and was the burden of my reflections for long, so profoundly, so touchingly generous did it appear in sense, so overpowering in expression. Perhaps my dearest and best friend outside of Shakespeare is D'Artagnan—the elderly D'Artagnan of the *Vicomte de Bragelonne*. I knew not a more human soul, nor, in his way, a finer; I shall be very sorry for the man who is so much of a pedant in morals that he cannot learn from the Captain of Musketeers. Lastly, I must name the *Pilgrim's Progress*, a book that breathes of every beautiful and valuable emotion.

But of works of art little can be said; their influence is profound and silent, like the influence of nature; they mould by contact; we drink them up like water, and are bettered, yet know not how. It is in books more specifically didactic that we can follow out the effect, and distinguish and weigh and compare. A book which has been very influential upon me fell early into my hands, and so may stand first, though I think its influence was only sensible later

on, and perhaps still keeps growing, for it is a book not easily outlived: the *Essais* of Montaigne. That temperate and genial picture of life is a great gift to place in the hands of persons of to-day; they will find in these smiling pages a magazine of heroism and wisdom, all of an antique strain; they will have their "linen decencies" and excited orthodoxies fluttered, and will (if they have any gift of reading) perceive that these have not been fluttered without some excuse and ground of reason; and (again if they have any gift of reading) they will end by seeing that this old gentleman was in a dozen ways a finer fellow, and held in a dozen ways a nobler view of life, than they or their contemporaries.

The next book, in order of time, to influence me, was the New Testament, and in particular the Gospel according to St. Matthew. I believe it would startle and move any one if they could make a certain effort of imagination and read it freshly like a book, not droningly and dully like a portion of the Bible. Any one would then be able to see in it those truths which we are all courteously supposed to know and all modestly refrain from applying. But upon this subject it is perhaps better to be silent.

I come next to Whitman's *Leaves of Grass*, a book of singular service, a book which tumbled the world upside down for me, blew into space a thousand cobwebs of genteel and ethical illusion, and, having thus shaken my tabernacle of lies, set me back again upon a strong foundation of all the original and manly virtues. But it is, once more, only a book for those who have the gift of reading. I will be very frank—I believe it is so with all good books except, perhaps, fiction. The average man lives, and must live, so wholly in convention, that gunpowder charges of the truth are more apt to discompose than to invigorate his creed. Either he cries out upon blasphemy and indecency, and crouches the closer round that little idol of part-truths and part-conveniences which is the contemporary deity, or he is convinced by what is new, forgets what is old, and becomes truly blasphemous and indecent himself. New truth is only useful to supplement the old; rough truth is only wanted to expand, not to destroy, our civil and often elegant conventions. He who cannot judge had better stick to fiction and the daily papers. There he will get little harm, and, in the first at least, some good.

Close upon the back of my discovery of Whitman, I came under the influence of Herbert Spencer. No more persuasive rabbi exists, and few better. How much of his vast structure will bear the touch of time, how much is clay and how much brass, it were too curious to inquire. But his words, if dry, are always manly and honest; there dwells in his pages a spirit of highly abstract joy, plucked naked like an algebraic symbol but still joyful; and the reader will find there a *caput mortuum* of piety,[1] with little indeed of its loveliness, but with most of its essentials; and these two qualities make him a wholesome, as his intellectual vigor makes him a bracing, writer. I should be much of a hound if I lost my gratitude to Herbert Spencer.

Goethe's Life, by Lewes, had a great importance for me when it first fell into my hands—a strange instance of the partiality of man's good and man's evil. I know no one whom I less admire than Goethe; he seems a very epitome of the sins of genius, breaking open the doors of private life, and wantonly wounding friends, in that crowning offence of *Werther,* and in his own character a mere pen-and-ink Napoleon, conscious of the rights and duties of superior talents as a Spanish inquisitor was conscious of the rights and duties of his office. And yet in his fine devotion to his art, in his honest and serviceable friendship for Schiller, what lessons are contained! Biography, usually so false to its office, does here for once perform for us some of the work of fiction, reminding us, that is, of the truly mingled tissue of man's nature, and how huge faults and shining virtues cohabit and persevere in the same character. History serves us well to this effect, but in the originals, not in the pages of the popular epitomizer, who is bound, by the very nature of his task, to make us feel the difference of epochs in-stead of the essential identity of man, and even in the originals only to those who can recognize their own human virtues and defects in strange forms, often inverted and under strange names, often interchanged. Martial is a poet of no good repute, and it gives a man new thoughts to read his works dispassionately, and find in this unseemly jester's serious passages the image of a kind, wise, and self-respecting gentleman. It is customary, I suppose, in reading Martial, to leave out these pleasant verses; I never heard of them, at least, until I found them for myself; and this partiality is one among a thousand things that help to build up our distorted and hysterical conception of the great Roman Empire.

This brings us by a natural transition to a very noble book—the *Meditations* of Marcus Aurelius. The dispassionate gravity, the noble forgetfulness of self, the tenderness of others, that are there expressed and were practised on so great a scale in the life of its writer, make this book a book quite by itself. No one can read it and not be moved. Yet it scarcely or rarely appeals to the feelings—those very mobile, those not very trusty parts of man. Its address lies further back: its lesson comes more deeply home; when you have read, you carry away with you a memory of the man himself; it is as though you had touched a loyal hand, looked into brave eyes, and made a noble friend; there is another bond on you thenceforward, binding you to life and to the love of virtue.

Wordsworth should perhaps come next. Every one has been influenced by Wordsworth, and it is hard to tell precisely how. A certain innocence, a rugged austerity of joy, a sight of the stars, "the silence that is in the lonely hills," something of the cold thrill of dawn, cling to his work and give it a particular address to what is best in us. I do not know that you learn a lesson; you need not—Mill did not—agree with any one of his beliefs; and yet the spell is cast. Such are the best teachers: a dogma learned is only a new error—the old one was perhaps as good; but a spirit communicated is a perpetual possession. These best teachers climb beyond teaching to the plane of art;

---

[1] *caput mortuum:* literally 'dead head.' skull. Stevenson probably means 'dry residue,' but the phrase doesn't suggest enthusiasm.

it is themselves, and what is best in themselves, that they communicate.

I should never forgive myself if I forgot *The Egoist*. It is art, if you like, but it belongs purely to didactic art, and from all the novels I have read (and I have read thousands) stands in a place by itself. Here is a Nathan for the modern David; here is a book to send the blood into men's faces. Satire, the angry picture of human faults, is not great art; we can all be angry with our neighbor; what we want is to be shown, not his defects, of which we are too conscious, but his merits, to which we are too blind. And *The Egoist* is a satire; so much must be allowed; but it is a satire of a singular quality, which tells you nothing of that obvious mote, which is engaged from first to last with that invisible beam. It is yourself that is hunted down; these are your own faults that are dragged into the day and numbered, with lingering relish, with cruel cunning and precision. A young friend of Mr. Meredith's (as I have the story) came to him in an agony. "This is too bad of you," he cried. "Willoughby is me!" "No, my dear fellow," said the author; "he is all of us." I have read *The Egoist* five or six times myself, and I mean to read it again; for I am like the young friend of the anecdote—I think Willoughby an unmanly but a very serviceable exposure of myself.

I suppose, when I am done, I shall find that I have forgotten much that was most influential, as I see already I have forgotten Thoreau, and Hazlitt, whose paper "On the Spirit of Obligations" was a turning-point in my life, and Penn, whose little book of aphorisms had a brief but strong effect on me, and Mitford's *Tales of Old Japan,* wherein I learned for the first time the proper attitude of any rational man to his country's laws—a secret found, and kept, in the Asiatic islands. That I should commemorate all is more than I can hope or the Editor could ask. It will be more to the point, after having said so much upon improving books, to say a word or two about the improvable reader. The gift of reading, as I have called it, is not very common, nor very generally understood. It consists, first of all, in a vast intellectual endowment—a free grace, I find I must call it—by which a man rises to understand that he is not punctually right, nor those from whom he differs absolutely wrong. He may hold dogmas; he may hold them passionately; and he may know that others hold them but coldly, or hold them differently, or hold them not at all. Well, if he has the gift of reading, these others will be full of meat for him. They will see the other side of propositions and the other side of virtues. He need not change his dogma for that, but he may change his reading of that dogma, and he must supplement and correct his deductions from it. A human truth, which is always very much a lie, hides as much of life as it displays. It is men who hold another truth, or, as it seems to us, perhaps, a dangerous lie, who can extend our restricted field of knowledge, and rouse our drowsy consciences. Something that seems quite new, or that seems insolently false or very dangerous, is the test of a reader. If he tries to see what it means, what truth excuses it, he has the gift, and let him read. If he is merely hurt, or offended, or exclaims upon his author's folly, he had better take to the daily papers; he will never be a reader.

And here, with the aptest illustrative force, after I have laid down my part-truth, I must step in with its opposite. For, after all, we are vessels of a very limited content. Not all men can read all books; it is only in a chosen few that any man will find his appointed food; and the fittest lessons are the most palatable, and make themselves welcome to the mind. A writer learns this early, and it is his chief support; he goes on unafraid, laying down the law; and he is sure at heart that most of what he says is demonstrably false, and much of a mingled strain, and some hurtful, and very little good for service; but he is sure besides that when his words fall into the hands of any genuine reader, they will be weighed and winnowed, and only that which suits will be assimilated; and when they fall into the hands of one who cannot intelligently read, they come there quite silent and inarticulate, falling upon deaf ears, and his secret is kept as if he had not written. [1887]

RANDOM MEMORIES

PULVIS ET UMBRA

We look for some reward of our endeavors and are disappointed; not success, not happiness, not even peace of conscience, crowns our ineffectual efforts to do well. Our frailties are invincible, our virtues barren; the battle goes sore against us to the going down of the sun. The canting moralist tells us of right and wrong; and we look abroad, even on the face of our small earth, and find them change with every climate, and no country where some action is not honored for a virtue and none where it is not branded for a vice; and we look in our experience, and find no vital congruity in the wisest rules, but at the best a municipal fitness. It is not strange if we are tempted to despair of good. We ask too much. Our religions and moralities have been trimmed to flatter us, till they are all emasculate and sentimentalized, and only please and weaken. Truth is of a rougher strain. In the harsh face of life, faith can read a bracing gospel. The human race is a thing more ancient than the ten commandments; and the bones and revolutions of the Kosmos, in whose joints we are but moss and fungus, more ancient still.

I

Of the Kosmos in the last resort, science reports many doubtful things and all of them appalling. There seems no substance to this solid globe on which we stamp: nothing but symbols and ratios. Symbols and ratios carry us and bring us forth and beat us down; gravity that swings the incommensurable suns and worlds through space, is but a figment varying inversely as the squares of distances; and the suns and worlds themselves, imponderable figures of abstraction, NH_3 and H_2O. Consideration dares not dwell upon this view; that way madness lies; science carries us into zones of speculation, where there is no habitable city for the mind of man. But take the Kosmos with a grosser faith, as our senses give it us. We behold space sown with rotatory islands, suns and worlds and the shards and wrecks of systems: some, like the sun, still blazing; some rotting, like the earth; others, like the moon, stable in desolation. All of these we take to be made of something we call matter: a thing which no analysis can help us to conceive; to whose incredible properties no familiarity can reconcile our minds. This stuff, when not purified by the lustration of fire, rots uncleanly into something we call life; seized through all its atoms with a pediculous malady; swelling in tumors that become independent, sometimes even (by an abhorrent prodigy) locomotory; one splitting into millions, millions cohering into one, as the malady proceeds through varying stages. This vital putrescence of the dust, used as we are to it, yet strikes us with occasional disgust, and the profusion of worms in a piece of ancient turf, or the air of a marsh darkened with insects, will sometimes check our breathing so that we aspire for cleaner places. But none is clean: the moving sand is infected with lice; the pure spring, where it bursts out of the mountain, is a mere issue of worms; even in the hard rock the crystal is forming.

In two main shapes this eruption covers the countenance of the earth: the animal and the vegetable: one in some degree the inversion of the other: the second rooted to the spot; the first coming detached out of its natal mud, and scurrying abroad with the myriad feet of insects or towering into the heavens on the wings of birds: a thing so inconceivable that, if it be well considered, the heart stops. To what passes with the anchored vermin, we have little clue: doubtless they have their joys and sorrows, their delights and killing agonies: it appears not how. But of the locomotory, to which we ourselves belong, we can tell more. These share with us a thousand miracles: the miracles of sight, of hearing, of the projection of sound, things that bridge space; the miracles of memory and reason, by which the present is conceived, and when it is gone, its image kept living in the brains of man and brute; the miracle of reproduction, with its imperious desires and staggering consequences. And to put the last touch upon this mountain mass of the revolting and the inconceivable, all these prey upon each other, lives tearing other lives in pieces, cramming them inside themselves, and by that summary process, growing fat: the vegetarian, the whale, perhaps the tree, not less than the lion of the desert; for the vegetarian is only the eater of the dumb.

Meanwhile our rotatory island loaded with predatory life, and more drenched with blood, both animal and vegetable, than ever mutinied ship, scuds through space with unimaginable speed, and turns alternate cheeks to the reverberation of a blazing world, ninety million miles away.

II

What a monstrous spectre is this man, the disease of the agglutinated dust, lifting alternate feet or lying drugged with slumber; killing, feeding, growing, bringing forth small copies of himself; grown upon with hair like grass, fitted with eyes that move and glitter in his face; a thing to set children screaming;—and yet looked at nearlier, known as his fellows know him, how surprising are his attributes! Poor soul, here for so little, cast among so many hardships, filled with desires so incommensurate and so inconsistent, savagely surrounded, savagely descended, irremediably condemned to prey upon his fellow lives: who should have blamed him had he been of a piece with his destiny and a being merely barbarous? And we look and behold him instead filled with imperfect virtues: infinitely childish, often admirably valiant, often touchingly kind; sitting down, amidst his momentary life, to debate of right and wrong and the attributes of the deity; rising up to do battle for an egg or die for an idea; singling out his friends and his mate with cordial affection; bringing forth in pain, rearing with long-suffering solicitude, his young. To touch the heart of his mystery, we find in him one thought, strange to the point of lunacy: the thought of duty; the thought of something owing to himself, to his neighbor, to his God: an ideal of decency, to which he would rise if it were possible; a limit of shame, below which, if it be possible, he will not stoop. The design in most men is one of conformity;

here and there, in picked natures, it transcends itself and soars on the other side, arming martyrs with independence; but in all, in their degrees, it is a bosom thought:—Not in man alone, for we trace it in dogs and cats whom we know fairly well, and doubtless some similar point of honor sways the elephant, the oyster, and the louse, of whom we know so little:—But in man, at least, it sways with so complete an empire that merely selfish things come second, even with the selfish: that appetites are starved, fears are conquered, pains supported; that almost the dullest shrinks from the reproof of a glance, although it were a child's; and all but the most cowardly stand amid the risks of war; and the more noble, having strongly conceived an act as due to their ideal, affront and embrace death. Strange enough if, with their singular origin and perverted practice, they think they are to be rewarded in some future life: stranger still, if they are persuaded of the contrary, and think this blow, which they solicit, will strike them senseless for eternity. I shall be reminded what a tragedy of misconception and misconduct man at large presents: of organized injustice, cowardly violence, and treacherous crime; and of the damning imperfections of the best. They cannot be too darkly drawn. Man is indeed marked for failure in his efforts to do right. But where the best consistently miscarry, how tenfold more remarkable that all should continue to strive; and surely we should find it both touching and inspiriting, that in a field from which success is banished, our race should not cease to labor.

If the first view of this creature, stalking in his rotatory isle, be a thing to shake the courage of the stoutest, on this nearer sight, he startles us with an admiring wonder. It matters not where we look, under what climate we observe him, in what stage of society, in what depth of ignorance, burdened with what erroneous morality; by camp-fires in Assiniboia, the snow powdering his shoulders, the wind plucking his blanket, as he sits, passing the ceremonial calumet and uttering his grave opinions like a Roman senator; in ships at sea, a man inured to hardship and vile pleasures, his brightest hope a fiddle in a tavern and a bedizened trull who sells herself to rob him, and he for all that simple, innocent, cheerful, kindly like a child, constant to toil, brave to drown, for others; in the slums of cities, moving among indifferent millions to mechanical employments, without hope of change in the future, with scarce a pleasure in the present, and yet true to his virtues, honest up to his lights, kind to his neighbors, tempted perhaps in vain by the bright gin-palace, perhaps long-suffering with the drunken wife that ruins him; in India (a woman this time) kneeling with broken cries and streaming tears, as she drowns her child in the sacred river; in the brothel, the discard of society, living mainly on strong drink, fed with affronts, a fool, a thief, the comrade of thieves, and even here keeping the point of honor and the touch of pity, often repaying the world's scorn with service, often standing firm upon a scruple, and at a certain cost, rejecting riches:—everywhere some virtue cherished or affected, everywhere some decency of thought and carriage, everywhere the ensign of man's ineffectual goodness:—ah! if I could show you this! if I could show you these men and women, all the world over, in every stage of history, under every abuse of error, under every circumstance of failure, without hope, without help, without thanks, still obscurely fighting the lost fight of virtue, still clinging, in the brothel or on the scaffold, to some rag of honor, the poor jewel of their souls! They may seek to escape, and yet they cannot; it is not alone their privilege and glory, but their doom; they are condemned to some nobility; all their lives long, the desire of good is at their heels, the implacable hunter.

Of all earth's meteors, here at least is the most strange and consoling: that this ennobled lemur, this hair-crowned bubble of the dust, this inheritor of a few years and sorrows, should yet deny himself his rare delights, and add to his frequent pains, and live for an ideal, however misconceived. Nor can we stop with man. A new doctrine, received with screams a little while ago by canting moralists, and still not properly worked into the body of our thoughts, lights us a step farther into the heart of this rough but noble universe.

For nowadays the pride of man denies in vain his kinship with the original dust. He stands no longer like a thing apart. Close at his heels we see the dog, prince of another genus: and in him, too, we see dumbly testified the same cultus of an unattainable ideal, the same constancy in failure. Does it stop with the dog? We look at our feet where the ground is blackened with the swarming ant: a creature so small, so far from us in the hierarchy of brutes, that we can scarce trace and scarce comprehend his doings; and here also, in his ordered polities and rigorous justice, we see confessed the law of duty and the fact of individual sin. Does it stop, then, with the ant? Rather this desire of well-doing and this doom of frailty run through all the grades of life: rather is this earth, from the frosty top of Everest to the next margin of the internal fire, one stage of ineffectual virtues and one temple of pious tears and perseverance. The whole creation groaneth and travaileth together. It is the common and the godlike law of life. The browsers, the biters, the barkers, the hairy coats of field and forest, the squirrel in the oak, the thousand-footed creeper in the dust, as they share with us the gift of life, share with us the love of an ideal: strive like us—like us are tempted to grow weary of the struggle—to do well; like us receive at times unmerited refreshment, visitings of support, returns of courage; and are condemned like us to be crucified between that double law of the members and the will. Are they like us, I wonder, in the timid hope of some reward, some sugar with the drug? do they, too, stand aghast at unrewarded virtues, at the sufferings of those whom, in our partiality, we take to be just, and the prosperity of such as, in our blindness, we call wicked? It may be, and yet God knows what they should look for. Even while they look, even while they repent, the foot of man treads them by thousands in the dust, the yelping hounds burst upon their trail, the bullet speeds, the knives are heating in the den of the vivisectionist; or the dew falls, and the generation of a day is blotted out. For these are creatures, compared with whom our weakness is strength, our ignorance wisdom, our brief span eternity.

And as we dwell, we living things, in our isle of terror and under the imminent hand of death, God forbid it should be man the erected, the reasoner, the wise in his own eyes—God forbid it should be man that wearies in well-doing, that despairs of unrewarded effort, or utters the language of complaint. Let it be enough for faith, that the whole creation groans in mortal frailty, strives with unconquerable constancy: surely not all in vain.

[1888]

BIBLIOGRAPHIES, NOTES, AND COMMENTS

SELECTED GENERAL BIBLIOGRAPHY

ASQUITH, H. H., *Some Aspects of the Victorian Age* (Romanes Lecture for 1918), Oxford, 1918. (Also in *Sketches and Studies*, New York, 1924.)

BATHO, EDITH, and DOBREE, B., *The Victorians and After, 1830-1914*, London, 1938.

BEER, MAX, *A History of British Socialism*, 2 vols., London, 1920.

BENN, A. W., *A History of English Rationalism in the Nineteenth Century*, London, 1906.

BENSON, E. F., *As We Were*, New York, 1931.

—— *Queen Victoria*, New York, 1935.

BEVINGTON, M. B., *The Saturday Review: 1855-1868*, New York, 1941.

BICKLEY, F., *The Pre-Raphaelite Comedy*, London, 1932.

BOLITHO, H., *Albert the Good, and The Victorian Reign*, New York, 1932.

—— *Victoria: The Widow and Her Son*, New York, 1934.

BRINTON, CRANE, *English Political Thought in the Nineteenth Century*, London, 1933.

BROWNELL, W. C., *Victorian Prose Masters*, New York, 1915.

BRYANT, ARTHUR, *English Saga: 1840-1940*, London, 1941.

BURDETT, OSBERT, *The Beardsley Period*, London, 1925.

BURTT, E. A. (ed.), *The English Philosophers from Bacon to Mill*, New York, 1939.

BURY, J. B., *The Idea of Progress*, New York, 1932.

Cambridge History of English Literature, vols. XII-XIV, New York, 1933.

Cambridge Modern History, vols. VIII-XII.

CHESTERTON, G. K., *The Victorian Age of Literature*, New York, 1913.

CHRISTIE, O. F., *The Transition to Democracy*, London, 1934.

CLAPHAM, J. H., *An Economic History of Modern Britain*, 3 vols., Cambridge, England, 1926-1937.

CLARK, KENNETH, *The Gothic Revival*, London, 1928.

COLE, G. D. H., *Chartist Portraits*, London, 1941.

—— and POSTGATE, R., *The Common People, 1746-1938*, London, 1938.

CORNISH, F. W., *The English Church in the Nineteenth Century*, 2 vols., London, 1910.

COURTNEY, JANET E., *Freethinkers of the Nineteenth Century*, New York, 1920.

CROWTHER, J. G., *British Scientists of the Nineteenth Century*, London, 1935.

CRUSE, AMY, *The Victorians and Their Reading*, Boston, 1935.

Eighteen-Sixties, The, Essays by Fellows of the Royal Society of Literature, ed. by John Drink-water, New York, 1932.

Eighteen-Seventies, The, Essays, etc. ed. by Harley Granville-Barker, Cambridge, England, 1929.

Eighteen-Eighties, The, Essays, etc. ed. by Walter De La Mare, Cambridge, England, 1930.

ELLIOT-BINNS, L. E., *Religion in the Victorian Era*, London, 1936.

ELTON, OLIVER, *A Survey of English Literature, 1780-1880*, 4 vols., New York, 1920.

ENGELS, F., *The Condition of the Working-Class in England in 1844*, London, 1926.

ENSOR, R. C. K., *England, 1870-1914*, Oxford, 1936.

ESCOTT, T. H. S., *England: Her People, Polity, and Pursuits*, London, 1885.

—— *Social Transformation of the Victorian Age*, London, 1897.

EVERETT, E. M., *The Party of Humanity: The Fortnightly Review and Its Contributors, 1865-1874*, Chapel Hill, N. C., 1939.

FAY, C. R., *Life and Labour in the Nineteenth Century*, Cambridge, England, 1933.

—— *Great Britain from Adam Smith to the Present Day*, New York, 1928.

GAMAGE, R. G., *History of the Chartist Movement*, Newcastle, 1894.

GAUNT, WILLIAM, *The Pre-Raphaelite Tragedy*, London, 1942.

—— *The Aesthetic Adventure*, London, 1945.

GOOCH, G. P., *History and Historians in the Nineteenth Century*, New York, 1913.

GRETTON, R. H., *A Modern History of the English People*, 2 vols., London, 1913.

GULLEY, E. E., *Joseph Chamberlain and English Social Politics*, New York, 1926.

HALÉVY, ÉLIE, *A History of the English People*, trans. from the French, New York, 1924-1934.

HAMMOND, J. L. and BARBARA, *Lord Shaftesbury*, London, 1923.

—— *The Town Labourer*, London, 1920.

—— *The Rise of Modern Industry*, New York, 1926.

—— *The Age of the Chartists: 1832-1854*, New York, 1930.

HARRISON, FREDERIC, *National and Social Problems*, New York, 1908.

—— *Autobiographical Memoirs*, London, 1911.

HEARNSHAW, F. J. C. (ed.), *Social and Political Ideas of the Age of Reaction and Reconstruction*, London, 1931.

—— *Social and Political Ideas of Some Representative Thinkers of the Victorian Age*, London, 1933.

HICKS, GRANVILLE, *Figures of Transition: A Study of British Literature at the End of the Nineteenth Century*, New York, 1939.

HIRST, F. W., *Early Life and Letters of John Morley*, 2 vols., London, 1927.

HOBHOUSE, CHRISTOPHER, *1851 and The Crystal Palace*, London, 1937.

HOUSE, HUMPHREY, *The Dickens World*, New York, 1941.

HOVELL, M., *The Chartist Movement*, Manchester, 1918.

HUNT, W. H., *Pre-Raphaelitism and the Pre-Raphaelite Brotherhood*, 2 vols., New York, 1906.

HUTCHINS, B. L., and HARRISON, A., *A History of Factory Legislation* (3rd ed.), London, 1926.

HUTTON, R. H., *Criticisms on Contemporary Thought and Thinkers*, 2 vols., London, 1894.

HYNDMANN, H. M., *The Record of an Adventurous Life*, New York, 1911.

—— *Further Reminiscences*, London, 1912.

INGE, W. R., *The Victorian Age*, Cambridge, England, 1922. (Also in *Outspoken Essays*, Second Series, New York, 1926.)

JACKSON, HOLBROOK, *The Eighteen Nineties*, New York, 1922.

KELLETT, E. E., *Religion and Life in the Early Victorian Age*, London, 1938.

KNICKERBOCKER, F. W., *Free Minds: John Morley and His Friends*, Cambridge, Mass., 1943.

LE GALLIENNE, R., *The Romantic '90s*, New York, 1946.

LIPPINCOTT, B. E., *Victorian Critics of Democracy*, Minneapolis, 1938.

LIPSON, E., *Europe in the Nineteenth Century, 1815-1914* (5th ed.), London, 1940.

LUBBOCK, SIR JOHN (BARON AVEBURY), *Fifty Years of Science, 1831-1881*, London, 1882.

LUDLOW, J. M., and JONES, L. L., *Progress of the Working Classes: 1832-1867*, London, 1867.

LYND, H. M., *England in the Eighteen-Eighties*, New York, 1945.

MACCOBY, S., *English Radicalism, 1832-1852*, London, 1935.

—— *English Radicalism, 1853-1886*, London, 1938.

MARCHAND, L. A., *The Athenaeum: A Mirror of Victorian Culture*, Chapel Hill, N. C., 1941.

MARRIOTT, SIR J. A. R., *Modern England, 1885-1932*, London, 1934.

—— *England Since Waterloo*, 7 vols., New York, 1913.

MARVIN, F. S., *The Century of Hope*, Oxford, 1921.

MASSINGHAM, H. J. and H., *The Great Victorians*, New York, 1932.

MEAD, G. H., *Movements of Thought in the Nineteenth Century*, Chicago, 1938.

MERZ, J. T., *A History of European Thought in the Nineteenth Century*, 4 vols., London, 1896-1914.

MILNER, G., *The Threshold of the Victorian Era*, London, 1934.

MORLEY, JOHN, *The Life of Gladstone*, 3 vols., New York, 1911.

—— (Viscount), *Recollections*, 2 vols., New York, 1917.

—— *Life of Richard Cobden*, 2 vols., London, 1881.

MORRIS, WILLIAM, and BAX, BELFORT, *Socialism: Its Growth and Outcome*, London, 1893.

MOWAT, R. B., *The Victorian Age*, London, 1939.

MUIR, RAMSEY, *A Short History of the British Commonwealth*, 2 vols., New York, 1924.

MURRAY, R. H., *Science and Scientists in the Nineteenth Century*, London, 1925.

—— *Studies in the English Social and Political Thinkers of the Nineteenth Century*, 2 vols., Cambridge, England, 1929.

NEVILL, RALPH, *The Gay Victorians*, London, 1930.

PATTISON, MARK, *Memoirs*, London, 1885.

PAUL, HERBERT, *A History of Modern England, 1846-1896*, 5 vols., New York, 1904-1906.

PEASE, E. R., *The History of the Fabian Society*, New York, 1916.

PECK, WILLIAM GEORGE, *The Social Implications of the Oxford Movement*, London, 1933.

PIMLOTT, J. A. R., *Toynbee Hall: Fifty Years of Social Progress, 1884-1934*, London, 1935.

QUENNELL, M., and C. H. B., *A History of Everyday Things in England, 1733-1851*, London, 1931.

QUENNELL, PETER, *Victorian Panorama*, New York, 1937.

RAVEN, C. R., *Christian Socialism*, London, 1920.

ROSE, J. H., *The Rise of Democracy*, London, 1897.

ROSENBLATT, F. F., *The Chartist Movement in Its Social and Economic Aspects: Part I*, New York, 1916.

ROTHENSTEIN, WILLIAM, *Men and Memories, A History of the Arts, 1872-1922*, 2 vols. in one, New York, n. d.

ROUTH, H. V., *England Under Victoria*, New York, 1930.

—— *Towards the Twentieth Century*, New York, 1937.

RUSSELL, G. W. E., *A Short History of the Evangelical Movement*, London, 1915.

SAINTSBURY, G., *A History of English Prose Rhythm*, London, 1922.

SANDERS, C. R., *Coleridge and the Broad Church Movement*, Durham, N. C., 1942.

SCUDDER, VIDA D., *Social Ideals in English Letters*, New York, 1923.

SHAW, B., WEBB, S., and OTHERS, *Fabian Essays in Socialism*, London, 1931.

SIMPSON, W. J. S., *The History of the Anglo-Catholic Revival from 1845*, London, 1932.

SLATER, GILBERT, *The Making of Modern England*, Boston, 1915.

SLOSSON, P. W., *The Decline of the Chartist Movement*, New York, 1916.

SOMERVELL, D. C., *English Thought in the Nineteenth Century*, New York, 1929.

SORLEY, W. R., *A History of English Philosophy*, Cambridge, England, 1937.

STAEBLER, WARREN, *The Liberal Mind of John Morley*, Princeton, 1943.

STEPHEN, LESLIE, *Some Early Impressions*, London, 1924.

STORR, V. F., *The Development of English Theology in the Nineteenth Century, 1800-1860*, New York, 1913.

STRACHEY, LYTTON, *Eminent Victorians*, New York, 1918.

—— *Queen Victoria*, New York, 1921.

THOMSON, J. A., and OTHERS, *Evolution in Modern Thought*, New York, n. d.

THRALL, M. M. H., *Rebellious Fraser's*, New York, 1934.

TREVELYAN, G. M., *The Life of John Bright*, London, 1913.

—— *British History in the Nineteenth Century, 1782-1901*, London, 1922.

—— *English Social History*, New York, 1943.

TUELL, A. K., *John Sterling, A Representative Victorian*, New York, 1941.

TULLOCH, J., *Movements of Religious Thought in Britain during the Nineteenth Century*, London, 1885.

TYNDALL, JOHN, *Fragments of Science*, 2 vols., New York, 1898.

WALKER, HUGH, *The Age of Tennyson*, London, 1914.

—— *The Literature of the Victorian Era*, Cambridge, England, 1910.

WALLACE, A. R., *The Wonderful Century*, New York, 1898.

—— and OTHERS, *The Progress of the Century*, New York, 1902.

WALPOLE, SPENCER, *The History of Twenty-Five Years*, 4 vols., New York, 1904-1908.

WARD, T. H. (ed.), *The Reign of Queen Victoria: A Survey of Fifty Years of Progress*, 2 vols., London, 1887.

WEBB, BEATRICE, *My Apprenticeship*, New York, 1926.

WEBB, C. C. J., *A Study of Religious Thought in England from 1850*, Oxford, 1933.

WEBB, S., *Socialism in England*, London, 1890.

WEBB, SIDNEY and BEATRICE, *A History of Trade Unionism*, London, 1920.

—— *Industrial Democracy*, London, 1920.

WELLS, H. G., *Experiment in Autobiography*, New York, 1934.

WHITE, A. D., *A History of the Warfare of Science with Theology in Christendom*, 2 vols., New York, 1898.

WILLIAMS, H. S., *The Story of Nineteenth Century Science*, New York, 1900.

WILLIAMS, S. T., *Studies in Victorian Literature*, New York, 1923.

WINGFIELD-STRATFORD, E., *The Victorian Tragedy*, London, 1931.

—— *The Victorian Sunset*, London, 1932.

WOODRUFF, L. L. (ed.), *The Development of Science*, New Haven, 1923.

WOODS, R. A., *English Social Movements*, New York, 1891.

WOODWARD, E. L., *The Age of Reform, 1815-1870*, Oxford, 1938.

YOUNG, G. M. (ed.), *Early Victorian England, 1830-1865*, 2 vols., London, 1934.

—— *Victorian England*, London, 1936.

THOMAS CARLYLE

SELECTED BIBLIOGRAPHY

I. STANDARD EDITIONS

People's Edition, 37 vols., London, 1871-1874.
Centenary Edition, 30 vols., London, 1896-1899; New York, 1898-1901.
Early Letters of Carlyle, ed. C. E. Norton, London, 1886.
Correspondence between Goethe and Carlyle, ed. C. E. Norton, London, 1887.
Letters of Carlyle, ed. C. E. Norton, London, 1888.
Reminiscences, ed. J. A. Froude, 2 vols., London, 1881; ed. C. E. Norton, 2 vols., London, 1887.
Correspondence of Carlyle and Emerson, ed. C. E. Norton, 2 vols., Boston, 1883.
Letters and Memories of Jane Welsh Carlyle, ed. J. A. Froude, London and New York, 1883.
Two Notebooks of Thomas Carlyle, ed. C. E. Norton, Grolier Club, New York, 1898.
New Letters and Memorials of Jane Welsh Carlyle, ed. A. Carlyle, 2 vols., London, 1903.
New Letters of Thomas Carlyle, ed. A. Carlyle, 2 vols., London, 1904.
Love Letters of Thomas Carlyle and Jane Welsh, 2 vols., ed. A. Carlyle, London, 1909.
Letters of Thomas Carlyle to J. S. Mill, Sterling, and Browning, ed. A. Carlyle, London, 1923.
Jane Welsh Carlyle: Letters to Her Family, ed. Leonard Huxley, London, 1924.

II. BIOGRAPHY AND CRITICISM

BROWNELL, W. C., *Victorian Prose Masters*, New York, 1901.
BURDETT, O., *The Two Carlyles*, Boston, 1931.
CAZAMIAN, L., *Carlyle*, Paris, 1913. Translated by E. K. Brown, New York, 1932.
CONWAY, MONCURE, *Thomas Carlyle*, London, 1881.
CRAIG, R. S., *The Making of Carlyle*, London, 1908.
CRICHTON-BROWNE, SIR JAMES, *The Nemesis of Froude*, London, 1903.
DREW, E., *Jane Welsh and Jane Carlyle*, New York, 1928.
DUFFY, GAVAN, *Conversations with Carlyle*, London, 1892.
DUNN, W. H., *Froude and Carlyle*, London, 1930.
EMERSON, R. W., *English Traits*, London, 1856.
—— "Impressions of Thomas Carlyle," *Lectures and Biographical Sketches*, London, 1884.
ESPINASSE, F., *Literary Recollections and Sketches*, London and New York, 1893.
FROUDE, J. A., *Thomas Carlyle: A History of the First Forty Years of His Life, 1795-1835*, 2 vols., London, 1882.
—— *A History of His Life in London*, 2 vols., London, 1884.
—— *My Relations with Carlyle*, London, 1903.
GARNETT, R., *Life of Thomas Carlyle*, London, 1887.
GOOCH, G. P., *History and Historians in the Nineteenth Century*, London, 1913.
HAMILTON, M. A., *Thomas Carlyle*, London, 1930.
HARROLD, C. F., *Carlyle and German Thought, 1819-1834*, New Haven, 1934.
JOHNSON, W. S., *Thomas Carlyle, A Study of His Literary Apprenticeship, 1814-1831*, New Haven, 1911.
LEA, FRANK A., *Carlyle: Prophet of To-Day*, London, 1943.
LEHMAN, B. H., *Carlyle's Theory of the Hero*, Durham, N. C., 1928.
MASSON, D., *Edinburgh Sketches and Memories*, London, 1892.
—— *Carlyle Personally and in His Writings*, London, 1885.
MAZZINI, J., *Essays*, London, 1887.
MORE, P. E., "The Spirit of Carlyle," *Shelburne Essays*, First Series, New York, 1905.
MORLEY, J., "Carlyle," *Critical Miscellanies*, London, 1871.
NEFF, E., *Carlyle*, New York, 1932.
—— *Carlyle and Mill*, New York, 1924.
NICHOL, J., *Thomas Carlyle*, London, 1892.
PERRY, BLISS, *Thomas Carlyle: How to Know Him*, Indianapolis, 1915.
RALLI, A., *A Guide to Carlyle*, 2 vols., London, 1920.
ROE, F. W., *Thomas Carlyle as a Critic of Literature*, New York, 1910.
—— *The Social Philosophy of Carlyle and Ruskin*, New York, 1921.
SAINTSBURY, G., *Corrected Impressions*, London, 1895.

SCUDDER, TOWNSEND, *Jane Welsh Carlyle*, New York, 1939.

SCUDDER, VIDA D., *Social Ideals in English Letters*, Boston, 1898.

SHINE, HILL, *Carlyle's Fusion of Poetry, History and Religion by 1834*, Chapel Hill, N. C., 1938.

STEPHEN, LESLIE, *Hours in a Library*, vol. III, London, 1892.

STERLING, JOHN, "On the Writings of Thomas Carlyle," *London and Westminster Review*, XXXIII (1829), 1-68.

STORRS, M., *The Relation of Carlyle to Kant and Fichte*, Bryn Mawr, 1929.

STRACHEY, LYTTON, *Portraits in Miniature*, London, 1931.

TREVELYAN, G. M., "Carlyle as a Historian," *Nineteenth Century*, XLVI (1899), 493-503.

VAUGHAN, C. E., "Carlyle and His German Masters," *Essays and Studies by Members of the English Association*, Oxford, 1910.

WILSON, D. A., *The Life of Thomas Carlyle*, 6 vols., London, 1923-34.

YOUNG, LOUISE M., *Carlyle and the Art of History*, Philadelphia, 1939.

YOUNG, N., *Carlyle: His Rise and Fall*, London, 1927.

NOTES AND COMMENTS

SIGNS OF THE TIMES

Written at Craigenputtock, "a green oasis in that desert of heath and rock," as Carlyle described his home, "among the granite mountains and black moors," and published in the *Edinburgh Review* for June, 1829. It was "the first of the essays in which he brought out his views of the condition of modern English society" (Froude). "Prime Minister Wellington and all the politicians were still shuddering at the French Revolution and hoping nothing like it would ever recur" (Wilson).

5a. 9. **Know'st thou Yesterday:** The verses are Carlyle's, though really a free transcription from the German of Goethe, whose lines in turn were "only a masterly paraphrase" of a French poem by Canon Maucroix (1619-1708) quoted in Voltaire's *Louis XIV*. Goethe's lines were first published in 1825, and later in *Zahme Xenien*, Group IV (See *Am. Journal of Philology*, 1920, v. 41, p. 379).

14. **large discourse of reason:** *Hamlet*, IV, iv, 36-7.

5b. 2. **prophets are not one, but many:** Religious sects and fanatics were active in Scotland. "They were now excited by the hope of the Second Coming of Christ, and distracted by the repeal of the Catholic disabilities" (Wilson).

17. **Aaron's rod of Truth:** *Numbers*, XVII.

6a. 16. **Titus Oates:** An imposter who in 1678 stirred up reports of a plot to murder Charles II and to establish Catholicism by force. On his evidence many persons were executed.

40. **Test Acts:** The Test and Corporation Acts (1673 and 1661, respectively), imposing civil disabilities upon Catholics and Dissenters, were repealed in 1828. Catholic emancipation, i.e., admission of Catholics to Parliament, came in 1829.

48. **slumbering Leviathan:** *Paradise Lost*, I, 200-208.

6b. 27. **Millennarians:** Believers in the coming millennium, a period of a thousand years "during which holiness is to be triumphant," as mentioned in *Rev*. XX.

30. **Fifth-monarchy men:** A fanatical sect in England at the time of the Commonwealth, who believed that the fifth monarchy, or the reign of Christ for a thousand years, was imminent. The four preceding eras were the Assyrian, Persian, Greco-Macedonian, and Roman.

31. **Utilitarians:** Followers of the ethical and social philosophy of Jeremy Bentham (1748-1832), who took as the principle of conduct and welfare *utility*, which he defined as "the greatest happiness of the greatest number," happiness being the equivalent of pleasure and pleasure being the opposite of pain. Bentham made happiness depend largely upon "circumstances."

40. **Delphic:** Referring to the ancient prophetic oracles uttered by the Pythian priestess at Delphi, in Greece.

7a. 38. **Camoens:** Luis de Camoëns (1524-80), Portuguese national poet, author of *The Luciads* (1572), an epic concerning the adventures of Portuguese voyagers, who with Vasco da Gama (1460?-1524) rounded the Cape of Good Hope in 1497.

7b. 31. **Lancastrian machines:** Allusion to the monitorial system of instruction adopted by Joseph Lancaster (1778-1838) of England, in which advanced pupils in a school taught the less advanced.

32. Hamiltonian machines: A reference to the special methods of teaching foreign languages, devised by James Hamilton (1769-1829).

8a. 26. Newton . . . the falling of an apple: The story that Sir Isaac Newton's speculations on the theory of gravitation were awakened by the sight of an apple falling in his garden is recorded by Voltaire in his *Philosophie de Newton.* Voltaire got the incident from Newton's step-niece.

40. Paternoster Row: A famous street in London, once the center of the book and publishing trade and so called because it had been the center of the makers of rosaries and prayer-books.

47. Queen Christina: The brilliant daughter (1626-89) of Gustavus Adolphus. As Queen of Sweden (1644-54) she drew to Stockholm a "choice circle of philosophers and literati," including the great French philosopher, René Descartes (1596-1650), who was in the Swedish capital 1649-50, where he died.

48. King Frederick: Frederick the Great (1712-86), King of Prussia (1740-86). He induced Voltaire to join him in Berlin, 1750-53.

9a. 6. Malebranche (1638-1715), Pascal (1623-62), Descartes (1596-1650), Fénelon (1651-1715) are eminent French thinkers of the 17th century, whose philosophy, broadly speaking, supported religion and an affirmative view of human life and destiny. Pascal and Descartes are world figures.

8. Cousins and Villemains: Victor Cousin (1792-1867), French philosopher of the Eclectic school, which selects from various systems according to the temperament of the eclectic. Cousin was rather a historian of philosophy than an original thinker. Abel-François Villemain (1790-1870) was both a politician and a man of letters who used the historical method in literary criticism; a forerunner of Sainte-Beuve.

9. in the department of physics: Carlyle was probably thinking of Laplace (1749-1827), the astronomer and mathematical physicist, famous for his nebular hypothesis and his great work, *Traité de Méchanique Céleste* (5 vols., 1799-1825). On his visit to Paris in 1824 Carlyle saw Laplace. He also saw the mathematician Legendre and the great naturalist Cuvier.

15. Professor Stewart: Dugald Stewart (1753-1828), professor of mathematics and (later) moral philosophy at the University of Edinburgh; rather a realist and empiricist than an intuitionist, whom Carlyle read and "derided . . . for magnifying Bacon."

28. LaGrange: Joseph Louis LaGrange (1736-1813), French mathematician and astronomer.

38. Archimedes and Plato: Archimedes (287-212 B.C.), Greek mathematician and inventor who lived at Syracuse in Sicily. —— Plato (427?-347 B.C.), Athenian philosopher, disciple of Socrates and founder of the Academy. His *Dialogues* have influenced speculation for over two thousand years.

40. French Institute: Established in 1795 as a national society to promote science, art, and literature. It is now in reality a union of five great French academies.

41. God geometrises: "God is a geometrician" is a saying traditionally attributed to Plato, according to Plutarch (ʽο Θεὸς γεωμετρεῖ) — 'God geometrises' — *Symposium,* 8, 2). cf. Sir Thomas Browne — "God is like a skilful Geometrician" (*Rel. Med.,* Part I, sec. 16).

44. Locke: John Locke (1632-1704), English philosopher, who is "known as the father of English empiricism" and whose thought was influenced by Bacon and Descartes. Carlyle refers to Locke's major work, *An Essay Concerning Human Understanding* (1690).

9b. 20. Reid: Thomas Reid (1710-96), Scottish philosopher, professor at the universities of Aberdeen and Glasgow; "chief of a philosophical school aiming to deliver philosophy from skepticism."

23. Hume: David Hume (1711-76), Scotland's greatest thinker, whose empirical and skeptical philosophy awakened even the great metaphysician Kant out of his dogmatic slumber; author of *A Treatise on Human Nature* (1739), besides other speculative essays, and a *History of England* (1754 ff.).

34. Hartley's, Darwin's, or Priestley's: David Hartley (1705-57) was rather a physiological psychologist than a philosopher, whose *Observations on Man* (1749) presented a doctrine of association that much influenced later Associationism. —— Erasmus Darwin (1733-1804), grandfather of Charles Darwin, physiologist, physician, poet, in whose *Zoönomia* (1794-96) the doctrine of evolution was anticipated. —— Joseph Priestley (1733-1804), English clergyman and chemist, famous for his discovery of oxygen (1774) and for his liberal ideas in a revolutionary era.

41. as the liver secretes bile: The quotation is from *Rapports* (or, rather, *Traité*, etc.), i.e., 'Treatise on the moral and physical nature of man,' 1802, by Pierre Cabanis (1757-1808), French physician, philosopher, and pioneer in physiological psychology. Much the same view was held by other French materialists of the period; La Mettrié, d'Holbach, Condillac, for examples.

52. Leuwenhoek: Anton van Leuwenhoek (1632-1723), a Dutch naturalist who made simple microscopes through which he observed micro-organisms, such as the red corpuscles of the blood.

10a. 9. Vauxhall: Place of pleasure gardens of that name in London on the south side of the Thames from 1661 to 1859.

15. Martinus Scriblerus: The imaginary author of the *Memoirs of Martinus Scriblerus* (1741), a satire on false tastes in learning, in the creation of which Dr. Arbuthnot had a hand. Carlyle also refers to the "Nuremberg man" in *Sartor*, and still earlier in his introductory sketch of Richter in *German Romance*.

22. Vaucanson: Jacques de Vaucanson (1709-82), French inventor, especially of silk-weaving machinery.

10b. 33. Hooker: Richard Hooker (1554?-1600), English country rector and theologian whose great work, *The Laws of Ecclesiastical Polity* (1594-97) is an eloquent plea for religious tolerance and the *via media*.

33. Taylor: Jeremy Taylor (1613-67), English rector, prelate, chaplain to Laud and Charles I, and author, whose best known works, *Holy Living* (1650) and *Holy Dying* (1651), reveal a profoundly religious nature.

38. Smith, DeLolme, Bentham: Adam Smith (1723-90), whose *Wealth of Nations* (1776) laid the foundations of political economy. — Jean Louis DeLolme (1740-1806), Swiss jurist of Geneva who wrote *The Constitution of England* (pub. in French, 1771; English trans. London 1775). — Jeremy Bentham—6b., 31.

12a. 8. Roger Bacons, Keplers, Newtons: Roger Bacon (1214?-94), a Franciscan monk and English philosopher and scientist, called 'Doctor Mirabilis,' because of his experiments and writings. Suspected of heresy, he was in confinement for many years. — The German Johannes Kepler (1571-1630) and the English Newton (1642-1727) are world-famous as mathematicians and mathematical astronomers.

9. the Fausts and the Watts: Dr. Johann Faust (1480?-1540) was a German magician, astrologer, soothsayer and teacher, who practised his magic in university cities and became the legendary Dr. Faustus. — James Watt (1736-1819), Scottish mechanical engineer and inventor of the modern condensing steam engine (1765). The watt, a unit of power, is named in his honor.

12b. 27. the passionate voice of one man: Peter the Hermit (1050?-1115), French hermit and monk, who, by his preaching, aroused thousands to join in the First Crusade; ... a motley crowd of enthusiasts, most of whom were "slaughtered on the plains of Bithynia."

37. English Revolution: The Puritan Revolution of 1642-60, involving civil war, the execution of Charles I (1649), and the Protectorate of Oliver Cromwell (1653-58).

13a. 17. the high priori road: The road of self-evident presuppositions not founded upon empirical knowledge.

31. Epictetus: Greek Stoic philosopher of the first century A.D. He was a slave at Rome in Nero's reign, but was freed, and taught there until expelled by Domitian with other philosophers in 89. He had a school at Nicopolis in Epirus until his death.

34. Las Casas: Bartolomé de Las Casas (1474-1566), Spanish Dominican missionary and historian, was the first priest to be ordained in the New World, where he spent his life in work for the Indians; known as the 'Apostle of the Indies.'

36. Cortés, Pizarro, Alba Ximenes: Hernando Cortés (1485-1547), famous Spanish conquistador, who conquered Mexico (1518-23). — Francisco Pizarro (1470?-1541), Spanish conqueror of Peru (1531-35). — Fernando Alvarez de Toledo, Duke of Alba, or Alva (1508?-83), Spanish general, who, under Philip II, was sent to the Netherlands to suppress revolt. His campaign (1567-73) was prosecuted with extreme cruelty. — Francisco Ximenes, or Jimenes, (1437-1517), Spanish prelate and statesman, primate of Spain (1495) and Cardinal (1507).

39. Inquisition: The Spanish Inquisition, established by the Catholic Church to stamp out heresy, was conducted in Spain during the reign (1556-98) of Philip II with fanatical cruelty.

43. Siege of Leyden: The Dutch city of Leyden was besieged by the Spaniards for many months (1573-74) until relieved in the nick of time, after one of the most heroic resistances in history.

44. William the Silent: Founder of the Dutch Republic, William the Silent (1533-84) led his countrymen in the "War of Liberation" against the Spanish armies, and was made hereditary stadholder (1579-84). He was assassinated at Delft.

44. Egmont or DeWitt: Lamoral, Count of Egmont (1522-68), Flemish general and statesman, who for his opposition to Alva in the Netherlands was executed at Brussels with his fellow countryman and patriot, Count Horn. — Jan DeWitt (1625-72), Dutch statesman and grand pensionary (magistrate) of Holland (1653-72).

53. Castlereagh: Robert Stewart, Viscount Castlereagh (1769-1822), prominent English reactionary statesman, Foreign Secretary and leader of the House of Commons (1812-22), and British representative at the Congress of Vienna (1814).

53. Burghley: William Cecil, first Baron Burghley (1520-98), was Queen Elizabeth's Secretary of State (1558-72) and Lord High Treasurer (1572-98). He was the Queen's most trusted adviser.

54. Sidney: Sir Philip Sidney (1554-86), poet, scholar, statesman, soldier, typical Renaissance figure, was for a time one of Elizabeth's favorites. He wrote the sonnet-sequence, *Astrophel and Stella* (1591), the pastoral romance *Arcadia* (1590), and *Defence of Poesie* (1595). He was sent to the Netherlands with his uncle, the Earl of Leicester, to fight against Spain, and he was mortally wounded at Zutphen (1586).

13b. 1. Knowles and Brummel: James Sheridan Knowles (1789-1862), British playwright, author of *Caius Gracchus* (1815), *Virginius* (1820), and other plays. — George Bryan Brummel (1778-1840), called Beau, was *the* English dandy of his time, friend of the Prince of Wales (afterward George IV), gambler and spender, who died in a French asylum for the insane.

14b. 3. Constant: Benjamin Constant de Rebecqué (1767-1830), French writer and politician, member of the *Chamber of Deputies* (1819-30).

4. Loyola: Saint Ignatius of Loyola (1491-1556), Spanish soldier and ecclesiastic; founder of the Society of Jesus, known as the Jesuit Order; canonized by Gregory XV (1622).

5. John Knox, a Wickliffe! John Knox (1505-72), Scottish reformer, writer, statesman, who spent an active life in an effort to establish Protestantism in Scotland. — John Wickliffe, or Wyclif (1320?-84), English religious reformer and theologian, who initiated the first complete translation of the Bible into English (carried through by John Purvey) and who is called "Morning Star of the Reformation."

8. Euphuist: Euphuists and Euphuism flourished in Elizabethan times, the names coming from John Lyly's romances, *Euphues* (1579) and *Euphues and His England* (1580). The Euphuist spoke and wrote a highly artificial and affected language.

21. Luther: Martin Luther (1483-1546), father of the Reformation in Germany, nailed (1517) his famous 95 theses to the church door at Wittenberg, attacking the Catholic sale of indulgences. He spent the rest of his life in warfare against the Church, which he saw as worldly and corrupt. During periods of forced retirement he translated the Bible into German.

15a. 2. Sir Hudibras: Burlesque hero of Samuel Butler's (1612-80) mock-heroic poem *Hudibras* (1663-78), in which Puritans are satirized.

15. Theories of Taste: Probably a reference to *Essays on the Nature and Principles of Taste* (1790) by Archibald Alison (1757-1839). Carlyle read the book in Dec. 1826, when he recorded in his notebook: "*Can* you believe that the Beautiful and Good have no deeper root in us than 'Association'?" Jeffrey enthusiastically reviewed a second edition in the *Edinburgh Review*.

21. Natural History of Religion: The first of *Four Dissertations* (1757) by David Hume is *The Natural History of Religion*. In 1779, three years after his death, *Dialogues concerning Natural Religion* appeared.

15b. 20. The true Church of England: Cf. the chapter on 'Organic Filaments' in *Sartor*,— "A Preaching Friar settles himself in every village; and builds a pulpit, which he calls a Newspaper."

45. Memnon statue: By this name the Greeks called a statue of Amenhotep III in ancient Thebes. Sounds were said to come from the statue when struck by rays of the rising sun.

53. Moloch: A Semitic deity in the worship of whom human sacrifices were made, especially of first-born children. (Cf. *Paradise Lost*, I, 392-405.)

16a. 40. Argus: In classical mythology a monster in human shape but with 100 eyes, of which some were always awake, until Hermes soothed them to sleep by a story and then slew Argus.

17a. 23. Heraclides and Pelasgi: The Heraclides were legendary descendants of Hercules, who fought for the possession of the Peloponnesus and in the fifth invasion succeeded. —— The Pelasgi, according to classical writers, were Hellenic dwellers in Greece and the eastern islands of the Mediterranean.

17b. 36. Carbonari: Literally, charcoal burners,—a secret political association organized in Italy about 1811 by agitators who first met among the charcoal burners of the mountains. The movement spread to other countries.

18b. 5. Hercules: "Spectroscopic studies and sky observations alike tell us that our sun and his family are all headed in a great migration across the sky toward a point between the constellations of Hercules and Lyra." (*National Geographic.*)

SARTOR RESARTUS

Sartor Resartus was the first original book of its author. It was written at Craigenputtock where Carlyle had moved from Edinburgh in 1828 for a period of productive thinking and writing. In his notebook on the 18th of September, 1830, he made the entry: "I am going to write— Nonsense. It is on 'Clothes.'" It had suddenly come to him that the conventions, creeds, laws, customs, and fashions of society were but so many changing forms, more properly to be called clothes, variously symbolical of the relatively unchanging soul of humanity beneath. He wrote out his meditations in the form of two articles and sent them to *Fraser's Magazine* with the title "Thoughts on Clothes,"—the first book of *Sartor*. Since Fraser did not publish the articles, Carlyle recalled them and expanded the material into a book by adding the second and third parts. With the completed manuscript he went to London to find a publisher, but he met with refusal on every hand. At last it was accepted for serial publication in *Fraser's Magazine,* where it came out from November 1833 to August 1834. After Emerson had brought out an American edition and Carlyle had won fame in 1837 with his *French Revolution, Sartor* was published in England as a book in 1838. It is Carlyle's spiritual autobiography, the fullest revelation of his personality given to the world. Teufelsdröckh and the "Editor" alike are the author in different moods.

I. The Everlasting No (Book II, Ch. VII)

"Carlyle often said it was his reflections on the death (June 9th, 1816) of his uncle that suggested to him the subject of his chapter on 'The Everlasting No'" (C. E. Norton). Of his Uncle Tom, Carlyle wrote: "He departed in my father's house in my presence: the first Death I had ever understood and laid with its whole emphasis to heart." (*Rem.* I, 34). 'The Everlasting No' is the spirit of negation: "it was God that said Yes. It is the Devil that forever says No," wrote the author in his notebook for January, 1827.

18a. 7. Son of Time: Translation of Goethe's phrase 'Söhne der Zeit' in the poem *Gott, Gemüth und Welt.*

18b. 28. Tartarean: Tartarus is the infernal regions of Homer, far below Hades. For Carlyle the word is synonymous with Hell.

19a. 1. Profit-and-Loss Philosophy: Bentham's utilitarianism.

21. absentee God: Carlyle's phrase for 18th century deism, the view that the universe was wound up like a watch by a God who exists apart from the mechanism He created.

28. Doctor Graham: James Graham (1745-94), a notorious quack doctor who invented a bed guaranteed to cure sterility.

30. Paul, Chief of sinners: *I Timothy,* I, 15.

32. Nero of Rome: The story of Nero's fiddling, while Rome was on fire, is told by Tacitus (*Annals*) and Suetonius (*Twelve Caesars*).

40. Prometheus Vinctus: 'Prometheus conquered.' Prometheus is the Titan who stole fire from heaven for the benefit of man and who was therefore chained by Zeus to a rock where a vulture daily consumed his liver, which grew again at night. Carlyle's phrase is the title of a drama by Aeschylus, based on the Greek myth.

19b. 9. Sibyl-cave: Allusion to the visit of Aeneas to the Sibyl, *Aeneid,* VI, 36 ff.

14. Pillar of Cloud and Pillar of Fire: See *Exodus,* XIII, 21.

21. Siècle de Louis Quinze: Title of a history by Voltaire, more exactly, *Précis du Siècle de Louis XV,*—the age of the *Encyclopédie.*

44. Lubberland: Land of plenty and idleness.

47. Handwriting: See *Daniel,* V, 5-28.

20a. 3. living without God: See *Ephesians,* II, 12.

15. As English Milton says: *Paradise Lost,* I, 157.

28. Know thyself: Γνῶθι σεαυτὸν, inscribed over the portico of the temple at Delphi.

48. practical Mystery: Here 'mystery' is used in the medieval sense of craft or occupation.

20b. 36. Golgotha: 'Place of skulls'—see *Matthew,* XXVII, 33.

21a. 4. From Suicide: Afflicted with "this infernal disorder in the stomach" (dyspepsia) and with spiritual depression, Carlyle sometimes thought of suicide: e.g. "Then why not kill yourself, sir?" (*Journal,* Dec. 31, 1823—Froude's *Life,* I, 200).

27. Selig der den, etc.: Inaccurately quoted from *Faust* I, iv, 1573-76.

51. Rue Saint-Thomas de l'Enfer: St. Thomas-of-Hell Street. Carlyle says that the "incident occurred quite literally to myself in Leith Walk (i.e. Edinburgh), during three weeks of total sleeplessness."

54. Nebuchadnezzar's Furnace: See *Daniel,* III, 19 ff.

21b. 40. Baphometic: From Baphomet, the name of an idol said to have been worshipped by the Knights Templars in certain secret rites. Carlyle's phrase means sudden spiritual illumination.

II. Centre of Indifference (Book II, Ch. VIII)

Teufelsdröckh has now overcome "the spirit of negation" and his intense morbid subjectivity, but he has not yet found "the spirit of affirmation" and healthy creative living. He passes through "the centre of indifference," when his mind is gradually taken from itself and comes to look with new interest upon the objective world. Carlyle symbolizes this experience by a metaphor from physics, i.e. the point exactly between the negative and positive poles of an electric cell where there is no potential.

22a. 12. Satanic School: Robert Southey's description of "the school" of Byron and Shelley, in satiric reference to the "audacious impiety" of their poetry.

15. Ernulphus-cursings: Ernulf was Bishop of Rochester (1114-24), whose curse was a form of excommunication of the Church of Rome (see Sterne's *Tristram Shandy,* III, Ch. 11).

21. method in their madness: Cf. *Hamlet,* II, ii, 206-7.

33. Not-me: A phrase from the philosopher Fichte, meaning the objective material world.

22b. 21. Cain and Tubalcain: See *Genesis,* IV, 2 and 22.

30. Schönbrunn, Downing Street, Palais Bourbon: Centers of government in Vienna, London, and Paris, respectively.

42. Armida's Palace: Palace of the Enchantress in the *Jerusalem Delivered* (Book XVI) of Tasso (1544-95).

23a. 27. pyramids of Geeza: Ghizeh and Sakkara, sites of great pyramids near Cairo.

33. Luther's Version: Luther's translation of the Bible into German was printed in 1534-35.

37. Wagram: On the plain of Marchfeld near Vienna, scene of Napoleon's defeat of the Austrians in 1809.

23b. 8. Stillfried: Also on the plain of Marchfeld and scene of a victory of Ottocar II of Bohemia over King Bela IV of Hungary in 1260; and in 1278 the scene of a victory of Rudolf I of Hapsburg over Ottocar II of Hungary who was slain.

30. Carcass of the Killer: *Judges,* XIV, 8-9.

37. Natural Enemies: Orangemen applied this phrase to members of the Catholic Association in 1824; the English frequently applied it to the French in the Napoleonic era.

51. South of Spain: Allusion to the Peninsular War (1808-14), when England was at war with Napoleon.

24a. 20. What devilry soever: See Horace, *Epistles,* I, ii, 14.

22. English Smollet: See *Count Fathom,* Ch. XLI, by Tobias Smollet (1721-71).

24b. 14. the great Hadrian: Hadrian (76-138), Roman Emperor, spent many years travelling over his empire.

20. Vaucluse: Valla Chiusa, near Avignon in southern France, home of Petrarch.

22. **Tadmor:** Ancient Palmyra, City of Palms, in the Syrian desert.

28. **Kings sweated-down:** In 1806 Napoleon issued the Berlin Decrees forbidding all trade with England. To Carlyle this meant making continental kings mere customs officers.

37. **birth-pangs of Democracy:** The July (1830) Revolution in Paris and the reform agitation in Britain.

25a. 2. **Treisnitz:** Triesnitz (correctly) near Jena, where Schiller and Goethe sometimes foregathered for conversation.

18. **Pope Pius:** Pius VII (Pope, 1800-23), who crowned Napoleon emperor at Paris (1804).

19. **Tarakwang:** Tao Kuang (1782-1850), Emperor of China (1820-50), whose reign was disturbed by rebellions and by the Opium War (1839-42) with Great Britain.

20. **Chinese Carbonari:** The "Water Lily" secret society in China (whose subversive activities lasted for several years) is likened to the secret political society in Italy, the Carbonari, or "Charcoal-burners."

42. **Enthusiasts:** Religious fanatics.

25b. 33. **Hyperborean:** Literally, beyond the North Wind, i.e. extreme north.

26a. 12. **Goliath:** *I Samuel*, XVII, 4-54.

28. **Hugo von Trimberg:** Schoolmaster, moralist, writer of several lost volumes and of one extant book of verse called *Der Renner* (The Runner) which "was finished in 1300" and "first printed in 1549" (see Carlyle's *Early German Literature*, 1831).

37. **Does Legion still lurk in him:** *Mark*, V, 9.

26b. 3. **caput-mortuum:** Literally, a dead-head; a term used by alchemists to denote the calcined residue after the escape of all volatile salts.

14. **Boy Alexander:** Juvenal's tenth satire has the incident (168-70), but Carlyle's version comes from Butler's *Hudibras*, I, iii, 1022 ff.

30. **Dog-cage of an Earth:** The allusion is to the old-fashioned spit turned by a wheel in a cage suspended above. Inside the cage a dog kept the wheel revolving. "No drudge or scullion can do the feat more cunningly." (Chamber's *Book of Days*, I, 490.)

III. THE EVERLASTING YEA (Book II, Ch. IX)

26b. 49. **Temptations in the Wilderness:** *Matthew*, IV, 1.

52. **old Adam:** Original sin. See *Ephesians*, IV, 22.

27a. 6. **Promethean:** Fire-bearing; Prometheus stole fire from Heaven.

27b. 47. **Harmattan wind:** Parching desert wind from the interior of Africa upon the West Coast.

28b. 1. **my mountain-seat:** From Dunscore Hill, near Craigenputtock, Carlyle says he "might see Dumfries with the cap of early kitchen-smoke, all shrunk to the size of one's hat, though there were 11,000 souls in it, far away to the right" (*Reminiscences*, ed. Norton, I, 168).

26. **Schreckhorn:** Peak of Terror, one of the high peaks of the Bernese Alps.

29a. 10. **wipe away all tears:** *Revelation*, XXI, 4.

23. **Sanctuary of Sorrow:** The phrase is Goethe's in *Wilhelm Meister*, III, xi (Carlyle's trans.). By this expression and the 'Divine Depth of Sorrow' Goethe (and Carlyle also) meant to suggest the essential spirit of Christianity. "All the *good* I ever got came to me rather in the shape of sorrow," wrote Carlyle to Thomas Erskine in 1847.

29b. 15. **Hochheimer:** A Rhenish wine, from Hochheim, near Mainz.

16. **Orphiuchus:** A constellation known as the Serpent-bearer, pictured in old charts as a man holding the serpent in his hands.

50. **hanged in a hair-halter:** "R. Cochrane (favorite of James III of Scotland) before his execution asked that his hands might be bound with silk instead of hemp.... To degrade him still further, his enemies procured a hair-halter and hanged him with that." (J. A. S. Barrett's ed. *Sartor*, 232 n.)

30a. 6. **the Wisest of our time:** Goethe, in *Wilhelm Meister*, III, xiv (Carlyle's trans.).

13. **because thou art not Happy:** "People want to be happy, and by happiness they mean pleasure, a series of passive enjoyments," said Carlyle (*Love Letters*, II, 304).

26. **Close thy Byron; open thy Goethe:** To Carlyle Byron was a symbol of ineffectual melancholy and discontent, while Goethe stood for creative living and a complete life.

27. **es leuchtet mir ein:** A phrase from Carlyle's favorite chapter (X) in *Wilhelm Meister*, III.

30b. 2. Zeno: Greek stoic philosopher (336?-?264 B.C.).

7. Worship of Sorrow: "Christianity, the 'Worship of Sorrow'" (Carlyle's *Voltaire*).

25. Baal-Priests: See *I Kings*, XVIII, 17-40.

29. Voltaire: For Carlyle Voltaire (1694-1778) symbolized the spirit of negation, as Goethe the spirit of affirmation.

31a. 9. Plenary Inspiration: The theological doctrine that the Bible is divinely inspired throughout.

11. One Bible I know: The "Bible of universal History" and of the visible world. "Authentic 'writings' of the Most High, were they found in old Books only? They were in the stars and on the rocks, and in the brain and heart of every mortal" (*Reminiscences*, ed. Norton, II, 206).

34. feast of shells: Shells were once used as drinking cups; hence the phrase. Carlyle, however, suggests also empty egg-shells.

43. Wissenschaftslehre: The philosopher Fichte's *Doctrine of Knowledge* (1794). It was Novalis who called it Applied Christianity (see Carlyle's essay, *Novalis*).

46. Whole Duty of Man: Title of a book published anonymously in 1659; also a phrase in *Ecclesiastes*, XII, 13.

31b. 5. Doubt of any sort: *Wilhelm Meister*, II, Bk. V, Ch. XVI (Carlyle's trans.).

12. Do the Duty: *Ibid.*, II, Bk. VII, Ch. I-III (Carlyle's trans.).

23. Lothario: *Ibid.*, Bk. VII, Ch. III.

45. Light: *Genesis*, I, 3.

45. Till the eye: Cf. *Matthew*, VI, 22-23.

32a. 15. Work while it is called Today: Cf. *Ecclesiastes*, IX, 10, and *John*, IX, 4.

IV. NATURAL SUPERNATURALISM (Book III, Ch. VIII)

Carlyle attached special significance to this chapter, since in it he summarized the central theme of *Sartor*, which was also the cornerstone of his own philosophy of life,—"the gist of my whole way of thought." In his *Journal* for Feb. 1, 1833 he wrote: "That the Supernatural differs not from the Natural is a great Truth, which the last century (especially in France) has been engaged in demonstrating. The philosophers went far wrong, however, in this, that instead of raising the natural to the supernatural, they strove to sink the supernatural to the natural." (Froude, *Life of Carlyle*, II, 330.)

32a. 41. Holy of Holies: See *Exodus*, XXVI, 33-4.

43. Transcendentalism: Carlyle's meaning of this term is summarized in his own phrase: "All visible things are appearances only; but also emblems and revelations of God."

47. Courage, then: Diogenes the Cynic, when a dull lecture was near the end, exclaimed: "Courage, friends! I see land." The incident is told in *Lives of Eminent Philosophers*, by Diogenes Laertius (Loeb Classics, *Lives*, II, 40). 'Our Diogenes' is of course Professor Teufelsdröckh.

32b. 11. Dutch King of Siam: Cf. Hume: "The Indian prince, who refused to believe the first relations concerning the effects of frost, reasoned justly" (*Inquiry*, sect. X, Of Miracles).

17. Open Sesame: The magical phrase used to open the door to the cavern of treasures in 'Ali Baba and the Forty Thieves,' a story in *The Arabian Nights*.

33. make Iron swim: See *Kings*, VI, 6.

46. Without variableness: See *James*, I, 17.

33a. 8. Did the Maker: Cf. *Job*, XXXVIII, 4-18.

19. Laplace's Book: *Traité de Méchanique Céleste* (5 vols., 1799-1825).

28. Hershel: Sir William Hershel (1738-1822), the English astronomer, attempted to count the stars of the Northern Hemisphere, and estimated that "in a dense part of the heavens 116,000 stars crossed the field of his stationary telescope in fifteen minutes."

37. System of Nature: Of this striking paragraph John Morley says: "The inalterable relativity of human knowledge has never been more fully illustrated" ("Carlyle" in *Miscellanies*).

47. Epicycle: In Ptolemaic astronomy "a circle in which a planet moves, the center of the circle being carried around at the same time on the circumference of a larger circle" (cycle).

33b. 19. here a line, there a line: Cf. *Isaiah*, XXVIII, 10.

34a. **34. Luther's Picture of the Devil:** Where Luther was translating the Bible in a castle at Wartberg, he saw an image before him on the wall. He took the spectre to be the Devil and flung his inkstand at him, whereupon the apparition disappeared (see *Heroes and Hero-Worship,* lecture IV).

47. Space and Time: "Time and Space are not external but internal entities; there is no time and no space out of the mind; they are mere forms of man's spiritual being, *laws* under which his thinking nature is constituted to act" (Carlyle's *Novalis*).

34b. **6. Fortunatus:** The hero of a European folk-tale, dramatized by Hans Sachs and Thomas Dekker (*Old Fortunatus,* II, 3), though Carlyle probably borrowed from *Phantasus* (1812) of Ludwig Tieck (1773-1853), German romanticist.

31. Paul and Seneca: Contemporaries in the first century A.D., who might have met. Both their meeting and their correspondence are legendary.

35b. **15. Orpheus or Amphion:** Great musicians in Greek mythology. Orpheus was the son of Apollo and the muse Calliope; Amphion was the son of Zeus and the Theban princess Antiope.

19. Steinbruch-Troglodyte: Quarry—cave-dweller (pre-historic man), respectively.

46. The stroke that came: If the first of a series of tangent balls, suspended from strings, be drawn away and then released, the energy will be transmitted through the middle spheres and only the last one will spring away.

36a. **15. Cock Lane:** A narrow street in the Smithfield district of London, where the ghost of a Mrs. Kent was said to have appeared in 1762. It was found to be a hoax. For Johnson's part in exposing the imposture see Boswell's *Life* for the year 1763.

39. squeak and gibber: *Hamlet,* I, i, 116.

43. Dance of the Dead: Probably an echo from Richter's allusion to the painter Holbein's frescoes at Basle, depicting Death dancing with the living to the grave.

43. scent of the morning air: *Hamlet,* I, v, 58.

48. Issus and Arbela: Battlefields (near ancient Antioch and in Assyria, respectively) where Alexander defeated the Persian armies under Darius, B.C. 333 and 331.

51. Moscow-Austerlitz: Napoleon retreated ingloriously from Moscow in 1812; he defeated the armies of Austria and Russia in 1805, at Austerlitz, a town in Moravia.

36b. **2. Made night hideous:** *Hamlet* I, iv. 54.

13. dust and shadow: Horace's *pulvis et umbra sumus* (*Odes,* IV, vii, 16).

25. plummet's sounding: *Tempest,* V, i, 56.

33. Cimmerian Night: The Cimmerians were a mythical people described by Homer (*Odyssey,* XI) as living far away in a region of mist and darkness. Carlyle may be remembering *Faust* rather than the *Odyssey* (Part II, Act III, 1. 9000).

37b. **4. We are such stuff:** *Tempest,* IV, i, 156-8.

HEROES AND HERO-WORSHIP: THE HERO AS POET

The third lecture in the last of a series of four lecture-courses which Carlyle delivered in London in the years 1837-40. In this course "On Heroes, Hero-Worship and the Heroic in History," there were six lectures, given in May, 1840 on Tuesday and Friday afternoons before audiences "aristocratic in rank and intellect." In 1841 the series appeared in book form with "Emendations and Additions," the only one of the four courses to be published by Carlyle. "The History of the world," he said in the first lecture, "is but the Biography of great men.... Could we see *them,* we should get some glimpses into the very marrow of the world's history."

37b. **9. Mirabeau:** Honoré Gabriel Victor Riqueti, Comte de Mirabeau (1749-1791), French orator and revolutionary leader. One of the most vivid figures in Carlyle's *French Revolution.*

19. Louis Fourteenth: Louis XIV (1638-1715), one of the most despotic and magnificent of monarchs, whose reign of 73 years is the longest in European history.

20. Turenne: Marshall Turenne (1611-75), one of France's greatest military leaders, surpassed only by Napoleon.

26. Petrarch and Boccaccio: Brilliant figures in the revival of classical learning in the 14th century; both were entrusted with diplomatic missions. Boccaccio (1313-75) is best known for his prose *Decameron* (1353), and Petrarch (1304-74) for his Italian lyrics, chiefly sonnets and odes written to a French lady of Avignon.

38a. **8. Whitechapel:** A large section of East London.

38. Fichte: Johann Gottlieb Fichte (1762-1814), German metaphysician and transcendentalist from whose lectures *On the Nature of the Scholar* Carlyle quotes.

50. Satirist: Carlyle.

38b. **40. Consider the lilies:** *Matthew*, VI, 28-29.

52. A saying of Goethe's: Unidentified. Carlyle records the same thought (as coming from Goethe and Schiller) in his journal for Oct. 28, 1830, and Feb. 7, 1831 (Froude's *Life*, II, 93-98).

39a. **3. I have said somewhere:** In his essay *Diderot*.

4. Vauxhall: Famous place of amusement in London on the south bank of the Thames from 1661 to 1859.

16. imagination that shudders: Carlyle quotes from his essay on Burns.

20. Saxo Grammaticus: Danish historian (1150?-?1220), author of *Gesta Danorum*, a history of Denmark to 1186.

41a. **3. Giotto:** Giotto di Bordone (1276?-?1337), Florentine painter, friend of Dante (1265-1321). What portrait Carlyle refers to is not known; certainly not the one discovered in July, 1840, on a wall of the Bargello in Florence.

38. mystic unfathomable song: The quotation is from Tieck on Novalis (see Carlyle's *Novalis*).

41b. **14. Beatrice Portinari:** The tradition that Beatrice was a member of the Portinari family originates in Boccaccio's *Memoir* of Dante. Modern scholars think that the real Beatrice may have been another lady or that she was a poetical ideal. Dante's 'account' of his meeting with her is told in his *La Vita Nuova* (The New Life), his first book.

29. far from happily: The source of this opinion is Boccaccio's *Memoir*. There is no mention of a wife in Dante's writings.

35. Prior: Dante *was* prior of Florence for one term (two months) in 1300; i.e. one of six magistrates then governing the city. Podestà, chief magistrate, was a higher office.

53. Guelf-Ghibelline: Names of two great political factions in Italy from the 12th to the 13th century. The Guelfs, or Church party, opposed the rule of the German emperors in Italy, while the Ghibellines upheld the authority of the emperors. The Guelfs were divided into two factions, Bianchi (Whites or moderates) and Neri (Blacks or extremists). Papal interference for the Blacks resulted in the banishment of Dante, who was a White.

42a. **13. a record:** Dated March 10, 1302.

31. come è duro calle: *Paradiso*, XVII, 59.

36. Can della Scala: Can Francesco della Scala (1291-1329), known as Can Grande, ruler of Verona, patron of the arts, friend of Dante. Carlyle's quotation is from Petrarch's *Rerum Memorandarum*.

42b. **43. Se tu sequi tua Stella:**

> "Se tu sequi tua Stella
> Non puoi fallire a glorioso porto."

(*Inferno*, XV, 55-6); the words of Brunetto Labini, Dante's schoolmaster, whom he finds in Hell.

50. which has made me lean:

> "If e'er it happen that the Poem Sacred,
>   To which both heaven and earth have set their hand,
>   So that it many a year hath made me lean,
> O'er come the cruelty that bars me out,
>   From the fair sheepfold"—etc.

(*Paradiso*, XXV, 1-5, Longfellow's trans.).

43a. **10. Hic claudor Dantes, etc.:** A line from the epitaph attributed to Dante himself.

43b. **11. canto fermo:** Fixed song—i.e., "the plain chant or simple Gregorian melody, prescribed as to form and use by ecclesiastical tradition; any melodic theme or subject for contrapuntal treatment" (Webster's *International*).

36. Eccovi l'uom, etc.: The incident is told in Boccaccio's *Memoir*.

48. to become perfect through suffering: *Hebrews*, II, 10.

44a. **32. Hall of Dite:** *Inferno*, VIII, 70-73.

38. Tacitus: Cornelius Tacitus (55?-cir. 117) Roman historian, author of *Annals, Life of Agricola, Germania*.

47. Plutus: The god of riches, who is stationed at the entrance into the fourth circle of Hell, guarding the prodigal and avaricious (*Inferno*, VII, 8-15).

51. 'face *baked*,' etc.: *Ibid.*, XV, 26-30.

52. a fiery snow: *Ibid.*, XIV, 28-30.

44b. 2. those Tombs: *Ibid.*, IX, 112 ff., and X, 1-18.

7. Farinata: Farinata degli Uberti was a Florentine leader of the Ghibelline faction. (*Ibid.*, X, 22-51.)

7. Cavalcante: The spirit of Cavalcante Cavalcanti, father of Dante's friend, Guido Cavalcante (c. 1250-1300), leading Florentine poet before Dante. Carlyle, by a slip, quotes 'fue' (was) for 'ebbe' (had). (*Ibid.*, X, 52-72.)

51. Raphael: Raffaello Santi, or Sanzio (1483-1520), one of the world's most famous Italian painters, best known for his religious pictures (e.g. the Sistine Madonna, now in the Dresden gallery) and for his frescoes in the Vatican.

45a. 8. Francesca and her Lover: The tragic story of Francesca da Rimini and Paolo is told by Dante, *Inferno*, V, 80-142.

27. terrestrial libel: "It (i.e. the *Divine Comedy*) was written in the purest spirit of justice," said Carlyle (*Lectures on the History of Literature*, 95).

41. These longings of his: Cf. *Purgatorio*, XXVII, 35-36; 40-45; 52-54.

42. their meeting together: Dante first meets Beatrice in the Earthly Paradise on the summit of the Mountain of Purgatory (*Purgatorio*, XXX).

43. transfigured eyes: Cf. the opening lines of *Purgatorio*, XXXII. In the *Paradiso* Beatrice is Dante's guide, whose face shines with increasing brilliancy and beauty as they proceed.

45b. 10. A Dio spiacenti, etc.: *Inferno*, III, 63. Non ragionam di lor: *ibid.*, III, 51. Non han speranza: *ibid.*, III, 46. All three lines describe

> "that caitiff choir
> Of Angels, who have not rebellious been
> Nor faithful were to God, but were for self."
> (*Inferno* III, 37-39).

42. tremolar dell' onde:

> "The dawn was vanquishing the matin hour
> Which fled before it, so that from afar
> I recognized *the trembling of the sea*."
> (*Purgatorio*, I, 115-17).

46a. 3. loves me no more: *Purgatorio*, VIII, 70-75.

4. bent-down like corbels: *Ibid.*, X, 130-135.

11. the whole Mountain shakes with joy: *Ibid.*, XX, 121-151, and XXI, 58-60.

47a. 21. Bastard Christianism: Mohammedanism, whose beginning is reckoned from the year of the hegira (622), or flight of Mohammed from Mecca to Medina.

42. Napoleon: Exiled to the island of St. Helena in 1815, where he died in 1821.

44. oldest Hebrew prophet: Carlyle means Job.

48b. 24. Tree Igdrasil: In Norse mythology the great ash tree symbolizing the universe.

28. Sir Thomas Lucy: The 'Warwickshire Squire' (1532-1600) who, according to a tradition reported by Nicholas Rowe (1674-1718), prosecuted Shakespeare for deer-stealing; he was reputedly caricatured by the dramatist as Justice Shallow.

49a. 16. St. Stephen's: The Houses of Parliament are so named, since at one time the Commons used to sit in St. Stephen's Chapel. The Chapel was destroyed by fire in 1834.

47. It has been said: By Carlyle in his essay on Burns.

51. *Novum Organum:* Bacon's 'new organ' or method of scientific investigation, written in Latin (1620) and intended to replace the deductive logic of Aristotle with the inductive method in the study of nature.

49b. 34. Fiat lux: Genesis, I. 3.

50a. 23. His characters are like watches: Johnson used a similar figure in his comparison of Richardson (whom J. preferred) with Fielding: "There was," he said, "as great a difference between them, as between a man who knew how a watch was made, and a man who could tell the hour by looking on the dial-plate." (Boswell's *Life* for 1768). Like some other editors, I am unable to locate the quotation in Goethe.

50b. 13. The crabbed old Schoolmaster: "An old blind Schoolmaster in Annan," whom Carlyle also quotes in a letter to Emerson, Dec. 2, 1838 (*Carlyle-Emerson Corr.* I, 205).

51.b. **3. Novalis' beautifully remarks:** In his essay on Novalis, Carlyle quotes the remarks from *Fragments* (*Blüthenstaub*, i.e. Pollen of Flowers).

47. a heedless notion, our common one: Common in the 17th and 18th centuries, as expressed, for example, by Gray, who called Shakespeare "Nature's Darling" (*Progress of Poesy*).

52a. **12. a 'good hater':** Said by Johnson of Dr. Richard Bathurst: "Dear Bathurst was a man to my very heart's content: he hated a fool, and he hated a rogue, and he hated a Whig; he was a very *good hater*" (Mrs. Piazzi's *Anecdotes*, ed. S. C. Roberts, 56; also, Hill's *Boswell*, I, 220 n. 2).

26. the crackling of thorns: *Eccles.* VII, 6.

29. Dogberry and Verges: *Much Ado*, especially III, iii.

42. Hamlet in *Wilhelm Meister*: *Meister's Apprenticeship*, Book IV, iii-v; xii.

44. Schlegel: August Wilhelm Schlegel (1767-1845), German man of letters, critic, member of the Romantic School. Carlyle refers to *Lectures on Dramatic Literature*.

48. Marlborough: John Churchill, the first Duke of Marlborough (1650-1722), victor of Blenheim (1704), made the remark in a discussion with Bishop Burnet (1643-1715), the historian (see Wolseley's *Life of Marlborough*, I, 33).

52b. **5. battle of Agincourt:** *Henry V*, Act IV.

11. Ye good yeomen: From the King's famous speech, *Ibid.*, III, i, 24-25.

50. *Disjecta membra*: Scattered parts.

53a. **5. We are such stuff:** *Tempest*, IV, i, 156-158.

6. That scroll: The words just quoted are inscribed on a scroll held in the left hand of a statue of Shakespeare in Westminster Abbey, the work of William Kent (1684-1748).

53b. **21. Aeschylus:** Eldest and, for Carlyle, greatest of Greek dramatists (525-456 B.C.), author of seven extant tragedies.

36. Koran: Sacred book of the Mohammedans, written in Arabic and containing the professed revelations of the prophet, Mohammed.

45. Manager of a Playhouse: Shakespeare was a stockholder in the Globe Theater and, later, in the Blackfriars; a member, too, of the Lord Chamberlain's Company of Players, who became the King's Men in 1603. The 3rd Earl of Southampton (Henry Wriothesley, 1573-1624) was his patron.

50. Treadmill: Carlyle's expression for punishment for poaching: "a mill worked by prisoners treading on steps on the periphery of a wide wheel having a horizontal axis" (Webster's *International*).

54a. **32. New Holland:** Early name for Australia.

54b. **14. Paramatta:** In New South Wales, Australia.

34. he cannot yet speak: Modern Russian literature had hardly begun when Carlyle was speaking in 1840-41.

PAST AND PRESENT

Past and Present "was written off," says Froude, "with singular ease in the first seven weeks of 1843. His heart was in his subject." While in the throes of composition, Carlyle wrote to John Sterling: "The thing I am upon is a volume to be called 'Past and Present.' It is a moral, political, historical, and a most questionable red-hot indignant thing, for my heart is sick to look at the things now going on in England." The book is the author's central utterance on the 'social question.' The selections are from Book III, Chs. iii, iv, xi, xii, xiii, respectively.

DILETTANTISM

55a. **3. Dilettantism:** Meaning for Carlyle the frivolous activity of an idle aristocracy rather than, specifically, a delight in the fine arts, the word's original denotation.

17. Corn-law: A law, or series of laws, regulating the import and export of corn (i.e. wheat). It was repealed in 1846, after prolonged agitation, especially from 1837.

55b. **21. Anselm, Becket:** Saint Anselm (1033-1109), scholastic philosopher, Archbishop of Canterbury (1093), canonized (1494) by Pope Alexander VI. — Thomas à Becket (1118?-70), English prelate of Norman parentage, Henry II's chancellor, Archbishop of Canterbury (1162); murdered in Canterbury Cathedral (1170).

51. changed into Apes: Sale's *Koran*—Introduction (Carlyle's note).

HAPPY

56a. 38. Worship of Sorrow: See "The Everlasting Yea," and notes.
56b. 14. Stomach: There is no basis for such etymology.
37. Greatest-Happiness Principle: Benthamite utilitarianism, or the principle that the greatest happiness of the greatest number is the standard of right and wrong in conduct. By happiness Carlyle here means enjoyment of the pleasant things of life, mainly material.
57a. 42. Rest, rest, perturbed spirit: *Hamlet*, I, v, 183.
57b. 15. Happiness our being's end and aim: Pope's *Essay on Man*, IV, 1.
34. eupeptic Curtis: Sir William Curtis (1752-1829), rich banker, member of parliament, lord mayor of London, close friend of George IV, and the butt of ridicule for his epicurean ways of life.
35. Epicurus: Greek philosopher (342?-270 B.C.), who taught in Athens; founder of Epicureanism, or the doctrine that pleasure is the only good. He put the emphasis, however, upon pleasures of the mind rather than of the body.
35. unhappy as Job: *Job*, II, 7-8.
36. Byron with Giaours: Byron's *The Giaour* is a typical expression of Byronic mélancholy and 'sensibility.'

LABOR

58a. 22. Know thyself: Words inscribed in Greek over the portico of the temple of Apollo at Delphi.
58b. 11. Prophet Ezechiel: There is no reference to the potter's wheel in *Ezekiel*. Probably Carlyle remembered the passage in *Jeremiah*, XVIII, 1-6 and ascribed it to the wrong prophet.
30. vessel of dishonour: *Romans*, IX, 21.
59a. 8. Doubt of whatever kind: See Goethe's *Wilhelm Meister's Apprenticeship*, II, bk. V, Ch. XVI (Carlyle's trans.).
18. Sir Christopher: Sir Christopher Wren (1632-1723), English architect and member of the Royal Society, who had a principal part in the rebuilding of London after the great fire (1666) and who rebuilt St. Paul's Cathedral (1675-1716) in spite of difficulties to which Carlyle refers.
26. Nell-Gwyn Defenders: Nell Gwyn (1650-87) was a popular actress and a mistress of Charles II. 'Defender of the Faith' is a title conferred by Pope Leo X upon Henry VIII for the King's answer to Luther, and ever since used by English sovereigns. Carlyle sweepingly alludes to Charles II and other kings of his kind.
54. monument: Wren's tomb in St. Paul's has the inscription: *'Si monumentum quaeris circumspice'*—If you seek his monument look around you.
59b. 12. Gideon: *Judges*, VI, 37.
31. "It is so," says Goethe: *Wilhelm Meister's Travels*, ch. XIV, par. 12.
46. Ursa Major: The Great Bear, a constellation near the North Pole, popularly called the Big Dipper.

REWARD

60a. 32. Brahmins, Antinomians, Dervishes: Brahmins (or Brahmans), members of the highest caste among the Hindus. —— Antinomians: ancient Christian sects who held that the moral law is not binding and that faith alone is necessary to salvation. —— Spinning Dervishes: Moslem friars who work themselves to a religious frenzy by whirling round and round until they collapse.
60b. 11. Shovel-hat: A broad-brimmed hat, turned up at the sides, worn by clergymen of the English Church; to Carlyle a symbol of religious conformity.
11. Talfourd-Mahon Copyrights: Sir Thomas Noon Talfourd (1795-1854), judge, poet, editor, and Philip Henry, 5th Earl of Stanhope (better known by his courtesy title, Lord Mahon, 1805-75), historian and parliamentarian, were authors of the Copyright Law of 1842.
20. Sinai thunders: *Exodus*, XIX, 16-19.
33. the Night cometh: *John*, IX, 4.

41. Kepler-Newton: Johannes Kepler (1571-1630), German mathematician and astronomer. —— Sir Isaac Newton (1642-1727) English mathematical physicist, author of *Principia* (1687), president of the Royal Society (1703-27).

44. Agony of bloody sweat: *Luke*, XXII, 44.

61a. **7. Spartan Mother:** Ἡ τὰν ἢ ἐπὶ τὰν; Greek saying, author unknown.

23. Mayfair: Aristocratic quarter of London, east of Hyde Park, so called from an annual fair that used to be held there in May.

37. unprofitable servants: *Luke*, XVII, 10.

40. 'much of my life': See Boswell's *Life of Johnson*, for August 5, 1763: "I have been an idle fellow all my life."

50. Eldorados: Lands of gold, imagined by Spanish explorers.

61b. **2. St. Stephens:** St. Stephen's Chapel, Westminster, where the House of Commons met until the Chapel was destroyed by fire in 1834.

5. Fair day's-wages: The demand of the Chartists.

20. Owen's Labor-bank: Robert Owen (1771-1858), manufacturer, philanthropist, and first English socialist, established in 1832 an unsuccessful 'Equitable Labor Exchange', in which 'Labor Notes' were the medium of exchange.

28. Downing-street: Location of many government offices in London, including residences of the Prime Minister and the Chancellor of the Exchequer.

62a. **11. as Burns said:** The quotation, free and not literal, is from a letter to George Thomson, 16 Sept., 1792 (*Letters of Robert Burns*, ed. Ferguson, II, 123).

31. bodies forth the form of Things Unseen: *A Midsummer-Night's Dream*, V, i, 14-15.

62b. **10. Mothers—Manes:** Goethe told Eckermann he "found in Plutarch that in ancient Greece mention was made of the Mothers as divinities" (*Conversations*, for Jan. 10, 1830: *Everyman's* trans., 342). By them the poet seems to have meant the mysterious, ideal, primeval forces (truth, beauty, etc.) "which manifest themselves through Genius in a manner inexplicable to all ordinary human consciousness." (Bayard Taylor's note). For Goethe's use of the idea see *Faust*, Part II, i, Sc. V (Dark Gallery). —— Manes: literally the 'good' gods in Roman religion; the spirits of the dead and gods of the lower world; or, finally, ancestral spirits, worshipped as gods.

10. Hercules-like: The twelfth and last task of Hercules was to bring to the upper world the three-headed dog Cerberus that guarded the entrance to Hades.

15. Lubberlands: Imaginary land of plenty and idleness.

17. Acheron: River of woe in Hades.

19. shall "make thee lean" etc.: *Paradiso*, XXV, opening lines.

36. Poet Dryden: "Great wits are sure to madness near allied" (*Absalom and Achitophel*, 163).

42. Eurydice: Loved by Orpheus, who went to Tartarus to bring her back to earth.

63a. **11. lath-and-plaster hats:** Used as advertisements.

15. Black or White Surplice: Sharp controversies were disturbing the English Church, at the time of the Oxford Movement, as to whether the preacher should wear the black gown or the white surplice.

16. Stuffed hair-and-leather Popes: See Ch. I of this third Book of *Past and Present*.

31. Great Taskmaster's eye: See Milton's sonnet, *How Soon Hath Time*. . . .

40. Midas-eared: In Greek mythology, Midas, king of Phrygia, decided a musical contest between Pan and Apollo in favor of Pan. Apollo then changed the ears of Midas into ass's ears. Dionysus once promised to grant Midas whatever he wished. He asked that all he touched be turned to gold. When his food became gold, he quickly begged that the favor be recalled. Midas is Carlyle's symbol for stupidity and greed.

48. Plugson of Undershot: Carlyle's typical manufacturer. 'Undershot' is a kind of mill-wheel moved by the power of water flowing under it.

48. Taillefer: Minstrel in the army of William the Conqueror who, at the Battle of Hastings (1066), rode in front of the troops singing the Song of Roland: he was the first to fall.

63b. **7. Antæus-like:** Antæus was a mythological giant who renewed his strength and was invincible every time he touched Earth, his mother. He was finally overcome by Hercules who lifted him above the ground and then strangled him.

36. Civil-List: In Great Britain a list of charges for the support of officers of the State.

In modern use, however, it means money voted by Parliament for the expenses of the sovereign and his household.

36. Goulburn—Baring: Chancellors of the Exchequer; Goulburn, 1841-46, and Baring, 1839-41.

64a. 27. Arms and the Man: *"Arma virumque cano"* (Aeneid, I, i).

DEMOCRACY

64b. 26. Stockport cellars—Poor-Law Bastilles: Stockport is a North-England manufacturing town. Bastilles are workhouses (see Bk. I, Ch. I, *P. and P.*).

37. *villani, bordarii, sochemanni:* Medieval names for serfs.

65a. 15. Phalaris' Bull: Phalaris was a tyrant of ancient Sicily, who punished criminals by roasting them alive in a bronze bull.

21. Irish widow: Carlyle is loosely quoting from Bk. III, Ch. II, where the incident is related.

39. Dahomey: A colony on the slave coast of West Africa.

41. Mungo Park: South African explorer (1771-1806), from whose *Travels in the Interior of Africa* (1799) Carlyle finds the incident described.

65b. 5. Gurth—Cedric: Characters in Scott's *Ivanhoe*.

6. Dryasdust: Satirical name for the ultra-dry, pedantic antiquarian or historian; an imaginary character also introduced by Scott in some of the prefaces to his novels.

66a. 42. William the Conqueror: William of Normandy, called the Conqueror (1027-87), invaded and conquered England (1066) and was king (1066-1087) until his death; because of his illegitimate birth Carlyle calls him "this big burly William the Bastard."

43. Tancred: Norman hero (1078?-1112), whose exploits in the First Crusade (1096-99) are celebrated in Tasso's *Jerusalem Delivered* (1575).

45. Champion of England: He appears at Coronation ceremonies dressed in full armour, as a survival of old custom. (See Bk. III, Ch. I, *P. and P.*)

66b. 3. Hereward: Saxon hero and outlaw, who in 1070 was the last to resist William the Conqueror in the Fen Country.

4. Earl of Waltheof: Saxon Earl of Northumberland, beheaded in 1076 for conspiracy against William.

45. to bush the partridges: Bushes were planted to protect game from the nets of poachers.

50. Joe-Manton: Joseph Manton (1766?-1835) was a London gunmaker, whose guns were much used by aristocratic game-hunters.

67a. 36. St. Mary Axe: A London church and parish. In the Church of England the vestry is a body of persons elected annually by the parish and charged with its temporal affairs, and hence, to Carlyle, a sign of democracy.

43. Teufeulsdröckh: Carlyle proceeds to speak in the freer language of the imaginary German hero of *Sartor* (i.e. himself).

67b. 5. Conservative Premier: Sir Robert Peel, who was Prime Minister for the second term (1841-46), when Carlyle was writing *Past and Present*. Under his leadership the corn laws were repealed (1846),—another sign of 'inevitable' democracy.

19. Malines-lace: Lace made in the Belgian city of Malines, or Mechlin.

22. Sumptuary Laws: Regulations to control the amount of money spent on private luxuries.

35. Cheruscan: The Cherusci were an ancient German tribe mentioned by Julius Caesar.

68a. 16. Sedan and Huddersfield: The first is a cloth-manufacturing town on the French frontier, better known as the place of Napoleon III's surrender to Germany in 1870. The second is a cloth-manufacturing town in Yorkshire, England.

68b. 9. Windsor Georges: Jewelled decorations, showing a figure of St. George, patron saint of England.

19. Heavy-wet: Strong ale or stout.

69a. 13. National Palaver: Parliament.

37. Pococurantism: Indifference, nonchalance. Pococurante is a character in Voltaire's *Candide* who has everything wealth can buy and is completely *blasé*.

38. Beau-Brummelism: Dandyism. Beau Brummel (1778-1840) was the typical dandy of his day, friend of the Prince of Wales, afterwards George IV.

SHOOTING NIAGARA : AND AFTER?

This essay is Carlyle's "last word" on the "condition of England question." It is, he said quite truly, "very fierce, exaggerative, ragged, unkempt, and defective;" but it is, nevertheless, a very powerful final blow struck against advancing democracy, as Carlyle then saw it. Disraeli had just come into power at the head of a Tory government and in August, 1867, had put through the second great Reform Bill,—"courting the votes of the mob," wrote Froude, interpreting Carlyle, "by the longest plunge yet ventured into the whirlpool of democracy." The essay appeared first in *Macmillan's Magazine* for August, 1867, and was published ("with some additions and corrections") as a pamphlet in the following September.

To economize space some paragraphs and sentences have been omitted from Carlyle's text without injury, it is believed, to the essential thought and structure of the essay.

70b. **23. Cheap and Nasty:** A colloquialism current among English tailors, referring to terrible sweat-shop conditions. The phrase 'Cheap Clothes and Nasty' was used as the title to one of Charles Kingsley's best known tracts, published in the *Christian Socialist* in 1850 over the *nom de plume* Parson Lot.

71a. **29. Herr von Bismarck:** Prince Otto von Bismarck (1815-1898) came into power in 1862, and promptly began his long career of aggression and imperialism. Prussianism found in him its most powerful champion, whose solution of German problems was, he said, by "blood and iron." In 1866 Bismarck formed the North German Federation under the leadership of Prussia, and in the summer of 1867 he brought to completion the drafting of its constitution. Carlyle said of Bismarck: "I always thought him the right man in the right place."

34. Niagara leap: That is, the Reform Bill of 1867.

46. Euclid: Greek geometer who lived about 300 B.C. and founded a school in Alexandria. He might be called the father of geometry, since his *Elements* is the basis of later works on the subject.

71b. **13. Cleon the Tanner:** Athenian demagogue and opponent of Pericles, leader of the democratic party, who demanded the continuation of the Peloponnesian War: killed in the battle of Amphipolis 422 B.C. He was brought up in the trade of a tanner, and is satirized by Aristophanes in *The Knights*.

13. Beales: Edmund Beales (1803-81), a political agitator and president of the Reform League, who organized the great popular demonstration in July, 1866, when the crowds, in anger at the government's refusal to permit a meeting in Hyde Park, broke down the railings and swarmed inside until armed forces drove them out.

13. John of Bromwicham: John Bright (1811-89), English orator, and liberal statesman, was a member of Parliament from Birmingham from 1857 to the end of his life. He strongly supported the Reform Bill of 1867.

72b. **40. Prytaneum:** In ancient Greek cities and towns the Prytaneum, built as the meeting place of the chief magistrates, was also used as a public hall in which hospitality was extended to distinguished citizens, Greek or foreign.

73b. **50. John of Leyden:** A Dutch Anabaptist fanatic (1509-36), who set up a 'Kingdom of Zion' in Münster, and introduced polygamy and community of goods, ruling with royal authority until he was imprisoned and executed.

50. Walter the Penniless: An eleventh century French knight who, with Peter the Hermit, led a mob of people through Europe in what is known as the Peasant's Crusade (1096); killed in 1097.

74a. **40. Saturnian time:** The golden age, in allusion to the classical myth that during the reign of the god Saturn peace and happiness were universal.

75b. **24. Jamaica and Dominica:** Island possessions of Great Britain in the West Indies. Carlyle alludes to insurrections among Negroes, especially the outbreak in Jamaica in 1865, when Governor Eyre by swift and rigorous measures suppressed a revolt and probably saved hundreds of whites from massacre. When Eyre was recalled in 1866 and tried for his harsh measures, Carlyle was vice-president of the Eyre Defence Committee, organized in London.

76a. **13. Orson:** Meaning 'bear'; one of the twin heroes in a 15th century romance, *Valentine and Orson*. Abandoned in infancy, Valentine is rescued by his uncle, Pepin, and brought up in court, while Orson is suckled by a bear, though eventually reclaimed. He is Carlyle's symbol of an 'unbred' nobleman or man of genius.

76b. 38. In 1789, for instance: Date of the fall of the Bastille in Paris, July 14, and the beginning of the French Revolution.

77a. 33. Copper-Captaincy: Napoleon III (1808-73), Emperor of France, (1852-71), because they thought him something of an imposter, was nicknamed by the English the "Copper Captain", from a bad shilling of copper silvered.

34. Russian Abolition, etc.: In 1815, at the Congress of Vienna, Poland was "erected into a constitutional kingdom under the Tzar" of Russia; in 1831 Russia suppressed a revolutionary outbreak and completely absorbed Poland; in 1863 another insurrection was "quickly and cruelly suppressed." Carlyle has these events in mind as he thinks of England's possible fate.

77b. 2. Comte-Philosophy-ing: Allusion to the 'positive philosophy' of Auguste Comte (1798-1857), which was being interpreted and disseminated in England during the 'sixties and 'seventies under the leadership of Frederic Harrison (1831-1923).

29. Oliver: Oliver Cromwell.

78b. 42. Paternoster-Rows: Paternoster Row, a London street, "long the center of the book and publishing trade of the city"; rosaries and prayer-books in still older days were made there.

79a. 24. Grub Street: A London street (now Bread Street) formerly inhabited by needy writers or literary hacks. In the 18th century the phrase became synonymous with 'small fry' literary folk, wherever they lived.

79b. 27. Blue Books: Authoritative reports, generally governmental, so called because in England such reports were issued in blue-paper covers.

80a. 28. Pandora's Box: Pandora, the all-gifted, was a beautiful woman to whom Zeus gave a box filled with evils, which overspread the earth when she opened it out of curiosity. Hope, alone, it was said, remained in the box.

52. Etruscan Pottery: The Etruscans were an ancient people living in Italy between the Tiber and the Arno, before the rise of Rome.

81a. 4. Overend-Gurney: 'Overend and Gurney Limited' was a prominent bill-broker firm (heads of the firm called themselves 'money-dealers') in Lombard Street, London. They "crashed to ruin" in 1866.

5. Chatham and Dover Railway: The line from London to Dover via Chatham became insolvent in the financial crisis of 1866.

82a. 8. Whit-Monday: The day after Whitsunday and a bank holiday in England.

83b. 2. Buncombe: Personified colloquialism, meaning one who speaks insincerely to gain popular applause.

THOMAS BABINGTON MACAULAY

SELECTED BIBLIOGRAPHY

I. STANDARD EDITIONS

The Works, 8 vols., ed. Lady Trevelyan, London, 1897.
The Complete Writings, 20 vols., Boston, 1899-1900.
Speeches, selected by G. M. Young, London, 1935.
Lays of Ancient Rome and Other Historical Poems, ed. G. M. Trevelyan, London, 1928.
Critical and Historical Essays Contributed to the Edinburgh Review, ed. F. C. Montagu, 3 vols., London, 1903.
Critical and Historical Essays, 2 vols., Everyman's Library.

II. BIOGRAPHY AND CRITICISM

ABBOTT, W. C., "Macaulay and the New History," *Yale Review,* XVIII (1929), 539-57.
ARNOLD, F., *The Public Life of Lord Macaulay,* London, 1862.
BAGEHOT, WALTER, *Literary Studies,* London, 1879.
BEATTY, R. C., *Lord Macaulay, Victorian Liberal,* University of Oklahoma Press, Norman, 1938.
BLAKELY, T. E., "Macaulay's English," *Harper's,* CV (1902), 529-33.
BRADFIELD, T., "Enduring Characteristics of Macaulay," *Westminster Review,* CXLV (1896), 152-66.
BRYANT, ARTHUR, *Macaulay,* London, 1932.

CHISLETT, W., Jr., "Macaulay's Classical Reading," *Classical Journal*, XI (1915), 142-50.

DICEY, A. V., "Macaulay and His Critics," *Nation*, LXXIV (1902), 388-89.

DOBREE, BONAMY, "Macaulay," *Criterion*, XII (1933), 593.

FIRTH, SIR CHARLES, *A Commentary on Macaulay's History of England*, London, 1938.

FROUDE, J. A., "Lord Macaulay," *Fraser's*, XCIII (1876), 675-94.

GLADSTONE, W. E., "The Life and Letters of Lord Macaulay," *Quarterly Review*, CXLII (1876), 1-50.

HARRISON, F., *Studies in Early Victorian Literature*, London, 1895.

JEBB, SIR R. C., *Macaulay*, London, 1900.

MILMAN, H. H., *A Memoir of Lord Macaulay*, London, 1862.

MORLEY, JOHN, *Critical Miscellanies*, I, London, 1904.

MORRISON, J. C., *Macaulay* (E.M.L.), London, 1882.

PATTISON, MARK, "Macaulay," *Encyclopaedia Britannica* (Eds. 9 and 11).

PAUL, H., *Men and Letters*, London, 1901.

SAINTSBURY, GEORGE, *Corrected Impressions*, New York, 1895.

SAMPSON, GEORGE, "Macaulay and Milton," *Edinburgh Review*, CCXLII (1925), 165-78.

SEDGWICK, H. D., *Essays on Great Writers*, Boston, 1903.

STEPHEN, LESLIE, *Hours in a Library*, III, London, 1907.

STRACHEY, LYTTON, *Portraits in Miniature*, London, 1931.

THACKERAY, W. M., *Roundabout Papers*, London, 1863.

THAYER, W. R., "Macaulay Fifty Years After," *North American Review*, CXC (1909), 735-42.

TREVELYAN, G. O., *The Life and Letters of Lord Macaulay*, 2 vols., London, 1876.

WILLIAMS, S. T., "Macaulay's Reading and Literary Criticism," *Philological Quarterly*, III (1924), 119-131.

WILLOUGHBY, D., "Lord Macaulay" in *The Great Victorians*, ed. by H. J. and H. Massingham, New York, 1932.

NOTES AND COMMENTS

SOUTHEY'S COLLOQUIES

The essay is a review of Robert Southey's *Sir Thomas More; or, Colloquies on the Progress and Prospects of Society*, 1829. Introductory and a few other paragraphs are omitted.

87a. 9. Catholic Claims: Southey's statement in the *Preface*, XIII, is as follows: "My opinions respecting the Roman Catholic claims to seats in Parliament and certain offices in the State have always been the same." In his early manhood Southey, like Coleridge and Wordsworth, was a revolutionary 'republican' or radical, but shortly after the turn of the century he changed into an 'Ultra-Tory,' contributing for thirty years articles to the great Tory periodical, the *Quarterly Review*. "Mr. Southey," said Hazlitt, "missed his way in Utopia; he has found it at old Sarum."

29. Jacobin: Originally the name was applied to Dominican friars, whose first convent in Paris was near the church of St. Jacques (Latin, Jacobus). During the French Revolution radical democrats who met in this old convent were called by their opponents *Jacobins*. Robespierre was their leader until his fall in 1794. In England, during these revolutionary times and after, radical thinkers were called Jacobins.

87b. 22. ride with darkness: *Paradise Lost*, IX, 63-64:—

> "The space of seven continu'd Nights he rode
> With darkness."

33. *Vision of Judgement:* A poem by Southey (then Poet Laureate) in hexameters (1821) on the apotheosis of George III: brilliantly satirized by Byron in *The Vision of Judgment* (1822).

36. Princess Charlotte: She was the only daughter (1796-1817) of the Prince of Wales, who became George IV in 1820.

88a. 40. Sir Thomas More: "The foremost Englishman of his time" (1478-1535), author of *Utopia* (in Latin, 1516), Lord Chancellor and Privy Counsellor under Henry VIII, by whose order he was beheaded in 1535 for refusing to support the king in his divorce from Catherine of Aragon and to take the oath of supremacy. Many regarded him as a martyr. He was canonized in 1935.

45. Cranmer: Thomas Cranmer (1489-1556), Archbishop of Canterbury under Henry VIII. He supported the King in the royal divorce from Queen Catherine (Queen Mary's mother) and in the Act of Supremacy. Under Mary he was imprisoned, but hoped to save his life by recantation of his Protestantism. Finding pardon impossible, he repudiated his recantation and was burned at the stake, holding his right hand "steadily in the flame," since this offending member had written in fear "contrary to my heart."

88b. **32. Laureate:** Southey became Poet Laureate in 1813.

36. Apocalypse: See *Revelation,* XX for prophecy of the thousand years of the reign of Christ and the subjugation of Satan.

42. Mr. Murray and Mr. Colburn: John Murray (1778-1843), prominent London publisher, who published the *Quarterly Review* (beginning 1809) and the works of Byron. Henry Colburn (d. 1855), London publisher, proprietor of the *Literary Gazette* (beginning 1817) and publisher of fashionable novels.

45. *Thalaba* (1801)—*Curse of Kehama* (1810): Romantic narrative poems by Southey.

89a. **5. the *Pucelle:*** Voltaire's *La Pucelle* (The Maid—1762) is a mock epic burlesquing Joan of Arc.

17. Carlile: Richard Carlile (1790-1843), English free thinker and reformer, printer of radical periodicals and publisher of Tom Paine's writings.

90a. **45. Amphion:** Son of Zeus and Antiope, a Theban princess. By the music of his lyre he charmed the stones into place for the walls of Thebes.

91a. **16. Montesinos:** Legendary Spanish hero, whose name is given to a cavern in *Don Quixote.* Southey's use of the name suggests his romantic interest in Spanish history and literature.

91b. **30. Teniers:** David Teniers, father (1582-1649), or son (1610-90), both of same name and both famous for their genre and landscape paintings.

93a. **16. Diafoirus:** Name of a quack doctor in Molière's *La Malade Imaginaire* (1673). The Latin line is from the Third Interlude of the play, which is an untranslatable medley of dog-Latin, French and Italian.

94a. **34. Lady Bountiful:** In Farquhar's comedy, *The Beaux' Stratagem* (1707), a country gentlewoman famous for her benevolence.

35. Paul Pry: Idle, meddlesome hero of a comedy, *Paul Pry* (1825), by John Poole (1786?-1872).

95a. **51. Tartarus:** In Greek mythology the infernal regions immeasurably below Hades, reserved especially for the rebel Titans.

52. Elysian Fields: Dwelling place of guiltless souls after death, a land of sunlight and gentle breezes on the western edge of the world (according to Homer).

54. Orestes-Midias: Allusions to *The Birds* of Aristophanes, in which Orestes is a notorious thief and Midias is an Athenian who "looks like a quail that has been hit hard on the head."

95b. **7. Brahmins:** Members of the highest caste among the Hindus.

96a. **37. Knights of Windsor:** "Members of an order of military pensioners, quartered within the precincts of Windsor Castle" (Webster's *International*).

97a. **4. *Relapse:*** *The Relapse,* or *Virtue in Danger* (1696), a comedy by Sir John Vanbrugh (1664-1726).

97b. **20. Arminian:** Referring to religious doctrines of Jacobus Arminius, Dutch reformed theologian (1560-1609), doctrines which were held by followers of John Wesley and by members of the English Church known as 'Low Church.'

98a. **2. Laud:** William Laud (1573-1645), Archbishop of Canterbury (1633-41), a High Churchman who supported Charles I and extreme Anglicanism, and who vigorously fought nonconformity: condemned and beheaded (1645) by the Long Parliament.

18. when the States-General met: The States-General was an assembly of the three chief estates or classes of France, the clergy, the nobility, the commons or 'third estate.' The assembly met first in 1302. When it was called at Versailles, May 5, 1789 (a prelude to the French Revolution), it had not met since 1614.

46. Another government arose: The Cromwellian Commonwealth, 1649-1660.

99a. **17. Rousseau never imposed:** An allusion to his doctrine of a 'return to nature' as meaning a return to the savage state. 'Nature' for Rousseau never meant primitive society, but rather an ideal state of human freedom and equality as opposed to the corruptions and inequalities which he saw in the artificial society of his day (see his *Discours sur l'origine de l'inégalité parmi les hommes,* 1755, and *Contrat Social,* 1762).

99b. 37. Edward the Sixth: King of England, 1547-53.

48. Harrison: William Harrison (1534-93), chronologist, antiquary, country clergyman, and author of *Description of England,* written for Holinshed's *Chronicles* (1577), and accounted "the truest picture that has come down to us of the England that Shakespeare knew and sang" (*Camb. Hist. Lit.* III, 368).

100a. 51. Sir Henry Halford—Dr. Butts: Sir Henry Halford (1766-1844) was physician to Kings George III and IV, William IV, and to Queen Victoria. —— Sir William Butts (d. 1545) was court physician to Henry VIII, to Anne Boleyn and Jane Seymour, and to Cardinal Wolsey.

100b. 4. Druids: A religious order in ancient Gaul, Britain, and Ireland.

101a. 37. Magendie: François Magendie (1783-1855), pioneer in experimental physiology.

101b. 30. Spitalfields: Section of East London, formerly center of silk weaving.

103a. 35. Thames: During the war with Holland in the reign of Charles II, the Dutch fleet sailed up the Thames to Gravesend unopposed (1667) and then withdrew, "masters of the Channel."

37. Charles the Fifth: Emperor of the Holy Roman Empire (1519-56) and King of Spain as Charles I (1516-56), who captured Francis I, King of France, in the battle of Pavia (1525), and kept him prisoner at Madrid for a year.

103b. 9. poorer than in 1790?: i.e. in the period of the French Revolution and the Napoleonic wars.

38. crash in 1720: i.e. the bursting of the South Sea Bubble, a fraudulent scheme of stock-jobbers (South Sea Company) to pay off the national debt "in return for the monopoly of trade to the South Sea" (1720). In 1721 the 'bubble' burst, causing widespread financial ruin.

104a. 11. the fee-simple of the revenue: i.e. the total landed estate (from which revenues were drawn) of the Plantagenets, without any condition or limitation whatsoever.

37. exclaimed Swift: The quotation, factually but not literally correct, is from Swift's *The Conduct of the Allies* (1711), a powerful pamphlet that helped to overthrow the Whigs and give power to the Tories to end the war of the Spanish Succession (1702-13).

104b. 1. Junius: Pseudonym of the author of a series of 69 political letters (21 Jan. 1769—21 Jan. 1772), written for the *Public Advertiser* and attacking prominent leaders in the Tory ministry, including the Dukes of Grafton and Bedford, Lord North, Lord Granby, and even George III. Authorship of the papers is unknown, though attributed to Sir Philip Francis or to the Earl of Shelburne in particular.

5. statesmen of 1783: Pitt, Fox, and Burke (as Macaulay says). William Pitt was Prime Minister 1783-1801 and 1804-06. Fox and Burke were the great liberal statesmen and orators during the stormy period of war with the American colonies and the period of the French Revolution.

SAMUEL JOHNSON

The occasion of this essay was the appearance of a new edition of Boswell's *Life of Johnson,* edited in five volumes by John Wilson Croker in 1831. The introductory pages are omitted, wherein the reviewer delivers a slashing attack upon Croker's edition as "ill compiled, ill arranged, ill written, and ill printed." Macaulay's essay was contributed to the *Edinburgh Review* for September, 1831.

104a. 5. Demosthenes: Athenian orator and statesman (385?-322 B.C.), most famous for his *Philippics,* a series of orations against Philip of Macedon.

6. Boswell: James Boswell (1740-95) first met Johnson May 16, 1763, when Johnson was in his 64th year and Boswell in his 23rd. He therefore saw Johnson at intervals for 21 years and was with him 180 days, or 276 days in all including the tour of the Hebrides (so estimates Croker). Whatever else Boswell may have been he was also a very conscious literary artist, who put seven years of labor upon the *Life,* after Johnson's death, and published it in 1791,—"the whole," he said, "exhibiting a view of literature and literary men in Great Britain for near half a century." "Johnson," said Burke, "is greater in Boswell's books than in his own."

9. Eclipse: A racehorse owned by Dennis O'Kelly (1720?-87), who made the boast at Epsom, May 3, 1769.

105a. 1. Dunciad: Pope's most ambitious satire (1728, 1st ed.; 1742, 2nd ed.), in which he attacked his enemies and the literary hacks of Grub Street.

2. Beauclerk: Topham Beauclerk (1739-80), descendant of Charles II and Nell Gwyn, was one of the brilliant younger members of Johnson's circle: "Johnson delighted in the good qualities of Beauclerk, and hoped to correct the evil" (Boswell).

16. Corsica Boswell: On his continental tour Boswell met General Pasquale Paoli (1725-1807), leader of revolts in Corsica for independence against the Genoese and, later, the French. His friendship with the Corsican patriot resulted in two books: *An Account of Corsica* (1768) and *British Essays in Favor of the Brave Corsicans* (1769).

16. Tour: Boswell's *Journal of a Tour of the Hebrides* (1785).

29. Tom Paine: Thomas Paine (1737-1809), political philosopher and revolutionary radical, author of *The Rights of Man* (1791-92) and *The Age of Reason* (1794-96).

47. took a hair of the dog that had bitten him: Old proverb used figuratively to mean another drink to cure the former one.

105b. 2. Lady Cork: Mary Monckton, Countess of Cork and Orrery (1746-1840), described as an 'English blue-stocking,' whose London house was a rendezvous of celebrities.

5. Duchess of Argyll: Elizabeth Gunning, wife of the 3rd Duke of Argyll. As told in the *Tour* for Oct. 25, 1773, the Duchess, at a dinner in the castle, treated Boswell with "stately contempt."

6. Colonel Macleod: See *Tour* for Sept. 16, 1773.

30. one of his contemporaries: Horace Walpole,—according to Boswell's note in the *Life* (year, 1763).

33. talked like poor Poll: One evening in Feb., 1774, at St. James's Coffee House in London, a company of wits started to write comic epitaphs upon one another. Garrick instantly dashed off the familiar couplet on Goldsmith:

> "Here lies Nolly Goldsmith, for shortness called Noll,
> Who wrote like an angel, but talked like poor Poll."

Unable to reply at once, Goldsmith later wrote several epitaphs which, after his death, were published under the title, *Retaliation*, the last thing from his pen.

36. La Fontaine: Jean de la Fontaine (1621-95), wayward and child-like in worldly affairs, was a genius in the art of French poetry. His *Fables* (1668-94) is a classic.

38. Hierocles: An Alexandrian neo-platonist of the fifth century A.D., under whose name there is extant a collection of jokes and amusing stories.

50. Paul Pry: An inquisitive character in a comedy of that name (1825) by John Poole (1786?-1872).

106a. 8. Tacitus-Clarendon-Alfieri: Cornelius Tacitus (55?-cir. 117 A.D.). Roman historian, author of *Agricola*, and *Annals*. —— Edward Hyde, first Earl of Clarendon (1609--74), author of *History of the Rebellion* (1702-4) and an autobiography, *Life of Edward, Earl of Clarendon* (1759). —— Count Vittorio Alfieri (1749-1803), Italian dramatist and patriot, author of an autobiography begun in 1790 and completed in 1803, the year of his death. This *Vita* is his only important prose work.

8. his own idol Johnson: An allusion to Johnson's *Lives of the Poets* (1778-81).

44. Justice Shallow: In *Merry Wives;* Dr. Caius and Fluellen: in *Henry V.*

106b. 5. Caesar Borgia or Danton: Cesare Borgia (1476-1507), son of Pope Alexander VI, was notorious for his cruelty and terrorism. —— George Jacques Danton (1759-94), French Revolutionary extremist, was a leader in the Reign of Terror (1793-94).

7. Alnaschar: An infatuated dreamer in *Arabian Nights;* Malvolio is a foolish egotist in *Twelfth Night.*

19. Palace of Truth: Allusion to *Le Palais de la Vérité*, by the Comtesse de Genlis (1746-1830), French novelist, dramatist, memoir-writer; author of more than 80 different works.

40. his son: Sir Alexander Boswell (1775-1822), antiquary, poet, member of parliament (1818-21), was the eldest son of Johnson's biographer.

107a. 32. Churchill-Kenrick: Charles Churchill (1731-64), English poet and satirist, caricatured Johnson as Pomposo in his poem *The Ghost* (1763). Johnson, in turn, called him "a blockhead." —— William Kenrick (1725?-79), miscellaneous writer and vicious satirist, who made several scurrilous attacks upon Johnson.

107b. 16. Reynolds and the Wartons: Sir Joshua Reynolds (1723-92) was, says Boswell, "the first proposer" of the Club in Feb., 1764; it had, however, "existed long without a name."

Sir Joshua painted the portraits of several members. —— Joseph Warton (1722-1800) and his brother, Thomas Warton (1728-90) were conspicuous figures in the literary life of their time as critics, poets, and editors or historians of literature. Thomas Warton was poet laureate (1785-90), and both were members of the Club.

18. Hamilton: William Gerard Hamilton (1729-96), English politician and member of parliament, who was nicknamed 'Single-speech' Hamilton because his first speech was his best. Johnson "maintained a long intimacy with him," says Boswell.

20. Langton: Bennett Langton (1737-1801), an original member of the Club. "The earth does not bear a worthier man than Bennett Langton," said Johnson.

21. Stowell, Jones, Windham: William Scott, Lord Stowell (1745-1836), English jurist and authority on maritime and international law, friend of Johnson. —— Sir William Jones (1746-94), orientalist and jurist, member of the Club. —— William Windham (1750-1810), statesman, member of parliament (1784-1810), Secretary for War (1794-1801) under Pitt; member of the Club.

23. Mrs. Thrale: Hester Lynch Thrale, later Piozzi (1741-1821), was for nearly twenty years hostess to Johnson at her home in Streatham, some seven or eight miles from London on the Surrey side. She published *Anecdotes of the late Samuel Johnson* (1786) and *Letters to and from the late Samuel Johnson* (1788).

50. Congreve and Addison: William Congreve (1670-1729), brilliant English Restoration dramatist in the field of comedy of manners. *The Way of the World* (1700) is his best play. — Joseph Addison (1672-1719), poet, essayist, statesman, a leading literary figure of the Queen Anne Age.

108a. 12. Congreve's first comedy: *The Old Bachelor* (1693), a stage success.

16. Smith: Edmund Smith (1671-2?-1710), classical scholar and critic of more promise than performance, whose failure to present to Lord Halifax the dedication of his play lost him "a place of three hundred pounds a year," says Johnson, who wrote his life.

19. Rowe: Nicholas Rowe (1674-1718), English poet and dramatist, first editor and biographer of Shakespeare (1709), poet laureate (1715-18).

23. Hughes: John Hughes (1677-1720), author of plays, (e.g. *Siege of Damascus,* 1720), contributor to *Tatler, Spectator, Guardian.*

25. Philips: Ambrose Philips (1675?-1749), called 'Namby-Pamby' because of some sentimental verses, minor poet and dramatist, friend of Addison, enemy of Pope.

26. Locke: John Locke (1632-1704), empirical English philosopher, whose *Essay Concerning Human Understanding* (1690) is a landmark in English philosophy.

28. Newton: Sir Isaac Newton (1642-1727), natural philosopher and mathematical genius, author of the famous *Principia* (1687).

29. Stepney and Prior: George Stepney (1663-1707), poet, member of the Kit-Cat Club, and envoy to Germany, Austria, and Holland successively. —— Matthew Prior (1664-1721), poet, diplomatist, writer of familiar verse and epigrams. In collaboration with Charles Montagne (afterwards first Earl of Halifax, 1661-1715), he wrote *The City Mouse and The Country Mouse* (1687), a parody of Dryden's *The Hind and The Panther.*

31. Gay: John Gay (1685-1732), poet and playwright, best known for *The Beggar's Opera* (1728).

38. Swift: Jonathan Swift (1667-1745), England's greatest satirist and for a few years (1710-1713) a powerful political figure, who spent the last half of his life in Dublin as Dean of St. Patrick's Cathedral.

40. Oxford: Robert Harley, first Earl of Oxford (1661-1724), Tory statesman, Chancellor of the Exchequer and head of the ministry (1710); Lord High Treasurer (1711), whose symbol of office was the white staff.

42. Parnell: Thomas Parnell (1679-1718), Anglo-Irish poet and clergyman, contributor to the *Spectator* and *Guardian,* friend of Pope and Swift; he became a Tory in 1710.

44. Steele: Sir Richard Steele (1672-1729), essayist and dramatist, started the *Tatler* (1709), the *Spectator* (1711), and the *Guardian* (1713); also active in political life.

46. Mainwaring: Arthur Mainwaring (1668-1712), wit, writer, member of the Kit-Cat Club, member of parliament and public official. Lord Godolphin in 1705 appointed him auditor of imprests (i.e. Office of loans to sailors and soldiers).

48. Tickell: Thomas Tickell (1686-1740), poet, editor, politician, secretary to the Lords Justices of Ireland from 1724.

51. Dorset: Charles Sackville (1638-1706), sixth Earl of Dorset, poet and courtier, patron of men of letters, including Dryden and Wycherley.

108b. 6. Harley and Bolingbroke: Harley is the Earl of Oxford noted above. —— Henry St. John, first Viscount Bolingbroke (1678-1751), statesman and orator, who shared leadership of the Tory party with Harley (1710-14); patron and friend of Swift and Pope. His deistic philosophy found expression in Pope's *Essay on Man*.

10. House of Hanover: Beginning with George I in 1714.

11. supreme power passed to a man: Sir Robert Walpole, first Earl of Orford (1676-1745), English statesman, master of finance, Prime Minister (1715-17; 1721-42), under whom political power was transferred from the House of Lords to the House of Commons.

25. Sir Charles Hanbury Williams: Satirical writer and diplomatist (1708-59), member of parliament, adherent of Walpole, "votary of wit and pleasure," said Burke.

27. Seasons-Pamela: James Thompson's *The Seasons* (1726-30); Samuel Richardson's *Pamela* (1740).

39. a foolish and unjust war: In 1739 an unsuccessful war was declared against Spain, which was soon followed by the War of the Austrian Succession (1740-48) and the Seven Years' War (1756-63). Walpole resigned in 1742, defeated by an opposition of Tories and 'Young Patriots' patronized by the King's son, Frederick, Prince of Wales. St. James's was the residence of the King; Leicester House, of Prince Frederick.

109a. 4. devoured the good ears: *Genesis*, XLI.

10. compters and spunging-houses: Debtors' prisons.

12. Common Side-Mount Scoundrel: The Common Side of the prison was the section given over to prisoners who could not pay fees or subsist without charity. —— Mount Scoundrel was the worst section, on a top floor. The old Fleet Prison was pulled down in 1846.

24. Grub Street: Once the name of a London street inhabited by needy hack writers.

27. bulk: A stall or counter projecting from a shop.

28. glass-house: Glass-factory. Johnson says of Richard Savage: "On a bulk, in a cellar, or in a glass-house among thieves and beggars, was to be found the author of *The Wanderer*" (*Lives of the Poets*: 'Savage').

33. Kitcat: Club of Whigs, politicians, and men of letters, so called from Christopher Cat in whose tavern members met.

33. Scriblerus Club: Authors' club, founded by Swift in 1714; Tory in politics.

35. High Allies: England, Austria, and the Empire, in the War of the Spanish Succession (1702-13).

38. Albemarle Street-Paternoster Row: Centers of London book and publishing trade.

109b. 2. a full third night: Proceeds of the third night's performance of a play went to the author.

11. Savage: Richard Savage (1697?-1743), minor poet and dramatist, who died in prison for debt. Johnson once shared his poverty and, later, wrote his biography (1744), which Macaulay seems to have had in mind as he wrote the paragraph.

12. Boyse: Samuel Boyse, or Boyce, (1708-49), minor poet, author of *The Deity: A Poem* (1739); he lived and died in wretchedness.

18. Betty Careless: A courtesan.

110a. 9. extended to his Homer: Pope earned financial independence with his translation of the *Iliad* (1715-20).

9. Young: Edward Young (1683-1765), dramatist, poet, author of *Night Thoughts* (1742-45). He received (1726) a pension of £200 a year.

15. Thomson-Mallet-Richardson: James Thomson (1700-48) received a pension of £100 a year (1738), through the influence of the Prince of Wales, and in 1744 was made surveyor general of the Leeward Islands, a sinecure from which "he received about £300 a year" (Johnson). —— David Mallet (1705?-65), minor poet and dramatist, whom the Prince of Wales made his under-secretary (1742). He is the reputed author of the patriotic song *Rule Britannia*. —— Samuel Richardson (1689-1761), the novelist, was a London printer by trade and became King's Printer and Master of the Stationers' Company.

29. all four arrested for debt: Johnson, in a letter (March 16, 1756) to Richardson, the novelist says: "I am now under an arrest for five pounds eighteen shillings" (*Life*, Hill's ed. I, 351 n). —— William Collins (1721-59), lyrical poet, remembered for his *Ode to Evening*, was once, says Johnson, "immured by a bailiff, that was prowling in the streets,"—a statement which probably means that the poet was under guard at home until the debt was paid. —— Henry Fielding (1707-54), playwright and "father of the English novel" (says Scott), was extravagant, improvident, and often in debt, but was probably never arrested. ——

James Thomson "is said to have been arrested for a debt of £70" (*Life, E. M. L.* 44).

42. a pension: In 1762 Johnson received from George III a pension of £300 a year at the hands of Lord Bute, Prime Minister.

110b. 5. Burke, Robertson, the Wartons, etc.: Of this group Burke, the Wartons, Gibbon, Adam Smith, Jones, and Goldsmith were members of the Club. —— William Robertson (1721-93), Scottish historian, author of *History of Scotland, 1542-1603* (1759), *History of Charles V* (1769), and *History of America* (1777). —— William Mason (1724-97), minor English poet and dramatist, author of *Life and Letters of Gray* (1774). —— James Beattie (1735-1803), Scottish poet, best known for his *Minstrel* (1771-4).

20. Curll and Osborne: Edmund Curll (1675-1747) and Thomas Osborne (d. 1767) were London booksellers. Both were lampooned in Pope's *The Dunciad.* Of Osborne Johnson says: "He was impertinent to me, and I beat him."

54. Streatham Park: Johnson met the Thrales in 1765, when he was 56; "he became one of the family," says Boswell.

111a. 1. St. John's Gate: The establishment of Edward Cave (1691-1754), printer and publisher, who founded and edited the *Gentleman's Magazine* (under the pseudonym of Sylvanus Urban), to which Johnson contributed for ten years. Boswell tells of an occasion at Cave's when Johnson was dressed so shabbily that he ate behind a screen (see *Life* for year 1744).

30. deferred hope which makes the heart sick: *Proverbs,* XIII, 12.

111b. 27. Lady Tavistock: See *Anecdotes of the late Samuel Johnson,* by Hester Lynch Piozzi, ed. S. C. Roberts (1925), 100-1.

42. to call him Holofernes: The newspapers had called Johnson and Goldsmith Holofernes and Dull, i.e. a pedant and his flatterer,—characters in *Love's Labour's Lost* (Piozzi's *Anecdotes, op. cit.,* 118).

43. Mrs. Carter: Elizabeth Carter (1717-1806), English poet, contributor to *Gentleman's Magazine,* translator of Epictetus. Johnson praised her Greek scholarship (for his quoted reply to her see Boswell's *Life* for April 20, 1781).

112a. 25. the fisherman in the Arabian tale: "The Fisherman and the Genie" in the *Arabian Nights.* One day the fisherman drew in with his net a vessel of yellow copper from which, when opened, there came a thick smoke ascending to the clouds and forming a great mist. The smoke presently reunited itself into the body of a genie, twice as high as the greatest of giants. The genie had been imprisoned in the vessel by the power of Solomon.

53. Hogarth: William Hogarth (1697-1764), English painter and engraver, famous for his pictorial satires of English low life (for his remark see Piozzi's *Anecdotes, op. cit.,* 90).

54. says in his haste: *Psalms,* CXVI, 11.

112b. 1. says Mrs. Thrale: For her remark and the incident of the "poor Quaker" see *Anecdotes, op. cit.,* 90-1.

13. earthquake at Lisbon: The Lisbon earthquake (Nov. 1, 1755) destroyed most of the houses of the city and upwards of 50,000 inhabitants (see *Anecdotes, op. cit.,* 92).

17. saw a ghost: See Boswell's *Life* for April 9, 1772.

19. ghost-hunt to Cock Lane: The story of the Cock Lane ghost (supposedly the apparition of a Mrs. Kent, appearing in 1762) was exposed by a company of men, including Johnson who wrote up the affair in *Gentleman's Magazine* (see Boswell's *Life* for June 25, 1763).

20. angry with John Wesley: John Wesley (1703-91), the founder of Methodism, and Johnson occasionally met. Johnson's account of Wesley's failure to "follow up another scent" is not told in anger but in mirth (see Boswell's *Life* for April 15, 1778).

29. Fingal: The reference is to poems which James Macpherson (1736-96) published as translations from a Gaelic bard called Ossian,—*Fragments of Ancient Poetry* (1760), *Fingal* (1762), and *Temora* (1763). Johnson vigorously denied the authenticity of the poems and found no merit in them.

34. Lord Roscommon: Wentworth Dillon, 4th Earl of Roscommon (1633?-85), British poet, author of *An Essay on Translated Verse* (1684) and translator of Horace's *Ars Poetica* (1680). Macaulay's reference is to early paragraphs in Johnson's sketch of Roscommon in the *Lives.*

113a. 3. arguments against showy dress: See Piozzi's *Anecdotes, op. cit.,* 72.

14. Hudibras or Ralpho: Sir Hudibras is the Presbyterian knight and Ralpho is his squire in Samuel Butler's mock-heroic poem *Hudibras* (1663-1664-1678), in which the Puritans are grotesquely satirized.

26. Campbell: John Campbell (1708-75), Scottish man of letters, author of *Military History of Prince Eugene and Duke of Marlborough* (1736). Johnson's characterization is from Boswell's *Life* for July 1, 1763.

113b. 16. Squire Western: The country squire in Fielding's *Tom Jones* (1749).

24. well-known lines: *The Traveller*, 429-30.

33. Rasselas: Hero in Johnson's didactic romance, *Rasselas, Prince of Abyssinia* (1759).

41. Sir Adam Ferguson: Scottish philosopher (1723-1816) and professor at Edinburgh. For the conversation see Boswell's *Life* for March 31, 1772.

114a. 8. Lord Bacon tells us: The anecdote is No. 221 of Bacon's *Apothegms* (*Works*, ed. Basil Montagu, I, 119). The philosopher is Thales. Bacon got the apothegm from the sketch of Thales in *Lives of Philosophers* by Diogenes Laertius, I, 37 (*Loeb Classical Lib.*).

42. schoolmen of the Middle Ages: The Schoolmen, or Scholastics, in philosophy did not question the truth or soundness of their general principles or their logic, the one being Christian and the other Aristotelian. On this basis they built a structure of thought known as scholasticism, and defended it with great skill and subtlety. Leading exponents of the system were Dun Scotus, Albertus Magnus, Thomas Aquinas, Abelard, and Peter Lombard. Not a little scholasticism ended in futile controversy and went down before the new learning and the new science.

114b. 49. Waller: Edmund Waller (1606-87), best known for his lyric, *Go, Lovely Rose,* was one of the first poets to use the closed couplet with so much art as to anticipate Dryden and Pope. "But he was rather smooth than strong," said Johnson, echoing Pope's opinion.

49. Denham: Sir John Denham (1615-69), remembered for his poem, *Cooper's Hill,* is another pioneer in the use of the couplet. "Denham and Waller," said Prior, "improved our versification, and Dryden perfected it" (quoted by Johnson).

115a. 2. *Aeneid* a greater poem than the *Iliad*: Macaulay seems to be in error here. "We must consider," says Johnson, "whether Homer was not the greatest poet, though Virgil may have produced the finest poem" (Boswell's *Life* for Sept. 22, 1777). Johnson evidently has in mind the thought of Homer and the style of Virgil: "In the comparison of Homer and Virgil," he says, "the discriminative excellence of Homer is elevation and comprehension of thought, and that of Virgil is grace and splendor of diction" (*Lives:* Dryden). And while Johnson described Pope's *Iliad* as "certainly the noblest version (i.e. translation) of poetry which the world has ever seen" (*Lives:* Pope), he did not place the translation *above* the original. In *interest* he ranked Homer with Shakespeare.

6. Hoole's translation of Tasso: John Hoole (1727-1803), playwright and translator, turned into heroic couplets Tasso's *Jerusalem Delivered* (1763) and Ariosto's *Orlando Furioso* (1783). For the former Johnson wrote the dedication to the Queen.

6. Fairfax: Edward Fairfax (d. 1635) translated the *Jerusalem Delivered* (1600) into the eight-line stanza of heroic verse (ottava rima). In his life of Waller, Johnson wrote: "Fairfax's work, after Mr. Hoole's translation, will perhaps not be soon reprinted."

10. Percy's fondness for them: Thomas Percy (1729-1811), English antiquary and poet, Bishop of Dromore, editor of *Reliques of Ancient English Poetry* (1765), the earliest collection of English ballads.

20. Sir Richard Blackmore: English physician and poetaster (1650?-1729). His *Creation: A Philosophical Poem* (1712) was praised by Johnson as placing its author "among the first favorites of the English muse" (*Lives:* Blackmore).

21. Gray a barren rascal: Johnson called Thomas Gray "a dull fellow" (Boswell's *Life* for March 28, 1775). Fielding was the "barren rascal" (*Life* for April 6, 1772).

42. Rymer: Thomas Rymer (1641-1713), archeologist, court historiographer, and critic, in whose *Tragedies of the Last Age* (1678) and *A Short View of Tragedy* (1692) the Elizabethans are roundly condemned for failure to respect the unities.

54. epitaph on Goldsmith: Several of Johnson's friends, including Burke, Reynolds, and Gibbon, addressed a Round Robin letter to Johnson, requesting him to make some changes in the epitaph and to write it "in English rather than in Latin." Johnson agreed to make any changes in the sense of it, but refused "to disgrace the walls of Westminster Abbey with an English inscription" (*Life* for 1776).

115b. 48. Country gentleman: See Boswell's *Journal of a Tour of the Hebrides* for Aug. 25, 1773.

116a. 3. The Athenians of the age of Demosthenes: Boswell's *Life* for April 3, 1773.

8. The boasted Athenians: *Life* for March 31, 1772.

32. Phidias and Zeuxis: Phidias, who created the Parthenon figures and the Olympian

Zeus, is considered the greatest of Greek sculptors. — Zeuxis was the greatest of Greek painters, though nothing of his art has survived. Both men belonged to the fifth century B.C.

36. *Shield of Achilles:* See *Iliad,* XVIII.

36. *Death of Argus:* See Aeschylus' *Prometheus Bound.*

116b. 31. **Dr. Moore's *Zeluco:*** John Moore (1729-1802), Scottish physician, traveller, writer, is best remembered for his novel *Zeluco* (1786), from the LXXIII chapter of which the quotation is taken.

44. **Johnson's visit to the Hebrides:** Johnson made the journey in 1773 with Boswell, who says: "His stay in Scotland was from the 18th of August till the 22nd of November." Johnson's *Journey to the Western Isles of Scotland* (1775) and Boswell's *Journal of a Tour to the Hebrides* (1786) are records of the visit.

117a. 13. **a snake in one of the pyramids of Egypt:** See Boswell's *Life* for May 11, 1778. James Caulfield, first Earl of Charlemont (1728-99), was a member of the Club.

15. **Lord Plunkett:** William Conyngham, first Baron Plunkett (1764-1854), eminent Irish lawyer, judge, and statesman.

18. **almanack-makers:** The suggestion that Johnson "would reduce all history to no better than an almanack" was made by Boswell (*Life* for April 11, 1775).

19. **Lord Hailes:** Sir David Dalrymple, Lord Hailes (1726-92), Scottish judge and antiquary, author of *Annals of Scotland* (1776) a work mentioned with high approval by Johnson, who also, on another occasion, alluded to "the foppery of Dalrymple" (*Life* for April 30, 1773).

21. **Robertson-Hume:** Johnson spoke of "the verbiage of Robertson" and his "cumbrous detail" (*Life* for April 30, 1773). "I have not read Hume," he said (*ib.*).

24. **Catiline's Conspiracy-Punic War:** See Piozzi's *Anecdotes, op. cit.* 55 and 54 respectively.

117b. 2. **Tom Dawson:** See second preceding paragraph and note on Dr. John Moore.

4. **Mr. Burke most justly observed:** "Burke affirmed that Boswell's *Life* was a greater monument to Johnson's fame than all his writings put together" (Boswell's *Life,* Hill's ed. I, 11 n. Quoted from the *Life of James Mackintosh*).

39. *The Rehearsal:* A burlesque play (1671) written, in part at least, by George Villiers, 2nd Duke of Buckingham (1628-87), as a satire on the heroic drama of the time, especially Dryden's. Buckingham, in turn, is damned as Zimri in *Absalom and Achitophel* (1681).

118a. 29. **Goldsmith said to him:** *Life* for April 27, 1773.

39. **Sir Piercy Shafton:** Character in Scott's *The Monastery* (1820), a euphuist.

41. **Euphelia, Rhodoclea, Cornelia, Tranquilla:** Imaginary figures in Johnson's *Rambler* papers. *The Rambler* appeared twice a week between March 20, 1750, and March 14, 1752.

42. **Imlac-Seged:** Characters in *Rasselas.*

118b. 14. **peard under her muffler:** *Merry Wives,* IV, ii, 192-3.

25. **omelet for Nugent:** Christopher Nugent (d. 1775), physician, was one of the "original members" of the Club and a Roman Catholic, who ordered an omelet at a Friday supper (Piozzi's *Anecdotes, op. cit.,* 62, 80).

MOORE'S LIFE OF LORD BYRON

The Letters and Journals of Lord Byron; with Notices of his Life, by Thomas Moore, was published in 1830. Macaulay's essay appeared in the *Edinburgh Review* for June, 1831.

119a. 7. *Life of Sheridan:* By Thomas Moore (1825).

119b. 38. **Duchess of Orleans:** Henrietta Anne, Duchess of Orleans (1644-70), sister of Charles II of England, wife of Phillipe I, Duc d'Orléans (brother of Louis XIV). Her son, Phillipe II, was Regent of France (1715-23) during minority of Louis XV. Macaulay (*History of England,* Ch. II) says the death of "the charming princess whose influence over her brother and brother-in-law had been so pernicious to her country...gave rise to horrible suspicions."

120a. 49. **His first poems:** *Hours of Idleness* (1807), severely assailed in the *Edinburgh Review.*

52. **The poem...on his return:** The first two cantos of *Childe Harold's Pilgrimage* (1812). "The effect," says Moore, "was electric." "I awoke one morning and found myself famous," said Byron.

120b. 29. lampooned the Prince Regent: In verses called *Windsor Poetics* (1812). On account of the insanity of George III his son (later George IV) was made Regent (1811-20).

49. There be that might an they list: *Hamlet,* I, v, 176-7.

121b. 30. Lord Nelson: Horatio Nelson, Viscount Nelson (1758-1805), one of England's greatest naval heroes, who died at the moment of victory in the battle of Trafalgar against the French fleet. He was the lover of Emma Hart, who as Lady Hamilton (1761?-1815) became his mistress.

122a. 2. True Jedwood justice: i.e. "hang in haste and try at leisure" (Scott's *Fair Maid of Perth*, Ch. XXXII). Jedwood, or Jedburgh, is a border town in Scotland, north of the Cheviot Hills.

19. Lewis Goldsmith: Political writer and journalist (1763?-1846), who spent some years in Paris, partly in the service of Napoleon, and later published books about the Emperor, charging him with debauchery and unscrupulousness.

42. enchantress in the Arabian Tales: Queen Labe of the City of Enchantments in the Story of Prince Beder and the Princess Jehann-Ara. As a sorceress she is the Arabic counterpart of the classical Circe.

122b. 23. He had fixed his home: In Venice.

48. rescued by a connection: i.e. with Countess Teresa Guiccioli (1801?-73), known for her liaison with Byron and for her book *My Recollections of Lord Byron* (1869, trans. from the French).

123a. 20. *The Liberal*: In the summer of 1822 Leigh Hunt arrived in Pisa (brought there at the suggestion of Shelley prompted by Byron) to start a periodical through which Byron's work and opinions might reach the public. The first number appeared Oct. 15, edited by Leigh Hunt in Italy, published by his brother, John Hunt, in London. *The Liberal* ran for four numbers only.

32. A nation: Greece had been under the yoke of Turkey since the end of the 15th century. In 1821 a war of independence broke out, under various leaders, of whom the most successful was Alexander Ypsilanti (1792-1828) and his brother Demetrius (1793-1832). With the aid of Britain, France, and Russia, Greece was finally freed and a prince of Bavaria was set up as King,—Otto I (1832-62).

123b. 15. He had when young: Byron left England in the summer of 1809 for a 'grand tour,' which lasted until July, 1811. He was in Greece for many months, spending the winters of 1809-10 and 1810-11 mostly in Athens.

23. to the Grecian camp: Byron sailed from Genoa for Greece July 23, 1823.

124a. 15. One died at Longwood: Napoleon, on the island of St. Helena, May 5, 1821.

16. the other at Missolonghi: Byron died there, April 19, 1824.

124b. 1. Parnell: Thomas Parnell (1679-1718), minor poet and essayist, member of the Scriblerus Club (with Pope, Arbuthnot, Swift, and Gay). He helped Pope in the translation of the *Iliad*.

28. Maximin: Emperor Maximin is a leading and ranting character in Dryden's 'heroic' drama *Tyrannic Love* (1669).

125a. 8. *Iphigénie*: *Iphigénie,* an imitation from Euripides, was first produced before the court of Louis XIV at Versailles in 1674. Neither Racine's Greeks nor Shakespeare's are Homer's Greeks; but Racine is the most 'correct' of the greater French dramatists because he followed the 'classical' rules more consistently.

18. quote Aristotle: In *Troilus and Cressida* (II, ii, 166-7) Hector quotes Aristotle incorrectly (cf. *Nicomachean Ethics*, I, 3).

22. Aulis: Harbor in Boeotia, ancient Greece, on the Euripos, the strait separating Euboea from the mainland; traditional place from which the Greeks sailed against Troy, and scene of the sacrifice of Iphigenia.

29. description of a moonlight: See Pope's translation of the last lines of the eighth *Iliad*, 542-561.

32. *Excursion*: The scene of Wordsworth's *Excursion* (1814) is among the mountains of the English Lake District.

33. *Cato*: Addison's *Cato*, a 'classical' tragedy, was produced at the Drury Lane theatre in 1713. —— Scott's *Lay of the Last Minstrel* (1805) is a narrative poem in which Wat Tinlinn and William Deloraine are characters.

47. Reynolds: Sir Joshua Reynolds (1723-92), eminent English portrait painter, friend of Dr. Johnson and member of the Club.

52. *Pursuits of Literature:* A poem satirizing contemporary writers, by Thomas James Mathias (1754?-1835).

54. **Mr. Gifford:** William Gifford (1756-1826), English literary critic, poet, and editor: first editor of the *Quarterly Review* (1809-24) and thought to be author of the magazine's savage attack on Keats's *Endymion* (1818).

125b. 4. **Hoole's translations:** John Hoole (1727-1803) translated Tasso's *Jerusalem Delivered* (1763) and Ariosto's *Orlando Furioso* (1783) into heroic couplets.

5. **Seatonian prize-poems:** Thomas Seaton (1684-1741), divine and hymn-writer, founded at Cambridge an annual prize for sacred poetry.

21. **Colley Cibber:** English author and dramatist (1671-1757); poet laureate from 1730; 'hero' of Pope's *Dunciad* (in 1743 revision).

30. **the unities:** "The unities of time and place," says Johnson, "(venerated) from the time of Corneille,... have given more trouble to the poet than pleasure to the auditor" (*Preface to Shakespeare*).

126a. 3. **Alfieri:** Conte Vittorio Alfieri (1749-1803) wrote some 19 tragedies, all 'classical' in structure.

8. **frightened at his own temerity:** From the *Preface to Shakespeare* (1765).

13. **Rymer:** In his own words Macaulay expresses the opinion of Thomas Rymer (1641-1713) in *A Short View of Tragedy* (1692) in which *Othello* is sweepingly condemned.

28. **While thus I called:** *Paradise Lost,* VIII, 283.

43. **As when we lived:** From "The Lady Jane Gray to the Lord Guilford Dudley," 55-6 (England's *Heroicall Epistles*, 1619).

126b. 3. **Such grief was ours:** The passage is from *Human Life,* 440-51, by Samuel Rogers (1763-1855), banker, poet, patron of artists and men of letters.

15. **Sir Roger Newdigate:** English antiquary (1719-1806), who founded at Oxford the Newdigate prize for English verse (1805).

46. **rivers Pison, etc.:** *Genesis,* II, 10-14.

52. **Tuilleries:** A royal palace in Paris, begun in 1564 and extended later by Henry IV and Louis XIV, and still later connected with the Louvre. Destroyed by the Commune in 1871.

127a. 17. **Hesperian fruit:** The golden apples guarded by nymphs (Hesperides) and the dragon; apples given by Gaea (Earth) as a wedding present to Hera.

35. **M. Jourdain:** A character in Molière's *Le Bourgeois Gentilhomme* (1670). The quotation is from Act III, iii.

39. **M. Tomès:** A character in Molière's *L'Amour Médecin* (1665), whose views are condensed from Act II, iii.

52. **Marshal Daun:** Count Leopold von Daun (1705-66), Austrian general who twice defeated Frederick the Great.

127b. 30. **Portcullis and Rouge Dragon:** Functionaries in the English Herald's College, who took their names from the armorial insignia of their lords.

49. **two strange old poems:** *Iliad* and *Odyssey.*

128a. 9. **Poetry is ... imitation:** Aristotle, in *Poetics.*

128b. 18. *Douglas:* A tragedy (1756) by John Home (1722-1808), Scottish clergyman and playwright, whose drama made a hit.

18. *Triumphs of Temper:* A poem (1781) in heroic couplets by William Hayley (1745-1820), a poetaster whose style Byron described as "Forever feeble and forever tame."

31. **Beattie and Collins:** James Beattie (1735-1803), Scottish professor and poet, is remembered for *The Minstrel* (1771-74) in Spenserian stanzas, in some few of which he anticipates the coming romanticism. —— William Collins (1721-59), a transitional poet between neo-classicism and romanticism, whose Odes (especially *To Evening*) keep their fame.

32. **Mason:** William Mason (1724-97), minor English poet and dramatist, friend and biographer of Thomas Gray.

129a. 3. **Lovelace ... Clarissa:** Lovelace is the libertine who accomplishes the ruin of Clarissa in Richardson's novel, *Clarissa Harlowe* (1747-48).

32. **separation from the see of Rome:** The Protestant Reformation.

33. **Anabaptists:** A religious sect that sprang up early in the 16th century, the members of which did not believe in infant baptism; called Anabaptists (i.e. rebaptists) by their persecutors.

36. **Jacobins:** Extreme radicals of the French revolutionary period.

37. Theophilanthropists: Literally, lovers of God and man; historically, members of a deistical society established in Paris during the period of the Directory (1795-99).

37. Macpherson: James Macpherson (1736-96), self-alleged translator of the Poems of Ossian, Gaelic bard.

38. Della Crusca: Pseudonym of Robert Merry (1755-98), English dilettante poet who lived in Florence, wrote affected verse, and was made a member of the Florentine Della Cruscan Academy, from which he adopted his fictitious name.

39. Knipperdoling—Clootz—Turgot: Bernhard Knipperdoling, fanatical German Anabaptist leader who was tortured and executed in 1536. —— Baron de Clootz, known as Anacharsis Clootz (1755-94), French Revolutionary fanatic of Prussian birth, who, with other leaders, set up the 'Worship of Reason' and was guillotined in 1794. —— Anne Robert Jacques Turgot, Baron de l'Aulne (1727-81), one of France's great statesmen,—economist, finance minister and reformer.

41. Chatterton's forgeries: Thomas Chatterton (1752-70), "the marvellous boy" of Wordsworth's poem, gained fame by the "Rowley Poems," a collection of verses purporting to be transcribed from the parchments of a 15th century monk named Thomas Rowley. The hoax was exposed by Tyrwhitt, Malone, and, later, by W. W. Skeat.

43. Ireland: William Henry Ireland (1777-1835), English forger of Shakespearean manuscripts, who confessed his impostures when challenged by the Shakespearean scholar, Edmund Malone.

51. Cowper: William Cowper (1731-1800), English poet and letter-writer who, in spite of temporary insanity and chronic religious melancholia, wrote poems and letters of sustained simplicity and charm; best known for *The Task* and *John Gilpin* (both, 1785).

53. Alfieri: Conte Vittorio Alfieri (1749-1803) in his earlier years spent much time in England, where in 1772 he fought a duel "with the injured husband of Lady Ligonier." Later in Florence, he formed an attachment with the Countess of Albany, wife of Charles Edward Stuart, the Young Pretender. Alfieri, man and poet, had a "passion for liberty" and revived "the national spirit of Italy."

129b. 4. Enoch: Patriarch who "walked with God" (*Genesis*, VI, 22).

6. who had not courage: Cowper was 'nominated' for the office of Clerk of the Journals in the House of Lords, but his timorous, hyper-sensitive nature brought on insanity and the 'nomination' had to be withdrawn.

9. favourite associates: Mary Unwin (1724-96) and John Newton (1725-1807), the curate of Olney. Mrs. Unwin lost her sight in 1792; Cowper alludes to the fact in his poem *To Mary* (1793).

27. The vision and the faculty divine: Wordsworth's *Excursion*, I, 79.

52. love-verses of Alfieri: To the Countess of Albany.

130a. 13. Manner is all in all, etc.: *Table-Talk* (1782), 542-3.

18. Made poetry a mere, etc.: *Ibid.*, 654-5.

34. creamy smoothness: *Ibid.*, 513.

130b. 18. Of Pope himself he spoke: E.g.—"I will show more *imagery* in twenty lines of Pope than in any equal length of quotation in English poetry." (Letter to Murray, March 1821.) —— "Pope, the most faultless of Poets, and almost of men." (To Murray, Oct. 9, 1820.) Cf. also, Byron's two letters to Murray on Bowles's *Strictures on the Life and Writings of Pope* (1821).

19. He did not venture to say: See the first letter to Murray on Bowles's *Strictures*.

25. Mr. Gifford: William Gifford (1756-1826) wrote *Baviad* (1791) and *Maeviad* (1795), satires in heroic verse, besides abusive essays in the *Quarterly Review* of which he was editor (1809-24).

37. clumsy, and frowsy, etc.:

> "A drowsy, frowsy poem, call'd *The Excursion*,
> Writ in a manner which is my aversion"
> (*Don Juan*, Canto III, st. 94).

38. *Peter Bell* excited his spleen: *Ibid.*, Canto III, st. 100.

44. *Imitation of Horace's Art of Poetry*: i.e. Byron's *Hints from Horace*, written in 1811, was published posthumously in 1831. Byron seems to have preferred it to *Childe Harold*.

51. In one of his works: "They (i.e. Byron's contemporaries) have raised a mosque by the side of a Grecian temple of the purest architecture . . . I *have* been amongst the builders of this Babel, attended by a confusion of tongues, but *never* amongst the envious destroyers of the classic temple of our predecessor" (Letter on Bowles's *Strictures*, Feb. 7, 1821).

131a. **6. in another letter:** To Murray, Sept. 15, 1817. Claudian, a Latin poet, born probably in Alexandria, who flourished in Rome about 395 A.D., was a prolific writer, whose work reflects the decadence of his age.

17. he preferred Pope's *Iliad*: "As a child I first read Pope's Homer with a rapture which no subsequent work could ever afford, and children are not the worst judges of their own language. As a boy I read Homer in the original, as we all have done, some of us by force, and a few by favor; under which description I come is nothing to the purpose, it is enough that I read him." (To Murray, Feb. 7, 1821.)

17. Mr. Moore confesses: In a note on Byron's letter to him (May 3, 1821) Moore, referring to the Bowles-Pope controversy, says that Byron in "the spirit of partisanship" was "led to place Pope *above* Shakespeare and Milton"; and in the concluding chapter of his *Life of Byron* he refers to "Byron's want of a due reverence for Shakespeare."

23. he places Tasso: See *Childe Harold*, IV, Stanzas 36-41.

26. Mr. Hunt is, we suspect: "Spenser he could not read; at least he said so.... I lent him a volume of the 'Fairy Queen,' and he said he would try to like it. Next day he brought it to my study-window, and said, 'Here, Hunt, is your Spenser. I cannot see anything in him.'" (Hunt's *Lord Byron and Some of His Contemporaries*, I, 77, 2nd ed., 1829.)

51. he must serve who fain would sway: Spoken by Manfred (*Manfred*, III, i, 117).

131b. **8. Donne:** John Donne (1573-1631) is best known for his 'metaphysical' poetry, which, underneath its 'quaintness,' is rich in passion and thought. Born a Catholic, Donne joined the Anglican Church, was made Dean of St. Paul's (1621-31), and became one of the greatest preachers of his time.

11. Bayes or Bilboa: In the Duke of Buckingham's burlesque drama *The Rehearsal* (1671), Bilboa was a satirical portrait of the dramatist Sir Robert Howard. Afterwards, the name was changed to Bayes, who became a caricature of Dryden.

33. *Essay on Man,... Excursion:* Pope's *Essay on Man* (1733-34); Wordsworth's *Excursion* (1814).

37. Voltaire: Voltaire (1694-1778), spans and reflects 18th century France, wrote verses during the last years of Louis XIV and was producing in the early years of Louis XVI's reign.

39. Lewis the Fourteenth: Louis XIV was King 1643 to 1715; Louis XVI, from 1774-1792.

40. Racine and Boileau: Racine's dramas fall mostly between 1664 and 1677. —— Boileau's poetry and criticism fall mostly between 1666 and 1683. The work of both writers was done in the reign of Louis XIV.

41. Condorcet and Beaumarchais: Condorcet (1743-94), philosopher, mathematician, politician, and Beaumarchais (1732-99), playwright and man of affairs (best known for his *Le Barbier de Séville*, 1775, and his *Le Mariage de Figaro*, 1784), did most of their work in the reign of Louis XVI.

48. Dryden: John Dryden (1631-1700) had many literary affinities with the 17th century, but much of his work anticipates the 18th.

51. Oromasdes and Arimanes: Spirits of Good and Evil, respectively, in the Persian religion of Zoroaster.

132a. **6. *Lyrical Ballads:*** By Wordsworth and Coleridge, first published in 1798; a second edition in 1800 contained Wordsworth's famous *Preface*.

35. All his characters: Harold, in *Childe Harold*; Giaour, in *The Giaour*; Conrad, in *The Corsair*; Lara, in *Lara*; Alp, in the *Siege of Corinth*; Manfred, in *Manfred*; Azzo and Ugo, in *Parisina*; Lambro, in *Don Juan*; Cain in *Cain, A Mystery*.

132b. **11. Sardanapalus:** Hero in *Sardanapalus: A Tragedy* (1821); historically, he was a ruler of Assyria (cir. 822 B.C.).

21. Juvenal-Otho: Decimus Junius Juvenalis (60?-?140 A.D.), Roman lawyer and author of sixteen extant satires. —— Marcus Salvius Otho (32-69), Emperor of Rome for three months (69). He brought about the death of his predecessor Galba, and committed suicide after his defeat by his successor Vitellius on the field of Bebriacum.

33. Prince Hal: In *Henry IV*, part I, Prince Hal (Henry, Prince of Wales), a comrade of Falstaff, is also a hero in the fight at Shrewsbury, where he kills Hotspur in single combat. In *Henry IV*, part II, the prince resumes companionship with Falstaff. Consistency of characterization is *not* sacrificed. Nor is it in the case of Mark Antony in *Antony and Cleopatra*.

133a. **11. Hermogenes:** In the *Poetaster* (1601) Hermogenes, a singer, refuses to sing at a supper-party until he is egged on by the singing of a rival; and then just as the 'banquet' is called he wishes the guests "to heare me sing another." Horace has two different men named Hermogenes (see *Satires* III-IV, Bk. I). Jonson seems to take from both for his character.

17. Peveril: Scott's *Peveril of the Peak* (1823) is a novel centering around the Popish Plot (1678) in the reign of Charles II. His Buckingham, based on Dryden's satirical portrait (i.e. Zimri in *Absalom and Achitophel*, I, 544-68) is an exaggerated, unhistorical figure.

25. Wharton: Philip, Duke of Wharton (1698-1731), profligate and adventurer, is satirized in Pope's *Moral Essays* (I, 179-207).

26. Lord Hervey: John, Lord Hervey (1696-1743), English politician and author of *Memoirs of the Reign of George II*, is satirized as Sporus in Pope's *Epistle to Dr. Arbuthnot* (305-33). Sporus, a eunuch, was a favorite of Nero's.

30. Haidee and Julia: In *Don Juan;* Leila, in *The Giaour;* Zuleika, in *The Bride of Abydos;* Gulnare and Medora, in *The Corsair.*

54. Clarendon: Edward Hyde, 1st Earl of Clarendon (1609-74), royalist statesman and historian, is the author of *History of the Rebellion* (pub. 1702-4), in which analytical characterization of the chief persons is the striking feature.

133b. **34. description of Rome:** *Manfred,* opening lines in III, iv.

36. Venetian revel: Speech of Lioni, *Marino Faliero,* opening part in IV, i.

37. concluding invective: *Marino Faliero,* V, iii.

51. To be or not to be: *Hamlet,* III, i, 56-90.

134a. **19. Lucifer and Cain:** *Cain,* I, i and II, i-ii.

37. hero of the *Rehearsal*: Bayes.

53. Description: "description is my forte" (Canto V, st. 52).

134b. **15. proverb of old Hesiod:** "Fools! who know not how much more is the half than the whole" (*Works and Days,* 40-1).

50. one dark and melancholy figure: Childe Harold, i.e. Byron.

54. Marah: When the Israelites passed through the Red Sea they stopped at Marah, whose waters were bitter (*Exodus,* XV, 23).

135b. **3. Ill may such contest, etc.:** *Childe Harold,* Canto II, st. XCIV, 6-7.

10. maiden speech: Byron's first speech was made Feb. 27, 1812. A few days later he wrote (March 5): "Lord Grenville remarked that the construction of some of my periods are very like Burke's!! And so much for vanity."

49. loves of Petrarch: Petrarch (1304-74) sings the praises of Laura, a French lady of Avignon, in his famous Italian sonnets and canzoni.

52. Rousseau: Tells of his sufferings in *Confessions* (pub. 1781 and 1788).

136a. **16. so dainty sweet as lovely melancholy:** From *The Nice Valour,* III, iii, by John Fletcher (1579-1625).

29. Master Stephen: Character in Jonson's *Every Man in his Humor.*

136b. **4. Minerva press:** A publishing house in Leadenhall Street, London, famous in early 19th century for its sentimental novels with complicated plots.

ENGLAND IN 1685

The three selections here given are from the famous third chapter of the first volume of *The History of England from the Accession of James II* (5 vols. 1848-61). Macaulay planned, he said, a history "from 1688 to the French Revolution," but he lived to bring it down only to the death of his hero, William III, in 1702. The work was at once immensely popular and sold in Great Britain and America by tens of thousands of copies.

136b. **9. Blackwall:** On the eastern edge of London.

137a. **13. Islington:** Now nearly in the center of London on north side of the Thames.

23. Dahomey: Colony in French West Africa.

36. the great fire: In 1666, destroying most of London.

137b. **6. Wren:** Sir Christopher Wren (1632-1723), the great architect, made the plans for rebuilding London. He designed and rebuilt St. Paul's Cathedral (1675-1716).

31. Lombard-Threadneedle: Financial and commercial centers of London, respectively.

138a. 11. Sir Robert Clayton: Very wealthy London merchant (1629-1707), politician, and a director of the Bank of England.

15. Sir Dudley North: Another wealthy London merchant (1641-91), who amassed a fortune in trade with the Levant.

34. age of Pericles: Pericles (495?-429 B.C.), Athenian statesman, orator, general, and patron of the arts. He was in power at Athens from 461-429 B.C.

138b. 4. Temple Bar: A stone gateway at the junction of Fleet Street and the Strand, which marked the boundary between the City and Westminster; so called because it stood before the ancient Church of St. Mary known as The Temple.

5. Guildhall: Council-hall of the city of London; badly damaged in Second World War.

139a. 15. Hampden and Pym: John Hampden (1594-1643) and John Pym (1584-1643), English statesmen and parliamentary leaders in the revolt against the tyranny of Charles I. They evaded the King's attempt to capture them on a charge of high treason (Jan. 1642), and were protected and returned to the House of Commons by the trainbands of the city.

19. to raise the siege of Gloucester: Sept. 6, 1643.

21. downfall of Richard Cromwell: Richard Cromwell (1626-1712) was Protector from Sept. 1658 to May, 1659. The government was unsettled until the return of Charles II in May, 1660.

37. Shaftesbury and Buckingham: The 1st Earl of Shaftesbury (1621-83) and the 2nd Duke of Buckingham (1628-87) were prominent figures in the Restoration period, both being members of the Cabal Ministry. The former is Achitophel and the latter Zimri in Dryden's *Absalom and Achitophel*.

139b. 20. Duke of Monmouth: An illegitimate son of Charles II and a popular favorite, who led an unsuccessful rebellion against James II and was beheaded on Tower Hill, 1685.

140b. 15. Lincoln's Inn mumper: A begging imposter.

141a. 48. dissolute young gentlemen: Macaulay refers to *Paradise Lost*, I, 498-502, and he says: "I am confident that he (Milton) was thinking of those pests when he dictated the noble lines."

141b. 31. Michaelmas to Lady Day: i.e. from 29th Sept. to 25th March, or from the third to the first 'quarter' day.

35. illuminations for La Hogue and Blenheim: Celebrations of the five-day naval battle against the French fleet ending in the bay of La Hogue (May 19-24, 1692), and of the victory of Marlborough at Blenheim (August 13, 1704).

47. Archimedes: Greek mathematician and inventor of Syracuse, Sicily (287?-212 B.C.), known for his work in mechanics and hydrostatics.

142a. 16. Carmelite Friars: Friars of the Order of Our Lady of Mt. Carmel, established on Mt. Carmel in Syria, in the 12th century. Since their habit included a white cloak and scapular, they were called White Friars.

47. Somers etc.: John, Baron Somers of Evesham (1651-1716), English lawyer and statesman, Lord Chancellor, author of the famous Declaration of Rights (1689). —— John Tillotson (1630-94), English preacher and prelate, Dean of St. Paul's (1689), Archbishop of Canterbury (1691). —— A chair in Will's coffeehouse in London was the throne from which Dryden (1631-1700) passed judgments upon writers and writings of his day. —— "The Royal Society of London for the Improvement of natural knowledge" received its charter from Charles in 1662. —— Sir Isaac Newton (1642-1727) became a Fellow of the Royal Society in 1672; his *Principia* was brought out by the Society in 1687.

142b. 8. The revolution: i.e. of 1688.

27. Walpole and Pelham: Sir Robert Walpole, 1st Earl of Orford (1676-1745), was Prime Minister for two terms (1715-17 and 1721-27) under George I, and for one term (1727-42) under George II. —— Henry Pelham (1695?-1754) was Prime Minister (1743-54) under George II.

36. born and bred on the Continent: Macaulay refers to William III, Prince of Orange, and to the sovereigns of the House of Hanover, two of whom, George I and II, were born in Germany, while George III, George IV, and William IV were as much German as English in their education, private lives, and national sympathy.

143a. 29. The levee: In the original meaning defined as "a reception held by a person of distinction on rising from bed," from the French, *se lever*, to rise.

41. flight from Worcester: After the defeat of the Royalists at Worcester (Sept. 3, 1651),

Charles was in flight and hiding (e.g. in the famous oak tree at Boscobel, in Shropshire) for several months before he made his escape to France.

43. a state prisoner in Scotland: In 1650 Charles II landed in Scotland, where he had been proclaimed king and where he was for a time under the complete control of Scotch Covenanters.

51. Marvell: Andrew Marvell (1621-78), poet, satirist, assistant to the Latin Secretary (Milton) of Cromwell, was both "an austere republican" and, because of his grace and wit, a favorite of Charles II.

143b. 16. John Sobiesky: John III Sobieski (1624-96), Polish soldier and King of Poland (1674-96), who in 1683 relieved the Turkish siege of Vienna and was "acclaimed hero of Christendom."

22. Halifax-Rochester: Sir George Savile, Marquis of Halifax (1633-95), a leading statesman in the reign of Charles II, was both Lord Privy Seal (1682-85, 1689-90) and Lord President of Council (1685). —— The 2nd Earl of Rochester (1647-80) was a dissolute favorite of the King and a writer of graceful lyrics.

144a. 17. Danby's administration: Thomas Osborne, 1st Earl of Danby (1631-1712), English statesman, was very powerful under Charles II until his fall in 1679. Later, under William III, he rose to power again for a time, until impeached in 1695, when his influence ceased.

54. Lord Foppington: Ridiculous coxcomb in Sir John Vanbrugh's comedy *The Relapse, or Virtue in Danger* (1696).

144b. 22. Perrault-Boileau: Charles Perrault (1628-1703), as author of *Le Siècle de Louis le Grand* (1687), took the side of the 'moderns' against the 'ancients' in the 'quarrel' of that period. —— Nicholas Boileau (1636-1711), in his *L'Art Poètique* (1674), was a champion of 'the ancients.'

27. *Venice Preserved:* Blank-verse tragedy (1682) by Thomas Otway (1652-85).

40. Bossu's treatise: René Le Bossu (1631-89) was the author of *Traité du Poème Epique* (1675).

45. Radcliffe: John Radcliffe (1650-1714) was physician of William III, Queen Mary, and Princess Anne.

145a. 30. *Hudibras:* Mock-heroic poem (1663-78) by Samuel Butler (1612-80).

30. *Baker's Chronicle:* Sir Richard Baker (1568-1645) wrote a much-read *Chronicle of the Kings of England* (from Roman period to 1625).

31. *Tarlton's Jests:* Richard Tarlton (d. 1588), English comedian and favorite clown of Queen Elizabeth, was the reputed author of a collection of anecdotes called *Tarlton's Jests* (1592?-?1611).

31. Seven Champions of Christendom: *The Famous Historie of the Seaven Champions of Christendom* (1596-7) by Richard Johnson (1573-?1659). Four of these romantic stories are the legends of St. George of England, St. Andrew of Scotland, St. Patrick of Ireland, and St. David of Wales.

145b. 22. now be ashamed to commit: One instance will suffice. Queen Mary had good natural abilities, had been educated by a bishop, was fond of history and poetry, and was regarded by very eminent men as a superior woman. There is, in the library of the Hague, a superb English Bible which was delivered to her when she was crowned in Westminster Abbey. In the title page are these words in her own hand: "This book was given the king and I, at our crownation. Marie R." (Macaulay's note.)

49. Jane Grey: Lady Jane Grey (1537-54), daughter of Henry Grey, Duke of Suffolk, ill-fated victim of a plot to make her queen on death of Edward VI, was a precocious student of languages, especially Greek. Roger Ascham in his *Schoolmaster* tells that in the summer of 1550 he found her reading Plato's *Phaedo*.

49. Lucy Hutchinson: Lucy Hutchinson (1620?-80), wife of the soldier and regicide, John Hutchinson (1615-64), wrote her husband's biography, *Life of Colonel Hutchinson* (pub. 1806), in which is drawn the character of a Puritan gentleman.

146a. 8. *Clelia* and the *Grand Cyrus:* French romances by Madeleine de Scudéry (1607-1701), in which the author depicts the adventures and passions of seventeenth century gallants and fine ladies.

19. Homer to Photius: Homer, the traditional name of the author of the *Iliad* and the *Odyssey*, may have lived anytime between 1200 and 850 B.C. —— Photius was Patriarch of Constantinople and author of *Myriobiblion*, a summary of 280 works of classical writers now mostly lost.

31. Epistles of Phalaris: Phalaris (d. 549 B.C.), a cruel Sicilian tyrant, was reputed to be the author of certain Greek epistles. They were shown to be spurious by Richard Bentley (1662-1742), a great classical scholar and Master of Trinity College, Cambridge. The controversy over the authorship of these letters evoked Swift's satire, *The Battle of the Books* (1704).

40. Raleigh and Falkland: Sir Walter Raleigh (1552?-1618), Elizabethan courtier, explorer, historian, poet. —— Lucius Cary, Viscount Falkland (1610?-1643), "that incomparable young man" (Clarendon), member of Parliament and Secretary of State, who was killed at Newbury fighting for Charles I.

43. Pitt, Fox, Windham, Grenville: Eminent English statesmen during the French Revolutionary period.

146b. 5. Virgil and Ovid: Virgil "celebrated the greatness of Augustus" (first Roman emperor 27 B.C.-14 A.D.) in several passages of his poetry, but especially in the sixth *Aeneid*, 792-808. —— Ovid "celebrated" Augustus in *Tristia*, especially in Bk. II.

27. Racine, Molière, La Fontaine, Bossuet: Four of the greatest figures in 17th century France, Racine and Molière for their dramas, La Fontaine for his *Fables* and *Contes,* and Bossuet for his pulpit oratory (e.g. *Oraisons Funèbres,* 1689).

147a. 12. Donne-Cowley: John Donne, (1573-1631) and Abraham Cowley (1618-67) are classed as 'metaphysical' poets, Donne being the great chief of the group and Cowley an imitator, unable to decide whether to write "with mystical fancy or clear common sense."

22. to use French words: The most offensive instance which I remember is in a poem on the coronation of Charles II by Dryden, who certainly could not plead poverty as an excuse for borrowing words from any foreign tongue:

> Hither in summer evenings you repair,
> To taste the faicheur of the cooler air

(Macaulay's note). The lines are from *To His Sacred Majesty*, 101-2 (1661).

47. Reformation to the Civil War: i.e. from about 1531, when Henry VIII was acknowledged 'Supreme Head of the Church of England,' to 1642.

53. Jack in the Green: A man or boy (chimney-sweep) covered with leaves and boughs on Mayday.

147b. 12. theatres were closed: From 1642 to 1660.

17. Cowley-Crashaw: Both were Cambridge men and both lost their fellowships because of royalist sympathies and refusal to accept the Solemn League and Covenant (1643). Crashaw (1613?-49) became a Catholic.

22. Supralapsarians: Calvinists who believed that the fall of man was a part of God's original purpose, decreed *before* man fell.

36. Roundhead: Puritans who wore their hair cut short were called Roundheads by the Cavaliers who wore long hair in ringlets.

148a. 21. Waller: Edmund Waller (1606-87), poet, political opportunist, and member of Parliament, best known for two or three lyrics (e.g. "Go, Lovely Rose").

27. A mightier spirit-Butler: Both Milton (1608-74) and Butler (1612-80) reached maturity before the excesses of the Restoration.

44. Durfey: Thomas D'Urfey (1653-1723), known as Tom Durfey, was a prolific producer of songs, satires, and dramas, including licentious comedies such as *Madame Fickle* (1667) and *The Virtuous Wife* (1680).

148b. 23. Hope-Rose: Philip Henslowe (d. 1616), "the first Englishman to make a fortune by the stage," built both the Rose theater (1586-7?) and the Hope (1613), on Bankside, London.

149a. 7. Calderon: Pedro Calderón de la Barca (1600-81), Spanish dramatist and poet, who wrote more than a hundred comedies.

9. Viola, etc.: Viola, in *Twelfth Night;* misanthrope, i.e. Alceste, in *Le Misanthrope;* Agnes, in *L'Ecole des Femmes.*

24. the *Fables*: Dryden's *Fables, Ancient and Modern* (1700) is mainly made up of paraphrases (called 'translations' by the author) from Chaucer and Boccaccio.

44. Southern: Thomas Southern (1660-1746) is remembered for two tragedies, *The Fatal Marriage* (1694) and *Oroonoko* (1696). Macaulay no doubt refers to the first, which held the stage for half a century.

45. Otway: *Don Carlos* (1676), a rhymed heroic drama by Thomas Otway (1652-85), won instant success and, according to Lord Rochester, filled the author's pockets.

47. Shadwell: Thomas Shadwell (1642?-92), dramatist, poet, and (after Dryden) poet-laureate (1689-92), was, in spite of Dryden's satirical portrait in *Mac Flecknoe,* a successful writer of plays.

149b. 2. Lucretius: Titus Lucretius Carus (96?-55 B.C.), Roman philosophical poet, author of *De Rerum Natura* in 6 books.

150a. 5. *Absalom and Achitophel:* Dryden's satire is an attack upon the Earl of Shaftesbury who led a conspiracy to give succession to the Duke of Monmouth, bastard son of Charles II. The poet uses the biblical story of Absalom's rebellion (II Samuel, XIII-XVIII) as the allegorical basis of his satire.

10. Exclusionists: Those who favored the Exclusion Bill, sponsored by Shaftesbury and his party, excluding the Duke of York (King's brother, afterwards James II) as a Catholic from the succession. The Bill was defeated in the House of Lords and Parliament was dissolved by the King.

150b. 2. Verulamian doctrine: Francis Bacon (1561-1626) was raised to the peerage (1618) as 1st Baron Verulam and Viscount St. Albans. Verulamium is the Latin name of a Roman town near the site of which was built the new town of St. Albans, named after the proto-martyr of Christianity in Great Britain. Bacon's home was here and here is his tomb in the ancient Church of St. Michael. The 'doctrine' is the Baconian inductive method of studying particular instances as the basis for generalization.

29. men of no common capacity and learning: See particularly Harrington's *Oceana* (Macaulay's note). *The Commonwealth of Oceana* (1656) by James Harrington (1611-77) is a utopian romance, written as a criticism of Hobbes' *Leviathan* (1651). Other political romances of the time are More's *Utopia* (1516) and Bacon's *New Atlantis* (1627). The Italian Campanella (1568-1639) published his *Civitas Solis* (City of the Sun) in 1623, which came to be widely known in England.

50. ascendancy of the new philosophy: The Royal Society for the Advancement of Science began as a dining club of men who met informally "to discuss the new or experimental philosophy." They 'organized' in 1660 and in 1662 received their charter from the King.

151a. 6. the Rota: A political club formed in 1659 by Harrington to discuss the plans set forth in his *Oceana.*

18. Cowley, in lines: i.e. *Ode to the Royal Society,* published in *Verses on Several Occasions* (1663).

25. Dryden . . . joined his voice: i.e. in stanzas 161-66 of *Annus Mirabilis,* or *The Year of Wonders* (1666). Dryden was elected a fellow of the Royal Society in 1662.

33. Ward-Wilkins: Seth Ward (1617-89), Bishop of Salisbury (1667), had been professor of astronomy at Oxford (1649-61) and was an original member of the Royal Society. —— John Wilkins (1614-72) was not only Bishop of Chester but an author of books on astronomy, e.g. *The Discovery of a World in the Moone* (1638).

38. Sprat: Thomas Sprat (1635-1713), Bishop of Rochester (1684) and Dean of Westminster (1683), was one of the founders of the Royal Society and published its history in 1667.

40. Hale . . . Guilford: Sir Matthew Hale (1609-76), eminent lawyer and jurist, was Chief Justice of the King's Bench from 1671 until shortly before his death. He wrote two books (described as of no scientific value): *An Essay touching the Gravitation or Non-Gravitation of Fluid Bodies* (1673), and *Observations touching the Torricellian Experiment* (1674). —— Francis North, 1st Baron Guilford (1637-85), Chief Justice of Common Pleas (1675-82), Lord Chancellor (1682) and Lord Keeper of the Great Seal, was not only a great lawyer but a man of broad culture, interested in art, music, science.

50. Buckingham: The brilliant and dissolute George Villiers, 2nd Duke of Buckingham (1628-87), a favorite of Charles II.

50. Rupert: Prince Rupert (1619-82), born in Prague, nephew of Charles I and leader of Royalist forces in the Civil War, rather improved than invented the processes of mezzotint and brought to England the glass drop known as 'Rupert's drop.'

151b. 9. Gresham curiosities: Sir Thomas Gresham (1519?-79), founder of the Royal Exchange, also founded Gresham College in London, which became the first home of the Royal Society, where the new scientific 'curiosities' and "fine experiments" (Pepys's phrase) were shown to aristocratic visitors.

54. Evelyn: John Evelyn (1620-1706), best known for his *Diary* (1640-1706), was a member of the Royal Society and its secretary (1672). He wrote, among other works, *Sylva,* a book on arboriculture (1664).

152a. 3. Temple: Sir William Temple (1628-99), statesman, diplomat, man of letters, retired from public service after the Revolution of 1688 and wrote his *Memoirs,* besides letters, and graceful essays on a variety of subjects. Swift for a time was his secretary.

11. Molière: Molière wrote several plays in which he ridiculed medical quackery, including *L'Amour Medécin* (1665), *Monsieur de Pourceaugnac* (1669), and *Le Malade Imaginaire* (1673), his last comedy.

14. Hippocrates and Galen: Hippocrates (460?-?377 B.C.), Greek physician, called the Father of Medicine, reputed author of the Hippocratic oath. —— Galen, Greek physician who settled in Rome (164 A.D.) and wrote many medical treatises which were accepted as authoritative for centuries.

32. Petty: Sir William Petty (1623-87), political economist and pioneer in the science of comparative statistics.

36. Boyle: Robert Boyle (1627-91) was a leading scientist of his day, both as physicist and chemist, and a founder of the Royal Society.

37. Sloane: Sir Hans Sloane (1660-1753), British physician and naturalist, collected hundreds of new species of plants in Jamaica (1687-89), succeeded Newton as President of the Royal Society (1727-41), and founded the Botanic Garden of London (1721).

51. Wallis: John Wallis (1616-1703), mathematician, was professor of geometry at Oxford (1649-1703) and author of *Arithmetica Infinitorum* (Arithmetic of Infinites, 1655), a first-class contribution to higher mathematics.

53. Halley: Edmund Halley (1656-1742), astronomer, best known for his study of comets, Astronomer Royal (1721), editor of Royal Society's *Transations* (1685-93), and publisher at his own expense of Newton's *Principia* (1687). In 1699-1700 he made a long and adventurous scientific voyage over the South Atlantic.

152b. 7. Flamsteed: John Flamsteed (1646-1719) became the first Astronomer Royal in 1675, and is best known for his work on stars, *Historia Coelestis Britannica* (1707 ff.).

30. Scotists and Thomists: Scotists were followers of John Duns Scotus (1266?-1308), Scottish scholastic theologian, known as the Subtle Doctor, and one of the great schoolmen whose conclusions provoked criticism of the system of the Thomists, followers of Saint Thomas Aquinas (1225?-74), the great Italian scholastic philosopher, known as the Angelic Doctor and Prince of Scholastics.

37. In the year 1685 his fame: In 1685 Newton verified by mathematical calculation the law of universal gravitation and began the *Principia,* described as "a treatise on theoretical and experimental physics. Never had the human intellect reached so noble a conception of things." While Halley paid for the printing, publication was authorized by the Royal Society, of which the diarist, Samuel Pepys, was then president.

153a. 4. Wren: Sir Christopher Wren (1632-1723), a charter member of the Royal Society, drew plans for rebuilding London after the great fire of 1666. While his greatest work is St. Paul's Cathedral, he built over fifty other churches in London, besides a number of famous edifices elsewhere.

31. Lely: Sir Peter Lely (1618-80), a Dutch painter, who went to England in 1641 and painted historical subjects and landscapes, but won his fame by portraits.

34. celebrated by Hamilton: Anthony Hamilton (1646?-1720), member of the old Scottish family of Hamilton, and a Jacobite who spent the later part of his life in France where he was known as 'Count Anthony.' He became an author of verses and tales, and wrote the *Mémoires du Comte de Grammont,* his brother-in-law (1713), a "work mainly occupied with 'amorous intrigues' at the court of Charles II during 1662-4; it is written with such brilliance and vivacity that it must always rank as a classic."

49. Kneller: Sir Godfrey Kneller (1646-1723) was born, not in Holland, but in Germany. He came to England in 1675 and won fame as a portrait-painter of celebrities.

153b. 1. Two Vandeveldes: William van de Velde (1611-93) and his son William (1633-1707), Dutch painters, lived in London from 1673 and painted, chiefly, marines and naval battles.

6. Varelst: It is not known when this painter came to England. Horace Walpole says that he "lived to a great age, certainly as late as 1710. His works were extremely admired, and his prices the greatest that had been known in this country." (*History of Painting,* III, 303-4).

8. Verrio: Antonio Verrio (1639?-1707), Italian painter, decorated Windsor Castle for Charles II and James II, and Hampton Court for William III and Queen Anne.

25. Cibber: Caius Gabriel Cibber (1630-1700), father of Colley Cibber, the actor and dramatist, was a Dane, living in London and best known for the two figures, Melancholy and Raving Madness, done for the Hospital of St. Mary of Bethlehem, an asylum for lunatics (called Bedlam).

28. Gibbons: Grinling Gibbons (1648-1720), born in Rotterdam, was a wood-carver and sculptor, who did work for the King and for Sir Christopher Wren.

35. a great painter: Sir Joshua Reynolds (1723-1792) had an established reputation before the end of George II's reign (1760).

154a. 6. Stafford: William Howard, 1st Viscount Stafford (1614-80), a leader of the Catholic party, was found guilty of high treason on the testimony of Titus Oates, and beheaded.

8. Russell: William Lord Russell (1639-83), Whig parliamentary leader, was accused of complicity in the Rye House Plot (to kill the King and his brother) and beheaded for high treason "in defiance of law and justice." (Macaulay)

19. Bridewell: A house of correction in Blackfriars, London, standing until 1864.

JOHN HENRY NEWMAN

SELECTED BIBLIOGRAPHY

I. STANDARD EDITIONS.

Collected Works, in separate volumes, published by Longmans, Green & Co., New York, various dates.

Letters and Correspondence of John Henry Newman, During his Life in the English Church, with a brief *Autobiography,* ed. Anne Mozley, 2 vols., London, 1890.

Correspondence of John Henry Newman with Keble and Others: 1839-1845, London, 1917.

Apologia pro Vita Sua, the two versions of 1864 and 1865, preceded by Kingsley's Pamphlets, with Introduction by Wilfred Ward, London, 1913.

Tract Ninety, reprinted with Commentary by A. W. Evans, London, 1933.

The Heart of Newman's Apologia, arranged by Margaret Grennan, New York, 1934.

Selections from the Prose Writings, ed. L. E. Gates, New York, 1895.

Selections from the Prose and Poetry of Newman, ed. M. F. Egan, Boston, 1907.

Literary Selections from Newman, ed. A Sister of Notre Dame, New York, 1923.

The Fine Gold of Newman, ed. J. J. Reilly, New York, 1931.

II. BIOGRAPHY AND CRITICISM

ABBOTT, E. A., *The Anglican Career of Cardinal Newman,* 2 vols., London, 1892.

ATKINS, G. G., *Life of Cardinal Newman,* New York, 1931.

BARRY, WILLIAM, *Newman* (Literary Lives Series), New York, 1904 (Revised Edition, London, 1933).

BREMOND, H., *The Mystery of Newman,* trans., by H. C. Corrance, London, 1907.

CASTLE, W. R., Jr., 'Newman and Coleridge,' *Sewanee Review,* XVII (1909), 139-52.

CHURCH, R. W., *The Oxford Movement,* London, 1894.

CRONIN, J. R., *Cardinal Newman: His Theory of Knowledge,* Washington, D. C., 1935.

CROSS, F. L., *John Henry Newman: with a Set of Unpublished Letters,* London, 1933.

DARK, SIDNEY, *Newman* (Great Lives Series), London, 1934.

DEVERE, AUBREY, "Some Recollections of Cardinal Newman," *Nineteenth Century,* XL (1896), 395-411.

FABER, G. C., *Oxford Apostles: A Character Study of the Oxford Movement,* London, 1933.

FLETCHER, J. B., "Newman and Carlyle," *Atlantic Monthly,* XCV (1905), 669-79.

FLOOD, J. M., *Cardinal Newman and Oxford,* London, 1933.

FROUDE, HURRELL, *Remains,* London, 1837-1839.

FROUDE, J. A., *The Nemesis of Faith,* New York, 1879.

—— "The Oxford Counter-Reformation" in *Short Studies,* IV, 231-360.

HARROLD, CHARLES F., *John Henry Newman,* New York, 1945.

HUTTON, R. H., *Cardinal Newman,* Boston, 1891.

HUXLEY, T. H., "Agnosticism and Christianity," *Nineteenth Century,* XXV, 1889.

INGE, W. R., "Cardinal Newman," *Outspoken Essays,* First Series, London, 1926.

MAY, J. LEWIS, *Cardinal Newman,* New York, 1930.

MOODY, JOHN, *John Henry Newman,* New York, 1945.

MORE, P. E., *The Drift of Romanticism,* Shelburne Essays, Eighth Series, Boston, 1913.

MOZLEY, T., *Reminiscences, Chiefly of Oriel College and the Oxford Movement*, 2 vols., London, 1882.

John Henry Newman: Centenary Essays, London, 1945.

PECK, W. G., *The Social Implications of the Oxford Movement*, New York, 1933.

REILLY, J. J., *Newman as a Man of Letters*, New York, 1925.

ROSS, J. E., *John Henry Newman: Anglican Minister, Catholic Priest, Roman Cardinal*, New York, 1933.

SAROLEA, CHARLES, *Cardinal Newman*, New York, 1908.

SHAFER, R., *Christianity and Naturalism*, New Haven, 1926.

SHAIRP, J. C., *Aspects of Poetry*, Boston, 1891.

STEPHEN, LESLIE, *An Agnostic's Apology*, London, 1893.

TIERNEY, MICHAEL, ed., *A Tribute to Newman: Essays on Aspects of His Life and Thought*, Dublin, 1945.

WARD, WILFRID, *The Life of Cardinal Newman*, 2 vols., London, 1912.

WEBB, C. C. J., *Religious Thought in the Oxford Movement*, London, 1928.

NOTES AND COMMENTS

APOLOGIA

This is the first chapter of Newman's *Apologia* (revised edition), 'apology for (justification of) his life,' which was written as a reply to Charles Kingsley, who in an article (on Froude's *History of England*), in *Macmillan's Magazine* for January, 1864 impugned Newman's intellectual honesty. "The original work," Newman says, "consisted of seven Parts, which were published in a series on consecutive Thursdays, between April 21 and June 2" (1864). It was republished the next year in book form, slightly revised, in five *Chapters*, with the first two parts omitted "excepting certain passages subjoined to the Preface."

160b. **8. *Remnants of Time*:** *Remnants of Time Employed in Prose and Verse* (1753), a collection of essays and verse by Isaac Watts (1674-1748), best known for his hymns (e.g. "Our God, our help in ages past," based on *Psalm* 90).

161a. **9. Littlemore:** Small village near Oxford, where Newman retired in 1842 to the cottage in which he became a Catholic in 1845.

27. Mrs. Radcliffe's or Miss Porter's: Mrs. Anne Ward Radcliffe (1764-1823) wrote popular 'Gothic' romances, the most famous of which is *The Mysteries of Udolpho* (1794). — Jane Porter (1776-1850) is remembered as the author of *Thaddeus of Warsaw* (1803) and *The Scottish Chiefs* (1810).

40. Paine's Tracts: *The Age of Reason* (1795) by Thomas Paine (1737-1809).

44. Hume's Essays: By David Hume (1711-76) Scotch philosopher, historian, essayist. Section X of *An Inquiry Concerning Human Understanding* (1758) is on miracles.

161b. **11. Calvin:** John Calvin (1509-64), French theologian and reformer, whose basic Protestant doctrines are known as 'Calvinism,' i.e. 'predestination, limited atonement, total depravity, irresistibility of grace, and perseverance of saints.'

12. Romaine: William Romaine (1714-95), clergyman of the English Church, "ablest exponent among the evangelicals of the highest Calvinistic doctrine." (D.N.B.)

47. Thomas Scott: Thomas Scott (1747-1821), Anglican clergyman, whose religious writings, including *The Force of Truth* (1779), were once extremely popular.

162a. **3. Daniel Wilson:** Daniel Wilson (1778-1858), Bishop of Calcutta (1832-58), an evangelical clergyman, prelate, and extensive writer on religious subjects.

19. Jones of Nayland: William Jones (1726-1800), eminent High Churchman, author of *On the Catholic Doctrine of the Trinity* (1756).

25. Athanasian Creed: "A Latin formulary, confession, or expression of faith beginning *Quicumque vult* ('Whosoever will [be saved]'), somewhat generally used in the churches of the West from the 9th century. It is of unknown authorship but originated probably in the 5th or 6th century" (Webster's *International*).

29. Antinomianism: The doctrine that faith alone, not the moral law ('works'), is necessary to salvation.

162b. **17. Law's *Serious Call*:** *A Serious Call to a Devout and Holy Life* (1728) by William Law (1686-1761), High Churchman and Tory, is a classic among books on Christian living. It had a profound influence upon John Wesley and Samuel Johnson.

32. Milner's *Church History*: *History of the Church of Christ* (1794-97), by Joseph Milner (1744-97), English clergyman of the evangelical school.

35. St. Augustine, St. Ambrose: Bishop of Hippo (354-430) and Bishop of Milan (340?-397), respectively; two great fathers of the Catholic Church.

39. Newton on the Prophecies: *Observations upon the Prophecies of Daniel and the Apocalypse* (1733) by Sir Isaac Newton (1642-1727), renowned mathematician and author of *Principia* (1687).

163a. 27. Mr. Whately: Richard Whately, student and Fellow of Oriel, Principal of St. Alban Hall (1825), Archbishop of Dublin (1831-1863). "He was credited with the authorship of the anonymous *Letters on the Church by an Episcopalian*" (1826)—which "contributed to the initiation of the tractarian movement." (D.N.B.)

33. St. Alban Hall: A separate hall of residence at Oxford in Newman's time but later (1881) taken over by Merton College.

36. Dr. Hawkins: Edward Hawkins (1789-1882), fellow of Oriel (1813), Provost of Oriel (1828-82), Vicar of St. Mary's (1823-28).

163b. 18. Sumner: John Bird Sumner (1780-1862), Bishop of Chester (1828-48), Archbishop of Canterbury (1848-62). His *Apostolical Preaching Considered in an Examination of St. Paul's Epistles* was published anonymously in 1815; a revised edition in 1817 came out with his name.

30. Blanco White: Joseph Blanco White (1775-1841) was born of an Irish father and a Spanish mother in Seville, where he became a Catholic priest. Later he renounced his Catholicism, escaped to England, entered the English church, and in 1826 settled at Oxford as a member of Oriel College, where for a time he was intimate with the Newman circle. He died a Unitarian.

164a. 27. Butler's *Analogy*: Joseph Butler (1692-1752), Bishop of Bristol (1738-50) and Durham (1750-52), published *The Analogy of Religion, Natural and Revealed, to the Constitution and Course of Nature* (1726) in an attempt to refute 18th century deism.

164b. 34. *London Review*: Newman's essay on *Poetry: With Reference to Aristotle's Poetics* appeared in the first number of the *London Review* in 1829, then under the editorship of Blanco White.

165a. 21. anti-Erastian views: Views opposed to the doctrines of Thomas Erastus (1524-83) Swiss physician and theologian, with whose name is associated the doctrine of supremacy of the state in ecclesiastical affairs—Erastianism.

25. Hurrell Froude: Richard Hurrell Froude (1803-36), fellow of Oriel College and one of Newman's closest friends and collaborators; brother of the historian.

165b. 25. Arianizing: Arius (280?-336), Greek Patriarch of Alexandria, who taught that Christ is not co-eternal with God nor of the same substance, though divine in a secondary sense,— i.e. neither truly God nor truly man. Arius was opposed by Athanasius (293?-373), and his creed was condemned at the great Church Council at Nicaea in 325.

27. Bull's *Defensio*: George Bull (1634-1710), Bishop of St. David's, was a defender of the Athanasian or trinitarian doctrine. His *Defensio Fidei Nicaenae* (Defense of the Nicene Creed) appeared in 1685.

33. Froude's *Remains*: The *Literary Remains* of Hurrell Froude appeared in 1838-39, with a preface by Newman.

38. Nicene Creed: A summary of the Christian faith as formulated and decreed by the First Council of Nicaea, A.D. 325. Essentially it is the creed of the Eastern and Western Churches.

49. Scripture Miracles: Newman wrote several articles for the *Encyclopaedia Metropolitana*, including the "Essay on the Miracles of Scripture" (1826). —— The *Ency. Metro.* was launched in 1818 as a 'Universal Dictionary of Knowledge,' suggested partly by S. T. Coleridge, who contributed an article for the first part. It continued until 1845, when it had reached 29 vols.

50. Middleton: Conyers Middleton (1683-1750), English divine, author of a *Life of Cicero* (1741) and *A Free Inquiry into the Miraculous Powers* (1748), a work which stirred up a storm of controversy.

166a. 2. liberalism of the day: *Vide* Note A, *Liberalism*, at the end of the volume (Newman's note).

5. bereavement: Death of his sister Mary.

8. Peel's re-election: Sir Robert Peel (1788-1850) was elected M. P. from Oxford in 1817. In the Wellington-Peel ministry (1828-30), the Catholic Emancipation Act was passed (1829) but both the Duke of Wellington and Peel were thrown out of office by the outraged Tories, and Peel lost his Oxford seat (though returned from Westbury). In '1828 or 1827' Newman, by voting 'in the minority' at Convocation had taken the 'liberal' side; in 1829 he opposed Peel and Catholic emancipation 'on a simple academical ground.' ('Convocation' is the assembly of graduates who constitute the final governing body of the University. At Oxford only graduates with the degree of M.A. whose names are on the University register may vote.)

28. Keble: John Keble (1792-1866), clergyman, poet, Professor of Poetry at Oxford (1831-41), author of *The Christian Year* (1827), a collection of sacred verse, and also author of seven of the famous *Tracts for the Times*.

166b. 18. Dr. Copleston: Dr. Edward Copleston (1776-1849), high churchman and Tory, Provost of Oriel (1814-28), Bishop of Llandaff and Dean of St. Paul's (1829-49).

24. Dr. Pusey: Edward Bouverie Pusey (1800-82), scholar, theologian, Regius Professor of Hebrew at Oxford; a high churchman and leader in Tractarianism, who did not go over to Rome.

167a. 11. Wilberforce: Robert Isaac Wilberforce (1802-57), son of the great philanthropist William Wilberforce, and younger brother of Bishop Samuel Wilberforce, was student and later fellow and tutor of Oriel (1826), and a member of the Newman circle. In 1854 he left the Church of England and was received into the Church of Rome.

37. Bowden: John William Bowden (1798-1844), member of Trinity College and active collaborator with Newman in the Oxford Movement; author of *Life of Gregory the Seventh* (1840).

167b. 8. Dr. Milman: Henry Hart Milman (1791-1868), poet, historian, scholar, Professor of Poetry at Oxford (1821-31), Dean of St. Paul's (1849-68), and author of *The History of Latin Christianity* (1855).

168a. 2. Berkleyism: The philosophical idealism of George Berkeley (1685-1753), Bishop of Cloyne (1733-53), according to which material things have no existence apart from a perception of them, whether in the individual mind or in the mind of God. There is no such entity as matter. (See *Principles of Human Knowledge*, 1710, and *Three Dialogues*, 1713.)

46. "I will guide thee with mine eye": *Psalms*, XXXII, 8-9.

168b. 5. Mr. Miller: John Cole Miller (1814-80), evangelical divine, honorary canon at Worcester College (1852) and canon and treasurer (1871-73); canon of Rochester (1873).

6. Bampton Lectures: The Bampton Lectures at Oxford were founded by John Bampton (d. 1751), Oxford graduate, and clergyman; they are eight divinity lecture-sermons, delivered annually "to confirm and establish the Christian faith." The first series began in 1779.

169b. 20. Day of Pentecost: Seventh Sunday after Christ's resurrection; see *Acts*, II, 1-41.

170b. 28. Ecumenical Councils: Councils convoked from the entire Catholic Church.

171a. 12. St. Ignatius and St. Justin: St. Ignatius (d. ?107), one of the Fathers of the Church, Bishop of Antioch, martyred at Rome under Trajan. —— St. Justin Martyr (100?-?165), Church Father in Palestine, probably martyred in Rome.

14. Hugh Rose: High Churchman and theologian (1795-1838), co-editor with Lyall of the Theological Library (vols. I-XIV, 1832-46). At his parsonage in Hadleigh, Suffolk, where Hurrell Froude and others met with Rose, the Tractarian Movement began.

14. Mr. Lyall: William Rowe Lyall (1788-1857), English divine and Dean of Canterbury (1845-57).

23. Church of Alexandria: Next to Rome Alexandria was the largest and most important city of the Roman Empire. When Christianity came into the city is not known, but by the middle of the second century Alexandria was becoming very active and influential in Church Councils.

40. ante-Nicene period: The period before the first great Ecumenical Church Council called by Constantine the Great at Nicaea in 325, when Arianism (the creed of the Alexandrian, Arius) was finally rejected. Nicaea was the capital of the Roman province of Bithynia in what is now northern Turkey.

46. Athanasius: St. Athanasius (293?-373) was one of the great churchmen at Alexandria, first a deacon, then for more than forty years a bishop; the head of anti-Arian Christians and author of many works.

49. Origen, Dionysius, Clement: Second century Fathers of the Church at Alexandria; Origen was the greatest theologian of the three and, indeed, of the Eastern Church.

172a. 42. Three Holy Children: Shadrach, Meshach, and Abednego (*Daniel*, III); the quotation is from the Catholic Bible. (Douai version of the Vulgate, *Daniel*, III, 57.)

172b. 13. Prophet Daniel: *Daniel*, X, 13.

16. Angels of the Seven Churches: *Rev.*, I, 20.

22. Justin, Athenagoras, etc.: For Justin see previous note; —— Athenagoras, Greek scholar of the late 2nd and early 3rd centuries A.D.; —— Irenaeus, Apostle of the Gauls, Bishop of Lyons (177), probably martyred; —— Clement (150?-?220), theologian who studied and taught at Alexandria; —— Tertullian (160?-?230), Latin ecclesiastical writer of Carthage, one of the great fathers of the Western Church; —— Origen (185?-?254), writer and teacher of the Eastern Church at Alexandria and Caesarea; —— Lactantius, teacher and writer, whom Constantine the Great sent to Gaul (cir. 306); —— Sulpicius (360?-?410), Christian writer and historian born in Aquitaine; —— Ambrose (340?-397), Bishop of Milan, foe of Arianism; —— Gregory of Nazianzen (329?-389), Bishop of Constantinople, great theologian of the Eastern Church.

42. Scylla and Charybdis: A rock and a whirlpool, respectively, in the Strait of Messina: in classical mythology both were represented as female monsters.

48. Hippoclides: Hippoclides, the favorite suitor of the daughter of King Cleisthenes, on the day of choosing danced in shameless fashion before his intended father-in-law, whereupon the outraged king cried out: "Son of Tisander, you have danced your wife away!" Newman quotes the youth's reply, which became a proverb (for the incident, see *Herodotus*, VI, 129).

173a. 1. Economy: Any special plan or dispensation of God in His government of the world.

17. Revolution in France: In July 1830, when the Bourbon King Charles X was dethroned, and the 'Citizen King' Louis Philippe was crowned in his place.

23. Reform Agitation: Resulting in the first great Reform Bill of 1832.

36. Blomfield: Charles James Blomfield (1786-1857) was Bishop of London (1828-56), a mediator in the Tractarian movement, and a classical scholar and editor of distinction.

45. Apostolical succession: Unbroken succession, or descent by successive ordination, from Apostles to Bishops, as held in the Roman Catholic, Eastern, and Anglican churches.

46. Non-Jurors: "Beneficed clergymen in England and Scotland who refused to take the oath of allegiance to William and Mary, or to their successors, after the Revolution of 1688" (Webster's *International*).

173b. 10. Primeval Mystery: The Incarnation of Christ.

13. Spiritual Mother: The Catholic Church.

19. Look on this picture and on that: *Hamlet*, III, iv, 53.

49. *Lyra Apostolica*: A collection of 179 sacred poems by Newman, Hurrell Froude, Keble, Williams, J. W. Bowden, and Wilberforce, published in 1836. They had first "appeared monthly in the *British Magazine*." Newman wrote 109 of them, and Keble 46.

174a. 32. Wiseman: Nicholas Patrick Stephen Wiseman (1802-65), Rector of the English College in Rome and later Archbishop of Westminster, and Cardinal (1850-65).

41. Tenebrae, at the Sistine: 'Darkness' (Latin plural)—"The matins and lauds for the last three days of Holy Week, commemorating the sufferings and death of Christ" (Webster's *International*). —— The Sistine Chapel in the Vatican, the walls of which are decorated with frescoes by great painters, chiefly Michaelangelo.

42. Miserere: Musical setting of the penetential 50th Psalm in the Vulgate (51st in A. V.).

50. Bill for the Suppression: A Bill introduced in Parliament in 1833, for the suppression of ten of the twenty-one sees of the Irish Protestant Church. It was this Bill that provoked Keble's Assize Sermon and precipitated the Tractarian Movement.

174b. 22. Dr. Arnold: Thomas Arnold (1795-1842), Headmaster of Rugby, Broad Churchman, historian, Regius professor of history at Oxford (1841), father of Matthew Arnold.

37. M. Bunsen: Christian Charles Josias Baron von Bunsen (1791-1860), Prussian diplomatist and scholar, ambassador at the Court of St. James (1842-54), when a young man was secretary to the Prussian envoy to the Papal Court (Niebuhr) at the time of Newman's visit to Rome.

39. "You shall know the difference": See *Iliad*, XVIII, 187-238.

175b. 23. Assize Sermon: Sermon preached before the judges of the assizes or superior courts.

THE TAMWORTH READING ROOM

"The Tamworth Reading Room," a series of seven letters, "was written," says Newman, "for the *Times* newspaper, and appeared in its columns in February, 1841, being afterwards published as a pamphlet." The letters were signed by 'Catholicus,' a pseudonym by which the author suggested the state of his mind in 1841, the year of *Tract Ninety,* when the Oxford Movement was at its height. The particular occasion of the letters was an address by Sir Robert Peel "delivered upon the establishment of a Library and Reading-room at Tamworth," a manufacturing town in Staffordshire. Newman could not accept secular knowledge as a substitute for personal religion: "Faith, not Knowledge or Argument," he insists, "is our principle of action."

177b. 21. Lord Brougham: Henry Baron Brougham and Vaux (1778-1868), Whig Statesman, scholar, author, one of the founders of the *Edinburgh Review* (1802) and of London University (1828), and Lord Chancellor (1830-34).

27. Pantheon: A temple dedicated to all the gods, especially the Pantheon at Rome, built by Hadrian about 120 A.D. It now means any building where rest the famous dead of a nation.

178a. 12. Democritus: Greek philosopher (B.C. 460?-?362) "who taught that all phenomena are to be explained by the incessant movement of atoms differing only in shape, order, and position" (Webster's *International*).

12. "The natural philosophies," etc.: from Bacon's *The Advancement of Learning* (1605). (Book II, vii, 7.)

178b. 1. Laplace: Pierre Simon, Marquis de Laplace (1749-1827), French astronomer and mathematician who formulated the *nebular hypothesis.*

31. the principles come of Faith: "This is too absolute; if it is to be taken to mean that the legitimate, and what may be called the objective, conclusion from the fact of Nature viewed in the concrete is not in favour of the being and providence of God. —— *Vide* 'Essay on Assent,' pp. 336-345, 369, and 'Univ. Serm.,' p. 194" (Newman's note).

179b. 5. not the Almighty God: "*Vide* 'University Education,' Disc. I, 2nd ed." (Newman's note).

19. it passes on to no prototype: "*Vide* 'Essays,' vol. I, p. 37, etc." (Newman's note).

WHAT IS A UNIVERSITY?

The second of a series of essays illustrating "the idea of a University," which "originally appeared in 1854 in the columns of the 'Dublin Catholic University Gazette,'" says Newman. In 1872 the series reappeared in the collection of *Historical Sketches* under "the more appropriate title" 'Rise and Progress of Universities.'

181a. 39. Sibyl: In the ancient world a woman inspired by the gods with a gift of prophecy, hence a prophetess. The most famous was the Cumaean Sybil, whose prophecies were written on leaves, and who was consulted by Aeneas before his descent into Hades.

46. sermons in stones, etc.: *As You Like It,* II, i, 16-17.

183a. 26. British Association: British Association for the Advancement of Science, founded in 1831.

184a. 21. Universities: London University was founded in 1828, but owing to religious opposition to a non-sectarian foundation, the institution was for years hardly more than "a board of administration." —— The beginnings of the University of Paris were early in the 13th century, and by 1215 "the university of masters was a legal corporation" (Rashdall, *Medieval Universities,* I, 298 n.). The University was suppressed in 1793. —— Rashdall assigns "the birth of Oxford as a *studium generale* to 1167 or the beginning of 1168" (*op. cit.,* III, 15). A *studium generale* "means, not a place where all subjects are studied, but a place where students from all parts are received" (*op. cit.,* I, 6). —— "By the year 1000 A.D. Bologna was famous as a studium of arts" (*op. cit.,* I, 108). —— The University of Salamanca was founded about 1227 (*op. cit.,* II, 75).

184b. 9. St. Irenaeus: Greek Bishop of Lyons (130?-?202), one of the greatest of early Church Fathers.

16. St. Anthony: Egyptian founder of Christian monasticism (251-?356), for many years a hermit in the solitudes of the desert.

19. Didymus: Theologian of Alexandria (309?-394), known as Didymus the Blind, due to loss of sight in childhood.

185b. 22. St. Patrick: Apostle and patron saint of Ireland (389?-?461), where he founded churches and established the faith.

THE IDEA OF A UNIVERSITY

The Idea of a University is a series of nine discourses on the "scope and nature of University Education" delivered by Newman at Dublin from May 10 to June 7, 1852. They were published later in the same year, and afterwards were republished along with a series of "Occasional Lectures and Essays on University Subjects," under the inclusive title, *The Idea of a University*. Written after he had been appointed in 1851 Rector of the proposed Catholic University in Dublin, Newman undertook to define "the *aims* and *principles*" of higher education. The book is now a classic exposition of 'liberal education.' 'Discourses' five and six are here reprinted.

KNOWLEDGE ITS OWN END

186a. 19. Butler's Analogy: Butler's *Analogy of Religion* (1736), by the greatest English theologian of his time. The book was widely accepted as a complete refutation of deism (see reference to Butler in the *Apologia*, together with note).

22. Pitt: William Pitt (1759-1806), English statesman, Prime Minister 1783-1801 and 1804-06, second son of the first Earl of Chatham, "the great Commoner."

25. Watson: Richard Watson (1737-1816), professor of chemistry and later professor of divinity at Cambridge; appointed to the see of Llandaff in Wales in 1782. He wrote an *Apology for Christianity* (1776) in reply to the historian Gibbon's treatment of the Early Church in the 15th and 16th chapters of his *History*. Gibbon wrote his *Vindication* (1779) as an answer.

31. Arcesilaus: Greek skeptical philosopher (315?-?241 B.C.), who established at Athens the New or Middle Academy and declared, said Newman, "first, that nothing can be known, and therefore nothing can be advanced." (See Cicero's *Academic Questions*, I, 12, from which N. quotes in his essay on *Cicero*.)

186b. 16. former Discourse: Discourse IV.

187a. 46. "selection from the records of Philosophy," etc.: Quoted from the Introduction to *Pursuit of Knowledge under Difficulties* (1830), by George Little Craik (1798-1866).

187b. 16. Cicero: The two quotations are from the *De Officiis* (Concerning Moral Duties); the first is from I, vi, 18, and the second, from I, iv, 13. A third quotation in the next paragraph is from I, vi, 19.

188a. 13. Baconian philosophy: The inductive method of reasoning from particulars to general principles or generalizations.

33. the elder Cato: Marcus Porcius Cato, the Censor (234-149 B.C.), statesman and patriot, one of the greatest characters of ancient Rome.

35. Carneades: Greek orator and skeptical philosopher (cir. 213-129 B.C.) of Cyrene, who, with Diogenes and Critolaus, was sent on an embassy to Rome in 155 B.C. Their philosophical discourses were so seductively attractive to Roman youth that the Senate, at the instance of Cato, abruptly dismissed them.

188b. 17. of which the poet speaks: In a note Newman refers to Aristotle's *Nicomachaean Ethics*, VI, iv: "art loves fate and fate loves art." The poet quoted is Agathon (Welldon's trans., 183).

46. Olympic games: For hundreds of years on every fourth year games were held at Olympia in ancient Elis, in the western Peloponnesus, including chariot races, and competitions in poetry and the fine arts. Victors were crowned with wild olive.

48. Xenophon: Greek historian and general (434?-?355 B.C.), author of *Anabasis, Cyropedia, Memorabilia* of Socrates, and other works.

189b. 23. the great Philosopher: Aristotle, *Rhetoric*, I, 5 (Newman's note).

190a. 23. Lycurgus: Famous lawgiver of Sparta in the 9th century B.C. When the Delphic oracle approved his reforms and institutions, he went into voluntary exile; where and when he died is unknown.

23. Seneca: Roman stoic philosopher and author (B.C. 4?-A.D. 65), who in one of his *Moral Epistles* (88, sec. 18) excludes wrestling from 'liberal' studies.

191a. 21. enthymeme: A syllogism in which one of the premises is omitted, as for example: he is too unimaginative to enjoy poetry.

192a. 45. Cicero: Marcus Tullius Cicero (106-43 B.C.), illustrious Roman statesman, orator, and philosopher, "was too easily elated by prosperity and too easily dejected by adversity."

47. Seneca: Formerly a preceptor to Nero, Seneca fell a victim to the wicked emperor's suspicion and jealousy, and was ordered to destroy himself.

48. Brutus: Marcus Junius Brutus (85-42 B.C.), one of the assassins of Julius Caesar, was defeated at the battle of Philippi and met death by suicide. Just before the battle he said to Cassius: "When I was young and unskillful in affairs, I was led, I know not how, into uttering a bold sentence in philosophy, and blamed Cato for killing himself, as thinking it an irreligious act" (Plutarch's *Life of Brutus*).

50. Cato: Marcus Porcius Cato (95-46 B.C.), the 'Younger' (great-grandson of Cato, the Censor), Roman patriot and philosopher, fell upon his sword at Utica rather than surrender to Julius Caesar.

50. his panegyrist: i.e. Cicero, who in his *Tusculan Disputations* said: "Cato departed from life with a feeling of joy in having found a reason for death; for the God who is master within us forbids our departure without permission" (I, xxx, 74, Loeb trans.).

53. Polemo: A rich young Athenian (314-cir. 276 B.C.) son of Philostratus, who was saved from a profligate life upon hearing Xenocrates lecture on intemperance. He reformed, and later succeeded Xenocrates as head of the Academy.

192b. 1. Anaxagoras: Greek philosopher (500?-428 B.C.), who renounced possessions in Asia Minor and devoted his life to philosophy at Athens. Among his pupils, it is said, were Pericles and Euripides and possibly Socrates.

3. *Rasselas:* Johnson's story of *Rasselas, Prince of Abyssinia* (1759) is really a series of reflections on "the vanity of human wishes." Quotations are from Ch. XVIII.

193a. 9. its Prophet: i.e. Bacon, who as Lord Chancellor was, in 1621, charged before the House of Lords with taking bribes. He confessed his guilt and was dismissed from his office, fined and imprisoned. Newman notes the practical or utilitarian side of Bacon's scientific studies.

16. "meanest": In his *Essay on Man*, IV, 282, Pope calls Bacon: "The wisest, brightest, meanest of mankind."

20. Idols of the den, etc.: Bacon (*Novum Organum, I*) distinguishes four kinds of false thinking, which he calls 'idols': *idols of the tribe*, due to the tribe or race, i.e. to human nature itself; *idols of the cave*, due to personal peculiarities; *idols of the market-place*, due to the loose thinking of men in society; *idols of the theatre*, due to traditional doctrines and dogmas, which, like dramas, are unreal.

22. His mission was the increase, etc.: "It will be seen that on the whole I agree with Lord Macaulay in his Essay on Bacon's Philosophy" (Newman's note). "The aim of the Platonic philosophy was to raise us far above vulgar wants. The aim of the Baconian philosophy was to supply our vulgar wants," said Macaulay.

48. the old mediciner in the tale: The quotation is from *The Unknown Patient* by Friedrich Fouqué (1777-1843), German romanticist.

193b. 15. Socrates or Seneca: Socrates (469-399 B.C.) was accused of corrupting Athenian youth and condemned to die by drinking hemlock. —— Seneca (4 B.C.?-65 A.D.), the moralist, condemned wealth, while Seneca, the servile flatterer, loved riches.

194b. 41. Scipio: There were several famous Scipios, but Newman probably refers to Publius Cornelius Scipio, *Africanus Major* (237-?183 B.C.), who subdued Spain and overcame Hannibal in Africa (battle of Zama, 202 B.C.).

41. Saladin: Celebrated Sultan of Egypt and Syria (1137-93), who fought against the Christians during the Crusades and took Jerusalem in 1187.

KNOWLEDGE VIEWED IN RELATION TO LEARNING

195b. 15. science has been appropriated: Since the word science comes from *sciens* (knowing), the present participle of the verb *scio*, Newman means that it should express a quality rather than the subject-matter of the intellect.

197a. 11. like the Egyptians: *Genesis*, XLI, 47-48.

198a. 9. For instance, let a person: "The pages which follow are taken almost *verbatim* from the author's 14th (Oxford) University Sermon, which, at the time of writing this discourse, he did not expect ever to reprint" (Newman's note).

198b. **43. "the world is all before it where to choose":** *Paradise Lost,* XII, 646.

199a. **3. king in the Tragedy:** Allusion to Pentheus, king of Thebes, in the *Bacchae* of Euripides. He opposed the worship of Bacchus and was in consequence torn to pieces by his mother and sisters.

199b. **17. St. Thomas:** St. Thomas Aquinas, called 'The Angelic Doctor' (1225?-1274), the great Catholic theologian, whose central purpose was "to form a synthesis of Christian theology and Aristotelian philosophy."

200a. **39. Pompey's Pillar:** A Corinthian column of red granite at Alexandria, Egypt, erected in the reign of Diocletian (302), whose statue it supported. It had nothing to do with Pompey.

202a. **7. Salmasius:** Claudius Salmasius (1588-1653), or Claude de Saumaise, great French scholar, who succeeded Scaliger at the University of Leyden, and who is remembered for his defense of Charles II which provoked a reply from Milton.

8. Burmann: The name applies to either of two eminent Dutch classical scholars; Peter, the elder (1668-1741), and his nephew, Peter, the younger (1714-78).

15. Tarpeia: "In Roman legend, a maiden (daughter of Tarpeius, governor of the citadel) who betrayed the citadel to the Sabines for the promise of 'what they wore on their arms,' meaning their gold bracelets. They threw their shields on her and killed her" (Webster's *International*).

29. Mosheim or Du Pin: Johann Lorenz von Mosheim (1694-1755), German Protestant theologian, whose *Ecclesiastical History* was written in Latin. — Louis Ellies Du Pin (1657-1719), French Catholic clergyman, ecclesiastical historian, and critic.

206a. **14. tongues in the trees, etc.:** *As You Like It,* II, i, 16-18.

206b. **5. as the village school, etc.:** Crabbe's *Tales of the Hall.* This Poem, let me say, I read on its first publication, above thirty years ago, with extreme delight, and have never lost my love of it; and on taking it up lately, found I was even more touched by it than heretofore. A work which can please in youth and age, seems to fulfil (in logical language) the *accidental definition* of a Classic. (A further course of twenty years has past, and I bear the same witness in favour of this Poem.) (Newman's note.)

LITERATURE

One of a series of lectures written by Newman, as he says, "while Rector of the Catholic University of Ireland" and delivered at various times between 1854 and 1858. They were published in 1858 under the general title 'University Subjects, Discussed in Occasional Lectures and Essays.' The lecture on 'Literature' was "read in the School of Philosophy and Letters, November, 1858." A few introductory paragraphs are here omitted.

208a. **26. the writer whose pages I have quoted:** i.e. Sermon XLII, from *Sermons of Mr. Yorick* (1760-69) by Laurence Sterne, the novelist (see pp. 331-335, vol. 2, of *Sermons of Mr. Yorick,* ed. W. L. Cross, New York, 1904).

208b. **14. in a public lecture elsewhere:** "Position of Catholics in England, pp. 101-2" (Newman's note). The learned scholar was White, professor of Arabic at Oxford, who engaged a Devonshire curate to turn his lectures "into ornamental English."

209a. **27. vision of Mirza:** No. 159, Addison's *Spectator,* for 1 September, 1711.

41. Aristotle ... the magnanimous man: *Nichomachaen Ethics,* bk. IV, Ch. VIII (Welldon, trans.).

209b. **16. Canst thou not minister:** *Macbeth,* V, iv, 40-45.

31. 'Tis not alone my inky cloak: *Hamlet,* I, ii, 77-83.

44. Cicero: Marcus Tullius Cicero (106-43 B.C.), Roman statesman, orator, philosopher, man of letters.

210a. **29. Neither Livy, nor Tacitus, etc.:** Titus Livius (B.C. 59-17 A.D.), Roman historian; — Publius Cornelius Tacitus (55?-cir. 117), Roman historian; — Publius Terentius Afer (190?-?159 B.C.), Roman writer of comedies; — Lucius Annaeus Seneca (B.C. 4?-64 A.D.), Roman Stoic philosopher and author; — Gaius Plinius, the Younger (62?-?114), Roman author and orator; — Marcus Fabius Quintilianus (35?-?100), Roman rhetorician and critic.

210b. **7. Isocrates:** Athenian orator (436-338 B.C.) and teacher of rhetoric.

8. sophists: Teachers of rhetoric, philosophy, and the art of living, in ancient Greece, who became prominent about the middle of the 5th century B.C.

35. **Michael Angelo:** Michelangelo Buonarroti (1475-1564), Italian painter, sculptor, architect, and poet.

36. **Raffaelle:** Raffaello Sanzio (1483-1520), Italian painter.

38. **Apollo Belvidere:** Famous statue of the god now in the Vatican, discovered in the 16th century near Anzio, a coast south of Rome.

211a. 1. **The poet's eye, etc.:** *A Midsummer Night's Dream,* V, i, 12-17.

21. **Demosthenes:** Athenian orator (384?-322 B.C.).

22. **Thucydides:** Athenian historian (471?-?400 B.C.).

24. **Herodotus:** (484?-425 B.C.), Greek historian, 'Father of History.'

28. **Addison:** Joseph Addison (1672-1719), essayist, dramatist, statesman. Newman probably refers to Addison's "fastidiousness" when Secretary of State: "In the office, says Pope, he could not issue an order without losing his time in quest of fine expressions" (Johnson, *Lives,* Life of Addison).

41. **Virgil wishes his Aeneid to be burned:** Before Virgil left for Greece for final work on the *Aeneid,* "if anything befell him," he instructed his friend, the poet Varius, to burn the poem. Virgil died on the return journey, but the manuscript was saved (see Suetonius' *Life of Virgil,* sec. 39—Loeb trans., II, 479).

45. **Gibbon:** Edward Gibbon (1737-94), whose *History of the Decline and Fall of the Roman Empire* (1766-88) is one of the greatest histories in the English language. In his *Memoirs* (1796) he says of it: "Three times did I compose the first chapter, and twice the second and third, before I was thoroughly satisfied with their effect."

212a. 19. **Beethoven:** Ludwig van Beethoven (1770-1827), German musician and composer. Newman's "favorite composer was Beethoven," says Wilfrid Ward, "to whom he was passionately devoted." "I had a good bout at Beethoven's quartettes," says Newman of one occasion, "and thought them more exquisite than ever—so that I was obliged to lay down the instrument (his 'fiddle') and literally cry out with delight." (Ward's *Life,* II, 350 and 76).

212b. 6. **Fra Angelico:** Giovanni da Fiesole (1387-1455), a Dominican monk and artist in the monastery of San Marco, Florence, better known as Fra Angelico (Angelic Brother) because of the beauty of the many angels which he painted and his devout religious nature.

6. **Francia:** Francesco Raibolini (1450-1518), called Francia, an Italian painter of Bologna, friend of Raphael.

JOHN STUART MILL

SELECTED BIBLIOGRAPHY

I. STANDARD EDITIONS

There is no complete standard edition of Mill's works. They are published in various editions and at various dates in England and America. There is a *Library Edition of the Miscellaneous Works* by Henry Holt and Company as follows:

Autobiography
Dissertations and Discussions, 4 vols.
Considerations on Representative Government.
Examination of Sir William Hamilton's Philosophy, 2 vols.
On Liberty; The Subjection of Women, 1 vol.
Comte's Positive Philosophy.

Other editions of individual Works and of Letters are:
Autobiography, with a Preface by J. J. Coss, Columbia University Press, 1924.
Autobiography, with an appendix of hitherto unpublished speeches and a preface by H. J. Laski, Oxford University Press, 1924.
A System of Logic, new impression, London, 1925.
On Liberty, Representative Government, The Subjection of Women; Three Essays, with introduction by M. G. Fawcett, Oxford University Press, 1940.
Principles of Political Economy, edited with an introduction by Sir W. J. Ashley, New York, 1923.
Utilitarianism, Liberty, and Representative Government, in Everyman's Library, New York, 1940.
The Subjection of Women, in Everyman's Library, (with *The Rights of Women* by Mary Wollstonecroft), New York, 1929.

Socialism: A Collection of his Writings on Socialism, Social Science Library, ed. W. D. P. Bliss, New York, 1891.

Three Essays on Religion, third edition, New York, 1885.

The Letters of John Stuart Mill, ed. Hugh Elliot, 2 vols., New York, 1910.

Correspondence inédite avec Gustave d'Eichthal, Paris, 1898.

II. BIOGRAPHY AND CRITICISM

BAIN, ALEXANDER, *John Stuart Mill: A Criticism with Personal Recollections,* New York, 1882.

BRANDES, G., *Creative Spirits of the Nineteenth Century,* New York, 1923.

CARLYLE, T., *Letters of, to John Stuart Mill, John Sterling, and Robert Browning,* ed. A. Carlyle, London, 1923.

COURTNEY, W. L., *Life of John Stuart Mill* (Great Writers Series), London, 1889.

—— *The Metaphysics of John Stuart Mill,* London, 1879.

DAVIDSON, W. L., *Political Thought in England: The Utilitarians,* Home University Library, New York, n.d.

DOUGLAS, C. M., *John Stuart Mill: A Study of his Philosophy,* Edinburgh, 1895.

ELTON, OLIVER, *A Survey of English Literature,* III, New York, 1920.

GRIBBLE, F., "John Stuart Mill," *Fortnightly Review,* LXXXVI (1906), 344-54.

HAMILTON, MARY AGNES, *John Stuart Mill* (Makers of New World Series), London, 1933.

HARRISON, F., *Tennyson, Ruskin, Mill,* London, 1899.

JENKS, E., *Thomas Carlyle and John Stuart Mill,* London, 1888.

MACCUNN, J., *Six Radical Thinkers,* London, 1907.

MASSON, DAVID, *Recent British Philosophy,* London, 1877.

MARTINEAU, JAMES, *Essays Philosophical and Theological,* New York, 1879.

MORLAN, G., *America's Heritage from John Stuart Mill,* New York, 1936.

MORLEY, JOHN, *Critical Miscellanies,* III and IV, New York, 1908.

NEFF, E., *Carlyle and Mill,* New York, 1924.

PRINGLE, G. O. S., "Mill's Humanity," *Westminster Review,* CL (1898), 159-62.

ROBERTSON, J. M., *Modern Humanists,* London, 1895.

—— *Modern Humanists Reconsidered,* London, 1927.

SCHERER, EDMOND, *Etudes Critiques sur la Littérature Contemporaine,* Paris, 1863.

SIMCOX, EDITH, "Influence of Writings of J. S. Mill," *Contemporary Review,* XXII (1873), 297-317.

STEPHEN, SIR JAMES F., *Liberty, Equality, Fraternity,* New York, 1873.

STEPHEN, SIR LESLIE, *The English Utilitarians,* Vol. 3, New York, 1900.

TAINE, H. A., *English Positivism:* (A Study of) J. S. Mill (a translation), London, 1870.

—— *A History of English Literature,* Vol. 4, London, 1873-1874.

TULLOCH, JOHN, *Movements of Religious Thought in Britain,* New York, 1893.

WARD, WILFRED, "John Stuart Mill," *Quarterly Review,* CCXIII (1910), 264-92.

WELLINGTON, S., "John Stuart Mill: The Saint of Rationalism," *Westminster Review,* CLXIII (1905), 11-30.

WILLIAMS, STANLEY, *Studies in Victorian Literature,* New York, 1923.

NOTES AND COMMENTS

AUTOBIOGRAPHY

John Stuart Mill's *Autobiography,* of which chapter V is reprinted from the edition published by his step-daughter, Helen Taylor, was written in the last years of his life, most of it probably from 1870. It was published soon after his death in 1873. Harold Laski describes it as "the most imperishable of his writings ... a document of the first importance in the intellectual history of the nineteenth century."

218a. 4. after this time: That is, he says, "when in the spring of 1828, I ceased to write for the *Westminster."* The *Westminster Review* was established by Jeremy Bentham as an organ of philosophical radicalism, the first number appearing in April 1824. Mill was a frequent contributor almost from the first.

21. Bentham: Jeremy Bentham (1748-1832), an indefatigable proponent of social and political reform in his day, was head and front of the utilitarianism and philosophical radicalism that so powerfully influenced British thought for two generations.

219a. **5. A grief without a pang, etc.:** *Dejection: An Ode,* 21-24.

28. words of Macbeth: *Macbeth,* V, iii, 40-45.

219b. **3. results of association:** i.e. the "Principle of Association" (as Mill called it), or the theory that the mental life is built up by the combination of simple sensations into complex wholes according to certain laws of association. Formulation of the doctrine goes back to Locke, Hume, and Hartley of the 18th century and to James Mill and his son, John Stuart Mill, of the 19th century.

220b. **43. Work without hope:** Coleridge, *Work Without Hope,* 13-14.

221a. **9. Marmontel:** Jean François Marmontel (1723-99), French dramatist and novelist, who contributed to the *Encyclopédie.* His *Mémoires d'un père* (4 vols.) came out after his death, in 1804.

49. theory of Carlyle: Carlyle's notion of "the unconscious" is set forth most fully in *Characteristics,* but it will be found in *Signs of the Times* and in *The Hero as Poet,* both of which are included in the present text.

222a. **40. Weber's *Oberon:*** Baron Karl Maria Friedrich Ernst von Weber (1786-1826), German composer and opera conductor, whose opera *Oberon* was first produced in the Covent Garden Theatre, April 12, 1826. The libretto was adapted from Wieland's poem, *Oberon* (1780), by the English playwright J. R. Planché (1796-1880).

222b. **8. Mozarts:** Wolfgang Amadeus Mozart (1756-91), Austrian composer of over 600 works, one of the world's great musical geniuses.

13. Laputa: The flying island of Swift's *Gulliver's Travels,* Part 3, home of impractical theorists.

223a. **38. Pyrenean:** In chapter II of the *Autobiography* Mill tells of spending a year in France (May 1820 to July 1821), during most of which time he was a guest of Sir Samuel Bentham, brother of the illustrious Jeremy. The family took him on "an excursion to the Pyrenees": "this first introduction to the highest order of mountain scenery made the deepest impression on me, and gave a color to my tastes through life."

223b. **28. Ode, falsely called Platonic:** In his famous note "to the famous Ode," Wordsworth dwells upon "that dreamlike vividness and splendour which invests objects of sight in childhood ... as a presumptive evidence of a prior state of existence"; and he recognizes this experience "as an ingredient in Platonic philosophy" (cf. the doctrine of reminiscence in Plato's *Phaedo*). But he nowhere says that the 'intimations' expressed in the poem came from Plato; in fact they are, he says, *"experiences* of my own mind."

224a. **9. Roebuck:** John Arthur Roebuck (1801-79), member of Parliament and reformer, was, along with Mill, one of the young "philosophical radicals" who for a number of years (1825-30) regularly met to debate questions both speculative and practical (cf. the later pages of Ch. IV, *Autobiography*).

27. Sterling: John Sterling (1806-44), British essayist and poet, friend of Coleridge, Mill, Emerson, and Carlyle; best revealed in Carlyle's *Life of Sterling* (1851).

38. vulgar notion of a Benthamite: Probably Mill has reference to Bentham's logical analysis of pleasure as the basis of his utilitarianism; i.e. pleasure depends only upon quantity and intensity, and when pleasures are equal in these respects one pleasure is as good as another,—"push pin is worth as much as poetry."

224b. **46. Frederick Maurice:** Frederick Denison Maurice (1805-72), English clergyman and theologian, leader of the Broad Church and of the Christian Socialist movement.

50. Hare: Julius Charles Hare (1795-1855), Archdeacon, editor and author of John Sterling's *Essays and Tales, with Life* (1848), the book which caused Carlyle to write a life of Sterling.

225a. **2. Eyton Tooke:** William Eyton Tooke is mentioned by Mill in the third chapter of the *Autobiography* as one of the members of the Utilitarian Society (1823-26), which Mill had organized: described there as "a young man of singular worth both moral and intellectual, lost to the world by an early death."

34. Thirty-nine Articles: The doctrines of the Church of England, originally forty-two (1553), were reduced to thirty-nine in 1563, and now comprise the articles of faith to which the clergy are required to assent.

52. Christian Socialist movement: "Christian Socialism" (1848-54) was organized by Maurice, Charles Kingsley, J. M. Ludlow, and Thomas Hughes, in an effort to socialize Christianity and Christianize society (see Introduction).

225b. **5. disciple of Coleridge:** Coleridge exerted a powerful influence upon Maurice and

Sterling. Carlyle's pen-portrait of the later Coleridge in his *Life of Sterling* (part I, ch. VIII) is justly famous.

226b. **12. Essay on Government:** *Essays on Government, etc.* (1828), by James Mill; reviewed by Macaulay in the *Edinburgh Review,* March, 1829.

21. Kepler, Newton, Laplace: Kepler, the German mathematical astronomer, was less bold as a generalizer than Newton and Laplace, less a 'philosophizing' scientist.

49. Hobbes: Thomas Hobbes (1588-1679), English philosopher, best known for his great work, *Leviathan* (1651), a treatise on the state.

227b. **7. Thomson's System of Chemistry:** Thomas Thomson (1773-1852), Scottish chemist, regius professor of Glasgow (from 1818), published his *System of Chemistry* in 1802, and founded the first chemical laboratory in Great Britain.

228a. **53. Goethe's device, 'many-sidedness':** A Goethean ideal of culture, e.g. *Laszt uns doch vielseitig sein*—let us then be many-sided (*Maximen und Reflektionen,* no. 1337).

228b. **6. St. Simonian school:** Allusion to the followers of Claude Henri Comte de Saint-Simon (1760-1825), French philosopher and social scientist, who is considered to be the founder of French socialism, in which the state would own all property and the worker would be rewarded according to the quality and quantity of his work. Mill, like Carlyle, was for a time much interested in the Saint-Simonians.

229a. **2. Fichte's Lectures:** Johann Gottlieb Fichte (1762-1814), German metaphysician and post-Kantian exponent of transcendental idealism, was also a writer and lecturer on popular subjects in which his philosophical idealism received practical application. One of these was *Grundzüge des gegenwärtigen Zeitalters* (1806), translated into English with the title given by Mill. The book is "a passionate arraignment of the frivolities" and skepticisms of the age.

18. Auguste Comte: Auguste Comte (1798-1857), the founder of positivism, a system of philosophy in which the 'theological' and 'metaphysical' stages of society are succeeded by the 'positive' stage, wherein the laws of science become the 'proper models' for the future structure of society; and the ideal of a progressive development of man's ethical nature becomes the positivist religion of humanity. Comte's central work is his *Système de Politique Positive* (4 vols., 1851-54), part of which (a first sketch of positivism with the same title) was published in 1822 and is the "early work" to which Mill refers. Mill also read articles in *Le Producteur,* an organ of the Saint-Simonians to which Comte con-tributed.

229b. **18. Gustave d'Eichthal:** Gustave d'Eichthal (1804-86) was a young Frenchman who first came to England in 1828, when he met Mill. On his return to France he joined the Saint-Simonians and sought to convert his English friends, including Carlyle whom he saw in London in 1832; later in his life he wrote in the fields of ethnology, archaeology, and biblical criticism.

21. Bazard and Enfantin: Saint-Amand Bazard (1791-1832) and Barthélemy Prosper Enfantin (1796-1864) were French socialists and followers of Saint-Simon. Enfantin set up in France a socialist community.

230a. **15. Owen and Fourier:** Robert Owen (1771-1858), philanthropist, industrialist, pioneer of co-operation and of English socialism. He founded several societies on the principle of co-operation and communal ownership, both in Great Britain and in America (e.g. New Harmony, Indiana). —— François Marie Charles Fourier (1772-1837), French communist, who proposed to organize society into small groups called phalansteries in which all property should be held in common and all living should be communal.

230b. **4. the wish of Fox:** Charles James Fox (1749-1806), English Whig statesman and orator, famous for his opposition to the ultra-conservative and repressive Tory governments and the absolutism of George III, and for his consistent liberal statesmanship and humani-tarianism.

231b. **13. French Revolution of July:** The Revolution of July 27-29, 1830, which resulted in the abdication of Charles X, an extreme Bourbon monarch, and the accession of Louis Philippe, a liberal Bourbon, known as "the Citizen King." In this crisis Lafayette (1757-1834) was made commander of the National Guard and, for a short period, held supreme control of the state.

24. Lord Grey's Ministery: Charles, 2nd Earl Grey (1764-1845), liberal Whig statesman, was Prime Minister of Great Britain (1830-34) during the period of parliamentary reform and passage of the Reform Bill of 1832.

28. Fonblanque: Albany Fonblanque (1793-1872), English journalist, who contributed articles to newspapers and periodicals, and was editor (1830-47) of the London *Examiner*, "chief organ of high-class intellectual radicalism."

232a. **5. The Spirit of the Age:** The articles under this title ran at intervals in the *Examiner* from Jan. 6 to May 29. They were recently collected with an introduction by Frederick A. von Hayek and published (1942) by the Univ. of Chicago Press.

22. a secluded part of Scotland: i.e. Craigenputtock (some 16 miles from Dumfries), where Carlyle lived from May 1828, until he made London his permanent home in the summer of 1834. When he came down to London in 1831 to arrange for the publication of *Sartor* he met (Sept. 2) Mill at the home of Mrs. John Austin: "We had almost four hours of the best talk I have mingled in for long," he wrote to his wife.

233a. **4. the elder Austin:** John Austin (1790-1859), English jurist, author of *Province of Jurisprudence Determined* (1832) and *Lectures on Jurisprudence* (1861-63).

234a. **45. Whately:** Richard Whately (1787-1863) published a text-book, *Elements of Logic* in 1826, which, while it awakened fresh interest in the subject, did not break new ground since it was concerned with deductive reasoning and not with an analysis of the inductive method, which was Mill's great contribution to the science.

51. Dugald Stewart: Dugald Stewart (1753-1828), Scotch philosopher and professor of moral philosophy for 25 years at Edinburgh, was author of *Elements of the Philosophy of the Human Mind* (3 vols., 1792, 1814, 1827), to which Mill here refers.

NATURE

This essay and two others, *Utility of Religion* and *Theism*, were first published in 1874 as *Three Essays on Religion*, a year after Mill's death. They were given to the public by his stepdaughter, Helen Taylor, who says that *Nature* and *Utility of Religion* "were written between the years 1850 and 1858," or before Darwin's *Origin*. Mill had intended to publish *Nature* in 1873, after having withheld the essay for some fifteen years or more in obedience to his determination not to be hurried in publishing his thoughts on such a subject.

235a. **27. Socratic Elenchus:** 'Elenchus' is literally a refutation and is defined as "a refutation cast in syllogistic form." The 'Socratic Elenchus' as used by Plato in his *Dialogues* is described in the text. Socrates, by skilful and logical questioning, exposes the loose and faulty thinking of his opponents and brings vague general terms down to precise definitions.

237a. **43. Justinian:** Justinian the Great (483-565), Emperor of the Eastern Roman Empire (527-565), administrator, builder, who appointed commissions to make a digest of all the writings of Roman jurists, including the *Institutes* (533), a textbook for students.

237b. **21. deistical moralists:** Anthony Ashley Cooper, 3rd Earl of Shaftesbury (1671-1713), was one of the leading deistical moralists of his time, though he is less philosophical than (e.g.) Tindal (1657-1733), Toland (1670-1722), and Collins (1676-1729). English deism, as a movement, belongs to the 17th and 18th centuries. As a religion it rejects all revelation and supernaturalism, and depends upon reason alone as sufficient to assure man of the being and goodness of God and of the truths of morality. The classical expression in English verse of deistical doctrines is Pope's *Essay on Man*,—e.g. "All are but parts of one stupendous whole, Whose body nature is, and God the soul" (I, 267-8).

28. Rousseau: Jean Jacques Rousseau (1712-1778) in *La nouvelle Héloïse* (1761) and *Emile* (1762) gives eloquent expression of the influence of 'nature' upon the human soul.

239a. **19. Montesquieu:** Mill refers to his *L'Esprit des Lois* (1748), a book that made literature out of jurisprudence.

29. George Combe: Scottish phrenologist (1788-1858), author of *The Constitution of Man* (1828).

242b. **11. à priori fallacies:** Fallacies due to reasoning from presuppositions or principles which are false or partial.

243b. **8. whatever is, is right:** *Essay on Man*, I, 294.

13. Shall gravitation cease, etc.: *Ib.*, IV, 128.

54. Nabis: Cruel tyrant of Sparta (207-192 B.C.). — — Domitian, Emperor of Rome (81-96 A.D.), took unnatural delight in the infliction of suffering and misery upon his subjects.

244a. **45. Carrier:** Jean Baptiste Carrier (1756-1794), French Revolutionist, was sent in 1793 to Nantes, on the Loire, to put down revolt. With inhuman cruelty he executed the sentences of the Revolutionary Tribunal, not only by the guillotine (which was set aside as inadequate), but by mass drownings of victims who were bound together on barges that were rowed to the middle of the river and there sunk. These were the infamous "noyades," i.e. judicial drownings.

49. Borgias: The Borgias in history are three: *Rodrigo Borgia* (1431?-1503), father of the other two, who as Pope Alexander VI (1492-1503) corruptly used his position and wealth to increase the temporal power of the papacy and the aggrandizement of his children; his son, *Cesare Borgia* (1475-6-1507), though one of the boldest military leaders of his age, was notoriously cruel, treacherous, and tyrannical; the daughter, *Lucrezia Borgia* (1480-1519), married three times to further her father's political interests, her third husband being the Duke of Ferrara, at whose court she received the homage of a brilliant group of artists and men of letters. While "the sins of the Borgias" are forever infamous, recent history has been unable to substantiate many accusations against them.

244b. 1. Reign of Terror: This French Revolutionary period of disorder and mass killings lasted from June 21, 1793 to the fall of Robespierre, July 27, 1794.

245a. 41. Monument: The Roman Doric column which commemorates the great fire of 1666 in London. It was built (1671-78) by Sir Christopher Wren, and on the pedestal there was cut in 1681 an inscription, now effaced, attributing the fire to a "horrid plott" by Catholics.

245b. 50. to him that hath shall be given: *Mark*, IV, 25.

246b. 5. vindicate the ways of God to man: Pope's *Essay on Man*, I, 16.

247b. 30. to believe with Plato: "It follows therefore that the good is not the cause of all things, but of good only.—Assuredly.—Then God, if he be good, is not the author of all things, as many assert, but he is the cause of a few things only, and not of most things that occur to men. For few are the goods of human life, and many are the evils, and the good is to be attributed to God alone; of the evils the causes are to be sought elsewhere, and not in him" (*Republic*, 379 b.).—"God desired that all things should be good and nothing bad, so far as this was attainable" (*Timaeus*, 30, Jowett's translation).

CHARLES DARWIN

SELECTED BIBLIOGRAPHY

I. STANDARD EDITIONS

Works, in 14 vols., New York and London, 1896-1897.
The Voyage of the Beagle, Harvard Classics, New York, 1909.
—— in World's Classics, New York, 1930.
—— in Everyman's Library, New York, 1920.
The Origin of Species, 2 vols., in one, 6th ed. New York, 1910; London, 1920.
—— in Everyman's Library, New York, 1934.
—— in The Modern Library, New York, 1936.
The Descent of Man, 2nd ed., New York and London, 1913.
The Living Thoughts of Darwin, presented by Julian Huxley, New York, 1939.
The Life and Letters of Charles Darwin, including an Autobiographical Chapter, 2 vols., ed. by Francis Darwin, New York and London, 1919.
More Letters of Charles Darwin, 2 vols., ed. by Francis Darwin and A. C. Seward, New York, 1903.

II. BIOGRAPHY AND CRITICISM

ALLEN, GRANT, *Charles Darwin*, (English Worthies Series), New York, 1885.
AMERICAN ASSOCIATION FOR THE ADVANCEMENT OF SCIENCE, *Fifty Years of Darwinism*, New York, 1909.
BALDWIN, J. M., *Darwin and the Humanities*, Baltimore, 1909.
BETTANY, G. T., *The Life of Charles Darwin*, (Great Writers Series), London, 1887.
BRADFORD, G., *Darwin*, Boston and New York, 1926.
DORSEY, G. A., *The Evolution of Charles Darwin*, New York, 1927.
HUXLEY, LEONARD, *Charles Darwin*, New York, 1927.
HUXLEY, T. H., *Darwiniana: Essays*, New York, 1896.
—— *Man's Place in Nature*, New York, 1908.
JORDAN, D. S., *Science Sketches*, Chicago, 1888.
—— *Darwinism*, Chicago, 1888.
KEITH, SIR ARTHUR, *Concerning Man's Origin*, New York, 1928.

—— *Darwinism and Its Critics,* London, 1935.

LITCHFIELD, H. E., Ed., *Emma Darwin: A Century of Family Letters, 1792-1896,* 2 vols., New York, 1915.

Memorial Notices, reprinted from *Nature: Charles Darwin,* with Introduction by T. H. Huxley, New York 1882.

MORGAN, T. H., *What Is Darwinism?,* New York, 1929.

OSBORN, H. F., *Impressions of Great Naturalists,* New York, 1924.

—— *From the Greeks to Darwin,* New York, 1913.

PEARSON, K., *Charles Darwin,* Cambridge, England, 1923.

ROMANES, G. J., *Darwin, and After Darwin,* Chicago, 1910.

THOMPSON, J. A., *Darwinism and Human Life,* London, 1919.

WALLACE, A. R., *Darwinism,* London and New York, 1889.

—— *My Life,* 2 vols., London, 1905.

—— *Letters and Reminiscences,* ed., James Marchant, 2 vols., London, 1916.

NOTES AND COMMENTS

AUTOBIOGRAPHY

260a. **25. my grandfather:** Erasmus Darwin (1731-1802), physician, physiologist, and poet, author of the poem *Botanic Garden; The Temple of Nature* (1803), and the prose work *Zoonomia* (1794-6), containing early views on evolution.

260b. **5. Abergele:** On the north shore of Wales.

261b. **11. Maer:** Maer Hall, in Staffordshire, the home of Darwin's maternal uncle, Josiah Wedgwood, second son of the great potter.

41. Dr. Butler's great school: Samuel Butler (1774-1839), Bishop of Litchfield and Coventry and a brilliant student at Cambridge, was headmaster of Shrewsbury School for 38 years (1798-1836).

262b. **20. Euclid:** The *Elements* by Euclid, Greek geometer (*cir.* 300 B.C.), is the basis of later works in geometry.

25. Galton: Sir Francis Galton (1822-1911), English scientist, best known for his studies in anthropology and heredity. His mother, the daughter of Erasmus Darwin by his second wife, was half-sister of Darwin's father. The "uncle" referred to is Samuel Tertius Galton (1783-1844), banker.

27. vernier of a barometer: A short sliding scale attached to the division of a graduated instrument, such as a barometer, to indicate parts of the division.

33. Thomson's *Seasons:* The *Seasons* (1726-30) by James Thomson (1700-48) is important in the history of English poetry as a forerunner of the Romantic Movement and the revival of interest in nature.

46. *Wonders of the World:* Darwin probably refers to *The Hundred Wonders of the World* (1818), by Rev. C. C. Clarke, the pseudonym of Sir Richard Phillips (1767-1840), who was known as a publisher of "cheap miscellaneous literature designed for popular instruction" and was said to have had "absurd scientific views." The Library of Congress has an American copy printed from the 10th London edition (1821).

263a. **44. White's *Selborne:*** Gilbert White (1720-93), English curate of his native village of Selborne, Hampshire, is known for his *Natural History and Antiquities of Selborne* (1789), a classic of its kind.

263b. **40. Hope:** Thomas Charles Hope (1766-1844), professor of chemistry in Edinburgh University (1795-1843); described as "a most successful teacher."

43. Dr. Duncan: Andrew Duncan, the younger (1773-1832), was professor of Materia Medica in Edinburgh University (1821-32).

264a. **44. Ainsworth:** William Francis Ainsworth (1807-96), English physician, geologist, and traveller, author of *Researches in Assyria* (1838) and other books of travel. He was a student of medicine at Edinburgh, graduating in 1827.

46. Wernerian geologist: One who accepts the theory that the strata of the earth's crust were formed by deposits from water; a theory now obsolete, but held and advocated by Abraham Gottlieb Werner (1750-1817), German geologist and mineralogist.

48. Dr. Coldstream: John Coldstream (1806-63), physician, Wernerian geologist, fellow of the Royal College of Physicians, and occasional lecturer at the University of Edinburgh.

54. Dr. Grant: Robert Edmund Grant (1793-1874), comparative anatomist, fellow of the Royal Society of Edinburgh, professor of comparative anatomy and zoology in the University of London (afterwards, University College), 1827-74.

264b. 11. Lamarck: French naturalist (1744-1829) and forerunner of Darwin, who developed the theory that changes in environment produce changes in structure of plants and animals, and that such changes or acquired characters are transmitted to offspring.

33. Newhaven fishermen: Newhaven is a fishing village a mile or two north of Edinburgh on the Firth of Forth, inhabited by fisher-folk of Scandanavian origin.

265a. 26. Kay-Shuttleworth: Sir James Kay-Shuttleworth (1804-1877), trained as a Medical student, became an English Liberal politician and educational leader and was prominent in health and education movements throughout his life.

31. Audubon: John James Audubon (1785-1851), American ornithologist and artist, author of *Birds of America* (1827-38).

34. Waterton: Charles Waterton (1782-1865), naturalist, was a wide-ranging student of animal life, travelling in North and South America, and author of *Wanderings in South America, the North-West of the U.S., and the Antilles in the years 1812, 1816, 1820, and 1824* (1825).

43. Sir Walter Scott: Scott was chosen President of the Royal Society in 1821. Lockhart, his biographer, says: "The new President soon began to take an interest in many of their discussions."

265b. 32. Salisbury Craigs: A rocky ridge near Arthur's Seat on the eastern edge of Edinburgh, from which one may get a view of the city.

266a. 50. Mackintosh: Sir James Mackintosh (1765-1832), Scottish philosopher and historian, author of *The Law of Nature and Nations* (1799), *Dissertation on the Progress of Ethical Philosophy* (1830), and a history of England in *Encyclopedia Britannica*, 7th ed. (1830).

267a. 7. Pearson on the Creeds: John Pearson (1613-86), English prelate and theologian, royalist, Bishop of Chester, and author of *Exposition of the Creed* (1659), long a standard work on the subject.

267b. 18. Little-Go: Slang name of the first examination for the B.A. degree (more commonly today, 'smalls'), called officially at Cambridge "The Previous Examination," and at Oxford, "Responsions."

26. Paley's *Evidences:* William Paley (1743-1805), English theologian, archdeacon of Carlisle, whose *Principles of Moral and Political Philosophy* (1785) and *View of the Evidences of Christianity* (1794) were textbooks at Cambridge.

268a. 3. Sedgwick's lectures: Adam Sedgwick (1785-1873), English geologist, who made special studies of the geology of Devon, Cornwall, the English Lake district, and Wales.

6. Henslow's lectures: John Stevens Henslow (1796-1861), English botanist, compiler of *Catalogue of English Plants* (1829) and *Dictionary of Botanical Terms* (1859), whose friendly interest in Darwin was of very great significance.

38. Senior Wrangler: At Cambridge a man placed first in the list of first class men who receive honors in mathematics is called senior wrangler.

42. Fitzwilliam Gallery: The Fitzwilliam Museum of art at Cambridge, in the Greek style of architecture, is named in honor of Viscount Fitzwilliam who bequeathed a collection of pictures to the University in 1816.

47. Reynolds' book: *Discourses* on painting before the Royal Academy, delivered at intervals from Jan. 2, 1769 to Dec. 10, 1790, during which time Sir Joshua was its President. The *Discourses* were published, complete, in 1794.

51. Sebastian del Piombo: Sebastiano Luciani, called S. del Piombo, (1485?-1547), Italian painter of the Venetian school, whose great picture, *Raising of Lazarus,* in the National Gallery, is probably the painting to which Darwin refers.

269a. 12. Albert Way: Albert Way (1805-74), English antiquary, graduate of Trinity College, Cambridge, fellow of the Society of Antiquaries, and founder in 1845 of the Archaeological Institute.

14. Thomson: Sir Harry Stephen Thomson (1809-74), graduate of Trinity, whose career included distinguished services to agriculture and to railroad management; author of many papers.

27. here at Down: Down, in Kent, a small village sixteen miles from London, was Darwin's home from 1842 until his death, in 1882.

270a. 23. Dr. Whewell: William Whewell (1794-1866), philosopher and mathematician, was professor of moral philosophy at Cambridge (1838-55), Master of Trinity (1841-66), and Vice-Chancellor of the University (1843-1856).

270b. 11. Humboldt's 'Personal Narrative': Alexander von Humboldt (1769-1859), German naturalist and traveller, eminent for the vast range of his interests in natural phenomena. He wrote many books, including *Cosmos* (5 vols., 1845-62), an encyclopedic study of the physical universe, and *Personal Narrative of Travels to the Equinoctial Regions of the New Continent during the years 1799-1804* (A. Bonpland, collaborator); this was translated from the French by H. M. Williams, 7 vols., 1814-29.

12. Hershel's 'Introduction': Sir John Frederick William Hershel (1792-1871), English astronomer, whose *Preliminary Discourse on the Study of Natural Philosophy* appeared in 1831.

271b. 27. Captain Fitz-Roy: Robert Fitzroy (1805-65), naval commander and meteorologist, who was captain of the *Beagle* and later Governor of New Zealand (1843-45), was a direct descendant of the 1st Duke of Grafton, 2nd son of Charles II by Barbara Villiers.

272a. 10. Lavater: Johann Kaspar Lavater (1741-1801), Swiss poet and mystic, "founder of the so-called science of physiognomy."

29. Lord Castlereagh: Robert Stewart, Viscount Castlereagh and 2nd Marquis of Londonderry (1769-1822), English statesman, who was leader of the House of Commons and Foreign Secretary (1812-22),—an extreme reactionary in time of revolution and change.

272b. 47. Lyell's *Principles*: The first volume was published in 1830.

273a. 14. Cirripedia: Darwin's monograph on the cirripedia, or barnacles, occupied his research activities for eight years, and was published in four volumes (1851-54).

274a. 54. Ascension: Small British island in the South Atlantic; used as an airplane and signal station in Second World War.

274b. 6. Lyell and Hooker: Sir Charles Lyell (1797-1875), geologist, and Sir Joseph Dalton Hooker (1817-1911), botanist, were leading British scientists and among Darwin's closest friends.

275a. 7. Baconian principles: The inductive method taught by Bacon, i.e. generalization only upon individual facts "collected on a wholesale scale."

25. 'Malthus on Population': Thomas Robert Malthus (1766-1834), English curate and economist, awakened controversy by his thesis in *An Essay on the Principles of Population* (1798; sec. ed., 1803), in which he argued that population, if unchecked, increases in a geometric ratio, while means of subsistence tend to increase in an arithmetical ratio.

49. Columbus and his egg: The story of Columbus and the egg goes back to Benzoni's *Historia del Mondo Nuovo* (1565). At a banquet given in 1493 by the Grand Cardinal of Spain in honor of Columbus upon his return from the first voyage to America, one of the guests said to the Admiral: "If you, sir, had not undertaken this great enterprise, we should have had a man here in Spain to do it." Columbus called for an egg, placed it upon the table, and asked the guests to make it stand without any support. None succeeded. Whereupon the Admiral took the egg and fixed it by pressing it down upon the table sufficiently to crush one end slightly: once a thing is done, all can do it. The anecdote is probably unhistorical; it was told of others even before it was told of Columbus.

275b. 22. Mr. Wallace: Alfred Russel Wallace (1823-1913), English naturalist, author of many books, spent several years (1854-62) in the Malay Archipelago: he was at Ternate, a small island in the Moluccas, when he wrote his paper.

276a. 8. Moor Park: In Surrey, some thirty-five miles southwest of London, famous as the place where Swift acted as secretary to Sir William Temple and met Stella.

THE ORIGIN OF SPECIES

The selection is chapter III of the *Origin*. Details of the writing and publication of this epochal work are to be found in Darwin's *Autobiography*.

STRUGGLE FOR EXISTENCE

279b. 28. expression often used by Spencer: "This survival of the fittest, which I have here sought to express in mechanical terms, is that which Mr. Darwin has called 'natural selection'" (*Principles of Biology*, 1864, I, pt. iii, ch. 12, sec. 165).

280a. 8. De Candolle: Augustin Pyrame de Candolle (1778-1841), Swiss botanist, much of whose work was done in France, at Paris, as director of the botanical gardens and at the University of Montpellier as professor of botany. His studies in plant classification attracted the interest of Cuvier and Lamarck, older contemporaries.

280b. 39. doctrine of Malthus: See note on Malthus under *Autobiography*.

281a. 2. Linnaeus: Carolus Linnaeus—latinized form of Carl von Linné (1707-78), great Swedish botanist, founder of the modern system of botanical nomenclature.

40. plains of La Plata: The Pampas de La Plata in Argentina to the west of Buenos Aires.

45. Dr. Falconer: Hugh Falconer (1808-65), Scotch paleontologist and botanist, discoverer of fossil mammals and reptiles in the Sewalik Hills, India (1832); professor of botany, Calcutta Medical College (1848-55).

45. Cape Comorin: Southern point of India.

284a. 18. carices: Carex is a genus of the sedge family; the plural, carices, are sedges of this genus.

284b. 17. Azara and Rengger: Felix de Azara (1746-1811), Spanish soldier and naturalist, who was sent to Paraguay (1781) on a commission to fix boundaries of Spanish and Portuguese territories; author of *Voyage dans l'Amérique Meridionale* (1809). —— Johann Rudolf Rengger (1795-1832), a Swiss zoologist, who was in South America, 1818-26.

285a. 37. Colonel Newman: Edward Newman (1801-76), English naturalist and publisher, who created *The Entomologist* (1840), which later became *The Zoologist,* edited by Newman until 1863; author of *History of British Moths* (1869), *Butterflies* (1870-71), and other works.

286b. 4. one species of charlock: Wild mustard.

NATURAL SELECTION

This is the last section of chapter IV, summarizing the theory of natural selection.

288b. 53. Ornithorhynchus: Name of a genus consisting only of the duck bill, a small aquatic animal, native of eastern and southern Australia and Tasmania.

53. Lepidosiren: Name of a genus of eel-shaped fishes containing only one species, found in the swamps of the Amazon and La Plata rivers and their tributaries.

JAMES ANTHONY FROUDE

SELECTED BIBLIOGRAPHY

I. STANDARD EDITIONS

There is no standard edition. Froude's *Works* have been published in London by Longman's, Green, and Co., and in New York by Scribners at various dates, as follows:

The History of England, 12 vols.
The English in Ireland in the Eighteenth Century, 3 vols.
Short-Studies on Great Subjects, 4 vols.
Oceana; or England and Her Colonies.
The English in the West Indies.
The Spanish Story of the Armada, and Other Essays.
The Divorce of Catherine of Aragon.
The Life and Letters of Erasmus.
The Council of Trent.
English Seamen in the Sixteenth Century.
Thomas Carlyle, 4 vols.
Jane Welsh Carlyle: Letters and Memorials, 2 vols.
Reminiscences of Thomas Carlyle.
Essays in Literature and History, Beaconsfield, and *History of England,* 10 vols., in Everyman's Library.
Short Studies on Great Subjects, first series, in Oxford World's Classics.

II. BIOGRAPHY AND CRITICISM

BIRRELL, A., "James Anthony Froude," *Scribner's Magazine,* XVII (1895), 149-153.
CLARKE, F., "Froude," *London Mercury,* XXII (1930), 314-323.
CARLYLE, A., and CRICHTON-BROWNE, *The Nemesis of Froude,* New York, 1903.

DAWSON, W. J., *The Makers of Modern Prose*, London, 1899.

DUNN, W. H., *Froude and Carlyle*, New York, 1930.

FREEMAN, E. A., "Mr. Froude's Life and Times of Thomas Becket," *The Contemporary Review*, XXXI (1878), 821-843.

—— "Last Words on Mr. Froude," *The Contemporary Review*, XXXV (1879), 214-237.

FROUDE, J. A., 'A Few Words on Mr. Freeman,' *Nineteenth Century*, V (1879), 618-637.

—— "Lord Macaulay," *Fraser's Magazine*, XCIII (1876), 675-694.

GOUCH, G. S., *History and Historians in the Nineteenth Century*, London, 1935.

HOLMES, T. RICE, "Mr. Froude and His Critics," *Westminster Review*, CXXXVIII (1892), 174-189.

HONE, J. M., "The Imperialism of Froude," *New Statesman*, XI (1918), 172-173.

ICELAND, MRS. A., "Recollections of James Anthony Froude," *Contemporary Review*, LXVII (1895), 17-28.

JEBB, R. C., *Essays and Addresses*, Cambridge, 1907.

KELLET, E. E., "James Anthony Froude," *London Quarterly Review*, CXLIV (1925), 107-11.

LILLY, W. S., "The New Spirit of History," *The Nineteenth Century*, XXXVIII (1895), 619-633.

PAUL, H., *The Life of Froude*, London, 1905.

POLLARD, A. F., "James Anthony Froude," *Dictionary National Biography*, Supplement II, 254-262.

SKELTON, JOHN, *The Table-Talk of Shirley*, Edinburgh and London, 1895.

SMITH, GOLDWIN, "Froude," *North American Review*, CLIX (1894), 677.

—— "Froude as a Historian," *Atlantic Monthly*, XCVII (1906), 715-717.

STEPHEN, LESLIE, *Studies of a Biographer*, III, 205-236.

STRACHEY, LYTTON, *Portraits in Miniature*, London, 1931.

NOTES AND COMMENTS

THE SCIENCE OF HISTORY

This essay was delivered as a lecture at the Royal Institution, Feb. 5, 1864. It was published as the first essay in *Short Studies on Great Subjects*, vol. I, a collection of essays (4 vols., 1867-83) "written at intervals," says Froude, in his preface (1882) to vol. IV, "during the last thirty years." The earliest appeared in 1850, the last in 1881.

294a. 30. **Mr. Buckle:** Henry Thomas Buckle (1821-62), author of *History of Civilization in England* (vol. I, 1857, vol. II, 1861). The work was unfinished, the two volumes being little more than introductory.

296a. 18. **Holbein:** Hans Holbein (1497?-1543), the younger, of Augsburg, Bavaria, portrait and historical painter, who spent his last years (from about 1536) in England as a court painter to Henry VIII; he painted portraits of the King, Erasmus, Sir Thomas More.

296b. 4. **Julius or Tiberius Caesar:** Gaius Julius Caesar (100-44 B.C.), Roman general and states-man, who became dictator from 49 B.C., until his assassination by a group of nobles in the senate house, March 15, 44 B.C. —— Tiberius Claudius Caesar (42 B.C.-37 A.D.), second emperor of Rome (14-37 A.D.), who began as an able and humane ruler, but became vicious and tyrannical in his last years.

17. **history of mankind is the history of its great men:** Carlyle's view: "Universal History, the history of what man has accomplished in this world, is at bottom the History of the Great men who have worked here." (*Heroes and H.W.*, 'The Hero as Divinity'; cf. also, *On History*, 1830.)

298a. 18. **Leibnitz:** Baron Gottfried Wilhelm von Leibnitz (1646-1716), German philosopher and mathematician, author of many essays and treatises, including *Theodicé* (1710), in which he says that ours is "the best of all possible worlds,"—a view which Voltaire satirized in *Candide* (1759).

299b. 18. **Sebastopol:** In the Crimean War (1854-56) between the Allies (England and France) and Russia, Sebastopol, besieged for a year, was finally taken in Sept., 1855.

20. **Inkermann:** On November 5, 1854 the Russians attacked the English position at Inker-mann in the Crimea, but were repulsed after bitter fighting. Thousands of wounded and sick were taken to Scutari, a town in Asia across the Bosporus from Constantinople, where Florence Nightingale (1820-1910) organized a barrack hospital, the first of its kind.

21. *Essays and Reviews:* A collection of essays (1860) on religious subjects by seven Broad Churchmen, which stirred up a storm of controversy, but which came to be recognized as a notable sign of liberty of thought within the Church of England.

300a. 14. Mormonism: Joseph Smith (1805-44) founded the Mormon Church (Church of Jesus Christ of Latter-Day Saints, at Fayette, N. Y.) in 1830. In 1847 under the leadership of Brigham Young (1801-77) the Church was settled at Great Salt Lake, Utah.

17. spirit-rapping: The Scottish spiritualist medium, Daniel Dunglas Home (1833-86), by his seances in London and elsewhere, provoked widespread interest and curiosity in spiritualism for two decades.

23. a certain detestable superstition: In his *Annales* (XV, 44) the Roman historian Tacitus (55?-117 A.D.), when describing the terrible Neronian persecution of 64 A.D., refers to the Christians as a class hated for their abominations and their pernicious superstition (*exitiabilis superstitio*).

30. stirrup of the Pontiff: The incident is the submission of Henry IV (1050-1106), King of Germany and Holy Roman Emperor (1056-1106), to Pope Gregory VII, known as Hildebrand (Pope, 1073-85). The King refused to recognize the papal decree suppressing simony and was excommunicated. Shunned as a man accursed, he finally crossed the Alps, sought the Pontiff in a castle in the Apennines (at Canossa), where he was obliged to wait for three days in sackcloth in the courtyard until admitted and forgiven (1077).

37. M. Comte: Auguste Comte (1798-1857), founder of Positivism, a system of philosophy in which the laws underlying society are considered to be as 'positive' as the laws underlying natural phenomena.

47. Tacitus and Thucydides: The works of Tacitus include *Historiae, Agricola, Germania, Annales.* —— Thucydides (471?-?400 B.C.), the greatest historian of antiquity, wrote a *History of the Peloponnesian War.*

300b. 10. Hegel's philosophy of history: Georg Wilhelm Friedrich Hegel (1770-1831), German metaphysician, was professor of philosophy, successively, at Jena, Heidelberg, and Berlin. His philosophy of history was presented in the form of lectures, published as *Vorlesungen über die Philosophie der Geschichte* (1837). Hegel's speculative world-view determined his conception of history: the World-Spirit unfolds itself "in the phenomena of the world's existence. This must present itself as the ultimate *result* of History.... God governs the world; the actual working of his government—the carrying out of his plan—is the History of the World.... (History, then, is the means which) the World-Spirit uses for realizing the Idea," i.e. Itself. (From 'Introduction to the Philosophy of History,' *Hegel: Selections,* ed. Loewenberg, Modern Student's Library, 1929.)

11. Schlegel's philosophy of history: Friedrich von Schlegel (1772-1829), poet, literary historian, author of *Geschichte der Alten und Neuen Litteratur* (1815), *Philosophie der Geschichte* (1829), and other works. He became a Roman Catholic in 1803 and his view of history reflects his religious faith: "The philosophy of History is not a theory standing apart and separated from history, but its results must be drawn out of the multitude of historical facts.... It must be the pure emanation of the great whole.... The Philosophy of History is ... to be found ... in the principles of social progress.... In the historical progress of nations ... is the visible guidance of an all-loving and all-ruling Providence.... (Without a faith) ... in this divine principle there could be no Philosophy of History." (From Lectures I and XV, *The Philosophy of History,* trans. by J. B. Robinson, 7th ed. rev., Bohn Lib.)

30. *Contrat Social:* In Rousseau's *Contrat Social* (1762) the phrase "state of nature" is rather "a term of controversy" than the concept of an ideal society. Nowhere does he soberly advocate a return to the "primeval simplicity" of the "noble savage."

23. When wild in woods, etc.: Dryden's *Conquest of Granada* (1670-1), I, i.

38. Goethe's novel: *Wilhelm Meisters Lehrjahre* (1796).

42. "What is history, but a fiction agreed upon?": From *Memoirs of the Life, Exile, and Conversations of the Emperor Napoleon,* by Las Cases, IV, 179 (4 vols., 1855).

43. said Faust to the student: Goethe's *Faust,* Part I, 221-26.

301a. 34. Adam Smith: Scotch economist (1723-90), professor of logic and moral philosophy, Glasgow (1751-64), member of Johnson's Club in London, author of the *Wealth of Nations* (1776). In economic life as he saw it, the motive that made for wealth was self-interest: "It is not from the benevolence of the butcher, the brewer, or the baker that we expect our dinner, but from their regard to their own interest. We address ourselves, not to their humanity but to their self-love, and never talk to them of our own necessities but of their advantages" (*Wealth of Nations,* bk. I, ch. II).

301b. 43. Kant, the philosopher: "Two things fill the mind with ever new and increasing admiration and awe, the oftener and more steadily we reflect on them: the starry heavens above and the moral law within." (*Kritik der Praktischen Vernunft*, 1788: 'Critique of Practical Reason', 260, trans. T. K. Abbott, 1909.)

302b. 31. Novalis: Pseudonym of Baron Friedrich von Hardenberg (1772-1801), German lyric poet and romanticist, author of *Hymnen an die Nacht* and an unfinished novel, *Heinrich von Ofterdingen*.

53. Fielding and Richardson: Henry Fielding (1707-54), novelist, author of *Joseph Andrews* (1742), *Tom Jones* (1749), and *Amelia* (1751). — Samuel Richardson (1689-1761), novelist, author of *Pamela* (1740), *Clarissa Harlowe* (1747-48), and *Sir Charles Grandison* (1753).

54. Jane Austen: Author (1775-1817) of six novels, of which *Pride and Prejudice* (pub. 1813) is the best known.

303a. 12. Gibbon: Edward Gibbon (1737-94), author of *The Decline and Fall of the Roman Empire*, died nearly two years before the emergence of Napoleon (Oct. 1795), who was made Emperor of France in Dec. 1804 and was at the height of his power in 1809, following his defeat of the Austrians at Wagram, July 6.

17. Crystal Palace: Formally opened May 1, 1851, by Queen Victoria.

19. Battles, bloody as Napoleon's: A reference to the American Civil War, as indicated at the end of the third succeeding paragraph.

303b. 4. Luther would have gone to work: Martin Luther (1483-1546), then a professor in the University of Wittenberg, nailed to the church door in 1517 his 95 theses in which he stated his views on indulgences and so started the Protestant Reformation. Little more than a century later (1618), the Thirty Years' War broke out between Protestants and Catholics, ending with the Peace of Westphalia (1648).

7. theology of Tübingen: The University of Tübingen, Germany, was the center of the new liberal theology and the higher criticism of the Bible. Ferdinand Christian Baur (1792-1860), professor of theology and church history there, was the founder of this new school, the influence of which profoundly stirred English religious thought.

8. Washington: he assumed command of the Continental armies at Cambridge, Mass., July 3, 1775.

304a. 17. Lessing: Gotthold Ephraim Lessing (1729-81), German dramatist and critic, confessedly wrote *Nathan der Weise* (1779) in the interest of toleration as a moral principle.

34. Cibber and others: Shakespeare "dominated the stage," during the 18th century, says Nichol Smith, but "from Betterton's days (1635?-1710) to Garrick's (1717-79), and later, his plays were commonly acted from mangled versions" (*18th Century Essays on Shakespeare*, Intro. XII). The 'adaptation' of *Richard III* by Colley Cibber (1671-1757) was played until 1821. Nahum Tate's (1652-1715) version of *Lear*, with a happy ending, held the stage (with some later changes by Garrick) until 1823. The Restoration version of *Hamlet* (Davenant's, 1676), which 'cut' about 800 lines from Shakespeare's text and altered words and phrases for increased 'clearness' and 'elegance' but remained structurally unchanged, held the stage until the time of Garrick, who, in an effort to make the drama conform to 18th century 'regularity,' omitted the funeral of Ophelia, "all the wisdom of the prince, and the rude jocularity of the grave-diggers." His version held the stage for only eight years, when the actor Kemble returned to the Davenant version. In no stage version were Hamlet and Ophelia married.

305a. 36. It has been said, etc.: By Aristotle. "Poetry is a more philosophical and a higher thing than history: for poetry tends to express the universal, history the particular" (*Poetics*, IX; Butcher's trans.). Wordsworth accepts Aristotle's dictum: "It is so: its object is truth, not individual and local, but general, and operative; not standing upon external testimony, but carried alive into the heart by passion . . . These passions and thoughts and feelings are the general passion and thoughts and feelings of men" (*Preface to Lyrical Ballads*).

39. We hear of poetic justice: Poetic justice is ideal justice, that is, the giving vice its proper punishment and virtue its proper reward. The term was first used by Thomas Rymer in his essay *Tragedies of the Last Age* (1678) and adopted by Dryden a year later in his *Preface to Troilus and Cressida* (1679), viz.: "We lament not, but detest a wicked man; we are glad when we behold his crimes are punished, and that poetical justice is done upon him."

52. speeches of Wolsey: According to modern scholarship, Henry VIII is the work of two, and possibly three, dramatists, Shakespeare, Fletcher, and (more conjecturally) Massinger. The speeches of Wolsey are thought to be Fletcher's and have their source in

George Cavendish's (1500?-62) *Cardinal Wolsey* (1557). Thomas Cardinal Wolsey (1475?-1530) was Henry VIII's Lord Chancellor, who fell from power in 1529, charged with high treason; he died on his way to London.

305b. 2. **Marlborough read Shakespeare:** John Churchill, 1st Duke of Marlborough (1650-1722), was one of England's greatest military commanders, famous for victories over the French in the War of Spanish Succession (1702-13). "In a discussion with Burnet upon some historical point, he (Marlborough) displayed so incorrect a conception of the subject, that the Bishop asked him the source of his information. He replied that it was from Shakespeare's play that he had learnt all he knew of English history." (*Life of John Churchill, Duke of Marlborough*, by Viscount Wolseley, I, 33). —— Burnet is Gilbert Burnet (1643-1715), Bishop of Salisbury and author of *History of the Reformation* and *History of my Own Time*. Professor Saintsbury (*Life of Marlborough*) calls the famous story "another of the anecdotes which only dulness takes literally."

6. **enough for Shakespeare:** The allusions are to *Henry IV*, parts I and II. The Mermaid was a famous tavern on Bread Street, London, where Elizabethan poets and wits foregathered.

306b. 4. **Bishop Butler says:** Joseph Butler (1692-1752), English prelate and theologian, author of *The Analogy of Religion* (1736) and *Fifteen Sermons* (1726). Froude's reference is to the second paragraph of the Preface to *Sermons:* For readers who have "no sort of curiosity to see what is true, . . . I have often wished that it had been the custom to lay before people nothing in matters of argument but premises, and leave them to draw conclusions themselves."

45. **Lichtenberg:** Georg Christoph Lichtenberg (1742-99), German physicist and satirist, and professor at Göttingen, who made two visits of some length to England and became familiar with English life and letters. He was influenced by Swift and wrote articles on Hogarth.

307b. 1. **Those obstinate questionings:** Wordsworth's *Ode: Intimations of Immortality* (1807), 141-47 and 148-55.

THE EXECUTION OF MARY QUEEN OF SCOTS

With the exception of the final four paragraphs the selection includes the last part of chapter 34, volume 12 of Froude's *History of England*. Mary Stuart had been a prisoner in England since she fled from Scotland 18 years before (1569). Most of this time she was kept at various places in the custody of George Talbot, 6th Earl of Shrewsbury (1528?-90). In 1586 she was removed to Fotheringay Castle in Northhamptonshire, where she was charged and found guilty of being an accomplice in the Babington plot to assassinate Queen Elizabeth, and was beheaded there, Feb. 8, 1587. In this dramatic account of Mary Stuart's execution Froude affords the reader a capital illustration of his idea of history as defined in the preceding essay. "He was not a chronicler," says Herbert Paul, his biographer, "but an artist, a moralist, and a man of genius."

The title of the earlier volumes of the history ran: "A History of England from the Fall of Wolsey to the Death of Elizabeth." But before he published the 11th volume, Froude came to the conclusion that the defeat of the Spanish Armada (1588) would be a more dramatic close, and altered the title accordingly (12 vols. as follows: I-II, 1856; III-IV, 1858; V-VI, 1860; VII-VIII, 1863; IX-X, 1866; XI-XII, 1870).

307a. 4. **they delivered:** The Earl of Kent and the Earl of Shrewsbury.

307b. 11. **Babington:** Anthony Babington (1561-1586), English Roman Catholic, former page to Mary Stuart, and one of several young men who had access, as courtiers, to Queen Elizabeth, was persuaded by John Ballard, a priest, to organize a plot to murder the Queen and liberate Mary. The plot was exposed by spies of Sir Francis Walsingham (1530?-90), Secretary of State (1573-90), whereupon Babington and the other conspirators were executed.

308a. 10. **Mendoza:** Don Bernardino de Mendoza, Spanish ambassador to England, who, after suspicious intrigues with Mary Stuart, was ordered to leave England (1584), and who then became ambassador to the court of Henry III, of Paris.

15. **Philip:** Philip II of Spain (1527-98).

21. **Arundel:** Philip Arundel (1557-95), 13th Earl of Arundel, was suspected of involve-

ment in Throgmorton's plot and, after an attempt to escape from England, was put into prison, where he died.

21. Paget: Thomas Paget (d. 1590), 3rd Baron Paget, Catholic conspirator, who fled to Paris after the discovery of Throgmorton's conspiracy (1583); he was attainted of treason by act of parliament and died in Brussels. —— His brother, Charles Paget (d. 1612), was also an exile and Catholic conspirator, who lived for many years in Paris as secretary to the Archbishop of Glasgow.

21. Morgan: Thomas Morgan (1543-?1606) was implicated in various plots to assassinate Elizabeth, especially in the Babington plot. For a time he was a secretary of the Archbishop of Glasgow, in Paris where he probably died in 1606.

22. Archbishop of Glasgow: James Beaton (1517-1603) was the last Roman Catholic Archbishop of Glasgow. He lived 45 years in Paris, where he served as Mary's Scottish ambassador at the French court. He died there, "leaving behind him an unblemished reputation."

22. Westmoreland: Charles Neville (1543-1601), 6th Earl of Westmoreland, had been involved in an attempt to release Mary in 1569.

23. Throgmorton: Francis Throgmorton (1554-84), a Catholic conspirator, active in Madrid and Paris with agents of Mary in a plot to raise an army of invasion and overthrow Elizabeth. He was executed at Tyburn. —— In the text Froude probably refers to the brother of Francis, Thomas Throgmorton (d. 1595), who was an active conspirator in Paris where he died.

23. Bishop of Ross: John Leslie (1527-96), Roman Catholic prelate, Bishop of Ross and stanch partisan of Mary, was banished from England (1573) for his part in an attempt (the Ridolfi plot) to marry Mary Stuart to the Duke of Norfolk and set her upon the English throne.

40. Cecil: William Cecil (1520-98), 1st Baron Burghley, was Queen Elizabeth's leading statesman, as Secretary of State (1558-72) and Lord High Treasurer (1572-98). He organized an elaborate spy-system to protect the Queen, and assumed responsibility for the execution of Mary Stuart.

41. Leicester: Robert Dudley (1532?-1588), 1st Earl of Leicester, was a great favorite of Elizabeth and entertained her in royal splendor at Kenilworth Castle (1575). The Queen once proposed him as a husband for Mary Stuart.

41. Walsingham: Sir Francis Walsingham (1530?-90), English statesman, Secretary of State (1573-90), a trusted member of Elizabeth's official family.

41. Huntington: Henry Huntington (1535-95), 3rd Earl of Huntington, was one of the custodians of Mary at Tilbury castle, on the Dove river near Derby (1569-70).

43. Paulet: Sir Amyas Paulet (1536?-88) was the Puritan keeper of Mary (succeeding Shrewsbury) during her last years of imprisonment, and at her trial was a commissioner.

44. Wade: Sir William Wade (1546-1623) was secretary of the Privy Council. With Paulet he had searched and seized Mary's papers at Chartley castle in Staffordshire (1586).

48. King of France: Henry III (1574-89).

308b. 33. Sir Robert: Robert Melville (1527-1621), 1st Baron Melville, had been representative of Mary Stuart at the English court, and, after sentence was passed, interceded with Elizabeth for Mary's life.

38. Commend me to my son: James VI of Scotland, Mary's son by Henry Lord Darnley. In 1603 he succeeded Elizabeth as James I of England.

309a. 8. the blood of Henry VII: Mary Stuart (1542-87) was the great-granddaughter of Henry VII, whose daughter, Margaret Tudor, married James IV of Scotland. Mary, the daughter of James V, succeeded to the throne of Scotland in 1542, when but six days old. She was brought up in France in the Roman Catholic faith and in 1558 she married Francis, who became Francis II of France (1559-60).

15. Curle's young wife: Curle was one of Mary's secretaries.

52. Beale...read the warrant: Robert Beale (1541-1601), diplomatist and antiquary, member of parliament, secretary to Walsingham; he carried the death warrant to Fotheringay.

309b. 8. Dr. Fletcher: Richard Fletcher (d. 1596), Dean of Peterborough, was chaplain at the execution of Mary, and later Bishop of Bristol, Worcester, and London, successively. He was the father of John Fletcher, the dramatist.

CARLYLE IN OLD AGE

The selection is from vol. II, ch. XXVI of *Carlyle's Life in London*. When Carlyle called upon Froude in the winter of 1861, Carlyle was sixty-six years old and Froude was forty-three. The *Life* was begun a few years before Carlyle's death in 1881. The next year Froude published *Thomas Carlyle: First Forty Years* (2 vols.), and in 1884, *Thomas Carlyle's Life in London* (2 vols.). "The drift of the whole," Froude said, "is that Carlyle was by far the most remarkable man of his time. . . . I loved and honored him above all living men, and with this feeling I have done my best to produce a faithful likeness of him."

311a. **10. Cheyne Row:** Carlyle had settled in London in 1834, at No. 5 Cheyne Row, Chelsea, where he lived for the remainder of his life. The house is now a Carlyle memorial, open to the public.

311b. **20. Whately:** Richard Whately (1787-1863), English logician and theologian, was Archbishop of Dublin (1831-63). Froude had known him at Oxford, where Whately was student and fellow of Oriel, and later principal of St. Alban Hall and professor of economics until called to Dublin.

312a. **42. *Latterday Pamphlets:*** Carlyle's outburst against "impending democracy and anarchy" was first published in the form of eight separate 'pamphlets,' appearing in 1850 from Feb. to Aug.

313a. **7. Kant's Categorical Imperative:** Kant's famous "basis of morals," viz.—"never to act on any maxim which could not without contradiction be also a universal law" (*Critique of Practical Reason*, trans. T. K. Abbott, 6th ed., 1909, p. 52).

25. Kepler: Johannes Kepler (1571-1630), German astronomer and mathematician, famous for his discovery of three laws of planetary motion, known as Kepler's laws.

35. Humboldt, Laplace: Alexander von Humboldt (1769-1859), German naturalist, traveller, and statesman, author of *Cosmos* (1845-62), a description of the physical universe (see note to Darwin's *Autobiography*). —— Pierre Simon de Laplace (1749-1827), French astronomer and mathematician, remarkable for his genius in celestial mechanics and for his 'nebular hypothesis.'

36. author of the 'Vestiges': Robert Chambers (1802-71), Scottish publisher and author, wrote *Vestiges of the Natural History of Creation* (1843-46), in which he advanced a theory of evolution and partly anticipated Darwin.

313b. **8. Lucretian Atheism:** Allusion to *De Rerum Natura* (Concerning the nature of things) by the Roman philosophical poet Lucretius (96?-55 B.C.), for whom the physical world, the only reality known to our senses, is made up of atoms, infinite in number, eternal, indivisible, always whirling. From the motion of these atoms is built up, by chance, the universe as revealed to our senses. There are gods (for Lucretius is an Epicurean) who dwell apart in the "interspaces between the worlds," unconcerned with nature or with man, whose soul, like nature, is composed of atoms and is mortal.

314a. **4. Hercules into Hades:** Hercules, the son of Zeus and Alcmene, famous hero in Greek mythology, was most famous for his twelve labors, the last of which was a descent into Hades to bring back the three-headed dog Cerberus. On another occasion he went to the underworld to restore the dead Alcestis to her husband, Admetus, king of Thessaly, as told in the *Alcestis* of Euripides.

45. Exodus from Houndsditch: Houndsditch was the center of the Jewish quarter in London, so named from an ancient foss or ditch around the city, into which dead dogs and other filth were thrown. By the phrase Carlyle meant abandonment of historical Christianity, more especially its supernaturalism. His own belief rested upon "natural supernaturalism."

314b. **22. Craigenputtock essays:** Craigenputtock is the name of Mrs. Carlyle's father's old estate in Scotland, some 16 miles northwest of Dumfries. Here Carlyle lived with his wife from 1828 to 1834, and here he wrote in part his essays, *Burns, Goethe, Voltaire, Diderot, Signs of the Times, Characteristics*, and also *Sartor Resartus*.

315b. **21. engaged with 'Frederick':** Carlyle began writing his history of Frederick the Great in 1852, and completed it in 1865. He travelled twice to Germany and went over all of Frederick's battle-fields. His literary gifts show best in the battle-scenes and sketches of great personalities, such as Froude mentions.

25. Voltaire: The writing and influence of Voltaire (1694-1778) nearly span the 18th century. He lived in Berlin at Frederick's court (1750-53).

25. **Maupertuis** (1698-1759), French mathematician, astronomer, supporter of Newtonian theory, was involved in a quarrel with Voltaire, who satirized him and thereby alienated King Frederick.

26. **Chatham:** William Pitt, Earl of Chatham (1708-78), known as 'the Elder Pitt' and 'the Great Commoner'; English statesman and orator.

26. **Wolfe:** James Wolfe (1727-59), British army officer, is best remembered as the commanding general in the conquest of Quebec against Montcalm (1759). He died on the battle-field.

JOHN RUSKIN

SELECTED BIBLIOGRAPHY

I. STANDARD EDITIONS

The Works of Ruskin, 39 vols., ed. Cook and Wedderburn, London, 1903-12; the Standard Edition, with introductions, notes, letters, appendices, and bibliography.

Letters of John Ruskin to Charles Eliot Norton, 2 vols., New York, 1905.

Selections from the Works of Ruskin, ed. C. B. Tinker, Boston, 1908.

Selections and Essays, ed. F. W. Roe, New York, 1918.

Selections, ed. A. C. Benson, New York, 1923.

Everyman's Library, New York, 17 vols., including principal works.

II. BIOGRAPHY AND CRITICISM

BALL, H. H. R., ed. *Ruskin as a Literary Critic; Selections,* Cambridge University Press, 1928.

BENSON, A. C., *Ruskin: A Study in Personality,* New York, 1911.

BROWNELL, W. C., *Victorian Prose Masters,* New York, 1901.

COLLINGWOOD, W. G., *The Life of John Ruskin,* Boston, 1902.

COOK, E. T., *The Life of Ruskin,* 2 vols., London, 1911.

—— *Studies in Ruskin,* London, 1890.

CROW, G. H., *Ruskin* (Great Lives Series), London, 1936.

EARLAND, ADA, *Ruskin and His Circle,* London, 1910.

EASTLAKE, C. L., *A History of the Gothic Revival,* London, 1892.

HARRISON, F., *John Ruskin* (E.M.L.), London, 1902.

—— *Tennyson, Ruskin, Mill, and Other Literary Estimates,* London, 1899.

HOBSON, J. A., *John Ruskin: Social Reformer,* London, 1898.

HOPE-SCOTT, EDITH, *Ruskin's Guild of St. George,* London, 1931.

KITCHIN, G. W., *Ruskin in Oxford and Other Studies,* London, 1904.

LADD, H. A., *The Victorian Morality of Art: An Analysis of Ruskin's Esthetic,* New York, 1932.

LARG, D., *John Ruskin,* London, 1932.

MACKAIL, J. W., *Studies in Humanism,* London, 1938.

MEYNELL, A. C., *John Ruskin,* London, 1900.

MILSAND, J., *L'esthétique anglaise,* Paris, 1864.

MOORE, C. H., "John Ruskin as an Art Critic," *Atlantic Monthly,* LXXXVI (1900), 438-50.

RAWNSLEY, H. D., *Ruskin and the English Lakes,* Glasgow, 1902.

REPPLIER, AGNES, "Ruskin as a Teacher," *The Catholic World,* XXXIX (1884), 642-49.

RITCHIE, A. T., *Records of Tennyson, Ruskin, Browning,* New York, 1892.

ROBERTSON, J. M., *Modern Humanists,* London, 1891.

ROE, F. W., *The Social Philosophy of Carlyle and Ruskin,* New York, 1921.

ROSSETTI, W. M., *Ruskin, Rossetti: Preraphaelitism Papers, 1854-62,* London, 1899.

SAINTSBURY, G., *Corrected Impressions: Essays on Victorian Writers,* London, 1895.

SHAW, G. B., *Ruskin's Politics,* London, 1921.

SIZERANNE, R. DE LA, *Ruskin et la Religion de la Beauté,* Paris, 1897; translation by the Countess of Galloway, London, 1899.

SPIELMAN, M. H., *John Ruskin, A Sketch of his Life,* etc., Philadelphia, 1902.

STEPHEN, LESLIE, *Studies of a Biographer,* III, London, 1907.

STURGIS, RUSSELL, "Art Criticism and Ruskin's Writings on Art," *Scribner's Magazine,* XXVII (1900), 509-12.

WALSTEIN, CHARLES, *The Work of John Ruskin: its Influence upon Modern Thought and Life*, New York, 1893.

WHISTLER, J. M., *The Gentle Art of Making Enemies*, London, 1936.

WHITEHOUSE, J. H., ed. *Ruskin The Prophet and Other Centenary Studies*, New York, 1920.

—— *Ruskin Centenary Addresses*, London, 1919.

—— *Ruskin and Brantwood*, Cambridge, 1937.

—— *Ruskin the Painter and His Works at Bembridge*, London, 1938.

WILENSKI, R. H., *John Ruskin: An Introduction to Further Study of His Life and Work*, London, 1933.

WILLIAMS-ELLIS, A., *The Exquisite Tragedy: An Intimate Life of John Ruskin*, New York, 1929.

NOTES AND COMMENTS

PRAETERITA

Praeterita ('Bygones'), or "Outlines of Scenes and Thoughts perhaps worthy of Memory in my past Life," is Ruskin's unfinished autobiography. It is his last writing and was first published in 28 chapters "at irregular intervals between 1885 and 1889. . . . I have written these sketches of effort and incident in former years for my friends; and for those of the public who have been pleased by my books," Ruskin says in his Preface. "I have written them, therefore, frankly, garrulously, and at ease." The first seven sections of Ch. I and nearly all of Ch. II are printed in the text.

THE SPRINGS OF WANDEL

320a. 1. **Wandel:** A small river whose sources are near the town of Croydon, some ten miles to the south of London, where Ruskin's mother had spent her girlhood and where he in turn spent many childhood days "to play by the river Wandel."

27. **Walter Scott . . . the Bible:** Ruskin's biographer and editor, E. T. Cook, says of his reading: "The Index to his Works gives a rough and ready way of comparing his literary preferences and the influence which different books had upon him. The Bible comes easily first. The index of his Bible references and quotations occupies 58 columns of small print. Sir Walter Scott comes second with 16; Shakespeare, third with 10; and Dante, fourth with 9. Other authors are by comparison nowhere. The next in order are Wordsworth, Milton, Plato, and Spenser; but none of these occupies so much as four columns. The Bible and Sir Walter were the food of Ruskin's youth, and the consolation of his age" (*Homes and Haunts of Ruskin*, 31-2).

42. **Johnson's English, or Gibbon's:** Ruskin has reference to the highly formal, stylized manners (each different from the other in particular effects) of Johnson in his *Rambler* essays (1750-52) and *Lives of the Poets* (1779-81), and of Edward Gibbon in his monumental *History of the Decline and Fall of the Roman Empire* (1776-88).

320b. 2. **Hooker and Herbert:** Richard Hooker in his *Ecclesiastical Polity* (1594-97) and George Herbert in his 'metaphysical' poetry (*The Temple*, 1633) wrote in styles yet farther from the free, informal, inartificial 19th century manner than the styles of Johnson and Gibbon.

17. **Tydides:** Son of Tydeus, i.e. Diomedes.

19. **Redgauntlet:** Principal character in Scott's novel of that name (1824).

321a. 36. **White Lady:** The White Lady (or Maid) of Avenel is a phantom character in Scott's *The Monastery* (1820). Glen Farg is a glen of the Ochil Hills, north of Kinross. Glendearg, in *The Monastery*, is imaginary.

39. **Loch Leven:** On an island in Loch Leven (about 25 miles north of Edinburgh across the Firth of Forth, Kinross being a small town on the lake) is an old castle in which Queen Mary was imprisoned in 1567, making her escape in 1568, as told in Scott's *The Abbot* (1820).

47. **Warwick Castle:** Warwick Castle is about ten miles to the north-east of Shakespeare's Stratford; the ancient home of the Earls of Warwick and described as "one of the finest and most picturesque feudal residences in England."

321b. 5. *Lady of the Lake:* James Fitzjames, the Knight of Snowdoun in Scott's *The Lady of the Lake* (1810), turns out to be James V of Scotland, whose court is at Sterling Castle, sometimes in old story called Snowdoun. Lord James of Douglas, banished favorite of the king, is father of Ellen, the Lady of the Lake.

6. *Marmion:* The Douglas in *Marmion* (1808) is Archibald Douglas, Earl of Angus (popularly named Bell-the-cat), whose principal castle was Tantallon, on "a high rock projecting into the German Ocean, about two miles east of North Berwick."

20. the 29th of May: The anniversary of the Restoration of Charles II in 1660. After the rout of the Royalist forces by Cromwell at Worcester (1651), Charles II hid in an oak tree at Boscobel (Shropshire); in memory of this incident many people wore "oak apples or sprigs of oak" on the 29th of May.

HERNE-HILL ALMOND BLOSSOMS

38. Standard in Cornhill: Ruskin refers to a water standard "built in 1582," from which "distances were formerly measured." Herne Hill is on the south side of the Thames, in Surrey. Cornhill is a street in central London, leading east past the Exchange.

323a. 33. Nasmyth: Alexander Nasmyth (1758-1840), Scottish portrait and landscape painter, who painted the portrait of Robert Burns in the Scottish National Gallery at Edinburgh.

38. Dr. Munro: Thomas Munro (1759-1833), physician and connoisseur, was an early patron of Turner, who, according to Ruskin, got "some practical teaching of that first patron." Dr. Munro possessed many drawings by Turner.

38. Turner: Joseph Mallord William Turner (1775-1851) is the great English landscape painter and water-colorist whom Ruskin defended in *Modern Painters.*

323b. 2. *Douglas:* A tragedy (1756) by John Home (1722-1808), Scottish clergyman and playwright.

3. *Castle Spectre:* A musical drama (1798) by Matthew Gregory Lewis (1775-1818), nicknamed 'Monk' Lewis, after his most famous romance *Ambrosio, or the Monk* (1796).

49. *Count Robert of Paris:* Scott was broken with illness when he wrote this novel (1831), the next to his last.

324a. 5. Ballantyne partnership: In 1805 Scott formed a secret partnership with the Scottish printer and publisher, James Ballantyne (1772-1833). At the height of his success as a writer, he found himself in debt for £130,000 as a result of the failure (1826) of Ballantyne and Co., and of the associated firm in London, Constable & Co.

324b. 30. "Shall any following spring," etc.: The quotation is from No. VIII of the "Translations and Paraphrases in Verse collected and prepared by a Committee of the General Assembly of the Church of Scotland, in order to be sung in Churches" (No. VIII is a paraphrase of *Job,* XIV, 1-15). The lines in the quotation were written by John Logan (1748-88), Scottish clergyman and poet, who was one of the committee on revision of the "Translations and Paraphrases," in 1775.

325b. 37. Mazzini: Guiseppe Mazzini (1805-72), Italian patriot, who became a revolutionary leader in the democratic movement in Italy, the aim of which was national unification under a republican form of government. For a time he lived in London where he was well known. In a note on this remark of Mazzini's (Letter 54 of *Fors Clavigera,* where several sections of this second chapter first appeared in 1875) Ruskin says: "Quite seriously said, yet perfectly feeling the joke also to the full."

MODERN PAINTERS

In 1842 Ruskin was vacationing in Switzerland after his final examinations at Oxford, when a savage critique on some of Turner's recent pictures reached him. The impetuous young enthusiast resolved to write a paper in defence of his idol and "blow the critics out of the water." He "found that *demonstration* in matters of art was no such easy matter, and the pamphlet turned into a volume. Before the volume was half way dealt with it hydrazied into three heads, and each head became a volume. Finding that nothing could be done except on such an enormous scale, I determined to take the hydra by the horns, and produce a complete treatise on landscape art." *Modern Painters* is a fragment, but it remains the most eloquent defence of an individual artist ever written.

NATURE

326a. 5. Friar's Crag: There is now on Friar's Crag, Derwentwater, in the English Lake country, a memorial of Ruskin in the form of a monolith wherein is fixed a medallion portrait in bronze.

327a. 15. Christie, Eustace, White Lady: Characters in *The Monastery*.

23. Kenilworth: The historical Kenilworth castle in Warwickshire, one of England's "most extensive baronial ruins," was founded in the 12th century, later belonged to John of Gaunt, and in 1563 was given to the Earl of Leicester by Queen Elizabeth.

51. I never thought of nature as God's work: Cf. "The supernatural charm of wild scenery to me was a spiritual joy in the thing itself and in nothing else" (*Works*, Lib. Ed., XXXV, 608).

327b. 38. Sanctity in the whole of nature: Cf. "I never climbed any mountain, alone, without kneeling down by instinct, on its summit to pray" (*Works*, Lib. Ed., IV, 350).

328a. 4. Stand upon the peak, etc.: "The description in the text was a reminiscence of a thing seen and recorded at the time—namely, in the middle of August 1835" (Cook's note, *Works*, Lib. Ed. III, 415).

17. Atlantis: Mythic island of the West, beyond the pillars of Hercules, said to have been sunk beneath the ocean by an earthquake.

328b. 8. the deep lake below: Lake Lucerne (Ruskin's note).

329b. 50. Ruysdael: Jacob Ruysdael, or Ruisdael (1628?-82), Dutch landscape painter and etcher.

330a. 37. Fall of Schaffhausen: In northern Switzerland, where the Rhine drops in a fall of 62 feet. Ruskin says: "The drawing of the fall of Schaffhausen, which I made at the time of writing this study, was one of the very few, either by other draughtsmen or myself, which I have seen Turner pause at with serious attention" (*Works*, Lib. Ed., III, 529 n). At a later date (1859) Ruskin was at Schaffhausen and wrote to C. E. Norton: "I was up at three to watch the dawn on the spray of the Fall."

331b. 9. "shape has none": *Paradise Lost*, II, 666.

332a. 8. Slave Ship: The descriptive title of this famous picture at the Exhibition was: "Slaver's throwing overboard the dead and dying—Typhoon coming on." Shortly after the publication and success of this first volume of *Modern Painters*, Ruskin says, "on January 1st, 1844, my father brought me in the 'Slaver' for a New Year's gift." In 1869 he sold the picture, finding that the "subject had become too painful to live with." It is now in the Boston Museum of Art.

332b. 1. incarnadines the . . . sea: Cf. *Macbeth*, II, ii, 62.

GREATNESS IN ART

332b. 6. In the 15th Lecture: Sir Joshua Reynolds (1723-92), English painter, friend of Samuel Johnson and member of the famous literary Club (founded at his suggestion), was most famous for his portraits. The *Discourses* on art, to the last of which Ruskin refers, "arose out of his appointment in 1768 as President of the newly-established Royal Academy of Arts." They were delivered at intervals from 1769 to 1790 and published complete in 1794.

In the 15th Discourse, the subject is mainly the art of Michelangelo, in whose genius Sir Joshua makes a distinction "between correctness of drawing and that part which respects the imagination," the one being "mechanical" and the other "poetical." In the 11th Discourse the same distinction furnishes a better illustration of Ruskin's reference: "For that power, which enables the artist to conceive his subject with dignity, may be said to belong to general education; and is as much the genius of a poet, or the professor of any other liberal art, or even a good critic in any of those arts, as of a painter. Whatever sublime ideas may fill his mind, he is a painter, only as he can put in practice what he knows, and communicate those ideas by visible representation."

48. It is not by the mode of representing, etc.: Ruskin adhered to this principle throughout his life, but he often felt that in the assertion of it here he was mistakenly understood to under-value execution or technique. In 1870 he said: "It was long before I myself understood the true meaning of the pride of the greatest men in their mere execution. . . . Inferior artists are continually trying to escape from the necessity of sound work, and either indulging themselves in their delights in subject, or pluming themselves on their noble motives for what they cannot perform; . . . whereas the great men always understand at once that the first morality of a painter, as of everybody else, is to know his business." (*Lectures on Art*, Lib. Ed., XX, 80-81).

333a. 13. Old Shepherd's Chief-mourner: By Sir Edwin Landseer (1802-73), English animal painter.

333b. 45. Rubens, Van Dyke, Rembrandt: Peter Paul Rubens (1577-1640) and Sir Anthony Van Dyke (1599-1641) are Flemish painters, the latter being the court painter to Charles I of England. Rembrandt van Rijn (1606-69) is the leading representative of the Dutch School of painters.

50. Cimabue and Giotto: Giovanni Cimabue (*cir.* 1240-*cir.* 1302), Florentine painter and mosaicist. —— Giotto di Bordone (1276?-?1337), Florentine painter, architect, and sculptor; a pupil of Cimabue. Both are famous Italian primitives.

334a. 20. Raffaelle: Raffaello Santi, or Sanzio (1483-1520), Italian painter, sometimes regarded as "one of the four greatest masters in the history of painting," Michelangelo, Leonardo da Vinci, and Titian being the others.

22. Carlo Dolci: Florentine painter (1616-86), whose religious canvases are described as "decidedly effeminate."

334b. 1. "things which the mind occupies," etc.: From *An Essay Concerning Human Understanding*, Bk. II, Ch. I (1690), by the English philosopher, John Locke (1632-1704).

20. Loggias: Galleries in the Vatican decorated with the arabesques of Raphael.

IDEAS OF TRUTH, BEAUTY, AND RELATION

Ruskin considers, altogether, five 'ideas' in art, two of which—'power' and 'imitation'—are here omitted, though much is said about imitation in the discussion of 'truth.' By 'power' Ruskin means the skill, mental or bodily, "necessary to the production of any work of art." By 'imitation,' i.e. deceptive imitation, he means "the immediate and present perception that something produced by art is not what it seems to be"; "mean and paltry" subjects may be imitated,—"a cat or fiddle,"—but nothing "really great."

Many years later Ruskin referred to his scheme of 'five ideas' in art as "affected and forced." "Now," he said, "I should say quite plainly—a picture must, first, be well painted; secondly, must be a true representation; thirdly, must be of a pretty thing; fourthly, must be of a pretty thing which there was some rational and interesting cause for painting" (*Works*, Lib. Ed., III, 93 n).

335b. 34. Claude's "Seaport": "The Embarkation of the Queen of Sheba" by Claude Lorrain (1600-82), French landscape painter, whose landscapes Turner undertook to rival.

337a. 13. I call in some way, or in some degree, beautiful: Cf. "The final definition of Beauty is, the power in anything of delighting an intelligent human soul by its appearance" (*The Laws of Fesole*, Lib. Ed. XV, 438).

338a. 32. Ideas of Relation: In addition to 'truth' and 'beauty' in art there must be design, which is here what Ruskin means by 'relation,'—i.e. "the visible operation of human intellect in the presentation of truth, the evidence of what is properly called design or plan in the work, no less than veracity. A looking-glass does not design." (*Works*, Lib. Ed., XVI, 285).

338b. 16. "Building of Carthage": "Dido building Carthage,"—one of the two Turners that hang in the National Gallery of London beside two Claudes, in accordance with the conditions of Turner's bequest by which he meant to challenge "his rival from the grave." The reference to Claude in the text is to "Seaport: Queen of Sheba," previously mentioned and one of the two Claudes hanging beside the two Turners.

339a. 7. Praxiteles: Athenian sculptor of the 4th century B.C., whose most famous extant statue is the Hermes, now in the museum at Olympia, Greece.

THE NATURE OF GOTHIC

This chapter on the Nature of Gothic in the second volume of *The Stones of Venice* (1853) was, said Ruskin, "precisely and accurately the most important in the whole book" (*Works*, Lib. Ed., XII, 101). Here is the turning-point of his thought from art to political economy and social reform. His mind, in recent months, and especially while in Venice at work on *Stones*, was becoming increasingly concerned, says his editor, Cook, "with the political and social mysteries of life —the inequalities of worldly fortune, the existence side by side of idle luxury and servile toil." The central pages of the present chapter on modern servile workers as contrasted with the free craftsmen of the Middle Ages "seemed to some of us," said William Morris in his introduction to the chapter in his separately printed Kelmscott Press edition (1892), "to point out a new road on which the world should travel. The lesson which Ruskin here teaches is that art is the expression of man's pleasure in labor; that it is possible for man to rejoice in his work, for, strange as it may seem to us today, there have been times when he did rejoice in it."

339a. 9. **Byzantine and Gothic forms:** The first was developed in the Byzantine Empire, especially in the 5th and 6th centuries, its chief characteristics being the domed basilica with richly incrusted walls and colored mosaics and capitals of greatly varied designs. St. Sophia in Istanbul and St. Marks in Venice are the most famous examples of Byzantine architecture in the world.—The best Gothic architecture, Ruskin thought, was created between 1250 and 1450, though there was important French and English Gothic earlier and though the later French and English periods extended nearly a century further.

341b. 7. **Dark Ages:** The period, loosely taken, from 400 to 1000, though the term, Dark Ages, has lost favor with historians.

343b. 4. **The workman was, in both systems, a slave:** The third kind of ornament, the Renaissance, is that in which the inferior detail becomes principal, the executor of every minor portion being required to exhibit skill and possess knowledge as great as that which is possessed by the master of the design; and in the endeavour to endow him with this skill and knowledge, his own original power is overwhelmed, and the whole building becomes a wearisome exhibition of well-educated imbecility. We must fully inquire into the nature of this form of error, when we arrive at the examination of the Renaissance schools (Ruskin).

345b. 34. **Come, and he cometh:** *Matthew*, VIII, 9.

346a. 1. **The Irish peasant:** At the time Ruskin wrote, agrarian crime had been prevalent in Ireland (Cook's note).

9. **"Another for Hector!":** *Vide* Preface to *Fair Maid of Perth* (Ruskin's note).

346b. 52. **vibration like hail:** Ruskin is no doubt describing what he had seen at the glass works of Murano (Cook's note). Murano is a northern suburb of Venice.

347a. 21. **a slave-driver:** The slave trade was abolished by Great Britain in 1807; slavery under the British flag was abolished in 1833. Slavery was an institution in the United States and elsewhere when Ruskin was writing *Stones of Venice*.

347b. 3. **Leonardo:** Leonardo da Vinci (1452-1519), probably the most versatile great genius on record, was painter, sculptor, architect, engineer, scientist. Ruskin was repeatedly extreme in his judgments of Leonardo, without being altogether wrong. The painter spent four years on his *Mona Lisa* and could not finish it. He is said to have destroyed much of his work because it failed to realize his demands for perfection. "Leonardo fretted his life away in engineering," says Ruskin again, "so that there is hardly a picture left to bear his name" (*Stones*, III, Lib. Ed., XI, 70).

348a. 24. **I have already defined:** i.e. in vol. I of *Stones* (Lib. Ed., IX, 290).

349a. 39. **human work...in its own bad way:** The Elgin marbles are supposed by many persons to be "perfect." In the most important portions they indeed approach perfection, but only there. The draperies are unfinished, the hair and wool of the animals are unfinished, and the entire bas-reliefs of the frieze are roughly cut. (Ruskin).

350a. 46. **Corinthian capitals:** A capital is the topmost member of a column or pilaster. The Greeks had three different capitals for their three different orders, columns, or units of style in architecture,—the Doric, simplest of all; the Ionic, slightly ornate; the Corinthian, highly ornate.

351a. 4. **Phidias:** Greek sculptor of the 5th century B.C. In the time of Pericles he was master of public works in Athens and executed many of the city's famous monuments, including the sculptures on the Parthenon.

6. **Titian:** Tiziano Vecelli (1477-1576), Italian painter, chief master of the Venetian school of painters.

352a. 54. **"love darkness rather than light":** *John*, III, 19.

353b. 11. **Seven Lamps of Architecture:** See *Works*, Lib. Ed., VIII, 101.

ARATRA PENTELICI: LECTURE I

Aratra Pentelici (Ploughs of Pentelicus) is the title of six lectures on the elements of sculpture, which Ruskin delivered at Oxford in Nov. and Dec. 1870, and published in 1872, "considerably" revised and changed. As to the title, he wrote: "Its meaning is that I have traced all the elementary laws of sculpture...to the right understanding of the power of incision or furrow in marble" (*Letters to C. E. Norton*, II, 33). Of Lecture I, the Division of Arts, the first twelve sections are printed in the text.

355a. 20. **iniquity the most reckless and monstrous:** Allusion to the Franco-Prussian War, which was declared in July, 1870.

355b. **3. yesterday or the day before:** While the Franco-Prussian War was in progress Bismarck "secretly stirred up Russia" to denounce those articles in the Treaty of Paris (at the end of the Crimean War, 1856) which prohibited Russia "from keeping warships or arsenals in the Black Sea." British indignation was aroused and suggestions of mobilization were made.

8. Soldiers of the Ploughshare, etc.: Ruskin's first use of this phrase was in *A Joy Forever* (1857)—the phrase in which, as he said in *Unto This Last* (1862) his "principles of Political Economy were all involved."

18. first four lectures: The first four, in *Lectures on Art*, Feb.-March, 1870.

356b. **1. this simple one, the ploughshare:** I had a real ploughshare on my lecture-table; but it would interrupt the drift of the statements in the text too long if I attempted here to illustrate by figures the relation of the coulter to the share, and of the hard to the soft pieces of metal in the share itself (Ruskin's note).

358a. **26. this peach:** One of William Hunt's peaches; not, I am afraid, imaginable altogether, but still less representable by figure (Ruskin's note).

358b. **30. replied Thackeray:** Mrs. Richmond Ritchie says that "of course my father never used the words directly addressed to anybody," but that she remembers "hearing him say something of the sort indirectly" (Cook's note, Lib. Ed., XX, 208).

34. second part of *Faust*: Act V, Sc. VI.

359a. **8. "to have pleasure rightly":** Aristotle's *Politics*, VIII, 5, 4.

QUEEN OF THE AIR: LECTURE III

The three lectures entitled *"Queen of the Air:* Being a Study of the Greek myths of Cloud and Storm" were published in 1869. The subject is treated very discursively, only the first having much to do with the Greek myths of Athena, the third, here printed in part, least of all, to which Ruskin added an explanation of the title: "'Athena the worker, or having rule over the worker.' The name was first given to her by the Athenians."

359a. **22. porches of Abbeville:** In the following paragraphs (i.e. up to "Thus far of Abbeville building") Ruskin inserted material which he had used earlier in the same year in a lecture on *The Flamboyant Architecture of the Valley of the Somme.*

359b. **36. that floral gable:** The elaborate pediment above the central porch at the west end of Rouen Cathedral, pierced into a transparent web of tracery, and enriched with a border of "twisted eglantine" (Ruskin's note).

37. Stonehenge: A group of upright stones, monoliths, near Salisbury, England, probably dating from a prehistoric period.

360a. **5. Bill Sykes, the Dodger:** Characters in Dickens's *Oliver Twist.*

53. Pharaoh, etc.: Official title of the sovereigns of ancient Egypt. Ruskin probably refers to the ruler who made Joseph governor and who oppressed and pursued the Israelites as recorded in *Exodus.* —— David: king of Judah and Israel (1013?-?973 B.C.). —— Leonidas: king of Sparta in the 5th century B.C., famous for his defense of the pass of Thermopylae against the Persians. —— Publius Valerius Publicola: Roman statesman, colleague of Lucius Junius Brutus as one of first two consuls and a legendary founder of the Roman Republic (509 B.C.). —— Frederick Barbarossa (1123?-1190): king of Germany and Holy Roman Emperor (1152-90), one of the greatest German leaders. —— Coeur de Lion, Lion-Hearted: Richard I (1157-99), king of England (1189-99), famous for his exploits in the Third Crusade. —— St. Louis: Louis IX (1214-70), king of France (1226-70), crusader in Sixth Crusade, canonized (1297) for his sanctity. —— Dandolo: Enrico Dandolo (1108-1205), doge of Venice (1192-1205), who led the Venetians when the Crusaders (Fourth Crusade) captured Constantinople (1203-4). —— Frederick the Great (1712-86): king of Prussia (1740-86), military genius and great administrator.

360b. **31. the foundation of moral character in war:** Ruskin, by and large, was inconsistent and contradictory in his treatment of war. He approved of just wars for defense, and he praised the heroism, discipline, and loyalty which wars brought out in men; he recognized, too, the calamities of war, its waste, corruption, injustice, etc.

361a. **39. Dürer:** Albrecht Dürer (1471-1528), German painter and engraver, who was born in Nuremberg, where much of his best work was done; reputed inventor of etching and of printing woodcuts in two colors.

LECTURES ON ART: LECTURE III

In 1869 Ruskin was made the first Slade Professor of Fine Art at Oxford. His first professorship (there was a second one in 1883 for a brief period) continued for three terms of three years each (1870-78). He delivered the first course of seven lectures in Feb. and March, 1870. They were published in the same year as *Lectures on Art,* the third of which, the first half, is included in the text.

363b. 38. Nisus and Lausus: *Georgics,* I, 404 ff., and *Aeneid,* X, 763 ff., respectively.

47. "Never elated," etc.: *Essay on Man,* IV, 323-24.

364a. 4. "exacted": Horace, *Odes,* III, xxx, 1.—*Exigi monumentum aere perennius:* I have 'exacted' a monument more lasting than bronze.

364b. 4. Mantegna: Andrea Mantegna (1431-1506), Italian painter and engraver, greatest name of the Paduan school, whose influence on Italian art was profound.

4. Veronese: Paulo Veronese, born Cagliari (1528-88), eminent painter of the Venetian school, whose art reflects the pomp and color of life in old Venice.

365a. 29. Bernard of Luino: Bernardino Luini (1475?-?1532), Italian painter of the Lombard school, who lived mostly in Milan, where he was influenced by Leonardo. "He joins the purity and passion of Angelico," says Ruskin, "to the strength of Veronese."

30. a Venetian: Vittore Carpaccio (b. before 1460-d. before 1526), Venetian painter, whom Ruskin 'discovered' in Venice in 1869: "This Carpaccio is a new world to me," he wrote to Burne-Jones. There was, however, a picture by Carpaccio in the National Gallery of London, purchased in 1865.

365b. 7. Apelles and Protogenes: Rival Greek painters of the fourth century B.C. Apelles was court painter of Philip of Macedon and of Alexander the Great. Protogenes lived at Rhodes. None of their works is extant. The story of their contest is told by Pliny (*Nat. Hist.,* XXXV, xxxvi),—"the rival painters alternately showing their skill by drawing a line of excessive fineness."

11. the circle of Giotto: The Pope sent one of his courtiers to Florence to see "what kind of man Giotto might be." The courteous painter, who was found in his workshop, "took a sheet of paper, and a pencil dipped in a red color; then, resting his elbow on his side, to form a sort of compass, with one turn of the hand he drew a circle, so perfect and exact that it was a marvel to behold. 'Here is your drawing,' said he, ... 'send it with the rest and you will see if it will be recognized.'" Whence the Pope and his intelligent courtiers "perceived how far Giotto surpassed all other painters of his time" (Vasari: *Lives of the Painters,* ed. Blashfield and Hopkins, I, 60-61).

17. Dürer: Raphael sent a drawing of two nude male figures to the German painter, on which Dürer wrote: "1515—Raffahell di Urbino, who is held in such high esteem by the Pope, he made these naked figures and sent them to Albrecht Dürer at Nürnberg to show him his hand" (Vasari, *op. cit.,* III, 183 n.).

366a. 13. Holbein: Hans Holbein, the Younger (1497?-1543), German painter, who spent his last years in England as court painter to Henry VIII; famous for his portraits of Erasmus and Thomas More.

THE CROWN OF WILD OLIVE: TRAFFIC

Traffic is the second of three lectures which Ruskin published in 1866 in a volume which he called *The Crown of Wild Olive.* The lectures were delivered at different places and times in 1864-5. *Traffic,* the one first read, was given in the Town Hall, Bradford, April 21, 1864. The text used is the revised text of the 1873 edition, to which was added a fourth lecture. A crown of wild olive was one of the prizes awarded to the victors in the great Olympian games of ancient Greece. To Ruskin it was used to suggest that honor in this life may be accepted as sufficient reward for all honest workers. We do not need to "share the degradation of the brute, because (we) are condemned to its mortality."

366a. 5. Exchange: At the time of the delivery of the lecture, no design had been chosen for the Exchange ... Ruskin had been invited to deliver it, not by the Directors of the Exchange, but by a special committee of citizens formed for the purpose (Cook's note, Lib. Ed., XVIII, 433).

367b. 22. hunger and thirst after justice: *Matthew,* V, 6.

32. Teniers: There are two Flemish genre painters, father and son, with this name, David

Teniers, the Elder (1582-1649), and David Teniers, the Younger (1610-90), whose picture *Flemish Tap-Room, Backgammon Players,* in the London National Gallery, is the one probably referred to.

368a. **9. a book:** *On Colour and on the Necessity for a General Diffusion of Taste among all Classes* (1858), by Sir John Gardner Wilkinson (1797-1875), English traveller and Egyptologist.

22. Newgate Calendar: An account of the prisoners in Newgate prison, with details of their crimes, formerly published in London. The prison was destroyed in 1902.

368b. **17. "They carved at the meal," etc.:** Scott, *The Lay of the Last Minstrel,* I, st. 4.

369a. **25. Armstrongs:** Big guns invented by Sir W. G. Armstrong (1810-1900), English inventor and armament maker.

30. black eagles: Allusion to the Order of the Black Eagle, a Prussian decoration (1701-1919), which conferred nobility upon royalty and high civil and military officers. Ruskin alludes to the unwillingness of Great Britain to arm in defence of Denmark against Prussia and Austria (1864).

369b. **7. Inigo Jones:** English architect (1573-1652), exponent of the classic style, who designed the banqueting hall at Whitehall, Lincoln's Inn Chapel, and the reconstruction of the old St. Paul's Cathedral.

8. Wren: Sir Christopher Wren (1632-1723), English architect, charter member of the Royal Society, who planned the rebuilding of London after the Great Fire (1666) and designed and rebuilt St. Paul's.

370a. **5. "How dreadful is this place":** *Genesis,* XXVIII, 17.

36. "Thou, when thou prayest": *Matthew,* VI, 6.

370b. **5. Lares:** Roman household gods.

21. good architecture: And all the other arts, for the most part; even of incredulous and secularly-minded commonalities (Ruskin's note).

371b. **22. to the Greeks—Foolishness:** *I Corinthians,* I, 23.

37. Gorgon: In Greek mythology one of the three sisters, whose snaky tresses and terrible faces turned beholders to stone; Medusa is the one most mentioned.

372a. **2. to do things evermore rightly and strongly:** It is an error to suppose that the Greek worship, or seeking, was chiefly of Beauty. It was essentially of Rightness and Strength, founded on Forethought: the principal character of Greek art is not beauty, but design: and the Dorian Apollo-worship and Athenian Virgin-worship are both expressions of adoration of divine wisdom and purity. Next to these great deities, rank, in power over the national mind, Dionysus and Ceres, the givers of human strength and life: then, for heroic example, Hercules. There is no Venus-worship among the Greeks in the great times: and the Muses are essentially teachers of Truth, and of its harmonies (Ruskin's note).

50. Tetzel's trading: Johann Tetzel (1465?-1519), German Dominican monk, appointed by the Catholic Church to sell papal indulgences. His preaching and selling of indulgences aroused Martin Luther and so brought on the Reformation.

372b. **6. The Virgin's temple:** The Parthenon, on the Acropolis, at Athens, "the most consummate building in the Doric Style," was built in the 5th century B.C. as a temple for worship of Pallas Athena, the virgin goddess of Wisdom.

9. The Revivalist: Allusion to the revival of the Roman classic style of architecture in the Renaissance, which finally degenerated (as Ruskin thought) into the rococo style of the palace at Versailles.

42. temple of Ephesus: At Ephesus in Asia Minor there was in ancient times a vast temple dedicated to the worship of Diana, who, for the Ephesians, was the goddess of fertility, a local form of the Great Mother of Anatolia, i.e. Nature.

373a. **29. His dislike of affairs of exchange:** *Matthew,* XXI, 12 ff.

52. compulsory comfort: Quite serious, all this, though it reads like a jest (Ruskin's note).

373b. **35. the loaves and fishes:** Please think over this paragraph, too briefly and antithetically put, but one of those which I am happiest in having written (Ruskin's note).

374a. **7. "In the best market":** Meaning, fully, "We have brought our pigs to it" (Ruskin's note. cf. *Matt.,* VIII, 28 ff.).

374b. **8. Olympus, Pelion, Ossa:** Mountains in northern Greece. In Greek mythology two giants, in an attempt to attack the Gods on Olympus, piled Pelion upon Olympus and Ossa upon Pelion; they were killed by Apollo.

9. Ossa like a wart: *Hamlet,* V, i, 306.

24. **Plutus:** God of wealth.

48. **When I was last here:** March 1, 1859, when Ruskin lectured at Bradford on Modern Manufacture and Design, published later in *The Two Paths*.

375a. 38. **"they should take who have the power,"** etc.: Wordsworth's *Rob Roy's Grave*, 39-40.

375b. 23. **Jerusalem as stones:** *I Kings*, X, 27.

51. **Bolton priory:** One of the most picturesque ruins in England on the banks of the river Wharfe in Yorkshire,—dating from the 12th century.

376a. 1. **". . . men may come,"** etc.: Tennyson's *The Brook*.

27. **last written words of Plato:** Plato's *Critias* is a fragmentary dialogue, probably belonging to the last period of the philosopher's life. Ruskin gives the reader his own translation,—120 E., to the end.

46. **daughters of men:** *Genesis*, VI, 2.

49. **"their spot was not,"** etc.: *Deut.*, XXXII, 5.

376b. 43. **The rest is silence:** *Hamlet*, V, ii, 372.

49. **plain of Dura:** *Daniel*, III, 1.

377a. 11. **which are pleasantness:** *Proverbs*, III, 17.

377b. 9. **temples not made with hands:** *Acts*, VII, 48.

SESAME AND LILIES: THE MYSTERY OF LIFE AND ITS ARTS

This lecture was delivered in Dublin before the Royal College of Science May 13, 1868. It was first printed in Dublin the next year with other lectures by other lecturers in the series, and in 1871 it was included in a revised edition of *Sesame and Lilies* ("the most popular of all Ruskin's books"). "I put into it all that I knew," said Ruskin; and Sir Leslie Stephen declared it "to be the most perfect of his essays."

377a. 4. **"I was not aware of a restriction":** That no reference should be made to religious questions (Ruskin's note).

377b. 24. **"What is your life?":** *James*, IV, 14.

378a. 9. **"man walketh in a vain shadow":** *Psalms*, XXXIX, 6.

27. **to water the garden:** *Genesis*, II, 6.

30. **"wells without water":** *II Peter*, II, 17.

378b. 23. **the greatest painter:** Turner.

50. **at Kensington:** The South Kensington Museum; the drawings are now in the National Gallery.

379a. 39. **Benjamin Woodward:** An architect of Irish birth (1815-61), member of a Dublin firm of architects (Deane, Woodward, and Deane), who built the library at Trinity College (Dublin) to which Ruskin refers, and who designed and built the Oxford Museum of Natural History (1855-58), in which Ruskin was deeply interested.

43. **Sir Thomas Deane:** Dublin architect and builder (1792-1871), senior member of the firm of architects referred to in the preceding note.

52. **an Irish sculptor:** O'Shea, whom Ruskin called "a most skilful carver," and who also worked on the Oxford Union, the interior walls of which were decorated by Rossetti, Morris, Burne-Jones, and other Pre-Raphaelites.

379b. 23. **palaces of crystal:** There were two such palaces to which Ruskin probably alluded: one was the famous Crystal Palace of London, built under the patronage of Prince Albert in 1851 in Hyde Park to house the International Exhibition (removed in 1854, destroyed by fire in 1936); the other was a similar building erected in Dublin for the Dublin International Exhibition of 1864, in the concert hall of which Ruskin delivered the present lecture.

45. **"Meanwhile opinion gilds,"** etc.: *Essay on Man*, II, 283-90.

380b. 41. **lest we should see with our eyes:** *Isaiah*, VI, 10.

381b. 38. **as grasshoppers:** *Isaiah*, XL, 22.

39. **the nations as the dust:** *Nahum*, I, 3.

382a. 36. **Hesiod's account:** Greek poet of the 8th century B.C., whose *Theogony* "is an account of the beginnings of the world and birth of the Gods."

54. **one dear Florentine:** Beatrice Portinari (1266-90), wife of Simone de Bardi, immortalized by Dante in his *Vita Nuovo* and *Divina Commedia*.

383a. 38. **this Achilles:** The son of Thetis and "taught" by Athena, Achilles lost his mistress, Briseis, to Agamemnon; his friend was Patroclus; he "dies at last" by the hand of Paris.

383b. 1. "by petty chance," etc.: Changing of foils in *Hamlet*, V; "by momentary folly": Cordelia's choice in *Lear*, I; "by broken message": *Romeo and Juliet*, IV; "by fool's tyranny": of Leontes in *Winter's Tale;* "by traitor's snare": Iago's in *Othello*.

10. visions of angels: *Henry VIII*, IV, 2.

10. the great soldier-king: *Henry V*, IV, viii, 108-15.

13. by many or by few: *I Samuel*, XIV, 6.

22. valley of the shadow of death: *Psalms*, XXIII, 4.

25. "the gods are just": *Lear*, V, iii, 171-72.

32. "there's a divinity": *Hamlet*, V, ii, 8-11.

384a. 5. weigh the earth: *Isaiah*, XL, 12.

52. taken home in the evening: I have sometimes been asked what this means. I intended it to set forth the wisdom of men in war contending for kingdoms, and what follows to set forth their wisdom in peace, contending for wealth (Ruskin's note).

384b. 54. the child'is father of the man: Wordsworth's *My heart leaps up when I behold*.

385a. 25. dress or keep the garden: *Genesis*, II, 15.

26. hewers of wood and drawers of water: *Joshua*, IX, 21.

385b. 1. Even Reynolds: In his *Discourses on Art*.

40. Alps on Alps arose: Pope, *Essay on Criticism*, II, 32.

386a. 19. Doré's art: Paul Gustave Doré (1833-83), French illustrator and painter, whose immense vogue in England as illustrator of the Bible, Milton, Tennyson, as well as of Dante, Rabelais, Cervantes, and Balzac, Ruskin regarded as "a sign and symptom of degradation in the taste of the time" (Cook, *Works*, Lib. ed., XVII, 344 n).

386b. 45. an Irish angel: See *The Two Paths*, §§ 28 *et seq*. (Ruskin's note).

387b. 41. in the sweat of their face: *Genesis*, III, 19.

46. "Do it with thy might": *Eccles.*, IX, 10.

388a. 5. being dead, have yet spoken: *Hebrews*, XI, 4.

15. the ground from which we were taken: *Genesis*, III, 23.

31. Garden of the Hesperides: In the Atlas Mountains the Hesperides, daughters of Atlas and Hesperis, guarded (with the aid of a dragon) "the golden apples of the tree that had sprung up to grace the wedding of Zeus and Hera."

39. perish of hunger: A reference to the terrible famine in 1866 in the Indian province of Orissa.

44. virgin goddess: Athena, who was not only goddess of wisdom but patroness of the arts, especially the art of weaving, i.e. Athena Ergane.

46. "She layeth her hands to the spindle," etc.: *Proverbs*, XXXI, 19-22, 24.

388b. 14. cast clouts and rotten rags: *Jeremiah*, XXXVIII, 11.

27. "I was naked, and ye clothed me not": *Matt.*, XXV, 43.

389a. 8. "I was a stranger": *Ibid*.

13. her untimely figs: *Rev.*, VI, 13.

14. desire of the eyes: *I John*, II, 16.

42. the imagination of our evil hearts: *Jeremiah*, XI, 8.

46. "as a vapor," etc.: *James*, IV, 14.

52. disquiets itself in vain, etc.: *Psalms*, XXXIX, 6; *Revelation*, XIV, 11.

389b. 1. no fear, no hope, no desire: *Eccles.*, IX, 10.

25. twinkling of an eye: *I Corinthians*, XV, 52.

28. "He maketh the winds His messengers": *Psalms*, CIV, 4.

42. He cometh with clouds: *Revelation*, I, 7.

46. the books opened: *Daniel*, VII, 10.

50. *Dies Irae:* Day of Wrath; opening words of the greatest of medieval hymns, describing the Last Judgment and closing with an appeal for the souls of the dead. The reputed author of the hymn is Thomas of Celano (1200?-?1255), a Franciscan monk.

390a. 17. sin of Ananias: *Acts*, V, 1-2.

20. taking up our cross: *Matt.*, X, 38.

23. "They that are His," etc.: *Galatians*, V, 24.

390b. 3. Levi's station in life: *Mark*, II, 14.

5. Peter's, the shore of Galilee: *Matt.*, IV, 18.

6. Paul's, the ante-chambers: *Acts*, IX, 1.

27. feed the hungry: *Isaiah*, LVIII, 7.

28. if any man will not work: *II Thes.*, III, 10.

391b. 51. "Lord, I thank Thee," etc.: *Luke*, XVIII, 11.
392b. 39. the greatest of these is Charity: *I Cor.*, XIII, 13.

MATTHEW ARNOLD
SELECTED BIBLIOGRAPHY

I. STANDARD EDITIONS

The Works of Arnold, 15 vols., London, 1903-4, including poetry, prose, letters, bibliography; also
    Works, New York, 12 vols., 1924; neither edition complete.
Letters of Matthew Arnold, ed. G. W. E. Russell, 2 vols., London, 1895.
The Letters of Matthew Arnold to Arthur Hough Clough, ed. H. F. Lowery, London and New
    York, 1932.
Unpublished Letters, ed. Arnold Whitridge, New Haven, 1923.
Matthew Arnold's Notebooks, pref. by Mrs. E. Wodehouse, London, 1902.
Essays Literary and Critical, Intro. G. K. Chesterton, Everyman's, New York, 1906.
Essays, including Essays in Criticism, 1865, On Translating Homer, and Five Other Essays, first
    time collected, Oxford Edition, New York, 1914.
Prose and Poetry, ed. A. L. Bouton, New York, 1927.
Essays and Poems, ed. F. W. Roe, New York, 1928.
Representative Essays, ed. E. K. Brown, New York, 1936.
Culture and Anarchy, ed. W. S. Knickerbocker, New York, 1925.
—— ed. J. Dover Wilson, Cambridge, England, 1932.

II. BIOGRAPHY AND CRITICISM

ADAMS, JAMES T., "Sweetness and Light—Sixty Years After," *Atlantic Monthly*, CXL, 1926, 629-37.
BLUNDEN, EDMUND, "Matthew Arnold," in *The Great Victorians*, New York, 1932.
BROWN, E. K., *Studies in the Text of Matthew Arnold's Prose Works*, Paris, 1935.
BROWNELL, W. C., *Victorian Prose Masters*, New York, 1901.
BURROUGHS, JOHN, *Indoor Studies*, Boston, 1889.
DAWSON, W. H., *Matthew Arnold and His Relation to the Thought of Our Time*, New York,
    1904.
ELIOT, T. S., "Arnold and Pater," in *Selected Essays*, London, 1932.
—— "Matthew Arnold," in *The Use of Poetry and the Use of Criticism*, Cambridge, Mass., 1933.
FRYE, PROSSER HALL, "Matthew Arnold," in *Visions and Chimeras*, Boston, 1929.
GARROD, H. W., "Matthew Arnold as Critic," in *Poetry and the Criticism of Life*, Cambridge,
    Mass., 1931.
GATES, L. E., *Three Studies in Literature*, New York, 1899.
HARRISON, FREDERIC, "Culture: A Dialogue," *Fortnightly Review*, VIII (1867), 603-14.
HARVEY, C. H., *Matthew Arnold: A Critic of the Victorian Period*, London, 1931.
JAMES, HENRY, "Matthew Arnold's Essays," in *Views and Reviews*, Boston, 1908.
KINGSWILL, HUGH, *Matthew Arnold*, New York, 1928.
MORE, P. E., "Criticism," *Shelburne Essays*, Vol. 7, New York, 1910.
PAUL, H. W., *Matthew Arnold* (English Men of Letters Series), London, 1902.
ROBERTSON, JOHN M., *Modern Humanists*, London, 1891.
—— *Modern Humanists Reconsidered*, London, 1927.
RUSSELL, G. E., *Matthew Arnold* (Literary Lives Series), New York, 1904.
SAINTSBURY, GEORGE, *Matthew Arnold*, New York, 1899.
—— *A History of English Criticism*, Edinburgh and London, 1911.
SELLS, I. E., *Matthew Arnold and France*, Cambridge, England, 1935.
SHAFER, ROBERT, *Christianity and Naturalism*, New Haven, 1926.
SHERMAN, STUART P., *Matthew Arnold: How to Know Him*, Indianapolis, 1917.
SIDGWICK, HENRY, "The Prophet of Culture," *Macmillan's Magazine*, XVI (1867), 271-280.
STANLEY, CARLTON, *Matthew Arnold*, Toronto, 1938.
TRILLING, LIONEL, *Matthew Arnold*, New York, 1939.
WHITRIDGE, ARNOLD, *Dr. Arnold of Rugby*, New York, 1928.
WILLIAMS, STANLEY, *Studies in Victorian Literature*, New York, 1923.
WOODBERRY, G. E., "Matthew Arnold," *Makers of Literature*, New York, 1900.

NOTES AND COMMENTS

SWEETNESS AND LIGHT

Sweetness and Light, now the first chapter in *Culture and Anarchy* (1869), was originally Arnold's last lecture as Professor of Poetry at Oxford, delivered June 15, 1867 and published in the *Cornhill Magazine* in July of the same year under the title *Culture and Its Enemies.*

396a.   22. **I have before now:** In *The Function of Criticism* (1864).

     32. *Quarterly Review:* For Jan. 1866.

396b.   11. **Montesquieu:** French jurist and political philosopher (1689-1755), best known for *Lettres Persanes* (1721) and *L'Esprit des Lois* (1748). Arnold quotes from *Discours sur les motifs qui doivent nous encourager aux sciences* (1725).

     49. **Bishop Wilson:** Thomas Wilson (1663-1775), Bishop of Sodor and Man, author of *Maxims,* and other religious writings. Arnold quotes from *Sacra Privata,* or, possibly, from *Maxim* 450 (see *Works,* V, 187 and 428, ed. 1860).

398a.   6. **Religion says:** *Luke,* XVII, 21.

     16. **As I have said on a former occasion:** In *A French Eton* (1864), third and concluding part (pp. 116-17 in 1892 ed.).

     47. **Bishop Wilson:** Quotation from *Sacra Privata* (*Works, op. cit.,* 39).

398b.   15. **Mr. Bright and Mr. Frederic Harrison:** John Bright (1811-89), English orator and statesman, member of Parliament, great political reformer. —— Frederic Harrison (1831-1923), essayist, author of many books, positivist philosopher. Arnold quotes from both men in his "Introduction" to C. and A. Harrison's article on *Culture: A Dialogue* appeared in the *Fortnightly Review,* Nov. 1867.

399a.   27. **I have . . . noticed Mr. Roebuck's stock argument:** In *The Function of Criticism.* John Arthur Roebuck (1801-79), member of Parliament for Sheffield, radical politician and one of Arnold's typical Philistines.

400b.   8. **"Bodily exercise profiteth little":** *I Timothy,* IV, 8.

     11. **Franklin:** *Poor Richard's Almanac,* for Dec. 1742.

     22. **Epictetus:** Greek Stoic philosopher (60?-?120 A.D.), originally a slave, who was freed and taught philosophy in Rome until expelled by the Emperor Domitian. Arnold quotes from his *Enchiridion,* Ch. XLI.

     39. **Swift.** *Battle of the Books* (1704); in the apologue of the Spider (modern writers) and the Bee (ancient writers), the Bee is made to say: "Instead of dirt and poison we have rather chose to fill our hives with honey and wax, thus furnishing mankind with the two noblest of things, which are sweetness and light."

401b.   18. *resist the devil: James,* IV, 7.

     18. *overcome the wicked one:* Cf. *I John,* V, 4.

     48. **Independents:** In the 17th and 18th centuries those Protestants who believed that each church group was a self-governing body; now known as Congregationalists.

     53. **"The Dissidence of Dissent":** From Burke's speech on *Conciliation with America.*

402a.   8. **"Finally, be of one mind":** *I Peter,* III, 8.

402b.   10. **Pilgrim Fathers' voyage:** After a long and difficult voyage in the Mayflower the Pilgrims anchored off Cape Cod in Nov. 1620, and later at Plymouth, Dec. 26.

     43. **Epsom:** Town in Surrey, near London, place of famous Derby horse races.

403a.   37. **the *Daily Telegraph:*** A London morning newspaper catering to the middle classes and voicing the characteristics of British philistinism.

404a.   32. **Mr. Beales and Mr. Bradlaugh:** Edmund Beales (1803-81), agitator and organizer of popular demonstrations in London, largest of which was one of Trafalgar Square and Hyde Park in 1866 in support of electoral reform; president of the Reform League in that year. —— Charles Bradlaugh (1833-91), freethinker, socialist, agitator, publisher of the *National Reformer* (1860); later (from 1880), for refusing to take his oath on the Bible, he faced a prolonged but successful struggle to assume his seat in Parliament.

404b.   13. **Liberalism:** For Newman's hostility to (and conception of) Liberalism see Note A in his *Apologia.*

     42. **Mr. Lowe:** Robert Lowe (1811-92), afterwards Viscount Sherbrooke, prominent middle-class liberal and parliamentarian, who opposed the Reform Bill of 1867 and feared the rise of the working-classes.

     48. **A new power:** Rise of the lower classes, whom Arnold called "the populace."

405b. 22. "See what you have done!" etc.: Arnold quotes loosely from Bright's speech of Dec. 4, 1866.

406a. 6. *Journeyman Engineer:* Pseudonym of Thomas Wright (1789-1875), an iron founder who devoted years of service to the reclamation of prison convicts; author of *Some Habits and Customs of the Working Classes* (1867), *Johnny Robinson* (1868), and *Our New Masters* (1873).

29. Comte: Auguste Comte (1798-1857), founder of Positivism, "a system of philosophy (based) on natural phenomena or properties of knowable things." It repudiates super-naturalism and metaphysical idealism, and substitutes for orthodox religion the worship of humanity.

30. Mr. Congreve: Richard Congreve (1818-99), English Positivist and essayist, translator (1858) of Comte's *Catéchisme Positiviste* (1852).

48. Bentham: Jeremy Bentham (1748-1832), leader of English Utilitarianism, whose prin-ciple of moral goodness was "the greatest happiness of the greatest number."

406b. 4. Preller: Ludwig Preller (1809-61), German classical philologist, Librarian at Weimar (1846-61), author of *Greek Mythology* (1854-55) and *Roman Mythology* (1858).

5. the Tarquins: Two legendary kings of early Rome, the fifth (616-578 B.C.) and the seventh (and last, 534-510 B.C.).

36. says Franklin: Arnold takes seriously one of Franklin's jokes: in *The Proposed New Version of the Bible* (included in *Bagatelles*, 1818), some verses in the *Book of Job* are rewritten in modern style as a satire on regal government, for the amusement of Franklin's friends. (See *Writings*, I, 177-78, ed. A. H. Smyth, 1905.)

407a. 1. *Deontology:* Or *The Science of Morality*, edited and published in 1834, after Ben-tham's death; for the passage see I, 39.

18. Mr. Buckle: Henry Thomas Buckle (1821-62), author of an unfinished *History of Civilization* (vol. I, 1857; II, 1861). For his theory of history see Froude's *The Science of History*.

21. "Be ye not called Rabbi": *Matt.*, XXIII, 8.

44. "The man of culture," etc.: From Harrison's "Our Venetian Constitution" in *Fort-nightly Review*, March 1, 1867.

408a. 26. Abelard: Pierre Abelard (1079-1142), famous French scholastic philosopher, theologian, and teacher; lover of Héloïse.

30. Lessing and Herder: Gotthold Ephraim Lessing (1729-81), German critic and drama-tist. —— Johann Gottfried von Herder (1744-1803), German philosopher and man of letters. Both Lessing and Herder were representative leaders of the German Aufklärung.

408b. 15. Saint Augustine: Early Christian church father and philosopher (354-430). Arnold quotes from his *Confessions*, XIII, xviii, 22.

LITERATURE AND SCIENCE

This essay, in the words of Arnold, "was originally given as the Rede Lecture at Cambridge." It was first published in the *Nineteenth Century* for August, 1882. In revised form it was the most popular of Arnold's three American lectures (1883-84), and was afterwards included in *Discourses in America* (1885), "the book by which, of all his prose-writings, he should most wish to be remembered," as he told Russell, the editor of *Letters of M. A.* (II, 327 n.).

408a. 4. Plato's absolute ideas: See his *Republic*, X, 596-97.

16. base mechanic arts: *Ibid.*, VI, 495.

408b. 19. picture of the working lawyer: Plato's *Theaetetus*, 172-73.

409a. 22. Emerson declares: "Literary Ethics," *Works*, Cent. ed., I, 179.

409b. 9. "An intelligent man," says Plato: *Republic*, IX, 591.

410a. 28. a phrase of mine: In *A Speech at Eton* and *The Function of Criticism*.

36. Huxley, in a discourse: Lecture on "Science and Culture," delivered Oct. 1, 1880 and reprinted in *Science and Culture and Other Essays* (Collected Works, III). It is included in the present text.

39. more words of mine: From *The Function of Criticism*.

410b. 37. "superficial humanism": See Renan's "L'Instruction superieur en France," in *Ques-tions Contemporaines*, Paris, 1868.

411a. 1. Wolf: Friedrich August Wolf (1759-1824), German classical scholar and critic.

53. Euclid: Greek geometer of about 300 B.C., whose *Elements* is the foundation of later geometry.

53. Newton: Sir Isaac Newton's *Principia* (1687), i.e. *The Mathematical Principles of Natural Philosophy,* is described as "the greatest single triumph of the human mind."

411b. 27. Copernicus: Nicolaus Copernicus (1473-1543), Polish astronomer, who established in place of the "Ptolmaic System" the since-called "Copernican System."

27. Galileo: Italian astronomer and physicist (1564-1642), who was denounced for defending the Copernican system and was forced by the Inquisition to abjure belief in it.

412a. 28. "the Levites of culture": The Levites were a priestly caste among the ancient Hebrews. Nebuchadnezzar, Chaldean King of Babylon (*cir.* 605-562 B.C.), a fierce enemy of the Hebrews.

412b. 27. British Association: British Association for the Advancement of Science, founded in 1831.

413b. 36. A certain Greek prophetess: Plato's *Symposium,* 201-206.

414a. 22. Sylvester: James Joseph Sylvester (1814-97), English mathematician who resigned a professorship at Johns Hopkins University in 1883 to accept one at Oxford (1883-97).

53. Darwin's famous proposition: In *The Descent of Man* (1871), pt. II, Ch. XXI.

415a. 1. Mr. Darwin once owned: See *Autobiography* in this text; also *Life and Letters,* by Francis Darwin, London, 1887 (I, 100-01).

21. Faraday: Michael Faraday (1791-1867), eminent English chemist and physicist. The Sandemanians are a small and narrow sect of Scottish Christians, followers of Robert Sandeman (1718-1771), a linen manufacturer and minister.

416a. 6. the Preacher's words: *Eccles.,* VIII, 17.

14. to say with Homer: *Iliad,* XXIV, 49.

22. Spinoza: Baruch (or Benedict) Spinoza (1632-67), Dutch Jewish philosopher; see *Ethics,* IV, prop. XVIII.

27. "What is a man," etc.: *Luke,* IX, 25.

417a. 12. Can'st thou not minister, etc.: *Macbeth,* V, iii, 40.

417b. 25. "has not an Englishman," etc.: From Huxley's *Science and Culture.*

49. Lady Jane Grey: (1537-54), daughter of the Duke of Suffolk, great-granddaughter of Henry VII, proclaimed queen in 1553 by a Protestant party led by the Duke of Northumberland; beheaded in 1554. A memorable account of her reading Plato's *Phaedo* in Greek is given in Roger Ascham's *Scholemaster* (1570).

POETRY AND THE CLASSICS

Published as a 'Preface' to *Poems* (1853), the first volume of poetry to appear with Arnold's name. A few months before the 'Preface' was composed, Arnold wrote to his mother: "I have never felt so sure of myself, or so *really* and *truly* at ease as to criticism, as I have done lately" (*Letters,* I, 35). The pronouncements in the essay are of primary importance in the study of Arnold as a critic.

419a. 10. volume published in 1852: i.e. *Empedocles on Etna, and Other Poems.* Empedocles was a Greek philosopher of the 5th century B.C., a disciple of Pythagoras; according to a tradition he died by throwing himself into the crater of Mt. Etna.

21. Orpheus and Musaeus: Orpheus was a legendary Thracian poet and musician, son of Apollo and the Muse Calliope. —— Musaeus was also a legendary Greek poet, son of Orpheus.

25. Sophists: Teachers of rhetoric, philosophy, and the art of successful living, who flourished in Greece in the fifth century B.C.

45. says Aristotle: *Poetics,* 4.

419b. 17. as Hesiod says: *Theogony,* 11, 54-56. Hesiod's *Theogony* is "the oldest literary monument of Greek mythology."

23. says Schiller: In introductory essay to *Die Braut von Messina* (The Bride of Messina), on the use of the chorus in tragedy ("Über den Gebrauch des Chors in der Tragödie").

420a. 25. said by an intelligent critic: In the *Spectator* of April 2, 1853. The words quoted were not used with reference to poems of mine (Arnold's note). Italics are Arnold's.

420b. 35. Achilles, Prometheus, etc.: Characters in the *Iliad, Prometheus Bound, Agamemnon* (both by Aeschylus), and the *Aeneid,* respectively.

47. *Hermann and Dorothea*, etc.: Narrative poems by Goethe, Byron, Lamartine, Wordsworth, respectively.

421a. 46. *grand style*: Arnold's first use of this famous phrase; described in his essay *On Translating Homer* as follows: "I think it will be found that the grand style arises in poetry *when a noble nature, poetically gifted, treats with simplicity or severity a serious subject.*" (*Last Words*, 1862.)

421b. 17. Orestes, Merope, Alcmaeon: Orestes, son of Agamemnon, avenged his father's murder by killing his mother, Clytemnestra; his story is dramatized by Aeschylus, Sophocles, and Euripides. —— Merope is the Greek queen who, with her son, killed her husband Polyphontes, King of Messenia, thus avenging the murder of her first husband, Cresphontes; the subject of a lost tragedy by Euripides and of tragedies by Voltaire and Arnold. —— Alcmaeon was the son of Amphiaraus (one of the Seven against Thebes) who in revenge of the death of his father killed his mother, Eriphyle; the subject of lost tragedies.

422a. 12. Polybius: Greek historian (*cir.* 205-123 B.C.).

29. Menander: Greek comic dramatist (*cir.* 343-291 B.C.).

422b. 40. "something incommensurable": See Eckermann's *Gespräche mit Goethe*, Jan. 3, 1830 (Everyman's trans., 341).

423b. 48. *Decameron*: By Boccaccio (1313-75), in 4th day, 5th novel.

424a. 29. Hallam: Henry Hallam (1777-1859), English historian; see his *Introduction to the Literature of Europe in the Fifteenth, Sixteenth and Seventeenth Centuries*, Ch. XXIII.

46. M. Guizot: French historian and statesman (1787-1874). Arnold refers to the preface of *Shakespeare and His Time:* "He is the most profound and dramatic of moralists; but he makes his personages speak a language which is often fastidious, strange, excessive, and destitute of moderation and naturalness" ("Preface," IV,—1852).

425b. 37. Niebuhr: German statesman and historian (1776-1831), author of *History of Rome* (3 vols., 1811-32), and other works. His judgments upon "the present age," as expressed in his letters, are many and various. Near the end of his life he wrote: "It is impossible not to perceive that the noble qualities which were the glory of our nation are disappearing— depth, sincerity, originality, heart, and affection—that shallowness and impudence are becoming universal" (19 Dec. 1830,—*Life and Letters*, N. Y. 1852, p. 530). For Goethe's opinions see (e.g.) Eckermann's *Gespräche* for Oct. 22, 1825 (Everyman's trans., 119-20).

426b. 1. Two kinds of *dilettanti*, says Goethe: From "Notes on Dilettantism" in *Die Propyläen* (1798-1800): also, in *Goethe's Literary Essays*, p. 78 (selected and arranged by J. E. Spingarn, N. Y., 1921).

THE STUDY OF POETRY

The essay was written as a general introduction to Ward's *The English Poets* (1880), for which Arnold also wrote introductions to the selections from Gray and Keats. It was published again as the first essay in *Essays in Criticism, Second Series* (1888).

426a. 3. "The future of poetry is immense," etc.: A shortened passage from the closing paragraph of Arnold's introduction to one of the volumes of *The Hundred Greatest Men*, 8 vols. (London, 1879).

426b. 23. does Wordsworth call poetry: Preface to *Lyrical Ballads* (2nd ed. 1800).

427a. 26. Sainte-Beuve: Charles Augustin Sainte-Beuve (1804-69), eminent French critic, whom Arnold described as "the finest critical spirit of our times" (*God and the Bible*, XXXII), and "one of my chief benefactors" (*Discourses in America*, 39). The quotation is from *Les Cahiers*, 51 (Paris, 1876).

427b. 2. poetry, as a criticism of life: A favorite and famous phrase, expressing a basic principle in Arnold's theory of poetry; for further use of it see his *On Translating Homer, Joubert, Wordsworth, Byron*.

428a. 35. Pellisson: Paul Pellisson (1624-93), French author, historiographer to Louis XIV.

42. d'Héricault: Charles-Joseph de Ricault (1823-99), historian, romance-writer, editor. —— Clement Marot (1496-1544) was court poet of Francis I.

429a. 51. the "Imitation" says: "When thou hast read and known many things, thou oughtest ever to return to the one principle" (*Imitation of Christ*, III, xliii, 2). Thomas à Kempis (1380-1471), German Augustinian monk, is the reputed author of *De Imitatione Christi*, a religious classic.

429b. 13. Caedmon: Religious poet, "father of English poetry," who flourished about 670 A.D., and who "paraphrased the history of the Old and New Testament" in Anglo-Saxon verse.

17. M. Vitet: Ludovic Vitet (1802-73), French dramatist, essayist, and politician, member of the French Academy; contributor to the *Revue des deux mondes*.

19. Chanson de Roland: French national epic, a *Chanson de geste*, composed in the eleventh century, whose hero is Roland, nephew of Charlemagne (King of Franks, 768-814, and Emperor of the West, 800-14).

23. Hastings: Channel town on the Sussex coast of England, where William the Conqueror overcame King Harold in 1066. For the story of Taillefer, see Freeman's *History of the Norman Conquest* (N. Y., 1873; III, 319-20).

29. One Turoldus or Théroulde: The Bodleian Library has the oldest manuscript of the poem, the last line of which gives the name Turoldus, thought to be the author but more likely the name of the minstrel or the transcriber.

430a. 38. touchstone: Defined as "a black siliceous stone allied to flint; ... so called because used to test the purity of gold and silver by the streak left on the stone when rubbed by the metal" (Webster's *International*). The 'poetic' touchstone, similarly, detects "the presence or absence of high poetic quality."

430b. 3. her brothers: Castor and Pollux.

431a. 1. "Wilt thou upon the high," etc.: *II Henry IV*, III, i, 18-20.

6. "If thou didst ever," etc.: *Hamlet*, V, ii, 357-60.

12. "Darken'd so," etc.: *Paradise Lost*, I, 599-602.

18. "And courage never," etc.: *Ibid.*, I, 108-09.

23. "which cost Ceres," etc.: *Ibid.*, IV, 271-72.

431b. 20. Aristotle's profound observation: *Poetics*, IX.

40. diction and movement: Cf. "The peculiar effect of a poet resides in his manner and movement, not in his words taken separately (153). . . . A poet's movement makes so large a part of his general effect" (210, *On Translating Homer*). Can we get a poet's "movement" from "single lines"?

432a. 24. *langue d'oïl—langue d'oc*: In Northern France 'yes' was *oïl*; in Southern France (Provence), it was *oc*.

31. Petrarch: Francesco Petrarcha (Eng. Petrarch,—1304-74), Italian poet, who wrote in Italian and Latin, and was crowned poet laureate at Rome in 1341; best known for his Italian sonnets and odes written to Laura, a French lady whom he met at Avignon.

432b. 3. Brunetto Latini: Florentine author and statesman (1212?-?1294), friend and counselor of Dante (*Inferno*, XV), whose prose work *Li Livres dou Trésor*, a treasury of medieval lore, was written in French because "its speech is more delightful and more common to all peoples."

8. Christian of Troyes: Chrétien or Chrestien de Troyes, French poet of the latter half of the 12th century, author of several Arthurian romances in verse, from one of which, *Le Roman de Cligès* (11, 30-39) the quotation is taken.

42. that stanza which the Italians used: The seven-line stanza (rime royal), invented by the Italians, and introduced into England by Chaucer, who also used the Italian ottava rima.

48. Wolfram: Wolfram von Eschenbach (1170?-?1220), Middle High German epic poet and minnesinger, author of *Parzival*, a metrical romance of the Holy Grail.

433a. 25. Dryden's comment: Both quotations are from *Preface to the Fables*, 1700.

39. "gold dew-drops of speech": The phrase is from John Lydgate (1370?-?1451), disciple and imitator of Chaucer, in his poem "The Life of Our Lady" (?1409-11); it may be found in the *Chaucer Society Publications: Five Hundred Years of Criticism*, I.

40. Johnson misses the point entirely: See Johnson's "History of the English Language" (*Dictionary*): "Dryden, who, mistaking genius for learning, and in confidence of his abilities, ventured to write of what he had not examined, ascribes to Chaucer the first refinement of our numbers, the first production of easy and natural rhymes, and the improvement of our language, by words borrowed from the more polished languages of the continent."

43. Gower: John Gower (1325?-1408), author of *Confessio Amantis*, his only poem in English (*cir.* 1390-93). Johnson calls him "the father of our poetry" (*op. cit.*), while Dryden describes Chaucer as "the father of English poetry" (*Fables*).

50. "well of English undefiled": Spenser's *Faerie Queene*, IV, ii, 32.

433b. 35. O Alma: From the Latin medieval hymn *Alma Redemptoris Mater*, 'Gracious (nourishing) mother of the Redeemer.'

434b. 9. Villon: François Villon, French poet, born in or near Paris in 1431. Stevenson has an essay on him, and Swinburne made an English version of *La Belle Heaulmière*.

11. La Belle Heaulmière: The name *Heaulmière* is said to be derived from a head-dress (helm) worn as a mark by courtesans. In Villon's ballad, a poor old creature of this class laments her days of youth and beauty. The last stanza of the ballad runs thus:—

> 'Ainsi le bon temps regretons
> Entre nous, pauvres vieilles sottes,
> Assises bas, à croppetons,
> Tout en ung tas comme pelottes;
> A petit feu de chenevottes
> Tost allumées, tost estainctes.
> Et jadis fusmes si mignottes!
> Ainsi en prend à maintz et maintes.'

'Thus amongst ourselves we regret the good times, poor silly old things, low-seated on our heels, all in a heap like so many balls; by a little fire of hemp-stalks, soon lighted, soon spent. And once we were such darlings! So fares it with many and many a one.' (Arnold's note.)

53. "that the sweetness of English verse," etc.: From *An Essay on Dramatic Poesy* (1688).

54. Cowley could see nothing at all in Chaucer's poetry: Cowley's opinion is cited by Dryden in *Preface to the Fables*.

435a. 6. "there is a rude sweetness," etc.: *Preface to the Fables.*

8. Addison: I can find no instance of direct comparison. In *An Account of the Greatest English Poets* (1694) Addison gives very qualified praise to Chaucer's "unpolish'd strain" (11, 9-16), and says of Dryden's muse: "She wears all dresses, and she charms in all."

21. Wordsworth and Coleridge denied it: See Wordsworth's *Essay, Supplementary to Preface* (1815). Coleridge's opinion of Dryden is less easy to fix; for various *obiter dicta* the indexes of *Table Talk* and Coleridge's *Miscellaneous Criticism* (ed. Raysor) may be consulted. For Coleridge on Pope, see *Bio. Lit.*, Chs. I, XVIII.

46. When we find Chapman: Arnold quotes from Chapman's "Commentarius" at the end of Bk. I of his translation of the *Iliad* (*The Iliad of Homer*, ed, Richard Hooper, I, 23; London, 1865).

50. Gades to Aurora and Ganges: Gades is the ancient name for the Spanish city of Cadiz, Spain; Aurora, the dawn; Ganges, a great river in India. The phrase means from farthest west to farthest east.

435b. 2. When we find Milton writing: In *An Apology for Smectymnuus.*

10. when we find Dryden telling us: Opening words of Dryden's "Postscript to the Reader" in his translation of *Virgil* (1697).

436a. 10. A milk-white Hind, etc.: Opening lines of the *Hind and the Panther* (1687).

18. To Hounslow Heath, etc.: *Imitations of Horace*, Bk. II, satire 2, 143-44.

436b. 33. Mark ruffian violence, etc.: From *Elegy on the Death of Robert Dundas, Esq.*

41. Clarinda: Burns as Sylvander corresponded with Mrs. Maclehose as Clarinda,—an Edinburgh woman with whom Burns for about a year exchanged letters.

43. "These English songs": Burns to George Thomson, Oct. 19, 1794.

437a. 35. Leeze me on drink: From *The Holy Fair.*

437b. 18. The sacred lowe: From *Epistle to a Young Friend.*

27. Who made the heart: From *Address to the Unco Guid.*

38. To make a happy fireside clime: From *Epistle to Dr. Blacklock.*

47. Xenophon tells us: I find no passage in *Memorabilia* exactly parallel with the passage from Burns. The reader may compare Xenophon's summary of the character of Socrates (IV, viii); and may consult *Oeconomicus*, VII

438a. 37. Had we never loved sae kindly: From *Ae Fond Kiss*, the usual title.

51. Thou Power Supreme: From *Winter: A Dirge.*

439a. 5. We twa hae paidl't: From *Auld Lang Syne.*

19. Pinnacled dim in the intense inane: Shelley's *Prometheus Unbound*, III, iv, last line.

41. On the brink of the night: *Ibid.*, II, v, first lines.

THE FUNCTION OF CRITICISM

The essay appeared first in *The National Review*, Nov., 1864. It was reprinted in *Essays in Criticism: First Series* (1865). "No man," said Swinburne, "has done so much to correct man's view of the higher criticism and its office."

439b. 43. I said: Quotation is from *On Translating Homer*, 2nd lecture, last paragraph.

440a. 9. Mr. Shairp's excellent notice: i.e. "Wordsworth: The Man and the Poet" in *The North British Review*, August, 1864, vol. 41; by John Campbell Shairp (1819-85), Scottish man of letters, critic, professor of poetry at Oxford, 1877-84. Some of his lectures were published in *Aspects of Poetry* (1881).

9. notice of Wordsworth: I cannot help thinking that a practice, common in England during the last century, and still followed in France, of printing a notice of this kind,— a notice by a competent critic,—to serve as an introduction to an eminent author's works, might be revived among us with advantage. To introduce all succeeding editions of Wordsworth, Mr. Shairp's notice might, it seems to me, excellently serve; it is written from the point of view of an admirer, nay, of a disciple, and that is right; but then the disciple must be also, as in this case he is, a critic, a man of letters, not, as too often happens, some relation or friend with no qualification for his task except affection for his author. (Arnold's note.)

15. Wordsworth says: In a letter to the Quaker poet, Bernard Barton (1784-1849; friend of Charles Lamb), Jan. 12, 1816. See *Memoirs of William Wordsworth* by Christopher Wordsworth (1851), II, 53.

26. "Wordsworth holds the critical power," etc.: Lady Richardson's words, quoted in Knight's *Life of Wordsworth* (1880), III, 438.

440b. 5. Johnson's *Irene:* A tragedy, written 1736-7, unsuccessfully produced at Drury Lane Theatre in 1749. His *Lives of the Poets* (1771-81) is Johnson's prose at its best.

10. Ecclesiastical Sonnets: A sonnet series in three parts (1821-22) on "the introduction, progress, and operation of the Church of England."

11. celebrated Preface: Preface to *Lyrical Ballads*, 2nd ed., 1800.

442a. 18. Pindar and Sophocles: Pindar (522?-443 B.C.), Greek lyric poet, author of 45 extant odes celebrating victories in great national games of Greece. —— Sophocles (496?-406 B.C.), Greek tragic poet, writer of many tragedies of which seven are extant.

52. Athens of Pericles: The Age of Pericles began with the great statesman's complete ascendancy over Athens (461-60) and ended with his death in 429.

52. England of Elizabeth: Queen Elizabeth's reign, 1558-1603.

443a. 14. The old woman: According to a doubtful tradition the woman was Jenny Geddes, who hurled her 'faulding stool' at the Dean of St. Giles's Church, when he began reading (July 23, 1637) the new liturgy recently prescribed for Scotland by Charles I.

443b. 29. Joubert: Joseph Joubert (1754-1824), French essayist and moralist. Quotation is from *Pensées*, Titre XXI, 2 (*Pensées, Essais, et Maxims*. I, ed. 1842).

444a. 42. Dr. Price: Richard Price, D.D. (1723-91), moral and political philosopher, Unitarian minister in London; a vigorous supporter of American and French revolutionists, and advocate of Paine's *Rights of Man*.

51. "to party gave up," etc.: From Goldsmith's epitaph on Burke in *Retaliation* (1774).

444b. 38. like Balaam: *Numbers*, XXII, 35, 38.

47. Lord Auckland: William Eden, first Baron Auckland (1745-1814), English statesman and diplomatist; ambassador at the Hague (1790-93).

445a. 51. like the traveller in the fable: Aesop's fable of "The Sun and the Wind."

446a. 27. *Revue des deux Mondes:* A leading French periodical, founded in Paris, 1831, by François Buloz (1803-77).

32. the *Edinburgh Review:* Founded in 1802.

35. the *Quarterly Review:* Founded in 1809.

38. the *British Quarterly Review:* Founded in 1845.

42. the *Times:* This great London daily newspaper was started in 1785 by John Walter (1739-1812) as *The Daily Universal Register*, which was renamed *The Times*, Jan. 1, 1788.

446b. 3. *Home and Foreign Review:* Published in London, 1862-64.

7. *Dublin Review:* Founded in 1836.

43. Sir Charles Adderley: First Baron Norton (1814-1905), Conservative statesman and churchman.

54. Mr. Roebuck: John Arthur Roebuck (1801-79), member of Parliament for Sheffield (1849-79), a leading advanced Liberal.

447a. 16. "Das wenige verschwindet," etc.: *Iphigenie auf Tauris*, I, ii, 91-92.

448a. 27. the Indian virtue: In Buddhism salvation means complete detachment from the world, annihilation of all desire and ambition. Buddhism "is practically extinct in India proper."

448b. 31. Lord Somers: John Somers, Baron Somers (1651-1716), English statesman, lord chancellor, chairman of committee that drew up Declaration of Rights (1689).

33. Cobbett: William Cobbett (1762-1835), pugnacious English agitator and pamphleteer, author of *The Political Register* (1802-35), and *Rural Rides* (1830).

40. Mr. Ruskin: Arnold no doubt had in mind *Unto This Last* (*Cornhill Magazine*, 1860), and *Munera Pulveris* (*Fraser's Magazine*, 1862-63).

449a. 35. To act is so easy: See Carlyle's translation of *Wilhelm Meister's Apprenticeship*, Bk. VII, Ch. ix.

43. Obermann: *Obermann* (1804) is a collection of highly subjective and romantic letters from Switzerland by Etienne Pivert Sénancour (1770-1846). The influence of this book upon Arnold was, at one time, very considerable (see his two poems on Obermann and his essay in *Essays in Criticism*, third series). He quotes from Letter XC: "Let us perish resisting."

49. Bishop Colenso: So sincere is my dislike to all personal attack and controversy, that I abstain from reprinting, at this distance of time from the occasion which called them forth, the essays in which I criticized Dr. Colenso's book; I feel bound, however, after all that has passed, to make here a final declaration of my sincere impenitence for having published them. Nay, I cannot forbear repeating yet once more, for his benefit and that of his readers, this sentence from my original remarks upon him; *There is truth of science and truth of religion: truth of science does not become truth of religion till it is made religious.* And I will add: Let us have all the science there is from the men of science; from the men of religion let us have religion (Arnold's note).

449b. 10. Dr. Colenso: John William Colenso (1814-83), Bishop of Natal, published in 1862 the first volume of *The Pentateuch and the Book of Joshua* (five vols. in all, 1862-79), in which he exposed the unhistorical character of the first six books of the Old Testament, and attacked belief in the literal inspiration of the Bible. Arnold's essay is *The Bishop and the Philosopher* (i.e. Spinoza) in *Macmillan's Magazine*, Jan., 1863.

16. says Joubert: Joubert's *Pensées*, Titre XXX (*op. cit.*, II, 109). Arnold has the following note on the entire sentence: It has been said I make it "a crime against literary criticism and the higher culture to attempt to inform the ignorant." Need I point out that the ignorant are not informed by being confirmed in a confusion?

26. Dr. Stanley: Arthur Penrhyn Stanley (1815-81), liberal churchman, Dean of Westminster, writer on ecclesiastical history, and biographer of Arnold's father, Dr. Thomas Arnold of Rugby. The book referred to is Stanley's *The Bible: Its Form and Its Substance* (1863), which Arnold discusses in his essay, *Dr. Stanley's Lectures on the Jewish Church* (*Macmillan's Magazine*, Feb., 1863).

41. eighty and odd pigeons: In his *Macmillan* essay on Colenso, Arnold alludes to an example of the Bishop's "arithmetical demonstration": " 'If three priests have to eat 264 pigeons a day, how many must each priest eat?' That disposes of Leviticus."

450a. 8. Miss Cobbe: Frances Power Cobbe (1822-1904), writer, lecturer, Unitarian, advanced Liberal. Arnold quotes from *Broken Lights* (1864), p. 134.

20. Dr. Strauss's book: David Friedrich Strauss (1808-74), German theologian and philosopher, author of *Das Leben Jesu* (1835-36), which was translated into English by George Eliot in 1846.

21. M. Renan's book: Ernest Renan (1823-92), French orientalist, author, and critic. Arnold refers to his *Vie de Jésus* (1863).

450b. 10. Coleridge's happy phrase: *Confessions of an Enquiring Spirit*, Letter 2.

451a. 4. Dr. Morrison: James Morrison (1770-1840), self-styled 'Hygeist,' was a merchant who, at the age of fifty, cured himself of illness, and renewed his youth by taking 'vegetable pills,' which he later marketed with great success to the British public as a panacea. His shop was called the British College of Health, in front of which, in 1856, a monument in the form of a lion was erected to his memory. Carlyle alludes to him in his chapter, "Morrison's Pill" (*Past and Present*, I, iv).

451b. **36. Luther's theory of grace:** According to Luther the efficacy of the Holy Sacraments depended upon the faith of those who received them, not upon the action or service independently (i.e. 'ex opere operato').

38. Bossuet's philosophy of history: Jacques-Benigne Bossuet (1627-1704), French bishop and pulpit orator, whose *Discours sur l'histoire universelle* (1681), "is a vindication of the ways of God in history, a theology of human progress. . . . By religion is meant Judaism and Christianity; by Christianity is meant the Catholicism of Rome."

40. Bishop of Durham: Charles Thomas Baring (1807-79), Bishop of Durham (1841-79).

42. Pope Pius the Ninth: Pope from 1846-78.

WORDSWORTH

The essay was first published in *Macmillan's Magazine* for July, 1879, and in the same year was used as a preface to Arnold's collection *The Poems of Wordsworth* in the *Golden Treasury Series;* later included in *Essays in Criticism, 2nd Series* (1888).

454a. **49. Rydal Mount:** Wordsworth's home, near Grasmere, 1813-50.

53. *Guide to the Lakes:* First published anonymously in 1809 as an introduction to a volume of 'Selected Views'; republished in expanded forms in later editions, and in 1835 in its present final form.

454b. **4. *Tennyson's decisive appearance:*** In 1842, with a 2-volume edition of his poems, containing *Ulysses, Morte d'Arthur, Locksley Hall,* etc.

35. *Mr. Palgrave:* Francis Turner Palgrave (1824-97), poet, critic, friend of Tennyson, Professor of poetry at Oxford (1885-95), editor of the widely-known anthology *Golden Treasury of the Best Songs and Lyrical Poems in the English Language* (1861).

48. "Glory," said M. Renan: Arnold quotes from *"Discours de Réception à l'Académie Française"* (3 Avril, 1879), in *Discours et Conférences,* 3rd ed., 1887, p. 3.

455a. **40. *"unrivalled happiness":*** The phrase is in a speech of Roebuck's from which Arnold quotes in Ch. III of *Culture and Anarchy* ("Barbarians, Philistines, Populace").

42. a candid friend: Arnold himself.

455b. **39. *Correspondant:*** The quotation is from "Un poète américain, Walt Whitman," by Henri Cochin (1854-1926), in *Le Correspondant* (Paris), Nov. 25, 1877, vol. CIX, 651-2.

456a. **5. Goethe says of Milton:** Quotations are from *Gespräche mit Goethe* for Jan. 31, 1830 (Everyman's trans., 346).

21. Amphictyonic Court: Representatives of an amphictyony, a league of States (or tribes) organized to protect religious centers or shrines, as the temple of Apollo at Delphi.

456b. **15. death of Molière:** In 1673.

19. for Germany: Klopstock (1724-1803); Lessing (1729-81); Schiller (1759-1805); Uhland (1787-1862); Rückert (1788-1866); Heine (1797-1856).

20. for Italy: Filicaja (1642-1707); Alfieri (1749-1803); Manzoni (1785-1873); Leopardi (1798-1837).

25. for France: Racine (1639-99); Boileau (1636-1711); Chénier (1762-94); Béranger (1780-1857); Lamartine (1790-1869); Musset (1810-57); Hugo (1802-85).

457b. **3. Wordsworth classified:** In his first collective edition of 1815.

458a. **48. Long ago. . . . I said:** See *On Translating Homer: Last Words* (1862).

458b. **4. On man, on nature, on human life:** *The Recluse,* 754. This was the first line of Wordsworth's "Prospectus" (conclusion of *The Recluse*), published in his Preface to the *Excursion* (1814).

12. Voltaire . . . remarked: In his *Siècle de Louis XIV* (Vol. I), *Oeuvres,* ed. Paris, 1878, XIV, 560.

41. Nor love thy life, nor hate, etc.: *Paradise Lost,* XI, 553-54.

459a. **1. We are such stuff:** *Tempest,* IV, i, 156-58.

22. criticism of life: See *The Study of Poetry* for further use of this definition, and the accompanying note.

50. Epictetus: *Discourses,* Bk. II, Ch. XXIII (Loeb Classics, 417).

459b. **32. Gautier:** Théophile Gautier (1811-72), French poet, novelist, critic, militant romanticist.

43. Of truth, of grandeur, etc.: *The Recluse,* 761-71.

460a. 31. Leslie Stephen: Sir Leslie Stephen (1832-1904), critic, biographer, editor, (first editor of *The Dictionary of National Biography*). Arnold quotes from "Wordsworth's Ethics," *Hours in a Library* (new ed., 1909, II, 250).

460b. 11. Immutably survive, etc.: *Excursion*, IV, 73-76.

29. One adequate support: *Ibid.*, IV, 10-17.

461a. 15. Thucydides says: *History of the Peloponnesian War*, Bk. I, Ch. I.

25. O for the coming, etc.: *Excursion*, IX, 293-302.

35. calls Voltaire dull: At the "immortal dinner" in the painter Haydon's studio (28 Dec., 1817) "Lamb soon got delightfully merry...'Now,' said Lamb, 'you old lake poet, you rascally poet, why do you call Voltaire dull?'" (*Autobiography of R. B. Haydon*, p. 231, ed. Penrose, N. Y., 1929).

51. "But turn we," etc.: *To the Lady Fleming*, st. IX.

461b. 42. the "not ourselves": From Arnold's definition of God as "the enduring power, not ourselves, which makes for righteousness" (*Literature and Dogma*, Ch. I).

52. as Goethe said himself: Goethe generally regarded himself as a poet whose powers were always in complete command; and he gave highest praise to the 'objective' as against the 'subjective' poet (see *Gespräche* for Mar. 20, 1830 and for Jan. 29, 1826). He praised Voltaire because his talent was "so completely at command every moment" (Dec. 16, 1828).

462a. 19. "This will never do": Opening sentence of Jeffrey's famous and slashing criticism of the *Excursion*, in the *Edinburgh Review*, for Nov. 1814 (No. 47). Jeffrey (1773-1850) was the first editor of the *E. R.* (1803-1829).

27. After life's fitful fever, etc.: *Macbeth*, III, ii, 23.

31. though fall'n on evil days: *Paradise Lost*, VII, 25-26.

48. the fierce confederate storm: *The Recluse*, 831-33.

462b. 20. The poor inhabitant below: *A Bard's Epitaph*.

463a. 10. *The Highland Reaper*: i.e. *The Solitary Reaper*.

463b. 40. They will cooperate: From Wordsworth's letter to Lady Beaumont, May 21, 1807 (*Letters of William and Dorothy Wordsworth*, The Middle Years, ed. De Selincourt, I, 131).

THOMAS HENRY HUXLEY

SELECTED BIBLIOGRAPHY

I. STANDARD EDITIONS

Collected Essays, 9 vols., London and New York, 1893-94: I. *Methods and Results*. II. *Darwiniana*. III. *Science and Education*. IV. *Science and Hebrew Tradition*. V. *Science and Christian Tradition*. VI. *Hume, with Helps to the Study of Berkeley*. VII. *Man's Place in Nature*. VIII. *Discourses, Biological and Geological*, IX. *Evolution and Ethics and Other Essays*.

American Addresses, with a lecture on the study of biology, New York, 1877.

The Advance of Science in the last Half-Century, New York, 1888.

Evolution and Ethics, and Other Essays, New York, 1899.

Mr. Balfour's Attack on Agnosticism (Huxley's last writing), *The Nineteenth Century*, XXXVII (1895), 527-40.

The Scientific Memoirs of Thomas Henry Huxley, 4 vols., ed. by Foster and Lankester, 1898-1902. Suppl. Vol. 1903.

Man's Place in Nature and Other Essays, with intro. by Sir Oliver Lodge, Everyman's Library, New York, 1908.

Lectures and Lay Sermons, with intro. by Sir Oliver Lodge, Everyman's Library, New York, 1910.

Autobiography and Selected Essays, ed. with intro. and notes, by Ada L. F. Snell, Boston, 1909 (Riverside Literature Series).

Readings from Huxley, ed. with intro. by Clarissa Rinaker, New York, 1920.

II. BIOGRAPHY AND CRITICISM

AINSWORTH, DAVIS, J. R., *Thomas H. Huxley* (English Men of Science), London, 1907.

AYRES, CLARENCE E., *Huxley*, New York, 1932.

BROOKS, WILLIAM K., *The Lessons of the Life of Huxley*, in *Smithsonian Institution, Annual Report*, Washington, 1900.

CHESTERTON, G. K., "The Art of Controversy: Macaulay, Huxley, and Newman," *Catholic World*, CV (1917), 446-56.

—— "Agnostic Defeat," *Living Age*, CCLXXII (1912), 777-83.

CLODD, EDWARD, *Thomas Henry Huxley*, New York, 1902.

Diary of the Voyage of H.M.S. Rattlesnake, ed. by Julian Huxley, Garden City, 1936.

FISKE, JOHN, "Reminiscences of Huxley," *Atlantic Monthly*, Feb., 1901.

FOSTER, M., "Huxley," *Living Age*, CCXLI (1904), 587-601.

GILL, THEODORE, "Huxley and His Works," in *Smithsonian Institution. Annual Report*, Washington, 1896.

HUXLEY, ALDOUS, *The Olive Tree and Other Essays* ("T. H. Huxley as a Literary Man"), London, 1936.

HUXLEY, LEONARD, *Life and Letters of Thomas Henry Huxley*, 2 Vols., New York, 1901.

—— "Carlyle and Huxley: Early Influences," *Cornhill Magazine*, LXXII (1932), 290-302.

—— "Home Memories. Personal Reminiscences of My Father," *Nature*, CXV (1925), 698-702.

HUTTON, R. H., "The Metaphysical Society, A Reminiscence," *The Nineteenth Century*, XVIII (1885), 177-196.

MIVART, ST. GEORGE, "Some Reminiscences of Thomas Henry Huxley," *The Nineteenth Century*, XLII (1897), 985-998.

MORE, P. E., *The Drift of Romanticism*, Shelburne Essays, Eighth Series, Boston, 1913.

OSBORN, H. F., *Impressions of Great Naturalists*, New York, 1924.

—— *Huxley and Education*, New York, 1910.

PETERSON, HOUSTON, *Huxley: Prophet of Science*, New York, 1932.

SCOTT, W. B., "An American Student in Huxley's Laboratory," *Cornhill Magazine*, CXLIX (1934), 679-93.

SHAFER, ROBERT, *Christianity and Naturalism*, New York, 1926.

SMALLEY, G. W., "Mr. Huxley," *Scribner's Magazine*, XVIII (1895), 514-24.

STEPHEN, LESLIE, *Studies of a Biographer*, III, New York, 1907.

WARD, WILFRID, "Thomas Henry Huxley, A Reminiscence," *The Nineteenth Century*, XL (1896), 274-92.

WILSON, D., "Huxley and Wilberforce at Oxford and Elsewhere," *Westminster Review*, CLXVII (1907), 311-16.

NOTES AND COMMENTS

AUTOBIOGRAPHY

First published as one of a series of biographical sketches by C. Engel, 1890. In a letter to his wife, March 2, 1889, Huxley says: "A man who is bringing out a series of portraits of celebrities, with a sketch of their career attached, has bothered me out of my life for something to go with my portrait, and to escape the abominable bad taste of some of the notices, I have done that" (*Life and Letters*, II, 245).

468a. 9. Bishop Butler: Joseph Butler (1692-1752), Bishop of Durham, author of *The Analogy of Religion* (1736).

15. Auckland: Auckland Castle, the episcopal palace of the bishops of Durham, about ten miles to the south of Durham on the river Wear.

24. the pre-Boswellian epoch: Boswell's *Life of Johnson* was first published in 1791.

469b. 9. Herbert Spencer: English philosopher (1820-1903), author of a *System of Synthetic Philosophy*, in several volumes. "One of few modern thinkers to attempt systematic account of all cosmic phenomena, including mental and social principles."

53. strangers in New South Wales: For many years criminals were "sent out" from England to Australia. Botany Bay on the east coast near Sidney was the site of the first penal settlement and still remains a general term for Australian convict settlements.

470b. 11. "Sweet south upon a bed of violets": *Twelfth Night*, I, i, 5-6—

> "O, it came o'er my ear like the sweet sound
> That breathes upon a bank of violets."

Huxley quotes from a text using Pope's conjectural substitution of 'south' for 'sound.'

50. my first scientific paper: "On a Hitherto Undescribed Structure in the Human Hair Sheath" (1845).

471a. 12. Sir Joseph Fayrer: English surgeon and writer (1824-1907); wrote on clinical surgery in India and tropical diseases.

15. Sir William Burnett: Scottish physician general of British Navy (1799-1861).

46. Nelson's old ship: Horatio Nelson (1758-1805), Viscount Nelson of the Nile, English admiral, who died on board his flag-ship, the Victory, at Trafalgar, Oct. 21, 1805.

47. Haslar Hospital: A marine hospital near Portsmouth.

51. Sir John Richardson: Scottish naturalist and arctic explorer (1787-1865), surgeon and naturalist to Sir John Franklin's polar expeditions.

472a. 37. Linnaean Society: Founded in 1788 to promote research in botany and zoology, and named after the Swedish naturalist, Linnaeus, 'father of modern systematic botany,' author of *Systema Naturae* (1737).

43. Royal Society: "Royal Society of London for the Advancement of Science," incorporated (1662) under Charles II, oldest scientific society in Great Britain and most famous (see Huxley's essay *On the Advisableness of Improving Natural Knowledge*).

472b. 16. Père Goriot: One of the best known novels of Balzac (1799-1850).

21. Professor Tyndall: John Tyndall (1820-93), eminent English physicist and lecturer.

53. Royal Institution: 'The Royal Institution of Great Britain' was "established under a charter by his majesty King George the Third, in the year 1800." Its foremost purpose was "to prosecute scientific and literary research." Many eminent British scientists have lectured at the Institution.

473b. 8. Presidency of the Royal Society: 1883-85.

19. New Reformation: In a letter to his wife in 1873, Huxley says: "We are in the midst of a gigantic movement greater than that which preceded and produced the Reformation, and really only the continuation of that movement" (*Life and Letters*, I, 427-28). He describes this movement in the preceding paragraph.

THE METHOD BY WHICH THE CAUSES OF THE PRESENT AND PAST CONDITIONS OF ORGANIC NATURE ARE TO BE DISCOVERED

The third lecture in a series of *Six Lectures to Working Men on Our Knowledge of the Causes of the Phenomena of Organic Nature*, delivered in London in 1863. Now published in *Collected Essays*, II.

474a. 9. Diogenes: Greek Cynic philosopher (412?-323 B.C.), noted "for his contempt for man's acts and motives," is said to have lived for a time in a tub. The incident in the text is told by Diogenes Laertius (3rd century A.D.) in his *Lives of Philosophers*. (Loeb Classics, II, 44,-Life of Diogenes.)

474b. 29. Baconian philosophy: The inductive method of scientific research, which Bacon described in his *Novum Organum* (1620),-the 'New Method,' intended to replace the deductive logic of Aristotle. Sir Francis Bacon (1561-1626), Baron Verulam, Viscount St. Albans, English philosopher, statesman, author, Lord Chancellor (1618-21).

475b. 32. one of Molière's plays: *Le Bourgeois Gentilhomme*, II, vi; the 'hero' is M. Jourdain.

478b. 16. Newton and Laplace: For Newton see following essay and note. — Pierre Simon Laplace (1749-1827), French astronomer and mathematician, who formulated the 'nebular hypothesis' as an explanation of the origin of the solar system.

ON THE ADVISABLENESS OF IMPROVING NATURAL KNOWLEDGE

A 'lay sermon' delivered at St. Martin's Hall, London, on Sunday, Jan. 7, 1866 (Huxley's note). It was published in the same month in the *Fortnightly Review*. "Science is, I believe, nothing but trained and organized common sense, differing from the latter only as a veteran may differ from a raw recruit: and its methods differ from those of common sense only so far as the guardsman's cut and thrust differ from the manner in which a savage wields his club" (1854: *Collected Essays*, III, 45).

479b. 3. The History of the Plague Year: *Journal of the Plague Year* (1722).

41. Republicans: Cromwellian Puritans.

480a. 14. Rochesters and Sedleys: Profligate satirists and poets of the Restoration: John Wilmot, 2nd Earl of Rochester (1647-80); Sir Charles Sedley (1639?-1701).

20. Laud: William Laud (1573-1645), Archbishop of Canterbury, High Churchman, vigorous foe of Puritanism. He was impeached and beheaded by the Long Parliament.

37. the words of one of the founders: John Wallis (1616-1703), eminent English mathematician, professor of geometry at Oxford (1649-1703), author of *Arithmetica Infinitorum* (1655), was one of the founders of the Royal Society. Huxley quotes from "Dr. Wallis's account of some passages of his own life" as he found it in *A History of the Royal Society*, vol. I, 31-32 (in two vols. by C. R. Weld, London, 1845).

50. Copernican hypothesis: The theory set forth by the Polish astronomer Nikolaus Copernicus (1473-1543) "who held that the earth rotated daily on its axis, and that the planets revolved in orbits around the sun."

480b. 8. Torricellian experiment: Torricelli (1608-47), Italian physicist, who improved the telescope and discovered the principle of the barometer (1643).

17. Galileo: Galileo Galilei (1564-1642), famous Italian astronomer who invented the thermometer and the telescope, and discovered the satellites of Jupiter and spots on the sun. His new views were condemned by the Pope, and in 1633 he was forced by the Inquisition to renounce the Copernican theory.

26. Dr. Wilkins: John Wilkins (1614-72), scientist, one of the founders of the Royal Society, Bishop of Chester.

40. Duke of Ormond: James Butler (1610-1688), 12th Earl and 1st Duke of Ormonde, Lord Lieutenant of Ireland before Cromwell's conquest and again after the Restoration (1661-69; 1677-82).

41. Chelsea College: Originally a theological college, later a hospital and even a prison, Chelsea College buildings were given to the Royal Society by a grant of the King in 1669; but the Society was unable to raise funds for new buildings and in 1681 sold grounds and buildings back to the King for £1300.

481a. 7. Newton: Sir Isaac Newton (1642-1727), celebrated mathematician and natural philosopher, who established the law of gravitation and explained it in his *Principia*, or "The Mathematical Principles of Natural Philosophy," published by the Royal Society in 1687.

33. Vesalius: Andreas Vesalius (1514-64), Belgian anatomist, one of the first to dissect the human body.

34. Harvey: William Harvey (1578-1657), English physician and anatomist, discoverer of the circulation of the blood.

35. grain of mustard seed: *Luke*, XIII, 19.

49. Schoolmen: Medieval scholastic philosophers, 'hair-splitters,' who often speculated over unimportant questions with excessive subtlety.

481b. 3. "writ in water": Allusion to the self-written epitaph on Keats's tombstone in the Protestant cemetery at Rome: "Here lies one whose name was writ in water."

5. First President: William, 2nd Viscount Brouncker (1620?-84), Irish mathematician; President of Royal Society (1662-77).

29. *revenant*: 'One who returns,' a ghost.

48. Mr. Hooke: Robert Hooke (1635-1703), English experimental philosopher, Gresham professor of geometry at Oxford (1665).

482a. 16. Boyle: Robert Boyle (1627-91), British chemist and natural philosopher, discoverer of Boyle's law of the elasticity of gases and founder (by his will) of the "Boyle Lectures" for the defense of Christianity.

16. Evelyn: John Evelyn (1620-1706), diarist and devoted churchman, and, like Boyle, a member of the Royal Society.

483a. 21. blind leaders of the blind: *Matt.*, XV, 14.

40. Aladdin's lamps: Aladdin is a youth in the *Arabian Nights*, who possesses a magic lamp and a magic ring,—"The Story of Aladdin; or, the Wonderful Lamp."

484a. 3. "When in heaven the stars," etc.: "Need it be said that this is Tennyson's English for Homer's Greek?" (Huxley's note): quoted from Tennyson's *Specimen of a Translation of the Iliad in Blank Verse* (*Iliad*, VIII, 555-59).

484b. 19. "increasing God's honor," etc.: From Bacon's *The Advancement of Learning*, I, v, 11.

485a. 4. ask for bread, etc.: Cf. *Matt.*, VII, 9.

31. Count Rumford: Benjamin Thompson, Count Rumford (1753-1814), physicist and adventurer, American by birth, invented or devised improvements in heating and lighting.

485b. 51. Altar of the Unknown: Cf. *Acts*, XVII, 23.

486b. 24. justification not by faith: Cf. *Romans*, III, 28.

A LIBERAL EDUCATION, AND WHERE TO FIND IT

An address delivered at the South London Workingmen's College, Jan. 4, 1868, and published later in the same year in *Macmillan's Magazine*.

487a. 31. **"You must educate," etc.:** After the passage of the Reform Bill of 1867, Robert Lowe, Viscount Sherbrooke (1811-92), English statesman, made the famous remark: "Now we must educate our masters."

42. **Ichabod:** *I Samuel*, IV, 21.

488a. 12. **senior wranglership, or a double first:** At Cambridge University an honors man placed in the first class in the final examination in mathematics is called a 'wrangler.' The first on the list was formerly called 'senior wrangler'; since 1909 the lists have been alphabetical. —— 'Double first' means first-class honors in two different subjects (e.g. classics and mathematics).

489a. 13. **Retzsch:** Moritz Retzsch (1779-1857), German painter, etcher, engraver, and designer. He illustrated works of Goethe, Schiller, and Shakespeare.

489b. 31. **Test Acts:** The Test Act of 1673 excluded from public office in England and Scotland all who refused to take oaths of allegiance and supremacy, to receive communion according to the usage of the Church of England, and to abjure belief in transubstantiation. It was repealed in 1828. The University Test Act was removed from Oxford and Cambridge in 1871.

37. **mass of mankind are the "Poll":** 'Poll' is an abbreviation from the Greek οἱ πολλοί, the many, the crowd; Cambridge slang for students who graduate with 'pass' degrees.

40. **plucked:** University slang for failure in examination.

490b. 26. **a map of the hundred:** Hundred is a division of an English shire or county; origin of the division is uncertain.

47. **Falstaff's bill:** *I Henry IV*, II, iv, 551-2.

491a. 37. **"circumbendibus":** Circumlocution, periphrasis; slang for 'big name.'

492a. 46. **Euclid:** Euclidean geometry, from the Greek geometer Euclid (*cir.* 300 B.C.).

492b. 14. **the great public schools:** Really great private schools, like Eton, Harrow, Rugby.

493a. 37. **Croesus:** King of Lydia, in Asia Minor (*cir.* 560 B.C.), "renowned for his vast wealth."

494a. 1. **Niebuhr, Gibbon, Grote:** Barthold Georg Niebuhr (1776-1831), German historian and philologist, author of *History of Rome* (3 vols., 1811-32). —— Edward Gibbon (1737-94), English historian, author of *The Decline and Fall of the Roman Empire* (5 vols., 1776-88) —— George Grote (1794-1871), English historian, author of *History of Greece* (8 vols., 1846-56).

494b. 4. **Cicero, Horace:** Marcus Tullius Cicero (106-43 B.C.), Roman orator, statesman, philosopher, man of letters. —— Quintus Horatius Flaccus (65-8 B.C.), Roman poet and satirist, author of *Ars Poetica*.

6. **Terence:** Publius Terentius Afer (190?-?159 B.C.), Roman writer of comedies.

495a. 11. **This is the stone, etc.:** *Matt.*, VII, 9.

23. **Rector of Lincoln College:** Mark Pattison (1813-84), Rector of Lincoln College (from 1861), scholar and author.

496a. 24. **Faraday, Brown, Lyell:** Michael Faraday (1791-1867), English chemist and physicist. —— Robert Brown (1773-1858), Scotch botanist. —— Sir Charles Lyell (1797-1875), British geologist.

496b. 39. **Bursch:** German university student.

45. **hot canvass:** Solicitation of votes from members, masters, and fellows of Oxford and Cambridge, who are eligible to vote in the university convocations.

SCIENCE AND CULTURE

An address delivered at the opening of Sir Josiah Mason's Science College, Birmingham, Oct. 1, 1880. It was published the next year in a volume of essays entitled *Science and Culture and Other Essays*. It should be compared with Arnold's *Literature and Science*. Introductory paragraphs are omitted.

498a. 6. **Levites:** Members of the tribe or family of Levi, who were charged by Moses with the care of the tabernacle and the sacred vessels; later, they had charge of the temple service (see *Numbers*, I, 48-53; *I Chron.*, XXIII, 24).

43. Once upon a time, a boy: Sir Josiah Mason (1795-1881), pen manufacturer and philanthropist, who began life by selling cakes and vegetables in the streets and who was shoemaker, carpenter, blacksmith, house-painter, carpet-weaver by turns. Later he took up pen-making and electro-plating, from which he acquired a fortune and built and endowed the College at Birmingham at a cost of £180,000.

499b. 25. our chief apostle of culture: Matthew Arnold.

501a. 23. as nature had been cursed: *Genesis,* III, 17.

501b. 39. Nemesis: Ancient Greek goddess of retributive justice.

502a. 50. Erasmus: Desiderius Erasmus (1466?-1536), great Dutch scholar and humanist of the Renaissance.

502b. 37. geometry from a book: Euclid's *Elements;* Euclid, 'the father of geometry,' lived in Alexandria about 300 B.C.

41. Hipparchus: Greek astronomer (160?-?125 B.C.), sometimes referred to as the founder of astronomy; discovered the procession of the equinoxes, catalogued over 1000 stars, founded trigonometry.

41. Ptolemy: Graeco-Egyptian astronomer, geometer, and geographer who flourished at Alexandria in the second century A.D. His theory of the earth as the fixed center of the solar system was received for ages, until superceded by the Copernican system in the 16th and 17th centuries.

42. Democritus and Archimedes: Democritus (460?-?362 B.C.), called "the laughing philosopher of Abdera" (in Thrace), best known for his atomic theory of matter. — Archimedes (287?-212 B.C.), Greek philosopher and mathematician of Syracuse, who is said to have discovered the principle of specific gravity and invented various mechanical instruments.

45. Aristotle, Theophrastus, Galen: Aristotle (384-322 B.C.), Greek philosopher, described as "the most comprehensive and systematic of all ancient thinkers." As a biologist he regarded each species of plant and animal as having its own characteristic 'form,' higher or lower, but immutable. — Theophrastus (372-4?-?287 B.C.), Greek philosopher and naturalist, disciple of Aristotle, author of *History of Plants* and *Theoretical Botany;* especially remembered for his sketches called *Characters.* — Galen (130?-?200 A.D.), Greek physician, native of Pergamos in Asia Minor, who spent many years in Rome; left numerous treatises on medicine and was regarded as an authority in the field up to the Renaissance.

504b. 8. withered by age, etc.: *Antony and Cleopatra,* II, ii, 240-41.

THE STRUGGLE FOR EXISTENCE IN HUMAN SOCIETY

Published in the *Nineteenth Century* for February, 1888, and republished in *Evolution and Ethics* (1893). In it, says Huxley, "the principles that, to my mind, lie at the bottom of the 'social question' are stated." The second half of the essay, in which the treatment becomes somewhat special and contemporary, is omitted.

505b. 13. à priori speculators: Who reason from assumed principles, deductively; à priori knowledge comes through reason, not through experience.

506b. 10. Eohippus: Extinct genus of the small primitive four-toed horses of the lower Eocene period.

12. Derby: Annual race for three-year-old horses, at Epsom, near London.

30. Diatom: A microscopic unicellular plant, species of algae.

31. Protococcus: Another species of microscopic algae, "containing red pigment and living in the upper layer of snow in arctic and alpine regions."

48. turn his thumbs down: In the Roman gladiatorial contests spectators expressed disapproval by turning their thumbs down.

507a. 13. John Howard: Famous Englishman (1726-90), who first exposed the "scandalous state of prisons at home and abroad" and introduced prison reform.

15. Istar: Chief goddess in the Babylonian and Assyrian pantheon; the Earth Mother and (with Assyrians) the goddess of war.

16. Aphrodite: Greek goddess of love and beauty (the Roman Venus).

17. Ares: Greek god of war (the Roman Mars).

20. Leibnitz: Gottfried Wilhelm Leibnitz (1646-1716), German mathmetician and philosopher, whose main doctrines are that ultimate reality is composed of 'monads' or spiritual entities, that these exist in a continuous gradation from lowest to highest (in man) and in harmony pre-established by God, that evil is not a positive reality, and that this is the best of all possible worlds.

21. Schopenhauer: Arthur Schopenhauer (1788-1860), German philosopher, who taught that ultimate reality is a blind power, manifesting itself as "the will to live," and "that life is an evil to be cured only by overcoming the will to live."

507b. **19. Ormuzd-Ahriman:** Ormuzd (or Ormazd) is supreme being and spirit of God, in Zoroastrian religion. —— Ahriman is the spirit of evil in that religion.

34. Tower of Siloam: *Luke*, XIII, 4.

508a. **5. setting limits to the struggle:** "The reader will observe that this is the argument of the Romanes Lecture, in brief" (Huxley's note,—1894).

35. Hobbesian war of each against all: Thomas Hobbes (1588-1679) in his *Leviathan* (1651), a treatise on the state, pictures man as innately selfish and naturally at war with his fellows,—his only hope of peace and freedom being in surrender to the absolute power ('leviathan') of a sovereign or dictator.

508b. **49. Atlantis:** A fabled island in the western ocean, mentioned by ancient writers. Bacon used this tradition in his *New Atlantis* (1627).

509a. **30. a very eminent physician:** "The late Sir W. Gull"—Huxley's note.

509b. **16. Arreoi societies:** Inhabitants of the Arroi, or Aru, Islands southwest of New Guinea, in the Dutch East Indies, who held their land communally.

510a. **25. Nemesis:** Greek goddess of retribution.

25. did not forget Croesus: Croesus, king of Lydia (560-546 B.C.), was renowned for his great wealth. He regarded himself as the happiest of men, when one night he dreamed that his son would die, "by the blow of an iron weapon." In spite of the most extreme precautions the son was accidentally killed in a boar-hunt by the spear of Adrastus, the Phrygian, a stranger whom the King had taken into his palace. Thus, says Herodotus, "a dreadful vengeance, sent of God, came upon Croesus, to punish him, it is likely, for considering himself the happiest of men" (*Herodotus*, I, 30-45).

27. There are now 36,000,000: "These numbers are only approximately accurate. In 1881, our population amounted to 35,241,482, exceeding the number in 1871 by 3,396,103. The average annual increase in the decennial period 1871-1881 is therefore 339,610. The number of minutes in a calendar year is 525,600" (Huxley's note).

45. insolent reproach of the first Napoleon: "L'Angleterre est une nation de boutiquiers," —England is a nation of shopkeepers,—a saying attributed to Napoleon by Sir Walter Scott in his *Life of Napoleon*, but without authority. Bertrand Barère, in a speech before the French National Convention, June, 1794, said: "Let, then, Pitt boast of his victory to his nation of shopkeepers."

510b. **9. the cotton famine:** During the American Civil War importations of cotton were stopped, owing to the blockade, and the Lancashire mills had to close, thus throwing thousands of textile workers out of their jobs.

47. wealth at the positive pole: "It is hard to say whether the increase of the unemployed poor, or that of the unemployed rich, is the greater social evil" (Huxley's note,—1894).

51. Sphinx: A monster, half-man, half-lion, whose riddle is said to have been: What creature goes on four feet in the morning, on two at noon, and on three in the evening? The answer is, man.

511a. **11. Oracle of Delphi:** The most famous oracle of the ancient world, at Delphi, Greece, on the slopes of Parnassus, and sacred to Apollo.

512b. **11. Lord Shaftesbury:** Anthony Ashley Cooper, 7th Earl of Shaftesbury (1801-85), English philanthropist and reformer, leader in factory reform.

27. moral coca: Coca is a South American shrub whose leaves are chewed by "natives of Peru and Bolivia to impart endurance."

WILLIAM MORRIS

SELECTED BIBLIOGRAPHY

I. STANDARD EDITIONS:

The Collected Works of William Morris, 24 vols., ed. by May Morris, London, 1910-1915.

William Morris: Artist, Writer, Socialist, 2 vols., ed. by May Morris, with introductions by May Morris and G. B. Shaw, Oxford, 1936.

William Morris: Poetry and Prose, Oxford University Press: London and New York, 1920.

Selections from the Prose Works of William Morris, ed. by Cambridge University Press, 1931.

William Morris: Selected Writings (Poetry and prose), ed. by G. D. H. Cole, Random House, New York, 1934.

Early Romances: The Life and Death of Jason, 2 vols., Everyman's.

The Works of Morris, in separate and cheap editions, Longmans, New York.

William Morris and E. Belfort Bax: *Socialism, Its Growth and Outcome*, London, 1893.

II. BIOGRAPHY AND CRITICISM:

Arts and Crafts Essays, with a Preface by William Morris, London, 1893.

BAINTON, GEORGE, *Letters on Socialism* by William Morris, London, 1894.

BAX, E. BELFORT, *Reminiscences and Reflections*, New York, 1920.

BLOOMFIELD, PAUL, *William Morris*, London, 1934.

BROOKE, S. A., *Four Victorian Poets*, New York, 1908.

CARY, ELIZABETH L., *William Morris, Poet, Craftsman, Socialist*, New York, 1902.

CHESTERTON, G. K., *Varied Types*, New York, 1909.

CLUTTON-BROCK, A., *William Morris: His Work and Influence*, London, 1914.

COMPTON-RICKETT, A., *William Morris: A Study in Personality*, London, 1913.

CRANE, WALTER, *William Morris to Whistler*, London, 1911.

CROW, GERALD H., *William Morris: Designer*, New York, 1934.

DAY, L. F., *The Decorative Art of William Morris and His Work*, London, 1899.

DRINKWATER, JOHN, *William Morris: A Critical Study*, New York, 1912.

ESHLEMAN, LLOYD W., *A Victorian Rebel*, New York, 1940.

EVANS, B. I., *William Morris and His Poetry*, London, 1925.

GLASIER, J. B., *William Morris and The Early Days of the Socialist Movement*, London, 1921.

GRENNAN, MARGARET B., *William Morris: Medievalist and Revolutionary*, New York, 1945.

JACKSON, HOLBROOK, *William Morris*, London, 1926.

HEARN, LAFCADIO, *Pre-Raphaelite and Other Poets*, New York, 1922.

HICKS, GRANVILLE, *Figures of Transition*, New York, 1939.

HOARE, A. D. M., *The Works of Morris and of Yeats in Relation to Early Saga Literature*, New York, 1937.

HUNT, WILLIAM HOLMAN, *Pre-Raphaelitism and the Pre-Raphaelite Brotherhood*, New York, 1906.

HYNDMAN, H. H., *The Record of An Adventurous Life*, New York, 1911.

LITZENBERG, KARL, *Contributions of the Old Norse Language and Literature to the Style and Substance of the Writings of William Morris, 1858-1876*, University of Michigan, Language and Literature, v. X.

—— *The Social Philosophy of William Morris and the Doom of the Gods*, Ann Arbor, 1933.

MACKAIL, J. W., *The Life of William Morris*, 2 vols., New York, 1911.

—— *William Morris and His Circle*, Oxford, 1907.

—— *William Morris, an Address*, The Doves Press, Hammersmith, 1902.

MORE, P. E., *Shelburne Essays*, Vol. VII, New York, 1910.

MURRY, J. M., "William Morris," in Massingham: *The Great Victorians*, New York, 1932.

—— *Heaven and Earth*, London, 1938.

NOYES, ALFRED, *William Morris*, London, 1908.

PHELAN, ANNA A. (Helmholz), *The Social Philosophy of William Morris*, Durham, N. C., 1927.

SAINTSBURY, GEORGE, *Corrected Impressions*, New York, 1895.

SHARP, WILLIAM, "William Morris, The Man and His Work," *Atlantic Monthly* LXXVIII (1896), 768-81.

SPARLING, H. H., *The Kelmscott Press and William Morris*, London, 1924.

VALLANCE, AYMER, *William Morris: His Art, His Writings, and His Public Life*, London, 1897.

WATTS-DUNTON, T., *Old Familiar Faces*, London, 1916.
WEEKLEY, M., *William Morris*, London, 1934 (Great Lives Series).
YEATS, W. B., *Ideas of Good and Evil*, London, 1903.

NOTES AND COMMENTS

THE LESSER ARTS

This lecture was the first that Morris ever gave in public. Under the title, "The Decorative Arts," it was delivered in London, Dec. 4, 1877, before the Trades Guild of Learning, and was published in 1878 as a pamphlet. In 1882 it was included in a volume of essays called *Hopes and Fears for Art*.

519a. 14. 'On the Nature of Gothic': Of the influence of Ruskin's chapter Morris's biographer, Mackail, says: "It was the first thing that, when Morris met with it long ago at Oxford, had set fire to his enthusiasm, and kindled the beliefs of his whole life." In 1892 Morris published the chapter separately in his Kelmscott Press, with a notable introduction.

519b. 25. Westminster Abbey . . . St. Sophia: Westminster Abbey, said to have been founded in the 7th century, and rebuilt by Edward the Confessor (king, 1043-66), is in its present form mainly the work of builders operating under the authority of Henry III (king, 1216-72), who demolished the Confessor's church and built a new one (1245-70). —— St. Sophia was built under the authority and direction of Justinian I, the Great (emperor of the Eastern Empire, 527-65), famous for his *Pandects,* a monumental digest of Roman Law, and for many great buildings, of which the best known and greatest is Santa Sophia (Holy Wisdom, erected 532-62). When the Turks conquered Constantinople in 1453 the Church was converted into a mosque.

520a. 19. Byzantium: Ancient name of Constantinople, changed in 330 by Constantine the Great.

522a. 30. scratchings on mammoth-bones: From 1840 to 1875, and later, many caves and rock-shelters in Southern France were explored and studied because of evidence in them of the art of pre-historic man. On the walls and on pieces of ivory (especially in caves along the Dordogne River) were found drawings, often artistic, of extinct mammoths and other animals.

524b. 21. the stupidity of the restoring architect: While Morris considered Westminster Abbey to be "the most beautiful of all English buildings, and unsurpassed in beauty by any building in the world" (*William Morris, Artist, Writer, Socialist,* ed. May Morris, I, 175), he thought the exterior "ruined" by the ugly towers of the west front (dating from 1722-40), and the "glorious interior . . . insulted" "by the pompous undertakers' lies" in the forms of numerous modern monuments and memorials, which he regarded as incongruous and unsightly.

26. matchless Hall near it: i.e. Westminster Hall, or Great Hall of the King's Palace, which dates from the 14th century. "From the time of the Confessor to the time of Henry VIII" the town of Westminster was "half monastery, half palace" (Lethaby's *Westminster Abbey*).

525a. 44. big houses . . . 'French and fine': In the 17th and 18th centuries Italian and French influences were dominant in the field of English domestic architecture. Many great country houses were built by English architects who had studied on the continent, and were decorated by Italian or French craftsmen. In 1665 when Sir Christopher Wren (1632-1723) was studying buildings in Paris, he wrote: "I shall bring you almost all France on paper." Morris had an unreasonable prejudice against all this 'classicism.'

525b. 6. "restoration": Throughout Morris's life ancient buildings were being mutilated or destroyed in the name of 'restoration,' that is, by replacing decayed or crumbling parts with new parts or wholes in the style of the old. And, to make a bad matter worse, the work was sometimes done by architects who had no guide but their "own individual whim" as to what was "admirable and what compatible." To Morris this meant the loss, from precious monumental buildings so treated, of all the "appearance of antiquity." He therefore urged "protection" instead of "restoration" and took a leading part in the organization (1877) and work of a Society for Protection of Ancient Buildings.

526b. 46. he who founded New College: William of Wykeham (1324-1404), English prelate, statesman, architect, Bishop of Winchester (1367-1404), was the founder and designer of

New College, Oxford (1379-1387), on which he placed the motto: "Manners makyth man."

THE ART OF THE PEOPLE

A lecture delivered before the Birmingham Society of Arts and School of Design, at Birmingham, Feb. 19, 1879, and published there as a pamphlet in the same year. It was included in *Hopes and Fears for Art* in 1882.

531a. 52. Byzantine Empire: In 284 A.D. the Roman Empire was reorganized by Diocletian into the Eastern and Western Empire, but the division was not realized until after the death of Theodosius the Great in 395, when his son Arcadius became Emperor in the East. The Eastern Empire, generally known as the Byzantine Empire, lasted until the fall of Constantinople to the Turks in 1453.

533b. 17. the presents which the native Princes gave: The Prince of Wales (who became King Edward VII, 1901-10) paid an official visit to India in 1875-76. Upon his return the objects of Indian art which the native Princes had lavishly given to him were exhibited for the season of 1876 at the South Kensington Museum (now called the Victoria and Albert Museum).

536a. 35. the great Plantagenet ... great Valois: The Plantagenets ruled England in direct line from 1154 (accession of Henry II) to 1399 (end of Richard II's reign). —— The House of Valois ruled France from 1328 (accession of Philip VI) to 1589 (death of Henry III). During these centuries in both countries Gothic art for the most part was supreme.

37. mass-john: The village mass-john was a *secular* priest of the Church, living in the world, as distinguished from the *regular* priest living in a monastery and withdrawn from the world. The name 'john' was added derisively as a stock epithet.

536b. 17. the countless laughter of the sea: The "*ἀνήριθμον γέλασμα*" of Aeschylus (*Prometheus Bound*, I, 89).

537a. 41. a very clever book of pictures: These were originally published in *Fun* (Morris' note).

THE BEAUTY OF LIFE

Delivered as a lecture before the Birmingham Society of Arts and Schools of Design, Feb. 19, 1880, one year later than the preceding lecture. It was given under the title "Labour and Pleasure versus Labour and Sorrow," and published as such at Birmingham in the same year. It was republished in 1882 in *Hopes and Fears for Art* under the present title.

544a. 33. literature since the time of George II: George II was King of England from 1727 to 1760, and by 1760 the new romanticism was well on its way. Blake's *Songs of Innocence* (1789) and *Songs of Experience* (1794), and Coleridge's *The Ancient Mariner* (1798), —poems that Morris probably had in mind—were sure signs that a new art had "happened in literature."

43. Walter Scott ... Gothic Architecture: Sir Walter Scott (1771-1832), "out-and-away King of the Romantics," as Stevenson called him, tells in his autobiography of his feeling for "the romance of external nature" when associated with historical incidents or traditional legends: "the love of natural beauty," he says, "more especially when combined with ancient ruins, or remains of our fathers' piety or splendor, became with me an insatiable passion." Gothic architecture in itself and not as a mass of picturesque and historic ruin was apt to appeal to him as "grotesque" and "wild." Ruskin, after visiting Abbotsford, came away convinced "that Scott ... had not the slightest feeling of the real beauty and application of Gothic architecture" (*Works*, XXXVI, 17; cf., also, V, 337-8). Eastlake in his *History of the Gothic Revival* (1872) doubted if Scott's knowledge of Gothic was more than "superficial."

544b. 15. that little knot of painters: The Pre-Raphaelites, who announced themselves as a 'brotherhood' in 1848. There were seven in the original group, the most prominent being the painters, Dante Gabriel Rossetti, William Holman Hunt, and John Everett Millais. Morris and his friend, Edward Burne-Jones, were for a time at least both in spirit and practice Pre-Raphaelites, and acknowledged Rossetti as their master. The 'P.R.B.' as a "knot of painters," however, lasted only a few years, certainly not beyond 1854; but they put new life into English art.

23. the name of John Ruskin: Morris's tributes to Ruskin are numerous and laudatory; "he retained towards him the attitude of a scholar to a great teacher and master, not only in matters of art, but throughout the whole sphere of human life" (Mackail, *Life of Morris*, I, 220).

545b. 15. Black Country: i.e. 'the Midlands,' including north Warwickshire and South Staffordshire,—the industrial center of England, black with smoke and grime.

22. "after me the deluge": "après moi le déluge," a saying attributed to Louis XV, king of France (1715-74).

546b. 12. let us work and faint not: *Galatians,* VI, 9.

547a. 12. Salamis: In the narrow straits between the island of Salamis and the shores of Attica, the Greeks defeated the Persians in a decisive naval battle in 480 B.C.

12. Thermopylae: A narrow pass between the mountains and the sea in ancient Locris (and a few miles from the modern town of Lamia), where Leonidas with 300 Spartans and some 700 Thespians held back the great Persian army for three or four days (480 B.C.), until all died but one, who escaped to tell the 'story.'

548a. 37. restoration of St. Mark's: "Sweeping restorations," says Mackail, "were proposed and already in progress at St. Mark's, Venice; and Morris was the soul of the movement of protest, which, though conducted in some quarters with more zeal than discretion in its attitude towards Italy and the Italian Government, at least had a powerful influence in preventing the proposed demolition and rebuilding of the western façade." (*Life of Morris*, II, 5).

548b. 22. on that convenience: "As I correct these sheets for the press, the case of two such pieces of destruction is forced upon me: first, the remains of the Refectory of Westminster Abbey, with the adjacent Ashburnham House, a beautiful work, probably by Inigo Jones; and second, Magdalen Bridge at Oxford. Certainly this seems to mock my hope of the influence of education on the Beauty of Life; since the first scheme of destruction is eagerly pressed forward by the authorities of Westminster School, the second scarcely opposed by the resident members of the University of Oxford" (Morris's note).

549b. 34. an Act in existence: The Public Health Act of 1875, in which the control of the smoke nuisance was left practically to the discretion of the manufacturers, who were mostly indifferent. Later acts were more effective.

550a. 1. Birmingham: "Since perhaps some people may read these words who are not of Birmingham, I ought to say that it was authoritatively explained at the meeting to which I addressed these words that in Birmingham the law is strictly enforced" (Morris's note).

3. Bradford ... Saltaire: Worsted and woolen manufacturing centers near Leeds. Saltaire is named for the river Aire and Sir Titus Salt (1803-76), a great industrialist, who made Saltaire a model manufacturing town.

10. Manchester: The metropolis of cotton manufacture, the largest industrial city in England.

44. Hampton Court: English royal palace on the Thames near London, built by Cardinal Wolsey, who turned it over to Henry VIII in 1526. It is now a show place, open to the public.

550b. 22. we always begin by clearing a site: "Not *quite* always: in the little colony at Bedford Park, Chiswick, as many trees have been left as possible, to the boundless advantage of its quaint and pretty architecture' (Morris's note).

553a. 14. Stamboul: French for Istanbul, the Turkish name for Constantinople; more exactly, it is the name of the city south of the Golden Horn.

553b. 32. Spanish pikes at Leyden: The defense and relief of the Dutch city of Leyden (1573-74) during the war of liberation against the "Spanish pikes" are among the most heroic incidents of history.

33. to have drawn sword with Oliver: Oliver Cromwell, Lord Protector of England (1653-58), at the outbreak of the Civil War (1642) organized the invincible Ironsides, men who, like the Dutch at Leyden, were ready "to die for a cause."

USEFUL WORK VERSUS USELESS TOIL

This essay was first published as a pamphlet, issued in 1885 by the Socialist League, which Morris and others had organized immediately upon their withdrawal from the Social Democratic Federation in December, 1884; its full title was: *Useful Work Versus Useless Toil: The Socialist Program.* The essay was included, with others, in *Signs of Change,* a collection published in 1888.

HOW I BECAME A SOCIALIST

This essay was written for *Justice* (June 16, 1894), "the Organ of Social Democracy," as it was called,—the official paper of the Social Democratic Federation, published weekly from January 9, 1884. The essay was re-issued as a pamphlet in 1896, in commemoration of Morris's death, with an introduction by H. N. Hyndman. It is included in vol. 23 of the *Collected Works*.

565a. 19. Adam Smith-Ricardo-Marx: Adam Smith (1723-90), Scottish economist, called 'the father of political economy,' because of his great work *The Wealth of Nations* (1776), which laid the foundations of the subject and had a world-wide influence. Smith was a member of Samuel Johnson's literary Club in London. —— David Ricardo (1772-1823), English economist, founder of 'the classical school of economics,' is best known for his *Principles of Political Economy and Taxation* (1817), a work accepted in its day as an authority. —— Karl Marx (1818-83), German political philosopher born in Prussia, is considered by many to be the founder of modern socialism. In collaboration with Friedrich Engels, he published the famous *Communist Manifesto* in 1847. More than half his life was spent as an exile in England where he wrote his great work *Das Kapital,* brought to completion by Engels (3 vols., 1867, 1885, 1895).

22. Mill: John Stuart Mill's papers on Socialism, which were written in the last period of his life as part of a projected work on the subject, were published after his death in the *Fortnightly Review,* Feb., March, April, 1879.

25. Socialism in its Fourierist guise: The French Socialist reformer, François Marie Charles Fourier (1772-1837), advocated the organization of society into co-operative, self-sustaining groups called phalansteries, of which the American Brook Farm (1841-47) was a famous example.

46. Bax, Hyndman, Scheu: Ernest Belfort Bax (1854-1926), English philosophical writer and socialist, was a friend and collaborator of Morris. Together they edited *The Commonweal,* organ of the Socialist League, and wrote *Socialism: Its Growth and Outcome* (1894). —— Henry Mayers Hyndman (1842-1921), English Socialist, founded the Democratic Federation (1881), afterwards The Social Democratic Federation, the first socialist organization in England, in the ranks of which Morris began activity as a Socialist. —— Andrew Scheu is described by May Morris as "the Austrian revolutionary, fiery and eloquent speaker, . . . not only a man of many adventures but of understanding concerning the relations of art and labor." He was a member of the Democratic Federation and followed Morris into the Socialist League.

566a. 39. Podsnap's: Mr. John Podsnap, a character in Dickens' *Our Mutual Friend,* a pompous, prudish, self-confident Philistine.

WALTER PATER

SELECTED BIBLIOGRAPHY

I. STANDARD EDITIONS

The Works of Walter Pater, 10 vols., London, 1910.
Uncollected Essays, Portland, Me. (T. B. Mosher), 1903.
Sketches and Reviews, New York, 1919.
Selections from Pater, ed. E. E. Hale, Jr., New York, 1901.
Selections from Walter Pater, ed. A. D. F. Snell, Boston, 1924.
Marius the Epicurean, 2 vols., ed. J. C. Squire, London, 1929.
—— ed. J. Sagmaster, New York, 1935.
The Renaissance and *Marius the Epicurean,* in the *Modern Library,* New York.

II. BIOGRAPHY AND CRITICISM

BARRY, W. F., *Heralds of Revolt,* London, 1904.
BENDZ, ERNEST P., *The Influence of Pater and Matthew Arnold in the Prose Writings of Oscar Wilde,* Gothenburg, 1914.
BENSON, A. C., *Walter Pater* (English Men of Letters Series), London, 1906.
BOCK, E. J., *Walter Pater's Einfluss auf Oscar Wilde,* Bonn, 1913.

CHANDLER, Z. E., *An Analysis of the Stylistic Technique of Addison, Johnson, Hazlitt, and Pater,* Iowa City, Iowa, 1928.

CHILD, RUTH C., *The Aesthetic of Walter Pater,* New York, 1940.

DOWDEN, E., *Essays Modern and Elizabethan,* London, 1910.

EAKER, J. G., *Walter Pater: A Study in Methods and Effects,* Iowa City, Iowa, 1933.

ELIOT, T. S., *Selected Essays,* London, 1932.

FARMER, A. J., *Walter Pater as a Critic of English Literature: A Study of 'Appreciations,'* Grenoble, 1931.

FRYE, P. H., *Visions and Chimeras,* Boston, 1929.

GOSSE, EDMUND, *Critical Kit-Kats,* London, 1896.

GREENSLET, FERRIS, *Walter Pater,* New York, 1903.

HUNEKER, JAMES, *The Pathos of Distance,* New York, 1913.

JOHNSON, LIONEL, "The Work of Mr. Pater," *Fortnightly Review,* LXII (1894), 352-67.

LEGALLIENNE, RICHARD, "On Rereading Walter Pater," *North American Review,* CXCV (1912), 214-24.

MORE, P. E., "The Drift of Romanticism," *Shelburne Essays,* Eighth Series, New York, 1913.

MORLEY, JOHN, "Mr. Pater's Essays," *Fortnightly Review,* XIX (1873), 471-77.

RALLI, AUGUSTUS, *Critiques,* New York, 1927.

ROSENBLATT, LOUISE, *L'Idée de l'art pour l'art dans la littérature anglaise pendant la Période Victorienne,* Paris, 1931.

SAINTSBURY, GEORGE, *A History of English Criticism,* London, 1911.

—— *Prefaces and Essays,* London, 1933.

SHAFER, ROBERT, *Progress and Science,* New Haven, 1923.

SHARP, WILLIAM, *Papers Critical and Reminiscent,* London, 1912.

SMITH, LOGAN P., *Reperusals and Recollections,* New York, 1937.

SQUIRE, SIR J. C., *Reflections and Memories,* London, 1935.

SYMONS, ARTHUR, *Studies in Prose and Verse,* London, 1904.

—— *Figures of Several Centuries,* New York, 1916.

—— *A Study of Walter Pater,* London, 1932.

THOMAS, EDWARD, *Walter Pater, A Critical Study,* London, 1913.

WARD, MRS. HUMPHREY, *A Writer's Recollections,* 2 vols., New York, 1918.

WELBY, T. EARLE, "Walter Pater," in *Revaluations: Studies in Biography,* London, 1931.

WRIGHT, THOMAS, *The Life of Walter Pater,* 2 vols., London, 1907.

YOUNG, HELEN H., *The Writings of Walter Pater, A Reflection of British Philosophical Opinions from 1860-1890,* Bryn Mawr College, 1933.

NOTES AND COMMENTS

THE RENAISSANCE

First published as *Studies in the History of the Renaissance* (1873), containing, besides the famous Preface and Conclusion, eight essays, of which five had been previously published in periodicals, four in *The Fortnightly Review,* and one—'Wickelmann'—in the *Westminster Review*). The essay on Giorgione was added in the third edition (1888). Pater's interest in the Renaissance was deep and lifelong: "the age of the Renaissance," he says, "—an age of which one may say, summarily, that it enjoyed itself, and found perhaps its chief enjoyment in the attitude of the scholar, in the enthusiastic acquisition of knowledge for its own sake" ("Raphael" in *Miscellaneous Studies,* 38).

PREFACE

The Preface was not published or written independently, but appeared with the complete volume.

570a. 27. **"To see the object as in itself it really is"**: Quoted from the concluding paragraph in the second of Arnold's lectures *On Translating Homer.* Arnold himself quotes the passage in the first paragraph of *The Function of Criticism.*

570b. 20. *La Gioconda:* See following selection.

20. hills of Carrara: The mountains near Carrara, Italy (province of Tuscany), from which the famous white statuary marble is quarried.

20. Pico of Mirandola: Giovanni Pico, Count of Mirandola (1463-94), brilliant young

Renaissance scholar and Platonist. He is the subject of Pater's second essay in *The Renaissance*.

571a. 13. William Blake: Pater is summarizing Blake's thought on "the ages" and "genius" in his "Descriptive Catalogue" of his painting of the Canterbury Pilgrims of Chaucer (see Blake's *Poetical Works*, Oxford Press, 433-35).

50. the history of the Renaissance: For Pater the spirit, or 'feeling,' peculiar to the Renaissance (i.e. "the free play of human intelligence around all subjects presented to it") found its earliest expression "in the end of the twelfth and the beginning of the following century" in France.

571b. 26. Joachim du Bellay: French poet (1524-60), member of "The Pléiade." He is the subject of Pater's eighth essay in *The Renaissance*.

572a. 23. the age of Pericles: i.e. 461-2-429 B.C., from the time that Pericles came into power until his death. In this period Athens reached the summit of her material and intellectual life.

24. Lorenzo: Lorenzo de' Medici (1449-92), called 'the Magnificent,' Prince of Florence, scholar, and patron of art and letters.

41. Winckelmann: Johann Joachim Winckelmann (1717-68), German classical archaeologist and art critic, author of *Geschichte der Kunst des Altertums* (History of Ancient Art, 1764).

LA GIOCONDA

From the essay "Leonardo da Vinci," first published in the *Fortnightly Review*, Nov. 1869, and sixth essay in *The Renaissance*. Leonardo da Vinci (1452-1519) "was the most universal genius of the Renaissance, perhaps of all time. He was painter, sculptor, architect, engineer, musician, philosopher, chemist, botanist, geologist."

572b. 3. La Gioconda: More often called "Mona Lisa," (i.e. Lady Lisa, now in the Louvre, Paris), the portrait of Lisa, "young third wife of Francesco del Giocondo," a Florentine aristocrat, whom she married in 1495. Vasari (*Lives of the Painters*) says that Leonardo, "after toiling over it (the portrait) for four years, left it unfinished."

6. Dürer: Albrecht Dürer (1471-1528), of Nuremberg, Germany; painter, engraver, "reputed inventor of etching and of printing woodcuts in two colors." "Melancholia" is a famous engraving.

13. time has chilled it least: Yet for Vasari there was some further magic of crimson in the lips and cheeks, lost for us (Pater's note).

18. Vasari: Giorgio Vasari (1511-74), Italian painter, architect, and biographer of artists from Cimabue to Michelangelo (*Vite*, etc., 1550).

19. Verrocchio: Andria de Verrocchio (1435-88), Italian sculptor and painter, or, as Pater says elsewhere in this essay, "carver, painter, and worker in metals," in whose workshop Leonardo was a student.

54. "the ends of the world are come": *I Corinthians*, X, 11.

573a. 17. Borgias: The best known are three, all notorious for sensuality and crime: Roderigo Borgia (1431-1503), who became Pope Alexander VI (1492-1503); his son, Cesare Borgia (1476-1507), cardinal, warrior; and his daughter, Lucrezia Borgia (1480-1519), Duchess of Ferrara.

CONCLUSION

The "Conclusion" to *The Renaissance* was written in 1868, thus preceding all of the "Studies" except the "Winkelmann." It was omitted in the second edition (1877) and replaced in the third (1888), with the following note: "This brief 'Conclusion' was omitted in the second edition of this book, as I conceived it might possibly mislead some of those young men into whose hands it might fall. On the whole, I have thought it best to reprint it here, with some slight changes which bring it closer to my original meaning. I have dealt more fully in *Marius the Epicurean* with the thoughts suggested by it."

573b. 22. gesture: 'Bearing, behavior.' Pater uses the original meaning of the word, now obsolete.

574b. 37. Comte: Auguste Comte (1798-1857), French thinker, founder of positivism, a religion of humanity that excludes all supernaturalism and treats social phenomena in the scientific spirit.

38. Hegel: Georg Wilhelm Friedrich Hegel (1770-1831), German metaphysician and post-Kantian idealist.

51. Rousseau: Jean-Jacques Rousseau (1712-78), French writer whose romantic and revolutionary ideals had a wide and profound influence. His *Confessions* was published in 1781-88.

575a. 9. Voltaire: Assumed name of François Marie Arouet (1694-1778), one of the great figures of 18th century Europe, philosopher, satirist, poet, dramatist, master of lucid French prose.
10. Victor Hugo: French poet, dramatist, novelist (1802-85) of the romantic period. Pater quotes from *Les Misérables*.
17. "children of this world": *Luke*, XVI, 8.

WORDSWORTH

This essay, an almost perfect illustration of Pater's method and spirit in literary criticism, was first published in the *Fortnightly Review*, April, 1874. It was included in *Appreciations*, 1889.

575a. 3. Some English critics: Coleridge and Wordsworth, particularly. In his essay on Coleridge in *Appreciations*, Pater says: "His prose works are one long explanation of all that is involved in that famous distinction between the Fancy and the Imagination" (*Lib. Ed.* 88). For Coleridge's general position, see *Biographia Literaria;* for Wordsworth's, the *Preface to the Poems of 1815.*

575b. 5. the excesses of 1795: A reference to the time when, after the fall of Robespierre on July 27, 1794, France turned from a "war of self-defense to one of conquest," an event which, in the opinion of Ernest De Selincourt, precipitated Wordsworth's "second moral crisis" and his reaction against the French Revolution. Wordsworth's political conservatism or Toryism came much later.

576b. 37. Senancour and Gautier, etc.: Senancour (1770-1846) in *Obermann* (1804); Gautier (1811-72) in some of his early poems; Rousseau (1712-78) in *la Nouvelle Héloïse* (1761); Chateaubriand (1768-1848) in *Atala* (1801); and Hugo (1802-85) in various volumes of poetry (e.g. *Les Voix Intérieures*, 1837, and *Les Contemplations*, 1856).—All reveal "in many forms" the influence of nature upon some of the great French Romantics.
52. Reynolds and Gainsborough: Sir Joshua Reynolds (1723-1792) and Thomas Gainsborough (1727-88) were both eminent English portrait-painters and members of the Royal Academy. Gainsborough excelled, also, in landscape.

577a. 23. the flower and its shadow: *So Fair, so sweet, withal so sensitive,* 5-6.
24. the cuckoo and its echo: *To the Cuckoo.*
34. "The pliant harebell": *Prelude*, X, 277-8.
36. "The single sheep ...": *Ibid.*, XII, 319-20.
39. "And in the meadows": *Ibid.*, IV, 329-30.
41. "And that green corn": *The Pet Lamb*, 28.
48. "noble sound as even moulding": *Three Years She Grew*, 29-30.
50. something actually "profaned": Cf. *Prelude*, II, 302-6.

577b. 15. "particular spots" of time: *Prelude*, XII, 208-33.
19. *The Recluse:* This poem was left by Wordsworth in manuscript and was not published until 1888 in an edition introduced by John Morley. It was meant to be the first book of the first part of a long philosophical poem (to be called *The Recluse*), which, if completed, would have consisted of three parts, the *Excursion* (1814) being the second part; with the *Prelude* (1850) as an autobiographical introduction to the whole. In a footnote concerning the publication of *The Recluse* Pater says: "It was well worth adding to the poet's great bequest to English literature. A true student of his work, who has formulated for himself what he supposes to be the leading characteristics of Wordsworth's genius, will feel, we think, a lively interest in testing them by the various fine passages in what is here presented for the first time"; and he quotes as "a sample" lines 129-51.
30. a moral or spiritual life: *Prelude*, III, 127-29.
35. the distant peak: *Ibid.*, I, 377-80.

578a. 11. "a sort of thought in sense": From Shelley's *Peter Bell the Third*, Pt. IV, 312.
18. an additional, accidental grace: *Prelude*, VIII, 256 ff.
42. the aged thorn: *The Thorn.*
43. the lichened rock: *Ibid.*, Sts. I-II.

578b. 1. The glories of Italy and Switzerland: For examples, in *Descriptive Sketches* and in the *Prelude*, VI.

30. "Grave livers" . . . stately speech: *Resolution and Independence*, st. XIV.

579a. 6. "related in a selection of language": Preface to *Lyrical Ballads*, par. 4.

12. select moments of vivid sensation: Cf. Preface to *L. B.*, par. 1.

44. George Sand: Pseudonym of Amandine Aurore Lucie, née Dupin (1803-76), French writer and novelist, best known for her lyrical, idyllic or humanitarian stories such as *Indiana* and *Valentine* (1832), *Lélia* (1839), *Consuelo* (1842), *La Mare au Diable* (1846), and *La Petite Fadette* (1848).

48. the sentiment of pity: This was conspicuous in Pater himself (see, for example, Ch. XXV in *Marius the Epicurean*).

49. Meinhold: Johann Wilhelm Meinhold (1797?-1851), German pastor, poet, and novelist; author of *The Amber Witch* (*Die Berstein Hexe*, 1843), which made a sensation and was translated into English. In the *Quarterly Review* for June 1844 it was described as "worthy of Defoe,"—a tale of superstition and supernaturalism told as if it were historical truth. Another of his novels of the same type is *Sidonia the Sorceress* (*Sidonia von Borck die Klosterhexe*, 1850).

49. Victor Hugo: (1802-25). Poet, novelist, dramatist, great leader in the French Romantic Movement.

51. the girl who rung her father's knell: *The Westmoreland Girl*, 1, 66.

52. unborn infant: *The Thorn*, st. XIII.

54. the instinctive touches of children: *Her Eyes are Wild*, st. IV.

579b. 2. tales of passionate regret: E.g., the story of Margaret, *Excursion*, I.

4. a heap of stones . . . that . . . outer world: *Michael* (also the story of Margaret).

10. carelessness for personal beauty: *Her Eyes are Wild*, st. VII.

12. the sailor . . . "half a shepherd": *The Brothers*, 45-46.

14. the wild woman: *Her Eyes are Wild*, st. VIII.

16. making of the shepherd's staff: *Michael*, 180-4.

17. the first stone of the sheepfold: *Ibid.*, 418-20.

580a. 5. "the little rock-like pile": *Prelude*, VII, 326.

22. the Platonists . . . Origen: In his note on "his famous *Ode*," Wordsworth says: "a pre-existent state has entered into the popular creeds of many nations; and . . . is known as an ingredient in Platonic philosophy" (cf. Plato's *Phaedo*, 72-76). He may have had in mind, also, the Neo-Platonists, chief of whom was Plotinus (206-270), who believed in pre-existence. —— Origen (185?-?254), described as "the most daring speculative genius of the Eastern Church," was a theologian of Alexandria, whose belief in pre-existence was only one of his several heresies, according to later theologians.

41. "the first diviner influence," etc.: *Prelude*, XII, 182.

45. moments of profound, imaginative power: Pater is referring to Wordworth's concept of imagination as a 'vivifying' and a 'visioning' power, whereby the mind seems to be "lord and master," and nature "but the obedient servant of her will," taking on a new unity and a new light. For illustrations see the *Prelude*, II, 362-74; VI, 592-616; XII, 208-33; XIV, 1-231.

580b. 3. At other times . . . the passive recipient: Cf. *Prelude*, II, 401-18; III, 127-32; and *Tintern Abbey*, 93-102.

17. *macrocosm* to Faust in his cell: In the opening scene of the drama (Part I), Faust perceives "the sign of the Macrocosmos" in the book of Nostradamus; it reveals to him "the powers of nature all around."

40. those two lofty books of *The Prelude:* XII and XIII.

581a. 38. With him, metre is but an additional grace: In the Preface to *L. B.*, Wordsworth speaks of the charm that exists in metrical language as "superadded"; and in the *Appendix to L. B.*, he says: "metre is but adventitious to composition."

581b. 15. a clause from one of Shakespeare's sonnets: Pater perhaps refers to line 26, bk. V of the *Prelude*, in which there is a phrase, 'weep to have,' from Shakespeare's sonnet LXIV.

18. its anticipator: Henry Vaughan, in *The Retreat* (Pater's note).

582a. 7. Grandet, or Javert: The old miser in Balzac's *Eugénie Grandet*, and the police officer in Hugo's *Les Misérables*, respectively.

14. Saint Catherine of Siena: Roman Catholic saint and mystic (1347-80), whose visions and revelations made her famous.

17. *House Beautiful:* See Pater's notion of this in following essay.

43. "antique Rachel" ... Beatrice: Rachel symbolizes the contemplative life in Dante (*Purgatorio*, XXVII), and in *Paradiso* (XXXII) she sits beside Beatrice enthroned.

54. said ... by one who had meditated: See an interesting paper, by Mr. John Morley, on "The Death of Mr. Mill," *Fortnightly Review*, June 1873 (Pater's note).

582b. 19. To treat life in the spirit of art: A favorite phrase of Pater's first used in *Diaphaneité* (1864), and meaning that the 'end' of life is contemplation.

34. "on the great and universal passions": Pater quotes from the Preface to *L. B.*

53. "of man suffering," etc.: *Prelude*, VIII, 165.

ROMANTICISM

The essay was first published in *Macmillan's Magazine*, Nov., 1876, and reprinted under the title "Postscript" as the concluding essay in *Appreciations* (1889).

583a. 41. House Beautiful ... Interpreter: Allusions to Bunyan's *Pilgrim's Progress.*

583b. 30. *Wuthering Heights:* This, the only novel of Emily Brontë (1818-48), was published in 1847.

40. Tieck: Johann Ludwig Tieck (1773-1853), poet, dramatist, novelist, editor and translater, one of the leaders of the German romantic movement.

41. Meinhold: Johann Wilhelm Meinhold (1797?-1851), a minor figure in the German romantic movement, whose sensational and supernatural novels seem to have much impressed Pater, as they did a good many other English readers (see reference to Meinhold in P's *Wordsworth*, and note).

46. Heine: Heinrich Heine (1797-1856), brilliant lyrical poet, critic, wit, and satirist; his *Die Romantische Schule* was first published in 1833.

48. Goethe: Johann Wolfgang von Goethe (1749-1832), Germany's leading literary figure, —poet, dramatist, critic,—whose *Götz von Berlichingen* (1773) was a powerful influence upon German romanticism.

49. Gautier: Théophile Gautier (1811-72), French poet, critic, and a leader in the French romantic movement, whose *L'Histoire du Romanticisme* (1854) is a critical account of the school.

54. *bizarrerie:* Extreme oddness.

584a. 34. Sainte-Beuve: Charles Augustin Sainte-Beuve (1804-69), eminent French literary historian and critic, whose *Causeries du Lundi* ('Monday Chats,'—15 vols., 1849-61) are among the great things in the field of literary criticism.

584b. 14. Stendhal: Pen-name of Marie Henri Beyle (1783-1842), French novelist and critic. Pater quotes from *Racine et Shakespeare* (1823), an "indictment of classical literature" (see *Racine et Shakespeare, Oeuvres*, 11 (1), Ch. III, 39—ed. 1925).

53. Racine: Jean Baptiste Racine (1639-99), poet and dramatist, greatest exemplar of French classicism.

585a. 15. Jean Paul: Jean Paul Richter (1763-1825), novelist, critic, humorist of the German romantic school. Carlyle, in a sympathetic appreciation, says of Richter's works: "They are a tropical wilderness, full of endless tortuosities."

22. Balzac: Honoré de Balzac (1799-1850), French novelist, author of many masterpieces, which he grouped together under the collective title *La Comédie Humaine:* "the gross bourgeois world was his special sphere."

53. the trees shrieking: See later note on Virgil.

54. Jean Valjean: Hero of Hugo's *Les Misérables.*

585b. 1. Redgauntlet: Hero of Scott's *Redgauntlet.*

14. Marius and Cosette: Characters in *Les Misérables.*

30. Madame de Staël: Anne Louise Germaine Necker, Baronne de Staël-Holstein (1766-1817), daughter of a famous minister of France, whose *De l'Allemagne* (1810) interpreted German romanticism to French readers and became a "pioneer in culture."

48. Strasbourg: Taken by the French in 1681, re-taken by Germany in 1871, and, again, in 1919 returned to France.

586a. 9. Murger: Henri Murger (1822-61), French man of letters, novelist and dramatist. The reference is to *Scènes de la Vie de Bohême* (1848), a collection of sketches of student and artist life: the book was the basis of Puccini's opera, *La Bohême* (1898).

36. Virgil describes the hazlewood: See *Aeneid*, III, 19 ff. Polydorus was the youngest son of Priam, king of Troy. For Dante's account of Polydorus and the bleeding twigs, see *Inferno*, canto XIII.

49. Provence: A district in south-eastern France where literature, especially the lyric poetry of the troubadours, flourished brilliantly from the eleventh century to the time of Dante. Pater touches on the love-poetry of Provence in his 'Two Early French Stories' (*Renaissance*).

586b. 13. Stothard: Thomas Stothard (1755-1834), English illustrator and painter.

14. Watteau: Jean Antoine Watteau (1684-1721), French painter of pastoral landscapes and court figures, whose work and character Pater describes in his imaginary portrait 'A Prince of Court Painters' (1885).

14. *Siècle de Louis XIV*: By Voltaire in 1751.

32. Rousseau's *Confessions*: The autobiography of Rousseau, written 1766-70, published 1781-88.

587a. 1. Werthers, Renés, Obermanns: Werther is the hero of Goethe's *Die Leiden des Jungen Werthers* (The Sorrows of Werther, 1774); René is the hero of Chateaubriand's romance of that name (first published in 1802, with *Génie du Christianisme*); Obermann is the hero of Senancour's *Obermann* (1804).

16. Quinet: Edgar Quinet (1803-75), poet, politician, historian. His *La Révolution* (2 vols., 1865) "attempts to replace the Revolutionary hero-worship, the Girondin and Jacobin legends, by a faithful interpretation of the meaning of events" (Dowden, *French Literature*, 423).

20. *Génie du Christianisme*: 'The Spirit of Christianity' (1802), a "poetic apology" of Christianity on sentimental rather than on rational grounds: "Of all religions that have ever existed," said the author, "the Christian Religion is the most poetic, most human, most favorable to liberty, to the arts and letters."

30. *Atala*: A romance (1801), or rather a prose poem, of American Indians; Atala, the heroine, is a chief's daughter.

39. Quasimodo: The hunchback in *Notre Dame de Paris* (1831).

39. Gwynplaine: The deformed boy in *L'Homme qui rit* ('The Man Who Laughs,' 1869).

43. Gautier's: *La Morte Amoureuse* (The Dead Lover, 1836); *Capitaine Fracasse* (1863).

48. Gilliatt with the devilfish: In *Les Travailleurs de la Mer* ('The Toilers of the Sea,' 1866).

52. *Quatre-Vingt-Treize*: 'Ninety-Three' (1874), Hugo's novel dealing with the French Revolution, including an episode of the National Convention (1792-95).

587b. 43. *Gaspard de la Nuit*: "Short poems in prose" by Louis Jacques Bertrand (1807-41), included in a volume published in 1842 called *Fantasies à la manière de Rembrandt et de Callot*, for which Saint-Beuve wrote an introduction, later included in *Portraits Littéraires*, II, from which Pater quotes: "Bertrand me fait l'effet d'un orfèvre ou d'un bijoutier de la Renaissance" ('Bertrand gives me the impression of a goldsmith or a jeweller of the Renaissance,'—348).

588a. 3. Stendhal argues: Pater states the general point of the "little treatise" throughout.

16. *Hernani*: Presented at the Théâtre Français, Paris, in 1830, where a fracas broke out during the performance between the spectators who shouted for the play (one of the maddest of whom was Gautier) and those who "represented the tyranny of tradition."

38. episode of Ugolino: *Inferno*, canto XXXIII.

588b. 23. " 'Tis art's decline, my son!": Browning's *Fra Lippo Lippi*, 233.

47. Phidias: Great Athenian sculptor of the fifth century B.C., whose gold and ivory statue of Athena was for centuries one of the glories of the Parthenon.

589a. 3. horses of Achilles: *Iliad*, XVII, 426-440.

589b. 30. "the style is the man": Famous maxim of Georges-Louis Leclerc, Comte de Buffon (1707-1788), French naturalist, who in his *Discours sur le Style* before the French Academy in 1753 said: "le Style est l'homme même."

THE CHILD IN THE HOUSE

First published in *Macmillan's Magazine*, August, 1878, with the title, 'Imaginary Portrait: The Child in the House.' It was reprinted in *Miscellaneous Studies* (1895). Florian Deleal is largely Pater himself.

590a. 9. a little place ... a great city: Enfield, a few miles to the north of London, was the home of Pater's aunt.

590b. 22. **Watteau:** See note on, preceding essay.
591a. 8. **thrum of colored silks:** Short threads, tufts, or fringes.
591b. 44. **"with lead in the rock forever":** *Job,* XIX, 24.
593a. 25. **"lust of the eye":** There is no such phrase in *Ecclesiastes* ('the Preacher'): cf. *I John,* II, 16.
593b. 12. **Marie Antoinette:** Guillotined, Oct. 16, 1793.
    13. **David:** Jacques Louis David (1748-1825), French painter to the court of Louis XVI, and later friend and painter of Napoleon.
596a. 3. **"resurrection of the just":** *Luke,* XIV, 14.
    8. **Joshua's Vision:** *Joshua,* V, 13-15.
596b. 4. *revenants:* 'Returners' from the dead, ghosts.
    39. **"lively hope":** *I Peter,* I, 3.
597a. 4. **the wrestling angel:** *Gen.,* XXXII, 24-30.
    5. **locked in his mysterious sleep:** *Ibid.,* XXVIII, 11-16.
    6. **bells and pomegranates:** *Exodus,* XXVIII, 33-35.
597b. 3. **Moses' tabernacle:** *Ibid.,* XXV-XXVII.
    6. **unction of the House of Bethany:** *John,* XII, 1-8.

DIVINE SERVICE

Chapter XVIII of *Marius the Epicurean* (1885), Pater's most important work. Many of the characteristics of Marius are Pater's also. The motto is from *Proverbs,* IX, 1-2.

598a. 9. *Zeus* of Olympia: A statue by Phidias in the great temple of Zeus at Olympia, at ancient Elis, in western Greece.
    11. *Acts of St. Francis:* Famous frescoes by Giotto (1276?-?1337), in the Church of St. Francis at Assisi, Italy.
598b. 2. **Cornelius:** A young Roman soldier, a Christian, whom Marius had met on his journey to Rome and who is now his friend.
    5. **Cecilian villa:** The Christian home of Cecilia, a wealthy Roman matron and widow. Pater's conception of her probably owes something to St. Cecilia, patron saint of musicians and of sacred music, a Christian martyr of the third century; and the conception may owe something to Raphael's painting of St. Cecilia.
    16. **Tusculum:** Ancient town some 12 or 15 miles southeast of Rome on a mountain. Cicero had a villa there.
599a. 28. **"the flaming rampart of the world":** "Flammantia moenia mundi" (Lucretius, *De Rerum Natura,* I, 73).
    46. **Catacombs:** Subterranean galleries, often of vast extent, used as places of burial and of worship by the early Christians.
600a. 36. **the Gradual, the "Song of Degrees":** "An antiphon or responsory, sung or recited with the Alleluia or the Tract between the Epistle and Gospel, originally from the steps of the altar" (Webster's *International*).
600b. 45. **a youthful "witness":** One who voluntarily suffered death as an expression of his fidelity to Christ. The Greek word for 'witness' is martyr.
601b. 11. **Aurelius:** Marcus Aurelius, Emperor of Rome (161-180). Marius is "an *amanuensis,* near the person of the philosophic emperor," and so comes into close contact with Stoicism.
    43. **foreseeing this very worship:** *Psalms,* XXII, 22-31 (Pater's note).
    49. **Saint Lewis:** Louis IX, King of France (1226-70); canonized as saint because of his almost perfect goodness. Voltaire said of him: "It is not given to man to carry virtue to a higher point."

ROBERT LOUIS STEVENSON

SELECTED BIBLIOGRAPHY

I. STANDARD EDITIONS

There are numerous editions of Stevenson's collected works. *The Edinburgh Edition,* 1894-98, in 28 vols., edited by Sir Sidney Colvin, was the first. Then came *The Pentland Edition,* 1906-7, in 20 vols., edited by Edmund Gosse, and *The Swanston Edition,* 1911-12, in 25 vols., edited by

Andrew Lang. In America Stevenson's publishers are Charles Scribner's Sons, whose *South Seas Edition*, 1925, in 32 vols., with introductions by Colvin, Lloyd Osborne, and Mrs. Stevenson, is the most available.

The Complete Poems of Robert Louis Stevenson, New York, 1923.
The Short Stories of Robert Louis Stevenson, New York, 1923.
The Day After To-morrow, by Robert Louis Stevenson, *Contemporary Review*, LI (1887), 472.
Selections from Robert Louis Stevenson, ed. by Canby and Pierce, New York, 1912.
Essays by Robert Louis Stevenson, ed. by Phelps (Modern Student's Library), New York, 1918.

II. BIOGRAPHY AND CRITICISM

ARCHER, WILLIAM, "Robert Louis Stevenson," *Critic* (N. Y.), VIII (1887), 225.
BAILDON, H. B., *Robert Louis Stevenson*, London, 1901.
BALFOUR, GRAHAM, *The Life of Robert Louis Stevenson*, 2 vols., New York, 1901.
BROWN, G. E., *A Book of R.L.S.*, London, 1919.
CANDLER, BEATRICE P., "Stevenson and Henley," *Putnam's Magazine*, VII (1909), 368.
CHESTERTON, G. K., *Robert Louis Stevenson*, London, 1927.
CLARK, W. E., "Robert Louis Stevenson in Samoa," *Yale Review*, X (1921), 275.
COLVIN, S., "Robert Louis Stevenson," *Memories and Notes of Persons and Places*, New York, 1921.
CORNFORD, L. C., *Robert Louis Stevenson*, New York, 1900.
DARK, SIDNEY, *Robert Louis Stevenson*, London, 1931.
EATON, CHARLOTTE, *Stevenson at Manasquan*, Chicago, 1921.
GARROD, H. W., "The Poetry of R. L. Stevenson," *The Profession of Poetry*, New York, 1929.
GOSSE, EDMUND, "Robert Louis Stevenson: Personal Memories," *Critical Kit-Kats*, London, 1896.
GWYNN, STEPHEN, *Robert Louis Stevenson*, London, 1939.
HAMILTON, CLAYTON, *On the Trail of Stevenson*, New York, 1915.
HELLMAN, GEORGE S., *The True Stevenson*, Boston, 1925.
HENLEY, W. E., "R.L.S.," *The Pall Mall Magazine*, XXV (Dec. 1901), 505.
JAMES, HENRY, *Partial Portraits*, New York, 1899.
KELMAN, JOHN, *The Faith of Robert Louis Stevenson*, Edinburgh, 1903.
LEE, VERNON, "The Handling of Words," *English Review*, IX (1911), 441.
LOW, W. H., *A Chronicle of Friendships*, New York, 1910.
MASSON, ROSALINE, *The Life of Robert Louis Stevenson*, Edinburgh, 1923.
MUIRHEAD, J. H., "Robert Louis Stevenson's Philosophy of Life," *Philosophy and Life*, London, 1902.
—— 'The Paradoxical Optimism of Stevenson,' *Current Literature*, XLI (1906), 49.
OSBOURNE, LLOYD, *An Intimate Portrait of R.L.S.*, New York, 1924.
RALEIGH, WALTER, *Robert Louis Stevenson*, New York, 1908.
RICE, RICHARD A., *Robert Louis Stevenson: How to Know Him*, Indianapolis, 1916.
SAROLEA, CHARLES, *Robert Louis Stevenson and France*, London, 1924.
SIMPSON, E. BLANTYRE, *Robert Louis Stevenson's Edinburgh Days*, London, 1913.
SNYDER, ALICE D., "Paradox and Antithesis in Stevenson's Essays," *Journal of English and Germanic Philology*, XIX (1920), 540.
STEPHEN, LESLIE, *Studies of a Biographer*, IV, New York, 1907.
STUART, JOHN A., *Robert Louis Stevenson, A Critical Biography*, 2 vols., Boston, 1924.
SWINNERTON, FRANK, *Stevenson: A Critical Study*, New York, 1923.

NOTES AND COMMENTS

PAN'S PIPES

This essay first appeared in the *London Magazine* for May 4, 1878, and was reprinted in *Virginibus Puerisque* (1881), Stevenson's earliest volume of collected essays.

606a. 13. Attila: King of the Huns (406?-453), called the "Scourge of God." Under his leadership the Huns overran Europe "from the Rhine to the Urals" (435-454).

18. the house of life: By the astrologers the heavens were divided into twelve parts, called 'houses,' numbered from the eastern horizon, which was known as the *first house*, or, *house of life*.

23. **Caesar's ashes:** *Hamlet*, V, i, 236-39.

38. **the fire of Rome:** Nero, Emperor of Rome (54-68), a monster of tyranny and cruelty was suspected of having kindled the fire which burned half of Rome in 64. Watching the conflagration from a tower, says the Roman historian, Suetonius, "he sang the whole of the 'Sack of Troy.'"

606b. 3. **Pan:** In Greek mythology Pan was the god of flocks and pastures, the god of the goatherd and the shepherd. He was part animal and was represented as having the legs, and sometimes the horns and hoofs, of a goat. He was the cause of sudden fright, *panic*, as from strange sounds heard in the fields or woods by night. He played upon the syrinx, 'Pan's pipes.'

607a. 11. **the young lambs bound as to a tabor:** Cf. Wordsworth's *Ode on Intimations of Immortality*, 20-21.

AES TRIPLEX

This essay was first published in the *Cornhill Magazine* for April, 1878, and afterwards included in the collection *Virginibus Puerisque* (1881). The title comes from Horace (*Odes*, I, iii, 9): "Illi robur et aes triplex circa pectus erat," etc.—'oak and triple bronze must have girt the breast of him who first committed his frail bark to the angry sea" (*Loeb Classics*, trans.).

608a. 28. **Thug:** Member of a former organization in northern India, worshipers of Kali (a goddess presiding over obscene rites), who murdered their victims by strangling, and lived on the loot.

42. **dule trees of mediæval Europe:** 'Dule' is a variation of the Scottish 'dool' or 'dole' (grief); dule trees mark a place of mourning.

609a. 12. **bluepeter:** Flag with a white center on a blue ground, raised on a ship as a signal for sailing.

47. **Balaclava:** Seaport in the Crimea, on the Black Sea,—scene, in the Crimean War (1854-56), of the famous charge of the Light Brigade on October 25, 1854.

51. **daring feat for Curtius:** Legendary Roman hero who leaped into a chasm in the Forum (362 B.C.), thus appeasing the anger of the gods and saving his country, when the chasm closed over him.

609b. 8. **the Derby:** Famous annual running race for horses, at Epsom, near London; instituted by the Earl of Derby in 1780.

10. **Caligula, etc.:** Mad emperor of Rome (37-41 A.D.). Baiae was a coast town and summer resort not far from Naples. The Praetorian guards formed the body-guard of Roman emperors; originally, under the Republic, they formed a guard of the Praetor. The incident mentioned may be found in the life of Caligula as told by Suetonius in his *Twelve Caesars*.

610a. 9. **the same stuff with dreams:** *The Tempest*, V, i, 156-58.

18. **Permanent Possibility of Sensation:** A phrase of John Stuart Mill, who said: "matter, then, may be defined, a Permanent Possibility of Sensation" (*Examination of Sir William Hamilton's Philosophy*, I, xi, 243).

610b. 19. **the Commander's statue:** In the famous legendary Spanish story Don Juan has killed the Commander, (i.e. governor, whose daughter D. J. has sought to seduce) and later holds a supper at the tomb of the slain man, to which he mockingly invites the statue of the Commander; whereupon the Statue carries off Don Juan to hell.

41. **a mere bag's end:** *cul de sac* (blind alley).

49. **Bath chair:** Invalid's chair, so named from the city of Bath, well-known health resort in west England.

611a. 4. **our respected lexicographer:** Dr. Samuel Johnson (1709-1784), whose Dictionary came out in 1755, and who went on a Highland tour with Boswell in 1773. Boswell's *Life* (1791) tells of Johnson's fear of death and fondness for tea.

28. **eminent chemist:** Joseph Black (1728-99), Scottish chemist and anatomist of Edinburgh, who was a victim of prolonged "feeble health."

48. **heart on his sleeve:** *Othello*, I, i, 63-65.

611b. 10. **mimmouthed friends:** Affectedly prim in speech; 'mim' is dialectic.

18. **"A peerage or Westminster Abbey":** The words of Admiral Nelson (1758-1905), spoken shortly before the Battle of the Nile (1798), when the English destroyed the French fleet.

25. **the nettle danger:** *I Henry IV*, II, iii, 10-11.

36. **Thackeray and Dickens in mid-course:** Both left unfinished novels, *Denis Duval* (1863), and *The Mystery of Edwin Drood* (1870), respectively.

612b. 8. **whom the gods love die young:** From the fragment of a lost play by the Greek comic dramatist, Menander, 343-291 B.C. (Menander, *Fragments*, 125 K, Loeb Classics, 345). Professor Phelps quotes Plautus, *Bacchides*, IV, vii, 816-17: *Quem di diligunt*, etc.,—"He whom the gods love dies young, while he has his strength and senses and wits" (Loeb trans.).

19. **trailing with him clouds of glory:** Wordsworth's *Ode on Intimations of Immortality*, 64-65.

A GOSSIP ON ROMANCE

This essay was first published in *Longman's Magazine* for November, 1882. It was later included in the collection *Memories and Portraits* (1887).

612a. 26. **Malabar coast:** Southwest coast of India.

612b. 7. **Jacobite:** A supporter of the Stuarts or their descendants after the Revolution of 1688. Highlanders in Scotland were mostly Jacobites.

12. **John Rann or Jerry Abershaw:** British highwaymen; Abershaw was hanged in 1795.

14. **"great North road":** Through eastern England to Edinburgh.

613a. 2. *What Will He Do with It?:* Novel (1858) by Bulwer-Lytton (1803-73).

19. **the horrors of a wreck:** Since traced by many obliging correspondents to the gallery of Charles Kingsley (Stevenson's note). The novel is *Two Years Ago* (1857).

36. **Conduct is three parts of life:** So said Matthew Arnold in *Literature and Dogma* (1873; ch. I, sec. I).

613b. 33. **"miching mallecho":** 'Skulking mischief,' *Hamlet*, III, ii, 147.

34. **Burford Bridge, etc.:** In Surrey, England, where Keats worked on Endymion in 1817. —— Emma is Lady Hamilton, loved by Admiral Nelson. —— Queen's Ferry is on the Firth of Forth, Scotland.

53. *Antiquary:* Novel (1816) by Sir Walter Scott.

614a. 29. **the inn at Burford:** Since the above was written I have tried to launch the boat with my own hands in *Kidnapped*. Some day, perhaps, I may try a rattle at the shutters (Stevenson's note).

614b. 6. **Crusoe . . . Achilles . . . Ulysses . . . Christian:** In Defoe's *Robinson Crusoe* (1719), when Crusoe first saw the footprints of Friday, he knew he was not alone. —— Achilles, after the death of Patroclus, shouted at the Trojans from the trenches of the Greeks (*Iliad*, XVIII, 217-21; cf. also, XX, 381-2). —— Ulysses bending the great bow (*Odyssey*, XXI, 404-10). —— Christian running (Bunyan's *Pilgrim's Progress*, 8th paragraph from opening).

44. **Ajax.** Leading character in Sophocles' *Ajax*.

615a. 9. **Trollope:** Anthony Trollope (1815-82), is best known for his 'Chronicles of Barset,' a series of six realistic novels on life in (or near) the small cathedral city of 'Barchester,' mostly concerned with the clergy. "Mr. Crawley's collision with the Bishop's wife" is in *The Last Chronicles of Barset* (1867). "Mr. Melnette dallying" is in *The Way We Live Now* (1875), but the name is Melmotte (see Ch. LIX for the incident).

17. **Rawdon Crawley's blow:** It is in Ch. LIII that Rawdon Crawley struck Lord Steyne "twice over the face with his open hand."

23. **the end of *Esmond*:** "the breaking of the sword" occurs in Bk. III, Ch. XIII of *Henry Esmond* (1852).

28. **the unblushing French thief:** Alexandre Dumas (1803-70), author *Les Trois Mousquetaires* (1844), *Le Comte de Monte Cristo* (1844) and other novels, took for his romances what he wanted where he could find it.

36. *Clarissa:* *Clarissa Harlowe* (1747-8) is the masterpiece of the novelist Samuel Richardson (1689-1761), who wrote his realistic novels in the form of letters. Stevenson really liked *Clarissa* and in a letter described it as "one of the rarest and certainly one of the best of books" (Dec. 1877).

615b. 47. *Arabian Nights:* The Arabian Nights' *Entertainments*, "a collection of Oriental tales, originally from various sources and existing in several variant Arabic collections" (Webster's *International*). There are several translations in English.

616a. 30. Lucy and Richard Feverel: Characters in *The Ordeal of Richard Feverel* (1859) by George Meredith (1828-1909).

616b. 11. Haydn and Consuelo: Characters in *Consuelo* (1842) by George Sand (1804-76).

21. "a joy forever": Keats's *Endymion*, first line: "A thing of beauty is a joy forever."

26. *The Sailor's Sweetheart:* Published in 1877, by William Clark Russell (1844-1911), English writer of sea tales; he produced 57 novels.

37. *Swiss Family Robinson:* English translation (1820) from the German of a children's story by J. R. Wyss (1781-1830). The story was first told orally by the writer's father, J. D. Wyss (1743-1818).

44. *Mysterious Island:* The author, Jules Verne (1828-1905), was in his time a writer of "enormously popular semi-scientific romances of adventure"; *l'Ile Mystérieuse* was published in 1870.

617a. 27. Eugène de Rastignac: Character in Balzac's *Le Père Goriot* (1834).

617b. 5. Walter Scott: *The Lady of the Lake* (1810); *The Pirate* (1821); *Guy Mannering* (1815).

618a. 7. Miss Braddon's idea of a story: Mary Elizabeth Braddon (1837-1915), English novelist who wrote "80 novels and many plays."

8. Mrs. Todgers: Character in Dickens' *Martin Chuzzlewit* (1843-44).

618b. 19. Elspeth: Character in the *Antiquary* (1816).

BOOKS WHICH HAVE INFLUENCED ME

This essay first appeared in the *British Weekly* for May 13, 1887. It was one of a series of papers on the subject, written by Gladstone, Ruskin, and others, and collected and published by the paper in the same year. Later it was included in a series of 'Essays on Literature' (vol. XXVII, *South Seas Edition*).

618b. 11. works of fiction: Stevenson means works of imagination, whether in prose or verse, as contrasted (generally speaking) with history, essays, biography, autobiography.

619a. 25. Mrs. Scott Siddons: An English actress of considerable reputation in Stevenson's time. She played Shakespeare parts, especially Juliet, Portia and Rosalind, and in 1881 assumed management of the Haymarket Theatre, London.

28. Kent's brief speech: *King Lear*, V, iii, 314-15.

36. *Vicomte de Bragelonne:* By Alexandre Dumas; sequel (1848) to *Vingt Ans Après* ('Twenty Years After,' 1845).

41. *Pilgrim's Progress:* Bunyan's (1628-88) great allegory of the Christian life of man was written in the Bedford jail in 1678.

619b. 2. *Essais* of Montaigne: Michel Eyquem Seigneur de Montaigne (1533-92) is the great original master of the personal essay. His *Essais* first appeared in 1580 (bks. I-II); in 1588 a fifth edition was published, to which a third book was added. They were translated into English (1603) by "resolute John Florio" (1553?-1625), Montaigne's Elizabethan contemporary.

8. "linen decencies": An echo from Milton's *Areopagitica:* "the ghost of a linen decency yet haunts me" (seventh-end par.).

31. *Leaves of Grass:* Published in 1855 by Walt Whitman (1819-92).

620a. 8. Herbert Spencer: Author (1820-1903) of a *System of Synthetic Philosophy* in several volumes. Up to 1887 (the date of the present essay) Stevenson might have read one or more of the following: *Social Statics* (1851), *Principles of Psychology* (1855), *First Principles* (1862), *Principles of Biology* (1864-67), *Principles of Sociology* (1st vol. 1876).

24. *Goethe's Life:* George Henry Lewes (1817-78) published his *Life of Goethe* in 1855.

32. *Werther:* *Die Leiden des jungen Werthers* ("The Sorrows of Werther," 1774).

620b. 6. Martial: Marcus Valerius Martialis (40?-?102 A.D.), Roman poet and epigrammatist; 14 books of epigrams are extant.

20. *Meditations:* Marcus Aurelius Antoninus (121-180), Roman emperor (161-180) and Stoic philosopher, wrote his *Meditations* in Greek, a classic.

42. "the silence that is in the lonely hills": Stevenson loosely quotes from Wordsworth's *Song at the Feast of Brougham Castle* (1807):

> "The silence that is in the starry sky,
> The sleep that is among the lonely hills" (163-64).

47. Mill did not: See Ch. V of Mill's *Autobiography* in this book.

621a. 4. *The Egotist:* Published in 1879 by George Meredith (1828-1909).

8. a Nathan for the modern David: *II Samuel*, XII, 1-7.

37. *Thoreau:* In 1880 Stevenson wrote an essay on Henry David Thoreau (1817-62), which appeared in the *Cornhill Magazine;* now included in *Familiar Studies.*

37. Hazlitt: The essays of William Hazlitt (1778-1830), like the essays of Montaigne, were high favorites of Stevenson, who called himself "a fervent Hazlittite" and at one time planned to write a life of Hazlitt. The essay referred to belongs to the collection called *The Plain Speaker* (1826).

39. Penn: The "little book of aphorisms," *Some Fruits of Solitude: in Reflections and Maxims relating to the Conduct of Human Life* (1693), by William Penn (1644-1718), was carried, said Stevenson, "in my pocket all about the San Francisco streets, read in street cars and ferryboats, when I was sick unto death, and (was) found in all times and places a peaceful and sweet companion" (Letter to H. F. Brown, from Davos, 1881).

41. *Tales of Old Japan:* By Algernon Bertram Freeman-Mitford, Baron Redesdale (1837-1916), who was attaché in Japan (1866-70) and who published *Tales of Old Japan* in 1871 "by A. B. Mitford."

PULVIS ET UMBRA

The essay first appeared in *Scribner's Magazine* for April, 1888 (where it was one of a series), and was reprinted in *Across the Plains* (1892). It is now in 'Random Memories' (vol. XIII, *South Seas Edition*). The title comes from Horace's *Odes*, IV, vii, 16: "pulvis et umbra sumus," —we are dust and shadow. "It is a mere sermon," said Stevenson.... "I wrote it with great feeling and conviction."

622a. 44. NH_3 and H_2O: Chemical formulas for ammonia and water, respectively.

46. that way madness lies: *King Lear*, III, iv, 21.

623a. 46. the heart of his mystery: Cf. *Hamlet*, III, ii, 370-1.

623b. 48. Assiniboia: Formerly a district of western Canada, now mostly in Saskatchewan. Calumet is the ceremonial pipe of peace used by North American Indians.

624a. 15. sacred river: The Ganges, into which, before the British stopped the practice, children were thrown as sacrifices to the gods.

20. touch of pity: *Richard III*, I, ii, 71.

35. jewel of their souls: *Othello*, III, iii, 156.

44. ennobled lemur: The lemur is a nocturnal, monkey-like mammal, "arboreal in his habits."

49. A new doctrine: Evolution.

624b. 23. the whole creation groaneth: *Romans*, VIII, 22.

36. double law of the members: *Ibid.*, VII, 23.

49. den of the vivisectionist: "I have never met anyone who hated cruelty of any kind with so lively a horror," says Stevenson's biographer, Balfour; "yet, with all his imagination and sensibility, he never ranged himself among the opponents of this method of inquiry," i.e. vivisection, properly controlled (*Life*, II, 216-17).

625a. 4. wise in his own eyes: *Proverbs*, III, 7.

6. wearies in well-doing: *Galatians*, VI, 9.